CONTENTS

Contents

Contents

FOREWORD

The publication of a second edition of this handbook is one of the indicators of current rapid progress of the science and teaching of health communication, a subject which was not even recognized, defined, or taught a half-century ago. When clinicians and scientists first called attention to the need for improvement of this aspect of health care delivery, there had been little scientific investigation or explicit attention to the subject. It was then considered part of the "art of medicine," which came naturally or not, depending on the personality of the professionals involved. The doctor–patient relationship was sacred, and could not be challenged and hence could neither be studied nor taught.

Ultimately, it took a more vocal, self-confident patient community, aware of its members' own rights, to come forward with criticisms of the way they were treated by their physicians (and surgeons). Since then there has been increasing dialogue in most professional and patient communities about this important issue. Just as the feminists have been congratulating one another on their progress in recent years, those of us involved in this area of study could proudly say: "We have come a long way, baby!"

At present, there is almost universal recognition that these communication issues must be addressed in the course of educating health professionals, and there have also been increasing efforts to educate patients, in order that they may have increased insight into communication issues, and so make their health care more comprehensive and more satisfying.

In this context, a new edition of the handbook is most welcome. As our health care delivery system is undergoing so many drastic changes and the context of health care is changing, I anticipate increasing needs for attention and support for education and research in the field of doctor–patient relationships and communication.

Barbara Korsch

PREFACE

Few if any areas in communication have seen as much intellectual growth in the past decade as has health communication. The first edition of the *Handbook of Health Communication* played a role in educating a new generation of health communication teachers and scholars, as well as adding depth and breadth of understanding about health communication for numerous teachers and researchers in medicine, public health, and other disciplines drawn to the field. This edition of the handbook reflects the growth in scholarship associated with health communication. It has been organized around seven areas to emphasize health communication as a discipline that has generated new knowledge. The first section of the handbook provides an introduction to the handbook and includes three chapters. The first chapter, authored by Parrott and Kreuter, reviews the rich landscape associated with health communication teaching and research. The authors introduce the multidisciplinary, interdisciplinary, and emerging transdisciplinary approaches to collaborating in health communication pursuits. The second chapter, authored by Babrow and Mattson, provides a metatheoretical lens to frame the theory, research, and practice undertaken within health communication as a discipline at the end of the first decade of the 21st century. The third chapter, authored by Sharf, Harter, Yamasaki, and Haidet enriches the meaning associated with the various collaborations in health communication and the macro metatheoretical and theoretical underpinnings. The authors emphasize narratives as holding an integral role in health communication, whoever may be conducting the research guided by whatever theoretical insights. This observation forms a core premise throughout the handbook, as highlighted in the next chapter.

The second section of the handbook focuses on "Delivery Systems of Formal Care." This section includes seven chapters. The first chapter in this section, which is authored by Roter and Hall, addresses interaction between physicians and patients. The authors provide a broad context for understanding the role of medical interaction in shaping and reflecting the patient–physician relationship and thereby directing patient care. The second chapter in this section, contributed by Clayton and Ellington, expands the examination of communication associated with formal health care. The chapter discusses health communication goals, similarities, and challenges among multiple members of the health care team including nurses, therapists (physical, occupational, speech, and recreational), social workers, pharmacists, genetic counselors, poison control specialists, specialty teams (dialysis, dental), office staff, and volunteers. The third chapter, authored by Whitten, Cook, and Cornacchione examines the interactions that occur as a result of telemedicine's ability to reduce the barriers associated with geography and access to caregivers. Barriers, advantages, and methodological challenges of telemedicine are discussed. Real and Poole then build on the previous two chapters through a focused examination of communication within health care teams conceptualized as primarily information exchange versus meaning construction. An input-process-output (IPO) framework is developed for communication and effectiveness in health care teams. Geist-Martin and Scarduzio's chapter summarizes how communication scholars are currently defining the notion of communicating health and wellness at work. They offer an expanded notion of wellness at work by reconsidering what it means to communicate health in organizations. Aldoory and Austin present the role of health public relations in the delivery systems of formal care, describing two theoretical approaches that have guided scholarship and practice in public relations and that apply to today's health public relations. This second section of the handbook concludes with a chapter by Turner, Skubisz, and Rimal that affords a framework to consider public health communication. This chapter provides a psychological overview of theory in risk communication with the ultimate goal of explaining why communicating risk is challenging. Literature on the affect heuristic, optimistic bias, and appraisal tendency theory are covered. Their look at the public health system and risk communication provides a nice transition to the book's next foci.

The third section of the handbook, "Health [Mis]information Sources," includes seven chapters that provide a purview of the research associated with understanding efforts to keep multiple audiences up-to-date on information relating to our health and well-being. The first chapter, coauthored by Galarce, Ramanadhan, and Viswanath, offers a framework for understanding health information-seeking. Sundar, Rice, Kim, and Sciamanna introduce research pertaining to online content associated with health information-seeking, patient-to-patient communication, and patient–physician dialogue. The authors provide questions framing technological and theoretical innovations in this area, including a roadmap for questions to be addressed in health communication as we face the next decade. Silk, Atkin, and Salmon present research and arguments to support a systematic and theoretically informed approach to developing media campaigns for health promotion. The chapter discusses essential components of media campaigns, including formative research, persuasive message strategies, channel and source selection, dissemination decisions, and evaluation of effects. Roberto, Murray-Johnson, and Witte enrich these principles by revealing both the consistencies and the challenges that emerge when undertaking international health campaigns. The chapter also includes a brief introduction to entertainment education and community mobilization literatures. Edgar, Volkman, and Logan convey the significance of social marketing as an approach to health communication. The authors emphasize communication as one component of social marketing, introducing hallmarks that distinguish health communication from social marketing. In the next chapter, Kline examines the role of poplar media in constructing the meaning of health. DeLorme, Huh, Reid, and An give a rich context for the role that advertising plays as a resource to health information and products. They focus on the nature and roles of the three forms of pharmaceutical advertising: direct-to-consumer prescription drug advertising, over-the-counter drug advertising, and dietary supplement advertising.

The fourth section of the handbook considers the state of knowledge about "Mediators and Moderators of Care and Understanding." The seven chapters included in this section open with Thompson, Whaley, and Stone's discussion of the importance of efforts to explain illness to patients and the effects. The chapter summarizes research on these topics and how the patient and care provider co-construct the illness explanation. The vital role of understanding continues to be emphasized, as Cameron, Wolf, and Baker, review the growth in awareness of the contributors to health literacy and illiteracy. This chapter demonstrates how tightly woven health literacy is to attaining access, comprehension, and assistance regarding one's health. A brief overview of the prevalence and consequences of low health literacy is presented. In the third chapter in this section, Dutta and Basu review the different approaches to culture in health communication theory, research, and praxis and provide a guiding framework for understanding and applying the different approaches to health communication. This is followed by a chapter by D. Goldsmith and Albrecht, who weave the tapestry associated with social networks and social support through an examination of four pathways that connect health to supportive conversations and social networks. They consider that relationships can communicate feedback, norms, and social control; communicate health information and facilitate access to care; coordinate tangible support and its relational meaning; and assist relational partners' coping assistance to buffer the otherwise negative effects of stress. Wright, Johnson, Bernrad, and Averbeck extend this discussion through an examination of online social support. Pecchioni and Keeley-Vassberg contribute arguments for why families matter to health communication and highlight some of the contingencies that can influence and be influenced by families and health. As a result, some of the facilitators and barriers to understanding physician explanations of illness, and the role of culture and the context in which social support may be sought and given emerge, bringing insight and understanding to the wide range of findings regarding the intersections of family and health communication. This section then closes with Cline's introduction to the role of everyday interpersonal interaction as an arena of health communication. The chapter presents a rationale and a social influence framework for exploring everyday interpersonal communication and health. Reviewing literature on the various roles of everyday interpersonal communication and HIV/AIDS clarifies the potentially powerful and often neglected influence of everyday interaction on health and provides road-signs for future research and practice.

The seven chapters in the fifth section address the "[Un]intended Outcomes of Health Communication." The first of these chapters, authored by Politi and Street, focuses on medical decision making. The authors discuss ways to improve the quality of the decision-making process through achieving shared mind on the clinical evidence, patients' values and preferences, and the implementation plan. Duggan and Thompson examine other outcomes in addition to decision making which persistently align with health communication during medical interaction. A distinction is drawn between relationship-centered and patient-centered care, and the role of emotions, social support, obstacles to care, disclosure, trust, bias, and knowledge/understanding on outcomes that include patient satisfaction, health, and adherence. Ray and Apker enlarge the scope of effects and effectiveness of health communication with an examination of its role on professionals in health organizations. Goldsmith, Wittenberg-Lyles, Ragan, and Nussbaum enrich the scope of health communication outcomes through an examination of end-of-life decisions. They identify palliative care in the landscape of health communication and discuss current deficits and challenges in communication within the frames of serious, chronic, and terminal illness. Smith follows with a chapter that examines stigma communication and health. For those facing health challenges, stigma processes are considered a leading barrier to health promotion and treatment, such as delays in seeking treatment, poor treatment adherence, and increased risks of health reoccurrence. Ndiaye, Krieger, Warren, and Hecht then examine health communication's contribution to the reduction of health disparities, and a cautionary tale about its potential to contribute to health disparities. Health disparities are a pervasive and significant social problem that impacts the lives of those most vulnerable and least able to overcome their effects. The section concludes with a chapter by Harris, Baur, Donaldson, LeFebvre, Dugan, and Arayasirikul who consider the history of teaching, scholarship, and practice in health communication that led to its inclusion as an essential component of national health promotion and disease prevention policy as expressed in *Healthy People*. The authors' review starts with the creation of the Health Communication Work Group in 1998 that resulted in the first set of health communication objectives in *Healthy People 2010*. They then describe how expanded health information technologies and social media guided the *Healthy People 2020* initiative involving hundreds of stakeholders in health communication and health IT from across the country in the development of the next version of health policy objectives.

The sixth section of this second edition of the handbook, "Methods in Health Communication," affords readers an opportunity to examine the utility of various approaches. The six chapters in this section start off with Robinson's introduction to conversation analysis (CA) and health communication. This chapter reviews: (a) how interactional forms of context shape the production and understanding of action during health care provider–client interaction; (b) the relationship between CA-derived patterns of interaction and postinteraction medical outcomes; and (c) efforts to translate CA research for providers and intervene in their practice for the purpose of improving medical outcomes. The second chapter, authored by Valente, stresses the importance of incorporating interpersonal communication into health promotion interventions in order to obtain enhanced campaign effects. The author examines strategies to include the use of naturally occurring social network structures in the analysis of health promotion messages. Du Pré and Crandall give us an overview of the powerful role that qualitative research methods play in advancing health communication knowledge. The authors explore the utility of grounded theory, phenomenology, ethnomethodology, ethnography, narrative analysis, and more, both as research methods and as guides to everyday practice. Dearing, Gaglio, and Rabin introduce community organizing, an approach to social change that can produce community-level capabilities which can be deployed again and again as new problems or opportunities arise. These capabilities include knowing who in each organization to contact to invite into new improvement efforts, knowing which organizations have technologies and infrastructure that can be accessed for a community-wide effort, and understanding who can best bring a broad range of stakeholders to focus on a topic and draw out their continued participation. Stephenson, Southwell, and Yzer provide a masterful review of the value that experimental designs sustain in health communication research. The authors focus on some of the prevalent methodological dilemmas that are not only resolvable, but that also help to point the way toward theory development. Three themes are addressed: measurement problems related to key variables, issues in model development and testing, and statistical issues. Morgan, King, and Ivic wrap up this section with a review of the powerful role that new technologies assume in the efforts to provide innovative tools that can be used to improve the research methods and observations made by researchers. This chapter explains how technological innovations have been used to improve the design, implementation, and evaluation of health communication interventions, as well as possible outlets for future utilizations, and discussion about potential issues in using these means for research in health contexts.

The final section of the *Handbook*, "Overarching Issues in Health Communication," includes three chapters. First, Kreps returns to the focus provided in the opening chapter of the book on translational research. Importantly, he talks about the impact of health communication research on issues in practice and the community. Next, Egbert, Query, Quinlan,

Savery, and Martinez provide a review of health communication and related interdisciplinary curricula. And to close the volume, Guttman reminds of us that identifying ethical issues in health communication is a critical challenge—whether in clinical settings, media campaigns, or local projects—precisely because it aims to benefit people. When closely scrutinized, decisions that relate to the goals and implementation of any health communication intervention involve ethical issues. This chapter presents an overview of ethical frameworks and a series of ethical issues to illustrate the types of ethical dilemmas that inadvertently emerge in the goals and tactics of persuasive health communication. It concludes with new and enduring challenges associated with recent developments in communication technologies, health policy, and new manifestations of infectious diseases.

The editors of this volume would like to thank all of the authors for their fine work and diligent efforts. Sincere thanks go also to Karen Gibson for her incredible organizational skills and great brain—you have kept Teri sane (well, at least something resembling sanity…)! Similarly, this book could not have come to fruition without the conscientious reference checking efforts of Sara Hoyt. Thank you! You will be much missed. And, finally, thanks to all of the people who have worked very hard with us at Routledge/Taylor & Francis and at EvS Communications, but especially Linda Bathgate, Kate Ghezzi, and Lynn Goeller.

RP, TT, and JFN

THE CONTRIBUTORS

Terrance L. Albrecht is Associate Center Director for Population Sciences and Leader of the Population Studies and Prevention Program at the Karmanos Cancer Institute and Professor, Department of Oncology, Wayne State University School of Medicine. Currently she leads transdisciplinary and translational research projects that include examining the role of interpersonal and environmental support as factors in epigenetic and behavioral studies of cancer health disparities.

Linda Aldoory is Associate Professor of Communication at the University of Maryland, founding director of the Center for Risk Communication Research, and former editor of the *Journal of Public Relations Research*. Her research focuses on health campaigns and audiences of women and adolescents. In addition to her teaching and research, Dr. Aldoory consults for various health and social service agencies, including the U.S. Centers for Disease Control and Prevention, the U.S. Food and Drug Administration, and the U.S. Department for Homeland Security.

Soontae An is Associate Professor of Advertising at Ewha Womans University, Seoul, Korea. Her recent research focuses on health communication issues such as pharmaceutical advertising and food marketing to children on the Internet.

Julie Apker is Associate Professor of Communication at Western Michigan University, where she teaches and conducts research in organizational and health communication. Prior to her academic career, Dr. Apker spent several years working as a public relations specialist and marketing communications associate.

Sean Arayasirikul served as the Health Literacy Fellow at U.S. Office of Disease Prevention and Health Promotion (ODPHP) during the development and writing of his chapter, and played an integral role in the Healthy People 2020 Health Communication and Health IT objectives' conceptualization and development process.

Charles K. Atkin chairs the Department of Communication at Michigan State University. He has published 160 journal articles and chapters dealing with media effects on health, political, and social behavior, and six books. The Decade of Behavior consortium recognized his work with the 2006 "Award for Applied Social Science Research," and he received the 2008 "Outstanding Health Communication Scholar Award" from the ICA and NCA Health Communication Divisions.

Lucinda Austin is a doctoral student and instructor of public relations in the Department of Communication at the University of Maryland, where she is also affiliated with the University's Center for Risk Communication Research. Her research focuses on the intersections of public relations with health and risk communication for campaigns and organization-public relationship building. Austin concurrently works as a communication specialist and researcher at ICF Macro in Rockville, Maryland, a firm offering communication research and support to government and non-profit organizations.

Joshua M. Averbeck is a doctoral student in the Department of Communication at the University of Oklahoma. His research focuses on language features and their effects on the persuasiveness of messages, particularly in the health domain. He has published 10 journal articles in such venues as *Communication Monographs, Communication, Methods and Measures,* and *Communication Studies.*

Austin S. Babrow is a Professor at Ohio University, where he studies health communication, with particular attention to problematic integration: the difficulties of synthesizing belief (e.g., uncertainty) and values/desires, ambivalence, and often painful certainty/ impossibility that characterize communication in the context of illness.

David W. Baker is Professor of Medicine and Chief of the Division of General Internal Medicine, at the Feinberg School of Medicine at Northwestern University. He was one of the developers of the Test of Functional Health Literacy in Adults (TOFHLA), and he was one of the Principal Investigators for the first major study examining health literacy using the TOFHLA. He was also the first to examine the relationship between literacy and health outcomes, including hospitalization and mortality. He has published extensively on the measurement of health literacy and the consequences of inadeqate health literacy. His current work focuses on developing interventions to improve health communication and to improve patient self-management skills and health behaviors, including use of multimedia and health information technology.

Ambar Basu is an Assistant Professor in the University of South Florida's Department of Communication. Dr. Basu's research explores the intersection of cultural issues and health communication. It locates culture as organic and fundamental in the framing of communicative patterns; and it examines how meanings are shared and health discourse is negotiated in the global-local context of multiple cultural, political, economic, and development agendas in marginalized spaces.

Cynthia Baur is the Senior Advisor for Health Literacy, Office of the Associate Director for Communication, Centers for Disease Control and Prevention, U.S. Department of Health and Human Services. Previously she served as Director, Division of Health Communication and Marketing, National Center for Health Marketing, CDC. She is a co-chair of the Healthy People 2020 Health Communication and Health Information Technology Workgroup and a co-chair of the HHS workgroup on health literacy.

Daniel R. Bernard is a doctoral student in the Department of Communication at The University of Oklahoma. His areas of research include the development of technology in theoretical and applied communication studies, risk and crisis communication, deception detection, and social influence in health contexts.

Kenzie A. Cameron is a Research Assistant Professor in the Division of General Internal Medicine at the Northwestern University Feinberg School of Medicine. Her research is informed by her background in persuasion and social influence, and focuses on message design, the reduction of health disparities, health communication and health promotion. Her research currently focuses on the development, evaluation, and implementation of theoretically based multimedia messages addressing preventive health issues such as colorectal cancer screening and influenza vaccination.

Margaret F. Clayton is a Family Nurse Practitioner and an Assistant Professor at the College of Nursing, University of Utah. She is also a member of the Huntsman Cancer Institute at the University of Utah. Dr. Clayton has an interdisciplinary program of research in cancer communications focusing primarily on adaptation to breast cancer survivorship. She has also conducted several studies of videotaped patient–provider interaction in family practice settings.

Rebecca J. Welch Cline is a Professor in the School of Communication Studies at Kent State University. Dr. Cline has authored more than 50 refereed publications and 20 chapters, technical reports, and reviews; and has delivered more than 170 research papers at scientific meetings. She is recognized in the communication, health education, and public health disciplines as a long-standing leader in health communication. In 2006, she received the Distinguished Career Award from the Public Health Education and Health Promotion Section, American Public Health Association.

David Cook is an Associate Professor in Health Policy and Management in the School of Medicine at The University of Kansas. His research interests primarily focus on the health of underserved populations, including health technology applications, workforce development, and emergency preparedness. Dr. Cook serves as the Executive Director of the Midwest Cancer Alliance at The University of Kansas Cancer Center and as the Associate Vice Chancellor for Outreach at The University of Kansas Medical Center.

Jennifer Cornacchione is a master's student in the Department of Communication at Michigan State University. Her research interests are in health and interpersonal communication, persuasion and social influence. Jennifer has worked on multiple research projects in the area of health and technology, including providing increased access to mental health care for rural cancer patients, and has also been involved with projects examining memorable messages.

Sonia J. Crandall is Director of the Leadership and Mentoring Program for the Women's Health Center of Excellence for Research, Leadership, Education at Wake Forest University School of Medicine. She is author or coauthor of articles related to medical student attitudes, cultural competency, and communication skills for health professions learners.

James W. Dearing is a behavioral researcher with Kaiser Permanente's Institute for Health Research in Colorado where he directs the Cancer Communication Research Center, a National Cancer Institute-designated center of excellence in cancer communication research. He conducts studies of how innovations spread through advice networks of intermediary service providers, such as physicians and nurses. He is involved in studying and diffusing innovations in climate change, tobacco quitlines, chemistry education, math education, construction worker safety, flexible scheduling in businesses, physical education, and progressive organizational uses of electronic medical records.

Denise E. DeLorme is Professor of Advertising in the Nicholson School of Communication at the University of Central Florida. Her recent research focuses on health communication, including pharmaceutical advertising and consumer health information seeking behavior.

Molla S. Donaldson is Professor of Medicine (Adjunct) at the George Washington University School of Medicine and Health Sciences in Washington, DC. Dr. Donaldson is founder and principal of MSD Healthcare Consulting Group, which helps clients design and implement new forms of health care delivery to create sustainable change and dramatic improvement in patient care. Her focus is the intersection of policy, practice, and clinical research, including coordination of cancer care across settings and stages of care. Her work includes the perspectives of clinicians, patients, senior clinical and administrative leaders, public health professionals, advocacy and business groups, and government agencies.

Emily Dugan is a Policy Coordinator within The Office of the National Coordinator for Health Information Technology. Her special projects include The College of Wooster Independent Study, "The Effects of Endurance Exercise Upon Short-Term Memory and Amyloid-Beta Deposition", and Carnegie Mellon University Systems Synthesis, "Programmatic Space Plan with the Children's Hospital of Pittsburgh."

Ashley P. Duggan is Associate Professor in the Communication Department at Boston College and adjunct faculty at Tufts University School of Medicine. Her research addresses the intersections of nonverbal and verbal communication processes, health, and relationships. She is currently working on projects that examine interpersonal control tactics about health behavior, emotional experience, and expression in provider–patient interactions, family communication about illness, and the influence of nonverbal behaviors in shaping conversations about physical and mental health.

Athena du Pré is director of the Strategic Communication & Leadership master's degree program and the Health Communication Leadership graduate specialization at the University of West Florida. She is author of *Communicating About Health: Current Issues and Perspectives* (3rd ed.) and *Humor and the Healing Arts* in addition to articles and chapters on communicating effectively in health care settings.

Mohan J. Dutta is Professor of Communication in the Department of Communication at Purdue University. Dr. Dutta's research on the culture-centered approach to health communication explores the role of culture in constituting communicative practices in marginalized spaces and the politics of resistance at the margins that seeks to challenge and transform unhealthy health policies, practices and interventions. In his work with indigenous tribes, rural populations, sex workers and migrant populations, Mohan Dutta continually explores the intersections of activism and health communication to co-construct culturally located solutions with communities at the margins.

Timothy Edgar is an Associate Professor and Director of the Graduate Program in Health Communication at Emerson College, where he teaches social marketing, research methods, and behavioral and communication theory. He has a secondary appointment as an Associate Adjunct Clinical Professor in the Department of Public Health and Community Medicine at the Tufts University School of Medicine. His career has been devoted to conducting research on the use of communication and social marketing strategies to motivate changes in health-related risk behaviors. His published work includes the edited volumes *AIDS: A Communication Perspective,* and *Communication Perspectives on HIV/AIDS for the 21st Century*.

Nichole Egbert is an Associate Professor in the School of Communication Studies at Kent State University. Her research interests focus predominantly on social support in health contexts, spirituality/religiosity and health behavior, and health literacy. She actively collaborates with a wide range of researchers, including those in the fields of nursing, public health, medicine, and communication.

Lee Ellington is a clinical psychologist and an Associate Professor at the College of Nursing and a member of the Huntsman Cancer Institute at the University of Utah. Dr. Ellington has an interdisciplinary program of research in patient–provider communication. She has studied health communication in a range of health care contexts and among diverse groups of health care providers. In particular, she is interested in the communication mechanisms in patient–provider interactions which predict attitudes, treatment decision making, adherence, health behaviors, and clinical outcomes.

Bridget Gaglio is a Senior Project Manager with the Institute of Health Research, and manager of the Center for Health Dissemination and Implementation Research, Kaiser Permanente Colorado. Her research interests include health literacy, health disparities, and the use of technology in health promotion in healthcare organizations and in communities.

Ezequiel M. Galarce is a Yerby Postdoctoral Fellow in the Harvard School of Public Health and Dana Farber Cancer Institute in Boston. His current work is focused on the integration of health disparities models with psychological perspectives on information processing and behavior change.

Patricia Geist-Martin is a Professor in the School of Communication at San Diego State University. Her research interests focus on narrative and negotiating identity, voice, ideology, & control in organizations, particularly in health and illness. She has published three books and over 50 articles and book chapters covering a wide range of topics.

Daena J. Goldsmith is Professor of Communication at Lewis and Clark College. Her research addresses social support in various contexts, including how couples communicate about one person's serious illness and how advice-givers and recipients manage threats to face. Her book, *Communicating Social Support,* won the Franklin Knower Award from the National Communication Association. With Dale Brashers, she edited *Managing Health and Illness: Communication, Relationships, and Identity.*

Joy Goldsmith is an Associate Professor and Chair of the Department of Communication Studies at Young Harris College. Her research addresses palliative and end-of-life communication among patient, family, and health providers/clinicians. Included in her program of study is the critique and intervention of medical school curriculum used to teach about palliative and end-of-life communication. She coauthored two sibling volumes *Communication as Comfort: Multiple Voices in Palliative Care* and *Dying in COMFORT: Family Illness Narratives and Early Palliative Care.*

Nurit Guttman is Chair of the Department of Communication and Head of the Herzog Institute of Media, Politics & Society at the Faculty of Social Sciences, Tel Aviv University, Israel. Her research focuses on employing participatory approaches to social marketing, ethics in health communication interventions, disseminating health rights information to the public, and using entertainment programs to advance social issues ("edutainment"). She is the author of *Public Health Communication Interventions: Values and Ethical Dilemmas.*

Paul Haidet is the Director of Medical Education Research and Professor of Medicine and Humanities at the Pennsylvania State University College of Medicine. A general internist and health services researcher by training, his research interests include cross-cultural communication and its relation to health care disparities, medical education around communication issues, innovative pedagogical methods, and the culture of medicine and medical education. He is the president-elect of the American Academy on Communication in Healthcare, and is a member of the European Association for Communication in Healthcare.

Judith A. Hall is Professor of Psychology at Northeastern University. Her current interests within the clinical research domain are on physician–patient communication with an emphasis on accuracy of interpersonal perception, as well as on ways in which physician and patient gender impact the nature and outcomes of medical interactions. Within the non-clinical domain, Dr. Hall's research includes the development of new methods for measuring communication accuracy, correlates of communication accuracy across different domains of judgment (e.g., judging emotions versus judging personality traits), and skill in expression.

Linda M. Harris is Senior Health Communication and e-health Advisor to the Deputy Assistant Secretary for Health, Disease Prevention and Health Promotion and Lead of the Health Communication and e-health Team in the Office of Disease Prevention and Health Promotion, Office of the Secretary, Health & Human Services. In this capacity she runs the National Health Information Center and oversees the management of healthfinder.gov. Prior to her government service Dr. Harris was the Director of Marketing and Corporate Communications at Concept Five Technologies, a systems integration and software development company and Director of Family Health Programs at the National Business Group on Health. Dr. Harris is the editor of *Health and the New Media: Technologies Transforming Personal and Public Health.*

Lynn M. Harter is the Steven and Barbara Schoonover Professor of Health Communication in the School of Communication Studies at Ohio University. Guided by narrative and feminist sensibilities, her scholarship focuses on the communicative construction of possibility as individuals and groups organize for survival and social change. Her research has encompassed a range of health care issues including pediatric cancer care, disability-related concerns, and the organizing of health care resources for underserved populations. She is Senior Editor of *Health Communication*.

Michael L. Hecht is a Distinguished Professor of Communication Arts and Sciences at the Pennsylvania State University. Dr. Hecht's collaboration with Dr. Michelle Miller-Day has resulted in the National Institute on Drug Abuse funded Drug Resistance Strategies project (1989–present) that was among the first to study the social processes of adolescent drug offers, including an examination of the role of ethnicity and acculturation in these processes. Dr. Hecht has received numerous awards including the National Communication Association's Gerald R. Philips Award for Distinguished Applied Communication Scholarship. In his current project, Dr. Hecht and his team are studying health message adaptation and developing a drug prevention curriculum for rural middle schools.

Jisu Huh is Associate Professor in the School of Journalism and Mass Communication at the University of Minnesota. Her research centers on advertising effects and consumer behavior. Areas of research include health communication (including DTC prescription drug advertising), indirect advertising effects (third-person effects and influence of presumed influence), and credibility and trust in interactive advertising.

Rebecca K. Ivic is a doctoral student in the Department of Communication at Purdue University. Her research focuses on social support within new technology paradigms, as well as e-health in general. Her past work focused on the role of online social support groups for people living with cancer.

Amy Janan Johnson is an Associate Professor in the Department of Communication at the University of Oklahoma. Her research interests include long-distance relationships and computer-mediated communication, friendships, stepfamilies, and interpersonal argument.

Maureen P. Keeley is a Professor in the Department of Communication Studies at Texas State University. Her research focuses on relational communication surrounding health challenges to reveal the verbal and nonverbal messages that help people to connect more fully with one another in the midst of strong emotions and life changes. Dr. Keeley teaches undergraduate and graduate courses focusing on relationships and the family.

Hyang-Sook Kim is a doctoral student at Penn State University's College of Communications. Kim has research background in message design for health campaigns. Her current research interests center on the effects of new media technology on users' perceptions, particularly those related to their own health.

Andy J. King is a doctoral student in the Department of Communication at Purdue University. His research focuses on health campaigns, with an emphasis on evaluation, message design, and research methods. Past work examined the impact of multiple campaigns promoting the Michigan Organ Donor Registry, as well as the role of theory and formative research on message evaluation and development.

Kimberly N. Kline is an Associate Professor in the Department of Communication at the University of Texas at San Antonio. Her primary research interest is the use of critical theories and methods to explore the influence of popular media on knowledge and ideologies related to health, illness, and medicine. Her published research has addressed topics such as the theoretical and methodological issues in the study of health and the mass media and the use of textual analysis to evaluate the persuasive potential of breast cancer education materials.

Gary L. Kreps is a University Distinguished Professor & Chair of the Department, where he also directs the Center for Health & Risk Communication at George Mason University. His research examines the role of communication in access and quality of care, reduction of health risks, promotion of health, and elimination of health disparities.

Matthew W. Kreuter is Professor of Social Work and Medicine, and a member of the Institute for Public Health at Washington University in St. Louis. He is Director of the Health Communication Research Laboratory, one of five NCI-designated Centers of Excellence in Cancer Communication Research. His research explores strategies to increase the reach and effectiveness of health information in low-income and minority populations to help eliminate health disparities.

Janice L. Krieger is an Assistant Professor in the School of Communication at Ohio State University where she teaches and conducts research in the areas of health communication and social influence. Her work focuses on how social identities shape the way individuals seek, process, and share health information.

R. Craig Lefebvre is an architect and designer of public health and social change programs. He is chief maven of socialShift, a social|design, marketing, and media consultancy and holds faculty appointments in the George Washington University, University of Maryland, and University of South Florida schools of public health. His current work focuses on the use of design thinking, social media and mobile technologies in social marketing, and organizational change. He has also been coordinating a global effort to establish a digital platform and professional association for social marketers. He is the author of over 70 peer reviewed articles and chapters on social marketing and health communication, community-based health promotion, and new media in public health.

Alison M. B. Logan works as a health writer and communication consultant for a variety of health and wellness institutions in Vermont. Ms. Logan's interests include nutrition and its role in disease prevention, social marketing and advocacy work.

Amanda R. Martinez is a doctoral student in the Department of Communication at Texas A&M University. Her graduate research focuses on the areas of health communication and mass media, with particular emphasis on race/ethnicity, culture, and identity

Marifran Mattson, Associate Professor, Purdue University, explores the intersection of health communication theory, campaign practice, and advocacy initiatives with emphasis on questions about the connections between communication processes and problems related to health and safety.

Susan E. Morgan, PhD, is Professor of Communication at Purdue University. Her research focuses on health campaigns, message design, and research methods. Past projects investigated the promotion of organ donation in diverse contexts, as well as message evaluations for campaign research. She has co-authored a book on how to report results in social scientific research called *From Numbers to Words: Reporting Statistical Results for the Social Sciences.*

Lisa Murray-Johnson is a Program Director for Patient Education at the Ohio State University Medical Center and Adjunct Faculty for the College of Nursing at The Ohio State University. Lisa is an expert who has published in the areas of health program research, design, and evaluation, and health education. Her work has led to domestic and international research in conjunction with the U.S. Agency for International Development (USAID), the Centers for Disease Control and Prevention (CDC), the National Institutes of Health (NIH), and the National Institute for Occupational Safety and Health (NIOSH).

Khadidiatou Ndiaye is an Assistant Professor in the Department of Communication at Michigan State University and a core faculty member in the African Study Center as well as the Center for Advanced Study of International Development. Her research explores how national and international cultures impact the understandings of health as well as individual and communities' behaviors. Dr. Ndiaye is also interested in addressing the inherent methodological challenges of international health communication research.

Jon F. Nussbaum is a Professor of Communication Arts & Sciences and Human Development & Family Studies at Penn State University. Nussbaum has published thirteen books and over eighty journal articles and book chapters, studying communication behaviors and patterns across the life span including research on family, friendship, and professional relationships with well and frail older adults. His current research centers on quality health care for older adults, healthcare organizations, and intimacy across the life span.

Roxanne Parrott is a Distinguished Professor at Penn State in the Department of Communication Arts & Sciences with a joint appointment in Health Policy & Administration. Over the past fifteen years, her funded research has focused on the design of health messages to promote behavioral adaptation in situations where individuals are unable, unwilling, or unlikely to avoid situations and practices that put their health at risk. She utilizes a community-based approach in the dissemination of behavioral adaptation messages, involving families, friends, and community organizations.

Loretta L. Pecchioni is an Associate Professor in the Department of Communication Studies at Louisiana State University. Her research interests focus on interpersonal relationships across the life span, particularly in relation to family care giving. Among the courses she teaches are a broad survey of health communication as well as one that focuses on the intersections between family and health communication.

Mary Politi is an Assistant Professor in the Department of Surgery, Division of Public Health Sciences at Washington University in St. Louis. Dr. Politi's research interests include the use of communication strategies to help patients make complex cancer prevention and treatment decisions. She has also been involved in an international effort to evaluate and improve the quality of existing decision support interventions for a broad range of medical decisions, and an international project examining ways to implement shared decision making training into continuing professional development programs.

Marshall Scott Poole is a Professor in the Department of Communication, Senior Research Scientist at the National Center for Supercomputing Applications, and Director of the Institute for Computing in the Humanities, Arts, and Social Sciences at the University of Illinois Urbana-Champaign. He is the author or editor of ten books and over 130 articles and book chapters. His research interests include group and organizational communication, organizational change, and information technology, particularly its implementation and impacts.

James L. Query, Jr. is a researcher whose scholarship examines communication competence, social support, and health outcomes across major life events such as cancer and hospice, Alzheimer's disease (AD), living with diabetes, AIDS/HIV, caregiving for Hispanic individuals with AD, retirement, online support groups, and returning to undergraduate education.

Margaret M. Quinlan (Ph.D., Ohio University, 2009) is an Assistant Professor of Communication and a Core Faculty Member of the Health Psychology Ph.D. Program at the University of North Carolina at Charlotte. Her scholarly work explores the organizing of health care resources and work opportunities for people with lived differences. She has published in *Health Communication, Text & Performance Quarterly,* and *Management Communication Quarterly.*

Borsika A. Rabin is the Research Coordinator for the Cancer Communication Research Center at the Institute for Health Research at Kaiser Permanente Colorado. Her research interests include cancer prevention, dissemination and implementation research, and chronic disease epidemiology.

Sandra Ragan is Professor Emerita of the Department of Communication, University of Oklahoma. She has coauthored five scholarly books, including *Communication as Comfort: Multiple Voices in Palliative Care* and its companion volume *Dying in COMFORT: Family Illness Narratives and Early Palliative Care.* Her published works focus on language in social interaction, notably in the context of health communication, especially women's health and palliative care communication.

Shoba Ramanadhan is a Research Scientist in the Center for Community-Based Research at the Dana-Farber Cancer Institute. Her work focuses on using social networks to improve the dissemination and implementation of evidence-based health promotion programs in community settings.

Eileen Berlin Ray is Professor in the School of Communication at Cleveland State University. Her research focuses on health and applied communication, with an emphasis on social support in organizational and interpersonal contexts. Current research includes patient perceptions of changes in oncologist communication from initial diagnosis to cancer recurrence, and uncovering the dialectics of hope for people facing life-altering crises.

Kevin Real is an Assistant Professor in the Department of Communication at the University of Kentucky. His teaching and research interests lie at the intersection of health and organizational communication. His current focus involves communication and health care organizations, occupational safety, and professional identity.

Leonard N. Reid is Professor of Advertising in the Grady College of Journalism and Mass Communications at the University of Georgia. He is a Fellow of the American Academy of Advertising and a past editor of the Journal of Advertising. His recent research focuses on pharmaceutical advertising, health information seeking, and cigarette advertising.

Ronald E. Rice is the Arthur N. Rupe Chair in the Social Effects of Mass Communication in the Department of Communication, and Co-Director of the Carsey-Wolf Center at University of California, Santa Barbara. He has published 100 refereed journal articles, sixty book chapters, and eleven books. Dr. Rice has conducted research and published widely in communication science, public communication campaigns, computer-mediated communication systems, methodology, organizational and management theory, information systems, information science and bibliometrics, social uses and effects of the Internet, and social networks.

Rajiv N. Rimal is Associate Professor in the Department of Health, Behavior & Society and Senior Evaluation Officer at the Center for Communication Programs at Johns Hopkins University. He studies the influence of risk perception and social norms on health behaviors. His projects have focused on understanding how first responders process risk information, and applying behavioral theories to promote HIV prevention in sub-Saharan Africa.

Anthony J. Roberto is Associate Professor in the Hugh Downs School of Human Communication at Arizona State University. His primary research and teaching interests are in the areas of social influence and health communication. He has received numerous awards for both research and teaching.

Jeffrey D. Robinson is an Associate Professor in the Department of Communication at Portland State University. Dr. Robinson's research involves both qualitative and quantitative examinations of the predictors, processes, and outcomes associated with healthcare provider-client interaction.

Debra L. Roter is Professor of Health, Behavior and Society at the Johns Hopkins Bloomberg School of Public Health. She is author of over 200 articles and is recognized by the Web of Science as among the most highly cited authors in the social sciences. Her work is especially notable in regard to its contribution to measurement of communication dynamics through worldwide adoption of her method of coding medical dialogue, the Roter Interaction Analysis System (RIAS).

Charles T. Salmon holds the Ellis N. Brandt Chair in Public Relations and is Past Dean of the College of Communication Arts and Sciences at Michigan State University. He has conducted health communication projects and research for the Minnesota Heart Health Program, the National AIDS Information and Education Program, the CDC's Division of Diabetes Translation, and the Kazakhstan office of UNICEF. His research focuses on the intersection of public relations, public health, and public opinion.

Carol A. Savery is a doctoral student in Communication Studies at Kent State University, focusing on interpersonal communication. Her research interests include supportive communication, grief, hospice volunteers, and communication instruction. Ms. Savery's recent publications focus on hospice volunteers as patient advocates, and utilizing storytelling in problem-based learning.

Jennifer A. Scarduzio is a doctoral student in the Hugh Downs School of Human Communication at Arizona State University. Her research examines the intersections of organizational and health communication. Her areas of interest include aging and the graying of the workforce, emotion in organizations, identity, work–life balance, and sexual harassment.

Chris N. Sciamanna is a Professor of Medicine and Public Health Sciences and Chief of the Division of General Internal Medicine. Dr. Sciamanna's research focuses on creating and testing web-based tools to help people control their weight and to control chronic illnesses, by helping them make changes and by helping them to negotiate treatment decisions with their provider.

Barbara F. Sharf is Professor of Communication at Texas A&M University where she teaches classes in health communication and interpretive methods. Her work has included patients' lived experience of illness; patient–physician communication; cultural understandings of health and illness; and communication related to health disparities of race, ethnicity, and geography. Current projects focus on food availability, preparation and consumption as forms of health agency and disparity, and experiences of practicing and undergoing complementary and alternative forms of healing.

Kami J. Silk is an Associate Professor in the Department of Communication, Michigan State University, where she has an appointment with the Michigan Agricultural Experiment Station. She conducts health and risk communication research, with specific interests in persuasive ant translational health message design, message effects, and health literacy issues. Dr. Silk also teaches courses that focus on formative research, communication theories, and campaign design.

Christine Skubisz is a doctoral candidate in the Department of Communication at the University of Maryland. She studies risk and health communication; specifically, she is studying the effects of individual difference factors on perceptions of numerical risk evidence.

Rachel A. Smith is an Assistant Professor in the Department of Communication Arts & Sciences and affiliated faculty with the Huck Institute for Life Sciences at The Pennsylvania State University. Her research investigates the impact of social phenomena (e.g., social networks, social support, social cognition, and stigma) on message diffusion and behavioral adoption in both domestic and international contexts. Her recent work focuses on optimizing network-based interventions and compliance dynamics.

Brian G. Southwell is a Senior Research Scientist at RTI International and Research Professor at the University of North Carolina at Chapel Hill. Previously, he was Associate Professor and Director of Graduate Studies at the University of Minnesota's School of Journalism and Mass Communication. He continues to hold an adjunct appointment in the University's School of Public Health. He has written and coauthored numerous articles relevant to health communication research on topics such as exposure measurement and the roles of interpersonal communication and social networks in media campaigns. He currently serves as Senior Editor for Health Communication.

Michael T. Stephenson is Professor in the Department of Communication and Associate Dean for Undergraduate and Interdisciplinary Programs in the College of Liberal Arts at Texas A&M University. He is past director of the communication core at the School of Rural Public Health's Center for Community Health Development at Texas A&M Health Science Center. His research focuses on media health interventions and persuasion, particularly in the area of substance use.

Anne M. Stone is a doctoral candidate in the Department of Communication at the University of Illinois, Urbana-Champaign. Her research focuses on the intersections of health and interpersonal communication in health care organizations.

Richard L. Street, Jr., is Professor and Head of Communication at Texas A&M University, and also serves as Director, Health Communication and Decision-Making Program in the Houston Center for Quality of Care and Utilization Studies, Baylor College of Medicine. Over the past 25 years, he has developed an extensive program of research examining issues related to health care provider–patient communication, medical outcomes, and strategies for increasing patient involvement in care. Street also has explored various ways information (e.g., interactive, multimedia programs) and telecommunication (e.g. the Internet) technology innovations can be used to enhance health services offered to patients. In 2003, he was named Outstanding Health Communication Scholar by both the National Communication Association and International Communication Association. In 2008, he received the Donohew Health Communication Scholar Award from the University of Kentucky.

S. Shyam Sundar is Distinguished Professor and Founding Director of the Media Effects Research Laboratory at Penn State University's College of Communications. He also serves as World Class University (WCU) Professor, Interaction Science at Sungkyunkwan University in Seoul, Korea. His research investigates social and psychological effects of technological elements unique to Web-based mass communication, ranging from websites to newer social media. Sundar has been identified as the most published author of Internet-related research in the field during the mediums first decade. He served as chair of the Communication & Technology Division of the International Communication Association from 2008 to 2010.

Teresa L. Thompson is Professor of Communication at the University of Dayton. She edits the journal *Health Communication,* and has authored or edited seven books and over 70 articles on various aspects of health communication. Her research focuses on concerns related to provider-patient interaction, organ donation, disability and communication, and gender issues. Her co-edited volume, *Handbook of Health Communication,* won the 2004 Distinguished Book Award jointly sponsored by the Health Communication Divisions of the National Communication Association and the International Communication Association. She was the 2009 National Communication Association Health Communication Scholar of the Year.

Monique Mitchell Turner is Associate Professor in the Department of Prevention and Community Health at the George Washington University Medical Center. She is the former Director of the Center for Risk Communication Research at the University of Maryland. She studies the intersection of emotion and cognition on perceptions of risk and health communication, and social marketing.

Thomas W. Valente is a Professor and Director of the Master of Public Health Program in the Department of Preventive Medicine, Keck School of Medicine, University of Southern California. Dr. Valente uses social network analysis, health communication, and mathematical models to implement and evaluate health promotion programs designed to prevent tobacco and substance abuse, unintended fertility, and STD/HIV infections. He is also engaged in mapping community coalitions and collaborations to improve health care delivery and reduce healthcare disparities. He is author of *Social Networks and Health: Models, Methods, and Applications*; *Evaluating Health Promotion Programs*; *Network Models of the Diffusion of Innovations*; and over 100 articles and chapters on social networks, behavior change, and program evaluation.

K. Viswanath is a faculty member in the Department of Society, Human Development, and Health at the Harvard School of Public Health, and in the Division of Population Sciences at the Dana-Farber Cancer Institute. His research interests include communication and social change in health with a particular focus on communication inequalities and health disparities, and the sociology of health journalism. His most recent work examined the impact of communication inequalities in health in the domains of tobacco use and cancer survivorship, social capital and health, digital divide, and occupational practices of health journalists. He has published more than 100 papers in peer-reviewed journals and edited volumes and is the editor of three books and monographs and was the editor of the Social and Behavioral section of the *International Encyclopedia of Communication*.

Julie E. Volkman is Assistant Professor in the Health Communication Graduate Program at Emerson College. Her research interests include an ecological view of health message design and health campaigns. She is currently researching the use of narrative evidence across cancer survivorship, organ donation and osteoporosis prevention.

Jennifer R. Warren is an Assistant Professor in the Department of Communication at Rutgers, The State University of New Jersey. As an interdisciplinary researcher, Dr. Warren investigates the interrelationships among communication processes, biopsychosocial factors, and health behavior/outcomes within underserved populations to inform the development and implementation of targeted community- and web-based interventions in the area of substance use.

Bryan B. Whaley is a Professor in the College of Arts and Sciences at University of San Francisco. His research interests concern the relationship between language/message variables and social influence, the linguistic and social cognitive factors related to illness explanation and compliance messages in health contexts, and the communicative strategies for explaining scientific or complex health-related information.

Pamela Whitten is Dean of the College of Communication Arts & Sciences at Michigan State University and a Professor in the Department of Telecommunication, Information Studies & Media. Her research focuses on the use of technology in health care with a specific interest in telehealth and its impact on the delivery of health care services and education. In addition to authoring/editing three books, she has more than 100 publications that have appeared in numerous journals and books. Prior to joining the faculty of MSU in 1998, Whitten ran the telemedicine program for the state of Kansas through the University of Kansas Medical Center.

Kim Witte is a former Professor at Michigan State University and senior research associate at Johns Hopkins University's Center for Communication Programs.

Elaine Wittenberg-Lyles is an Associate Professor in the Department of Communication Studies at the University of North Texas. Her research program entails an examination of the interpersonal processes occurring in the context of death and dying, specifically in hospice and palliative care. She is a coauthor of *Communication as Comfort: Multiple Voices in Palliative Care* **and** *Dying in COMFORT: Family Illness Narratives and Early Palliative Care.*

Michael S. Wolf is an Associate Professor of Medicine and Learning Sciences, and Associate Division Chief of Research in the Division of General Internal Medicine at the Feinberg School of Medicine at Northwestern University. Dr. Wolf is a behavioral scientist and health services researcher with primary interests in adult literacy and learning, cognitive factors, and the management of chronic disease. He has received numerous national awards for his work in the field of health literacy and medication safety. As a Fulbright Faculty Scholar to the United Kingdom, he has facilitated international collaborations in health communication and disparities research, and continues to serve on relevant advisory committees for the U.S. Food and Drug Administration, U.S. Pharmacopeia, and the Agency for Healthcare Research and Quality.

Kevin B. Wright is a Professor in the Department of Communication at the University of Oklahoma. His research focuses on life span communication, developmental psychology, interpersonal communication, family communication, social support and health outcomes, and computer-mediated relationships. He coauthored the book *Life Span Communication*, and his work has appeared in over forty-five book chapters and journal articles.

Jill Yamasaki is an Assistant Professor in the Valenti School of Communication at the University of Houston. Her research interests focus on narrative inquiry and practice in health communication and aging, particularly in the contexts of long-term care and community.

Marco Yzer is an Associate Professor at the University of Minnesota's School of Journalism and Mass Communication and an adjunct associate professor at the University of Minnesota's School of Public Health. His research focuses on health behavior as a function of interpersonal and mass-mediated information. His work has focused on behavior change in the context of STDs, smoking, drug use and obesity.

SECTION I

Introduction

1

MULTIDISCIPLINARY, INTERDISCIPLINARY, AND TRANSDISCIPLINARY APPROACHES TO HEALTH COMMUNICATION

Where Do We Draw the Lines?

Roxanne Parrott and Matthew W. Kreuter

There is a classic poem that illustrates what happens when something large is reduced to smaller parts in order to describe it. In the poem, six blind men feel different parts of an elephant to describe what an elephant is like. After feeling the elephant's broad and sturdy side, one man concludes that the elephant is like a wall. A second, who feels the tusk, concludes the elephant is more like a spear. A third, who feels the squirming trunk declares that the elephant resembles a snake, as a fourth asserts that the elephant appears to be like a tree—this after feeling the elephant's knee. The fifth blind man felt an ear and declared the elephant to be like a fan, while the sixth man, feeling the tail, compared the elephant to a rope (Saxe, 1873). Each blind man contributed to understanding about what an elephant is like, but in a reductionist fashion that makes it difficult to imagine the whole as a sum of these parts. And so it appears at times in regard to health communication, where the discipline of communication has been involved in various ways for several decades, emerging in public health programs with increased frequency, and aligned with competencies in medical education as well. New technologies and patient education together with many other disciplines have been involved in health communication, so that putting the pieces together into a coherent image and making sense of it is a challenge.

Our task in this chapter is to represent the meaning, similarities, and differences of health communication conducted from multidisciplinary, interdisciplinary, and transdisciplinary approaches. Multidisciplinary approaches to health communication reflect research in which a common problem is addressed *independently* with the research proceeding from the specific disciplinary lens of individuals working on it. This happens sometimes simultaneously without awareness or even interest in each other's activities, and sometimes sequentially such that one discipline's insights lead to another discipline's uptake of the issue. Interdisciplinary approaches reflect *collaborative* health communication approaches. The work is conducted through the collaboration of individuals from two or more disciplines or subdisciplines working together to form research questions and problem solutions that reflect and respect the various domains of knowledge. Much of the work that we have done in health communication has been interdisciplinary. Transdisciplinary approaches reflect health communication research conducted jointly as well, but these efforts work toward *integration* of theories, methods, and systems in innovative ways that include individual, professional, organizational, and societal systems. This may lead to the formation of a shared conceptual framework that includes a model in which the constructs being tested reflect two or more theories from two or more disciplines or subdisciplines and systems.

One dilemma facing academics from different disciplines who are in pursuit of health communication is a lack of awareness of what other disciplines are doing. More than two decades ago, Thompson (1984) pointed to the reality that too much research duplicates the findings of other work due to a lack of awareness of what has been done. The value of replication is thus overshadowed by this reality, which relates to the myriad of approaches and disciplines involved in health communication. In approaching this chapter, we draw on our own educational backgrounds which frame our health communication pursuits, with Parrott earning a doctorate in Communication with a minor in Health Policy, and Kreuter earning a doctorate in Health Behavior and Health Education, as well as a Master's of Public Health degree. We also draw on our professional experiences, including the fact that we both have served on the National Academies of Sciences' Institute of Medicine (IOM) Board of Population Health and Public Health Practice. Through such service, we have gained awareness and appreciation for the place that health communication holds in views about how to solve health problems.

What and Why a Discipline? "What's In a Name?"

Academic disciplines form organizing frameworks related to competencies, promotion and tenure, and professional standards, thus forming identities. In terms of disciplinary identities, health communication aligns with a number of disciplines all making significant contributions to the body of knowledge that represents health communication. The beginning of efforts to address more systematically the roles of the social and behavioral science disciplines in health has been aligned with the World Health Organization (WHO) and UNICEF sponsored conference in the 1970s that set the goal of "Health for All" (HFA) by the year 2000. The HFA 2000 strategy has been identified as a catalyst for linkages between the medical and social sciences in the 1980s (Rosenfield, 1992), the era that saw the birth of these interests aligned with health in sociology, psychology, and communication. Moreover, intradisciplinary approaches reflect the reality that many of these disciplines include subdisciplines, illustrated in this chapter by specific reference to our experiences with public health and communication.

Disciplinary identities often guide the development of publication outlets based on islands of knowledge. The journal *Sociology of Health and Illness*, for example, was first published in 1978; the journal *Health Psychology* was first published in 1981; and the journal *Health Communication* was first published in 1989. Research published in these outlets reflects a biopsychosocial approach to health and illness, indicating roles for biological, psychological, and social factors. Health communication literature appears in all of the journals just named and many others, challenging health communicators to keep pace with relevant research. The *Journal of Health and Mass Communication's* inaugural edition appeared in 2009, suggesting the growing emphasis on understanding the role of mass communication, an example of a subdiscipline within communication which makes significant contributions to health communication.

Disciplinary identities frame insights about theory and systems that contribute possible solutions to health problems. The communication discipline, for example, often appears in university settings as a department within a college affiliated with social science and the humanities, or it appears in a college uniting such departments as public relations, advertising, and media effects. This institutional framework describes both the University of Georgia's and Penn State's approaches to organizing departments related to communication, sites where Parrott has had academic appointments. Health communication research and training is conducted under the auspices of both academic units. The "health" part of health communication also links it to a wide range of long-standing disciplines like public health, health promotion, health education, and patient education, as well as more recent and emerging disciplines like social marketing, medical decision making, and e-health.

Disciplinary identities form criteria by which individuals gain access to knowledge that makes them an asset in settings where health communication problems will be addressed. These identities matter within the institutional frameworks that define programs of study (e.g., Calhoun, Ramiah, Weist, & Shortell, 2008; Edgar & Hyde, 2005) and programs of research aligned with tenure and promotion in academic settings (Kreps, 1989). These identities are less important, some would even say meaningless, when it comes to doing the work associated with health communication, but in order to get to the benefits that health communicators hope to contribute, the former must be traversed. As discussed in Egbert et al.'s chapter in this volume, these programs in relation to health communication have primarily emerged in schools of public health and communication departments. The foci within these programs give a sense of core competencies. In addition to the formal programs that focus on training health communication scholars, individual faculty members, research centers, or selected coursework often carry the flag for health communication in various academic units throughout the world. In such cases, individuals and collectives bring their own educational backgrounds and experiences to the table to guide health communication pursuits.

Each program or individual discipline involved in the training of health communication scholars has the responsibility to consider how to frame goals and priorities which inevitably vary along the lines of disciplinary identities. In reflecting on "what's in a name," then, different disciplines involved in health communication research and practice represent various perspectives about issues such as, "Can we validly talk about health communication processes without identifying the 'health' situation?" "Can we validly talk about health communication processes without identifying the verbal *and* nonverbal behaviors, or life stage of participants in the communication event?" Or, "Can we validly talk about health communication processes without considering the policies that limit behavior, the economic status of individuals and families or communities, and the access to and competencies for using a host of technologies linked to communication and to health?" The titles of many articles cited throughout this handbook suggest that principles of health communication remain constant, standing without reference to condition or communication content or life stage. Disciplinary identities would suggest otherwise, however, as health communication is pursued from multiple approaches.

Multidisciplinary Approaches to Health Communication

Multidisciplinary pursuits in health communication represent a large body of literature. This literature reflects the fact that many disciplines focus on communication in efforts to tackle health-related issues, with communication often seen as a *tool* to address a problem rather than a discipline guided by theory and practice. Communication may be examined as one dimension of a health problem, the communication dimension may be addressed by different disciplines acting independently in search of understanding, or the communication dimension may comprise the focus of a number of subdisciplines within larger disciplines—still without collaboration and too often unaware of each other's pursuits.

Multiple Disciplines Independently Address Multiple Dimensions of a Health Issue

Multidisciplinary pursuits in health communication reveal that in addition to approaches that reflect economic, genetic, environmental, and any number of other disciplinary efforts to address a health issue, communication is pursued as one dimension of a health issue. This may happen sequentially, building on the scientific knowledge of one discipline's findings to spark a hypothesis or research question in another discipline. For example, medical research revealed a role for folic acid in neural tube and other birth defects (Brundage, 2002). In turn, the March of Dimes began to promote folic acid to women of reproductive age. Health communication researchers sought to understand the effects of communicating about a role for folic acid on women's health practices. In other research, findings that sensation-seekers respond differently to drug prevention messages (Donohew et al., 1999) preceded research designed to examine whether high versus low sensation-seekers vary in the likelihood of carrying gene variants (Limosin, Loze, Rouillon, Ades, & Gorwood, 2003).

Multidisciplinary approaches to tackle the many dimensions of a health issue may also happen simultaneously. This may be reflected in research that reveals communication to be one dimension of many being pursued, sometimes in the same timeframe, especially as an issue reaches the public agenda. These efforts to resolve a problem are also undertaken without direct linkages among the approaches and too little if any insights about the various undertakings. Efforts to understand the increase in childhood obesity, for example, have been simultaneously examined from the purview of many disciplines without collaboration or recognition of one another's activities. An economic perspective (Wolf & Colditz, 1998) has considered families' food budgets and linked eating energy-dense foods, which include refined grains, fats, and added sugars, to their low cost, thereby revealing an implicit link to obesity (Drewnowski & Specter, 2004). At the same time, researchers examined the positive relationships between time spent being inactive—operationalized in terms of the number of hours spent watching TV, obesity, and hypertension rates (Pardee, Norman, Lustig, Preud'homme, & Schwimmer, 2007). Other approaches have considered how to promote physical activity via leveraging various channels to disseminate the promotion message. These included comparisons of local media, websites, workplace projects, and schools (De Cocker, De Bourdeaudhuij, Brown, & Cardon, 2007). Each project contributes to the understanding about contributors to obesity from the purview of a different field. The latter study suggests that the communication dimension of the issue could be addressed by many disciplines, including mass communication, information sciences, organizational studies, and education, each with disciplinary driven insights about research questions or hypotheses.

Multiple Disciplines Independently Address the Communication Dimension of a Health Issue

A second multidisciplinary approach to health communication to address a problem reflects

6

"who" undertakes the work designed to address the communication dimension. Someone with a medical background may undertake efforts to address communication between doctors and patients. A pediatrician, for example, Dr. Barbara Korsch is credited with bringing a core focus on communication into clinical practice. In the 1960s, Korsch identified some traditional barriers to effective communication in medical interactions, including doctors' use of medical jargon (Korsch, Gozzi, & Francis, 1968) during pediatric consultations. In the inaugural issue of the journal *Health Communication*, Korsch (1989) summarized the status of research relating to medical interactions that had taken place since her ground-breaking studies in the 1960s, emphasizing the research findings to support the importance of respecting a patient's autonomy and goals. Building on this foundation, someone might undertake research with an emphasis on how nonverbal behaviors communicate respect for autonomy. Someone else might tackle the autonomy issue by considering the physical layout of a room and its accessibility when a door opens, revealing or not revealing a patient in the room.

Approaches to address communication as one dimension of a health issue might be undertaken by psychologists, sociologists, communication scientists, or specialists in new technologies—to name but a few. In this era when genomics has a role in health care, for example, health policy makers consider the ethics of direct-to-consumer (DTC) advertising of genetic testing, advertising researchers consider the effects of DTC ads on consumer behavior, and genetic counselors consider the effects of DTC ads on clients' understanding, to name but a few of the disciplines with an interest in the communication effects of DTC ads. Each path leads to conclusions that become grist for the health communication mill, as revealed in the DeLorme et al. chapter in this volume. All can and often are conducted in relative isolation from each other, which challenges health communication researchers to keep pace with the work.

Academics in public health approach health communication as influenced by their particular disciplinary background as well. Public health curricula have aligned around training in biostatistics, epidemiology, environmental health sciences, health services administration, and the social and behavioral sciences, with informatics and communication, as well as genomics enriching the scope of training (Gebbie, Rosenstock, Hernandez, & Committee on Educating Public Health Professionals, 2003). This educational background has, for example, guided health policy researchers to explore effects of warning labels and nutrition labels mandated for use on consumer products. Epidemiologists and biostatisticians have examined whether such risk information has differential effects when it is presented in absolute versus relative terms. Other epidemiologists conduct mapping studies to determine whether exposure to information about dangerous products varies based on where you live or demographic characteristics. A multidisciplinary approach to the communication dimension of a health issue may thus develop a richer understanding based on the frames formed from different disciplinary approaches. This may be the result of pursuits based on the work of various subdisciplines as well.

Subdisciplines of Various Disciplines Independently Address the Communication Dimension of a Health Issue

Multidisciplinary pursuits also occur within subdisciplines of broader disciplines that pursue health communication. Public relations researchers, as one unit within a college of communication, for example, may study the images of health care organizations, while advertising researchers within the same college consider how advertising the services of health care organizations relates to credibility perceptions. Relational or family communication scholars, whose home is more likely to be within a college of liberal arts and a department devoted to "communication," might consider whether marital partners tell one another their impressions about health care organizations based on seeing such ads. These pursuits may build on one another sequentially, as when the relational scholar reads the advertising research and then frames a research hypothesis regarding couples' treatment decisions—but without collaboration with the advertising researchers. Or the work may happen simultaneously without linking to others' research, as when a relational scholar pursues understanding about treatment decisions and learns that advertisements are one variable relating to choices made, while advertising scholars examine audience perceptions of organizational credibility and discern the ads' influence on couples.

The possibility of a range of perspectives to guide health communication is also evident within the core disciplines that form public health or medicine as overarching disciplines. Within departments of social and behavioral sciences, one of the core disciplines of public health, reside psychologists, sociologists, anthropologists, as well as those from education, communication, community development, and a host of health science disciplines such as nursing, nutrition and dietetics, and physical therapy. When a single department is devoted to one of these disciplines, such as nutrition, the proximity of other nutritionists supports the likelihood of greater awareness of the scope of nutrition approaches to health communication. When a unit includes one nutritionist and a half dozen other social and behavioral scientists representing different subdisciplines, the proximity of those researchers supports the likelihood of greater awareness of a range of research across these areas but perhaps less conversation about varied approaches to nutrition. In either situation, pursuit of health communication without collaboration with others risks redundancies and inefficiencies based on the challenges common to multidisciplinary pursuits.

When health communicators adhere strictly to the content of a single discipline or subdiscipline without awareness of other approaches, they too often make "discoveries" that other disciplines have long known about and create inconsistent vocabularies which limit the translation of research into benefits. A multidisciplinary review of the research relating to continuity of care, for example, reveals that efforts to describe the problem and advance solutions face the use of inconsistent vocabulary in which "continuum of care," "coordination of care," "discharge planning," "case management," and "integration of services" appear to be used interchangeably (Haggerty et al., 2003). A lack of awareness may be more likely in the conduct of multidisciplinary pursuits, where the "lone wolf" researcher functions in isolation to build "novel" insights based on a single discipline's or subdiscipline's theories and published research. Fortunately, multidisciplinary teams frequently share findings with one another, or in efforts to be aware of the ongoing research in an area, researchers discover one another, which contributes to interdisciplinary pursuits.

Interdisciplinary Approaches to Health Communication

That health communication is interdisciplinary has not escaped the notice of several of the best scholars within health communication...questions linking the communication process and the health setting are not the sole domain of health communication scholars....

(Nussbaum, 1989, p. 36)

Reasons to collaborate in pursuit of interdisciplinary health communication are numerous. Interdisciplinary research broadens the research agenda, increasing the likely validity of the conclusions related to the research. Additionally, these linkages increase the likelihood that effective health programs and health promotion strategies will be institutionalized. To pursue interdisciplinary health communication research requires collaborators to bring their view to the table as *a* contribution but not *the* contribution (Parrott & Steiner, 2003). Interdisciplinary research thus requires respect for the contributions that other disciplines offer to understanding. Health communicators pursuing interdisciplinary research often face the need to become competent in new vocabularies (Parrott, 2008). The goal is not to become expert but rather to understand others who are expert and ask intelligent questions, a pursuit that requires time and commitment, which can be barriers to such scholarly engagement. As with multidisciplinary pursuits, the ways to view interdisciplinary research vary.

Multiple Disciplines Collaboratively Address Multiple Dimensions of a Health Issue

One view of health communication as an interdisciplinary pursuit advances communication as *one* dimension of a health issue that should be addressed collaboratively. As a team, different disciplines work together to plan, implement, and evaluate efforts to improve individual and public health. As such, they bring different strengths, perspectives, and weaknesses to health communication endeavors. Parrott is part of such a team that is addressing the human papillomavirus (HPV) from the perspectives of basic clinical research to "type" the virus, epidemiological research to determine incidence and prevalence, educational research to inform college-age women about HPV, and informed consent research to communicate about the goals of participating in HPV clinical trials. Recruitment to clinical trials is a complex health communication issue that has layered nuances linked to the type of trial and the condition of focus in the trial, as well as cultural, social, and personal views.

In some situations, interdisciplinary health communication research helps all involved to avoid wasting resources. The "lone wolf" communication scientist who does not collaborate with public health or medical researchers, for example, may design an intervention that the public health or medical system would never adopt because it overlooks a well-accepted practice linked to informed consent, a law relating to liability and disclosure, or is impractical given the real-world constraints of public health practice settings. The "lone wolf" public health or medical researcher who does not collaborate with someone whose expertise comes from the discipline of communication may design an intervention that asks for disclosures which the communication researcher would never recommend because of the face wants and privacy needs of the person being asked the questions.

Multiple Disciplines Collaboratively Address the Communication Dimension of a Health Issue

It is widely accepted that communication leads to understanding or influence related to health across all levels of an ecological model (i.e., individual, interpersonal, institutional, community, society). The core content of different disciplines, however, reveals a range of approaches to prioritizing the role of individual and societal level theories in explaining communication processes and outcomes, and thus different points of entré in the communication process. Disciplines may also "disagree" about the role of societal versus individual responsibility in a situation, and the priorities for research and practice based on the "evidence." In collaboration, various disciplinary views may represent communication in research that more holistically represents processes related to a health issue.

Public health and medical priorities may lead to the solicitation of personal information to guide priorities in collecting data for disease registries, allocating resources to health and health care needs, and recognizing gaps in policy and health law. Our cooperation with disclosure of personal information in medical and public health settings is frequently an important part of achieving personal and societal health priorities. Communication theory and research provides a framework for understanding and predicting individual feelings of privacy violations associated with these disclosures, complicated by computerization of health information. Researchers from psychology may emphasize the effects of disclosure on individual self-concept, while health policy researchers may acknowledge that disclosures can impact health insurance coverage. Working in collaboration, these disciplinary insights into the communication process suggest barriers that should be addressed before attempting to gain personal disclosures.

Subdisciplines of Various Disciplines Collaboratively Address the Communication Dimension of a Health Issue

Parent disciplines often encompass a range of subdisciplines that offer their own theories and views about priorities linked to communication which may be applied to health issues. When intradisciplinary groups are working collaboratively to address the communication dimension of a health issue, they must make decisions about: (a) collecting and interpreting formative data at the individual versus dyadic versus group versus societal levels; (b) working with diverse audiences and groups, ranging from patients to parents to policy makers and opinion leaders representing the various levels; (c) reframing issues as personal, social, cultural, *and* societal, rather than *or*; and (d) analyzing and formulating findings with an eye toward standards of care and public policy (Maibach, Parrott, Long, & Salmon, 1994).

Intradisciplinary pursuits aimed at the communication dimension of a health issue afford a greater likelihood of considering a fuller spectrum of both rewards and challenges associated with health communication. In the public health realm, for example, strong evidence exists that the HPV vaccine reduces the risk of cervical cancer for many girls and young women. Viewed from the perspective of protecting the public's health or from the profit motive perspective of a vaccine manufacturer, the role of communication might be to reach as many women as possible with persuasive messages about getting vaccinated. Alternatively, others will see the role of communication in HPV vaccination as informed decision making, not widespread promotion. Still others will study public discourse about the vaccine, including media coverage, advertising, and policy debates. Taken together, researchers who collaborate to approach HPV prevention from the perspectives of family, medical, and public health systems provide a richer understanding of the challenges of communicating about the HPV vaccine and also a broader set of options for cancer control professionals. The contribution of different areas of communication, public health, medicine, or other parent disciplines toward understanding these processes is both exciting and sobering. Such endeavors also increase the likelihood that health communication will make advances in efforts to conduct transdisciplinary research.

Transdisciplinary Health Communication Research: Strategic Efforts to Leverage Serendipity

The hallmark of transdisciplinary science is *intellectual integration*, including cross-fertilization of theoretical perspectives (Stokols et al., 2003). In health communication, for example, integrative models that include medical and epidemiological approaches in concert with behavioral science approaches lead to novel innovations and insights that go beyond a single discipline's theories and systems. Transdisciplinary approaches to research thus aim to *transcend* disciplinary boundaries and to reach for innovations beyond those more narrowly constructed fields defined by various departments in academic settings. A growing number of transdisciplinary health communication undertakings, for example, focus on urban planning perspectives. One project that promotes physical activity proposes to unite urban planning with personal level perspectives aimed at motivation and physical activity literature to advance a model that includes urban design, transportation planning, and land use as variables related to self-determination, stages of change, and reasoned action (King, Stokols, Talen, Brassington, & Killingsworth, 2002).

The broad aim of transdisciplinary research relates to removing barriers to thought about what might be possible if we harnessed all knowledge, without regard to disciplinary borders, in generating solutions to health issues. "Think tanks," academic funded research teams, online virtual groups, and consulting practices offer alternative organizational formats to traditional academic departments in efforts to promote transdisciplinary initiatives. Transdisciplinary health communication research is thus not about approaching communication as one dimension of a health issue, or representing numerous disciplinary or subdisciplinary approaches to communication. While fewer models exist to support insights about transdisciplinary undertakings, some lessons may be gleaned from existing efforts and might be applied when considering the utility of this approach to a problem.

Lessons Learned from Transdisciplinary Endeavors

Case studies afford one way to reveal how transdisciplinary endeavors evolve and may be sustained (Scholz, Lang, Wiek, Walter, & Stauffachwer, 2006). The Community Health Research Unit (CHRU), for example, illustrates two common realities: (a) these endeavors likely involve many organizations, and (b) funding supports formal linkages to encourage and enable the activities (Maclean, Plotnikoff, & Moyer, 2000). CHRU received funding from the Ontario Ministry of Health and cosponsorship with the University of Ottawa's Department of Epidemiology and Community Medicine, together with the School of Nursing and the Ottawa-Carleton Health Department (Maclean et al., 2000). The perspectives evident in this unit cross multiple disciplines and systems of public health and health care to reflect an innovative approach to community health.

Practical concerns that align with transdisciplinary efforts include some of the same associated with interdisciplinary research. These include the need to find a common vocabulary, harness the time to collaborate, establish an egalitarian group climate, and gain members' commitment (Maclean et al., 2000). To address the need for a common vocabulary requires the same desire and respect to learn from each other that interdisciplinary pursuits engender. One approach to address the "time" commitment involves use of a *collaboratory*, in which engineering and computer science focus on designing systems for purposes of supporting scientific collaboration (Bly, 1998). Such groups develop digital libraries to enlarge the scope of research being shared with each other, and enable data collection and analysis across multiple sites, reducing the lack of awareness of ongoing work across and within various disciplines. Synchronous audio- or videoconferencing extends the opportunities for interaction which may enhance more equal participation by all in a group. Leadership that sets some boundaries for involvement in transdisciplinary initiatives has an explicit opportunity to define the concrete parameters of a member's commitment to such an endeavor.

One of the most recognized benefits associated with transdisciplinary research is a higher quality solution to a health issue (Maclean et al., 2000). There is, however, also worry expressed about transdisciplinary efforts contributing to the dilution of disciplines, resulting in the inability of individuals to explain a discipline's unique contribution to knowledge generation (Maclean et al., 2000). When academic institutions' survival is threatened by an economic downturn, departments may be required to present such arguments regarding the uniqueness of contributions, but even in settings where financial worries do not predominate, individuals frequently must present evidence of the unique role they play and justify its merits. An irony arises around innovation in the face of tensions linked to tough economic times, as these are often the result of institutional environments placing greater rather than less emphasis on innovation with the hope of sparking scientific revolution, which appears more likely to occur in the presence of transdisciplinary endeavors.

Innovative methodologies and new technologies afford opportunities for transdisciplinary pursuits that simply were not possible in the past. For example, Rimer and Kreuter (2006) argue that major improvements in computing power and the emergence of desktop publishing in the early 1990s made possible the revolution in tailored health communication. Tailoring is a clear product of transdisciplinary convergence among epidemiology (identifying behavioral risk factors and calculating personal risk estimates), communication (analyzing and segmenting audiences), and behavioral science (using stage theories to identify individuals more and less ready to change health behaviors). It would not have been feasible without these technologies. More recently, the use of geographic information systems (GIS) is making possible myriad new transdisciplinary collaborations in health communication (Parrott et al., 2010). For example, to help eliminate breast cancer disparities among African American women, Kreuter and colleagues (Kreuter, Alcarez, Pfeiffer, & Christopher, 2008; Kreuter, Black et al., 2006) used touch-screen computer information kiosks to deliver an evidence-based mammography intervention in six different community settings—beauty salons, laundromats, churches, health centers, social service agencies, and public libraries. To determine which settings were most promising for cancer education outreach, the evaluation drew upon outcomes from communication (e.g., reach) and public health (e.g., need for breast cancer screening), but also used GIS to determine where women lived relative to where they used the kiosk. Use of this technology, as discussed by Morgan et al. in this volume, contributed to findings which showed laundromats to be the most promising setting for community outreach, reaching more women who needed mammograms than any other setting, but also reaching the most geographically localized population. In turn, this GIS finding will lead to new transdisciplinary collaborations between health communicators and cancer surveillance systems, to identify and address areas with high concentrations of breast cancer incidence and mortality.

Examples of Organized Transdisciplinary Health Communication Research

The translation of research into benefits for society has motivated funders to focus on transdisciplinary activities, as illustrated by the National Institute of Drug Abuse and National

Cancer Institute's (NCI) commitment of resources to transdisciplinary tobacco use research centers (Morgan et al., 2003) and NCI's commitment of resources to Centers of Excellence for Cancer Communication Research. These Centers support transdisciplinary science, and provide training and career development to prepare a next generation of researchers to conduct this type of science. The University of Pennsylvania's Transdisciplinary Tobacco Use Research Center, for example, aims to improve treatment for nicotine dependence via translation of findings from neuroscience, pharmacology, genetics, and behavioral science, as illustrated by looking at smokers' reactions to advertising that promotes low nicotine cigarettes.

The Center of Excellence in Cancer Communication Research at Washington University in St. Louis directed by Kreuter aims to help eliminate cancer disparities by increasing the reach and effectiveness of health information to low income and minority populations and using communication technologies to connect them to cancer control services in their community. These efforts are led by transdisciplinary research teams from public health, journalism, marketing, clinical medicine, social services, psychology, and a range of other disciplines. For example, one study proposes that people living in poverty often need help meeting basic needs before prevention can emerge as a priority (*i.e., hierarchy of needs from psychology*). Therefore, it may be necessary to first link them to programs designed to address these needs (*i.e., community-based public assistance programs from social service*), then provide access to systems of cancer prevention and control that do not require insurance or resources (*i.e., screening and prevention programs from public health*), and finally, provide tangible support to help them overcome obstacles and navigate complex systems to receive needed cancer control services (*i.e., case management from social work*). The resulting solution to be tested involves integrating proactive cancer risk assessment and referral to control services into the United Way's "2-1-1 Information and Referral System." These transdisciplinary examples serve as sites for transdisciplinary education as well.

Other models of experience with and exposure to transdisciplinary research have emerged as well, with many university settings, including colleges that are comprised exclusively of centers that tenure line faculty affiliate with based on teaching and research interests, without any supervisory department affiliations. Faculty members in these settings have often been hired since the dawn of the 21st century and are approaching promotion and tenure decisions. Having served as reviewers in some of these cases for various institutions across the nation, we have identified a set of reflections around transdisciplinary health communication research. To advance these, we look to a case study published in the late 1950s to frame them.

Rules for the Road in Conducting Transdisciplinary Research

A review of the researchers, research, and organizational paradigms in which transdisciplinary research is being conducted reveals that this is not an approach to be used for every research question or hypothesis. The resources needed are extensive and the investment is intensive. We look to the case of the floppy-eared rabbits told by Barber and Fox, published in 1958, to suggest several principles to guide reflection about undertaking health communication transdisciplinary endeavors. This case emphasizes how the disciplinary lens through which one views the world may lead to the viewer forming blinders, contributing to instances of serendipity lost—failure to take advantage of the element of chance in an unexpected outcome to unveil an innovative insight (Barber & Fox, 1958, p. 128). Two scientists observed that after injecting the enzyme papain, rabbits experienced the collapse of their ears, but only one scientist made a new scientific discovery related to the cartilage of rabbit ears as a result of the observation. In the analysis by Barber and Fox (1958), the course of discovery reveals a path that in today's era could be used to guide an intentional transdisciplinary undertaking. Perhaps the overall integrative message in the Barber and Fox analysis and this chapter is that *where one places priority in the examination of an issue often leads to different outcomes.* While this statement seems patently obvious and overly simplistic, its reality cannot be lost in considering the various approaches to health communication discussed in this chapter and the goal to transcend disciplinary boundaries in order to advance understanding.

Transdisciplinary researchers must be willing to step outside not only the theoretical realm in which they are most comfortable but also to go beyond their usual methods, whatever these might be. In extracting insights from the Barber and Fox (1958) analysis, it is telling to start with the observation that in-depth qualitative research led to these revelations. Barber and Fox (1958) conducted extensive interviews of the "scientists," Thomas and Kellner, in the floppy-eared rabbit case. The use of qualitative research, as well as new technologies, social network analysis, and community organizing are among the methods available to engender integrative insights to link disciplines that work in health communication. Through qualitative research, Barber and Fox learned that both Thomas and Kellner had experienced serendipitous discoveries in their own research in the past. In fact, each could identify specific situations in which they had used an unexpected outcome to make a new scientific discovery. They could also recall situations in which they missed the opportunity to make a discovery. Their reflections support several conclusions.

The first reason to undertake transdisciplinary approaches relates to the reality that an explanation of an event falls (a) *outside the boundaries of our traditional disciplinary explanations.* At the outset, both Thomas and Kellner pursued the floppy-eared rabbit result, unexpected as it was, through the view of their own disciplines. Thomas, guided by his training and disciplinary experiences, cut sections of the rabbit ears to observe them, but found no change in the connective tissue and no inflammation or tissue damage. Not judging the issue to be related to the cartilage of the rabbit's ear, he only superficially examined the cartilage, letting his preconceived though "expert" expectations guide his efforts. Kellner's scientific training related to muscle tissue, so he, too, paid little attention to changes in cartilage. In communication science applications to health issues, efforts to promote regular health screenings have sometimes revealed that some in an intended audience respond as desired and others do not. A look at the availability of care might reveal no differences between those who had health insurance and those who did not, but among those who live within a certain distance of screening sites, differences in uptake may emerge. A map of the topographic characteristics could reveal that some literally have to go over a mountain to reach a site for screening, which suggests that a transdisciplinary approach to explain screening behavior could render novel explanations that communication science alone would not provide.

Transdisciplinary approaches also appear to be best utilized to explain an event (b) *which occurs with such regularity that it rules out randomness as an explanation.* Both Thomas and Kellner observed the floppy-eared rabbit phenomenon time and again, contributing to a desire to explain what caused the ears to flop. Similarly, health communicators observe time and again that patients are unable to recall details about their family health histories. This continues to occur despite repeated public health and clinical efforts encouraging us to know our family health histories. Most of us do not know the kinds of details doctors could use to guide informed choices for genetic testing linked to our health in this era of genomic health care. This reality presents an opportunity that might frame the focus of a group brought together from many disciplines to consider how to integrate their insights to form an innovative approach to understanding barriers and motivators linked to communicating about family health histories.

Transdisciplinary approaches also appear to be best utilized to explain an event (c) *in which we sustain interest and want to discuss with colleagues from many backgrounds to inform our own thoughts;* or (d) *that we use to demonstrate a phenomenon to students in service of learning.* The scientist Thomas, who made the serendipitous discovery relating to floppy-eared rabbits, observed that he found himself over *years* of thought about the unexplained phenomenon never losing interest in it and sometimes even demonstrating it to doubters. These informal dialogues guided his thoughts, eventually leading to a novel hypothesis and explanation. Thomas also talked about the floppy-eared rabbit event and demonstrated it in teaching pathology to second-year medical students. In the case of health communication research, the phenomenon relating to widening gaps between knowledge and behavior after an intervention has been planned and delivered guided conversations and generated insights that resulted from interdisciplinary efforts. Still, this event continues to occur with unfortunate regularity, we find ourselves talking to colleagues about it—colleagues from different disciplines who afford us insights that might eventually lead to an integrative transdisciplinary approach.

Other insights derived from the case study of the floppy-eared rabbits that transcend the event to afford insights about health communication research include the realities that transdisicplinary research may best be pursued when: (e) *we have time;* and (f) *we have money.* Thomas had many trials and failures relating to the floppy-eared rabbit event, but when funds for rabbits to repeat trials ran out, Thomas temporarily stopped pursuing an explanation for the unexpected event. Thomas had other ongoing research that was proving to derive expected results and thus spent his time on that work. Health communication researchers and supporters who are considering transdisciplinary research should realize that it often takes funding to pursue research in novel ways with input from numerous disciplines and it always takes time to pursue research related to an unexpected finding. Having only so much time, we pursue research that we have some confidence will lead to a productive end.

Conclusion

Health communicators are challenged to keep pace with all the research being published that relates to their own areas of interest. This arises in response to the reality that health communication research is not limited to any specific disciplinary boundaries. Communication researchers may, however, act independently without consultation with health researchers when addressing communication related to a health issue. Health researchers may also act independently without consultation with communication researchers when addressing communication related to a health issue. While this creates conflict and confusion among theorists and practitioners alike, the stage is also set for us to benefit from taking stock of the theories used across multiple disciplines with intention to integrate them. These pursuits may form transdisciplinary visions which demand that we get out of our comfort zones when often we are challenged to maintain our research programs as evidence of having harnessed some small corner of expertise that not only we but also others can claim in justifying our positions.

Collaboration between communication and health professionals requires a willingness to be flexible about or even to compromise on closely held disciplinary values. As an example, public health applications of health communication often place a greater premium on pragmatism, while applications from communication scientists may emphasize fidelity with theory. If the ultimate goal of health communication is to help improve the health of individuals and populations, health communicators representing various disciplines and subdisciplines may need to adapt their expectations to make the most progress toward that goal. Just as highly practical research need not ignore theory, nor should we insist on a pure application of theory if it may compromise effectiveness and limit our motivation to integrate perspectives or generate a serendipitous discovery.

References

Barber, B., & Fox, R. C. (1958). The case of the floppy-eared rabbits: An instance of serendipity gained and serendipity lost. *The American Journal of Sociology, 64,* 128–136.

Bly, S. (1998). Collaboratories. *Interactions, 5,* 31.

Brundage, S. C. (2002). Preconception health care. *American Family Physician, 65,* 2507–2514.

Calhoun, J. G., Ramiah, K., Weist, E. M., & Shortell, S. M. (2008). Development of a core competency model for the master of public health degree. *American Journal of Public Health, 98,* 1598–1607.

De Cocker, K., De Bourdeaudhuij, I. Brown, W., & Cardon, G. (2007). Effects of "10,000 steps Ghent": A whole-community intervention. *American Journal of Preventive Medicine, 33,* 455–463.

Donohew, R. L., Hoyle, R. H., Clayton, R. R., Skinner, W. F., Colon, S. E., & Rice, R. E. (1999). Sensation seeking and drug use by adolescents and their friends: Models for marijuana and alcohol. *Journal of Studies on Alcohol, 60,* 622–631.

Drewnowski, A., & Specter, S. E. (2004). Poverty and obesity: The role of energy density and energy costs. *The American Journal of Clinical Nutrition, 79,* 6–16.

Edgar, T., & Hyde, J. N. (2005). An alumni-based evaluation of graduate training in health communication: Results of a survey on careers, salaries, competencies, and emerging trends. *Journal of Health Communication, 10,* 5–25.

Gebbie, K., Rosenstock, L., Hernandez, L., & Committee on Educating Public Health Professionals for the 21st Century (2003). *Who will keep the public healthy? Educating public health professionals for the 21st century.* Washington, DC: National Academies of Sciences Press.

Haggerty, J. L., Reid, R. J., Freeman, G. K., Starfield, B. H., Adair, C. E., & McKendry, R. (2003). Continuity of care: A multidisciplinary review. *British Medical Journal, 327,* 1219–1221.

King, A. C., Stokols, D., Talen, E., Brassington, G. S., & Killingsworth, R. (2002). Theoretical approaches to the promotion of physical activity: Forging a transdisciplinary paradigm. *American Journal of Preventive Medicine, 23*(2 Supplement), 15–25.

Korsch, B. (1989). Current issues in communication research. *Health Communication, 1,* 5–9.

Korsch, B. M., Gozzi, E. K., & Francis, V. (1968). Doctor–patient interaction and patient satisfaction. *Pediatrics, 42,* 855–871.

Kreps, G. L. (1989). Setting the agenda for health communication research and development: Scholarship that can make a difference. *Health Communication, 1,* 11–15.

Kreuter, M. W., Alcaraz, K. I., Pfeiffer, D., & Christopher, K. (2008). Using dissemination research to identify optimal community settings for tailored breast cancer information kiosks. *Journal of Public Health Management, 14,* 160–169.

Kreuter, M. W., Black, W. J., Friend, L., Booker, A. C., Klump, M. P., Bobra, S., & Holt, C. L. (2006). Use of computer kiosks for breast cancer education in five community settings. *Health Education & Behavior, 33,* 625–642.

Limosin, F., Loze, J., Rouillon, F., Ades, J., & Gorwood, P. (2003). Association between dopamine receptor D1 gene Dde l polymorphism and sensation seeking in alcohol-dependent men. *Alcoholism: Clinical & Experimental Research, 27,* 1226–1228.

Maclean, L. M., Plotnikoff, R. C., & Moyer, A. (2000). Transdisciplinary work with psychology from a population health perspective: An illustration. *Journal of Health Psychology, 5,* 173–181.

Maibach, E., Parrott, R. L., Long, D. M., & Salmon, C. T. (1994). Competencies for the health communication specialist of the 21st century. *American Behavioral Scientist, 38,* 351–360.

Morgan, G. D., Kobus, K., Gerlach, K. K., Neighbors, C., Leman, C., Abrams, D. B., & Rimer, B. K. (2003). Facilitating transdisciplinary research: The experience of the transdisciplinary tobacco use research centers. *Nicotine & Tobacco Research, 5,* S11–S19.

Nussbaum, J. (1989). Directions for research within health communication. *Health Communication, 1,* 35–40.

Pardee, P. E., Norman, G. J., Lustig, R. H., Preud'homme, D., & Schwimmer, J. B. (2007). Television viewing and hypertension in obese children. *American Journal of Preventive Medicine, 33,* 430–443.

Parrott, R. (2008). A multiple discourse approach to health communication: Translational research and ethical practice. *Journal of Applied Communication Research, 36,* 1–7.

Parrott, R., & Steiner, C. (2003). Lessons learned about academic and public health collaborations in the conduct of community-based research. In T. L. Thompson, A. M. Dorsey, K. Miller, & R. L. Parrott (Eds.), *Handbook of Health Communication* (pp. 637–650). Mahwah, NJ: Erlbaum.

Parrott, R., Volkman, J., Lengerich, E., Ghetian, C., Chadwick, A., & Hopfer, S. (2010). Community involvement: Use of geographic information systems for comprehensive cancer control. *Health Communication, 25,* 276–285.

Rimer, B. K., & Kreuter, M. W. (2006). Advancing tailored health communication: A persuasion and message effects perspective. *Journal of Commununication, 56*(Supplement), 184–201.

Rosenfield, P. L. (1992). The potential of transdisciplinary research for sustaining and extending linkages between the health and social sciences. *Social Science & Medicine, 35,* 1343–1357.

Saxe, J. G. (1873). *Poems of John Godfrey Saxe.* Boston, MA: James R. Osgood.

Scholz, R. W., Lang, D. J., Wiek, A., Walter, A. I., & Stauffachwer, M. (2006). Transdisciplinary case studies as a means of sustainability learning: Historical framework and theory. *International Journal of Sustainability in Higher Education, 7,* 226–251.

Stokols, D., Fuqua, J., Gress, J. Harvey, R., Phillips, K., Baezconde-Garbanati, L., ... Trochim, W. (2003, December). Evaluating transdisciplinary science. *Nicotine and Tobacco Research, 5*(Supplement 1), S21–S39.

Thompson, T. L. (1984). The invisible helping hand: The role of communication in the health and social service professions. *Communication Quarterly, 32,* 148–163.

Wolf, A. M., & Colditz, G. A. (1998). Current estimates of the economic cost of obesity in the United States. *Obesity Research, 6,* 97–106.

2

BUILDING HEALTH COMMUNICATION THEORIES IN THE 21ST CENTURY

Austin S. Babrow and Marifran Mattson

Recent reviews in the health communication literature might be taken by the unwary reader to reveal that theorizing and theory-based research are exceptional activities rather than the rule in this area. For instance, Beck et al. (2004) found that only 23% of 852 communication articles published in 19 journals in the years 1989 through February 2001 made explicit reference to theory within their abstracts. T. L. Thompson (2006) reported that only 13% of the 914 articles identified in William Evans's bibliographies published in *Health Communication* between 2005 and the first issue of the journal in 2006 were classified in his "Health Communication Theory and Research" category. These estimates surely understate the presence of theory in health communication scholarship. Many of the pieces that Evans places in the other categories within his organizing scheme are clearly theory-informed or informing, although perhaps not "health communication theory" per se (e.g., risk, health belief, planned behavior, narrative, metaphor, conversation analytic). Moreover, given the field's pragmatic interests, we should not be surprised if authors deemphasize theory in their abstracts. So these observations are surely lower (perhaps quite low) bounds of theory-informed/informing activity in this area. We can just as surely conclude that health communication scholars are not preoccupied with theory-building. In writing this chapter, we are motivated by the belief that theoretically informed/informing work is of the greatest importance in this late- or postmodern age.

This second edition of *The Routledge Handbook of Health Communication*, broadened by inclusion of 10 more chapters than the first edition, and produced less than a decade after that edition, bears striking testimony to perhaps the most significant characteristic of scholarship in the first decade of the 21st Century: the ongoing, accelerating expansion of the universe of knowledge. Although social constructionists abjure prediction, a working postpositivist might be tempted to say that this characteristic of scholarship was predicted by the constructionist claim that nothing in the material world requires it to be understood in any particular way (Gergen, 2009). We can understand the world in whatever ways we find meaningful, and our meanings are limited as much by creativity/habits of thought as by unyielding materiality.

The expanding universe of knowledge creates challenges. As knowledge expands, our grasp of it recedes. As new voices enter, dialogue becomes dissonance. The selectivity of all seeing and saying becomes all the more striking in the unseen and unsaid. And, of course, the more ambitious the assertion, the more inadequate it is likely to be—even as we are ever more needful of synthesis and summation.

Given these considerations, we have chosen to write this chapter on theorizing about health communication in ways that respect diversity and encourage mutually enriching dialogue across perspectives and interests. For instance, we understand meaningful health communication theory quite broadly as *consciously elaborated, justified, and uncertain understanding developed for the purpose of influencing practice related to health and illness* (Babrow & Mattson, 2003, discuss specific elements of this definition). We aim to foster such theorizing by (a) identifying several generative tensions in health communication and (b) reviewing various alternative conceptions of communication that can be put into fruitful dialogue with one another to further illuminate the tensions in health communication (also see Babrow & Mattson, 2003).

Generative Tensions in Health Communication Theory

Interplay of the Body and Communication

Health communication is significant for the pronounced and profound tensions and interplay between the realms of communication and the body. Zook's (1994) discussion of the biopsychosocial turn notes two aspects of this interplay: "the material existence of biochemical pathways between mind and body, and the effect of psychological, social, and cultural variables on personal health behaviors" (p. 354). As a powerful example of the former, Melzack's (2005) neuromatrix theory of pain suggests that communication processes and practices along with a variety of other inputs shape the neural network that produces sensations of pain. Another intriguing example is Floyd et al.'s (2007) demonstration that "communicating affection following exposure to an acute stressor accelerates adrenocortical recovery" (p. 130). But on reflection, the distinction between direct pathways and presumably indirect influences of communicative practices on the body and health behavior is hard to sustain (see Zook, 1994).

Physical disease shapes communication, from a pointed cry of pain to grumbling complaints, and from information- to diagnosis- to support-seeking. As noted above, these communication acts and processes in turn influence bodily states (e.g., generalized or specific distress, or relief; again see Floyd, et al., 2007; also see Lazarus, 1991, ch. 10), and so on. Moreover, these specific and local experiences of the interplay of communication and the body are shaped by:

> Powerful social and cultural forces influencing individuals' behavior.... Communities form individuals' behavior symbolically and tangibly.... As agents of the dominant culture, communities transmit values and norms that symbolically circumscribe some behavioral choices and encourage others. As systems of exchange and influence ... communities establish opportunities for people to behave in some ways, but not in others.
>
> (Finnegan & Viswanath, 1990, p. 20)

Hence, the communicative interweaving of bodily sensation, cognitive-emotional sense-making, and various layers of social structures and practices fabricate the social meaning of physical states and the physical meaning of social states.

The interplay of body and communication is powerfully illustrated in the processes by which physical sensations and diseases are conceptualized and labeled. For example, cultural variations in the language we use to talk about our bodily states are revealing. Culture shapes how we label our physical states, and clearly we react to and treat ailments differently depending on how they are labeled. This dilemma was noted in Cassell's (1985) landmark work on doctor–patient talk: "How do doctors ever make a diagnosis? How can we distinguish between a 'terrible' (Jewish) pain and an 'annoying' (Irish) pain?" (pp. 53–54). Obviously, then, the interplay of language and bodily sensations shapes illness experience; these interactions are themselves shaped by historically bound socio-cultural processes.

Studies of metaphor also reveal the interplay of body and communication. For instance, consider analyses of metaphor in domains such as cancer (Harrow, Wells, Humphris, Taylor, & Williams, 2008; Sontag, 1978), infectious disease (Sontag, 1989; Wallis & Nerlich, 2005), and death and dying (Rallison, Limacher, & Clinton, 2006). Such work reveals that figurative conceptualizations of the body and bodily processes, such as disease and dying, shape understanding, attitudes, experiences of the body, and action.

In a curious turn, Sontag's (1978) analysis of the role of metaphorical conceptualizations of illness led her to "call for a kind of linguistic cleansing of medical and lay attitudes toward disease such that the true biological core of disease can be apprehended and distinguished from its metaphorical extensions" (Aronowitz, 1998, p. 13). Sontag's turn is curious because medical historians have demonstrated repeatedly the difficulty of apprehending "the biological core of disease unadulterated by attitudes, beliefs, and social conditions" (Aronowitz, 1998, p. 13). Indeed, our labels and conceptualizations of disease are continually reconfigured by developments in social attitudes (e.g., homosexuality and a host of women's conditions), diagnostic tests, and treatments (see Caplan, McCartney, & Sisti, 2004). For instance, Aronowitz (1998) discusses "the increasing number of new diseases rendered discoverable by our advanced technological capacity … [including] 'diseases' that have no corresponding phenomenological basis until a patient is found or 'constructed' by screening tests" (p. 37). Similarly, new drugs affect not only bodily states but also disease categories, and therefore our understanding of emotional and physical health. This is powerfully illustrated in the ways that psychoactive drugs have reconfigured conceptions of mental illnesses and treatment and in debates about these drugs, their uses, and their effects on conceptions of illness and health care (Kramer, 1993; also see Babrow & Mattson, 2003).

In short, diagnostic criteria, disease labeling, treatment, as well as associated reimbursement, sick role, and myriad other aspects of illness are shaped in communicative constructions of the social, cultural, political, economic, and material worlds. For instance, consider the process by which a panel of medical experts reached consensus on a narrow, "objective" definition of and diagnostic criteria for Lyme disease.

> The panel was not unaware that this definition would sever the diagnosis from many patients whom Lyme disease specialists would rather not treat, including those who questioned medical authority, did not play by the sick role rules, had depression or other psychiatric conditions, had low thresholds for seeking medical care, had heightened awareness of their own bodily processes, or worst of all, did not improve with known treatments. The critical appraisal of medical evidence could not be separated from knowledge of who would be the likely winners and losers if Lyme disease were defined one way or another. To no one's surprise, attempts such as this one to keep symptom clusters out of the Lyme disease definition have been controversial.
>
> (Aronowitz, 2004, p. 71)

Thus, in many ways, health communication is significant for the pronounced and profound interplay of the body and communication. Theories of health communication ought to at least recognize this interplay. Theories that emphasize this interdependence have the potential to illuminate one of the signal characteristics of health communication.

Science and Humanism

A second distinctive and generative characteristic of health communication is the pronounced tension between scientific and humanistic assumptions, values, aspirations, and limitations. What we have in mind here are the sometimes discordant interests people have in the power and potentialities of science and the desire to recognize and actualize our human being. This tension has many manifestations; it is evident in debates about biomedical vs. biopsychosocial models, disease vs. illness, technique vs. meaning, conflicts about alternative therapies, and medical ethics. For instance, the movement toward biopsychosocial models has not only recognized the interplay between the body and communication, but the debate also has exemplified tensions between the traditional scientific imperatives of materialism and reductionism on the one hand and efforts to understand the significance of mental or ideational human realities on the other (see Anderson, 1996, ch. 2). In saying this, we do not mean to equate humanistic and biopsychosocial models, for the latter can be thought of as scientific. Rather, we mean to say that this approach, more so than traditional biomedical health care, attempts to recognize the human meanings of disease.

A poignant illustration of the contrast and tensions between scientific and humanistic orientations is found in contemporary attitudes and practices related to death and dying (see Ariès, 1981; Kuhse, 2002). One of the most provocative analyses in this area is Ernest Becker's (1984) contention that human society is the result of our inability to face the fact of our mortality; seen in this view, both science and humanism are elaborate systems of meaning constructed to sublimate our fear of death.

Certainly, in much of the "developed" world, changes in nutrition, sanitation, engineering safety, and medical technology have caused a shift in the nature of our dying, from death shortly after the abrupt onset of an acute illness or injury, to death after lengthy, often multiple chronic illnesses (Callahan, 2000). Ethicist Daniel Callahan (2000) has argued that these changes have created a practical paradox in health care; as medical science and technology have gained control over a widening array of assaults on our lives, the process of dying has become more agonizing. Contemporary medicine has replaced the certainty of death from a given illness, at a given hour, with the uncertainty of a vanishing line between life and death (Callahan, 2000). Yet despite the uncertainty, encouraged by scientific discoveries and technological innovation, we have become a death avoidant culture (Nuland, 1993). Callahan contends that we have lost the willingness and perhaps the capacity to talk openly about death except in the bloodless technical terms of medicine and the law. And while there have been some encouraging developments in discourse on the process of dying and meaning of death (e.g., Keeley & Yingling, 2007), even in the literature one would expect to be most open to and searching in its consideration of the meaning of death, such as work on palliative care, there persists an emphasis on the biomedical to the near exclusion of the meanings of dying and death (Ragan, Wittenberg, & Hall, 2003; also see Ragan, Wittenberg-Lyles, Goldsmith, & Sanchez-Reilly, 2008).

In short, Callahan (2000) argues, we have been attempting to control death through monomaniacal scientific and technological efforts. As a result, death has lost much of its meaning. We have become insensitive to the most profound challenges posed by critical illness and death—the ancient and unanswered questions about human existence raised by dying. Most notably, in the blinkered pursuit of control, we have obscured a fundamental, age-old question that embodies our deep ambivalence about death: whether it "should be fought or accepted" (Callahan, 2000, p. 89; O'Hair et al., 2003). Since we cannot and should not go back to a time when we were powerless to deal with mortal illness and death, Callahan argues, we must find ways to deal more forthrightly with this ancient question. We must, in short, face and refashion our understandings of nature and death, and ultimately, of what it means to live human life. Science cannot do this, but neither can we undertake the necessary private and public discussion without recognizing the powerful imperatives of science. Hence, as revealed in this most basic example, a profoundly significant characteristic of health communication is the pronounced tension between scientific and humanistic assumptions, values, aspirations, and limitations.

Idiosyncrasy and Commonality

A third characteristic of health communication is the tension between idiosyncrasy and commonality. Of course, this tension reflects the challenge of intersubjectivity or identification in all communication. That is, if meaning is inescapably experiential, and if no two people share a common history, then shared meaning is a problematic notion. However, what we want to say about health communication is that it is distinct because of the ways that it magnifies the tension between our uniqueness and commonality.

One of the ways that this occurs is in debates between advocates of two major models of disease/illness.

> Historians of medicine have labeled as "ontological" the view that diseases are specific entities that unfold in characteristic ways in the typical person. In this framework, diseases exist in some platonic sense outside their manifestations in a particular individual. The other compelling account of illness, the "physiological" or "holistic," stresses the individual and his or her adaptation, both psychological and physical, to a changing environment. In this framework, illness exists only in individuals. These ideal-typical notions have been in a state of dynamic tension since antiquity.
>
> (Aronowitz, 1998, p. 8)

Ontologically inclined thinkers "question whether one has to treat the 'whole person' if one can rid him or her speedily and painlessly of disease and hence prevent the necessity of a long-term 'association' with the medical professional" (Jenkins, 1998, p. 354). Although some people would like to see such practices enforced with boot leather applied to the rear of recalcitrant patients, those more inclined toward the holistic orientation respond by arguing that disease/illness is frequently not that simple to treat, and that the force of medical authority is often countered by reactance (Fogarty, 1997; also see the discussion of "noncompliance" below); more generally, "physiologic, psychological, and social processes are uniquely combined in any single person to constitute illness" (Aronowitz, 2004, p. 71).

The debate between ontological and holistic models of disease/illness reflects the basic tension between idiosyncrasy and commonality in health communication. This tension constitutes a fault line in scholarly conceptions of health care and promotion, within the interactions of patients and care providers, and in the conceptions of risk as they are understood by health communicators and their audience members. For example, the tension is reflected in the ever-present possibility of debates over relative expertise, what counts as legitimate evidence, the meanings of (relative) risk, decision making, and so on.

In addition to the varying models of disease/illness, the tension between idiosyncrasy and commonality is also manifested in the values of affirming the personal meanings of an illness (and by extension our life and being) on the one hand and affirming our common humanity on the other. For instance, illness is at once a private and public matter. We strip illness of its public significance when we promote patients' individual autonomy as if it were the only significant human value (Callahan, 2000; Smith, 1996). Indeed, we strip ourselves of our humanity when we promote autonomy as our cardinal value. "Human beings will and must be a burden on one another; the flight from dependency is a flight from human-ity" (Callahan, 2000, p. 127). Of course, we also stand to lose when we deny the individual significance of illness. While we all become sick and eventually die, each pain—particularly in the way it is expressed—marks out our individuality, and each death is the loss of a voice that will never speak again.

One other subtle but profoundly important manifestation of the tension between idio-syncrasy and commonality arising in health communication is reflected in the dialectic of the human propensity toward routinization and mindlessness on the one hand and mind-ful sense-making on the other (see Babrow, 2007). For example, Ellingson (2007) has described the competing movements toward routinization and adaptation in dialysis care. This tension reflects among the most basic characteristics of mind, as conceived in Piaget's (1985) theory of the dialectic of assimilation and accommodation in cognitive development; it is also undoubtedly related to our sense of uncertainty/certainty (see Babrow, Kasch, & Ford, 1998, for a discussion related to "medicine as the management of uncertainty," and particularly "(un)certainty (un)seen"; also see next tension). But even though these mani-festations of tension between idiosyncrasy and commonality are not distinctive features of health communication, the values at stake in illness make the tension uniquely significant. To further develop this idea, we turn to one more vital tension in health communication.

(Un)Certainties and Values (e.g., Expectations and Desires)

Uncertainty is central to illness experiences (Atkinson, 1995; Katz, 1984). In their review of the meanings of uncertainty in illness, Babrow et al. (1998) identified literature on the role of uncertainty in relation to producing, labeling, recovery from, and prevention of illness; in relation to stress and coping; and in relation to helplessness and perceived control (also see Duggan, 2006; McGrath, 2005; Rosen & Knauper, 2008).

Given its pervasiveness, it is not surprising to note that uncertainty intertwines with tensions between the realms of communication and the body, scientific and humanistic assumptions and aspirations, and idiosyncrasy and commonality. Indeed, some perspec-tives take uncertainty as their focal point and, based largely on mechanistic or biomedical frames, emphasize accurate communication of knowledge and uncertainty (e.g., models of judgment under uncertainty, rational choice and decision analysis, theories of risk and uncertainty reduction).

Others take uncertainty as a starting point for more open-ended analysis. In particular, a number of writers have been developing theory and research on the relationship between communication and uncertainty management (Brashers, 2007; DeLorme & Huh, 2009; Dillard & Carson, 2005; Jones, Denham, & Springston, 2007; S. Thompson & O'Hair, 2008). And, in a related vein, problematic integration theory argues that uncertainty is at most only half of the heart of illness (Babrow, Hines, & Kasch, 2000; Cohen, 2009;

Dorgan, Williams, Parrott, & Harris, 2003; Gill & Babrow, 2007; Matthias, 2009; Polk, 2005). More specifically, problematic integration theory suggests that uncertainties take on meaning only relative to the values at stake in health and illness, just as values are themselves responsive to (un)certainties (e.g., the value of life and death move with chances of survival; Babrow, 2007). Moreover, PI theory counters a wide variety of common misconceptions about uncertainty: that it has a single or narrowly homogeneous meaning—for instance, it is necessarily bad or the result of insufficient information; that the main response to uncertainty is information seeking; the aim and significant outcome of any encounter with uncertainty is its reduction (or frustration of this aim), and the frequent assumption that its reduction is possible; that uncertainty and its attendant problems are resolved exclusively by managing the level of uncertainty (as opposed to reappraisal of value or more holistic transformations); that any one resolution of an unpleasant uncertainty is the final punctuation of experience, or for that matter that any dilemma involving expectation and desire has a clear first cause; and that the course of such dilemmas is predictable in any specific and robust sense (Babrow, 2007; also see Babrow & Matthias, 2009). Indeed, problematic integration theory strongly suggests that overemphasis of uncertainty in our research and theory distracts researchers' attention from equally vital, interrelated phenomena, such as the nature of value, diverging expectation and desire, ambivalence, and certainty/impossibility in health and illness.

In summary, much recent theorizing about health communication has emphasized that uncertainty pervades illness experiences and communication about health and illness. A subset of that work further suggests that the meaning of uncertainty in general (i.e., in any of its particular forms) is profoundly dependent on the values at stake.

Some of this work, particularly based on problematic integration theory, recognizes as well that our evaluation of whatever is at stake depends on how we formulate uncertainty or make sense of what we know. This occurs, for example, as we cope with chronic illness, irreversible losses from aging and illness, traumatic injuries, and approaching death (also see Geist-Martin, Ray, & Sharf, 2003). Our sense of possibilities, our construction of the unknown, of the knowable, and of the nature of what it means to know (Babrow, 2007; Babrow & Matthias, 2009), condition what we value and the extent to which we value it; so too what we value shapes what we take to be possible, both by compelling us to cling to possibility and to act in ways that are intended to affect objective chances. A heroic example of these ideas is the pursuit of a cure for a child's illness depicted in the 1992 movie *Lorenzo's Oil*. Examples of these ideas that are both more profound and wide ranging actually constitute ongoing debates in the United States over the potentialities and aims or values of health care reform. In these debates we ask: What is possible? What is desirable? To what extent, and in what ways, should we be guided by our current sense of what is possible? Or, rather than being constrained by apparent "realities" and "impossibilities," should we be guided more by our sense of what would be right or just, under the belief that aspiration sets the boundaries not only of human experience but our humanity. In short, health communication is largely an ongoing matter of (un)certainty motivating the rearticulation of values and values compelling the rearticulation of (un)certainty (Babrow, 2007).

Summary and Implications

With the growth of scholarship, which appears to be particularly vigorous in our area as communication is ever more widely recognized as an essential process in experiences with health and illness, there arises a commensurate need for ways of building bridges, dams, lakes, shelters—some form of ecology that can support life in common, shared understanding, and mutual enrichment. We offer the four tensions noted above not as boundary markers that can or should constrain health communication scholarship. Rather, we offer these ideas as a variety of paths toward broader, more integrative thinking about the nature of communication and health/illness. Any concept or set of concepts is, as Burke (1935/1984) observed, both a way of seeing and of not seeing. We hope that the tensions noted here remind researchers to look not only in front of them but look behind, not just to the left but to the right as well, not only down at the ground but up at the sky. Whether or not binocular vision gives us a more accurate picture of an objective reality, it most certainly gives us a deeper and more enriched and enriching view than seeing with only one lens. In this same spirit, we offer what we believe is yet another enlivening perspective on health communication theory and theorizing.

Traditions of (Health) Communication Theory and Research

Although there are a myriad of potential organizing frameworks to categorize health communication theories and research (see Babrow and Mattson, 2003), we believe Craig's (1999) metamodel is most attractive for the purposes of this chapter. Craig identifies seven distinct traditions or ways of conceptualizing and problematizing communication (also see Craig, 2008).[1] Our reasons for adopting this model are consistent with Craig's three arguments for developing a constitutive model of communication: this approach (a) considers communication to be a practical discipline (i.e., a discipline that "recursively cultivates the very social practices that constitute the discipline's specific subject matter" [p. 9]), (b) suggests varied ways of constituting the communication process symbolically (Craig, 1999), and (c) fosters discourse about communication by identifying ways that each tradition of communication theory can be used to engage with everyday practice and create spaces for argument across traditions (see Craig, 1999, Table 2). From this perspective, health communication theory is understood to emerge from practical efforts. For example, consider efforts to foster patient autonomy, such as the doctrine of informed consent; efforts such as this give rise to theory building, which in turn is intended to inform and refine these practices (Olufowote, 2008, 2009).

Rhetorical Tradition

According to Craig (1999), the rhetorical tradition theorizes communication as a practical art of persuasive discourse. Rhetorical theory has enormous implications across the spectrum of public deliberation over health care policies. And, as traditional boundaries have been challenged, scholars have developed analyses of ever-wider forms and contexts of suasory texts and discourse in the rhetorical tradition (e.g., Carmack, Bates, & Harter, 2008; Kline, 2006; Sharf, 1990).

From nearly its inception, the rhetorical tradition has grappled with the role of discourse in arriving at probabilistic judgments and also with the tensions between reason and emotion (Bitzer, 1981; Craig, 1999). Hence, it is well-suited to studies of the communicative framing of uncertainty and values and the tension between expectations and desires. Moreover, rhetorical theory has important implications for understanding the mutual interdependence of the symbolic and physical realms (Chesebro, 1982) and tensions between scientific and humanistic orientations (Harter, Stephens, & Japp, 2000; Segal, 2005).

The rhetorical tradition also offers resources for bridging theory and practice. Craig (1999) discussed ways that rhetorical theory both appeals to the commonsense of everyday discourse (e.g., the value of informed judgment, improvability of practice) and challenges metadiscursive commonplaces (e.g., mere words are not actions, appearance is not reality, style is not substance, opinion is not truth). Consider, for instance, Kline's (2007) rhetorical criticism of breast cancer pamphlets designed for African American women. Guided by the PEN-3 model of cultural sensitivity, Kline determined that although some pamphlets acknowledged cultural values important to the target audience, other pamphlets and health promotion efforts more generally must pay more attention in messaging to culturally nuanced meanings, arguments and evidence, and ambiguity.

Rhetorical theory also can be used to challenge policy makers, insurers, and practitioners who wish to maintain that these profound changes in the *style* of health communication and care are not also profound changes in the *substance* of communication and care (see Conrad & McIntush, 2003; Quick, Bates, & Quinlan, 2009).

Semiotic Tradition

According to Craig (1999), the semiotic tradition theorizes communication as intersubjective mediation by signs and sign systems. Semiotics problematizes the nature of individual signs and meanings, positing instead that signs are meaningful only in relation to other signs. Intersubjectivity, then, arises to the extent that webs of relationships are shared by communicators.

Semiotics has important implications for the distinctive tensions in health communication described above. For instance, consider the tension between the realms of communication and the body. Johnny and Mitchell (2006) deconstructed the underlying assumptions of World AIDS Campaign posters and determined that although some of the images projected redefined HIV/AIDS infection other aspects of the posters may have reinforced stigma and discrimination. Semiotic insights also can be used to promote positive innovations in health communication practice. Craig (1999) noted ways that semiotic theory both appeals to some commonsense postulates of everyday discourse (e.g., understanding requires common language; the omnipresent danger of miscommunication), and challenges other metadiscursive commonplaces (e.g., words have correct meanings and stand for thoughts; codes and media are neutral). Consider, for instance, the widespread (though sometimes reluctant) embrace of new technologies as media for health communication. Websites sanctioned by medical authorities convey not only accurate content but also, inescapably, the medical establishment's imprimatur on patients' self-directed study of disease, self-diagnosis, and self-treatment. Although these authoritative sites may urge visitors to consult a physician, these cautionary notes cannot remove the inclination toward an initial judgment by the web visitor of health status and lay treatment. Semiotic theory thus suggests important issues that must be managed by would-be sources and users of health information.

Phenomenological Tradition

As Craig (1999) characterized it, the phenomenological tradition theorizes communication as dialogue or experience of otherness.

> Authentic communication, or dialogue, is founded on the experience of direct, unmediated contact with others.... Hence, phenomenology challenges the semiotic notion that intersubjective understanding can be mediated only by signs...as well as the rhetorical notion that communication involves artful or strategic uses

of signs.... Among the paradoxes of communication that phenomenology brings to light is that conscious goal seeking, however benevolent one's intentions may be, annihilates dialogue by interposing one's own goals and strategies as a barrier against one's direct experience of self and other.

(Craig, 1999, pp. 138–139)

Outside of Rogerian psychotherapy, phenomenological approaches to health communication continue to be rare (for exceptions, see Fuchs, 2005; Mattson, 2000). Nonetheless, this tradition can be used to derive important ideas about the tensions that characterize health communication. For instance, consider the tension between the realms of communication and the body. Zook (1994) argued that both the biomedical and biopsychosocial models are based on dualistic conceptions of mind and body that misapprehend both the nature of health/illness and communication. In the biomedical model, illness is reduced to biological pathology (i.e., disease), whereas the biopsychosocial model admits to the interdependence of psychological, social, and physiological factors. A phenomenological theory of health and communication opens the way to a truly holistic conception of health as a state of being-in-the-world.

The phenomenological tradition also offers avenues to inform health communication and care practice. Notably, Craig (1999) identified ways that the tradition appeals to the common sense of everyday discourse (e.g., we all need human contact; we should treat others as persons, respect differences) and challenges other common beliefs (e.g., communication is a skill, facts are objective, and values subjective). For one example, phenomenology contests widespread practice by suggesting that skill instruction, strategy, and artifice, rather than improving communication, create barriers to authentic contact between patients and care providers. Rather than imposing preconceived understandings, care providers and patients should be encouraged to cultivate sensitivity and openness (D'Cruz, 2004; Mattson, 2000).

Cybernetic Tradition

Craig (1999) contended that, in the cybernetic tradition, communication is theorized as information processing by which systems are able to function (and often malfunction). Communication involves encoding, transmission, and decoding. Moreover, depending on the focus and complexity of the particular theory, communication also can include feedback and more or less complex system regulation and environmental impact. Theories in the cybernetic tradition are clearly suited to studying characteristic tensions in health communication (see Donohew & Ray, 1990). For instance, theories in this tradition have much to tell us about the tensions between the realms of communication and the body insofar as they are conceived as distinguishable yet interrelated systems. Moreover, family systems theories (Minuchin, 1974; Watzlawick, Beavin, & Jackson, 1967) are applicable to the tension between idiosyncrasy and commonality (Northouse & Northouse, 1998). Interdependence forges a common experience among family members. However, individuals are themselves open systems and are elements within many systems in addition to the family. The particular, unique configuration of each individual's relationships to these other systems creates idiosyncratic experiences and meanings of the very illness that disturbs the entire family. Recently, an interdisciplinary group of experts on family communication during cancer care recommended that, in keeping with the cybernetic tradition, future research should pay more attention to the broader family system rather than focusing exclusively on couples and family caregivers (Harris et al., 2009).

The cybernetic tradition also offers resources for bridging theory and practice. Craig (1999) discussed several ways that such theory appeals to the commonsense of everyday discourse (e.g., the identity of mind and brain; the value of information and logic; complex systems can be unpredictable) and challenges other commonplace notions (e.g., humans and machines differ; emotion is not logical; cause and effect are linear). For instance, systemic theory counters the linear effects notion that patient "noncompliance" is a function of some characteristic of the patient (e.g., ignorance, irresponsibility) or physician (e.g., inadequate compliance-gaining behavior). Systems thinking, instead, offers that control and resistance are mutually conditioning features of the traditional hierarchical relationship. Fadiman's (1997) depiction of the "collision" between the Hmong and the American medical establishment provides a poignant example of this dynamic. Although health promoting change might be accomplished to some degree by first-order changes, such as the physician pressing less or the patient complying more, the fundamental dynamic can only change by a second-order transformation in the nature of the relationship (see Watzlawick, Weakland, & Fisch, 1974).

Sociopsychological Tradition

The essence of communication in the sociopsychological tradition is "a process in which the behavior of humans or other complex organisms expresses psychological mechanisms, states, and traits and, through interaction with similar expressions of other individuals, produces a range of cognitive, emotional, and behavioral effects" (Craig, 1999, p. 143). Although this tradition has implications for all four of the tensions in health communication, the most obvious are related to the tension between (un)certainty and values. A wide range of theories and foci illustrate this point. For instance, theories of health beliefs (Mattson, 1999), risk perceptions (Rimal, Böse, Brown, Mkandawire, & Folda, 2009), fear appeals (Morrison, 2005; Nabi, Roskos-Ewoldsen, & Carpentier, 2008; Witte, 1992), compliance (Burgoon, Birk, & Hall, 1991), social support (Dennis, Kunkel, & Keyton, 2008), uncertainty management (Brashers, 2007), and problematic integration (see above) all grapple in some way with uncertainties and values. Ultimately, each of these theories will have to confront the complex interdependencies between expectations and uncertainties on the one hand, and values, desires, and wishes on the other (Babrow, 2007).

The sociopsychological tradition also has both commonsensical and unapparent implications for health communication practice. Craig (1999) noted that these theories appeal to commonly accepted ideas: that communication reflects personality, beliefs and feelings bias judgments, and people in groups affect one another. These models also counter familiar notions: that humans are rational beings, we know our own minds, and we know what we see. For example, explaining illness is more than merely processing clear and thorough information; rather, it is working out health beliefs and uncertainties within the context of related beliefs and values that constitute our sense of self, roles, and relationships through interaction with care providers, loved ones, and others (Mattson, 1999; Whaley, 2000).

Sociocultural Tradition

Craig (1999) described the sociocultural perspective on communication as "a symbolic process that produces and reproduces shared sociocultural patterns" (p. 144). In other words, shared systems of beliefs, values, language, political economy, and various other institutional arrangements make communication possible (see Geist-Martin et al., 2003; Zoller &

Kline, 2008). Moreover, our communication reproduces these very arrangements. Still, as Craig notes, in given interactions and across time, there is need and opportunity for improvisation and hence for the production of new sociocultural arrangements.

Although the sociocultural tradition is relevant to all four distinctive tensions in health communication, one very important connection is to the tension between scientific and humanistic assumptions, values, and aspirations. In particular, cross-cultural studies reveal the enormous difficulties of reconciling the perspective of Western allopathic medicine with that of indigenous healing. Fadiman (1997) provides compelling illustrations including when a Hmong mother saw a life-threatening act in the removal of a soiled string around a baby's wrist when she was admitted for emergency treatment; in the mother's view, an evil spirit, or *dab*, might steal the child's spirit once the securing string was removed. In other words, the most basic assumption of Western medicine—that well-established medical science trumps all other forms of knowledge—may be overturned when cultures interact (also see Airhihenbuwa, 1995; Geist, 1994).

Like the other traditions, sociocultural theory can be linked in important ways to practice. Craig (1999) suggests that such theories can appeal to commonsense notions such as the idea that the individual is a product of society, every society has a distinct culture, and social actions have unintended effects. He also notes that these theories challenge belief in individual agency and responsibility, the absolute identity of self, and the naturalness of the social order. In a richly layered narrative, Sharf (2009) described not only her inside experiences grappling with the death of a beloved pet and her outside experiences struggling to comprehend the sudden death of a seemingly healthy neighbor, but also what it means to witness and be incorporated into the healing narratives of others. In so doing, Sharf continues to assist others in understanding the power of narratives to cocreate and reframe meanings of culture, health, survival, and mortality (for other pertinent examples of health as narrative refer to companion articles in Harter & Bochner's [2009] Special Issue of the *Journal of Applied Communication Research* [2009] and Harter, Japp, & Beck's [2005] seminal book on health narratives).

Critical Tradition

In the critical tradition, genuine communication occurs in the process of discursive reflection, but material and ideological social practices often preclude or distort discursive reflection and prevent authentic communication (Craig, 1999). Critical theorists and researchers attempt to uncover the material practices and hegemonic ideologies that distort communication (see Zoller & Kline, 2008). For example, Ellingson's (2005) feminist ethnography of interdisciplinary teams in a geriatric oncology unit problematizes the communication of gender, power, and privilege within patient, health care provider, and family relationships.

Like the other six traditions Craig (1999) identifies, critical theory is highly relevant to the various distinctive tensions in health communication. For instance, the tensions between scientific and humanistic assumptions and values and between idiosyncrasy and commonality appear to be consistent with key tensions in critical thought (Zoller & Kline, 2008). These same dialectical oppositions are illustrated in Babrow and Kline's (2000) application of problematic integration theory to critique the "ideology of uncertainty reduction" that ignores or delegitimizes women's experiences of breast self-exams. As one additional example, Mattson, Clair, Sanger, and Kunkel (2000) illuminate the tension between idiosyncrasy and commonality in a case study of a woman's search for social support.

The relevance of critical theory to distinctive features of health communication also suggests significant opportunities to address practice. Craig (1999) noted that the critical tradition both appeals to the common sense of everyday discourse (e.g., the self-perpetuation of power and wealth; the values of freedom, equality, and reason; and the notion that discussion produces awareness and insight) and challenges metadiscursive commonplaces (e.g., the naturalness and rationality of the traditional social order, the objectivity of science and technology). The most important of these challenges arises in the critical analysis of power relationships in health-related institutions and practices (Foucault, 1973). For a pointed example, consider King's (2006) controversial analysis, *Pink Ribbons, Inc.*, of the popular campaign to raise breast cancer awareness and resources. From a critical lens, King challenges the commercialization of breast cancer by suggesting that the large corporations that have joined the bandwagon in the chase for a cure are perhaps more interested in promoting their philanthropic public image than supporting prevention efforts and asking important questions about the reason why breast cancer is so rampant in our society. As another example, Mattson and Basnyat (2008) argued in favor of reframing HIV test counseling practice by infusing harm reduction theory "which when applied to disease prevention practice suggests movement away from traditional, one-way medical approaches of counselor-to-client interviewing in favor of more realistic, nonjudgmental, client-involved collaborative sessions" (p. 140; also see Waitzkin, 1991). These projects problematize current health communication assumptions and practices and offer alternative ways of understanding and addressing crucial health issues.

Conclusion

In this chapter, we have tried to offer not so much a review of extant health communication theory as vantage points from which to view what we take to be vitally important issues for building theory in the area. Although health communication theory building and research will no doubt proceed with great vigor and largely independent of our suggestions, we offer this chapter in the conviction that attention to its contours will promote greater opportunities for the most salutary sorts of innovation and synthesis.

The four tensions identified here are central to the experience of health and illness, and indeed to our humanity; for these reasons, the implications of these tensions extend to every aspect of these experiences. And as we have tried to point out in various places, the four tensions also intersect with one another in interesting and important ways. Moreover, by using Craig's schema as a way to organize specific theories, we have joined him in emphasizing distinctions based on differences in conceptions of *communication* rather than variations in *epistemology*. We also have briefly noted some of the many ways that these traditions in conceptualizing communication intersect with the four central tensions in communicating about health and illness.

In all of these efforts, our hope is to respect diversity while at the same time promoting reflective syntheses. As health communication scholarship in the 21st Century reaches ever farther into, out from, and across the infinite reaches and dimensions of human sense-making, grasping anything will require just this sort of dance between differentiation and integration. While the dialectic of differentiation and integration, or analysis and synthesis, has animated theory, research, and practice since the dawn of human inquiry, it has never been more important than it is now, and it is now not as important as it will be as the pace of inquiry and the accumulation of knowledge continue to accelerate. As we respond to this challenge, so will we constitute experience of human health and illness, the theories we construct to understand these experiences, and the practices that embody our understandings.

Note

1. Russill (2004, 2008) suggested adding an eighth tradition to Craig's scheme: a pragmatist tradition; for a response, see Craig (2007). For health communication exemplars, see Mattson and Basu (2010a, b).

References

Airhihenbuwa, C. O. (1995). *Health and culture: Beyond the western paradigm*. Thousand Oaks, CA: Sage.

Anderson, J. A. (1996). *Communication theory: Epistemological foundations*. New York: Guilford.

Ariès, P. (1981). *The hour of our death*. New York: Vintage Books.

Aronowitz, R. A. (1998). *Making sense of illness: Science, society, and disease*. Cambridge, UK: Cambridge University Press.

Aronowitz, R. A. (2004). When do symptoms become a disease? In A. L. Caplan, J. J. McCartney, & D. A. Sisti (Eds.), *Health, disease, and illness* (pp. 65–72). Washington, DC: Georgetown University Press.

Atkinson, P. (1995). *Medical talk and medical work*. London: Sage.

Babrow, A. S. (2007). Problematic integration theory. In B. B. Whaley & W. Samter (Eds.), *Explaining communication: Contemporary theories and exemplars* (pp. 181–200). Mahwah, NJ: Erlbaum.

Babrow, A. S., Hines, S. C., & Kasch, C. R. (2000). Illness and uncertainty: Problematic integration and strategies for communicating about medical uncertainty and ambiguity. In B. B. Whaley (Ed.), *Explaining illness: Messages, strategies and contexts* (pp. 41–67). Hillsdale, NJ: Erlbaum.

Babrow, A. S., Kasch, C. R., & Ford, L. A. (1998). The many meanings of "uncertainty" in illness: Toward a systematic accounting. *Health Communication 10*, 1–24.

Babrow, A. S., & Kline, K. N. (2000). From "reducing" to "coping with" uncertainty: Reconceptualizing the central challenge in breast self-exams. *Social Science & Medicine, 51*, 1805–1816.

Babrow, A. S., & Matthias, M. S. (2009). Generally unseen challenges in uncertainty management: An application of problematic integration theory. In T. Afifi &. W. Afifi (Eds.), *Uncertainty and information regulation in interpersonal contexts: Theories and applications* (pp. 9–25). London: Routledge.

Babrow, A. S., & Mattson, M. (2003). Theorizing about health communication. In T. Thompson, A. M. Dorsey, K. I. Miller, & R. Parrott (Eds.), *Handbook of health communication* (pp. 35–61). Mahwah, NJ: Erlbaum.

Beck, C. S., Benitez, J. L., Edwards, A., Olson, A., Pai, A., & Torres, M. B. (2004). Enacting "Health Communication": The field of health communication as constructed through publication in scholarly journals. *Health Communication, 16*, 475–492.

Becker, E. (1984). *Denial of death*. New York: Free Press.

Bitzer, L. (1981). Political rhetoric. In D. D. Nimmo & K. R. Sanders (Eds.), *Handbook of political communication* (pp. 225–248). Beverly Hills, CA: Sage.

Brashers, D. E. (2007). A theory of communication and uncertainty management. In B. Whaley & W. Samter (Eds.), *Explaining communication theory* (pp. 201–218). Mahwah, NJ: Erlbaum.

Burgoon, M.., Birk, T. S., & Hall, J. R. (1991). Compliance and satisfaction with physician–patient communication: An expectancy theory interpretation of gender differences. *Human Communication Research, 18*, 177–208.

Burke, K. (1984). *Permanence and change*. Berkeley: University of California Press. (Original work published 1935)

Callahan, D. (2000). *The troubled dream of life: In search of a peaceful death*. Washington, DC: Georgetown University Press.

Caplan, A. L, McCartney, J. J., & Sisti, D. A. (Eds.). (2004). *Health, disease, and illness*. Washington, DC: Georgetown University Press.

Carmack, H., Bates, B. R., & Harter, L. M. (2008). Narrative constructions of health care issues and policies: The case of President Clinton's apology-by-proxy for the Tuskegee Syphilis Experiment. *Journal of Medical Humanities, 29*, 89–109.

Cassell, E. J. (1985). *Talking with patients: Vol. 1. The theory of doctor–patient communication*. Cambridge, MA: MIT Press.

Chesebro, J. W. (1982). Illness as a rhetorical act: A cross-cultural perspective. *Communication Quarterly, 30*, 321–331.

Cohen, E. L. (2009). Naming and claiming cancer among African American women: An application of problematic integration theory. *Journal of Applied Communication Research, 37*, 397–414.

Conrad, C., & McIntush, H. G. (2003). Communication, structure and health care policymaking. In T. Thompson, A. M. Dorsey, K. I. Miller, & R. Parrott (Eds.), *Handbook of health communication* (pp. 403–422). Mahwah, NJ: Erlbaum.

Craig, R. T. (1999). Communication theory as a field. *Communication Theory, 9*, 119–161.

Craig, R. T. (2007). Pragmatism in the field of communication theory. *Communication Theory, 17*, 125–145.

Craig, R. T. (2008). Communication in the conversation of disciplines. *Russian Journal of Communication, 1*, 7–23.

D'Cruz, P. (2004). *Family care in HIV/AIDS: Exploring lived experience*. Thousand Oaks, CA: Sage.

DeLorme, D. E., & Huh, J. (2009). Seniors' uncertainty management of direct-to-consumer advertising usefulness. *Health Communication, 24*, 494–503.

Dennis, M. R., Kunkel, A., & Keyton, J. (2008). Problematic integration theory, appraisal theory, and the Bosom Buddies breast cancer support group. *Journal of Applied Communication, 36*, 415–436.

Dillard, J. P., & Carson, C. L. (2005). Uncertainty management following a positive newborn screening for cystic fibrosis. *Journal of Health Communication, 10*, 57–76.

Donohew, L., & Ray, E. B. (1990). Introduction: Systems perspectives on health communication. In E. B. Ray & L. Donohew (Eds.), *Communication and health: Systems and applications* (pp. 3–8). Hillsdale, NJ: Erlbaum.

Dorgan, K. A., Williams, S. L., Parrott, R. L., & Harris, T. M. (2003).Hope and despair in Pandora's box: Perceiving reproductive reward and risks of genetics technologies and information. *Women's Studies in Communication, 26*, 88–117.

Duggan, A. (2006). Understanding interpersonal communication processes across health contexts: Advances in the last decade and challenges for the next decade. *Journal of Health Communication, 11*, 93–108.

Ellingson L. L. (2005). *Communicating in the clinic: Negotiating frontstage and backstage teamwork*. Creskill, NJ: Hampton Press.

Ellingson, L. L. (2007). The performance of dialysis care: Routinization and adaptation on the floor. *Health Communication, 22*, 103–114.

Fadiman, A. (1997). *The spirit catches you and you fall down: A Hmong child, her American doctors, and the collision of two cultures*. New York: Farrar, Straus, and Giroux.

Finnegan, J. R., & Viswanath, K. (1990). Health communication: Medical and public health influences on the research agenda. In E. B. Ray & L. Donohew (Eds.), *Communication and health: Systems and applications* (pp. 9–24). Hillsdale, NJ: Erlbaum.

Floyd, K. Mikkelson, A. C., Tafoya, M. A., Farinelli, L., La Valley, A. G., Judd, J., ... Wilson, J. (2007). Human affection exchange: XIII. Affectionate communication accelerates neuroendocrine stress recovery. *Health Communication, 22*, 123–132.

Fogarty, J. S. (1997). Reactance theory and patient noncompliance. *Social Science and Medicine 45*, 1277–1288.

Foucault, M. (1973). *The birth of the clinic*. London: Tavistock.

Fuchs, T. (2005). Corporealized and disembodied minds: A phenomenological view of the body in melancholia and schizophrenia. *Philosophy, Psychiatry, & Psychology, 12*, 95–107.

Geist, P. (1994). Negotiating cultural understanding in health care communication. In L. A. Samovar & R. E. Porter (Eds.), *Intercultural communication: A reader* (7th ed, pp. 311–321). Belmont, CA: Wadsworth.

Geist-Martin, P., Ray, E. B., & Sharf, B. F. (2003). *Communicating health: Personal, cultural, and political complexities*. Belmont, CA: Wadsworth/Thompson.

Gergen, K. J. (2009). *An invitation to social construction* (2nd ed.). London: Sage.

Gill, E. A., & Babrow, A. S. (2007). To hope or to know: Coping with uncertainty and ambivalence in women's magazine breast cancer articles. *Journal of Applied Communication Research, 35*, 133–155.

Harris, J., Bowen, D. J., Badr, H., Hannon, P., Hay, J., & Sterba, K. R. (2009). Family communication during the cancer experience. *Journal of Health Communication, 14*, 76–84.

Harrow, A., Wells, M., Humphris, G., Taylor, C., Williams, B. (2008). "Seeing is believing, and believing is seeing": An exploration of the meaning and impact of women's mental images of their breast cancer and their potential origins. *Patient Education and Counseling, 73*, 339–346.

Harter, L. M., & Bochner, A. P. (Eds.). (2009). Health as narrative [Special issue]. *Journal of Applied Communication Research, 37(2)*.

Harter, L. M., Japp, P. M., & Beck, C. S. (2005). *Narratives, health, and healing: Communication theory, research, and practice*. Mahwah, NJ: Erlbaum.

Harter, L. M., Stephens, R. J., & Japp, P. M. (2000). President Clinton's apology for the Tuskegee syphilis experiment: A narrative of remembrance, redefinition, and reconciliation. *Howard Journal of Communication, 11*, 19–34.

Jenkins, D. J. A. (1998). [Book review] Making sense of illness: Science, society, and disease, by Robert A. Aronowitz. *New England Journal of Medicine, 339*, 354.

Johnny, L., & Mitchell, C. (2006). "Live and Let Live": An analysis of HIV/AIDS-related stigma and discrimination in international campaign posters. *Health Communication, 11*, 755–767.

Jones, K. O., Denham, B. E., & Springston, J. K. (2007). Differing effects of mass and interpersonal communication on breast cancer risk estimates: An exploratory study of college students and their mothers. *Health Communication, 21*, 165–175.

Katz, J. (1984). *The silent world of doctor and patient*. New York: Free Press.

Keeley, M. P., & Yingling, J. M. (2007). *Final conversations: Helping the living and the dying talk to each other*. Acton, MA: VanderWyk & Burnham.

King, S. (2006). *Pink ribbons, inc: Breast cancer and the politics of philanthropy*. Minneapolis: University of Minnesota Press.

Kline, K. N. (2006). A decade of research on health content in the media: The focus on health challenges and sociocultural context and attendant informational and ideological problems. *Journal of Health Communication, 11*, 43–59.

Kline, K. N. (2007). Cultural sensitivity and health promotion: Assessing breast cancer education pamphlets designed for African American women. *Health Communication, 21*, 85–96.

Kramer, P. D. (1993). *Listening to Prozac*. New York: Viking Press.

Kuhse, H. (Ed.). (2002). *Unsanctifying life: Essays on ethics*. Malden, MA: Wiley-Blackwell.

Lazarus, R. S. (1991). *Emotion and adaptation*. New York: Oxford University Press.

Matthias, M. S. (2009). Problematic integration in pregnancy and childbirth: Contrasting approaches to uncertainty and desire in obstetric and midwifery care. *Health Communication, 24*, 60–70.

Mattson, M. (1999). Toward a reconceptualization of communication cues to action in the health belief model: HIV test counseling. *Communication Monographs, 66*, 240–265.

Mattson, M. (2000). Empowerment through agency-promoting discourse: An explicit application of Harm Reduction Theory to reframe HIV test counseling. *Journal of Health Communication, 5*, 333–347.

Mattson, M., & Basnyat, I. (2008). Infusing HIV test counseling practice with harm reduction theory. In T. Edgar, S. M. Noar, & V. S. Freimuth (Eds.), *Communication Perspectives on HIV/AIDS for the 21st Century* (pp. 137–167). New York: Erlbaum.

Mattson, M. & Basu, A. (2010a). Center for Disease Control's DES update: A case for effective operationalization of messaging in social marketing practice. *Health Promotion Practice, 11*, 580–588.

Mattson, M. & Basu, A. (2010b). The message development tool: A case for effective operationalization of messaging in social marketing practice. *Health Marketing Quarterly, 27*, 275–290.

Mattson, M., Clair, R., Chapman, P. A., & Kunkel, A. W. (2000). A feminist reframing of stress: Rose's story. In P. M. Buzzanell (Ed.), *Rethinking organizational communication from feminist perspectives* (pp. 157–174). Thousand Oaks, CA: Sage.

McGrath, P. (2005). Developing a language for nonreligious spirituality in relation to serious illness through research: Preliminary findings. *Health Communication, 18*, 217–235.

Melzack, R. (2005). Evolution of the neuromatrix theory of pain. The Prithvi Raj lecture. Presented at the Third World Congress of the World Institute of Pain, Barcelona 2004. *Pain Practice, 5(2)*, 85–94.

Miller, G., & Mitchell, D. (Producers), & Miller, G. (Director). (1992). *Lorenzo's oil* [Motion picture]. United States: Universal Pictures.

Minuchin, S. (1974). *Family and family therapy*. Cambridge, MA: Harvard University Press.

Morrison, K. (2005). Motivating women and men to take protective action against rape: Examining direct and indirect persuasive fear appeals. *Health Communication, 18*, 327–356.

Nabi, R. L., Roskos-Ewoldsen, D., & Carpentier, F. D. (2008). Subjective knowledge and fear appeal effectiveness: Implications for message design. *Health Communication, 23,* 191–201.

Northouse, L. L., & Northouse, P. G. (1998). *Health communication: Strategies for health professionals* (3rd ed.). Stamford, CT: Appleton & Lange.

Nuland, S. B. (1993). *How we die: Reflections on life's final chapter.* New York: Knopf.

O'Hair, D., Villagran, M. M., Wittenberg, E., Brown, K., Ferguson, M., Hall, H. T., & Doty, T. (2003). Cancer survivorship and agency model: Implications for patient choice, decision making, and influence. *Health Communication, 15,* 193–202.

Olufowote, J. O. (2008). A structurational analysis of informed consent to treatment: Societal evolution, contradiction, and reproductions in medical practice. *Health Communication, 23,* 292–303.

Olufowote, J. O. (2009). A structurational analysis of informed consent to treatment: (Re)productions of contradictory sociohistorical structures in practitioners' interpretive schemes. *Qualitative Health Research, 19,* 802–814.

Piaget, J. (1985). *The equilibration of cognitive structures: The central problem of intellectual development.* Chicago, IL: University of Chicago Press.

Polk, D. M. (2005). Communication and family caregiving for Alzheimer's dementia: Linking attributions and problematic integration. *Health Communication, 13,* 257–273.

Quick, B. L., Bates, B. R., & Quinlan, M. M. (2009). The utility of anger in promoting clean indoor air policies. *Health Communication, 24,* 548–561.

Ragan, S. L., Wittenberg, E., & Hall, H. T. (2003). The communication of palliative care for the elderly cancer patient. *Health Communication, 15,* 219–226.

Ragan, S. L., Wittenberg-Lyles, E. M., Goldsmith, J., & Sanchez-Reilly, S. (2008). *Communication as comfort: Multiple voices in palliative care.* New York: Routledge.

Rallison, L., Limacher, L. H., & Clinton, M. (2006). Future echoes in pediatric palliative care: Becoming sensitive to language. *Journal of Palliative Care, 22,* 99–104.

Rimal, R. N., Böse, K., Brown, J., Mkandawire, G., & Folda, L. (2009). Extending the purview of the risk perception attitude framework: Findings from HIV/AIDS prevention research in Malawi. *Health Communication, 24,* 210–218.

Rosen, N. O., & Knauper, B. (2008). A little uncertainty goes a long way: State and trait differences in uncertainty interact to increase information seeking but also to increase worry. *Health Communication, 24,* 228–238.

Russill, C. (2004). *Toward a pragmatist theory of communication* (Doctoral dissertation). Pennsylvania State University, University Park, PA.

Russill, C. (2008). Through a public darkly: Reconstructing pragmatist perspectives in communication theory. *Communication Theory, 18,* 478–504.

Segal, J. Z. (2005). *Health and the rhetoric of medicine.* Carbondale: Southern Illinois University Press.

Sharf, B. F. (1990). Physician–patient communication as interpersonal rhetoric: A narrative approach. *Health Communication, 2,* 217–231.

Sharf, B. F. (2009). Observations from the outside in: Narratives of illness, healing, and mortality in everyday life. *Journal of Applied Communication Research, 37,* 132–139.

Smith, D. H. (1996). Ethics in the doctor–patient relationship. *Medical Ethics, 12,* 179–197.

Sontag, S. (1978). *Illness as metaphor.* New York: Farrar, Straus and Giroux.

Sontag, S. (1989). *AIDS and its metaphors.* New York: Farrar, Straus Giroux.

Thompson, S., & O'Hair, H. D. (2008). Advice-giving and the management of uncertainty for cancer survivors. *Health Communication, 23,* 340–348.

Thompson, T. L. (2006). Seventy-five (Count 'em—75!) issues of Health Communication: An analysis of emerging trends. *Health Communication, 20,* 117–122.

Waitzkin, H. (1991). *The politics of medical encounters.* New Haven, CT: Yale University Press.

Wallis, P., & Nerlich, B. (2005). Disease metaphors in new epidemics: The UK media framing of the 2003 SARS epidemic. *Social Science & Medicine, 60,* 2629–2639.

Watzlawick, P., Beavin, J. H., & Jackson, D. D. (1967). *Pragmatics of human communication: A study of interpersonal patterns, pathologies, and paradoxes.* New York: Norton.

Watzlawick, P., Weakland, J., & Fisch, R. (1974). *Change: Principles of problem formation and problem resolution.* New York: Norton.

Whaley, B. B. (Ed.). (2000). *Explaining illness: Research, theory, and strategies.* Hillsdale, NJ: Erlbaum.

Witte, K. (1992). Putting the fear back into fear appeals: The extended parallel process model. *Communication Monographs, 59,* 329–349.

Zoller, H., & Kline, K. N. (2008). Theoretical contributions of interpretive and critical research in health communication. In C. Beck (Ed.), *Communication yearbook 32* (pp. 89–135). New York: Routledge.

Zook, E. G. (1994). Embodied health and constitutive communication: Toward an authentic conceptualization of health communication. In S. Deetz (Ed.), *Communication yearbook 17* (pp. 344–377). Thousand Oaks, CA: Sage.

3

NARRATIVE TURNS EPIC

Continuing Developments in Health Narrative Scholarship

Barbara F. Sharf, Lynn M. Harter, Jill Yamasaki, and Paul Haidet

Cancer is an uninvited life guest, disrupting daily routines, straining relationships, and shifting one's sense of self. Instead of forming bone on her growth plates, sixteen-year-old Caitlin Shoup grew a two by two inch tumor on the end of her left distal femur, biopsied and diagnosed as osteosarcoma in June, 2004. Within ten days, she began a triple drug chemotherapy regimen. While her classmates chose between co-curricular activities, Caitlin weighed the comparative benefits and risks of limb salvage surgery versus amputation. She completed most of her junior year in the oncology ward at Akron Children's Hospital, and though she returned to Perry High to complete her senior year, starkly visible markers of her cancer remained. She continues to bear the twelve-inch scar between her thigh and calf with dignity. "I wear my scar with pride and am honest about it most times, unless people approach me rudely, in which case the scar is from a shark attack!" In addition to hair loss and permanent hearing damage, though, Caitlin lost patience for the melodramas of teenage life. "I have a low tolerance for B.S. and immaturity," Caitlin shared. "... It's amazing how few people actually appreciate their life and don't want to waste it."

With a femur replaced with titanium and a new plastic knee, the range of motion in Caitlin's knee remains limited, she walks slower than most people her age and with a visible limp. Her left leg is disfigured from numerous surgeries and, due to nerve damage in her foot, multiple surgeries, and staph infections, she has on occasion relied on leg braces, crutches, wheelchairs, and immobilizers to ward off infections, reduce the impact of "foot drop," and increase mobility. A blue tag hanging from Caitlin's rearview mirror marks her as disabled, a welcome moniker that limits the distance she must walk to her apartment, class, and restaurants. Even so, she resists the marginal position that too often accompanies living with a disability. "Although I am legally handicapped, I don't consider myself that. I just say I am different-abled. I'm proud of everything I had to overcome and it makes me who I am today."

Narrative Roots in Health Communication

The late Don Hewitt, legendary television news producer for CBS, said that his format for his famous show *60 Minutes* was simple; namely four words that every child knows—"Tell me a story!" This anecdote is a layman's version of rhetorician Walter Fisher's (1987) claim that humans are inherent storytellers (and hearers). In other words, each of us, to varying degrees, makes use of our narrative tendencies in a wide array of communicative activities, including how we talk about health, illness, and medicine. Thus we begin with a brief overview of the basic elements and purposes of narratives in health-related contexts. This

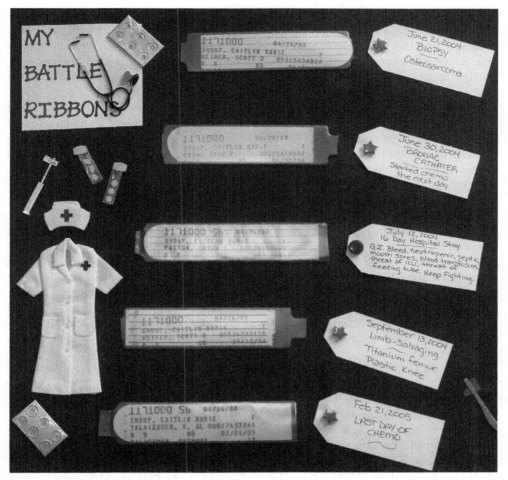

Figure 3.1   Battle ribbons: Caitlin's hospital wristbands.

is knowledge that is foundational to health communication scholarship conducted as narrative inquiry.

The story of Caitlin and her family, which we have introduced and will continue to relate throughout this essay, clearly illustrates all the classic features that constitute the communicative form widely recognized as a health narrative. It is in large part an illness narrative insofar as it was prompted by the life-threatening, life-altering personal rupture (Bruner, 1990) that is cancer. As this tale unfolds, it becomes a story of healing and hopefulness. In some ways it is a quest for the deeper meanings of this illness experience (Frank, 1995), as well as an enactment of resilience, courage, coping, family love, and community solidarity. The main protagonist and narrator, naturally, is Caitlin, but several other characters—her mom, dad, younger sister, and a hometown journalist—co-construct, narrate, and enrich this account. Each voices motives, fears, desires, and choices that work to emplot the series of events in which they find themselves; that is, to form connections among actions and ideas, to attribute agency to self and others, and to come to grips with changing circumstances and storylines (Mattingly, 1998). As with all narratives, the plotline extends through time (Ricoeur, 1984–1988). There is a seemingly faraway past depicting a happy family prior to cancer; a series of frightening, near past episodes in which pain, diagnosis, treatments, and treatment repair predominate; an energetic, thankful, and optimistic present, tempered by ongoing challenges, lessons learned, and an altered way of living; and, thankfully, a foreseeable future, open with possibilities. The story that is eventually layered and pieced together occurs through changing scenes of home, hospital, and the public sphere. What begins as intensely personal interactions among members of Caitlin's family evolves to include friends, health practitioners, and eventually a dialogue with a larger audience of well-wishers and interested others. We should also assume that there are deliberate silences, parts of the lived story that individual narrators have chosen not to disclose (Poirier & Ayres, 1997). As unique as the content of this particular health narrative, so is its telling through the several texts through which it unfolds, in many voices, through multiple perspectives. It is visual and verbal; oral and written; conversational, journalistic, poetic, and deliberative.

In addition to the grammar or constituent parts, foundational narrative scholarship has spoken to the functions or applications of health narratives. Health narratives may occur as individual stories (or as in our example, a pastiche of individual stories constituting a family narrative), but there are also socially constructed stories or master narratives that arise from and exist within the larger culture; for example, exemplary depictions of what it means to live with cancer. Previous research (Sharf & Vanderford, 2003) has identified several major functions of health narratives. Stories are a way of making sense of an uncertain or chaotic set of circumstances (Bruner, 1990), which are frequently set in motion by a serious diagnosis, among other life events (Frank, 1995). The stories we create or ascribe to are both a by-product of our cultural life (Morris, 1998) and a further construction of social reality; for example, stories such as Caitlin's enable people to understand cancer as a survivable, chronic disease rather than a death sentence. Narratives provide implicit explanations (Kleinman, 1988) that reveal ideas of causation, remedy, and future possibilities, infer warrants for decisions made, and enable a sense of control in the face of threat and disorder (Beck, 2001; Sharf, 2005). Life-altering illness or disability necessarily brings about changes in personal identity in terms of how individuals view themselves and how they are perceived by others (Frank, 1995). Narratives can help to create identification (Burke, 1950) among people experiencing similar health problems, thus building a sense of community in place of social isolation. Finally, narratives may result in beneficial health outcomes (Pennebaker, 2000).

Moving on from these fundamental understandings of what health narratives are and what purposes they serve, we now transition to the current landscape of health communication scholarship. We emphasize how the robustness of narrative theory rests in part in its focus on webs of interwoven social (and material) forces. No story is solely personal, organizational, or public; personal stories cannot escape the constraints of institutional interests, nor are they separate from cultural values, beliefs, and expectations. Meanwhile, institutional structures and scripts intertwine to form the social milieu in which performances unfold. In their seminal compilation of narrative analyses from various vantage points of health-related concerns, Harter, Japp, and Beck (2005) encapsulate the scholarly challenges of negotiating tensions between knowing and being, continuity and disruption, creativity and constraint, and the partial and the indeterminate. In what follows we account for newer directions in inquiry, and ways in which this work is enriching contemporary understandings of health, medicine, and illness.

Enlarging the Landscape of Health Narratives

Humanizing Health Care

After a routine CT scan revealed a suspicious mass on her left lung, Caitlin's oncologist feared a worst case scenario—osteosarcoma had metastasized to her chest wall. Even after a basic explanation from the surgeon, the process and techniques of a transthoracic needle aspiration biopsy remained opaque to common sense. "I wanted to know what was going on in my own body. [The doctor] was telling me, but I couldn't see it, I couldn't visualize it," stressed Caitlin. "Oftentimes they take photos for medical reasons, so I just asked him to take my camera in to my surgeries. And he did. He always had one of his medical students, that was their job for the day, to take pictures." The transformation of Caitlin's body was rendered seeable as well as sayable as her surgical team snapped photos, dramatizing the biopsy process, and preserving a fragment of narrative experience that might otherwise be lost. "I learned a lot about my body. Like this picture here [a photo of her chest cavity open], I thought it was cool at first, because I didn't know what a lung looked like. I thought it looked like a tongue. But, the opening is so huge. I couldn't believe they could do that. Unbelievable." Images can activate patterned integrations of our remembered past, perceived present, and envisioned future, and in so doing function as anchors to transitory moments and living memories (Reismann, 2008). Three years later, the photo elicits conflicting emotions for Caitlin, a mnemonic device beckoning her to remember and reflect on a punctuated moment. "I feel angry when I look at that picture, because I told [the doctors] it had not metastasized. I knew my body, and they didn't listen. But I also feel relief, the relief that came from the pathology report, from knowing with confidence that it had not spread."

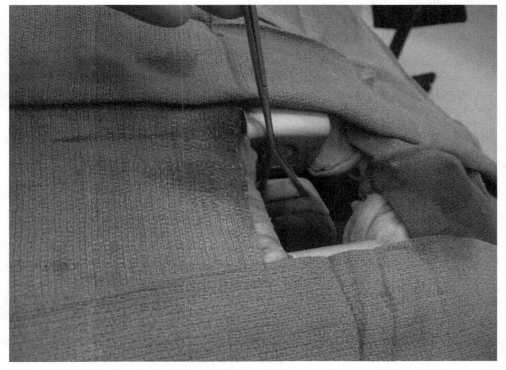

Figure 3.2   Caitlin's chest cavity during surgery.

The provision of health care would be impossible if not for our human capacity to organize and embody lived experience in narrative form (Hunter, 1991). Diagnosis and treatment are narratively inflected enterprises consumed with emplotment processes (Charon, 2006). A central difficulty arises, though, when the singularities of a patient's case are juxtaposed with the generalities of a science-using practice. Caitlin's providers followed warning signs to detect potential problems, search for patterns of causality, and chart courses of action. They were trained and legitimated to do so by the language and practices of technology, complex and esoteric terminology and techniques. The Shoup family had not heard of a solitary pulmonary nodule (SPN). Caitlin's doctors were faced with a narrative challenge: to help the family comprehend and contemplate "the shadow" on the CT scan of Caitlin's lungs, and the potential consequences of a malignant mass. Extraordinary health care providers are endowed with the gift of plot—those who understand how clinical practice relies on narrative activity to not only facilitate treatment but also build relationships with patients and probe what it means to be sick and well.

Narrative sense-making is not new in medical practice. Even so, the fact that information from patients often arrives in narrative form usually goes unrecognized. Until recently, the explicit acknowledgment of narrative activity in clinical work was whispered on the fringes of mainstream medicine. The growing interest in narrative activity in health contexts is evident in scholarship on the narrative nature of clinical judgment and health care (e.g., Ellingson, 2005; Hunter, 1991; Montgomery, 2006), and the emergence of the narrative medicine movement (e.g., Charon, 2006, 2009; Greenhalgh & Hurwitz, 1998). Loosely coupled, these research and praxis trajectories emphasize the role of narrative practices in humanizing health care.

Cultural Stories: Moving between Public and Private

Of course, you have to be careful. You hear a lot of stories on ACOR [online cancer list-serv]. We have buried a lot of kids. Sometimes you have to filter what you read, 'cause it can create a lot of "what ifs" and it can take a toll on you. But, we've made life-long friends through ACOR.—Tricia, Caitlin's mom

Narratives rarely, if ever, have a solitary existence. They operate concurrently in relation to other stories, and may reinforce, indirectly compete with, or actively confront or resist one another (Lindemann-Nelson, 2001) in ways that shape our understandings of disease, illness, healthiness, care, healing, survival, and mortality, among other issues. This is the case even with master narratives, stories that underlie, reflect, and perpetuate predominant cultural values and assumptions about how the world is constituted and how society functions. For example, at present the master narrative that the U.S. health care system is the best in the world, albeit that it has grown too expensive, is being challenged by other versions of what is at stake and how reform should occur: stories that illustrate a health care system whose outcomes lag far behind those of other national systems that are less costly and technologically dependent, is inaccessible to large groups of working people, and unfair in terms of who benefits and who is omitted. The saliency, vividness, clarity, and resonance of these competing, sometimes colliding, narrative accounts now circulating in the public sphere is likely to determine how U.S. health care will be reshaped for generations to come. Making sense out of the multiplicity of overlapping but frequently contradictory stories told about specific health concerns is a challenging aspect of health literacy. Some issues that come into play in considering how health narratives are communicated, shared, and understood in the public sphere include intertextuality, narrative transformations, and instrumental, as well as expressive, functions. We'll discuss each of these factors in turn.

Intertextuality. This term refers to the processes through which discrete narrative meanings influence one another (Harter et al., 2005), and even give rise to newly derived significance not intended or implied in preexisting stories. Perhaps the most important interface is between private and public versions of illness narratives. Upon diagnosis of a life-changing or life-threatening condition, one struggles to revise one's autobiography to make sense of an altered identity and why this has happened, and to accommodate ensuing changes in body, lifestyle, and social relations, amongst others. In Caitlin's case, her revision is, by necessity, sudden, radical, and unavoidable: "I was worried about school because I was on the fast track to being valedictorian.... Life just seemed to change in an instant." The difficulty of this transition was in part lessened by exchanging stories with Michelle, another girl undergoing similar experiences: "Cancer brought me a new best friend. She understood in ways that my other friends from school couldn't." Caitlin's mother Tricia found a similar enhanced meaning through participation on a cancer web site in which stories are shared.

However, Tricia also points out a more problematic side of intertextuality in this venue, in which hopeful, positive meanings are superseded by tragic ones. Another intertextual difficulty is what happens when there is a breach or outright contradiction between one's personal narrative and a more public version. Caitlin's father, Doug, commented on the pros and cons of making their personal story public: "It was nice that people thought to donate to us. But a lot of the time, I didn't feel like I needed it, there were probably people who needed it worse. I donated a lot to churches, soup kitchens, 'cause we didn't have a need for it." Japp and Japp (2005), examining experiences with Chronic Fatigue Syndrome, describe the additional suffering brought about when one's private illness narrative is at odds with the dominant public version; in this case the biomedical master narrative of what constitutes a legitimate disease, necessitates the evolution of the "legitimacy narrative" in which an individual's account of illness must attempt to establish moral, medical, and public legitimization for the suffering s/he experiences (p. 109). A more optimistic trajectory may occur when going public with one's private account is voluntary and provides positive functions for both the storyteller and her audience. Beck (2005) emphasizes how readers or listeners became collaborators in the co-construction of an illness story, thus broadening a support community.

Narrative Transformations. When Caitlin's experiences with cancer were communicated to the people of Massilon, Ohio through a series of articles in the local newspaper, she and her family received many responses, though how exactly the readers were affected is difficult to know. A question of great interest that has been investigated through several theoretical vantage points is how the narrative process works. Some of this work is distinctly psychological in nature, theorizing how comprehension of stories impacts individuals and mass audiences, including narrative transportation or how respondents are psychologically transported out of the here-and-now through story (Green & Brock, 2000), authenticity as a necessary quality of effective narrative content in public health (Petraglia, 2009), and education-entertainment in which mass-mediated stories are used purposively to instill ideas, values, and ideologies (Singhal & Rogers, 1999; Slater, 2002). Alternative conceptualizations posit mediated characters and plots as role models (Sharf,

Freimuth, Greenspon, & Plotnick, 1996) and representative anecdotes (Workman, 2005) that enable viewers to work through problematic health scenarios encountered in real time. In sum, current research looks to cultural health narratives as conduits for transforming viewers/listeners, shaping their understandings, feelings, attitudes, and perhaps behaviors in particular ways.

The connection between the personal and public runs both ways. A different perspective on transformation focuses on how personal health narratives are changed through media and other forms of cultural exposure. One of the likely outcomes of the publication of Caitlin's story was public education about the illness experience, cancer diagnosis, and treatment. Since she has been in remission, Caitlin is active in writing and speaking publicly about cancer: "My experience with cancer has been life altering and now it is my duty as a survivor to help good come from this bad chapter in the book of life." However, making personal accounts public may have much more complicated consequences.

The sad, extremely difficult story of Terri Schiavo, a young woman in a persistent vegetative state, is a case in point. The private family disagreement between Terri's parents and her husband over whether life-sustaining treatment should be withdrawn became a national narrative and counternarrative that was portrayed repeatedly on television, through the Internet, and other journalistic outlets. Members of Congress weighed in with contrasting opinions, religious beliefs about the nature of life were invoked, and conversations about advance directives were sparked among ordinary people. How did the popularization of the Schiavo case affect the personal relations among Terri's various advocates? Could the argument have been negotiated with less rancor had the story remained private? What purposes were served by the public debate that ensued from opening this conflict to public scrutiny? What costs were engendered? Was the human dignity of Terri in her compromised state honored or degraded by the public retelling and interpretation of her story?

Narrative Functionality Continued. The aforementioned functions of sense-making, exerting control, warranting decisions, and coping with changing identity are especially pertinent to the communication of personal health narratives (even if this occurs in a public setting). Building community, to which we have now added increasing public awareness and education, are necessarily narrative functions that must transpire in the public sphere. There are two more potential functions connected to public communication we would like to mention. Counternarratives that challenge widely ascribed master narratives are primary and necessary aspects of health advocacy and social activism (Sharf, 2001; Zoller, 2005); for example, poet Audre Lorde's (1980) prescient and memorable image of one-breasted women descending upon Congress to change what was a climate of secrecy and invisibility surrounding breast cancer. Thus, closely related, is the use of narrative to propel changes in social and governmental health care policies (Sharf, 2001). As our scholarship moves more in the direction of these newer functions, we envision a parallel continuum of stories of illness to stories of prevention, healing, and mobilization of resources.

The Narrative Nature of Clinical Judgment and Health Care

What knowledge is necessary to practice medicine, mused Kathryn Montgomery Hunter (1991), an English professor then on the faculty of Morehouse Medical School. Scientific and instrumental logics remain central to the practice of Western medicine, reasoning skills powerfully equipped to address certain dilemmas even as they obscure other ways of knowing. The almost unquestioned assumption that medicine is a science is misleading to the extent that it fails to acknowledge how clinical success also depends on a provider's interpretive capacities to make clinical judgments in inescapably uncertain and contingent moments (Montgomery, 2006). Montgomery enlarged dominant notions of rationality by positioning narrative sense-making as vital for the provision of health care (see also Greenhalgh & Hurwitz, 1998; Mattingly, 1998).

Medicine is far from an unmediated representation of reality. Health care participants construct understandings of experience and use those interpretive frames to guide future actions. Providers and patients alike read physical symptoms narratively and contextually, urged by the impulse to emplot events befalling a character, search for causality, and develop actionable interventions. Individuals offer storied accounts of symptoms, side-effects, and, if invited or supported, their experience of illness in the diverse scenes that compose their lives. But in health care contexts, narratives also take the form of cultural scripts and even performances which create as well as comment upon prior experiences. Norms characterizing the biomedical model (e.g., detached concern) represent institutionalized scripts about how people, labor, and health care delivery should be arranged and performed. The biomedical model itself can be understood as a grand narrative, an ongoing structure of values and beliefs including a hierarchy of characters, archetypal plots, and sacred spaces (Morris, 1998). For example, drawing on ethnographic fieldwork, Morgan-Witte (2005) positioned nurses' stations as backstage storytelling hubs, webs of narrative activity endorsing (and dismissing) value structures, and Ellingson (2005) emphasized the interconnectedness between backstage and frontstage role performances among providers interacting with patients being served by an interdisciplinary oncology team. Of course, personal narratives and cultural scripts are told and lived in material circumstances that shape performances. In reporting on fieldwork with a mobile health clinic serving families in rural Appalachia, Harter, Deardorff, Kenniston, Carmack, and Rattine-Flaherty (2008) illustrated the difficulty of sustaining the taken-for-granted script of patient–provider confidentiality amidst shifting material and social circumstances that call it into question (e.g., paper-thin doors separating exam rooms from waiting areas).

From a performance perspective, clinical action itself is an ever-emerging story, what Mattingly (1994, 1998) termed *therapeutic emplotment*. "Therapists and patients not only tell stories, sometimes they create story-like structures through their interactions," argued Mattingly (1998, p. 19), story-making that is integral to healing. To envision clinical action as an unfolding story reaches beyond looking at narrative as raw material offered by patients and family members. Mattingly's performative stance assumes narratives are lived before they are told (see also, Langellier, 2009). In recounting her immersion with occupational therapists, Mattingly described how they are motivated to locate themselves and patients in an intelligible plot in the midst of interaction. The success of occupational therapy rests with what the therapist and patient accomplish together; "One could say that a therapist's clinical task is to create a therapeutic plot which compels a patient to see therapy as integral to healing" (Mattingly, 1994, p. 813).

In summary, scientific rationality is a limited conception of reason. Isolating a physiological problem and situating it in a realm of its own disconnects illness from the scenes of everyday experience.

Continuing the Conversation

Broadening Narrative Scholarship

I've been scrapbooking a long time. So, anything of significance in our family deserves its own book, be it a prom or birth of a baby or wedding. Each of my kids have scrapbooks from birth to present day. In terms of scrapbooking our cancer experience, initially, I just had to preserve everything. I had to preserve every second and every nuance in case she wasn't here anymore. I had to. I had to. And, but as it went on and she fought harder and got stronger, then it became a book of her victory. When I wrote the letter on the back, I said I was just proud of her and I thanked her for letting me go on the journey with her because I learned so much from her, from humility to humor. Normally, you don't learn those things from your children. And she taught me all those things. So it came from preserving her life into her victory.—Tricia, Caitlin's mom

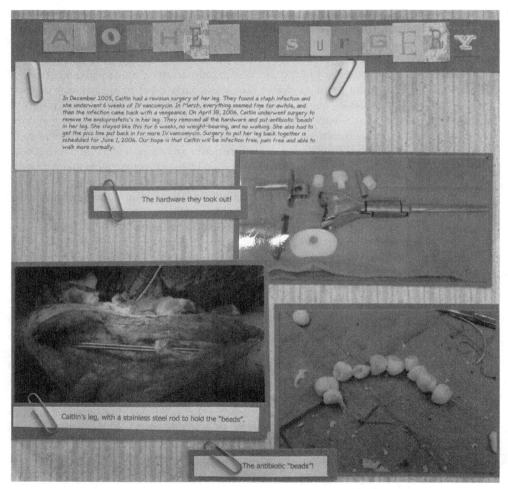

Figure 3.3   Another surgery: Treating staph infection.

Communication scholars naturally gravitate toward linguistic narrative in oral or written form, but individuals use many ways to express their stories of health and illness in everyday life. Scrapbookers like Tricia, for example, serve as memory curators, storytellers who function as what Langellier and Peterson (2006) term *keepers of the kin*. By highlighting special occasions and everyday rituals, individuals make meaning and extend family culture to future generations. The events memorialized in Caitlin's scrapbook mirror moments of importance to most teens—prom, birthday parties, and graduation. In Caitlin's case, however, movie tickets are placed alongside photos of her left lung and leg during surgical procedures, hardware used during reconstructive surgery, and Caitlin's "battle ribbons": plastic ID bracelets from every hospital stay. Obituaries of friends who succumbed to cancer rest beside photos of benefits and blood drives in Caitlin's honor. All told, the scrapbook offers an aesthetic, imaginative representation of Caitlin's storied experiences as a teenager living with cancer.

Narrative frameworks that reflect the multisensorial sense-making of individuals in health and illness (Ellingson, 2009; Harter, 2009; Sharf, 2009) provide voice to individuals who are disenfranchised or otherwise unable to verbally articulate their points of view, and offer opportunities for "representing participants in ways that challenge social conventions" (Cole, Quinlan, & Hayward, 2009, p. 81). Narrative scholars have turned to documentary (Cole et al., 2009), poetic transcription (Carr, 2003), choreographed movement (Joseph, 2008), quilting (Jones & Dawson, 2000), and performance (Gray & Sinding, 2002), in their work with individuals living with AIDS, cancer, or other physical and mental disabilities. These narrative forms offer different ways of understanding the lived experiences of others while also challenging conventional representations and prevailing assumptions. For example, the director and producers of *Plan F* documented the ways in which an auto mechanic's work influences and is influenced by his blindness through particular aesthetic choices (Cole et al., 2009). The short film is shot in the garage with a camera lens that causes only a fraction of the image to be in focus at any given time and resists standard plots of disability by instead depicting the 71-year-old mechanic's life as "thoroughly ordinary, save for his living with a disability" (Cole et al., 2009, p. 85). Such sensibilities ultimately enlarge traditional research rationalities to include "knowledge derived from storied, emotive, and embodied experience" (Harter, Ellingson, Dutta, & Norander, 2009, p. 35).

Aesthetic sensibilities extend to creative and collaborative analytic practices, as well. Ellingson (2009) advocates crystallization methodology as a framework for blending social scientific analyses with creative representations of data into a coherent text or series of related texts. Crystallization manifests in qualitative projects that (a) represent multiple, contrasting ways of knowing on a continuum anchored by art and science; (b) offer complexly rendered interpretations of meanings; (c) utilize more than one genre of writing or other medium; (d) include a significant degree of reflexive consideration on the researcher's role; and (e) embrace knowledge as partial, embodied, constructed, and situated (Ellingson, 2009, p. 10). Given the interactive nature of qualitative research, much of narrative inquiry has expanded to include the researcher's actions for co-constructing meaning with participants, as well. Narrative scholars endorse dialogic ways of knowing that emphasize "how researcher and participant came together in some shared time and space and had diverse effects *on each other*" (Frank, 2005, p. 968).

The turn toward a relational and coconstructive approach to narrative sense-making recognizes narrativity as an inherently social and dialogic communicative process (Harter et al., 2005). Tricia's unconventional representation of Caitlin's lived experiences, for example, ends with a letter included in the back cover of the scrapbook. "May this book be a reminder to you of your strength, determination, and quest for life," writes Tricia to Caitlin. "Thank you for letting me take this journey with you." In similar fashion, participatory research methods such as photovoice (Wang & Burris, 1997; Yamasaki, 2009) and readers' theater (Schneider et al., 2004) can empower and situate ordinary community members as coresearchers in the design, participation, and implementation of scholarly projects. For example, Yamasaki's (2009) narrative analysis of late life in community settings incorporates the photographs of 34 elderly participants who live in the small town and the assisted living facility at the center of the project. The participants chose which pictures to take; titled and described them in in-depth interviews; and selected their favorites for display in local community and online exhibits. In another project (Schneider et al., 2004), individuals with schizophrenia chose a topic (experiences with clinicians), conducted in-depth interviews with each other, and then developed and performed a readers' theater presentation of their results and recommendations for medical professionals.

Practicing Narrative Medicine

Institutional and cultural narratives articulate possibilities and preferences that social actors invoke, orientations that lead to trained incapacities and fossilized institutions (Burke, 1935/1984). In the dominant culture of medicine, patients' experiences deemed notable (and chartable) typically appear as depersonalized abstractions imprinted by the omnipresent voice of the medical enterprise (Poirier et al., 1992). Even so, professional cultures are contested terrains—dynamic, situated, and indeterminate webs of sense-making (Gubrium & Holstein, 2009). The rise of narrative medicine signifies growing acknowledgment that clinical judgment is an interpretive act drawing on narrative skills to integrate overlapping stories told by patients, clinicians, and diagnostic taxonomies.

Dr. Rita Charon, Professor of Clinical Medicine at Columbia University, is a widely recognized, pioneering authority in the practice of narrative medicine. She is Founding Director of the Program in Narrative Medicine at Columbia, and has written extensively on possibilities and difficulties of practicing medicine with narrative sensibilities (e.g., Charon, 2006, 2009). Charon characterizes narrative medicine as practiced with the competence to recognize, absorb, interpret, and be moved by stories of illness. Practicing narrative medicine does not require providers to reject scientific logics, or to privilege personal anecdotes over randomized control trials. Instead, it presupposes that patients experience illness in unique ways that must be juxtaposed with the generalities of a science-using practice (Haidet & Paterniti, 2003). Narrative activity provides meaning, context, and perspective for a patient's predicament, sense-making that clinicians can draw on to understand the plight of the patient and recast it into a medical story coupled with appropriate treatment (Greenhalgh & Hurwitz, 1998).

How is narrative medicine practiced? In the realities of clinical interactions, patients' stories frequently fail to be fully articulated, let alone understood. Why? The achievement of what we refer to as an "aligning moment," an experience of genuine shared understanding, must overcome formidable obstacles. First, doctors must be open to hearing a personal narrative that runs parallel to their own biomedical narratives. Second, patients must be willing and empowered to tell their own stories. In an ideal situation, the inclusion of patients' storied concerns can provide a "narrative jolt," creating a pause in the scripts of biomedical practice and focusing both the doctor and patient on the fully contextualized health issue. There is still much work to be done to realize such an ideal, however, as patients' role expectations often present barriers to telling their own stories, and physicians who have the capacity to hear and understand such stories may still not have the training to know how to respond to and incorporate into decision making what they have heard (Waitzkin, 1991).

At the 2007 National Communication Association convention, Dr. Charon, delivering the Vice-Presidential Plenary Lecture, emphasized that, at a minimal level, all clinical inter-actions possess a narrative structure; that said, some clinical moments are more narrative than others. Serious illness is a breach of the commonplace, moving individuals through disorienting terrain. In such cases, attending to human suffering involves witnessing tran-sitions and transformations. Charon (2006) draws on her literary background to develop future physicians' capacities to join with another who suffers and act on that person's behalf. As students learn to closely read literature (i.e., form, genre, frame, plot, time), one may hope that they become better equipped to listen to patients, read symptoms contextually, and represent what is heard in a form that honors the patients' meanings. Charon also coaches students to write parallel charts and reflect on what they themselves undergo in the care of individuals. As suggested by their name, parallel charts remain separate from official medical records, and articulate socio-emotional aspects of care that may otherwise remain unspoken. Although a literary background has oriented Charon to narrative practices that contextualize and personalize care, other aesthetic experiences provide similar inspiration. Notable examples include Dr. Paul Haidet's translation of jazz improvisation in clinical con-texts (Haidet, 2007) and Dr. Pete Anderson's use of photography in coconstructing medical records with patients and family members (see Harter, 2009).

Responses to Charon spawned an intellectual exchange that continued in a special issue of the *Journal of Applied Communication Research* (Harter & Bochner, 2009). In that issue, several narrative scholars explored the vulnerability (Bochner, 2009), moral dilemmas (Thompson, 2009; Zaner, 2009), and ethos of friendship (Rawlins, 2009) that can accom-pany narrative medicine. Authors encouraged scholars and practitioners to enlarge narra-tive frameworks to reflect aesthetic and performative concerns (Harter, 2009; Langellier, 2009; Sharf, 2009). Collectively, authors remind us that narratives represent *equipment for living*—symbolic resources that allow individuals to size up circumstances and chart future actions (Burke, 1935/1984). Storytelling in health care reflects the narrative impulse and is a powerful form of experiencing and expressing suffering, loss, and healing. Several first tier medical journals (see *Journal of the American Medical Association, Annals of Internal Medi-cine, Health Affairs*) over the past several years have instituted sections for narrative writing. Joining them, *Health Communication*, starting with Volume 24, Issue 7, will publish a regular narrative feature titled "Defining Moments." For the first time within the communication discipline, members of our academic community will be invited to submit essays illustrating the power of narrative to foster health-related commentary and social action.

Reaching Out and Carrying On

For all Dr. Charon's successes—in addition to her extensive scholarship and teaching, her work has been featured on National Public Radio and in the New York Times—she still struggles to be understood and influential within her own profession. Likewise, it is incumbent upon narrative scholars engaged in health communication scholarship and practice to develop ways of extending their work beyond academic journals into actionable outcomes. Consider the range of stakeholders who may benefit from our work—general publics, patients and families, practitioners, medical schools, activist organizations, policy makers. Whatever inroads we have made in this regard are slight and open to improvement.

The concept of "translational research," a mandate to make theoretical and esoteric studies accessible to practitioners and publics that can put such knowledge to everyday use, has been emphasized in medicine and public health, but not in health communication. For narrative scholars, a move in this direction sets the stage for learning from storied cultural and socio-economic diversification (e.g., Dutta, 2004), working toward broader systemic changes, and striving to enrich individuals' lives.

Throughout this whole process, strangers have contacted me, friends have prided me, my parents have stood by me, and my whole community has helped me. They all say that I am an inspiration to everyone due to my strength and perseverance. I enjoy the praise knowing that people believe in my ability to get better, but I do not feel that I am an inspiration at all. I just look at it as if I did what I had to do.—Caitlin Shoup, 2005

Figure 3.4 Caitlin's commentary.

Acknowledgment: The authors are indebted to Caitlin Shoup and her family for permitting their story to become a significant part of this essay.

References

Beck, C. S. (2001). *Communicating for better health: A guide through the medical mazes.* Boston, MA: Allyn & Bacon.

Beck, C. S. (2005). Becoming the story: Narratives as collaborative, social enactments of individual, relational, and public identities. In L. M. Harter, P. M. Japp, & C. S. Beck (Eds.), *Narratives, health and healing: Communication theory, research, and practice* (pp. 61–82). Mahwah, NJ: Erlbaum.

Bochner, A. P. (2009). Vulnerable medicine. *Journal of Applied Communication Research, 37,* 159–166.

Bruner, J. (1990). *Acts of meaning.* Cambridge, MA: Harvard University Press.

Burke, K. (1950). *A rhetoric of motives.* Englewood Cliff, NJ: Prentice-Hall.

Burke, K. (1984). *Permanence and change* (3rd ed.). Berkeley: University of California Press. (Original work published 1935)

Carr, J. M. (2003). Poetic expressions of vigilance. *Qualitative Health Research, 13,* 1324–1331.

Charon, R. (2006). *Narrative medicine: Honoring the stories of illness.* New York: Oxford University Press.

Charon, R. (2009). Narrative medicine as witness for the self-telling body. *Journal of Applied Communication Research, 37,* 118–131.

Cole, C. E., Quinlan, M., & Hayward, C. (2009). Aesthetic projects engaging inequities: Documentary film for social change. In L. M. Harter, M. J. Dutta, & C. E. Cole (Eds.), *Communicating for social impact: Engaging theory, research and pedagogy* (pp. 79–90). Cresskill, NJ: Hampton Press.

Dutta, M. (2004). The unheard voices of Santalis: Communicating about health from the margins of India. *Communication Theory, 14*(3), 237–263.

Ellingson, L. L. (2005). *Communicating in the clinic: Negotiating frontstage and backstage teamwork.* Cresskill, NJ: Hampton Press.

Ellingson, L. L. (2009). *Engaging crystallization in qualitative research: An introduction.* Thousand Oaks, CA: Sage.

Fisher, W. R. (1987). *Human communication as narration: Toward a philosophy of reason, value, and action.* Columbia: University of South Carolina Press.

Frank, A. W. (1995). *The wounded storyteller: Body, illness, and ethics.* Chicago, IL: University of Chicago Press.

Frank, A. W. (2005). What is dialogical research, and why should we do it? *Qualitative Health Research, 15,* 964–974.

Gray, R., & Sinding, C. (2002). *Standing ovation: Performing social science research about cancer.* Walnut Creek, CA: AltaMira Press.

Green, M. C., & Brock, T. C. (2000). The role of transportation in the persuasiveness of public narratives. *Journal of Personality and Social Psychology, 79,* 701–721.

Greenhalgh, T., & Hurwitz, B. (Eds.). (1998). *Narrative based medicine: Dialogue and discourse in clinical practice.* London: BMJ Books.

Gubrium, J. F., & Holstein, J. A. (2009). *Analyzing narrative reality.* Thousand Oaks, CA: Sage.

Haidet, P. (2007). Jazz and the "art" of medicine: Improvisation in the medical encounter. *Annals of Family Medicine, 5,* 164–169.

Haidet, P., & Paterniti, D. (2003). "Building" a history rather than "taking" one: A perspective on information sharing during the medical interview. *Archives of Internal Medicine, 163,* 1134–1140.

Harter, L. M. (2009). Narratives as dialogic, contested, and aesthetic accomplishments. *Journal of Applied Communication Research, 37,* 140–150.

Harter, L. M., & Bochner, A. (2009). Healing through stories. *Journal of Applied Communication Research, 37,* 113–117.

Harter, L. M., Deardorff, K., Kenniston, P. J., Carmack, H., & Rattine-Flaherty, E. (2008). Changing lanes and changing lives: The shifting scenes and continuity of care in a mobile health clinic. In H. Zoller & M. Dutta-Bergman (Eds.), *Emerging issues and perspectives in health communication: Interpretive, critical, and cultural approaches to engaged research* (pp. 313–334). Mahwah, NJ: Erlbaum.

Harter, L. M., Ellingson, L. L., Dutta, M. J., & Norander, S. (2009). The poetic is political ... and other notes on engaged scholarship. In L. M. Harter, M. J. Dutta, & C. E. Cole (Eds.), *Commu-*

nicating for social impact: Engaging theory, research and pedagogy (pp. 33–46). Cresskill, NJ: Hampton Press.

Harter, L. M., Japp, P. M., & Beck, C. S. (2005). Vital problematics about narrative theorizing about health and healing. In L. M. Harter, P. M. Japp, & C. S. Beck (Eds.), *Narratives, health, and healing: Communication theory, research, and practice* (pp. 7–30). Mahwah, NJ: Erlbaum.

Hunter, K. (1991). *Doctors' stories: The narrative structure of medical knowledge.* Princeton, NJ: Princeton University Press.

Japp, P. M., & Japp, D. K. (2005). Desperately seeking legitimacy: Narratives of a biomedically invisible disease. In L. M. Harter, P. M. Japp, & C. S. Beck (Eds.), *Narratives, health and healing: Communication theory, research, and practice* (pp. 107–130). Mahwah, NJ: Erlbaum.

Jones, C., & Dawson, J. (2000). *Stitching a revolution.* San Francisco, CA: HarperCollins.

Joseph, S. (2008, February 6). These vets are moved to action: Former soldiers with stress disorders join with a choreographer to tell their stories through dance. *Los Angeles Times,* p. E2.

Kleinman, A. (1988). *The illness narratives: Suffering, healing, and the human condition.* New York: Basic Books.

Langellier, K. M. (2009). Performing narrative medicine. *Journal of Applied Communication Research, 37,* 151–158.

Langellier, K. M., & Peterson, E. E. (2006). Family storytelling as communication practice. In L. H. Turner & R. West (Eds.), *The family communication sourcebook* (pp. 109–128). Thousand Oaks, CA: Sage.

Lindemann-Nelson, H. (2001). *Damaged identities, narrative repair.* Ithaca, NY: Cornell University Press.

Lorde, A. (1980). *The cancer journals.* Argyle, NY: Spinsters Ink.

Mattingly, C. (1994). The concept of therapeutic "emplotment." *Social Science & Medicine, 38,* 811–822.

Mattingly, C. (1998). *Healing dramas and clinical plots: The narrative structure of experience.* Cambridge, UK: Cambridge University Press.

Montgomery, K. (2006). *How doctors think: Clinical judgment and the practice of medicine.* Oxford, UK: Oxford University Press.

Morgan-Witte, J. (2005). Narrative knowledge development among caregivers: Stories from the nurses' station. In L. M. Harter, P. M. Japp, & C. S. Beck (Eds.), *Narratives, health, and healing* (pp. 217–236). Mahwah, NJ: Erlbaum.

Morris, D. B. (1998). *Illness and culture in the postmodern age.* Berkeley: University of California Press.

Pennebaker, J. W. (2000). Telling stories. The health benefits of narrative. *Literature and Medicine, 19,* 3–18.

Petraglia, J. (2009) The importance of being authentic: Persuasion, narration, and dialogue in health communication and education. *Health Communication, 24,* 176–185.

Poirier, S., Rosenblum, L., Ayres, L., Brauner, D. H., Sharf, B. F., & Stanford, A. F. (1992). Charting the chart—An exercise in interpretation(s). *Literature and Medicine, 11,* 1–22.

Poirier, S., & Ayres, L. (1997). Endings, secrets, and silences: Overreading in narrative inquiry. *Research in Nursing and Health, 20,* 551–557.

Rawlins, W. K. (2009). Narrative medicine and the stories of friends. *Journal of Applied Communication Research, 37,* 167–173.

Reismann, C. (2008). *Narrative methods for the human sciences.* Thousand Oaks, CA: Sage.

Ricoeur, P. (1984–1988). *Time and narrative* (Vols. 1-3; K. McLaughlin & D. Pellaver, Trans.). Chicago, IL: University of Chicago Press.

Schneider, B., Scissons, H., Arney, L., Benson, G., Derry, J., Lucas, K., … Sunderland, M. (2004). Communication between people with schizophrenia and their medical professionals: A participatory research project. *Qualitative Health Research, 14,* 562–577.

Sharf, B. F. (2001). Out of the closet and into the legislature: The impact of communicating breast cancer narratives on health policy. *Health Affairs 20,* 213–218.

Sharf, B. F. (2005). How I fired my surgeon and embraced an alternate narrative. In L. M. Harter, P. M. Japp, & C. S. Beck (Eds.), *Narratives, health and healing: Communication theory, research, and practice* (pp. 325–342). Mahwah, NJ: Erlbaum.

Sharf, B. F. (2009). Observations from the outside in: Narratives of illness, healing, and mortality in everyday life. *Journal of Applied Communication Research, 37,* 132–139.

Sharf, B. F., Freimuth, V. S., Greenspon, P., & Plotnick, C. (1996). Confronting cancer on thirty-something: Audience response to health content on entertainment television. *Journal of Health Communication, 5,* 141–160.

Sharf, B. F., & Vanderford, M. L. (2003). Illness narratives and the social construction of health. In T. L. Thompson, A. M. Dorsey, K. I. Miller, & R. Parrott (Eds.), *Handbook of health communication* (pp. 9–34). Mahwah, NJ: Erlbaum.

Shoup, C. (2005, Spring). From behind a cancer teen's eyes. *CCCF Newsletter,* p. 9 (The National Office of Candlelighters Childhood Cancer Foundation). Retrieved from http://candlelighters.org/Information/cancerteen/tabid/325/Default.aspx

Singhal, A., & Rogers, E. M. (1999). *Entertainment-education: A communication strategy for social change.* Mahwah, NJ: Erlbaum.

Slater, M. D. (2002). Entertainment education and the persuasive impact of narratives. In M. C. Green, J. J. Strange, & T. C. Brock (Eds.), *Narrative impact: Social and cognitive foundations* (pp. 157–182). Mahwah, NJ: Erlbaum.

Thompson, T. L. (2009). The applicability of narrative ethics. *Journal of Applied Communication Research, 37,* 188–195.

Waitzkin, H. (1991). *The politics of medical encounters.* New Haven, CT: Yale University Press.

Wang, C. C., & Burris, M. A. (1997). Photovoice: Concept, methodology, and use for participatory needs assessment. *Health Education & Behavior, 24,* 369–387.

Workman, T. (2005). Death as the representative anecdote in the construction of the collegiate "binge-drinking" problem. In L. M. Harter, P. M. Japp, & C. S. Beck (Eds.), *Narratives, health and healing: Communication theory, research, and practice* (pp. 131–148). Mahwah, NJ: Erlbaum.

Yamasaki, J. (2009). *Community connectedness and long-term care in late life: A narrative analysis of successful aging in a small town* (Unpublished doctoral dissertation). Texas A&M University, College Station, TX.

Zaner, R. M. (2009). Narrative and decision. *Journal of Applied Communication Research, 37,* 167–173.

Zoller, H. M. (2005). Health activism: Communication theory and action for social change. *Communication Theory, 15,* 341–364.

SECTION II

Delivery Systems of Formal Care

4

HOW MEDICAL INTERACTION SHAPES AND REFLECTS THE PHYSICIAN–PATIENT RELATIONSHIP

Debra L. Roter and Judith A. Hall

Interaction is the fundamental instrument by which the doctor–patient relationship is shaped and through which medical care is directed. By interaction we mean talk—what is said in the verbal sense—the words that are used, the facts exchanged, the advice given, and the social amenities that tie the conversation together. But we also mean communication beyond words, the whole repertoire of nonverbal expressions and cues within which verbal transactions are embedded. The smiles and head nods of agreement, the grimaces of pain, the high-pitched voice of anxiety, the rapid fire delivery of questions critical to a differential diagnosis, or the calm soothing tones of comfort and reassurance are all indicative of the communicated, but unsaid. These nonverbal expressions give context and enhanced meaning to the words spoken. It is here in the intersection of the said and the unsaid that the relationship between patient and physician is forged and interpersonal dominance, respect, liking, or trust are established.

Though physicians conduct physical exams and use blood tests, X-rays, medications, and other tools to achieve therapeutic goals, the value of these activities is limited without the interactions that put them in a meaningful context for both the patient and the physician. High regard for the role of communication is far from universally accepted. Historians of modern medicine have tracked an undeniable decline in the centrality of communication to the care process through the latter half of the 20th century. In his study of the history of doctors and patients, Shorter (1985) attributes the denigration of communication to the ascendancy of the molecular- and chemistry-oriented sciences as the predominant medical paradigm. This change was fundamental in directing medical inquiry away from the person of the patient to the biochemical and pathophysiology of the patient. It was not coincidental that the practice of interviewing patients from a written outline designed around a series of yes-no hypothesis testing questions replaced unstructured medical histories at this point in the history of medicine. The patient's talk was largely curtailed by these changes and was restricted to answering the questions asked. One important effect of these changes was to recast the medical interview as wholly scientific and objective. It can be further argued that the scientific recasting of the medical dialogue contributed to a loss of physician confidence in the significance of any but the most explicit hypothesis-driven exchanges and quantified findings.

The tide, however, may be turning. National reports, including two issued by the Institute of Medicine (IOM, 1999, 2001) and one by the American College of Physicians' Charter on Medical Professionalism (ABIM Foundation, ACP-ASIM Foundation, European Federation of Internal Medicine, 2003) have focused attention on the centrality of patient-centered communication to the safe delivery of quality medical care and the practice of ethical medicine. Within this context, patient-centeredness has become the shorthand reference to the inclusion of patients' perspective and preferences in care, as well as the provision of as much information to patients as they need in order to participate, to the extent they would like, in medical decision making (Gerteis, Edgman-Levitan, Daley, & Delbanco, 1993; Laine & Davidoff, 1996). Supported by a growing literature that links communication to a host of valued outcomes (see Duggan & Thompson, this volume), patient-centered communication is increasingly regarded as a critical area of medical practice (Lipkin, Putnam, & Lazare, 1995). Indeed, key US medical accrediting and licensing bodies have set 2020 as the point by which patient-centered communication skills will be redefined as a domain of professional practice for which a demonstration of proficiency will be demanded and assessed (see Egbert et al., this volume).

Even with increasing recognition of communication's role in quality of care, attention to emotion and its role in the care process remains largely unexamined (Roter, Frankel, Hall, & Sluter, 2006). Using the terms *high-* and *low context culture* coined by anthropologist Edward T. Hall (1976), medicine can be seen as having undergone a shift in its nature from a high- to a low communication context endeavor. High context communication depends on sensitivity to nonverbal behaviors and environmental cues to decipher meaning, while low context exchanges are more verbally explicit with little reliance on the unstated or nuanced. It is our premise that the doctor–patient relationship is an intrinsically high context phenomenon within which the communication of expert knowledge as well as emotion are central (Roter & Hall, 2006).

The purpose of this chapter is to provide a broad context for understanding the role of both verbal and nonverbal medical interactions in shaping and reflecting the patient–physician relationship and the delivery of high quality medical care. We will describe the elements of patient-centered communication and its relationship to the communication of emotion through nonverbal behavior.

Patient-Centered Communication

As noted, patient-centered communication is widely valued as a conceptual marker of quality care. However, the term has been so broadly used as to be ascribed to phenomena as disparate as a communication style (Byrne & Long, 1976; Roter, 2000), a clinical method (McWhinney, 1989), a philosophy of medicine (Engel, 1977), a type of therapeutic relationship (Gerteis et al., 1993), a quality of care indicator (IOM, 2001), and a professional and moral imperative (ABIM foundation et al., 2002). Despite wide reference to the concept of patient-centeredness, there is agreement on only its broadest dimensions. For instance, the IOM (2001, p. 3) definition of patient-centered care as being "respectful of and responsive to individual patient preferences, needs and values, and ensuring that patient values guide all clinical decisions" is more philosophic than operational. Other definitions are similarly broad, including the provision of as much information as needed for patients to participate to the extent desired in medical decision making (Laine & Davidoff, 1996); in making it easier for patients to express concerns, be involved in the design of their care, and be supported in patient self-management (Bergeson & Dean, 2006); beyond all else the slogan emerging from an international retreat of multidisciplinary clinicians and researchers, "nothing about me without me" (Delbanco et al., 2001).

What all this means in regard to explicit verbal exchange can be equally broad and focused in the eye of the beholder. Nevertheless, some communications are better matched to these descriptions than others. In our meta-analyses on the subject of physician gender and medical communication, we sorted over 150 communication variables into categories consistent with the literature describing patient-centeredness, and were able to organize them by the functions of the medical interview, including those related to data gathering, patient education and counseling, emotional responsiveness, and partnership-building (Roter & Hall, 2004).

In terms of data gathering, we included physician communication that furthers the patient's ability to tell the story of his or her illness through disclosure of information that the patient may deem meaningful (e.g., use of open-ended questions, particularly in the psychosocial domain), as well as all forms of patient questions useful in directing physician instruction to patient-defined areas of informational need. Patient education and counseling communication includes information in the biomedical and psychosocial realm that assists patients in making sense of their condition and coping with the medical regimen and lifestyle demands of treatment. From the patient perspective, as suggested by Sharf et al. in the preceding chapter, the opportunity to relate the illness narrative and reflect on experience, perspective, and interpretation of symptoms and circumstances may hold therapeutic value, and, consequently, patients' disclosure, especially in the psychosocial realm, can be viewed as an indicator of the visit's patient-centered focus. Partnership-building communication assists patients in assuming a more active role in the medical dialogue, either through active enlistment of patient input (e.g., asking for the patient's opinion and expectations, use of interest cues, paraphrasing and interpreting the patient's statements to check for [physician] understanding, and explicitly asking for patient understanding) or passively by assuming a less dominating stance within the relationship (e.g., being less verbally dominant). Patients' participatory communication reflects components of active enlistment that include facilitation of physician input through requests for opinion, understanding, paraphrase and interpretations, and verbal attentiveness.

Statements that explicitly convey emotion include empathy, legitimation, reassurance, or concern. In addition, positive and negative statements also convey emotional content. Positive talk captures the general positive atmosphere created in the visit through verbal behaviors such as agreements, approvals, compliments, joking, and laughter. Social conversation defined as nonmedical exchanges are largely social pleasantries and greetings, usually functioning as a linguistic bridge from the social opening or closing of the visit to the business of the visit. Social talk is not as emotionally charged as positive talk, but does convey friendliness and personal regard. Negative emotion is captured in statements reflecting disagreement and criticism. While the type of verbal exchanges just described captures the "what" of patient-centered communication, the nonverbal channel provides the "how" by which interaction is delivered.

Nonverbal Communication of Patient-Centeredness

We define nonverbal behavior to include a variety of communicative behaviors that do not carry linguistic content (Knapp & Hall, 2010). Briefly, these include (among others) facial expressivity, smiling, eye contact, head nodding, hand gestures, postural positions (open or closed body posture and forward to backward body lean); paralinguistic speech characteristics such as speech rate, loudness, pitch, pauses, and speech dysfluencies; and dialogic behaviors such as interruptions. Nonverbal behavior is widely recognized as conveying affective and emotional information, though it has other functions as well (such as regulating turn-taking in conversation) (Knapp & Hall, 2010). As examples, a frown may convey disapproval or a smile may convey approval or agreement. A blank expression may also convey an affective message to a perceiver, such as aloofness, boredom, or dismissal. Nonverbal behaviors often (although not always) accompany words and thereby give words meaning in context (for example, by amplifying or contradicting the verbal message). So, a verbal message of agreement ("Sure, that's fine") may be interpreted differently depending on whether the statement is accompanied by a frown or a smile or a blank expression.

Considering its centrality to the care process, nonverbal behavior has received surprisingly little attention in the medical communication literature (Hall, Harrigan, & Rosenthal, 1995; Heath, 1986; Schmid Mast, 2007). For this reason, the remainder of this chapter will focus primarily on the role of nonverbal behavior and its transmission of emotion in patient-centered care.

Emotions and the Medical Care Process

There are three interrelated ways that emotions play a part in the process of medical care: patients and physicians have emotions, they show emotions, and they judge the emotions of others. The pathways by which each of these is communicated will be briefly described.

First, physicians and patients are influenced by emotions they have experienced in the past, by emotions they experience in interaction with each other in the present, and by the anticipation of emotions in the future. We often think of patients as the ones having emotions. For example, they may have anxiety or depression, and they are likely to have positive or negative feelings about their physicians. Physicians' emotions receive less study, though physicians inevitably bring their emotional lives into medical visits and have emotional responses to patients. An antagonistic, frustrating, or demanding patient may anger or exasperate a physician (Levinson, 1993), while a pleasant, healthy, or cooperative patient may be liked more than others (Hall, Epstein, DeCiantis, & McNeil, 1993; Hall, Horgan, Stein, & Roter, 2002). A patient or physician may try to orchestrate the visit so that emotionally demanding or arousing situations do not occur by bypassing discussion of such contentious topics as weight or smoking, missed appointments or medication adherence.

Also relevant to the discussion of patient and physician emotion are the concepts of transference and countertransference. Well described in the psychiatric literature, transference is a phenomenon in which patients displace or "transfer" to the doctor strong emotional feelings that are engendered by others with whom they have intense relationships, such as a parent, spouse, or child. When this occurs, the patient may experience an emotional response to a clinical situation that seems out of proportion with the situational context. Countertransference works in a similar way but refers to the physician's "transfer" of strong emotions based on his or her own personal relationships to the patient. The experience of transference and countertransference goes beyond a sentiment like "you remind me of my daughter" to intense feelings, positive or negative, including protectiveness, love, or manipulation (Cohen-Cole, 1991).

It is difficult to pinpoint the origin of intense emotional reaction and this is particularly true within the context of transference and countertransference. Personal awareness training, clinical supervision, and individual therapy may be useful in helping physicians more accurately identify transference in their patients and better understand their own motivations and tendencies in this regard (Cohen-Cole, 1991; Novack, 1987).

Second, both physicians and patients show emotions, sometimes in spite of efforts at suppression or masking. As noted by Schmid Mast (2007), one only need consider the widespread acceptance of the necessity for double-blind studies in drug trials to appreciate the implications of inadvertent nonverbal cueing. Not only must a patient be blind to the active/inert status of a drug to guard against the well documented placebo effect, but blinding a physician to the drug status is equally necessary to guard against an expectation bias. The show of positive anticipation through an eager smile or nod, or the expression of disappointment in a downward gaze may bias results. Some of the emotional cues that are conveyed by patients reflect their illness state. These include cues relating to physical pain (Patrick, Craig, & Prkachin, 1986; Prkachin, 1992) and to physical and psychological distress (Hall, Roter, Milburn, & Daltroy, 1996). Coronary disease is associated with distinctive vocal and facial expressions (Hall, Friedman, & Harris, 1986). Among patients with coronary illness, episodes of ischemia correspond with facial movements associated with anger, suggesting that anger can trigger coronary events (Rosenberg, Ekman, Jiang, et al., 2001). Some of the cues expressed by patients are inadvertently conveyed, while others are part of deliberate efforts to convey the experience of symptoms and suffering to the physician—experiences that are difficult to express in words (Heath, 2002).

Third, the evidence that emotions are shown in the medical visit implies that both physicians and patients judge each other's emotions. Physicians use patients' affective cues in the diagnostic process, as well as in evaluating clinical progress and overall well-being. For example, physicians may elicit emotions to help make a diagnosis such as expressive aphasia, or may look for certain nonverbal cues when concerned about a patient's possible depression or when estimating how much pain the patient is experiencing. Patients may also use physicians' affective cues in a sort of parallel diagnostic process to draw conclusions about the doctor, as well as about the veracity and seriousness of the information that is conveyed. Using information derived from both what the doctor says and how he or she says it, patients may judge the kind of a person the doctor is and the nature of the doctor's attitudes, intentions, and trustworthiness. Thus, even a doctor who is bland in expression and who spends all his or her time on medical business may still inspire good feelings in a patient because the patient values being taken seriously. Further, physicians who provide adequate information are likely to be interpreted as being competent and caring, and these interpretations may be a major influence on the relationship and the entire course of illness; these interpretations may be more important even than the information itself (Hall, Roter, & Rand, 1981).

In a somewhat different way, patients use emotion to look to physicians for "information behind the information" in an attempt to come to terms with the uncertainty and anxiety that so often accompany health-threatening or life-threatening conditions. Is there yet more bad news to come? Is there reason to hope? Has the doctor given up on me? The judgments physicians and patients make of each other's emotional cues may be right or wrong, but, either way, such judgments are likely to lead to behavioral choices and possibly to health consequences.

Shared Emotional Experience

Like all people who forge relationships, patients and physicians are influenced by a shared emotional experience that defines, at least in part, the nature of their relationship. To the extent that the experience of an emotion–that is, the feeling of an emotion–is distinct from an awareness of the emotion, it is reasonable to question if patients and physicians are consciously aware of the emotional contours of their relationship. We suggest that they are. We will draw support for our conclusion from two studies in which this idea of shared emotion has been explored. The first of these is a study of patient and physician liking and the second is a study of respect.

In our study of liking (Hall, Horgan et al., 2002), physicians and patients were asked to independently rate how much they liked one another. Liking was defined as feelings of warmth and friendliness, and enthusiasm for seeing someone. From the patient's perspective two questions were asked (responses were on a 5-point Likert scale): "All in all, I like this doctor a lot" (mean = 4.53, SD = .69) and "I really think this doctor liked me a lot" (mean = 4.09, SD = .80). Liking was rated by the physicians with two parallel questions, using the same 5-point scale: "All in all, I like this patient a lot" (mean = 4.05, SD = .78) and "This patient likes me a lot" (mean = 3.89, SD = .74). The correlations among the liking variables shed light on actual mutuality of liking, assumed mutuality of liking, and accuracy of liking in the physician–patient relationship. *Actual mutuality of liking* was significantly positive, although the correlation was small in magnitude (r = .23) (correlation of "I like patient" with "I like physician"), meaning that how much the physician liked the patient was positively related to how much the patient liked the physician. *Assumed mutuality of liking* was much stronger than actual mutuality of liking, for both the patient (r = .66) (correlation of "I like doctor" with "Doctor likes me"), and the physician (r = .68) (correlation of "I like patient" and "Patient likes me"). Finally, *accuracy of liking* was significantly positive, and equally so for both the patient and the physician, meaning that both patients and physicians were similarly aware of how much they were liked by the other. The patient's accuracy, captured by the correlation between "Doctor likes me" and "I like patient," was significant, but small in magnitude (r = .21) and the physician's accuracy, captured by the correlation between "Patient likes me" and "I like doctor," was similarly significant and small (r = .21).

This study found that liking is indeed part of the physician–patient relationship, as much for the physician as for the patient. First, we found that how much each liked the other was related to how much each was liked, and this mutuality-of-liking effect was equally present for both the physician and the patient. Thus, there appears to be reciprocity in terms of liking. We can speculate that one of the many possible ramifications of this mutuality is that, when the patient and physician like each other, they both behave in ways that reflect this. For example, each may show greater responsiveness to the needs of the other: patients may pay greater attention to what the physician says and be more likely to adhere to appointments and his/her treatment recommendations; and physicians may listen more to what the patient says and be more willing to explain why certain tests were done and participate in decision making. And, of course, these influences can feed back, such that (as an example) a more-liked patient might express more positive affect, which in turn might increase further the physician's liking for that patient.

We also found that liking for the other was even more strongly related to the *perception* of being liked, which we referred to as assumed mutuality. Considering that perceptions comprise the psychological reality within which people function, this finding, too, has potential implications, and all the more so in light of our finding that both physicians and patients were significantly accurate in their assessment of how much they were liked. Though these accuracy correlations were not strong in absolute magnitude, they did demonstrate that the physicians were not fully able to disguise or conceal how much they liked or disliked their patients, and indeed they were no more successful in doing so than their patients were. It is obvious that accuracy in perceiving liking could contribute to the reciprocal processes described above.

Although individuals may make explicit reference to the quality of their relationship in words, this is rare and we believe it is much more common for feelings of liking, warmth, and enthusiasm to be conveyed, and reciprocated, indirectly through verbal or nonverbal behavior that carries meaning for the participants. We did not have observational measures in the study, but we did asked patients to report on how the physician acted during the visit, asking, for example, about instrumental behaviors (e.g., the doctor answered my questions, the doctor told me exactly why certain tests would be done) and socioemotional behaviors (e.g., the doctor seemed annoyed, the doctor made me feel important). We found that physicians were significantly less well liked when patients perceived them to have communicated less than optimally (on both instrumental and socioemotional dimensions).

A second study of shared emotional experience explores perceptions of respect (Beach, Roter, Wang, Duggan, & Cooper, 2006). In that "respectful" features as the first definitional element in the IOM definition of patient-centered care, we wondered about the extent to which physicians vary in how much they respect their patients, and if patients accurately perceive levels of physician respect. As in the liking study, physicians and patients were asked for independent ratings. Patients were asked one item (responses were on a 5-point Likert scale): "This doctor has a great deal of respect for me." Physicians were asked a parallel question, using the same 5-point scale, to assess the level of respect for that patient: "Compared to other patients, I have a great deal of respect for this patient." Physician-reported respect varied across patients; physicians *strongly* agreed that they had a great deal of respect for about 33% of their patients, agreed for 45%, and were either neutral or disagreed for 21%. On the whole, patients accurately perceived physician respect, and the relationship was significant but small in magnitude ($r = .18$); 38% reported respect precisely as rated by the physician, 45% overestimated their physicians' rating, and 16% underestimated physician respect.

In this study, the medical visits were recorded and we were able to identify communication correlates of visits in which the doctor reported respecting the patient. Physicians were significantly more affectively positive (based on raters' judgments of emotional tone), and provided more statements of information to highly respected compared with more moderately respected patients during medical visits. The findings suggest that there are measurable ways in which physician attitudes of respect toward patients are communicated during medical encounters. Moreover, this communication appears to be both in the instrumental realm through greater provision of information and in the socioemotional realm through greater positive affect. Although not measured, it is likely that the affective ratings present a parallel channel to other nonverbal behaviors, such as nodding, smiling, making eye contact, or leaning forward (Hall, Harrigan, & Rosenthal, 1995).

Emotional Self-Awareness and Nonverbal Sensitivity

Although emotional self-awareness, and the related concept of mindfulness, are recognized as attributes of the reflective practitioner, with some authors asserting that awareness of one's own feelings is a prerequisite for insight into the feelings of others and an indication of empathic ability, it has received relatively little attention in the research literature (Cohen-Cole, 1991; Holm & Aspegren, 1999; Krasner et al., 2009; Novack, 1987).

An unusual study of emotional self-awareness in medical students was undertaken as part of a communication skills training program (Holm & Aspegren, 1999). Prior to training, male and female medical students scored equally on the study's measure of emotional self-awareness. Both male and female students showed improvement as a result of the training program; however, female students were able to describe their emotional reactions to videotape clips of patients with greater awareness of complex and ambivalent feelings than their male counterparts. The authors suggest that increased communication proficiency in the verbal domain (stressed in the training curriculum) enhanced female students' empathic abilities and consequently awareness of their patients' as well as their own emotions. The gender advantage for female students may be attributed to their generally higher levels of comfort in talking about feelings and emotion.

In contrast to studies of emotional awareness, there is a large research literature and a number of well-established tools for measuring nonverbal sensitivity (Hall & Bernieri, 2001), although its application within the context of medicine is similarly sparse. Most measures of nonverbal sensitivity assess accuracy in the recognition of emotions as expressed by others, known broadly as decoding skill. While less often measured because of its cost and complexity, an assessment of an individual's ability to convey emotional messages as intended is also an important nonverbal communication skill.

Physicians' nonverbal skills in terms of encoding (the ability to accurately convey emotional messages as intended) and decoding (the ability to accurately recognize emotions of others) have been investigated in several studies (DiMatteo, Hays, & Prince, 1986; DiMatteo, Taranta, Friedman, & Prince, 1980; Friedman, DiMatteo, & Taranta, 1980; Hall, Roter, Blanch, & Frankel, 2009). Physicians who are more skilled on the expressive task of emotional encoding have patients who rate their physician as listening more and being more caring and sensitive than other doctors. Also, patients of physicians who are more accurate at decoding body movements receive higher satisfaction ratings from their patients, and patients of physicians who are better able to decode voice tone cues are less likely to cancel medical appointments.

Whether physicians' nonverbal skill has a causal impact on these outcomes (as opposed to other, unmeasured variables) cannot be determined from correlational studies. However, if a causal relation is established it is important to consider the mechanisms through which physicians' nonverbal skill may be translated into higher satisfaction and appointment keeping. We can speculate that nonverbally skilled physicians engage in more appropriate nonverbal behaviors, are more sensitive to patient nonverbal cues of distress or confusion, and are more effective in conveying emotional messages of caring and sincerity to their patients.

In our study of medical students (Hall, Roter, Blanch, et al., 2009), we have noted that male students who were more nonverbally sensitive reported greater ability to identify their own emotions and were more patient-centered in their communication with simulated patients during an OSCE exercise. Unlike the findings of Holm and Aspegren (1999), we found these relationships were only evident for male students; female students' nonverbal sensitivity appeared unrelated to either emotional self-clarity or communication performance.

Clues to Emotion in Thin Slices of Interaction

People can accurately judge others' emotions at above chance levels, as well as judging personality traits, intelligence, status, and social attitudes (such as racial prejudice), based on surprisingly small amounts of behavioral information, often called "thin slices" of behavior (Ambady & Rosenthal, 1992; Hall & Bernieri, 2001). Sometimes the thin slices that are investigated are less than one second in duration, but more often they are several seconds up to several minutes long.

Several thin slice studies of electronically filtered speech (speech that is altered so that the words cannot be understood) have found that physicians' feelings toward patients, reflected in how they talked about them in interviews when the patient was not present, were highly related to the physicians' tone of voice during medical visits (Rosenthal, Blanck, & Vannicelli, 1984). An interesting study of alcoholic patients showed the effect of voice tone on patient utilization behavior (Milmoe, Rosenthal, Blane, Chafetz, & Wolf, 1967). Milmoe and colleagues asked physicians to talk about their feelings toward alcoholic patients seen in an emergency room. Measures of hostility in the physician's tone of voice during these interviews predicted the physician's subsequent failure to have patients follow through on referrals to treatment centers for alcoholics. Presumably, the patient noticed the physician's hostile and rejecting voice tone during the medical visit and responded by rejecting the physician's suggestion for further treatment, even though that treatment was with other doctors in a different facility.

In our own thin slice studies, a combination of the physician's words and voice tone predicted patient satisfaction in a counterintuitive way; negative affect (irritation and anxiety) conveyed through the physician's voice when coupled with positive words (sympathetic and calming) was associated with more patient satisfaction and better appointment keeping over a 6-month period (Hall, Roter, & Rand, 1981). We speculate that anxiety (and even irritation) in the physician's voice tone may be heard as conveying seriousness and concern for the patient's well-being and future health. The presence of positive verbal messages may help moderate the negativity of the voice tone and reinforce the attribution of physician sincerity. This may be especially true when the patient and physician have a longstanding relationship, or may act to encourage the continuation of the relationship.

In another study of filtered speech using simulated patients, additional intriguing relationships were found between nonverbal communication and role-playing subjects' satisfaction ratings (Roter, Hall, & Katz, 1987). Physicians who were more informative and less social in their interactions were judged to have more interested and anxious vocal qualities than other physicians. These visits were also rated by role-playing subjects as being more satisfying than the more social visits. From these studies, it appears that medical encounters with some degree of negative affect (especially anxiety in the physician's voice), when coupled with comforting words, may be viewed by patients as positive for the relationship, probably reflecting perceived sincerity, dedication, and competence.

Some researchers have speculated that physicians who get sued for medical malpractice may communicate differently, both verbally and nonverbally, from those who do not. Voice analysis of a sample of routine surgical visits—half with physicians who had had at least two previous malpractice claims against them and half with no malpractice claim history—found that the emotional tone of the physician's voice distinguished these two groups (Ambady, LaPlante et al., 2002). The physicians judged by raters to convey higher levels of dominance and lower levels of concern or anxiety in their voice tones were much more likely to have been sued than other physicians in the sample. This result has interesting parallels to the findings mentioned above in which affect in the physician's voice was linked to patient satisfaction.

In the previously described study of liking, physicians' liking of patients was inversely related to the patient's consideration of changing doctors a year later; the greater the liking, the less likely was the patient to contemplate switching physicians (Hall, Horgan, et al., 2002). It is possible that warmth and liking transmitted through voice tone reinforced patients' commitment to not switching doctors. However, direct evidence linking physicians' nonverbal communication and health consequences is sparse. Especially noteworthy in this regard is a study by Ambady and colleagues which links physical therapists' patterns of nonverbal communication and their therapeutic efficacy (Ambady, Koo, Rosenthal, & Winograd, 2002). Independent raters' judgments of videotaped samples of therapists' nonverbal behavior were correlated with clients' physical, cognitive, and psychological functioning at admission, discharge, and at 3-month follow-up. Therapists' distancing behaviors, defined as not smiling and looking away from the client, were strongly correlated with short- and long-term decreases in physical and cognitive functioning. In contrast, facial expressiveness reflected in smiling, nodding, and frowning was associated with short- and long-term improvements in functioning. Physicians who appear to exhibit more emotionally expressive nonverbal behaviors, which are perhaps related to nonverbal sensitivity—including facial expressiveness, eye contact, head nods, body posture, and voice tone—are generally viewed more favorably by patients.

Griffith and colleagues addressed the question of whether nonverbal behaviors carry greater significance for patients with psychosocially complex complaints rather than more purely somatic complaints (Griffith, Wilson, Langer, & Haist, 2003). In their study, medical residents were assigned to one of three standardized encounters: a primarily medical problem of chest pain, a primarily psychosocial problem of depression with a history of sexual abuse, or a counseling problem involving risk reduction for an HIV patient. The standardized patients rated the residents using a multi-item checklist on: (a) general verbal communication skills (including use of open ended questions and summarization); (b) case-specific information gathered and information counseled; (c) a seven-element nonverbal index (facial expressivity ranging from unexpressive, blank to very expressive, emotional; frequency of smiling; eye contact and nodding both ranging from infrequent to very frequent; body lean ranging from backward to forward; body posture ranging from closed to open; and tone of voice ranging from unexpressive, monotone, to very expressive, emotional); and (d) a 5-item general satisfaction measure.

Findings revealed that patient satisfaction was strongly associated with more emotionally expressive nonverbal behavior scores of physicians, regardless of medical scenario. This relationship was equally evident in the biomedical chest pain scenario as well as the psychosocial and behavioral scenarios of depression and HIV compliance, suggesting that the nature of the medical problem does not moderate the effect of the physician's nonverbal behavior on patient satisfaction. Moreover, the correlation between general satisfaction and the nonverbal score was substantially stronger than the correlations between satisfaction and general verbal communication skills or information scores. Nonverbal communication explained more patient satisfaction variance than the verbal performance of the study residents.

Future Directions and New Challenges

In many respects, and especially in regard to the provision of medical information, the Internet, as many commentators have noted, has changed everything. This applies in spades to health information. According to the Pew Internet and American Life Project (Fox & Fallows, 2003), fully half of the American adult population has used the Internet at least once to search for health information. Among people who are regular Internet users, 80% say that they use online sources to seek health or medical information. This is not an everyday activity but something that is undertaken when health issues or questions arise.

Health information obtained online is used in a variety of ways, including: to research a diagnosis or prescription, prepare for surgery or to find out how best to recover from surgery, to get tips from other caregivers and patients about dealing with a particular symptom, and to obtain emotional support from others sharing a common health or medical problem. The great majority of those who look for health information online say that what they find is useful, at least most of the time, and that what they learn is new to them (Fox & Fallows, 2003). Even more impressive is that the information obtained online is reported to have improved the way the survey respondents take care of themselves, especially in terms of what they eat and how they exercise. Almost 70% indicated that their last online health search affected their decision about how they might treat an illness, whether to visit a doctor, ask new questions, or get a second opinion. Indeed, one in three of online health seekers who find relevant health information bring it to their doctor for a "quality check" (Fox & Fallows, 2003).

As more and more patients come to their medical visits well informed, or at least well supplied with advice and information pertinent to their medical problems, physicians are confronted with the task of trying to establish which pieces of information are valid and which are not. This can be, of course, a time consuming endeavor. How time consuming this activity is may vary depending on the physician's specialty and the kinds of information patients are likely to bring. Within the context of oncology visits, a survey of practicing oncologists estimated that physicians spend 10 additional minutes discussing the online health information that patients bring with them (Helft, Hlubocky, & Daugherty, 2003). The oncologists expressed mixed feelings in regard to this information, reporting that it can simultaneously affect patients in both positive (more hopeful and knowledgeable) and negative (confused and anxious) ways. It also has a mixed effect on physicians. Forty-four percent of the oncologists in the survey reported that they have had difficulty, even if only occasionally, discussing Internet information with patients, and 9% reported that they have occasionally felt uncomfortable when patients brought Internet information to them for discussion (Helft et al., 2003). Patients reported mixed physician receptivity to their presentations of online information; some physicians were reported to welcome it, while others expressed irritation and defensiveness (Fox & Fallows, 2003).

As a result of Internet access, as well as the information dissemination efforts of many patient advocacy groups, patients are sometimes better informed than their physicians. This is particularly evident when the patient's medical condition is rare. As noted by one respondent to the Pew survey, "as the parent of a child with a very rare neurological syndrome, the Internet was vital to putting the pieces of a puzzle together. It saved my son months of struggle when I found a diagnosis prior to the neurologist he was seeing, who openly admitted she had only heard of the syndrome but never treated a child with [Landau-Kleffner syndrome]" (Fox & Fallows, 2003, p. 7).

Of course the Internet has done more than increase patient access to health information. It has increased patient access to their physician. Many observers of cyberspace suggest that e-mail access to physicians will in time become as critical and commonplace as the telephone (Delbanco & Sands, 2004; Ferguson, 1998). It is this possibility that Kassirer regards as having the potential to induce cultural changes in the delivery of care more revolutionary than any restructuring of the medical care system (Kassirer, 2004).

Enthusiasm for e-mail has also been dampened by a fear that it may diminish the social, emotional, and psychosocial dimensions of care that are central to patient-centered medicine by reducing communication to brief, task-specific electronic exchanges (Baur, 2000). Baur argues that e-mail has the potential to reinforce an already shifting tide toward consumerism and away from patient-centeredness in American medicine. It is not clear, however, that consumerism is inextricably tied to a decrease in medicine's ability to be patient centered. There is some reason to suggest that the asynchronicity of place afforded by e-mail may free patients from the social constraints of the patient role and enable them to convey sensitive, embarrassing, or especially distressing information that may be withheld in face-to-face visits (Lazare, 1987; Smyth, Stone, & Hurewitz, 1999; Strasser, Fisch, Bodurka, Sivesind, & Bruera, 2002).

The physical distance e-mail affords may also help some patients feel less emotionally constrained in conveying embarrassing or especially distressing information (Lazare, 1987; Strasser et al., 2002). The disinhibition and increased candor characteristic of e-mail generally may in part account for the high level of emotional investment patients demonstrated in their text, including both the expression of criticisms as well as needs for support and reassurance (Smyth et al., 1999). For instance, based on in-depth interviews with physician users of e-mail, Patt and colleagues conclude that while physicians were wary of inadvertent breaches of confidentiality through e-mail, they also noted that this form of communication had a positive effect on their relationships with patients by increasing rapport and keeping lines of communication open (Patt, Houston, Jenckes, Sands, & Ford, 2003). Delbanco and Sands (2004) have noted that the use of e-mail in their practice has been effective in building trust and drawing together patients and their physicians.

The implications of these changes are tremendous and they must be given full and serious consideration in conceptualizing how the patient–physician relationship may be shaped in the future. Important strides have been made in understanding the nature of this very powerful, and often therapeutic, relationship that connects patients and physicians. Challenges, however, remain. The most significant of these is to use our conceptual and methodological imagination—as well as our heart—to approach these important questions in meaningful ways.

References

ABIM Foundation, ACP-ASIM Foundation, & European Federation of Internal Medicine. (2002). Charter on medical professionalism. *Annals of Internal Medicine, 136*, 243–246.

Ambady, N., Koo, J., Rosenthal R., & Winograd, C. H. (2002). Physical therapists' nonverbal communication predicts geriatric patients' health outcomes. *Psychology of Aging, 17*, 443–452.

Ambady, N., LaPlante, D., Nguyen, T., Rosenthal, R., Chaumeton, N., & Levinson, W. (2002). Surgeons' tone of voice: A clue to malpractice history. *Surgery, 132*, 5–9.

Ambady, N., & Rosenthal, R. (1992). Thin slices of expressive behavior as predictors of interpersonal consequences: A meta-analysis. *Psychological Bulletin, 111*, 25–274.

Baur, C. (2000). Limiting factors on the transformative powers of e-mail in patient–physician relationships: A critical analysis. *Health Communication, 12*, 239–259.

Beach, M. C., Roter, D. L, Wang, N-Y., Duggan, P. S., & Cooper, L. A. (2006). Are physicians' attitudes of respect accurately perceived by patients and associated with more positive communication behaviors? *Patient Education and Counseling, 62*, 347–354.

Bergeson, S. C., & Dean, J. D. (2006). A systems approach to patient-centered care. *Journal of the American Medical Association, 296*, 2848–2851.

Byrne, J. M., & Long, B. E. L. (1976). *Doctors talking to patients*. London: Her Majesty's Stationary Office.

Cohen-Cole, S. A. (1991). *The medical interview: The three-function approach*. St. Louis, MO: Mosby Year Book.

Delbanco, T., Berwick D. M., Boufford, J. I., Edgman-Levitan, S., Ollenschläger, G., Plamping, D., & Rockefeller, R.G. (2001). Healthcare in a land called PeoplePower: Nothing about me without me. *Health Expectations, 4*, 144–150.

Delbanco, T., & Sands, D. Z. (2004). Electrons in flight—e-mail between doctors and patients. *New England Journal of Medicine, 350,* 1705–1707.

DiMatteo, M. R., Hays, R. D., & Prince, L. M. (1986). Relationship of physicians' nonverbal communication skill to patient satisfaction, appointment noncompliance, and physician workload. *Health Psychology, 5,* 581–594.

DiMatteo, M. R., Taranta, A., Friedman, H. S., & Prince, L. M. (1980). Predicting patient satisfaction from physicians' nonverbal communication skills. *Medical Care, 18,* 376–387.

Engel, G. L. (1977). The need for a new medical model: A challenge for biomedicine. *Science, 196,* 129–136.

Ferguson, T. (1998). Digital doctoring-opportunities and challenges in electronic–physician communication. *Journal of the American Medical Association, 280,* 1361–1362.

Fox, S., & Fallows, D. (2003). Health searches and email have become more commonplace, but there is room for improvement in searches and overall Internet access. Retrieved from http://www. pewinternet.org.

Friedman, H. S., DiMatteo, M. R., & Taranta, A. (1980). A study of the relationship between individual differences in nonverbal expressiveness and factors in personality and social interaction. *Journal of Research in Personality, 14,* 351–364.

Gerteis, M., Edgman-Levitan, S., Daley, J., & Delbanco, T. L. (1993). *Through the patient's eyes.* San Francisco, CA: Jossey-Bass.

Griffith, C., Wilson, J. F., Langer, S., & Haist, S. A. (2003). House staff nonverbal communication skills and standardized patient satisfaction. *Journal of General Internal Medicine, 18,* 170–174.

Hall, E. T. (1976). *Beyond culture.* Garden City, NY: Anchor Press/Doubleday.

Hall, J. A., & Bernieri, F. J. (Eds.). (2001). *Interpersonal sensitivity: Theory and measurement.* Mahwah, NJ: Erlbaum.

Hall, J. A., Epstein, A. M., DeCiantis, M. L., & McNeil, B. J. (1993). Physicians' liking for their patients: More evidence for the role of affect in medical care. *Health Psychology, 12,* 140–146.

Hall, J. A., Friedman, H. S., & Harris, M. J. (1986). Nonverbal cues, the Type A behavior pattern, and coronary heart disease. In P. D. Blanck, R. Buck, & R. Rosenthal (Eds.), *Nonverbal communication in the clinical context* (pp. 144–168). State College, PA: Pennsylvania State University Press.

Hall, J.A., Harrigan J.A., & Rosenthal R. (1995). Nonverbal behavior in clinician–patient interaction. *Applied and Preventive Psychology, 4,* 21–37.

Hall, J. A., Horgan, T. G., Stein, T. S., & Roter, D. L. (2002). Liking in the physician–patient relationship. *Patient Education and Counseling, 48,* 69–77.

Hall, J. A., Roter, D. L., Blanch, D. C., & Frankel, R. M. (2009). Nonverbal sensitivity in medical students: Implications for clinical interactions. *Journal of General Internal Medicine, 24,* 1217–1222.

Hall, J. A., Roter, D. L., Milburn, M. A., & Daltroy, L. H. (1996). Patients' health as a predictor of physician and patient behavior in medical visits: A synthesis of four studies. *Medical Care, 34,* 1205–1218.

Hall, J. A., Roter, D. L., & Rand, C. S. (1981). Communication of affect between patients and physicians. *Journal of Health and Social Behavior, 11,* 18–30.

Heath, C. (1986). *Body movement and speech in medical interaction.* Cambridge, UK: Cambridge University Press.

Heath, C. (2002). Demonstrative suffering: The gestural (re)embodiment of symptoms. *Journal of Communication, 52,* 597–616.

Helft, P. R., Hlubocky, F., & Daugherty, C. K. (2003). American oncologists' views of internet use by cancer patients: A mail survey of American Society of Clinical Oncology members. *Journal of Clinical Oncology, 21,* 942–947.

Holm, U., & Aspegren, K. (1999). Pedagogical methods and affect tolerance in medical students. *Medical Education, 33,* 14–18.

Institute of Medicine. (1999). *To err is human: Building a safer health system.* Washington, DC: National Academy Press.

Institute of Medicine. (2001). *Crossing the quality chasm: A new health system.* Washington, DC: National Academy Press.

Kassirer, J. (2004). The next transformation in the delivery of health care. *New England Journal of Medicine, 332,* 52–54.

Knapp M. L., & Hall, J. A. (2010). *Nonverbal communication in human interaction* (7th ed.). Belmont, CA: Wadsworth.

Krasner, M. S., Epstein, R. M., Beckman, H., Suchman, A. L., Chapman, B., Mooney, C. J., & Quill, T. E. (2009). Association of an educational program in mindful communication with burnout, empathy, and attitudes among primary care physicians. *Journal of the American Medication Association, 302,* 1284–1293.

Laine, C., & Davidoff, F. (1996). Patient-centered medicine: A professional evolution. *Journal of the American Medical Association, 275,*152–156.

Lazare, A. (1987). Shame and humiliation in the medical encounter. *Archives of Internal Medicine, 147,* 1653–1658.

Levinson, W. (1993). Mining for gold. *Journal of General Internal Medicine, 8,* 172–173.

Lipkin, M., Putnam, S. M., & Lazare, A. (1995). *The medical interview: Clinical care, education, and research.* New York: Springer-Verlag.

McWhinney, I. (l989). The need for a transformed clinical method. In M. Stewart & D. Roter (Eds.), *Communicating with medical patients* (pp. 25–40). Newbury Park, CA: Sage.

Milmoe, S., Rosenthal, R., Blane, H. T., Chafetz, M. E., & Wolf, I. (1967). The doctor's voice: Postdictor of successful referral of alcoholic patients. *Journal of Abnormal Psychology, 72,* 78–84.

Novack, D. H. (1987). Therapeutic aspects of the clinical encounter. *Journal of General Internal Medicine, 2,* 347–354.

Patrick, C. J., Craig, K. D., & Prkachin, K. M. (1986). Observer judgments of acute pain: Facial action determinants. *Journal of Personality and Social Psychology, 50,* 1291–1298.

Patt, M. R., Houston, T. K., Jenckes, M. W., Sands, D. Z., & Ford, D. E. (2003). Doctors who are using e-mail with their patients: A qualitative exploration. *Journal of Medical Internet Research, 5,* e9.

Prkachin, K. M. (1992). Dissociating spontaneous and deliberate expressions of pain: Signal detection analyses. *Pain, 51,* 297–306.

Rosenberg, E. L., Ekman, P., Jiang, W., … Blumenthal, J. A. (2001). Linkages between facial expressions of anger and transient myocardial ischemia in men with coronary artery disease. *Emotion, 1,* 107–115.

Rosenthal, R., Blanck, P. D., & Vannicelli, M. (1984). Speaking to and about patients: Predicting therapists' tone of voice. *Journal of Consulting and Clinical Psychology, 52,* 679–686.

Roter, D. (2000). The enduring and evolving nature of the patient-physician relationship. *Patient Education and Counseling, 39,* 5–15.

Roter, D. L., Frankel, R. M., Hall, J. A., & Sluyter, D. (2006). The expression of emotion through nonverbal behavior in medical visits: Mechanisms and outcomes. *Journal of General Internal Medicine, 21,* S28–34.

Roter, D. L., & Hall, J. A. (2004). Physician gender and patient-centered communication: A critical review of empirical research. *Annual Review of Public Health, 25,* 497–519.

Roter, D. L., & Hall, J. A. (2006). *Doctors talking to patients/Patients talking to doctors: Improving communication in medical visits* (2nd ed.)..Westport, CT: Praeger.

Roter, D. L., Hall, J. A., & Katz, N. R. (1987). Relations between physicians' behaviors and analogue patients' satisfaction, recall, and impressions. *Medical Care, 25,* 437–451.

Schmid Mast, M. S. (2007). On the importance of nonverbal communication in physician-patient interaction. *Patient Education and Counseling, 67,* 315–318.

Shorter, E. (l985). *Bedside manners.* New York: Simon and Schuster.

Smyth, J. M., Stone, A. A., & Hurewitz, A. (1999). Effects of writing about stressful experiences on symptom reduction in patients with asthma or rheumatoid arthritis: A randomzied trial. *Journal of the American Medication Association, 281,* 1304–1309.

Strasser, F., Fisch, M., Bodurka, D. C., Sivesind, D., & Bruera, E. (2002). E-emotions: Email for written emotional expression. *Journal of Clinical Oncology, 20,* 3352–3355.

5

BEYOND PRIMARY CARE PROVIDERS

A Discussion of Health Communication Roles and Challenges for Health Care Professionals and Others

Margaret F. Clayton and Lee Ellington

When a patient receives health care she/he interacts with a multitude of individuals who collectively comprise the health care team. Although much of the current literature focuses on communication between patient and provider, other licensed professionals, staff, and even volunteers play a critical role in a patient's experience. Families of patients also interact with the health care team, giving and receiving information and often receiving social support. Currently, a patient-centered (also referred to as client-centered or family focused) style of communication is advocated to promote optimal patient outcomes. This approach encompasses both patients and families and addresses individualized health related concerns. In general, most disciplines advocate this holistic style of health care, citing communication skills (i.e., interviewing, listening, eliciting goals) as a necessary part of health care delivery. These skills not only facilitate patient and family involvement (at their desired level of participation) but also optimize communication between members of the health care team.

Despite the benefits of implementing a patient-centered approach to health communication, many challenges to implementing this approach are recognized across disciplines. This chapter will discuss health communication goals, similarities, and challenges for many members of the health care team but cannot be considered inclusive of all possible health care professionals. For example, psychologists are seen as integral members of healthcare teams (e.g., chronic pain teams) yet, because their direct patient communication is considered a psychotherapeutic treatment rather than health communication, this profession is not discussed.

Nurses

Nurses are consistently ranked as one of the most trusted health care professions (Gallup, 2008). Registered nurses typically hold an associate's or a bachelor's degree in nursing. Some older nurses may hold a diploma from a hospital school of nursing although these programs have now been phased out. All registered nurses are licensed for practice in their state, functioning under a legal scope of practice document. The scope of practice is extensive, but does not include prescriptive privileges or diagnostic responsibilities.

Nurses interact with patients more than do providers from any other discipline, providing emotional and physical care. Despite multiple definitions of patient-centered communication, the encompassing nature of this communication style is consistent with the holistic approach of nursing care that embraces the needs of the patient as a person rather than focusing solely on the illness and treatment process. Anecdotally, the literature and media abound with patient stories reflecting the value of nursing care. Empirically, nurses have identified seven dimensions that define professional nursing practice: caring, compassion, spirituality, community outreach, providing comfort, crisis intervention, and going the extra distance (Hudacek, 2008). Nursing care has been shown to facilitate adherence to treatment, improve patient health outcomes, facilitate quality of life, and enhance satisfaction (McLellan, 2009; Suhonen, Valimaki, Katajisto, & Leino-Kilpi, 2007). In nonemergency situations, key nursing communication tasks are to create a therapeutic relationship, provide information, offer empathy, understanding, and support, assess patient/family values and preferences, describe care options, confirm understanding, and respond to emotions (Back et al., 2007; Epstein & Street, 2007; Kruijver, Kerkstra, Francke, Bensing, & van de Wiel, 2000). The communication between nurse and patient therefore assumes the utmost importance as part of providing quality patient care (McCabe, 2004).

Hospital or office nurses are often the first health care professionals that patients or their families encounter in both inpatient and outpatient settings when seeking care for acute or chronic problems. Registered nurses are responsible for obtaining a great deal of information, such as eliciting the reason for the office visit or hospital admission, obtaining a relevant history of the problem, and evaluating personal or contextual factors that may influence diagnosis and treatment. Nurses also give information to patients, families, and other members of the health care team. Examples include instructing patients and families about critical information such as when to report symptoms and how to take medications, explaining events, and helping to interpret and reinforce information about diagnoses and prognoses. Other examples of information giving include teaching clinical skills such as intravenous medication administration and dressing change methods to caregivers in the homecare environment. Nurses also communicate information to other health care team members. These tasks require communication proficiency (e.g., interviewing and listening skills) and professional judgment (Charlton, Dearing, Berry, & Johnson, 2008; Lein & Wills, 2007).

Unfortunately, there is a widely held assumption that nurses are innately skilled communicators, given their reputation for empathy and their need to interface with other health care providers, patients, and families (Wilkinson, Perry, Blanchard, & Linsell, 2008). However, many communication issues challenge nurses when interacting with patients. For example, nurses have identified discussing spirituality as one of the most challenging communication issues they face (Delgado, 2007; Molzahn & Sheilds, 2008).

An integral part of nursing communication is eliciting and addressing the psychosocial and emotional needs of patients and families. It has been shown that patients are less likely to share information regarding psychosocial concerns if they believe their feelings will be dismissed or unacknowledged (Arora, 2003). While physicians may be on a tight time schedule, staff nurses can often spend more time with patients, allowing discovery of psychosocial issues. For example, hospital nurses spend time talking with patients during bathing times or during wound care dressing changes; office nurses talk with patients during the initial assessment interview eliciting the reason(s) for the office visit. Time spent during these interactions facilitates communication on a personal level, and is consistent with the holistic approach of nursing care (Clayton, 2006). Finally, nurses also need to be alert to situations where patients and families prefer not to communicate at a specific time, while remembering that this may change in the future. For example, at any given time patients may not want to disclose emotional feelings, and patients may not desire information that would extinguish their hope of a cure (Brashers et al., 2000; Kvale, 2007). To assist nurses with these communication challenges, communication skills have been incorporated into nursing education and post-employment structured practitioner education (American Association of Colleges of Nursing, 2005; Beckman & Frankel, 2003).

Nurse Practitioners and Nurse Clinical Specialists

Advanced practice nurses (APRNs) are nurses who have obtained either a master's degree (MS) or a clinical doctorate (DNP) in nursing. In addition to their nursing license, states require these nurses to pass a national certification exam in their specialty area (for example, midwifery or family nurse practitioner). APRNs function under a legal scope of practice document that includes among other aspects the privilege to prescribe medications and to diagnose and treat patient illnesses, in addition to other nursing duties.

APRNs face communication challenges that more closely resemble those of physicians. The same patient outcomes that have been reported in positive patient–physician relationships apply to advanced practice nurse–patient relationships, namely satisfaction, malpractice suits, treatment adherence, emotional and physical health, and diagnostic accuracy (Fortin, 2002; Roter, 2000; see also Duggan & Thompson chapter, this volume). Moreover, advanced practice nurses must adhere to the same time limits as physicians when diagnosing and treating patients in a managed care office setting. These nurses do not have the luxury of frequent or regularly scheduled periods of time to interact with patients as do hospital staff nurses (during tasks such as dressing changes or bathing) or office nurses (during telephone triage, telephone provision of lab results, initial discovery of the reason for the visit). However, some research suggests that advanced practice nurses employ patient-centered communication approaches more often than physicians do, even though advanced practice nurses experience the same time constraints (managed care visit length) as physicians (Cunningham, 2004). A patient-centered communication style from the APRN provider perspective has been shown to incorporate the realization that patients have unique communication goals despite similar diagnoses and may not want a collaborative or active partnership with their provider at a particular time (Clayton, Dudley, & Musters, 2008). In addition, this style facilitates the flexibility to address patient concerns throughout the visit, rather than following a prescribed "script" for visit temporal structure (Clayton & Dudley, 2009).

Certified Nursing Assistants

Very little research has been conducted on the communication processes between patients and certified nursing assistants (CNAs). CNAs provide supportive patient care—their education varies by state but usually consists of a training course and a competency exam. A high school diploma may or may not be required. Existing research has mainly been conducted in nursing home/extended care settings where CNAs deliver 80 to 90% of routine care to nursing home residents (as opposed to professional care such as giving medications which must be done by a licensed LPN or RN; Burgio et al., 2001; Curry, Porter,

Michalski, & Gruman, 2000; Pennington, Scott, & Magilvy, 2003). As in any health care setting, communication between disciplines is important, but this is a known communication challenge for CNAs. Reasons for interdisciplinary communication difficulties are grounded in the attitudes of other staff toward the relative merit of the CNA contribution to patient outcomes and occasionally denial of clinical information to CNAs (Colon-Emeric et al., 2007; Curry et al., 2000).

Interventions promoting CNA communication skills training have been shown to be successful in fostering positive CNA communication behaviors toward residents of extended care facilities, although resident outcomes have been mixed (Burgio, Allen-Burge, et al., 2001; Burgio, Stevens, et al., 2002). One study found that improved CNA communication behaviors reduced resident agitation (Burgio, Stevens et al., 2002). Another positive finding of CNA communication skills training was that the time required to deliver care was not increased by changing communication behaviors, supporting other literature that has noted this finding (Burgio, Allen-Burge, et al., 2001; Cegala, Post, & McClure, 2001).

Physician Assistants

Physician Assistants (PAs) are not licensed providers although they do possess graduate education and have passed a certification exam. Similarly to APRNs, PAs provide primary care or work alongside a physician in specialty practice. While there is a vast literature on patient–PA communication, overall communication benefits and challenges for PAs can be considered similar to those of APRNs and physicians (see Duggan & Thompson chapter this volume).

Therapists

Physical, occupational, speech, and recreational therapists have been encouraged to adopt a patient-centered approach, involving patients and their families as much as possible (Edwards, Millard, Praskac, & Wisniewski, 2003; Potter, Gordon, & Hamer, 2003; Sumsion & Law, 2006). In fact, one of the core competencies for recreation therapy is effective interpersonal communication with patients and has been emphasized as essential to the development, implementation, and evaluation of the course of treatment in recreation therapy (Austin, 2009; Corey, 2008).

Therapists often work in concert as part of a health care team, shifting emphasis from one therapy specialty to another as the needs of the patient change, working simultaneously to assist patients to maximize function (Clayton, 1996; Wottrich, von Koch, & Tham, 2007). Similar to other disciplines, the therapeutic process is dependent on building a relationship with the patient in order to tailor interventions to meet patient specific problems and concerns (Sylvester, Voelkl, & Ellis, 2001). Moreover, because most therapy is a process that involves more than one encounter, effective communication with the patient allows feedback on the course of the treatment (Corey, 2008). However, difficulties arise when goals of the patient, family, and therapist differ (Sumsion & Smyth, 2000). Truly adopting a patient-centered or family-centered communication approach that respects patient and family values may be exceedingly difficult in these circumstances (Clayton, 1996).

Physical, occupational, speech, and recreational therapists face multiple communication challenges such as setting goals with patients who may not be able to fully participate in the discussion due to physical or cognitive incapacity. For example, aphasic patients and stroke patients present such unique communication challenges as ensuring understanding and eliciting patient preferences (Leach, Cornwell, Fleming, & Haines, 2009; Liechty, 2006). Those who have lost normal speech (possibly due to a cerebral vascular accident or traumatic brain injury) may require extra time to allow them to form words (Nordehn, Meredith, & Bye, 2006). Further, those with paralysis, especially facial paralysis, may not be able to offer the nonverbal cues so integral to communication processes (Vanswearingen, 2008).

Therapists working in the home environment as opposed to a residential facility have the advantage of being able to place the patient and family in context, and can therefore suggest very specific and individualized treatment approaches (Wottrich et al., 2007). Yet in the home setting therapists also face situations where the primary goal is not to restore functioning but to find alternative ways to meet patient goals, such as the ability to communicate when the capacity to restore speech is no longer an option or the ability to restore mobility when muscle function is lost. Utilizing a patient-centered approach and identifying patient goals can dramatically improve patient well-being and quality of life in these circumstances (Clayton, 1996).

Social Workers

Social workers have consistently been at the forefront of teams assisting special needs populations, such as those who have suffered from sexual abuse. Communication challenges between these patients and members of the health care team must be overcome to successfully meet the legal mandates and health care needs of these patients. Social workers with special training often fill this role (Havig, 2008). Social workers are also integral to critical care environments, helping patients and families to avoid excessive health care costs, serving as a patient or family advocate, and facilitating discharge planning (Carr, 2009). Finally, social workers provide a vital link between inpatient care and supportive community services, assisting other health care disciplines to minimize disruption of patient care during a transition to the home environment or between acute and residential treatment facilities. To assist patients, families, and other health care disciplines, social workers must have communication skills that enable them to identify and prioritize patient, family, and administrative goals in such as way as to minimize disruption of patient care, maximize patient satisfaction, and minimize costs.

Chaplains

Pastoral care is an integral part of many patients' illness experiences. Even those who do not normally attend religious services may turn to hospital chaplains in times of acute distress. This requires hospital chaplains to be able to step out of their individual religious traditions and at times offer support to those not of their faith (Byrne, 2007). Much of pastoral health care communication research has been reported in the end of life or palliative care literature, when individual culture, religion, and preference must be respected (Ragan, Wittenberg, & Hall, 2003). Indeed, chaplains have long been recognized as a vital part of any hospice or palliative care team (Mularski, Bascom, & Osborne, 2001; Taylor, 1994). Other units, such as intensive care units and pediatric units, have also recognized the contribution made by chaplains when promoting patient or family centered styles of health care delivery (Titone, Cross, Sileo, & Martin, 2004).

Because discussing spirituality with patients is an acknowledged communication challenge for many nurses, they may consult with a chaplain or refer a patient to a chaplain to meet a patient's spiritual needs (Delgado, 2007; Molzahn & Sheilds, 2008). Yet, meeting spiritual needs may present communication challenges such as ascertaining and meeting the needs of those with dementia or aphasia. Patients with early dementia especially may be very aware of their circumstances and possibly very frightened, requesting spiritual comfort. These patients are particularly well served by a patient-centered approach (Jackson, 2002). For those patients with more advanced dementia, research suggests that a patient-centered communication approach can be used to elicit the life stories of these patients, using individualized examples to meet their religious needs (Ryan, Martin, & Beaman, 2005). Aphasic patients may be equally anxious, angry, and sometimes depressed. Patient-centered pastoral communication adapted to the aphasic patients' needs can be beneficial to these individuals (Liechty & Heinzekehr, 2008).

In addition to supporting the religious needs of patients, chaplains may also support individual members of the health care team. For example, it can be emotionally distressing for nurses to care for very ill or dying newborns, and by extension the newborn's parents, in a neonatal intensive care unit. Chaplains can help nurses cope with these types of difficult and often repetitive events (Downey, Bengiamin, Heuer, & Juhl, 1995).

Pharmacists

Pharmacists interact with virtually any patient taking a medication. Recognition of the pharmacist–patient relationship has created a flurry of television commercials where information and patient reassurance are provided by the pharmacist, demonstrating the supportive and informative nature of the pharmacist–patient relationship. Recent emphasis on a patient-centered approach to pharmacist–patient communication has fostered a renewed interest in the evaluation of these interactions (de Oliveira & Shoemaker, 2006). While some research suggests positive patient-centered pharmacist–patient interactions, other research indicates that patients perceive a less than adequate pharmacist–patient relationship (Keshishian, Colodny, & Boone, 2008; Worley, 2006). In concert with a patient-centered model, pharmacists suggest there are communication responsibilities for both pharmacist and patient; while pharmacists possess a relatively unified understanding of these communication responsibilities, patients appear less sure of their role in this relationship, suggesting multiple avenues for further research (Worley et al., 2007).

Counselors

Genetic Counselors

The role of a genetic counselor is to work with individuals and families to help them understand the implications of genetic contributions to health and disease (Resta et al., 2006). Counseling sessions typically consist of one to two visits, require the presentation of dense, abstract genetic information, and are met with client anxiety and uncertainty about disease vulnerability. How words are used in these emotionally laden situations becomes especially important; for example, consider the emotional valence of these terms: *abortion* versus *termination*; *mental retardation* versus *global developmental delay*, giving *bad* news versus discussing *unexpected* news; possessing a genetic *mutation* versus a genetic *alteration*; and quantifying the *risk* of an event versus the *chance* of an event. With the rapid advancement of genetic technical language, there has been increased interest and focus on the genetic counseling process (Biesecker & Peters, 2001; Meiser, Irle, Lobb, and Barlow-Stewart, 2008).

Genetic counseling impacts clients and families in profound ways, requiring specialists to possess a firm grasp of personal, familial, and social ethical issues (Parker, 1994). It is common for clients and family members to attend a counseling session together since genetic testing is likely to have risk implications beyond the client, yet little research has been conducted on the role of family members in the session or counselor engagement of them (Ellington et al., 2005). Overall, the challenges that genetic counselors face are similar to those of many other healthcare professionals (Smets , van Zwieten, & Michie, 2007) in that they require listening and the provision of emotional and informational support during this potentially difficult consultation (Roter et al., 2006).

Traditionally, genetic counseling practice has been examined in light of two different professional models of care: teaching and counseling (Kessler, 1997). The teaching or educational approach is considered essential to genetic counseling because counselors transmit unfamiliar, highly complex, and probabilistic genetic risk information. However, the counseling model aligns with a client-centered approach, addressing psychosocial concerns and facilitation of personal or familial congruent decision making. Despite a professional call to fuse these two models in practice (Weil, 2003), research suggests that counselors predominantly practice with an educational, directive approach, paying much less attention to client psychosocial and emotional issues (Ellington et al., 2005; Pieterse, van Dulmen, Ausems, Beemer, & Bensing, 2005; Roter, Ellington, Erby, Larson, & Dudley, 2006). Interestingly, Pieterse et al. (2005) found that even when counselors were informed of clients' previsit needs, most counselors did not tailor their approach except to provide more information.

A relatively unaddressed but promising intervention opportunity for genetic counselors is the promotion of health behaviors. It is somewhat surprising that facilitation of health behaviors has not received much attention by genetic counselors, given that a professional goal is to help individuals at genetic risk take action to prevent and to screen for disease (Marteau & Lerman, 2001). From the long line of health behavior research, it is evident that provision of risk information alone will not motivate preventive or screening behaviors. Given that genetic counselors have a window of opportunity to encourage health behaviors, the genetic counseling profession faces a challenge, consistent with all healthcare professions, to adopt and promote skills which increase the likelihood of client engagement in necessary health behaviors (Smets et al., 2007).

Given the rapid evolution of genetic technology, the novelty of genetic information and terminology to the lay public, and the tendency for genetic counselors to use a didactic approach with a large volume of mathematical statements, health literacy is an important challenge for this profession. Based on findings of a national sample of 152 counselors conducting simulated genetic counseling sessions, Roter and colleagues (2007) concluded that genetic counselors need to simplify their vocabulary and sentence structure, and engage in a more interactive dialogue to increase client understanding. These recommendations are especially important given that clients with low levels of education have been found to be less knowledgeable about genetic testing and made genetically related decisions that were inconsistent with their personal values (Dormandy, Michie, Hooper, & Marteau, 2005; van den Berg, Timmermans, Ten Kate, van Vugt, & van der Wal, 2005)

Health Communication by Telephone

There has been a growth in health care delivery and communication delivered via a distance mode such as by telephone. Call-in centers range from local suicide hotlines to national centers such as 1-800-CANCER sponsored by the National Cancer Institute. On a worldwide basis, consumers are rapidly increasing their use of telephone health advice, and they report satisfaction with the care/recommendations they receive (Bunn, Byrne, & Kendall, 2004; Rutenberg, 2000). The use of telephone health services and telephone triage is likely to continue to grow and merge with the use of telehealth and the Internet, especially since 98.1% of U.S. households have telephone service using either land lines or cellular services (Bloomberg & Luke, 2008; Reisman, 2002). Numerous challenges and opportunities for scholars are posed by investigating the use and effectiveness of health communication by phone.

Poison Control Centers

Poison control services are provided by pharmacists and nurses with special education in clinical toxicology. These specialists staff the 61 North American Poison Control Centers (Institute of Medicine, 2004). A toll-free number can connect a caller to a local center 24 hours/day. Poison control centers were originally developed to aid parents in responding to child exposures to toxic substances. Their mission has rapidly broadened to handle the increasing demands of a wide range of poisonings including those caused by bioterrorism (Institute of Medicine, 2004). Yet, while these poison control specialists receive extensive toxicology education and earn certification, they receive little formalized training in, or evaluation of, communication skills and competencies (personal communication, AAPCC Managers' Listserve, L. Ellington, October 18, 2009).

Because specialized poison control nurses and pharmacists assess acute poisonings, taking an accurate and effective history is critical to determining the nature of the poison exposure. Information is typically collected while simultaneously reassuring and calming the caller. Detailed information is required: the nature of the exposure (e.g., topical or oral), substance(s) involved, amount, time since initial exposure, and cause (e.g., accidental vs. intentional). Additionally, the specialist collects relevant data on the identified client's health status (e.g., chronic health condition, current symptoms, other medications) and factors that may influence the poison exposure (e.g., age, weight). Based on this information, the specialist determines the potential severity of the exposure and makes treatment recommendations.

Nurses and pharmacists who staff poison control centers face multiple unique challenges when compared to other health care professionals. Given that these specialized nurses and pharmacists deliver emergency care via telephone they must be particularly astute at gathering all critical information through questioning and listening (Rothwell, Ellington, Planalp, & Crouch, under review). Without visual cues, misunderstandings can occur. Additionally, the vast majority of calls made to poison control centers are routine or informational so specialists must remain vigilant for the less frequent, but potentially high severity cases. Potentially serious cases may require the specialist to instruct a caller or their family/friend (i.e., nonexperts) to take immediate action (Broadhead, 1986; Wezorek, Dean, & Krenzelok, 1992), to calm a panicked caller (White, 1997), or to sort through a complex medication regime when medication administration errors have occurred (Cobaugh & Krenzelok, 2006; Skarupski, Mrvos, & Krenzelok, 2004).

Poison control center specialists indicate that they are particularly stressed during periods of surge (Ellington et al., 2009). Surge capacity is when call volume to the center exceeds the ability of specialists to immediately respond (i.e., when multiple calls are on hold). Unlike an emergency room where patients can be visually triaged, a poison control specialist has no visual cues regarding the unanswered calls lined up in an electronic queue.

Relatively brief periods of routine surge occur on a daily basis, but extended periods occur during medical disasters. From focus groups conducted with poison control specialists it is evident that communication patterns are altered (i.e., shortened call length, decreased psychosocial assessment, interrupting or talking over the caller) during busy or stressful periods (Ellington et al., 2009; Rothwell et al., in press).

Supporting recognition of the communication challenges that telephone emergency services impose on poison control specialists, a survey conducted with 537 poison control specialists and directors from the United States and Canada found that respondents indicated a strong desire for communication skills training to improve caller outcomes (Planalp, Crouch, Rothwell, & Ellington, 2009). Poison control specialists reported that they learned communication skills by trial and error and noted that they received little guidance during initial training at their center. Improving poison control specialists' communication skills may lead to increased efficiency, improved specialist satisfaction, improved caller satisfaction, and ultimately better patient (caller) outcomes.

Office Staff

First impressions last: Medical office staff often create a first impression, leaving a patient with a positive or negative impression of the care they are about to receive (Weiss, 2003). Recognizing the importance of front office staff, one medical practice advocated monthly staff meetings of office staff that included role playing of difficult communication issues (Rowan, 2008). Moreover, positive interactions with office staff can influence the choice of primary care practitioners, influence patient satisfaction with their physician, and improve patient–provider communication (Anderson, Barbara, & Feldman, 2007; Arora, Singer, & Arora, 2004; Nye, 2001). Special populations such as those who are hard of hearing place emphasis on the importance of interactions with office staff, citing communication difficulties that include receiving long phone messages, and interacting with front desk staff while in the waiting room (Iezzoni, O'Day, Killeen, & Harker, 2004).

Housekeeping

Housekeeping staff employed by hospitals, nursing home/extended care facilities, and rehabilitation centers interact with patients on a regular basis. Anecdotal evidence indicates that housekeeping staff often provide companionship to patients and offer necessary quality of life related care such as adjusting TV channels, volume levels, temperature settings, getting a blanket, and repositioning a bedside table. If housekeeping staff simply talk to patients while cleaning a room it can reduce patients' feelings of anonymity. For example, one housekeeper mentioned that she always called the nursing home resident in 414B "Dr." because "that is his title, he earned it, and I can respect him. Besides he likes it, and it makes him smile!" (personal communication M. Clayton, June 20, 2009). This comment reflected the personal nature of her interactions with the resident, getting to know him, and trying to make him feel valued. It also reflects an individualized communication approach by the housekeeper toward this resident. Although empirical literature on housekeeper communication is lacking, the valuable contributions to patient quality of life of this group of health care related employees should not be overlooked. Indeed, hospital management teams have noted the importance of housekeeping as part of the overall health care delivery system when addressing patient-centered administrative approaches (Dreachslin, Hunt, & Sprainer, 1999, 266–268).

Volunteers

Volunteers serve in both hospital and community settings providing needed services and support to patients and families. Regardless of the setting or service, what volunteers have in common is a willingness to interact with patients and families through sharing their expertise or their time. Volunteers read to children, sit with patients and families at the end of life, check on homebound patients and deliver meals, assist sexual assault victims, and even partner with aphasic patients to aid in the development of communication skills (Beatty, Oxlad, Koczwara, & Wade, 2008; Ceribelli, Nascimento, Pacifico, & de Lima, 2009; Claxton-Oldfield, MacDonald, & Claxton-Oldfield, 2006; Hellman & House, 2006; Planalp & Trost, 2008; Rayner & Marshall, 2003). Many other foundations and organizations have diagnosis specific volunteer programs. For example, the Breast Cancer Foundation solicits cancer survivors to assist newly diagnosed cancer patients, and the Lupus Foundation of America enrolls volunteers to interact with lupus patients (Breast Cancer Foundation, 2009; Lupus Foundation of America, Inc., 2009). These volunteers have an important health communication role in information giving, social support, and acting as a link to help patients and families receive the health care services they need.

Specialty Teams

Many specialties emphasize the importance of communication between the health care team and the patient as well as communication between health care team members (e.g., technicians and providers), for improved patient outcomes. Dialysis teams, radiation departments, dental services, and many others all advocate interdisciplinary communication and patient-centered communication (Desai et al., 2008; Kahng, 2006, discussion 194–185; Thommen & Emery, 2006). In ophthalmology, one innovative intervention explored the use of prerecorded instructions in patients' native Hebrew language rather than using interpreters during an exam to assess visual fields (Nesher, Ever-Hadani, Epstein, Stern, & Assia, 2001). This study reported no increase in the length of time it took technicians to provide services and no compromise in the quality of services provided, suggesting methods for communicating basic information in multilingual settings (Nesher et al., 2001). Another facility has piloted an innovative software program that utilizes pictures to help patients and providers identify medications since patients often remember size and color but not name or dosage (Lowrey, Lee, & Gerber, 2003). This communication aid has the potential to reduce medication errors and has shown positive results; it could be used by any member of a health care team.

Conclusion

Many different individuals and professionals interact with patients and families as they navigate the health care system. Using a communication approach that recognizes individual goals, needs, and priorities is virtually universally recommended. Similarly, the overall challenges of communicating in this fashion are not necessarily unique to a particular discipline, although many disciplines have identified areas of particular difficulty. As health care evolves yet more challenges will be identified. Telemedicine, where patients and providers can interact via webcams, provides an example of how health communication is being revolutionized by technology (see Whitten et al., this volume). Health communication by e-mail is another emerging challenge. Regular electronic communication of patient data sent from a device such as a pacemaker may require health care professionals to initiate a systematic program of patient contact to provide reassurance and alleviate uncertainty. Clearly, the health communication challenges for those involved in patient care are many, and continue to evolve. By utilizing and continuously updating health communication skills training and educational programs for all those who interact with patients, the delivery of quality patient care and, by extension, professional, staff, and volunteer satisfaction can be attained.

References

American Association of Colleges of Nursing. (2005). *Standards for accreditation of baccalaureate and graduate nursing programs.* Washington DC: Commission on Collegiate Nursing Education.

Anderson, R., Barbara, A., & Feldman, S. (2007). What patients want: A content analysis of key qualities that influence patient satisfaction. *The Journal of Medical Practice Management, 22,* 255–261.

Arora, N. (2003). Interacting with cancer patients: The significance of physicians' communication behavior. *Social Science & Medicine, 57,* 791–806.

Arora, R., Singer, J., & Arora, A. (2004). Influence of key variables on the patients' choice of a physician. *Quality Management in Health Care, 13,* 166–173.

Austin, D. R. (2009). *Therapeutic recreation: Processes and techniques.* Champaign, IL: Sagamore.

Back, A. L., Arnold, R. M., Baile, W. F., Fryer-Edwards, K. A., Alexander, S. C., Barley, G. E., ... Tulsky, J. A. (2007). Efficacy of communication skills training for giving bad news and discussing transitions to palliative care. *Archives of Internal Medicine, 167,* 453–460.

Beatty, L., Oxlad, M., Koczwara, B., & Wade, T. D. (2008). The psychosocial concerns and needs of women recently diagnosed with breast cancer: A qualitative study of patient, nurse and volunteer perspectives. *Health Expectations: An International Journal of Public Participation in Health Care and Health Policy, 11,* 331–342.

Beckman, H. B., & Frankel, R. M. (2003). Training practitioners to communicate effectively in cancer care: It is the relationship that counts. *Patient Education and Counseling, 50,* 85–89.

Biesecker, B. B., & Peters, K. F. (2001). Process studies in genetic counseling: Peering into the black box. *American Journal of Medical Genetics, 106,* 191–198.

Bloomberg, S., & Luke, J. (2008). Wireless substitution: Early release of estimates from the National Health Interview Survey July–December 2008. Retrieved from http://www.cdc.gov/nchs/data/nhis/earlyrelease/wireless200905.htm#Status

Brashers, D. E., Neidig, J. L., Haas, S. M., Dobbs, L. K., Cardillo, L., & Russell, J. A. (2000). Communication in the management of uncertainty: The case of persons living with HIV or AIDS. *Communication Monographs, 67,* 63–84.

Breast Cancer Foundation. (2009). Be a BCF volunteer. Retrieved from http://www.bcf.org.sg/joinBcf/beABcfVolunteer.html

Broadhead, R. S. (1986). Directing intervention from afar: The telephone dynamics of managing acute poisonings. *Journal of Health and Social Behavior, 27,* 303–316.

Bunn, F., Byrne, G., & Kendall, S. (2004). Telephone consultation and triage: Effects on health care use and patient satisfaction. *Cochrane Database of Systematic Reviews, 3,* 1469–1493. Art. No.: CD004180. DOI: 10.1002/14651858.CD004180.pub2.

Burgio, L. D., Allen-Burge, R., Roth, D. L., Bourgeois, M. S., Dijkstra, K., Gerstle, J., ... Bankester, L. (2001). Come talk with me: Improving communication between nursing assistants and nursing home residents during care routines. *Gerontologist, 41,* 449–460.

Burgio, L. D., Stevens, A., Burgio, K. L., Roth, D. L., Paul, P., & Gerstle, J. (2002). Teaching and maintaining behavior management skills in the nursing home. *Gerontologist, 42,* 487–496.

Byrne, M. (2007). Spirituality in palliative care: What language do we need? Learning from pastoral care. *International Journal of Palliative Nursing, 13,* 118–124.

Carr, D. D. (2009). Building collaborative partnerships in critical care: The RN case manager/social work dyad in critical care. *Professional Case Management, 14,* 121–132.

Cegala, D. J., Post, D. M., & McClure, L. (2001). The effects of patient communication skills training on the discourse of older patients during a primary care interview. *Journal of the American Geriatric Society, 49,* 1505–1511.

Ceribelli, C., Nascimento, L. C., Pacifico, S. M., & de Lima, R. A. (2009). Reading mediation as a communication resource for hospitalized children: Support for the humanization of nursing care. *Revista Latino-Americana Enfermagem, 17,* 81–87.

Charlton, C. R., Dearing, K. S., Berry, J. A., & Johnson, M. J. (2008). Nurse practitioners' communication styles and their impact on patient outcomes: An integrated literature review. *Journal of the American Academy of Nurse Practitioners, 20,* 382–388.

Claxton-Oldfield, S., MacDonald, J., & Claxton-Oldfield, J. (2006). What palliative care volunteers would like to know about the patients they are being asked to support. *American Journal of Hospice and Palliative Care, 23,* 192–196.

Clayton, M. (1996). Caring for Carl at home. *Home Health Care Nurse, 14,* 605–608.

Clayton, M. F. (2006). Communication: An important part of nursing care. *American Journal of Nursing, 106,* 70–71.

Clayton, M. F., & Dudley, W. N. (2009). Patient-centered communication during oncology follow-up visits for breast cancer survivors: Content and temporal structure. *Oncology Nursing Forum 36 Online Exclusive,* E69–79.

Clayton, M. F., Dudley, W. N., & Musters, A. (2008). Communication with breast cancer survivors. *Health Communication, 23,* 207–221.

Cobaugh, D. J., & Krenzelok, E. P. (2006). Adverse drug reactions and therapeutic errors in older adults: A hazard factor analysis of poison center data. *American Journal of Health-System Pharmacy: AJHP: Official Journal of the American Society of Health-System Pharmacists, 63,* 2228–2234.

Colon-Emeric, C. S., Lekan, D., Utley-Smith, Q., Ammarell, N., Bailey, D., Corazzini, K.,... Anderson, R. A. (2007). Barriers to and facilitators of clinical practice guideline use in nursing homes. *Journal of the American Geriatric Society, 55,* 1404–1409.

Corey, G. (2008). *The theory and practice of group counseling.* Belmont, CA: Brookes/Cole.

Cunningham, R. S. (2004). Advanced practice nursing outcomes: A review of selected empirical literature. *Oncology Nursing Forum, 31,* 219–232.

Curry, L., Porter, M., Michalski, M., & Gruman, C. (2000). Individualized care: Perceptions of certified nurse's aides. *Journal of Gerontological Nursing, 26,* 45–51.

Delgado, C. (2007). Meeting clients' spiritual needs. *Nursing Clinics of North America, 42,* 279–293.

de Oliveira, D. R., & Shoemaker, S. J. (2006). Achieving patient-centeredness in pharmacy practice: Openness and the pharmacist's natural attitude. *Journal of the American Pharmacists Association, 46,* 56–64..

Desai, A. A., Bolus, R., Nissenson, A., Bolus, S., Solomon, M. D., Khawar, ...Speigel, B. (2008). Identifying best practices in dialysis care: Results of cognitive interviews and a national survey of dialysis providers. *Clinical Journal of the American Society of Nephrology, 3,* 1066–1076. DOI: 10.2215/CJN.04421007

Dormandy, E., Michie, S., Hooper, R., & Marteau, T. M. (2005). Low uptake of prenatal screening for Down syndrome in minority ethnic groups and socially deprived groups: A reflection of women's attitudes or a failure to facilitate informed choices? *International Journal of Epidemiology, 34,* 346–352.

Downey, V., Bengiamin, M., Heuer, L., & Juhl, N. (1995). Dying babies and associated stress in NICU nurses. *Neonatal Network, 14,* 41–46.

Dreachslin, J. L., Hunt, P. L., & Sprainer, E. (1999). Communication patterns and group composition: Implications for patient-centered care team effectiveness. *Journal of Healthcare Management, 44,* 252–266..

Edwards, M., Millard, P., Praskac, L. A., & Wisniewski, P. A. (2003). Occupational therapy and early intervention: A family-centred approach. *Occupational Therapy International, 10,* 239–252.

Ellington, L., Roter, D., Dudley, W. N., Baty, B. J., Upchurch, R., Larson, S., & Botkin, J. R. (2005). Communication analysis of BRCA1 genetic counseling. *Journal of Genetic Counseling, 14,* 377–386.

Ellington, L., Sheldon, L. K., Matwin, S., Smith, J. A., Poynton, M. M., Crouch, B. I., & Caravati, E. M. (2009). An examination of adherence strategies and challenges in poison control communication. *Journal of Emergency Nursing, 35,* 186.

Epstein, R. M., & Street, R. L. (2007). *Patient-centered communication in cancer care: Promoting healing and reducing suffering* (NIH Publication No. 07-6225). Bethesda, MD: National Cancer Institute.

Fortin, A. H. (2002). Communication skills to improve patient satisfaction and quality of care [Supplement]. *Ethnicity and Disease, 12*(3), 58–61.

Gallup. (2008). Nurses shine, bankers slump in ethics ratings: Annual honesty and ethics poll rates nurses best of 21 professions. Retrieved from http://www.gallup.com/poll/112264/nurses-shine-while-bankers-slump-ethics-ratings.aspx

Havig, K. (2008). The health care experiences of adult survivors of child sexual abuse: A systematic review of evidence on sensitive practice. *Trauma Violence Abuse, 9,* 19–33.

Hellman, C. M., & House, D. (2006). Volunteers serving victims of sexual assault. *Journal of Social Psychology, 146,* 117–123.

Hudacek, S. S. (2008). Dimensions of caring: A qualitative analysis of nurses' stories. *Journal of Nursing Education, 47,* 124–129.

Iezzoni, L. I., O'Day, B. L., Killeen, M., & Harker, H. (2004). Communicating about health care: Observations from persons who are deaf or hard of hearing. *Annals of Internal Medicine, 140,* 356–362.

Institute of Medicine. (2004). Forging a poison prevention and control system. Retrieved from http://www.nap.edu/openbook.php?isbn=0309091942.

Jackson, G. A. (2002). Person-centered care in dementia. *Nursing Times, 98,* 30–32.

Kahng, L. S. (2006). Patient-dentist-technician communication within the dental team: Using a colored treatment plan wax-up. *Journal of Esthetic and Restorative Dentistry, 18,* 185–193.

Keshishian, F., Colodny, N., & Boone, R. T. (2008). Physician–patient and pharmacist–patient communication: Geriatrics' perceptions and opinions. *Patient Education and Counseling, 71,* 265–284.

Kessler, S. (1997). Psychological aspects of genetic counseling: IX. Teaching and counseling. *Journal of Genetic Counseling, 6,* 287.

Kruijver, I. P., Kerkstra, A., Francke, A. L., Bensing, J. M., & van de Wiel, H. B. (2000). Evaluation of communication training programs in nursing care: A review of the literature. *Patient Education and Counseling, 39,* 129–145.

Kvale, K. (2007). Do cancer patients always want to talk about difficult emotions? A qualitative study of cancer inpatients communication needs. *European Journal of Oncology Nursing, 11,* 320–327.

Leach, E., Cornwell, P., Fleming, J., & Haines, T. (2009). Patient-centered goal-setting in a subacute rehabilitation setting. *Disability & Rehabilitation, 32*(2), 1–14.

Lein, C., & Wills, C. E. (2007). Using patient-centered interviewing skills to manage complex patient encounters in primary care. *Journal American Academy of Nurse Practitioners, 19,* 215–220.

Liechty, J. A. (2006). The sounds of silence: Relating to people with aphasia. *Journal of Psychosocial Nursing & Mental Health Services, 44,* 53–55.

Liechty, J. A., & Heinzekehr, J. B. (2008). Finding God without words: A guide to pastoral care for persons with aphasia. *Journal of Pastoral Care & Counseling, 62,* 297–300.

Lowrey, G., Lee, E., & Gerber, B. (2003). Evaluation of the medication sketch artist: A new method of determining unknown patient medications. *AMIA Annual Symposium Proceedings,* 401–404.

Lupus Foundation of America Inc. (2009). Get involved. Retrieved from http://www.lupus.org/webmodules/webarticlesnet/templates/new_actionvolunteer.aspx?articleid=200&zoneid=52

Marteau, T. M., & Lerman, C. (2001). Genetic risk and behavioural change. *BMJ (Clinical Research Ed.), 322*(7293), 1056–1059.

McCabe, C. (2004). Nurse–patient communication: An exploration of patients' experiences. *Journal of Clinical Nursing, 13,* 41–49.

McLellan, A. (2009). The nurse–patient relationship will prove key to effective medication adherence. *Nursing Times, 105,* 29.

Meiser, B., Irle, J., Lobb, E., & Barlow-Stewart, K. (2008). Assessment of the content and process of genetic counseling: A critical review of empirical studies. *Journal of Genetic Counseling, 17,* 434–451.

Molzahn, A. E., & Sheilds, L. (2008). Why is it so hard to talk about spirituality? *Canadian Nurse, 104*(1), 25–29.

Mularski, R. A., Bascom, P., & Osborne, M. L. (2001). Educational agendas for interdisciplinary end-of-life curricula [Supplement]. *Critical Care Medicine, 29*(2), N16–23.

Nesher, R., Ever-Hadani, P., Epstein, E., Stern, Y., & Assia, E. (2001). Overcoming the language barrier in visual field testing. *Journal of Glaucoma, 10,* 203–205.

Nordehn, G., Meredith, A., & Bye, L. (2006). A preliminary investigation of barriers to achieving patient-centered communication with patients who have stroke-related communication disorders. *Topics in Stroke Rehabilitation, 13,* 68–77.

Nye, L. G. (2001). Office staff savvy: Quality staff–patient communications as a loss prevention strategy. *The Journal of Medical Practice Management, 17,* 21–24.

Parker, L. S. (1994). Bioethics for human geneticists: Models for reasoning and methods for teaching. *The American Journal of Human Genetics, 54,* 137–147.

Pennington, K., Scott, J., & Magilvy, K. (2003). The role of certified nursing assistants in nursing homes. *Journal of Nursing Administration, 33,* 578–584.

Pieterse, A. H., van Dulmen, A. M., Ausems, M. G., Beemer, F. A., & Bensing, J. M. (2005). Communication in cancer genetic counseling: Does it reflect counselees' previsit needs and preferences? *British Journal of Cancer, 92,* 1671–1678.

Planalp, S., Crouch, B., Rothwell, E., & Ellington, L. (2009). Assessing the need for communication training for specialists in poison information. *Clinical Toxicology, 47,* 584–589.

Planalp, S., & Trost, M. R. (2008). Communication issues at the end of life: Reports from hospice volunteers. *Health Communication, 23,* 222–233.

Potter, M., Gordon, S., & Hamer, P. (2003). The physiotherapy experience in private practice: The patients' perspective. *Australian Journal of Physiotherapy, 49,* 195–202.

Ragan, S. L., Wittenberg, E., & Hall, H. T. (2003). The communication of palliative care for the elderly cancer patient. *Health Communication, 15,* 219–226.

Rayner, H., & Marshall, J. (2003). Training volunteers as conversation partners for people with aphasia. *International Journal of Language & Communication Disorders, 38,* 149–164.

Reisman, A. B. (2002). Overview of telephone medicine. In A. B. Reisman & D. L. Stevens (Eds.), *Telephone medicine: A guide for the practicing physician* (pp. 3–18). Philadelphia, PA: American College of Physicians.

Resta, R., Biesecker, B. B., Bennett, R. L., Blum, S., Hahn, S. E., Strecker, M. N., & Williams, J. L. (2006). A new definition of genetic counseling: National society of genetic counselors' task force report. *Journal of Genetic Counseling, 15,* 77–83.

Roter, D. (2000). The medical visit context of treatment decision-making and the therapeutic relationship. *Health Expectations: An International Journal of Public Participation in Health Care and Health Policy, 3,* 17–25.

Roter, D., Ellington, L., Erby, L. H., Larson, S., & Dudley, W. (2006). The genetic counseling video project (GCVP): Models of practice. *American Journal of Medical Genetics. Part C, Seminars in Medical Genetics, 142,* 209.

Roter, D. L., Erby, L. H., Larson, S., & Ellington, L. (2007). Assessing oral literacy demand in genetic counseling dialogue: Preliminary test of a conceptual framework. *Social Science & Medicine, 65,* 1442–1457.

Rothwell, E., Ellington, L., Planalp, S., & Crouch, B. I. (in press). Identifying communication challenges of specialists in poison information through focus groups. *Qualitative Health Research.*

Rowan, K. E. (2008). Monthly communication skill coaching for health care staff. *Patient Education and Counseling, 71,* 402–404.

Rutenberg, C. D. (2000). What do we really KNOW about telephone triage? *Journal of Emergency Nursing, 26,* 76–78.

Ryan, E. B., Martin, L. S., & Beaman, A. (2005). Communication strategies to promote spiritual well-being among people with dementia. *Journal of Pastoral Care & Counseling, 59,* 43–55.

Skarupski, K. A., Mrvos, R., & Krenzelok, E. P. (2004). A profile of calls to a poison information center regarding older adults. *Journal of Aging and Health, 16,* 228–247.

Smets, E., van Zwieten, M., & Michie, S. (2007). Comparing genetic counseling with non-genetic health care interactions: Two of a kind? *Patient Education and Counseling, 68,* 225–234.

Suhonen, R., Valimaki, M., Katajisto, J., & Leino-Kilpi, H. (2007). Provision of individualized care improves hospital patient outcomes: An explanatory model using LISREL. *International Journal of Nursing Studies, 44,* 197–207.

Sumsion, T., & Law, M. (2006). A review of evidence on the conceptual elements informing client-centred practice. *Canadian Journal of Occupational Therapy, 73,* 153–162.

Sumsion, T., & Smyth, G. (2000). Barriers to client-centredness and their resolution. *Canadian Journal of Occupational Therapy, 67,* 15–21.

Sylvester, C, Voelkl, J. E., & Ellis, G. (2001). *Therapeutic recreation: Theory and practice.* State College, PA: Venture.

Taylor, C. (1994). Ministering to persons who face death. Practical guidance for care givers of persons making end-of-life treatment decisions. *Health Progress, 75,* 58–62.

Thommen, P. J., & Emery, R. J. (2006). An analysis of 20 years of radiation-related health care complaints in Texas for the purposes of quality improvement [Supplement]. *Health Physics, 90* (5), S62–S66.

Titone, N. J., Cross, R., Sileo, M., & Martin, G. (2004). Taking family-centered care to a higher level on the heart and kidney unit. *Pediatric Nursing, 30,* 495–497.

van den Berg, M., Timmermans, D. R. M., Ten Kate, L. P., van Vugt, J. M. G., & van der Wal, G. (2005). Are pregnant women making informed choices about prenatal screening? *Genetics in Medicine: Official Journal of the American College of Medical Genetics, 7,* 332–338.

Vanswearingen, J. (2008). Facial rehabilitation: A neuromuscular reeducation, patient-centered approach. *Facial Plastic Surgery, 24,* 250–259.

Weil, J. (2003). Psychosocial genetic counseling in the post-nondirective era: A point of view. *Journal of Genetic Counseling, 12,* 199–211.

Weiss, R. (2003). Don't forget about the office staff. *Marketing Health Services, 23,* 10–11.

Wezorek, C. M., Dean, B. S., & Krenzelok, E. P. (1992). Factors influencing non-compliance with poison center recommendations. *Veterinary and Human Toxicology, 34,* 151–153.

White, N. C. (1997). Poisons and panic! *Veterinary and Human Toxicology, 39,* 170–172.

Wilkinson, S., Perry, R., Blanchard, K., & Linsell, L. (2008). Effectiveness of a three-day communication skills course in changing nurses' communication skills with cancer/palliative care patients: A randomized controlled trial. *Palliative Medicine, 22,* 365–375.

Worley, M. M. (2006). Testing a pharmacist–patient relationship quality model among older persons with diabetes. *Research in Social & Administrative Pharmacy, 2,* 1–21.

Worley, M. M., Schommer, J. C., Brown, L. M., Hadsall, R. S., Ranelli, P. L., Stratton, T. P., & Uden, D. L. (2007). Pharmacists' and patients' roles in the pharmacist–patient relationship: Are pharmacists and patients reading from the same relationship script? *Research in Social & Administrative Pharmacy, 3,* 47–69.

Wottrich, A. W., von Koch, L., & Tham, K. (2007). The meaning of rehabilitation in the home environment after acute stroke from the perspective of a multiprofessional team. *Physical Therapy, 87,* 778–788.

6

TELEMEDICINE

Reviewing the Past, Looking Toward the Future

Pamela Whitten, David Cook, and Jennifer Cornacchione

Erika, a diabetic patient, has trouble managing her glucose levels and lives 120 miles away from a medical specialist. Through the use of a handheld mobile device, she can electronically submit her sugar levels to a nurse practitioner at another location to manage her condition. Genevieve, an elderly cancer patient, lives in a rural community 300 miles away from her oncologist. In her condition, driving 5 hours to the cancer center would be exhausting, and she likely would not routinely make her visits. Over Interactive Tele-Video (ITV) augmented with a digital stethoscope, she can drive across town in 10 minutes and have a teleconsultation. Matthew gets in a serious car accident on his way to work. The emergency physician is able to access vital patient information from Matthew's online health record through a health information exchange to provide him with the best care possible. These scenarios are all examples of what is commonly referred to as telemedicine. This chapter will discuss telemedicine's past, present, and future beginning with an overview of telemedicine followed by a discussion of advantages and barriers. Then, methodological challenges will be addressed. Finally, opportunities for communication scholars will be highlighted.

Telemedicine Defined

The American Telemedicine Association (ATA) defines telemedicine as the use of technologies to provide health care over a distance to individuals (ATA, 2009). Telemedicine interactions deliver health care via either asynchronous technologies (store and forward, such as e-mail) or synchronous technologies (real time, such as videoconferencing). For almost 50 years, the use of telemedicine has slowly become more commonplace in the United States and worldwide. With the continual advancements of health technology and its ability to revolutionize how health care is delivered, the still untapped myriad uses of telemedicine are guaranteed to progressively be identified and applied as a critical part of the solution to the problem of health care access, cost, and quality.

The first telemedicine application using ITV communications occurred in 1959 between the Nebraska Psychiatric Institute and the Norfolk State Hospital. Over a distance of 112 miles, telepsychiatry consultations occurred via microwave technology using closed-circuit television (Whitten & Sypher, 2006). This early pilot project sparked tremendous interest, and the decade of the 1970s witnessed an abundance of activity. Much of this early work focused on using some kind of ITV or videoconferencing technology to connect physicians with their patients. However, despite the early surge in activity, almost all projects ended in the 1980s because the soft dollar funding base came to an end, and the telecommunications infrastructure at the time was not sophisticated enough to provide cost-effective solutions. For example, early telemedicine systems could easily cost $125,000 to $150,000 for technology for which we currently pay $5,000 to $10,000 today. Telemedicine began growing again in the 1990s as a result of increasing health care costs, advances in technology, lowered technology costs, and the availability of more federal funding for projects (Maheu, Whitten, & Allen, 2001). In particular, telecommunication infrastructures became more prevalent in urban and some rural communities across the United States, facilitating opportunities for broader connectivity. The initial infrastructures commonly resembled phone systems from the early 20th century, which were dedicated networks requiring centralized scheduling and coordination, limitations that made telemedicine more cumbersome than desirable.

The 1990s also realized a shift in the way telemedicine was conceptualized and defined. In prior decades, telemedicine was primarily described as consultations that took place between a physician and a patient for medical purposes. To broaden this focus to include nursing and allied health professionals, as well as educational applications, telehealth became part of the common nomenclature (ATA, 2009). One of the premiere academic journals changed its name from the *Journal of Telemedicine* to the *Journal of Telemedicine and Telehealth*. Additionally, a leading trade association emerged as the Association for Telehealth Service Providers (ATSP). Today, the terms *telemedicine* and *telehealth* are used interchangeably. During this decade, innovative delivery models that extended beyond hospitals became more prevalent, and a natural evolution occurred where networks began to be used to connect patients to health care in their homes, at long-term care facilities, schools, and jails. The next phase in the telemedicine movement, which began in the late 1990s and early 2000s shifted to utilization of the World Wide Web to provide e-health services. The term *e-health* refers to providing the general public with health care and health related services via the Internet (Maheu et al., 2001; see also Sundar et al., this volume). Without question, the Internet has assumed increased prominence in providing information, education, and other health related services and resources. Fox and Jones (2009) found that over 60% of American adults looked online for health information. There are clear concerns with the quality of some of the information and the credibility of so-called experts online, but consumers continue to see the value in e-health applications to access information on a variety of topics such as weight loss or chronic disease management (Krukowski, Harvey-Berino, Ashikaga, Thomas, & Micco, 2008). This change has led to a paradigm shift from a more medically dominant patient care model to one where patients are more informed and engaged in their health care.

In the 1990s, telemedicine scholars began focusing on the role of technology in sharing patient information, including insurance and billing data, through Health Information Exchanges (HIE). At the present time, HIEs are broadly defined without a standardized technical platform to bridge these information systems across states or regions. An example of an HIE includes a hospital with an electronic health record (EHR) that is linked with other health care providers, pharmacies, insurers, and possibly local businesses. The value of HIEs is that they can provide efficiencies across a health care system while improving the quality of care provided. HIEs may prevent dangerous drug interactions or abuse by automatically cross-checking patient history with the range of medications being prescribed (Shapiro, 2007; Shapiro, Kannry, Kushniruk, & Kuperman, 2007). Considerable energy is being invested nationwide in growing the HIE industry while addressing critical challenges such as promoting interoperability standards and ensuring privacy and security. Although telemedicine's evolution over the past half century has been significant, telemedicine consultations still only constitute a fraction (.005%) of the overall health care activity in the country. Some of the most recent statistics from the Agency for Health care Research and Quality (AHRQ) indicated that 48,194 telemedicine consultations (excluding teleradiology) were performed in 2003 in 46 states. In comparison, according to the U.S. Department of Health and Human Services (HHS), approximately 820 million traditional office visits occur per year across the United States during a similar time frame. It is important to keep telemedicine's volume of activity in perspective while considering its impact. As the evolving role of technology transforms health care on a routine basis, telemedicine will undoubtedly be an important part of health care delivery for decades to come.

Types of Telemedicine

As discussed in the previous section, the way telemedicine has been conceptualized has changed, and will continue to change over time. The categories outlined below are not mutually exclusive, but are meant to help better understand the different types of telemedicine.

Identification by Technology

Practitioners frequently define telemedicine simply by the technology used to facilitate interactions. The most common distinction is between synchronous and asynchronous delivery methods. The term asynchronous refers to store and forward applications, such as teleradiology where an X-ray is sent digitally to a radiologist at a distant location for a diagnosis. Teleradiology is commonly used by practitioners in different countries and enables a radiologist to review a slate of X-rays during the evening so diagnoses can be received the following morning in another country. The term synchronous refers to real-time interactions where a physician consults with a patient over a videoconferencing system. Depending on the specialty, these consultations are often augmented with the appropriate peripheral device such as a telestethoscope, dermascope, or otoscope.

Discussions of telemedicine technology also refer to the availability of bandwidth supporting the connection. The term *bandwidth* refers to the amount of information that can be sent through a particular technical connection. An analog telephone line provides 14.4mbps, whereas T-1 lines provide up to 1 mg, or 20 times the bandwidth capacity (Horak, 2008). The greater the bandwidth, the more information can be sent, and in a more timely fashion. This is particularly important if large images, such as pathology slides, need to be shared between providers. With the emergence of broadband technology, more and more applications are able to access high-end bandwidth, which facilitates higher quality images and more synchronous communications. However, practitioners sometimes have to weigh the perceived value of a certain bandwidth versus its associated cost. As bandwidth increases, so too does the cost of the connection. Wireless networks further define and shape the way telemedicine is described. Over the past decade wireless networks have become more prevalent, providing greater access to geographically isolated communities. Early wireless applications often connected rural areas for medical consultations when land telecommunication lines were difficult to access. More recent innovations involve using technologies such as handheld devices or even wearable applications to exchange patient information in a timely fashion. Hong et al. (2009) recently evaluated the performance of wireless electrocardiogram (ECG) devices worn by the patient, finding ECG signal detection and transmission similar to conventional methods.

Identification by Context

The location or context of delivery also varies widely, with each model having notable implications for the type of service and care provided. Contexts may include hospitals, nursing homes, prisons, home health settings, or schools to name only a few (Alverson et al., 2008; Maheu et al., 2001). For example, the goal of a home health project that is targeting congestive heart failure (CHF) patients may be to monitor their vital signs to ensure that they are stable and stay out of the emergency room. A nurse manager may likely be the primary health care provider in this model, focusing on ensuring patient compliance. Telemedicine may involve sharing medical data about key clinical indicators between the nurse and the patient's home through an online portal. When outliers persist, the nurse telephones the patient to assess the situation (Whitten, Bergman, Meese, Bridwell, & Jule, 2009; Whitten & Mickus, 2007). In an elementary school setting, nurses may target children with acute conditions to connect patients over ITV with pediatricians for more direct patient care. Similar to the traditional setting, a stethoscope and otoscope would augment the care provided (Whitten & Cook, 1999). With these examples a telehome health project for CHF patients is quite different from a teleschool project for children. By including the context in their telemedicine descriptor, practitioners provide some insight into the type of program in which they are involved.

Advantages of Telemedicine

Research across a number of programs and states has identified the benefits of telemedicine, including increased patient access, decreased health care transportation expenses, and decreased disparities between urban and rural health care (Gray, Stamm, Toevs, Reischl, & Yarrington, 2006). The following section highlights a few of these key issues.

Access

Researchers and practitioners alike overwhelmingly highlight one of telemedicine's greatest strengths as enabling the provision of access to care where it is otherwise not likely to be available. Perhaps the greatest advantage of telemedicine is its ability to transcend geographic and socioeconomic barriers. We have known for years that telemedicine provides greater access to health care for individuals in underserved communities, especially for rural residents (Bashshur, 1997). These patients often struggle to obtain treatment because of a lack of transportation or inability to take time off from work.

Potential Cost Savings

Numerous economic analyses have compared several telemedicine specialties such as teleradiology and telemental health, and supporting technologies such as echocardiographic image transmission, and have found telemedicine to be a cost-effective alternative to in-person health care (Hailey, Roine, & Ohinmaa, 2002). One study assessed telecardiology in a neonatal ICU and pediatric ICU and found an estimated savings of $150,000 and $172,000, respectively (Marcin, Nesbitt, Struve, Traugott, & Dimand, 2004; Rendina, Carrasco, Wood, Cameron, & Bose, 2001).

The Health Care Financing Administration (HCFA, now the Center for Medicare and Medicaid Services [CMS]) recognized that telemedicine may save health care expenditures for beneficiaries, providers, and payers through reduced costs for patient or health professional travel, medical education, interhospital patient transfer, and patient record keeping (Kumekawa et al., 1997). One study investigating potential cost-savings of telemedicine patients in rural Arkansas revealed that without telemedicine access, 94% of patients would travel greater than 70 miles for medical care, 84% would miss one day of work, and 74% would spend $75 to $150 for additional family expenses. Telemedicine access saved $32 in fuel costs for 92% of patients and $100 in wages for 84% of patients (Bynum, Irwin, Cranford, & Denny, 2003). Telemedicine's ability to remotely monitor patients for preventative care can potentially save money by detecting problems before they become critical. Despite a number of research studies focusing on cost, greater rigor needs to be applied to determine the true economic impact of telemedicine (Whitten, Mair, et al., 2002).

Barriers to Telemedicine

There are a number of issues that are a challenge in providing telemedicine. Two of the most commonly identified, reimbursement and licensure, are discussed below.

Reimbursement

Reimbursement has been at the epicenter of telemedicine policy discussions from the beginning. The primary struggle involves some insurance companies refusing to reimburse physicians for nontraditional consults, and Medicaid coverage for telemedicine not being consistent across states (Whitten & Buis, 2007). This issue dates back to the Balanced Budget Act (BBA) of 1997, which mandated that the Health Care Financing Administration (now CMS) begin reimbursing for select telehealth consultations on January 1, 1999. Although the act provided some reimbursement, limitations to the policy are typically viewed as undermining telemedicine adoption.

Coverage by Medicare was expanded in 2001 with considerably more favorable reimbursement mechanisms. A number of states have developed more flexible policies with state Medicaid offices and private insurers. Five states have passed legislation requiring private insurance coverage of health care services provided through telemedicine (California, Kentucky, Texas, Louisiana, and Oklahoma). Despite this progress, federal expenditures for telehealth services remain extremely low. In 2006, for example, the total Medicare payment for telehealth services (including the originating site facility fee) was approximately $2 million. Previous expansions to Medicare telehealth services have also not resulted in significant federal increases in Medicare expenditures. Similarly, states where telemedicine insurance coverage was mandated by law have not seen significant federal increases in expenditure activity once the new policies were initiated. Although there has been some progress at the federal, state, and private insurance levels, reimbursement continues to be a critical issue for telemedicine practitioners and a perceived barrier to its acceptance into mainstream medicine.

Licensure

Licensure is another critical issue for telemedicine. Doctors are licensed by the individual state, which creates a challenge in providing telemedicine services across state borders (Stanberry, 2006). In this case, telemedicine's advantage of overcoming geographic barriers is also one of its limitations—particularly between states. If a physician practices in California and sees a patient via telemedicine in Nevada, where does the consult occur and which state policy practices should have precedence? To address this question, some physicians who routinely practice telemedicine across borders get licensed in both states. While some policy experts believe this strategy should address the licensure concern, legal precedent on this issue is extremely limited. Until case law provides better guidance on this topic, practitioners will continue to struggle with determining best practice. A great advantage of telemedicine is its use for second opinion services. If a cancer patient in Kansas wants a second opinion from a leading specialist in another state, he or she can connect via telemedicine. Specialists, however, are at times reluctant to provide consults for limited or acute televisits in part because of the licensure issue. It is also unlikely that a physician would become licensed in a distant state for only a handful of second opinion consults.

Other Barriers

A variety of barriers to telemedicine have been detailed in the literature. One centers on patient privacy concerns where a broader range of nonhealth care practitioners have access to patient records as they become digitized (Matusitz & Breen, 2007). Practitioners' dislike of technology can also be a barrier to the use of telemedicine. There are basic struggles with fundamental changes in delivery when care is provided over telemedicine (Whitten & Holtz, 2008; Whitten & Mackert, 2005). Where telecare is perceived as second-rate or lacking the clinical rigor of traditional medicine, there can also be concerns related to quality. These issues have created a barrier for complete acceptance, utilization, and satisfaction with telemedicine.

Satisfaction and Utilization

Much of the early research focused on patient and provider satisfaction, and it continues to be a common research area today. Overall, the research has provided fairly positive results. In 2001, Williams, May, and Esmail reviewed 93 patient satisfaction studies, finding satisfaction levels higher than 80% and frequently at 100%. Still, they cited a variety of methodological limitations including small sample sizes and the multiple ways telemedicine was defined. In some cases satisfaction research has shown more positive outcomes for telemedicine than traditional settings. A more recent study found that the majority of clinicians were satisfied with telemonitoring patients during acute trauma resuscitations, citing patient benefits and improved collegiality as important factors (Al–Kadi et al., 2009). However, Whitten and Love (2005) caution against positive satisfaction findings by citing methodological issues, such as using invalidated measurement tools.

Acceptance and utilization of health communication technologies is another interest to many telemedicine scholars. Buck (2009) outlines nine human factors that are necessary for telemedicine acceptance, among which are that the advantages of the telemedicine application must be understood and clear to participants, and patients and doctors should be able to maintain control and respect by being able to fulfill their normal duties. However, even if users accept a telemedicine program, organizational factors such as unsupportive management impede utilization (Whitten, Holtz, Meyer, & Nazione, 2009).

Clinical Outcomes

Research relating to clinical outcomes has frequently focused on diagnostic accuracy, comparing telemedicine to traditional settings. In a review of 160 studies, Heinzelmann and colleagues found most clinically oriented studies to focus on diagnosis, clinical management, and patient clinical outcomes (Heinzelmann, Williams, Lugn, & Kvedar, 2005). Across these studies, the light microscope and film radiology were most commonly compared. For specialty care, diagnostic equipment unique to that area was most commonly used (e.g., dermatology and cardiology peripherals). Overall, 69% of the studies supported the diagnostic accuracy of telemedicine whereas only 5% were unsupportive. Research relating to clinical outcomes in general, however, remains inconsistent. For example, positive clinical outcomes have been observed with obese children receiving teleconsultations with an endocrinologist (Shaikh, Cole, Marcin, & Nesbitt, 2008), but DelliFraine and Dansky (2008) found no link between home telecare and diabetes outcomes.

Cost Research

Cost effectiveness is another popular area of telemedicine research, although very few studies contain any true cost–benefit data (Hailey, 2005; Whitten, Mair, et al., 2002). Shore and colleagues suggest that as transmission costs continue to decrease, telemedicine will continue to decrease health care costs (Shore, Brooks, Savin, Manson, & Libby, 2007). Telemedicine has been found to be cost effective for some projects, such as treating retinopathy of prematurity for low birth weight infants (Jackson et al., 2008), but not for other applications, such as blood glucose self-monitoring (Farmer, Gibson, Tarassenko, & Neil, 2005). Overall, a need exists for more cost–benefit studies in telemedicine research because evidence is not strong enough to state with certainty that telemedicine is a cost-effective means of health care delivery (Whitten, Mair, et al., 2002).

Communication

Communication is at the core of every telemedicine project with many researchers focusing on organizational and interpersonal communication. The provider–patient relationship is the most frequently studied relationship in telemedicine research. Some researchers argue that the technologies depersonalize the provider–patient relationship and limit nonverbal cues because the participants are not in the same location (Miller, 2003). Although this is a common fear in telemedicine projects, data do not always suggest this actually occurs; some patients and providers are satisfied with the services (Whitten & Buis, 2008). Researchers should continue to study how health communication technologies impact interpersonal relationships.

Organizational

Various studies have examined the organizational components that affect telemedicine projects. A project champion, who is a current staff member interested in supporting the project and motivating other staff members to use the equipment, is critical in implementing and sustaining a telemedicine intervention. Because providers are oftentimes cited as the gate-keepers to telemedicine use in organizations (Whitten & Holtz, 2008; Whitten & Mackert, 2005) another member of the organization is necessary to facilitate the project's use. Besides having a project champion, other organizational factors are important for success. For example, one study cited support from upper management and feedback as important factors for telemedicine success (Whitten, Holtz, Young, & Davis, 2009). Perceptions of technology usefulness were also found to be an important characteristic. In general, telemedicine success is strongly dependent on organizational acceptance.

Implementation and Evaluation

Methodological issues abound in telemedicine implementation and evaluation because the field as a whole does not adhere to agreed-upon guidelines (Whitten, Johannessen, Søerensen, Gammon, & Mackert, 2007). Theory-driven interventions are necessary to implement telemedicine initiatives and conduct evaluations. Theories inform projects by highlighting some of the key constructs that are necessary for organizational, provider, and patient acceptance, utilization, and satisfaction (Gammon, Johannessen, Søerensen, Wynn, & Whitten, 2008). Unfortunately, theory is scarce in telemedicine research, with projects being service delivery oriented rather than research oriented. Very few studies make any mention of a paradigmatic or theoretical approach, and many do not test any hypotheses or research questions (Whitten, Johannessen et al., 2007). Therefore, conclusions cannot be drawn about the effectiveness of telemedicine projects.

Other methodological challenges include small sample sizes, difficulty accessing rural populations, and difficulty in having control groups for comparison. Because telemedicine aims to improve access to health care for underserved populations, it is sometimes difficult to recruit these patients for the programs because of low socioeconomic status and limited access to transportation (Nelson & Palsbo, 2006). It is also difficult to include control groups because it requires recruiting even more participants. Thus, sample sizes are usually small, and may not be adequate for generalization from the results. Small sample sizes affect statistical power, making it less likely that the null hypotheses can be rejected because a small sample increases the standard error (Cohen, 1988). Overall, telemedicine research can be strengthened by addressing these methodological issues, which would validate the generalizability of satisfaction, utilization, outcomes, and cost–benefit findings.

Six "Truths" about Telemedicine that Nobody Tells You

The previous sections outlined the traditional issues raised in discussions of the strengths of telemedicine and the challenges that arise. The following list focuses on critical issues, some of which are not typically found in the telemedicine literature.

1. *Physicians are too busy for telemedicine.* Practitioners discuss a wide range of critical issues when describing the challenges of and barriers to the effective use of telemedicine. These discussions are important because they outline impediments that must be addressed to ensure the long-term success of telemedicine. Perhaps the biggest hurdle of all relates to physicians' complicated schedules and overwhelming workloads. Physicians who try telemedicine generally recognize its value and do not typically believe that quality is compromised. One of their biggest challenges is that their clinical or

professional time is monitored more closely than ever before. Squeezing something new into their schedule, such as an ad hoc telemedicine consult, is extremely difficult. While there are exceptions, the majority of physicians struggle with finding time to try something new because they have so little time to meet the demands of their traditional clinic schedule. Unfortunately, this issue is one over which telemedicine practitioners have very little control.

2. *Physicians don't want to see patients with a lower payer mix.* Over the past several decades physicians have faced increasing pressures to generate revenue to support their practices. Every minute of every day is scrutinized. Unfortunately, underserved areas—where telemedicine could be most beneficial—lose out in this situation. Typically, rural and underserved communities have a payer mix well below that of other populations. Therefore, initiating a telemedicine practice becomes less appealing because it does not offer the opportunity to generate greater or even comparable revenue for physicians' practices. Even in academic settings—where telemedicine initiatives tend to prosper—it is difficult to garner support from physicians who are increasingly under tremendous pressure to generate dollars. For this reason, physicians are often persuaded to participate in telemedicine use by other means (such as research interests), rather than from an economic incentive.

3. *Telemedicine use has grown more slowly than practitioners would like you to believe.* Telemedicine has a unique and exciting history within the United States and abroad. For decades, it has steadily grown and become more widespread. Practitioners have preached about its potential to revolutionize health care delivery, and have forced us to rethink the way we conceptualize health care. However, true adoption has been much slower than many suggest. In assessing its future, scholars must recognize that for all its successes, telemedicine still constitutes a mere fraction of care being delivered. This is something to be considered as the next telegeneration is championed by clinicians and practitioners alike.

4. *There is a research and funding conflict of interest inherent in telemedicine.* Conflict of interest is prevalent across the telemedicine discipline and ultimately undermines much of what has been written and researched on the subject. Major federal agencies, academic journals, and conferences have at their core the mission to advance the use of telemedicine. In funding and supporting major initiatives for decades, their success is undeniably linked to the success of the programs they fund or promote. For example, if a grantee is not effective, it reflects poorly on the funder. This dilemma has undermined the rigor required to advance the field, and ultimately has created a proinnovation bias in some cases. Reviews of the literature reflect a broad range of conflicts. Programs must show their success if they are to garner ongoing funding from a variety of sources. In these cases the evaluators are often tied to the programs themselves (Krupinski et al., 2006). For telemedicine to evolve, it must demand a higher academic standard. Evidence of this evolution is becoming realized as more funding is being directed toward telemedicine by the National Institutes of Health (NIH), which grants opportunities for research where proinnovation biases are not as inherently present.

5. *You don't have to see patients in person … ever.* One of the greatest telemedicine myths is that practitioners must see patients in person first, followed by telemedicine consults: examples abound across the globe that prove this is not the case (e.g., Poropatich, DeTreville, Lappan, & Barrigan, 2006). In fact, telemedicine clinics can create efficiencies not realized in a traditional setting when patients are initially seen over a telemedicine

system. There are plenty of clinics where patients are never seen in person at all (e.g., Jameson, Zygmont, Newman, & Weinstock, 2008). Psychiatry clinics are prime examples where physicians may serve telemedicine populations without also seeing them in traditional settings. With the shortage of mental health professionals nationwide, this is one of the strategies that has worked for the discipline and enabled patients in communities or regions where no mental health care alternative exists to get the care they need (Keane, 2007).

6. *Telemedicine is style over substance.* Telemedicine does many amazing things. On the one hand, it truly deserves the attention it receives; however, on the other hand, its value is frequently overstated. There are a variety of reasons that help explain this dilemma. In regions where telemedicine is funded by a state budget, it is politicized by politicians and policy makers as being a savior for rural and underserved regions. It is often oversold, with the best of intentions, because it has such potential to make a profound impact. Rural health care administrators also buy into this rhetoric. Having telemedicine available to link a small community hospital to an urban core is an excellent marketing tool. When margins are thin, and market share is difficult to gain, telemedicine can make a tremendous difference. At the end of the day, telemedicine initiatives are sometimes supported because of their emotional appeal rather than their true clinical advantage.

Opportunities for Communication Scholars

An abundance of opportunities await communication scholars in the field of telemedicine. A starting point is to apply theory or seek new models to implement and evaluate telemedicine programs. Scholars with a variety of communication interests have many opportunities to enhance their area of research through telemedicine studies.

Interpersonal Communication

Telemedicine would benefit from research in interpersonal and computer mediated communication (CMC). Patient–provider communication has been extensively studied in face-to-face contexts (Thompson & Parrott, 2002). With the continued growth of telemedicine, this provides an excellent opportunity to study the effects of health communication technologies on patient–provider and provider–provider communication. The literature is extant on the effects of patient satisfaction as a result of patient–provider communication. One study found that patient consultations with an electronic medical record (EMR) have both positive and negative effects on patient–provider communication (Margalit, Roter, Dunevent, Larson, & Reis, 2006). Patients tend to disclose more medical information while the physician is typing on the keyboard, but physicians tend to contribute fewer statements while gazing at the computer screen (Margalit et al., 2006).

Scholars should also study the differences between face-to-face and mediated interactions, pulling from interpersonal and CMC theories to determine how these different mediums affect communication amongst providers and between patients and providers. Many asynchronous technologies, such as e-mail, deprive interactions of any nonverbal cues that are often important in social situations (Matusitz & Breen, 2007). Breen and Matusitz (2007) suggest examining telemedicine through the lens of three common interpersonal and CMC theories: social penetration (Altman & Taylor, 1973), uncertainty reduction (Berger

& Calabrese, 1975), and social presence (Short, Williams, & Christie, 1976). Exploring these theories would help explain why some telemedicine visits are impersonal, and offer suggestions on how to overcome these barriers.

Numerous theoretical models exist that describe the development, deployment, and adoption of new technologies in organizations. Diffusion of innovations (Rogers, 1995) can be used to demonstrate how innovations spread across social networks, especially in organizations. The technology acceptance model (Davis, 1989) posits that perceived usefulness and perceived ease of use determine how and when new technologies will be used. Finally, the unified theory of acceptance and use of technology (Venkatesh, Morris, Davis, & Davis, 2003) explains how organizational and individual issues impact successful implementation. These models are starting points for communication scholars to study organizational issues involved with telemedicine implementation and sustainability. Telemedicine would greatly benefit from scholars studying the effects of health communication technologies on interpersonal relationships, and, in turn, how these relationships affect health care.

Organizational Communication

Organizations are at the core of every telemedicine program, and projects fail if the organization is not invested in the project. Organizations must support telemedicine programs to ensure their sustainability once the funding ends. Videophones have been underutilized in telehospice programs because management has not mandated or encouraged their use (Whitten, Holtz, Meyer et al., 2009). Provider utilization is one of the major barriers to telemedicine acceptance (Whitten & Holtz, 2008), and scholars should seek to understand how this situation can be changed by better communicating the advantages of the field. One study identified several organizational elements that are important for sustainable telemedicine programs, including support from senior management (Whitten, Holtz, Young, et al., 2009).

Intercultural Communication

Opportunities in the telemedicine field also await intercultural scholars. Researchers should study cocultural factors within their home country. Both patients and providers come from a variety of cultural backgrounds, and these differences could affect the interaction between the health practitioner and the patient. To date, very few programs have examined intercultural projects; instead, either domestic or international projects are investigated, but not their interface. It is imperative to examine how people from various backgrounds conceptualize using communication technologies for health care. In addition, telemedicine programs in developing countries have not been sustainable due to funding issues as well as project rejection (Edirippulige, Marasinghe, Dissanayake, Abeykoon, & Wootton, 2009). Therefore, communication scholars should investigate these projects to determine how to make them more effective. Formative research and recruitment of community-based health care workers (CBHW) are two ways to target these problems (Kar, Alcalay, & Alex, 2001). The inclusion of CBHW helps develop champions for the project—they understand the community's needs and can help with user interface, patient recruitment, and retention (Iluyemi, 2009). Incorporating CBHW into the development and implementation of telemedicine interventions paves the way for sustainable programs in developing countries. Intercultural scholars should seek to determine the key constructs in implementing and sustaining telemedicine interventions across the globe.

Future Trends in Telemedicine

Primary Care

A troubling health care trend nationwide is the growing shortage of primary care physicians to support rural and underserved communities, which are without access to basic medical services. To address this concern, policy makers currently are working diligently on defining the medical home care model to bring primary care physicians more centrally into health care delivery. Practitioners supporting this agenda cite research that shows that medical outcomes are significantly better when physicians are intimately involved with the care of patients and their families (Rosenthal, 2008). This model of care paves the way for health information technology to play a critical role in helping physicians track a wide range of patient data to encourage a higher standard of care while facilitating more preventive health services. Telemedicine will likely have a critical role within this approach, helping to tie patients to critical resources and better link primary care with specialists.

Home Health

Utilizing telemedicine to facilitate home health is far from a new concept. Its roots are decades old with significant practices thriving in pockets all across the United States (Krupinski, 2008). Activity continues to grow as aging populations receive even more care in the home than ever before. In a review of the home health industry, Engle (2009) forecasts that the use of home telehealth will double in the next year, and anticipates that telemedicine will become an integral and inseparable part of the health care industry. Reductions in hospitalizations and the demand to create efficiencies in health care delivery are encouraging the adoption of home-based delivery models. The greatest opportunities are seemingly for populations with chronic conditions. The evolution of technology and the changing role of primary care home health point to a bright future for telemedicine innovation.

Evolving Technology

Since its beginning, telemedicine growth has been tied to evolving technology, often with the promise that greater technical sophistication and reduced costs will equate to its widespread adoption. Although it is important to be cautious of this rhetoric, it is difficult to deny the impact of these trends. The past decade has witnessed tremendous progress in these areas. The development of hand-held devices with greater data capacity than is possible today will likely change the way patients manage their care. The growing ubiquity of wireless networks will transcend geography in completely new ways, and the acceptance of technological advancements by younger generations will further encourage the use of telemedicine.

HIT and HIE

Health Information Technology (HIT) is defined as information systems specific to the health care domain. Systems may include computer equipment, programs, procedures, and other types of data. Health Information Exchange (HIE) is defined as the electronic movement of health-related information among organizations according to nationally recognized standards (State Alliance for E-Health, 2008, p. 8). HIE is at the forefront of health care reform policy discussions at the national level. The U.S. health care system is viewed as being the most advanced in the world, with the best cutting edge technologies and best-trained practitioners. However, we spend more per capita than any other developed country and rank lower on quality outcomes and access to services (Peterson & Burton, 2007). A central failing of the system is the lack of HIT and HIE in addressing issues of efficiency across the system. Remarkably, 31% of total health care spending in the United States is spent on administrative costs, which is almost double Canada's rate (Woolhandler, Campbell, & Himmelstein, 2003). The benefits of HIE speak volumes. It can improve patient care and increase efficiency by reducing duplicative treatments and tests, creating administrative efficiencies, helping with disease management, and providing greater adherence to treatment protocols (State Alliance for E-Health, 2008, p. 6). Undoubtedly, the emergence of HIE/HIT provides a plethora of opportunities for telemedicine researchers and practitioners to better understand how this trend will affect the future of health care delivery.

Conclusion

This chapter reviewed the evolution of various aspects of telemedicine over the past half-century. HIE appears to be the most recent trend to be explored for its potential role in addressing many of the problems facing our health care system today. Decades of telemedicine have provided practitioners with the experience and understanding of how to effectively implement a broad range of services. Although progress has been made, research is still lagging behind. Opportunities exist to address a broad range of questions ranging from patient satisfaction to cost to specific clinical outcomes, providing fertile ground for future inquiry. Communication scholars have an excellent opportunity to provide value in investigating questions across all of these contexts. Those who are able to take the lessons learned from decades of telemedicine research and apply them to burgeoning research questions with an HIE focus will be at the forefront of the health care industry.

References

Al-Kadi, A., Dyer, D., Ball, C. G., McBeth, P. B., Hall, R., Lan, S., ... Kirkpatrick, A. W. (2009). User's perceptions of remote trauma telesonography. *Journal of Telemedicine and Telecare, 15,* 251–254.

Altman, I., & Taylor, D. I. (1973). *Social penetration: The development of interpersonal relationships.* New York: Holt, Reinhart, & Winston.

Alverson, D., Holtz, B., D'Iorio, J., DeVany, M., Simmons, S., & Poropatich, R. (2008). One size doesn't fit all: Bringing telehealth services to special populations. *Telemedicine and e-Health, 14,* 957–963.

American Telemedicine Association. (2009). *Telemedicine defined.* Retrieved from http://www.americantelemed.org/i4a/pages/index.cfm?pageid=3333

Agency for Health care Research and Quality. (n.d.). U.S. Department of Health and Human Services. Retrieved from http://www.ahrq.gov/

Bashshur, R. L. (1997). Telemedicine and the health care system. In R. L. Bashshur, J. H. Sanders, & G. W. Shannon (Eds.), *Telemedicine: Theory and practice* (pp. 5–35). Springfield, IL: Thomas.

Berger, C. R., & Calabrese, R. J. (1975). Some explorations in initial interaction and beyond: Toward a developmental theory of interpersonal communication. *Human Communication Research, 1,* 99–112.

Breen, G., & Matusitz, M. (2007). An interpersonal interaction of telemedicine: Applying relevant communication theories. *eHealth International Journal, 3,* 18–23.

Buck, S. (2009). Nine human factors contributing to the user acceptance of telemedicine applications: A cognitive–emotional approach. *Journal of Telemedicine and Telecare, 15,* 55–58.

Bynum, A. B., Irwin, C. A., Cranford, C. O., & Denny, G. S. (2003). The impact of telemedicine on patients' cost savings: Some preliminary findings. *Telemedicine and e-Health, 9,* 361–367.

Cohen, J. (1988). *Statistical power analysis for the behavioral sciences* (2nd ed.). Hillsdale, NJ: Erlbaum.

Davis, F. C. (1989). Perceived usefulness, perceived ease of use, and user acceptance of information technology. *MIS Quarterly, 13,* 319–340.

DelliFraine, J. L., & Dansky, K. H. (2008). Home-based telehealth: A review and meta-analysis. *Journal of Telemedicine and Telecare, 14,* 62–66.

Edirippulige, S., Marasinghe, R. B., Dissanayake, V. H. W., Abeykoon, P., & Wootton, R. (2009). Strategies to promote e-health and telemedicine activities in developing countries. In R. Wootton, N. G. Patil, R. E. Scott, & K. Ho (Eds.), *Telehealth in the developing world* (pp. 79–87). Ottawa, Ontario: Royal Society of Medicine Press.

Engle, W. (2009). The approaching telehealth revolution in home care. Retrieved from The Telemedicine Information Exchange, http://tie.telemed.org/articles/article.asp?path=articles&article=telehealthRevolution_wengle_tie09.xml

Farmer, A., Gibson, O. J., Tarassenko, L., & Neil, A. (2005). A systematic review of telemedicine interventions to support blood glucose self-monitoring in diabetes. *Diabetic Medicine, 22,* 1372–1378.

Fox, S., & Jones, S. (2009). Pew Internet: The social life of health information. Retrieved from http://www.pewinternet.org/Reports/2009/8-The-Social-Life-of-Health-Information.aspx

Gammon, D., Johannessen, L. K., Søerensen, T., Wynn, R., & Whitten, P. (2008) An overview and analysis of theories employed in telemedicine studies. A field in search of an identity. *Methods of Information in Medicine, 47,* 260–269.

Gray, G. A., Stamm, B. H., Toevs, S., Reischl, U., & Yarrington, D. (2006). Study of participating and nonparticipating states' telemedicine reimbursement status: Its impact on Idaho's policymaking status. *Telemedicine and e-Health, 12,* 681–690.

Hailey, D. (2005). The need for cost-effectiveness studies in telemedicine. *Journal of Telemedicine and Telecare, 11,* 379–383.

Hailey, D., Roine, R., & Ohinmaa, A. (2002). Systematic review of evidence for the benefits of telemedicine. *Journal of Telemedicine and Telecare, 8,* S1–S7.

Heinzelmann, P. J., Williams, C. M., Lugn, N. E., & Kvedar, J. C. (2005). Clinical outcomes associated with telemedicine/telehealth. *Telemedicine and e-Health, 11,* 329–347.

Hong, S., Yang, Y., Kim, S., Shin, S., Lee, I., Jang, Y., … Lee, J. (2009). Performance study of the wearable one-lead wireless electrocardiographic monitoring system. *Telemedicine and e-Health, 15,* 166–175.

Horak, R. (2008). *Telecommunications and data communications handbook.* Hoboken, NJ: Wiley.

Iluyemi, A. (2009). Community-based health workers in developing countries and the role of m-health. In R. Wootton, N. G. Patil, R. E. Scott, & K. Ho (Eds.), *Telehealth in the developing world* (pp. 43–54). Ottawa, Ontario: Royal Society of Medicine Press.

Jackson, K. M., Scott, K. E., Zivin, J. G., Bateman, D. A., Flynn, J. T., Keenan, J. D., & Chiang, M. F. (2008). Cost-utility analysis of telemedicine and ophthalmoscopy for retinopathy of prematurity management. *Archives of Ophthalmology, 126,* 493–499.

Jameson, B. C., Zygmont, S. V., Newman, N., & Weinstock, R. S. (2008). Use of telemedicine to improve glycemic management in correctional institutions. *Journal of Correctional Health Care, 14,* 197–201.

Kar, S. B., Alcalay, R., & Alex, S. (2001). *Health communication: A multicultural perspective.* Thousand Oaks, CA: Sage.

Keane, M. G. (2007). Review of the use of telemedicine in South America. *Journal of Telemedicine and Telecare, 13,* S34–S35.

Krukowski, R. A., Harvey-Berino, J., Ashikaga, T., Thomas, C. S., & Micco, N. (2008). Internet-based weight control: The relationship between web features and weight loss. *Telemedicine and e-Health, 14,* 775–782.

Krupinski, E. A. (2008). Telemedicine for home health and the new patient: When do we really need to go to the hospital? In R. Latifi (Ed.), *Current principles and practices of telemedicine and e-health* (pp. 179–189). Washington, DC: IOS Press.

Krupinski, E. A., Dimmick, S., Grigsby, J., Mogel, G., Puskin, D., Speedie, S., … Yellowlees, P. (2006). Research recommendations for the American Telemedicine Association. *Telemedicine and e-Health, 12,* 579–589.

Kumekawa, J., Puskin, D. S., Morris, T., Brink, L., England, W., Greberman, M., ... Tunanidas, E. (1997, January 31). Telemedicine report to Congress. Retrieved from http://www.ntia.doc.gov/reports/telemed/index.htm

Maheu, M. M., Whitten, P., & Allen, A. (2001). *E-health, telehealth, and telemedicine.* San Francisco, CA: Jossey-Bass.

Marcin, J. P., Nesbitt, T. S., Struve, S., Traugott, C., & Dimand, R. J. (2004). Financial benefits of a pediatric intensive care unit base telemedicine program to a rural adult intensive care unit: Impact of keeping acutely ill and injured children in their local community. *Telemedicine and e-Health, 10* (Supplement 2), 1–5.

Margalit, R. S., Roter, D., Dunevant, M. A., Larson, S., & Reis, S. (2006). Electronic medical record use and physician–patient communication: An observational study of Israeli primary care encounters. *Patient Education and Counseling, 61,* 134–141.

Matusitz, J., & Breen, G. (2007). Telemedicine: Its effects on health communication. *Health Communication, 21,* 73–83.

Miller, E. A. (2003). The technical and interpersonal aspects of telemedicine: Effects on doctor–patient communication. *Journal of Telemedicine and Telecare, 9,* 1–7.

Nelson, E., & Palsbo, S. (2006). Challenges in telemedicine equivalence studies. *Evaluation and Program Planning, 29,* 419–425.

Peterson, C., & Burton, R. (2007). U.S. health care spending: Comparing with other OECD countries. Congressional research service report to Congress. Retrieved from OpenCRS. (Document ID: RL34175).

Poropatich, R. K., DeTreville, R., Lappan, C., & Barrigan, C. R. (2006). The U.S. Army telemedicine program: General overview and current status in Southwest Asia. *Telemedicine and e-Health, 12,* 396–408.

Rendina, M.C., Carrasco, N., Wood, B., Cameron, A., & Bose, C. (2001). A logit model for the effect of telecardiology on acute newborn babies. *International Journal of Technology Assessment in Health Care, 17,* 244–249.

Rogers, E. M. (1995). *Diffusion of innovations* (4th ed.). New York: Free Press.

Rosenthal, T. C. (2008). The medical home: Growing evidence to support a new approach to primary care. *Family Medicine and the Health Care System, 21,* 427–440.

Shaikh, U., Cole, S. L., Marcin, J. P., & Nesbitt, T. S. (2008). Clinical management and patient outcomes among children and adolescents receiving telemedicine consultations for obesity. *Telemedicine and e-Health, 14,* 434–440.

Shapiro, J. S. (2007). Evaluating public health uses of health information exchange. *Journal of Biomedical Informatics, 40,* S46–S49.

Shapiro, J. S., Kannry, J., Kushniruk, A. W., & Kuperman, G. (2007). Emergency physicians' perceptions of health information exchange. *Journal of the Medical Informatics Association, 14,* 700–705.

Shore, J., Brooks, E., Savin, D., Manson, S., & Libby, A. (2007). An economic evaluation of telehealth data collection with rural populations. *Psychiatric Services, 58,* 830–835.

Short, J. A., Williams, E., & Christie, B. (1976). *The social psychology of telecommunication.* New York: Wiley.

Stanberry, B. (2006). Legal and ethical aspects of telemedicine. *Journal of Telemedicine and Telecare, 12,* 166–175.

State Alliance for E-Health. (2008). Accelerating progress: Using health information technology and electronic health information exchange to improve care:First annual report and recommendations from the state alliance for e-health. Retrieved from http://www.nga.org/portal/site/nga/menuitem.9123e83a1f6786440ddcbeeb501010a0/?vgnextoid=403666a956b8c110VgnVCM1000001a01010aRCRD

Thompson, T. L., & Parrot, R. (2002). Interpersonal communication and health care. In M. L. Knapp & J. A. Daly (Eds.), *Handbook of interpersonal communication* (pp. 680–725). Thousand Oaks, CA: Sage.

Venkatash, V., Morris, M. G., Davis, F. D., & Davis, G. B. (2003). User acceptance of information technology: Toward a unified view. *MIS Quarterly, 27,* 425–478.

Whitten, P. Bergman, A., Meese, M. A., Bridwell, K., & Jule, K. (2009). St. Vincent's home telehealth for congestive heart failure patients. *Telemedicine and e-Health, 15,* 158–153.

Whitten, P., & Buis, L. (2007). Private payer reimbursement for telemedicine services in the United States. *Telemedicine and e-Health, 13,* 15–23.

Whitten, P., & Buis, L. (2008). Use of telemedicine for haemodialysis: Perceptions of patients and health-care providers, and clinical effects. *Journal of Telemedicine and Telecare, 14,* 75–78.

Whitten, P., & Cook, D. (1999). School-based telemedicine: Using technology to bring health-care to inner city children. *Journal of Telemedicine and Telecare, 5*(Suppplement 1), 23–25.

Whitten, P., & Holtz, B. (2008). Provider utilization of telemedicine: The elephant in the room. *Telemedicine and e-Health, 14,* 995–997.

Whitten, P., Holtz, B., Meyer, E., & Nazione, S. (2009). Telehospice: Reasons for slow adoption in home hospice care. *Journal of Telemedicine and Telecare, 15,* 187–190.

Whitten, P., Holtz, B., Young, R., & Davis, S. (2009, April). *The organizational structure and architecture of telemedicine: Keys to success.* Paper presented at the American Telemedicine Association Conference in Las Vegas, Nevada.

Whitten, P., Johannessen, L. K., Søerensen, T., Gammon, D., & Mackert, M. (2007). A systematic review of research methodology in telemedicine studies. *Journal of Telemedicine and Telecare, 13,* 230–235.

Whitten, P., & Love, B. (2005). Patient and provider satisfaction with the use of telemedicine: Overview and rationale for cautious enthusiasm. *Journal of Postgraduate Medicine, 51,* 294-300.

Whitten, P., & Mackert, M. (2005). Addressing telehealth's foremost barrier: Providers as initial gatekeepers. *Journal of Telemedicine and Telecare, 21,* 517–521.

Whitten, P., Mair, F., Haycox, A., May, C. R., Williams, T. L., & Hellmich, S. (2002). Systematic review of cost effectiveness studies of telemedicine interventions. *British Medical Journal, 324,* 316–319.

Whitten, P., & Mickus, M. (2007). Home telecare for COPD/CHF patients: Outcomes and perceptions. *Journal of Telemedicine and Telecare, 13,* 69–73.

Whitten, P., & Sypher, B. (2006). Evolution of telemedicine from an applied communication perspective in the United States. *Telemedicine and e-Health, 12,* 590–600.

Williams, T. L., May, C. R., & Esmail, A. (2001). Limitations of patient satisfaction studies in tele-healthcare: A systematic review of the literature. *Telemedicine and e-Health, 7,* 293–316.

Woolhandler, S., Campbell, T., & Himmelstein, D. U. (2003). Costs of health care administration in the United States and Canada. *New England Journal of Medicine, 349,* 768–775.

7

HEALTH CARE TEAMS

Communication and Effectiveness

Kevin Real and Marshall Scott Poole

A growing body of empirical research suggests that the success of health care teams can be improved when health care professionals communicate effectively as they work together (Grumbach & Bodenheimer, 2004; Haynes et al., 2009; Lemieux-Charles & McGuire, 2006; Lingard, Regehr, et al., 2008; Williams et al., 2007). National studies of medical safety have found that health care teams have communication problems linked to patient safety, medical errors, and other adverse events (Baker, Gustafson, Beaubien, Salas, & Barach, 2005; Institute of Medicine, Kohn, Corrigan, & Donaldson, 1999). Communication is particularly important in health care teams given the complex nature of medical care (Nussbaum & Fisher, 2009). Much research in this area recognizes that communication in health care teams depends on situated language practices (Lingard, Reznick, DeVito, & Espin, 2002) and discursive constructions that guide and constrain the increasingly complex and evolving roles important to the enactment of teamwork (Apker, Propp, & Ford, 2005; Eisenberg et al., 2005; Ellingson, 2003). Other research examines crucial information exchange in health care teams and how communication is essential to effective patient care (Haynes et al., 2009; Lingard, Regehr, et al., 2008).

As observed in Parrott and Kreuter's chapter (this volume), health communication is primarily interdisciplinary and much scholarship draws from a broad array of scholarly disciplines and intellectual traditions. This is also the case with group research, which has a long tradition of interdisciplinary scholarship (Poole & Hollingshead, 2005). In this chapter, we review recent research on communication in health care teams from many scholarly disciplines in order to both understand how communication is conceptualized and how it relates to team effectiveness. We then highlight an input-process-output framework for communication and effectiveness in health care teams derived from classic research in group dynamics (McGrath, 1984), small-group communication (Hirokawa & Poole, 1996), and recent health care team research (Fernandez, Kozlowski, Shapiro, & Salas, 2008; Reader, Flin, Mearns, & Cuthbertson, 2009). Before delving into these two areas, it is first important to understand the nature of health care teams.

The Nature of Health Care Teams

There are many ways in which health care teams are characterized in the literature. In our chapter in the previous edition of this handbook (Poole & Real, 2003), we explicitly delineated teams from groups, suggesting that teams were those groups that were high on interaction, interdependence, boundedness, commonality, and motivation. Increasingly, *health care team* has become the normative construct referring to group modes of work in the literature, describing research and practice across a wide variety of health care contexts and organizations. However, it is important to understand that *team* is also a rhetorical construct (Lingard, Espin, Evans, & Hawryluck, 2004; Simpson, 2007) that connotes a level of collaboration and cooperation that may be an aspiration that is not actually achieved in particular health care groups. Nevertheless, because much research in health care uses *team* as the primary construct, we employ the aspirational term, keeping in mind that not all health care "teams" have achieved a high level of teamwork. In this chapter, we build on our prior definition of health care teams by suggesting that a health care team can be defined as *an intact group of health care providers motivated to communicate with each other regarding the care of specific patients* (Grumbach & Bodenheimer, 2004; Poole & Real, 2003; Starfield, 1992; Wagner, 2000). This definition underscores the importance of communication in health care teams.

Poole and Real (2003) focused their review on how different types of health care teams are structured and how communication typically occurs in such groups. From this perspective, teams can be considered on a continuum based on such factors as boundedness, interdependence, and collaboration. Teams at the simpler end of this continuum include *ad hoc, nominal care,* and *unidisciplinary* teams, where communication may vary but typically involves information sharing. More complex groups include *multidisciplinary, interdisciplinary,* and *transdisciplinary teams,* which describe greater degrees of collaboration, boundedness, and interdependence. Communication in these groups varies but often goes beyond information sharing to include informal, backstage, and interaction influential to the construction of meaning. Readers interested in understanding the nature of health care teams (HCTs) from a group perspective would be well-served by reviewing Poole and Real (2003). Beyond this brief summary, we refer you to that earlier chapter and will focus here on new findings and trends since it was published.

Communication Research in Health Care Teams

A number of empirical studies of communication in health care teams have been published since the first chapter was completed. This section is devoted to empirical research that explicitly examined communication in health care teams between 2001 and 2009. This is not an exhaustive review of all studies that examined communication in health care teams in some form or another. Rather, described here and presented in Table 7.1 are good examples of different ways in which communication has been studied in health care teams.

Moreover, given the interdisciplinary nature of health care team research as well as broad concerns for patient safety that have arisen over the past decade (Baker et al., 2005; Institute of Medicine et al., 1999; Lemieux-Charles & McGuire, 2006), many of the studies presented here are from outside the communication discipline. However, the communication discipline is well represented and many studies have been published that demonstrate the robust nature of communication research in health care teams. Research in communication has examined nurse team communication in various ways (Apker, Propp, & Ford, 2005, 2009; Apker, Propp, Ford, & Hofmeister, 2006): backstage communication in an oncology team (Ellingson, 2003); the use of narrative in children's mental health care teams (Davis, 2008); forms of communicative rationality in emergency medicine teams (Eisenberg et al., 2005); occupational biases (Grice, Gallois, Jones, Paulsen, & Callan, 2006); intergroup

Table 7.1 Exemplary Studies of Communication in Health Care Teams (2001–2009)

First Author and Year	Medical Focus	Sample	Method	Findings
Anderson, 2001	Patients' View of HCTs	87 student-patients in Study 1 (U.S); 62 student-patients in Study 2 (Hong Kong)	Survey (open and closed-ended items)	Content analysis of patient stories revealed that different HCT roles engaged in distinct communication foci and culture mattered. For example, U.S. and H.K. MDs both engaged in technical competence, information giving, and information seeking, but U.S. MDs also focused on socio-emotional communication
Apker, Propp, & Ford, 2005	Nurse Roles in HCTs	50 healthcare workers (primarily RNs)	Interviews (individual and focus group) and Observations	RNs face a number of communicative challenges in HCTs, including role dialectics related to hierarchy, status, and professional identity. RNs need to develop a repertoire of communication strategies to manage role-based contradictions and tensions
Apker, Propp, Ford, & Hofmeister, 2006	Nurse Comm Skills	50 healthcare workers (primarily RNs)	Interviews (individual and focus group) and Observations	Four communication skill sets exemplify nurse professionalism to members of HCTs: collaboration, credibility, compassion, and coordination. Authors argue that these need to be part of nurse education and training
Apker, Propp, & Ford, 2009	Nurse Retention	201 hospital nurses	Survey	Analysis revealed three nurse–team communication processes: promoting team synergy, ensuring quality decisions, and individualizing communication. Team synergy was related to intent to leave, but was mediated by team/organizational identification
Awad et al., 2005	Surgical Teams	Nurses, surgeons, and anesthesiologists (sample size not indicated)	Pre-Post Interventions at 4 points in time (baseline plus 3)	Briefings developed through interactive training increased communication scores of surgeons, anesthesiologists but not nurses; implementation of specific patient safety procedures also increased as a result of preoperative team briefings
Bleakley, 2006	Patient Safety	400 hospital safety reports	Rhetorical	Providers maintain professional boundaries related to identity by stereotyping the "other" professions on the team. Suggests that reports based on "fearless speech" can lead to increased safety and newer forms of identity construction

First Author and Year	Medical Focus	Sample	Method	Findings
Coopman, 2001	Hospice Care	52 members of 7 hospice teams from 3 hospice organizations	Survey	Perceptions of democracy are important to team outcomes; team involvement in decisions associated with cohesion, productiveness, satisfaction with team, team communication, and desire to stay with team
Davis, 2008	Children's Mental Health	118 child and family team meetings	Ethnography	Leaders and members used narratives and counternarratives in the meetings to advocate for either system of care or medical model principles and values
Donnison et al., 2009	Mental Health	7 clinician members of two teams	Qualitative: Interviews / Thematic analysis	Communication in community mental health teams is challenging and "compounded by increased focus on managing complex needs and risk management" (p. 314)
Ellingson, 2003	Geriatric Oncology	Long-term field study (>2 years) of oncology team: 2 MDs, 1 NP, 2 RNs, 1 PharmD, and 1 LCSW	Ethnography: Observations Interviews and Analysis of Audio Recordings of Initial Patient Visits	Reveals the importance of backstage communication to HC teamwork. Seven types of communication occur: informal impression and information sharing; checking clinic progress; relationship building; space management; training students; handling interruptions; and formal reporting. These embedded team practices are crucial to HCTs
Eisenberg et al., 2005	Emer-gency Medicine and Patient Safety	Year-long field study of HCTs in two Emergency Departments (ED)	Qualitative: Primarily Structured Observations	Analysis revealed four communication processes:triage, testing/evaluating; handoffs, admitting. Narrative rationality (the patient's story) was consistently subjugated to technical rationality (actionable lists). These have implications for patient safety and need attention by ED HCTs
Frankel, 2007	Health care teams in general	In development using simulations	Behavioral Observations	Pilot program assessing communication and teamwork behaviors for feedback to clinicians
Gardezi et al., 2009	Surgery	>700 procedures from 3 hospitals of teams of surgeons, OR nurses, anesthesiologists, and trainees	Critical Ethnography: Observation	Identified three forms of recurring "silences": absence of communication; not responding to queries or requests; and speaking quietly. These silences may be defensive or strategic, and they may be influenced by larger institutional and structural power dynamics as well as by the immediate situational context

(continued)

Table 7.1 Continued

First Author and Year	Medical Focus	Sample	Method	Findings
Grice et al., 2006	Health care teams and work teams in general	142 HCT members (MDs, RNs, LCSWs etc)	Survey	Occupational/ingroup biases shape perceptions of team communication patterns and ratings of communication effectiveness. Members of the same occupation are perceived to interact better than others on team
Haynes et al., 2009	Surgical Teams	3,733 patients pre-intervention 3,955 pts post-intervention	Pre-Post Intervention	Patients' postsurgical rate of complications decreased after introduction of 19-item communication checklist in surgical teams
Hewett et al., 2009	Gastro-enterology	227 medical records	Qualitative: Thematic Induction	MDs used medical records to express specialty identity and negotiate intergroup conflict. Interspecialty conflict represented a threat to the quality of patient care
Lingard, Reznick, Regehr, et al., 2002	General Surgery, Urology, Otolar-yngology, Cardiac Surgery	35 procedures, 15 surgeons, 28 RNs, 10 anesthetists, 30+ novices (3rd-yr students to sr. residents)	Ethnographic Observation and Interviews	Communication in the OR followed recurrent patterns. Each procedure had one to four "higher-tension" events, which often had a ripple effect, spreading tension to other participants and contexts. Surgical trainees responded to tension by withdrawing from the communication or mimicking the senior staff surgeon. Both responses had negative implications for their own team relations
Lingard, Reznick, DeVito, et al. 2002	Surgery	14 Focus Groups: 13 surgeons, 19 RNs, 9 anesthetists, 11 trainees	Qualitative: Focus Groups	Interpretations of communication scenarios differed by profession. Constructions of other professions' roles, values, and motivations differed from self-constructions. Trainees tend to simplify/distort others' roles and motivations which has implications for identity formation
Lingard, Espin, Whyte, et al., 2004	Surgery: General and Vascular	48 procedures, 35 surgeons, 31 RNs, 25 anesthetists, 3 clerks	Ethnographic Observation	129 of 421 communication events were coded as failures, which were categorized as "occasion" (poor timing), "content" (missing or inaccurate information), "purpose" (issues not resolved) and "audience" (key individuals excluded). 36% of these failures resulted in effects which jeopardized patient safety

First Author and Year	Medical Focus	Sample	Method	Findings
Lingard, Reznick, et al., 2004	Intensive Care Unit	7 focus groups from 2 hospitals, 27 RNs, 6 Residents, 4 MDs	Qualitative: Focus Groups	Two mechanisms by which team collaboration was achieved or undermined in a complex and high-pressure context were described: the perception of "ownership" (of specialized knowledge, technical skills, equipment, clinical territory and even the patient) and the process of "trade" (of equipment/resources, respect, goodwill and knowledge)
Lingard, Espin, Rubin, et al., 2005	Vascular Surgery	18 cases; 33 OR team members (MDs, RNs)	Ethnographic Observation, Interviews	Development and pilot of a preoperative checklist facilitated a preoperative discussion that included provision of detailed case-related information, confirmation of details, articulation of concerns, and team building
Lingard, Whyte, et al., 2006	Surgery	302 preoperative checklist briefings, 11 surgeons, 24 surgical trainees, 41 RNs, 28 anesthesiologists, 24 anesthesia trainees	Ethnographic Observation, Phased Implement of Preoperative Team Briefing	Two-part model of communicative "utility" was developed. "Informational utility" involved new information, explicit confirmation, reminders, or education. "Functional utility" represented direct communication–work connections, such as identifying problems, prompting decision making, and following-up of actions
Lingard, Regehr, et al., 2008	Surgery	172 OR procedures (86 preinter-vention, 86 postintervention)	Intervention, Observation, Exit Survey	Average number of communication failures per procedure declined from 3.95 before the intervention to 1.31 after the intervention ($p<.001$)
Martin et al., 2008	Geriatric and Adult Medicine	5 MDs and 8 NPs	Qualitative: Semi-Structured Interviews	Contradictions and dialectical oppositions revealed through communication bet MDs-NPs. NPs want autonomy but believe that MDs limit their potential; MDs want NPs to be proactive yet limit their decision-making leading to frustration in the relationship
Mills et al., 2008	Surgery	384 surgical staff members in 6 facilities	Survey	Discrepancies among physicians and nurses: Surgeons perceived stronger organizational culture, better communication, and better teamwork than either nurses or anesthesiologists

continued

Table 7.1 Continued

First Author and Year	Medical Focus	Sample	Method	Findings
O'Connor et al., 2009	Intensive Care Unit	106 ICU staff: 66 RNs, 18 RTs, 9 clerks, 4 MDs, 4 leaders, 2 PharmD, 1 LCSW, 2 NR	Post-Intervention Survey	After implementation of a wireless e-mail system, ICU HCT members were assessed for their perceptions of its impact on communication. ICU staff perceived wireless e-mail to improve communication, team relationships, staff satisfaction, and patient care
Paulsel et al., 2006	Patient Satis-faction and Perception	358 patients of a large medical clinic	Survey	Patients' perceptions of medical team competence and caring were positively correlated with patients' satisfaction with care and MD
Reader et al., 2007	Intensive Care	48 MDs and 136 RNs	Survey	Differing perceptions of HCT communication existed between RNs, MDs; RNs perceived lower levels of communication openness, which was found to be important to patient care goals
Reddy & Jansen, 2008	Surgery and Emer-gency Medicine	2 health care teams (MD, RN, PharmD)	Ethnography: Interviews, Observations	Information seeking in HCTs is a collaborative, not individual, enterprise that shapes how individuals interact with each other, the complexity of the information need, and the role of information technology
Reddy & Spence 2008	Emer-gency Medicine	1 ED HCT (MD, RN, Paramedics, Technicians, Clerical)	Ethnography: Interviews, Observations	Information seeking in ED HCTs is collaborative and triggered by (1) lack of expertise, (2) lack of immediately accessible information, and (3) complex information needs. Colocation of ED members leads to increased face-to-face interaction and also the potential for an "interruptive" workplace
Reeves et al., 2009	General and Internal Medicine	47 interviews: MDs, RNs, Administrators, Allied Health Professionals	Ethnography: Interviews, Observations	MD communication with other professionals was terse and directive whereas RN and other professionals' communication were richer, lengthier, and consisted of negotiations related to both clinical and social content
Shaw et al., 2005	Primary Care	48 interviews: 19 GPs, 2 NPs, 10 PNs, 17 PMs, from 21 practices	Qualitative: Semi-structured interviews	Some participants felt teams helped provide improved patient care while others suggested teamwork was limited by issues related to goals, recruitment, inadequate communication, and hierarchical structures

First Author and Year	Medical Focus	Sample	Method	Findings
Sinclair et al., 2009	Physical Medicine and Rehab-ilitation	14 meetings, 40–45 staff: RNs plus physio-therapists, occupational therapist, social workers and more	Ethnographic Observations and Interviews	Descriptive approach found two major themes. Team Culture (leadership, care philosophy, relationships, and the context of practice) and Communication Structures (both formal and informal). This site's culture encouraged open communication in the HCT
Sutcliffe et al., 2004	Medical Error/ Mishaps	26 randomly selected residents stratified by specialty, year of residency, and gender in a teaching hospital	Qualitative: Semi-structured interviews	Medical mishaps linked to faulty communication; not simply poor transmission or exchange of information. "Communication failures are far more complex and relate to hierarchical differences, concerns with upward influence, conflicting roles and role ambiguity, and interpersonal power and conflict" (p. 186)
Tschan et al., 2009	Medical Decision Making	20 groups of physicians	Behavioral Observations	In simulations involving communication and decision making in ambiguous diagnostic situations, physicians often failed to report pivotal information after reading in the patient chart. MD teams that discussed reasons for taking a specific course of action had better patient outcomes but this was influenced by confirmation biases of physicians
Weingart et al., 2009	Patient-Oriented Approach to HCT	203 patients at baseline, 118 at 2-month and 83 at 3-month follow-up	Survey	Multifaceted campaign aimed at encouraging patients to (1) check for hazards in the environment, (2) ask questions of clinicians, and (3) notify staff of safety concerns found no changes in patients' behavior but some changes reported by those exposed to campaign
Williams et al., 2007	Surgery	15 focus groups at 5 medical centers of 59 surgical residents, 36 attending MDs; and 42 surgical RNs	Qualitative: Focus Groups	Communication errors that lead to adverse events include blurred boundaries of responsibility, decreased surgeon familiarity with patients, diversion of surgeon attention and distorted or inhibited communication. These errors led to delays in patient care, wasted time, and serious adverse patient consequences

HCT=Health Care Team; MD=Medical Doctor; RN=Registered Nurse; NP=Nurse Practitioner; PharmD=Clinical Pharmacist; LCSW=Licensed Clinical Social Worker; ED=Emergency Department; GP=General Practitioner; PM=Practice Manager; PN=Practice Nurse; RT=Respiratory Therapist; NR=No Report (of Occupation); OR=Operating Room conflict (Hewett, Watson, Gallois, Ward, & Leggett, 2009); dialectical tensions (Martin, O'Brien, Heyworth & Meyer, 2008); democracy (Coopman, 2001); patients' perceptions of health care team interactions (Anderson, 2001); and patients' satisfaction with and perceptions of medical team competence and caring (Paulsel, McCroskey, & Richmond, 2006). Additionally, a whole series of studies by Lingard and her colleagues, detailed below, have been conducted that examine communication in health care teams from a variety of communication perspectives.

While there are many ways to examine communication in health care teams, such as focusing on the medical context or research methodology, our aim here is to describe empirical studies in terms of how communication was conceptualized in empirical research. Based on the studies examined for this chapter, we found two primary ways in which to consider communication: as information exchange and as the construction of meaning. Certainly there are other ways to conceptualize communication, but we make this distinction based on the empirical research described in Table 7.1. Moreover, this is not to imply a strict dichotomy, but rather a continuum in which to think about communication in health care teams. Before describing these approaches to how communication is conceptualized in health care teams research, a brief note on methodology is appropriate.

Methodological Approaches

As seen in Table 7.1, a variety of methodological approaches were used to examine communication in health care teams in the studies examined for this chapter. Most of these, by far, were qualitative studies (22) and the particular approaches included ethnography (observation, shadowing, interviews, over-time designs), interviews (individual and focus group), interviews and observations, and one thematic analysis of medical records. The second most common approach described here includes quantitative approaches (14) such as surveys, interventions based on experimental design approaches, and behavioral observations. In addition, one study used a rhetorical analysis and there were also elements of rhetorical analysis in some of the qualitative studies, particularly those conducted by Lingard and colleagues. While these methodological approaches were similar to those discussed in Poole and Real (2003), there appear to be an increasing number of interpretive approaches aimed at understanding how communication operates in health care teams. In the following sections, we examine how communication is conceptualized in these studies and how communication relates to effectiveness.

Communication as Information Exchange

An information exchange perspective suggests that communication can be employed to address practical problems facing health care teams. In this view, communication is a phenomenon by which information is exchanged between members of a team so that all members are clear as to their role, the patient's diagnosis, the care that will be delivered, and more. This research typically examines the role of briefings, checklists, communication errors, or information sharing in reducing adverse events, delays in patient care, and communication failures (Lingard, Regehr, et al., 2008; Williams et al., 2007). Examples of these studies are provided below.

An international study of information exchange in surgical teams (Haynes et al., 2009) examined the impact of a 19-item communication checklist intervention in eight global hospitals. The checklist required teams to perform a number of communication activities prior to and during operations such as orally confirming the patient's identity, verbally noting that the surgical site was marked (if applicable), and orally confirming that members of the team were aware of the patient's allergies. The checklist also required, before incision, that all members of the team orally review any concerns they had related to the procedure. Researchers found that use of the communication checklist significantly decreased negative outcomes for patients (more specific details of this study are discussed in the section below on effectiveness). This study provided evidence that a formal structure for information exchange was important to clinical effectiveness.

Lingard and colleagues conducted a series of studies examining the implementation and assessment of a preoperative checklist designed to support team briefings in the operating room (Lingard, Espin, Rubin, et al., 2005; Lingard, Regehr, et al., 2008; Lingard, Whyte, et al., 2006). Lingard, Espin, Rubin, et al. (2005) found that the development and piloting of a preoperative checklist facilitated a preoperative discussion that included provision of detailed case-related information, articulation of concerns, and team building interaction. Lingard, Whyte, et al. (2006) observed the implementation of a formal preoperative team briefing and found that communication in team briefings could be considered as two forms of "utility": "informational" (new information, confirmations) and "functional" (identifying problems, decision making), each of which had implications for patient care. In a later study, Lingard, Regehr, et al. (2008) assessed whether the briefings, structured by a checklist, improved surgical team communication and found that communication failures declined significantly after the checklist/briefing intervention. This series of studies provides a body of evidence suggesting that the formal communication structures (e.g., briefings, checklists) act to improve the exchange of clinical information and increase clinical team effectiveness.

Mills, Neily, and Dunn (2008) used surveys to gauge perceptions of communication, teamwork, and organizational culture among members of surgical teams. The conceptualization of communication in this study involved information-related items such as "Our team routinely briefs procedures before starting them." The study found that surgeons had more positive perceptions of communication, culture, and teamwork than did nurses or anesthesiologists. Mills et al. suggest that understanding these discrepancies can identify hidden communication problems in surgical teams that can be addressed in formal team training.

Taking a different approach, one that involved patients, Weingart et al. (2009) used a multifaceted campaign aimed at encouraging patients to (1) check for hazards in the environment, (2) ask questions of clinicians, and (3) notify staff of safety concerns. Using teamwork and communication principles developed from prior research, these researchers worked with patients on situational awareness and assertiveness. For example, they asked patients whether they would feel comfortable asking clinicians if they had washed their hands. They also asked patients how often they clarified unclear instructions or explanations from providers. Including patients (and their advocates) on health care teams is an innovative approach aimed at increasing the flow of information in patient care teams. Although the study found no changes in overall behavior, a substantial group of patients who reported campaign awareness also reported behavior/communication changes (e.g., more assertive in their communication with providers).

Communication as Meaning Construction

Another perspective on communication in HCTs is one that examines the socially constructed nature of interaction in health care teams. In this view, much of what occurs in the work of teams is constituted through communication practices. Identity, tensions, work processes, status, and patient safety are discursively constructed in ways that generate particular meaning to members of health care teams. This constitutive perspective views communication as the product of human relations and discursive practices that are already in place in teams. For example, in a year-long study of teams in emergency departments in two hospitals, Eisenberg et al. (2005) discovered that meaning was constructed through communication in two distinct ways. Patients would often describe their situations in story form (narrative rationality), but these stories were then translated and subjugated to meaning constructions that worked best for emergency teams, such as lists (technical rationality). As patients were processed, miscommunication occurred in team processes such as triage, evaluations, handoffs, and admissions, where the construction/translation of patient stories into technical lists failed to capture the whole meaning of patients' descriptions. This phenomenon has implications for patient care and safety.

Ellingson (2003), in a long-term field study of communication and teamwork in an oncology team, illustrated in important ways how backstage communication (outside of team meetings) was critical to health care teamwork. Ellingson demonstrated a number of embedded team practices (e.g., relationship building, informal information sharing, handling interruptions, formal reporting) that operated in dyads and triads of team members in the normal process of a working day rather than in formal meetings. These discursive practices provided flexibility for team members to enact clinical work within a medical system steeped in hierarchy. In this sense, the social construction of teamwork is dependent on the beliefs and attitudes of team members, the context where the team works, and the extent to which discipline-specific knowledge claims can be reinforced, negotiated, or resisted through communication.

Lingard, Reznick, DeVito, et al. (2002) examined the situated language practices of health care team members (surgeons, nurses, anesthesiologists, and residents) through interpretations of field-based communication scenarios developed from observations of team interaction. The researchers found that team members' constructions of other professions' roles, discourse, values, and motivations often differed from their self-constructions. Team members constructed an identity of the "other" in the operating room using harsh language ("shift worker") while ascribing favorable motives to their own group ("patient advocate"). The researchers suggested that professional identity construction is often the result of years of discipline-specific training that can be contradictory to working in health care teams.

Apker, Propp, and Ford (2005) examined the meaning of role contradictions that emerged in health care team communication and the discursive processes by which nurses manage role tensions. The researchers revealed three nurse role dialectics related to medical hierarchy, status, and professional identity. Nurses' communication in health care teams reflects the increasingly complex and evolving roles they are asked to fill that involve patients, physicians, and other health care providers. In this sense, communication acts to both attenuate and amplify contradictions that nurses face in health care teams.

Communication and Effectiveness in HCTs

A number of factors and processes influence team effectiveness and communication figures prominently among them. Before examining how communication operates in effective health care teams, it may be useful to examine *ineffective* communication among health care providers, which has been cited as a contributing factor to medical errors (Baker et al., 2005; Institute of Medicine et al., 1999). For example, communication failure has been identified as a leading factor for medical error in surgical teams (Gawande, Zinner, Studdert, & Brennann, 2003; Lingard, Espin, Whyte, et al., 2004) and medical mishaps in hospitals (Sutcliffe, Lewton, & Rosenthal, 2004). Outcomes of these errors and mishaps range from no consequences to team tension to permanent disability to patient death. On the other hand, successful teamwork and effective communication have been found to be critical to quality performance and effective outcomes in health care teams (Awad et al., 2005; Haynes et al., 2009; Lingard, Regehr, et al., 2008; Williams et al., 2007). Findings from these studies highlight the importance of communication to health care team effectiveness.

A particularly good example of the importance of communication in health care team success is the Haynes et al. (2009) study, where patients' negative outcomes (postsurgical rate of complications, in-hospital death rate, rates of surgical-site infection, and unplanned reoperation) declined significantly after the introduction of a communication checklist. In this study, conducted in hospitals across the globe from different socioeconomic environments, specific and structured communication was effective in reducing patient morbidity and mortality. In another study, Lingard, Regehr, et al. (2008) examined how the implementation of a briefing structured by a checklist reduced failures in communication in surgery. They found that the average number of communication failures per procedure declined from 3.95 before the intervention to 1.31 after the intervention ($p < .001$). These failures had observable consequences, including inefficiency, team tension, resource waste, delays, and procedural errors, all of which had implications for patient safety.

Sutcliffe et al. (2004) examined how communication failures contributed to medical mishaps in a teaching hospital. Medical mishaps were characterized by a variety of incidents, from close calls (switching of patients orders that were subsequently corrected) to major incidents (inserting a chest tube in the wrong side). Sutcliffe et al. found faulty communication to be an "insidious" contributor to medical mishaps. Communication problems resulted not only from faulty information exchanges (inadequate information sharing, poor timing, or incorrect medium) but also from hierarchical differences, concerns with upward influence, role conflict, role ambiguity, and interpersonal conflict.

The empirical studies described here and presented in Table 7.1 demonstrate specific ways in which communication is conceptualized and important to teams in health care. The final section of the chapter illustrates a framework in which researchers and practitioners can consider communication in health care teams.

A Framework for Communication and Effectiveness

There are a number of ways in which to envision how communication operates in health care teams. One framework that illustrates the systemic properties of health care teams is the classic input-process-output model (McGrath, 1984). A manifestation of this framework, derived primarily from the studies reviewed in this chapter, is provided in Figure 7.1. The focus of this input-process-output (IPO) framework is to illustrate the communication structures that shape communication processes and how these processes can influence health care team outcomes.

This IPO framework is situated within clinical (e.g., surgical, geriatric, primary care), team (e.g., multidisciplinary, interdisciplinary), and organizational (e.g., hospital, nursing homes) contexts (Ramanujam & Rousseau, 2006). Certainly a primary care team differs from a surgical team and communication in a transdisciplinary team is likely distinct from that in unidisciplinary teams. Moreover, teams that work in hospitals differ from geriatric care teams in nursing homes and the characteristics of inputs, processes, and

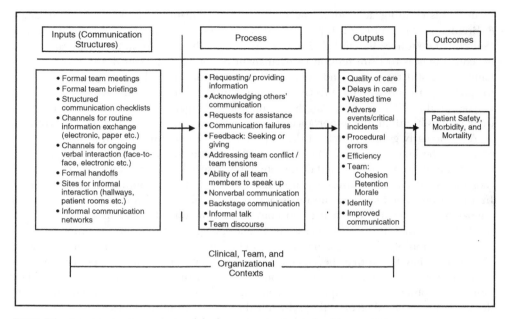

Figure 7.1   Input–output–process model of communication in health care teams.

outputs will be affected by these contexts. The presentation of this framework is designed to generate thinking about communication and effectiveness in health care teams and is not a comprehensive review of prior research on each facet of the framework. Our goal is to provide practical insight into how communication structures and processes operate in health care teams in order to provide an accessible approach to understanding communication and effectiveness in health care teams.

Inputs (Communication Structures)

Clinical teams are comprised of many different "inputs" that are not communicative, such as professions, roles, hierarchies, experience, attitudes, motivation, training, task structures, task complexity, time pressures, and more (Reader et al., 2009). Yet often overlooked are the communication structures that act as inputs to team communication processes. As seen in Figure 7.1, there are a number of communication structures, including formal briefings (Awad et al., 2005; Lingard, Whyte, et al., 2006) and structured checklists (Haynes et al., 2009; Lingard, Regehr, et al., 2008), that shape communication and team effectiveness.

Communication structures provide for the seemingly mundane but critical flow of information and construction of meaning in health care teams. Routine information exchange (patient data, medical records) can occur through a number of communication channels, including paper charts or newer forms of electronic medical records or clinical management information technologies. Face-to-face communication can be both formal and informal and the sites where they occur include formal team meetings, handoffs, patient rooms, hallways, and the like. Communication network structures, such as strength of ties, cohesion, density, and multiplexity, can also shape team communication. Each of these inputs/communication structures act to influence communication processes in teams.

Process

There are a number of distinct health care team processes (patient care, distribution of work), and many relate to communication. A number of processes involve information exchange, such as information sharing, requests for assistance, and acknowledging of others' communication (Reddy & Jansen, 2008; Reddy & Spence, 2008). Failure to share information can cause groups to be ineffective and lead to poorer outcomes (Gawande et al., 2003; Tschan et al., 2009). Information and feedback that address team conflict, team tensions, and critical patient care are important processes in teams (Apker, Propp, & Ford, 2005; Grumbach & Bodenheimer, 2004; Lingard, Reznick, Regehr, et al., 2002).

Ellingson's (2003) research has illustrated an important process vital to teamwork by examining the informal talk and discursive practices that occur outside the formal meetings that are traditionally believed to be the center of team communication. Other researchers have noted this phenomenon as well, where health care provider communication occurs primarily through "minute-to-minute conversations rather than lengthy meetings" (Grumbach & Bodenheimer, 2004, p. 1248). These points are valuable because they underscore how the processes that make teams effective often stem from informal talk and discourse. Informal communication highlights the discursive practices that constitute much of what teams do. This is an interesting area rich with potential for future research.

Outputs

The empirical studies examined above and in Table 7.1 provide a good picture of the type, quality, and variety of outcomes examined in research on communication in health care teams. Quality of care is a major clinical category in which to consider the effectiveness of team communication, both negative and positive. Specific ways in which communication problems have affected the quality of care include adverse events (Gawande et al., 2003; Sutcliffe et al., 2004; Williams et al., 2007) as well as delays in care, wasted time, procedural errors, inefficiency, or resource waste (Lingard, Regehr, et al., 2008; Williams et al., 2007). On the other hand, well-designed forms of team communication have lead to improved clinical outcomes for patients (Awad et al., 2005; Haynes et al., 2009).

Beyond clinical outcomes, communication also impacts team outcomes, which are important to such team functions as cohesion, retention, and morale (Apker, Propp, & Ford, 2009; Coopman, 2001). There is a long tradition in group dynamics research that demonstrates the importance of these factors (McGrath, 1984; Poole & Hollingshead, 2005). Identity, particularly professional identity, is also an important issue in health care teams and a number of researchers have examined this phenomenon. Lingard, Reznick, DeVito et al. (2002) found that identity constructions in health care teams affected patient care. Apker, Propp, and Ford (2005) found that identity was one of a number of communicative challenges that nurses face in teams, suggesting that nurses need to develop a repertoire of communication strategies to manage role-based identity tensions. Bleakely (2006) and Hewett et al. (2009) describe how professional identity shapes communication in medical records and how this has implications for patient care and safety.

Outcomes

The principal outcomes for health care teams are patient safety, morbidity, and mortality and research suggests that communication is directly linked to each of these (Baker et al.,

2005; Institute of Medicine et al., 1999). Haynes et al.'s (2009) study is a good example of how a communication intervention significantly reduced negative patient outcomes.

Conclusion

In this chapter, we explore communication in health care teams with the aim of understanding how communication influences team effectiveness. As Parrott (2004) has advocated, our aim is "communication" in health care team research. We found communication in health care team research to be practical, robust, interdisciplinary, and outcome-oriented. Communication is crucial to both the flow of critical information and the construction of situated meaning and is important to health care team effectiveness. The IPO framework provides a useful model for understanding and organizing the communication factors that facilitate or inhibit team effectiveness.

Future research could examine the dynamic nature of this model, in which distinct communication practices and team processes are examined episodically and temporally in order to understand which processes are critical depending on the team's task (Arrow, Poole, Henry, Wheelan, & Mooreland, 2004; Fernandez et al., 2008). Theories are needed which account for the complexity of health care team interaction in order to better understand communication and effectiveness in health care teams.

References

References marked with an asterisk indicate studies included in Table 7.1

*Anderson, C. M. (2001). Communication in the medical interview team: An analysis of patients' stories in the United States and Hong Kong. *The Howard Journal of Communications, 12*, 61–72.

*Apker, J., Propp, K. M., & Ford, W. Z. (2005). Negotiating status and identity tensions in health care team interactions: An exploration of nurse role dialectics. *Journal of Applied Communication Research, 33*, 93–115.

*Apker, J., Propp, K. M., & Ford, W. Z. (2009). Investigating the effect of nurse-team communication on nurse turnover: Relationships among communication processes, identification, and intent to leave. *Health Communication, 24*, 106–114.

*Apker, J., Propp, K. M., Ford, W. Z., & Hofmeister, N. (2006). Collaboration, credibility, compassion, and coordination: Professional nurse communication skill sets in health care team interactions. *Journal of Professional Nursing, 22*, 180–189.

Arrow, H., Poole, M. S., Henry, K. B., Wheelan, S., & Mooreland, R. L. (2004). Time, change, and development: The temporal perspective on groups. *Small Group Research, 35*, 73–105.

*Awad, S. S., Fegan, S. P., Bellows, C., Albo, D., Green-Rashed, B., De La Garza, M., & Berger, D. H. (2005). Bridging the communication gap in the operating room with medical team training. *American Journal of Surgery, 190*, 770–774.

Baker, D. P., Gustafson, S., Beaubien, J., Salas, E., & Barach, P. (2005). *Medical teamwork and patient safety: The evidence-based relation (AHRQ Publication No. 05-0053). Rockville, MD: Agency for Health Care Research and Quality.* Retrieved from http://www.ahrq.gov/qual/medteam/

*Bleakley, A. (2006). You are who I say you are: The rhetorical construction of identity in the operating theatre. *Journal of Workplace Learning, 17*, 414–425.

*Coopman, S. J. (2001). Democracy, performance and outcomes in interdisciplinary health care teams. *Journal of Business Communication, 38*, 261–284.

*Davis, C. S. (2008). Dueling narratives: How peer leaders use narrative to frame meaning in community mental health care teams. *Small Group Research, 39*, 706–727.

*Donnison, J., Thompson, A. R., & Turpin, G. (2009). A qualitative exploration of communication within the community mental health team. *International Journal of Mental Health Nursing, 18*, 310–317.

*Ellingson, L.L. (2003). Interdisciplinary health care teamwork in the clinic backstage. *Journal of Applied Communication Research, 31*, 93–117.

*Eisenberg, E., Murphy, A., Sutcliffe, K., Wears, R., Schenkel, S., Perry, S., & Vanderhoef, M. (2005). Communication in emergency medicine: Implications for patient safety. *Communication Monographs, 72*, 390–413.

Fernandez, R., Kozlowski, S. W. J., Shapiro, M. J., & Salas, E. (2008). Toward a definition of teamwork in emergency medicine. *Academic Emergency Medicine, 15*, 1104–1112.

*Frankel, A., Gardner, R., Maynard, L., & Kelly, A. (2007). Using the Communication and Teamwork Skills (CATS) Assessment to measure health care team performance. *The Joint Commission Journal on Quality and Patient Safety, 33*, 549–558.

*Gardezi, F., Lingard, L., Espin, S., Whyte, S., Orser, B., & Baker, G. R.. (2009). Silence, power and communication in the operating room. *Journal of Advanced Nursing, 65*, 1390–1399.

Gawande, A. A., Zinner, M. J., Studdert, D. M., & Brennann, T. A. (2003). Analysis of errors reported by surgeons at three teaching hospitals. *Surgery, 133*, 614–621.

*Grice, T., Gallois, C., Jones, E., Paulsen, N., & Callan, V. (2006). "We do it, but they don't": Multiple categorizations and work team communication. *Journal of Applied Communication Research, 34*, 331–348.

Grumbach, K., & Bodenheimer, T. (2004). Can health care teams improve primary care practice? *Journal of the American Medical Association, 291*, 1246–1251.

*Haynes, A. B., Weiser, T. G., Berry, W. R., Lipsitz, S. R., Breizat, A. S., Dellinger, E. P., ... Gawande, A. A. (2009). A surgical safety checklist to reduce morbidity and mortality in a global population. *New England Journal of Medicine, 360*, 491–499.

*Hewett, D. G., Watson, B. W., Gallois, C., Ward, M, & Leggett, B. A. (2009). Communication in medical records: Intergroup language and patient care. *Journal of Language and Social Psychology, 28*, 119–138.

Hirokawa, R. Y., & Poole, M. S. (Eds.) (1996). *Communication and group decision-making* (2nd ed.). Thousand Oaks, CA: Sage.

Institute of Medicine, Kohn, L. T., Corrigan, J. M., & Donaldson, M. S. (Eds.). (1999). *To err is human: Building a safer health system.* Washington, DC: National Academy Press.

Lemieux-Charles, L., & McGuire, W. L. (2006). What do we know about health care team effectiveness? A review of the literature. *Medical Care Research and Review, 63*, 263–300.

Lingard, L., Espin, S., Evans, C., & Hawryluck, L. (2004b). The rules of the game: Interprofessional collaboration on the intensive care unit team. Critical Care, 8, 403–408.

*Lingard, L., Espin, S., Rubin, B., Whyte, S., Colmenares, M., Baker, G. R., ... Reznick, R. (2005). Getting teams to talk: Development and pilot implementation of a checklist to promote safer operating room communication. *Quality and Safety in Health care, 14*, 340–346.

*Lingard, L., Espin, S., Whyte, S., Regehr, G., Baker, G. R., Reznick, R., ... Grober, E. (2004). Communication failures in the operating room: An observational classification of recurrent types and effects. *Quality and Safety in Health care, 13*, 330–334.

*Lingard, L., Regehr, G., Orser, B., Reznick, R., Baker, G. R., Doran, D., ... Whyte, S. (2008). Evaluation of a preoperative checklist and team briefing among surgeons, nurses, and anesthesiologists to reduce failures in communication. *Archives of Surgery, 143*, 12–17.

*Lingard, L., Reznick, R., DeVito, I., & Espin, S. (2002). Forming professional identities on the health care team: Discursive constructions of the "other" in the operating room. *Medical Education, 36*, 728–734.

*Lingard, L., Reznick, R., Regehr, G., DeVito, I., & Espin, S. (2002). Team communications in the operating room: Talk patterns, sites of tension, and implications for novices. *Academic Medicine, 77*, 232–237.

*Lingard, L., Whyte, S., Espin, S., Baker, G. R., Orser, B., & Doran, D. (2006). Towards safer interprofessional communication: Constructing a model of "utility" from preoperative team briefings. *Journal of Interprofessional Care, 20*, 471–483.

*Martin, D. R., O'Brien, J. L., Heyworth, J. A., & Meyer, N. R. (2008). Point counterpoint: The function of contradictions on an interdisciplinary health care team. *Qualitative Health Research, 18*, 369–379.

McGrath, J. E. (1984). *Groups: Interaction and performance.* Englewood Cliffs, NJ: Prentice-Hall.

*Mills, P., Neily, J., & Dunn, E. (2008). Teamwork and communication in surgical teams: Implications for patient safety. *Journal of the American College of Surgeons, 206*, 107–112.

Nussbaum, J., & Fisher, C. L. (2009). A communication model for the competent delivery of geriatric medicine. *Journal of Language and Social Psychology, 28*, 190–208.

*O'Connor, C., Friedrich, J. O., Scales, D. C., & Adhikari, N. K. J. (2009). The use of wireless email to improve health care team communication. *Journal of the American Medical Informatics Association, 16,* 705–713.

*Paulsel, M. L., McCroskey, J. C., & Richmond, V. P. (2006). Perceptions of health care professionals' credibility as a predictor of patients' satisfaction with their medical care and physician. *Communication Research Reports, 23,* 69–76.

Parrott, R. (2004). Emphasizing "communication" in health communication research. *Journal of Communication, 54,* 751–787.

Poole, M. S., & Hollingshead, A. V. (Eds.) (2005). *Theories of small groups: Interdisciplinary perspectives.* Thousand Oaks, CA: Sage.

Poole, M.S., & Real, K. (2003) Groups and teams in health care: Communication and effectiveness. In T. L. Thompson, A. M. Dorsey, K. I. Miller, & R. Parrott (Eds.), *Handbook of health communication* (pp. 369–402) Mahwah, NJ: Erlbaum.

Ramanujam, R., & Rousseau D. (2006). The challenges are organizational not just clinical. *Journal of Organizational Behavior, 27,* 811–827.

*Reader, T. W., Flin, R., Mearns, K. & Cuthbertson, B. H. (2007). Interdisciplinary communication in the intensive care unit. *British Journal of Anaesthesia, 98,* 347–352.

Reader, T. W., Flin, R., Mearns, K. & Cuthbertson, B. H. (2009). Developing a team performance framework for the intensive care unit. *Critical Care Medicine, 37,* 1787–1793.

*Reddy, M. C., & Jansen, B. J. (2008a). A model for understanding collaborative information behavior in context: A study of two health care teams. *Information Processing & Management, 44,* 256–273.

*Reddy, M. C., & Spence, P. R. (2008b). Collaborative information seeking: A field study of a multidisciplinary patient care team. *Information Processing & Management, 44,* 242–255.

*Reeves, S., Rice, K., Conn, L. G., Miller, K. L., Kenaszchuk, C., & Zwarenstein, M. (2009). Interprofessional interaction, negotiation and non-negotiation on general internal medicine wards. *Journal of Interprofessional Care, 99999;* 1; DOI: 10.1080/13561820902886295

*Shaw, A., De Lusignan, S., & Rowlands, G. (2005). Do primary care professionals work as a team: A qualitative study. *Journal of Interprofessional Care, 19,* 396–405.

Simpson, A. (2007). The impact of team processes on psychiatric case management. *Journal of Advanced Nursing, 60,* 409–418.

*Sinclair, L., Lingard, L., & Mohabeer, R. (2009). What's so great about rehabilitation teams? Documenting interprofessional collaboration in practice. *Archives of Physical Medicine and Rehabilitation, 90,* 1196–1201.

Starfield, B. (1992). *Primary care: Concept, evaluation, and policy.* New York: Oxford University Press.

*Sutcliffe, K. M., Lewton, E., & Rosenthal, M. M. (2004). Communication failures: An insidious contributor to medical mishaps. *Academic Medicine, 79,* 186–194.

*Tschan, F., Semmer, N. K., Gurtner, A., Bizzari, L., Spychiger, M., Breuer, M., & Marsch, S. U. (2009). Explicit reasoning, confirmation bias, and illusory transactive memory: A simulation study of group medical decision making. *Small Group Research, 40,* 271–300.

Wagner, E. H. (2000). The role of patient care teams in chronic disease management. *British Medical Journal, 320,* 569–572.

*Weingart, S. N., Simchowitz, B., Eng, T. K., Morway, L., Spencer, J., Zhu, J., ... Horvath, K. (2009). The you CAN campaign: Teamwork training for patients and families in ambulatory oncology. *The Joint Commission Journal on Quality and Patient Safety, 35,* 63–71.

*Williams, R.G., Silverman, R., Schwind, C., Fortune, J. B., Sutyak, J., Horvath, K. D., ... Dunnington, G. L. (2007). Surgeon information transfer and communication: Factors affecting quality and efficiency of inpatient care. *Annals of Surgery, 245,* 159–169.

8

WORKING WELL

Reconsidering Health Communication at Work

Patricia Geist-Martin and Jennifer A. Scarduzio

The boundaries between work and life are navigated through communication (Clark 2000; Kirby, Golden, Medved, Jorgenson, & Buzzanell, 2003). The challenge for organizations is to design and implement programs that assist employees in navigating these boundaries effectively. The purpose of this chapter is fourfold. The first goal is to summarize how communication scholars define the notion of communicating health and wellness at work. The second goal is to describe the evolution of wellness programs. The third goal is to offer an expanded notion of wellness at work by reconsidering what it means to communicate health in organizations. Fourth and finally, our goal is to recommend directions for future research on health communication and wellness programs through four theoretical lenses. In essence, this chapter is directed toward understanding employees' navigation of work–life boundaries by turning toward health communication research. In the process, we will discover how topics in organizational communication research offer enhanced understanding of health communication in work settings.

The Centrality of Communicating Health at Work

Communication is central to the social environment created at work: it influences interactions among co-workers, the impact of what we do on who we are, the ways our work interfaces with our personal lives, and people's overall experience of wellness and disease at work and at home. Therefore, the promotion of healthy workplaces and employees should be focused on communication and the ways we organize our work practices (Mattson, Clair, Sanger, & Kunkel, 2000). As Parrott (2004) points out, the reality is "that people's physical and mental well-being depends far more on our ability to manage health day-to-day than on the teachable moments that occur via health promotion and education via medical interaction" (p. 751). As a result, we need to consider and improve the social and environmental conditions that promote the well-being of the whole person in the context of his or her workplace through effective communicative practices (Geist-Martin, Horsley, & Farrell, 2003; Thompson & Swihart, 2008).

Previously, health communication researchers have examined how managers gain compliance for participation from employees (see Freimuth, Edgar, & Fitzpatrick, 1993; Rogers, 1996). These studies focused on the outcomes of workplace programs, but did not emphasize the communicative processes that impact these results. Recently, health communication researchers have considered meaning-centered approaches to health initiatives (see Farrell & Geist-Martin, 2005; Parrott & Lemieux, 2003; Zoller, 2003, 2004; Zook, 1994). For example, Zook (1994) called for "a broader conception of communication wherein instrumental interests are balanced by emancipatory interests" (p. 345). As suggested by Ratzan and Parker (2006), the term health literacy "reminds health communicators of the need to tailor information, messages, and advice while choosing the appropriate media to enhance quality decision-making" (p. 715). Clearly, there is a need to employ communicative practices throughout the process of designing wellness programs that addresses both company goals and employee needs. The challenge in addressing diverse employee needs is to be innovative and culturally sensitive, designing initiatives so that people can access and use the information (Parker, Ratzan, & Lurie, 2003). So, what are the health needs of employees at work? How should communication be designed to address these needs?

Recent trends have considered the health of employees both inside and outside the "box" of the organization (Cheney, Zorn, Planalp, & Lair, 2008). Suggesting that what falls outside the domain of work influences work life and vice versa, researchers focus on the ways organizations communicate with employees to influence their work–life balance (Cowan & Hoffman, 2007; Edley, 2001, 2003; Golden, Kirby, Jorgenson, 2006; Hoffman & Cowan, 2008; Medved & Kirby, 2005), friendships inside and outside of work (Sias & Cahill, 1998), family–work interface (Medved, Brogan, McClanahan, Morris, & Shepherd, 2006; Parrott & Lemieux, 2003), and general well-being (Harris, Daniels, & Briner, 2003). Navigating the boundaries between work and life necessitates considering the ways these boundaries are permeable. Cheney et al. suggest that

> concerns about the physical well-being of workers have shifted significantly toward this more subjective domain in the wake of significant improvements to the material conditions of workplaces in many industrialized societies since the early 1970s.... The attainment of meaningful work goals contributes to subjective well being.
>
> (p. 141)

Too often the focus is only on the objective features of the organization or job (e.g., work environment, hours, salary, benefits, and technology), when instead consideration should also be given to communication about subjective well-being (e.g., the ways that we discuss, interpret, and frame our work as meaningful).

Meaningful work is the umbrella term describing a constellation of factors that contribute to working well, including job satisfaction, job enrichment, work–life balance, career path, leisure, and life satisfaction (Cheney et al., 2008). As we consider the permeable nature of the boundaries between our life and our work, questions arise about the best way to communicate information to the public and about changing people's behaviors to make healthier choices (Pohl & Freimuth, 1983). With a broader conceptualization of health communication at work that is centered on meanings of physical, psychological, social, and spiritual health (Geist-Martin, Ray, & Sharf, 2003; Lips-Wiersma, 2002) we may enhance our understanding of the ways that employees navigate the boundaries between their work and personal lives. For instance, while seemingly separate from the institutional context, the family of an employee may have a large impact on the way that an employee perceives and responds to the communication of health initiatives in organizations. Parrott and Lemieux (2003), in researching the collision between work and wellness, describe how the involvement of family members in giving health information often facilitates health and the performance of health behaviors. In their view, the social support behavior of family members must be taken into account in the planning and communication of prevention programs.

At the same time, questions arise about ways to encourage healthy behaviors, the limits of managerial involvement in employees' personal lives, and the limits to employee participation. It is clear that behavior change is not always easy to achieve—especially when one of the most challenging components of designing a wellness program is achieving reasonable levels of employee participation (Johnson, 2008). In the next sections, this chapter discusses the evolution of wellness initiatives and the need to reconsider health communication at work. We end this chapter by describing communication theories that might offer a more complex perspective on communicating health in organizations.

The Evolution of Wellness Initiatives in Organizations

With most Americans spending almost 50% of their lives at work, organizations undoubtedly play a large role in constructing the conditions of people's lives and, consequently, their experiences of health and disease. At the same time, employee health problems are extremely expensive for the United States as a whole and for organizations in particular. It is estimated that job stress costs the United States over $300 billion annually (American Institute on Stress, 2009). Employee abuse of alcohol and drugs costs American business about $80 billion a year (Johnson, 2008). In addition, American businesses lose $6 billion due to decreased productivity from employee difficulties in personal relationships (Turvey & Olson, 2006). Ten percent of employees are impaired enough to need behavioral health intervention (Poverny & Dodd, 2000). Across industries, organizations often report savings on medical costs for employees of as much as $3.00 to $5.00 for every dollar invested in health risk reduction programs and close to $3.00 in savings in absenteeism costs (Baicker, Cutler, & Song, 2010).

Not surprisingly, the number of wellness initiatives and programs in U.S. businesses has risen substantially over the past ten years (Fitch & Pyenson, 2008). In 1950, there were fewer than 100 employee assistance programs (EAPs), in companies in the United States. However, by 2008, 76% of public sector employees and 46% of private sector employees had EAPs at their workplaces (U.S. Bureau of Labor Statistics, 2009). Historically, EAPs started by offering occupational alcoholism programs that saved money, increased production, and "rehabilitated" skilled employees (Coshan, 1991). EAPs continued to develop, targeting the most extreme and expensive health issues, such as psychological counseling needs, smoking, alcohol abuse, and high stress levels (Pelletier, 1984). As the popularity of EAPs has grown, so too have the types of services they offer and communicate to their employees, including the broadening of alcoholism programs to reach out and communicate to families of alcoholic workers and persons facing other personal life issues (Dickman, 1985).

Numerous surveys from 2007 reported that 77% to 89% of mid- to large-sized companies in the United States offer wellness programs (Fitch & Pyenson, 2008). Furthermore, the government has become involved through the creation and communication of initiatives by the Centers for Disease Control and Prevention, the National Chronic Disease Prevention Agenda, and school and community based health programs ("Essential Elements," 2007). While all the communication developed through these programs shares the original goals of EAPs, such as improving job performance, family life, and health (Shain & Groenveld, 1980), EAPs have evolved from an emphasis on communication about existing problems to programs focusing on health promotion, wellness, quality of work-life, and work engagement (Attridge, 2009; Coshan, 1991). In addition, more recent research reveals an effort to create standardized outcomes and reporting formulas so that the EAP profession provides efficient, effective, and standardized services to employees (Jacobson & Jones, 2010).

The most cutting-edge health initiatives being communicated in organizations have evolved into a vision of overall wellness, integrating employee assistance programs, work–life, and wellness programs. According to Thompson and Swihart (2008), this attempt is one of sending messages that educate employees about ways to change unhealthy behaviors and develop healthy habits. For example, the University of Arizona's Life and Work Connections program focuses on an integrated model of wellness. The goal of communication in this program is to "facilitate a developmental process that helps the employee not only resolve the problem at hand, but better equips him or her to manage future issues" (Thompson & Swihart, 2008, p. 152). Additionally, the program communicates about employee resilience, sending messages that ask employees to look beyond their present health status to strategies that would improve health and their resistance to illness.

While the types of programs have changed, there still is a need to understand the communication surrounding the design, implementation, and follow-up of worksite health promotion programs and activities. An organization's communication related to innovative programs plays a major role in employees' acceptance of and participation in such programs (Corman & Poole, 2000). It is clear, for example, that employees do not always participate in the wellness initiatives or EAPs designed to help them. Past research has suggested that this could be due to feelings of embarrassment (Johnson, 2008), uneasiness about the employer's involvement in their personal affairs (Murphy, Hurrell, & Quick, 1992), or a lack of trust in the confidentiality of counseling (Stainbrook & Green, 1989). More recently, scholars have proposed that employees do not always participate in these initiatives because they "are not terribly sophisticated in their evaluations of sources of health and wellness information" (Johnson, 2008, p. 264). In other words, employees are not motivated toward or trusting of wellness initiatives in their workplaces, and some lack the health education to know when they need assistance. As we gain a clearer sense of the limitations of communicating health at work, it becomes evident that we need to reconsider health communication at work.

Reconsidering Health Communication at Work

Working well in organizations and participating in worksite health promotion programs is complicated by the cultural diversity of our workforce, the increasing numbers of temporary workers, and the occupational stress that has come from all directions—demands for technological proficiency, downsizing and rightsizing, the struggle to balance work and life stressors, and employees' quest for meaningful, healthy, well-balanced, and spiritual lives. What all of this reveals is the need to reconsider worksite health promotion in a way that recognizes the significant role that communication plays in creating and sustaining a healthy workplace. In the following subsections we articulate some of the ways that we may describe wellness initiatives through health communication, reconsidering (a) the medicalization of work, (b) the definition of health communication, and (c) the context of communicating health at work.

Reconsidering the Medicalization of Work

The rising costs of health benefits and wellness programs can lead to the medicalization of work, which occurs when corporations pay closer attention to employees' health, inside and outside the workplace (May, 1998). Concerns have been raised about the ethical and legal implications of this increased focus upon health and wellness inside and outside the workplace and the social processes that lead to claims that a problem is a medical one (Conrad, 2007). It seems as if during this process the managerial role is transformed from supervisor to lay doctor, as managers, with little or no training in medicine, are responsible for identifying troubled workers, referring them to appropriate EAPs, and then taking disciplinary action when workers do not comply with the EAP.

May (1998) describes six other concerns about the medicalization of work and the pathologizing of worker productivity, suggesting that, first, employee assistance programs expand the problems that require medical attention and redefine organizational life through a disease metaphor. Second, managerial control surrounding EAPs mandates that workers speak more openly about their problems in the context of work in order to be "cured." Third, EAPs locate the worker as the focus of intervention, rather than environmental conditions in the workplace that may contribute to worker stress, psychological maladjustment, or substance abuse. Fourth, EAPs create labeling processes wherein a worker is rarely able to escape the label, the accompanying continual observation, or the ability to define him- or herself as well, rather than being seen as in denial. Fifth, medicalization of the workplace increases the number of health-related personnel whose livelihood depends upon the proliferation of EAPs. Sixth, EAPs have rewritten the employer–employee contract so that the boundaries between public and private, work and family, labor and leisure, medical and non-medical are blurred.

Reconsidering the medicalization of work does not translate to foregoing EAPs or eliminating worksite health promotion. Instead, it means shifting to a wellness model of health communication where the focus is not on naming illnesses that must be addressed medically, but on employing communication to engage and involve people in their work as a form of preventative medicine. As was suggested by previous research, the medicalization of work raises issues that can be addressed through a reconsideration of how we define and incorporate communication into organizational wellness (Geist-Martin et al., 2003). In the following section, we discuss the importance of reconsidering the definition of health communication.

Reconsidering the Definition of Health Communication

Much of the work in the area of worksite health promotion focuses on health communication from either a biological or psychological perspective—communicating to change unhealthy behaviors to healthy behaviors or counseling to cope with or resolve psychological trauma associated with difficult professional and personal life events. While biology and psychology are key components of our health, it is also essential to reconsider a definition of health communication that balances concern for biological survival with concerns of personal, social, societal, and spiritual well-being. By using a definition of health communication as "the symbolic processes by which people, individually and collectively, understand, shape, and accommodate to health and illness" (Geist-Martin et al. 2003, p. 3), we expand our understanding of worksite health promotion.

This reconsideration of health and communication implies that we include an individual's biography with their biology. Employees' biographies include ruptures at work and at home which disintegrate or throw out of balance any part of our biological, psychological, social, or spiritual health (Gonzalez, 1994). Such events may include an injury, a death, a family crisis, a new assignment, or a new supervisor. For example, differences in the ways that employees of various cultures define and treat health in a multicultural organization, affect the appeal of wellness initiatives. Reconsideration of health and communication moves away from either a medicalized (via occupational health interventions) or individualized (via EAPs) conceptualization to a broader approach based on workplace well-being that addresses the challenges faced in particular organizational contexts (Bates & Thompson, 2007).

When employees have the opportunity to talk with co-workers and supervisors about unhealthy work or home-life situations, they are not just telling someone about their disease, they are asking others to construct new ways of interpreting and coping with these unhealthy dilemmas. In the process of communicating with one another, a number of things can occur that reinforce participation in worksite health promotion: (a) employees learn something from others' perspectives (e.g., perceived benefits, self-efficacy) (Alexy, 2007); (b) employees provide support to one another for continuing participation (Alexy, 2007; Bungum, Orsak, & Chng, 1997); and (c) disclosure of discomfort or traumatic events is physically beneficial—communicating with other people actually contributes to the health of the immune system (Pennebaker, 1990, 1995). When we begin to consider the multiple discourses that employees are audience to we begin to see health communication at work as not solely an individual issue.

Reconsidering the Focus on Individuals

While the costs of illness and disease are clear for both the individual and the organization, accountability for and participation in the causes and treatments of such diseases are not so equally spread. Companies are working at cross-purposes when, on the one hand, they offer programs which they believe will enhance the health of employees and thus reduce the number of health insurance claims, but at the same time do nothing to change the working conditions or organizational culture that are inherently stressful.

In contrast, some companies are developing organizational change initiatives, which may contribute to employees' health from an organizational structure or roles perspective. For example, the University of Arizona (UA) Life and Work Connections Program employs systems theory to incorporate a whole-person view of employees. The program centers on synergy, differentiation, and resilience, and provides attention to both the life- and work cycle (Thompson & Swihart, 2008). Emphasis on the life- and work cycle may offer increased understanding of the forms of communication that facilitate or constrain employees' participation in organizational wellness programs.

Reconsidering the Context of Communicating Health at Work

There are several limitations to the current wellness programs in organizations today. First, it is difficult to tell if a program is actually promoting change in behavior because many of these programs are not measurable. In fact, because wellness programs often target people who are at risk but not sick, it "may take years for the risk to materialize (if it ever does)" (Fitch & Pyenson, 2008, p. 39). The Employee Assistance Research Foundation (EARF) indicates that little behavioral research exists to document the value of employee assistance programs (Pompe & Sharar, 2008). Second, employee turnover impacts the ability to tell how a program is affecting the organization. Additionally, lack of a common definition of what an EAP is supposed to accomplish contributes to organizations' inability to track the impact of the programs they develop (Shar & Hertenstein, 2005). Third, public education, disease management, and changes in medical practice throughout the course of the programs also make results difficult to detect. Fourth, participation in wellness programs is voluntary and participants often self-select (Fitch & Pyenson, 2008). In other words, the employees that actually decide to participate in the programs are probably the ones most likely to change their negative health behaviors.

Previous research measures frequency of intent to participate or frequency of participation but fails to research the political complexities of communication in worksite contexts that might facilitate or restrict employees' participation in programs designed to help them to sustain or improve their health (Hutter, 2001). More research is needed to follow up on communication issues surrounding the context of participation—why are some individuals unaware of wellness centers and benefits? Why do people choose not to participate even if they are aware of the benefits? Why do people participate once or twice, but do not consistently participate?

The messages often designed and imparted from a top-down model may not represent what makes employees feel comfortable in talking about disease, illness, or wellness or what draws them together in fellowship and commonality (Carey, 1989). Sustaining viable worksite health promotion may be deeply dependent upon matching the complexity of communication with the complexity of the workforce in a particular industry. We clearly need to understand how forms of talk about health and illness may or may not be appropriate, comfortable, or beneficial for specific employees, and the meanings they have developed for health, illness, and meaningful work.

New directions for considering health communication at work necessarily turn our focus toward workplace well-being. Thus, we move away from the medicalized and individualized approaches toward a broader, more contextualized approach that focuses on communication, problem solving, and well-being (Bates & Thompson, 2007).

Directions for Future Conceptual Ties to Communicating Health in Organizations

Communicating health and wellness in organizational contexts is a process that can be informed through a wide range of theoretical lenses. Indeed, in order to understand the challenges and benefits of communicating about health and wellness in organizations, it is essential to consider the insight gleaned from these theoretical lenses. In the following sub-sections, we describe the ties between four theoretical concepts and communicating health in organizations: (a) work–life border, (b) identity, (c) emotional labor, and (d) structuration theory.

Communicating across the Work–Life Border

Work–life balance is a process that is negotiated through communication. Some research-ers have termed the relationship that exists between work and life as a conflict (WLC) and explored the ways that communication about work and life impacts workplace rela-tionships with supervisor/supervisee and co-worker relationships and family relationships with spouses, partners, or dependents (Kirby, Wieland, & McBride, 2006). Furthermore, researchers have argued that the communication discipline is uniquely situated to study work–life issues through a focus on meaning-centered and process-oriented approaches (Kirby, 2003). The way that individuals communicate about work and life, both at home and in their workplaces, is a process that influences their health and wellness (Cowan & Hoffman, 2007).

Past research has suggested that there are two responses that organizations have to the spheres of work and life—integrated or separated (Kanter, 1977). As the names imply, separation suggests that there is no interaction between work and life, and interaction acknowledges that some interaction does occur (Cowan & Hoffman, 2007). The work–life border theory (Clark, 2000) was created to explain how individuals "manage work and life domains in order to obtain balance" (p. 37).

Not surprisingly, organizations have an enormous impact on how their employees negotiate the domains of health and wellness in work and life. Starting in the 1990s, organizations appealed to potential employees through initiatives such as substance abuse treatment, counseling, and exercise programs (Hoffman & Cowan, 2008). The way companies present the ideology of work and life usually manifests today in one of four ways: "work is the most important element of life, life means family, individuals are responsible for managing the relationship between paid work and the rest of life, and organizations control work–life programs" (Hoffman & Cowan, p. 239). Indeed, the way an organization constructs and communicates about work–life balance ultimately enhances or detracts from the wellness of its employees and communicates how each organization values health.

Permeability is a concept that also reveals the challenges of navigating health issues in both work and life. Permeability is defined as the amount of influence that each domain, both work and life, has upon individuals' communication in the opposite setting (Clark, 2000). In other words, permeability is the degree of "spillover," or attitudes, emotions, stressors, concerns, and beliefs that spill over from one domain to the other. The concept of spillover highlights the challenges that employees face as they communicate to navigate between the boundaries of work and life. Furthermore, the permeability of one's work and life domains has the ability to influence one's wellness because it regulates how much an individual can communicate about each domain in either location. For example, Ward and Winstanley (2003) studied the work–life challenges of lesbian and gay individuals, finding that as compared to heterosexual employees, they are usually more restricted from talking about their private lives.

Balancing work and life translates to finding ways to communicate about the issues of health and illness that are central to our identities and which cannot be boxed as inside or outside the boundaries of an organization. At the same time, the ways that an organization communicates about health and illness may validate, threaten, or even nullify our identities.

Communicating Identity

An employee's sense of self and his or her identity are influenced by the ways health and wellness are communicated in the organization. Wellness programs have been based on substance-abuse models of treatment (Trethewey, Tracy, & Alberts, 2006), influencing employee identities through (a) the creation of policies (Kirby & Krone, 2002), (b) the definitions of wellness they promote (Farrell & Geist-Martin, 2005), and (c) the expectations developed by the organization (Newton, 1995). Communication scholars are uniquely situated to examine how the current language of work–life wellness positions "the individual as the locus of work-life problems" (Trethewey et al., 2006, p. 3). In order to untangle the relationship between health, wellness, and identity, it is essential to explore various conceptualizations of the term.

Identity is discursively constructed through the interactions that occur during an individual's life. Previous research suggests that the self is "seen as neither fixed nor essential, but instead, as a product of competing, fragmentary, and contradictory discourses" (Tracy &

Trethewey, 2005, p. 168). Early theories of identity from both pragmatists and social interactionists focused on the self as fixed and stable (Blumer, 1969). Recently, however, postmodern theorists have suggested that focusing on an essential self is problematic because the self is "nothing more than an image among countless other images" (Tracy & Trethewey, 2005, p. 171).

As an alternative to the real self–fake self dichotomy, Tracy and Trethewey (2005), proposed the crystallized self, which is not real, fake, flattened, suffocated, or colonized. Instead, crystallized selves have "different shapes depending on the various discourses through which they are constructed and constrained" (Tracy & Trethewey, p. 186). The crystallized self allows individuals to recognize that multiple parts of their identity are shaped through discourse and none are more "real" or "fake" than the others.

This metaphor of a crystallized self can be applied to the communication of health and wellness in frames of work and life. Trethewey et al. (2006) suggest that a crystallized approach "suggests the need to study the management of various spheres and identities through multiple levels of communication—including micro-level negotiations" (p. 4). Furthermore, a crystallized approach to identity, wellness, and health proposes that the ability to manage multiple identities is varied for each individual, and the intersections and implications of wellness at work need to be explored through their relationships to employee identities.

The next theoretical tie examines situations where the emotions mandated by employers do not match the emotional expression of employees, another process that influences the communication of wellness and health at work.

Communicating Emotional Labor

Emotional labor has direct implications on the health and wellness of employees both in their work and life. These health consequences can result in either positive benefits or negative costs that influence an employee's relationship with the organization and his or her personal sense of well-being. *Emotional labor*, a term originally proposed by Hochschild (1983), refers to "the display of largely inauthentic emotions, emotions that ... can be controlled, trained, and prescribed, in employee handbooks" (Miller, Considine, & Garner, 2007, p. 233). In other words, emotional labor is mandated by the norms, or rules, of the organization and is not always consistent with employees' feelings.

The requirement of emotional labor by employers has direct implications for wellness and health communication—both positive and negative. Initially, Hochschild (1983) suggested that the consistent pressure of emotional labor could lead to "drug use, excessive drinking, headaches, absenteeism, and sexual dysfunction" (Rafaeli & Sutton, 1987, p. 31). Scholars have found that surface acting is related to stress (Grandey, 2003) and that there are harmful but limited psychosocial costs to emotional labor (Erickson & Wharton, 1997). Wharton (1993) explained that emotional labor could produce a fusion between people's self and their work role or a feeling of estrangement between the two. Frequently, these feelings of estrangement are blamed on emotional dissonance, or "clash[es] between 'real' feelings and 'fake' display" (Tracy, 2005, p. 262).

Other scholars have explicated the positive effects and strategic use of emotional labor. Fineman (2008) explained that emotional labor "can be self-enhancing and stimulating for the worker" in some situations (p. 677). Schuler and Sypher (2000) proposed that emergency call takers were excited by the emotional demands of remaining neutral or responding to challenging situations. Moreover, Scott and Myers (2005) described the positive consequences of emotional labor in the socialization process of firefighters. They suggested that emotional labor should be viewed as a "valuable workplace skill" that is necessary and productive in some organizational contexts (Scott & Myers, p. 85).

The communication employees engage in on a day-to-day basis to negotiate work–life balance, identity, and emotional labor inevitably impact macro issues, such as the ways that policies are structured or restructured. Structuration theory offers an enhanced understanding of health communication in organizational contexts by attending to micro- and macro-level intersections.

Communicating Structuration Theory

Structuration theory has been frequently used to examine work–life issues because it highlights the relationship between structure and action (Golden et al., 2006; Kirby & Krone, 2002; Tracy & Rivera, 2010). Past work–life scholarship has successfully "used structuration theory to explore the taken-for-granted ways that communication in the workplace influences policies and practices" (Tracy & Rivera, 2010, p. 6). Structuration theory specifically relates to health communication because it reveals the rules and resources that employees use in the workplace that influence their daily well-being.

The central idea of structuration theory is that social life is constrained and enabled through the social interaction of everyday life. Giddens (1984) stated that the "basic domain of the social sciences … is neither … the individual actor, nor … societal totality, but social practices" (p. 2). Giddens (1979) described structuration as the "fundamental recursiveness of social life," meaning that the application of this theory highlights the relationships between macro- and micro-social action and practices (p. 69). For example, a conversation at the water cooler about whether an employee will utilize the paternity leave policy is influenced by the way the policy has been utilized in the past and is constrained and enabled by the larger macro structures that inform cultural perceptions of paternity leave.

Structure involves both rules and resources (Rose, 2006). More specifically, structure is "reinterpreted in structuration theory to mean the constellation of rules and resources that people draw on that simultaneously enable and constrain social interaction" (Bastien, McPhee, & Bolton, 1995, p. 88). Individuals access rules, "techniques or generalizable procedures," in social interactions as a means to understand or sanction others (Rose, 2006, p. 175). In other words, employees use rules as a way to understand and also punish other employees for their health choices at work (see Kirby & Krone, 2002). Alternatively, resources include advantages or capabilities that individuals use within interactions to influence others.

A central process of structuration is the dual nature of structures, also called the duality of structure. According to Giddens (1976), the duality of structure means that systems are "constantly actualized, displayed, and modified" through individuals' ability to make sense of them (p. 113). In other words, employees are dependent on the structure of wellness programs in order to participate in daily organizational life, while at the same time the structures themselves are being constructed and maintained by the employees through everyday talk.

One specific example of how structuration theory could inform our current understanding of health and wellness communication at work is through a consideration of sustainability and the sustainable self. As scholars interested in the health of employees in organizations, it is important to ask "what happens if our organizations and homes are sustainable, but the people within those places are not" (Montoya & Trethewey, 2009, p. 1)?

In relation to structuration theory, at the micro level many employees are provided with wellness and success tips at work, yet at that macro level the organizations in which they work do not provide policies and practices that facilitate employees' health. Montoya and Trethewey propose that organizations should attempt to remedy this disconnect through the creation of policies that could facilitate individuals and companies that are self-sustaining. They suggest that employees "connect and willingly listen to different part[s] of one's mind, body, and soul in an effort to engage in new types of decision making [and that they] recognize where one has privilege based on his/her own social identities and work to not oppress others" (Montoya & Trethewey, 2009, p. 8). As this example reveals, sustainability highlights the interaction between rules and resources and also depicts how successful health communication at work needs to consider both micro- and macro communication to enhance the health and wellness.

Summary of Communicating Health at Work

In the past few years, wellness initiatives and programs have changed and developed. Some companies are incorporating alternative and complementary medicine such as yoga, meditation, and acupuncture. Other employers are attempting to integrate EAPs, work–life issues, and wellness programs in a more comprehensive view of wellness (Thompson & Swihart, 2008). Yet, it also appears as if wellness is still viewed as a disposable expense in some organizational contexts, particularly when economic downturns arise (Fitch & Pyenson, 2008). As wellness programs continue to flourish, the future of "well" employees may be well-intentioned to center on a whole-person view.

The expectation that employees completely leave their home relationships, health problems, or needs of their family members outside of the workplace is not realistic. Prior wellness initiatives have acknowledged the existence of these multiple domains in employees' lives, yet they often have failed to consider how the navigation between these domains impacts employees' daily health. A whole-person view of wellness goes beyond acknowledgment and instead recognizes that there are "*interactions* between domains" (Thompson & Swihart, 2008, p. 149). A wellness program that incorporates this view recognizes these interactions through the inclusion of synergy. According to Thompson and Swihart:

> Synergy … spills over into service offerings that produce more broad-based knowledge, are often unique, and have a tighter, better fit to equip employees to manage their real-world life and work situations.

(p. 150)

Through the inclusion of the whole-person view and synergy, employers are treated as assets instead of budget lines. Companies become focused on positive emotional experiences for employees, such as resilience, compassion, and generosity instead of only preventing negative experiences. Successful wellness programs may be better served by considering the whole-person view as well as including explorations of effective health communication at work (Fitch & Pyenson, 2008).

Vision, empowerment, harmony, balance, creativity, learning, and *sustainability* are all words used to describe an emerging organizational culture that values a communal quest for transforming organizational dialogues, relations, structures, and paradoxes. Employees in today's organizations genuinely want to be a part of this transformation. However, a focus only on the body, the individual, or the medicalized model of treatment leaves out the significance of communicating to shape and transform employees' health and wellness. Without a doubt, well-being in the workforce today is clearly tied to communication and interdependence between dialogue and evolving organizational practices that support people and convince them that what they contribute matters.

References

Alexy, B. B. (2007). Factors associated with participation or nonparticipation in a workplace wellness center. *Research in Nursing and Health, 14,* 33–40. DOI: 10.1002/nur.4770140106

American Institute on Stress. (2009). Job stress. Retrieved from http://www.stress.org/job.htm

Attridge, M. (2009). Measuring and managing employee work engagement: A review of the research and business literature. *Journal of Workplace Behavioral Health, 24,* 383–398. DOI: 10.1080/15555240903188398

Baicker, K, Cutler, D., & Song, Z. (2010). Workplace wellness programs can generate savings. *Health Affairs, 2,* 304–311. DOI: 10.13777/hlthaff.2009.0626

Bastien, D. T., McPhee, R. D., & Bolton, K. A. (1995). A study and extended theory of the structuration of climate. *Communication Monographs, 62,* 87–109. DOI: 10.1080/03637759509376351

Bates, J., & Thompson, N. (2007). Workplace well-being: An occupational social work approach. *Illness, Crisis, and Loss, 15,* 273–284. Retrieved from http://baywood.metapress.com/link. asp?id+q3r7u20067772q2

Blumer, H. (1969). *Symbolic interactionism: Perspective and method.* Englewood Cliffs, NJ: Prentice-Hall.

Bungum, T. J., Orsak, K. C., & Chng, C. L. (1997). Factors affecting exercise adherence at a worksite wellness program. *American Journal of Health Behavior, 21,* 59–66. DOI: 10. 1998032538

Carey, J. W. (1989). *Communication as culture: Essays on media and society.* Boston, MA: Unwin Hyman.

Cheney, G., Zorn, T. E., Planalp, S., & Lair, D. L. (2008). Meaningful work and personal/social well-being: Organizational communication engages the meanings of work. In C. Beck (Ed.), *Communication yearbook 32* (pp. 137–186). New York: Routledge.

Clark, S. C. (2000). Work–family border theory: A new theory of work–family balance. *Human Relations, 53,* 747–770. DOI: 10.1177/0018726700536001

Conrad, P. (2007). *The medicalization of society: On the transformation of human conditions into treatable disorders.* Baltimore, MD: The John Hopkins University Press.

Corman, S. R., & Poole, M. S. (Eds.). (2000). *Perspectives on organizational communication: Finding common ground.* New York: Guilford.

Coshan, M. (1991). Enlarging the concept of employee assistance. *Employee Assistance Quarterly, 7,* 25–44. DOI: 10.1300/J022v07n01_04

Cowan, R., & Hoffman, M. F. (2007). The flexible organization: How contemporary organizations construct the work/life border. *Qualitative Research Reports in Communication, 8,* 37–44. DOI: 10.1080/17459430701617895

Dickman, F. J. (1985). Employee assistance programs: History and philosophy. In F. J. Dickman, W. G. Emener, Jr., & W. S. Hutchinson, Jr. (Eds.), *Counseling the troubled person in industry* (pp. 7–12). Springfield, IL: Charles C. Thomas.

Edley, P. (2001). Technology, employed mothers, and corporate colonization of the lifeworld: A gendered paradox of work and family balance. *Women and Language, 24,* 28–35. Retrieved from http://go.galegroup.com.ezproxy1.lib.asu.edu/ps/i.do?id=GALE|A82352863&v=2.1&u=asuniv &it=r&p=LitRC&sw=w

Edley, P. (2003). Entrepreneurial mothers' balance of work and family: Discursive constructions of time, mothering, and identity. In P. M. Buzzanell, H. L. Sterk, & L. H. Turner (Eds.), *Gender in applied communication contexts* (pp. 255–273). Thousand Oaks, CA: Sage.

Erickson, R. J., & Wharton, A. (1997). Inauthenticity and depression: Assessing the consequences of interactive service work. *Work and Occupations, 24,* 188–213. DOI: 10.1177/0730888497024002004

Essential elements of effective workplace programs and policies for improving worker health and wellbeing. (2007). NIOSH WorkLife Initiative. Retrieved from http://www.cdc.gov/niosh/ worklife/essentials.html

Farrell, A., & Geist-Martin, P. (2005). Communicating social health: Perceptions of wellness at work. *Management Communication Quarterly, 18,* 543–592. DOI: 10.1177/0893318904273691

Fineman, S. (2008). Emotion and organizing. In S. Clegg, C. Hardy, & W. Nord (Eds.), *Handbook of organization studies* (pp. 675–700). London: Sage.

Fitch, K., & Pyenson, B. (2008). Taking stock of wellness. *Benefits Quarterly, 34–40.* Retrieved from http://www.mcgohanbrabender.com/documents/content/361.pdf

Freimuth, V. S., Edgar, T., & Fitzpatrick, M. A. (1993). Introduction: The role of communication in health promotion. *Communication Research, 20,* 509–516. DOI: 10.1177/009365093020004001

Geist-Martin, P., Horsley, K., & Farrell, A. (2003). Working well: Communicating individual and collective wellness initiatives. In T. L. Thompson, A. M. Dorsey, K. I. Miller, & R. Parrott (Eds.), *Handbook of health communication* (pp. 423–443). Mahwah, NJ: Erlbaum.

Geist-Martin, P., Ray, E. B., & Sharf, B. F. (2003). *Communicating health: Personal, cultural, and political complexities.* Belmont, CA: Wadsworth.

Giddens, A. (1976). *New rules of sociological method.* New York: Basic Books.

Giddens, A. (1979). *Central problems in social theory.* Berkeley: University of California Press.

Giddens, A. (1984). *The constitution of society.* Berkeley: University of California Press.

Golden, A. G., Kirby, E. L., & Jorgenson, J. (2006). Work–life research from both sides now: An integrative perspective for organizational and family communication. In C. S. Beck (Ed.), *Communication yearbook 30* (pp. 143–195). Mahwah, NJ: Erlbaum.

Gonzalez, M. C. (1994). An invitation to leap from a trinitarian ontology in health communication research to a spiritually inclusive quatrain. In S. A. Deetz (Ed.), *Communication yearbook 17* (pp. 378–387). Thousand Oaks, CA: Sage.

Grandey, A. (2003). When "the show must go on": Surface acting and deep acting as determinants of emotional exhaustion and peer-rated service delivery. *Academy of Management Journal, 46,* 86–96. Retrieved from http://www.jstor.org/stable/30040678

Harris, C., Daniels, K., & Briner, R. B. (2003). A daily diary study of goals and affective well-being at work. *Journal of Occupational and Organizational Psychology, 76,* 401–410. DOI: 10.1348/096317903769647256

Hochschild, A. (1983). *The managed heart.* Berkeley: University of California Press.

Hoffman, M. F., & Cowan, R. (2008). The meaning of work/life: A corporate ideology of work/life balance. *Communication Quarterly, 56,* 227–246. DOI: 10.1080/01463370802251053

Hutter, B. M. (2001). *Regulation and risk: Occupational health and safety on the railways.* Oxford, England: Oxford University Press.

Jacobson, J. M., & Jones, A. L. (2010). Standards for the EAP profession: Isn't it time we all started speaking the same language? *Journal of Workplace Behavioral Health, 25,* 1–18. DOI: 10.1080/15555240903538741

Johnson, J. D. (2008). Employee assistance programs: Sources of assistance relations to inputs and outputs. *Journal of Workplace Behavioral Health, 23,* 263–282. DOI: 10.1080/15555240802242866

Kanter, R. M. (1977). *Work and family in the United States: A critical review and agenda for research and policy.* New York: Sage.

Kirby, E. L. (2003). Bob's dilemma. In J. Keyton & P. Shockley-Zalabak (Eds.), *Organizational communication: Understanding communication processes* (pp. 287–294). Los Angeles, CA: Roxbury.

Kirby, E. L., Golden, A. G., Medved, C. E., Jorgenson, J., & Buzzanell, P. M. (2003). An organizational communication challenge to the discourse of work and family research: From problematics to empowerment. In P. J. Kalbfleishch (Ed.), *Communication yearbook 27* (pp. 1–43). Mahwah, NJ: Erlbaum.

Kirby, E. L., & Krone, K. J. (2002). "The policy exists but you can't really use it": Communication and the structuration of work-life policies. *Journal of Applied Communication Research, 30,* 50–77. DOI: 10.1080/00909880216577

Kirby, E. L., Wieland, S., & McBride, M. C. (2006). Work-life conflict. In J. Oetzel & S. Ting-Toomey (Eds.), *Handbook of conflict communication* (pp. 327–357). Thousand Oaks, CA: Sage.

Lips-Wiersma, M. (2002). The influence of spiritual "meaning-making" on career behavior. *The Journal of Management Development, 21,* 497–520.

Mattson, M., Clair, R. P., Sanger, P. A. C., & Kunkel, A. D. (2000). A feminist reframing of stress. In P. M. Buzzanell (Ed.), *Rethinking organizational & managerial communication from feminist perspectives* (pp. 157–174). Thousand Oaks, CA: Sage.

May, S. K. (1998). Health care and the medicalization of work: Policy implications. In *Marriner S. Eccles Policy Yearbook* (pp. 6–35). Salt Lake City: University of Utah.

Medved, C. E., Brogan, S. M., McClanahan, A. M., Morris, J. F., & Shepherd, G. J. (2006). Family and work socializing communication: Messages, gender, and ideological implications. *Journal of Family Communication, 6,* 161–180. DOI: 10.1207/s15327698jfc0603_1

Medved, C. E., & Kirby, E. L. (2005). Family CEOs: A feminist analysis of corporate mothering discourses. *Management Communication Quarterly, 18,* 435–478. DOI: 10.1177/0893318904273690

Miller, K. I., Considine, J., & Garner, J. (2007). "Let me tell you about my job": Exploring the terrain of emotion in the workplace. *Management Communication Quarterly, 20,* 231–260. DOI: 10.1177/089331890629358

Montoya, Y. J., & Trethewey, A. (2009). Rethinking good work: Developing sustainable employees and workplaces (white paper). Retrieved from http://humancommunication.clas.asu.edu/aboutus/Rethinking%20Work%20DevelopingaSustainableSelf.pdf

Murphy, L. R., Hurrell, J. J., & Quick, J. C. (1992). Work and well-being: Where do we go from here? In J. C. Quick, L. R. Murphy, & J. J. Hurrell, Jr. (Eds.), *Stress and well-being at work: Assessments and interventions for occupational mental health* (pp. 331–347). Washington, DC: American Psychological Association.

Newton, T. (1995). *"Managing" stress: Emotion and power at work.* London: Sage.

Parker, R. M., Ratzan, S. C., & Lurie, N. (2003). Health literacy: A policy challenge for advancing high-quality health care. *Health Affairs, 22,* 147. Retrieved from https://www.sicklecelldisease.net:4430/cbo/documents/v22n4s26.pdf

Parrott, R. (2004). Emphasizing "communication" in health communication. *Journal of Communication, 54,* 751–787. Retrieved from http://login.ezproxy1.lib.asu.edu/login?url=http://search.ebscohost.com.ezproxy1.lib.asu.edu/login.aspx?direct=true&db=ufh&AN=15413351&site=ehost-live

Parrott, R., & Lemieux, R. (2003). When the worlds of work and wellness collide: The role of familial support on skin cancer control. *Journal of Family Communication, 3,* 95–106. DOI: 10.1207/S15327698JFC0302_02

Pelletier, K. R. (1984). *Healthy people in unhealthy places: Stress and fitness at work.* New York: Merloyd Lawrence.

Pennebaker, J. W. (1990). *Opening up: The healing power of confiding in others.* New York: Morrow.

Pennebaker, J. W. (Ed.). (1995). *Emotion, disclosure, and health.* Washington, DC: American Psychological Association.

Pohl, S. N., & Freimuth, V. S. (1983). Foods for health: Involving organizations in planned change. *Journal of Applied Communication Research, 11,* 17–27. DOI: 10.1080/00909888309365228

Pompe, J. C., & Sharar, D. A. (2008). Preparing for the challenges of the employee assistance research foundation: A response to Carl Tisone's call to action. *Journal of Workplace Behavioral Health, 23,* 217–226. DOI: 10.1080/15555240802241587

Poverny, L. M., & Dodd, S. J. (2000). Differential patterns of EAP service utilization: A nine year follow-up study of faculty and staff. *Employee Assistance Quarterly, 15,* 29–42. DOI: 10.1300/J022v15n04_03

Rafaeli, A., & Sutton, R. I. (1987). Expression of emotion as part of the work role. *Academy of Management Review, 12,* 23–37. Retrieved from http://www.jstor.org/stable/257991

Ratzan, S. C., & Parker, R. M. (2006). Health literacy—Identification and response. *Journal of Health Communication, 11,* 713–715. DOI: 10.1080/10810730601031090

Rogers, E. M. (1996). The field of health communication today: An up-to-date report. *Journal of Health Communication, 1,* 25–41. DOI: 10.1080/108107396128202

Rose, R. A. (2006). A proposal for integrating structuration theory with coordinated management of meaning theory. *Communication Studies, 57,* 173–196. DOI: 10.1080/10510970600666867

Schuler, S., & Sypher, B. D. (2000). Seeking emotional labor: When managing the heart enhances work experience. *Management Communication Quarterly, 14,* 50–89. DOI: 10.1177/0893318900141003

Scott, C., & Myers, K. K. (2005). The socialization of emotion: Learning emotion management at the fire station. *Journal of Applied Communication Research, 33,* 67–92. DOI: 10.1080/00909880042000318521

Shain, M., & Groenveld, J. (1980). *Employee-assistance programs: Philosophy, theory, and practice.* Lexington, MA: Lexington.

Shar, D. A., & Hertenstein, E. (2005). Perspectives on the integration of employee assistance programs and work-life programs: A survey of key informants in the EAP field. *Journal of Workplace Behavioral Health, 21,* 53–65. DOI: 10.1300/J490V21n01_05

Sias, P. M., & Cahill, D. J. (1998). From coworkers to friends: The development of peer friendships in the workplace. *Western Journal of Communication, 62,* 273–299. DOI: 10.1080/10570319809374611

Stainbrook, G. L., & Green, L. W. (1989). Measurement and evaluation methods for worksite stress-management programs. In L. R. Murphy & T. F. Schonfeld (Eds.), *Stress management in work settings* (pp. 101–134). New York: Praeger.

Thompson, D. A., & Swihart, D. L. (2008). University of Arizona life and work connections: A synergistic strategy for maximizing whole-person productivity over the employees' life-cycle/work-cycle. *Journal of Workplace Behavioral Health, 22,* 145–160. DOI: 10.1300/J490v22n02_10

Tracy, S. J. (2005). Locking up emotion: Moving beyond dissonance for understanding emotion labor discomfort. *Communication Monographs, 72,* 261–283. DOI: 10.1080/03637750500206474

Tracy, S. J., & Rivera K. D. (2010). Endorsing equity and applauding stay-at-home moms: How male voices on work-life reveal aversive sexism and flickers of transformation. *Management Communication Quarterly, 24,* 3–43. DOI: 10.1177/0893318909352248

Tracy, S. J., & Trethewey, A. (2005). Fracturing the real-self fake-self dichotomy: Moving toward crystallized organizational identities. *Communication Theory, 15,* 168–195. DOI: 10.1111/j.1468-2885.2005.tb00331.x

Trethewey, A., Tracy, S. J., & Alberts, J. K. (2006). Crystallizing frames for work-life. *The Electronic Journal of Communication, 16*(3/4). Retrieved from http://www.cios.org/www/ejc/v16n34.htm

Turvey, M. D., & Olson, D. H. (2006). *Marriage and family wellness: Corporate America's business?* Minneapolis, MN: Live Innovations.

U.S. Bureau of Labor Statistics. (2009). *Access to wellness and employee assistance programs in the U.S.* Washington, DC: U.S. Department of Labor. Retrieved from www.bls.gov/opub/cwc/cm20090416ar01pl.htm

Ward, J., & Winstanley, D. (2003). The absent presence: Negative space within discourse and the construction of minority sexual identity in the workplace. *Human Relations, 56,* 1255–1280. DOI: 10.1177/00187267035610005

Wharton, A. S. (1993). The affective consequences of service work: Managing emotions on the job. *Work and Occupation, 20,* 205–232. DOI: 10.1177/0730888493020002004

Zoller, H. M. (2003). Working out: Managerialism in workplace health promotion. *Management Communication Quarterly, 17,* 171–205. DOI: 10.1177/0893318903253003

Zoller, H. M. (2004). Manufacturing health: Employee perspectives on problematic outcomes in a workplace health promotion initiative. *Western Journal of Communication, 68,* 278–301. DOI: 10.1080/10570310409374802

Zook, E. G. (1994). Embodied health and constitutive communication: Toward an authentic conceptualization of health communication. In S. A. Deetz (Ed.), *Communication Yearbook* (Vol. 17, pp. 378–387). Thousand Oaks, CA: Sage.

9

RELATIONSHIP BUILDING AND SITUATIONAL PUBLICS

Theoretical Approaches Guiding Today's Health Public Relations

Linda Aldoory and Lucinda Austin

Health public relations is defined for this chapter as the strategic planning, implementation, and evaluation of communication tactics for purposes of influencing health attitudes, knowledge, behaviors, and decision making. While typically the practice of public relations is constrained within an organizational domain, Bardhan (2002) asserted that today's global health arena has reconstituted health public relations as any planned communicative action that aims to develop mutually beneficial relationships between multiple stakeholders (p. 224). Some relevant stakeholders include national governments, international health organizations, pharmaceutical companies, activist groups, health service facilities, people living with a health risk or disease, and family and friends.

The scope of tactics used in health public relations is quite broad, and the typical ones are topics of other chapters in this *Handbook*: mass media campaigns; media advocacy; social marketing; advertising; community relations; and worksite/employee safety campaigns. Therefore, for this chapter, instead of focusing on any one tactic, we describe two theoretical approaches that have guided scholarship and practice in public relations and that apply to today's health public relations. The two theories—organization–public relationship theory and the situational theory of publics—are empirically and heuristically strong and have contributed to research in health public relations over the last 10 years.

Health public relations became a professional label in the 1960s when hospitals and pharmaceutical companies began competing for patients and using communication tactics such as media campaigns and community relations to boost their reputations (Berkowitz, 2007; Gordon & Kelly, 1999). However, the profession has expanded exponentially and is now part of government, business, and consumer contexts (Henderson, 2005); subsequently, health care has been recognized as one of the predominant areas of work in public relations today (Kirdar, 2007; Rotarius, Wan, & Liberman, 2007). Due to the surge in health costs, government attention toward health policy, and consumer advocacy and activism, the need for strategic public relations in the public health sector "has never been higher" (Springston & Weaver-Lariscy, 2005, p. 218). Scholars and practitioners have had to revise how public relations is defined and conducted within health organizations. In particular, a two-way paradigm of communication emerged, and health public relations turned to segmenting and addressing publics according to public needs and building long-term relationships with these publics.

This chapter begins with an explanation of the two-way paradigm that has influenced much of public relations today and that offers context for the development of the two theories highlighted here. We then describe organization–public relationship theory and the situational theory of publics. For both theoretical approaches, we indicate the research in health public relations that has applied the theory and real-world cases of the theory in use. The chapter concludes with some suggestions for the future that would integrate the theoretical approaches into global and digital contexts, which are redefining the field of health public relations.

A Two-Way Paradigm for Health Public Relations

In the 1980s, when consumers became increasingly aware of governmental and corporate failures in communication, a cultural and ideological shift began in public relations (Ferguson, 1984; Ledingham, 2008). The field understood the role of participatory, engaged communication in public relations effectiveness. When organizations collaborated with publics and included negotiation and compromise in their communication objectives, they were more successful at accomplishing their goals.

Ultimately, a two-way paradigm for communication emerged as the desired perspective for public relations (Berkowitz, 2007). The two-way paradigm in public relations considers public needs as much as organizational goals. The only satisfying end state, according to a two-way paradigm, is one that is mutually beneficial for both organization and stakeholders; thus, dynamic and ethical communication takes precedence.

Importantly, a two-way paradigm does not suggest solely relying on two-way communication methods (Berkowitz, 2007; Grunig, 2001). This worldview considers various one-way and two-way tactics of communication, appropriate for reaching short-term objectives and long-term goals, all within a larger view toward helping build relationships with stakeholders over time (L. A. Grunig et al., 2002). Traditional "one-way" public information, persuasion messages, and promotional tools are used. Organizations that function with a two-way worldview for their public relations integrate collaborative decision-making and compromise with persuasion and public information goals. As Grunig (2001) put it, "If persuasion occurs, the public should be just as likely to persuade the organization's management to change attitudes or behavior as the organization is likely to change the public's attitudes or behavior" (p. 13).

Within the two-way paradigm, health public relations functions as long-term strategic planning and management of communication based on research with stakeholders (Grunig, 1992, 2001; Grunig & Hunt, 1984; Kelly, Thompson, & Waters, 2006). However, researchers have acknowledged the role of one-way communication (Bachand, 1960; Derryberry, 1950; Falck, 1960; Getting, 1949; Hetherington, Ekachai, & Parkinson, 2001; Tiboni, 1965). Kelly et al. (2006), for example, supported using a two-way paradigm of public relations for hospices and physicians to improve end-of-life care. The authors cautioned though that the two-way paradigm "does not promise to resolve all conflicts," but "both parties at least engage in a dialogue" (p. 610). Bardhan (2002) stated that the "global discourse" about AIDS/HIV is "leaning toward" the two-way paradigm, and that co-participation is not changing the stakeholders, but is allowing the powerful stakeholders to "be more inclusive of the lived experiences of those most affected by the pandemic" (p. 226). With AIDS/HIV, Bardhan argued, this is accomplished by identifying points of conflict between stakeholders and by working toward communicative relationship building and maintenance.

Organization–Public Relationship Theory

Organization–public relationship (OPR) theory emerged out of the evolutionary turn in public relations toward a two-way paradigm of communication (J. E. Grunig, 2000; L. A. Grunig et al., 2002; Ledingham, 2003, 2008). The main theoretical premise is that an organization will increase the likelihood of achieving certain goals if its public relations efforts emphasize building and maintaining mutually beneficial relationships with publics (Bruning & Ledingham, 2000; Ledingham, 2003; Ledingham & Bruning, 2001; Wise, 2007). Mutual benefit can include "economic, social, political, and/or cultural benefits to all parties involved, and is characterized by mutual positive regard" (Ledingham & Bruning, 1998, p. 62).

Just in the last 10 years, OPR theory has become one of the most investigated areas within public relations, and scholars in health public relations have applied it to health care settings (Berkowitz, 2007; Lucarelli-Dimmick, Bell, Burgiss, & Ragsdale, 2000; Springston & Weaver-Lariscy, 2005; Wise, 2001, 2007). Research has illuminated several criteria for building and maintaining good relationships. These criteria have helped describe (a) antecedents to relationships, (b) maintenance strategies, (c) outcomes or qualities of good relationships, and (d) different types of relationships (Bruning, DeMiglio, & Embry, 2006).

Few studies have examined antecedents to organization–public relationships, and the work that has been done has focused on reputation and credibility as key factors for organizations. Yang (2007) found that favorable organizational reputation was significantly related to positive relationship building efforts by publics. Other antecedents he found relevant are prior personal experience with the other party involved, familiarity with the other party, and former experiences communicating with each other. Kim (2007) studied internal publics and found that organizational structure and perceived organizational justice influenced employee–organization relationships.

Maintenance strategies are those that help manage the dialectical tensions between parties in a relationship. The available evidence suggests that these strategies are the most important elements in managing relationship tensions. The strategies include access to organizational representatives and to leaders of engaged publics; openness and willingness to disclose opinions as well as facts; assurances of legitimacy and commitment to maintain the relationship; networking with similar third-party groups by all parties in the relationship; and the sharing of tasks (L. A. Grunig et al., 2002; Hon & Grunig, 1999; Ki & Hon, 2006). In the context of conflict resolution, stakeholders should seek out common interests and seek to solve problems together through joint compromise (L. A. Grunig et al., 2002).

The outcomes and qualities of relationships often depend on the type or nature of the relationship between stakeholders. Grunig and Huang (2000) distinguished between symbolic relationships, which are communication driven, and behavioral relationships, which are action-based. In addition, studies have found exchange relationships, where one party engages in a relationship only to gain a benefit; and communal relationships, where both parties provide benefit to the other out of concern for the other's welfare (Hon & Brunner, 2002). The degree to which a public perceives a communal relationship with an organization is a key measure of satisfaction, and hence, public relations effectiveness (L. A. Grunig et al., 2002). In addition to satisfaction, there are three outcomes that are considered relevant to understanding a good relationship. These outcomes are (a) trust, which includes several dimensions, such as perceived integrity, dependability, and perceived competence; (b) commitment, which is the extent to which the parties expend energy on the relationship; and (c) control mutuality, the degree of power that each party has and other parties agree to (Grunig & Huang, 2000; Ledingham, 2003, 2008). Yang and Grunig (2005) found empirical support for the assumption that these specific qualities of a relationship have a direct effect on positive evaluations of organizational performance.

OPR Theory in Health Contexts

Several authors have espoused the value of OPR theory for health public relations, as the theory explains how two-way communication helps achieve long-term health outcomes (Berkowitz, 2007; Lucarelli-Dimmick et al., 2000; Meath, 2006; Springston & Weaver-Lariscy, 2005; Wise, 2003, 2007, 2009). Muturi (2005) argued that current reproductive health campaigns in Africa have been unsuccessful and that OPR theory applied to the development and implementation of campaigns would improve chances for behavior change. In her research in Kenya, Muturi found that OPR theory contributed to community understanding and maintenance of newly adopted behaviors and practices regarding HIV/AIDS prevention.

The theoretical approach has also been useful for those who examine health corporations and hospitals. Lucarelli-Dimmick et al. (2000) examined the characteristics of OPR theory for physician–patient relationships and included a set of characteristics necessary for strong communication linkages: symmetry, intensity, frequency, duration, valence, and content. Guy, Williams, Aldridge, and Roggenkamp (2007) examined how public relations can build relationships between organ transplant organizations and hospitals: authors showed that interactions with publics were regular and consistent, and that the publics were involved in co-creating messages and methods to achieve mutual goals (p. 16). Finally, Wan and Schell (2007) examined types of relationships and measured whether a health corporation can build trust with its publics so that it will move from a symbolic relationship to a behavioral one. In a post-crisis scenario, authors found that a behavioral relationship is possible if publics initially trust the corporation and perceive their goals to be congruent with those of the organization. Springston and Weaver-Lariscy (2005) concluded that building positive relationships with stakeholders was one major element of effective public relations in public health.

Building Relationships by Hospital Public Relations

Hospital public relations—one of the oldest types of health public relations—offers a case context for how OPR theory can apply to the field. Most of the early literature in health public relations focused on hospital settings (Guy et al., 2007). Gordon and Kelly (1999) found that a typical public relations department for a hospital housed two to four people, and about half the departments in their survey had access to their hospital's CEO. Today, the increased competition among hospitals due to privatization and health costs has resulted in public relations becoming one of the most important activities for a hospital (Kirdar, 2007; Tengilimoglu, Yesiltas, Kisa, & Dziegielewski, 2007). One study indicated that public relations activities were a crucial factor in determining consumers' hospital choice (Tengilimoglu et al., 2007). Specifically, hospitals are required to use public relations for purposes of building enduring relationships with key publics in order to maintain a consumer base.

Hospital public relations departments that practice two-way communication and plan strategically are more likely to contribute to organizational effectiveness and to be viewed as being valuable to the hospital (Gordon & Kelly, 1999). These departments focus on relationship building, which benefits the hospital when controversy affects the organization. More recently, Berkowitz (2007) showed how hospitals have used the Internet for purposes of building relationships with key publics. The author emphasized blogging, which not only encourages dialogue among key publics, but more importantly, also allows public problems to emerge and be addressed in real time. Guy et al. (2007) supported hospital executives using two-way communication because it achieves "better health outcomes for the communities they serve" (p. 16) and places the focus on the community publics rather than just on the organizational goals. This focus on publics is uniquely situated within the scholarship of public relations and is the emphasis of one of the most useful theories in the field, that of the situational theory of publics.

The Situational Theory of Publics

The situational theory of publics (STP) explains why publics communicate and when they are most likely to do so. Grunig (1989, 1992; Grunig & Hunt, 1984) spent three decades testing STP in various professional settings using several topics of public concern. Vasquez and Taylor (2001) labeled Grunig's work in this arena "the most systematic investigation of social-psychological concepts for segmentation of a public" (p. 143).

The situational theory is based on the conceptualization of a public provided by Dewey (1927). A public is a group of people who share an interest in an organization, its functioning, and its impacts on their welfare (Guy et al., 2007). A public forms expectations about an organization, and may have members who communicate with an organization, who demonstrate varying degrees of activity or passivity, and who interact with others concerning their relationship with the organization (Guy et al., 2007). Ultimately, a public is a type of stakeholder group that has the power to potentially change or constrain an organization. Public relations practitioners identify and segment publics to increase the possibility of achieving communication goals and building mutually beneficial relationships with targeted groups important to the organization (Kim, Ni, & Sha, 2008).

However, members of a public could be unaware that they share a certain issue with others, even though the potential is always there for them to organize and actively communicate with each other and with organizations. From an organizational point of view, this potential for public energy and expression can be advantageous or disadvantageous depending on organizational goals. For example, a pharmaceutical corporation might communicate in ways that are intended to prevent a public from becoming active and protesting the company's products. On the other hand, if awareness of a health risk is a goal, then understanding how to move a public from being unaware to actively seeking information would benefit an organization as well as the public in question. Conceptualizing publics as dynamic and contextual is a central premise to the STP.

Three Key Factors

The theory suggests that three factors can influence whether a public passively processes information from a campaign or actively seeks further information and is more likely to change attitudes or behaviors resulting from the information. The three factors are problem recognition, constraint recognition, and level of involvement (Grunig, 1997). Problem recognition is the extent to which someone recognizes an issue as a problem to be considered or addressed. If problem recognition occurs, then people may either seek out reinforcing information or brand new data (Aldoory & Sha, 2007). Problem recognition, by means of attention gaining messages and tactics, tends to be the easiest of STP factors to achieve.

Constraint recognition is the extent to which individuals perceive barriers that inhibit their ability to move to action (Grunig, 1997). Perceived constraints could derive from everyday physical barriers in a person's life, such as lack of transportation to access health care or lack of technology in order to seek further information on the web. However, constraints might also derive from psychological and emotional sources. Low self-efficacy, for example, is a well-documented constraint to people increasing healthful behavior. Grunig and Ipes (1983) concluded, "For a campaign to move people to develop organized cognitions and perhaps to change their behavior, it must show people how they can remove constraints to their personally doing anything about the problem" (p. 51).

Unlike constraint recognition and problem recognition, level of involvement is influenced less by external cues from communication efforts. Level of involvement is a measure of how personally relevant a particular problem is, and how emotionally connected to a problem a person perceives her- or himself to be. When involvement is high, people actively seek out information and pay attention to information that comes to them with little effort, which they process passively. When involvement is low, people may still process information passively if they have time available, but will not engage in intentional searches for information relevant to the situation (Grunig, 1997). The way that involvement is conceptualized here is unique in relation to other theories in marketing and psychology. Instead of involvement being a component of a message to be manipulated, involvement is a psychological trait within individuals that varies according to an individual's former experiences, family history, or socialization (Aldoory & Sha, 2007). Involvement is particularly relevant in the context of health and in the face of traumatic personal and familial experiences with illness and disease. For example, an individual whose mother died of lung cancer might find messages about tobacco control personally salient even though he or she never smoked cigarettes.

Communication Behavior

The three factors are situational because they describe perceptions that publics have of specific situations that might be problematic or unresolved and may lead to conflict. The theory predicts communication behavior as a response to the three factors described earlier. Because situations, problems, and issues change over time, the theory maintains, publics communicate differently in different situations. A public may seek information to further understand a problem and communicate actively—this involves intentional and often strategic scanning of the environment for messages about the specified topic. For example, individuals may use traditional media, the Internet, and friends to gather information about global warming in order to become more personally active in communicating on their community listservs and with neighbors about how to address the problem at a local level. Information seeking leads people to develop more organized cognitions and stronger attitudes regarding the issue. Otherwise, a public may rely on information processing—the unplanned discovery of a message followed by continued processing of it (Grunig, 1997). Information processing occurs when people pay attention to a message and absorb some of it even when not intentionally doing so. A public often seeks information through a variety of specialized media and interpersonal contacts, whereas a public more likely processes information only from mass media (Grunig, 1980). These two types of communication behavior have effects, in turn, on cognitions, attitudes, and individual and collective behaviors (Grunig, 1997).

Research has indicated that high problem recognition and low constraint recognition increase both active information seeking and passive information processing (Aldoory, 2001; Hamilton, 1992). Level of involvement increases information seeking, but it has less effect on information processing (Grunig, 1997). Stated differently, people seldom seek information about situations that do not involve them. Yet, they will randomly process information about low-involvement situations, especially if they also recognize the situation as problematic. Because people participate more actively in information seeking than in information processing, people communicating actively develop more organized cognitions, are more likely to have attitudes about a situation, and more often engage in a behavior that will affect the situation (Grunig, 1992; Grunig & Ipes, 1983).

Segmenting by Type of Publics

The situational theory of publics is useful because it helps health practitioners segment publics in ways that allow for greater communication effects. There are four general types of publics: active, aware, latent, and non-public (Grunig, 1997). Non-publics are not organized in any meaningful way with respect to the issue at hand. They are not involved or at risk with the particular issue. At the other extreme are active publics, which have low constraint recognition, high problem recognition, and high involvement. This type actively seeks information about a health problem, potentially shares information, and could become activist. Active publics can be beneficial or detrimental to an organization depending on goals. On one hand, an active public could advocate for an organization's efforts and act as promoter of the health messages that an organization is espousing. On the other hand, an active public could constrain an organization by building resistance to its work and facilitating protest against it.

The aware public has high problem recognition and high involvement as well, but also high constraint recognition. If their perceived constraints are either reduced or eliminated, aware publics could become active publics. Sometimes, health public relations efforts focus on aware publics so they become active: participatory approaches that attempt to empower publics lead them to seek out useful information and "let their voice be heard" (Servaes & Malikhao, 2010). In their examination of health advocacy, Servaes and Malikhao suggested that public relations not just attempt to increase problem recognition and lower constraints, but that it also help publics to comprehend the health problem, and maintain control of the health problem over time. In the context of HIV and AIDS, for example, an aware public might become active after gaining knowledge of the virus and disease and the ways in which its impact has changed over time in different audiences.

Latent publics have low problem recognition, but their level of involvement is still moderate to high. Issues do not prompt their interests until they discover and acknowledge the personal connections. Latent publics are often designated as targets of health campaigns (Grunig, 1989; Grunig, Clifford, Richburg, & White, 1988). At-risk publics fall in this category: those that have a high level of involvement due to a predisposed condition or engagement in risky behavior. The public may be latent in that it is unaware of its connections to the health threat. Health campaigns and messages would be designed to increase their problem recognition and lower their perceived constraints. In other cases, however, corporations might wish to communicate in ways that prevent a latent public from becoming aware and active. In one case, Howell and Miller (2006) found that a major asbestos producing company worked to keep the media from asking questions and confined the story of asbestos poisoning so that publics would not become active.

Hot Issue Publics. Many studies have discovered a hot issue public, a type of active public that is pertinent to health public relations (Ristino, 2007). A hot issue public forms around a single issue and has little interest in related issues. Hot issue publics typically result from extensive media coverage of a single health crisis, and the new public usually involves nearly everyone in the population (Grunig, 1997). One illustration of a U.S. hot issue public is the one that formed from the intense media coverage of the 2009 H1N1 flu outbreak and vaccine availability. In addition to the news of incidence and individual cases, state and local governments and health agencies promoted preventive health information as well as locations for vaccine clinics. The hot issue public comprised Americans who had high involvement and high problem recognition, but then reacted to the public relations messages based on varying levels of constraint recognition. Those with low constraint recognition were actively communicating about locations for local vaccination clinics and were traveling miles to get their children vaccinated. Those with high constraint recognition perceived limited access or time to acquire vaccines.

Researchers have studied hot issue publics involved in the energy shortage, air pollution, and deregulation of natural gas (Grunig, 1983); toxic waste and acid rain (Grunig, 1989); the Clinton health care initiative (Grunig, 1997); and a predicted earthquake (Major, 1993). More recently, Ristino (2007) illustrated a case study of the emergence of a hot issue public that affected the Rhode Island Department of Health. The state and local media covered the news of two deaths among children who had contracted meningitis, and, as Ristino (2007) described it, "panic spread across the state." At one urgent health care center, parents who were trying to get their children vaccinated, rioted. The overall incidence and severity of meningitis cases in the state at that time were not enough to warrant mass immunization, but nonetheless, the health department launched a free program for purposes of settling the panic among the hot issue public. A multi-channel public relations campaign was implemented to reduce the anxiety among state residents and to eliminate the pressure on physician offices and other health service settings. Evaluation of the public relations campaign indicated that more than 160,000 children and young adults were immunized and that awareness and recall of key campaign messages were high (Ristino, 2007). The body of research on hot issue publics has indicated that when the initial, heightened media and public relations attention goes away, the hot issue public dissipates, yet remains in a primed cognitive and emotional state. Thus, if there is a second wave of media attention on the same issue, this public is more likely to jump to an active phase than remain aware or latent.

Media as Public. As with all public relations, working with media is a primary responsibility in health public relations, and current research suggests that health journalists are aware or active publics (Brunner & Bruner, 2010; Cho & Cameron, 2007; Comrie, 1997; Len-Rios, Hinnant, & Park, 2009; Lumpkins, Bae, & Cameron, 2010). Servaes and Malikhao (2010), for example, argued that media are a public that should be activated, to build public support and pressure for any necessary policy decisions. According to Springston and Weaver-Lariscy (2007), the aware and active nature of media is not only because of the professional role of journalism, but because of the expert and detailed knowledge in health and medicine that is necessary for health journalists and health public relations professionals. Recent research has shown that health public relations practitioners who build close relationships with media are recognized as experts and are contacted more frequently by reporters (Cho, 2006; Cho & Cameron, 2007; Tanner, 2004). In another study, local TV health reporters stated that most of their story ideas were derived from their personal contacts with health public relations practitioners (Tanner, 2004).

The Situational Theory in Health Contexts

Over the last few years, the situational theory of publics has been applied to health contexts, and evidence supports the theory's ability to understand strategic publics of health communication efforts (Aldoory, 2001; Dimitrov, 2008; Grunig & Ipes, 1983; Muturi, 2005; Pavlik, 1988; Springston, 1997; Thomas, Smith, & Turcotte, 2009). One early study found that level of involvement and constraint recognition mediated between a heart health campaign and its resulting increases in heart health knowledge (Pavlik, 1988). More recently, Thomas et al. (2009) analyzed a campaign that distinguished between latent and active publics of health practitioners and at-risk citizens, in order to increase information seeking related to risks to radioactive iodine in the environment. Their communication messages successfully revived interest among community members "who had become apathetic" and increased the number of people who sought information about their potential risk of exposure. Wise (2009) examined international health agencies as aware and active publics and described their efforts in health diplomacy. He found that the public relations function was in the "unique position" to assist with international collaboration for purposes of improving global health outcomes (p. 128). In general, the research on health and the situational theory of publics shows that health messages can be developed to raise problem recognition or lower constraint recognition or both, but publics should be categorized by their level of involvement prior to campaign message design (Aldoory & Sha, 2007).

Aldoory (2001) examined women's level of involvement with health campaigns that the women found most relevant to their everyday lives: the campaigns addressed diabetes, heart disease, and eating disorders. The women shared several antecedent factors that influenced their involvement: source preference, self-identity, a consciousness of personal health, and cognitive complexity of message content. Another study that focused on women found that perceptions about mammography screening related to level of involvement and constraint recognition (Springston, 1997).

Communicating about Pandemic Flu Using the Situational Theory

The U.S. Department of Health and Human Services' (USDHHS, 2007) pandemic influenza preparedness campaign, a "Symphony of Encouragement," highlights a collaborative public relations initiative that utilized the situational theory of publics to develop distinctive messages for different publics (Ogilvy Public Relations, 2009; Weinberg, 2008). As the potential of pandemic influenza became more realistic but the severity of such an outbreak was unknown, USDHHS saw the increasing importance of encouraging personal preparedness. A national communication strategy was developed to empower community leaders not traditionally prepared for health emergencies to engage their communities in pandemic influenza preparedness.

USDHHS and Ogilvy Public Relations used formative research to segment community leaders by type of public. In particular, USDHHS desired community leaders who already had high involvement and medium to high problem recognition, but potentially had constraints, such as lack of knowledge about how to prepare and lack of efficacy in their perceived ability to promote preparedness. Four priority groups of community leaders were identified that were concerned about the issue but not yet actively engaged in encouraging community preparedness (aware publics): health care providers, faith-based leaders, business employers and human resource managers, and other local community leaders (USDHHS, 2007).

Focus groups and interviews were then conducted to further examine problem recognition, level of involvement, and constraint recognition among the participants representing the four aware publics. In a first phase of research, community leaders' perceptions of pandemic influenza and their willingness and ability to take an active role in pandemic flu preparedness for their constituents were evaluated. A second round of research tested specific messages and materials about pandemic influenza preparedness that these publics might receive, encouraging them to participate and assisting them in educating community members. Many of the community leaders expressed low self-efficacy regarding how they could have a role in preparedness. They needed more information to increase their problem recognition and lower their constraints before they reached out to their community members. Individuals felt they would be more encouraged to be a part of this effort if others like them were also involved.

Using this research, a Pandemic Flu Leadership Forum was convened with leaders from the four groups. The forum featured information about preparedness and enumerated the ways in which these individuals could have a collaborative role with USDHHS and others in their own groups or groups with a similar cause. Before the forum, a participatory blog titled the "Pandemic Flu Leadership Blog" was created to foster discussion and generate interest online (USDHHS, 2007). Ogilvy PR and USDHHS undertook additional efforts for alliance building and development of collateral materials. A large majority of the desired participants attended the Leadership Forum, and the leadership blog generated strong interest (Ogilvy Public Relations, 2009). Ultimately, Ogilvy PR and USDHHS exceeded their goals and were able to negotiate functional partnerships with empowered community leaders who engaged their communities in pandemic influenza preparedness.

Implications for the Future

This chapter focused on how public relations can contribute to health outcomes by framing communication within a participative, relational context and by segmenting publics according to their needs and abilities to actively communicate and change their behavior. Two theoretical approaches, organization–public relationship theory and the situational theory of publics, have been utilized in health public relations research and practice to impact organizational goals. However, the potential for these two theories to contribute to health public relations is much greater than realized, and certain trends in health will allow for future application.

For example, one potential area for theoretical growth is the growing prevalence of research on the Internet and digital health (see chapter 6, this volume). Scholars have been studying the effectiveness of digital communication on improving health outcomes, and have found that the impact of the digital landscape on individual and community health is significant (Berkowitz, 2007). At this time, there has been limited research on how organization–public relationship theory and the situational theory of publics can apply to digital health communications. However, for organizations, the cost advantages of the Internet for global communication outweighs most other traditional forms of health communication, and consumer publics are becoming more global and aware due to their ever growing

Internet presence and activity. These factors will lead organizations to consider the participatory strength of the Internet for relationship building needs. Berkowitz (2007) found that blogs and podcasts offer a method for dialogue and encouraging active engagement in health for global publics. The situational theory of publics will help segment online publics by their level of digital activity and communication as well as their level of traditional communication activity. Constraint recognition may end up focusing on access restrictions to technology and the web. Berkowitz (2007) concluded that the Internet "...opens avenues of possibilities for better understanding of how to build relationships with key constituencies and for the institution to respond in a proactive fashion" (p. 127).

A second area for theoretical application is in global health communication and international collaboration among nations and health organizations. Indigenous social, cultural, and economic factors of different countries moderate the communication interventions often planned by international organizations. Muturi (2005) acknowledged that a participatory paradigm has already changed international health communication, and many campaigns involve community members in the problem definition, data collection, and implementation processes (p. 82). However, the participatory approach, while "a big leap," has not overruled the traditional approach that aims at reaching a wide audience through one-way campaigns and media (Muturi, 2005, p. 83). The organization–public relationship theory would take into consideration indigenous cultural factors and empower local community leaders to make communication decisions. Furthermore, the theory suggests a long-term process in relationship building and maintenance, and health behavior change seldom occurs in the short term (Muturi, 2005). Wise (2009) envisioned how public relations can contribute to the burgeoning field of health diplomacy. Health diplomacy attempts to improve global health while maintaining and strengthening international relations between the U.S. and other countries. Understanding level of involvement and constraint recognition among countries and international organizations can assist with health diplomacy goals. Finally, Bardhan (2002) suggested that there has been a lack of cohesiveness and clarity in the direction of global planning to address the AIDS/HIV pandemic. A relational perspective that involves the private sector and local organizations is necessary in addressing today's pandemic, and OPR theory considers local context and its impact on health initiatives (Bardhan, 2002). If today's global health arena has reconstituted health public relations as any planned communicative action that aims to develop mutually beneficial relationships between multiple stakeholders, then understanding the theoretical approaches to building those relationships is critical for tomorrow's health public relations.

References

Aldoory, L. (2001). Making health communications meaningful for women: Factors that influence involvement and the situational theory of publics. *Journal of Public Relations Research, 13,* 163–185.

Aldoory, L., & Sha, B.-L. (2007). The situational theory of publics: Practical applications, methodological challenges, and theoretical horizons. In E. L. Toth (Ed.), *The future of excellence in public relations and communication management: Challenges for the next generation* (pp. 339–355). Mahwah, NJ: Erlbaum.

Bachand, A. (1960). Health departments and their public relations. *Canadian Journal of Public Health, 51,* 272–277.

Bardhan, N. R. (2002). Accounts from the field: A public relations perspective on global AIDS/HIV. *Journal of Health Communication, 7,* 221–244.

Berkowitz, E. N. (2007). The evolution of public relations and the use of the Internet: The implications for health care organizations. *Health Marketing Quarterly, 24,* 117–130.

Brunner, B. R., & Bruner, L. R. B. (2010). 101 ways to improve health reporting: A comparison of the types and quality of health information in men's and women's magazines. *Public Relations Review, 36,* 84–86.

Bruning, S. D., DeMiglio, P. A., & Embry, K. (2006). Mutual benefit as outcome indicator: Factors influencing perceptions of benefit in organization–public relationships. *Public Relations Review, 32,* 33–40.

Bruning, S. D., & Ledingham, J. A. (2000). Perceptions of relationships and evaluations of satisfaction: An exploration of interaction. *Public Relations Review, 26,* 85–95.

Cho, S. (2006). The power of public relations in media relations: A national survey of health PR practitioners. *Journalism & Mass Communication Quarterly, 83,* 563–580.

Cho, S., & Cameron, G. T. (2007). Power to the people—Health PR people that is! *Public Relations Review, 33,* 175–183.

Comrie, M. (1997). Media tactics in New Zealand's Crown Health Enterprises. *Public Relations Review, 23,* 161–176.

Derryberry, M. (1950). Health education and public relations: A symposium. *American Journal of Public Health and the Nation's Health, 40,* 251–259.

Dewey, J. (1927). *The public and its problems.* Athens, OH: Swallow Press.

Dimitrov, R. (2008). Gender violence, fan activism and public relations in sport: The case of "Footy Fans Against Sexual Assault." *Public Relations Review, 34,* 90–98.

Falck, H. S. (1960). Public relations in public health. *The Canadian Nurse, 56,* 409–412.

Ferguson, M. A. (1984, August). *Building theory in public relations: Inter-organizational relationships.* Paper presented to the Association for Education in Journalism and Mass Communication, Gainesville, FL.

Getting, V. A. (1949). Public relations in public health. *American Journal of Public Health, 39,* 1561–1566.

Gordon, C. G., & Kelly, K. S. (1999). Public relations expertise and organizational effectiveness: A study of U.S. hospitals. *Journal of Public Relations Research, 11,* 143–165.

Grunig, J. E. (1980). Communication of scientific information to nonscientists. In B. Dervin & M. J. Voigt (Eds.), *Progress in communication sciences* (Vol. 2, pp. 167–214). Norwood, NJ: Ablex.

Grunig, J. E. (1983). Communication behaviors and attitudes of environmental publics: Two studies. *Journalism Monographs, 81,* 1–47.

Grunig, J. E. (1989). Sierra club study shows who become activists. *Public Relations Review, 15,* 3–24.

Grunig, J. E. (Ed.). (1992). *Excellence in public relations and communication management.* Hillsdale, NJ: Erlbaum.

Grunig, J. E. (1997). A situational theory of publics: Conceptual history, recent challenges and new research. In D. Moss, T. MacManus, & D. Verčič (Eds.), *Public relations research: An international perspective* (pp. 3–48). London: International Thomson Business Press.

Grunig, J. E. (2000). Collectivism, collaboration, and societal corporatism as core professional values in public relations. *Journal of Public Relations Research, 12,* 23–48.

Grunig, J. E. (2001). Two-way symmetrical public relations: Past, present, and future. In R. L. Heath (Ed.), *Handbook of public relations* (pp. 11–30). Thousand Oaks, CA: Sage.

Grunig, J. E., Clifford, L., Richburg, S. J., & White, T. J. (1988). Communication by agricultural publics: Internal and external orientations. *Journalism Quarterly, 65,* 26–38.

Grunig, J. E., & Huang, Y.-H. (2000). From organizational effectiveness to relationship indicators: Antecedents of relationships, public relations strategies, and relationship outcomes. In J. A. Ledingham & S. D. Bruning (Eds.), *Public relations as relationship management: A relational approach to public relations* (pp. 23–54). Mahwah, NJ: Erlbaum.

Grunig, J. E., & Hunt, T. (1984). *Managing public relations.* New York: Holt, Rinehart & Winston.

Grunig, J. E., & Ipes, D. A. (1983). The anatomy of a campaign against drunk driving. Public Relations Review, 9, 36–51.

Grunig, L. A., Grunig, J. E., & Dozier, D. M. (2002). Excellent public relations and effective organizations. Mahwah, NJ: Erlbaum.

Guy, B., Williams, D., Aldridge, A., & Roggenkamp, S. (2007). Approaches to organizing public relations functions in healthcare. *Health Marketing Quarterly, 24,* 1–18.

Hamilton, P. K. (1992). Grunig's situational theory: A replication, application, and extension. *Journal of Public Relations Research, 4,* 123–149.

Henderson, J. K. (2005). Evaluating public relations effectiveness in a health care setting. *Journal of Health and Human Services Administration, 28,* 282–322.

Hetherington, L. T., Ekachai, D., & Parkinson, M. G. (2001). Public relations in the health care industry. In R. L. Heath (Ed.), *Handbook of public relations* (pp. 571–581). Thousand Oaks, CA: Sage.

Hon, L. C., & Brunner, B. R. (2002). Measuring public relationships among students and administrators at the University of Florida. *Journal of Communication Management, 6,* 227–238.

Hon, L. C., & Grunig, J. E. (1999). *Guidelines for measuring relationships in public relations.* Gainesville, FL: Institute for Public Relations.

Howell, G., & Miller, R. (2006). Spinning out the asbestos agenda: How big business uses public relations in Australia. *Public Relations Review, 32,* 261–266.

Kelly, K. S., Thompson, M. F., & Waters, R. D. (2006). Improving the way we die: A coorientation study assessing agreement/disagreement in the organization-public relationship of hospices and physicians. *Journal of Health Communication, 11,* 607–627.

Ki, E.-J., & Hon, L. C. (2006). Relationship maintenance strategies on Fortune 500 company web sites. *Journal of Communication Management, 2,* 27–43.

Kim, H.-S. (2007). A multilevel study of antecedents and a mediator of employee-organization relationships. *Journal of Public Relations Research, 19,* 167–197.

Kim, J.-N., Ni, L., & Sha, B.-L. (2008). Breaking down the stakeholder environment: Explicating approaches to the segmentation of publics for public relations research. *Journalism and Mass Communication Quarterly, 85,* 751–768.

Kirdar, Y. (2007). The role of public relations for image creating in health services: A sample patient satisfaction survey. *Health Marketing Quarterly, 24,* 33–53.

Ledingham, J. A. (2003). Explicating relationship management as a general theory of public relations. *Journal of Public Relations Research, 15,* 181–198.

Ledingham, J. A. (2008). A chronology of organization-stakeholder relationships with recommendations concerning practitioner adoption of the relational perspective. *Journal of Promotion Management, 14,* 243–262.

Ledingham, J. A., & Bruning, S. D. (1998). Relationship management in public relations: Dimensions of an organization-public relationship. *Public Relations Review, 24,* 55–65.

Ledingham, J. A., & Bruning, S. D. (2001). Managing community relationships to maximize mutual benefit: Doing well by doing good. In R. L. Health (Ed.), *Handbook of public relations* (pp. 527–534). Thousand Oaks, CA: Sage.

Len-Rios, M. E., Hinnant, A., & Park, S.-A. (2009). Understanding how health journalists judge public relations sources: A rules theory approach. *Public Relations Review, 35,* 56–65.

Lucarelli-Dimmick, S., with T. E. Bell, S. G., Burgiss, & C. Ragsdale (2000). Relationship management: A new professional model. In J. A. Ledingham & S. D. Bruning (Eds.), *Public relations as relationship management: A relational approach to public relations* (pp. 117–136). Mahwah, NJ: Erlbaum.

Lumpkins, C. Y., Bae, J., & Cameron, G. T. (2010). Generating conflict for greater good: Utilizing contingency theory to assess Black and mainstream newspapers as public relations vehicles to promote better health among African Americans. *Public Relations Review, 36,* 73–77.

Major, A. M. (1993). Environmental concern and situational communication theory: Implications for communicating with environmental publics. *Journal of Public Relations Research, 5,* 251–268.

Meath, M. (2006). Taking time to care: Best practices in long-term care communications. *Corporate Communications, 11,* 336–352.

Muturi, N. W. (2005). Communication for HIV/AIDS prevention in Kenya: Social-cultural considerations. *Journal of Health Communication, 10,* 77–98.

Ogilvy Public Relations. (2009). *U.S. Department of Health and Human Services: HHS pandemic influenza.* Retrieved from http://www.ogilvypr.com/en/case-study/hhs-pandemic-influenza.

Pavlik, J.V. (1988). Audience complexity as a component of campaign planning. *Public Relations Review, 14,* 12–20.

Ristino, R. J. (2007). Communicating with external publics: Managing public opinion and behavior. *Health Marketing Quarterly, 24,* 55–80.

Rotarius, T., Wan, T. T. H., & Liberman, A. (2007). A typology of health marketing research methods—Combining public relations methods with organizational concern. *Health Marketing Quarterly, 24,* 201–211.

Servaes, J., & Malikhao, P. (2010). Advocacy strategies for health communication. *Public Relations Review, 36,* 42–49.

Springston, J. K. (1997). Application of public relations theory to breast cancer screening: A worksite study. In J. Biberman & A. Alkhafaji (Eds.), *Business research yearbook: Global business perspectives* (pp. 762–766). Slippery Rock, PA: International Academy of Business Disciplines.

Springston, J. K., & Weaver-Lariscy, R. (2005). Public relations effectiveness in public health institutions. *Journal of Health and Human Services Administration, 28,* 218–245.

Springston, J. K., & Weaver-Lariscy, R. (2007). Health crises and media relations: Relationship management-by-fire. *Health Marketing Quarterly, 24,* 81–96.

Tanner, A. H. (2004). Agenda building, source selection, and health news at local TV stations: A nationwide survey of local television health reporters. *Science Communication, 25*(4), 350–363.

Tengilimoglu, D., Yesiltas, M., Kisa, A., & Dziegielewski, S. F. (2007). The role of public relations activities in hospital choice. *Health Marketing Quarterly, 24,* 19–31.

Thomas, G. D., Smith, S. M., & Turcotte, J. A. (2009). Using public relations strategies to prompt populations at risk to seek health information: The Hanford Community Health Project. *Health Promotion Practice, 10,* 92–101.

Tiboni, E. A. (1965). What you can do to improve public relations for public health. *American Journal of Public Health, 54,* 2083–2084.

U.S. Department of Health and Human Services (DHHS). (2007, July). *Pandemic flu leadership blog.* Retrieved from http://blog.pandemicflu.gov.

Vasquez, G. M., & Taylor, M. (2001). Research perspectives on "the public." In R. L. Heath (Ed.), *Handbook of public relations* (pp. 139–154). Thousand Oaks, CA: Sage.

Wan, H.-H., & Schell, R. (2007). Reassessing corporate image—An examination of how image bridges symbolic relationships with behavioral relationships. *Journal of Public Relations Research, 19,* 25–45.

Weinberg, L. (2008). *Creating a "Symphony of Encouragement" to motivate Americans to take steps to personally prepare for a possible influenza pandemic.* Paper presented to the World Social Marketing Conference, Brighton and Hove City, England.

Wise, K. (2001). Opportunities for public relations research in public health. *Public Relations Review, 27,* 475–487.

Wise, K. (2003). Linking public relations processes and organizational effectiveness at a state health department. *Journal of Health and Human Services Administration, 26,* 473–501.

Wise, K. (2007). The organization and implementation of relationship management. *Health Marketing Quarterly, 24,* 151–166.

Wise, K. (2009). Public relations and health diplomacy. *Public Relations Review, 35,* 127–129.

Yang, S.-U. (2007). An integrated model for organization-public relational outcomes, organizational reputation, and their antecedents. *Journal of Public Relations Research, 19,* 91–121.

Yang, S.-U., & Grunig, J. E. (2005). Decomposing organizational reputation: The effects of organization-public relationship outcomes on cognitive representations of organizations and evaluations of organizational performance. *Journal of Communication Management, 9,* 305–325.

10

THEORY AND PRACTICE IN RISK COMMUNICATION

A Review of the Literature and Visions for the Future

Monique Mitchell Turner, Christine Skubisz, and Rajiv N. Rimal

When Monica was in the 18th week of pregnancy with her first child, her doctor ordered the quad screening test, which examines for four particular substances in maternal blood to identify pregnancies at risk for Down syndrome. A week after the test Monica received the results: Low levels of AFP and abnormal levels of hCG and estriol. The medical aide on the phone said very calmly, "This test may indicate that the developing baby has Trisomy 21 (Down syndrome). Your baby has a 1 in 200 chance of being born with Down syndrome." The purpose of explaining these results was clear; it was to help Monica and her spouse make an effective decision among many options: Pursue potential interventions that may exist, begin planning for a child with special needs, address potential lifestyle changes, look for support groups, or make a decision about carrying the child to term. Monica had important information to digest and share with her husband. And, both had to understand that the baby might not have any special needs at all (in fact, the baby did not have Down syndrome)—indeed, uncertainty was high. This kind of risk information is vital to health-related decision making, though some individuals may not pursue interventions or additional testing regardless of the risk information. Perhaps they will have the baby regardless of the results; maybe aborting the pregnancy is not an option; and some parents choose not to allow any testing that poses a risk of harming the baby. In other words, receiver characteristics also play a substantial role in responses to risk information. This intersection between message and receiver, theory and practice, and their effect on risk decision making is the focus of this chapter.

Communicating about public health often means communicating risk, which in turn involves particular challenges due to its complex and multi-dimensional nature. Elucidating the difficulties associated with risk communication starts with understanding the word *risk*. To us, risk is the perceived probability of negative consequences of a hazard occurring and the perceived magnitude of those consequences (Lofstedt & Boholm, 2009; Witte, 1992, 1994). It is possible for one, but not the other to be high enough to warrant attention from any particular individual or group of individuals. For example, Rimal, Böse, Brown, Mkandawire, and Folda (2009) found that in Malawi, where the HIV prevalence is close to 12%, most individuals believed that AIDS was a severe disease, but they also believed they were unlikely to get it. By contrast, many people feel susceptible to the common cold during the flu season, but do not perceive the common cold to be very severe. Thus, we will be assuming that risk incorporates both the susceptibility and the severity dimensions of any given threat, as is consistent with contemporary understanding of this term (Witte, 1992).

Hence, our concern in this chapter revolves around *perceived risk*. This is for both practical and theoretical reasons. From a practical standpoint, for many of the risk factors of concern in this Handbook, which include various diseases and health conditions, calculating the probabilistic risk for any given individual is virtually impossible. Doing so would mean taking into account information at the population level from multiple sources, whose predictive ability is far from precise, and making judgments about individual persons. Sources of information include those about one's genetic structure, family history, behavior, and environmental conditions, to name just a few. The second reason why we focus on perceived risk is theoretical: theories of behavior change have a long history of showing that individuals' perceptions of risk are more important in determining their course of action than what their actual risks might be. Perceptions of risk are sometimes driven by actual risks (as, for example, when individuals with a family history of heart disease come to believe that they, too, are susceptible to the disease), but the behaviors people engage in to reduce risk are mostly driven by perceptions.

Effective risk communication is vital to individuals' health. People weigh the pros and cons of medications, treatments, and prevention and detection options so that they can live longer and healthier lives. Risk communicators must relay risks and benefits of these health decisions effectively so that individuals can make sound decisions. As such, risk communication is not about telling people what to do, but it is about providing people with information aimed at helping them make informed decisions. Risk communication, seen from this angle, is a multi-directional conversation between, but not limited to, risk analysts, risk managers, and decision makers about the known and unknown information regarding risks with the goal of fostering informed and effective decision making (Lofstedt & Boholm, 2009).

Communication is an interactive process in which sources and receivers negotiate meanings they derive from the exchange of information (see Politi & Street's chapter on collaborative decision making in this volume). This feature of the communication process is acknowledged in the definition of risk communication proposed by the National Research Council (1989, p. 2): "an interactive process of exchange of information and opinion among individuals, groups, and institutions." This definition implies that a careful study of risk communication should acknowledge the importance of understanding the role of receivers, messages, and sources. In communicating about risk, sources need to pay special attention not only to what they say, but also to how their messages are formulated and framed, and how those messages affect receivers differently, depending on receiver characteristics, perceptions, and beliefs. In this chapter, we focus on each of these elements of the communication process.

Therefore, we organized this chapter by first examining the receiver's perspective. We review the relevant literature in state and traits that affect perceptions of risk as well as risk information seeking. Second, we look at the message perspective. We lay out the relevant challenges for risk communicators in developing their messages and follow up with the research on how to communicate risk numerically and visually.

The Receiver Perspective

Risk Perception

Scholars of risk perception understand that it is, in large part, due to the perceptions of knowledge and dread with regard to the risk. This thinking originated from Fischhoff, Slovic, Lichtenstein, Read, and Coombs (1978), who found that such a 2-factor model fit their data on the acceptability of distinct risks. Fischhoff et al. (1978) surveyed lay people with regard to 30 distinct risk topics, asking them about the benefits and risks of each. Their data showed that nuclear power was rated the highest in terms of severity of consequences; it was viewed as having high risks and low benefits. Skiing, though, was viewed as having many benefits and few risks, and, skiing was rated below the mid-point of the scale for severity of consequences. Regarding the acceptability of risks, Fischhoff et al.'s data indicated that individuals judged d the acceptability of risks differently for voluntary activities (like skiing) versus involuntary activities (living in a community with a nuclear power facility). Their data also indicated that as perceived risks increased, perceived benefits decreased (see Slovic, Finucane, Peters, & MacGregor, 2007); a fascinating finding given that often the benefits and risks of an issue or innovation are totally uncorrelated. For example, consuming alcoholic beverages can cause risks such as reaction time or have a negative effect on decision-making quality. But, alcohol consumption (in moderation) can decrease risks such as diabetes (for beer) or heart disease (red wine). Alhakami and Slovic (1994) found that the inverse relationship between perceived risk and perceived benefit of an activity (e.g., using pesticides) was related to the strength of affect (positive or negative) linked with that activity.

Slovic (1987) used Fischhoff et al.'s data to assess the public's attitudes toward risks. Slovic's (1987) factor analysis indicated that most risks break down into two continuous factors: dread risk and unknown risk. High dread risk is defined by perceptions of low control, high dread, high catastrophic potential, fatal consequences, high risk to future generations, low mitigation rates, low voluntariness, increasing in riskiness, and the inequitable distribution of risks and benefits. Nuclear weapons, nerve gas accidents, nuclear weapons fallout, and radioactive waste among others scored high on dread risk. Unknown risk is defined by perceptions that hazards are unobservable, hazard is unknown to those exposed, hazard is unknown to scientists, hazard is new, and effects of hazard are delayed in their manifestation. Chemical technologies scored high on unknown risk, as did cadmium usage and radioactive waste.

In explaining these findings, Slovic et al. (2007) argued that humans are more likely to process risk information experientially (Epstein, 1994) rather than rationally. Epstein (1994) posited that "There is no dearth of evidence in everyday life that people apprehend reality in two fundamentally different ways, one variously labeled intuitive, automatic, natural, nonverbal, narrative, and experiential, and the other analytical, deliberative, verbal, and rational" (p. 710). Experiential processing tends to be a quicker, easier, and more efficient way to navigate in a complex, uncertain, and sometimes dangerous world (Slovic et al., 2007). Epstein (1994) also noted that

> The experiential system is assumed to be intimately associated with the experience of affect ... which refer[s] to subtle feelings of which people are often unaware ... the experiential system automatically searches its memory banks for related events, including their emotional accompaniments.... If the activated feelings are pleasant,

they motivate actions and thoughts anticipated to reproduce the feelings. If the feelings are unpleasant, they motivate actions and thoughts anticipated to avoid the feelings.

(p. 716)

Optimistic Bias

Interestingly, Epstein's quote may also explain the optimism bias. We noted above that people's subjective judgments of risk tend to differ—sometimes substantially—from objective risks. There is now a well established literature on optimistic bias arguing that this discrepancy tends to manifest in one particular direction: people underestimate their own risks. Optimistic bias is the tendency to perceive that one is at lesser risk of a disease or event in comparison to the average person (Weinstein, 1980, 1982, 1983, 1984) and it has shown to be a fairly robust finding across cultures and across a number of countries, including Belgium, Morocco, Poland (Peeters, Cammaert, & Czapinski, 1997), Canada, and Japan (Heine & Lehman, 1995).

There are a number of explanations for the optimism bias, one of which is that believing that one is at *greater* risk than others (i.e., being pessimistically biased) is more anxiety provoking and thus less likely to occur (Kirscht, Haefner, Kegeles, & Rosenstock, 1966). Another explanation, one based on the social attribution literature, holds that individuals are egocentrically biased (Allison, Messick, & Goethals, 1989; Jones & Nisbett, 1971) in that positive outcomes that happen in one's own life are attributed to internal factors (e.g., expended effort), but comparable outcomes that happen in others' lives are attributed to external factors (e.g., happenstance). According to this view, individuals perceive the world in a self-serving manner, one example of which is to view oneself as invulnerable, or, at the very least, less vulnerable than others. Rimal and Morrison (2006) posited that optimistic biases may also be based, at least partially, on the nature of the image that individuals conjure up when they are asked to make judgments about their own risks, relative to the risks incurred by others. Individuals deliberately choose a dissimilar other (and one more prone to risk) as a frame of reference for evaluating their own risk and thus conclude that they are at lower risk than others. A final explanation would be one based on the affect heuristic: people feel positively about their own behaviors and therefore experience positive affect with regard to them. Since positive affect is related to decreases in risk perceptions, it would lead to the optimism bias.

Although these explanations differ in the underlying mechanism that would explain how or why optimistic bias exists, the overall implication of this collective body of work has important implications for risk communication and intervention efforts. To the extent that self-protective behaviors are driven by underlying motivations to reduce risk, as the optimistic bias literature suggests, such behaviors are less likely to occur if individuals tend to minimize their risks in the first place. Hence, interventions based on risk reduction strategies have enormous hurdles to overcome: Individuals have to be convinced that they are at risk and that taking the recommended steps will mitigate the risks.

Emotion Appraisals

So, scholars have explained the discrepancy between probabilistic risk and perceived risk with the notion of affect—what Slovic refers to as the faint whisper of emotion (e.g., Slovic et al., 2007). Yet, sometimes risks correspond with distinct and specific emotions, such as anger or fear. Appraisal theorists believe emotions are initiated by appraisal of events in the

149

environment in relation to individuals' well-being and the things that they care about, and that these appraisals also affect the consequences of emotions. Smith and Ellsworth (1985) identified six cognitive dimensions that could be combined to distinguish among discrete emotions: certainty, pleasantness, attentional activity, control, anticipated effort, and responsibility. Of particular interest to risk communication researchers are the dimensions of *certainty* (degree to which future events seem predictable and comprehensible); *control* (degree to which events seem brought about by individual agency [high] vs. situational agency [low]); and *responsibility* (degree to which someone or something other than oneself [high] vs. oneself [low] seem responsible for the events). According to Lerner and Keltner (2001), these dimensions map directly onto the two cognitive meta-factors about which the risk-psychometrics literature talks: unknown risk and "dread" risk. For example, if a lifetime smoker is diagnosed with lung cancer, she may perceive high certainty of the cause of the disease, individual control, and self-responsibility. In this case, the smoker might feel some level of guilt. But, imagine that a non-smoking bartender (in a bar where smoking is legal and prevalent) is diagnosed with lung cancer. In this case the bartender might also perceive high certainty and individual control; but, *other*-responsibility. The bartender would be more likely to experience anger.

Two commonly experienced emotions in risk-related situations, anger and fear, are clearly differentiated by these two dimensions: Anger arises from appraisals of negative events as (a) predictable (certainty) and (b) under the control of and brought about by others (other-responsibility/control), whereas fear arises from perceptions of negative events as (a) unpredictable and (b) under situational control. Lerner and Keltner (2001) found that these two distinct emotions influenced individuals' risk judgments: Fearful people expressed pessimistic risk estimates and risk-averse choices, whereas angry people expressed optimistic risk estimates and risk-seeking choices. Indeed, distinct emotions are tied to distinct action (i.e., behavioral) tendencies. This research suggests that whether people are pessimistically or optimistically biased depends on the emotion they are experiencing with regard to that risk.

We have established that people appraise risks and these appraisal patterns can cause distinct emotions, which in turn lead to unique action tendencies. Action tendencies are biologically based behavioral responses that allow people to cope with emotion-arousing events. The specific emotion that people experience due to a risk is critical because, just as each emotion is associated with a distinctive set of appraisals, it will be associated with particular action tendencies that are automatic and impulsive, but are not necessarily advisable for effectively coping with the risk. Coping draws heavily on perceptions about what is possible and likely to be effective in the specific context and what one is capable of doing (Lazarus, 1991). The innate action tendencies may be augmented or inhibited by such perceptions. The effects of emotions on information seeking and processing, for example, may be mediated or moderated by factors such as information sufficiency and efficacy.

The Importance of Risk Information Seeking and Processing

Although the goal of risk communication is to foster a better understanding by experts and non-experts alike of the actual and perceived risks, the possible solutions, and the related issues and concerns regarding the risk (Oleckno, 1995), the risk communication literature reveals a mostly passive construction of "audiences" of risk information that examines how people react to manipulations of various contents or formats of risk messages. Scholars of risk communication must have a better understanding of risk information seeking, those times when an audience strategically seeks out such content.

Risk information seeking has been linked to preventive behaviors, improved coping mechanisms (Brashers, Neidig, & Goldsmith; 2004, Carver, Scheier, & Weintraub, 1989), and quality-of-life improvements (Ransom, Jacobsen, Schmidt, & Andrykowski, 2005). Yet, these outcomes are dependent upon understanding individuals' abilities and motivations to seek information, the depth of their processing of this information, and how those variables mediate the risk judgment and decision-making processes—the focus of theory in this area.

The RISP Model. One information seeking model applied to risk issues is the Risk Information Seeking and Processing (RISP) model developed by Griffin and colleagues. They have applied this model, using cross-sectional surveys, to citizens' information seeking and processing on such topics as Great Lakes fish contamination, floods, climate change, and a parasite in drinking water (e.g., Griffin, Neuwirth,, Dunwoody, & Giese, 2004). The primary application of RISP has been to issues on which people might seek and process information from various sources, as measured through self-reported information seeking (though one study from outside the Griffin et al. team has applied the RISP model to hypothetical emissions from a factory using a sample of industry neighbors [Johnson, 2005]).

Figure 10.1 shows the main elements of the RISP model pertinent to information seeking,[1] based mostly on the heuristic–systematic model of information processing (HSM; Eagly & Chaiken, 1993), but also incorporating the subjective-norms concept from the theory of planned behavior (TPB; Ajzen, 1991). The RISP also includes perceived hazard characteristics and affective response from the risk perception literature, and channels beliefs and information seeking from communication literature.

The RISP model suggests that information seeking is the joint outcome of the belief that one has less knowledge than needed for one's purposes (motivation of information insufficiency), one has the capacity to seek and find needed information (internal communication efficacy), and that potential information sources provide needed information (external efficacy). Individual differences affect both capacity and channel beliefs, but their effect on information insufficiency is moderated by beliefs about hazard characteristics that produce affective responses and by beliefs about how informed and important others think one should be about the topic. Empirical survey data so far tend to support the model, particularly with regard to the role of information insufficiency.

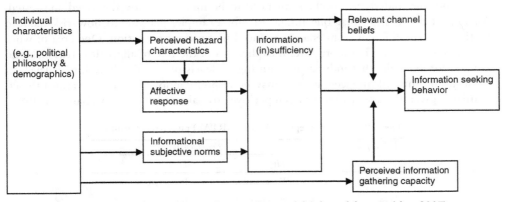

Figure 10.1 Risk information seeking and processing model (adapted from Kahlor, 2007).

The RISP model has yet to be adopted by scholars of health communication, unfortunately. This may be due to limitations to the model. First, the RISP model is not able to predict how much information will be *retained*. Second, the model has not included as part of its formal theorizing the role of emotion. And, the RISP model has only been studied with survey data; therefore, causal claims cannot be made with it. We turn to an alternative risk information seeking model, the Risk Perception Attitude Framework, which has been studied both with survey data and with experimentation, and has measured information retention as well as the role of anxiety.

The Risk Perception Attitude (RPA) Framework. The risk perception attitude (RPA) framework (Rimal & Real, 2003) posits that perceptions of risk are motivators for behavioral action, and that efficacy beliefs are critical for facilitating changes in behaviors. According to the RPA framework, whether individuals will take action to mitigate impending risks is dependent on both risk perception and efficacy beliefs. When low risk perceptions are coupled with weak perceptions of personal efficacy, people are least motivated to act and tend not to take initiatives to change because they do not believe they are capable of changing. At the other extreme, when high perceptions of risk accompany strong efficacy beliefs, individuals tend to be much more willing to act.

With some exceptions (Rimal & Real, 2003,Study 1; Turner, Rimal, Morrison, & Kim, 2006), studies testing central propositions of the RPA framework do tend to find that high risk perceptions and strong efficacy beliefs are associated with highest levels of protective action, and low risk perceptions with weak efficacy beliefs are associated with the lowest levels of protective action (Rimal et al., 2009).

Two important implications for future research emerge from this body of work. First, the extant literature has not made fine distinctions among different kinds of outcomes that are likely to be more or less affected by risk and efficacy perceptions. Turner et al. (2006), for example, focused explicitly on information seeking as an outcome, whereas many of the RPA-framework based studies have focused on other health behaviors (e.g., sun-safety behaviors, HIV prevention behaviors, breast cancer screening behaviors). Clearly, different behaviors have different underlying configurations of attributes—some are enacted in public settings, whereas others are not; some have severe consequences, whereas others do not—and it is likely that the RPA framework applies more to some behaviors than to others. Carefully delineating the boundary conditions of the relevant behaviors will be an important next step.

Second, the underlying mechanisms need to be more explicitly theorized and tested. An important question that one might ask, for example, pertains to how risk-induced motivations are different from efficacy-induced motivations for action. One area of work that explores this idea is a more careful explication of the role of affect. It is reasonable to assume, for example, that individuals with higher levels of risk also have higher levels of anxiety, and this risk-induced anxiety may be responsible for greater motivations to act. Similarly, given the association between positive arousal and self-efficacy (Bandura, 1986),

Table 10.1 Risk Perception Attitude (RPA) Framework Groups

Efficacy Beliefs	Perceived Risk	
	High	Low
High	Responsive	Proactive
Low	Anxious	Indifference

it may be that efficacy-induced change occurs when individuals experience positive affect. These are hypotheses worthy of test in future efforts.

Emotion and Information Seeking

Affect and emotion have become increasingly important in understanding risk perception and risk communication (e.g., Lerner, Gonzalez, Small, & Fischhoff, 2003; Loewenstein, Weber, Hsee, & Welch, 2001; Peters & Slovic, 1996), but their role in information seeking has just begun to be explored. Although the original version of RISP did not explicitly propose discrete emotions as a key part of the model, subsequent studies have attempted to look at affective responses in various ways. Griffin et al. (2008) applied the RISP model to flooding in Milwaukee, adding a single item on "how much anger they felt because managing agencies had not done more to minimize flood risks" (p. 297; three other emotions were rated as well, but this paper did not report on their effects). Anger correlated with political intentions on flooding (lobbying, voting, etc.), and seemed related to lower trust and judged likelihood of future flooding, as well as to ascription of flood damages to poor government management rather than to the actions of those living near the river. Subjective norms and anger appeared to be direct motivators of information seeking and processing, stronger than the indirect effect predicted via cognitive need for more information.

Powell, Dunwoody, Griffin, and Neuwirth (2007), in a secondary analysis of RISP-related data, found that an index combining worry and anger strongly predicted perceived uncertainty about the personal health risks of eating fish from the Great Lakes, although perceived knowledge and need to know also were factors. Powell et al. (2007) acknowledged the limitations of their one-item measure of uncertainty, but argued it was important to understand whether and how people themselves feel uncertain, in addition to the public response to scientific uncertainties otherwise well covered in the literature (e.g., Johnson, 2003; Johnson & Slovic, 1995, 1998). Powell et al. (2007) briefly discussed the role of actual knowledge, but only measured the effect of perceived knowledge. Additionally, Valentino, Hutchings, Banks, and Davis (2008) found that induced anger, anxiety, and enthusiasm are antecedents to reported intention to attend to a political campaign, but in this case, anger reduced information seeking. Anxiety also was associated with greater learning, and thus, in the view of Valentino, Hutchings, Banks, and Davis (2007), with the *quality* of information seeking.

Rimal and Real's RPA data contradict the idea that anxiety leads to higher quality information seeking. In their RPA research on information seeking, Rimal and Real (2003) proposed the idea of *affective interference*. As information seeking is one mechanism available to individuals to relieve their anxiety, those who perceive high risk and low efficacy (i.e., members of the avoidance group) should seek more information. Anxiety, however, is not conducive to information processing, so the prediction is that anxiety should reduce ability to remember the information that one encounters and suppress information retention. This prediction was tested by Turner et al. (2006). Risk perceptions and efficacy beliefs about skin cancer (Study 1) and diabetes (Study 2) were manipulated to determine whether people with high risk and low efficacy sought greater amounts of information to reduce anxiety. Such individuals indeed displayed elevated levels of anxiety, but the rate of information acquisition (amount of information retained per unit of time spent seeking it) was low among this group. These findings led the researchers to conclude that reduction of anxiety among members of the avoidance group was the primary motivation underlying information-seeking behaviors; however, their motivation did not translate into retention of information.

As noted above, seeking information does not necessarily mean that individuals will retain or understand that information; yet, understanding one's risk is vital to making effective risk decisions. Neither the RISP nor the RPA consider the effect of trait variables in understanding risk information. However, research is clear in indicating that health literacy can have a substantial effect on understanding and decision making about health. We turn to one particular sub-component of literacy, numeracy, which has a robust effect on understanding risk information.

Numeracy

Regardless of how much risk information seeking people engage in, to understand risk information, people must understand basic terms, including risk and probability. In addition to familiarity with general terms, people must also grasp more specific concepts to which risk information refers (e.g., mean, median, mode). Finally, receivers must also understand the basic process of science from which risk information is derived. These skills fall under the category of functional literacy; the ability of use written materials to accomplish tasks (Rudd, Moeykens, & Colton, 1999). In this volume, Cameron, Baker, and Wolf thoroughly review health literacy and its subcomponents.

Two specific types of literacy are directly related to the understanding of risk information—scientific literacy (Jenkins, 1994) and health literacy (see Cameron et al. this volume). Risk communication often includes scientific language and information. Evolving scientific advances require people to have some understanding of the scientific process. One sub-dimension of health literacy is numeracy: A person's ability to understand, use, and attach meaning to numbers (Nelson, Reyna, Fagerlin, Lipkus, & Peters, 2008). The ability to understand the numerical information that is presented in a risk message varies within message receivers. Individuals possess different levels of proficiency in numeracy depending on their background and experiences (Adelsward & Sachs, 1996; Fagerlin et al., 2007; Grimes & Snively, 1999; Lipkus, Samsa, & Rimer, 2001; Peters, Västfjäll et al., 2006).

The pervasiveness of low numeracy and the effects of low numeracy on comprehension, decision making, and behavior have been well documented. According to the most recent National Assessment of Adult Literacy (Kutner, Greenberg, Lin, Paulsen, & White, 2006), 22% of adults performed below a basic quantitative skill level, 66% performed at a basic or intermediate skill level, and only 13% performed at a proficient level. Although these findings are startling, numeracy is more complicated than basic quantitative skills. Numeracy is a unique construct from general intelligence or level of education. Even well educated people may understand very little about mathematics and use intuitions about numbers that do not conform to simple mathematical rules (Paulos, 1988). Lipkus et al. (2001) measured the performance of participants with a high school education or above. Sixteen percent were unable to correctly determine risk magnitude (i.e., what represents a larger risk: 1%, 5%, or 10%). Sheridan and Pignone (2002) investigated the numeracy skills of medical students and found that almost 25% of first year medical students could not manage basic numerical calculations. The medical students who had difficulty with the numeracy questions also experienced challenges with interpreting the treatment benefit of a hypothetical disease.

Individuals with low numeracy, who are unable to perform simple tasks with numbers, are less likely to handle more complicated manipulations and risk assessments. Numeracy is related to health outcomes, cognition, and risk perception. Low numeracy skills predict poorer health outcomes, less accurate perceptions of health risks, and compromised ability to make medical decisions (Reyna & Brainerd, 2007). For example, Lobb, Butow, Kenny, and Tattersall (1999) investigated the ability of women to understand breast cancer risk information. In this research, 53% of the women could not calculate how therapy would reduce their risk, and 73% did not understand the statistical term *median* when researchers used it to describe how long it takes for cancer to return. People with low numeracy trust numerical information less and are more likely to reject numerical data, compared to people with high numeracy (Gurmankin, Baron, & Armstrong, 2004b; Peters, Hibbard, Slovic, & Dieckmann, 2007). In addition, people with lower numeracy over estimate the benefits of tests or treatment options (Schwartz, Woloshin, Black, & Welch, 1997) and are more influenced by irrelevant non-numeric sources of information (Peters, Västfjäll et al. 2006).

Importantly, less numerate people are more likely to be influenced by how numerical information is presented. People with higher numeracy should have more access to all numerical formats (Peters,Västfjall et al., 2006). For example, when presented with frequency information, the highly numerate should be able to calculate a percentage. Thus, risk communication presentation format should have less influence on outcomes for highly numerate people and more influence on outcomes for less numerate people who do not have access to all formats. In research conducted by Peters, Västfjäll et al. (2006), participants were shown two pictures of bowls with colored and white jelly beans and told to imagine that they could select one bean. If they selected a colored jelly bean, they would win five dollars. The first bowl was larger, contained 100 jelly beans, 9 of which were colored, and was labeled as having "9% colored jelly beans" and represented the inferior choice. The second bowl was smaller, contained 10 jelly beans, 1 of which was colored, and was labeled as having "10% colored jelly beans." These data indicated that lower numeracy was associated with inferior choices. Less numerate participants were more likely to choose the bowl with 100 jelly beans than participants who scored higher on the numeracy scale. Further support for the influence of presentation format was found by Galesic, Gigerenzer, and Staubinger (2009) who examined the role of natural frequencies in improving outcomes for people with lower numeracy skills. Participants were given information as a natural frequency or a conditional probability and asked to estimate a positive predictive value for a medical screening procedure. Overall, the number of accurate estimates was low, but accuracy was higher when natural frequencies were provided, regardless of age group or numeracy level. It might be that people with lower health literacy, and numeracy in particular, mandate different kinds of risk messages than those with higher levels of these traits. We turn to the message perspective next.

The Message Perspective

Risk communication is a challenging enterprise. Many of those challenges are in no small part due to the lack of clear understanding regarding the nature of risk, particularly as it relates to scientific innovations and public safety. Risk communication is made further challenging by the fact that humans rarely perceive probabilistic risk in an objective manner. Subjectivity prisms that people use to perceive their risk often mean that there may be considerable divergence in risk assessments between perceptions and reality (Fischhoff et al., 1978; Slovic, 1987). Notions of uncertainty, pros and cons, as well as doubt and ambiguity are inherent in the concept of risk. Therefore, when we talk about risk, we have to recognize that there are numerous psychological and emotional factors affecting the way key audiences perceive risk. We highlight some of the specific challenges in communicating risk.

Uncertainty

Fessenden-Raden and colleagues (1987) wrote, "No matter how accurate it is, risk information may be misperceived or rejected if those who give information are unaware of the complex, interactive nature of risk communication and the various factors affecting the reception of the risk message." (p. 100). Uncertainty is an ever-present backdrop in which risk-related decisions have to be made and communicated. In fact, Politi and Street (this volume) thoroughly discuss the importance of collaborative decision making in managing uncertainty in their chapter. We recommend examining that chapter for a detailed review on the how people manage uncertainty in health decision making.

For risk communicators, information is never completely precise, with regard to hazard occurrences or their consequences. Physicians, as discussed in the Politi and Street chapter, for example, have to communicate information to patients about risk factors when only estimates about the risk at the population level may be available. Similarly, government agencies often have to warn the larger public about impending hazards when only a few cases may have occurred (as was the case immediately following the 2009 HI1N1 flu outbreak). Receivers of risk information, too, have to act under conditions of uncertainty. Contradictory information emanating from government and other sources can further exacerbate the public's understanding and confusion. A real world example of this phenomenon can be seen in the public's perception of the risk associated with the global avian flu epidemic. The risk from avian influenza is generally low for most people, because the viruses do not usually infect humans. But, a study released at the World Economic forum, titled "Global Risks" claimed that avian flu was a more significant threat than terrorism and that, given the right circumstances, could kill between 40 and 50 million people worldwide (Marsh and McLennan Companies, Inc., Merrill Lynch, Swiss Re, & the Risk Management and Decision Processes Center of the Wharton School at the University of Pennsylvania, 2006). Such contradictory information highlights the complexity of the risk, but it may also lead to a great deal of frustration and doubt on the part of the public. The goal is to reduce uncertainty by communicating in a confident, credible and assertive manner while ensuring that key audiences respond appropriately to new and evolving information. This does not imply that communicators act as though they know more than they do; in fact, communicators should always admit what they do not know. Unfortunately, there is scant evidence on how to communicate uncertainty. According to the National Research Council (1989) communicators should not avoid or lie about the uncertainty inherent in risk.

Communicating Numerical Risk

The same numerical information can be presented in a range of formats, including frequencies, probabilities, percentages, population size required for one expected event, decimal proportion, odds, and verbal expressions. How numerical information is presented does not make a mathematical difference (that is, 5% is mathematically equivalent to 5 out of 100), but it does make a perceptual difference for message receivers (Hoffrage, Lindsey, Hertwig, & Gigerenzer 2000; Slovic, Monahan, & MacGregor, 2000). The choice of a numerical format can influence the understanding and decisions of a message receiver (Edwards, Elwyn, & Gwyn, 1999; Gigerenzer & Edwards, 2003; Sackett, 1996).

Some general conclusions can be drawn regarding the disadvantages and advantages of the various formats of risk information. Verbal labels such as "probably," "likely," or "rarely" have a number of strengths and weaknesses. These labels increase fluidity in the communication, are easy to use, express the imprecision of risk, encourage one to think of reasons why an event will or will not occur, and can show directionality (Lipkus, 2007; Renooij & Witteman, 1999). However, message receivers may interpret verbal labels in vastly different ways depending on the context of the message. For example, if receivers interpret verbal expressions as representing frequencies that are higher or lower than reality, their interpretations could cause serious implications for health decisions and behavior. Gurmankin, Baron, and Armstrong (2004a) presented participants with one of three cancer risk scenarios: verbal only, verbal plus a percentage, or verbal plus a fraction. The data showed that the messages that included numerical statements of risks led to less variation in risk perception than the message that included a verbal expression only.

Fischer and Jungermann suggested that numbers are better than words and people should be told what each verbal label means numerically (1996). In addition, when they have to interpret a risk people prefer to receive risk information in a numerical format, as opposed to a verbal format (Lion & Meertens, 2001; Mazur, Hickman, & Mazur, 1999; Teigen & Brun, 1999). In studies comparing numerical information to verbal probability information, numerical information was trusted more (Gurmankin, Baron, & Armstrong, 2004b), participants reported being more satisfied with the information (Berry, Raynor, Knapp, & Bersellini, 2004), and numerical information was better understood (Marteau et al., 2000). Thus, providing information verbally is not the best method to facilitate understanding and comprehension (Thomson, Cunningham, & Hunt, 2001) leading researchers to conclude that the most effective presentation of risk magnitude is through the use of numbers (see Schwartz, Woloshin, & Welch, 1999).

In particular, a number of studies have linked frequency information to positive outcomes. Gigerenzer and Hoffrage (1995) argued that people make more accurate judgments when given frequency formats. Participants were assigned to receive natural frequency or percentage information about the occurrence of fifteen health and accident risks and were asked to estimate the probability that one person would experience each specific event. The natural frequency format stimulated and facilitated statistical reasoning, operationalized as use of Bayesian algorithms, compared to the percentage information. In a series of experiments conducted by Slovic, Monahan, and MacGregor (2000), psychologists and psychiatrists were asked to evaluate the likelihood that a mental patient, Mr. Jones, would commit an act of violence within six months of being discharged from a hospital. Participants were provided with the patient's risk of violence as a frequency ("of every 100 patients similar to Mr. Jones, 10 are estimated to commit an act of violence") or as a probability with a percentage ("patients similar to Mr. Jones are estimated to have a 10% chance of committing an act of violence") and asked to make a decision to either discharge or not discharge Mr. Jones from the hospital. Participants who received frequency information evaluated Mr. Jones as more dangerous than participants who received probability information.

Further support for the superiority of the frequency format was found by Brase (2002). In this study, four statistical formats were compared: a simple frequency (e.g., 1 in 3), a single event probability (e.g., 0.33), a relative frequency (e.g., 33%), and an absolute frequency for the U.S. population (e.g., 90 million). Topic was also manipulated; participants received information in one of four contexts (disease prevalence, education, marketing, or drug efficacy). Participants received one format and evaluated the clarity of the information. Significant differences in clarity were reported: simple frequencies and relative frequencies were rated clearer than single event probabilities and absolute frequencies.

Visual Format

The advantages of visual presentation of data are debated. On one hand, visual messages such as pie charts, Venn diagrams, bar charts, or paling scales exploit automatic visual perception skills and reduce the need for mental processing (Cleveland & McGill, 1985). Large amounts of numerical data can be overwhelming and visual displays can be used to change a numerical, computational task into a perceptual one (Lipkus, 2007). Visual displays can summarize much information, show patterns in data (e.g., interaction effects, regression lines), facilitate mathematical operations, and attract and hold attention by displaying information in concrete, visual terms (Lipkus, 2007; Lipkus & Hollands, 1999). In terms of risk perception, visual formats have been found to be more effective than numerical formats for increasing risk avoidant behavior (Chua, Yates, & Shah, 2006; Stone, Sieck et al., 2003; Stone, Yates, & Parker, 1997). Pictures were found to intensify the sense of riskiness by utilizing both cognitive and affective mechanisms. Pictures have been found to elicit stronger, more aversive associations between a risk and an outcome (Chua et al., 2006).

On the other hand, research has indicated that visual representations do not always provide assistance to message receivers (Lipkus, 2007; Parrott, Silk, Dorgan, Condit, & Harris, 2005). These displays may require more effort if receivers lack the skills to interpret the visual. Also, people may interpret graphs in ways that are not intended. Graphs can be misleading by amplifying the effects of certain elements and diminishing the effects of others (Huff, 1954). Visual displays may discourage people from considering such details as the numbers themselves (Lipkus, 2007). To date, the research exploring the effects of visual representations is inconclusive. It is unclear if visual displays are as effective as other formats and it is unclear which visuals are more effective and why. Although visual formats may enhance the risk communication process, we know little about how these formats affect risk-related behaviors (see Civan, Doctor, & Wolf, 2005).

The research and study of visual design has been in existence since the 1700s; yet, this body of work is largely unscientific. Most of this work provides lists of "do's and don'ts" based upon commonsense rules and visual appeal (e.g., Edwards, Elwyn, & Mulley, 2002; Paling, 2003). Few researchers have developed theory in this area or have developed principles of visual perception of quantitative information.

Conclusion

The study of risk communication is a vibrant and dynamic field. The job of a risk communicator would be simple if he or she could simply relay the known facts. Let's take the example we presented in the beginning of the chapter. Imagine if the medical aide calling Monica, the expectant mother, could have said "Your baby certainly has/does not have Down syndrome." But, the actuality is that risk is inextricably tied to uncertainties. The medical aide in this scenario could only relay the probabilities of Down syndrome with the hope of helping the parents make an effective decision. The mother and father had to sit with the anxiety and wonder, "Is *this* baby the one out of 200 to be born with Down syndrome?" But, what health decision was to be made depended upon their values, culture, and personality. It depended on how they interpreted the numbers. It depended on their information seeking and comprehension of that information. It also depended upon how the numbers were communicated.

Fischhoff, in his historical analysis of risk communication, noted that it was once believed that just providing people with numbers would foster understanding and informed risk management decisions (Fischhoff, 1995). Unfortunately, even in the face of information, humans experience a discrepancy between their probabilistic risk and their perception of their risk. McGregor (2006) referred to risk perception as the lens through which individuals view risk; in fact, Brewer, Weinstein, Cuite, and Herrington (2004), for example, found that people with higher initial risk perceptions were more likely than people with lower risk perceptions to get vaccinated.

The "holy grail" for the risk communicator, then, is to develop a message that can aid in closing the gap between perceived risk and probabilistic risk. In this chapter, we covered the relevant research on risk communication including the predictors of risk perception and risk information seeking and retention/comprehension. We then discussed the relevant research on message development, which included communicating uncertainty, numerical risk, and visual depictions of risk. There is much more to be learned about the communication of risk information.

First, with regard to receiver dimensions, we need to better understand personality traits that may interfere with the reception of risk information. For example, Donohew and colleagues' research on sensation seeking and its role in the reception of public service announcements with high message sensation value is important (see Donohew, Palmgreen, & Duncan, 1980; Donohew, Palmgreen, & Lorch, 1994; Stephenson, 2002). This research indicates that the personality trait sensation seeking makes people more likely to pay attention to and be persuaded by high sensation messages. In addition to sensation seeking, Ulleberg and Rundmo (2003) examined several personality characteristics, including aggression, altruism, anxiety, and normlessness, that may affect the reception of risk information. They found that the relationships between the personality traits and risky driving behavior were mediated through attitudes about the risk. In this research, personality primarily influenced behavior indirectly by affecting attitudinal determinants.

Second, researchers must begin to focus on the communication of uncertainty, which is inherent in the communication of risk information. Yet, little is known about how to communicate in uncertain situations and if particular message features will be perceived as more credible than others under conditions of uncertainty. It could be that uncertainty is better tolerated when communicators provide a contextualized understanding of why the uncertainty exists. Risk information is often based on science and risk communicators must acknowledge that there is information that is not yet known. Evolving scientific advances require people to have some understanding of the scientific process, what Zarcadoolas, Pleasant, and Greer (2006) call scientific literacy. At times, risk messages may need to include information about the evolving science that is involved. Research is needed to understand when and how this may be useful. In addition, research on metaphors, analogies, and other figurative language may aid in the communication of emerging risks (see Sopory & Dillard, 2002). Perhaps risk messages might be more effective if they likened a new type of uncertainty to other kinds of uncertainty that people have accepted and with which they are familiar. For example, a message discouraging people from talking on a cell phone while driving could inform the public that they are just as impaired when talking on a cell phone while driving as they would be if they were driving while intoxicated at the legal .08 limit. The use of analogy to explain a new, uncertain risk with information about an established risk is a potentially useful risk communication technique and an area that needs further research attention.

Third, there are relatively few theories of risk communication compared to other areas in the discipline, such as persuasion, interpersonal communication, and organizational communication. Research is needed to understand the process through which risk information is sought out, comprehended, and used. For example, there is currently no comprehensive theoretical explanation describing the relationships between numerical information, emotion, risk perception, and risk-related decisions. Although it is interesting to know that frequencies are more persuasive than percentages, for example, it would also be important to understand the theoretical underpinnings of such effects.

Finally, risk communication scholars need to take a more dynamic and process-oriented approach. Risk communication is received in an active communication environment. For example, during the H1N1 flu crisis of 2009, the Centers for Disease Control, National Institutes of Health, Food and Drug Administration, as well as numerous local health departments were all communicating information to the public. Meanwhile, parents and other stakeholders were communicating about the issue via social networking tools such as Facebook and Twitter. It is likely the case that our studies of risk communication do not reflect how people really receive communication. In addition, risk communication often takes place as a risk evolves. People are exposed to new information (and perhaps contradictory information) constantly. We do not have a full understanding of how people integrate information from multiple sources and make sense of it.

The field of risk communication provides an opportunity to do research that has an immeasurable and immediate influence on the lives of real people. This scholarship may be employed by practitioners to improve their risk communication plans and activities. Hence, we believe that there is not only an opportunity to deeply engage in this research, but an obligation to do so.

References

Adelsward, V., & Sachs, L. (1996). The meaning of 6.8: Numeracy and normality in health information talks. *Social Science Medicine, 43,* 1179–1197.

Ajzen, I. (1991). The theory of planned behavior. *Organizational Behavior and Human Decision Processes, 50,* 179–211.

Alhakami, A. S., & Slovic, P. (1994). A psychological study of the inverse relationship between perceived risk and perceived benefit. *Risk Analysis, 14,* 1085–1096.

Allison, S. T., Messick, D. M., & Goethals, G. R. (1989). On being better but not smarter than others: The Muhammad Ali effect. *Social Cognition, 7,* 275–295.

Bandura, A. (1986). *Social foundations of thought and action.* Englewood Cliffs, NJ: Prentice-Hall.

Berry, D., Raynor, T., Knapp, P., & Bersellini, E. (2004). Over the counter medicines and the need for immediate action: A further evaluation of European Commission recommended wordings for communicating risk. *Patient Education and Counseling, 53,* 129–134.

Brase, G. (2002). Which statistical formats facilitate what decisions? The perception and influence of different statistical information formats. *Journal of Behavioral Decision Making, 15,* 381–401.

Brashers, D. E., Neidig, J. L., & Goldsmith, D. J. (2004). Social support and the management of uncertainty for people living with HIV. *Health Communication, 16,* 305–331.

Brewer, N. T., Weinstein, N. D., Cuite, C. L., & Herrington, J. (2004). Risk perceptions and their relation to risk behavior. *Annals of Behavioral Medicine, 27,* 125–130.

Carver, C. S., Scheier, M. F., & Weintraub, J. K. (1989). Assessing coping strategies: A theoretically based approach. *Journal of Personality and Social Psychology, 56,* 267–283.

Chua, H. F., Yates, F., & Shah, P. (2006). Risk avoidance: Graphs vs. numbers. *Memory and Cognition, 34,* 399–410.

Civan, A., Doctor, J. N., & Wolf, F. M. (2005). What makes a good format: Frameworks for evaluating the effect of graphic risk formats on consumers' risk-related behavior. *Proceedings of the AMIA Annual Fall Symposium.* Washington, DC, 927. Retrieved from http://www.ncbi.nlm.nih.gov/pmc/articles/PMC1560820/pdf/amia2005_0927.pdf

Cleveland, W. S., & McGill, R. (1985). Graphical perception: Theory, experimentation, and application to the development of graphical methods. *Journal of the American Statistical Association, 79,* 531–554.

Donohew, L., Palmgreen, P., & Duncan, J. (1980). An activation model of information exposure. *Communication Monographs, 47*, 295–303.

Donohew, L., Palmgreen, P., & Lorch, E. P. (1994). Attention, sensation seeking, and health communication campaigns. *American Behavioral Scientist, 38*, 310–332.

Eagly, A. H., & Chaiken, S. (1993). *The psychology of attitudes.* Fort Worth, TX: Harcourt Brace.

Edwards, A., Elwyn, G., & Gwyn, R. (1999). General practice registrar responses to the use of different risk communication tools in simulated consultations: A focus group study. *British Medical Journal, 319*, 749–752.

Edwards, A., Elwyn, G., & Mulley, A. (2002). Explaining risks: Turning numerical data into meaningful pictures. *British Medical Journal, 324*, 817–830.

Epstein, S. (1994). Integration of the cognitive and the psychodynamic unconscious. *American Psychologist, 49*, 709–724.

Fagerlin, A., Zikmund-Fisher, B. J., Ubel, P. A., Jankovi, A., Derry, H. A., & Smith, D. M. (2007). Measuring numeracy without a math test: Development of the subjective numeracy scale. *Medical Decision Making, 27*, 672–680.

Fessenden-Raden, J., Fitchen, J. M., & Heath, J. S. (1987). Providing risk information in communities: Factors influencing what is heard and accepted. *Science, Technology, and Human Values, 12*, 94–101.

Fischer, K., & Jungermann, H. (1996). Rarely occurring headaches and rarely occurring blindness: Is rarely = rarely? *Journal of Behavioral Decision Making, 9*, 153–172.

Fischhoff, B. (1995). Risk perception and communication unplugged: Twenty years of progress. *Risk Analysis, 15*, 137–145.

Fischhoff, B., Slovic, P., Lichtenstein, S., Read, S., & Combs, B. (1978). How safe is safe enough? A psychometric study of attitudes toward technological risks and benefits. *Policy Sciences, 9*, 127–152.

Galesic, M., Gigerenzer, G., & Staubinger, N. (2009). Natural frequencies help older adults and people with low numeracy to evaluate medical screening tests. *Medical Decision Making, 29*, 368–371.

Gigerenzer, G., & Edwards, A. (2003). Simple tools for understanding risk: From innumeracy to insight. *British Medical Journal, 327*, 741–744.

Gigerenzer, G., & Hoffrage, U. (1995). How to improve Bayesian reasoning without instruction: Frequency formats. *Psychological Review, 102*, 684–704.

Griffin, R.J., Neuwirth, K., Dunwoody, S., & Giese, J. (2004). Information sufficiency and risk communication. *Media Psychology, 6*, 23–61.

Griffin, R. J., Yang, Z., ter Huurne, E., Boerner, F., Ortiz, S., & Dunwoody, S. (2008). After the flood. *Science Communication, 29*, 285–315.

Grimes, D. A., & Snively, G. R. (1999). Patients' understanding of medical risks: Implications for genetic counseling. *Obstetrics and Gynecology, 93*, 910–914.

Gurmankin, A. D., Baron, J., & Armstrong, K. (2004a). Intended message versus message received in hypothetical physician risk communications: Exploring the gap. *Risk Analysis, 24*, 1337–1347.

Gurmankin, A. D., Baron, J., & Armstrong, K. (2004b). The effect of numerical statements of risk on trust and comfort with hypothetical physician risk communication. *Medical Decision Making, 24*, 265–271.

Heine, S. J., & Lehman, D. R. (1995). Cultural variation in unrealistic optimism: Does the West feel more vulnerable than the East? *Journal of Personality and Social Psychology, 68*, 595–607.

Hoffrage, U., Lindsey, S., Hertwig, R., & Gigerenzer, G. (2000). Communicating statistical information. *Science, 22*, 2261–2262.

Huff, D. (1954). *How to lie with statistics.* New York: Norton.

Jenkins, E. W. (1994). Scientific literacy. In T. Husen & T. N. Postlethwaite, (Eds.), *The International encyclopedia of education* (2nd ed., Vol. 9, pp. 5345–5350). Oxford, England: Pergamon Press.

Johnson, B. B. (2003). Further notes on public response to uncertainty in risks and science. *Risk Analysis, 23*, 781–789.

Johnson, B. B. (2005). Testing and expanding a model of cognitive processing of risk information. *Risk Analysis, 25*, 631–650.

Johnson, B. B., & Slovic, P. (1995). Presenting uncertainty in health risk assessment: Initial studies of its effects on risk perception and trust. *Risk Analysis, 15*, 485–494.

Johnson, B. B., & Slovic, P. (1998). Lay views on uncertainty in environmental health risk assessment. *Journal of Risk Research, 1*, 261–279.

Jones, E. E., & Nisbett, R. E. (1971). *The actor and the observer: Divergent perceptions of the causes of behavior.* New York: General Learning Press.

Kahlor, L. A. (2007) An augmented risk information seeking model: The case of global warming. *Media Psychology, 10,* 414–435.

Kirscht, J. P., Haefner, D. P., Kegeles, S. S., & Rosenstock, I. M. (1966). A national study of health beliefs. *Journal of Health and Human Behavior, 7,* 248–254.

Kutner, M., Greenberg, E., Lin, Y., Paulsen, C., & White, S. (2006). *The health literacy of America's adults: Results from the 2003 national assessment of health literacy* (NCES 2006–483). Washington, DC: U.S. Department of Education.

Lazarus, R. S. (1991). *Emotion and adaptation.* New York: Oxford University Press.

Lerner, J. S., Gonzalez, R. M., Small, D. A., & Fischhoff, B. (2003). Effects of fear and anger on perceived risks of terrorism: A national field experiment. *Psychological Science, 14,* 144–150.

Lerner, J. S., & Keltner, D. (2001). Fear, anger, and risk. *Journal of Personality and Social Psychology, 81,* 146–159

Lion, R., & Meertens, R. M. (2001). Seeking information about a risky medicine: Effects of risk-taking tendency and accountability. *Journal of Applied Social Psychology, 31,* 778–795.

Lipkus, I. M. (2007). Numeric, verbal, and visual formats of conveying health risks: Suggested best practices and future recommendations. *Medical Decision Making, 27,* 696–713.

Lipkus, I. M., & Hollands, J. G. (1999). The visual communication of risk. *Journal of the National Cancer Institute Monographs, 25,* 149–163.

Lipkus, I. M., Samsa, G., & Rimer, B. K. (2001). General performance on a numeracy scale among highly educated samples. *Medical Decision Making, 21,* 37–44.

Lobb, E. A., Butow, P. N., Kenny, D. T., & Tattersall, H. N. (1999). Communicating prognosis in early breast cancer: Do women understand the language used? *Medical Journal of Australia, 171,* 290–294.

Loewenstein, G., Weber, E. U., Hsee, C. K., & Welch, N. (2001). Risk as feelings. *Psychological Bulletin, 127,* 267–286.

Lofstedt, R. E., & Boholm, A. (2009). The study of risk in the 21st century. In R. E. Lofstedt & A. Bonolm (Eds.), *The earthscan reader on risk.* Sterling, VA: Earthscan.

Marsh and McLennan Companies, Inc., Merrill Lynch, Swiss Re, & the Risk Management and Decision Processes Center of the Wharton School at the University of Pennsylvania (2006). *Global risks 2006:* A world economic forum report. Washington, DC. Retrieved from http://74.125.93.132/search?q=cache:pxwvlzTDDeoJ:www.weforum.org/pdf/CSI/Global_Risk_Report.pdf+world+economic+forum+global+risks+2006&cd=1&hl=en&ct=clnk&gl=us

Marteau, T. M., Saidi, G., Goodburn, S., Lawton, L., Michie, S., & Bobrow, M. (2000). Numbers or words? A randomized controlled trial of presenting screen negative results to pregnant women. *Prenatal Diagnosis, 20,* 714–718.

Mazur, D., Hickman, D., & Mazur, M. (1999). How patients' preferences for risk information influence treatment choice in a case of high risk and high therapeutic uncertainty. *Medical Decision Making, 19,* 394–398.

McGregor, S. L.T. (2006). Reconceptualizing risk perception: Perceiving majority world citizens at risk from "Northern" consumption. *International Journal of Consumer Studies, 30,* 235–246.

National Research Council. (1989). *Improving risk communication.* Washington, DC: National Academy Press.

Nelson, W., Reyna, V. F., Fagerlin, A., Lipkus, I., & Peters, E. (2008). Clinical implications of numeracy: Theory and practice. *Annals of Behavioral Medicine, 35,* 261–274.

Oleckno, W. A. (1995). Guidelines for improving risk communication in environmental health. *Journal of Environmental Health, 58,* 20–23.

Paling, J. (2003). Strategies to help patients understand risks. *British Medical Journal, 327,* 745–747.

Parrott, R., Silk, K., Dorgan, K., Condit, C., & Harris, T. (2005). Risk comprehension and judgments of statistical evidentiary appeals: When a picture is not worth a thousand words. *Human Communication Research, 31,* 423–452.

Paulos, J. A. (1988). *Innumeracy: Mathematical illiteracy and its consequences.* New York: Hill & Wang.

Peeters, G., Cammaert, M., & Czapinski, J. (1997). Unrealistic optimism and positive-negative asymmetry: A conceptual and cross-cultural study of interrelationships between optimism, pessimism, and realism. *International Journal of Psychology, 32,* 23–34.

Peters, E., Hibbard, J., Slovic, P., & Dieckmann, N. F. (2007). Numeracy skill and the communication, comprehension, and use of risk-benefit information. *Health Affairs, 26,* 741–748.

Peters, E., & Slovic, P. (1996). The role of affect and worldviews as orienting dispositions in the perception and acceptance of nuclear power. *Journal of Applied Social Psychology, 26,* 1427–1453.

Peters, E., Västfjäll, D., Slovic, P., Mertz, C. K., Mazzocco, K. & Dickert, S. (2006). Numeracy and decision making. *Psychological Science, 17,* 407–413.

Powell, M., Dunwoody, S., Griffin, R., & Neuwirth, K. (2007). Exploring lay uncertainty about an environmental health risk. *Public Understanding of Science, 16,* 323–343.

Ransom, S., Jacobsen, P. B., Schmidt, J. E., & Andrykowski, M. A. (2005). Relationship of problem-focused coping strategies to changes in quality of life following treatment for early stage breast cancer. *Journal of Pain and Symptom Management, 30,* 243–253.

Renooij, S., & Witteman, C. (1999). Talking probabilities: Communicating probabilistic information with words and numbers. *International Journal Approximate Reasoning, 22,* 169–194.

Reyna, V. F., & Brainerd, C. J. (2007). The importance of mathematics in health and human judgment: Numeracy, risk communication, and medical decision making. *Learning and Individual Differences, 17,* 147–159.

Rimal, R. N., Böse, K., Brown, J., Mkandawire, G., & Folda, L. (2009). Extending the purview of the risk perception attitude (RPA) framework: Findings from HIV/AIDS prevention research in Malawi. *Health Communication, 24,* 210–218.

Rimal, R. N., & Morrison, D. (2006). A uniqueness to personal threat (UPT) hypothesis: How similarity affects perceptions of susceptibility and severity in risk assessment. *Health Communication, 20,* 209–219.

Rimal, R. N., & Real, K. (2003). Perceived risk and efficacy beliefs as motivators of change. *Human Communication Research, 29,* 370–400.

Rudd, R., Moeykens, B., & Colton, T. C. (1999). Health and literacy: A review of the medical and public health literature. In J. Comings, B. Garner, & C. Smith (Eds.), *Annual Review of Adult Learning and Literacy* (pp. 158–199). San Francisco, CA: Jossey-Bass.

Sackett, D. L. (1996). On some clinically useful measures of the effects of treatment. *Evidence-Based Medicine, 1,* 37–38.

Schwartz, L. M., Woloshin, S., Black, W., C., & Welsh, H. G. (1997). The role of numeracy in understanding the benefit of screening mammography. *Annals of Internal Medicine, 127,* 966–972.

Schwartz, L.M., Woloshin, S., & Welch, H.G (1999). Risk communication in clinical practice: Putting cancer in context. *Journal of the National Cancer Institute Monographs, 25,* 124–133.

Sheridan, S. L., & Pignone, M. (2002). Numeracy and the medical student's ability to interpret data. *Effective Clinical Practice, 5,* 35–40.

Slovic, P. (1987). Perception of risk. *Science, 236,* 280–285.

Slovic, P., Finucane, M. L., Peters, E., MacGregor, D. G. (2007). The affect heuristic. *European Journal of Operational Research, 177,* 1333–1352.

Slovic, P., Monahan, J., & MacGregor, D.G. (2000). Violence risk assessment and risk communication: The effects of using actual cases, providing instruction, and employing probability versus frequency formats. *Law and Human Behavior, 24,* 271–296.

Smith, C. A., & Ellsworth, P. C. (1985). Patterns of cognitive appraisal in emotion. *Journal of Personality and Social Psychology, 48,* 813–838.

Sopory, P., & Dillard, J. P. (2002). Figurative language and persuasion. In J. P. Dillard & M. Pfau (Eds.), *The Persuasion handbook* (pp. 407–426). Thousand Oaks, CA: Sage.

Stephenson, M. T. (2002). Sensation seeking as a moderator of the processing of anti-heroin public service announcements. *Communication Studies, 53,* 358–380.

Stone, E. R., Sieck, W. R., Bull, B. E., Yates, J. F., Parks, S. C., & Rush, C. J. (2003). Foreground background salience: Explaining the effects of graphical displays on risk avoidance. *Organizational Behavior and Human Decision Processes, 90,* 19–36.

Stone, E. R., Yates, J. F., & Parker, A. M. (1997). Effects of numerical and graphical displays on professed risk-taking behavior. *Journal of Experimental Psychology: Applied, 3,* 243–256.

Teigen, K. H., & Brun, W. (1999). The directionality of verbal probability expressions: Effects on decisions, predictions, and probabilistic reasoning. *Organizational Behavior and Human Decision Processes, 80,* 155–190.

Thomson, A. M., Cunningham, S. J., & Hunt, N. P. (2001). A comparison of information retention at an initial orthodontic consultation. *European Journal of Orthodontics, 23,* 169–178.

Turner, M. M., Rimal, R. N., Morrison, D., & Kim, H. (2006). The role of anxiety in seeking and retaining risk information: Testing the risk perception attitude framework in two studies. *Human Communication Research, 32,* 130–156.

Ulleberg, P., & Rundmo, T. (2003). Personality, attitudes and risk perception as predictors of risky driving behaviour among young drivers. *Safety Science, 41,* 427–443.

Valentino, N. A., Hutchings, V. L., Banks, A. J., & Davis, A. K. (2007, August). *Selective exposure in the Internet age: Emotional triggers of political information seeking.* Paper presented at the annual meeting of the American Political Science Association, Chicago, IL.

Valentino, N. A., Hutchings, V. L., Banks, A. J., & Davis, A. K. (2008). Is a worried citizen a good citizen? Emotions, political information seeking, and learning via the Internet. *Political Psychology, 29,* 247–273.

Weinstein, N. D. (1980). Unrealistic optimism about future life events. *Journal of Personality and Social Psychology, 39,* 806–820.

Weinstein, N. D. (1982). Unrealistic optimism about susceptibility to health problems. *Journal of Behavioral Medicine, 5,* 441–460.

Weinstein, N. D. (1983). Reducing unrealistic optimism about illness susceptibility. *Health Psychology, 2,* 11–20.

Weinstein, N. D. (1984). Why it won't happen to me: Perceptions of risk factors and susceptibility. *Health Psychology, 3,* 431–457.

Witte, K. (1992). Putting the fear back in to fear appeals: The extended parallel process model. *Communication Monographs, 59,* 329–349.

Witte, K. (1994). Fear control and danger control: A test of the extended parallel process model. *Communications Monographs, 61,* 113–134.

Zarcadoolas, C., Pleasant, A. F., & Greer, D. S. (2006). *Advancing health literacy: A framework for understanding and action.* San Francisco, CA: Jossey-Bass.

SECTION III

Health [Mis]information Sources

11

HEALTH INFORMATION SEEKING

Ezequiel M. Galarce, Shoba Ramanadhan, and K. Viswanath[1]

Introduction

When does a parent decide whether a child's fever is high and persistent enough to go to the emergency room? Is that allergy medicine shown on TV commercials effective? How does a patient decide which available treatment option is better for her? The growing complexity of the information environment and the choices one is expected to exercise have set the bar high for public and patient health engagement. Engagement implicitly assumes a Jeffersonian notion of an informed citizenry and an advanced level of knowledge necessary to making health decisions. Health knowledge, in turn, implies active health information seeking. For this reason, health information seeking, along with its determinants and consequences, has become a major subject of scientific interest. This growing attention to health information seeking behaviors (HISBs) can be traced to two related phenomena. For more than a decade, there has been a growing reliance on patients' active participation in treatment choices, self-monitoring, and self-care, leading to a shift from a paternalistic model of patient–provider interaction to a shared decision-making paradigm (Institute of Medicine, 2001). This transition has been accompanied by a rapid increase in the availability of treatment options and health information in the environment (Viswanath, 2005). Health information has become ubiquitous, constantly appearing in pharmaceutical advertisements, health news, entertainment media, health websites, and, more recently, in user-generated Internet content, such as blogs and microblogs through a variety of information delivery platforms—as discussed in multiple chapters in this *Handbook*.

Accessing and correctly using health information has an enormous influence on health-related lifestyle factors, early detection and diagnosis, coping with disease, managing symptoms, engaging in active medical decision making, understanding different treatment options, and ultimately, facing end-of-life challenges (van der Molem, 1999; Viswanath, 2005). Historically, the task of health information provision has been placed in the hands of physicians. Today, patients are increasingly relying on other sources to complement health information obtained from providers, either because of dissatisfaction with what is being provided, or a perception of an unfulfilled need for more information (Fallowfield, Ford, & Lewis, 1995).

In this context, understanding and promoting HISB is essential to improve health outcomes. This chapter is not intended to be an in-depth analysis of HISB, but to provide a broad approach to this concept, discuss the factors that may facilitate or hinder its occurrence, and present a brief review of its consequences. We start with a definition of HISB and its scope and boundaries, followed by a characterization of the barriers to HISB, and also entities that facilitate it, including social and structural determinants that may be influential. We also briefly outline the likely health consequences of HISB. Throughout, we draw connections between HISB and communication inequalities, thus placing health information seeking behavior in a social and structural context.

Definition of HISB

An HISB is a purposive act intended to satisfy a perceived need for health information (Johnson, 1997). Consequently, other forms of information acquisition, which are more passive in nature, such as incidental exposure or scanning, are not usually considered to be HISBs (e.g., Shim, Kelly, & Hornik, 2006). An HISB can be defined by its trigger, channel, source, search strategy, type of information sought, and outcomes. These components are mutually dependent and are determined by a complex array of sociodemographic, situational, personal, and structural factors.

Triggers

An HISB is usually triggered by an external stimulus. For example, it could be because of an information need that arises when a person, or someone close to him/her, is experiencing a stressful event, such as a disease (Lenz, 1984). Yet the generation of an information need is not always followed by an HISB. The interpretations of both a health threat and the subsequent information need are constructed in a context- and history-dependent manner (Johnson, 1997; Pinquart & Duberstein, 2004). In other words, the conscious awareness of a need and preference for health information arises from the interaction between health status, type of health problem or disease, psychological processes, and social context. As a result, how much information patients actively seek may vary greatly from some who regularly seek information on health topics to those who may avoid any information (Case, Andrews, Johnson, & Allard, 2005; Echlin & Rees, 2002; Feltwell & Rees, 2004). Some argue that the elicitation of an HISB from an information need ultimately depends on a cost–benefit evaluation in which the effort put into seeking health information is gauged against an anticipated outcome (Lenz, 1984).

Once a person is determined to engage in an HISB he/she will opt for a search strategy, or a specific set of actions to obtain the desired health information. This may include choosing to discuss information directly with other people, attending workshops, reading, relying on another person to perform the search, or other strategies. The selected strategy will become an important determinant of the channel and the source used to obtain the desired information.

Channels

Health information channels are usually classified as either personal (health care provider, family, or friends) or impersonal (pamphlets, magazines, books, radio, or television). The Internet can be placed in either category depending on the way it is used. For example, when searching for information on health websites the Internet can be considered an impersonal channel. When using online forums or social media, however, this channel should be defined as a personal one. It is also common to categorize channels of information as interpersonal or mass media. Others have grouped these channels as less or more intentional depending on the degree of effort required to seek information (Duncan, White, & Nicholson, 2003). People may use more than one channel in an attempt to acquire more information, or to validate the information they have already obtained (Muha, 1998).

The Internet is quickly becoming an important channel of health information. Not only is it constantly available, and able to provide massive amounts of health information, it also provides anonymity (Viswanath, Ramanadhan, & Kontos, 2007). This is especially important when people are seeking sensitive health information which they find difficult or embarrassing to discuss in an interpersonal context (Maguire, Faulkner, Booth, Elliott, & Hillier, 1996). A recent report revealed that 61% of American adults were searching the Internet for health and medical information (Fox & Jones, 2009). It must be noted, however, that access to and capacity to use the Internet varies significantly among social groups, with deep divides amongst social classes and amongst racial/ethnic groups (Viswanath et al., 2006; Viswanath & Kreuter, 2007).

Sources

Health information sources are usually chosen depending on their perceived characteristics pertaining to their accessibility, familiarity, trustworthiness, attractiveness, and reliability. As mentioned above, the choice of a source largely depends on the type of information sought. For instance, when faced with a serious disease, such as cancer, most people prefer their health care professionals as the main source of health information (Johnson & Meischke, 1991). This is especially true when the information sought is factual and related to an immediate health problem. Health care providers may be preferred when seeking information related to the pros and cons of different treatment options. This choice reflects the trust people tend to have in health care providers as sources of objective and reliable information (Hesse et al., 2005).

If confronted with a medical emergency, such as the sudden appearance of a pandemic disease, people may choose to gather health information from newscasters, government officials, or reputable health institutions. This choice, in turn, will affect the selected channel as people will use those with the capacity to deliver information in a constant and immediate manner, such as the radio, television, or the Internet.

A recent study by our group found that 80% of cancer patients rely on family members or friends to assist them with information and decision making. These informal third-party assistants or "Proxy Information Agents (PIAs),"[2] can be defined as social contacts that are asked or volunteer to obtain cancer-related information on behalf of a patient (Echlin & Rees, 2002). The role of PIAs, as both source or channel is important to understand as communications technologies and the availability of information about health are rapidly changing their role and as they become critical in the delivery of health information (see Sundar et al. in this volume).

Health information sources are as varied as sources for any other type of information. For example, a study of female cancer patients found that 60% of patients sought information to complement that provided by their medical team. Among this group of seekers, almost two-thirds (64%) sought information from current and former patients, 55% sought information from people working in a medical environment, 65% sought information from mass media sources, including television and newspapers, and 13% used the Internet to find additional information (Serin et al., 2004).

Even though the vast majority of reports stress the role of sources as separate entities, some studies have focused attention on the way different sources interact. Of great interest is the way patients share information with their doctors that they have sought from nonclinical sources. It is likely that this cross-source phenomenon provides a synergistic benefit that exceeds the added benefit of each separate source and could very well be a reflection of patient engagement with their health (Lewis, Gray, Freres, & Hornik, 2009). However, it is also possible that different sources may conflict in content, which may either favor critical thinking or, on the contrary, induce confusion and stress that potentially lead to communication inequalities.

Types of Information Sought

Health information types vary along several dimensions. Some are medical in nature (e.g., treatment options), whereas others are related to health situations in a more indirect manner (e.g., coping with relationship issues while ill, or financial information after losing a job due to illness). Most research on HISB, however, is focused on medical information. This type of information is often described in the context of a novel health-threatening situation, patient and health-provider communication, shared decision making, symptom management, treatment options, prognosis, preventive behaviors, survivorship, and end-of-life issues (Borgers et al., 1993; Butow, Maclean, Dunn, Tattersall, & Boyer, 1997). A few studies have also focused on patients' HISB patterns regarding doctor and institution choices, and on health-related financial and work issues (Squiers, Rutten, Treiman, Bright, & Hesse, 2005). Even though specific information needs might lead to seeking a limited range of health-information topics, most people will look for different health topics at different stages of their disease. There is evidence to suggest these changes are not only qualitative but quantitative, as patients' HISBs decrease as their condition becomes less acute (Eheman et al., 2009).

Measurement of HISB

Given the complex nature of HISB and its breadth, HISB measurement varies greatly from study to study. For instance, while most researchers may capture the sources of health information, they may or may not tap into other dimensions such as types of health information sought, frequency and intensity, and changes over time, among others.

This situation is the natural consequence of a construct with no universally agreed upon conceptual definition and, most importantly, without any consensual attempts to operationalize it. Moreover, sometimes HISB may be reported as an equivalent to information needs, or preference for information. We argue that "needs" and "preferences" are distinct from and are only early stages in HISB and do not necessarily guarantee that an HISB will take place.

In other circumstances, attempts have been made to measure HISB using scales that were originally created to measure related constructs. For instance, this is the case with the Miller Behavioral Style scale (MBSS) (Miller, 1987), which was designed to measure overall information seeking or avoidance under several hypothetical stressful scenarios. Even though this scale has proven to be both reliable and valid, it does not directly measure people's real HISB patterns.

Current measurement shortcomings are understandable given the relatively recent attention to this subject and the radical changes in the information environment and in information delivery platforms. The current situation will only be remedied with more conceptual and methodological research efforts.

Psychosocial Determinants

Whether a person's information needs are going to be followed by an HISB depends in part on his/her psychosocial traits. These include personality factors that may influence whether a person will be prone to avoid actions that are expected to induce negative emotions. Research has also shown that a person's conviction about his/her capacity to successfully seek information (i.e., self-efficacy), has a great influence on the probability that an information need will be followed by an HISB (Bass et al., 2006). More recent work has offered an integration of a number of individual level psychosocial variables drawn from a variety of models to argue that it is a deliberative or planned behavior that cuts across several health contexts (Kahlor, 2010).

Psychological Traits and Coping Styles

As suggested in the measurement section, the concept of HISB is closely related to Miller's (1987) notions of *monitoring* and *blunting*. From a coping style perspective, the trigger for an HISB is always a stressful event. Therefore, a proclivity toward monitoring (seeking) or blunting (avoiding) is assessed in the context of a stressor. Miller's constructs are not equivalent to HISB, but are widely used to study and understand HISB (e.g., Rees & Bath, 2001). Blunters tend to focus on the predicted negative emotional consequences of engaging in HISB. They avoid health information because they fear that, if found, health information might be scary, negative, or depressing (Rees & Bath, 2001). Blunting, from a purely psychological perspective, however, may be a successful coping strategy. Indeed, one study found that blunters usually felt less distressed than those seeking information (Miller, 1995).

In the case of a serious illness, such as cancer, decisions about seeking or avoiding health information usually take place as a patient is experiencing negative emotions, such as fear, shame, impotence, or worthlessness (Irving & Lloyd-Williams, 2010; Whetten, Reif, Whetten, & Murphy-McMillan, 2008). Therefore, avoiding and seeking health information can be understood as intentional attempts to minimize negative emotions. This choice depends on the interaction of psychological traits (e.g., self-esteem) and contextual factors (Radecki & Jaccard, 1995). When a perceived threat is high, the chances of avoidance also rise. A recent study, for example, found that one third of people with a history of cancer had never looked for cancer-related information (Ramanadhan & Viswanath, 2005). Nonetheless, it is important not to over-attribute the lack of information seeking to personality or health factors without taking into consideration an individual's contextual circumstances, such as access to information and the capacity to use it.

It is noteworthy that when people engage in HISB once, they are more likely do so in the future (Borgers et al., 1993; Czaja, Manfredi, & Price, 2003). Even though the influence of an initial HISB on subsequent HISB attempts is not yet understood in detail, it may be especially important when designing interventions to promote HISB in patient populations. Interventions on certain modifiable psychosocial factors, such as self-efficacy, health beliefs, and social norms, appear to be promising ways to increase HISB in both patient and general populations.

Self-Efficacy and Perceived Norms

A person's beliefs regarding his/her capacity to seek health information (i.e., HISB self-efficacy) are associated with a higher probability of HISB (Bandura & Cervone, 1983; Bass et al., 2006). Self-efficacy has been a central concept in many health behavior change theories (e.g., social cognitive theory) and some recent studies support its relevance to understanding why some people engage in HISB while others do not (Bass et al., 2006). Some have even extended the construct of self-efficacy into HISB, characterizing it as "information efficacy" (Arora et al., 2008).

Beliefs relating to HISB (such as potential costs and benefits of the action and perceptions of engaging in HISB) are important drivers of engaging in HISB (Fishbein et al., 2002). Similarly, perceived behavioral control (assessment of how difficult or easy it will be to engage in HISB) is an important predictor (Ajzen, 1991), and the discussion of self-efficacy is directly relevant to it.

Self-efficacy is measured in terms of specific contexts and domains. For example, a person might show high self-efficacy about asking his/her doctor for treatment options, but low self-efficacy when it comes to finding that same information on the Internet. Change can be induced with specific interventions aimed at boosting self-efficacy and may also naturally change after successful experiences in HISB. In this way, the relationship between self-efficacy and HISB is bidirectional. Self-efficacy is not a purely mental construct. Self-efficacy is also, at least in part, the outcome of an objective resource evaluation. When resources such as access to information are scarce, perceived barriers (e.g., access to Internet) may be disappointingly real and tangible. Thus, self-efficacy-focused interventions must consider and address real barriers to HISB.

Perceived social norms may also act as critical factors in facilitating or undermining HISB attempts. Knowing that family and friends are willing to share and discuss information, or feel that it is important, promotes further HISBs. On the other hand, when an individual feels that there is no interest among people in his/her immediate social context to talk about health issues, he/she might be discouraged and will refrain from seeking further information (Brashers, Goldsmith, & Hsieh, 2002; Loiselle, Lambert, & Cooke, 2006).

Health Beliefs

We have previously argued that health information seeking tends to be avoided when a person fears the negative consequences of learning more about a health problem, such as an aggressive cancer, HIV, or when approaching end-of-life decisions. Negative feelings may arise, ranging from shame and impotence to fear of social stigma. These emotions, however, are not likely to appear when searching for a less threatening health problem, such as a mild toothache. Thus, the occurrence of HISB depends on the nature of a health threat and beliefs regarding such concerns as its risk, prognosis, or stigma. Our focus group research found that cancer patients' likelihood of engaging in HISB varies according to their specific cancer diagnosis. Patients with chronic diseases are more likely to seek health information than are those with acute illnesses (Tu & Hargraves, 2003).

While psychosocial determinants of HISB are important, we contend that for a more complete understanding of HISB, one must also account for social determinants that constrain HISB. Understanding the mutual influence between social and individual factors is essential to improve our understanding of HISBs and their consequences.

Social Determinants

Disparities in health are a major focus of attention among scientists, advocates, and policy makers (Berkman & Kawachi, 2000; Institute of Medicine, 1999; U.S. Department of Health and Human Services, 2000). As discussed in the health disparities chapter of this volume (see Ndiaye, Krieger, Warren, and Hecht, this volume), differences in the quality of clinical care may be one major contributor to health disparities though other non-clinical factors such as socioeconomic status (SES), education, age, and structural factors, such as neighborhoods and social policies, play important roles as well. Differences in information seeking may play a role in creating and perpetuating disparities in health care and health outcomes, a hypothesis that has been discussed in the broader context of *communication inequalities* (Viswanath et al., 2006). Recent studies have shown that communication inequalities are associated with differences in knowledge on smoking and skin cancer, cancer screening, smoking behaviors, and environmental health risks (Ackerson & Viswanath, 2009; Cairns & Viswanath, 2006; Taylor-Clark, Koh, & Viswanath, 2007; Viswanath et al., 2006). Significant inequalities in the degree to which patients from different socioeconomic and racial/ethnic groups actively seek information may lead to disparate health outcomes (Ramanadhan & Viswanath, 2006).

This macrosocial perspective differentiates itself from prevailing viewpoints which tend to associate motivation for health information seeking with psychosocial coping styles, such as monitoring or blunting. Seminal studies, such as those by Cassileth et al. (Cassileth, Zupkis, Sutton-Smith, & March, 1980), and more recent work on communication inequalities, have exposed significant differences in HISB among different social classes and racial and ethnic groups. However, the differences and inequalities in health information seeking among different social groups are poorly understood (Ramanadhan & Viswanath, 2006).

The Structural Influence Model

Recent work has shown that social determinants shape access to and use of information channels, attention to and the ability to process health information, recollection and comprehension of health information, and the capacity to act upon that knowledge (Viswanath, 2006). From this perspective, the health disparities existing between higher and lower SES groups are considered to be, at least partly, a product of underlying inequalities in communication.

The Structural Influence Model (SIM) proposes that health outcomes, including health disparities, are the consequence of social determinants, sociodemographic moderating factors, and health communication outcomes (Viswanath et al., 2007). Social determinants are mostly understood as factors related to socioeconomic position, such as education, income and occupation, and physical context (Ramanadhan & Viswanath, 2006; Viswanath, 2006). The moderating factors in health outcomes are related to sociodemographic dimensions like gender, age and race/ethnicity, as well as such social network characteristics as social capital and network resources. Both social determinants and mediating factors such as psychosocial variables lead to specific health communication outcomes, including HISBs, which subsequently influence health outcomes that incorporate cognitive (health knowledge and beliefs), behavioral (capacity for action, preventive behaviors), and medical outcomes (treatment, survivorship, and end-of-life care).

Thus, SIM conceives health outcomes and health disparities as the product of the cumulative influence of social determinants, sociodemographic factors, and communication outcomes. The relationships among health communication dimensions and health outcomes are likely to be bidirectional. Health communication outcomes influence health outcomes, and some health outcomes' dimensions, such as knowledge and health beliefs, also determine the nature of health media attention, use, and processing. Furthermore, health outcomes may have a direct impact on social determinants, such as employment and income.

Sociodemographic Factors

The association between sociodemographic variables and HISB has been extensively examined (Duggan & Bates, 2008; Eakin & Strycker, 2001; Mayer et al., 2007; Rutten, Squiers, & Hesse, 2006). This relationship has been almost always found to be very robust. Most studies tend to come to similar conclusions: being white, young, female, well-educated, and in a good financial position will favor the chances of someone being an active information seeker. The following examples will help illustrate this point.

Age. Several studies have shown that people aged 65 or older tend to be infrequent information seekers (Duggan & Bates, 2008; Lambert & Loiselle, 2007; Rutten et al., 2006). The reason for this is not yet clear, but there is evidence to suggest that older people face specific barriers to accessing health information (Cotten & Gupta, 2004). This is especially true when attempting to use the Internet as a channel of health information. Another explanation may be that older people tend to rely more on health care providers and have a lower interest in actively participating in the medical decision-making process than do young people. However appealing it may be, this hypothesis has yet to be tested.

Gender. Most studies examining HISB find that women are much more likely to seek health information than are men (e.g., Rutten et al., 2006). The reasons underlying this phenomenon are not entirely clear. Possible explanations may range from general statements about sociocultural gender differences to assumptions about role responsibilities that lead them to engage in HISBs.

Race. Whites tend to engage more in HISBs than any other ethnic/racial group (Nguyen & Bellamy, 2006). Like older people, members of minority groups tend to rely on their health care providers to make decisions for them (Maliski, Connor, Fink, & Litwin, 2006). This has been demonstrated both among African Americans and Spanish-speaking Hispanics (Levinson, Kao, Kuby, & Thisted, 2005; Vanderpool, Kornfeld, Finney Rutten, & Squiers, 2009). Among Spanish-speaking Hispanics who attempted to engage in HISBs, some reported having a hard time understanding cancer information, putting a lot of effort into it, and experiencing overall feelings of frustration (Levinson et al., 2005; Vanderpool et al., 2009).

While the difference in HISB between whites and other racial/ethnic minorities is extensively documented, the reasons for the difference are not clear. Several plausible hypotheses may be offered. It is possible that some minority groups, especially recent immigrants, are less likely to take an active role in decision making and hence feel less of a need for health information seeking. It is also possible that the effects of a less active role in medical decision making on HISBs may be confounded by effects of language barriers or education levels. This suggests that in many cases it may not be race or ethnicity *per se* that mediates HISB but possibly other nativity or SES factors.

Education and Health Literacy. The role of education in HISB is paramount. The majority of studies stressing the role of sociodemographics in HISB have found a strong association between education and HISBs (Arora et al., 2008; Kelly, Sturm, Kemp, Holland, & Ferketich, 2009; Sullivan & Finney Rutten, 2009). Our own studies have found that when including education in an HISB model, the effects of race, as well of income on HISB become less relevant (Galarce et al., 2010). Not understanding health content may be one of the strongest barriers to HISB. In recent years, the association between health literacy, HISB, and health has become more apparent (Institute of Medicine, 2004; Shieh, Mays, McDaniel, & Yu, 2009). Further details regarding issues of health literacy can be found in the chapter by Cameron et al. in this book

Measurement issues are of prime importance in studying the impact of education on HISB. Researchers usually use *years of education* (or degrees obtained) as the main education variable. Though this measure allows for demonstration of the impact of education on HISB, it only accounts for *quantity* of education, not for *quality*, which varies greatly in the United States. Thus, measuring actual numeracy, reading and comprehension skills may help better understand the relationship between education and health behaviors. The precise pathways connecting education with health outcomes, either through communication or through other resources that education endows, is yet to be fully explored.

Financial Status. Monetary wealth can provide access to many resources, including health information. The effects of income on HISB are especially evident when comparing low-income with middle- and high-income people (Mayer et al., 2007; Ramanadhan & Viswanath, 2006). With the increasing role of the Internet as a major channel for the delivery of health information, this difference has become more apparent, and has been coined by some as the *digital divide*. Even though computers are becoming more affordable, Internet access is still outside the reach of many low-income people. To make matters worse, most new websites require broadband Internet speeds to run properly, which can only be afforded by people in a comfortable financial position (Viswanath, 2005). Additionally, individuals with low levels of wealth may face competing demands that leave them with little time or motivation to engage in any form of HISB.

HISB Outcomes

HISBs not only serve an instrumental function but provide the emotional support necessary for reducing feelings of uncertainty and anxiety and for engaging in successful coping styles and in preventive behaviors (Johnson, 1997). Health knowledge gained from information seeking is associated with increased self-efficacy to manage health, and may, in turn, encourage further HISB (Bandura & Cervone, 1983; Lee, Hwang, Hawkins, & Pingree, 2008). An extensive body of work shows a strong association between HISBs and outcomes such as cancer screening, reducing unhealthy behaviors, promoting self-care management and treatment compliance, participation in medical decision making, greater satisfaction with the treatment, and coping with their diagnoses (Briss et al., 2004; Cassileth et al., 1980; Gray et al., 2009; Hiatt & Rimer, 1999; Manfredi, Czaja, Price, Buis, & Janiszewski, 1993; Rutten et al., 2006; Shi, Nakamura, & Takano, 2004; Warner & Procaccino, 2004; Yu & Wu, 2005).

Conclusion

In this chapter we attempted to provide a broad description of health information seeking, the social and individual determinants that are associated with it, and its consequences. The subject of health information seeking is becoming more important than ever before. Patients are expected to make more informed decisions about their medical treatments, and this trend is expected to grow exponentially for a variety of reasons that include the revolutionary developments in biomedical sciences such as genomics and proteomics and systems biology, which will lead to greater numbers of treatment choices. These advances in biomedical sciences are occurring in parallel with the communication and informatics revolution that provides more information on a variety of information delivery platforms. Taming the tide of this information and making choices that can have positive health outcomes is an important capacity to cultivate among patients and families coping with illness and disease.

Equally critical is to ensure that this capacity to cope with the information and make informed choices is not limited to the privileged but is more democratically available to all. Future research will improve our knowledge of channels and formats through which information is sought and how this may vary among different SES, racial, and ethnic groups. This should include better understanding of what channels are used across the SES continuum to obtain different types of health information, of how people process and use different aspects of health-related messages, and ultimately, what specific demands for health information needs are unmet. In this way, a broader picture of the impact of social determinants on information-seeking processes could lead to the development of more effective interventions.

Improvement of information support is critical to the care process, yet information is one of the care categories with the highest unmet need (Cassileth et al., 1980; Duggan & Bates, 2008; Mayer et al., 2007). Ultimately, a deeper understanding of not just whether patients and survivors seek information but also of *what* they are looking for, as well as patterns of information-seeking across social groups is vital to improve the delivery of information to these groups and thereby bridge existing disparities in health outcomes.

Notes

1. Acknowledgments: We gratefully acknowledge funding support from the Lance Armstrong Foundation and the National Cancer Institute (CA122894) to the senior author, Viswanath.
2. The term *proxy information agent* (PIA) was coined by Dr. Eric Schneider, a physician and health services researcher at Rand.

References

Ackerson, L. K., & Viswanath, K. (2009). Communication inequalities, social determinants, and intermittent smoking in the 2003 Health Information National Trends Survey. *Preventing Chronic Disease, 6*, A40.

Arora, N. K., Hesse, B. W., Rimer, B. K., Viswanath, K., Clayman, M. L., & Croyle, R. T. (2008). Frustrated and confused: The American public rates its cancer-related information-seeking experiences. *Journal of General Internal Medicine, 23*, 223–228.

Ajzen, I. (1991). The theory of planned behavior. *Organizational Behavior and Human Decision Processes, 50*, 179–211.

Bandura, A., & Cervone, D. (1983). Self-evaluative and self-efficacy mechanisms governing the motivational effects of goal systems. *Journal of Personality and Social Psychology, 45*, 1017–1028.

Bass, S., Ruzek, S., Gordon, T., Fleisher, L., McKeown-Conn, N., & Moore, D. (2006). Relationship of internet health information use with patient behavior and self-efficacy: Experiences of newly diagnosed cancer patients who contact the national cancer institute's cancer information service. *Journal of Health Communication, 11,* 219–236.

Berkman, L. F., & Kawachi, I. (Eds.). (2000). *Social epidemiology.* New York: Oxford University Press.

Borgers, R., Mullen, P. D., Meertens, R., Rijken, M., Eussen, G., Plagge, I., ... Blijham, G. H. (1993). The information-seeking behavior of cancer outpatients: A description of the situation. *Patient Education & Counseling, 22,* 35–46.

Brashers, D. E., Goldsmith, D. J., & Hsieh, E. I. (2002). Information seeking and avoiding in health contexts. *Human Communication Research, 28,* 258–271.

Briss, P., Rimer, B., Reilley, B., Coates, R. C., Lee, N. C., Mullen, P., ... Lawrence, R. (2004). Promoting informed decisions about cancer screening in communities and healthcare systems. *American Journal of Preventive Medicine, 26,* 67–80.

Butow, P. N., Maclean, M., Dunn, S. M., Tattersall, M. H. N., & Boyer, M. J. (1997). The dynamics of change: Cancer patients' preferences for information, involvement and support. *Annals of Oncology, 8,* 857–863.

Cairns, C., & Viswanath, K. (2006). Colorectal cancer screening among the uninsured: Data from the Health Information National Trends Survey. *Cancer Causes and Control, 17,* 1115–1125.

Case, D. O., Andrews, J. E., Johnson, J. D., & Allard, S. L. (2005). Avoiding versus seeking: The relationship of information seeking to avoidance, blunting, coping, dissonance, and related concepts. *Journal of the Medical Library Association, 93,* 353–362.

Cassileth, B. R., Zupkis, R. V., Sutton-Smith, K., & March, V. (1980). Information and participation preferences among cancer patients. *Annals of Internal Medicine, 92,* 832–836.

Cotten, S. R., & Gupta, S. S. (2004). Characteristics of online and offline health information seekers and factors that discriminate between them. *Social Science & Medicine, 59,* 1795–1806.

Czaja, R., Manfredi, C., & Price, J. (2003). The determinants and consequences of information seeking among cancer patients. *Journal of Health Communication, 8,* 529–562.

Duggan, C., & Bates, I. (2008). Medicine information needs of patients: The relationships between information needs, diagnosis and disease. *Quality and Safety in Health Care, 17,* 85–89.

Duncan, D. F., White, J. B., & Nicholson, T. (2003). Using internet-based surveys to reach hidden populations: Case of non abusive illicit drug users. *American Journal of Health Behavior, 27,* 208–218.

Eakin, E., G., & Strycker, L. A. (2001). Awareness and barriers to use of cancer support and information resources by HMO patients with breast, prostate, or colon cancer: Patient and provider perspectives. *Psycho-Oncology, 10,* 103–113.

Echlin, K. N., & Rees, C. E. (2002). Information needs and information-seeking behaviors of men with prostate cancer and their partners: A review of the literature. *Cancer Nursing, 25,* 35–41.

Eheman, C. R., Berkowitz, Z., Lee, J., Mohile, S., Purnell, J., Rodriguez, E. M., ... Morrow, G. (2009). Information-seeking styles among cancer patients before and after treatment by demographics and use of information sources. *Journal of Health Communication, 14,* 487–502.

Fallowfield, L., Ford, S., & Lewis, S. (1995). No news is not good news: Information preferences of patients with cancer. *Psycho-Oncology, 4,* 197–202.

Feltwell, A. K., & Rees, C. E. (2004). The information-seeking behaviours of partners of men with prostate cancer: A qualitative pilot study. *Patient Education and Counseling, 54,* 179–185.

Fishbein, M., Cappella, J., Hornick, R., Sayeed, S., Yzer, M., & Ahern, R. K. (2002). The role of theory in developing effective anti-drug public service announcements. In W. D. Crano & M. Burgoon (Eds.), *Mass media and drug prevention: Classic and contemporary theories and research* (pp. 89–118). Mahwah, NJ: Erlbaum.

Fox, S., & Jones, S. (2009). The social life of health information. Washington, DC: Pew Internet & American Life Project.

Galarce, E. M., Ramanadhan, S., Crisostomo, J., Alexander-Molloy, J., Weeks, J., Schneider, E. C., & Viswanath, K. (2010, April). *Barriers to accessing internet health information among cancer patients and survivors.* Paper presented at the Society of Behavioral Medicine, Seattle, USA.

Gray, S. W., O'Grady, C., Karp, L., Smith, D., Schwartz, J. S., Hornik, R. C., & Armstrong, K. (2009). Risk information exposure and direct-to-consumer genetic testing for BRCA mutations among women with a personal or family history of breast or ovarian cancer. *Cancer Epidemiology Biomarkers & Prevention, 18,* 1303–1311.

Hesse, B. W., Nelson, D. E., Kreps, G. L., Croyle, R. T., Arora, N. K., Rimer, B. K., & Viswanath, K. (2005). Trust and sources of health information: The impact of the internet and its implications for health care providers: Findings from the first Health Information National Trends Survey. *Archives of Internal Medicine, 165,* 2618–2624.

Hiatt, R. A., & Rimer, B. K. (1999). A new strategy for cancer control research. *Cancer Epidemiology Biomarkers & Prevention, 8,* 957–964.

Institute of Medicine. (1999). *The unequal burden of cancer.* Washington, DC: National Academy Press.

Institute of Medicine. (2001). *Crossing the quality chasm: A new health system for the 21st century.* Washington, DC: National Academy Press.

Institute of Medicine. (2004). *Health literacy: A prescription to end confusion.* Washington, DC: National Academy Press.

Irving, G., & Lloyd-Williams, M. (2010). Depression in advanced cancer. *European Journal of Oncology Nursing: The Official Journal of European Oncology Nursing Society.*

Johnson, J. D. (1997). *Cancer-related information seeking.* Cresskill, NJ: Hampton Press.

Johnson, J. D., & Meischke, H. (1991). Women's preferences for cancer information from specific communication channels. *The American Behavioral Scientist, 34,* 742–755.

Kahlor, L. (2010). PRISM: A Planned Risk Information Seeking Model. *Health Communication, 25*(4), 197–211.

Kelly, K. M., Sturm, A. C., Kemp, K., Holland, J., & Ferketich, A. K. (2009). How can we reach them? Information seeking and preferences for a cancer family history campaign in underserved communities. *Journal of Health Communication, 14,* 573–589.

Lambert, S. D., & Loiselle, C. G. (2007). Health information seeking behavior. *Qualitative Health Research, 17,* 1006–1019.

Lee, S. Y., Hwang, H., Hawkins, R., & Pingree, S. (2008). Interplay of negative emotion and health self-efficacy on the use of health information and its outcomes. *Communication Research, 35,* 358–381.

Lenz, E. (1984). Information seeking: A component of client decisions and health behavior. *Advances in Nursing Science, 6,* 59–71.

Levinson, W., Kao, A., Kuby, A., & Thisted, R. A. (2005). Not all patients want to participate in decision making. *Journal of General Internal Medicine, 20,* 531–535.

Lewis, N., Gray, S. W., Freres, D. R., & Hornik, R. C. (2009). Examining cross-source engagement with cancer-related information and its impact on doctor-patient relations. *Health Communication, 24,* 723–734. doi: 10.1080/10410230903264030

Loiselle, C. G., Lambert, S. D., & Cooke, A. (2006). The searching, processing, and sharing of breast cancer information by women diagnosed with the illness. *Canadian Journal of Nursing Research, 38,* 82–104.

Maguire, P., Faulkner, A., Booth, K., Elliott, C., & Hillier, V. (1996). Helping cancer patients disclose their concerns. *European Journal of Cancer Care, 32A,* 78–81.

Maliski, S. L., Connor, S., Fink, A., & Litwin, M. S. (2006). Information desired and acquired by men with prostate cancer: Data from ethnic focus groups. *Health Education & Behavior, 33,* 393–409.

Manfredi, C., Czaja, R., Price, J., Buis, M., & Janiszewski, R. (1993). Cancer patients' search for information. *Journal of the National Cancer Institute Monographs, 14,* 93–104.

Mayer, D. K., Terrin, N. C., Kreps, G. L., Menon, U., McCance, K., Parsons, S. K., & Mooney, K. H. (2007). Cancer survivors' information seeking behaviors: A comparison of survivors who do and do not seek information about cancer. *Patient Education and Counseling, 65,* 342–350.

Miller, S. M. (1987). Monitoring and blunting: Validation of a questionnaire to assess styles of information seeking under threat. *Journal of Personality and Social Psychology, 52,* 345–353.

Miller, S. M. (1995). Monitoring versus blunting styles of coping with cancer influence the information patients want and need about their disease. Implications for cancer screening and management. *Cancer, 76,* 167–177.

Miller, S. M. (1987). Monitoring and blunting: Validation of a questionnaire to assess styles of information seeking under threat. *Journal of Personality and Social Psychology, 52,* 345–353.

Muha, C. (1998). The use and selection of sources in information seeking: The cancer information service experience. Part 8. *Journal of Health Communication, 3,* 109–120.

Nguyen, G. T., & Bellamy, S. L. (2006). Cancer information seeking preferences and experiences: Disparities between Asian Americans and whites in the Health Information National Trends Survey (HINTS) [Supplement]. *Journal of Health Communication, 11*(1), 173–180.

Pinquart, M., & Duberstein, P. R. (2004). Information needs and decision-making processes in older cancer patients. *Critical Reviews in Oncology/Hematology, 51*, 69–80.

Radecki, C. M., & Jaccard, J. (1995). Perceptions of knowledge, actual knowledge, and information search behavior. *Journal of Experimental Social Psychology, 31*, 107–138.

Ramanadhan, S., & Viswanath, K. (2005, December). *Disparities in information-seeking among persons with a history of cancer: Evidence from a national survey.* Paper presented at the American Public Health Association, Philadelphia, PA.

Ramanadhan, S., & Viswanath, K. (2006). Health and the information nonseeker: A profile. *Health Communication, 20*, 131–139.

Rees, C. E., & Bath, P. A. (2001). Information-seeking behaviors of women with breast cancer. *Oncology Nursing Forum, 28*, 899–907.

Rutten, L. J. F., Squiers, L., & Hesse, B. (2006). Cancer-related information seeking: Hints from the 2003 Health Information National Trends Survey (HINTS). *Journal of Health Communication, 11*, 147–156.

Serin, D., Dilhuydy, J. M., Romestaing, P., Guiochet, N., Gledhill, J., Bret, P., ... Flinois, A. (2004). "Parcours de femme 2001": A French opinion survey on overall disease and everyday life management in 1870 women presenting with gynecological or breast cancer and their caregivers. *Annals of Oncology, 15*, 1056–1064.

Shi, H.-J., Nakamura, K., & Takano, T. (2004). Health values and health-information-seeking in relation to positive change of health practice among middle-aged urban men. *Preventive Medicine, 39*, 1164–1171.

Shieh, C., Mays, R., McDaniel, A., & Yu, J. (2009). Health literacy and its association with the use of information sources and with barriers to information seeking in clinic-based pregnant women. *Health Care for Women International, 30*, 971–988.

Shim, M., Kelly, B., & Hornik, R. (2006). Cancer information scanning and seeking behavior is associated with knowledge, lifestyle choices, and screening. *Journal of Health Communication, 11*, 157–172.

Squiers, L., Rutten, L. J. F., Treiman, K., Bright, M. A., & Hesse, B. (2005). Cancer patients' information needs across the cancer care continuum: Evidence from the cancer information service. *Journal of Health Communication, 10*, 15–34.

Sullivan, H. W., & Finney Rutten, L. J. (2009). Cancer prevention information seeking: A signal detection analysis of data from the cancer information service. *Journal of Health Communication, 14*, 785–796.

Taylor-Clark, K., Koh, H., & Viswanath, K. (2007). Perceptions of environmental health risks and communication barriers among low-sep and racial/ethnic minority communities. *Journal of Health Care for the Poor and Underserved 4*, 165–183.

Tu, H. T., & Hargraves, J. L. (2003). Seeking health care information: Most consumers still on the sidelines. *Issue Brief (Center for Studying Health System Change), 61*, 1–4.

U.S. Department of Health and Human Services. (2000). *Healthy people 2010: Understanding and improving health and objectives for improving health* (2nd ed.). Washington, DC: U.S. Government Printing Office.

van der Molem, B. (1999). Relating information needs to the cancer experience: 1. Information as a key coping strategy. *European Journal of Cancer Care, 8*, 238–244.

Vanderpool, R. C., Kornfeld, J., Finney Rutten, L., & Squiers, L. (2009). Cancer information-seeking experiences: The implications of Hispanic ethnicity and Spanish language. *Journal of Cancer Education, 24*, 141–147.

Viswanath, K. (2005). The communications revolution and cancer control. *Nature Reviews Cancer, 5*, 828–835.

Viswanath, K. (2006). Public communications and its role in reducing and eliminating health disparities. In G. E. Thomson, F. Mitchell, & M. B. Williams (Eds.), *Examining the health disparities research plan of the national institutes of health: Unfinished business* (pp. 215–253). Washington, DC: Institute of Medicine.

Viswanath, K., Breen, N., Meissner, H., Moser, R. P., Hesse, B., Steele, W. R., & Rakowski, W. (2006). Cancer knowledge and disparities in the information age. *Journal of Health Communication, 11,* 1–17.

Viswanath, K., & Kreuter, M. W. (2007). Health disparities, communication inequalities, and ehealth [Supplement]. *American Journal of Preventive Medicine, 32,* S131–S133.

Viswanath, K., Ramanadhan, S., & Kontos, E. Z. (2007). Mass media and population health: A macrosocial view. In S. Galea (Ed.), *Macrosocial determinants of population health* (pp. 275–294). New York: Springer.

Warner, D., & Procaccino, J. D. (2004). Toward wellness: Women seeking health information. *Journal of the American Society for Information Science and Technology, 55,* 709–730.

Whetten, K., Reif, S., Whetten, R., & Murphy-McMillan, L. K. (2008). Trauma, mental health, distrust, and stigma among HIV-positive persons: Implications for effective care. *Psychosomatic Medicine, 70,* 531–538.

Yu, M. Y., & Wu, T. Y. (2005). Factors influencing mammography screening of Chinese American women. *Journal of Obstetric, Gynecologic, and Neonatal Nursing, 34,* 386–394.

12

ONLINE HEALTH INFORMATION

Conceptual Challenges and Theoretical Opportunities

S. Shyam Sundar, Ronald E. Rice, Hyang-Sook Kim, and Chris N. Sciamanna

"Tectonic shift": That is how the architects of the first Health Information National Trends Survey characterized recent changes in the way we seek and consume health information (Hesse et al., 2005). Thanks to the dramatic diffusion of the Internet and widespread availability of health information and services online, the majority of Americans now conduct increasing amounts of their health communication via online channels. The latest Pew survey found that 61% of adults had used the Internet for health information (Hesse et al., 2005, reported 63%), up from 25% in 2000 (Fox & Jones, 2009). The most frequent searches were for a specific disease or medical problem (49%) and a medical treatment or procedure (41%). Searching for exercise and fitness information increased the most from 2002, up to 38%. Quite noteworthy is that two-thirds talk about the results with someone else, typically a spouse or friends, and that just over half of all online inquiries are done for the benefit of someone else. More and more, users are also reading someone else's experiences (41% via news group, website or blog), rankings of doctors or health care providers, and rankings of hospitals or other medical facilities (both 24%), receiving health or medical updates (19%), or listening to a health or medical issue podcast (13%).

While the digital divide is still a reality, with e-health usage tempered by access issues (e.g., Beckjord et al., 2007), sociodemographic, psychological, and health factors (e.g., McNeill, Puleo, Bennett, & Emmons, 2007; Rice, 2006), the trend toward posting and seeking health information online continues, especially globally. In Europe, 44% of the adult population of Norway, Denmark, Germany, Greece, Poland, Portugal, and Latvia (71% of Internet users in these countries) report going online for health information (Andreassen et al., 2007) in order to read up on medical conditions and prepare for or follow up on doctor visits. Similar patterns have been observed in less developed parts of the world, especially among the younger generation. For example, Borzekowski, Fobil, and Asante (2006) report that two-thirds of the in-school youth and over half (54%) of out-of-school adolescents in Ghana's capital city of Accra had gone online, with 53% of them seeking health information on the Internet with "great interest" and "high levels of efficacy" (p. 450).

An Overview of e-Health

The increase in and diversification of users are matched only by the tremendous variety and scope of health information and services available online. The landscape of e-Health has become a vast one, with individual and population health technologies that have been deployed in clinical as well as nonclinical areas for a range of stakeholders, with the overall goal of enabling and improving health and health care (Eng, 2001). It includes access to and provision of content (health information, health behavior change, decision making); connectivity (across functions, organizations, actors, providing research results); community (messaging, online support); commerce (products, medical equipment and supplies, medications, insurance); and care (self-care, electronic health records, disease management, telemedicine/tele-Health) (e.g., Eng, 2001; Gibbons, 2007; Wallis & Rice, 2006). See Tables 12.1 and 12.2 for a summary of the advantages and disadvantages of e-Health, as well as facilitators of and barriers to the development of e-Health.

Health Websites

Websites remain the mainstay of health information on the Internet. Websites are remarkably versatile tools for mass communication of health information and advice. For example, the Dietary Approaches to Stop Hypertension (DASH) program found that sustained use of materials on nutrition education, delivered totally via the Internet, involving no person-to-person contact with health professionals, resulted in significant dietary improvements and lowering of weight and blood pressure after 12 months (Moore et al., 2008). In general, health websites have been shown to be quite effective in promoting self-help (Farvolden, Denisoff, Selby, Bagby, & Rudy, 2005) and preparing patients for doctor appointments (Hartmann et al., 2007).

Health websites are not only repositories of information, but also vibrant forums for discussion. While research on social support has historically examined chat rooms and bulletin boards on health sites, newer studies have focused on Web 2.0 media such as blogs and wikis. As Denecke and Nejdl (2009) note, some medical weblogs and question and answer portals provide rich information on diseases and medications, and some wikis deal with information on anatomy and procedures. Patients and nurses tend to dwell on personal and emotional aspects while doctors fill their blog posts with information. Both of them are picked up by search engines and therefore enter the mainstream of online health information, given that most people tend to start their quest for health information via search engines (e.g., Eysenbach & Kohler, 2002). Despite the free-floating nature of content, studies show that health blogs are seen as credible sources of information. Medical bloggers tend to be highly educated and devoted to sharing practical knowledge and skills (Kovic, Lulic, & Brumini, 2008). Sundar, Edwards, Hu, and Stavrositu (2007) argue that blogs have the real potential to put the public back into public health by allowing patients an active, dynamic space for dealing with their illness and informing as well as influencing others along the way. As part of their coping, patient bloggers not only connect with others in similar situations, but also construct their identity, in an effort to assert agency (Sundar, 2008). In the blogosphere, the receiver is the source of both personal and mass communication. In addition, other receivers also serve as sources through their own blogs or by commenting on others' blogs. In this manner, blog technology operationalizes the concept of "receiver sources" (Sundar & Nass, 2001) at both the individual and collective levels.

Table 12.1 Advantages and Disadvantages of e-Health

Advantages

- allow anonymity and reduced social cues, to increase honest discussions and disclosure, for posting personal health information and problems and less risk in online self-disclosure
- allow some who are not comfortable posting messages to "lurk"
- awareness and management of one's own health records
- better informed patients for physicians
- broader access on demand (more times and places)
- broader range of health information
- collaborative health decision making
- connect patients and health care providers who are geographically or professionally isolated
- convenient and efficient learning environments for medical training
- cost-containment or cost-reduction strategies
- emotional support
- encyclopedic breadth of information
- expanded choice and autonomy
- faster diffusion of medical research and knowledge (i.e., rare conditions)
- finding/communicating with/evaluating health providers
- foster development of online communities
- foster development of social and professional health care networks beyond patients/individuals and beyond system users
- greater access to diverse sources of health information
- greater communication with others sharing the health problems, and with health professionals
- greater provision at lower cost in residential and rural homes
- healthier communities
- healthier employees
- healthier population more capable of self-care
- help patients make sense of their medical experience (such as cancer)
- improve access to alternative medicine products and information
- improve and update dissemination of health information
- improve doctor–patient communication (through e-mail, and bringing in printouts of Internet health information)
- improve patient empowerment and self-care
- improve self-presentation in discussing medical conditions with others
- increase access to emotional and social support from broad range of others who share same experience and concerns
- increase access to health information
- increase interaction with others dealing with the same problem
- increase personalization
- increase the capacity of health care providers to promote, treat, monitor, and discuss health conditions
- match the modes used to the intervention purposes of the users' learning styles
- message tailoring and stages of readiness assessed through interactive choices
- more adherent and satisfied patients
- more efficient service
- more interactivity
- more personalized and customized information and interactions
- not just receive but also provide social support or the more broad experience of generalized reciprocity and sharing
- provide clinical support (such as medical education, diagnoses, and best practices) to nonphysicians
- provide convenient support for peer counseling
- provide more health services to underserved populations, reducing health disparities
- provide online health insurance applications and registration
- reduce costs
- reduce errors and delays (such as in prescriptions, medications, obtaining personal medical records)
- reduce health care costs
- reduce obstacles to interpersonal communication
- support groups
- sustained use of e-Health products
- switch from telephone calls to online information provision
- tailor health information
- tailoring
- therapeutic value of self-disclosure
- time, place, and space flexibility in taking online medical education courses
- wider access for at-risk groups through online health campaigns and interactive interventions
- wider markets for products

(Continued)

Table 12.1 Continued

Disadvantages	
• access to unregulated drugs and risk of bypassing checks for drug interactions	• inaccurate and unknown quality of information (especially through online support groups)
• access to unverified information and alternative medicines or treatments	• inappropriate access by third parties
• allow some to "lurk" and "free ride"	• may require additional procedures and effort to use a new system
• altering perceived expertise and authority of physician	• may require important financial investments over time
• applications misuse	• missing or misleading website links
• barriers to access, worsening digital and cultural divide	• narrow and self-reinforcing information and interactions
• benefits require technical expertise, skills and medical knowledge	• overload, confusion, and even fright, from online health information
• challenges to physicians by patients with Internet information	• overwhelming number of sites and resources
• commercial biases in health and prescription sites not always identified	• presentation of opinion as fact
• complexity and difficulty in understanding online medical information	• pressure on physicians to prescribe Internet-advertised medicines
• decrease public trust in health providers and practices	• privacy and confidentiality risks
• email interaction with patients generates considerable demands on staff and raises liability issues	• risk of frauds or severe health damages
	• search results are difficult to filter
• enormous barriers to access in developing countries	• self-diagnosis and prescribing
• fraud	• unknown authorship, lack of source citation
• improper use of personal information	• unreliable networks or storage
	• use of social media to bypass bans or restrictions on advertising

Sources: Eng (2001), Fox (2006), Freeman & Chapman (2008), Morahan-Martin (2004), Murero & Rice (2006), Neuhauser & Kreps (2003), Vance, Howe, & Dellavalle (2009).

Health websites do, however, vary in their content and features, especially across commercial and nonprofit sites. A content analysis of 20 commercial and 11 government health sites in 1999 (Rice, Peterson, & Christie, 2001) compared 74 specific features in seven major categories: Non-Interactive Substantive Content, e-Commerce, Multimedia Content, Navigation or Assistance, Search Methods, Interactivity, and Policy. Scientific/Medical/Academic materials were slightly more frequent on government sites (especially notices of clinical trials, and medical library databases) than on commercial sites. Alternatively, commercial sites had somewhat more Educational/Journalistic/PR/Publicity features than did government sites, but only in the area of prevention/wellness information. Obviously, commercial sites had far more e-commerce features, especially in the form of advertising banners, sponsors, online pharmacies, and health or life insurance quotes. Commercial sites also used multimedia features more frequently, especially moving icons/animation or pictures/illustrations. Government sites provided more navigation and assistance features, and search methods and tools, especially in the use of topic headings, but with far less use of pull-down or scrolling menus. Commercial sites provided extensive support for interactivity among users compared to government sites, especially chat rooms and news groups, and also for interactivity with the website. Government sites provided noticeably fewer policy features, particularly with respect to copyright (to be expected, as most, but not all, government information is not copyrighted), advertising policy, and disclaimers. On average, commercial sites offered 22.5 of the 74 features compared to 14 by government sites.

One decade later, West and Miller (2009) conducted a rigorous content analysis of the top 44 commercial websites, top 30 nonprofit health websites, and each state's department of public health website. Few commercial sites displayed health information quality certification seals, and generally had low levels of sponsor disclosure, while government sites presented clear disclosure. Accessibility (e.g., color contrasts, text "alt" tags for images, text telephones or telecommunications devices for the deaf tools, navigation tools) was provided by just over half of government sites, but less than 20% of commercial or nonprofit sites. The mean reading grade level of the text on the sites was 11.4 for government, 9.6 for nonprofit, and 8.7 for commercial sites. Commercial and nonprofit sites offered more interactivity (newsletters, e-mail messages, updates, tailoring, mobile devices) than government sites. Security policies were provided by 84% of commercial, 56% of government, and 40% of nonprofit sites, though privacy policies were more abundant (98%, 56%, and 77%, respectively). Although many of the policies were weak or ambiguous, 77% of commercial sites stated they would not share personal information, with 44% of governmental and 60% of nonprofit sites doing so. Information quality (comparing coverage of breast cancer, strokes, and kidney stones) varied widely across these three major categories of sites, and across nations and cultures (Baek & Yu, 2009).

Health Devices

In addition to web-based technologies, health communication online takes place through a number of devices. Given increasing acceptance of self-service technology and the readiness for medical self-diagnosis (Lanseng & Andreassen, 2007), a suite of online as well as offline applications, using a variety of media from telephones to kiosks, has emerged to provide automated health care. Electronic mail, for example, is proving to be a cost-effective tool, both for directing attention and traffic toward health websites (Woodall et al., 2007) and for reminding users to adopt healthy behaviors. An e-mail intervention called *Alive!*, featuring weekly goal-setting, individualized feedback, tips, reminders, and promotion of social

Table 12.2 Facilitators of and Barriers to e-Health

Facilitators	
• appropriate regulation (i.e., Health Insurance Portability and Accountability Act [HIPAA] standards) and reliable web content • broadband infrastructure • collaboration and cooperation among agencies • computer skills and Internet proficiency for nonmedical public and health care providers • cultural and psychological dimensions • facilitating cultural agents and media support • government promotion of access and infrastructures for e-Health • interconnectivity across systems and channels • mobile/wireless devices and interconnections • more familiarity with and use of general Internet resources	• multicultural expertise and teamwork for development of telemedicine projects, including cooperation and coordination among service, infrastructure providers, and health care providers • patients' willingness to be involved in medical decisions • physician recommendations of health sites • positive perceptions of technology and online service attributes • positive attitude reinforcement and satisfaction from previous online experience (word of mouth) • private investments • reimbursement for online time and services (such as e-mail communication, or medical record exchanges) • support by national and international medical associations

(Continued)

Table 12.2 Continued

Barriers

- access and knowledge
- accountability and responsibility
- applying technical standards for interoperability and clinical/care protocols
- appropriate infrastructure
- appropriate usability design
- attracting users to a site
- computer fears
- computer/ICT skills
- contention for system usage between administrators and health care providers
- cultural divides concerning technology use and social norms toward health behaviors
- developing sufficient privacy protections
- differences in data conceptualization by physicians (narratives) and administrators (structured data entry)
- differences in procedures for reimbursement and health coverage across economic sectors and national boundaries
- difficulties in assessing online knowledge acquisition
- disparities in Internet (especially broadband) access and knowledge (digital divide), especially for the very groups that need it most
- ethical conflicts (private sites promoting products and services by sponsors
- fragmented and conflicting jurisdiction (across federal, state, regulatory agencies, and technical standards)
- high costs of technology overwhelm low cost of access and communication
- HIPAA regulations
- implementation costs
- individuals' perceptions of current medical information rights
- insufficient and varying levels of health and technology literacy
- insufficient bandwidth
- insufficient control or awareness of third party access to personal medical records
- insufficient health staff

- insuring quality information and care
- interoperability (different standards imposed by regulatory agencies)
- joint involvement by local service providers/physicians/patients
- lack of basic infrastructure
- lack of insurance reimbursement codes for online treatment
- lack of interconnection
- lack of standard evaluation criteria
- lack of support for sustainability of online interventions and health projects
- large gap between those with Internet access and those with many kinds of chronic health problems (such as HIV/AIDS)
- legal issues such as cross-state pharmacy licenses
- limited vision by government and health care agencies as to potential applications
- low commitment to and engagement with online health material
- low interest in learning about health topics
- majority of health sites in English language
- need for anonymity (especially for stigmatizing or deviant topics)
- norms for mediated patient-physician relationships
- overcoming people's avoidance of relevant health information
- physician resistance/hesitancy
- political divisions, with varying motives
- poor management of ICT personnel and projects
- reimbursement uncertainty
- standard codes for practices and protocols
- state licensing laws
- sustainability (costs, updating, link stability)
- time required to learn new systems
- usability
- varying national and cultural norms and policies

Sources: Lieberman, Lloyd-Kolkin, Kreuter, Chea, & Benter (2004), Murero & Rice (2006).

support resulted in significant improvements in diet, physical activity, self-efficacy, and quality of life (Block et al., 2007).

The latest trend, however, is the use of mobile devices. A recent intervention employing a wrist-worn accelerometer, with real-time feedback via the Internet, led to significant increases in, and maintenance of, level of physical activity (Hurling et al., 2007). Another study showed that diary monitoring and behavioral coaching via digital assistance devices were quite feasible and well accepted by migraine sufferers (Sorbi, Mck, Houtveen,

Kleiboer, & van Doornen, 2007). Other studies have explored the feasibility of SMS (short messaging service) on mobile phones for disease management, from submitting asthma diary data (Anhøj & Møldrup, 2004) to recording blood glucose level of diabetics (e.g., Kim & Kim, 2008) to reporting routine pill intake (Cocosila, Archer, Haynes, & Yuan, 2009), with encouraging results. The widespread diffusion of mobile phones among youth has provided prevention scientists with a new channel for reaching their target audiences. Several elaborate multimedia mobile-phone smoking cessation interventions have been launched (e.g., Whittaker et al., 2008), with significant impact on abstinence (Brendryen, Drozd, & Kraft, 2008).

Bundled Interventions

Of course, the success of such interventions via newer media is contingent upon the characteristics, preferences, and abilities of target groups. There is evidence to suggest that older media centered around printed text are more effective with certain populations, especially when the intervention is purely informational and designed for mass dissemination (e.g., Kroeze, Oenema, Campbell, & Brug, 2008). However, when the technological affordances of newer media are leveraged to provide value-added advantages such as tailoring (discussed below), they can be quite effective, especially when they are deployed in tandem rather than in isolation.

An emerging theme is the importance of supplementing web-based interventions with other technologies that are more personal in their reach. For example, An et al. (2008) found that adding peer e-mail support to smoking cessation messages in an online college-life magazine served to increase abstinence. Even when compared to an interactive control condition, interventions tend to be more successful when bundled with tailored e-mails, journaling activities, and small-group motivational interviewing (Norman, Maley, Li, & Skinner, 2008), thus lending new meaning to the notion of "multi-media." As Zbikowski, Hapgood, Barnwell, and McAfee (2008) found, integrating phone counseling to tailored e-mails and printed *Quit Guides* promoted adherence to their web-based tobacco cessation treatment. Richardson, Brown, Foley, Dial, and Lowery (2005) reported similar success when they enhanced pedometer feedback with tailored nutritional counseling for increasing walking activity among those at high risk for cardiovascular disease. In their weight management intervention, Ware et al. (2008) noted that the "use of monitoring devices to capture and send data to the automated Web-based coaching program may have influenced the high levels of engagement" (p. 1).

One technology often serves as a triage mechanism for health information delivered via another. Nijland, van Gemert-Pijnen, Boer, Steehouder, and Seydel (2008) call for research that focuses on web-based triage mechanisms for medical complaints while simultaneously developing interactive technologies for patients. The key to bundling interventions appears to be effective integration of various online and offline technologies. The Comprehensive Health Enhancement Support System (CHESS) developed by Gustafson et al. (2008) is a good example of integrating information with patient support and analysis as well as decision tools. When compared to control subjects who were given ready access to high-quality breast-cancer websites, CHESS subjects were more likely to log in and access health resources, experienced greater social support, and reported better quality of life and health care competence both during and after the intervention. The value of integration is quite obvious when one considers the multi-dimensional nature of the quality criteria specified by patients and caregivers for Internet interventions. As Kerr, Murray, Stevenson, Gore, and

Nazareth (2006) found out, health care recipients not only have detailed expectations for content (e.g., practical, updated, deep, mention of scientific controversies, accurate, non-commercial) but also for design (e.g., easy access, attractive layout) and functionality (e.g., interactivity, personalization, navigational ease), thereby making the intervention more than merely informational and motivating health communicators to think creatively about leveraging the unique technological capabilities of newer digital media.

Technological Features

The ability of the interface to interact with the user is perhaps the most important and distinctive feature of online health. Numerous studies have shown that interactive features in health systems are favored by patients, both for keeping track of preventive regimens (Hurling, Fairley, & Dias, 2006) and for making disease-related decisions (e.g., Evans et al., 2007). Technological features of new media have given rise to a number of tools that are associated with pro-health behavioral outcomes (e.g., An et al., 2008).

Interactivity

The power of interactivity lies in its ability to engage the user. As interventionists know all too well, getting users to pay attention to health messages has been a major challenge for campaigns using traditional media. But, with interactive media, this does not appear to be an issue. Engagement with content has been theorized as a critical outcome of interface interactivity. Several studies have demonstrated the heightened user engagement generated by interactive tools (e.g., Ware et al., 2008). In his model of interactivity effects, Sundar (2007) identifies three species of interactivity corresponding to source, medium, and message, the central elements of all communication. Interactivity as a *source* feature is the ability of the interface to allow the user to serve as creator or source of content. This is particularly evident in Web 2.0 outlets such as social networking sites and blogs, where users contribute health information. It is available to a somewhat lesser degree in web portals and other customizable interfaces where the user is given opportunities to gatekeep and organize health information. Even simpler interfaces, like the CD-ROM program used by Hornung et al. (2000), allow the user to play source by letting them select the order in which three versions of sun-safety behavior episodes are viewed with three variations of cartoon characters. Interactivity as a *medium* feature refers to the various tools available for interaction with an interface, from mouse-overs to downloads to sliders, each serving to enhance the perceptual representation of health content provided by the system. As a *message* feature, interactivity is the degree to which the interface affords users the ability to have a sustained, threaded interaction with some part of the system, be it in a message board or an online tool that calls for back-and-forth interaction from the user. Health-risk assessment tools are a good example of message-based interactivity because their output is contingent upon user input. As Strecher et al. (2008) found, a Web-based cessation program that delivers information sequentially (as user interaction progresses) leads to greater engagement with the intervention.

Tailoring

The contingency of user–system interaction is best realized when an online health system *actively* tailors content based on each individual user's needs and preferences. Tailoring, as discussed by Parrott and Kreuter in this volume, targets the individual based on characteristics salient in a health situation and has the potential to provide personalized care in a manner that is more feasible and efficient than face-to-face health communication. Tailored systems provide messages appropriate for specific individuals depending on their responses (Hartmann et al., 2007; Huang et al., 2009; Lieberman, Lloyd-Kolkin, Kreuter, Chea, & Benter, 2004). According to Hawkins, Kreuter, Resnicow, Fishbein, and Dijkstra (2008, p. 454), "tailoring involves either or both of two classes of goals (enhancing cognitive preconditions for message processing and enhancing message impact through modifying behavioral determinants of goal outcomes) and employs strategies of personalization, feedback and content matching" leading to a 2 × 3 matrix in which some strategies and their component tactics match better to some goals than to others. This framework has led to different kinds of tailoring (e.g., Kreuter et al., 2004) such as Behavioral Construct Tailoring (BCT) and Culturally Relevant Tailoring (CRT). Widely deployed for promoting a variety of health behaviors (Oenema, Brug, Djikstra, de Weerdt, & Vries, 2008), tailoring is found to be generally more effective than generic messages (Neuhauser & Kreps, 2003). Rimal and Adkins (2003) reviewed studies showing the positive outcomes (exposure, attention, use, recall, credibility, behavior change) of campaigns using tailored messages in general, and online or digital media-based tailored messages in particular. These positive outcomes seem to be due largely to increased relevance, self-monitoring, perceived risk, self-efficacy, and even the process of entering one's own data, all enhanced through feedback, in some cases fostered through regular prompts. Computer-based interactivity, narrowcasting, and tailoring are good matches with the transtheoretical (stages of change) model (Prochaska & Velicer, 1997) as the system can ask questions that identify the user's stage of change (and thus potential motivators such as intention, attitude, self-efficacy, subjective norms, etc.), and then provide appropriate information and activities (see Huang et al., 2009).

Use Patterns of Online Health

A principal attribute of online health technologies is that their content is intrinsically related to user behavior. Both the design and effectiveness of online health information strategies depend heavily on a clear understanding of users and their use patterns. In general, research has focused on three broad uses—information seeking, patient-to-patient (p2p) communication, and patient–physician dialogue.

Information Seeking

Most individuals begin most of their health information-seeking online by entering keywords into search engines such as Google and Yahoo (Eysenbach & Köhler, 2002; Fox, 2006), and it takes high Internet self-efficacy to persevere in this task and locate relevant health information (Hong, 2006). As Lau and Coiera (2008) note, although searching across a variety of quality sites can improve consumers' accuracy in answering health questions, their confidence in an answer is not a good indicator of its accuracy. Studies have shown that people, especially students, take away predominantly incorrect information about medical topics when they search online (e.g., Kortum, Edwards, & Richards-Kortum, 2008).

That said, they seek health information online all the time, from looking up symptoms to checking if they qualify for a clinical trial (Atkinson et al., 2007). Perceived and behavioral outcomes of online health information seeking are receiving more research attention, with somewhat contradictory results (e.g., Baker, Wagner, Singer, & Bundorf, 2003; Harris

Interactive, 2003; Morahan-Martin, 2004; Pastore, 2000). Half or more of the 61% of online health information seekers in a Pew 2008 survey said that online health information has affected their health treatment decision (60%) or their overall approach to maintaining their own or others' health (56%), prompted them to ask their doctor new questions or obtain a second opinion (53%), or changed their thinking about diet, exercise, or stress management (59%). Just under 40% reported it influenced whether they saw a doctor or not, or how they coped with a chronic condition or pain (Fox & Jones, 2009).

Rice (2006) summarized various outcomes identified in seven Pew surveys from 2000 to 2002. In 2000, 91% said they had learned something new, 55% improved how they got medical and health info, 48% indicated that online advice had improved the way they take care of themselves, and 47% who had looked for health information for themselves during their last Internet search said it affected decisions about care and treatments. In 2001, 16% said it had a major impact and 52% a minor impact on their own health care routine or way they helped care for someone else, and 80% found most or all of what they were looking for online. In 2002, 73% said the Internet improved the health and medical information and services they received, and a quarter of Internet users who helped another person deal with a major illness, or who dealt with a major illness themselves, said the Internet played a crucial or important role. Rice's (2006) analyses concluded that across those surveys, the primary influences on reported outcomes were the extent of health information seeking, the number of such searches, the extent of engagement in other Internet activities, and time since first going online. Other influences included participating in online support groups, perceived credibility of the information, difficulties in gaining access to a doctor, being non–white or Asian, looking for sensitive topics that are difficult to talk about, and making one's own diagnoses.

Wantland, Portillo, Holzemer, Slaughter, and McGhee (2004) provided one of the first meta-analyses that compared behavioral change outcomes of web-based vs. non-web-based interventions. Twenty-two articles, involving nearly 12,000 participants, reported effect sizes from -.01 to .75. Outcomes involved exercise time, nutritional status knowledge, asthma treatment knowledge, health care participation, reduced decline in health, perception of body shape, and maintenance of weight loss. Rains and Young (2009) provided a very rigorous meta-analysis of 28 studies (involving over 4,000 participants and 12 health conditions) of health-related outcomes related to formal computer-mediated support group interventions (online sites that provide both an educational and a group interaction aspect, with membership registration, a limited duration, and moderating or expert leadership). Positive outcomes, across the studies, from participating included increased social support (average effect size $r = .16$), decreased depression (.23), increased quality of life (.14), and increased self-efficacy in managing one's health condition (.15). Other reviews of online/digital media interventions are provided by Griffiths, Lindenmeyer, Powell, Lowe, and Thorgood (2006), Neuhauser and Kreps (2003), and Rice and Atkin (2009).

P2P Communication

The rising importance of "patient expertise" (Tuckett, Boulton, Olson, & Williams, 1985) has benefited from online media, which offer a variety of tools for peer interactions about health topics. Sites such as patientslikeme.com help users share their symptoms, find similar others, and learn from each others' experiences (Frost & Massagli, 2008). Online peer communication involves four dimensions of health behavior influence (Ancker et al., 2009): information, emotional support, instrumental support, and peer modeling. A rigorous analysis of participants on a Taiwanese Post-Traumatic Therapy (PTT) psychosis support bulletin board found that the most exchanged types of support were information and specific linkages (threaded responses) (Chang, 2009). Social media websites, such as YouTube, Facebook, MySpace, Twitter, and Second Life are increasingly popular sources of health information, especially for teens and young adults (Vance, Howe, & Dellavalle, 2009). Social media may be especially appropriate for support groups (Ancker et al., 2009), as they provide ways for individuals to describe their identities, conditions, concerns, and interests, which in turn allows others and groups to connect with each other based on those entries, and to develop multiple networks. Features such as tags, comments, initiating connections, links to other sites and services, and privacy controls, offer both a sense of community and control. Many non-contributing "participants" can benefit, and postings and threads are archived for later users, allowing both extended access as well as, unfortunately, persistence of outdated information. The English Wikipedia is a prominent source of online health information compared to the other online health information providers studied (Laurent & Vicker, 2009). RSS feeds are already being used in campaigns such as the Johns Hopkins Bloomberg School of Public Health's Center for Communication Programs to distribute up-to-date changes and new entries about health information. Blogs allow users with similar health information needs and concerns to share their views and experiences. Podcasts are another, portable means of providing relevant audio or video information to target audiences at their convenience, while wikis (or collaboratively created online documents) support collaboration among project members (Haylock & Rabi, 2007).

While information and advice are sought significantly more than emotional or esteem support, for issues involving spiritual or partner matters, patients express greater interest in communicating with others who share their values even if they are not particularly knowledgeable (Bunde, Suls, Martin, & Barnett, 2006). They obtain valuable advice on a number of intangible issues, including how to communicate with health care providers (Meier, Lyons, Frydman, Forlenza, & Rimer, 2007). In general, as Barak, Boniel-Nissim, and Suler (2008) note, patients derive a host of benefits by way of social interactions and improved feelings—all non-specific but psychologically important in that they lead to personal empowerment, which can be useful for dealing with certain health conditions. They also point out that participation has potential costs, such as dependence, distancing from physical contacts, and exposure to unpleasant experiences typical of social engagement online.

Patient–Physician Dialogue

A growing number of online health seekers have approached their physicians specifically because of, or to mention, information they found on the Internet (Rice & Katz, 2006). Available statistics indicate relevant numbers at anywhere from 8 to 24% of patients (e.g., Murray, Lo, Pollack, Donelan Catania, White, et al., 2003). Murray, Lo, Pollack, Donelan Catania, Lee, et al. (2003) found that 85% of a national random sample of physicians reported that patients had brought Internet information to an office visit. If physicians felt that the quality of information the patient brought was accurate and relevant, they judged it to be beneficial. Even early on, from the physician's perspective, 93% said that they want their patients to discuss Internet information with them, and 62% even said it is a good idea for the physicians to explore the Internet in order to familiarize themselves with the information patients find (Hollander & Lanier, 2001). Sixty-two percent of patients believed that the doctor should recommend specific websites to patients so that they could learn more, yet only 3% reported that a doctor had done this in the past 6 months (Diaz, Sciamanna, Evangelou, Stamp, & Ferguson, 2005). In general, research overwhelmingly indicates that the increased patient health-seeking behavior does not necessarily lead to patients desiring to replace or challenge their physician, nor to decreased telephone contacts with or visits to physicians (e.g., Baker et al., 2003). However, Murray, Lo, Pollack, Donelan, Catania, Lee, et al. (2003) reported that inaccurate or irrelevant information was judged to harm health outcomes and the physician–patient relationship. The most consistent predictor of a perceived deterioration in the physician–patient relationship, the quality of health care, or in the health outcome, was physicians' feeling that patients were challenging their authority. A substantial number of physicians (38%) believed that the patient bringing in information made the visit less time efficient, particularly if the patient wanted something that the physician considered inappropriate.

Rice and Katz (2006) analyzed responses from the same national random sample of 2000 physicians providing at least 20 hours a week of direct patient care, stratified by medical specialty, about their patients' bringing Internet health information to the appointment with the doctor. Their integrated model reported on levels and predictors of influences on physicians' perceptions of, and reactions to, their patients' discussing Internet health information, and of their own and patients' perceptions of the outcomes associated with those discussions. For example, they were more likely to assess this information as relevant to the patient's disease or condition if they had more positive assessments of the effects of Internet health information, felt that public health information was more accurate, and spent fewer hours per week on patient-related care. Overall, the strongest influences on outcomes were physicians' use of e-mail to communicate with their patients, their evaluations of the accuracy and relevance of the online health information about which their patients talk, and how good their patients are at assessing health websites.

Patient–health care provider communication through the Internet is still infrequent. Less than 4% of people in 2005 had used online systems to interact with health care providers, though most indicated they would like to, for activities such as using e-mail to schedule or receive reminders for appointments, communicating with their doctors, receiving test results, managing one's medical record, and sending self-monitoring results to doctors (PR Newswire, 2006). Another study observed that there were fewer than 1 in 10 outpatient visits in 2001 (9.2%) to physicians who reported doing Internet or e-mail consults, and this did not increase in 2002 (5.8%) or 2003 (5.5%) (Sciamanna, Rogers, Shenassa, & Houston, 2007). Overall, most studies have found positive outcomes from online mediated health care provider–patient relations (Miller, 2001), including reductions in visits to the doctor's office (Bergmo, Kummevold, Gammon, & Dahl, 2005).

Conceptual Challenges and Theoretical Opportunities

As the influence of online health information continues to rise, medical practitioners and health communicators alike are asking questions that require greater scientific understanding of the nature, uses, and effects of online health media. Traditional communication concepts such as "source" and "credibility" are undergoing revision in light of the new technologies introduced by online media, thereby challenging researchers to formulate new theories of health communication that take into account the importance of emergent technological affordances. In particular, the following discussion considers issues of sources, sourcing, and source-layering, agency and customization, and credibility.

Sources, Sourcing, and Source-Layering

The sender or source is the originator of communication and therefore quite central to any consideration of user reception of mediated information. While the source is quite obvious when we receive information via traditional media, it is quite murky in online media (Sundar & Nass, 2001). In addition to the "original source" (i.e., the person providing new information), there are various "selecting sources" that edit and disseminate information via the Internet. Let us suppose that a doctor commented about certain new risks of skin cancer on a blog run by a medical organization, but you got to read it as a Facebook entry posted by one of your friends who picked it from delicious.com, a social bookmarking site, based on the number of tweets it received there. Who or what is the source here? Some would argue that it is the doctor (original source) while others would say that it came from Facebook (selecting source). In their typology of online selecting sources, Sundar and Nass (2001) distinguish between *visible sources* (those that are visually seen as delivering the information—doctor or medical organization in the example provided above); *technological sources* (medium or media that the user psychologically perceives as source, such as Facebook or delicious.com or even the Internet); and *receiver sources* (users themselves either individually or collectively—your friend who posted this on Facebook, in this case, or an online support group via a bulletin board). Depending on which of these sources is salient during the course of communication, online users are likely to perceive the content differently because they apply different decision rules (or heuristics) when they encounter different sources. A doctor or journalist may trigger the "expertise heuristic," whereas reminding consumers that other users of the health website rated this as the most important item may lead to application of a "bandwagon heuristic" (Sundar, 2008).

In confirmation of such distinctions, Hu and Sundar (2010) found that an identical piece of health information was more likely to lead to behavioral outcomes if it was sourced to a website or a bulletin board than to a blog, homepage, or Internet in general. This effect was mediated by perceptions of gatekeeping. Study participants perceived information on websites as being controlled by editors and that on bulletin boards as being monitored by moderators. This, in addition to perception of information completeness (influenced by expertise and related heuristics), seems to reassure users sufficiently to motivate healthy behaviors. Based on these findings, the authors proposed a new typology of online health sources (see Figure 12.1).

While each source can be aligned along any one dimension (e.g., level of professional gatekeeping; medical expertise) in an ordinal fashion, multiple sources pose a particular challenge to researchers, given their widespread prevalence online. As Sundar and Nass (2001) noted, we receive information through a chain of sources, with an implicit hierarchy, but often varying sequence (Stephens, Sørnes, Rice, & Browning, 2008), among them. While each source can individually have effects on user perceptions and actions, "source layering" of multiple online sources can lead to combination effects. For example, Hu and Sundar (2010) found that a health message from a doctor was rated as more credible when it appeared on a website than on a homepage; whereas the same message attributed to a layperson was considered more credible when it appeared on a homepage than on a website. Therefore, appropriate combinations of sources are critical for fostering credibility of online health information. Given the multiplicity of sources online, it is imperative that scholars theorize about ways in which sources come together to influence users.

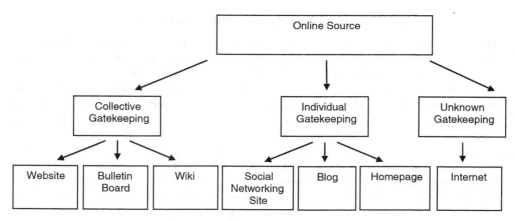

Figure 12.1   Online health source typology proposed by Hu & Sundar (2010).

Agency and Customization

One of the key innovations of online media, especially Web 2.0 media, is that receivers are now able to act as sources, creators, and producers of information. In the health domain, this has dramatically transformed the role of the user, making the patient more proactive about his/her health care and putting the "public" back in "public health." In proposing their experiential health information processing model, O'Grady, Witteman, and Wathen (2008) stress the importance of collaboration and shared understanding of health issues. Several scholars have noted the sense of community built by social media such as blogs because of participation by other users. At an individual level, these technologies can be quite powerful in building a sense of agency by producing such metrics as number of site visits. Both sense of community and sense of agency are associated with psychological empowerment (Stavrositu & Sundar, 2008). As the next section notes, however, user sources also create considerable challenges to online health information accuracy and credibility.

Even without contributing to a public forum, modern-day patients can become empowered by participating in interactive programs related to their personal health. As Lai, Larson, Rockor, and Bakken (2008) found out, even the simple act of generating a self-care plan is quite empowering for persons living with HIV and AIDS. When patients enter their own data, they feel agentic as evidenced by positive attitudinal and behavioral outcomes. For example, when Anhøj and Møldrup (2004) asked asthma patients to enter their daily information through SMS, rates of compliance with their medicines and treatment went up. When the system pushes users toward entering information for obtaining tailored services, the results tend to be positive (e.g., van Straten, Cuijpers, & Smits, 2008).

However, as Sundar, Marathe, and Kang (2009) argue, simply providing tailored communication does not appear to be sufficient for breeding a strong sense of agency among health users. When the system tailors information for users, the locus of control is located in the system, not the user, therefore making him/her a somewhat passive receiver of health information (though more active than with traditional mass media sources or even some physicians) instead of an active consumer. Given that the information is not expressly solicited by the user, it may be relevant to the user (as determined by the profile), but not quite relevant to his/her needs at the time. Therefore, in order to feel truly agentic, the user, not the system, should perform the tailoring, as argued by the agency model of customization (Sundar, 2008). Applications of the transtheoretical (stages of change) model to interactive interventions have served to increase the convergence between system content and user agency (Prochaska & Velicer, 1997; Rice & Atkin, 2009).

Results across the health literature lend support to this notion by emphasizing the strong motivational component underlying the success of tailoring interventions (e.g., Stoddard, Augustson, & Moser, 2008). In general, motivated patients are most likely to benefit from tailoring systems because they tend to put more of their personal information into it. Theoretically, this would suggest the incorporation of motivational mechanisms in inferring the effects of online health information. One strategy would be to identify drivers of intrinsic motivation and accordingly target users who are likely to score high on autonomy, competence, and relatedness, the three predictors of self-determination. As Resnicow et al. (2008) determined, the impact of tailored messages was higher for those who prefer an autonomy-supportive style of communication. A different strategy would be to creatively deploy the tools of online technology to build motivation among users. Several studies have shown that the use of e-mail and other forms of mediated communications to reach patients tend to increase their motivation to adhere to health regimens (e.g., Napolitano et al., 2003). The next step is to theorize which aspects of technology can systematically influence which predictors of self-determination en route to building intrinsic motivation among users. Customization tools can be used to imbue a sense of autonomy whereas navigational aids on the interface can build competence and interactivity tools can promote relatedness, thus offering rich potential for proposing theory-based approaches to deploying online technologies for promoting health-related motivations, which appear to be critical for changing behaviors.

Credibility

A consistent topic of concern about online health information is the accuracy and quality of the content (see Rice [2001], for a review of health information credibility assessments and experiments; see also Morahan-Martin [2004]; for an extensive program of research on web credibility, see Flanagin & Metzger [2007]; Metzger [2007]). An analysis of 79 studies involving nearly 6000 health websites and over 1300 health web pages concerning users' credibility criteria found that users emphasized accuracy, completeness, readability, design, disclosures, and references, with completeness of content being the most important (Eysenbach, Powell, Kuss, & Sa, 2002). Nearly three-quarters (70%) of the studies concluded that information quality was a problem, with only 9% reporting a positive evaluation. Despite this focus and concern about credibility, most users have reported that they would use the retrieved information or felt the information was helpful; and most had positive evaluations, found what they were searching for, and believed the information was trustworthy, helpful, valuable, and accurate (e.g., Murero, D'Ancona, & Karamanoukian, 2001; Zeng, Kogan, Plovnick, Crowell, Lacroix, & Greenes, 2004). Some hope comes from a LaurusHealth.com survey (Pastore, 2000), which indicated that users felt the most credible health websites are those recommended by users' physicians (67%) or a local hospital (56%), while the least credible are those sponsored by a company that sells products or surveys on that site (9%); even those recommended by friends were perceived as not very credible (32%). Some users, however, do tend to feel that the online health information search process is complex and unsuccessful, leading to overload and confusion; they report having limited search and evaluation skills, ignore credibility indicators, and do not compare across sites (e.g., Morahan-Martin, 2004; Murero et al., 2001).

A key challenge for researchers is to understand how users evaluate credibility of online messages, and leverage this information for designing interventions as well as launching media literacy campaigns. While credibility cues abound in the content of health communication, Sundar (2008) suggests that non-content attributes of the interface can influence credibility as well. He posits that four classes of "affordances" (or action possibilities) in digital media— modality, agency, interactivity, and navigability—could cue cognitive heuristics about the perceived quality and credibility of online health information. This means websites and interventions can be strategic about the design of interface tools, especially in terms of triggering specific heuristics. Theoretically, this argues for greater elaboration of dual-process models in social psychology for examining the effects of technology on perceived credibility of online health information. Researchers have long noted that Internet users do not methodically undertake the information-verification steps recommended by credibility checklists (e.g., Metzger, 2007), preferring instead to let design and other surface features affect their trust in online content. The Elaboration Likelihood Model and related theoretical approaches (Petty & Cacioppo, 1986; Chen & Chaiken, 1999) can be effectively applied to leverage this tendency to rely on interface features. We could segment audiences for tailoring as well as design interfaces for the express purpose of motivating greater audience involvement in health content.

Conclusion

By featuring an increasingly diverse array of digital and online technologies, the Internet has not only changed assumptions about the role of individuals in their health care, but also vastly expanded the domain of health information, health services, and health communication research. Even a partial coverage of issues related to e-Health in this chapter has revealed a broad range of technologies, characteristics of health websites, the development of (especially mobile) health devices, bundled interventions (combined as well as sequential), technological features (source, medium and message interactivity, and tailoring), usage patterns (information seeking and patient–physician dialogue), and conceptual challenges (relating to interactions of sources, agency and customization, and accuracy and credibility), foregrounding the numerous theoretical, empirical, social, economic, and technological challenges that lie ahead as we find ways and means to use new media technologies for improving health throughout society. The Internet has become the preferred source of health information, yet we find a lot of variability across various venues on the Internet, with different sources exerting different kinds of influence, based in part on their differential technical abilities and the affordances that they offer to users. While interactivity has vastly aided health communication on a number of levels, it has served to highlight the importance of user agency in realizing the rich potential of the Internet. Therefore, future theorizing ought to consider the interactive nature of technological features and psychological factors in influencing the nature, uses, and effects of health communication online. This would imply a variable-centered approach to studying technology (Nass & Mason, 1990) by including different levels of a given affordance (e.g., low, medium, and high levels of interactivity) rather than simply comparing online with offline means of communicating a particular piece of health communication. The vast majority of studies in online health communication do not systematically vary technological factors such as interactivity or tailoring. They simply compare the existence of some interactivity against a control condition that has no interactivity, with the former being administered online and the latter through offline means, thus introducing confounds and precluding a clear understanding of technology's impact on health communication. Future research can rectify this by minimizing the tendency to compare across media and taking seriously the individual affordances of technology that are offered to different degrees by different media. Furthermore, it ought to explore how specific psychological variables related to motivations, attitudes, and social cognition are both influenced by and interact with technological factors en route to predicting behavioral outcomes of online health communication.

References

An, L. C., Klatt, C., Perry, C. L., Lein, E. B., Hennrikus, D. J., Pallonen, U. E., … Ehlinger, E. P. (2008). The RealU online cessation intervention for college smokers: A randomized controlled trial. *Preventive Medicine, 47,* 194–199.

Ancker, J. S., Carpenter, K. M., Greene, P., Hoffman, R., Kukafka, R., Marlow, L. A. V., … Quillin, J. M. (2009). Peer-to-peer communication, cancer prevention and the Internet. *Journal of Health Communication, 14,* 38–46.

Andreassen, H. K., Bujnowska-Fedak, M. M., Chronaki, C. E., Dumitru, R. C., Pudule, I., Santana, S., … Wynn, R. (2007). European citizens' use of E-health services: A study of seven countries. *BMC Public Health, 7,* 53. DOI:10.1186/1471-2458-7-53.

Anhøj, J., & Møldrup, C. (2004). Feasibility of collecting diary data from asthma patients through mobile phones and SMS (short message service): Response rate analysis and focus group evaluation from a pilot study. *Journal of Medical Internet Research, 6*(4), e42. Retrieved from http://www.jmir. org/2004/4/e42/

Atkinson, N. L., Massett, H. A., Mylks, C., Hanna, B., Deering, M. J., & Hesse, B. W. (2007). User-centered research on breast cancer patient needs and preferences of an Internet-based clinical trial matching system. *Journal of Medical Internet Research, 9*(2), e13. Retrieved from http://www.jmir. org/2007/2/e13/

Baek, T. H., & Yu, H. (2009). Online health promotion strategies and appeals in the USA and South Korea: A content analysis of weight-loss websites. *Asian Journal of Communication, 19*(1), 18–38.

Baker, L. C., Wagner, T. H., Singer, S. J., & Bundorf, M. K. (2003). Use of the Internet and e-mail for health care information: Results from a national survey. *Journal of the American Medical Association, 289,* 2400–2406.

Barak, A., Boniel-Nissim, M., & Suler, J. (2008). Fostering empowerment in online support groups. *Computers in Human Behavior, 24,* 1867–1883.

Beckjord, E. B., Finney-Rutten, J. J., Squiers, L., Arora, N. K., Volckmann, L., Moser, R. P., & Hess, B. W. (2007). Use of the Internet to communicate with health care providers in the United States: Estimates from the 2003 and 2005 Health Information National Trends Surveys (HINTS). *Journal of Medical Internet Research, 9*(3), e20. Retrieved from http://www.jmir.org/2007/3/e20/

Bergmo, T. S., Kummervold, P. E., Gammon, D., & Dahl, L. B. (2005). Electronic patient–provider communication: Will it offset office visits and telephone consultations in primary care? *International Journal of Medical Informatics, 74,* 705–710.

Block, G., Sternfeld, B., Block, C. H., Block, T. J., Norris, J., Hopkins, D., … Clancy, H. A. (2008). Development of Alive! (a lifestyle intervention via e-mail), and its effect on health-related quality of life, presenteeism, and other behavioral outcomes: Randomized controlled trial. *Journal of Medical Internet Research, 10*(4), e43. Retrieved from http://www.jmir.org/2008/4/e43/

Borzekowski, D. L. G., Fobil, J. N., & Asante, K. O. (2006). Online access by adolescents in Accra: Ghanaian teens' use of the Internet for health information. *Developmental Psychology, 42,* 450–458.

Brendryen, H., Drozd, F., & Kraft, P. (2008). A digital smoking cessation program delivered through Internet and cell phone without nicotine replacement (happy ending): Randomized controlled trial. *Journal of Medical Internet Research, 10*(5), e51. Retrieved from http://www.jmir.org/2008/5/e51/

Bunde, M., Suls, J., Martin, R., & Barnett, K. (2006). Hystersisters online: Social support and social comparison among hysterectomy patients on the Internet. *Annals of Behavioral Medicine, 31,* 271–278.

Chang, H-J. (2009). Online supportive interactions: Using a network approach to examine communication patterns within a psychosis social support group in Taiwan. *Journal of the American Society for Information Science & Technology, 60,* 1504–1518.

Chen, S., & Chaiken, S. (1999). The Heuristic-Systematic Model in its broader context. In S. Chaiken & Y. Trope (Eds.), *Dual-process theories in social psychology* (pp. 73–96). New York: Guildford.

Cocosila, M., Archer, N., Haynes, R. B., & Yuan, Y. F. (2009). Can wireless text messaging improve adherence to preventive activities? Results of a randomized controlled trial. *International Journal of Medical Informatics, 78,* 230–238.

Denecke, K., & Nejdl, W. (2009). How valuable is medical social media data? Content analysis of the medical Web. *Information Sciences, 179,* 1870–1880.

Diaz, J. A., Sciamanna, C. N., Evangelou, E., Stamp, M. J., & Ferguson, T. (2005). Brief report: What types of Internet guidance do patients want from their physicians? *Journal of General Internal Medicine, 20,* 787–788.

Eng, T. R. (2001). *The e-health landscape: A terrain map of emerging information and communication technologies in health and health care..* Princeton, NJ: The Robert Wood Johnson Foundation.

Evans, R., Elwyn, G., Edwards, A., Watson, E., Austoker, J., & Grol, R. (2007). Toward a model for field-testing patient decision-support technologies: A qualitative field-testing study. *Journal of Medical Internet Research, 9*(3), e21. Retrieved from http://www.jmir.org/2007/3/e21/

Eysenbach, G., & Kohler, C. (2002). How do consumers search for and appraise health information on the World Wide Web? Qualitative study using focus groups, usability tests, and in-depth interviews. *British Medical Journal, 324,* 573–577.

Eysenbach, G., Powell, J., Kuss, O., & Sa, E. (2002). Empirical studies assessing the quality of health information for consumers on the World Wide Web. *Journal of the American Medical Association, 287,* 2691–2700.

Farvolden, P., Denisoff, E., Selby, P., Bagby, R. M., & Rudy, R. (2005). Usage and longitudinal effectiveness of a web-based self-help cognitive behavioral therapy program for panic disorder. *Journal of Medical Internet Research, 7*(1), e7. Retrieved from http://www.jmir.org/2005/1/e7

Flanagin, A. J., & Metzger, M. J. (2007). The role of site features, user attributes, and information verification behaviors on the perceived credibility of web-based information. *New Media & Society, 9,* 319–342.

Fox. S. (2006). *Online health search 2006.* Pew Internet and American Life Project. Retrieved from http://www.pewInternet.org/Reports/2006/Online-Health-Search-2006.aspx

Fox, S., & Jones, S. (2009, June 11). *The social life of health information* (online health information use). Retrieved from http://www.pewInternet.org/Reports/2009/8-The-Social-Life-of-Health-Information.aspx

Frost, J. H., & Massagli, M. P. (2008). Social uses of personal health information within PatientsLikeMe, an online patient community: What can happen when patients have access to one another's data. *Journal of Medical Internet Research, 10*(3), e15. Retrieved from http://www.jmir.org/2008/3/e15/

Gibbons, M. C. (2007). *e-Health solutions for health care disparities.* New York: Springer.

Griffiths, F., Lindenmeyer, A., Powell, J., Lowe, P., & Thorogood, M. (2006). Why are health care interventions delivered over the Internet? A systematic review of the published literature. *Journal of Medical Internet Research, 8*(2), e10. Retrieved from http://www.jmir.org/2006/2/e10/

Gustafson, D. H., Hawkins, R., McTavish, F., Pingree, S., Chen, W. C., Volrathongchai, K., … Serlin, R. C. (2008). Internet-based interactive support for cancer patients: Are integrated systems better? *Journal of Communication, 58,* 238–257.

Harris Interactive. (2003). e-Health's influence continues to grow as usage of the Internet by physicians and patients increases. *Health Care News, 3*(6), 1–7.

Hartmann, C. W., Sciamanna, C. N., Blanch, D. C., Mui, S., Lawless, H., Manocchia, M., … Pietropaoli, A. (2007). A website to improve asthma care by suggesting patient questions for physicians: Qualitative analysis of user experiences. *Journal of Medical Internet Research, 9*(1), e3. Retrieved from http://www.jmir.org/2007/1/e3/

Hawkins, R.P., Kreuter, M., Resnicow, K., Fishbein, M., & Dijkstra, A. (2008). Understanding tailoring in communicating about health. *Health Education Research, 23,* 454–466.

Haylock, C., & Rabi, M. (2007, November). *Wikis, RSS, blogs, podcasts: How Web 2.0 technologies can enhance public health websites.* Paper presented at 135th American Public Health Association conference, Washington, DC.

Hesse, B. W., Nelson, D. E., Kreps, G. L., Croyle, R. T., Arora, N. K., Rimer, B. K., & Viswanas, K. (2005). Trust and sources of health information: The impact of the Internet and its implications for health care providers: Findings from the first Health Information National Trends Survey. *Archives of Internal Medicine, 165,* 2618–2624.

Hollander, S., & Lanier, D. (2001). The physician–patient relationship in an electronic environment: A regional snapshot. *Bulletin of the Medical Library Association, 89,* 397–399.

Hong, T. (2006). The Internet and tobacco cessation: The roles of Internet self-efficacy and search task on the information-seeking process. *Journal of Computer-Mediated Communication, 11,* 536–556

Hornung, R. L., Lennon, P. A., Garrett, J. M., DeVellis, R. F., Weinberg, P. D., & Strecher, V. J. (2000). Interactive computer technology for skin cancer prevention targeting children. *American Journal of Preventive Medicine, 18,* 69–76.

Hu, Y., & Sundar, S. S. (2010). Effects of online health sources on credibility and behavioral intentions. *Communication Research, 37,* 105–132.

Huang, S-J., Hung, W-C, Chang, M., & Chang, J. (2009). The effect of an Internet-based, stage-matched message intervention on young Taiwanese women's physical activity. *Journal of Health Communication, 14,* 210–227.

Hurling, R., Catt, C., Boni, M.D., Fairley, B. W., Hurst, T., Murray, P., ... Sodhi, J. S. (2007). Using Internet and mobile phone technology to deliver an automated physical activity program: Randomized controlled trial. *Journal of Medical Internet Research, 9*(2), e7. Retrieved from http://www.jmir.org/2007/2/e7/

Hurling, R., Fairley, B. W., & Dias, M. B. (2006). Internet-based exercise intervention systems: Are more interactive designs better? *Psychology & Health, 21,* 757–772.

Kerr, C., Murray, E., Stevenson, R., Gore, C., & Nazareth, I. (2006). Internet interventions for long-term conditions: Patient and caregiver quality criteria. *Journal of Medical Internet Research, 8*(3), e13. Retrieved from http://www.jmir.org/2006/3/e13/

Kim, S. I., & Kim, H. S. (2008). Effectiveness of mobile and Internet intervention in patients with obese type 2 diabetes. *International Journal of Medical Informatics, 77,* 399–404.

Kortum, P., Edwards, C., & Richards-Kortum, R. (2008). The impact of inaccurate Internet health information in a secondary school learning environment. *Journal of Medical Internet Research, 10*(2), e17. Retrieved from http://www.jmir.org/2008/2/e17/

Kovic, I., Lulic, I., & Brumini, G. (2008). Examining the medical blogosphere: An online survey of medical bloggers. *Journal of Medical Internet Research, 10*(3), e10. Retrieved from http://www.jmir.org/2008/3/e28/

Kreuter, M. W., Skinner, C. S., Steger-May, K., Holt, C. L., Bucholtz, D. C., Clark, E. M., & Haire-Joshu, D. (2004). Responses to behaviorally vs. culturally tailored cancer communication among African American women. *American Journal of Health Behavior, 28,* 195–207.

Kroeze, W., Oenema, A., Campbell, M., & Brug, J. (2008). Comparison of use and appreciation of a print-delivered versus CD-Rom-delivered, computer-tailored intervention targeting saturated fat intake: Randomized controlled trial. *Journal of Medical Internet Research, 10*(2), e12. Retrieved from http://www.jmir.org/2008/2/e12/

Lai, T-Y., Larson, E. L., Rockor, M. L., & Bakken, S. (2008). User acceptance of HIV TIDES—Tailored Interventions for management of depressive symptoms in persons living with HIV/AIDS. *Journal of the American Medical Informatics Association, 15,* 217–226.

Lanseng, E. J., & Andreassen, T. W. (2007). Electronic health care: A study of people's readiness and attitude toward performing self-diagnosis. *International Journal of Service Industry Management, 18,* 394–417.

Lau, A. Y. S., & Coiera, E. W. (2008). Impact of web searching and social feedback on consumer decision making: A prospective online experiment. *Journal of Medical Internet Research, 10*(1), e9. Retrieved from http://www.jmir.org/2008/1/e2/

Laurent, M., & Vicker, T. J. (2009).Seeking health information online: Does Wikipedia matter? *Journal of the American Medical Informatics Association, 16,* 471–479.

Lieberman, D., Lloyd-Kolkin, D., Kreuter, M. Chea, W., & Benter, D. J. (2004, September). *Design strategies and effectiveness of prevention content online: Current research findings.* Contract 0404CT74655 prepared for Office of Disease Prevention and Health Promotion, Washington, D.C. Bethesda, MD: Abt Associates.

McNeill, L. H., Puleo, E., Bennett, G. G., & Emmons, K. M. (2007). Exploring social contextual correlates of computer ownership and frequency of use among urban, low-income, public housing adult residents. *Journal of Medical Internet Research, 9*(4), e35. Retrieved from http://www.jmir. org/2007/4/e35/

Meier, A., Lyons, E. J., Frydman, G., Forlenza, M., & Rimer, B. K. (2007). How cancer survivors provide support on cancer-related Internet mailing lists. *Journal of Medical Internet Research, 9*(2), e12. Retrieved from http://www.jmir.org/2007/2/e12/

Metzger, M. J. (2007). Making sense of credibility on the Web: Models for evaluating online information and recommendations for future research. *Journal of the American Society for Information Science and Technology, 58,* 2078–2091.

Miller, E. A. (2001). Telemedicine and doctor-patient communication. *Journal of Telemedicine and Telecare, 7,* 1–17.

Moore, T. J., Alsabeeh, N., Apovian, C. M., Murphy, M. C., Coffman, G., A., Cullum-Dugan, D., ... Cabral, H. (2008). Weight, blood pressure, and dietary benefits after 12 months of a web-based nutrition education program (dash for health): Longitudinal observational study. *Journal of Medical Internet Research, 10*(4), e52. Retrieved from http://www.jmir.org/2008/4/e52/

Morahan-Martin, J. (2004). How Internet users find, evaluate, and use online health information: A cross-cultural review. *CyperPsychology & Behavior, 7,* 497–510.

Murero, M., D'Ancona, G., & Karamanoukian, H. (2001). Use of the Internet by patients before and after cardiac surgery: Telephone survey. *Journal of Medical Internet Research, 3*(3), e27. Retrieved from http://www.jmir.org/2001/3/e27/

Murero, M., & Rice, R. E. (2006). E-health research. In M. Murero & R. E. Rice (Eds.), *The Internet and health care: Theory, research and practice* (pp. 3–26). Mahwah, NJ: Erlbaum.

Murray E., Lo, B., Pollack, L., Donelan, K., Catania, J., Lee, K., ... Turner, R. (2003). The impact of health information on the Internet on health care and the physician–patient relationship: National U.S. Survey among 1,050 U.S. physicians. *Journal of Medical Internet Research 2003, 5*(3), e17. Retrieved from http://www.jmir.org/2003/3/e17/

Murray, E., Lo, B., Pollack, L., Donelan, K., Catania, J., White, M., ... Turner, R. (2003). The impact of health information on the Internet on the physician–patient relationship: Patient perceptions. *Archives of Internal Medicine, 163,* 1727–1734.

Napolitano, M. A., Fotheringham, M., Tate, D., Sciamanna, C., Leslie, E., Owen, N., ... Marcus, B. (2003). Evaluation of an Internet-based physical activity intervention: A preliminary investigation. *Annals of Behavioral Medicine, 25*(2), 92–99.

Nass, C., & Mason, L. (1990). On the study of technology and task: A variable-based approach. In J. Fulk & C.W. Steinfield (Eds.), *Organizations and communication technology* (pp. 46–68). Newbury Park, CA: Sage.

Neuhauser, L., & Kreps, G. L. (2003). Rethinking communication in the e-Health era. *Journal of Health Psychology, 8,* 7–22.

Nijland, N., van Gemert-Pijnen, J., Boer, H., Steehouder, M. F., & Seydel, E. R. (2008). Evaluation of Internet-based technology for supporting self-care: Problems encountered by patients and caregivers when using self-care Applications. *Journal of Medical Internet Research, 10*(2), e13. Retrieved from http://www.jmir.org/2008/2/e13/

Norman, C. D., Maley, O., Li, X. Q., & Skinner, H. A. (2008). Using the Internet to assist smoking prevention and cessation in schools: A randomized, controlled trial. *Health Psychology, 27,* 799–810.

O'Grady, L. A., Witteman, H., & Wathen, C. N. (2008). The experiential health information processing model: Supporting collaborative web-based patient education. *BMC Medical Informatics and Decision Making, 8,* 58. Retrieved from http://www.biomedcentral.com/1472-6947/8/58

Oenema, A., Brug, J., Dijkstra, A., de Weerdt, I., & de Vries, H. (2008). Efficacy and use of an Internet-delivered computer-tailored lifestyle intervention, targeting saturated fat intake, physical activity and smoking cessation: A randomized controlled trial. *Annals of Behavioral Medicine, 35,* 125–135.

Pastore, M. (2000). Consumers choose health sites with doctors' input. *CyberAtlas.* Retrieved from http://cyberatlas.Internet.com/markets/health care/print/0,,5931_335121,00.html

Petty, R. E., & Cacioppo, J. T. (1986). *Communication and persuasion: Central and peripheral routes to attitude change.* New York: Springer/Verlag.

PR Newswire. (2006, September 22). Few patients use or have access to online services for communicating with their doctors. Retrieved from www.prnewsire.com

Prochaska, J. O., & Velicer, W. F. (1997). The transtheoretical model of health behavior change. *American Journal of Health Promotion, 12,* 38–48.

Rains, S. A., & Young, V. (2009). A meta-analysis of research on formal computer-mediated support groups: Examining group characteristics and health outcomes. *Human Communication Research, 35,* 309–336.

Resnicow, K., Davis, R., Zhang, G., Konkel, J., Strecher, V., Shaikh, A., ... Wiese, C. (2008). Tailoring a fruit and vegetable intervention on novel motivational constructs: Results of a randomized study. *Annals of Behavioral Medicine, 35,* 159–169.

Rice, R. E. (2001). The Internet and health communication: A framework of experiences. In R. E. Rice & J. E. Katz (Eds.), *The Internet and health communication: Expectations and experiences* (pp. 5–46). Thousand Oaks, CA: Sage.

Rice, R. E. (2006). Influences, usage, and outcomes of Internet health information searching: Multivariate results from the Pew surveys. *International Journal of Medical Informatics, 75,* 8–28.

Rice, R. E., & Atkin, C. K. (2009). Public communication campaigns: Theoretical principles and practical applications. In J. Bryant & M. B. Oliver (Eds.), *Media effects: Advances in theory and research,* 3rd ed. (pp. 436–468). Hillsdale, NJ: Erlbaum.

Rice, R. E., & Katz, J. E. (2006). Internet use in physician practice and patient interaction. In M. Murero & R. E. Rice (Eds.), *The Internet and health care: Theory, research and practice* (pp. 149–176). Mahwah, NJ: Erlbaum.

Rice, R. E., Peterson, M., & Christie, R. (2001). A comparative features analysis of publicly accessible commercial and government health database websites. In R. E. Rice & J. E. Katz (Eds.), *The Internet and health communication: Expectations and experiences* (pp. 213–231). Thousand Oaks, CA: Sage.

Richardson, C. R., Brown, B. B., Foley, S., Dial, K. S., & Lowery, J. C. (2005). Feasibility of adding enhanced pedometer feedback to nutritional counseling for weight loss. *Journal of Medical Internet Research, 7*(5), e56. Retrieved from http://www.jmir.org/2005/5/e56/

Rimal, R. N., & Adkins, A. D. (2003). Using computers to narrowcast health messages: The role of audience segmentation, targeting, and tailoring in health promotion. In T. L. Thompson, A. M. Dorsey, K. I. Miller, & R. Parrott (Eds.), *Handbook of health communication* (pp. 497–513). Mahwah, NJ: Erlbaum.

Sciamanna, C. N., Rogers, M. L., Shenassa, E. D., & Houston, T. K. (2007). Patient access to U.S. physicians who conduct Internet or e-mail consults. *Journal of General Internal Medicine, 22,* 378–381.

Sorbi, M. J., Mck, S. B., Houtveen, J. H., Kleiboer, A. M., & van Doornen, L. J. P. Mobile web-based monitoring and coaching: Feasibility in chronic migraine. *Journal of Medical Internet Research, 9*(5), e38. Retrieved from http://www.jmir.org/2007/5/e38/

Stavrositu, C., & Sundar, S. S. (2008, May). *Psychological empowerment derived from blogging: Is it agency or is it community?* Paper presented at the International Communication Association, Montreal, Canada.

Stephens, K., Sørnes, J. O., Rice, R. E., & Browning, L. (2008). Discrete, sequential, and follow-up use of information and communication technology by advanced ICT users. *Management Communication Quarterly, 22,* 197–231.

Stoddard, J. L., Augustson, E. M., & Moser, R. P. (2008). Effect of adding a virtual community (bulletin board) to smokefree.gov: Randomized controlled trial. *Journal of Medical Internet Research, 10*(5), e53.

Strecher, V. J., McClure, J., Alexander, G., Chakraborty, B., Nair, V., Konkel, J., ... Pomerleau, O. (2008). The role of engagement in a tailored web-based smoking cessation program: Randomized controlled trial. *Journal of Medical Internet Research, 10*(5), e10. Retrieved from http://www.jmir.org/2008/5/e36/

Sundar, S. S. (2007). Social psychology of interactivity in human–website interaction. In A. N. Joinson, K. Y. A. McKenna, T. Postmes, & U.-D. Reips (Eds.), *The Oxford handbook of internet psychology* (pp. 89–104). Oxford, England: Oxford University Press.

Sundar, S. S. (2008). The MAIN model: A heuristic approach to understanding technology effects on credibility. In M. J. Metzger & A. J. Flanagin (Eds.), *Digital media, youth, and credibility* (pp. 72–100). Cambridge, MA: MIT Press.

Sundar, S. S., Edwards, H. H., Hu, Y., & Stavrositu, C. (2007). Blogging for better health: Putting the "public" back in public health. In M. Tremayne (Ed.), *Blogging, citizenship and the future of media* (pp. 83–102). New York: Routledge.

Sundar, S. S., Marathe, S., & Kang, H. (2009, November). *Beyond tailoring: Customization in health websites.* Paper presented at the 95th annual convention of the National Communication Association, Chicago, IL.

Sundar, S. S., & Nass, C. (2001). Conceptualizing sources in online news. *Journal of Communication, 51,* 52–72.

Tuckett, D., Boulton, M., Olson, C., & Williams, A. (1985). *Meetings between experts.* London: Tavistock.

Vance, K., Howe, W., & Dellavalle, R. P. (2009). Social Internet sites as a source of public health information. *Dermatological Clinics, 27,* 133–136.

van Straten, A., Cuijpers, P., & Smits, N. (2008). Effectiveness of a web-based self-help intervention for symptoms of depression, anxiety, and stress: Randomized controlled trial. *Journal of Medical Internet Research, 10*(1), e7. Retrieved from http://www.jmir.org/2008/1/e7/

Wallis, K., & Rice, R. E. (2006). Technology and health information privacy: Consumers and the adoption of digital medical records technology. In M. Murero & R. E. Rice (Eds.), *The Internet and health care: Theory, research and practice* (pp. 279–311). Mahwah, NJ: Erlbaum.

Wantland, D. J., Portillo, C. J., Holzemer, W. L., Slaughter, R., & McGhee, E. M. (2004). The effectiveness of web-based vs. non-web-based interventions: A meta-analysis of behavioral change outcomes. *Journal of Medical Internet Research, 6*(4), e40. Retrieved from http://www.jmir.org/2004/4/e40/

Ware, L. J., Hurling, R., Bataveljic, O., Fairley, B. W., Hurst, T. L., Murray, P., ... Foreyt, J. P. (2008). Rates and determinants of uptake and use of an Internet physical activity and weight management program in office and manufacturing work sites in England: Cohort study. *Journal of Medical Internet Research, 10*(4), e56. Retrieved from http://www.jmir.org/2008/4/e56/

West, D. M., & Miller, E. A. (2009). *Digital medicine: Health care in the internet era.* Washington, DC: Brookings Institute Press.

Whittaker, R., Maddison, R., McRobbie, H., Bullen, C., Denny, C., Dorey, E., ... Rodgers, A. (2008). A multimedia mobile phone-based youth smoking cessation intervention: Findings from content development and piloting studies. *Journal of Medical Internet Research,* 10(5), e49. Retrieved from http://www.jmir.org/2008/5/e49/

Woodall, W. G., Buller, D. B., Saba, L., Zimmerman, D., Waters, E., Hines, J. M., ... Starling, R. (2007). Effect of emailed messages on return use of a nutrition education website and subsequent changes in dietary behavior. *Journal of Medical Internet Research, 9*(3), e27. Retrieved from http://www.jmir.org/2007/3/e27/

Zbikowski, S. M., Hapgood, J., Barnwell, S. S., & McAfee, T. (2008). Phone and web-based tobacco cessation treatment: Real-world utilization patterns and outcomes for 11,000 tobacco users. *Journal of Medical Internet Research, 10*(5), e41. Retrieved from http://www.jmir.org/2008/5/e41/

Zeng, Q., Kogan, S., Plovnick, R., Crowell, J., Lacroix, E-M., & Greenes, R. (2004). Positive attitudes and failed queries: An exploration of the conundrums of consumer health information retrieval. *International Journal of Medical Informatics, 73,* 45–55.

13

DEVELOPING EFFECTIVE MEDIA CAMPAIGNS FOR HEALTH PROMOTION

Kami J. Silk, Charles K. Atkin, and Charles T. Salmon

Improving utilization of seatbelts or mammogram services; raising awareness about AIDS, cancer risks, or cardiovascular disease; educating about sudden infant death syndrome or the H1N1 vaccine; reducing uptake of tobacco, alcohol, or drugs—media campaigns are used to influence and communicate about a range of health issues and behaviors. In their comprehensive review of communication campaigns, Rogers and Story (1987) extracted four essential elements across definitions, including: (a) a campaign is intended to generate outcomes or effects, (b) in a relatively large number of individuals, (c) usually within a specified period of time, and (d) through an organized set of communication activities. Campaigns have a long, well-established and respected heritage as an instrument for achieving social change (Paisley, 2001) as well as an apparatus for promoting public health (Hornik, 2002). In this chapter, we discuss the essential components to media campaigns, including formative research, persuasive message strategies, channel and source selection, dissemination decisions, and evaluation of effects.

Approaching Campaign Design

Today's savvy media consumers expect campaigns to have high quality graphics and creative ideas, but a fundamental understanding of communication theory is also necessary to maximize audience assessment, message content, and evaluation strategies. The essence of a campaign involves a systematic approach that requires campaign planners to perform a thorough situational analysis, develop a pragmatic strategic plan, and create and place messages in accordance with principles of effective media campaign practices. To maximize the effectiveness of any campaign endeavor it is advantageous to rely on research inputs at each phase of the campaign process, including the primary phases of planning, implementation, and evaluation.

The first step for planning is to conduct a conceptual analysis of the situation to understand the behavioral aspects of the health problem and to determine which actions should be performed by which people in order to improve health outcomes. The campaign team needs to specify *focal segments* of the population whose health-related practices are to be changed and the bottom-line *focal behaviors* that the campaign ultimately seeks to influence. The next step is to trace backwards from the focal behaviors to identify the proximate and distal determinants and then create *models* of the pathways of influence via attitudes, beliefs, knowledge, social influences, and environmental forces. For example, we may decide that kids are a primary focal segment because they need to eat more fruits and vegetables each day, and we might identify that they need to have more fruits and vegetables available to them at home.

The next step is to assess the model from a communication perspective, specifying *intended audiences* and *intended responses* that can be directly influenced by campaign messages. The communication campaign can then be designed to impact the most promising pathways, and measurable campaign objectives can then be created to inform further planning, implementation, and later evaluation of effects. For example, to get kids to increase fruit and vegetable consumption we might decide that mothers are the key audience (Andrews, Silk, & Eneli, 2010). Thus, we create objectives and campaign messages that promote the purchase of more fruits and vegetables by mothers. A comprehensive plan is necessary so that strategic decisions can be made about different campaign components.

A practical consideration is the allocation of resources for the campaign, and strategists are faced with a range of issues to consider. Should the campaign seek to change fundamental behaviors or chip away at more readily altered behaviors? Should the most resistant or most receptive audience segments be the focus of the campaign? What proportion of the resources should be devoted to direct and indirect pathways of influence on the focal segment? Who should be targeted? What is the optimum combination of awareness messages, instructional messages, and persuasive messages? How many messages should attack the *competition* (the unhealthy behavior) and how many promote the healthy alternative? Is it more effective to disseminate the messages via expensive TV channels or primarily utilize free new media like YouTube, blogs, or social network sites? Should the campaign messages be scheduled in concentrated bursts or spread out over a lengthy period of time? Strong formative research at the planning stage informs these questions.

Strategists also must anticipate audience reactions to campaign messages and they should not underestimate what it takes to get audience members to respond at all. In responding to media stimuli, individuals proceed through the basic stages of exposure and processing before effects can be achieved at the learning, yielding, and action levels. *Exposure* includes both the initial reception and degree of attention to the campaign messages, which can be amplified by subsequent campaign-instigated seeking of further information or sensitization to other relevant media messages that are encountered. *Processing* encompasses mental comprehension, interpretive perceptions, pro and con arguments, and cognitive connections and emotional reactions produced by the campaign message along with subsequent interpretation of other relevant stimuli, particularly the development of resistance to countermessages. Audience predispositions play a crucial role in determining responses to campaign messages.

As message concepts are designed and refined, qualitative reactions to message concepts should be assessed through focus group testing (Silk, Bigsby, Volkman, Kingsley, Atkin, Ferrara, & Goins, 2006), and quantitative ratings should be assessed in message-testing labs or online experimental testing (Maddock, Silbanuz, & Reger-Nash, 2008). Pretest feedback prior to final production and dissemination of campaign messages is particularly helpful in assessing whether the audience regards the content and style as informative, believable, motivating, convincing, useful, on-target, and enjoyable, and not be too preachy, disturbing, confusing, irritating, or dull. A focus group approach was used extensively by the U.S. Centers for Disease Control and Prevention in its "America Responds to AIDS" campaigns of the early 1990s. Focus groups were conducted at shopping malls around the country to generate concepts, offer reactions to storyboards and potential campaign themes, and for other campaign-related research (Salmon & Jason, 1992). In one instance, health officials sought to gain understanding of the public's concern about a case where a young woman allegedly contracted AIDS from visiting a dentist. Focus group participants talked about their fears and the cues they used to assess their risk when visiting a doctor's or dentist's office, one of which was the absence or presence of a wedding ring on the finger of their primary care physician. Although this particular finding did not become the focus of a campaign, it did create an impetus for new campaigns to counter stereotypes and misconceptions about the disease.

Formative research evidence is crucial to resolve disputes between sponsoring organization officials, health experts, communication strategists, and creative professionals. Feedback from audience research can reveal whether the tone of a message is too righteous (admonishing unhealthy people about their incorrect behavior); the recommendations too extreme (rigidly advocating unpalatable ideals of healthy behavior); the execution too politically correct (staying within prescribed boundaries of propriety to avoid offending certain groups); and the execution too self-indulgent (letting creativity and style overwhelm substantive content). In particular, research helps bridge the gap between health specialists who differ substantially from their target audiences in knowledge, values, priorities, and level of involvement.

Intended Audiences

A typical health campaign might subdivide the population by age, sex, ethnicity, stage of change, susceptibility, self-efficacy, values, personality characteristics, social context, or media usage variables (Rodgers, Chen, Duffy, & Fleming, 2009), and each dimension has multiple levels that could ultimately create thousands of potential subgroups that might be specially targeted with individually tailored messages. There are two major strategic advantages of segmenting groups into larger subsets. First, message efficiency can be maximized if subsets of the audience are ordered according to importance (Who is most in need of change?) and receptivity (Who is most likely to be influenced?). Second, effectiveness can be increased if message content, form, and style are tailored to the predispositions and abilities of the distinct subgroups (Atkin & Freimuth, 2001; Dervin & Frenette, 2001). Defining and segmenting audiences based on psychographics, demographics, geographics, and other relevant theoretical constructs and variables increases campaign designers' ability to tailor messages to the needs of the intended primary and secondary audiences. Slater (1996) provides a review and critique of commonly used audience segmentation strategies.

Campaign designers can choose to collect background data about audience predispositions, channel usage, and other necessary information (Atkin & Freimuth, 2001), or they may choose to use an available research program that has developed standard inventories of demographic and psychographic variables for use in campaign development. For example, the Centers for Disease Control and Prevention (CDC) licenses the annual American Healthstyles survey for audience analysis (CDC, 2009), and the Health Information National Trends Survey (HINTS) provides research on a representative U.S. sample of adults specific to cancer and includes information on channel usage, risk perceptions, and use of information as well as demographic information (National Cancer Institute, 2009). These research programs help campaign designers segment their audiences across relevant variables so that messages can be tailored to audience characteristics.

Three basic types of audiences can be targeted in media health campaigns. First, messages may be aimed directly to the focal segments whose behavior is to be changed; second, the campaign might target individuals who are in a position to influence the focal segments; and third, messages might focus on policy makers who can shape policy that can alter the environments within which health decisions occur. For example, campaigners might target adolescents directly in an antidrug campaign, but focus on legislators to increase funding for more drug resistance education. The nature of the health problem dictates the broad parameters of the focal audience to be influenced.

Campaigns often focus on receptive or favorably disposed audiences because they are ready to be influenced to perform the practice (Proschaska & DiClemente, 1983), which will increase the likelihood the campaign will achieve some impact. A less receptive but important target audience is composed of "at risk" people who might try an unhealthy behavior in the near future—for example, teenagers who might experiment with drugs. On the other hand, those committed to unhealthy practices are not readily influenced by campaigns that target them directly. So, a heavy investment of resources to get smokers to quit smoking immediately is likely to yield a marginal payoff. Campaigners also need to consider other demographic, social, and psychological-based subgroups such as high- and low-income groups or sensation-seekers (see Palmgreen, Donohew, & Harrington, 2001). Influencing these varied population segments requires a complex mix of narrowly customized messages and broadly applicable, multitargeted messages that use diverse appeals and optimally ambiguous recommended actions.

Intended Responses

Campaigns should be designed with measurable objectives that define an intended response by audience members. In the health arena, the focal behavior is usually a specific behavioral practice or discrete action like "eat five servings of fruits and vegetables each day" or "wear a seatbelt when you drive." However, there are numerous intermediate responses that might be targeted, such as awareness, knowledge, salience priorities, beliefs, expectancies, values, and attitudes to help facilitate behavior change. The two fundamental approaches for campaigns are to promote healthy behavior or to reduce or prevent unhealthy behavior. The promotion of desirable practices works better for certain topic areas and a negatively oriented prevention approach is more potent for topics where harmful outcomes are genuinely threatening. Other types of target responses come into play when campaigns are aimed at influencers and social policy makers.

Prevention campaign messages often focus on the harmful consequences of the unhealthy practice rather than positive alternatives to it. Health campaigners typically attack the competition by threatening dire consequences for performing the proscribed behavior—for example, the "Truth Campaign" relied heavily on images of dead teens in front of tobacco industry corporate offices to illustrate the death toll associated with tobacco use (Farrelly, Davis, Haviland, Messeri, & Healton, 2005). Although threats can be effective if handled skillfully, a heavy reliance on negative attacks tends to restrict the strategic arsenal. A softer tactic is to discount the perceived benefits of the unhealthy practice like assertions that smoking doesn't really impress peers, for example. In campaign messages that promote a positive product directly to a focal segment, there is a continuum of prospective target responses that can be explicitly recommended for adoption. These actions can vary in their acceptability to the audience, based primarily on the effort and sacrifice required to perform the behavior and the monetary expense. Barriers can be overcome with smaller or softer products that demand lower investment and generate fewer drawbacks. For example, it may be fruitless to advocate for a sizable degree of change like asking smokers to quit smoking because it is beyond their latitude of acceptability; however, an incremental "foot in the door" strategy that asks smokers to cut back on smoking may be more effective for resistant audiences.

A major challenge in prevention campaigns is that the positive product or outcome is essentially "nothing." For example, terminology and imagery such as "drug-free lifestyle" and "abstinence" have not been overwhelmingly effective in the alcohol, tobacco, and drug domains because "nonuse" is not an appealing option—creative labeling and packaging is necessary in these instances. Some campaigns might instead promote modestly demanding products such as prebehaviors (e.g., sign pledge card, state intentions publicly, wear red ribbon) or limited forms of abstaining (e.g., keep drug free for a week, delay use until later). Again, realistic expectations of intended campaign responses are developed from strong formative research with the focal behavior and audience segments.

Message Types

Awareness, instruction, and persuasion messages are the three basic communication processes used to influence target audiences. Awareness messages inform people about what to do, specify who should do it, and provide cues about when and where it should be done. Instruction messages present "how to do it" information. Persuasive messages feature convincing reasons why the audience should adopt the advocated action or avoid the proscribed behavior. For audiences that are favorably inclined, the campaign has the easier persuasive task of strengthening a positive attitude, promoting behavioral consolidation, and motivating behavioral maintenance over time. The relative emphasis on the three types of messages will vary at different points of the campaign and for different target audiences because the pathways to impact depend on the existing pattern of knowledge and attitudes of the audience.

Persuasive Message Strategies

The most central and fundamental element of media campaigns is the content, form, and style of individual messages. Sophisticated message design includes strategic selection of substantive material, systematic construction of message components, and creative execution of stylistic features. Our discussion here begins with incentives, which are central to persuasive media messages. For most of the pathways of influence, there are several additional message qualities that increase effectiveness. *Credibility,* the extent to which the message content is believed to be accurate and valid, is primarily conveyed by the trustworthiness and competence of the source and the provision of convincing evidence. Whether it is Michael J. Fox for Parkinson's disease or the American Cancer Society for lung cancer, perceptions of source credibility impact the believability and influence of a message. Campaign messages can be made *engaging* by using stylistic features that are superficially attractive and entertaining (and less pleasing features that are nevertheless arresting or refreshing) and including substantive content that is interesting, mentally stimulating, or emotionally arousing. To influence behavior, the presentation must be personally *involving* and *relevant* so receivers regard the recommendation as applicable to their situation and needs. Finally, the *understandability* of the message contributes to recipient processing and learning. In sum, the messages should be simple, explicit, sufficiently detailed, comprehensive, and understandable.

Incentive Appeals

The approaches used in media campaigns generally have corresponding positive or negative incentive appeals. Message content that links desired health behavior to positive incentives like valued attributes or outcomes (or unhealthy behavior with negative incentives) is preferable to direct appeals to act in a specified way. The classic incentive strategy in health messages is to build on the existing values of the target audience and offer a series of substantive arguments for or against a particular behavior, buttressed by credible evidence or source assertions. Messages for high-involvement health practices tend to emphasize incentives, presenting persuasive arguments supported by credible messengers and evidence to move the audience through a hierarchy of output steps such as attention, attitude change, and action (McGuire, 1994).

The most widely used frameworks (theory of reasoned action, protection motivation theory, and health belief model) employ a basic expectancy-value mechanism, wherein attitudinal and behavioral responses are contingent upon each individual's valuation of outcomes promoted in campaign messages. Appeals can emphasize the subjective probability of a consequence occurring or the degree of positive or negative valence of that outcome (vulnerability x severity). The prime communication strategies are to either change beliefs regarding the probability component or intensify the valence of the messages by emphasizing negative consequences, positive benefits, or already salient advantages to engaging in recommended practices. For example, a breast cancer prevention campaign message may strive to increase women's perceived vulnerability by citing a statistic that one in eight women will be diagnosed with breast cancer in their lifetime; and the same message might address severity by focusing on the fact that early detection via mammograms increases survival rates, while late detection can lead to death.

Incentives can focus on physical health, time/effort, economic, psychological, and social dimensions, with each one having both negative and positive value associated with them. The most frequently used dimension is physical health, with negatively valued unhealthy outcomes like death, illness, and injury featured more often than positive reinforcements. There is a need to diversify the negative incentive strategies to include appeals not directly related to physical health per se (e.g., psychological regret or social rejection in antiobesity messages) and to give greater emphasis to reward-oriented incentives (e.g., valued states or consequences such as well-being, altruism, and attractiveness as rewards for exercise).

Negative Appeals. Health campaigns rely heavily on loss-framed messages designed to motivate behavior change by threatening the audience with harmful outcomes from initiating or continuing an unhealthy practice. Beyond strong fear appeals, messages should include threats of a less severe nature, negative incentives beyond the physical health domain, and positive incentives. For many health topics it might be best to select a mildly valenced incentive that is highly probable. In the case of drug campaigns, for example, minor negative physical incentives might be loss of stamina, weight gain, and physiological addiction, while negative social incentives might include looking uncool, alienating friends, incurring peer disapproval, losing the trust of parents, or deviating from social norms. Psychological incentives might include reduced ability to concentrate, low grades, feeling lazy and unmotivated, losing control, and making bad decisions, as well as anxiety about getting caught or experiencing harm, guilt, and loss of self-respect. Among the economic incentives related to drugs are diminished job prospects, fines, the cumulative cost of purchasing drugs, and inability to spend money on other needs and desires. Finally, messages might highlight penalties for violating laws and policies, such as incarceration, loss of driver's license, or suspension from school.

Positive Appeals.   Campaigns should diversify by presenting a high proportion of gain-framed incentives. For most negative consequences of performing a recommended practice, there is usually a mirror-image positive outcome that can be promised for performing the healthy alternative (e.g., avoiding drugs or enjoying a drug-free lifestyle). In the physical health dimension, messages can offer incentives ranging from a longer lifespan to enhanced athletic performance. Similarly, social incentives might include being cool, gaining approval and respect, forming deeper friendships, building trust with parents, and being a good role model, while psychological incentives might promise outcomes like gaining control over one's life, achieving a positive self-image, attaining one's goals, or feeling secure. Exaggerated rewards may work well as motivators even though their actual likelihood is small. While negative strategies using long-shot prospects of severe harm are often dismissed by defensive receivers, positive approaches may attain greater success by promising lottery-type payoffs that are more believable to optimists.

Multiple Appeals.   There are dozens of persuasive appeals that are potentially effective, and the degree of potency is roughly equivalent in many cases. Rather than relying on a handful of incentives, it is advantageous to use multiple appeals across a series of messages in a campaign to influence different segments of the target audience (especially in media channels where precise targeting is difficult) and to provide several reasons for the individual to comply. In selecting incentives, the key criteria are the salience of the promised or threatened consequences, the malleability of beliefs about the likelihood of experiencing these outcomes, and the potential persuasiveness of the arguments that can be advanced (see Cappella, Fishbein, Hornik, Ahern, & Sayeed, 2001). For messages about familiar health subjects, it is important to include novel appeals to complement the standard arguments.

Evidence

It is typically necessary to provide evidence to support claims made in campaign messages, particularly when belief formation is a central mechanism and when the message source is not highly credible. The type of evidence featured varies according to each audience as research demonstrates that individuals subjectively interpret different types of evidence, often preferring written over visual representations (Parrott, Silk, Condit, Dorgan, & Harris, 2005). Highly involved individuals are more influenced by messages that cite statistics, provide documentation, and include quotations from experts, whereas those who are less involved are more influenced by dramatized case examples and testimonials by respected sources. The message should demonstrate how the evidence is relevant to the situation experienced by the target audience. Special care should be taken with the presentation of extreme claims (rare cases, implausible statistics, overly dramatic depictions of consequences) as well as biased and misleading information. These elements may strain credulity and trigger counterarguing among audience members and may be challenged by critics in rebuttal messages. Reinard (1988) provides a comprehensive review of the evidence literature.

One-Sided versus Two-Sided Content

Compliance with campaign message recommendations is impeded by a variety of disadvantages perceived by the audience, such as obstacles, drawbacks, and forsaken alternatives. The strategist is faced with the question of how to handle these disadvantages. A one-sided message strategy presents only the case favoring the desired behavior or against the competition and ignores the drawbacks. In a two-sided message, the elements of the opposing case are strategically raised and discounted in order to counteract current and future challenges. The three basic techniques for addressing drawbacks are *refutation, diminution,* and *tactical concession.* First, supposed advantages of the unhealthy behavior or disadvantages of the promoted behavior can be directly refuted by contrary evidence or emotional attacks. In other words, messages can acknowledge that the competition has certain attractive aspects and then argue that each seemingly positive consequence is either unlikely to occur, not so positive after all, or relatively unimportant. Second, drawbacks of the focal behavior can be mentioned and then downplayed by arguing that these factors are relatively unimportant compared with the beneficial features. Third, minor disadvantages of engaging in the recommended behavior can simply be conceded as a tactic for enhancing credibility, which may increase the believability of the overall message.

Two-sided messages are more persuasive if the audience is sophisticated and knowledgeable about the topic, predisposed against the position being advanced, wary of a manipulative intent, and already aware of the pro arguments or likely to be exposed to them in the future. The main weakness of a two-sided presentation is that it may heighten the salience of certain drawbacks that may not have been considered by audience members when they weighed their decisions. Formative research is useful in determining which of these factors are predominant in a particular health campaign situation.

Awareness and Instruction Strategies

In addition to motivational appeals, media campaigns typically include awareness and instruction messages that highlight the health problem and solution, trigger appropriate behaviors, and teach coping skills.

Awareness Messages. Awareness messages may be designed to: create *recognition* of the topic or practice for a large portion of the public; trigger *activation* among favorably predisposed audiences; use interpersonal influences or environmental forces as motives for *compliance*; encourage further *information-seeking* about the topic; and to *sensitize* individuals to subsequently encountered messages. Information-seeking is a crucial function because campaign messages with the broadest reach are not tailored to carefully segmented audiences and are generally superficial in content. Thus, awareness messages aim to stimulate interest and motivate audience members to actively seek further information elaboration from additional sources like websites, hotline numbers, counselors, parents, and opinion leaders. In the mass media, there are news stories, advertisements, entertainment portrayals, online stimuli, and other public service campaigns that may present content that is consistent with campaign goals. Similarly, individuals may not be conscious of social norms, interpersonal influences, behavioral models, or social conditions relevant to the focal behavior. Thus, some campaign messages can sensitize audiences to attend to additional stimuli related to the campaign topic.

Instruction Messages. In many media campaigns, there is a need to provide information that produces *knowledge gain* and *skills acquisition*. If the behavioral components are elaborate or complex, messages can educate the audience by providing a detailed blueprint. If the focal segment is subject to peer pressure or exposed to unhealthy media portrayals, instruction messages can teach *peer resistance* and *media literacy* skills. And messages can provide encouragement or training to enhance *personal efficacy*. Given the potentially detrimental health effects of commercial advertising, entertainment media portrayals, and certain websites, it may be wise to devote a modest proportion of campaign messages to *inoculating* viewer and listeners against influences that might undermine the campaign.

Influential Source Messengers

The *messenger*, the model or character in the message that delivers information, demonstrates behavior, or provides a testimonial, is distinct from the institutional sponsor and the message creator. Atkin (1994) provides an elaborate discussion of the strengths and weaknesses of various types of messengers. Messengers can enhance the content of the message by being engaging, credible, and relevant; increase exposure by attracting attention; facilitate comprehension through personalization or modeling of recommended actions; elicit positive cognitive responses through message evaluation; heighten emotional arousal through identification and transfer affect (from messenger to message content); and increase retention by being memorable.

Five key dimensions to source selection include: expertise and trustworthiness (source credibility) and familiarity, similarity, and likability to the target audience (facets of attractiveness). Expertise makes a surprisingly small contribution to persuasive impact of a message, while trustworthiness is more effective as audiences perceive the messenger as honest in character, sincere, or lacking self-interest. Low-involvement audiences rely on this "credibility heuristic" to judge message claims rather than investing elaborate processing efforts. Messenger attractiveness can produce greater influence because the audience admires or identifies with the engaging or appealing messenger. Similarity, typically based on target audience demographics, shared attitudes, and common experiences, is used as a strategy when modeling message recommendations or demonstrating consequences is necessary. Peer models are most important for youth, minority, and other nonmainstream audiences as they may not trust conventional sources. Likability seems to be an influential factor when the arguments are weak or the target response is regarded as unappealing.

Eight types of messengers are often featured in campaign messages, including: celebrities, public officials, expert specialists (e.g., doctors/researchers), organizational leaders (e.g., hospital administrator), professional performers (e.g., models/actors), average people (e.g., blue-collar males), especially experienced people (e.g., victim/survivor), or unique characters (e.g., animated/costumed characters). Selection of the messenger depends on the predispositions of the target audience, persuasion mechanism underlying the strategy, and type of message. Awareness messages tend to present celebrities, characters, and public officials; instruction messages rely on experts; and persuasion messages are more likely to feature ordinary people and organizational leaders. Professional performers appear in all types of messages. Each source has its advantages and disadvantages.

For example, a medical authority would strengthen the expertise dimension, but would be less engaging due to the complex information typically featured in authority-based messages. In contrast, a message that features a well-known celebrity can bring great interest to a campaign message, especially if the celebrity has special competence or relevant experience as victims or survivors of the health problem. For example, basketball star Magic Johnson's disclosure of his HIV status along with his celebrity status helped garner greater attention to AIDS as a public health threat. Many celebrities are highly respected and perceived as trustworthy on a broad array of topics, while other celebrities may promote skepticism, distract from message content, lose their luster, or be perceived as unhealthy role models. Despite certain drawbacks, the personalized, credible, and engaging qualities of a source figure offer clear advantages over presenting message material without a manifest messenger or only with attribution to an impersonal organization. Multiple messengers can increase the odds of success in some cases, but this tactic may risk information overload and undermine continuity across message executions. Again, formative evaluation research is helpful for informing selection of messengers.

Selecting Appropriate Channels and Formats

In disseminating messages, media campaigns have traditionally relied on television, radio, newspapers, and printed materials, especially broadcast spots, press releases, and pamphlets. This is supplemented by secondary channels and vehicles (e.g., billboards, posters, theater slides); entertainment-education materials (e.g., songs, program inserts, comics; Singhal & Rogers, 1999); and interactive technology (e.g., blogs, websites, computer games). In recent years, the Internet has become a primary source of information provision and seeking, e-mail has been used to extend the interpersonal components of campaigns as in the Digital Heroes Campaign (DHC; Rhodes, Spencer, Saito, & Sipe, 2006), and mobile phones have become well-suited to offer tailored, wide-reaching, interactive, and continuing campaign interventions. Although channel selection is dictated by usage patterns, limited resources play a pragmatic and pivotal role.

In assessing each option for channeling campaign messages, designers can consider myriad advantages and disadvantages along a number of communicative dimensions. Specifically, designers can channel differences in terms of entities such as these:

- *reach* (proportion of community exposed to the message),
- *specialization* (targetability for reaching specific subgroups),
- *intrusiveness* (ability to overcome selectivity and command attention),
- *safeness* (avoidance of risk of boomerang or irritation),
- *participation* (active receiver involvement while processing stimuli),
- *meaning modalities* (array of senses employed in conveying meaning),
- *personalization* (human relational nature of source–receiver interaction),
- *decodability* (mental effort required for processing stiumuli),
- *depth* (channel capacity for conveying detailed and complex content),
- *credibility* (believability of material conveyed),
- *agenda-setting* (potency of channel for raising salience priority of issues),
- *accessibility* (ease of placing messages in a channel),
- *economy* (low cost for producing and disseminating stimuli), and
- *efficiency* (simplicity of arranging for production and dissemination).

Atkin (1994) provides a consideration of key strengths and weaknesses associated with each of these communicative dimensions.

Table 13.1 Features of Media Channels and Modes for Disseminating Health Messages

Channel & Mode	Access[a]	Reach[b]	Target[c]	Depth[d]	Credibility[e]	Agenda-Setting[f]
TV						
PSA spots	0	++	+	+	+	+
Paid ads	++	++	+	+	+	+
News Coverage	+	+	+	+	++	++
Feature stories	+	+	+	++	++	+
Public service shows	++	0	++	++	++	0
Talk/magazine shows	0	++	+	++	+	+
Entertainment inserts	0	++	+	+	+	+
Radio						
PSAs	+	++	++	0	+	+
Paid spots	++	++	++	0	+	+
News coverage	+	+	++	0	+	+
Talk/call in	++	+	++	++	+	+
Newspaper						
Ads	0	++	+	++	+	+
News coverage	++	++	+	++	++	++
Feature stories	+	++	+	++	+	+
Editorial comment	+	+	++	++	+	+
Letters to editor	++	+	+	+	+	+
Magazine ads/stories	+	+	++	++	+	0
Internet Web pages	++	+	++	++	+	+
Billboards/posters	+	++	++	0	0	0
Theater shorts/slides	+	+	++	+	0	0
Film, tape and slide shows	++	0	++	++	+	0
Pamphlets/booklets	+	0	++	++	+	0
Direct mail material	+	+	++	++	+	0

Note. ++ = high; + = medium; 0 = low.
[a]Degree of campaign's accessibility to channel distribution.
[b]Proportion of general public exposed to the message in channel.
[c]Reaching of specialized target audience segments via channel.
[d]Channel capacity for conveying detailed and complex content.
[e]Believability of message content carried in the channel.
[f]Channel potency for raising perceived significance of topic.

To achieve an impact on the audience, there are several advantages of public relations messages over prepackaged stimuli such as PSAs and web pages. Messages appearing in the informational media tend to have greater credibility than packaged messages that utilize an advertising format, and their credibility facilitates the formation of beliefs regarding health consequences and the acceptance of recommended behaviors. Messages placed in the mainstream media can attract the attention of key informal influencers, who can exert an indirect influence on the focal individuals. Health issues that gain visibility in the news media can benefit from the agenda-setting effect (e.g., the obesity epidemic in the United States), whereby problems and solutions are perceived as more urgent and significant. This is particularly important in media advocacy strategies targeted at opinion leaders and policy makers.

Entertainment-education, the practice of embedding health-related material in entertainment programming or creating entertainment programming as a vehicle for health education, attracts large audiences and conveys information in a relevant and credible manner. This approach has proved to be quite successful in promoting health in less developed countries (Singhal & Rogers, 1999), and it also has been used in the United States to promote safety belts, use of designated drivers, safe sex, and drug abstinence as well as deal with child-oriented topics such as alcohol and obesity prevention. Kline (this volume) considers this strategy in more depth.

There are thousands of websites and CD-ROMs offering a wide variety of health materials, and many campaigns utilize these channels. In addition to providing prepackaged pages and streaming video, these technologies have an interactive capacity that gives them an advantage over standard media (see the VERB campaign, Wong et al., 2004). Screening questionnaires can assess each individual's capabilities, stage of readiness, stylistic taste, knowledge level, and current beliefs, and then direct the individual to narrowly targeted customized messages. Not only does this approach increase the likelihood of learning and persuasion, but it decreases the possibility of boomerang effects. Furthermore, entertaining interactive formats such as games are particularly well suited to youthful focal segments (Lieberman, 2001).

Influencers and the Environment

It is often valuable for media campaigns to supplement the direct approach (educating and persuading the focal segment) by influencing other target audiences who can exert interpersonal influence or help reform environmental conditions that shape the behaviors of the focal segment. Mass media campaigns have considerable potential for producing effects on institutions and groups at the national and community level as well as motivating personal influencers in close contact with individuals in the focal segment. These influencers can provide positive and negative reinforcement, exercise control (by making rules, monitoring behavior, and enforcing consequences), shape opportunities, facilitate behavior with reminders at opportune moments, and serve as role models. Furthermore, influencers can customize their messages to the unique needs and values of the individual.

Interpersonal Influencers

An important goal of campaigns is to stimulate interpersonal influence attempts by inspiring, prompting, and empowering influencers. For example, a variety of peer and authority figures are in a position to personally educate, persuade, or control adolescents: parents, siblings, friends, coworkers, bosses, teachers, club leaders, coaches, medical personnel, and police officers. These influencers are likely to be responsive to negative appeals that arouse concern about harmful consequences to those they are trying to help behave appropriately. Thus, some campaign messages should be designed to motivate facilitators and enforcers to take action.

Social Policy Makers

Individuals' decisions about health practices are strongly shaped by the constraints and opportunities in their social environment, such as monetary expenses, laws, entertainment role models, commercial messages, social forces, and community services. Through the interventions of government, business, educational, medical, media, religious, and community organizations, many of these influential factors can be engineered to increase the likelihood of healthy choices or discourage unhealthy practices (e.g., banning of smoking in public spaces). These initiatives include direct service delivery, restrictions on advertising and marketing practices, and the imposition of taxes. More fundamental long-range approaches might seek to restructure basic socioeconomic conditions by reducing poverty, improving schools, broadening access to the health care system, and enhancing employment opportunities.

Reformers have refined techniques that combine community organizing and media publicity to advance healthy public policies through *media advocacy* (see Wallack & Dorfman, 2001). News coverage of health can shape the public agenda and the policy agenda pertaining to new initiatives, rules, and laws. An important element is changing the public's beliefs about the effectiveness of policies and interventions that are advanced, which leads to supportive public opinion (and direct pressure) that can help convince institutional leaders to formulate and implement societal constraints and opportunities.

Maximizing Quantity of Dissemination

Strategic dissemination considerations encompass the volume of messages, the amount of repetition, the prominence of placement, and the scheduling of message presentation. A substantial *volume* of stimuli is needed to attain adequate reach and frequency of exposure, along with comprehension, recognition, and image formation. Moreover, maximum saturation conveys the significance of the problem and thus facilitates agenda-setting. Moderate *repetition* of specific executions may be needed to force low-involvement receivers to attend to and process the message, but high repetition leads to message fatigue and diminishing returns.

Prominent placement of messages in conspicuous positions within media vehicles (e.g., prime time, back page) serves to enhance both exposure levels and perceived significance. To provide a common thread unifying the varied messages, the campaign should feature *continuity devices* (e.g., logo, slogan, jingle, messenger). These devices increase memorability and enable the audience to cumulatively integrate material across multiple exposures. Another quantitative consideration is the *scheduling* of a fixed number of presentations. Depending on the situation, campaign messages may be most effectively concentrated over a short duration, dispersed thinly over a lengthy period, or distributed in intermittent bursts.

The *length* of the campaign is a final consideration. Perpetual campaigning is often necessary because focal segments are in constant need of influence. There are always newcomers who move into the "at risk" stage of vulnerability, backsliders who revert to prior misbehavior, evolvers who gradually adopt the recommended practice, waverers who need regular doses of reinforcement to stay the course, and latecomers who finally see the light after years of unhealthy habits. Resources determine the ability of media campaigns to maximize dissemination of messages.

215

Determining Campaign Effectiveness

Depending upon the objectives of the sponsoring organization, campaigns can seek to influence outcomes at different levels, ranging from the individual to the societal. Campaigns that seek to influence individual-level outcomes focus on knowledge (awareness, consciousness raising, familiarity, recognition, recall), attitudes (affect, disposition, inclination, opinion), or behavior (behavioral decision, trial behavior, repeat behavior). Societal level outcomes, however, usually focus on policy changes like gaining approval for health care reform or shaming local municipalities to increase the number of homeless shelters. Researchers have assessed the impact of media-based health campaigns using survey and experimental designs over the past several decades. The findings from a range of studies have been summarized in literature reviews by Atkin (1981, 2001), Backer, Rogers, and Sopory (1992), and Dejong and Winston (1990) and in a meta-analysis by Snyder (2001). The preponderance of the evidence shows that conventional campaigns typically have limited direct effects on most health behaviors; specifically, data suggest that campaigns are capable of exerting moderate to powerful influence on cognitive outcomes, less influence on attitudinal outcomes, and still less influence on behavioral outcomes. Further, the conventional wisdom is that behavioral outcomes are more likely to occur in proportion to such factors as dose of information, duration of campaign activities, integration of mass and interpersonal communication systems, and integration of social-change strategies (enforcement, education, engineering).

There are a number of reasons why a campaign may not have a strong impact. Audience resistance barriers arise at each stage of response, from exposure to behavioral implementation. Perhaps the greatest challenge is reaching the audience and gaining its attention. Other key barriers include misperception of susceptibility to negative outcomes, deflection of persuasive appeals, denial of applicability to self, rejection of unappealing recommendations, and inertial lethargy. Given the many links in the effects chain necessary to lead an individual from initial exposure to sustained behavioral change (McGuire, 1994), it is small wonder that expectations regarding campaign effectiveness have become modest.

In addition to expected outcomes, campaigns also are capable of producing outcomes that are either undesirable or serendipitous or both. These outcomes are not necessarily indicators of boomerang effects that occur when a message elicits the opposite reaction intended by the campaign. For example, antidrug messages may heighten rather than discourage interest in illegal drugs and designated driver campaigns may encourage greater amounts of drinking among individuals who know they have a safe ride home. Although the obvious remedy would seem to suggest conducting more extensive pretesting, unintended effects are simply unavoidable. Mass audiences are heterogeneous by definition, chock full of sensation seekers and risk avoiders, precontemplators and contemplators, health zealots, and health resisters.

Campaign effectiveness typically is defined in relative rather than absolute terms. If a campaign meets the objectives set by its planners, then it is labeled "effective," and if it does not, then it is labeled "ineffective." It is little wonder, therefore, that prescriptions for improving campaign effectiveness frequently have suggested that campaign planners set readily attained goals and objectives. Lowering the bar does not improve campaign performance per se, but it lowers expectations and thereby increases the odds that the campaign will be viewed as a success. For instance, two campaigns could induce the same level of behavioral change, but one might be judged effective and the other ineffective on the basis of the idiosyncratic goals and objectives that were set for each (see Salmon &

Murray-Johnson, 2001). Fishbein (1996) further elaborates on effectiveness by arguing that small effect sizes should be set for media campaigns so that obtaining effects is achievable.

Most of the published evaluations of campaign effects provide little useful information about which components of the campaign contributed to the effect that was measured. For example, a typical field experiment simply compares treatment communities that receive a full multifaceted campaign intervention and control communities that receive no intervention. This design does not permit examination and isolation of "what works." Secular trends also impact the ability to detect media campaign effects. Populations are more knowledgeable about health issues due to ongoing public health initiatives and changes in clinical knowledge, as well as increases in news coverage of health issues and increases in the number of channels disseminating similar stories (Viswanath & Finnegan, 2002).

Conclusion

Drawing on this substantial body of scholarship, we know that many media health campaigns have attained a rather modest impact because of meager resources, poor conceptualization, and narrow strategic approaches. The limited potency of the media has several implications for campaigns. It is advisable to have realistic expectations, especially when attempting to influence fundamental behaviors in the short run. Campaigns should be prepared for the long haul, because many campaigns will take years to achieve a significant impact. More emphasis should be given to relatively attainable effects by aiming at more receptive focal segments and by creating or promoting more palatable positive products with a favorable cost-benefit ratio. Campaigns should play to the evident strengths of media channels by imparting new knowledge (e.g., a TV spot informing people about the nutritional value of soy), enhancing salience (e.g., news publicity stressing the importance of reducing drunk driving), providing instruction (e.g., a website describing protective sexual behaviors), triggering action (e.g., a radio announcement reminding drivers to buckle up during a snowstorm), and stimulating information-seeking (e.g., a Facebook ad linking to a website). Media messages should be augmented by supplementary education, persuasion, and control via classroom instruction, physician advice, social influence, and environmental constraints, using the media campaign to shape and energize these forces. The use of these approaches improves the likelihood of campaign effectiveness.

Health campaign researchers have ample opportunities to expand the theoretical and applied literature on the processes and effects of campaigns, particularly as the channels of dissemination rapidly evolve. Future investigations will help us gain a better understanding of the complex combination of factors that determine campaign effectiveness. In particular, greater priority should be given to campaign-level analyses rather than a narrow focus on message variables. Researchers should address the impact of various quantities of campaign messages (e.g., point of diminishing return for total volume of messages, wear-out point for specific message repetition), the optimum mix of incentives across a diverse range of messages over the course of a campaign (e.g., physical health vs. nonhealth dimensions, gain vs. loss frame), the appropriate ratio of direct vs. indirect pathways (e.g., for simple vs. complex behavioral responses, willingness vs. apathy of potential influencers), and the relative impact of varied combinations of channels and modes of directly disseminating key types of campaign messages. In each case, careful attention must be given to differential effectiveness contingent upon the characteristics and predispositions of audience segments.

There is also a need for transdisciplinary models for conducting research related to translation and dissemination of health messages in larger campaign contexts, as discussed in the Parrott and Kreuter chapter (this volume). Transdisciplinary teams should include communication scientists, public relations specialists, scientists from the basic sciences, new media and design experts, and health advocates who can work together to better address how to develop, implement, and evaluate health media campaigns (Breast Cancer and Environment Research Centers, 2010). Opportunities for these types of research endeavors will continue to emerge as funding agencies strive to communicate research findings to the lay public as effectively as possible.

Finally, ongoing research is needed to keep pace with the rapidly changing technological landscape and to assess the ever changing potential of new technologies for enhancing health campaigns. Investigators can identify the most efficient approaches for utilizing traditional and emerging media to drive key audiences to Internet sites featuring information-rich content, individually tailored messages, or immediate opportunities for behavior enactment. Moreover, campaign strategists have promising avenues for exploiting social media connectivity in order to stimulate interpersonal influence processes. Finally, researchers will continue pursuing the elusive endeavor of harnessing interactive entertainment formats, particularly video games, to promote health-related learning and behavioral enactment.

References

Andrews, K., Silk, K., & Eneli, I. (2010). Parents as health promoters: A theory of planned behavior perspective on the prevention of childhood overweight and obesity. *Journal of Health Communication, 15,* 95–107.

Atkin, C. (1981). Mass media information campaign effectiveness. In R. Rice & W. Paisley (Eds.), *Public communication campaigns* (pp. 265–280). Beverly Hills, CA: Sage.

Atkin, C. (1994). Designing persuasive health messages. In L. Sechrest, T. Backer, E. Rogers, T. Campbell, & M. Grady (Eds.), *Effective dissemination of clinical health information* (AHCPR Publication No. 95-0015, pp. 99–110). Rockville, MD: U.S. Public Health Service, Agency for Health Care Policy and Research.

Atkin, C. (2001). *Impact of public service advertising: Research evidence and effective strategies* (Report to Kaiser Family Foundation). Retrieved from www.kff.org/entmedia/upload/PSAs-in-a-New-Media-Age-Background-Paper.pdf.

Atkin, C., & Freimuth, V. (2001). Formative evaluation research in campaign design. In R. E. Rice & C. K. Atkin (Eds.), *Public communication campaigns* (3rd ed., pp. 125–145). Thousand Oaks, CA: Sage.

Backer, T., Rogers, E., & Sopory, P. (1992). *Designing health communication campaigns: What works?* Newbury Park, CA: Sage.

Breast Cancer and the Environment Research Centers (BCERC). (2010). *Emerging topics in breast cancer and the environment.* Bethesda, MD: National Institutes of Health. Retrieved from http://www.bcerc.org/

Cappella, J., Fishbein, M., Hornik, R., Ahern, R. K., & Sayeed, S. (2001). Using theory to select messages in anti-drug media campaigns: Reasoned action and media priming. In R. E. Rice & C. K. Atkin (Eds.), *Public communication campaigns* (3rd ed., pp. 214–230). Thousand Oaks, CA: Sage.

Centers for Disease Control and Prevention. (2009). Health marketing. Retrieved from http://www.cdc.gov/healthmarketing/entertainment_education/healthstyles_survey.htm

Dejong, W., & Winston, 1. (1990). The use of mass media in substance abuse prevention. *Health Affairs, 2,* 30–46.

Dervin, B., & Frenette, M. (2001). Applying sense-making methodology: Communicating communicatively with audiences as listeners, learners, teachers, confidantes. In R. E. Rice & C. K Atkin (Eds.), *Public communication campaigns* (3rd ed., pp. 69–87). Thousand Oaks, CA: Sage.

Farrelly, M. C., Davis, K. C., Haviland, M. L., Messeri, P., & Healton, C. G. (2005). Evidence of a dose–response relationship between "truth" antismoking ads and youth smoking prevalence. *American Journal of Public Health, 95,* 425–431.

Fishbein, M. (1996). Editorial: Great expectations, or do we ask too much from community-level interventions? *American Journal of Public Health, 86,* 1075–1976.

Hornik, R. C. (2002). *Public health communication: Evidence for behavior change.* Mahwah, NJ: Erlbaum.

Lieberman, D. (2001). Using interactive media in communication campaigns for children and adolescents. In R. E. Rice & C. K. Atkin (Eds.), *Public communication campaigns* (3rd ed., pp. 373–388). Thousand Oaks, CA: Sage.

Maddock, J., Silbanuz, A., Reger-Nash, B. (2008). Formative research to develop a mass media campaign to increase physical activity and nutrition in a multiethnic state. *Journal of Health Communication, 13,* 208–215.

McGuire, W. (1994). Using mass media communication to enhance public health. In L. Sechrest, T. Backer, E. Rogers, T. Campbell, & M. Grady (Eds.), *Effective dissemination of clinical health information* (AHCPR Publication No. 95-0015, pp. 125–151). Rockville, MD: U.S. Public Health Service, Agency for Health Care Policy and Research.

National Cancer Institute. (2009). *Health information national trends survey.* Retrieved from http://hints.cancer.gov/dataset.jsp

Paisley, W. 1. (2001). Public communication campaigns: The American experience. In R. E. Rice & C. K. Atkin (Eds.), *Public communication campaigns* (3rd ed., pp. 3–21). Thousand Oaks, CA: Sage.

Palmgreen, P., Donohew, L., & Harrington, N. (2001). Sensation seeking in anti-drug campaign and message design. In R. E. Rice & C. K. Atkin (Eds.), *Public communication campaigns* (3rd ed., pp. 300–304). Thousand Oaks, CA: Sage.

Parrott, R. L., Silk, K. J., Condit, C. M., Dorgan, K., & Harris, T. M. (2005). Risk comprehension and judgments of statistical evidentiary appeals: When a picture is not worth a thousand words. *Human Communication Research, 31,* 423–452.

Prochaska, J. O., & DiClemente, C. C. (1983). Stages and processes of self change of smoking: Toward an integrative model. *Journal of Consulting and Clinical Psychology, 1*(Supplement), 390–395.

Reinard, J. (1988). The empirical study of the persuasive effects of evidence: The status after fifty years of research. *Human Communication Research, 15,* 3–59.

Rhodes, J., Spencer, R., Saito, R., & Sipe, C. (2006). Online mentoring: The promise and challenges of an emerging approach to youth development. *The Journal of Primary Prevention, 27,* 493–513.

Rodgers, S., Chen, Q., Duffy, M., & Fleming, K. (2009). Media usage as health segmentation variables. *Journal of Health Communication, 12,* 105–119.

Rogers, E., & Storey, D. (1987). Communication campaigns. In C. Berger & S. Chaffee (Eds.), *Handbook of communication science* (pp. 817–846). Newbury Park, CA: Sage.

Salmon, C., & Jason, J. (1992). A system for evaluating the use of media in CDC's National AIDS Information and Education Program. *Public Health Reports, 106,* 639–645.

Salmon, C., & Murray-Johnson, L. (2001). Communication campaign effectiveness. In R. E. Rice & C. K. Atkin (Eds.), *Public communication campaigns* (3rd ed., pp. 168–180). Thousand Oaks, CA: Sage.

Silk, K. J., Bigsby, E., Volkman, J., Kingsley, C., Atkin, C., Ferrara, M., & Goins, L. A. (2006). Formative research on adolescent and adult risk factors for breast cancer. *Social Science and Medicine, 63,* 3124–3136.

Singhal, A., & Rogers, E. (1999). *Entertainment-education: A communication strategy for social change.* Mahwah, NJ: Erlbaum.

Slater, M. (1996). Theory and method in health audience segmentation. *Journal of Health Communication, 1,* 267–283.

Snyder, L. (2001). How effective are mediated health campaigns? In R. E. Rice & C. K. Atkin (Eds.), *Public communication campaigns* (3rd ed., pp. 181–190). Thousand Oaks, CA: Sage.

Viswanath, K., & Finnegan, J. R. (2002). Reflections on community health campaigns: Secular trends and the capacity to effect change. In R. C. Hornik (Ed.) *Public health communication: Evidence for behavior change* (pp. 289–312). Mahwah, NJ: Erlbaum.

Wallack, L., & Dorfman, L. (2001). Putting policy into health communication: The role of media advocacy. In R. E. Rice & C. K. Atkin (Eds.), *Public communication campaigns* (3rd ed., pp. 389–401). Thousand Oaks, CA: Sage.

Wong, F., Huhman, M., Heitzler, C., Asbury, L., Bretthauer-Mueller, McCarthy, S., & Londe, P. 2004). VERB—A social marketing campaign to increase physical activity among youth. *Prevention of Chronic Disease.* Retrieved from www.cdc.gov/pcd/issues/2004/jul/toc.htm

14

INTERNATIONAL HEALTH COMMUNICATION CAMPAIGNS IN DEVELOPING COUNTRIES

Anthony J. Roberto, Lisa Murray-Johnson, and Kim Witte

Over the past 25 years, scholars who study health communication and related areas have learned a considerable amount about designing, implementing, and evaluating health communication campaigns in developing countries. One overarching lesson is that there is no single path to success when undertaking this type of endeavor. Each community requires differing levels of community involvement, resource sustainability, and organizational support. Data may or may not be available on prior successes, and when available, the explanatory evidence may be mixed. Threaded among campaign populists will be dissenting voices. For each success, failures will be noted. Health communication scholars may be asked to plan interventions without a clear understanding of preexisting communication differences within and among the target audiences they are there to serve. In short, health communication planners working in developing countries are global adventurers. The purpose of this chapter is to review some of the important resources that have been developed to increase the likelihood of creating successful health communication messages in this context.

With the above in mind, this chapter will begin by defining and discussing the importance of formative evaluation when developing international health communication campaigns in developing countries. Next, we will briefly review a variety of health communication theories and provide examples of how each of these theories has been applied in this area. Then, we will define, briefly review the relevant bodies of literature for, and provide examples of two important trends regarding international health communication campaigns: entertainment education and community mobilization. Finally, the chapter will conclude with a discussion of the importance of considering both intended and unintended consequences when conducting international campaigns in developing countries.

The Importance of Formative Evaluation

Formative evaluation can be conducted either before (preproduction) or after (postproduction) health communication messages or program materials have been created, but before they are completed and implemented on a large scale (Atkin & Freimuth, 1989). The primary goals of *preproduction* formative evaluation are to gain insight into and input from target audience members, and to refine existing ideas and to generate new ideas. For example, preproduction formative research might be conducted to get a better understanding of the target audience's current knowledge, perceptions, and motivations, or to get feedback on a program or materials before the development phase. Researchers often ask questions about variables from multiple theoretical perspectives during the preproduction formative evaluation phase of a campaign to help them select the theory or theories that seem best suited to the topic and target audience. The primary goals of *postproduction* formative evaluation are to obtain feedback from target audience members after draft materials are created but before they are finalized. For example, postproduction formative research could be conducted to show target audience members a draft of the message you want to disseminate in an effort to make sure all important aspects of the message are appealing and clear. Any problems that are identified would then be addressed or fixed before the message is finalized and widely disseminated.

Both quantitative and qualitative data can provide important information during the formative stages of a campaign. For example, surveys can be used to get a quantitative estimate of important theoretical variables (i.e., current behavior, attitudes, perceptions, etc.), and small experiments can be conducted to pilot test messages to see if they are having the desired effect on these or other key dependent variables. When possible, such efforts are also an excellent way to pretest surveys and pilot test procedures. Similarly, focus groups and in-depth interviews with target audience members or local experts can provide rich qualitative data about what terminology might be most effective, if messages are being interpreted as intended, and if the message is culturally sensitive.

In short, formative evaluation provides program designers with an opportunity to try out one or more aspects of the program *before* it is fully implemented. The key goal of formative evaluation is to identify and correct potential problems before the campaign is implemented to increase the likelihood of success. Because researchers may not be members of the culture or audience for which the campaign is being developed, formative research is particularly important when developing messages for health communication campaigns in developing countries.

The Role of Previous Health Communication Theory

Few health communication scholars or practitioners would disagree with the premise that interventions should be theory based. In the previous edition of this handbook, Murray-Johnson and Witte (2003) provide a general overview of the role several theories play in the design and evaluation of health messages in general. In this section, we will extend this discussion by providing a brief review of how these and several other theories are commonly used by researchers designing international health communication campaigns in developing countries. We also discuss at least one example of how each of these theories has been used to guide message design or evaluation in this setting.

Social Cognitive Theory

According to social cognitive theory (SCT), people learn through both direct experience and by observing others (Bandura, 1997). Bandura (2004) notes that, "trial-and-error learning [through direct experience] is not only tedious but hazardous when errors produce costly or injurious consequences. This process is short cut by [observational] learning from the successes and mistakes of others" (p. 78). Many international health communication campaigns include messages designed to help the audience learn important lessons by observing role models who face the realistic consequences of adopting or not adopting the recommended behavior. For example, characters in entertainment-education programming are often designed to serve as *positive role models* (i.e., individuals who engage in the recommended behavior and are rewarded or experience some positive outcome), *negative role models* (individuals who do not engage in recommended behaviors and are punished or experience some negative outcome), or *transitional role models* (individuals who start out as negative role models but turn into positive role models by the end of the story). According to Bandura (2004), self-efficacy is the driving force of human behavior change: "[A]mong the mechanisms of self-influence, none is more central or pervasive than beliefs in one's efficacy to exercise control over one's functioning and events that affect one's life" (pp. 78–79). Modeling can increase self-efficacy by demonstrating how to perform the recommended response, and by demonstrating how certain behaviors can lead to certain outcomes (i.e., outcome expectations or response-efficacy).

Journey of Life (Witte, 2003) was an entertainment-education radio serial designed to deliver prosocial educational messages about the importance of modern family planning methods and the dangers of HIV/AIDS and how to avoid them to 15- to 30-year-old Ethiopians. Though this program was guided largely by the extended parallel process mode (discussed below), it also incorporated several important elements from social cognitive theory. For example, the main message of *Journey of Life* was *yichalal* ("it is possible"), meaning that it was possible for Ethiopians to improve their quality of life by planning their families, and that it was possible to control the HIV/AIDS epidemics by taking appropriate measures to limit the spread of these diseases. Efficacy messages about family planning and HIV/AIDS prevention were intermingled throughout the various plots of the radio serial. Further, characters were created to serve as positive role models, negative role models, or transitional role models. More information about the *Journey of Life* appears later in this chapter.

Perceived Collective Efficacy.   Collective efficacy is "the degree to which members of a system believe they have the ability to organize and execute actions required to produce desired results" (Singhal & Rogers, 2003, p. 314). The main difference between self-efficacy and collective efficacy is that the former focuses on an individual's perceptions of his or her abilities to achieve a particular outcome, whereas the latter concerns perceptions of a group's ability to do so (Bandura, 1997). Bandura (2004) argues that, "many of the challenges of life involve common problems that require people to work together with a collective voice to change their lives for the better" (p. 80). Many international health communication campaigns in developing countries deal with issues where it would be particularly difficult for individuals to exercise control over the health threat entirely on their own (i.e., issues like HIV/AIDS prevention and family planning include many challenges that require collective effort from families or communities to solve).

Papa et al. (2000) conducted a study in an Indian village looking at the effects of an entertainment-education radio soap opera on the villagers' sense of collective efficacy to address a variety of social issues facing the community. Results of in-depth interviews indicated that informal groups that had formed to listen to the program had gradually become formalized into clubs with regular members. Members of the clubs would listen to the programs and then collectively discuss the content and come up with a course of action to address the issues emphasized in the program. The villagers appeared to have developed a sense of collective efficacy to address problems facing the community as a result of this entertainment-education effort.

Elaboration Likelihood Model

According to the elaboration likelihood model (ELM; Petty & Cacioppo, 1981), there are two "routes" to persuasion. Individuals who have *both* the motivation (e.g., personal involvement or relevance) *and* the ability (e.g., cognitive capability) to process a persuasive message will do so via the *central route*. These individuals will carefully examine and critically evaluate the information and arguments presented in the message, and they will be persuaded by arguments that they perceive to be strong. Notably, persuasion through the central route should lead to longer-lasting change that is more resistant to counterinfluence. Individuals who lack *either* the motivation *or* the ability to process a message will process it via the *peripheral route*. In this instance, little effort or thought is put into evaluating the message arguments and instead individuals base their decision on simple decision rules, or heuristics, that are not directly related to the substance or quality of the message. Example heuristics include social proof, liking, authority, and number (rather than quality) of arguments. An extension of the model (E-ELM) by Slater and Rouner (2002) argues that individuals watching entertainment-education programs will be less critical and produce fewer counterarguments. For example, individuals watching entertainment-education programming may not realize that the message is being used to try to persuade them regarding a particular point, and therefore they do not react as they might do if the message were presented in a more traditional way.

Though a fair amount has been written regarding the ELM and E-ELM in an entertainment-education context, we were unfortunately unable to find a study that explicitly tested either theory in this context. However, Sood (2002) looked at the relationship between audience involvement and self-efficacy, collective efficacy, and interpersonal communication among listeners to a radio soap opera in India. Results indicate that involvement was positively related to both self-efficacy and collective efficacy. Further, at least in some instances, individuals who scored higher on involvement were more likely to engage in interpersonal communication about the radio soap opera. So, while involvement seems to be related to these three important outcome variables, future research is needed to more thoroughly ascertain the role of the ELM and its recent extension in the entertainment-education arena.

Extended Parallel Process Model

The extended parallel process model (EPPM; Witte, 1992) focuses on the effects of perceived threat (susceptibility and severity) and perceived efficacy (i.e., response-efficacy and self-efficacy) on changes in attitudes, intentions, and behavior. According to the EPPM, three outcomes are possible depending on one's levels of perceived threat and efficacy. First, when perceived threat is low, *no response* will occur (i.e., the person will not be motivated to pay attention to the message and, therefore, will not respond to it). Second, when perceived threat is high and perceived efficacy is low, an individual will engage in *fear control* (i.e., the person will take steps to reduce the fear—such as defensive avoidance, denial, or reactance—that do not decrease the actual danger or risk). Third, when both perceived threat and perceived efficacy are high, an individual will engage in *danger control* (i.e., the person will think carefully about the recommended response, which should lead to attitude, intention, and behavior changes in the advocated direction). In short, "perceived threat motivates action; perceived efficacy determines the nature of that action—specifically, whether people attempt to control the danger or control their fear. This critical point, when perceived efficacy exceeds perceived threat, is an important concept in the development of effective applied communication messages" (Witte & Roberto, 2009, p. 586). The reader is referred to Witte and Allen's (2000) meta-analysis regarding the effectiveness of fear appeals, and to Rimal and Real (2003) for information on the risk perception attitude framework, which is closely related to the EPPM and has been applied to several health communication campaigns in developing countries.

As noted above, though the *Journey of Life* radio serial contained several important components from social cognitive theory, the EPPM served as the primary theoretical underpinning for this entertainment-education radio soap opera. The choices of the EPPM to guide the development of the intervention, and radio to disseminate the message, were based on formative evaluation results. *Journey of Life* was designed to provide education about the use of modern family planning methods, the dangers of HIV/AIDS, and how to prevent HIV/AIDS. The radio serial contained 26 20-minute episodes, which aired one per week for 6 months. Outcome evaluation results (Witte, 2003) indicate that the *Journey of Life* was perceived positively by listeners, and also increased listeners' perceived susceptibility, response-efficacy, and self-efficacy. Furthermore, perceived severity, which was high in the baseline, decreased slightly; this was deemed important since it increased the likelihood that listeners would follow the danger control rather than the fear control path (i.e., because perceived severity was too high and was causing fear control outcomes). In tandem, these and other outcome evaluation results suggest that the EPPM-based *Journey of Life* had positive and desired behavioral and perceptual effects on audience members.

Perceived Collective Efficacy.   Roberto, Goodall, and Witte (2009) and Smith, Ferrara, and Witte (2007) argue that perceived collective efficacy should also have implications for EPPM. For example, Smith et al. tested the usefulness of adding collective efficacy to the EPPM to predict willingness to help individuals affected by HIV in Namibia. These authors argued that even if an individual is high in self-efficacy, low collective efficacy may discourage community dialogue, collective action, and persistence of collective action in the face of barriers. Results indicate that individuals with a greater sense of collective efficacy had greater beliefs that members of their community would take in AIDS orphans. Readers can read more about collective efficacy and perceived societal risk (introduced next) in Roberto et al. (2009).

Perceived Threat to Others.   Traditional EPPM research focuses on personal physical threats to the message recipient. However, some research suggests that social threats (Murray-Johnson, Witte, Liu et al., 2001) and threats to others can also motivate behavior change. Whereas personal threat perceptions refer to beliefs about how a risk will impact the individual, perceived threat to others includes beliefs and concerns about the impact the threat may have on known and unknown others. Recent experiments in the United States suggest that messages emphasizing threat to others (rather than just threat to self) can be used to motivate behavior change on behalf of those who are actually at risk (e.g., Lindsey, 2005; Roberto, Goodall, West, & Mahan, 2010). Though typically not an explicit aspect of many international health communication campaigns in developing countries, these and related studies suggest messages focusing on threat to others might be worth exploring in this setting in the future.

Theories of Reasoned Action and Planned Behavior

According to the theory of reasoned action (TRA; Fishbein & Ajzen, 1975), the best predictor of behavior (i.e., what a person actually does) is behavioral intention (i.e., a person's intention to perform or not perform the behavior). Behavioral intention, in turn, is a joint function of a person's attitude toward performing the behavior (i.e., the individual's favorable or unfavorable predispositions toward the behavior) and subjective norms (i.e., the individual's perception of the behavior expected by relevant significant others). The theory of planned behavior (TPB; Ajzen, 1985) extends the TRA by adding a direct link from perceived behavioral control (i.e., the degree to which a person believes he or she can control the behavior in question) to both behavior intention and behavior. Several meta-analyses offer consistent support for the ability of one or both theories to predict intentions and behavior (e.g., Albarracin, Johnson, Fishbein, & Muellerleile, 2001).

Molla, Astrøm, and Berhane (2007) assessed the ability of the TPB to predict condom use intentions and behaviors in a sample of young adult men and women in rural Ethiopia. Though the TPB model was generally supported for this topic and target population, the authors conclude that the TPB was much more accurate at predicting intentions (explaining 36% of the variance) than behavior (explaining 5.3% of the variance). Based on TRA recommendations, Kane, Gueye, Speizer, Pacque-Margolis, and Baron (1998) explicitly targeted attitudes and intentions when developing and evaluating a multimedia family planning campaign in Bamako, Mali. Outcome evaluation results indicated significant shifts in the desired direction for both of these variables.

Descriptive and Injunctive Norms. Piotrow and de Fossard (2004) note that a key advantage of entertainment-education programs is their ability to change social norms. At least two types of norms play an important role in influencing human behavior: *Injunctive norms*, which refer to an individual's perceptions of what others approve or disapprove in a given situation, and *descriptive norms*, which refer to an individual's perceptions about what most others do (Cialdini, Reno, & Kallgren, 1990). In the United States, research indicates that people often overestimate the prevalence or approval of risky behaviors and underestimate the prevalence or approval of protective behaviors, and such misperceptions have been the target of numerous social norms campaigns (Borsari & Carey, 2003; Scholly, Katz, Gascoigne, & Holck, 2005).

The potential benefit of targeting norms in international health communication campaigns in developing countries is illustrated by the following two studies. First, in a correlational study, Kamal (2000) found that Bangladeshi women's use of modern contraceptive techniques was significantly and positively related to perceived husband approval or disapproval (i.e., injunctive norms) of this behavior. On a related note, Terefe and Larson (1993) conducted an experiment to determine the effects of a family planning intervention that did and did not include husband participation, and found that including husbands nearly doubled modern contraception use by Ethiopian couples at both the 2- and 12-month follow-up.

Stage-Based Models

At least two stage-based models of behavior change have been used with some regularity to guide the development of health communication campaigns in developing countries:

diffusion of innovations and the transtheoretical model. Rogers (2003) defines diffusion as "the process by which an innovation [i.e., a new idea or behavior] is communicated through certain channels over time among the members of a social system" (p. 5). The innovation–decision process consists of five steps (Rogers, 2003): (a) *knowledge* (i.e., when an individual is first exposed to or becomes aware of the recommended behavior and why it should be adopted); (b) *persuasion* (i.e., the process of forming a positive or negative attitude about the recommended behavior); (c) *decision* (i.e., seeking additional information to that will help the individual decide whether or not he or she should engage in the recommended behavior); (d) *implementation* (i.e., the point at which an individual chooses to start engaging in the recommended behavior); and (e) *confirmation* (i.e., when an individual seeks information that supports the decision to engage in the recommended behavior). Notably, some individuals may not go through these stages in order. For example, some individuals may skip one or more stages altogether, and some individuals will go back and forth between stages before implementation and confirmation are achieved.

Rogers (2003) identifies five attributes of an innovation that help explain its rate of adoption: relative advantage, compatibility, complexity, trialability, and observability. Behaviors that are perceived as *high* in relative advantage, compatibility, trialability, and observability, and *low* in complexity, should be adopted more quickly than behaviors that are not. Rogers (2003) also presents five adopter categories designed to describe when individuals first begin to use a new behavior (i.e., innovators, early adopters, early majority, late majority, and laggards), with innovators being among the first to adopt a behavior and laggards being among the last to do so. Finally, as Vaughan and Rogers (2000) note, diffusion of innovation "stresses the importance of interpersonal communication via peer networks as the mechanism motivating the adoption of a new idea" (p. 207). *Opinion leaders* are highly trusted individuals within a social network who are able to informally influence others. Not surprisingly, these individuals can play an important role in whether or not individuals in a social network adopt or reject a recommended behavior.

The transtheoretical model (a.k.a., stages of change) also sees behavior change as a five-step process (Prochaska & DiClemente, 1983) that closely parallels the diffusion of an innovation process: *precontemplation* (i.e., when individuals have no intention to change their behavior within six months, and may be unaware that a need to change their behavior exists); *contemplation* (i.e., when individuals are aware of a problem and consider the pros and cons of initiating a change within six months); *preparation* (i.e., when individuals plan to change their behavior within a month); *action* (i.e., when individuals have actively engaged in behavior changes for less than six months); and *maintenance* (i.e., when individuals have adopted a behavior and regularly engage in it for more than six months). Vaughn and Rogers (2000) note that, "individuals have been found to cycle through the SOC [stages of change], often several times, before the maintenance state is achieved" (p. 206). Research has shown that stage-appropriate health communication messages are more likely to be effective than those that are not.

To illustrate, Valente and Saba (1998) evaluated a family planning and reproductive health campaign in Bolivia that was guided by both diffusion of innovations theory and the transtheoretical model. The campaign consisted of 11 different television and radio spots broadcast over a 7-month period, and then again over a 3-month period approximately a year later. The campaign was broadcast over 1,000 times in each of the four major cities of Bolivia, and over 300 times in each of the three next smaller cities. The authors derived a series of behavioral change stages based on diffusion of innovation theory and the transtheoretical model, and compared the relative influence of mass media and interpersonal communication on movement through these stages. As predicted, mass media campaign exposure was positively related to the earlier (i.e., information-related) stages, whereas personal network exposure was more strongly related with actual behavior change.

Summary

This section of the chapter introduced and reviewed several theoretical perspectives and constructs that play an important role in the design, implementation, and evaluation of health communication campaigns in developing countries today. The continued application and testing of theory and research allows for a more systematic and efficient advancement of both theory and practice in this important area. The next two sections of this chapter discuss the entertainment education and community mobilization literatures—two important areas where these theories are often applied by health communication scholars interested in this context.

Entertainment-Education

Singhal and Rogers (2004) define *entertainment-education* as, "the process of purposefully designing and implementing a media message to both entertain and educate, in order to increase audience members' knowledge about an educational issue, create favorable attitudes, shift social norms, and change overt behavior" (p. 5). Approximately 200 entertainment-education projects have been implemented in dozens of countries around the world (Piotrow & de Fossard, 2004; Singhal & Rogers, 2004). Examples range from national campaigns to messages designed for local audiences, and from a few lines of dialogue in an existing media program to an entire long-running series (Greenberg, Salmon, Patel, Beck, & Cole, 2004; Singhal & Rogers, 2004).

Entertainment-education programming is typically theory-based (Sood, Menard, & Witte, 2004), and guided by formative evaluation with the intended audience. Key goals typically include changing, shaping, or reinforcing individuals' knowledge, attitudes, and behavior, as well as the social/external environment. For example, Piotrow and de Fossard (2004) discuss meta-analytic data suggesting that the effects of entertainment-education programming "are comparable to various health campaigns in the United States; on average, the number of individuals who adopted the desired behavior change increased by about 7 percentage points" (p. 43). Because these messages are designed to entertain as well as to educate, key advantages of the entertainment-education strategy include higher receiver interest and involvement, emotional engagement, and enhancing an audience's willingness to attend to prevention messages.

Types of Entertainment-Education

As noted above, traditional definitions of entertainment-education often focus on efforts involving some form of media message (Moyer-Gusé, 2008; Singhal & Rogers, 2003, 2004). This is not surprising since, as Singhal (2004) notes, "most past entertainment-education interventions have utilized mass media vehicles (television, radio, films, videos, or comic books) to tackle issues of development and social change" (pp. 396–397). However, while mass media may be the primary channel (and drama the primary vehicle) for many past entertainment-education efforts, "today there exist multiple types of E-E [entertainment-education]" (Singhal & Rogers, 2004, p. 8), and "E-E comes in many different sizes and shapes" (Piotrow & de Fossard, 2004, p. 43). For example, many entertainment-education programs involve live (i.e., nonmediated) theatrical performances. To illustrate, Guttman, Gasser-Edelsburg, and Israelashvili (2008) investigated Israeli adolescents' views regarding live antidrug abuse entertainment-education dramas that were implemented as part of their school's drug prevention program. Similarly, Roberto (in preparation) recently helped design a live musical theater performance based on the EPPM in an effort to increase breast-cancer awareness among women and men in rural Bangladesh. Finally, Singhal (2004) describes participatory theater programs in South Africa, Brazil, and India "as an alternative application of the entertainment-education strategy" (p. 379).

Glik, Nowak, Valente, Sapsis, and Martin (2002) argue that entertainment-education programs based on live performances draw upon the strength of both mass and interpersonal communication by reaching many people at once while at the same time involving direct and immediate interactions with target audience members. These authors go on to argue that, "live audiences are also usually more emotionally attuned to the performers and messages, thus creating an environment that is more conducive to learning and behavior change" (p. 41). Singhal (2004) calls for "adding participatory theatrical practices to the entertainment-education arsenal ... [to] transform entertainment-education interventions from being a one-way 'monolog' into a two-way 'dialog' between audience and actors" (p. 397).

In sum, given the wide variety of forms and channels that have been used to disseminate entertainment-education interventions, traditional definitions of entertainment-education should be broadened to include all types of messages that are designed to both entertain and educate, regardless of the communication channel used to disseminate such messages. Future research might also look at whether or not the advantages and influence processes of entertainment-education messages are similar across these various message types and communication channels. Receiver involvement is one variable that is commonly studied in this context that also seems particularly relevant to any comparisons between mediated and live entertainment-education programming. An overview of the role receiver involvement in entertainment-education programming is presented next.

The Role of Involvement

In a recent theoretical piece about entertainment-education, Moyer-Gusé (2009) provides a detailed discussion of the role of two types of involvement in entertainment-education messages. *Narrative involvement* concerns engagement in the storyline: "involvement in this sense refers to the interest with which viewers follow the events as they unfold in the story" (p. 409). *Involvement with characters* is, "an overarching category of concepts related to how viewers interact with characters" (p. 409). Specifically, Moyer-Gusé separates involvement with characters into five related subcategories: (a) *identification with characters*—when viewers forget about their own reality and temporarily takes on the role of a character; (b) *wishful identification*—when a viewer looks up to, wants to be like, or emulates a character; (c) *similarity*—when individuals believe they have something in common with a character (e.g., physical, demographic, or psychographic variables); (d) *parasocial interaction*—when individuals view a character as a friend or as part of their social world; and (e) *liking*—when individuals view a character positively, or feel a social attraction or affinity for a character.

Moyer-Gusé (2009) advances a series of propositions regarding how these types of involvement affect numerous theoretically important variables that have been shown to facilitate or inhibit behavior change during entertainment-education programming. Specifically, Moyer-Gusé argues that narrative structure, parasocial interaction, and liking will all reduce reactance and therefore increase the likelihood of story-consistent attitude and behavior change. Similarly, she argues that parasocial interaction will reduce counterarguing, identification and enjoyment will reduce selective avoidance, perceived similarity and identification will increase perceived vulnerability, and parasocial interaction will change perceived norms. Notice how many of these constructs are important mediating or outcome variables according to several of the theories discussed earlier in this chapter.

The Pathways to Change Tool

There are often conflicts between the "entertainment" and "education" goals of entertainment-education program (i.e., it can be difficult to incorporate health communication theory and research into storylines and scripts designed to entertain). Petraglia, Galavotti, Harford, Pappas-DeLuca, and Mooki (2007) suggest, "this is largely due to the lack of tools that bridge the divide between the artistic world of storytelling and the demands of a structured, science-based, public health intervention" (p. 384). To help bridge this gap, Petraglia et al. (2007) developed the *Pathways to Change* tool, which is designed to help practitioners and researchers more successfully and systematically integrate health communication theory and research into entertainment-education scripts. This approach is guided by multiple theoretical perspectives, including social cognitive theory and the transtheoretical model, both of which were discussed earlier in this chapter.

In short, the *Pathways to Change* training tool is comprised of three elements designed to help scriptwriters better understand and incorporate health communication theory and research into their scripts. In the *game phase*, teams of scriptwriters (a) play a board game designed to expose them to a series of personal, social, and environmental barriers and facilitators identified via formative research, and (b) write a brief story about their character that incorporates these barriers and facilitators. The *chart phase*, "reminds team members that behavior change is a process that occurs in stages and that their goal is to create a realistic model of behavior change with which the audience can identify" (p. 388). Based explicitly on the transtheoretical model, this chart helps scriptwriters develop characters that move through the stages of change in a realistic manner (i.e., in a nonlinear fashion, and incorporating barriers and facilitators identified by the target audience via formative evaluation). Finally, the *behavior change adherence routine phase* is designed help to project managers and scriptwriters monitor and evaluate the quality of scripts using two main steps: (a) track transitional characters' behavioral trajectory over time, and (b) develop dialog that reveals a character's progress through the stages of change. In tandem, Petraglia et al. (2007) argue that these three phases "help writers articulate and integrate many technical aspects of behavior change that are often ignored" (p. 392).

Community Mobilization

Health communication campaigns can be challenging in developing countries. Patterns of stigma, disenfranchisement, lack of sustainable access to resources, and avoidance of social responsibility are often uncovered (Hogan & Palmer, 2005; Hogan & Salmon, 2005). Community mobilization is one option often used to cocreate a reality of investment and action. Community mobilization, also referenced as social mobilization, is a people-centered development process (see Dearing, Gaglio, and Rabin in this volume for more details). It garners internal support for a health program by empowering the target audience and related community members to contribute to integration and sustainability of campaign outcomes (Babalola et al., 2001). The approach has been well documented as an empowering strategy for many health communication campaigns, such as nutrition projects in South Asia (Jonsson, 1997); reducing seroprevalence for HIV in Namibia (Mchombu & Mchombu, 2007); family planning (Babalola et al., 2001); food security in Sri Lanka (Bigdon & Sachithanandam, 2003); and polio eradication in Pakistan (Cheng, 2004).

Community Mobilization in Namibia

One health communication campaign for HIV/AIDS prevention in Namibia, funded by the US Agency for International Development, illustrates the use of community mobilization. Namibia is a language diverse and culturally complex country. Although English is the official language, Namibians may speak one of 140 native languages. To strengthen a common campaign ideology, 80 partners were involved to manage campaign needs across 20 urban and rural regions of the country (Murray-Johnson, Witte & Keulder, 2003). A baseline community survey was employed within each region. Trained surveyors who spoke the native languages interviewed a sample of 5,000 persons per region using a hierarchical multistage sampling frame (Witte, Murray-Johnson, & Keulder, 2001). The survey focused on knowledge, skills, attitudes, and behaviors for HIV prevention, family planning, care of orphans and vulnerable children, community involvement, participation in urban/ rural government, faith-based membership, and perceived barriers or gaps in social services. Simultaneously, a social network survey was used to map campaign strategies with partner organization involvement (Smith & Nguyan, 2008). Both surveys provided a valuable opportunity to identify respected opinion leaders, who were then invited to partner with health experts in developing effective campaign messages. These individuals and groups served as both a measure of campaign progress and decisional empowerment about how to reduce HIV infection and care for people living with AIDS.

While community mobilization may take multiple forms in a health communication campaign, each requires careful planning, execution and evaluation. By anticipating the roles and relationship of partners in advance, assessing community members' vulnerabilities and support, and developing action plans that are responsive to timelines and resources, most efforts are rewarded with some level of success.

Campaign Effects vs. Effectiveness

Salmon and Murray-Johnson (2001) argue that while "the terms campaign 'effects' and 'effectiveness' have long been treated as interchangeable and synonymous ... they are conceptually quite distinct" (p. 175). We believe these distinctions are particularly relevant to international health campaigns in developing countries. A campaign would be viewed as having *both effects and effectiveness* if it reached its intended goal, but as having *no effects and no effectiveness* if it did not reach its intended goal and did not have any other unintended consequences (i.e., the prototypical campaign failure). A campaign would be viewed as having *effects but not effectiveness* if it did not reach its intended goal, but had some other positive or negative unintended consequence (e.g., a fear appeal that focuses too much on threat or not enough on efficacy might lead to a fear control rather than a danger control response—see the discussion of the EPPM above). The reader is referred to Cho and Salmon (2007) for a thorough discussion of 11 potential unintended effects of health communication campaigns. Finally, a campaign may be seen has having *no effects but effectiveness* when it does not reach its goal but meets some other criteria of success (i.e., "reinforcement of existing nonsmoking rates rather than actual reduction—or other types of seemingly 'null' effects—could be considered a type of victory" [Salmon & Murray-Johnson, 2001]).

We have two main reasons for devoting a section of this chapter to the discussion of campaign effects and effectiveness. First, sampling error and measurement error often make it harder to find effects when evaluating health communication campaigns in international settings. For example, it is often difficult or impossible to employ random sampling procedures or have large sample sizes. Further, typical measurement issues are compounded by the facts that evaluators are often not native speakers of the language or part of the culture being studied, and study participants may not fully understand standard survey items and techniques. In other words, extreme care has to be taken to make sure key conceptual and operational definitional issues literally do not get lost in translation. If not carefully addressed, these and a host of related issues are likely to attenuate effects, making it less likely that a campaign's outcomes will be accurately identified. Second, numerous language and cultural issues might increase the chances that unintended consequences will occur, so special care must be taken to minimize such effects, especially if they might be negative. Earlier in this chapter we discussed the important role of formative evaluation in campaign development, and the potential for the types of problems outlined in this section further reinforces the vital role of pretesting campaign messages and study measures and procedures with target audience members prior to full implementation.

Conclusion

The primary goal of this chapter was to provide an overview of recent theory, research, and practice regarding health communication campaigns in developing countries. According to the *World Development Indicators 2009* (World Bank, 2009), more than a billion people live in slums of developing countries' cities without adequate food or health care. Developing countries continue to have an acute need for health promotion and disease prevention efforts. Health campaigns have the ability to make a lasting and significant impact on public health and quality of life indicators. And, as illustrated throughout this chapter, health communication scholars have been and continue to play an important role in understanding and responding to these important issues.

References

Ajzen, I. (1985). From intentions to actions: A theory of planned behavior. In J. Kuhl & J. Beckman (Eds.), *Action control: From cognition to behavior* (pp. 11–39). Berlin, Germany: Springer-Verlag.

Albarracin, D., Johnson, B. T., Fishbein, M., & Muellerleile, P. A. (2001). Theories of reasoned action and planned behavior as models of condom use: A meta-analysis. *Psychological Bulletin, 127,* 142–161.

Atkin, C. K., & Freimuth, V. (1989). Formative evaluation research in campaign design. In R. E. Rice & C. K. Atkin (Eds.), *Public communication campaigns* (2nd ed., pp. 131–150). Newbury Park, CA: Sage.

Babalola, S., Sakolsky, N., Vondrasek, C., Mounlom, D., Brown, J., & Tchupo, J. P. (2001). The impact of a community mobilization project on health related knowledge and practices in Cameroon. *Journal of Community Health, 26,* 459–477.

Bandura, A. (1997). *Self-efficacy: The exercise of control.* New York: Freeman.

Bandura, A. (2004). Social cognitive theory for persona and social change by enabling media. In A. Singhal, M. J. Cody, E. M. Rogers, & M. Sabido (Eds.), *Entertainment-education and social change: History, research, and practice* (pp. 75–96). Mahwah, NJ: Erlbaum.

Bigdon, C., & Sachithanandam, S.A. (2003). *Community mobilization principles and practice guidebook.* Trincomalee, Sri Lanka: Integrated Food Security Program.

Borsari, B., & Carey, K. B. (2003). Descriptive and injunctive norms in college drinking: A meta-analytic integration. *Journal of Studies on Alcohol, 64,* 331–341.

Cheng, W. (2004). *Reaching the unreached: Communication support for the Pakistan polio eradication initiative.* New Delhi, India: United Nations Children's Fund Regional Office for South East Asia.

Cho, H., & Salmon, C. T. (2007). Unintended effects of health communication campaigns. *Journal of Communication, 47,* 293–317.

Cialdini, R. B., Reno, R. R., & Kallgren, C. A. (1990). A focus theory of normative conduct: Recycling the concept of norms to reduce littering in public places. *Journal of Personality and Social Psychology, 58,* 1015–1026.

Fishbein, M., & Ajzen, I., (1975). *Belief, attitude, intention, and behavior.* Reading, MA: Addison-Wesley.

Glik, D., Nowak, G., Valente, T., Sapsis, K., & Martin, C. (2002). Youth performing arts entertainment-education for HIV/AIDS prevention and health promotion: Practice and research. *Journal of Health Communication, 7,* 39–57.

Greenberg, B. S., Salmon, C. T., Patel, D., Beck, V., & Cole, G. (2004). Evolution of an E-E research agenda. In A. Singhal, M. J. Cody, E. M. Rogers, & M. Sabido (Eds.), *Entertainment-education and social change: History, research, and practice* (pp. 191–206). Mahwah, NJ: Erlbaum.

Guttman, N., Gesser-Edelsburg, A. & Israelashvili, M. (2008). The paradox of realism and "authenticity" in entertainment-education: A study of adolescents' views about anti-drug abuse dramas. *Health Communication, 23,* 128–141.

Hogan, T. P., & Palmer, C. L. (2005). Information preferences and practices among people living with HIV/AIDS: Results from a nationwide survey. *Journal of the Medical Library Association, 93,* 431–439.

Hogan, D. R., & Salmon, J. (2005). Prevention and treatment of human immunodeficiency virus/ acquired immunodeficiency syndrome in resource-limited settings. *Bulletin of the World Health Organization, 83,* 135–143.

Jonsson, U. (1997). Success factors in community-based nutrition oriented programmes and projects. In S. Gillespie (Ed.), *Malnutrition in South Asia: A regional profile* (Publication No. 5, pp. 161–189). Kathmandu, Nepal: UNICEF Regional Office for South Asia.

Kamal, N. (2000). The influence of husbands on contraceptive use by Bangladeshi women. *Health Policy and Planning, 15,* 43–51.

Kane, T. T., Gueye, M., Speizer, I., Pacque-Margolis, S., & Baron, D. (1998). The impact of a family planning multimedia campaign in Bamako, Mali. *Studies in Family Planning, 29,* 309–323.

Lindsey, L. L .M. (2005). Anticipated guilt as behavioral motivation: An examination of appeals to help unknown others through bone marrow donation. *Human Communication Research, 31,* 453–481.

Mchombu, K., & Mchombu, C. (2007, August 19–23). *Overview and information issues concerning the HIV/AIDS situation in Africa.* Paper presented at the World Library and Information Congress: 73 IFLA General Conference and Council, Durban, South Africa.

Molla, M., Astrøm, A. N., & Berhane, Y. (2007). Applicability of the theory of planned behavior to intended and self-reported condom use in a rural Ethiopian population. *AIDS Care, 19,* 424–431.

Moyer-Gusé, E. (2008). Toward a theory of entertainment persuasion: Explaining the persuasive effects of entertainment-education messages. *Communication Theory, 18,* 407–425.

Murray-Johnson, L., & Witte, K. (2003). Looking toward the future: Health message design strategies. In T. L. Thompson, A. M. Dorsey, K. I. Miller, & R. Parrott (Eds.), *Handbook of health communication* (pp. 473–496). Mahwah, NJ: Erlbaum.

Murray-Johnson, L., Witte, K., Liu,W-Y, Hubbell, H. P., Sampson, J., & Morrison, K. (2001). Addressing cultural orientation sin fear appeals: Promoting AIDS-protective behaviors among Mexican immigrant and African American adolescents in American and Taiwanese college students. *Journal of Health Communication, 6,* 335–358.

Murray-Johnson, L, Witte, K., & Keulder, E. (2003). *A baseline report of the USAID Namibia individual community survey: Phase 2.* (Unpublished USAID report)

Papa, M. J., Singhal, A. Law, S., Pant, S., Sood, S., Rogers, E. M., & Shefner-Rogers, C. (2000). Entertainment-education and social change: An analysis of parasocial interaction, social learning, collective efficacy, and paradoxical communication. *Journal of Communication, 50,* 31–55.

Petraglia, J., Galavotti, C., Harford, N., Pappas-DeLuca, K. A., & Mooki, M. (2007). Applying behavioral science to behavior change communication: The *Pathways to Change* tools. *Health Promotion and Practice, 8,* 384–393.

Petty, R. E., & Cacioppo, J. T. (1981). *Attitudes and persuasion: Classic and contemporary approaches.* Dubuque, IA: William C. Brown.

Piotrow, P. T., & de Fossard, E. D. (2004). Entertainment-education as public health intervention. In A. Singhal, M. J. Cody, E. M. Rogers, & M. Sabido (Eds.), *Entertainment-education and social change: History, research, and practice* (pp. 39–60). Mahwah, NJ: Erlbaum.

Prochaska, J. O., & DiClemente, C. C. (1983). Stages and processes of self-change in smoking: Toward an integrative model of change. *Journal of Consulting and Clinical Psychology, 51,* 390–395.

Rimal, R. N., & Real, K. (2003). Perceived risk and efficacy beliefs as motivators of change: Use of the risk perception attitude (RPA) framework to understand health behaviors. *Human Communication Research, 29,* 370–399.

Roberto, A. J. (in preparation). *A randomized trial of a live breast cancer entertainment education performance guided by the extended parallel process model in rural Bangladesh.*

Roberto, A. J., Goodall, C. E, West, P., & Mahan, J. D. (2010). Persuading physicians to test their patients' level of kidney functioning: The effects of framing and point of view. *Health Communication, 25,* 107–118.

Roberto, A. J., Goodall, C. E., & Witte, K. (2009). Raising the alarm and calming fears: Perceived threat and efficacy during risk and crisis. In R. Heath & D. O'Hair (Eds.), *Handbook of risk and crisis communication* (pp. 287–303). Washington, DC: Routledge.

Rogers, E. M. (2003). *Diffusion of innovations* (5th ed.). New York: Free Press.

Salmon, C. T., & Murray-Johnson, L. (2001). Communication campaign effectiveness: Critical distinctions. In R. E. Rice & C. K. Atkin (Eds.), *Public communication campaigns* (3rd ed., pp. 168–180). Thousand Oaks, CA: Sage.

Scholly, K., Katz, A. R., Gascoigne, J., & Holck, P. S. (2005). Using social norms theory to explain perceptions and sexual health behaviors of undergraduate college students: An exploratory study. *Journal of American College Health, 53,* 159–166.

Singhal, A. (2004). Entertainment-education through participatory theater: Freirean strategies for empowering the oppressed. In A. Singhal, M. J. Cody, E. M. Rogers, & M. Sabido (Eds.), *Entertainment-education and social change: History, research, and practice* (pp. 377–398). Mahwah, NJ: Erlbaum.

Singhal, A., & Rogers, E. M. (2003). *Combating AIDS: Communication strategies in action.* New Delhi, India: Sage.

Singhal, A., & Rogers, E. M. (2004). The status of entertainment-education worldwide. In A. Singhal, M. J. Cody, E. M. Rogers, & M. Sabido (Eds.), *Entertainment-education and social change: History, research, and practice* (pp. 3–20). Mahwah, NJ: Erlbaum.

Slater, M. D., & Rouner, D. (2002). Entertainment-education and elaboration likelihood: Understanding the processing of narrative persuasion. *Communication Theory, 12,* 173–191.

Smith, R. A., Ferrara, M., & Witte, K. (2007). Social sides of health risks: Stigma and collective efficacy. *Health Communication, 21,* 55–64.

Smith, R. A., & Nguyen, L. (2008). Searching for a "generalized *social* agent" to predict Namibians' intentions to prevent sexual transmission of HIV. *AIDS Care, 20,* 1266–1275.

Sood, S. (2002). Audience involvement and entertainment-education. *Communication Theory, 12,* 153–172.

Sood, S., Menard, T., & Witte, K. (2004). The theory behind entertainment-education. In A. Singhal, M. J. Cody, E. M. Rogers, & M. Sabido (Eds.), *Entertainment-education and social change: History, research, and practice* (pp. 117–149). Mahwah, NJ: Erlbaum.

Terefe, A., & Larson, C. P. (1993), Modern contraception use in Ethiopia: Does involving husbands make a difference? *American Journal of Public Health, 83,* 1567–1671.

Valente, T. W., & Saba, W. P. (1998). Mass media and interpersonal influence in a reproductive health communication campaign in Bolivia. *Communication Research, 25,* 96–124.

Vaughan, P. W., & Rogers, E. M. (2000). A staged model of communication effects: Evidence from an entertainment-education radio sop opera in Tanzania. *Journal of Health Communication, 5,* 203–227.

Witte, K. (1992). Putting the fear back into fear appeals: The extended parallel process model. *Communication Monographs, 59,* 329–349.

Witte, K. (2003, September). *Preventing HIV/AIDS through entertainment education in Ethiopia.* Speech presented to the Africa Studies Center, Michigan State University, East Lansing.

Witte, K., & Allen, M. (2000). A meta-analysis of fear appeals: Implications for effective public health campaigns. *Heath Education Behavior, 27,* 591–614.

Witte, K, Murray-Johnson, L., & Keulder, E. (2001). *A baseline report of the USAID Namibia individual community survey: Phase 1 Oshikuku, Rehoboth and Onandjokwe.* (Unpublished USAID report)

Witte, K., & Roberto, A. J. (2009). Fear appeals and public health: Managing fear and creating hope. In L. R. Frey & K. N. Cissna (Eds.), *Handbook of applied communication research* (pp. 584–610). New York: Routledge.

World Bank (2009). Chapter 1: Worldview. In *World Development Indicators 2009.* Retrieved from http://web.worldbank.org/WBSITE/EXTERNAL/DATASTATISTICS/0,,contentMDK:2172 5423~pagePK:64133150~piPK:64133175~theSitePK:239419,00.html

15

SOCIAL MARKETING

Its Meaning, Use, and Application for Health Communication

Timothy Edgar, Julie E. Volkman, and Alison M. B. Logan

Introduction

While preparing the manuscript for this chapter, the first author sat down at his computer one morning to check e-mail. In his list of messages, he discovered a response to a post that appeared earlier in the day on the *Social Marketing Listserv* sponsored by Georgetown University. A graduate student in health communication had posted a query in which she said that she was working on a project for a local high school that had asked her to develop a communication plan to reduce heavy marijuana use among students. In her posting, she said that she intended to use "strategies to execute some sort of campaign, or materials (video ad, posters, class activities) to use at the high school." Within a few hours, she received a response from Michael Rothschild, one of the leading scholars of social marketing, in which he suggested that she read a recent publication in the *American Journal of Public Health* that reported on the results of the evaluation of the National Youth Anti-Drug Media Campaign for which the U.S. Congress appropriated nearly $1 billion (Hornik, Jacobsohn, Orwin, Piesse, & Kolton, 2008). Professor Rothschild noted that the results showed no positive behavior change as a result of the campaign. He remarked that "If they couldn't do anything with $1 billion, your desired communications campaign may not fare any better. May I encourage you to consider *marketing* [our emphasis] rather than *messages* [also our emphasis] as a way to change target behaviors?"[1]

We certainly do not want to introduce this story to suggest that message strategies cannot be used to effect behavior change related to personal health, but the listserv exchange does help to illustrate one of the primary points that we wish to make in this chapter. That is, although health communication and social marketing have a close relationship, they are not the same thing. Health communication scholars and practitioners use the term *social marketing* with great frequency as articles in our journals frame initiatives under a social marketing umbrella, and many presentations have been made at academic conferences in the field of health communication in the last decade that label the effort under investigation as social marketing. We believe, however, that social marketing has reached the status of a buzz term and has lost its meaning to a certain degree because of overuse and misuse. Health communicators often talk about planning, evaluating, and studying social marketing campaigns by equating social marketing with any activity that involves using various media to communicate to a population about health issues, but using *health communication* and *social marketing* as interchangeable synonyms is not appropriate or accurate. Although social marketing relies heavily on the incorporation of a communication strategy (or promotion strategy in the parlance of social marketing) as part of an overall approach to behavior change, social marketing as a framework goes beyond the creation and dissemination of messages. The editors of this volume asked for this chapter to be written to help clarify what exactly social marketing is. In the original *Handbook of Health Communication* that appeared in 2003, there was no mention of social marketing in the subject index at all.

In this chapter, we describe how social marketing differs from similar approaches, and we use detailed examples from the academic literature to highlight the characteristics of the framework. Because this chapter appears in a volume intended primarily for students and scholars of health communication, we also examine how behavioral and communication theory have guided social marketing initiatives in the past, and we offer suggestions for how communication theory can inform future social marketing efforts.

How Is Social Marketing Unique?

History and Definition

Overviews on the history of social marketing (see, for example, Andreasen, 2003) typically trace the genesis of the perspective to an article in *Public Opinion Quarterly* published by G. D. Wiebe in the early 1950s in which he asked the question, "Why can't you sell brotherhood like you sell soap?" (Wiebe, 1951–1952, p. 679). The approach then received its name two decades later when Kotler and Zaltman (1971) discussed how to use commercial marketing as a technology that could be applied to social issues. Although it has been linked to a wide variety of topics, social marketing's deepest penetration has focused upon behaviors related to personal health (Andreasen, 2002). Social marketing is not a theory in and of itself or a unique set of techniques (Edgar & Palamé, 2009), but can be described as a process for effecting change modeled on the processes used in private sector marketing (Andreasen, 2002). Others have characterized it as a tool or framework that "relies on multiple scientific disciplines to create programs designed to influence human behavior on a large scale" (Smith, 2006, p. 138).

Primacy of Behavior Change

Regardless of whether social marketing is labeled as a process, tool, or framework, one defining characteristic about which there is almost universal agreement is that behavior change is the bottom line for social marketing. Andreasen (2002), for instance, has stated that "If you don't move the needle, you're not being a successful marketer. Simply gaining acceptance of an idea without inducing action is not success" (p. 7). Andreasen noted that health communicators in particular often concentrate on the goals of increasing knowledge, awareness, or attitude change. Although changes in thinking are stepping-stones to a behavior shift, initiatives with these types of goals should not be considered social marketing.

Other perspectives, too, share the intent of a behavioral shift, but social marketing provides a unique approach to achieving the end goal. In a seminal essay, Rothschild (1999) sought to explicate the core characteristics of social marketing by contrasting them with other orientations to behavior change. Rothschild developed a tripartite classification system in which he compared education/communication, law, and a marketing-based approach. According to Rothschild, *education/communication* "refers to messages of any type that attempt to inform and/or persuade a target to behave voluntarily in a particular manner but do not provide, on their own, direct and/or immediate reward or punishment" (p. 25).[2] He acknowledged that education/communication can increase awareness and present arguments about behavior change, but it does not have the power on its own to explicitly deliver the benefits. *Law* within Rothschild's framework involves the use of coercion to prompt behavior change in a nonvoluntary manner or using the threat of punishment for noncompliance or inappropriate behavior (e.g., fines for not wearing seat belts). *Social marketing*, on the other hand, involves attempts to change behavior by offering reinforcing incentives or consequences in a context that provides opportunities for voluntary exchange. The social marketer finds ways to make the environment more favorable for the desired behavior through the development of choices with comparative advantage, favorable cost–benefit relationships, and time and place utility enhancement. Positive reinforcement exists when the transaction becomes complete.

Expanding on Rothschild's classification scheme, Maibach (2002) offered an explanation of how the three approaches to behavior change can best be used by placing them on a continuum where "prone to behave as desired" is at one end and the other end is bounded by "resistant to behave as desired." Maibach argued that education/communication by itself can be very effective when targeting audiences who sit at the "prone to behave" end of the continuum. He believed that individuals who fall into this category will understand why the recommended change in behavior is in their best interest and will respond readily to attempts to influence them, especially when the barriers to performance are minor or when alternative behaviors offer relatively less attractive benefits (e.g., telling parents to place their babies on their backs while sleeping to prevent Sudden Infant Death Syndrome). Maibach placed the force of law at the "resistant to behave" end of the continuum noting that legal enforcement has the potential for greatest influence when those who are promoting behavior change have little to offer the target audience that will convince them that change is in their best interest or that the health benefit might not be realized for many years (e.g., banning the sale of cigarettes to minors). For Maibach, social marketing falls in the middle of the continuum and has the greatest chance of success with people for whom behavior change might not be easy but who are "open to good offers" (p. 10). Social marketers develop an approach in which they embed within their overall strategy a mechanism for increasing benefits, reducing barriers, and providing opportunities that encourage a particular behavior. Maibach identified the obesity epidemic as a health issue ripe for intervention through social marketing. Compelling people to change their eating and physical activity habits through force of law is virtually impossible, and education/communication alone has proven ineffective in combating the competition (i.e., ubiquitous messages about tempting food offerings that flood our senses coupled with increased opportunities to spend time in sedentary pursuits). He argued that social marketing has a greater chance for success because the approach at its core seeks to restructure the environment and offer a more attractive package of benefits.

Integrated Marketing Mix

Beyond the primacy of behavior change, the distinguishing principle of social marketing is that campaign planners incorporate an integrated strategy that foregoes a message-only approach. Andreasen (2002) argued that initiatives "that are purely communications campaigns are not social marketing. Indeed, it is when campaigns move beyond mere advertising that the power of the approach is manifested" (p. 7). At the heart of the integrated strategy is what is known as the marketing mix or the four Ps (i.e., product, price, place, and promotion). Borrowed from commercial marketing, the four Ps provide a framework for designing an intervention that complements messages with product innovation, environmental restructuring, and the deliverance of attractive rewards that result in an acceptable exchange. Because the mix forms the core of social marketing and because the four Ps are frequently misunderstood, we now devote considerable space in the following pages to detailed explanations of each of the four strategy components. We depend heavily on the academic literature that chronicles past initiatives for examples that illuminate the components and process.

Product. Development of an integrated strategy typically begins with identification of the product. According to Kotler and Lee (2008), three levels of products comprise the product strategy: actual, core, and augmented. The actual product is the specific behavior that the social marketer wants the target audience to adopt or "buy"; the core product is the benefit that the audience should expect in exchange for performing the behavior; and an augmented product includes any goods or tangible products or services that the social marketer might develop, distribute, sell, or promote to support behavior change.

The distinction between the first two types of products (i.e., core and actual) can be illustrated through the *Think Again* initiative conducted throughout Canada (Lombardo & Léger, 2007). The goal of the campaign was to reduce the number of new cases of HIV infection amongst gay men who engage in anal intercourse. Planners identified the core product as the benefit of avoiding the personal trauma associated with HIV infection, while the actual product that they promoted was talk amongst gay men and their partners about the risks of engaging in unprotected sex.

The key role of the third level of product strategy—the augmented product—is often overlooked in the research literature on social marketing. In the vast majority of articles that have been published describing social marketing initiatives, detailed description of a product strategy rarely goes beyond a quick reference to the desired behavioral outcome of the actual product. Because an augmented product provides tangible assistance for engaging in a new behavior, careful attention to the creation and introduction of an augmented product can greatly enhance the chances of success by taking social marketing beyond mere messaging. Inclusion of an augmented product as part of a larger strategy also provides a physical "tool" to enable action.

A prime example of an augmented product comes from the VERB™ campaign, which was launched by the Centers for Disease Control and Prevention (CDC) in 2002. One of the largest social marketing campaigns ever implemented in the United States, the initiative focused on the sedentary lifestyles of young adolescents. Created in response to the alarming data about the increase of obesity and type 2 diabetes among youth, the CDC targeted *tweens* (i.e., children aged 9 to 13 years old), parents, and key influencers (e.g., teachers, youth program leaders) in an attempt to increase physical activity among the kids (Wong et al., 2004). The multiethnic campaign included a very comprehensive approach to behavior change, but one of the most innovative aspects of the initiative was the introduction of the augmented product known as the Yellowball. The CDC created the Yellowball to support a variety of physical activities (i.e., the actual product) by allowing tweens to invent their own unique activities that included the use of the play object. CDC distributed over 500,000 of the yellow-colored balls throughout the United States (the balls were slightly smaller than a volleyball and had the VERB logo and a code number printed on the side) and encouraged tweens to discover a variety of ways to use the balls as part of their daily play activities.

Another key component of an overall product strategy is *positioning*. As described by Kotler and Lee (2008), "positioning is the act of designing the organization's actual and perceived offering in such a way that it lands on and occupies a distinctive place in the mind of the target market—where you want it to be" (p. 185). The social marketing framework places great emphasis on understanding the perceptual maps that specific audiences have for individual behaviors. That is, the social marketer strives through audience research to see how individuals frame an actual product (i.e., the targeted behavior) in their own minds with respect to the different dimensions of the behavior as well as how perceptions map vis-à-vis competing behaviors. Using the VERB campaign again as an example, the CDC prior to the design of the initiative carefully mapped physical activity in the minds of tweens along the dimensions of social connections, fun, control, self-esteem, creativity, expertise, and inspiration (Wong, Greenwell, Gates, & Berkowitz, 2008). Their formative research told them that successful "selling" of the product required a careful integration of the different dimensions so that physical activity would be positioned in the minds of the children as a pleasurable act instead of a painful one. Reviews of previous initiatives taught them that prior attempts to increase physical activity among this age group often failed because the product became positioned in the minds of kids as something negative and reflected a loss of control. In contrast, the VERB approach to positioning emphasized the rewards of empowerment (Wong et al., 2008).

Price. The price strategy lies at the core of what Smith (2006) refers to as social marketing's principal contribution to behavior change. That is, voluntary behavior is achieved through an exchange of value wherein the social marketer and the target audience engage in a sophisticated game of "Let's make a deal." Guided by the principles of exchange theory (more on this in the section on theory), social marketers assume people will change their behavior not just because they are well informed but because they believe that they will get something of value in return. The goal of a price strategy is to show members of the target audience that "buying" the product is advantageous, because even though there might be costs associated with the adoption of a behavior, the benefits of the transaction provide an attractive outcome (Lefebvre & Flora, 1988). As described in the literature, a price strategy may take many forms. For instance, in much of the social marketing work that has been done internationally, especially in countries with high levels of poverty, the price strategy for campaigns focuses heavily on subsidizing the monetary costs of an augmented product so that people have the ability to buy it and use it to engage in the recommended behavior. Examples of this approach can be seen in initiatives where iron-fortified soy sauce was made available at a reasonable cost for women in the Guizhou province in China (Sun, Guo, Wang, & Sun, 2007) and folic acid supplements to prevent anemia were sold to rural village women in Cambodia at a nominal price (Kanal et al., 2005). The monetary value of an augmented product can also come into play in a price strategy by framing a tangible good as a relative bargain in comparison to other everyday purchases. In a family planning campaign in Bangladesh, for example, planners highlighted consumer benchmarks such as the price of a cup of tea, a box of matches, and single cigarettes when selling condoms (Schellstede & Ciszewski, 1984).

The more typical approach seen in the literature to developing a price strategy involves the identification of nonmonetary barriers to behavior and then either introducing information that reframes the perceived barrier or supplies augmented products that make it easier for the target audience to overcome the barrier. For example, Fraze, Rivera-Trudeau, and McElroy (2007) reported the results of a campaign sponsored by the CDC called *Prevention IS Care* that attempted to change the behavior of physicians so that they (a) routinely delivered HIV prevention messages to their patients who were HIV negative and (b) screened the same population of patients to find out if they were engaging in behaviors that would prevent transmission to others. To lower perceived costs for the physicians (i.e., lack of time to screen and deliver prevention messages, doubts about the efficacy of behavioral screening, and discomfort in discussing sexual behaviors), the CDC provided a host of intervention tools (e.g., influential speakers at professional meetings, a video that included patient testimonials, skill-building workshops, a published scientific article that provided evidence for the effectiveness of screening behavior) that made it easier for the physicians to view the behavioral product as a reasonable "purchase."

The task of offering an exchange that has perceived significant value can be very challenging, especially when dealing with behaviors related to one's own health. The social marketer might only be able to offer benefits that may be realized years down the line, are intangible, or both. When making behavioral choices, individuals default to behaviors that bring the most immediate pleasure. Data from the evaluation literature on social marketing suggests the greatest chance for behavior change occurs when campaign planners have the ability to offer attractive short-term benefits as the core of their price strategy (Rothschild, 1999). Although providing immediate benefits might require substantial resources that add to the overall budget of an initiative, there is evidence that innovative approaches can lead to meaningful change and can be funded, at least in part, through partnerships. A perfect example of innovation in offering short-term benefits through partnerships comes from the *Quit and Win* smoking cessation campaign that has been implemented in over 80 countries around the world and has helped an estimated 150,000 smokers to quit (Lavack, Watson, & Markwart, 2007). Originating in Minnesota in 1975, the *Quit and Win* approach is grounded in a price strategy focused on a contest format in which participants have the opportunity to win expensive prizes if they stop smoking. At the end of a contest period, winners are randomly selected from a computer-generated list of entrants. Those whose names are selected are contacted and asked to report on their smoking status. Verification of abstinence requires a written statement signed by witnesses and often biochemical verification is required for those selected for a major prize such as cars and exotic vacations donated by businesses in exchange for publicity (Lavack et al., 2007).

Place. For the sake of consistent alliteration, social marketers use the term *place* as the key word to label the third piece of the marketing mix, but the word *convenience* might serve as a more apt descriptor. As Kotler and Lee (2008) have acknowledged, individuals "live in a convenience-oriented world in which many of us place an extremely high value on our time, trying to save some of that for our families, friends, and favorite leisure activities" (p. 247). In the development of a place strategy, the goal of the social marketer is to make the enactment of the desired behavior as convenient as possible for the target audience. Smith (2000) explained that the concept of place "refers to the system through which the 'products' (commodities, messages, and health services) flow to users and the quality of service offered where these products are made available. Place focuses largely on overcoming important structural obstacles to easy access" (p. 15). The social marketer identifies the key barriers, both perceived and real, that prevent individuals from adopting behaviors that can benefit their health. Campaign planners then either must convince the audience that the behavior is actually more convenient than originally perceived or find ways to restructure the environment so that audience members associate the behavior with convenience and ease.

The exact characteristics of the place strategy often have been misunderstood and inaccurately identified, and campaign planners often confuse place with other strategies by simply relegating place to channel selection. That is, the place strategy inappropriately becomes equated with the decision-making process about the most effective communication channels for reaching the intended audience (e.g., should campaign planners rely on print, broadcast, or computer technologies to disseminate their message?). Overall success typically is dependent (at least in part) on effective channel selection, but many social marketing experts believe that decisions about channels fall under the promotion strategy umbrella (Kotler & Lee, 2008). When place becomes relegated to channel selection, then the power of environmental restructuring can become at the very least diminished and at worst completely lost.

There are several innovative examples from the literature that illustrate the forms a place strategy can take. For instance, part of the place strategy might include making an augmented product available to a population by working cooperatively with businesses that become distribution points. Warnick et al. (2004), for example, reported on a social marketing initiative in Bolivia aimed at increasing the use of multivitamin and mineral supplements among resource-poor women. Program planners succeeded in placing the multivitamin *VitalDía* in 90 percent of pharmacies in urban areas and 58 percent of pharmacies in rural areas so that women could easily find the product after learning about it through promotional efforts (as part of the price strategy, the team also was able to provide the multivitamin at an affordable cost).

Improving access to services also can be part of the place strategy. Williams, Dewapura, Gunawardene, and Settinayake (1998) showed how this can work through an initiative in Sri Lanka created to eliminate leprosy in that country. One of the greatest obstacles that program planners faced was an insufficient number of health care professionals in the country who knew how to properly diagnose the disease. In response, they trained 4,000 paramedical workers and over 1,000 medical officers in outpatient departments of hospitals to detect leprosy and refer people with suspicious lesions to the primary leprosy staff. Thus, individuals throughout the country had access to a convenient first-point-of-contact without having to compete initially for the time of the limited number of leprosy experts in the nation.

Through a very clever and multipronged use of a place strategy, Ludwig, Buchholz, and Clarke (2005) described how social marketers at a university campus in the southeastern United States sought to increase the use of helmets among bicyclists on campus by providing motivational information at the moment that the intended audience members obtained the augmented product (i.e., a free bicycle helmet) at the point of distribution. As a first step, trained peer agents on campus approached individuals they observed not wearing a helmet while riding a bicycle. The agents asked the bicyclists to participate in the program in which they would receive a coupon for a free helmet if they signed a pledge to commit to wearing a helmet in the future. When the bicyclists went to a designated store participating in what was known as *The Grateful Head* initiative, they had to redeem the coupon at the store counter. Before handing the free helmet to the bicyclists, the store clerks, who also had been trained by project staff, provided personal accounts about the benefits of helmet use (e.g., a story about a friend who had been hurt in an accident while not wearing a helmet).

Increasing behavioral convenience can even include social marketers providing a mechanism for removing some of the burden of making a key decision at a crucial moment when an individual is least able to make sound choices. As part of a successful initiative called *Road Crew*, program planners sought to reduce the number of fatalities among 21- to 34-year-olds living in rural parts of Wisconsin (Rothschild, Mastin, & Miller, 2006). Because there is limited or no public transportation for people leaving bars in sparsely populated regions, the high-risk default behavior for many individuals is to drive their own cars. Through formative research, the planning team learned that bar goers did not want to leave their cars behind; they were not interested in a ride program that would prohibit continued drinking on the way home; and they wanted to be able to pay for ride options at the beginning of the evening so that they reduced the risk of running out of cash at the bar. The *Road Crew* team restructured the environment by developing a place strategy with a round-trip ride system. For an upfront cost of $10 to $15, project personnel picked up patrons at their homes in older luxury vehicles, drove them to the bar of their choice, and then provided transportation back home at the end of the evening. If local ordinances allowed, riders also could continue drinking in the cars.

Promotion.   The fourth P, which is known as promotion, is the part of the marketing mix that is best known and understood by health communication scholars and practitioners because it is the strategic component that entails message creation and channel selection. Promotion is also the P that receives the most attention in published articles within the social marketing literature. As we discussed earlier, promotion frequently is mistaken for the whole of social marketing. Although numerous social marketing scholars have commented on this trend in the past (Maibach, 2002; Sublet & Lum, 2008), the authors of this chapter were further struck by this pattern when reviewing the literature for the preparation of this manuscript. As we conducted our literature search, we frequently found published articles that used the term *social marketing* in the title and referred to the described effort with the same label throughout the article, but a close reading of a substantial number of these publications often revealed that promotion stood alone as the strategic guide for specific initiatives. In many cases, what authors called a *social marketing campaign* appears, at least within the pages of a publication, as no more than the creation of a message intended to increase awareness or encourage behavior change. Either the authors did not truly use the social marketing framework or they failed to report how they incorporated the entire marketing mix.

One possible reason why so much emphasis is placed on promotion in the literature might be the inherent fascination that it attracts. Promotion undoubtedly represents the glitz and glamour of social marketing. It is not uncommon to hear professionals—even those who have a thorough understanding of the needed integrative relationship of the total market- ing mix—refer to promotion as "the fun part." Clever slogans, cute cartoon spokespersons, well-produced television spots, and colorful posters become the face of a campaign in a way that the other components of the marketing mix typically do not. For example, explaining the details in print about the mechanisms for making a behavioral choice more accessible to an audience likely provides less allure for readers. On the other hand, as the visible, final product (not to be confused with product strategy) of an initiative, the promotion piece is the easiest to highlight and lends itself most readily to visual presentation. When prepar- ing articles or books for publication, authors might have a tendency to devote the greatest amount of word space to promotion because they suspect that portion will garner the most attention from both reviewers and the readership. As more publications appear over time with promotion highlighted, professionals who read the literature or hear presentations at conferences might begin to equate social marketing only with messaging.

None of these concerns about an overemphasis on promotion should detract, however, from the innovative promotional work that has been conducted in the past within the context of an integrated approach. Many examples exist of high-quality campaigns that have carefully developed targeted promotional strategies grounded in rigorous formative research and thorough concept and message testing.[3] To illustrate approaches that strategically incorporated multiple channels to communicate the message of the campaign complemented by equitable attention to the other three Ps, we offer two diverse examples from Australia and the United States.[4] The Australian campaign conducted in the western part of the country was called *Freedom From Fear* and had the goal of reducing violence against women by their partners. The specific behavioral focus was to get the perpetrators and men at risk to voluntarily attend counseling programs. The primary medium for reaching the target audience was television and radio advertising, especially during sporting events. Program planners also developed extensive public relations activities with groups such as counseling professionals, the police, and other government departments in the hope that they would function as influencers. In addition, they created publications for professionals, employers, victims, and for the men themselves. With the assistance of trade unions, these publications were combined into campaign information packets that were distributed to work sites. Other packets were distributed by mail, and posters advertising a help line were placed at work sites around the region. The strategy behind the campaign message was to avoid threats of imprisonment and other legal sanctions and instead focus on feelings of remorse related to the effects of domestic violence on children (Donovan, Paterson, & Francas, 1999).

The American example comes from the *Healthy Penis* campaign developed by the San Francisco Department of Public Health to increase testing for syphilis. The initiative primarily was promoted in neighborhoods with a large concentration of gay and bisexual men and in businesses frequented by the same population. The campaign included posters on the streets, in bars and commercial sex venues, and bus shelters; advertising on buses; palm cards; advertising in gay publications; and banner advertisements on a popular Internet site for meeting sexual partners. Through community outreach, the campaign team also used a 7-foot Healthy Penis costume, T-shirts, and a Healthy Penis stress grip. They also relied on the use of a humorous cartoon strip that featured the Healthy Penis character that provided information on syphilis transmission, symptoms, and prevention (Montoya et al., 2005).

With this understanding of social marketing, its differentiation from health communication, and the core concepts of the four Ps, we turn our attention to the theoretical frameworks and uses within social marketing. Because the primary readership for this volume will be students and scholars who are devoted to the development and application of theory, we assume that the link between social marketing and theory will be of utmost interest.

Theoretical Considerations

Although there are a few instances in the literature where authors refer to "social marketing theory," scholars generally agree, even if they are avid proponents of social marketing principles, that social marketing is not a theory in and of itself. As we mentioned earlier in this chapter, it most commonly is labeled as a process, framework, or tool. Because it lacks theoretical status, social marketing often has been viewed with a skeptical eye (Edgar, 2008). One of the authors of this chapter, for instance, recalls a conversation where a colleague described social marketing as "just a practice of throwing everything against a wall and seeing what sticks for an audience without any theoretical logic or framework." Although not a stand-alone theory, we will show in this section that theory has been used to ground social marketing practices, and we believe that behavioral and communication theory has the potential to further inform it.

Exchange Theory

Since its inception, the driving theoretical force behind social marketing has been exchange theory (Edgar, Boyd, & Palamé, 2009), which is derived from psychological and economic principles and "assumes that we are need-directed beings with a natural inclination to try and improve our lot" (Hastings & Saren, 2003, p. 309). In order for a successful exchange to occur, both parties act primarily to fulfill their own interests. If a new behavior's benefits outweigh its barriers, the theory predicts that change is likely to occur.

In an example of exchange theory driving social marketing strategy, Bellows, Anderson, Davies, and Kennedy (2009) described a Colorado campaign to combat rising rates of obesity in preschool children. They found that for teachers, pressure from school administrators who prioritized other academic enrichment activities was a major barrier to increasing physical activity in preschoolers. Other identified barriers were lack of adequate space and equipment. Under the guidance of exchange theory, social marketers overcame barriers by developing comprehensive lessons that required little preparation time, were designed for small classroom spaces and did not require gymnasiums and playgrounds.

Although reference to exchange theory is ubiquitous in the social marketing literature, the theory is limited and often oversimplifies the process by which individuals engage in new behaviors. Craig Lefebvre, one of the leading scholars in the area of social marketing, discussed the limitations of the theory in an interview for *Social Marketing Quarterly* in which he said, "One of the things about social marketing that does need reexamination … is having exchange theory as the central theoretical element to social marketing" (Bryant, 2004, p. 21). Social marketers who rely only on exchange theory risk missing the complexity, variability, and even irrationality of human health behavior, which exchange theory cannot elegantly predict. However, dropping exchange theory completely from the social marketing framework likely would incite significant pushback from social marketing purists. Lefebvre explained the dilemma by stating, "We are at a point where most social marketers implicitly believe that exchange theory does not have lot of robustness to help us think through behavioral determinants and change" but "there are other people who would argue that once you walk away from exchange theory that you've walked away from the central element of marketing" (p. 22). Lefebvre argued that the principle of the exchange is central to the framework, but "theoretical eclecticism makes social marketing a stronger, more vibrant approach" (p. 21). In the next section, we examine these considerations.

Other Theories Guiding Previous Social Marketing Initiatives

A review of the literature shows that psychological, behavioral, and communication theories and models beyond exchange theory have been used by social marketers with social cognitive theory, the transtheoretical model, diffusion of innovation, the theories of reasoned action and planned behavior, and the health belief model as the conceptual frameworks most frequently cited. These theories have informed strategy both throughout the integrated marketing mix as well as in individual strategic components. For example, to guide social marketers on audience segmentation, the transtheoretical model has been very useful. Gallivan, Lising, Ammary, and Greenberg (2007) employed the model to determine how likely patients with diabetes were to take control of and manage their conditions. This social marketing team developed two different behavioral products for members depending on whether they were in the precontemplation stage (not quite ready to change) or the contemplation stage (more ready to change than not).

In other efforts, behavioral theories have informed the development of specific components of the marketing mix. For example, social cognitive theory and diffusion of innovation are theories that have been used to enhance the promotional strategies of campaigns (Bellows, Cole, & Anderson, 2006; Dearing, Maibach, & Buller, 2006). In particular, concepts from these theories that have been successfully used to promote positive health changes by helping social marketers to better understand how interpersonal influence can impact the adoption of a behavior.

The theories of reasoned action and planned behavior are two other behavioral theories that have been used in the development of all components of a social marketing plan. These theories are often employed to explain determinants of behavior that can range from pressure of social norms about a health behavior, to perceptions of severity and susceptibility about the health risk, to feelings of whether an individual will succeed in the health behavior change. As we have seen in the explanation of the marketing mix, determinants of behavior are integral to the development of all four P strategies. For instance, Kelly, Comello, and Slater (2006) took the notion of social norms from the theories of reasoned action and planned behavior into account when developing an initiative to combat drug abuse in young adults. During the formative research stage, they found that a widespread perceived barrier to abstaining from substance abuse was potentially jeopardizing friendships and staying "cool" in social circles. However, members of this audience also perceived themselves to be independent and rarely admitted to following the crowd. Knowing that social norms were an obstacle to abstaining from substance abuse, social marketers developed their product, price, place, and promotional strategies to reinforce the notion that one can be his or her own influence and avoid drug abuse.

These campaigns in combination with theoretical frameworks have provided much benefit toward societal gain. Given the importance of identifying the benefits and rewards among target audiences, however, we feel more can be done in social marketing in the use of theory. This last section thus focuses on recommendations for future theoretical incorporations.

Future Theoretical Directions for Social Marketing

In this chapter, our goal has been to provide readers with a thorough understanding of what is (and is not) social marketing. As part of this goal, we included details about social marketing's foundation in exchange theory and the limitations of this theory to equip readers with a full understanding of the intricacies involved in social marketing endeavors. However, given the importance of identifying the benefits and rewards among target audiences, we feel that theory should be used more consistently in the development of social marketing initiatives. Although the application of the social cognitive theory, theory of reasoned action, and other traditional theories is commendable, we feel that social marketers can benefit greatly from communication theories in particular. We have argued repeatedly that social marketing casts a much wider net than strategizing about message construction and delivery, but we also recognize that communication theory is the most obvious and easy fit for the promotional portion of an initiative. In addition, we believe that communication theory has the potential to inform all components of the marketing mix by helping predict the determinants of behavior change through insights into the cognitions, reactions, and roles that are a part of the human experience. We acknowledge that the perspectives presented in this concluding section are not exhaustive, but rather a preliminary glance at what health communication scholars and practitioners might contribute to social marketing efforts.

Uncertainty and Information Seeking.   Throughout this chapter, we have alluded to the unique evaluations, considerations, and attributes that individuals assign to particular products or behaviors, and how these perceptions influence each part of the marketing mix in social marketing. A fundamental appraisal that may influence a social marketing effort revolves around the level of uncertainty individuals may experience with regard to a newly presented health situation. In particular, this experience of uncertainty can determine information-seeking behaviors. The relationship between uncertainty and information-seeking is not new. For decades, scholars having been striving to understand how individuals manage and cope with their uncertainties regarding health and disease and have determined that mechanisms range from seeking information to alleviate uncertainty, to avoiding specific health information and maintaining chronic uncertainty (Hogan & Brashers, 2009). Consequently, one theoretical perspective for social marketers to consider is uncertainty management theory (UMT) (Brashers, 2001) as it helps elucidate why individuals seek or avoid information about a health issue. Grounded in understanding uncertainty in illness, UMT provides social marketers with a window into how individuals appraise their uncertainty as either an opportunity or danger (Brashers, 2001; Hogan & Brashers, 2009). Based on the uncertainty appraisal, individuals choose to manage their uncertainty through seeking ambiguous information (opportunity to remain uncertainty) or seeking information to alleviate their uncertainty (uncertainty is a danger) (Brashers, 2001).

We believe that understanding the audience's uncertainty and information seeking behaviors regarding a health issue is pertinent in the formative research stage of a social marketing campaign. For example, when developing a price strategy, understanding individuals' appraisals of uncertainty can help determine how to best inform the audience of the costs and benefits of a product or behavior. As information is conveyed about the costs and benefits by the price strategy, the level of uncertainty associated with an issue may indicate whether individuals will seek or avoid further information based on their uncertainty appraisal. The latter scenario certainly would present a challenge for social marketers. Thus, it is important for social marketers to know the specific issues (costs) about which individuals may be uncertain, and the information they may see as a benefit to alleviate uncertainty when developing the price strategy.

Communication Competence.   In addition to uncertainty appraisal, other communication concepts are important social determinants to be incorporated into the development of social marketing endeavors. When selecting messengers of a promotion strategy or individuals who carry out a place strategy, social marketers should monitor the communication skills and competence of individuals or groups while they are communicating with the target audience. Health communication efforts and research continue to study the communication competence of health care providers and caregivers within the health care system (Nussbaum & Fisher, 2009; Thompson & Parrott, 2002) and their efforts to improve overall health outcomes. Such consideration should also be evaluated by social marketers. Evaluations of the competence and skillfulness of individuals can span interpersonal sensitivity (Street, 2003) to satisfaction (Spitzberg, 2003).

For social marketers, assessing communication competence of individuals who play a role in carrying out the social marketing initiative can occur during several stages of the marketing mix. For instance, social marketers could assess which individuals the target audience perceives as competent to deliver the messages of the promotion strategy, as well as whether or not the target audience feels the location and individuals as part of the place strategy can enable skillful communication to occur. For example, a target audience's behavior (or product) may include signing an organ donation card. Lack of perceived politeness from individuals at the site where audience members sign the card may impair the effectiveness of the campaign. Similarly, if the spokesperson for the campaign is thought to be unclear, future problems may result for social marketers.

Narratives and Exemplars. Another avenue that social marketers can use to incorporate communication theory is in the development of the promotion strategy of a social marketing campaign. The concept of sharing an experience or personal testimonial is often studied in health communication (Kreuter et al., 2007). Many efforts have employed personal stories (Reinard, 1988; Reynolds & Reynolds, 2002) or exemplars (Zillmann, 1999) as illustrations to audiences of how behaviors can be adopted and performed. Within social marketing efforts, the use of an example story or narrative often occurs when individuals communicate their own experiences as a motivation for target audience members to perform the desired behavior. This could occur at the point at which campaign personnel ask for the desired behavior to be performed (e.g., my daughter was saved by an organ donation, so thanks for signing this card), or as part of the promotional strategy when a story is told while distributing promotional materials to encourage behavior change in audience members (e.g., spokesperson telling his or her experience in a television spot). We find there are several theoretical frameworks that social marketers may utilize when developing these strategies.

One perspective to consider is exemplification theory (Zillmann, 1999). Social marketers can use this theory to employ individuals who serve as positive role models with primary and secondary characteristics that comprise what's known as an exemplar (Zillmann, 1999). Social marketers should assess the primary features of the exemplar with which the audience might identify, as well as the secondary characteristics that highlight differences that members of the target audience lack and can subsequently model (Zillmann, 1999). As a result, social marketers should be able to reinforce the audience's intentions to partake in the recommended behavior with the use of exemplars. Furthermore, when considering the examples to be shared, social marketers should reflect on how these examples are conveyed. For example, a personal testimonial or secondhand experience can be communicated as examples to support and motivate for the target audience.

To guide social marketers, Schank and Berman (2002) offer several different types of narratives (e.g., firsthand, secondhand, official) to be used as evidence in support of messages surrounding the behavior within the promotion strategy, and each has unique properties that may elicit more or less identification and interest by the target audience. Furthermore, social marketers should assess the level of consistency and fidelity of the narrative, as argued by Fisher's (1987) narrative theory to ensure the narrative is reliable and truthful. In addition, social marketers should follow Ochs and Capps's (1996) assertion that narratives need elements of temporality and point of view. Remaining true to the structure of the narrative and selecting the appropriate narrative to use as evidence for the target audience can only increase the likelihood of target behaviors.

In sum, this section offers different theoretical perspectives that could be pursued by social marketers to enhance their efforts. The authors feel that each part of the marketing mix of social marketing could be enhanced with the application of different theoretical frameworks. Again, these are not the only theoretical applications that can be used, but may provide a starting point for future social marketing endeavors.

Conclusion

In the beginning of this chapter, we stated that we believe that social marketing has become inappropriately equated with health communication. We sought to provide clarification on what social marketing was intended to be in order to guide more accurate application in the future. Social marketing has borrowed from commercial marketing strategies and focused on voluntary behavior change, to provide health communication scholars and practitioners with another perspective to consider when looking for guidance on changing behaviors related to personal health. Social marketing has been theoretically grounded in the fundamentals of exchange theory and use of various behavioral theory frameworks for specific efforts, but health communication experts have ample opportunity to expand social marketing with the use of communication theories. Consequently, much more remains to be achieved with social marketing and its use for improving the health of multiple populations. We hope readers take this challenge and that we see the use of social marketing increase in both scholarship and practice.

Notes

1. The National Youth Anti-Drug Media Campaign, which was supervised by the White House Office of National Drug Control Policy, has at times been referred to as a *social marketing effort* (for example, Hornik et al., 2008, used that term), but most of the campaign activity was devoted to advertising on television, radio, websites, magazines, movie theaters, and other outlets. The evaluation revealed that the campaign was successful in exposing a large percentage of the target audience to the advertising (i.e., youths aged 9 to 18 years, their parents, and other influential adults), but there was no evidence to support the claim that exposure affected the marijuana use of the youths as desired.

2. In the interest of accuracy, Rothschild (1999) used the term *education* in his original essay as a stand-alone umbrella term for the first category in his classification system for approaches to behavior change. In the next paragraph in which we discuss how Maibach (2002) expanded on Rothschild's ideas, Maibach also used education by itself as the descriptor. Rothschild did, however, follow his initial definition of education with an acknowledgment that his intended meaning for the term is very similar to how others have used the terms *persuasion* and *health communication*. Because this chapter appears in a volume devoted to health communication, we are taking the liberty of using the term *education/communication* as the label for this particular approach when presenting the ideas of both Rothschild and Maibach.

3. In an effort to provide the reader with a wide variety of examples (both in terms of health topic and geographic location of implementation) to illustrate the various components of the social marketing framework, we wish to minimize the use of repeated examples from campaigns. However, we believe that more information has been published in the academic literature about the VERB campaign than almost any other social marketing initiative ever conducted. At least 15 different articles have been published about VERB in academic journals, including those appearing in 2008 in a special issue of the *American Journal of Preventive Medicine* devoted to the campaign. We refer the reader to the article by Berkowitz et al. (2008) in which program

personnel devoted great detail to explaining how they used formative research to develop their promotion strategy. The CDC also provides access to their unpublished internal reports on their approach to concept and message testing during campaign development. Rather than try to provide an overview of testing principles within this chapter, we refer the reader to the complete CDC reports that can be found at http://www.cdc.gov/youthcampaign/research/report. htm. Understanding the role of formative research in social marketing is crucial, because as Andreasen (2002) noted, one of the defining characteristics of social marketing is that it is "fanatically customer-driven" (p. 7).

4. Both the *Healthy Penis* and *Freedom from Fear* campaigns developed their promotional strategies within the context of a total marketing mix. For the sake of economy of space in this chapter, we refer the reader to the original publications for the details.

References

Andreasen, A. R. (2002). Marketing social marketing in the social change marketplace. *Journal of Public Policy & Marketing, 21,* 3–13.

Andreasen, A. R. (2003). The life trajectory of social marketing. *Marketing Theory, 3,* 293–303.

Bellows, L., Anderson, J., Davies, P., & Kennedy, C. (2009). Integration of social marketing elements in the design of a physical activity program for preschoolers. *Social Marketing Quarterly, 15,* 2–21.

Bellows, L., Cole, K., & Anderson, J. (2006). Assessing characteristics, needs, and preferences of a secondary audience for the development of a bilingual parent component to the Food Friends social marketing campaign. *Social Marketing Quarterly, 12,* 43–57.

Berkowitz, J. M., Huhman, M., Heitzler, C. D., Potter, L. D., Nolin, M. J., & Banspach, S. W. (2008). Overview of formative, process, and outcome evaluation methods used in the VERB™ campaign [Supplement]. *American Journal of Preventive Medicine, 34,* S222–S229.

Brashers, D. E. (2001). Communication and uncertainty management. *Journal of Communication, 51,* 477–497.

Bryant, C. (2004). An interview with R. Craig Lefebvre. *Social Marketing Quarterly, 10,* 17–30.

Dearing, J. W., Maibach, E. W., & Buller, D. B. (2006). A convergent diffusion and social marketing approach for disseminating proven approaches of physical activity promotion [Supplement]. *American Journal of Preventative Medicine, 31,* S11–S23.

Donovan, R. J., Paterson, D., & Francas, M. (1999). Targeting male perpetrators of intimate partner violence: Western Australia's "Freedom From Fear" campaign. *Social Marketing Quarterly, 5,* 127–144.

Edgar, T. (2008). Social marketing. In W. Donsbach (Ed.), *The international encyclopedia of communication* (pp. 3686–3689). Oxford, England: Blackwell.

Edgar, T., Boyd, S., & Palamé, M. J. (2009). Sustainability for behaviour change in the fight against antibiotic resistance: A social marketing framework. *Journal of Antimicrobial Chemotherapy, 63,* 230–237.

Edgar, T., & Palamé, M. J. (2009). Social marketing campaigns. In W. Eadie (Ed.), *21st century communication: A reference handbook* (pp. 822–829). Thousand Oaks, CA: Sage.

Fisher, W. R. (1987). *Human communication as narration: Toward a philosophy of reason, value, and action.* Columbia: University of South Carolina Press.

Fraze, J. L., Rivera-Trudeau, M., & McElroy, L. (2007). Applying behavioral theories to a social marketing campaign. *Social Marketing Quarterly, 13,* 2–14.

Gallivan, J., Lising, M., Ammary, N. J., & Greenberg, R. (2007). The National Diabetes Education Program's "Control Your Diabetes. For Life." campaign: Design, implementation, and lessons learned. *Social Marketing Quarterly, 13,* 65–82.

Hastings, G., & Saren, M. (2003). The critical contribution of social marketing: Theory and application. *Marketing Theory, 3,* 305–322.

Hogan, T. P., & Brashers, D. E. (2009). The theory of communication and uncertainty management: Implications from the wilder realm of information behavior. In T. D. Afifi & W. A. Affifi (Eds.), *Uncertainty, information management and disclosure decisions: Theories and applications* (pp. 45–66). New York: Routledge.

Hornik, R., Jacobsohn, L., Orwin, R., Piesse, A., & Kalton, G. (2008). Effects of the National Youth Anti-Drug Media Campaign on youths. *American Journal of Public Health, 98,* 2229–2236.

Kanal, K., Busch-Hallen, J., Cavalli-Sforza, T., Crape, B., Smitasiri, S., & the Cambodian Weekly Iron-Folic Acid Program Team. (2005). Weekly iron-folic acid supplements to prevent anemia among Cambodian women in three settings: Process and outcomes of social marketing and community mobilization [Supplement]. *Nutrition Review, 63*, S126–S133.

Kelly, K. J., Comello, M. L., & Slater, M. D. (2006). Development of an aspirational campaign to prevent youth substance use: "Be under your own influence." *Social Marketing Quarterly, 12*, 14–27.

Kotler, P., & Lee, N. R. (2008). *Social marketing: Influencing behaviors for good.* Thousand Oaks, CA: Sage.

Kotler, P., & Zaltman, G. (1971). Social marketing: An approach to planned social change. *Journal of Marketing, 35*, 3–12.

Kreuter, M. W., Green, M. C., Cappella, J. N., Slater, M. D., Wise, M. E., Storey, D., ... Woolley, S. (2007). Narrative communication in cancer prevention and control: A framework to guide research and application. *Annals of Behavioral Medicine, 33*, 221–235.

Lavack, A. M., Watson, L., & Markwart, J. (2007). Quit and win contests: A social marketing success story. *Social Marketing Quarterly, 13*, 31–52.

Lefebvre, R. C., & Flora, J. A. (1988). Social marketing and public health intervention. *Health Education & Behavior, 15*, 299–315.

Lombardo, A. P., & Léger, Y. A. (2007). Thinking about "Think Again" in Canada: Assessing a social marketing HIV/AIDS prevention campaign. *Journal of Health Communication, 12*, 377–397.

Ludwig, T. D., Buchholz, C., & Clarke, S. W. (2005). Using social marketing to increase the use of helmets among bicyclists. *Journal of American College Health, 54*, 51–58.

Maibach, E. (2002). Explicating social marketing: What is it, and what isn't it? *Social Marketing Quarterly, 8*, 7–13.

Montoya, J. A., Kent, C. K., Rotblatt, H., McCright, J., Kerndt, P. R., & Klausner, J. D. (2005). Social marketing campaign significantly associated with increases in syphilis testing among gay and bisexual men in San Francisco. *Sexually Transmitted Disease, 32*, 395–399.

Nussbaum, J. F., & Fisher, C. L. (2009). A communication model for the competent delivery of geriatric medicine. *Journal of Language and Social Psychology, 28*, 190–208.

Ochs, E., & Capps, L. (1996). Narrating the self. *Annual Review of Anthropology, 25*, 19–43.

Reinard, J. C. (1988). The empirical study of the persuasive effects of evidence: The status after 50 years of research. *Human Communication Research, 15*, 3–59.

Reynolds, R. A., & Reynolds, J. L. (2002). Evidence. In J. P. Dillard & M. Pfau (Eds.), *The persuasion handbook: Developments in theory and practice* (pp. 427–444). Thousand Oaks, CA: Sage.

Rothschild, M. L. (1999). Carrots, sticks, and promises: A conceptual framework for the management of public health and social issue behaviors. *Journal of Marketing, 63*, 24–37.

Rothschild, M. L., Mastin, B., & Miller, T. W. (2006). Reducing alcohol-impaired driving crashes through the use of social marketing. *Accident Analysis & Prevention, 38*, 1218–1230.

Schank, R. C., & Berman, T. R. (2002). The persuasive roles of stories in knowledge and action. In M. C. Green, J. J. Strange, & T. C. Brock (Eds.), *Narrative impact: Social and cognitive foundations* (pp. 287–313). Mahwah, NJ: Erlbaum.

Schellstede, W. P., & Ciszewski, R. L. (1984). Social marketing of contraceptives in Bangladesh. *Studies in Family Planning, 15*, 30–39.

Smith, W. A. (2000). Social marketing: An evolving definition. *American Journal of Health Behavior, 24*, 11–17.

Smith, W. A. (2006). Social marketing: An overview of approach and effects. *Injury Prevention, 12*, i38–i43.

Spitzberg, B. H. (2003). Methods of interpersonal skill assessment. In J. O. Greene & B. R. Burleson (Eds.), *Handbook of communication and social interaction skills* (pp. 93–194). Mahwah, NJ: Erlbaum.

Street, Jr., R. L. (2003). Interpersonal communication skills in health care contexts. In J. O. Greene & B. R. Burleson (Eds.), *Handbook of communication and social interaction skills* (pp. 909–934). Mahwah, NJ: Erlbaum.

Sublet, V. H., & Lum, M. R. (2008). Use of health communication and social marketing principles in planning occupational safety and health interventions. *Social Marketing Quarterly, 14*, 45–70.

Sun, X., Guo, Y., Wang, S., & Sun, J. (2007). Social marketing improved the consumption of iron-fortified soy sauce among women in China. *Journal of Nutrition Education and Behavior, 39*, 302–310.

Thompson, T. L., & Parrott, R. (2002). Interpersonal communication and health care. In M. L. Knapp & J. A. Daly (Eds.), *Handbook of interpersonal communication* (3rd ed., pp. 680–725). Thousand Oaks, CA: Sage.

Warnick, E., Dearden, K. A., Slater, S., Butrón, B., Lanata, C. F., & Huffman, S. L. (2004). Social marketing improved the use of multivitamin and mineral supplements among resource-poor women in Bolivia. *Journal of Nutrition Education and Behavior, 36,* 290–297.

Wiebe, G. D. (1951–1952). Merchandising commodities and citizenship on television. *Public Opinion Quarterly, 15,* 679–691.

Williams, P. G., Dewapura, D., Gunawardene, P., & Settinayake, S. (1998). Social marketing to eliminate leprosy in Sri Lanka. *Social Marketing Quarterly, 4,* 27–31.

Wong, F., Huhman, M., Heitzler, C., Asbury, L., Bretthauer-Mueller, R., McCarthy, S., & Londe, P. (2004). VERB™—A social marketing campaign to increase physical activity among youth. *Preventing Chronic Disease, 1,* 1–7.

Wong, F., Greenwell, M., Gates, S., & Berkowitz, J. (2008). It's what you do! Reflections on the VERB™ campaign [Supplement]. *American Journal of Preventive Medicine, 34,* S175–S182.

Zillmann, D. (1999). Exemplification theory: Judging the whole by some of its parts. *Media Psychology, 1,* 69–94.

16

POPULAR MEDIA AND HEALTH

Images and Effects

Kimberly N. Kline

Violet has just found out she's pregnant; she wasn't planning on this and she doesn't know which of the two sexual partners she's been with in the past few months is the father. Obviously, Violet hasn't been using a condom. This is particularly surprising since this Harvard-educated psychiatrist works at a clinic that specializes in sexual health. Both of her sexual partners are doctors, one of whom has previously owned an infectious diseases practice (he's recently had another sexual partner who is also a physician just returned to the US from Ghana). It seems like all of these individuals would be aware that, in addition to the possibility of unplanned pregnancy, each year in the United States alone around 19 million men and women of all economic levels are affected by sexually transmitted illnesses (STIs; http://www.womenshealth.gov/faq/sexually-transmitted-infections.cfm#b). The good news is that Violet is a character in the highly acclaimed television show *Private Practice*. Good news, that is, except that the take home message for over 9 million viewers was that even physicians, presumably the most credible of all sources for health information, don't find it necessary to use condoms to protect their sexual health. As detailed in this chapter, that these physicians were virtual role models does not ameliorate the impact on social understandings of health.

As the use of health, illness, and medicine to attract audiences and advertising revenue escalates (Radley, Lupton, & Ritter, 1997), advertisement, entertainment, and news media are increasingly saturated with health messages. Health communication scholars have long recognized that the mass media serve as a powerful socializing agent (Croteau & Hoynes, 1997) and it has been well-established that it is crucial to understand how values, beliefs, and norms associated with health, illness, and medicine are affected by interaction with mass mediated messages. Indeed, mass mediated messages are an integral part of health promotion; however, reference to *popular* mass media presumes nothing other than the absence of communication identifiably and strategically designed for a definable health campaign goal and thus refers to the domains of advertising, news, and entertainment (Kline, 2003). Since popular health media research debuted in the mid-1980s (Freimuth, Greenberg, DeWitt, & Romano, 1984; Gerbner, Gross, Morgan, & Signorielli, 1981; Turow & Coe, 1985), there has been a proliferation of popular media research related to health, illness, and medicine

(Kline, 2003, 2006). In this chapter, I review research on health in the entertainment and journalistic popular media in terms of representation and audience effects.

Health Images in the Popular Mass Media

The preponderance of research devoted to the role of the popular mass media in meaning-making related to health, illness, and medicine focuses on the messages to which people are being exposed. Grounded in the assumption that the mass media have at least some cognitive, affective, or behavioral influence, this approach asks the question, "What is being said in these depictions?" An assessment of messages to which people are being exposed helps us understand at least some of the knowledge and experiences people have had with regard to health issues.

The Informational Value of Popular Media Health Messages

Given our culture's heavy emphasis on science as a source of knowledge, we typically think of information as a collection of facts or data derived from scientific study. When it comes to health issues, we generally think of "facts" as credentialed information about such issues as the severity of a disease, a person's susceptibility to that disease including risk factors, disease symptoms, or details about the recommended response to reduce the health threat. The informational value of a discourse may be influenced by the depiction of role models who provide clues about appropriate or desirable health practices, perhaps considered "'rules for living' or implicit instructions on how to do something" (Grossberg, Wartella, & Whitney, 1998, p. 150). A mainstay of health media research, Social Learning Theory (Bandura, 1977) suggests that people often learn by observing what other individuals do rather than by their own trial-and-error actions.

Notably, role models do not have to be "real" people. Fictional characters can become "media role models, unobtrusively teaching the viewing public about [a] disease, especially the psychological and social difficulties it engenders" (Sharf & Freimuth, 1993, p. 145). Thus, we may tend to think of news as information, relegating the content of entertainment to fiction and advertisements to persuasion, but entertainment and advertising provide information about health, illness, and medicine as well. As Sharf and Freimuth (1993) suggest, entertainment television provides people with health information in the form of narrative portrayals of illness (p. 141). Information, then, is a product of a variety of mass-mediated discourse, and those who analyze mass media texts often do so to assess their information value in terms of relevance, accuracy, and sufficiency.

To some extent, media research has identified some positive health representations, as when Jensen and Jensen (2007) found that the television show *Sex and the City* was more likely to portray "healthy sex," or "intercourse between established partners (rather than between partners who had just met) and ... depictions of sexual risks and responsibilities (i.e., sexual patience, precaution, and risks/negative consequences)" (p. 282). Unfortunately, a more common finding was that the information value of health messages was often seriously compromised by misrepresentations, omissions, and inappropriate role modeling.

Inferior Information. Less common than might be assumed, some mass media research exposed factual inaccuracies in health information. For instance, Pruitt and Mullin (2005) found that newspapers consistently confused emergency contraception with medical abortion. This misrepresentation was patently incorrect since, "Emergency contraception works by preventing ovulation, fertilization or implantation and does not disturb an implanted egg" whereas "medications or devices acting after implantation are regarded as abortifacients rather than contraceptives" (Pruitt & Mullen, 2005, p. 15). The authors' concern was that this error "may have contributed to incorrect beliefs about a form of contraception that is used or offered infrequently, despite its potential to deter unintended pregnancy and abortion" (p. 19).

A more common finding than gross inaccuracy, however, was that mass mediated health information was potentially misleading because of the manner in which the issue was framed. The concept of framing refers to the way writers represent a particular story (see, for example, Clarke, 2005). As Wallack and colleagues (1993) pointed out, "Everything cannot be said about every issue in every story in the short space of a newspaper article or television broadcast. Certain things are included in the package, while other aspects are left out" (p. 68). The way in which certain aspects of issues were selected and emphasized in recounting led to a number of different types of framing dilemmas.

One framing issue frequently commented upon was the *incomplete coverage or avoidance* of certain health topics. For example, when breast cancer was discussed in television and print news stories, information about environmental risks from pharmaceuticals such as Hormone Replacement Therapy (HRT) was often provided. On the other hand, information about risks related to lifestyle practices and other environmental contaminants (i.e., tobacco smoke or other chemical contaminants) was neglected (Atkin, Smith, McFeters, & Ferguson, 2008). Likewise, newspaper reports of genetic research, though accurate, tended to overemphasize behavioral genetics such as genes for sexual orientation, alcoholism, mental illness, or criminality (Bubela & Caulfield, 2004). Reports related to the Human Papilloma Virus (HPV) vaccine did not acknowledge the disease was sexually transmitted and avoided discussion of the need to continue cervical cancer screening after being vaccinated (Kelly, Leader, Mittermaier, Hornik, & Cappella, 2009). Television news reports about organ donation were overall positive, but did not provide enough information about current shortage of organs or how to become an organ donor (Quick, Kim, & Meyer, 2009).

Misrepresentation (i.e., over- or under-reporting) was especially common when reporting about the prevalence of certain health threats. The mass media selectively cover certain health topics so the "scope of illnesses attended to in the media do not reflect prevalent health threats" (for UK journalistic selectivity, see Harrabin, Coote, & Allen, 2003; Kline, 2006, p. 46). Breast cancer, for example, was over-represented in comparison to lung cancer in newspapers, magazines, and TV news (Slater, Long, Bettinghaus, & Reineke, 2008) and in comparison to cardio-vascular disease (CVD) in popular magazines (Blanchard, Erblich, Montgomery, & Bovbjerg, 2002). Possibly the greatest sin of omission, however, was the disregard for the health information needs of various socio-demographic groups. One study (Armstrong, Carpenter, & Hojnacki, 2006) found that print and broadcast media attend less to diseases that disproportionately burden blacks relative to whites (Cohen et al., 2008), and that stories did not accurately reflect the impact of different cancers on African American mortality, regardless of whether the media were mainstream or targeted to African Americans. In cases where information was incomplete or absent, the problem was not so much that the information provided was inaccurate or even problematic; rather the problem was that additional information about the subject was needed in order for individuals to make truly informed health decisions.

Negative Role Modeling. Though there seem to be fewer studies that address role models, research indicates that characters in television shows and movies *role model unhealthy behaviors* and *downplay possible negative effects.* For instance, in youth oriented films, problem foods like oils, solid fats, and foods with added sugars were over-represented (Greenberg, Rosaen, Worrell, Salmon, & Volkman, 2009) in terms of being offered and consumed, and under-represented were injury safety practices such as safety belt, helmet, and personal flotation device use, or the use of a crosswalk and looking both ways when crossing a street (Pelletier et al., 2000). In top grossing films from 1999 to 2001, teen characters often smoked cigarettes, drank alcohol, and used illicit drugs, typically without consequence (Stern, 2005); GLBT newspapers and magazines glamorized tobacco use, associating smoking with celebrities (E. A. Smith, Offen, & Malone, 2006); and in men's magazines such as *Maxim, Men's Health,* and *GQ* "the smoking man is sensuous, mysterious, independent, and in some other place that is different from the mundane locales of everyday life" (Dutta & Boyd, 2007, p. 261).

Textual analysis has been useful in pointing out the information deficits and defects in a variety of media, and, in some cases, identifying potentially health promoting depictions. However, many contemporary scholars of health-related popular mass media are concerned with social, political, and economic influences on health, illness, and medical issues. In particular, these scholars address the ways in which health discourses participate in the constitution, reflection, and re-creation of cultural ideologies and hegemonies.

Ideological Hegemony in Popular Media Health Messages

Most media analysts recognize that the mass media are not just suppliers of information, but are made up of a group of institutions which wield at least some power to influence emotions, beliefs, attitudes, and behaviors. Contemporary media scholars acknowledge that the power of the mass media extend well beyond suppliers of information and role modeling and into the realm of politics and ideology. In part, mass media serve an agenda-setting function (P. A. Collins, Abelson, Pyman, & Lavis, 2006). By repeatedly covering certain issues, the mass media focus attention on some issues and deflect attention away from others, effectively setting the agenda for public debate (McCombs, 1994) and, consequently, contributing to public policy outcomes (e.g., Feeley & Vincent, 2007; Turow & Coe, 1993). By assessing the content of mass media, we may identify which issues are being promoted, the range of viewpoints depicted, and the solutions being proposed, and the implications if public policy follows from these representations.

Other media theorists conceptualize the mass media as having more substantial power in that it constitutes, maintains, and perpetuates, that is, cultivates, dominant cultural ideologies (Gerbner, Gross, Morgan, & Signorielli, 1994). Discourse does not describe the material world; rather, people use symbolic constructs to give meaning to their world. Lupton (2000) summarized the constructionist perspective with regard to health issues thus:

> For most social constructionists, the types of knowledges that are developed and brought to bear upon health, illness, and medical care may be regarded as assemblages of beliefs that are created through human interaction and preexisting meanings. This perspective contrasts with the traditional view of medicine, which sees disease as being located in the body as a physical object of physical state that can be objectively identified and treated as a physiological condition by scientific medical knowledge.
>
> (p. 50)

Essentially, meanings associated with health, illness, and medicine are not fixed and static entities waiting to be discovered and documented. Rather, they are a function of the complex and dynamic personal and social values of all interactants and "must be considered and made explicit if illness and health-care problems are to be satisfactorily dealt with" (Conrad & Kern, 1990).

Scholars interested in the political and ideological function of popular media often seek to identify the meanings and ideologies related to health, illness, and medicine fostered by the mass media, explicate the way the media constitute and reflect related meanings, and pinpoint the hegemonic arrangements that are instantiated by mass media representations. A common thread in critical analysis was the identification of the ideological themes that are constituted, maintained, and perpetuated by health discourses. These themes included the professionalizing and technologizing of health care whereby the contemporary medical establishment laid claim to legitimate power in the realm of health and illness; the medicalization of the body in order to expand the purview of medical establishment control; the individualization of health and illness, which fostered condemnation of those who succumbed to a health threat; and gender stereotyping, which positions women and men as differentially accountable for social health problems. Overall, research suggests that mass media portrayals are, at best, inappropriate and unethical, and at worst, socially, mentally, and physically threatening.

Professionalizing and Technologizing. So well-accepted are contemporary medical practices that most people forget that such practices are relatively new. Analysts distressed that the preeminence of medical authority constitutes a medical hegemony (see Foucault, 1973) have focused a number of their studies on the way in which representations legitimize the authority of practitioners schooled in institutionally accepted medical practices. Critics continue to be troubled with the tendency to cite purported experts rather than those who have suffered from a particular problem (Clarke & Binns, 2006), activists, or health care providers who might offer less mainstream explanations. Likewise, scholars lament the reliance on a biomedical paradigm with its corollary emphasis on technological (Harter & Japp, 2001) and pharmacological solutions to health problems.

Medicalizing. While the concept of professionalization suggests that the domain of health care has been claimed by an elite collective of medical professionals, the concept of *medicalization* suggests that the medical institution continuously strives to broaden its reach (Zola, 1972). Critiques of medicalizing discourse refer to the need to pathologize women's normal bodily processes in order to claim medical jurisdiction (Kline, 2007; Metzl & Angel, 2004). Other scholars introduce new realms of medicalization such as sleep "disorders" (Coveney, Nerlich, & Martin, 2009; Seale, Boden, Williams, Lowe, & Steinberg, 2007; Williams, Seale, Boden, Lowe, & Steinberg, 2008a, 2008b). Critical interpretive research suggests that popular media medicalize health and illness via nearly exclusive reference to medical models without portraying the role of politics in decision making and deflecting attention from non-medical strategies for resolution.

Individualizing. The concept of individualizing refers to the presumption that individuals are responsible for the cause and cure of health threats (Becker, 1986). For instance, Roy's (2008, p. 63) analysis revealed that English-Canadian women's magazines "consistently present health as an important individual responsibility and a moral imperative which creates an entrepreneurial subject position for women" (see also Campo & Mastin, 2007;

Gattuso, Fullagar, & Young, 2005). Kim and Willis (2007) echo this concern, but also note that more recently with regard to news framing of obesity there is an increase of references to societal causes. In part, the concern with an individualizing approach is that it may reinforce the castigation of individuals for health problems over which they have little or no control. In other words, it allows for the moralization of illness which concomitantly allows illness sufferers to be stigmatized based on their disease. Insofar as diseases are thought to be biological threats which exist independently of the body, unlike illness which is typically understood as the subjective experience of a disease, diseases are not generally regarded as subject to ethical evaluation. Yet, numerous critical studies have illustrated the manner in which "diseases are given meanings and carry attributions in the media" (Clarke, 1992, p. 115) including mental illness (Olstead, 2002; Wahl, Wood, Zaveri, Drapalski, & Mann, 2003) and drug addiction during pregnancy (Meyers, 2004). Even with childhood cancer, there is a certain stigma attached as "it may be that the fact that there is an overwhelming emphasis on the polarized differences between normal childhood and family life before cancer serves to separate the social world into normal children with normal families and others" (i.e., not normal) (Clarke, 2005, p. 602).

Gender Stereotyping. Another common ideological theme censured by scholars was the persistent gender stereotypes associated with health representations; perhaps most interesting were the contrasts in gender representations. With regard to health in general, it appears that men take responsibility for their own well-being (Crawshaw, 2007), whereas women maintain the caretaking feminine stereotype (Barnett, 2006). With regard to portrayals of people with cancer, for men it was "a test of pre-existing character," while for women it was an opportunity to demonstrate their skills "in the emotional labour of self-transformation" (Seale, 2002, p. 107). When it came to dieting, men were naïve and vulnerable, while women were experts (see also Gough, 2006, 2007). Similarly, traditional gender stereotypes were reinforced in sexual health content where men sought sex and women were responsible for birth control (Hust, Brown, & L'Engle, 2008). Indeed, Crawshaw's (2007) analysis of the United Kingdom magazine *Men's Health* revealed that representations promoted the idea that having regular sex was necessary for male health, so much so that men were encouraged to have casual sex (despite the public health goal of raising awareness of the risks associated with casual sex).

Popular Mass Media Audiences

Though it is reasonable and valid for researchers to "investigate media content as a gauge of social norms, values, and the interests of society in general" (Croteau & Hoynes, 1997, p. 136), it is also the case that these are inferential assessments of potential effects on both society and the individual. As Signorielli (1993) cautioned, "these comparisons tell us how the [media] world deviates from reality and helps us ascertain what consequences these deviations might have for action, thinking, and policy" (p. 4). Still, these studies rely on an assumption of probabilistic effects of popular media messages in the "real world." More specifically, health communication scholars are interested in how actual audiences make sense of health-related popular media representations.

General Observations about Audience Effects

In general, audience reception research is equivocal with regard to whether popular media undermine or contribute to health. In the past, the overall consensus was that popular media, especially entertainment media, had detrimental effects on audiences (Signorielli, 1993). Certainly, research continues to find popular media troubling from a public health perspective. Television and cinema representations can foster early-onset of risky behaviors including the use of alcohol (Sargent, Wills, Stoolmiller, Gibson, & Gibbons, 2006), smoking (Primack, Land, & Fine, 2008; Tanski et al., 2009), and sexual activity (Brown et al., 2006; R. L. Collins et al., 2004). Children demonstrate reduced nutritional knowledge as a result of watching TV (Harrison, 2005). Magazines promote tobacco use through attractive smoking imagery (MacFadyen, Amos, Hastings, & Parkes, 2003) and encourage a desire to be thin (Sung-Yeon, 2005), which can lead to eating disorders.

However, it appears that the audience effects of popular media health representations are not all bad; that is, popular media can advance public health goals. News reports of the connection between the Human Papilloma Virus (HPV) and cervical cancer were associated with greater HPV knowledge (Kelly et al., 2009). When the popular television show *ER* included a storyline of an African American teen who was diagnosed with hypertension and then given diet and exercise advice, audiences reported, among other effects, walking or exercising more and eating more fruits and vegetables (Valente et al., 2007). When this same show aired two storylines about syphilis in men who have sex with men (MSM), audience members reported intentions to get screened and to tell others to get screened (Whittier, Kennedy, St. Lawrence, Seeley, & Beck, 2005). The often positive impact of breast cancer media representations has been explored in a number of studies. Breast cancer genetics storylines on popular television shows *ER* and *Grey's Anatomy* had a modest impact on viewers' knowledge, attitudes, and behaviors related to breast cancer (Hether, Huang, Beck, Murphy, & Valente, 2008). Even as family members, friends, and the medical community were major sources for breast cancer information, a number of "memorable messages" about breast cancer detection, awareness, treatment, and prevention are taken from journalistic media (S. W. Smith et al., 2009). Moreover, journalistic media contributed to mammography utilization, especially for women who had no regular contact with a physician (Yanovitzky & Blitz, 2000).

In short, research has consistently found that health depictions which run contrary to public health concerns are likely to encourage detrimental health knowledge, attitudes/ beliefs, and behaviors; pro-health messages tend to have beneficial audience effects. Certainly, any effect is tempered by the veracity of the content presented. When researchers compared audience response data to media content analyses, they found that audience knowledge generally mirrored the media messages (Stryker, Moriarty, & Jensen, 2008). Yet, even acknowledging that variation in media content can alter audience effects still implies a fairly direct effects model and this appears to be far too simplistic. Current audience effects research has become increasingly more nuanced, recognizing that numerous individual and social variables confound the effects of mediated health messages.

Moderating Variables Associated with Audience Effects

As I mentioned above, textual analytic research focuses on the messages to which people are being exposed. Audience effects researchers take this issue one step further and consider whether audiences are paying attention to these messages. As Slater, Hayes, and Ford (2007) point out, "exposure may be a necessary, but not sufficient, condition for media to affect individual beliefs" (p. 357). Moreover, in an era of diverse and ubiquitous mass media influences, scholars recognize that not all media formats are used equally (Pollard,

2003; Purvis Cooper, Burgoon, & Roter, 2001). In other words, various audiences are likely to glean health understandings from different media. As Dutta-Bergman (2004; see also Dutta, 2007) demonstrated, health-conscious individuals use active media channels, including print media and the Internet, whereas less health-oriented individuals tend to use passive consumption channels such as television and radio. More to the point, a number of individual and social variables moderate the effects of popular media on even attentive audiences.

Scholars recognize that *individual differences* alter understandings of mediated messages. Interpersonal relationships influence audience interpretations. For instance, parent involvement can impinge on the way that adolescents negotiate mediated messages related to alcohol (Austin & Chen, 2003) and condoms (R. L. Collins, Elliott, Berry, Kanouse, & Hunter, 2003). Audience member personal attitudes and beliefs, too, are brought to bear on interpretations. Though news coverage about the health risks of marijuana use to some extent influences adolescent abstinence, personal disapproval of marijuana is a mediating variable (Stryker, 2003). When it comes to adolescent judgments of alcohol-related risks as represented in accident and crime news stories, sensation seeking and negative personal experiences with alcohol are individual factors that mediate attention to the stories (Slater et al., 2007). Moreover, individual circumstances that relate to the specific health threat represented can affect understandings. Thus, when women were asked how they understood fish consumption safety messages, they indicated that personal relevance of eating fish and barriers to eating fish were taken into consideration when assessing the threat to their families (Vardeman & Aldoory, 2008).

In addition to individual differences, the social context of mediated messages can factor into effects on audiences. Studies show that rather than a direct causal association between media coverage of a particular health risk and audience perceptions, public policy actions are a mediating factor. Thus, media coverage is associated with changes in public policy actions which, in turn, are associated with public perception. Yanovitzky (2002), for example, demonstrated that news coverage contributes to drunk driving related policy actions, which then contributes to reduced drunk driving among young and high-risk drivers (see also Yanovitzky & Stryker, 2001 with regard to binge drinking). This path from media coverage to public policy to audience effects is even more complicated when considering how public policy is influenced by media coverage. Slater, Lawrence, and Comello (2009) suggest that attention to stories about violent crime and accidents leads to greater concern about alcohol-related injuries due to assault and accidents, which then leads to perceptions of alcohol's contribution to these injuries, and this, in turn, leads to support for various alcohol control policies. The implications for media advocacy are less elaborate; rather than attempting to influence thematic media coverage, media advocates must encourage reporting of crime and injury news that "more accurately reflects the possible causal role of alcohol in the incident" (Slater et al., 2009, p. 273).

Overall, research focused on the audiences of popular mass media indicates that the mass media do impinge on health, illness, and medically oriented understandings and behaviors. Still, if it is the case that popular mass media have great potential to advance the cause of health promotion, judging by the popular media research it is a potential that has yet to be fully realized. Despite the intuitive appeal of popular mass media as a venue for advancing health, any efforts to commandeer the mass media for health promotional use will encounter significant institutional obstacles.

Institutional Processes and Competing Agendas Entertainment and Health

The relationship between the popular mass media and health promotion is fraught with conflicting priorities (Wallack, 1990). Increasingly, scholars have detailed the institutional expectations that have led to troubling health representations in popular media. Each domain—journalism, entertainment, and advertising—is characterized by certain problems and possibilities. To counteract these problems, health promotion experts actively seek to influence the producers of health messages in the popular media. Today, there is perhaps no better evidence of the widespread concern with the ways in which popular media influence public health concerns than the debut of such groups as the Association of Health Care Journalists http://www.healthjournalism.org) and Hollywood, Health and Society (HH&S; http://www.learcenter.org/html/projects/?cm=hhs).

When health promotion specialists attempt to influence journalistic representations, it is called "media advocacy." As Glik (2004) explained, "Important components in this process include framing the health problems as social justice issues rather than individual tragedies, as well as networking with news media writers to 'pitch' stories and get issues of interest in the local press." The CDC has been a leader in working to influence journalistic media representations of public health issues, with more (Mebane, Temin, & Pravanta, 2003) or less (Barrett, 2005) success.

Alternatively, when health promotion specialists endeavor to integrate pro-health messages in entertainment media, it is called "entertainment-education" (EE).[1] It stands to reason that if entertainment media can have a negative influence on health behaviors, they should also be able to have a positive influence. That is the premise on which health promoters who advocate entertainment-education are banking. EE, as defined in Roberto et al.'s chapter, focuses on the strategic use of entertainment media to educate an audience. Until recently, most entertainment-education activities have been conducted in resource-poor countries, rather than the United States (see chapter 14 for a review of EE in international contexts).

There have been some EE initiatives conducted in the United States with varying degrees of success. Singhal et al.'s (2004) edited volume on entertainment-education includes brief mentions of *Maude* (one of the first sitcoms to address a social issue when 47-year-old Maude decided to obtain an abortion), the Harvard Alcohol Project for Designated Drivers (which prompted 77 prime-time programs to promote the designated-driver concept), *Sesame Street* (which introduced numerous pro-social messages to children aged 2 to 5), and the two series *Cancion de la Raza* and *Que Pasa, U.S.A.* (which addressed social issues relevant to Mexican Americans and Cuban Americans, respectively). HH&S also has consulted on such television shows as *Bones, Crossing Jordon, CSI Miami, Grey's Anatomy, House, Law and Order, Malcolm in the Middle, Numbers, Bold and the Beautiful, General Hospital, The Young and the Restless, Telemundo, Desperate Housewives,* and *ER.*

While health promotion experts are identifying strategies for facilitating more successful EE interventions in the United States (Beck, 2004; Glik, 2004), US EE initiatives still face numerous barriers (Glik, 2004; Glik et al., 1998; Wilson & Beck, 2002). In their case study of HH&S's work with the primetime drama *Numbers*, for example, Movius and colleagues (2007) explained that despite efforts to educate the writer that a black market for organ donations does not exist in the United States, the storyline was based on this premise. However, due largely to the EE effort, the show "provided considerable accurate information about the number of people on the transplant waiting list … the computer system for organ matching [and] an extensive discussion about the importance of organ donation around the detectives' family dinner table" (Movius et al., 2007, n.p.). Such successes motivate health promoters to continue efforts to collaborate with the entertainment industry.

There are challenges associated with the use of EE as a strategic approach to health promotion. Wallack (1990) argued that it is precisely the narrative elements that are necessary for this storytelling medium (Glik et al., 1998) that undercut the potential for integrating pro-social messages in entertainment programming. "Television takes social and health issues and reduces them to personal emotional dramas," contended Wallack (1990, p. 45). This may contribute stigma and victim-blaming and, again, may deflect attention from larger social, political, and economic influences, thereby limiting understanding of causes and solutions of health problems. Consequently, attempts to utilize entertainment media to forward public health agendas should be tempered by the realization that such activities might exacerbate existing problems. Despite this caveat, popular health media scholars can provide media producers with advice on how to develop health promoting messages. For instance, in their analysis of women's magazine representations of coping with breast cancer, Gill and Babrow (2007) acknowledge that "to conjure cancer in language is necessarily to construct terrifying uncertainty and heart-rending ambivalence" (p. 150). They then suggest ways that observations from their analysis and "relevant theory can be used to suggest less problematic, more helpful constructions" (p. 150).

Future Directions for Research in Popular Media and Health

As this chapter has illustrated, there is considerable interest regarding the relationship between the popular media and social understandings of health issues. Numerous scholars have detailed the informational and ideological shortcomings of the popular media, while others have advocated the strategic use of popular programming to advance public health agendas. All agree that the pervasiveness and influence of the popular mass media are not to be ignored. Scholars must continue the project of identifying the manner in which discourse impinges on the meanings and behaviors related to health and illness, employing a variety of methodologies and perspectives.

It is important that scholars continue delineating the symbolic content of media messages because "locating the repeated biases in modes of delivering messages may assist media consumers in becoming media literate, granting the skills necessary to 'read' health care messages in a critical and productive fashion" (Parrott & Condit, 1996, p. 7). However, even as scholars continue to describe the ways that the mass media invite individuals to understand health issues, scholars must be careful not to fall into the trap of presuming the possibility of what Edward Schiappa (2008) refers to as "representational correctness." The standard of representational correctness presumes that "popular culture texts have a primary, or at least a preferred or dominant, meaning that a discerning critic can *independently* determine and analyze" (p. 10), "that socio-politically good texts cause good effects, and that socio-politically bad texts cause bad effects" (p. 11), and that it is feasible to simultaneously avoid stereotyping, ideological contradictions, and insulting groups depicted (p. 9). Schiappa argues that meeting all these expectations is impossible.

As this review confirms, research concerned with media representations of health and illness issues generally take two different approaches: They either identify whether the media messages provide appropriate and accurate coverage of available research and health recommendations or address the social and political implications of media representations. Either way, there is a tendency to reduce analyses to dichotomous assessments. With regard to informational value, representations are right/wrong, good/bad, or accurate/inaccurate;

with regard to critical assessments, representations privilege/marginalize voices. The problem is that these approaches assume "there is such a thing as a 'correct' representation... to which [media producers] ought to aspire" (p. 6). Schiappa counsels media scholars to pay closer attention to how audience members make meaning from the representations. In their audience analytic study of how individuals with multiple sclerosis (MS) interpret depictions of MS in the primetime television show *The West Wing*, Zoller and Worrell (2006) found that there were diverse responses and these were often linked to the individual's own illness experience. Davin (2003) compared audience reactions to parallel illness narratives in a soap opera and a documentary and found that audiences "produce complex, multi-layered, sometimes contradictory and/or unexpected interpretations" (p. 674). Thus, in addition to pursuing research which focuses on the textual elements of popular media representations, scholars must address the manner in which these discourses affect the lived experiences of audience members.

Audience analytic research must also take care not to reduce assessments to simple direct effects—bad/good role models lead to bad/good health behaviors, more information leads to more knowledge. Audiences are increasingly more diverse, faced with a multiplicity of health threats, and bombarded with health messages from a proliferation of media. A growing body of research demonstrates that interpersonal, individual, and social influences impinge on the interpretation of mediated messages. Or, as Condit (1989) explained, audiences are polyvalent. That is, audience members may share understandings of a particular denotative message in a mediated text, but because of individual differences they may value the messages in such a way that they generate markedly distinct interpretations. If health promoters hope to employ popular media to forward health agendas, they must carefully attend to audience variability.

Whether engaging in textual or audience analysis or some combination of both, scholars of popular health discourse must strive to develop theories which can be used not only to describe discursive situations, but also to explain the relationships between health discourse, people, and society. Ultimately, theoretical projects should contribute to prescriptions of more ethical and effective approaches to addressing health issues in the popular media. Thus far, the primary focus of extant research on popular health discourse has been on describing discourses specific to a particular health issue (e.g., smoking, diet, HIV/AIDS, breast cancer, etc.). Yet, for most scholars concerned with health discourse, the ultimate goal is to prompt improvement of the discourse, whether such improvement refers to increasing the informational value or the persuasiveness with regard to individual behavior and social/public policy changes, or to emend ideological instantiations constituted by the discourse. Therefore, research projects should begin to synthesize the approaches and concepts generated from diverse studies to develop broader, more systematic explanations for the observations being made. As scholars begin to develop these theories, they should do so with a keen awareness of the potential for uniting theory and praxis not only to promote better health, but to promote better health discourses.

Note

1. Occasionally, health media researchers refer to health messages that are not necessarily intended to be promotional as EE initiatives. For instance, Gray (2007) refers to the breast cancer storyline on *Sex and the City* as entertainment-education, but there is no evidence that health promoters influenced the producers.

References

Armstrong, E. M., Carpenter, D. P., & Hojnacki, M. (2006). Whose deaths matter? Mortality, advocacy, and attention to disease in the mass media. *Journal of Health Politics, Policy & Law, 31*, 729–772.

Atkin, C. K., Smith, S. W., McFeters, C., & Ferguson, V. (2008). A comprehensive analysis of breast cancer news coverage in leading media outlets focusing on environmental risks and prevention. *Journal of Health Communication, 13*, 3–19.

Austin, E. W., & Chen, Y. J. (2003). The relationship of parental reinforcement of media messages to college students' alcohol-related behaviors. *Journal of Health Communication, 8*, 157–169.

Bandura, A. (1977). *Social learning theory.* Englewood Cliffs, NJ: Prentice-Hall.

Barnett, B. (2006). Health as women's work: A pilot study on how women's magazines frame medical news and femininity. *Women & Language, 29*, 1–12.

Barrett, M. S. (2005). Spokespersons and message control: How the CDC lost credibility during the anthrax crisis. *Qualitative Research Reports in Communication, 6*, 59–68.

Beck, V. (2004). Working with daytime and prime-time television shows in the United States to promote health. In A. Singhal, M. J. Cody, E. M. Rogers, & M. Sabido (Eds.), *Entertainment-education and social change: History, research, and practice* (pp. 207–224). Mahwah, NJ: Erlbaum.

Becker, M. H. (1986). The tyranny of health promotion. *Public Health Reviews, 14*, 15–25.

Blanchard, D., Erblich, J., Montgomery, G. H., & Bovbjerg, D. H. (2002). Read all about it: The over-representation of breast cancer in popular magazines. *Preventive Medicine, 35*, 343–348.

Brown, J. D., L'Engle, K. L., Pardun, C. J., Guang, G., Kenneavy, K., & Jackson, C. (2006). Sexy media matter: Exposure to sexual content in music, movies, television, and magazines predicts black and white adolescents' sexual behavior. *Pediatrics, 117*, 1018–1027.

Bubela, T. M., & Caulfield, T. A. (2004). Do the print media "hype" genetic research? A comparison of newspaper stories and peer-reviewed research papers. *CMAJ: Canadian Medical Association Journal, 170*, 1399–1407.

Campo, S., & Mastin, T. (2007). Placing the burden on the individual: Overweight and obesity in African American and mainstream women's magazines. *Health Communication, 22*, 229–240.

Clarke, J. N. (1992). Cancer, heart disease, and AIDS: What do the media tell us about these diseases? *Health Communication, 4*, 105–120.

Clarke, J. N. (2005). Portrayal of childhood cancer in English language magazines in North America: 1970–2001. *Journal of Health Communication, 10*, 593–607.

Clarke, J. N., & Binns, J. (2006). The portrayal of heart disease in mass print magazines, 1991–2001. *Health Communication, 19*, 39–48.

Cohen, E. L., Caburnay, C. A., Luke, D. A., Rodgers, S., Cameron, G. T., & Kreuter, M. W. (2008). Cancer coverage in general-audience and Black newspapers. *Health Communication, 23*, 427–435.

Collins, P. A., Abelson, J., Pyman, H., & Lavis, J. N. (2006). Are we expecting too much from print media? An analysis of newspaper coverage of the 2002 Canadian healthcare reform debate. *Social Science & Medicine, 63*, 89–102.

Collins, R. L., Elliott, M. N., Berry, S. H., Kanouse, D. E., & Hunter, S. B. (2003). Entertainment television as a healthy sex educator: The impact of condom-efficacy information in an episode of Friends. *Pediatrics, 112*, 1115–1121.

Collins, R. L., Elliott, M. N., Berry, S. H., Kanouse, D. E., Kunkel, D., Hunter, S. B., & Miu, A. (2004). Watching sex on television predicts adolescent initiation of sexual behavior. *Pediatrics, 114*, 280–289.

Condit, C. M. (1989). The rhetorical limits of polysemy. *Critical Studies in Mass Communication, 6*, 103–122.

Conrad, P., & Kern, R. (1990). *The sociology of health and Illness: Critical perspectives* (3rd ed.). New York: St. Martin's Press.

Coveney, C. M., Nerlich, B., & Martin, P. (2009). Modafinil in the media: Metaphors, medicalisation and the body. *Social Science & Medicine, 68*, 487–495.

Crawshaw, P. (2007). Governing the healthy male citizen: Men, masculinity and popular health in *Men's Health* magazine. *Social Science & Medicine, 65*, 1606–1618.

Croteau, D., & Hoynes, W. (1997). *Media/society: Industries, images, and audiences.* Thousand Oaks, CA: Pine Forge.

Davin, S. (2003). Healthy viewing: The reception of medical narratives. *Sociology of Health and Illness, 25*, 662–679.

Dutta, M. J. (2007). Health information processing from television: The role of health orientation. *Health Communication, 21*, 1–9.

Dutta, M. J., & Boyd, J. (2007). Turning "smoking man" images around: Portrayals of smoking in men's magazines as a blueprint for smoking cessation campaigns. *Health Communication, 22*, 253–263.

Dutta-Bergman, M. J. (2004). Primary sources of health information: Comparisons in the domain of health attitudes, health cognitions, and health behaviors. *Health Communication, 16*, 273–288.

Feeley, T. H., & Vincent, D., III. (2007). How organ donation is represented in newspaper articles in the United States. *Health Communication, 21*, 125–131.

Freimuth, V. S., Greenberg, R. H., DeWitt, J., & Romano, R. M. (1984). Covering cancer: Newspapers and the public interest. *Journal of Communication, 34*, 62–73.

Gattuso, S., Fullagar, S., & Young, I. (2005). Speaking of women's "nameless misery": The everyday construction of depression in Australian women's magazines. *Social Science and Medicine, 61*, 1640–1648.

Gerbner, G., Gross, L., Morgan, M., & Signorielli, N. (1981). Health and medicine on television. *New England Journal of Medicine, 305*, 901–904.

Gerbner, G., Gross, L., Morgan, M., & Signorielli, N. (1994). Growing up with television: The cultivation perspective. In J. Bryant & D. Zillmann (Eds.), *Media effects: Advances in theory and research* (pp. 17–42). Hillsdale, NJ: Erlbaum.

Gill, E. A., & Babrow, A. S. (2007). To hope or to know: Coping with uncertainty and ambivalence in women's magazine breast cancer articles. *Journal of Applied Communication Research, 35*, 133–155.

Glik, D. C. (2004). Health communication in popular media formats. *Public Health & Prevention*. Retrieved from http://cme.medscape.com/viewarticle/466709

Glik, D. C., Berkanovic, E., Stone, K., Ibarra, L., Jones, M. C., Rosen, B., ... Richards, D. (1998). Health education goes Hollywood: Working with prime-time and daytime entertainment television for immunization promotion. *Journal of Health Communication, 3*, 263–282.

Gough, B. (2006). Try to be healthy, but don't forgo your masculinity: Deconstructing men's health discourse in the media. *Social Science & Medicine, 63*, 2476–2488.

Gough, B. (2007). "Real men don't diet": An analysis of contemporary newspaper representations of men, food and health. *Social Science & Medicine, 64*, 326–337.

Gray, J. B. (2007). Interpersonal communication and the illness experience in the *Sex and the City* breast cancer narrative. *Communication Quarterly, 55*, 397–414.

Greenberg, B. S., Rosaen, S. F., Worrell, T. R., Salmon, C. T., & Volkman, J. E. (2009). A portrait of food and drink in commercial TV series. *Health Communication, 24*, 295–303.

Grossberg, L., Wartella, E., & Whitney, D. C. (1998). *Mediamaking: Mass media in a popular culture.* Thousand Oaks, CA: Sage.

Harrabin, R., Coote, A., & Allen, J. (2003). *Health in the news: Risk, reporting and media influence.* London: King's Fund.

Harrison, K. (2005). Is "fat free" good for me? A panel study of television viewing and children's nutritional knowledge and reasoning. *Health Communication, 17*, 117–132.

Harter, L. M., & Japp, P. M. (2001). Technology as the representative anecdote in popular discourses of health and medicine. *Health Communication, 13*, 409–425.

Hether, H. J., Huang, G. C., Beck, V., Murphy, S. T., & Valente, T. W. (2008). Entertainment-education in a media-saturated environment: Examining the impact of single and multiple exposures to breast cancer storylines on two popular medical dramas. *Journal of Health Communication, 13*, 808–823.

Hust, S. J. T., Brown, J. D., & L'Engle, K. L. (2008). Boys will be boys and girls better be prepared: An analysis of the rare sexual health messages in young adolescents' media. *Mass Communication & Society, 11*, 3–23.

Jensen, R., & Jensen, J. (2007). Entertainment media and sexual health: A content analysis of sexual talk, behavior, and risks in a popular television series. *Sex Roles, 56*, 275–284.

Kelly, B. J., Leader, A. E., Mittermaier, D. J., Hornik, R. C., & Cappella, J. N. (2009). The HPV vaccine and the media: How has the topic been covered and what are the effects on knowledge about the virus and cervical cancer? *Patient Education and Counseling, 77*, 308–313.

Kim, S. H., & Willis, L. A. (2007). Talking about obesity: News framing of who is responsible for causing and fixing the problem. *Journal of Health Communication, 12,* 359–376.

Kline, K. N. (2003). Popular media and health: Images, effects, and institutions. In T. L. Thompson, A. M. Dorsey, K. I. Miller, & R. Parrott (Eds.), *Handbook of health communication* (pp. 557–581). Mahwah, NJ: Erlbaum.

Kline, K. N. (2006). A decade of research on health content in the media: The focus on health challenges and sociocultural context and attendant informational and ideological problems. *Journal of Health Communication, 11,* 43–59.

Kline, K. N. (2007). Midwife attended births in prime-time television: Craziness, controlling bitches, and ultimate capitulation. *Women & Language, 30,* 20–29.

Lupton, D. (2000). The social construction of medicine and the body. In G. L. Albrecht, R. Fitzpatrick, & S. C. Scrimshaw (Eds.), *The handbook of social studies in health and medicine* (pp. 50–63). Thousand Oaks, CA: Sage.

MacFadyen, L., Amos, A., Hastings, G., & Parkes, E. (2003). "They look like my kind of people"— Perceptions of smoking images in youth magazines. *Social Science & Medicine, 56,* 491–499.

McCombs, M. (1994). News influence on our pictures of the world. In J. Bryant & D. Zillman (Eds.), *Media effects: Advances in theory and research* (pp. 1–15). Hillsdale, NJ: Erlbaum.

Mebane, F., Temin, S., & Pravanta, C. F. (2003). Communicating anthrax in 2001: A comparison of CDC information and print media accounts [Supplement 1]. *Journal of Health Communication, 8,* 50–82.

Metzl, J. M., & Angel, J. (2004). Assessing the impact of SSRI antidepressants on popular notions of women's depressive illness. *Social Science & Medicine, 58,* 577–584.

Meyers, M. (2004). Crack mothers in the news: A narrative of paternalistic racism. *Journal of Communication Inquiry, 28,* 194–216.

Movius, L., Cody, M., Huang, G., Berkowitz, M., & Morgan, S. (2007). Motivating television viewers to become organ donors. *Cases in Public Health Communication & Marketing,* Retrieved from http://www.casesjournal.org/volume1/peer-reviewed/cases_1_08.cfm

Olstead, R. (2002). Contesting the text: Canadian media depictions of the conflation of mental illness and criminality. *Sociology of Health & Illness, 24,* 621–643.

Parrott, R., & Condit, C. (Eds.). (1996). *Evaluating women's health messages: A resource book.* Thousand Oaks, CA: Sage.

Pelletier, A. R., Quinlan, K. P., Sacks, J. J., Van Gilder, T. J., Gilchrist, J., & Ahluwalia, H. K. (2000). Injury prevention practices as depicted in G-rated and PG-rated movies. *Archives of Pediatrics & Adolescent Medicine, 154,* 283–286.

Pollard, W. E. (2003). Public perceptions of information sources concerning bioterrorism before and after Anthrax attacks: An analysis of national survey data. *Journal of Health Communication, 8,* 93.

Primack, B. A., Land, S. R., & Fine, M. J. (2008). Adolescent smoking and volume of exposure to various forms of media. *Public Health, 122,* 379–389.

Pruitt, S. L., & Mullen, P. D. (2005). Contraception or abortion? Inaccurate descriptions of emergency contraception in newspaper articles, 1992–2002. *Contraception, 71,* 14–21.

Purvis Cooper, C., Burgoon, M., & Roter, D. L. (2001). An expectancy-value analysis of viewer interest in television prevention news stories. *Health Communication, 13,* 227.

Quick, B. L., Kim, D. K., & Meyer, K. (2009). A 15-Year Review of ABC, CBS, and NBC news coverage of organ donation: Implications for organ donation campaigns. *Health Communication, 24,* 137–145.

Radley, A., Lupton, D., & Ritter, C. (1997). Health: An invitation and introduction. *Health, 1,* 5–21.

Roy, S. C. (2008). "Taking charge of your health": Discourses of responsibility in English-Canadian women's magazines. *Sociology of Health & Illness, 30,* 463–477.

Sargent, J. D., Wills, T. A., Stoolmiller, M., Gibson, J., & Gibbons, F. X. (2006). Alcohol use in motion pictures and its relation with early-onset teen drinking. *Journal of Studies on Alcohol, 67,* 54–65.

Schiappa, E. (2008). *Beyond representational correctness: Rethinking criticism of popular media.* Albany, NY: SUNY Press.

Seale, C. F. (2002). Cancer heroics: A study of news reports with particular reference to gender. *Sociology, 36,* 107–126.

Seale, C. F., Boden, S., Williams, S., Lowe, P., & Steinberg, D. (2007). Media constructions of sleep and sleep disorders: A study of UK national newspapers. *Social Science & Medicine, 65,* 418–430.

Sharf, B. F., & Freimuth, V. S. (1993). The construction of illness on entertainment television: Coping with cancer on *thirtysomething*. *Health Communication, 5*, 141–160.

Signorielli, N. (1993). *Mass media images and impact on health*. Westport, CT: Greenwood.

Singhal, A., Cody, M. J., Rogers, E. M., & Sabido, M. (Eds.). (2004). *Entertainment-education and social change: History, research, and practice*. Mahwah, NJ: Erlbaum.

Slater, M. D., Hayes, A. F., & Ford, V. L. (2007). Examining the moderating and mediating roles of news exposure and attention on adolescent judgments of alcohol-related risks. *Communication Research, 34*, 355–381.

Slater, M. D., Lawrence, F., & Comello, M. L. (2009). Media influence on alcohol-control policy support in the U.S. adult population: The intervening role of issue concern and risk judgments. *Journal of Health Communication, 14*, 262–275.

Slater, M. D., Long, M., Bettinghaus, E. P., & Reineke, J. B. (2008). News coverage of cancer in the United States: A national sample of newspapers, television, and magazines. *Journal of Health Communication, 13*, 523–537.

Smith, E. A., Offen, N., & Malone, R. E. (2006). Pictures worth a thousand words: Noncommercial tobacco content in the lesbian, gay, and bisexual press. *Journal of Health Communication, 11*, 635–649.

Smith, S. W., Nazione, S., LaPlante, C., Kotowski, M. R., Atkin, C., Skubisz, C. M., & Stohl, C. (2009). Topics and sources of memorable breast cancer messages and their impact on prevention and detection behaviors. *Journal of Health Communication, 14*, 293–307.

Stern, S. R. (2005). Messages from teens on the big screen: Smoking, drinking, and drug use in teen-centered films. *Journal of Health Communication, 10*, 331–346.

Stryker, J. E. (2003). Media and marijuana: A longitudinal analysis of news media effects on adolescents' marijuana use and related outcomes, 1977–1999. *Journal of Health Communication, 8*, 305–328.

Stryker, J. E., Moriarty, C. M., & Jensen, J. D. (2008). Effects of newspaper coverage on public knowledge about modifiable cancer risks. *Health Communication, 23*, 380–390.

Sung-Yeon, P. (2005). The influence of presumed media influence on women's desire to be thin. *Communication Research, 32*, 594–614.

Tanski, S. E., Stoolmiller, M., Sonya Dal, C., Worth, K., Gibson, J., & Sargent, J. D. (2009). Movie character smoking and adolescent smoking: Who matters more, good guys or bad guys? *Pediatrics, 124*, 135–143.

Turow, J., & Coe, L. (1985). Curing television's ills: The portrayal of health care. *Journal of Communication, 35*, 36–51.

Turow, J., & Coe, L. (1993). Curing television's ills: The portrayal of health care. In B. C. Thornton & G. L. Kreps (Eds.), *Perspectives on health communication* (pp. 130–145). Prospect Heights, IL: Waveland.

Valente, T. W., Murphy, S., Huang, G., Gusek, J., Greene, J., & Beck, V. (2007). Evaluating a minor storyline on ER about teen obesity, hypertension, and 5 a day. *Journal of Health Communication, 12*, 551–566.

Vardeman, J. E., & Aldoory, L. (2008). A qualitative study of how women make meaning of contradictory media messages about the risks of eating fish. *Health Communication, 23*, 282–291.

Wahl, O., Wood, A., Zaveri, P., Drapalski, A., & Mann, B. (2003). Mental illness depiction in children's films. *Journal of Community Psychology, 31*, 553–560.

Wallack, L. (1990). Mass media and health promotion: Promise, problem, and challenge. In C. K. Atkin & L. Wallack (Eds.), *Mass communication and public health: Complexities and conflicts* (pp. 41–51). Newbury Park, CA: Sage.

Wallack, L., Dorfman, L., Jernigan, D., & Themba, M. (1993). *Media advocacy and public health: Power for prevention*. Newbury Park, CA: Sage.

Whittier, D. K., Kennedy, M. G., St. Lawrence, J. S., Seeley, S., & Beck, V. (2005). Embedding health messages into entertainment television: Effect on gay men's response to a syphilis outbreak. *Journal of Health Communication, 10*, 251–259.

Williams, S. J., Seale, C. F., Boden, S., Lowe, P., & Steinberg, D. L. (2008a). Medicalization and beyond: The social construction of insomnia and snoring in the news. *Health: An Interdisciplinary Journal for the Social Study of Health, Illness & Medicine, 12*, 251–268.

Williams, S. J., Seale, C. F., Boden, S., Lowe, P., & Steinberg, D. L. (2008b). Waking up to sleepiness: Modafinil, the media and the pharmaceuticalisation of every day/night life. *Sociology of Health & Illness, 30*, 839–855.

Wilson, K. E., & Beck, V. H. (2002). Entertainment outreach for women's health at CDC. *Journal of Women's Health & Gender-Based Medicine, 11*, 575–578.

Yanovitzky, I. (2002). Effect of news coverage on the prevalence of drunk-driving behavior: Evidence from a longitudinal study. *Journal of Studies on Alcohol, 63*, 342–352.

Yanovitzky, I., & Blitz, C. L. (2000). Effect of media coverage and physician advice on utilization of breast cancer screening by women 40 years and older. *Journal of Health Communication, 5*, 117–134.

Yanovitzky, I., & Stryker, J. (2001). Mass media, social norms, and health promotion efforts. *Communication Research, 28*, 208.

Zola, I. K. (1972). Medicine as an institution of social control. *Sociological Review, 20*, 487–504.

Zoller, H. M., & Worrell, T. (2006). Television illness depictions, identity, and social experience: Responses to multiple sclerosis on among people with MS. *Health Communication, 20*, 69–79.

17

ADVERTISING IN HEALTH COMMUNICATION

Promoting Pharmaceuticals and Dietary Supplements to U.S. Consumers

Denise E. DeLorme, Jisu Huh, Leonard N. Reid, and Soontae An

Pharmaceutical companies and dietary supplement manufacturers use consumer advertising to market and sell prescription (Rx) medicines, over-the-counter (OTC) drugs, and dietary supplements (DS). Spending on consumer-targeted advertising for pharmaceuticals and supplements is substantial, and advertising for these products is an important source of public health information and a significant influence on consumer behavior (DeLorme, Huh, & Reid, 2007a). Pragmatically speaking, pharmaceutical advertising is used to produce specific communication effects, and the communication tasks assigned to consumer advertising always work in relation to the other elements of integrated marketing communication (public relations, sales promotion, personal selling). However, pharmaceutical advertising is intended to influence purchase behavior by moving consumers through a series of hierarchical steps; for example, leading them from attention → comprehension → yielding to conclusion → retention of the belief → behaving (see McGuire, 1978; Menon, Deshpande, Zinkhan, & Perri, 2004).

As a marketing communication tool, advertising is designed and placed to bring about two basic consumer-targeted actions: (1) to help presell drug products to end-users and (2) to help persuade distribution channel agents to stock and sell the products for end-user consumption. The presell function occurs as part of a pull promotion strategy and advertising's role is to pull drug products through the distribution channel by stimulating demand at the end-user level (e.g., to move consumers to ask for a drug). In the pull promotion strategy, advertising typically plays a dominant role in product marketing. When used to influence distributors, consumer advertising works as part of a push promotion strategy and is used to convince distributors and retailers that advertising is being directed at consumers to stimulate end-user demand for drug products. In the push promotion strategy, consumer advertising's role is typically less prominent, and the focus is on building market penetration and product availability at the distribution level.

In this chapter, we focus on the nature and roles of the three forms of pharmaceutical advertising—direct-to-consumer prescription drug advertising (DTCA), over-the-counter (OTC) drug advertising, and dietary supplement (DS) advertising. Though not studied as extensively as other health communication subjects, pharmaceutical advertising is an important area of research where communication motives are driven by concerns ranging from pragmatic profit pressures to society's well-being (e.g., education and informed decision making). We begin by first describing the regulatory environment of pharmaceutical advertising, and then reviewing the publicly available research on each advertising form.

U.S. Regulation of Pharmaceutical and Dietary Supplement Advertising

The practice of advertising pharmaceuticals and dietary supplements to consumers has a long history in the United States. During the 18th and 19th centuries, patent medicines were heavily advertised in newspapers, often with outrageous and blatantly false claims. Patent medicines were available without a prescription and Congress did not draw a distinction between Rx and OTC medicines at that time. Such practice was completely unregulated until 1906 when Congress passed the Pure Food and Drug Act, a precursor to today's regulatory procedures. The Act, however, had little impact on deceptive patent medicine advertising, as it addressed product labels only (Schwartz, Silverman, Hulka, & Appel, 2009).

In 1938, Congress passed the federal Food, Drug, and Cosmetic Act (FDCA), providing the framework for contemporary pharmaceutical advertising regulation. The FDCA included a Food and Drug Administration (FDA) premarket notification requiring that all new drugs be proven safe before being marketed and to carry a label of adequate use directions, which was a major advance in regulation of pharmaceuticals (Institute of Medicine, 2006). In 1951, Congress enacted the Durham-Humphrey Amendments to the FDCA, creating the two drug categories, Rx and OTC drugs. In 1962, the Kefauver-Harris Drug Amendments transferred jurisdiction of Rx drug advertising from the Federal Trade Commission (FTC) to the FDA and this jurisdictional distinction remains in effect today. Currently, the United States and New Zealand are the only two countries allowing DTCA.

In the United States, pharmaceutical advertising has been protected under the First Amendment (*Virginia State Board of Pharmacy* v. *Virginia Citizens Consumer Council*, 1976). Any state or federal regulation of pharmaceutical advertising should survive the First Amendment challenge. While some scholars suggest a relaxation of FDA rules to accelerate the dissemination of drug information (see Calfee, 2002), others argue for strengthening the FDA's regulatory authority, especially postmarketing surveillance (Institute of Medicine, 2006).

Direct-to-Consumer (DTC) Prescription Drug Advertising

Rx drugs are drugs available only with a written prescription from a doctor. Due to the nature of the product, most pharmaceutical marketing until the mid-1980s concentrated on creating and maintaining supply-chain demand toward physicians and pharmacists. DTC advertising (DTCA), defined as, "any promotional effort by a pharmaceutical company to present prescription drug information to the general public in the lay media" is relatively new (Wilkes, Bell, & Kravitz, 2000, p. 112). However, in the past two decades it has radically changed the way Rx drugs are promoted.

Consumer advertising has long played a pivotal role in the marketing of pharmaceuticals and supplements. However, DTCA dramatically altered the buyer–seller dynamic. DTCA is unique compared to other advertising. The purchase decision, while made by the patient, is not possible without physician approval. Before DTCA, manufacturers relied on promotional tools, such as direct-to-physician advertising and detailing, to stimulate drug brand demand by selling only to physicians. DTCA brought the patient into the equation, eroding some of the physician's market control and giving drug manufacturers more power. Though the physician retained authority to prescribe or not, DTCA empowered the patient with information, once exclusive to physicians (Deshpande, Menon, Perri, & Zinkhan, 2004). If DTCA performed as designed, the patient, armed with ad-supplied information, was now in a position to engage the doctor in a discussion about a drug brand and even ask that it be prescribed or an existing Rx changed. DTCA gave the drug manufacturer the opportunity to stimulate patient demand and thereby, as noted earlier, pull the promoted brand through the distribution channel.

Federal Regulation of DTC Advertising

Within the FDA, the Division of Drug Marketing, Advertising, and Communications (DDMAC), under the Center for Drug Evaluation and Research (CDER), regulates DTCA. Drug companies must submit final DTC ad materials to DDMAC at the time of initial publication of the advertisement (21 C.F.R. § 314.81(b)(3)(i)). However, the FDA does not currently mandate a premarket review of DTC ads unless the drug was approved on an accelerated basis. Drug companies may voluntarily submit draft versions of DTCA materials for advisory comments. If the DDMAC finds a disseminated DTC ad that does not comply with FDA guidelines, it may issue: (1) a Notice of Violation (NOV) or "untitled letter" for minor violations, or (2) a warning letter for more serious violations. More recently, the Food and Drug Administration Amendments Act of 2007 (FDAAA) authorized the FDA to impose civil penalties for false and misleading ads (FDAAA, 2007).

Although Congress differentiated advertising of Rx drugs from that of OTC drugs in 1951, there were no formal regulations that distinguished DTCA from direct-to-physician advertising (Palumbo & Mullins, 2002). Until the early 1980s, health care professionals were the primary target of promotional activities of Rx drugs, and the FDA did not have an explicit policy about DTCA. As patients' influence over health decisions increased, the first DTCA was launched in 1981 by Boots Pharmaceuticals for the ibuprofen product, Rufen (Palumbo & Mullins, 2002). The FDA requested a voluntary moratorium on DTCA in 1983, soon after pharmaceutical companies started advertising directly to consumers. Two years later the moratorium was lifted without substantive changes. In fact, the FDA required DTC ads to meet the same legal requirements as direct-to-physician ads, including: (a) the "brief summary" of the drug's side effects, contraindications, warnings, and precautions and (b) "fair balance" between the drug's risks and benefits (FDA/DHHS, 1985).

The FDA differentiates three types of DTC ads: (a) "reminder" ads containing no reference to the drug's purpose, benefits, or risks, with the drug's brand name only, (b) "help-seeking" ads containing information about a disease or medical condition without mentioning the drug's brand name, and (c) "product-claim" ads containing both the drug's brand name and medical conditions (FDA/DHHS, 1995). The third type ("product-claim" ads) is regulated by the FDA and must include the brief summary and "fair balance" (Palumbo & Mullins, 2002). Product claim advertising, which is usually what is referred to as DTCA, is the most common and controversial. Meeting FDA requirements for product claim advertising was difficult, especially in broadcasting, so until the late 1990s the pharmaceutical industry communicated to consumers mainly through reminder or help-seeking ads.

However, DTCA took an important turn in 1997 when the FDA loosened broadcast DTCA requirements. The new rules required that DTCA in broadcast media need only contain information about "major risks" instead of a full "brief summary." Under the "major risks" requirement, ads must disclose the drug's major risks and most common adverse effects in the audio or audio and visual parts of the presentation. Also, instead of a "brief summary," DTC ads may make "adequate provision" for dissemination of package labeling information by referring consumers to: (a) a toll free number, (b) a website, (c) print ads, and (d) health care professionals (FDA, 1999).

DTC Advertising Growth

Since the FDA's regulatory change, DTCA has continued to expand and broadcast ad expenditures have soared. DTCA became one of the fastest growing advertising categories in the 2000s. In 2006, at the height of spending, DTCA reached almost $5 billion. However, expenditures dropped to $4.8 billion in 2007 and $4.4 billion in 2008 due to the overall economic downturn and because companies began waiting longer to bring to market new drugs with more limited indications (in medical terminology, a drug's "indication" refers to the use of that drug for treating a particular disease; "Ad Spend Dips," 2009; Arnold, 2009a, 2009b). A limited number of blockbuster brands tend to account for a large share of DTCA spending: the top 25 DTCA brands accounted for 62% of total DTCA spending in 2008 (Gebhart, 2009). These brands are also concentrated on a few chronic disease types such as depression, asthma, coronary artery disease, insomnia, and erectile dysfunction (ED) (Arnold, 2009b).

In addition to the phenomenal increase in ad spending, DTCA has also shown media diversification. Until the FDA's 1997 guidance allowed broadcast advertising without "brief summary" information, most DTCA was in print media. However, TV ad spending quickly surpassed print and now the lion's share of spending goes to TV. In 2006, TV ad spending accounted for 56.3% of the pharmaceutical industry's total DTCA expenditure; TV expenditures reached 57.6% in 2007 and 62.5% in 2008, making TV advertising the fastest growing form of DTCA (Arnold, 2009b). Pharmaceutical advertisers have also increased use of the Internet (Huh & Cude, 2004).

The potential consumer benefits of DTCA cannot be ignored, but drug manufacturers' increased commitment to DTCA has generated controversy among legislators, health care professionals, regulatory organizations, ad experts, and consumer advocates. Opponents call for more stringent oversight to protect consumers from detrimental and socially undesirable DTCA effects. Among their claims are that DTCA confuses and misleads consumers, interferes with the physician–patient relationship, stimulates unnecessary drug demand (especially for costly brands over generics), leads to inappropriate Rx drug use, and contributes to rising health care costs (e.g., Auton, 2004, 2006; Stange, 2007). Proponents claim that, despite these concerns, DTCA can be helpful. It informs and educates consumers, primes consumers to see physicians and ask more informed questions, leads to identification and treatment of undiagnosed medical conditions, enhances physician–patient dialogue, and results in better patient compliance and decreased adverse medical events (Calfee, 2002; Pfizer, 2001, 2005).

Stakeholder Views about DTC Advertising

The issues involved in research being conducted on DTCA include questions of public health, health care costs, corporate responsibility, advertising ethics, physician–patient dynamics, and consumers' ability to understand and use medical information. Detailed reviews of the DTCA literature are published elsewhere (e.g., Auton, 2004, 2006; Taylor,

Capella, & Kozup, 2007). This section discusses viewpoints of different stakeholders (government, pharmaceutical industry, health insurance industry, health care professionals, and consumers) on these issues and relevant research.

Government (FDA) Challenges

The FDA is an important DTCA stakeholder. However, due to financial and human resource limitations, the FDA can review only a small portion of the DTCA materials it receives, and the agency cannot ensure that all DTC ads comply with regulatory guidelines (Government Accountability Office [GAO], 2006). To better understand DTCA and help policy makers and regulatory agencies, a number of content analyses have been conducted. These studies address issues of DTC ad information quality and presentation by examining how well the ad content complies with FDA regulations and if current regulations are sufficient. Of the 12 DTCA content analyses identified in the literature, three analyzed TV commercials, five analyzed print media, and four examined branded websites.

Most of the studies have found DTC ads in different media are not complying satisfactorily with FDA guidelines and raised concerns about: the high volume of DTC ads on TV (Brownfield, Bernhardt, Phan, Williams, & Parker, 2004; Frosch, Krueger, Hornik, Cronholm, & Barg, 2007); information quality (Frosch et al., 2007; Parker & Delene, 1998); and fair balance between benefit and risk information (Kaphingst, DeJong, Rudd, & Daltroy, 2004). Specific concerns related to DTCA information presentation style include: overuse of emotional appeals; portraying lifestyle changes as insufficient (Frosch et al., 2007); emphasizing drug benefits more than risks (Kaphingst et al., 2004); potentially creating health information disparities among racial/ethnic groups (Mastin, Andsager, Choi, & Lee, 2007); ad readability and ease of understanding (Sheehan, 2006); and questionable visual cues (Cline & Young, 2004).

The newest area of DTCA regulatory-related research is Internet DTCA. The FDA stipulates no special web-based DTC ad regulations if the site does not mention a drug brand name. However, when a brand is mentioned, the site must meet the standards applied to print advertising (Frangos, 2001). Four studies analyzing content of DTC brand websites suggested that the nature of the Internet necessitates specific regulations (Huh & Cude, 2004; Macias & Lewis, 2003, 2006; Sheehan, 2007).

With increasing evidence of DTCA regulation compliance problems and market withdrawal of heavily advertised drugs (e.g., Vioxx), concerns about DTCA have been intensifying and the FDA's enforcement capacity has been under attack (Donohue, Cevasco, & Rosenthal, 2007). A recent GAO report about the FDA's DTCA oversight identifies three areas needing improvement: (a) the FDA reviews only a small portion of DTC ads and cannot ensure it is the highest priority material; (b) after the 2002 policy change, the FDA's process for issuing regulatory letters took longer and the number of issued letters declined; and (c) effectiveness of FDA letters at halting dissemination of noncompliant DTC materials was limited (GAO, 2008). The growing body of DTCA research will not only improve understanding of positive and negative effects, but will also help policy makers and regulatory agencies develop more efficient and effective consumer protection strategies.

Pharmaceutical Industry Support

Pharmaceutical companies are the most ardent supporters of DTCA. They embraced the FDA's 1997 regulation change and have demonstrated continued advocacy for more relaxed

DTCA regulations. From the industry viewpoint, DTCA provides an important marketing tool that offsets increasing competition and declining impact of direct-to-physician marketing efforts. Pharmaceutical companies argue they have not only a right to free speech, but also a responsibility to educate individuals about drug treatments and inform them about new products (Holmer, 1999). They assert that DTCA is an opportunity to provide consumers with important information about diseases and treatments, and to encourage them to speak with physicians and seek necessary care (Calfee, 2002; Pfizer Inc., 2005). To support their arguments for DTCA benefits, pharmaceutical companies have conducted consumer studies demonstrating that DTCA educates and empowers patients (e.g., Pfizer, 2001, 2005; Pharmaceutical Research and Manufacturers of America [PhRMA], 2002); they have also presented these findings at the FDA's public hearings. However, much of the research conducted by pharmaceutical companies is proprietary and access to findings is limited.

Health Insurance Industry View

Situated opposite the pharmaceutical industry on the spectrum of DTCA stance is the health insurance industry. The health insurance industry has opposed DTCA because health care spending is rising faster than ever and it is believed that the increase in drug advertising expenditures is partly to blame (Arxcel, 2008). A Kaiser Family Foundation (2008) report revealed that U.S. Rx drug spending has risen sharply and the trend is likely to continue. Managed care organizations (MCOs) have complained that DTCA encourages excessive prescribing or leads consumers to prefer pricier brands over generics (Blue Cross Blue Shield Association, 2002; National Institute for Health Care Management [NIHCM], 2000).

Annual surveys of corporate executives in employee benefits departments conducted by Arxcel have reported that 46% of respondents chose DTCA as the key determinant of escalating Rx benefit costs in 2007. The percentage dropped to 33% in 2008 but DTCA was still the most frequently mentioned cost-driving factor (Arxcel, 2008). While pharmaceutical costs are indeed rising, the economic impact of DTCA on overall U.S. health care spending requires more investigation. Existing literature provides only correlational evidence that DTCA is an increasingly important factor driving the expanded use of newer and pricier drugs and thus, health care costs (Findlay, 2001, 2002; GAO, 2006). Based on a thorough review of existing literature on the economic impact of DTCA, the GAO found that increases in DTCA were significantly correlated to overall increases in spending on both the advertised drug itself and on other drugs treating the same conditions. The estimated increases in sales ranged from little or no change in sales to an increase of more than $6 for every $1 spent on DTCA (GAO, 2006). However, the impact of DTCA on the sales of an individual drug brand depends on many factors, such as spending on other promotional tools, marketing efforts and sales of other drugs treating the same condition, and increases in outbreak and diagnosis of a certain medical condition. Whether or not the economic effects are positive or negative is yet to be determined (GAO, 2006).

Health Care Professionals' Attitudes

Historically, health care professionals have exhibited negative attitudes toward DTCA. Early studies reported that the majority of physicians perceived DTCA would produce negative outcomes for themselves and their patients, increase demand for advertised drugs, or raise drug costs. They viewed DTCA as a challenge to their medical authority and were concerned it might undermine the physician–patient relationship (Hollon, 1999; Lipsky & Taylor, 1997; Wilkes, Bell, & Kravitz, 2000).

However, as research has accumulated, more positive or mixed views have been reported. Physicians seem to acknowledge DTCA benefits such as educating patients about diseases (Allison-Ottey, Ruffin, & Allison, 2002; Weissman et al., 2004) and making patients more informed and confident in talking with doctors (FDA, 2004; Murray, Lo, Pollack, Donelan, & Lee, 2003). Although physicians believe DTCA can prompt patients to ask for unnecessary prescriptions and cause confusion over risks and benefits, most believe little or no interpersonal tension is created (FDA, 2004; Weissman et al., 2004).

Most physicians do not believe their prescribing practice is affected by DTCA, but surveys of physicians have provided some intriguing findings. Murray et al. (2003) found that most physicians filled requests for new Rxs. Physicians were ambivalent about drug choice for requested vs. nonrequested drugs, especially for DTCA-related requests. In another survey, Weissman et al. (2004) reported most physicians did not prescribe DTCA-induced patient-requested drugs, but 39% prescribed requested DTCA drugs. Huh and Langteau (2007) demonstrated that while physicians' responses to patients' requests for an advertised drug were mixed, greater presumed detrimental effects of DTCA predicted refusal of patient requests, even after other physician demographic and attitudinal variables were controlled. This finding is in line with the 2003 survey with clinicians that reported that when a patient's request was based on DTC advertising, clinicians were more likely to respond negatively (Zachry, Dalen, & Jackson, 2003). Both studies shed light on the rather unknown role of prejudgment of the doctor about DTCAs' detrimental effects.

Although the literature suggests physicians are responsive to patients' requests to a degree, more research is needed to determine if DTCA is a main cause of physicians' more frequent writing of Rxs for advertised drug brands. A few studies examining and comparing the influence of direct-to-physician promotions and DTCA on physicians' prescribing have found direct-to-physician promotions had a much greater impact than did DTCA (Donohue & Berndt, 2004; Wosinska, 2005). Both Donohue and Berndt (2004), and Wosinska (2005) conducted econometric analyses of physicians' prescription drug choice comparing the impact of DTCA and direct-to-physician detailing. Product-specific expenditures on DTCA and detailing were entered as predictors to a model predicting physicians' choice of specific drug brands. The analysis results revealed that the detailing expenditure variable had much greater predictive power of physicians' brand choice than the DTCA expenditure variable.

Consumers/Patients' Attitudes and Behaviors

Compared to physicians, consumers demonstrate more positive attitudes toward DTCA. They believe DTCA can provide useful drug information and education about new treatments (e.g., FDA, 2004; Huh, DeLorme, & Reid, 2004). Nevertheless, there are indications that consumer views may be changing, showing increased skepticism toward DTCA and negative perceptions of its educational value (Diehl, Mueller, & Terlutter, 2008; Spake & Joseph, 2007).

Despite the increasingly skeptical views among consumers, DTCA has been found to impact consumer behavior and physician–patient interaction by motivating consumers to seek more information and to initiate discussions with doctors. Some consumers ask their doctors to prescribe advertised brands or change prescriptions (An, 2007; DeLorme, Huh, & Reid, 2007b; GAO, 2006). Based on an extensive review of survey research, Mintzes

(2001) reported that between 23% and 29% of respondents spoke to their doctor for the first time about a drug or condition in response to DTCA; between 6% and 9% requested a particular brand in response to DTCA. More recently, GAO (2006) reported that, on average, about 30% of consumers who had seen DTCA discussed with their physician the ad-featured medical condition or drug; among them, about 25% requested a Rx.

Studies about DTCA effects suggest both positive and negative effects on consumers: DTC ads have been found to encourage consumers to talk to their doctors about previously undiagnosed conditions and obtain treatment (e.g., Weissman et al., 2004). However, in some cases, DTC ads are related to: increases in Rxs for advertised drugs when alternatives may be more appropriate (e.g., Spence, Teleki, Cheetham, Schweitzer, & Millares, 2005), viewing advertised drugs as a primary treatment option (An, Jin, & Brown, 2009), and cultivating perceptions of disease prevalence (e.g., An, 2008; Park & Grow, 2008). Based on existing literature, Taylor, Capella, and Kozup (2007) concluded that research generally supports the idea that DTCA is beneficial by helping patients become more informed and better able to communicate more effectively with doctors. However, other scholars argue DTCA is mostly harmful and needs to be banned or tightly regulated (Stange, 2007), and the heated debate continues.

Over-the-Counter (OTC) Drug Advertising

Consumer advertising has long been important to the success or failure of OTC drugs in the highly competitive nonprescription drug market (Smith, 1983). Today, advertising is especially important because of two market drivers—the growth of self-medication and the emergence of Rx-to-OTC drug switching. Since 1972, numerous drugs once available only by Rx have joined old standards (e.g., aspirin, cough syrups, allergy medicines) on retail shelves, and consumers are more empowered today to participate in their health care than ever before (Kittinger & Herrick, 2005).

OTC drugs are medicines that can be purchased without a doctor's prescription. Also known as nonprescription drugs, OTC medications are used to self-treat mild transitory symptoms, conditions, and illnesses and do not require physician approval and supervision. OTC medicines have been screened and approved as reasonably safe and effective for self-medication and must have little or no abuse potential (Palumbo & Mullins, 2002). There are two OTC drug categories in the United States: unrestricted and restricted. Unrestricted OTC drugs can be bought without pharmacist intervention and can be found on self-service shelves of convenience stores, supermarkets, and gas stations, not just at pharmacies. Restricted OTC drugs are kept behind the pharmacy counter and passed to the consumer with pharmacist approval. Restricted OTC drugs, sometimes called behind-the-counter (BTC) drugs, are sold by pharmacies only.

The purpose of OTC drug advertising is no different from other forms of consumer advertising. Pharmaceutical companies use advertising to perform three basic communication functions—to inform, to persuade, and to remind consumers about OTC drug attributes, functions, and benefits. Specifically, OTC drug advertising is used to: (a) promote self-medication; (b) increase awareness of health conditions and symptoms; (c) communicate product advantages (e.g., ingredients, functions); and (d) influence purchase by positioning brands as the best relief solutions (Smith, 1983).

Advertising is used to target two segments: users and nonusers of OTC products. It exerts its influence in two contexts: before purchase and after purchase. Before purchase, OTC drug ads target nonusers of OTC drugs (e.g., acetaminophen) or users of other brands (e.g., Tylenol vs. new brand) to affect first purchase (i.e., trial). After purchase, ads target OTC drug users to remind, reinforce, and legitimize learned user behaviors. Except for the introduction of new products and brands, OTC drug advertising does most of its work after purchase to promote continued use, prevent product/brand-switching, and build product/brand loyalty.

In either context, OTC drug advertising's influence can be direct or indirect. The direct influence is one step—ad exposure directly influences nonuser/user behavior. The indirect influence is a two-step process and involves an interpersonal moderator—ad exposure influences an agent who in turn affects nonuser/user behavior. OTC drug advertising's indirect influence is especially important to understand. Despite what many believe, the direct power of OTC drug advertising is limited. Ads that produce interpersonal interactions between health professionals and consumers are particularly effective. As one industry executive has noted, millions spent to advertise a drug cannot accomplish what a doctor or pharmacist can do in one day (Reynolds, 1992, p. 18).

Federal Regulation of OTC Drug Advertising

The FTC regulates OTC drug advertising under section 5 of the Federal Trade Commission Act, which labels "unfair or deceptive acts or practices" as unlawful. The principle is that all advertising should be truthful and not misleading and all claims substantiated. As such, typical OTC drug ad cases stem from the FTC's deception doctrine and advertising substantiation doctrine (Watts & Wilkenfeld, 1992).

The FTC defines deceptive advertising as an ad containing a representation or omission that is likely to mislead reasonable consumers. Proof that consumers were deceived or misled is not required and the FTC examines the ad in its totality, rather than individual ad elements, when evaluating deception likelihood. That is, even if the ad claim of an OTC drug is literally true, when the ad conveys a false or misleading impression the FTC will interpret it as deceptive. The omission of or failure to provide material information also constitutes deceptive advertising.

In addition, the FTC's advertising substantiation doctrine requires that all objective product claims, either express or implied, should be adequately substantiated. If an ad claims the drug has been proven effective for a particular condition, the company should be able to produce evidence to support the statement. Often, the FTC collaborates with the FDA to determine if there is a "reasonable basis" for ad claims of OTC drugs (Watts & Wilkenfeld, 1992). The FTC considers six factors to assess a "reasonable basis": (a) type of claim, (b) nature of the product, (c) benefits of a truthful claim, (d) consequences of a false claim, (e) cost of developing substantiation, and (f) amount of substantiation that experts in the field believe is reasonable.

OTC Drug Advertising Spending

According to *OTC Perspectives* (2009), just under $3 billion was spent to advertise OTC brands in 2008, a drop of 9% from 2007 ($3.2 billion). The biggest 2008 spenders were Tylenol ($155.7 million), Claritin ($153.6 million), Zyrtec ($118.9 million), and Advil ($102.6). Network TV ($834.5 million), national magazines ($684.7 million), and cable TV ($668.2 million) received the lion's share of 2008 ad dollars, though OTC advertisers shifted significant expenditures from network (-14.4%) and cable TV (-28.9%) to spot TV

(+27.9%), coupons (+15.9%), and national Sunday supplements (+13.8%) (*OTC Perspectives*, 2009).

Billions are spent on OTC drugs each year, and sales have increased steadily since 2004 ($14.1 billion). In 2008, $16.8 billion was spent to buy OTC drugs, up from $16.1 billion in 2007. As a rule, OTC sales have been fairly recession-proof and sales' peaks and valleys have been minimal (Consumer Healthcare Products Association, 2009; "Allergies," 2009). Private label sales were up 8.2% in 2007–2008, driven primarily by private label substitutes for Prilosec OTC (omeprazole) and Zyrtec (certirizine). Rx-to-OTC drug switches resulted in significant sales growth for two drug types: allergy, asthma, and sinus medications were up 17.3% and feminine products grew 7.3% ("Allergies," 2009; Miley, 2009). The growth of private-label OTC drugs suggests more Americans are seeking value for their money. To counter sales erosion, many advertisers have turned to "value" messages in their ads.

The OTC drug market is expected to continue to expand for several reasons. First, self-medication is growing among Americans, and OTC drugs provide a convenient and inexpensive way to treat minor health problems ("Allergies," 2009; Consumer Healthcare Products Association, 2009). Second, Rx-to-OTC switching (transference of drugs from Rx to nonprescription status upon FDA approval) is not likely to abate, making more medications available without a prescription. Third, use of OTC medications is encouraged by medical gatekeepers (e.g., HMOs, insurance companies) as a cost-saving option to expensive Rx drugs. Fourth, health literacy is likely to increase, especially as Internet use for self-medication information grows.

Research on OTC Drug Advertising

OTC drug advertising has been the focus of limited academic study, though extensive proprietary research certainly exists. Studies have appeared sporadically in the public research literature since the mid-1970s, and have generally focused on separate, unrelated questions of inquiry making it difficult to draw definite conclusions about OTC advertising.

Message Placement and Content

OTC drug ads are placed in various media, but only one study has investigated their quantity and placement. Brownfield et al. (2004) analyzed OTC drug commercials in 504 hours of network TV programs from 2001. OTC commercials accounted for 4.8% of the total 18,906 ads, were more prevalent than DTC commercials, and most commonly aired in midafternoon and early evening.

Research on OTC drug ad content is more abundant, but also scarce. Six content analyses have appeared in the literature. OTC drug print ads have been the subject of most of the research. One study analyzed OTC drug ad content by gender orientation in popular consumer magazines and found more ads appeared in female-oriented magazines, and most of those emphasized "appearance" concerns (Vener & Krupka, 1984). Most ads in men's magazines focused on raising energy levels with stimulants. The social portrayal of people in OTC drug magazine ads was investigated in another study which found that depictions of men and women did not differ significantly from those in general ads (Rallapalli, Smith, & Stone, 1994). Other researchers studied product claim accuracy and side effect information in OTC drug ads and found that 50% contained inaccurate claims and only one presented side effect information (Sansgiry, Sharp, & Sansgiry, 1999).

OTC drug TV ad content has been analyzed in two studies. The first study analyzed 150 OTC drug commercials and found product awareness was the primary communication goal, information emphasized user benefits, and performance was featured as simple solutions for relief (Tsao, 1997). The second studied health content of OTC drug commercials in child-oriented prime-time network programs and concluded that TV advertising cultivates a "magic of medicine" belief in OTC drugs as the rapid, easy, and risk-free way of relieving health problems (Byrd-Bredbenner & Grasso, 1999).

Consumer Response and Message Effects

Attitudes and Perceptions. Though not overwhelming in volume, evidence suggests attitudes toward OTC drug advertising are generally unfavorable. Studies have reported that consumer attitudes toward OTC drug advertising are less favorable than attitudes toward advertising in general (Diehl, Mueller, & Terlutter, 2008), even though consumers appear to be less skeptical of OTC drug advertising than advertising in general (Diehl, Mueller, & Terlutter, 2007). A study of the attitudes of pharmacy professionals reported that they also view OTC drug advertising unfavorably. The research indicates that pharmacists are unfavorable toward OTC advertising because they consider the ads to be untruthful and to omit important product information (Mackowiak, O'Connor, Geller, Nguyen, & Wilkes, 1997).

Message Effects. Only two experiments have manipulated variables to establish causal links between OTC drug advertising and consumer responsiveness to message content. One experiment examined the effects of ad credibility and ad format (direct comparative vs. noncomparative) on consumer beliefs, attitudes, and behavioral intention and found that direct comparative/high credibility formatted ads consistently produced the most favorable responses to OTC medicines (Kavanoor, Grewal, & Blodgett, 1997). Ad credibility was not found to moderate format effects. The other experiment tested the effect of instructions in TV commercials which urged consumers to read in-store warnings about OTC drugs and product packages, discovering that a message combining a concrete verbal action instruction with a visual of the action produced a short-term increase in package inspection and reading of in-store warning signs (Wright, 1979).

Advertising Information and Decision Making. Advertising is thought to play a role in consumer decision making regarding OTC drugs, and one group, The Nonprescription Drug Marketing Association (NDMA), has claimed Americans rely on advertising as a major OTC drug information source. However, evidence indicates that OTC advertising exerts limited influence on OTC drug decisions (Kim & King, 2009).

A study of information search for both Rx and OTC drugs found that consumers rely on similar sources for both Rx and OTC drug information, though source importance varied by drug type. Physicians and pharmacists were viewed as most important for both types; however, physicians were significantly more important for Rx than OTC drugs. Interpersonal, mass media, and package sources were more important for OTC drugs; Internet sources were more important for Rx drugs; and no advertising form was rated important for OTC drug information (see Kim & King, 2009).

Age-based differences in consumer decision making have been investigated in three studies, all of which also challenge the NDMA's claim about the importance of OTC advertising. An investigation of the relationship between source characteristics and likelihood of source use for decisions among college students found that TV ads for OTC medicines were judged as convenient, inexpensive, and efficient information sources but received the lowest likelihood of use rating of five information sources (Portner & Smith, 1994). Another study compared decision making of older and younger adults and found older adults recalled less information from TV advertising, and recalled fewer brand name cold/allergy drugs relative to younger adults (Stephens & Johnson, 2000). However, TV commercials did not prime OTC drug information search or purchase decisions of either older or younger adults, suggesting that OTC drug advertising is not a strong decisional influence. Research on decision processes of the elderly specifically found media advertising was rarely or never used for OTC drug information, suggesting that it is not very important in older adults' medicinal decision making (Reisenwitz & Wimbush, 1997).

Use, Misuse, and Abuse: Unintended Effects. Like all advertising, OTC drug advertising has unintended consequences beyond its pragmatic communication effects. OTC drug advertising's association with the use, misuse, and abuse of both proprietary and illicit drugs among children and teens has been the subject of most research on unintended effects. Research has consistently found little or no connection between children's and teens' OTC drug ad exposure and use, misuse, and abuse of proprietary or illicit drugs (e.g., Rossano & Butter, 1987; Rossiter & Robertson, 1980).

Economic Impact

In addition to microconsiderations, OTC drug advertising also plays a role in the larger American economy. Market competition and advertising's economic contributions are closely associated, though the jury is empirically out on whether the associations involving OTC drugs are good or bad for the consumer. Proponents argue that advertising allows pharmaceutical companies to compete with one another more effectively. Such competition, it is argued, produces new and better OTC medicines, and at competitive prices. Critics counter that OTC drug advertising is anticompetitive, resulting in higher prices, barriers to market entry, and wasteful economic resources.

Though the research is not extensive, the evidence is revealing. A study of the order-of-entry effects and other outcomes relative to marketing efforts and Rx-to-OTC switching found that pioneering OTC drug brands enjoy order-of-market entry advantages (e.g., Tylenol, Advil), but that first-mover advantages are not insurmountable for later entrants (Ling, Berndt, & Kyle, 2002). Additionally, marketing efforts have positive spillover effects from Rx to OTC drugs but not from OTC to Rx drugs. The findings suggest that drug advertising for Rx versions influences sales of OTC drug versions, but not vice versa.

Dietary Supplement Advertising

Americans have been increasingly seeking information not only for traditional medicine but also for complementary and alternative medicine, including dietary supplements (DS). A DS is a product (other than tobacco) that is intended to supplement the diet, contains one or more dietary ingredients (including vitamins, minerals, herbs or other botanicals, amino acids, and other substances) or their constituents, and is labeled on the front panel as being a DS (National Institutes of Health, 2006). As many medical conditions are linked to nutrition, supplements are believed to help prevent disease and maintain health. However, they are not intended to treat or cure illnesses and there is debate on their efficacy and safety (Sadovsky, Collins, Tighe, Brunton, & Safeer, 2008).

Competitive pressures have forced more companies to seek to establish unique claims for their products. Health-related claims are often used to create perceptions that products are healthful and entice purchase. These claims are commonly within the context of consumer testimonials (e.g., "before" and "after" photos), "expert" endorsements, and celebrity endorsements (McCann, 2005). While it is crucial that DS advertising be truthful and nonmisleading, the promotion of these products has been plagued by many issues and concerns.

Federal Regulation of Dietary Supplement Advertising

The FTC has jurisdiction over dietary supplement advertising regulation, while the FDA has regulatory authority for DS claims made in labeling (i.e., affixed label, packaging, inserts, point of sale materials). However, the distinction between advertising and labeling is not always clear, leading to controversies (Villafranco & Lustigman, 2007). In principle, if the information accompanies the product at the point of sale, it is labeling; otherwise, it is considered advertising (Abood, 2008). Because claims on labels and ads are subject to different rules by two separate agencies, regulation can become quite complicated (Nestle, 2002). The issue of jurisdiction may delay appropriate actions and cause a public health hazard, given that dietary supplements are typically taken without professional supervision.

To comply with FTC guidelines, supplement ad claims must be truthful, nonmisleading, and adequately substantiated, as must other ad claims. In addition, the FTC issued *Dietary Supplements: An Advertising Guide for Industry* in 1998. To constitute adequate substantiation, a reasonable claim based on competent and reliable scientific evidence should be made. The FTC interprets "competent and reliable scientific evidence" as any "tests, analyses, research, studies, or other evidence based on the expertise of professionals in the relevant area that have been conducted and evaluated in an objective manner by persons qualified to do so, using procedures generally accepted in the profession to yield accurate and reliable results" (FTC, 1998, p. 9). However, DS ads do not have to be approved by the FTC prior to dissemination (Ashar, Miller, Pichard, Levine, & Wright, 2008).

The FDA has the statutory authority to regulate DS claims on product labels. The Dietary Supplement Health and Education Act of 1994 (DSHEA) is the key federal statute governing the FDA's role in that process. There are four types of label claims: (a) "health claims" that describe the efficacy of a supplement or ingredient for a disease or other health-related condition, (b) "qualified health claims" that discuss emerging evidence of a supplement or ingredient on a disease or other health-related condition, (c) "nutrient content claims" describing the level of a nutrient, and (d) "structure/function claims" explaining how a dietary ingredient affects the human body physiologically.

The FDA must approve health claims, qualified health claims, and nutrient content claims. However, structure/function claims do not require the FDA's preapproval and need only be accompanied by the disclaimer: "This statement has not been evaluated by the Food and Drug Administration. This product is not intended to diagnose, treat, cure or prevent any disease." However, the disclaimer does not relieve the advertiser from the substantiation requirement for any claims made in the ad (Dickinson, 1999). The DSHEA changed the way supplements are regulated, affecting ad practices, and will be discussed further in this section.

Dietary Supplement Advertising Spending

Ad spending by DS marketers has increased steadily, reaching $904 million in 2008, which is about a 10% increase from the $826.5 million spent in 2007 (TNS Media Intelligence Ad Spender Data, 2009). Of the total ad media expenditures in 2008, 40.3% was spent on magazines, reflecting DS marketers' reliance on magazine ads and advertorials (TNS Media Intelligence Ad Spender Data, 2009).[1]

Among factors explaining the dramatic increase in DS ad spending are the signing into law of two federal Acts in the 1990s: the Nutritional Labeling and Education Act (NLEA) and the Dietary Supplement Health and Education Act (DSHEA). The NLEA clarified definitions of nutritional terms and enabled food companies to utilize standardized nutritional labeling information, leading possibly to greater consumer interest in food labeling, more reliance on nutritional label information for purchase decisions, and a stronger association between food and health conditions resulting in acceptance of DS ad claims (Stroube, Rainey, & Tanner 2002). The passage of the DSHEA was a more direct driving force behind the DS ad surge and related issues.

Major Driver of Dietary Supplement Advertising and Key Issues

The DSHEA

Prompted by industry lobbying and consumer pressures, Congress passed the 1994 Dietary Supplement Health and Education Act (DSHEA) to improve consumer access to and information flow about supplements. The DSHEA contained four basic provisions: (a) it broadened the legal definition of dietary supplements to encompass not only vitamins and minerals but also botanical and herbal products; (b) it mandated that DS manufacturers do not need to prove the safety, efficacy, and quality of their products to the FDA before putting them on the market; (c) it specified that the FDA is responsible for demonstrating that products are unsafe before removing them from the market; and (d) it allowed manufacturers to label their products with a new type of claim called a "structure/function claim" that does not require FDA approval: (a) if the manufacturer notified the FDA within 30 days of first marketing the product, (b) has on file some substantiation for the statement, and (c) if the DSHEA disclaimer is included on the label (Nestle, 2002).

The DSHEA has sparked controversy among various stakeholders. Critics say the DSHEA allows too many unsubstantiated claims while restricting the FDA's regulatory ability. Further, they argue the FDA does not have resources for adequate enforcement. Proponents, however, stress the industry's self-regulatory ability, that manufacturers must have evidence on hand to substantiate claims, and that the mandated "structure/function" disclaimer alerts consumers about the product's lack of FDA review (Triplett, 2004). Some acknowledge that the recent Dietary Supplement and Nonprescription Drug Consumer Protection Act requiring manufacturers to report to the FDA all serious supplement-related adverse events is progress toward stricter regulation (Ashar, Miller, Pichard, Levine, & Wright, 2008). Yet the debate is ongoing.

Issues in Dietary Supplement Advertising

The DSHEA has had a number of advertising-related implications. First, since the DSHEA's expansion of the DS definition, the quantity and diversity of products marketed to consumers has skyrocketed (Ashar et al., 2008); most of these are thought to pose no serious harm and many seem to help maintain or improve health. However, since supplements are usually taken without medical supervision, instructions for proper use and risk awareness may be lacking (Balluz, Kieszak, Philen, & Mulinare, 2000).

Second, the DSHEA's loosening of premarket approval regulation seems to have compounded potential problems by exposing consumers to supplements that may be ineffective or dangerous due to lack of standardization of ingredients or adulteration or contamination. Additionally, some supplement manufacturers have been marketing substances with pharmaceutical-like properties and effects to avoid FDA drug regulations (Crawford & Leventis, 2005).

A third issue results from the DSHEA's "structure/function" claim category, as manufacturers have been boldly making health-related claims, some of which may be exaggerated or untrue. Fourth, while the Act has generated health information, it may have created confusion as well, resulting in unnecessary, inappropriate, or dangerous uses of supplements (Mason, 1998; Mason & Scammon, 2000).

A fifth DSHEA consequence is that the volume and variety of DS advertising has increased dramatically (FTC, 1998). The DSHEA relaxed the FDA's regulation of DS labeling, but did not alter the FTC's regulation of advertising. The FTC holds health-related claims in supplement ads to more rigorous standards than FDA labeling requirements, and hundreds of actions for allegedly false or misleading claims in DS ads have been filed over the years (Mason, 1998; Sopher, 2005). Nonetheless, there has been "a proliferation of advertisements which, despite FTC guidelines, contain misleading, erroneous, or unsubstantiated information" under the DSHEA (Ashar et al., 2008, p. 23). Consequently, there have been many calls for stricter DS ad regulation. The FTC's 1998 booklet *Dietary Supplements: An Advertising Guide for Industry,* noted earlier, was one effort in response.

There are also Internet-related issues because many questionable supplements have been promoted unethically or illegally through e-mails and websites. For example, research has found that many sites make prohibited "disease claims" or fail to disclose potential adverse effects (Ashar, Miller, Getz, & Pichard, 2003; Morris & Avorn, 2003). While FTC truth-in-advertising standards also apply to the Internet, claims in the medium are difficult to control (Ashar et al., 2003). To address these challenges, the FTC published Internet marketing guidelines and the FTC and FDA have been collaborating to better regulate fraudulent DS Internet marketing, including periodic online searches to identify sites and ads with unsubstantiated claims (Crawford & Leventis, 2005).

Research on Dietary Supplement Advertising

To date, there has been little empirical research on DS advertising. Most of the literature has involved discussions about DSHEA and associated regulatory issues from the viewpoints of medical, legal, and supplement industry professionals. Findings of the few relevant studies of consumer perceptions suggest that they are confused about the roles of the FDA and FTC in DS regulation (e.g., Ashar et al., 2008; Blendon, DesRoches, Benson, Brodie, & Altman, 2001; Miller & Russell, 2004).

Research on the process and effects of DS advertising is rare. A small stream of work has studied use of different information sources for DS decision making. While some studies have found consumers consult with health care professionals about supplements (e.g., Peters, Shelton, & Sharma 2003; Rowe & Toner, 2003), others indicate consumers are hesitant to disclose use because they perceive that these experts are biased against alternative therapies (e.g., Blendon et al., 2001; Greger, 2001).

Though the evidence is limited, advertising appears to have some influence on consumers' DS decision making, especially among certain groups such as older adults (Mason & Scammon, 1999; Peters et al., 2003; Snyder, Dundas, Kirkpatrick, & Neill, 2009). Overall, findings suggest that consumers use multiple sources including interpersonal contacts (family, friends, store clerks, personal trainers), printed materials (books, newsletters, scientific journals), media reports, health-related websites, and advertising (e.g., Peters et al., 2003; Rowe & Toner, 2003; Snyder et al., 2009). Identifying and evaluating information quality in advertising has been the focus of another vein of DS research. Content analyses of magazine ads (e.g., Kava, Meister, Whelan, Lukachko, & Mirabile, 2002; Philen, Ortiz, Auerbach, & Falk, 1992; Shaw, Zhang, & Metallinos-Katsaras, 2009) and websites (e.g., Jordan & Haywood, 2007) have documented that certain DS ads and sites fail to contain complete and accurate information. Consumer evaluation of DS information in different sources, including advertising, has been the focus of only a few studies. The findings suggest that consumers are not critical in their assessment of source objectivity. In contrast to traditional medications, DS-related decisions may be influenced more by social interaction and personal beliefs stemming from anecdotal evidence and product promotion (Crawford & Leventis, 2005; Mason & Scammon, 1999).

Further, there is some indication that DS users and nonusers evaluate DS-related information differently. Specifically, Blendon et al. (2001) found that DS users were more likely than nonusers to believe advertising claims. They also found that many consumers believed so strongly in the supplements they were taking that they reported they would continue taking them even if scientific evidence demonstrated they were ineffective. These findings suggest that regular DS users may be especially susceptible to DS-related persuasion. The problem of susceptibility is compounded for vulnerable consumers (e.g., being older, in chronic pain) such that they may be eager to try products with little or no valid support of safety or effectiveness (Mason & Scammon, 2000; Philen et al., 1992).

Conclusion

From this overview, several broad observations about pharmaceutical and dietary supplement advertising can be made. First, advertising plays a significant role in the U.S. pharmaceutical and DS markets. Ad spending has increased substantially in recent years and continues to grow. Advertising appears to be a prominent and important driver of the purchase and consumption of pharmaceuticals and supplements. Second, Americans are more empowered in their personal health care today than ever before. They are seeking more knowledge about traditional as well as alternative medicines. Advertising serves to help fulfill consumers' informational needs, along with other sources. However, advertising in this public health domain is especially complex compared to other types of consumer advertising and not without challenges. All three product categories are surrounded by ongoing, advertising-related controversies and regulatory concerns.

Third, many gaps remain in regard to understanding pharmaceutical and DS advertising and further research is needed. The specific gaps vary by product type, but significant research opportunities exist for positively impacting U.S. public health. Despite a substantial amount of study on DTCA, questions remain, especially regarding outcomes. For DTCA, there is a lack of evidence about potential health benefits or to exclude potential harm. There is also limited investigation of how physicians respond to patients' inquiries and requests for an advertised drug. Further, studies are needed to explore DTC ad effects on: appropriateness of drug use, compliance with drug instructions, preventative health measures, use of health care services, and changes in pharmaceutical costs. As most studies have relied on self-report surveys, other research methods should also be pursued.

The OTC drug advertising literature stream is small, fragmented, and dated. New evidence should be gathered about ad content characteristics including information/persuasive balance, prevalence of health/nonhealth claims, and human portrayals. Importantly, studies should scrutinize the accuracy of product claims and side effects in ads. Research should also examine how the average consumer responds to OTC drug ad content, including its role in information seeking and decision making for specific OTC drug categories and Rx-to-OTC drug switches. Additionally, studies are needed on how OTC drug advertising influences patient/health care provider interactions to determine how ads affect advice seeking and giving that relates to OTC medications. Previous work on OTC drug advertising's influence on socially disadvantaged consumers should be replicated and extended to other populations. Finally, more information on advertising's role in the OTC drug market is required at both the aggregate and product category levels. Among other things, research should focus on questions of advertising as information or persuasion, market entry, price competition, and regulatory impacts.

Dietary supplement advertising is a subject that is also ripe for research. Although there is some existing literature on physician–patient communication about supplements (e.g., Kemper et al., 2003; Roberts et al., 2005), the area is virtually unexplored. For DS advertising, content analyses of ads directed to different target audiences and across all major media types that identify patterns in ad characteristics, claims, and creative approaches would provide important benchmark data for possible message improvements. Development of a typology of DS ads is also recommended. Studies which aim to better understand consumers' perceptions and opinions of DS advertising and comprehension of health-related claims should be another priority, especially studies which compare DS users and nonusers. Closer investigation of consumers' use and evaluation of different DS information sources, including advertising, is also advocated, as is inquiry on DS ad effects. Research comparing Rx, OTC drug, and DS advertising would make a valuable contribution as well.

There are a number of similarities across the three product types. However, not all pharmaceutical and supplement products are permitted to be promoted in the same way. While the underlying purpose and process of advertising is essentially the same (i.e., to inform, persuade, help sell), there are some important contextual distinctions in additional goals and processes and each has unique controversial issues and regulatory restrictions that warrant attention from health communicators and researchers.

Because advertising is a biased, sponsor-controlled information source, appropriate and socially responsible consumer education programs are needed. Thus, the development and implementation of health-literacy programs that educate consumers about current limitations of government oversight for pharmaceuticals and supplements and how to critically assess advertising's persuasive influences are recommended. In addition, education to facilitate effective communication with consumers should be considered for health care providers. Though consumers must be actively involved in self-education, it is especially important that health communicators and policy officials carefully consider advertising's role in health contexts; monitor the surrounding issues and dynamic regulatory environment; and gain a deeper understanding of consumers' perceptions, motivations, and uses of pharmaceutical and supplement advertising. Truthful and responsible advertising for the three product types can contribute to quality of life and more informed and empowered consumers.

Note

1. The advertising spending total for each year was calculated by summating advertising expenditures for three product categories—vitamins and minerals, weight loss and gain aids, and nutritional supplements.

References

Abood, R. R. (2008). *Pharmacy practice and the law.* Sudbury, MA: Jones & Barlett.

Ad spend dips; Pharma pulls back on media as wallets get thinner. (2009, April). *Pharmaceutical Executive,* p. 18.

Allergies: Private-label OTC drugs post solid gains in 2008, according to Kline. (2009, April 24). *Drug Week,* p. 1674.

Allison-Ottey, S. D., Ruffin, K., & Allison, K. B. (2002). To do no harm, survey of the physicians of the National Medical Association regarding perceptions on DTC advertisements. *Journal of the National Medical Association, 94*(4), 194–202.

An, S. (2007). Attitude toward direct-to-consumer advertising and drug inquiry intention: The moderating role of perceived knowledge. *Journal of Health Communication, 12,* 567–580.

An, S. (2008). Antidepressant direct-to-consumer advertising and social perception of the prevalence of depression: Application of the availability heuristic. *Health Communication, 23,* 499–505.

An, S., Jin, H. S., & Brown, J. (2009). Direct-to-consumer antidepressant ads and young adults' beliefs about depression. *Health Marketing Quarterly, 26,* 259–278.

Arnold, M. (2009a, January). DTC spending lagged in '08, says TNS. *Medical Marketing & Media,* p. 28.

Arnold, M. (2009b, April). Between screens: A shift in DTC. *Medical Marketing & Media,* pp. 40–47.

Arxcel Inc. (2008, September*). Arxcel 2008 prescription benefits management research survey.* Williamsville, NY: Arxcel. Retrieved from http://www.arxcel.com/research/2008_Survey.pdf.

Ashar, B., Miller, R. G., Getz, K. J., & Pichard, C. P. (2003). A critical evaluation of Internet marketing of products that contain ephedra. *Mayo Clinic Proceedings, 78,* 944–946.

Ashar, B. H., Miller, R. G., Pichard, C. P., Levine, R., & Wright, S. M. (2008). Patients' understanding of the regulation of dietary supplements. *Journal of Community Health, 33,* 22–30.

Auton, F. (2004). The advertising of pharmaceuticals direct to consumers: A critical review of the literature and debate. *International Journal of Advertising, 23,* 5–52.

Auton, F. (2006). Direct-to-consumer advertising (DTCA) of pharmaceuticals: An updated review of the literature and debate since 2003. *Institute of Economic Affairs, 26*(3), 24–32.

Balluz, L., Kieszak, S. M., Philen, R. M., & Mulinare, J. (2000). Vitamin and mineral supplement use in the United States: Results from the third national health and nutrition examination survey. *Archives of Family Medicine, 9,* 258–262.

Blendon, R. J., DesRoches, C. M., Benson, J. M., Brodie, M., & Altman, D. E. (2001). Americans' views on the use and regulation of dietary supplements. *Archives of Internal Medicine, 161,* 805–810.

Blue Cross Blue Shield Association. (2002, March 7). Business leaders identify healthcare cost drivers. News Release. Chicago, IL: Blue Cross Blue Shield Association.

Brownfield, E., Bernhardt, J., Phan, J., Williams, M., & Parker, R. (2004). Direct-to-consumer drug advertisements on network television: An exploration of quantity, frequency, and placement. *Journal of Health Communication, 9,* 491–497.

Byrd-Bredbenner, C., & Grasso, D. (1999). Prime-time health: An analysis of health content in television commercials broadcast during programs viewed heavily by children. *International Electronic Journal of Health Education, 2*(4), 159–169.

Calfee, J. E. (2002). Public policy issues in direct-to-consumer advertising of prescription drugs. *Journal of Public Policy and Marketing, 21,* 174–193.

Cline, R. J. W., & Young, H. N. (2004). Marketing drugs, marketing health care relationships: A content analysis of visual cues in direct-to-consumer prescription drug advertising. *Health Communication, 16,* 131–157.

Consumer Healthcare Products Association. (2009). OTC retail sales 1964–2008. Retrieved from www.chpa-info.org/pressroom/Retail_Sales.aspx.

Crawford, S. Y., & Leventis, C. (2005). Herbal product claims: Boundaries of marketing and science. *Journal of Consumer Marketing, 22,* 432–436.

DeLorme, D., Huh, J., & Reid, L. N. (2007a). Seniors' perceptions of prescription drug information sources. *International Journal of Pharmaceutical and Healthcare Marketing, 1,* 107–127.

DeLorme, D., Huh, J., & Reid, L. N. (2007b). "Others are influenced, but not me": Older adults' perceptions of DTC prescription drug advertising effects. *Journal of Aging Studies, 21,* 135–151.

Deshpande, A., Menon, A., Perri, M., & Zinkhan, G. M. (2004). Direct-to-consumer advertising and its utility in health care decision-making: A consumer perspective. *Journal of Health Communication, 9,* 499–513.

Dickinson, A. (1999). New FTC guidelines on dietary supplement advertising: A valuable restatement and explanation of current enforcement policy. *Journal of Nutrition Education, 31,* 276–277.

Diehl, S., Mueller, B., & Terlutter, R. (2007). Skepticism toward pharmaceutical advertising in the U.S. and Germany. *Cross-Cultural Buyer Behavior: Advances in International Marketing, 18,* 31–60.

Diehl, S., Mueller, B., & Terlutter, R. (2008). Consumer responses towards non-prescription and prescription drug advertising in Germany. *International Journal of Advertising, 27,* 99–131.

Dietary Supplement Health and Education Act of 1994, Pub. L. 103-417, 108 Stat. 4325 (1994)

Dietary Supplement and Nonprescription Drug Consumer Protection Act of 2006, Pub. L. 109-462, 120 Stat. 3469 (2006)

Donohue, J. M., & Berndt, E. R. (2004). Effects of direct-to-consumer advertising on medication choice: The case of antidepressants. *Journal of Public Policy & Marketing, 23,* 115–127.

Donohue, J. M., Cevasco, M., & Rosenthal, M. B. (2007). A decade of direct-to-consumer advertising of prescription drugs. *The New England Journal of Medicine, 357,* 673–681.

Durham-Humphrey Amendments of 1951, Pub. L. 82-215, 65 Stat. 648 (1951)

Federal Trade Commission (FTC). (1998). *Dietary supplements: An advertising guide for industry.* Retrieved from http://www.ftc.gov/bcp/edu/pubs/business/adv/bus09.shtm

Findlay, S. D. (2001). Direct-to-consumer promotion of prescription drugs: Economic implications for patients, payers, and providers. *Pharmacoeconomics, 19,* 109–119.

Findlay, S. D. (2002). Do ads really drive pharmaceutical sales? The true effects of DTC advertising remain a mystery. *Marketing Health Services, 22*(1), 21–25.

Food and Drug Administration. (1999, August). Guidance for industry: Consumer-directed broadcast advertisements, Washington, DC: Author. Retrieved from http://www.fda.gov/downloads/RegulatoryInformation/Guidances/ucm125064.pdf).

Food and Drug Administration. (2004, November 19). *Patient and physician attitudes and behaviors associated with DTC promotion of prescription drugs—Summary of FDA survey research results* (Final Report). Washington, DC: Author.

Food and Drug Administration Amendments Act of 2007 (FDAAA). Pub. L. No. 110-85, § 901, 121 Stat. 823, 939-42.

Food and Drug Administration, Department of Health and Human Services (FDA/DHHS). (1985). Direct to consumer advertising moratorium for prescription drugs ended. *Federal Register, 50,* 36677–36678.

Food and Drug Administration, Department of Health and Human Services (FDA/DHHS). (1995). Direct to consumer promotion: Public hearing. *Federal Register, 60,* 42581–42583.

Food, Drug, and Cosmetic Act of 1938, Pub. L. 75-717, 52 Stat. 1040 (1938)

Frangos, A. (2001, April 23). E-commerce: Prescription for change: Drug companies are slowly starting to warm up to the web as a place to advertise [A special report]. *The Wall Street Journal,* p. R24. (Reprint from Recent Food and Drug Administration warning letters. *Drug Information Journal, 41,* 281–289)

Frosch, D., Krueger, P. M., Hornik, R. C., Cronholm, P. F., & Barg, F. K. (2007). Creating demand for prescription drugs: A content analysis of television direct-to-consumer advertising. *Annals of Family Medicine, 5,* 6–13.

Gebhart, F. (2009, April 27). DTC ad spending decreased last year. *Modern Medicine.* Retrieved from http://www.modernmedicine.com/modernmedicine/Chains+%26+Business/DTC-ad-spending-decreased-last-year/ArticleStandard/Article/detail/595223.

Government Accountability Office (GAO). (2006, November). *Prescription drugs: Improvements needed in FDA's oversight of direct-to-consumer advertising.* Washington, DC: Author.

Government Accountability Office (GAO). (2008, May). *Prescription drugs: Trends in FDA's oversight of direct-to-consumer advertising.* Washington, DC: Author.

Greger, J. L. (2001). Dietary supplement use: Consumer characteristics and interests [Supplement]. *Journal of Nutrition, 131,* 1339S–1343S.

Hollon, M. F. (1999). Direct-to-consumer marketing of prescription drugs: Creating consumer demand. *Journal of the American Medical Association, 281*, 382.

Holmer, A. F. (1999). Direct-to-consumer prescription drug advertising builds bridges between patients and physicians. *Journal of the American Medical Association, 281*, 380–382.

Huh, J., & Cude, B. J. (2004). Is the information "fair and balanced" in direct-to-consumer prescription drug websites? *Journal of Health Communication, 9*, 529–540.

Huh, J., DeLorme, D. E., & Reid, L. N. (2004). The information utility of DTC prescription drug advertising. *Journalism and Mass Communication Quarterly, 81*, 788–806.

Huh, J., & Langteau, R. (2007). Presumed influence of direct-to-consumer (DTC) prescription drug advertising on patients: The physicians' perspective. *Journal of Advertising, 36*, 305–326.

Institute of Medicine. (2006). *The future of drug safety: Promoting and protecting the health of the public.* Washington, DC: National Academy Press.

Jordan, M. A., & Haywood, T. (2007). Evaluation of Internet websites marketing herbal weight-loss supplements to consumers. *Journal of Alternative and Complementary Medicine, 13*, 1035–1043.

Kaiser Family Foundation (2008, September). *Prescription drug trends.* Washington, DC: Author.

Kaphingst, K. A., DeJong, W., Rudd, R. E., & Daltroy, L. N. (2004). A content analysis of direct-to-consumer television prescription drug advertisements. *Journal of Health Communication, 9*, 515–528.

Kava, R., Meister, K. A., Whelan, E. M., Lukachko, A. M., & Mirabile, C. (2002). Dietary supplement safety information in magazines popular among older readers. *Journal of Health Communication, 7*, 13–23.

Kavanoor, S., Grewal, D., & Blodgett, J. (1997). Ads promoting OTC medications: The effect of ad format and credibility on beliefs, attitudes, and purchase intentions. *Journal of Business Research, 40*, 219–227.

Kefauver-Harris Drug Amendments of 1962, Pub. L. 87-781, 76 Stat. 781 (1962)

Kemper, K. J., Amata-Kynvi, A., Dvorkin, L., Whelan, J. S., Woolf, A., Samuels, R. C., & Hibberd, P. (2003). Herbs and other dietary supplements: Healthcare professionals' knowledge, attitudes, and practices. *Alternative Therapies in Health and Medicine, 9*, 42–49.

Kim, W. J., & King, K. W. (2009). Product category effects on external search for prescription and nonprescription drugs. *Journal of Advertising, 38*, 5–19.

Kittinger, P., & Herrick, D. (2005, August 22). Patient power: Over-the-counter drugs. *National Center for Policy Analysis, Brief Analysis, 524*, 1–2.

Ling, D. C., Berndt, E. R., & Kyle, M. K. (2002). Regulating direct-to-consumer marketing of prescription drugs: Effects on prescription and over-the-counter product sales. *Journal of Law & Economics, 45*, 691–723.

Lipsky, M. S., & Taylor, C. A. (1997). The opinions and experiences of family physicians regarding direct-to-consumer advertising. *Journal of Family Practice, 45*, 495–499.

Macias, W., & Lewis, L. S. (2003). A content analysis of direct-to-consumer (DTC) prescription drug web sites. *Journal of Advertising, 32*, 43–56.

Macias, W., & Lewis, L. S. (2006). How well do direct-to-consumer, DTC, prescription drug web sites meet FDA guidelines and public policy concerns? *Health Marketing Quarterly, 22*(4), 45–71.

Mackowiak, E. D., O'Connor, T. W., Geller, H., Nguyen, J., & Wilkes, W. (1997). A survey of pharmacists' and pharmacy students' attitudes toward OTC advertising. *Journal of Pharmaceutical Marketing & Management, 12*(1), 33–49.

Mason, M. J. (1998). Drugs or dietary supplements: FDA's enforcement of DSHEA. *Journal of Public Policy and Marketing, 17*, 296–302.

Mason, M. J., & Scammon, D. L. (1999). Consumers and nutritional supplements: Could this be me? This is me! *Advances in Consumer Research, 26*, 107–112.

Mason, M. J., & Scammon, D. L. (2000). Health claims and disclaimers: Extended boundaries and research opportunities in consumer interpretation. *Journal of Public Policy & Marketing, 19*, 144–150.

Mastin, T., Andsager, J. L., Choi, J., & Lee, K. (2007). Health disparities and direct-to-consumer prescription drug advertising: A content analysis of targeted magazine genres, 1992–2002. *Health Communication, 22*, 49–58.

McCann, M. A. (2005). Dietary supplement labeling: Cognitive biases, market manipulation, & consumer choice. *American Journal of Law and Medicine, 31*, 215–268.

McGuire, W. J. (1978). An information processing model of advertising effectiveness. In H. L. Davis & A. J. Silk (Eds.), *Behavioral and management science in marketing* (pp.156–180). New York: Ronald Press.

Menon, A. M., Deshpande, A. D., Zinkhan, G. M., & Perri, M. (2004). A model assessing the effectiveness of direct-to-consumer advertising: Integration of concepts and measures from marketing and healthcare. *International Journal of Advertising, 23*, 91–118.

Miley, M. (2009, February 2). Consumers flock to private labels. *Advertising Age*, p. 27.

Miller, C. K., & Russell, T. (2004). Knowledge of dietary supplement label information among female supplement users. *Patient Education and Counseling, 52*, 291–296.

Mintzes, B. (2001). *An assessment of the health system impacts of direct-to-consumer advertising of prescription medicines (DTCA): Volume 2, Literature review direct-to-consumer advertising of prescription drugs: What do we know thus far about its effects on health and health care services?* Vancouver, Canada: University of British Columbia Press.

Morris, C. A., & Avorn, J. (2003). Internet marketing of herbal products. *Journal of the American Medical Association, 290*, 1505–1509.

Murray, E., Lo, B., Pollack, L., Donelan, K., & Lee, K. (2003). Direct-to-consumer advertising: Physicians' views of its effects of quality of care and the doctor–patient relationship. *Journal of the American Board of Family Practice, 16*, 513–524.

National Institute for Health Care Management (NIHCM). (2000). *Prescription drugs and mass media advertising, 2000.* Washington, DC: National Institute for Health Care Management Research and Educational Foundation. Retrieved from http://www.nihcm.org/~nihcmor/pdf/DTCbrief.pdf.

National Institutes of Health, Office of Dietary Supplements. (2006). *Dietary supplements: Background information.* Bethesda, MD: Author.

Nestle, M. (2002). *Food politics: How the food industry influences nutrition and health.* Berkeley: University of California Press.

Nutrition Labeling and Education Act of 1990, Pub. L. 101-535, 104 Stat. 2353 (1990) *OTC Perspectives.* (2009, June). Spending review: The latest spending data from Nielsen Monitor-Plus. *OTC Perspectives, 1*(1), 10.

Palumbo, F. B., & Mullins, D. (2002). The development of direct to consumer prescription drug advertising regulation. *Food and Drug Law Journal, 57*, 423–443.

Park, J. S., & Grow, J. (2008). The social reality of depression: DTC advertising of antidepressants perceptions of the prevalence and lifetime risk of depression. *Journal of Business Ethics, 79*, 379–393.

Parker, B. J., & Delene, L. M. (1998). Direct-to-consumer prescription drug advertising: Content analysis and public policy implications. *Journal of Pharmaceutical Marketing & Management, 12*(4), 27–42.

Peters, C. O., Shelton, J., & Sharma, P. (2003). An investigation of factors that influence the consumption of dietary supplements. *Health Marketing Quarterly, 21*(1/2), 113–135.

Pfizer. (2001, July). *Direct-to-consumer advertising: How it benefits consumers,* New York: Pfizer.

Pfizer. (2005). *2005 Patient empowerment study.* New York: Pfizer.

Pharmaceutical Research and Manufacturers of America (PhRMA) (2002, April). *Direct-to-consumer advertising of prescription drugs: Myths and facts.* Washington DC: Author.

Philen, R. M., Ortiz, D. I., Auerbach, S. B., & Falk, H. (1992). Survey of advertising for nutritional supplements in health and bodybuilding magazines. *Journal of the American Medical Association, 268*, 1008–1011.

Portner, T. S., & Smith, M. C. (1994). College students' perceptions of OTC information source characteristics. *Journal of Pharmaceutical Marketing & Management, 8*(1), 161–185.

Rallapalli, K. C., Smith, M. C., & Stone, G. W. (1994). The social portrayal of people in OTC drug advertising: A content analysis of magazine advertisements. *Journal of Pharmaceutical Marketing & Management, 8*(2), 111–126.

Reisenwitz, T. H., & Wimbush, G. J. (1997). The purchase decision process and involvement of the elderly regarding nonprescription drugs. *Health Marketing Quarterly, 15*(1), 49–68.

Reynolds, W. J. (1992). Trends in advertising pharmaceuticals: A publisher's perspective. *Journal of Pharmaceutical Marketing & Management, 7*(1), 5–22.

Roberts, C. S., Baker, F., Hann, D., Runfola, J., Witt, C., McDonald, J.,...Blanchard, C. (2005). Patient–physician communication regarding use of complementary therapies during cancer treatment. *Journal of Psychosocial Oncology, 23*, 35–60.

Rossano, M. J., & Butter, E. J. (1987). Television advertising and children's attitudes toward proprietary medicines. *Psychology & Marketing, 4*, 213–224.

Rossiter, J. R., & Robertson, T. S. (1980). Children's dispositions toward proprietary drugs and the role of television advertising. *Public Opinion Quarterly, 44*, 316–329.

Rowe, S., & Toner, C. (2003). Dietary supplement use in women: The role of the media [Supplement]. *Journal of Nutrition, 133,* 2008S–2009S.

Sadovsky, R., Collins, N., Tighe, A. P., Brunton, S. A., & Safeer, R. (2008). Patient use of dietary supplements: A clinician's perspective. *Current Medical Research and Opinion, 24,* 1209–1216.

Sansgiry, S., Sharp, W. T., & Sansgiry, S. S. (1999). Accuracy of information on printed over-the-counter drug advertisements. *Health Marketing Quarterly, 17*(2), 7–18.

Schwartz, V. E., Silverman, C., Hulka, M. J., & Appel, C. E. (2009). Marketing pharmaceutical products in the twenty-first century: An analysis of the continued viability of traditional principles of law in the age of direct to consumer advertising. *Harvard Journal of Law and Public Policy, 32,* 333–362.

Shaw, P., Zhang, V., & Metallinos-Katsaras, E. (2009). A content analysis of the quantity and accuracy of dietary supplement information found in magazines with high adolescent readership. *Journal of Alternative & Complementary Medicine, 15,* 159–164.

Sheehan, K. (2006). Consumer friendly or reader hostile? An evaluation of the readability of DTC print ads. *Health Marketing Quarterly, 23*(4), 1–16.

Sheehan, K. (2007). Direct-to-consumer (DTC) branded drug web sites. *Journal of Advertising, 36,* 123–135.

Smith, M. C. (1983). *Principles of pharmaceutical marketing,* Philadelphia, PA: Lea & Febiger.

Snyder, F. J., Dundas, M. L., Kirkpatrick, C., & Neill, K. S. (2009). Use and safety perceptions regarding herbal supplements: A study of older persons in Southeast Idaho. *Journal of Nutrition for the Elderly, 28,* 81–95.

Sopher, J. (2005). Weight-loss advertising too good to be true: Are manufacturers or the media to blame? *Cardozo Arts & Entertainment Law Journal, 22,* 933–964.

Spake, D. F., & Joseph, M. (2007). Consumer opinion and effectiveness of direct-to-consumer advertising. *Journal of Consumer Marketing, 24,* 283–292.

Spence, M. M., Teleki, S. S., Cheetham, T. C., Schweitzer, S. O., & Millares, M. (2005). Direct-to-consumer advertising of COX-2 inhibitors: Effect on appropriateness of prescribing. *Medical Care Research and Review, 62,* 544–559.

Stange, K. C. (2007). Time to ban direct-to-consumer prescription drug marketing. *Annals of Family Medicine, 5,* 101–104.

Stephens, E. C., & Johnson, M. (2000). Dr. mom and other influences on younger and older adults' OTC medication purchases. *Journal of Applied Gerontology, 19,* 441–459.

Stroube, W. B., Rainey, C., & Tanner, J. T. (2002). Regulatory environment in the advertising of dietary supplements. *Clinical Research & Regulatory Affairs, 19,* 109–114.

Taylor, C. R., Capella, M. L., & Kozup, J. C. (2007). Does DTC advertising provide information or create market power? Evidence from the U.S. and New Zealand. *Advances in International Marketing, 18,* 9–30.

TNS Media Intelligence Ad Spender Data. (2009). New York: TNS Media Intelligence. Retrieved from University of Minnesota Library, http://www.lib.umn.edu/

Triplett, W. (2004). Dietary supplements: Is tougher regulation needed to protect consumers? *CQ Researcher, 14*(30), 709–732.

Tsao, J. C. (1997). Informational and symbolic content of over-the-counter drug advertising on television. *Journal of Drug Education, 27,* 173–197.

Vener, A. M., & Krupka, L. R. (1984). Over-the-counter drug advertising in gender oriented popular magazines. *Journal of Drug Education, 16,* 367–381.

Villafranco, J. E., & Lustigman, A. B. (2007). Regulation of dietary supplement advertising: Current claims of interest to the Federal Trade Commission and National Advertising Division. *Food and Drug Law Journal, 62,* 709–725.

Virginia State Board of Pharmacy v. *Virginia Citizens Consumer Council Inc.,* 425 U.S. 748 9 (1976).

Watts, M. R., & Wilkenfeld, J. D. (1992). The role of the Federal Trade Commission in regulating non-prescription drug advertising and promotion. *Journal of Drug Issues, 22,* 265–276.

Weissman, J. S., Blumenthal, D., Silk, A. J., Newman, M., Zapert, K., Leitman, R., & Felbelmann, S. (2004). Physicians report on patient encounters involving direct-to-consumer advertising. *Health Affairs, 23,* W4219–4233.

Wilkes, M. S., Bell, R. A., & Kravitz, R. L. (2000). Direct-to-consumer prescription drug advertising: Trends, impact and implications. *Health Affairs, 19,* 110–128.

Wosinska, M. (2005). Direct-to-consumer advertising and drug therapy compliance. *Journal of Marketing Research, 42*, 323–332.

Wright, P. (1979). Concrete action plans in TV messages to increase reading of drug warnings. *Journal of Consumer Research, 6*, 256–269.

Zachry, W. M., Dalen, J. E., & Jackson, T. R. (2003). Clinicians' responses to direct-to-consumer advertising of prescription medications. *Archives of Internal Medicine, 163*, 1808–1812.

SECTION IV

Mediators and Moderators of Care and Understanding

18

EXPLAINING ILLNESS

Issues Concerning the Co-Construction
of Explications

Teresa L. Thompson, Bryan B. Whaley, and Anne M. Stone

The central function of all medical systems is to give meaning to illness by naming and defining its cause (Stoeckle & Barsky, 1980). The goal of much health communication, then, is explaining illness. There is much to be said about this topic (see Whaley, 2000). One critical issue that arises in regard to explaining illness that has received recent scholarly attention is how providers and patients co-construct the explaining illness interaction. The present analysis will describe the need for illness explanations to provide a framework for better understanding the role of co-construction of explanations between providers and patients. The chapter concludes with attention to future directions for research on explaining illness.

Need for Illness Explanations

To understand the process of explaining illness, one must begin with an understanding of the need for such explanations (Thompson, 2000). This necessity is made apparent in several ways, but most notable amongst these is the *lack* of explanations reported by most patients. Receiving explanations is not, however, associated with such feared negative effects as treatment refusal or increased side-effects (Quaid, Faden, Vining, & Freeman, 1990). The research indicates that health care providers typically underestimate patients' demands for information and overestimate the quantity, completeness, and effectiveness of the explanations they provide (Strull, Lo, & Charles, 1984; Waitzin, 1985). The same lack of reception of illness explanation is reported by patients' family members; this is especially true of parents of ill children. Illness explanation needs are well documented in the literature in that study after study demonstrates the multitudinous needs for additional information on the part of patients (Thompson, 2000). This is true across almost all health problems and provider types. Cultural factors do, however, moderate the perceived need for explanations. Individuals from some cultures and in some age groups desire less complete information than do others (Thompson, 2000).

A second factor leading to an apparent need for explanations of illness may be seen in the research that documents the effects of receiving them. Those patients who receive more adequate explanations are more likely to adhere to treatment recommendations. They also recover more quickly, experience less postoperative vomiting and anxiety, need less anesthesia and pain medication, and are healthier, amongst many other positive outcomes (see Thompson, 2000 for a more complete discussion of this issue; see also Duggan and Thompson, this volume). The importance of the patients' perception of an illness, regardless of where it comes from, is indicated by data showing that such perceptions are key determinants of adjustment and coping (Dorian, Dempster, & Adair, 2009). Also, there are no associations between receiving illness explanations and treatment refusal or increased side-effects (Thompson, 2000).

Scholars have also examined how a patient's medically unexplained symptoms affect the provider–patient relationship (Fishchoff & Wessely, 2003; Greer & Halgin, 2006; Seaburn et al., 2005) and thus have implications for explaining illness. Specifically, Peters, Stanley, Rose, and Salmon (1998) examined the connection between lay and medical beliefs when a patient presents physical symptoms that the health care provider cannot diagnose. The authors suggested, contrary to other research findings, that patients view the physician as an ally and that patients do not adopt a biomedical model to describe their symptoms. Furthermore, Ogden et al. (2002) were interested in predictors of agreement on symptom etiology for patients with ambiguous symptoms. The authors found that physicians were more likely to define the illness as psychological if the patient was female, had a history of psychotropic medication use, and if the symptoms could not clearly be linked to a medical explanation.

Explanations that are provided to patients are also influenced by care providers' expectations and cultural/racial biases (Perloff, Bonder, Ray, Berlin Ray, & Siminoff, 2006). Racial biases must also be understood within the context of literacy level, however. Controlling for literacy levels does help moderate disparities in health function based on race (Sentel & Halpin, 2006). Similarly, the gender of both the explainer and the subject of the explanation influence explanations and attributions that are offered (Benrud & Reddy, 1998).

Research has highlighted uncertainty as a familiar experience across a variety of illnesses, including Alzheimer's disease (Stone & Jones, 2009), cancer (e.g., Clayton, Mishel, & Belyea, 2006), heart disease (Jurgens, 2006), and chronic pain (Johnson, Zautra, & Davis, 2006). Scholars have described the complexity of uncertainty experiences in illness in a number of ways. Following Mishel's (1988, 1990) work on uncertainty in acute and chronic illness, Brashers et al. (2003) identified three sources of uncertainty in the HIV illness context (i.e., medical, personal, and social sources). As Mishel (1988, 1990) described, medical uncertainty is related to insufficient information about diagnosis, ambiguous symptom patterns, complex systems of treatment and care, and unpredictable disease progression. Given that patients report that they do not receive the amount of information that they want in medical encounters, and that the information given is not clear, it is important to consider the important role that managing uncertainty may play in explaining illness.

Other theories of uncertainty have also described the complexity of the experience of uncertainty. For example, Babrow (1992, 2001) developed Problematic Integration theory to help explain how people experience uncertainty in illness. Babrow, Hines, and Kasch (2000) argued that the answers to people's questions take the form of "probabilistic orientations." For example, patients may question the likelihood of a drug helping them cope with the physical manifestations of an illness. According to Problematic Integration theory, people also evaluate their experiences. These "evaluative orientations" refer to the assessments people make after they consider the likelihood of a particular occurrence.

In addition to considering the psychosocial contextual features of explaining illness, it is important to consider the clarity of information that is used to explain illness. Problems with research on the information communicated during explanations of illness has been noted by such scholars as Tuckett and Williams (1984), whose review of this scholarship indicated that a considerable amount of work has focused on how much information is given rather than the content or value of that information. It is more important to examine how illuminating, relevant, or helpful the information might be to patients than it is to just examine how much information is communicated. The small amount of research that has attempted to examine information offered in illness explanations has generally asked patients to rate the value of the information. While these data are useful, one might question the patient's ability to assess such value. The patient's assessment is of interest in terms of what the patient does with the information and how the patient uses it, but might not correspond with a broader perspective on the value of the information.

Patient understanding of disease fluctuates somewhat with age and with culture, with children and adults from some Asian cultures accepting magical causality, although most adults prefer biological causality (Nguyen & Rosengren, 2004). Other research has identified the role that perceived genetic causality plays in the process of understanding and explaining illness (Parrott et al., 2004).

Third, the need for explanations of illness is also determined by the difficulty of providing them. Patients generally have poor recall of explanations, provide their own interpretation of illness, and have many misconceptions about illnesses. Many patients demonstrate little understanding of the medical jargon on which most explanations rely, making the explanation process even more difficult. While it may be assumed by some that patient understanding of medical terminology has improved over time, the data fail to document such an improvement. Indeed, much medical terminology is not even understood by care providers themselves. Reliance on medical terminology by care providers results in a lack of understanding on the part of the patient and social "one-upmanship," mystification, and control. Patients sometimes sue or seek ethics consultations just to receive an understanding of the language that has been used by care providers. The literature is replete with examples of apparently simple terms used by providers that are not appropriately understood by patients (Thompson, 2000).

Research that focuses on how much information is recalled or remembered by patients, however, also generally does not take into account the sense that patients make of that information. It may well be more important to examine how useful and convincing patients find explanations provided by care providers compared to their own lay conceptions, for instance (Tuckett & Williams, 1984) than it is just to look at the objective nature of the information.

Building on this foundational understanding of the need for illness explanation, various health care providers have shared suggestions based on their experience of the types of information that should be included in explanations and the ways in which explanations should be communicated (Thompson, 2000). Such suggestions are consistent with much else that will be found throughout the present volume, in that they include the value of adapting to the patient's knowledge, literacy levels, and concerns. The patient should be put at ease and explanations should be simply expressed; the patient's explanatory model of illness should be elicited.

The act of explaining illness serves more than an instrumental function—it should also be accompanied by emotional support. The message can and should communicate interest and caring as well as information. Some explanations documented in the research, however, function to control patients rather than to provide valuable information or social support (Rabinowitz, Beckman, Morse, & Naumburg, 1994). Experimental studies of the effects of different approaches to explanation provision indicate that both sensory and procedural information are helpful. The best explanations, however, elucidate for the patient both the procedures that he or she will be experiencing *and* the sensations that will be experienced (Thompson, 2000). Such explanations are associated with decreased pain. When sensory and procedural explanations are combined with coping suggestions, patients experience even more positive effects. This effect is especially notable with sicker, less well-educated, and poorer patients (Chwalow et al., 1990).

Given the importance of empathy in communication between providers and patients with regard to both provider and patient outcomes (Hojat et al., 2002; Larson & Yao, 2005), it is important to consider the role of empathy in explaining illness. Other research has provided in-depth observation of care providers who seem to be especially good at providing explanations. These care providers combine their explanations with empathy and humor and use much repetition, pauses, ask tag questions, and use reinforcement. Those providers are also observed to validate the patient's understanding and to switch from the voice of medicine to the voice of the lifeworld. Patients are likely to experience a variety of emotions during a visit with their health care provider. It is essential, then, that, while communicating with the patient, the provider demonstrates empathy via her or his message. Research has suggested that demonstrating empathy helps the patient to better comprehend the situation and avoids situations where emotions take over (Ptacek & Eberhardt, 1996; Quill & Townsend, 1991). Observational studies further document the lack of communication about risk information, side-effects, and medication in most provider–patient interactions.

The Co-Construction of Illness Explanations

The work just reviewed focused primarily on the need for illness explanations and suggestions in addressing those needs by health care providers when they explain illness to patients. The actual process, however, is of course, much more complicated than depicted. During medical interaction, illness explanations are *co-constructed*. Some physicians and researchers argue that shared decision making is really only appropriate in instances of medical uncertainty (Dominick, Frosch, & Kaplan,1999), and others articulate various conditions under which patient preferences should be taken into account (c.f., Kassirer, 1994). In actuality, both the provider and the patient work together, implicitly or explicitly, to generate *any* explanation that is ultimately created. Even the use of the term "ultimately created," however, is misleading. That terminology implies that there is an end-point to illness explanation. As the research to be reviewed below makes clear, however, the explanation process is instead an ongoing one.

Essential to understanding the co-construction of illness explanation is an appreciation for the *process* of medical interaction. Initially, of course, the patient arrives at the medical interaction with some preconceived ideas about his or her medical problem. Self-reported patient health is determined by many variables beyond physical and mental symptoms (Singh-Manoux et al., 2006). These initial conceptions are rather tenacious and long-lasting. The preliminary conceptualization of illness must move through an interpretive process during which the patient begins to label sensations that she or he is experiencing as potential symptoms. This process involves determining which sensations a person must pay attention to—which sensations could be problems. These are interpretive decisions that are influenced by cultural ideas about vulnerability, sensation duration, and interference with activities (Hay, 2008).

Culturally plausible conceptualizations of illness are important considerations for understanding the explanation process (Garro, 2000). Indeed, it has been argued that cultural differences in explanatory models become key determinants of differences in health service availability and subsequent mortality (Furnham & Baguna, 1999). "Suffering" is defined differently in various cultures (Shweder, 2008). Socio-demographic and ethnic differences have also been observed, in that individuals from lower-class and some ethnic backgrounds are less likely than others to define a particular sensation as a health problem (Stoeckle, Zola, & Davidson, 1963). Some studies have found that over 90% of those preselected as "healthy" individuals in research that compares healthy and unhealthy patients are not healthy at all—they, too, have diseases and conditions that are amenable to diagnosis and treatment (Stoeckle et al., 1963). Patients differ in the triggers that lead them to seek health care.

The initial interpretation, however, of the individual experiencing the "sensation" is tentative; it is frequently discussed with others to determine whether or not it should be seen as a "symptom." Conversations help an individual decide if it should be pathologized and socially legitimated as an illness or health problem (Hay, 2008). These initial beliefs also include conceptualizations of potential harm and side effects of treatment possibilities (Aikens, Nease, & Klinkman, 2008). Many of these explanatory models are also metaphorical (Mabeck & Olesen, 1997). These initial ideas/models, called "lay ideas" (Leventhal, Meyer, & Nerenz, 1980, p. 7; see also Leventhal, Leventhal, & Cameron, 2001), help patients understand and cope with that threat.

Another depiction of patients' explanatory models of illness is offered in Mill's (2000, 2001) participatory action research on HIV positive Aboriginal and Ghanaian women. This work indicated that the women's explanatory models combined both traditional and biomedical conceptualizations of illness. The women had their own views on the etiology, pathophysiology, symptomology, course of illness, and methods of treatment for their illness. Mill's research indicated that care providers who did not take these initial explanatory models held by the patients into account were not able to treat the patients effectively. The significance of a patient's explanatory model is also evidenced by the findings that patient health beliefs determine the degree of distress experienced by those receiving chemotherapy (Thuné-Boyle, Meyers, & Newman, 2006) and suffering from severe allergy and asthma symptoms (Knibb & Horton, 2008)

Because physicians and patients often have different perspectives on medical interactions scholars have noted that it is increasingly important to understand explanatory models of health and illness. Haidet et al. (2009) described the importance of identifying specific dimensions of explanatory models to develop an instrument to measure patients' and physicians' explanatory models (see Haidet et al. for The CONNECT instrument, a 19-item scale focusing on six dimensions of explanatory models).

The patient has, of course, made only a tentative decision about defining a sensation as a symptom at the time that a medical interaction begins. Some of the most promising work that focuses on what happens during the co-construction of the explanation that occurs within the medical interaction has been discourse or conversation analytic in nature (see also Robinson, this volume). Some related work, however, is based on writing by physicians or other care providers and is more "how-to." For instance, Galland's (2005) work on patient-centered care takes a very dyadic approach as it provides such guidelines for doctors as, "The importance of understanding the patient's experience of his/her illness cannot be overemphasized" (p. 62).

To actualize Galland's (2005) suggestions, care providers need to allow patients to explain their symptoms and perceptions in their own words. Doing so has been termed "patient exposition" by Orth, Stiles, Scherwitz, Hennrikus, and Vallbona (1987, p. 29), whose research indicated that patients who are allowed do this demonstrate reductions in both systolic and diastolic blood pressure. By contrast, physician exposition of the patient's problem is associated with only lower diastolic blood pressure.

As noted above, patients enter a medical interaction with an explanatory model of which care providers are typically unaware. Research by Lang, Floyd, and Beine (2000) has identified cues that indicate such explanatory models, however. Their work indicates that (a) expression of feelings (especially concern or worry), (b) attempts to understand or explain symptoms, (c) speech clues that underscore the patient's particular concerns, (d) personal stories that link the patient with medical conditions or risks, and (e) behaviors suggestive of unresolved concerns or unmet expectations may communicate to care providers that the patient does indeed have an explanatory model in mind that should be explored because of its likely impact on subsequent treatment responses.

Patient–provider co-construction of explanations requires the examination of the messages offered by both and how each responds to the other. For instance, does each elaborate on what the other has said? Does each question try to clarify what the other has said? Is disagreement offered? Does the provider pick up on the patient's attempts at explanation and encourage elaboration? All of these indicate the co-construction process.

The patient's initial response to the physician's diagnostic statement is determined by the way in which the evidence supporting the diagnostic statement is presented by the physician. In those instances in which the evidence is verbally explicated, patients respond by then talking about the diagnosis. In situations where the physician does not verbally explicate the diagnosis, the patient does not go on to talk about the diagnosis. When patients do talk about the diagnosis, four types of responses have been observed: straight agreements, symptom descriptions, rejections of the proposed diagnosis, and actions related to the interpretation of evidence (Peräkylä, 2002). Rarely do patients explicitly disagree with a physician's diagnosis, however (Heath, 1992). Patients are more likely to remain silent or produce a minimal acknowledgment. Patients who disagree are likely to instead refer to the subjective experience of suffering or indirectly or cautiously encourage the physician to reconsider the assessment. Some patients, however, explicitly communicate agreement and occasionally disagreement with the other in co-construction.

Patient participation is encouraged by diagnoses (a) formatted as questions, (b) presented as uncertain, or (c) showing implicitly or explicitly that the doctor's view of the condition differs from what the patient expected. More thorough explication of the diagnosis through explanation also leads to more discussion of the diagnosis with the provider. The provider may need to make explicit the desire to share participation in decision making in order for it to be evident to the patient. Online commentary during an examination, may also invite co-construction.

Additionally, the dyadic nature of the explanation process is affected by patients' information seeking and verifying behavior. Patients vary on these behaviors both as individuals and in response to the behaviors of their doctors. Research by Cegala, Post, and McClure (2001), however, has indicated that patient training in information seeking and verifying behaviors can impact patient effectiveness and the amount of information that patients obtain.

Tuckett and Williams's (1984) review noted that "patients can manipulate doctors to do what they want by limiting what they tell them" (p. 571). However, lack of patient participation is also created by the structure of the medical interaction. Medical interactions operate according to a consistent pattern, which typically does not explicitly include patient co-creation of the explanation. Most medical interactions operate by following four simple steps: (a) establishing the reason for the visit; (b) gathering of additional information on the part of the provider (history taking, physical exam); (c) deliverance of the diagnosis; and (d) suggestions for treatment recommendations. This is the pattern of interaction that providers are taught and it is the pattern with which patients are familiar. As can be seen, it leaves little room for patient participation in co-creation.

How patients respond to interruptions by the provider is a crucial part of co-creation. For instance, does the patient allow the provider to change the direction of the conversation or does that patient continue with the narrative, perhaps after answering the question? Co-creation may involve the patient drawing attention to particular symptoms or past history. Co-construction is also indicated by the mention of unasked for information and symptoms.

Just as examining what the patient brings to the interaction is foundational to the co-construction process, the predispositions that the care provider brings to the interaction are also relevant. Those care providers who are generally more open to discussions of feelings are more likely to explore patients' experience of illness, whereas those providers who perceive that medical interaction should be more rule-bound (Chapman, Duberstein, Epstein, Fiscella, & Kravitz, 2008) involve the patient less in treatment decisions. These doctors may, however, still explore patients' psycho-social and life experiences. Physicians who themselves report more anxious vulnerability also involve patients less in decision making (Chapman et al., 2008).

Part of the co-construction of the explanation is the patient's presentation of the narrative—telling the story of the reason that she/he is there (see Sharf et al., this volume). Narratives allow patients to maintain control over the content and trajectory of the talk. Telling the story may, thus, be used by the patient in preference to just answering the provider's questions. The story may include explication of what the patient has already tried to do to address the problem. The patients' communication of the narrative may invite the provider to reassure, as well. The patient may also bring in the opinions of others as part of the co-creation of the explanation (e.g., "my husband thought...." "I heard on the news that..."). The story may include such statements as "...and I thought" or "first I thought.... So I tried ... and then it seemed...." The story is likely to describe the time line of the health problems and various attempts at treatment. The introduction of new details by the patient during the exam and diagnosis may indicate implicit disagreement with the provider. Similarly, patient repetition and emphasis of symptoms are frequently indications that the provider's explanation is not adequately taking into account the severity of the symptoms.

Understanding the nature of the co-construction of illness explanation requires examining the outcomes of the interaction in terms of subsequent patient perceptions of the information that was communicated and how these relate to actual recordings of the interaction as well as chart records. DiMatteo, Robinson, Heritage, Tabarrah, and Fox (2003) did just that in an analysis of 17 physicians and 77 of their patients. Their results indicated great inconsistency between patients' recollections and chart records, but better although not complete correspondence between patients' recollections and videotapes of the interactions. An understanding of the explanation process must take into account that the "explanation" that is understood by the patient may not correspond to either what actually occurred or what the care provider perceived.

The goal of the medical interaction is, in part, to name the problem (Brown, 1990). For both interactants, naming helps in sense making. The care provider wants the certainty and control which comes from naming the problem; to a certain degree, the patient also wants this certainty and control (Brown, 1990). This is an organizing process (Balint, 1957). But diagnosis is also "an arena of struggle" (Brown, 1990, p. 402). Although Brown characterized diagnosis as a "power-linguistic approach to categorization, in which patient subjectivity is sacrificed to clinical objectivity" (p. 400), he also noted the dynamic and interactive nature of the process—"certain bits of information are sought or offered, leading to decisions to ask for other bits" (p. 400).

Going beyond what takes place in the medical interaction itself, however, it is important to note, as mentioned above, that the process of illness explanation is an ongoing one. It begins prior to the medical interaction, evolves during that interaction, but, importantly, continues well beyond the actual interaction. Perhaps the most interesting work articulating this process-oriented view of illness explanation comes from Hunt, Jordan, and Irwin (1989). Hunt et al. began their work by hypothesizing that the medical diagnosis plays a key role in determining patients' assessments of what is wrong with them. Their longitudinal interviews with patients, however, indicated that the medical diagnosis and the opinions/explanations provided by the physicians played a relatively minor role in patients' actual perceptions of their illness condition. The physicians' diagnosis is only one small determinant of patients' explanations of their illnesses. Patients constantly restructure their understandings of their illness as their lives evolve and change. Hunt et al.'s interviewees showed great fluctuation in the explanations they provided of their illness over time, and these reformulations were typically not prompted by the medical consultation. Daily circumstances and aspects of the social environment played a large role in these reformulations. Information came to patients from other doctors, popular literature, and the media (Gill & Babrow, 2007), their own interpretations of biology and psychology, and the advice and experiences of family and friends.

Stoeckle, Zola, and Davidson (1963) discussed a similar "lay referral system" (p. 975). Pharmacists are yet another source helping in the construction of the illness explanation (Schommer, 2000; Schommer et al., 2006). Varying environmental circumstances, such as a move, job change, or change in marital status, were reconstructed by patients to help explain their illness. These factors eventually came to be seen as more important than the physicians' original diagnosis. A related example of how such change is seen as key to explaining illness may be found in the findings of Emami and Torres (2005) that health problems in Iranian immigrants who moved to Sweden late in life are perceived by the patients as more directly related to their recent move than to any other explanatory factor.

Rarely were the initial diagnoses provided by the physicians completely rejected by patients in Hunt et al.'s (1989) research. Instead, the patient's conceptualization of his or her illness typically evolved over time so that, while it still incorporated some elements from the physician's diagnosis, it also returned to the patient's original view of the health care problem. Hunt et al.'s findings confirm the notion mentioned above about the tenacity of patients' preconceptions of illness. The explanation, they found, was shaped to function usefully in the life of the patient. Some explanations were constructed to give the patients social recognition for their hardships and stress; some functioned to solicit social support. All were used to marshal resources needed by the patient.

The additional social factors that impact explanations of illness are also emphasized in such perspectives as those offered in this volume by Cline, focusing on the role of everyday health communication, and by Parrott (2004a), emphasizing the informal and less intentional communication processes relating to health. Similarly, Parrott's (2004b) work on the impact of religious faith and spirituality in understanding the health communication process should remind us of the broader context in which explanations are constructed and the other important factors that impact them beyond the medical interaction. Parrott's exhortation is also consistent with the findings of Schnoll, Harlow, and Brower (2000), which indicated the positive role of spirituality in adjustment to and coping with cancer.

The finding noted above that patients frequently reject care providers' explanations and, subsequently, treatment recommendations, has been studied in further detail by Sharf, Stelljes, and Gordon (2005). Their findings help us interpret the conclusions of Hunt et al. (1989) that patients reconstruct the explanations provided by caregivers. Sharf et al. studied lung cancer patients who had refused the treatment recommended by their doctor; the rationales for these decisions offered by patients fit with the reconstructions noted by Hunt et al. (1989). They included such arguments as patient reports that, having heard that exercising is good for lung cancer, they were exercising instead of engaging in the doctor-recommended treatment. Another patient noted, "I just seen a spot on the X-ray. A little bitty spot and I'm a big man. It'd take a lot to pull me down" (Sharf et al., p. 639). There was much minimization of threat and focus instead on self-efficacy amongst the patients who were interviewed. Reliance on faith or fatalism was also noted. Such findings yield further light on the co-construction and re-construction of explanations. All of these patients had received explanations of their lung cancer and explicit treatment recommendations, which they had chosen not to follow. Similarly, Moore et al.'s (2004) large scale, multiethnic survey of patients who delayed treatment found associations between avoidance or delay of treatment and patients' satisfaction with the time spent with the provider, along with the respect, understanding, and listening provided by their physicians.

Explanations that are provided to patients are also influenced by care providers' expectations and cultural/racial biases (Perloff et al., 2006). Racial biases must also be understood within the context of literacy level, however. Controlling for literacy levels does help moderate disparities in health function based on race (Sentel & Halpin, 2006). Similarly, the gender of both the explainer and the subject of the explanation influence explanations and attributions that are offered (Benrud & Reddy, 1998). The importance of the patients' perception of an illness, regardless of where it comes from, is indicated by data showing that such perceptions are key determinants of adjustment and coping (Dorian et al., 2009).

Future Directions

Health care providers, patients, and families are faced with a unique challenge in medical interactions. The move from a paternalistic model of patient care to a more patient-centered approach that considers communication suggests several avenues for future research. Scholars have long demonstrated that communication is purposeful and have described theoretical frameworks that help to elucidate the complexities of communicative interactions. Theories of multiple goals, in particular, have been useful in highlighting the importance of both content and form of messages. A multiple goals perspective is a principled way of identifying message features that are likely to be effective in explaining illness. Because individuals may have different needs during the interaction, there are almost certain to be various goals present when creating illness explanations; messages that address multiple goals should be more effective. Various theories of multiple goals have demonstrated worth in communication literature (e.g., Clark & Delia, 1979; Goldsmith, 2004; O'Keefe, 1990). Clark and Delia (1979) discussed goals in terms of relational, identity, and task goals. One of these goals may be the predominant feature of a message or multiple goals may be negotiated within the co-creation of messages. Another theory suggested that messages are constructed using different design logics (O'Keefe, 1990). Most recently, Goldsmith (2004) suggested that rather than thinking in terms of "goals," perhaps communication scholarship should consider the multiple purposes that a message needs to address in order to be considered effective. For example, when health care providers are faced with an instrumental goal of explaining illness (i.e., comprehension) and, say, the task of delivering bad news within the same interaction sequence (a task that is reportedly one of the most difficult a medical professional faces), health care providers must consider the amount of information the patient already has in addition to how that message should be communicated to attend to relational and identity goals.

As scholars have suggested elsewhere (Thompson, 2000; Whaley, 2000) explaining illness needs to be examined at content and relational levels. It is essential to communicate information that meets patients' needs while maintaining a sense of their emotional capacity for integrating that information into decision making. This chapter provides further evidence that improving illness explanations and the relationship between providers and patients requires attention to the multitude of factors present in each health care interaction.

References

Aikens, J. E., Nease, D. E., & Klinkman, M. S. (2008). Explaining patients' beliefs about the necessity and harmfulness of antidepressants. *Annals of Family Medicine, 6,* 23–29.

Babrow, A. S. (1992). Communication and problematic integration: Understanding and diverging probability and value, ambiguity, ambivalence, and impossibility. *Communication Theory, 2,* 95–130.

Babrow, A. S. (2001). Uncertainty, value, communication, and problematic integration. *Journal of Communication, 51,* 553–573.

Babrow, A. S., Hines, S. C., & Kasch, C. R. (2000). Managing uncertainty in illness explanation: An application of problematic integration theory. In B. B. Whaley (Ed.), *Explaining illness: Messages, strategies and contexts* (pp. 41–67). Hillsdale, NJ: Erlbaum.

Balint, M. (1957). *The doctor, his patient and the illness.* London: Tavistock.

Benrud, L. M., & Reddy, D. M. (1998). Differential explanations of illness in women and men. *Sex Roles, 38,* 375–386.

Brashers, D. E., Neidig, J. L., Russell, J. A., Cardillo, L. W., Haas, S. M., Dobbs, L. K., ... Nemeth, S. (2003). The medical, personal, and social causes of uncertainty in HIV illness. *Issues in Mental Health Nursing, 24,* 497–522.

Brown, P. (1990). The name game: Toward a sociology of diagnosis. *The Journal of Mind and Behavior, 11,* 385–406.

Cegala, D. J., Post, D. M., & McClure, L. (2001). The effects of patient communication skills training on the discourse of older patients during a primary care interview. *Journal of the American Geriatric Society, 49,* 1505–1511.

Chapman, B. P., Duberstein, P. R., Epstein, R. M., Fiscella, K., & Kravitz, R. L. (2008). Patient-centered communication during primary care visits for depressive symptoms. What is the role of physician personality? *Medical Care, 46,* 806–812.

Chwalow, A. J., Mamon, J., Crosby, E., Grieco, A. J., Salkever, D., Fahey, M., & Levine, D. M. (1990). Effectiveness of a hospital-based cooperative care model on patients' functional status and utilization. *Patient Education and Counseling, 15,* 17–28.

Clark, R. A., & Delia, J. G. (1979). Topoi and rhetorical competence. *Quarterly Journal of Speech, 65,* 187–206.

Clayton, M., F., Mishel, M. H., & Belyea, M. (2006). Testing a model of symptoms, communication, uncertainty and well-being in older breast cancer survivors. *Research in Nursing and Health, 29,* 18–39.

DiMatteo, M. R., Robinson, J. D., Heritage, J., Tabarrah, M., & Fox, S. A. (2003). Correspondence among patients' self-reports, chart records, and audio/videotapes of medical visits. *Health Communication, 15,* 393–413.

Dominick L., Frosch, B, A., & Kaplan, R. M. (1999). Shared decision making in clinical medicine: Past research and future directions. *American Journal of Preventive Medicine, 17,* 285–294.

Dorian, A., Dempster, M., & Adair, P. (2009). Adjustment to inflammatory bowel disease: The relative influence of illness perceptions and coping. *Inflammatory Bowel Disease, 15,* 47–55.

Emami, A. & Torres, S. (2005). Making sense of illness: Late-in-life migration as a point of departure for elderly Iranian immigrants' explanatory models of illness. *Journal of Immigrant Health, 7*, 153–164.

Fishchoff, B., & Wessely, S. (2003). Managing patients with inexplicable health problems. *British Medical Journal, 326*, 595–597

Furnham, A., & Baguna, P. (1999). Cross-cultural differences in explanations for health and illness: A British and Uganda comparison. *Mental Health, Religion, and Culture, 2*, 121–134.

Galland, L. (2005). *Textbook of functional medicine.* Gig Harbor, WA: Institute for Functional Medicine.

Garro, L. C. (2000). Remembering what one knows and the construction of the past: A comparison of cultural consensus theory and cultural schema theory. *Ethos, 28*, 275–319.

Gill, E. A., & Babrow, A. S. (2007). To hope or to know: Coping with uncertainty and ambivalence in women's magazine breast cancer articles. *Journal of Applied Communication Research, 35*, 133–155.

Goldsmith, D. J. (2004). *Communicating social support.* New York: Cambridge University Press.

Greer, J., & Halgin, R. (2006). Predictors of physician–patient agreement on symptom etiology in primary care. *Psychosomatic Medicine, 68*, 277–282.

Haidet, P., O'Malley, K. J., Sharf, B. F., Gladney, A. P., Greisinger, A. J., & Street, R. L. (2009) Characterizing explanatory models of illness in healthcare: Development and validation of the CONNECT instrument. *Patient Education & Counseling, 72*, 232–239.

Hay, M. C . (2008). Reading sensations: Understanding the process of distinguishing "fine" from "sick." *Transcultural Psychology, 48*, 198–229.

Heath, C. (1992). The delivery and reception of diagnosis and assessment in the general practice consultation. In P. Drew & J. Heritage (Eds.), *Talk at work* (pp. 235–267).Cambridge, England: Cambridge University Press.

Hojat, M., Gonnella, J. S., Nasca, T. J., Mangione, S., Vergare, M., & Magee, M. (2002). Physician empathy: Definition, components, measurement, and relationship to gender and specialty. *American Journal of Psychiatry, 159*, 1563–1569.

Hunt, L. M., Jordan, B., & Irwin, S. (1989). Views of what's wrong: Diagnosis and patients' concepts of illness. *Social Science & Medicine, 28*, 945–956.

Johnson, L. M., Zautra, A. J., & Davis, M. C. (2006). The role of illness uncertainty on coping with fibromyalgia symptoms. *Health Psychology, 25*, 696–703.

Jurgens, C. Y. (2006). Somatic awareness, uncertainty, and delay in care-seeking in acute heart failure. *Research in Nursing Health, 29*, 74–86.

Kassirer, J. P. (1994). Incorporating patients' preferences into medical decisions. *New England Journal of Medicine, 330*, 1895–1896.

Knibb, R. C., & Horton, S. L. (2008). Can illness perceptions and coping predict psychological distress amongst allergy sufferers? *British Journal of Health Psychology, 13*, 103–119.

Lang, F., Floyd, M. R., & Beine, K. L. (2000). Clues to patients' explanations and concerns about their illnesses. *Archives of Family Medicine, 9*, 222–227.

Larson, E. B., & Yao, X. (2005). Clinical empathy, emotional labor and acting in the patient–physician relationship. *Journal of the American Medical Association, 29*, 1100–1106.

Leventhal, H., Leventhal, E. A., & Cameron, L. (2001). Representations, procedures and affect in self-regulation: A perceptual-cognitive model. In A. Baum, T. A. Revenson, & J. E. Singer (Eds.), *Handbook of health psychology* (pp. 19–48). Mahwah, NJ: Erlbaum.

Leventhal, H., Meyer, D., & Nerenz, D. (1980). The common sense model of illness danger. In S. Rachman (Ed.), *Contributions to medical psychology* (Vol. 2, pp. 7–30). Oxford, England: Pergamon.

Mabeck, C. E. & Olesen, F. (1997). Metaphorically transmitted diseases. How do patients embody medical explanations? *Family Practice, 14*, 271–278.

Mill, J. E. (2000). Describing an explanatory model of HIV illness among Aboriginal women. *Holistic Nursing Practice, 15*, 42–56.

Mill, J. E. (2001). I'm not a "basabasa" woman: An explanatory model of HIV illness in Ghanaian women. *Clinical Nursing Research, 10*, 254–274.

Mishel, M. H. (1988). Uncertainty in illness. *Image: Journal of Nursing Scholarship, 22*, 225–232.

Mishel, M. H. (1990). Reconceptualization of the uncertainty in illness theory. *Image: Journal of Nursing Scholarship, 22*, 256–262.

Moore, P. J., Sickel, A. E., Malat, J., Williams, D., Jackson, J., & Adler, N. E. (2004). Psychosocial factors in medical and psychological treatment avoidance: The role of the doctor–patient relationship. *Journal of Health Psychology, 9*, 421–433.

Nguyen, S. P., & Rosengren, K. S. (2004). Causal reasoning about illness: A comparison between European and Vietnamese-American children. *Journal of Cognition & Culture, 4,* 51–78.

Ogden, J., Fuks, K., Gardner, M., Johnson, S., McLean, M., & Martin, P., ... Shah, R. (2002). Doctors' expressions of uncertainty and patient confidence. *Patient Education and Counseling, 48,* 171–176.

O'Keefe, B. J. (1990). The logic of regulative communication: Understanding the rationality of message designs. In J. P. Dillard (Ed.), *Seeking compliance: The production of interpersonal influence groups* (pp. 87–104). Scottsdale, AZ: Gorusch Scarisbrick.

Orth, J. E., Stiles, W. B., Scherwitz, L., Hennrikus, D., & Vallbona, C. (1987). Patient exposition and provider explanation in routine interviews and hypertensive patients' blood pressure control. *Health Psychology, 6,* 29–42.

Parrott, R. (2004a). Emphasizing "communication" in health communication. *Journal of Communication, 54,* 751–787.

Parrott, R. (2004b). "Collective amnesia": The absence of religious faith and spirituality in health communication research and practice. *Health Communication, 16,* 1–5.

Parrott, R., Silk, K., Weiner, J., Condit, C., Harris, T., & Bernhardt, J. (2004). Deriving lay models of uncertainty about genes' role in illness causation to guide communication about human genetics. *Journal of Communication, 54,* 105–121.

Peräkylä, A. (2002) Agency and authority: Extended responses to diagnostic statements in primary care encounters. *Research on Language and Social Interaction, 35,* 219–247.

Perloff, R. M., Bonder, B., Ray, G. B., Berlin Ray, E., & Siminoff, L. A. (2006). Doctor–patient communication, cultural competence, and minority health. *American Behavioral Scientist, 49,* 835–852.

Peters, S., Stanley, I., Rose, M., & Salmon, P. (1998). Patients with medically unexplained symptoms: Sources of patients' authority and implications for demands on medical care. *Social Science and Medicine, 46,* 559–565.

Ptacek, J. T., & Eberhardt, T. L. (1996). Breaking bad news: A review of the literature. *Journal of the American Medical Association, 276,* 496–502.

Quaid, K. A., Faden, R. R., Vining, E. D., & Freeman, J. M. (1990). Informed consent for a prescription drug: Impact of disclosed information on patient understanding and medical outcomes. *Patient Education and Counseling, 15,* 249–259.

Quill, T. E., & Townsend, P. (1991). Bad news: Delivery, dialogue, and dilemmas. *Archives of Internal Medicine, 151,* 463–468.

Rabinowitz, B., Beckman, H. B., Morse, D., & Naumburg, E. H. (1994). Discussing preventive services with patients: Can we make a difference? *Health Values, 18*(4), 20–26.

Schnoll, R. A., Harlow, L. L., & Brower, L. (2000). Spirituality, demographic and disease factors, and adjustment to cancer. *Cancer Practice, 8,* 298–304.

Schommer, J. C. (2000). Pharmacists' new communicative role: Explaining illness and medicine to patients. In B. B. Whaley (Ed.), *Explaining illness: Research, theory, and strategies* (pp.209–233). Mahwah, NJ: Erlbaum.

Schommer, J. C., Pedersen, C. A., Worley, M. M., Brown, L. M., Hadsall, R. S., Ranelli, P. L. ... Chewning, B. A. (2006). Provision of risk management and risk assessment information: The role of the pharmacist. *Research in Social and Administrative Pharmacy, 2,* 458–478.

Seaburn, D. B., Morse, D., McDaniel, S. H., Beckman, H., Silberman, J., & Epstein, R. (2005). Physician responses to ambiguous patient symptoms. *Journal of General Internal Medicine, 20,* 525–530.

Sentel, T. L., & Halpin, H. A. (2006). The importance of adult literacy in understanding health disparities. *Journal of General Internal Medicine, 21,* 862–866.

Sharf, B. F., Stelljes, L. A., & Gordon H. S. (2005). "A little bitty spot and I'm a big man": Patients' perspectives on refusing diagnosis or treatment for lung cancer. *Psycho-Oncology, 14,* 636–646.

Shweder, R. C. (2008). The cultural psychology of suffering: The many meanings of health in Orissa, India (and elsewhere). *Ethos, 36,* 60–75.

Singh-Manoux, A., Martikainen, P., Ferrie, J., Zins, M., Marmot, M., & Goldberg, M. (2009). What does self-rated health measure? Results from the British Whitehall II and French Gazel cohort studies. *Journal of Epidemiological Community Health, 60,* 364–372.

Stoeckle, J. D., & Barsky, A. D. (1980). Attributions: Use of social science knowledge in the doctoring of primary care. In L. Eisenberg & A. Kleinman (Eds.), *The relevance of social science for medicine* (pp. 223–240). Dordrecht, Netherlands: D. Reidel.

Stoeckle, J. D., Zola, I. K., & Davidson, G. E. (1963). On going to the see the doctor: The contributions of the patient to the decision to seek medical aid. *Journal of Chronic Diseases, 16,* 975–989.

Stone, A. M., & Jones, C. L. (2009). Sources of uncertainty: Experiences of Alzheimer's disease. *Issues in Mental Health Nursing, 30,* 677–686.

Strull, W.M., Lo, B., & Charles, G. (1984). Do patients want to participate in medical decision making? *Journal of the American Medical Association, 252,* 2990–2994.

Thompson, T. L. (2000). The nature and language of illness explanations. In B. B. Whaley (Ed.), *Explaining illness: Research, theory and strategies* (pp. 3–39). Mahwah, NJ: Erlbaum.

Thuné-Boyle, I. C. V., Meyers, L. B., & Newman, S. P. (2006). The role of illness beliefs, treatment beliefs, and perceived severity of symptoms in explaining distress in cancer patients during chemotherapy treatment. *Behavioral Medicine, 32,* 19–29.

Tuckett, D., & Williams, A. (1984). Approaches to the measurement of explanation and information-giving in medical consultations: A review of empirical studies. *Social Science & Medicine, 18,* 571–580.

Waitzin, H. (1985). Information giving in medical care. *Journal of Health and Social Behavior, 26,* 81–101.

Whaley, B. B. (2000). (Ed.). *Explaining illness: Research, theory, and strategies.* Mahwah, NJ: Erlbaum.

19

INTEGRATING HEALTH LITERACY IN HEALTH COMMUNICATION

Kenzie A. Cameron, Michael S. Wolf, and David W. Baker

Introduction

The public today is exposed to more health information than at any previous time in human history. Health care professionals provide advice, television and radio programs broadcast stories about health and well-being, the Internet delivers nearly unlimited information on numerous health topics, and patients manage communication with their physicians via clinic and hospital Web portals. Exposure to such health information has the potential to assist individuals in managing their health; however, such information may be ineffective, or even counterproductive, if an individual is unable to access, understand, or apply the information. The field of health communication is well situated to play a crucial role in closing the gap in health literacy via development of carefully and creatively crafted messages, interventions, and communication techniques. To do so, communication scholars first must understand the definition, measurement, prevalence, and consequences of low health literacy.

What Is Health Literacy?

In 1991, the federal National Literacy Act defined literacy as, "an individual's ability to read, write, and speak in English, and compute and solve problems at levels of proficiency necessary to function on the job and in society, to achieve one's goals, and develop one's knowledge and potential" (National Literacy Act, 1991). This emphasis on the practical use of verbal skills is often referred to as *functional* literacy.

Functional literacy may vary depending on a reader's familiarity with the subject. Health-related materials may be particularly problematic because of the ubiquitous use of unfamiliar terms and concepts. Therefore, health care professionals and health educators discuss *functional health literacy* as an entity distinct from general literacy, defining it as "the ability to read and comprehend prescription bottles, appointment slips, and the other essential health-related materials required to successfully function as a patient" (Ad Hoc Committee on Health Literacy, American Medical Association [AMA], 1999, p. 552). *Healthy People 2010* defined health literacy more broadly as, "the capacity to obtain, interpret, and understand basic health information and services and the competence to use such information and services to enhance health" (U.S. Department of Health and Human Services,

2000). The World Health Organization (WHO) defined health literacy as, "the *cognitive and social skills* which determine the motivation and ability of individuals to gain access to, understand and use information in ways which promote and maintain good health" (Nutbeam, 1998, p. 10).

As the field of health literacy has expanded in scope and depth, the term "health literacy" has come to mean different things to various audiences and has become a source of some confusion and debate. Definitions that emphasize the degree to which individuals have the capacity to obtain, process, understand, and use basic health information present health literacy as a set of *individual capacities* that allow the person to acquire and use new information. Some view *health knowledge* as part of health literacy. For example, an Institute of Medicine (IOM, 2004) report divided the domain of "health literacy" into (a) cultural and conceptual knowledge, (b) oral literacy, including speaking and listening skills, (c) print literacy, including writing and reading skills, and (d) numeracy. Others have argued that if health literacy is the ability to function in the health care environment, it must depend upon characteristics of both the individual and the health care system. From this perspective, health literacy is a *dynamic state* of an individual during a health care encounter. An individual's health literacy may vary depending upon the medical problem being treated, the health care provider, and the system that is providing the care.

Baker (2006) developed a conceptual model of health literacy and the relationship of health literacy to health outcomes and suggested possible terms to describe the relevant concepts and domains. An expanded version that includes cognitive abilities and social skills is presented in Figure 19.1. The first domain is individual capacity: the set of resources that a person has to deal effectively with health information, health care personnel, and the health care system. The three subdomains of capacity are reading fluency, prior knowledge, and

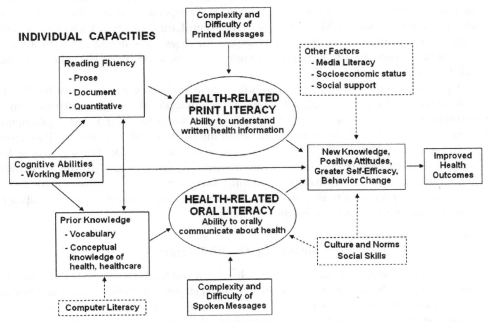

Figure 19.1 Revised conceptual model of the relationship between individual capacities, health-related print and oral literacy, cognitive and social skills, and health outcomes.

cognitive abilities. Reading fluency is the ability to mentally process written materials and form new knowledge; prior knowledge is composed of vocabulary (knowing what individual words mean), and conceptual knowledge (understanding aspects of the world, e.g., what cancer is and how it injures the body). Both are described in further detail in Baker's (2006) original presentation of the model. Although some of the more expansive definitions of health literacy include conceptual knowledge, this model views conceptual knowledge as a resource a person has that facilitates health literacy but does not in itself constitute health literacy.

Reading fluency allows one to expand one's vocabulary and gain conceptual knowledge. Vocabulary and background knowledge of the general topics covered in written materials also improve reading fluency of these materials, as shown by the double-headed arrow between the two individual capacity boxes in Figure 19.1. It is easier to read and comprehend materials that contain familiar vocabulary and concepts. Two individuals with similar general reading fluency may have different abilities to read and understand health-related material as a result of differences in their baseline knowledge of health vocabulary and concepts.

Both reading fluency and prior knowledge are affected by more fundamental cognitive processes, including working memory: a theoretical construct conceptualizing how we temporarily store and manipulate information in short-term memory. Working memory is vital for readers if they are to focus on particular elements of what they read, and keep track of and monitor information in texts. Other cognitive processes affect how much information is remembered (i.e., long-term memory), retrieval of information in long-term memory, and the ability to fully comprehend and use complex conceptual information.

The second major domain in the model is health literacy. The IOM report divided health literacy into health-related print literacy and health-related oral literacy, although the true distinction between the two is unclear. Both depend upon an individual's health-related reading fluency, health-related vocabulary, familiarity with health concepts, and the complexity and difficulty of printed and spoken messages encountered in the health care environment. Thus, health literacy is determined by characteristics of both the individual and the health care system.

A person's culture, norms, and social skills will affect her interactions with health care professionals, willingness to ask questions, and confidence in asking for clarification of instructions. People unable to use computer hardware and software (i.e., lacking computer literacy) may have less access to important health information and messages. Similarly, people lacking the ability to critically understand mass media (i.e., media literacy) may be less likely to resist inaccurate or unhealthy media portrayals and messages (Austin & Johnson, 1997). It is important conceptually to distinguish these domains, but it is particularly salient for researchers who want to measure these domains precisely and investigate the relationships and causal pathways between these elements.

Measuring Health Literacy

Health literacy and general literacy are closely related and likely to be highly correlated for most individuals. Nevertheless, the distinction between general reading fluency and health-related reading fluency is important for research because measures of an individual's ability to read and understand health-related materials should be more closely related to health outcomes than a measure of general literacy. Hence, a study using a measure of health-related reading fluency as a predictor variable will have greater power to detect associations with health outcomes than a study using a measure of general reading fluency. For this reason, we will restrict our discussion to measures of health literacy. Our purpose is not to advocate for any specific measurement, but rather to provide an overview of available options. Choice of measurement should be directly related to the goals of the specific research: a more comprehensive measure will be of utility if health literacy is a primary predictor or outcome; a shorter measure may be sufficient if health literacy is included as a descriptive element.

The Rapid Estimate of Adult Literacy in Medicine (REALM) (Davis et al., 1993) and the Test of Functional Health Literacy in Adults (TOFHLA) are the most widely used measures of health literacy (Baker, Williams, Parker, Gazmararian, & Nurss, 1999; Parker, Baker, Williams, & Nurss, 1995). The REALM is a 66-item word recognition and pronunciation test that measures health-related vocabulary. The 67-item TOFHLA measures reading fluency; it consists of a reading comprehension section to measure prose literacy and a numeracy section assessing individuals' capacity to read and understand actual hospital documents and labeled prescription vials. The two tests are highly correlated ($r = 0.80$; Parker et al., 1995) and both are highly correlated with general vocabulary tests (i.e., the Wide Range Achievement Test, Revised; Jastak & Wilkinson, 1984). The Newest Vital Sign (NVS) consists of six questions about the information contained in an ice-cream nutrition label (Weiss et al., 2005). The first four questions require document and quantitative skills, including the ability to calculate percentages.

Several other measures focus on quantitative abilities. The 18-item Medical Data Interpretation Test measures patients' ability to interpret and use risk and rates presented in medical contexts, including calculating relative and absolute risk reduction and comparing risks from different treatments (Schwartz, Woloshin, & Welch, 2005). These are tasks that patients may rarely perform, but the test is correlated with performance on the quantitative and document literacy questions from the NALS (Schwartz et al., 2005). Lipkus, Samsa, and Rimer (2001) published a 10-item scale covering similar content. Others have developed tests more focused on patients' ability to perform relevant clinical tasks requiring numeracy abilities. For example, the Diabetes Numeracy Test asks patients to use a "sliding scale" to determine how much insulin they would need to inject for a given blood sugar level (Huizinga et al., 2008).

Shortened Measures

Shorter measures designed for use in both research and clinical settings include a short version of the TOFHLA (the S-TOFHLA), which includes two reading passages plus numeracy items (Baker, Williams, et al., 1999). An even shorter version that includes only the two reading passages can also be used (Kandula et al., 2009). An eight-item version of the REALM has been developed and reported to be reasonably well correlated with tests of general literacy (Bass, Wilson, & Griffith, 2003); further validation of this instrument is needed.

Self-Report Measures

An alternative approach to directly measuring individual capacity is to ask patients to rate their self-reported difficulty in understanding health care professionals and the written materials they encounter in their health care. Self-report directly assesses the mismatch between an individual's capacities and the communication demands faced from the patient's perspective. Chew, Bradley, and Boyko (2004) found three questions with reasonably high predictive value for identifying individuals with inadequate health literacy: (a) "How often do you have someone help you read hospital materials?" (b) "How confident are you filling out medical forms by yourself?" and (c) "How often do you have problems learning about your medical condition because of difficulty understanding written information?" The second of these questions has been identified as a potential single-item measure (Wallace et al., 2007). By asking individuals "how often," rather than "if" they have difficulties reading or completing forms normalizes the need for assistance, and thus may be less likely to induce shame and anxiety in respondents.

Measuring Health Literacy in Individuals with Limited English Proficiency

Spanish versions of the TOFHLA, S-TOFHLA, and NVS are available. The REALM and other word pronunciation tests are not valid in Spanish because of the phoneme–grapheme correspondence: words are generally pronounced as they look, so people can read and pronounce a word even though they do not know its meaning (Lee, Bender, Ruiz, & Cho, 2006). Lee et al. (2006) overcame this challenge by developing the *Short Assessment of Health Literacy for Spanish-speaking Adults* (SAHLSA), a word recognition test that tests examinees' comprehension of the medical terms by having them associate each term to a related word. Reading fluency tests also are being developed in other languages and should be available soon (Kim, 2009).

Prevalence and Distribution of Limited Health Literacy

In the United States, the National Assessment of Adult Literacy (NAAL) of 2003 reported that 14% of U.S. adults possess skills in the lowest level of prose and document literacy ("below basic"); 22% are at the lowest level for quantitative literacy (Kutner, Greenberg, & Baer, 2005). These individuals can perform only the most simple and concrete tasks associated with each domain. Individuals with "basic" literacy proficiency are likely to be hindered in routine daily activities. When considering individuals with basic and below basic skills combined, as many as 34% to 55% of adults in the United States have limited literacy skills.

These general estimates may not give the full picture. Reading fluency and the full range of literacy skills is likely to vary with an individual's familiarity with content (Rudd, Kirsch & Yamamoto, 2004). Health materials and encounters may contain unfamiliar and difficult medical terms (Castro, Wilson, Wang, & Schillinger, 2007); estimates of limited health literacy based on general functional literacy surveys are likely to underestimate the problem. The NAAL 2003 included the first national health literacy assessment, results of which showed the average health literacy scores of Americans to be lower than average adult NAAL general literacy scores. Only 12% of adults were identified as having "proficient" health literacy skills; most (53%) fell into an intermediate classification. The NAAL report concluded that large numbers of U.S. adults—especially the elderly, socioeconomically disadvantaged, and those belonging to racial/ethnic minority groups or living in rural areas—lack the health literacy skills to effectively access, understand, and use health materials to accomplish challenging health-related tasks.

Consequences of Low Health Literacy

Low health literacy can have a significant negative impact on one's health and well-being. Two decades of empirical data have demonstrated both plausible mechanisms by which literacy may directly affect health behaviors as well as the impact that inadequate health literacy may have on a patient's health and utilization of health care (Paasche-Orlow & Wolf, 2007). Limited health literacy has been associated with lower levels of health knowledge (Gazmararian, Williams, Peel, & Baker, 2003) and reports of psychological aspects such as shame, stigma, and denial (Parikh, Parker, Nurss, Baker, & Williams, 1996). Shame about divulging one's level of health literacy can become a significant barrier to effective patient–provider communication. Individuals with poor health literacy skills tend to ask fewer questions during medical encounters and to be less capable of describing their condition to medical personnel than people with higher health literacy. Further, many patients do not see their literacy level as relevant to their health and do not disclose their literacy status to providers (Roter, 2000).

Limited health literacy has been associated with lower self-management skills, particularly related to chronic diseases such as diabetes, asthma, and HIV/AIDS (Schillinger et al., 2002; Williams, Baker, Honig, Lee, & Nowlan, 1998; Wolf, Davis, Cross et al., 2004). Higher rates of misunderstanding of medication instructions and warnings among those with limited literacy is associated with lower adherence to medical recommendations and prescribed medication (Wolf, Davis, Osborn. et al., 2007).

Limited health literacy has been associated with higher hospitalization rates (Baker, Parker et al., 1998), increased health care costs (Friedland, 1998), poorer health (Wolf, Gazmararian, & Baker, 2005), and higher mortality (Sudore et al., 2006). In fact, literacy is more strongly associated with these outcomes than is years of education (Wolf, Gazmararian, & Baker, 2005). For further information, readers are referred to recent systematic reviews of literacy and health outcomes (DeWalt, Berkman, Sheridan, Lohr, & Pignone, 2004; Pignone, DeWalt, Sheridan, Berkman, & Lohr, 2005).

With more than 1600 health literacy-related studies to date, and nearly half of these documenting various consequences across an array of health conditions and contexts, the magnitude of the economic impact of health literacy presumably is large. Two seminal reports estimated that the cost of low health literacy to the U.S. economy ranges from $106 to $230 billion annually (Friedland, 1998; Vernon, Trujillo, Rosenbaum, & DeBuono, 2007).

Approaches to Decrease the Consequences of Limited Health Literacy

Over the past decade, the majority of interventions have focused on rewriting health materials at a simpler reading level or following other design techniques to improve patient reading comprehension (Pignone et al., 2005). While there is a need for additional research on how to appropriately respond to limited health literacy, certain health communication "best practices" have been recommended. These are relatively simple steps to assist health care providers in identifying patients at risk for limited health literacy and potentially poor health outcomes, to improve the quality and effectiveness of communication during clinical encounters, and to improve patients' ability to retain that information. Targets for intervention generally include health materials, oral communication skills of health care providers, and health care practices themselves.

Enhancing Print Materials

The value of print health materials is that they are tangible and ideally can reinforce verbal communication or information provided by other, less tangible sources (i.e., video). However, many print materials utilized in health care settings today are written at a level too complex for the majority of patients to comprehend. Printed materials such as fact sheets, brochures, and booklets should be created in a format that promotes patient understanding. Numerous resources that describe best practices for writing health care materials are available; Table 19.1 describes some key techniques identified by prominent practitioners (Doak, Doak, & Root, 1996). Studies have shown that the majority of patients, even those with adequate health literacy, prefer to have print materials provided in clear and concise formats. Ensuring that print materials are simplified is a practice that should be universally adopted.

Utilizing Visual Aids. Health care providers also should consider using visual aids within print materials and during clinical encounters to help patients remember and process health information. One study demonstrated that subjects who listened to medical instructions

Table 19.1 Techniques to Simplify Print Materials

Technique	Explanation
Write in short sentences	Short sentences tend to be easier to read and understand for patients. Sentence length should be less than 15 words, and ideally less than 10 words. Sentences should be written in a conversational style.
Print in large, Sans-Serif font	Text should be written in Sans-Serif font (i.e. Arial) with a minimum font size of 12 pt. Use of all capital letters should be avoided; only the first letter of words in text should be capitalized.
Include sufficient white space	Large margins and adequate spacing between sentences and paragraphs will provide sufficient white space and prevent a document from appearing to be solid text. In general, text should be left-justified for easy reading.
Select simple words	Words that are commonly used in conversation are the best to include in health messages. Shorter words tend to be easier to understand and more familiar to patients.
Provide information in bulleted lists	Bullets help to separate information from the rest of the text. Information provided in lists is often easier and faster for patients to read and comprehend.
Highlight or underline key information	Bolding and highlighting phrases or words can draw attention to essential information for patients. It should be used sparingly to differentiate key sentences or phrases from the rest of the text.
Design passages to be action and goal oriented	Written passages should be action and goal-oriented, and should provide readers with a clear explanation of the purpose of the written material. Passages should clearly define what actions should be taken by the reader and why these actions are necessary.
Group and limit instructional content	Consider grouping information under common headings to promote understanding. Place key information in the beginning of a paragraph and be sure to limit the amount of instructional content that is given to what is essential for the patient to know and understand.
Use active voice	Information written using active voice is easier to understand and more likely to motivate the patient to action.
Avoid unnecessary jargon	Unnecessary jargon can be distracting to patients and often provides little information. Medical terminology should be used as infrequently as possible and, if used, should always be clearly defined and explained to the patient.

accompanied by a pictograph remembered 85% of what they heard, in contrast to 14% for patients who did not receive a visual aid (Houts, Witmer, Egeth, Loscalzo, & Zabora, 2001). Visual materials are useful to teach patients about health conditions that cannot be seen easily (for example, cholesterol in the blood vessels) and to demonstrate how to follow steps to complete a task. Visual materials should be tailored to reflect the culture, age, and background of the patient population and should be simple, recognizable, and clear.

Improving Oral Communication Skills

It may not always be possible to identify patients with limited health literacy. A best practice for health communication is to adopt a universal approach: Always use plain language with all patients, and try to avoid the use of medical jargon (Paasche-Orlow, Schillinger et al., 2006). Rudd (n.d.) defines plain language as "a clear, simple, conversational style and one that presents information in a logical order" (p. 3). It is not always possible to use plain language and avoid jargon, so terms and concepts should be defined and clarified when they arise. Health care providers should verify that information provided verbally has been understood by the patient by incorporating interactive communication strategies during clinical encounters with patients.

The "teach back" technique is a particularly useful and simple way to confirm patient understanding during the encounter (Schillinger, Piette et al., 2003). After describing a diagnosis or recommending treatment, the health care provider asks the patient to reiterate the core elements of the encounter. The provider should be specific about what the patient should teach back, and should limit instruction to 1 or 2 main points. If a patient provides incorrect information, the provider reviews the information again and gives the patient another opportunity to demonstrate understanding. In this manner, the provider can gain assurance that the patient has adequately understood the health information presented.

Guided imagery requires the patient to not only teach back information and instructions, but to describe how a recommended behavior (i.e., medication use) will be specifically performed within the patient's own situation. This approach might include explicitly asking a patient when he will take a prescribed medicine, where he will store the medicine, and how he will remind himself of the activity. One study found the use of guided imagery to significantly improve adherence (Park, Gutchess, Meade, & Stine-Morrow, 2007).

Integrating Health Literacy into the Field of Health Communication

As a starting point for integration, it is important for health communication scholars to recognize that health literacy is an integral, if unexplored, part of theoretical models we already employ. Many theories, particularly those used when attitude or behavior change is desired, identify some form of knowledge as a causal factor. An individual's knowledge or understanding of a given health issue, treatment option, or recommended preventive behavior is the foundation on which one's attitudes and future behaviors are built. Individuals with limited health literacy may lack critical knowledge needed to be an active participant in their medical care.

Consider an individual who has only rudimentary knowledge about breast cancer and mammography, is unable to read printed health materials, and has difficulty communicating orally about her health concerns. Upon receipt of a recommendation for a mammography, she may turn to trusted friends and family to assist her in making the decision to complete the recommended screening or not. Her perception of normative beliefs and her motivation

313

to comply with others, as described by the Theory of Reasoned Action/Theory of Planned Behavior (Ajzen & Fishbein, 1980; Fishbein & Ajzen, 1975), may become paramount as she looks for assistance in making a health decision she feels ill-equipped to make on her own. Should she not have had previous experience with such preventive screening, she may give more weight to subjective norms than her own attitudes.

Similarly, it is critical to consider the context (e.g., print material, audio, in-person, online) in which a health message is conveyed to the receiver. What background knowledge may be presumed by the creators of the message? Many behavioral models used in the development of health communication messages, such as the Health Belief Model (HBM; Becker, 1974) and the Extended Parallel Process Model (EPPM; Witte, 1992, 1994) note that one must perceive oneself to be susceptible to a severe threat before one considers processing information regarding actions to reduce or remove the threat. However, if the receiver is unable to adequately understand risk information presented to her, then it seems nonsensical to expect that individual to feel an increased level of susceptibility toward the health threat. Both the Transtheoretical Model (Prochaska & Diclemente, 1983) and Weinstein's Precaution Adoption Process Model (PAPM; Weinstein, 1988) chart a course of behavior change for an individual that rely on an understanding and acceptance that change is needed. These models allow for change to occur through multiple stages, or processes, with the expectation that one has the ability to move through the various stages once convinced that change is necessary. As we continue to use these models in the development of health communication interventions, we must recognize that a lack of progression through the stages of change may not be due to a lack of desire for change, but rather a lack of basic knowledge needed to make the changes. If one cannot understand risk perception, then even materials designed to meet some common universal standards, such as the use of everyday or living room language, may still be necessary but not sufficient to effect attitude and behavior change.

Integrating Health Communication into Health Care Systems

Health care systems should target several key areas to improve health communication in general and to ameliorate the problems faced by patients with limited health literacy (Paasche-Orlow, Schillinger, et al., 2006).

Screening for Health Literacy versus Addressing Communication Difficulties for All Patients

With the availability of several short tests of health literacy, should patients be screened to identify those with low health literacy? Benefits have not been found (Seligman et al., 2005), and many experts have serious concerns that screening will cause embarrassment to many patients by exposing a secret that many have tried to hide their whole life. Thus, screening is not recommended (Paasche-Orlow & Wolf, 2008).

Instead, we advocate that providers assume all patients experience some degree of difficulty in understanding complex health information, and all should be treated with a uniform approach to ensure understanding. This approach has sometimes been called "universal precautions," a term originally coined in infectious diseases. Providers should be taught how to provide clear communication using plain language and a minimum of jargon, and to utilize communication tools where available (e.g., multimedia). Providers should always confirm patient understanding (i.e., teach back), and where there are gaps, providers should provide tailored teaching around points not understood or remembered and then reassess comprehension until all key points are mastered ("teach to goal").

Expand Communication beyond the Clinical Encounter

Busy clinicians have limited time to discuss health issues with patients during the clinical encounter. To address this challenge, health care systems must employ strategies to improve communication before and after the visit. Providers should anticipate patients' information needs and provide them with print or audiovisual materials prior to their visit about issues to be addressed (e.g., the need to start a cholesterol-lowering medication, the need for colorectal cancer screening). Providing background information prior to the visit should allow clinicians to focus their time on what patients do not understand, and, more important, spend more time helping patients make decisions.

Few practices have systematically implemented this type of "previsit" education, although it has been advocated for many years by the Chronic Care Model (Wagner, 1998). In the General Internal Medicine clinic of the Northwestern Medical Faculty Foundation, we are conducting pilot projects using the electronic health record to identify patients who are about to reach the age when they need a clinical service (e.g., age 50 for colorectal cancer screening) and send print and audiovisual materials about the service prior to their visit. The effectiveness of this approach is under investigation.

Improving communication after the visit is also critical. Electronic health record systems can generate patient information to reinforce key messages, send standardized follow-up letters, and allow clinicians to contact patients via e-mail. However, to date these tools have been underutilized, and many of the commercial educational materials available are not properly designed to be easily understood by individuals with limited health literacy. Portals allowing patients to see their electronic health records, view patient education materials, and review written instructions from a previous visit create incredible opportunities to improve communication. Handheld devices also are being investigated, but have met with limited success to date (Forjuoh, Reis, Couchman, & Ory, 2008; Jones & Curry, 2006). More research is needed before concrete guidance can be given on how to incorporate these tools into routine practice.

Future Health Literacy Research

Over the last two decades, we have learned that inadequate health literacy is common, adversely affects communication in medical encounters and patients' ability to learn about their diseases and self-management behaviors, and is associated with higher hospitalization and mortality rates. More recently, investigators have examined ways to improve communication with low literate patients, both within and outside of medical encounters. Yet, research lacunae still exist in several key areas, with targets ranging from the individual, the provider–patient dyad, groups of patients, and health care systems.

For example, when considering how to improve individuals' ability to obtain health information, future research can explore how Web sites may be designed to facilitate use by low-literate patients, particularly considering the increasing use of electronic health record systems, some of which allow patients to view their health information via secure portals. We can further explore how patients with limited health literacy may be activated and empowered to ask more questions of their providers and to ask for clarification when the information provided is unclear. In addition to patient activation, more research is needed to understand what providers can do to improve long-term recall of essential information by patients of all levels of literacy, and whether or not electronic health record systems that incorporate multimedia communication tools may be able to assist providers in explaining medical conditions and self-care to patients. When considering the use of multimedia, we must also be cognizant that audio and video messages can go by quickly, and individuals with slower information processing speed, particularly the elderly, may have difficulty comprehending information presented this way. Research can explore if print and multimedia can be combined to greater benefit, to allow learners to review written information augmented by visual presentation of difficult key concepts. Learning how to most effectively use communication tools such as cell phones, hand-held devices, and social networking sites outside of the more traditional patient–provider encounter to improve care of all patients, regardless of literacy ability, is a critical avenue of future research.

Conclusion

Health literacy is an integral part of the study of health communication. If people are unable to access, understand, and apply the health-related information they receive, then whether or not the "best" message is reaching the population is no longer an important question. The question becomes much more basic: whether or not a message, any message, is reaching the population. Communication scholars need to pair with researchers well versed in the field of health literacy to identify where we—as scholars, as health care professionals, as public health researchers and educators—can seamlessly integrate health literacy into our current scholarship. The medical field has become well aware of the prevalence and the challenge of health literacy, and how it may affect patients seen (or cause them to not be seen) within the health care system. This awareness provides an opportunity for health communication researchers to join those in medicine and public health to address this challenge, which affects well over half of the U.S. population.

This chapter provides an overview of health literacy and explores how health communication, and health communication researchers, can and should address health literacy barriers. By providing the background to the concept of health literacy, and discussing its evolution, this chapter demonstrates how tightly woven the concept of health literacy is to attaining access, comprehension, and assistance regarding one's health. Suggestions presented for addressing health literacy inadequacies through health communication are only the start to an exciting, rewarding, and necessary venture for health communication professionals.

Acknowledgments

We appreciate and acknowledge the contributions of Jay M. Bernhardt, coauthor of the health literacy chapter in the first edition of this handbook (Bernhardt & Cameron, 2003); Mark V. Williams, for assistance in brainstorming the structure and content of the current chapter; and Sara Hauber for editing assistance.

References

Ad Hoc Committee on Health Literacy, American Medical Association. (1999). Health literacy: Report of the Council on Scientific Affairs. *Journal of the American Medical Association, 281,* 552–557.

Ajzen, I., & Fishbein, M. (1980). *Understanding attitudes and predicting social behavior.* Englewood Cliffs: Prentice-Hall.

Austin, E. W., & Johnson, K. K. (1997). Immediate and delayed effects of media literacy training on third graders' decision making for alcohol. *Health Communication, 9,* 323–349.

Baker, D. W. (2006). The meaning and the measure of health literacy. *Journal of General Internal Medicine, 21,* 878–883.

Baker, D. W., Parker, R. M., Williams, M. V., & Clark, W. S. (1998). Health literacy and the risk of hospital admission. *Journal of General Internal Medicine, 13,* 791–798.

Baker, D. W., Williams, M. V., Parker, R. M., Gazmararian, J. A., & Nurss, J. (1999). Development of a brief test to measure functional health literacy. *Patient Education and Counseling, 38,* 33–42.

Bass, P. F., III, Wilson, J. F., & Griffith, C. H. (2003). A shortened instrument for literacy screening. *Journal of General Internal Medicine, 18,* 1036–1038.

Becker, M. H. (1974). The health belief model and personal health behavior. *Health Education Monographs, 2,* 324–508.

Bernhardt, J. M., & Cameron, K. A. (2003). Accessing, understanding, and applying health communication messages: The challenge of health literacy. In T. L. Thompson, A. M. Dorsey, K. I. Miller, & R. L. Parrott (Eds.), *Handbook of health communication* (pp. 583–605). Mahwah, NJ: Erlbaum.

Castro, C. M., Wilson, C., Wang, F., & Schillinger, D. (2007). Babel babble: Physicians' use of unclarified medical jargon with patients [Supplement 1]. *American Journal of Health Behavior, 31,* S85–S95.

Chew, L. D., Bradley, K. A., & Boyko, E. J. (2004). Brief questions to identify patients with inadequate health literacy. *Family Medicine, 36,* 588–594.

Chew, L. D., Griffin, J. M., Partin, M. R., Noorbaloochi, S., Grill, J. P., & VanRyn, M. (2008). Validation of screening questions for limited health literacy in a large VA outpatient population. *Journal of General Internal Medicine, 23,* 561–566.

Davis, T. C., Long, S. W., Jackson, R. H., Mayeaux, E. J., George, R. B., Murphy, P. W., & Crouch, M. A. (1993). Rapid estimate of adult literacy in medicine: A shortened screening instrument. *Family Medicine, 25,* 391–395.

DeWalt, D. A., Berkman, N. D., Sheridan, S., Lohr, K. N., & Pignone, M. P. (2004). Literacy and health outcomes: A systematic review of the literature. *Journal of General Internal Medicine, 19,* 1228–1239.

Doak, C. C., Doak, L. G., & Root, J. H. (1996). *Teaching patients with low literacy skills* (2nd ed.). Philadelphia, PA: J. B. Lippincott.

Fishbein, M., & Ajzen, I. (1975). *Belief, attitude, intention, and behavior: An introduction to theory and research.* Reading, MA: Addison-Wesley.

Forjuoh, S. N., Reis, M. D., Couchman, G. R., & Ory, M. G. (2008). Improving diabetes self-care with a PDA in ambulatory care. *Telemedicine Journal and e-Health, 14,* 273–279.

Friedland, R. (1998, October). *New estimates of the high costs of inadequate health literacy.* Paper presented at the Pfizer Conference, Promoting Health Literacy: A Call to Action, Washington, DC.

Gazmararian, J. A., Williams, M. V., Peel, J., & Baker, D. W. (2003). Health literacy and knowledge of chronic disease. *Patient Education and Counseling, 51,* 267–275.

Houts, P. S., Witmer, J. T., Egeth, H. E., Loscalzo, M. J., & Zabora, J. R. (2001). Using pictographs to enhance recall of spoken medical instructions II. *Patient Education and Counseling, 43,* 231–242.

Huizinga, M. M., Elasy, T. A., Wallston, K. A., Cavanaugh, K., Davis, D., Gebretsadik, T., ... Rothman, R. L. (2008). Development and validation of the Diabetes Numeracy Test (DNT). *BMC Health Services Research, 8,* 96–117.

Institute of Medicine (IOM). (2004). *Health literacy: A prescription to end confusion* (L. Nielsen-Bohlman, A. Panzer, & D. A. Kindig, Eds.). Washington, DC: National Academies Press.

Jastak, S., & Wilkinson, G. S. (1984). *WRAT-R, Wide Range Achievement Test: Administration manual* (Rev. ed.). Wilmington, DE: Jastak Assessment Systems.

Jones, D., & Curry, W. (2006). Impact of a PDA-based diabetes electronic management system in a primary care office. *American Journal of Medical Quality, 21,* 401–407.

Kandula, N. R., Nsiah-Kumi, P. A., Makoul, G., Sager, J., Zei, C. P., Glass, S., ... Baker, D. W. (2009). The relationship between health literacy and knowledge improvement after a multimedia type 2 diabetes education program. *Patient Education and Counseling, 75,* 321–327.

Kim, S. H. (2009). Health literacy and functional health status in Korean older adults. *Journal of Clinical Nursing, 18,* 2337–2343.

Kutner, M., Greenberg, E., & Baer, J. (2005). *A first look at the literacy of America's adults in the 21st century.* Washington, DC: National Center for Education Statistics, U.S. Department of Education.

Lee, S. Y., Bender, D. E., Ruiz, R. E., & Cho, Y. I. (2006). Development of an easy-to-use Spanish Health Literacy test. *Health Services Research, 41*(4 Pt 1), 1392–1412.

Lipkus, I. M., Samsa, G., & Rimer, B. K. (2001). General performance on a numeracy scale among highly educated samples. *Medical Decision Making, 21,* 37–44.

National Literacy Act of 1991. PL 102-73 (1991).

Nutbeam, D. (1998). Health promotion glossary. Retrieved from http://www.who.int/hpr/docs/glossary.pdf

Paasche-Orlow, M. K., Schillinger, D., Greene, S. M., & Wagner, E. H. (2006). How health care systems can begin to address the challenge of limited literacy. *Journal of General Internal Medicine, 21,* 884–887.

Paasche-Orlow, M. P., & Wolf, M. S. (2007). The causal pathways linking health literacy to health outcomes. *American Journal of Health Behavior, 31,* S19–S26.

Paasche-Orlow, M. K., & Wolf, M. S. (2008). Evidence does not support clinical screening of literacy. *Journal of General Internal Medicine, 23,* 100–102.

Parikh, N. S., Parker, R. M., Nurss, J. R., Baker, D. W., & Williams, M. V. (1996). Shame and health literacy: The unspoken connection. *Patient Education and Counseling, 27,* 33–39.

Park, D. C., Gutchess, A. H., Meade, M. L., & Stine-Morrow, E. A. (2007). Improving cognitive function in older adults: Nontraditional approaches. *Journal of Gerontology Series B: Psycholological Sciences and Social Sciences, 62*(Spec. No 1), 45–52.

Parker, R. M., Baker, D. W., Williams, M. V., & Nurss, J. R. (1995). The Test of Functional Health Literacy in Adults (TOFHLA): A new instrument for measuring patients' literacy skills. *Journal of General Internal Medicine, 10,* 537–542.

Pignone, M., DeWalt, D. A., Sheridan, S., Berkman, N., & Lohr, K. N. (2005). Interventions to improve health outcomes for patients with low literacy. A systematic review. *Journal of General Internal Medicine, 20,* 185–192.

Prochaska, J. O., & Diclemente, C. C. (1983). Stages and processes of self-change of smoking: Toward an integrative model of change. *Journal of Consulting and Clinical Psychology, 51,* 390–395.

Roter, D. L. (2000). The outpatient medical encounter and elderly patients. *Clinical Geriatric Medicine, 16,* 95–107.

Rudd, R. E. (n.d.) Guidelines for creating materials: Resources for developing and assessing materials. Retrieved December 1, 2010, from http://www.hsph.harvard.edu/healthliteracy/files/resources_for_creating_materials.pdf

Rudd, R. E., Kirsch, I., & Yamamoto, K. (2004). *Literacy and health in America.* Princeton, NJ: Princeton University Press.

Schillinger, D., Grumbach, K., Piette, J., Wang, F., Osmond, D., Daher, C., ... Bindman, A. B. (2002). Association of health literacy with diabetes outcomes. *Journal of the American Medical Association, 288,* 475–482.

Schillinger, D., Piette, J., Grumbach, K., Wang, F., Wilson, C., Daher, C., ... Bindman, A. B. (2003). Closing the loop: Physician communication with diabetic patients who have low health literacy. *Archives of Internal Medicine, 163,* 83–90.

Schwartz, L. M., Woloshin, S., & Welch, H. G. (2005). Can patients interpret health information? An assessment of the medical data interpretation test. *Medical Decision Making, 25,* 290–300.

Seligman, H. K., Wang, F. F., Palacios, J. L., Wilson, C. C., Daher, C., Piette, J. D., ... Schillinger, D. (2005). Physician notification of their diabetes patients' limited health literacy. A randomized, controlled trial. *Journal of General Internal Medicine, 20,* 1001–1007.

Sudore, R. L., Yaffe, K., Satterfield, S., Harris, T. B., Mehta, K. M., Simonsick, E. M., ... Schillinger, D. (2006). Limited literacy and mortality in the elderly: The health, aging, and body composition study. *Journal of General Internal Medicine, 21,* 806–812.

U.S. Department of Health and Human Services. (2000). *Healthy people 2010: Understanding and improving health.* Retrieved August 2, 2006 from, http://www.healthypeople.gov/2010/Document/pdf/uih/2010uih.pdf

Vernon, J. A., Trujillo, A., Rosenbaum, S., & DeBuono, B. (2007). *Low health literacy: Implications for National Policy* (2000). Retrieved January 17, 2011 from http://www.gwumc.edu/sphhs/departments/healthpolicy/dhp_publications/pub_uploads/dhpPublication_3AC9A1C2-5056-9D20-3D4BC6786DD46B1B.pdf

Wagner, E. H. (1998). Chronic disease management: What will it take to improve care for chronic illness? *Effective Clinical Practice, 1*, 2–4.

Wallace, L. S., Cassada, D. C., Rogers, E. S., Freeman, M. B., Grandas, O. H., Stevens, S. L., & Goldman, M. H. (2007). Can screening items identify surgery patients at risk of limited health literacy? *Journal of Surgical Research, 140*, 208–213.

Weinstein, N. D. (1988). The precaution adoption process. *Health Psychology, 7*, 355–386.

Weiss, B. D., Mays, M. Z., Martz, W., Castro, K. M., DeWalt, D. A., ... Hale, F. A. (2005). Quick assessment of literacy in primary care: The newest vital sign. *Annals of Family Medicine, 3*, 514–522.

Williams, M. V., Baker, D. W., Honig, E. G., Lee, T. M., & Nowlan, A. (1998). Inadequate literacy is a barrier to asthma knowledge and self-care. *Chest, 114*, 1008–1015.

Witte, K. (1992). Putting the fear back into fear appeals: The extended parallel process model. *Communication Monographs, 59*, 329–349.

Witte, K. (1994). Fear control and danger control: A test of the extended parallel process model. *Communication Monographs, 61*, 113–134.

Wolf, M. S., Davis, T. C., Cross, J. T., Marin, E., Green, K., & Bennett, C. L. (2004). Health literacy and patient knowledge in a Southern US HIV clinic. *International Journal of STD & AIDS, 15*, 747–752.

Wolf, M. S., Davis, T. C., Osborn, C. Y., Skripkauskas, S., Bennett, C. L., & Makoul, G. (2007). Literacy, self-efficacy, and HIV medication adherence. *Patient Education and Counseling, 65*, 253–260.

Wolf, M. S., Gazmararian, J. A., & Baker, D. W. (2005). Health literacy and functional health status among older adults. *Archives of Internal Medicine, 165*, 1946–1952.

20

CULTURE, COMMUNICATION, AND HEALTH

A Guiding Framework

Mohan J. Dutta and Ambar Basu

In her editorial in the *American Journal of Public Health*, Freimuth (2004) called for efforts to understand and incorporate complexities of culture beyond surface level cultural codes such as race and ethnicity in designing, implementing, and evaluating health communication strategies that seek to touch people's lives. Cultural nuances derived from members of a target population factored into the design, implementation, and evaluation of health campaign efforts (Airhihenbuwa & Obregon, 2000) lead to more effective health interventions (Dutta, 2007). A campaign that seeks to promote healthy eating habits among African Americans, for example, may locate oral communication as a predominant communication pattern among members of the target population. Instead of labeling this cultural trait as a barrier to promoting healthy eating habits through written scripts, a culturally sensitive campaign will plan to use oral modes of communication to promote such healthy eating habits as consuming five servings of fruits and vegetables a day.

In this chapter, we propose a guiding framework for organizing the various approaches to culture in health communication on the basis of how culture is conceptualized in these approaches and the desired objectives of the proposed health communication solutions these approaches offer. It is our goal to demonstrate in this chapter that there are fundamental variations in conceptualizations of culture, and the ways in which culture is conceptualized shapes the communicative practices that are envisioned in cultural approaches to health. Also, the conceptualization of communicative practices in relationship to the broader distribution of health resources frames the ways in which health communication scholars and practitioners working on culture enter into the field. The historical roots of the earliest health communication scholarship on campaigns have been contextualized in international settings often involving the intersections of cultures. Nonetheless, the topic of culture has historically been omitted from studies of health communication that have operated under universalist notions of health and communication (Airhihenbuwa, 1995; Dutta, 2008; Dutta-Bergman, 2004a, 2004b). This approach, also traditionally referred to as the *dominant approach* to health communication, takes culture for granted in its assumptions of the overarching role of the biomedical model in problematizing health and in offering solutions to health problems (Dutta, 2008). In the last decade, the topic of culture in health communication began receiving greater attention, with scholars attempting to incorporate culture into how health communication is conceptualized, theorized, and practiced.

Cultural Approaches in Health Communication: A Guiding Framework

Drawing upon Craig (1999), we offer a theoretical framework for organizing the various approaches to culture in health communication. The theoretical framework builds upon two dialectical tensions that have defined the area of culture and health communication: social change versus status quo, and the conceptualization of culture as static versus the conceptualization of culture as dynamic. The status quo/social change dialectic draws upon the role of communication knowledge, research, and practice in working within the existing social configurations in contrast to seeking to bring about transformations in these social configurations. Health communication scholarship that works to reify social structures describes health practices, seeks to understand health meanings, and develops health solutions to problems conceptualized at the individual level. Health communication focused on social change locates health problems at the level of social structures and seeks to bring about changes in these structures in order to address health problems. The culture-as-static versus culture-as-dynamic axis of health communication scholarship is drawn upon the ontological and epistemological treatment of culture. The culture-as-static framework conceptualizes culture as a conglomeration of values, beliefs, and practices contained within a defined space; culture is categorized based on essential characteristics that are used to guide perception, motivation, and attitudes (Prentice & Miller, 2007). The culture-as-dynamic framework treats culture as transformative and contextually situated, as an interpenetrating web of meanings that is continuously in motion, informed by the local context. Although such an approach does note the transmission function of culture in passing values and beliefs through generations, it also emphasizes the notion that cultures are dynamic and are continuously constituted communicatively in shifting contexts.

The intersection of the status quo/social change and static/dynamic axes in the study of culture in health communication produces four different approaches. The *cultural sensitivity approach* treats culture as a static entity and works within the status quo. Culture is theorized as a set of values and beliefs, and cultural characteristics are extracted in order to assist in the development of health communication solutions that are tailored to the characteristics of the culture. Such an approach works within the status quo because it focuses on individual behavior as the locus of health problems and therefore offers individual level solutions rather than looking at the structural contexts of health experiences. The *ethnographic approach* to health communication also typically works within the status quo as it seeks to describe the cultural practices through which meanings and experiences of health are constructed. Treating culture as dynamic, such an approach emphasizes the meanings of health, and the ways in which cultural members come to understand meanings of health through communicative practices (see the chapter by du Pré and Crandall in this volume to further frame the meaning of this approach).

On the social change side of the spectrum, the *structure-centered approach* emphasizes the resource-based configurations within which health experiences are constructed, and seeks to transform those that adversely impact health outcomes. Culture is typically treated as a static entity and characteristics of the culture are extracted at the community level, demonstrating the role of aggregate community characteristics such as social networks, social ties, community participation, and sources of social support in the realm of health. The *culture-centered approach* further builds on the social change emphasis of the structure-centered approach and locates health experiences in the realm of social structures; it articulates communicative processes through which unhealthy structures can be changed. However, it differs from the structure-centered approach in noting the nature of culture as dynamic, and therefore, emphasizing the meaning-making nature of culture in shifting contexts. The culture-centered approach suggests participatory strategies and dialogic processes as tools for engaging with cultural voices and foregrounding cultural meanings with the ultimate goal of transforming the structures of inequity that constitute health experiences.

Cultural Sensitivity

Calls by scholars such as Lupton (1994) and Airhihenbuwa (1995) to recenter global health efforts such that they include cultural traits of target communities at their core led to what we know today as the notion of being culturally sensitive in health communication. Cultural sensitivity is theorized and practiced across communication contexts and health scenarios in today's increasingly multicultural society (see Tables 20.1–20.3). For instance, it is generally believed that cultural values and practices of people of Asian and African origin are likely to lead them to organize health and healing around cultural values such as collective identity, belief in indigenous healing processes, and the role of nature and spirituality in health and illness. Similarly, for some groups of people of Latin American birth, health and illness negotiation practices are often framed around notions of the family and the gender-based roles that influence family and public discourse. People of European origin are more likely to construct health around individualistic notions of prevention and responsibility even as they differ about logics and universalities of health care systems. The instances cited above are not to be taken as any attempt to generalize; they are mere illustrative examples used for the purposes of clarification. Furthermore, scholarly studies of cross-cultural interactions in mainstream health care settings draw attention to the diverse cosmologies of health that come face-to-face in these intersections. For example, the Ayurvedic approach to health and healing constitutes health in the overall balance between mind, body, and the spirit, whereas the biomedical model approaches health in terms of curing individual-level problems identified in the body through reductionist technologies (Dutta, 2008). Scholarly studies also draw attention to the communicative fractures in interpretation and meaning making that happen in cross-cultural interactions in physician–patient settings in the realms of both verbal and non-verbal communications (Cole & Bird, 2000; Luckman, 2000).

Cultural sensitivity is one of the most widely accepted principles of research and praxis in disciplines such as public health, communication, education, psychology, nursing, and medicine. Resnicow, Soler, Braithwaite, Ahluwalia, and Butler (2000) note that cultural

Table 20.1 Foreign-Born Population of the United States (2007)

	Number	*Percentage*
Total population of the United States	**301,621,159**	**100.0**
Foreign-born population	**38,059,555**	**12.6**
Born in Europe	4,990,294	13.1
Born in Asia	10,184,906	26.8
Born in Africa	1,419,317	3.7
Born in Oceania	216,701	0.6
Born in Latin America	20,409,676	53.6
Born in Northern America	838,661	2.2

Source: 2007 American Community Survey and Census Data on the foreign born by state.

Table 20.2 Foreign-Born Population of the United States—Detail (2007)

	Number	Percentage
Total Foreign-Born Population	38,059,555	100.0
Europe	4,990,294	13.1
Northern Europe	939,589	2.5
United Kingdom	681,285	1.8
United Kingdom, excluding England	315,276	0.8
England	366,009	1.0
Ireland	135,722	0.4
Other Northern Europe	122,582	0.3
Western Europe	1,008,989	2.7
France	154,786	0.4
Germany	631,990	1.7
Other Western Europe	222,213	0.6
Southern Europe	863,290	2.3
Italy	417,511	1.1
Portugal	198,119	0.5
Other Southern Europe	247,660	0.7
Eastern Europe	2,166,658	5.7
Poland	484,777	1.3
Russia	403,072	1.1
Other Eastern Europe	1,278,809	3.4
Europe, n.e.c.4	11,768	0.0
Asia	10,184,906	26.8
Eastern Asia	3,339,300	8.8
China	1,930,202	5.1
China, excluding Taiwan	1,570,532	4.1
Taiwan	359,670	0.9
Japan	352,933	0.9
Korea	1,042,580	2.7
Other Eastern Asia	13,585	0.0
South Central Asia	2,470,619	6.5
India	1,501,782	3.9
Iran	326,205	0.9
Other South Central Asia	642,632	1.7
Southeastern Asia	3,542,850	9.3
Philippines	1,701,126	4.5
Vietnam	1,100,833	2.9
Other Southeastern Asia	740,891	1.9
Western Asia	790,145	2.1
Israel	134,438	0.4
Lebanon	124,187	0.3
Other Western Asia	531,520	1.4
Asia, n.e.c. 4	41,992	0.1
Africa	1,419,317	3.7
Eastern Africa	386,225	1.0
Northern Africa	274,951	0.7
Western Africa	505,619	1.3
Middle and Southern Africa	137,651	0.4
Africa, n.e.c. 4	114,871	0.3

(continued)

Table 20.2 Continued

	Number	Percentage
Oceania	216,701	0.6
Australia and New Zealand Subregion	103,860	0.3
Oceania, n.e.c. 4	112,841	0.3
Americas	21,248,337	55.8
Latin America	20,409,676	53.6
Caribbean	3,387,004	8.9
Cuba	983,454	2.6
Jamaica	597,940	1.6
Other Caribbean	1,805,610	4.7
Central America	14,450,476	38.0
Mexico	11,738,537	30.8
El Salvador	1,104,390	2.9
Other Central America	1,607,549	4.2
South America	2,572,196	6.8
Brazil	338,853	0.9
Colombia	604,527	1.6
Other South America	1,628,816	4.3
Northern America	838,661	2.2
Canada	830,388	2.2
Other Northern America	8,273	0.0

Source: 2007 American Community Survey and Census Data on the foreign born by state.

sensitivity has several labels—cultural competence, cultural relevance, cultural appropriate-ness, cultural consistency, multiculturalism, cultural legitimacy, ethnical sensitivity, cultural diversity, cultural pluralism, cultural tailoring, and cultural targeting. They define cultural sensitivity as:

> The extent to which ethnic/cultural characteristics, experiences, norms, values, behavioral patterns, and beliefs of a target population as well as relevant historical, environmental, and social forces are incorporated in the design, delivery, and evaluation of targeted health promotion materials and programs.
>
> (p. 272)

Similarly, Dutta (2007) writes that the cultural sensitivity approach focuses on creating effective health messages that are responsive to the values and beliefs of the culture. The advocacy for cultural sensitivity in health communication is based on the notion that communication about health ought to adapt to the characteristics of a culture in order to be most effective (Sue & Sue, 1999; Ulrey & Amason, 2001).

The promotion of cultural sensitivity as a theoretical framework in health communication research and praxis has primarily been a result of immigration patterns into the United States, the critiques of the dominant paradigm of health communication in its inability to meet the specific health needs of cultural communities, and the gaps in access to health services and prevention measures that vary by culture (Airhihenbuwa, 1995, 2007; Dutta, 2007, 2008; Geist-Martin, Ray, & Sharf, 2003; Kreps & Thornton, 1992). In the realms of interpersonal communication between patients and health experts, Sharf and Kahler (1996)

Table 20.3 Language Other than English Spoken at Home among Foreign-Born Population in the United States (2007).

	Total	Percentage
Total Household Population, Age 5 and Older	**280,950,438**	**100.0**
Speak language other than English	55,444,485	100.0
Spanish or Spanish Creole	34,547,077	62.3
French (including Patois and Cajun)	1,355,805	2.4
French Creole	629,019	1.1
Italian	798,801	1.4
Portuguese or Portuguese Creole	687,126	1.2
German	1,104,354	2.0
Yiddish	158,991	0.3
Other West Germanic languages	270,178	0.5
Scandinavian languages	134,925	0.2
Greek	329,825	0.6
Russian	851,174	1.5
Polish	638,059	1.2
Serbo-Croatian	276,550	0.5
Other Slavic languages	312,109	0.6
Armenian	221,865	0.4
Persian	349,686	0.6
Gujarathi	287,367	0.5
Hindi	532,911	1.0
Urdu	344,942	0.6
Other Indic languages	616,147	1.1
Other Indo-European languages	420,896	0.8
Chinese	2,464,572	4.4
Japanese	458,717	0.8
Korean	1,062,337	1.9
Mon-Khmer, Cambodian	185,056	0.3
Hmong	181,069	0.3
Thai	144,405	0.3
Laotian	149,045	0.3
Vietnamese	1,207,004	2.2
Other Asian languages	625,148	1.1
Tagalog	1,480,429	2.7
Other Pacific Island languages	358,644	0.6
Navajo	170,717	0.3
Other Native North American languages	200,560	0.4
Hungarian	91,297	0.2
Arabic	767,319	1.4
Hebrew	213,576	0.4
African languages	699,518	1.3
Other and unspecified languages	117,265	0.2

Source: 2007 American Community Survey and Census Data on the foreign born by state.

theorize culturally sensitive communication as one that takes into account the several layers of meaning that each participant in the communication encounter brings to her/his relationship and conversation about health and illness. These layers of meaning typically include ideology, sociopolitical context, institutional/organizational norms and cultures, community and familial meanings of health and illness, and interpersonal notions of communicating about health. In the same context, Ulrey and Amason (2001) conceptualize cultural sensitivity in physician–patient interaction situations in terms of variables such as using culturally appropriate language, having cultural knowledge, understanding cultural values, considering culture in assessment of patients, and adapting treatment according to the cultural knowledge physicians have about a patient.

In some health communication projects, such as the one reported by Ulrey and Amason, cultural sensitivity is operationalized by developing scales to measure it and correlating it with outcome factors. Ulery and Amason found that cultural sensitivity has a positive correlation with satisfactory doctor–patient communication outcomes, and Bresnahan, Lee, Smith, Shearman, and Yoo (2007) developed a culturally sensitive spirituality scale to predict why research participants from Korea, Japan, and the United States were willing or reluctant to register as organ donors. In addition to developing scales to theorize cultural sensitivity in health communication, Dutta (2007) notes that cultural sensitivity in health communication is also theorized and practiced by extrapolating certain aspects of cultures into extant theories and applications of health communication. Models built on this approach identify cultural variables and use them to predict a variety of health outcome variables. For instance, Lee, Hubbard, O'Riordan, and Kim (2006) incorporate cultural traits of independence and interdependence into the theory of planned behavior to predict smoking cessation intentions among a multi-cultural college student community in Hawaii.

Health interventions, such as those related to smoking cessation, take the shape of mass mediated campaigns as well, and here, too, the notion of cultural sensitivity is valued and promoted. Kline (2007) discusses the implications of cultural sensitivity for the rhetorical choices in breast cancer education materials developed for African American audiences by national organizations. Kline uses the PEN-3 model of cultural sensitivity (Airhihenbuwa, 1995) as an analytic framework to report that while some pamphlets acknowledged African American cultural values related to community, such as self-reliance, spirituality, and distrust of the medical establishment, several messages were lacking in terms of providing a balanced, comprehensive, and audience-specific discussion of the breast cancer issue.

The PEN-3 model developed by Airhihenbuwa (1995) is one of the earliest theorizations of cultural sensitivity in health communication. It aims to "offer a space within which cultural codes and meanings can be centralized in the development, implementation, and evaluation of health promotion programs" (p. 28). The PEN-3 model states that three dynamically related facets of health beliefs and behavior influence how health is communicated, each with three categories labeled to form the PEN-3 acronym: (a) cultural identity (person, extended family, neighborhood), (b) relationships and expectations (perceptions, enablers, nurturers), and (c) cultural empowerment (positive, existential, negative).

Airhihenbuwa advocates the institution of localized identity at the core of health promotion efforts. He notes that the meanings one ascribes to one's self and one's group are not just a function of one's choice of identity; these meanings are anchored in one's history, experiences with and within extant social arrangements such as one's self, one's family, and one's community. Thus, identity is a process of constructing the self in relation to one's context. And this context influences and is influenced by one's perceptions (knowledge, attitudes, values, and beliefs that have an impact on how one is able and willing to change behavior), enablers (social and cultural systems that may enhance or act as barriers to health behavior change), or nurturers (behaviors and beliefs in family and community that influence individual-level behavior change). Tied to identity and relationships, according to Airhihenbuwa (1995), are positive, existential, or negative health behaviors that should either be encouraged or discouraged through messages that empower cultural participants to enact healthful behaviors without being displaced from the context of their history, politics, and cultural meaning systems. Airhihenbuwa and Webster (2004) apply the model to explain how culture plays a vital role in determining the level of health of the individual, the family, and the community, particularly in the context of HIV or AIDS in Africa, where values of extended family and community influence individual-level behavior.

According to Dutta (2007), the cultural sensitivity approach typically begins by setting up an agenda for the health communication program; cultural variables of interest are then defined, following which the cultural variables are measured in formative research. Finally, health communication solutions that respond to the cultural variables identified in formative research are developed. The program is then evaluated based on the criteria developed by the experts; the pathway for the health communication program is also defined by these experts. It is the central role of the outside expert in a culturally sensitive health communication initiative, however, that opens it up for critique (see section on the culture-centered approach).

Structure-Centered Approach

The structure-centered approach to health communication situates health in the realm of the social structures that constitute it (Dutta-Bergman, 2003, 2004c; Kawachi & Kennedy, 1999; Viswanath, Finnegan, Hannan, & Luepker, 1991). Therefore, health outcomes, access to and quality of health services, technologies, and products are studied against the backdrop of the organizing structures within which health care systems are delivered. By situating health services, health technologies, health products, and health services in the realm of broader structures, the structure-centered approach problematizes health in the realm of the systems of organizing within which it is delivered, and seeks to transform these underlying structures as solutions for health care problems of communities (Dutta, 2008; Zoller, 2005). Drawing upon a Marxist approach to health and communication, the structure-centered approach typically treats culture as a static entity, extracting characteristics of the community in order to theorize about the role of structures in shaping health communication processes, and to develop processes of social change directed at changing the underlying structures. In addition to work on the structure-centered approach within health communication, the allied fields of public health and health sociology offer multiple examples of structure-centered health communication theory, scholarship, and application development (see Kawachi & Kennedy, 1999).

Structure refers to the systems of organizing social systems, within which resources are made available or unavailable to communities (Dutta, 2008). Structures are embedded within an economic base, but also are connected to the forms of community networks and community ties that are available to the members of the community; these, in turn, are also economically constituted (Dutta-Bergman, 2003, 2004c). At an aggregate level, therefore, structure reflects community characteristics such as social networks, social ties, and community organizations; and at a more fundamental level, structure also reflects economic access and abilities. The material foundation of structures constitutes the economic resources for the community, and the extent to which a community has access to economic resources determines the community's access to other forms of resources. From a communicative standpoint, the sorts of communicative opportunities that are available to individuals and communities depend upon their positions within social structures (Dutta, 2008). This is further developed in the chapter by Ndiaye et al. in this volume.

Structures have been systematically absent from the dominant conversations of health communication, which have typically explored individual level solutions to health problems. In this framework, health campaigns have been proposed as solutions to health problems. Individuals have been asked to modify their lifestyles and behaviors, leaving structures intact (Lupton, 1994). Health communication scholars increasingly explore the role of social structures in the realm of access to health services, preventive services, and health solutions (Dutta-Bergman, 2003, 2004c). Of note are the knowledge gap studies that examine the gaps between higher and lower SES segments of the population brought about by health intervention campaigns (Viswanath et al., 1991), an ethical dilemma discussed by Guttman in this volume. Structures are directly addressed as the causes of poor health outcomes, and strategies are put in place for remedying lack of access.

Beyond the application-driven emphasis on exploring solutions to health disparities, as discussed in the chapter by Ndiaye et al. in this volume, health communication scholars have also theoretically examined the role of social structures in the context of health. For instance, based upon aggregate characteristics drawn out at the community level, health communication scholars have theorized about the role of social capital in the realm of health experiences (Basu & Dutta, 2008b; Dutta-Bergman, 2003, 2004c). Communities with high social capital are those communities that have strong social networks and high levels of community participation as compared to low social capital communities that lack these amenities. The literature suggests that high social capital communities are likely to enjoy better health outcomes because of their strong networks for diffusing health information, because of their greater capacities to articulate community needs and secure resources, and because of the strong bonds within such communities that act as buffers against life stressors.

This line of research goes on further to point out the linkages between socioeconomic status of communities and social capital (Kawachi & Kennedy, 1999). Lower socioeconomic status communities are likely to have weaker bonds and lower levels of social capital as compared to those with higher socioeconomic status. Furthermore, communities with higher levels of inequities are also likely to score lower in social capital as compared to more equitable communities. These findings point toward the constitutive role of socioeconomic indicators and community structures in shaping health experiences, access to health care, quality of health care experienced by community members, as well as health outcomes. Furthermore, communication scholars point out the absence of adequate communication infrastructures in underserved communities (Dutta, 2008). Individuals and communities that have lower socioeconomic status are less likely to use those channels of communication that are typically used by campaign planners and health information programs (Dutta-Bergman, 2004d). The gap between the channel use patterns of individuals from lower socioeconomic status and those of communication campaigns contributes to knowledge gaps and increasing health-related disparities, too often linked back to culture.

Based on the examination of the differential patterns of communication channel access and usage, structure-centered communication scholars emphasize the creation of communication infrastructures in underserved communities in order to create points of information dissemination. Such infrastructure-based communication scholarship is evident in the development within underserved communities of telecommunication systems, traditional communication channels such as radio and television, as well as new media channels such as wireless technologies and the Internet. We also see evidence of structure-centered health communication in the works of scholars such as Zoller (2005) and Kreps (2006), who articulate the importance of addressing issues of policy in health communication scholarship. Ultimately, structure-centered health communication scholarship seeks to bring about changes in social structures in order to create access to health care among the underserved segments of the population.

Culture-Centered

The culture-centered approach to health communication is founded on a historical deconstruction of the field of health communication, noting the absence of cultural sensitivity in health communication and the Eurocentric biases of theory and praxis that take for granted the cultural bases and value-based constructions of the biomedical model and the social-cognitive theories that explain human behaviors (Dutta, 2008). This absence of cultural considerations is accompanied by the absence of the voices of cultural communities that have typically been treated as the subjects of health communication interventions, drawing upon a top-down Westcentric biomedical narrative (Dutta, 2008; Dutta-Bergman, 2004a, 2004b). Noting the absence of cultural voices as a starting point and drawing from the post-colonial and subaltern studies projects, the culture-centered approach utilizes the tools of dialogue, narrative co-construction, solidarity building, and participatory communication in order to engage with voices of cultural communities, to listen to these voices, and to seek out spaces of change based on conversations with marginalized voices (Basu & Dutta, 2008a, 2009; Villagran, Collins, & Garcia, 2008; Wood, Hall, & Hasian, 2008).

The culture-centered approach is theoretically rooted in the subaltern studies project, with an emphasis on the examination of the communicative processes and structures through which the margins are created and erased from the dominant discursive spaces (Dutta, 2008; Wood et al., 2008). Subaltern studies, as a discipline of inquiry, is interested in interrogating the erasures in the dominant configurations of knowledge (Beverly, 2004; Guha, 1997). In doing so, subaltern studies turns the lens on the dominant *epistemic* structures and questions the underlying privileges of the elite that are maintained by these structures through processes of erasure of subaltern voices in policy platforms, in discursive spaces of knowledge, and in communication interventions (DeSouza, Basu, Kim, Basnyat, & Dutta, 2008; Villagran et al., 2008).

Politicizing the knowledge production processes in health communication, the culture-centered approach questions the ways in which dominant discourses of health communication erase the voices of certain groups and communities, and create conditions of subalternity through propagation of social inequities (DeSouza et al., 2008; Dutta, 2007; Dutta-Bergman, 2004a, 2004b). It focuses on examining the taken-for-granted assumptions in the dominant theories of health communication and the ways in which these taken-for-granted assumptions continue to undermine the agency of cultural participants in re-creating the structural inequities, fixing them as recipients of messages of enlightenment, and continuing to serve the structural inequities that constitute subalternity (Dutta, 2008). The culture-centered approach argues that the undermining of the agency of subaltern groups is quintessential to the erasures of these groups from the dominant epistemic structures, from policy platforms, and from spaces of campaign design and development.

Knowledge here is intrinsically connected to praxis, as the applications of health communication that are developed in the mainstream continue to erase the voices of subaltern communities by consistently categorizing them as deviant and as the subjects of health care interventions (see Dutta & Basnyat, 2008). In this sense, the marginalized community or culture is located in a fixed category imbued with "undesirable" characteristics (such as illiteracy, ignorance, primitive beliefs, etc.), and interventions are developed to change the "undesirable" characteristics of the subaltern groups. By interrogating the absences of subaltern voices in health care policies, programs, and evaluation strategies, the culture-centered approach creates discursive openings for co-constructing narratives of health through dialogue with subaltern communities (Basu & Dutta, 2007, 2008a, 2009; Dutta-Bergman, 2004a, 2004b). It calls for shifts in health care policies and the ways in which policies are presented and represented through the voices of the subaltern participants engaged in dialogue with the scholar (Wang, 1999).

The culture-centered approach is built upon three key concepts and the interactions among these concepts: structure, culture, and agency. Structure refers to those aspects of social organization that constrain and enable the capacity of cultural participants to seek out health choices and engage in health-related behaviors. On one hand, structures limit the opportunity for securing health care in marginalized contexts by determining the range of health care choices that are available or unavailable to cultural members; on the other hand, they create opportunities for change by challenging the frameworks within which health is constituted. The concept of culture refers to the local contexts within which health meanings are constituted and negotiated.

Culture provides the communicative framework for health meanings such that the ways in which community members come to understand health and illness are embedded within beliefs, values, and practices. These beliefs, values, and practices are also contextual and health meanings become localized within these contexts. It is this contextual nature of health meanings that contributes to the dynamic nature of culture, suggesting that cultural meanings continually shift. Culture is constituted by the day-to-day practices of its members as they come to develop their interpretations of health and illness and engage in their day-to-day practices. Furthermore, cultural meanings provide the locally situated scripts through which structures influence the health choices of cultural participants.

Agency refers to the capacity of cultural members to enact their choices and to actively participate in negotiating the structures within which they find themselves. In other words, the concept of agency reflects the active processes through which individuals, groups, and communities participate in a variety of actions that directly challenge the structures that constrain their lives and simultaneously work with the structures in finding healthful options. From a health communication standpoint, participatory spaces are created and sustained that allow health communicators the opportunity to engage with the agency of cultural participants, listen to subaltern voices, and create transformative opportunities through the co-construction of narratives (Basu & Dutta, 2008a; Wang, 1999; Wang & Burris, 1994).

The three concepts of structure, culture, and agency are intertwined. Structures within social systems are played out through the culturally situated contexts in communities. Structural constraints become meaningful through the lived experiences of cultural members and through the sharing of these lived experiences. Simultaneously, culture offers the substratum for structure, such that structures are both reified and challenged through the cultural meaning systems that are in circulation within the culture. It is through the articulation of new meanings that cultures create points of social change. For instance, when cultural members in a marginalized context start sharing their stories of deprivation, greater awareness is created and opportunities are introduced for changes in the health care infrastructures (Wang & Burris, 1994).

Agency is enacted in the lives of individuals and communities as they struggle with the structural constraints they face. Given the emphasis of the culture-centered approach on marginalized settings, much of the discussion of the approach ties in to the lack of basic resources and economic capacities in these contexts (Dutta-Bergman, 2004a, 2004b). Agency offers an opportunity to situate the lives of marginalized individuals, groups, and communities in the realm of their active engagement in living with and challenging the structures that constrain their lives (Camacho, Yep, Gomez, & Velez, 2008). Members of marginalized communities continually interact with the structures within which they live, simultaneously working within these structures and participating in avenues that seek to change them (Basu & Dutta, 2008a, 2009; Camacho et al., 2008; Dutta-Bergman, 2004a, 2004b). Ultimately, agency offers the opportunity for social change by challenging the structures that limit health care capacities in marginalized communities through community mobilization and activism, performance, and dialogic avenues for social change.

From the standpoint of praxis, the culture-centered approach stresses the need to develop respect for the capability of members of marginalized communities to define their health needs and to seek out solutions that fulfill these needs. Voices of community members are presented through the dialogical engagement with the community. In this context, the researcher does not claim to be the expert on the so-called lay theories articulated by the participants, nor does he/she seek to completely remove himself/herself from the dialogue, knowing that this is neither possible nor desirable. The voices of marginalized communities are therefore played out through the dialogues between the researcher and the community members. This perspective takes us outside the realm of wanting to change people and to teach them how to better live their lives through one-way transmission-based models to a framework that is built on the goal of developing an understanding of people and their cultures (Beverly, 2004; Dutta-Bergman, 2004; Foss & Griffin, 1995; Mokros & Deetz, 1996). The researcher here is a listener and a participant who engages in dialogue with the members of the community. Dialogue introduces voices of cultural participants into the discursive space, which has largely omitted them or treated them as absent. Noting the moral commitment required for the dialogical process to occur, Freire (1970) articulated that "being dialogic is not invading, not manipulating, not imposing orders. Being dialogic is pledging oneself to constant transformation of reality" (p. 46). Fundamental to the culture-centered approach is the understanding that members of communities actively participate in interpreting, interacting with, and seeking to transform the social structures that encompass them. The culture-centered approach seeks to narrate these dialogic encounters and partake in social change by the very introduction of marginalized voices into the dominant discursive space.

Opportunities for learning in this case are not only opened up to the participating members of the culture, but also to the researcher/scholar that engages in dialogue with the culture (see for instance, Villagran et al., 2009). The traditional construction of the receivers of the message is expanded, moving from the realm of the target communities for diffusion of innovations to the inclusion of funding agencies, policy makers, researchers/scholars, community members, and other stakeholders involved in the project that continually switch between the roles of sender and receiver as they engage in dialogue, identify problems, and propose structural solutions to these problems (see Basu & Dutta, 2008a, 2009).

Conclusion

With this increasing interest in culture, the field has witnessed diverse approaches to the study and practice of culture in health communication. The four different approaches to the study of culture highlighted here share a great many commonalities even as they demonstrate points of departure from each other. One of the goals of this chapter was to outline the parameters of the different approaches to the scholarship of culture in health communication. The cultural sensitivity approach is perhaps the most widely circulated approach in health communication, seeking to develop communication solutions that are tailored for or targeted toward the multicultural population. In this approach, the role of the researcher is to identify the most salient characteristics of the culture that would aid in the tooling of the communication practice to the characteristics of the culture. Scholarship on cultural sensitivity ranges from developing cultural competence training programs for physicians to avoid miscommunication to creating culturally sensitive campaign messages directed at persuading potential multicultural audiences to engage in health promoting behaviors. The structure-centered approach also emphasizes extracting the key characteristics of the culture and developing resource-based solutions on the foundations of these characteristics. Structure-centered health communication scholarship examines the communication infrastructures, community characteristics, participatory resources, and community capacities that contribute to positive health outcomes in communities. In both these approaches, culture is treated as an aggregate of characteristics, and the emphasis is on working with the characteristics to develop health communication solutions.

The ethnographic approach to culture in health communication emphasizes the dynamic nature of culture, and seeks to engage with the local contexts within which cultural meanings are constituted. The focus therefore is on understanding the ways in which health meanings are constituted and negotiated in health care interactions, processes, and settings. Similarly, the culture-centered approach also treats culture as a dynamic entity embedded in local cultural contexts, and emphasizes the development of participatory processes and platforms for listening to the voices of the local cultural communities as opposed to the top-down communication processes in traditional health campaigns. Whereas the emphasis of the ethnographic approach is on describing and interpreting health care interactions, processes, and meanings, the emphasis of the culture-centered approach is on listening to the voices of local cultural communities as entry points to changes in structural configurations that marginalize the resource-poor sectors.

It is worth mentioning, however, that even as the outline presented here suggests boundaries between these approaches, the approaches often interpenetrate in their treatment of health communication. The topic of culture is increasingly becoming relevant in health communication with the escalating flow of people across nation states and the interpenetration of issues of health across geographic boundaries. It is our hope that the next generation of health communication scholars will respond to this global cultural flow not only in terms of finding ways of adapting health communication scholarship to the changing global cultural landscape, but also in terms of creating openings for questioning the hegemony of the biomedical model and exploring other ways of knowing that offer alternative readings and interpretations of health (Dutta, 2008).

References

Airhihenbuwa, C. O. (1995). *Health and culture. Beyond the Western paradigm.* Thousand Oaks, CA: Sage.

Airhihenbuwa, C. O. (2007). *Healing our differences: The crisis of global health and the politics of identity.* Lanham, MD: Rowman & Littlefield.

Airhihenbuwa, C. O., & Obregon, R. (2000). A critical assessment of theories/models used in health communication for AIDS [Supplement]. *Journal of Health Communication, 5,* 5–15.

Airhihenbuwa, C., & Webster, J. D. (2004). Culture and African contexts of HIV/AIDS prevention, care, and support. *Journal of Social Aspects of HIV/AIDS Research Alliance, 1,* 4–13.

Basu, A., & Dutta, M. (2007). Centralizing context and culture in the co-construction of health: Localizing and vocalizing health meanings in rural India. *Health Communication, 21,* 187–196.

Basu, A., & Dutta, M. (2008a). Participatory change in a campaign led by sex workers: Connecting resistance to action-oriented agency. *Qualitative Health Research, 18,* 106–119.

Basu, A., & Dutta, M. (2008b). The relationship between health information seeking and community participation: The roles of motivation and ability. *Health Communication, 23*(1), 70–79

Basu, A., & Dutta, M. (2009). Sex workers and HIV/AIDS: Analyzing participatory culture-centered health communication strategies. *Human Communication Research, 35,* 86–114.

Beverly, J. (2004). *Subalternity and representation: Arguments in cultural theory.* Durham, NC: Duke University Press.

Bresnahan, M., Lee, S. Y., Smith, S., Shearman, S. W., & Yoo, J. H. (2007). Reservations of the spirit: The development of a culturally sensitive spiritual beliefs scale about organ donation. *Health Communication, 21,* 45–54.

Camacho, A., Yep, G., Gomez, P., & Velez, E. (2008). El Poder y la fuerza de la passion: Toward a model of HIV/AIDS education and service delivery from the bottom-up. In H. M. Zoller & M. J. Dutta (Eds.), *Emerging perspectives in health communication* (pp. 224–246). New York: Routledge.

Cole, S. A., & Bird, J. (2000). *The medical interview: The three-function approach.* St. Louis, MO: Mosby.

Craig, R. T. (1999). Communication theory as a field. *Communication Theory, 9,*119–161.

DeSouza, R., Basu, A., Kim, I., Basnyat, I., & Dutta, M. (2008). The paradox of "fair trade": The influence of neoliberal trade agreements on food security and health. In H. Zoller & M. Dutta (Eds.), *Emerging perspectives in health communication: Interpretive, critical and cultural approaches* (pp. 411–430). Mahwah, NJ: Erlbaum.

Dutta, M. (2007). Communicating about culture and health: Theorizing culture-centered and cultural-sensitivity approaches. *Communication Theory, 17,* 304–328.

Dutta, M. (2008). *Communicating health: A culture-centered approach.* Cambridge, England: Polity.

Dutta, M., & Basnyat, I. (2008). Interrogating the Radio Communication Project in Nepal: The participatory framing of colonization. In H. Zoller & M. Dutta (Eds.), *Emerging perspectives in health communication: Interpretive, critical and cultural approaches* (pp. 247–265). Mahwah, NJ: Erlbaum.

Dutta-Bergman, M. (2003). Demographic and psychographic antecedents of community participation: Applying a social marketing model. *Social Marketing Quarterly, 9,* 17–31.

Dutta-Bergman, M. (2004a). Poverty, structural barriers and health: A Santali narrative of health communication. *Qualitative Health Research, 14,* 1–16.

Dutta-Bergman, M. (2004b). The unheard voices of Santalis: Communicating about health from the margins of India. *Communication Theory, 14,* 237–263.

Dutta-Bergman, M. (2004c). An alternative approach to social capital: Exploring the linkage between health consciousness and community participation. *Health Communication, 16,* 393–409.

Dutta-Bergman, M. (2004d). Primary sources of health information: Comparison in the domain of health attitudes, health cognitions, and health behaviors. *Health Communication, 16,* 273–288.

Foss, S. K., & Griffin, C. L. (1995). Beyond persuasion: A proposal for an invitational rhetoric. *Communication Monographs, 62,* 2–18.

Freimuth, V. (2004). The contributions of health communication to eliminating health disparities. *American Journal of Public Health, 94,* 2053–2055.

Freire, P. (1970). *Pedagogy of the oppressed.* New York: Herder and Herder.

Geist-Martin, P., Ray, E. B., & Sharf, B. (2003). *Communicating health: Personal, cultural, and political complexities.* Belmont, CA: Wadsworth.

Guha, R. (1997). Introduction. In R. Guha (Ed.), *A subaltern studies reader* (pp. ix–xii). Minneapolis, MN: University of Minnesota Press.

Kawachi, I., & Kennedy, B. (1999). Income inequality and health: Pathways and mechanisms. *Health Services Research, 34,* 215–227.

Kline, K. N. (2007). Cultural sensitivity and health promotion: Assessing breast cancer education pamphlets designed for African American women. *Health Communication, 21,* 85–96.

Kreps, G. L. (2006). Communication and racial inequalities in health care. *American Behavioral Scientist, 49,* 760–744.

Kreps, G. L., & Thornton, B.C. (1992). *Health communication: Theory and practice* (2nd ed.). Prospect Heights, IL: Waveland Press.

333

Lee, H., Hubbard, A. S. E., O'Riordan, C. K., & Kim, M. (2006). Incorporating culture into the theory of planned behavior: Predicting smoking cessation intentions among college students. *Asian Journal of Communication, 16,* 315–332.

Luckman, J. (2000). *Transcultural communication in health care.* Albany, NY: Delmar.

Lupton, D. (1994). Toward the development of a critical health communication praxis. *Health Communication, 6,* 55–67.

Mokros, H. B., & Deetz, S. (1996). What counts as real? A constitutive view of communication and the disenfranchised in the context of health. In E. B. Ray (Ed.), *Communication and disenfranchisement: Social issues and implications* (pp. 29–44). Mahwah, NJ: Erlbaum.

Prentice, D., & Miller, D. (2007). Psychological essentialism of human categories. *Current Directions in Psychological Science. 16,* 202–206.

Resnicow, K., Soler, R., Braithwaite, R. L., Ahluwalia, J. S., & Butler, J. (2000). Cultural sensitivity in substance use prevention. *Journal of Community Psychology, 28*(3), 271–290.

Sharf, B. F., & Kahler, J. (1996). Victims of the franchise: A culturally sensitive model for teaching patient-physician communication in the inner city. In E. B. Ray (Ed.), *Communication and the disenfranchised: Social health issues and implications* (pp. 95–115). Mahwah, NJ: Erlbaum.

Sue, D. W., & Sue, D. (1999). *Counseling the culturally different: Theory and practice* (3rd ed.). New York: Wiley.

Ulrey, K. L., & Amason, P. (2001). Intercultural communication between patients and health care providers: An exploration of intercultural communication effectiveness, cultural sensitivity, stress, and anxiety. *Health Communication, 13,* 449–463.

Villagran, M., Collins, D., & Garcia, S. (2008). Voces de las colonias: Dialectical tensions about control and cultural identification in Latina's communication about cancer. In H. M. Zoller & M. J. Dutta (Eds.), *Emerging perspectives in health communication: Interpretive, critical and cultural approaches* (pp. 203–223). New York: Routledge.

Viswanath, K., Finnegan, J. R., Hannan, P. J., & Luepker. R. V. (1991). Health and knowledge gaps: Some lessons from the Minnesota Heart Health Program. *American Behavioral Scientist, 34,* 712–726.

Wang, C. C. (1999). Photovoice: A participatory action research strategy applied to women's health. *Journal of Women's Health, 8,* 185–192.

Wang, C. C., & Burris, M. (1994). Empowerment through photo novella: Portraits of participation. *Health Education Quarterly, 21,* 171–186.

Wood, R., Hall, D. M., & Hasian, M., Jr. (2008). Globalization, social justice movements, and the human genome diversity debates. In H. M. Zoller & M. J. Dutta (Eds.), *Emerging perspectives in health communication: Interpretive, critical and cultural approaches* (pp. 431–445). New York: Routledge.

Zoller, H. M. (2005). Health activism: Communication theory and action for social change. *Communication Theory, 15,* 341–364.

21

SOCIAL SUPPORT, SOCIAL NETWORKS, AND HEALTH

A Guiding Framework

Daena J. Goldsmith and Terrance L. Albrecht

Almost four decades ago, in *Illness, Immunity, and Social Interaction*, Moss (1973) described the function of social support as providing

> general social therapy for all types of incongruities one may encounter.... Social support provides each person with a communication network that is a safe base. Here he [sic] can be accepted whether he succeeds or fails in other networks. Here he can retreat to take stock of himself and prepare to meet "life." Here he is accepted as a "whole person," and all his various qualities, roles, desires, and the like are of interest.
>
> (pp. 236–237)

Though the specific terminology has changed over the years, researchers across the social sciences, epidemiology, public health, and medicine recognize the importance of supportive communication as a necessary condition for the quality of life and for healthful living. The links between psychosocial and biomedical processes are now widely accepted and we recognize that the resources (or lack of resources) in a community affect health outcomes (Berkman & Glass, 2000). The study of social support is as timely today as it ever has been.

"Social support" is an umbrella term for various theories and concepts that link involvement in social relationships to health and well-being. As Moss's description of support as social therapy demonstrates, communication plays a central role in many of these processes. Social support is communicated in the structures of ordinary relationships enabling us to build a safe base from which to confront the hassles of daily life (Goldsmith, 2004). Social support is also the foundation for extraordinary deeds in situations of extreme distress, such as the rescue of the Jews during the Holocaust (Albrecht, 1994a).

This chapter surveys research on supportive communication from the vantage point of health communication. Other reviews have examined support in the domains of inter-personal communication (e.g., Burleson & MacGeorge, 2002), sociology (e.g., Smith & Christakis, 2008), epidemiology (e.g., Berkman & Glass, 2000), and social psychology (Sarason & Sarason, 2001). We begin by briefly reviewing the history of the social support concept.

History and Origins of Social Support

At about the same time that Moss (1973) was exploring the linkages between illness, immunity, and social interaction, other prominent scholars were also recognizing the importance of social support. John Cassel's (1976) presidential address to the American Public Health Association identified social support as a health protective feature of the environment.

In his 1976 presidential address to the Society for Psychosomatic Medicine, physician Sidney Cobb termed social support as information that "led the subject to believe that he/ she 1) is cared for and loved; 2) is esteemed and valued; and 3) belongs to a network of communication and mutual obligation" (Cobb, 1976, p. 300).

Empirical studies gathered momentum during the 1980s. Evidence mounted for the causal link between support and health, and longitudinal epidemiological studies showed that support had profound consequences for mental and physical well-being (for a review, see House, Landis, & Umberson, 1988). The notion that network structures and communication processes could impact health outcomes was conceptually groundbreaking and provided a much needed explanation for the relationship between social behavior and biomedical problems (Moss, 1973).

Measures and methodologies began to be refined and conceptual debates flourished. Was social support a buffer against the otherwise negative effects of stress or an ongoing positive influence on health behavior and mental outlook, independent of stressful events? Cohen and Wills (1985) proposed that perceiving that support is available has a stress-buffering effect whereas integration in diverse types of relationships affects health by providing coherence, positive affect, and social control (see also Cohen, Gottlieb, & Underwood, 2000).

In 1987, Albrecht and Adelman encouraged scholars to conceptualize support as "verbal and nonverbal communication between recipients and providers that helps [manage][1] uncertainty about the situation, the self, the other or the relationship and functions to enhance a perception of personal control in one's life experience" (p. 19). This challenged a view of social support as an individual difference in personal perception (cf. Sarason, Sarason, & Pierce, 1990) and, instead, emphasized how support could vary in more or less functional patterns based on differences in social interaction. It also gave a theoretical explanation for the well-established link between social support and positive health outcomes. This enabled scholars to identify features of messages and networks that facilitated uncertainty management and also to recognize that patterns of communication could have negative effects.

Social support is describable now as a vast, multidisciplinary body of theory and empirical findings. Large scale, prospective mortality studies show a consistent effect of social support on health, comparable to other well-known risk factors such as smoking, blood pressure, blood lipids, obesity, and physical activity (House et al., 1988, p. 541). Experimental studies demonstrate how support blunts cardiovascular reactivity (Uchino, Cacioppo, & Kiecolt-Glaser, 1996), improves neuroendocrine and immune functioning (Uchino, 2006), and can even protect us from the common cold (Cohen, Doyle, Skoner, Rabin, & Gwaltney, 1997). Those with social support live longer and healthier lives (Uchino, 2006), are more likely to follow medical regimens (DiMatteo, 2004), and recover more successfully from illness and surgery (Kulick & Mahler, 1989).

Three decades of research have demonstrated that "social support" is not a single, unified construct. *Supportive conversations* and *social networks* are of particular relevance to health communication research. Supportive conversations seek to communicate reassurance, validation, and acceptance; offer perspective shifts on cause–effect contingencies; enhance another's training or skills; coordinate sharing resources and assistance; and enable disclosure of thoughts and emotions (Albrecht & Adelman, 1987). Attention to support networks reminds us that these conversations occur within a web of relationships. We turn now to the multiple pathways that link supportive conversations and networks to health.

How Do Supportive Conversations and Networks Enhance Health?

The study of supportive *conversations* focuses on the actions that relational partners (e.g., friends, family members, peers, neighbors, acquaintances, co-workers) undertake with the intention of helping one another cope. Enacted support (a.k.a., received support, supportive behaviors, support transactions) includes informational support (e.g., giving advice or sharing information), emotional support (e.g., expressing caring and acceptance), tangible support (e.g., providing resources or assisting in tasks), and appraisal support (e.g., helping interpret an event or assess coping options). Enacted support research explores the conditions under which communication has beneficial outcomes, including features of interaction that make some attempts more beneficial than others. Enacted support is typically measured through self-reports of how frequently different kinds of support occur (for a review, see Wills & Shinar, 2000) or by coding behaviors observed in laboratory conversations (for a review, see Reis & Collins, 2000).

The correlations between enacted support and health outcomes vary widely (Goldsmith, 2004). Sometimes individuals benefit from more enacted support, but these effects are usually only evident for some types of support under some conditions. Some studies show more enacted support is associated with *worse* health. This might be because in cross-sectional designs, those with the greatest need receive the most support, but it could also occur because enacted support provokes resistance to health regimens or undermines self-efficacy. Further, measuring amount or frequency of support overlooks quality and appropriateness (Goldsmith, 2004). For example, advice about a health problem could turn out to be uninformed, critical, or condescending, and even well-intentioned efforts can produce relational conflict or increase uncertainty. Communication scholars are well-positioned to move beyond counting and correlating behaviors with outcomes and, instead, to theorize how specific features of conversations produce the health-relevant processes through which benefits accrue.

Supportive interactions occur in the context of *support networks* (i.e., sets of overlapping relational linkages, Penner, Dovidio, & Albrecht, 2000). Network research focuses on the patterns of communication that are most likely to create health protective social environments and enhance access to health resources. These patterns are characterized by structural indices including size (e.g., the number of support providers an individual perceives) and density (the extent to which network members are connected to one another). Multiplex ties link relational partners through multiple roles whereas uniplex ties involve a weak tie or singular role relationship with a more limited context, scope, and character. Reciprocity includes attributes such as whether both people in a network identify one another as linked or whether a person reports giving and receiving support from others. Finally, homogeneity taps network member similarity (e.g., sociodemographic characteristics, communication styles, character traits). Research on supportive conversations and networks shows how health is embedded in the content and structure of relational life outside the clinic and alongside the media message. Social support studies reveal how we come to hold some of our health beliefs, where we obtain some of our information, and the social pressures and resources that reinforce or undermine what health care providers or campaigns tell us to do. We turn now to four ways that conversations and networks may enhance health: (a) by giving feedback and exercising social control, (b) communicating health information and

337

referral to care, (c) coordinating assistance with health behaviors and care, and (d) helping cope with stress.

Communicating Feedback and Social Control

Involvement in a network of relationships can regulate risky behavior and encourage healthful behavior (Umberson, 1987). Social isolates have no one to tell them when their drinking is out of control and family life can impose an orderly schedule of sleeping and eating. Friends can make exercise an enjoyable occasion for companionship. Parenthood entails obligations to care for others and model behavior, providing an incentive to choose healthful behaviors and avoid risks.

Social networks can promote healthful norms and provide resources for following them. For example, among elderly Japanese American men, support from the network was a better predictor of colorectal cancer screening than the men's own attitudes toward screening (Honda & Kagawa-Singer, 2006). Turkish mothers who made good on their intention to breastfeed were embedded in social networks that valued breastfeeding and gave information and instrumental support (Göksen, 2002). In a community sample with a variety of health goals, support predicted perceived motivation to comply with subjective norms, perceived control, and behavioral intentions; it also had a unique, positive impact upon *achieving* health-related goals three months later (VonDras & Madey, 2004).

Networks sometimes encourage unhealthy behavior (Smith & Christakis, 2008). Drug use and needle sharing have been linked to how many members of one's network also engage in those behaviors (e.g., Latkin, Wallace, Vlahov, Oziemkowska, & Celantano, 1996). Diabetic teens who were highly satisfied with their social support were *less* successful in managing their diabetes, perhaps because an active social life and peer pressure discouraged healthful choices or distracted them from attending to symptoms (Kaplan, Chadwick, & Schimmel, 1985). Christakis and Fowler (2007) made news by demonstrating that obesity clusters in social networks, such that having a friend of a friend of a friend who was obese increased an individual's likelihood of being overweight. Simply measuring the size or general supportiveness of a network does not reveal what norms, behaviors, and messages circulate in that social environment. Among individuals with chronic illness, measuring support for self-care and healthful lifestyle is a better predictor of behavior and health than assessing general levels of social support (Gallant, 2003).

We must also consider *how* relational partners talk about health behavior. In a study of patients recovering from a cardiac event, the frequency, directness, and framing of marital conversations about diet and exercise shaped whether talk was interpreted as caring, helpful, and empowering versus critical, controlling, and emphasizing loss (Goldsmith, Gumminger, & Bute, 2006; Goldsmith, Lindholm, & Bute, 2006). In turn, how patients interpret those conversations can impact heart healthy behaviors six months later (Franks et al., 2006). A partner's encouragement that is interpreted positively is more likely to promote healthful behavior whereas negative or controlling attempts are associated with ignoring the partner, doing the opposite of a desired behavior change, and hiding unhealthful behaviors (e.g., Tucker & Anders, 2001).

Communicating Health Information and Seeking Care

Social support can help patients make more informed decisions and assist in negotiating complex health care systems. Social support is linked to more effective utilization of health care among persons with HIV (Uphold & Mkanta, 2005) and to fewer hospitalizations among those with severe mental illness (Albert, Becker, Mccrone, & Thornicroft, 1998). Fear of troubling others may delay seeking treatment for a heart attack, but when patients reveal their symptoms, network members are instrumental to seeking emergency treatment (Khraim & Carey, 2009). Integration in the community can improve women's knowledge of cancer treatments and increase their likelihood of having mammograms (Klassen & Washington, 2008). Having a confidant with whom they can discuss HIV and sex makes it more likely young men who have sex with men will seek HIV testing (Sumartojo et al., 2008).

Others may help us find and evaluate information about illness or collaborate in avoiding unwanted information (Brashers, Goldsmith, & Hiseh, 2002). Similarly, support networks can aid in managing uncertainty, but sometimes requires coordinating uncertainty management and coping with the burden of others' uncertainty (Brashers, Neidig, & Goldsmith, 2004). Support also helps integrate complex information such as the likelihood of side effects or whether a treatment is worth the risk (Ford, Babrow, & Stohl, 1996).

Support networks are involved in our health care decisions. Partners of cancer patients helped initiate treatment, handle information, choose treatments, carry out treatments, interact with health care providers, manage patient outlook, and evaluate treatment (Goldsmith & Moriarty, 2008). Patients utilize treatment information from their informal networks and family members are instrumental in obtaining and evaluating this network input (O'Rourke & Germino, 1998). Families have a significant impact on patient treatment decision making (e.g., Zhang & Siminoff, 2003) and the quality of interaction between family members and health care providers has been linked to patient outcomes (Rees & Bath, 2000).

Support networks are also important for preventive care such as prenatal care. Supportive interactions shape a mother's information, knowledge, experience, feelings, and perceptions about herself and the pregnancy. Informational support may help her recognize the symptoms of pregnancy (Maternal and Child Health Services, 1996), understand reasons to seek care, and overcome negative perceptions of exam procedures (Byrd, Mullen, Selwyn, & Lorimor, 1996). Support also helps low-income women learn when and where to obtain prenatal care services, which physicians accept Medicaid patients (and treat them respectfully), and whether care can be initiated while awaiting Medicaid eligibility approval (Omar & Schiffman, 1995).

Different types of links afford different advantages for seeking information and care. Dense, homogeneous networks can create trust in information and referrals whereas weak links to dissimilar others provide novel health information and access to resources not available in one's immediate circle (Derose & Varda, 2009). Network structures affect the diffusion of all kinds of health information, including physicians learning about new drugs; campaigns disseminating information about birth control, family planning, and HIV; and researchers sharing results and training (for a review, see Luke & Harris, 2007).

Communicating Tangible Support for Health

Enacting health behaviors, seeking care, and adhering to medical advice can require tangible aid (e.g., money, transportation, child care, food preparation). Social networks extend an individual's own resources and provide instrumental assistance. Tangible aid is also symbolic behavior that can convey care and concern as well as obligation, control, or judgment (Albrecht & Adelman, 1987; Goldsmith, 2004).

Reciprocity of aid may influence its usefulness. Chandola, Marmot, and Siegrist (2007) found poorer physical and mental health were associated with failed reciprocity in marriage, with one's children, or in community life. Piferi and Lawler (2006) concluded that giving and receiving support are beneficial through different pathways: receiving support reduces blood pressure and symptoms of illness by lowering stress whereas giving support improves health by increasing efficacy (which, in turn, reduces stress). The elderly may find their interactions with family tilt toward unreciprocated instrumental aid, so a network that includes peer interactions based on reciprocal companionship is important for positive affect and continuing self-esteem (Rook, 1990).

Support is involved when communities cope with shared hardship. The exchange of support, the confidence that support is forthcoming, a sense of community, informal community ties, and attachment to place are among the resources that enable resilient communities to adapt to natural disasters, large scale accidents, or violence (Albrecht, 1994a; Norris, Stevens, Pfefferbaum, Wyche, & Pfefferbaum, 2008). Resilient communities are more than simply collections of resilient individuals; instead, they may be conceptualized as "a set of networked adaptive capacities" (Norris et al., 2008, p. 135).

Communicating Coping Assistance

Individuals cope more effectively with stress when they have social support, thereby avoiding the otherwise negative effects of stress on health (for a review, see Lakey & Cohen, 2000). This chain of effects has been observed for numerous types of stressors, from everyday work stress and the transition to new parenthood (Terry, Rawle, & Callan, 1995) to the challenges of caring for a partner with arthritis (Revenson & Majerowitz, 1991). Conversely, unsupportive responses from significant others are associated with poorer coping with cancer (Manne & Glassman, 2000). Communication research in the stress-buffering tradition has examined an intermediary link in this chain of effects, namely the features of support messages that recipients deem helpful and comforting (for a review, see Burleson & MacGeorge, 2002).

Problem-focused support (e.g., advice, information, tangible aid) and emotion-focused support (expressions of concern, belonging, esteem, and comforting) are preferred under different circumstances (Horowitz et al., 2001). Emotion-focused support is perceived positively in a wider variety of situations (e.g., Cutrona & Suhr, 1994), whereas the benefits of problem-solving support are more contingent on the nature of the problem (e.g., whether or not it is controllable), the recipient's own needs and resources, the provider's expertise, and the quality of information or aid (Goldsmith, 2004; MacGeorge, Lichtman, & Pressey, 2002).

Within the categories of problem-solving or emotion-focused support, there are more and less effective support attempts. Emotional support messages that acknowledge, elaborate, and legitimate the feelings of a distressed other are seen as more sensitive and effective than messages that reject, deny, or attempt to draw attention away from feelings (Burleson, 1994). Elaborating feelings promotes reappraisal of the situation and coping options and this can reduce distress (Burleson & Goldsmith, 1997; Jones & Wirtz, 2006). Advice is a common type of problem-solving support but recipients react poorly to advice when they perceive it as critical or controlling (Goldsmith & Fitch, 1997). Recipients find advice more helpful when the content, form, and sequence attend to the recipient's face wants (i.e., desires for acceptance and autonomy; Goldsmith, 2004).

Helpful coping assistance also depends on conversational coordination. Talking about problems can create challenges that include how to respond to intrusive questions (Bute,

2007), introduce problem topics (Jefferson, 1984), handle painful self-disclosures (Coupland, Coupland, & Giles, 1991), license an extended problem narrative (Metts, Backhause, & Kazoleas, 1995), and eventually transition from problem talk to other, lighter topics (McDermott, 2004). What kind of support one receives is influenced by how one discloses a problem or asks for help (Barbee & Cunningham, 1995; Caughlin et al., 2009). Research on dyadic coping examines how interdependent partners not only cope with a stressor but also with the strains of coordinating their individual coping (for reviews, see Berg & Upchurch, 2007; Goldsmith, 2009).

This interdependence of stress and coping extends beyond the dyad. In a dense network, members who know one another can coordinate support for someone in crisis, especially when tangible aid is required over long periods of time. In contrast, when coping requires new information, skills, or identity, weak links outside of dense family or neighborhood connections are critical (Hirsch, 1980). A loosely coupled network, in which pockets of high density co-exist with weaker, low density links, may be optimal for individual coping and may also protect networks from a contagion of distress that makes it difficult to support one another (Albrecht & Adelman, 1987).

The network context is particularly important in a health crisis. Many cancer patients experience a reduction in network size that can limit access to coping assistance during treatment and may continue to diminish opportunities for social integration even after recovery (Bloom, 2008). For some illnesses, such as HIV, changes in network size and structure are associated with stigma (Rintamaki, 2003). HIV service organizations, activist associations, and peer support groups become invaluable for individuals whose links to friends, family, and acquaintances undergo dramatic changes with the discovery of illness. Mobilizing the family network for caregivers of Alzheimer's patients improves caregiver outcomes and delays nursing home placement for the patient (Joling et al. 2008).

Can We Intervene to Improve Social Support?

The practical implications of social support have widespread appeal and there are numerous studies of social support interventions (for reviews, see Cattan, White, Bond, & Learmouth, 2005; Gottlieb & Wachala, 2007; Hogan, Linden, & Najarian, 2002). Of particular interest for health communication are those interventions that seek to (a) train individuals to seek and utilize social support more effectively, (b) improve the quality of supportive interactions in a primary relationship, (c) alter community norms surrounding the communication of support, or (d) communicate support in the context of a professionally facilitated support group or peer led self-help group. We point to examples of each of these types of interventions.

Major life stresses (including illness) create new demands that prompt support seeking and may require locating new sources of support. The HIV Uncertainty Management Project (Brashers, Neidig, & colleagues; described in Goldsmith & Brashers, 2008) utilizes peer support to help persons newly diagnosed with HIV to develop communication skills needed to manage illness uncertainty. A peer with HIV works one-on-one with the newly diagnosed person on a curriculum that covers how to disclose one's HIV status, seek help from the social network and community resources, talk with health care providers, find and evaluate information on the web, and understand treatment and care. Another support seeking intervention taught drug-abusing incarcerated women how to seek social support upon release from prison (El-Bassel et al., 1995). The women were also encouraged to reflect on their network, identifying who would support healthful behavior and who was likely to discourage it. One month after the intervention, participants were 3.8 times more likely than control group members to report safe sex behavior, improved coping skills, and more perceived emotional support.

Communication is also a focus in interventions that focus on improving supportive interactions in a primary relationship. The Partners for Life program (Sher et al., 2002) invites couples coping with heart disease to discuss how to implement a heart healthy lifestyle, including how to communicate with one another about changes in diet, exercise, smoking, and stress management. The FAMCON program (Shoham, Rohrbaugh, Trost, & Muramoto, 2006) helps health compromised smokers who have been unable to quit smoking. A therapist works with the family to discover how smoking has become embedded in family interaction patterns and then develop alternative ways of relating.

Interventions may focus on improving the health protective functioning of a network or community. The Community Helpers Project (e.g., D'Augelli & Ehrlich, 1982) gave informal helpers in rural communities (e.g., hairdressers, clergy, housewives) training in communication skills such as nonverbal attending, active listening, assisting others in assessing goals and plans, and helping in a crisis. Community members served on the advisory board and conducted training so the intervention could adapt to local concerns, build trust, and leave knowledgeable resources in the community after the program concluded. Trained helpers reported greater confidence in their skills and diary reports indicated that in one week, the 37 helpers interacted with over 150 different people for an average of 25 minutes per person, including relatives, friends, co-workers, and neighbors. Eggert and her colleagues (1994) offered a life skills class (including seeking and giving support) to at-risk high school students. Teachers modeled supportive communication and encouraged it among students. Over a 10-month follow-up, participants felt more bonded with their school and women experienced less bonding with deviant peers. As a result, students in the class had fewer drug problems and improved GPA and self-esteem compared to a control group.

Talk is a primary activity in face-to-face support groups and participation can improve mental and physical health (Hogan et al., 2002). However, some people decline to join a support group or drop out after a meeting or two (Gottlieb & Wachala, 2007) and some individuals may experience worse outcomes for having participated (Galinsky & Schopler, 1994; Helgeson, Cohen, Schulz, & Yasko, 2000). Few studies have probed what transpires in groups (Cline, 1999) and how different patterns of communication might shape the outcomes of participation. Notable exceptions include Hsieh's (2004) study of how members of a transplant support group used narratives to socialize, ask for help, bolster their self-image, assert their beliefs, and manage uncertainty. Golden and Lund (2009) examined how conversations in support groups for caregivers of persons with dementia provided a sense of options through talking about balance, sameness, and individuality. Communication theory has much to offer future research on how group interaction promotes trust, identification, disclosure, mutual aid, and friendship (Goldsmith & Brashers, 2008; see also Wright et al. in this volume for discussion of computer-mediated support groups).

Directions for Future Research

The communication of support in social networks is clearly important for health. Over 30 years of empirical research documents a consistent effect of social support and recent advances reveal the pathways through which the risks and benefits of support occur. Under the right conditions, social support interventions can benefit participants. We conclude by identifying some distinctive contributions health communication researchers can make to future research.

Previous studies have theorized what features of messages and conversations participants tend to find helpful; future research might explore how these features are linked to health outcomes. Do those who report helpful advice from their networks engage in better self-care, health care utilization, or treatment decision making than those who are plagued by critical or condescending advice? Do the distress-reducing properties of sophisticated comforting messages translate into beneficial changes in hormonal stress markers (cf. Floyd & Rigoriati, 2008) or to reduced visits to a campus health center (cf. Pennebaker, 1993)? Research on health outcomes tends to utilize global reports of received support that lack detail about interactions, or laboratory conversations coded for positive versus negative behaviors. By providing nuanced measurement of conversations, communication scholars can explain the processes that underlie support effects and suggest how to improve health by changing how we talk.

Conceptualizations of social support usually focus on laypersons, rather than health care or social service providers, as sources of support. Future research might explore similarities between the attributes of effective social support and dimensions of provider-patient interaction. For example, low income women with HIV consider health care providers important sources of emotional support (Peterson, 2003). Supportive messages from providers can enable cancer patients to cope with their lack of technical understanding of medical terms and facilitate their ability to move forward with treatment decisions in a positive frame of mind (Albrecht, Blanchard, Ruckdeschel, Coovert, & Strongbow, 1999). Supportive behaviors also influence treatment choices for experimental cancer therapy (Albrecht et al., 2008). At the very least, health care providers should include assessment of a patient's social isolation as a factor that affects adherence, decision making, and recovery (Mookadam & Arthur, 2004).

Future research should explore the intersection of support conversations and networks to better understand how social structure contextualizes messages. This is also important for the design of interventions; for example, the effects of a support group differ for those who are relatively isolated compared to those who are well-integrated (Gottlieb, 2000). The ability of any particular relationship to provide novel health information or referrals, to sustain high levels of tangible support, or to effectively give comfort without becoming distressed, may depend upon the surrounding network structure.

Support interventions are needed that are theoretically based, grounded in assessment of needs and resources, and rigorously evaluated (Gottlieb, 2000). Health communication scholars are underrepresented in support intervention research but we have a significant role to play in theorizing and measuring the communication processes that are central to many support interventions (Goldsmith & Brashers, 2008). In addition to their importance for improving health, interventions can also test theorized causal relationships.

Finally, studying social support entails considering ethical issues. Supportive communication and networks embody some of what is best and most altruistic in human beings (Albrecht, 1994a). Observing the human needs that inspire social support should also force us to confront societal inequities and disparities in work conditions, access to health care and health information, distribution of resources, and vulnerability to stress and disease (Pilisuk & Minkler, 1985). The origins of the social support concept reflect both a moral agenda to improve life and some potentially questionable sociopolitical pressures to do so in ways that are inexpensive (e.g., by utilizing people's own networks rather than costly professional services) and least likely to disrupt the status quo (e.g., by changing the individuals who suffer from stress rather than changing the environmental conditions that create it). Theory and practice related to social support should occur with an eye toward social justice, too.

Note

1. We emphasize the notion that supportive communication functions to help "manage uncertainty," rather than reducing uncertainty (as originally conceived by Albrecht & Adelman, 1987), given recent research that shows ambiguity about otherwise certain outcomes (e.g., death and dying) can provide hope and maintain motivation.

References

Albert, M., Becker, T., Mccrone, P., & Thornicroft, G. (1998). Social networks and mental health service utilization: A literature review. *International Journal of Social Psychiatry, 44*, 248–266.

Albrecht, T. L. (1994a). Social support and community: An historical account of the rescue networks in Denmark. In B. Burleson, T. Albrecht, & I. Sarason (Eds.), *Communication of social support: Messages, interactions, relationships, and community* (pp. 267–280). Newbury Park, CA: Sage.

Albrecht, T. L., & Adelman, M. A. (1987). *Communicating social support*. Newbury Park, CA: Sage.

Albrecht, T. L., Blanchard, C., Ruckdeschel, J. C., Coovert, M., & Strongbow, R. (1999). Strategic physician communication and oncology clinical trials. *Journal of Clinical Oncology, 17*, 3324–3332.

Albrecht, T., Eggly, S., Gleason, M., Harper, F., Foster, T., Peterson, A., Ruckdeschel, J. (2008). The influence of clinical communication on patients' decision making on participation in clinical trials. *Journal of Clinical Oncology, 26*, 2666–2673.

Barbee, A. P., & Cunningham, M. R. (1995). An experimental approach to social support communications: Interactive coping in close relationships. In B. Burleson (Ed.), *Communication yearbook 18* (pp. 381–413). Thousand Oaks, CA: Sage.

Berg, C. A., & Upchurch, R. (2007). A developmental-contextual model of couples coping with illness across the adult life span. *Psychological Bulletin, 133*, 920–954.

Berkman, L. F., & Glass, T. (2000). Social integration, social networks, social support, and health. In L. F. B. I. Kawachi (Ed.), *Social epidemiology* (pp. 137–173). New York: Oxford University Press.

Bloom, J. R. (2008). Improving the health and well-being of cancer survivors: Past as prologue. *Psycho-Oncology, 17*, 525–532.

Brashers, D. E., Goldsmith, D. J., & Hsieh, I. (2002). Information seeking and avoiding in health contexts. *Human Communication Research, 28*, 258–271.

Brashers, D. E., Neidig, J. L., & Goldsmith, D. J. (2004). Social support and the management of uncertainty for people living with HIV or AIDS. *Health Communication, 16*, 305–331.

Burleson, B. R. (1994). Comforting messages: Significance, approaches, and effects. In B. R. Burleson, T. L. Albrecht, & I. G. Sarason (Eds.), *Communication of social support: Messages, interactions, relationships, and community* (pp. 3–28). Thousand Oaks, CA: Sage.

Burleson, B. R., & Goldsmith, D. J. (1997). How comforting messages work: Some mechanisms through which messages may alleviate emotional distress. In P. A. Anderson & L. K. Guerrero (Eds.), *Handbook of communication and emotion: Research, theory, applications, and contexts* (p. 245–280). Orlando, FL: Academic Press.

Burleson, B. R., & MacGeorge. E. L. (2002). Supportive communication. In M. L. Knapp & J. A. Daly (Eds.), *Handbook of interpersonal communication* (3rd ed., pp. 374–424). Thousand Oaks, CA: Sage.

Bute, J. (2007). *Talking about infertility: A conceptual model.* (Unpublished doctoral dissertation). University of Illinois at Urbana-Champaign, Urbana, IL.

Byrd, T. L., Mullen, P. D., Selwyn, B. J., & Lorimor, R. (1996). Initiation of prenatal care by low-income Hispanic women in Houston. *Public Health Reports, 111*, 536–540.

Cassel, J. (1976). The contribution of the environment to host resistance. *American Journal of Epidemiology, 104*, 107–123.

Cattan, M., White, M., Bond, J., & Learmouth, A. (2005). Preventing social isolation and loneliness among older people: A systematic review of health promotion interventions. *Ageing and Society, 25*, 41–67.

Caughlin, J. P., Bute, J. J., Donovan-Kicken, E., Kosenko, K. A., Ramey, M. E., & Brashers, D. E. (2009). Do message features influence reactions to HIV disclosures? A multiple-goals perspective. *Health Communication, 24,* 270–283.

Chandola, T., Marmot, M., & Siegrist, J. (2007). Failed reciprocity in close social relationships and health: Findings from the Whitehall II study. *Journal of Psychosomatic Research, 63,* 403–411.

Christakis, N. A., & Fowler, J. H. (2007). The spread of obesity in a large social network over 32 years. *New England Journal of Medicine, 357*(4), 370–379.

Cline, R. J. W. (1999). Communication in support groups. In L. R. Frey, D. S. Gouran, & M. S. Poole (Eds.), *The handbook of group communication theory and research* (pp. 516–538). Thousand Oaks, CA: Sage.

Cobb, S. (1976). Social support as a moderator of life stress. *Psychosomatic Medicine, 38,* 300–314.

Cohen, S., Doyle, W. J., Skoner, D. P., Rabin, B. S., & Gwaltney, J. M. (1997). Social ties and susceptibility to the common cold. *Journal of the American Medical Association, 277,* 1940–1944.

Cohen, S., Gottlieb, B. H., & Underwood, L. G. (2000). Social relationships and health. In S. Cohen, L. G. Underwood, & B. H. Gottlieb (Eds.), *Social support measurement and intervention: A guide for health and social scientists* (pp. 3–25). Oxford, England: Oxford University Press.

Cohen, S., & Wills, T. A. (1985). Stress, social support, and the buffering hypothesis. *Psychological Bulletin, 98,* 310–357.

Coupland, N., Coupland, J., & Giles, H. (1991). *Language, society, and the elderly: Discourse, identity, and ageing.* Oxford, England: Blackwell.

Cutrona, C. E., & Suhr, J. A. (1994). Social support communication in the context of marriage: An analysis of couples' supportive interactions. In B. R. Burleson, T. L. Albrecht, & I. G. Sarason (Eds.), *Communication of social support: Messages, interactions, relationships, and community* (pp. 113–135). Thousand Oaks, CA: Sage.

D'Augelli, A. R., & Ehrlich, R. P. (1982). Evaluation of a community-based system for training natural helpers. II. Effects on informal helping activities. *American Journal of Community Psychology, 10,* 447–456.

Derose, K. P., & Varda, D. M. (2009). Social capital and health care access: A systematic review. *Medical Care Research and Review, 66,* 272–306.

DiMatteo, M. R. (2004). Social support and patient adherence to medical treatment: A meta-analysis. *Health Psychology, 23,* 207–218.

El-Bassel, N., Ivanoff, A., Schilling, R. F., Gilbert, L., Borne, D., & Chen, D. R. (1995). Preventing HIV/AIDS in drug-abusing incarcerated women through skills building and social support enhancement: Preliminary outcomes. *Social Work Research, 19*(3), 131–141.

Eggert, L. L., Thompson, E. A., Herting, J. R., Nicholas, L. J., & Dicker, B. G. (1994). Preventing adolescent drug abuse and high school dropout through an intensive school-based social network development program. *American Journal of Health Promotion, 8,* 202–215.

Floyd, K., & Riforgiate, S. (2008). Affectionate communication received from spouses predicts stress hormone levels in healthy adults. *Communication Monographs, 75,* 351–368.

Ford, L. A., Babrow, A. S., & Stohl, C. (1996). Social support messages and the management of uncertainty in the experience of breast cancer: An application of problematic integration theory. *Communication Monographs, 63,* 189–207.

Franks, M. M., Stephens, M. A. P., Rook, K. S., Franklin, B. A., Keteyian, S. J., & Artinian, N. T. (2006). Spouses' provision of health-related support and control to patients participating in cardiac rehabilitation. *Journal of Family Psychology, 20,* 311–318.

Galinsky, M. J., & Schopler, J. H. (1994). Negative experiences in support groups. *Social Work in Health Care, 20,* 77–95.

Gallant, M. P. (2003). The influence of social support on chronic illness self-management: A review and directions for research. *Health and Education Behavior, 30,* 170–195.

Göksen, F. (2002). Normative vs. attitudinal considerations in breastfeeding behavior: Multifaceted social influences in a developing country context. *Social Science & Medicine, 54,* 1743–1753.

Golden, M. A., & Lund, D. A. (2009). Identifying themes regarding the benefits and limitations of caregiver support group conversations. *Journal of Gerontological Social Work, 52,* 154–170.

Goldsmith, D. J. (2004). *Communicating social support.* Cambridge, England: Cambridge University Press.

Goldsmith, D. J. (2009). Uncertainty and communication in couples coping with serious illness. In T. Afifi & W. Afifi (Eds.), *Uncertainty and information regulation: Theories and applications* (pp. 203–225). New York: Routledge.

Goldsmith, D. J., & Brashers, D. E. (2008). Communication matters: Developing and testing social support interventions. *Communication Monographs, 75,* 320–330.

Goldsmith, D. J., & Fitch, K. (1997). The normative context of advice as social support. *Human Communication Research, 23,* 454–476.

Goldsmith, D. J., Gumminger, K., & Bute, J. J. (2006). Communication about lifestyle change between cardiac patients and their partners. In B. LePoire & R. M. Dailey (Eds.), *Socially meaningful applied research in interpersonal communication* (pp. 95–118). New York: Lang.

Goldsmith, D. J., Lindholm, K. A., & Bute, J. J. (2006). Dilemmas of talking about lifestyle changes among couples coping with a cardiac event. *Social Science & Medicine, 63,* 2079–2090.

Goldsmith, D. J., & Moriarty, C. M. (2008 May). *Partner involvement in cancer treatment decision-making.* Paper presented at the meeting of the International Communication Association, Montreal, QC.

Gottlieb, B. H. (2000). Selecting and planning support interventions. In S. Cohen, L. G. Underwood, & B. H. Gottlieb (Eds.), Social support measurement and intervention: A guide for health and social scientists (pp. 195–220). New York: Oxford University Press.

Gottlieb, B. H., & Wachala, E. D. (2007). Cancer support groups: A critical review of empirical studies. *Psycho-Oncology, 16,* 379–400.

Helgeson, V. S., Cohen, S., Schulz, R., & Yasko, J. (2000). Group support interventions for women with breast cancer: Who benefits from what? *Health Psychology, 19,* 107–114.

Hirsch, B. J. (1980). Natural support systems and coping with major life changes. *American Journal of Community Psychology, 8,* 159–172.

Hogan, B. E., Linden, W., & Najarian, B. (2002). Social support interventions: Do they work? *Clinical Psychology Review, 22,* 381–440.

Honda, K., & Kagawa-Singer, M. (2006). Cognitive mediators linking social support networks to colorectal cancer screening adherence. *Journal of Behavioral Medicine, 29,* 449–460.

Horowitz, L. M., Krasnoperova, E. N., Tatar, D. G., Hansen, M. B., Person, E. A., Galvin, K. L., & Nelson, K. L. (2001). The way to console may depend on the goal: Experimental studies of social support. *Journal of Experimental Social Psychology, 37,* 49–61.

House, J. S., Landis, K. R., & Umberson, D. (1988). Social relationships and health. *Science, 241,* 540–544.

Hsieh, E. (2004). Stories in action and the dialogic management of identities: Story telling in transplant support group meetings. *Research on Language and Social Interaction, 37,* 39–70.

Jefferson, G. (1984). On stepwise transition from talk about a trouble to inappropriately next-positioned matters. In M. Atkinson & J. Heritage (Eds.), *Structures of social action: Studies in conversation analysis* (pp. 191–222). Cambridge, England: Cambridge University Press.

Joling, K. J., van Hout, H. P. J., Scheltens, P., Vernooij-Dassen, M., van den Berg, B., Bosmans, J., … van Marwijk, H. W. J. (2008). (Cost)-effectiveness of family meetings on indicated prevention of anxiety and depressive symptoms and disorders of primary family caregivers of patients with dementia: Design of a randomized controlled trial. *BMC Geriatrics, 8.* doi:10.1186/1471-2318-8-2.

Jones, S. M., & Wirtz, J. G. (2006). How *does* the comforting process work? An empirical test of an appraisal-based model of comforting. *Human Communication Research, 32,* 217–243.

Kaplan, R. M., Chadwick, M. W., & Schimmel, L. E. (1986). Social learning intervention to promote metabolic control in Type I diabetes mellitus: Private experiment results. *Diabetes Care, 8,* 152–155.

Khraim, F. M., & Carey, M. G. (2009). Predictors of pre-hospital delay among patients with acute myocardial infarction. *Patient Education and Counseling, 75,* 155–161.

Klassen, A. C., & Washington, C. (2008). How does social integration influence breast cancer control among urban African-American women? Results from a cross-sectional survey. *BMC Women's Health, 8*(4). doi:10.1186/1472.6874.8.4. Retrieved from www.biomedcentral.com.

Kulik, J. A., & Mahler, H. I. (1989). Social support and recovery from surgery. *Health Psychology, 8,* 221–238.

Lakey, B., & Cohen, S. (2000). Social support theory and measurement. In S. Cohen, L. G. Underwood, & B. H. Gottlieb (Eds.), *Social support measurement and intervention: A guide for health and social scientists* (pp. 29–52). Oxford, England: Oxford University Press.

Latkin, C., Wallace, M., Vlahov, D., Oziemkowska, M., & Celentano, D. (1996). People and places: Behavioral settings and personal network characteristics as correlates of needle sharing. *Journal of Acquired Immune Deficiency Syndromes and Human Retrovirology, 13,* 273–280.

Luke, D. A., & Harris, J. K. (2007). Network analysis in public health: History, methods, and applications. *Annual Review of Public Health, 28,* 69–93.

MacGeorge, E. L., Lichtman, R., & Pressey, L. (2002). The evaluation of advice in supportive interaction: Effects of facework, evaluator sex, target responsibility and effort, and advice content. *Human Communication Research, 28,* 451–463.

Manne, S., & Glassman, M. (2000). Perceived control, coping efficacy, and avoidance coping as mediators between spouses' unsupportive behaviors and cancer patients' psychological distress. *Health Psychology, 19,* 155–164.

Maternal and Child Health Services, Oklahoma State Department of Health. (1996). Initiation of prenatal care among women having a live birth in Oklahoma. *Journal of the Oklahoma State Medical Association, 89,* 328–332.

McDermott, V. M. (2004). *The structure of troubles talk in conversations among close relational partners* (Unpublished doctoral dissertation). University of Illinois at Urbana-Champaign, Urbana, IL.

Metts, S., Backhaus, S., & Kazoleas, P. (1995, February). *Social support as problematic communication.* Paper presented at the meeting of the Western Speech Communication Association, Portland, OR.

Mookadam, F., & Arthur, H. A. (2004). Social support and its relationship to morbidity and mortality after acute myocardial infarction: Systematic overview. *Archives of Internal Medicine, 164,* 1514–1518.

Moss, G. E. (1973). *Illness, immunity, and social interaction.* New York: Wiley Interscience.

Norris, F. H., Stevens, S. P., Pfefferbaum, B., Wyche, K. F., & Pfefferbaum, R. L. (2008). Community resilience as a metaphor, theory, set of capacities, and strategy for disaster readiness. *American Journal of Community Psychology, 41,* 127–150.

Omar, M. A., & Schiffman, R. F. (1995). Pregnant women's perceptions of prenatal care. *Maternal Child Nursing Journal, 23,* 132–142.

O'Rourke, M. E., & Germino, B. B. (1998). Prostate cancer treatment decisions: A focus group exploration. *Oncology Nursing Forum, 25,* 97–104.

Pennebaker, J. W. (1993). Putting stress into words: Health, linguistic, and therapeutic implications. *Behavioral Research and Therapy, 31,* 539–548.

Penner, L. A., Dovidio, J. F., & Albrecht, T. L. (2000). Helping victims of loss and trauma: A social psychological perspective. In J. H. Harvey & E. D. Miller (Eds.), *Handbook of loss and trauma* (pp. 62–85). Philadelphia, PA: Brunner/Mazel.

Peterson, J. (2003). *The development of a normative model of social support for women living with HIV* (Unpublished doctoral dissertation). University of Illinois at Urbana-Champaign, Urbana, IL.

Piferi, R. L., & Lawler, K. A. (2006). Social support and ambulatory blood pressure: An examination of both receiving and giving. *International Journal of Psychophysiology, 62,* 328–336.

Pilisuk, M., & Minkler, M. (1985). Social support: Economic and political considerations. *Social Policy, 15,* 6–11.

Rees, C. E., & Bath, P. A. (2000). Exploring the information flow: Partners of women with breast cancer, patients, and healthcare professionals. *Oncology Nursing Forum, 27,* 1267–1275.

Reis, H. T., & Collins, N. (2000). Measuring relationship properties and interactions relevant to social support. In S. Cohen, L. G. Underwood, & B. H. Gottlieb (Eds.), *Social support measurement and intervention: A guide for health and social scientists* (pp. 136–192). New York: Oxford University Press.

Revenson, T. A., & Majerovitz, S. D. (1991). The effects of chronic illness on the spouse: Social resources as stress buffers. *Arthritis Care and Research, 4,* 63–72.

Rintamaki, L. S. (2003). *HIV identity trajectories and social interaction* (Unpublished doctoral dissertation). University of Illinois at Urbana-Champaign, Urbana, IL.

Rook, K. S. (1990). Social relationships as a source of companionship: Implications for older adults' psychological well-being. In B. R. Sarason, I. G. Sarason, & G. R. Pierce (Eds.), *Social support: An interactional view* (pp. 219–250). New York: Wiley.

Sarason, B. R., Sarason, I. G., & Pierce, G. R. (1990). Social support: The sense of acceptance and the role of relationships. In B. R. Sarason, I. G. Sarason, & G. R. Pierce (Eds.), *Social support: An interactional view* (pp. 97–128). New York: Wiley.

Sarason, B. R., & Sarason, I. G. (2001). Ongoing aspects of relationships and health outcomes: Social support, social control, companionship, and relational meaning. In J. Harvey & A. Wenzel (Eds.), *Close romantic relationships: Maintenance and enhancement* (pp. 277–289). Mahwah, NJ: Erlbaum.

Sher, T. G., Bell, A. J., Braun, L., Domas, A., Rosenson, R., & Canar, W. J. (2002). Partners for life: A theoretical approach to developing an intervention for cardiac risk reduction. *Health Education Research, 17*, 597–605.

Shoham, V., Rohrbaugh, M. J., Trost, S. E., & Muramoto, M. (2006). A family consultation intervention for health-compromised smokers. *Journal of Substance Abuse Treatment, 31*, 395–402.

Smith, K. P., & Christakis, N. A. (2008). Social networks and health. *Annual Review of Sociology, 34*, 405–429.

Sumartojo, E., Lyles, C., Choi, K., Clark, L, Collins, C., Grey, G., … City Study Team (2008). Prevalence and correlates of HIV testing in a multi-site sample of young men who have sex with men. *AIDS Care, 20*, 1–14.

Terry, D. J., Rawle, R., & Callan, V. J. (1995). The effects of social support on adjustment to stress: The mediating role of coping. *Personal Relationships, 2*, 97–124.

Tucker, J. S., & Anders, S. L. (2001). Social control of health behaviors in marriage. *Journal of Applied Social Psychology, 31*, 467–485.

Uchino, B. N. (2006). Social support and health: A review of physiological processes potentially underlying links to disease outcomes. *Journal of Behavioral Medicine, 29*, 377–387.

Uchino, B. N., Cacioppo, J. T., & Kiecolt-Glaser, J. K. (1996). The relationship between social support and physiological processes: A review with emphasis on underlying mechanisms and implications for health. *Psychological Bulletin, 119*, 488–531.

Umberson, D. (1987). Family status and health behaviors: Social control as a dimension of social integration. *Journal of Health and Social Behavior, 28*, 306–319.

Uphold, C. R., & Mkanta, W. N. (2005). Use of health care services among persons living with HIV infection; State of the science and future directions. *AIDS Patient Care and STDs, 19*, 473–485.

VonDras, D. D., & Madey, S. F. (2004). The attainment of important health goals throughout adulthood: An integration of the theory of planned behavior and aspects of social support. *International Journal of Aging and Human Development, 59*, 205–234.

Wills, T. A., & Shinar, O. (2000). Measuring perceived and received social support. In S. Cohen, L. G. Underwood, & B. H. Gottlieb (Eds.), *Social support measurement and intervention: A guide for health and social scientists* (pp. 86–135). New York: Oxford University Press.

Zhang, A. Y., & Siminoff, L. A. (2003). Silence and cancer: Why do families and patients fail to communicate? *Health Communication, 15*, 415–429.

22

COMPUTER-MEDIATED SOCIAL SUPPORT

Promises and Pitfalls for Individuals Coping with Health Concerns

Kevin B. Wright, Amy Janan Johnson, Daniel R. Bernard, and Joshua Averbeck

The communication of social support has been predominantly studied as a phenomenon that occurs in face-to-face interaction. Although face-to-face communication is certainly an important source of social support, this traditional focus on face-to-face support neglects the fact that social support frequently occurs in a variety of communication modalities and computer-mediated supportive discourse may even be preferred in some circumstances (Walther & Parks, 2002). The advent of the Internet has had a significant impact on support-seeking behaviors (Neuhauser & Kreps, 2003). Online support groups have proliferated in the past decade: An estimated 90 million Americans have participated in some type of computer-mediated support group. It appears that the growth of online support groups will continue to be an important context for social support interactions.

Most researchers have acknowledged that computer-mediated social support (CMSS), although there are many definitions of it, includes informational, emotional, appraisal, and instrumental support (Barrera, 1986; Pull, 2006). Online support group users typically share opinions, insights, experiences, and perspectives about health concerns with each other during online interaction (Sarasohn-Kahn, 2008). Computer-mediated supportive interactions differ from face-to-face supportive interactions in that online interactions are primarily text-based, computer-mediated communication allows for relatively anonymous interactions, and online forums offer the opportunity to expand one's social network beyond what would be possible in the face-to-face world (Tanis, 2008).

Participants in computer-mediated support groups tend to be peers with similar concerns and experiences (Tanis, 2008). These groups provide convenient communication opportunities, span time and geographic constraints, and provide anonymity (if desired) for discussion of sensitive issues (Tanis, 2008). Most groups tend to be egalitarian, relying on a peer moderator who voluntarily serves in a leadership role. However, some computer-mediated support groups also seek the expertise of a health care professional, who may or may not serve in a leadership role for the group. The popularity and utility of using online social support groups to deal with health concerns will be the focus of this chapter.

Growth and Prevalence of Computer-Mediated Support

In recent years, many support groups for people with health conditions (including alcoholism) have moved online, and they continue to be an influential source of social support and health information. A 2008 study estimated that one in three Americans used some type of online social network when dealing with health issues (Sarasohn-Kahn, 2008). Research that has examined individuals with cancer illustrates the ubiquity of the online support group. Monnier, Laken, and Carter (2002) found that 58% of individuals living with cancer use the Internet as a source of cancer information and emotional support. More than 200,000 cancer-related support groups can be found on the Internet (Im et al., 2007). Moreover, individuals facing other health concerns have also become frequent users of computer-mediated support groups. For example, Houston, Cooper, and Ford (2002) examined depressed individuals who used online support groups and found that over 50% of the users reported participating in a support group for more than five hours over a two week period. In addition, Darcy and Dooley (2007) found that individuals coping with eating disorders reported using online eating disorder groups more than eight hours a week. Also, caregivers of people facing health issues appear to be attracted to computer-mediated social support (Madden & Fox, 2006).

Given the proliferation of computer-mediated support groups, it is important for researchers to conduct theoretically based studies of the phenomenon. Such efforts may help to extend and refine theory as it applies to this context. The following section highlights key theoretical approaches that have been used by researchers in previous studies.

Theoretical Approaches to the Study of Computer-Mediated Social Support

Researchers have drawn both from general theories about social support and theories about computer-mediated communication to understand how individuals utilize online support groups. This section will explore some of these theories to examine their contributions to understanding communicative behavior in this specific context.

Weak Tie/Strong Tie Network Support

One theoretical framework that has been used to explain many advantages of face-to-face and computer-mediated support networks is Granovetter's (1973) theory of weak ties (Adelman, Parks, & Albrecht, 1987). According to Adelman et al. (1987), *weak ties* refer to a "wide range of potential supporters who lie beyond our circle of family and friends" (p. 136). These relationships often lack the frequency of interaction and intimacy associated with closer ties (i.e., close friends and family members). Despite less frequent interaction and lower levels of intimacy, weak ties can often be important sources of social support (Adelman et al., 1987; Granovetter, 1973), especially in contexts such as the computer-mediated support group (Walther & Boyd, 2002).

Prior to the Internet, individuals facing health concerns were somewhat limited in terms of their options for finding potential weak tie support. Computer-mediated support groups make it possible for people to gain access to a plethora of individuals with similar health concerns who may serve as supportive weak ties—regardless of how rare the condition is or how unique people's questions are.

According to Granovetter (1983), "whether one uses weak or strong ties for various purposes depends not only on the number of ties one has at various levels of tie strength but also on the utility of ties of different strengths" (p. 209). The utility of the particular social network individuals choose when disclosing problems and seeking social support is influenced by a number of factors, including the type of stressful situation they are facing, the degree of stigma or potential for embarrassment surrounding their problem, the need for emotionally meaningful relationships, the desire for new or novel information, the perceived understanding and competencies of potential support providers in their network, their judgments about role obligations, and the perceived resources and social capital of social network members (Granovetter, 1983).

Online support groups may be particularly important for those individuals who lack strong ties or wish to supplement those that they already have. Houston et al. (2002) found that 18% of participants using online depression support groups reported they had no one available to provide them with tangible support. They also found that after a year, their participants reported receiving between one quarter and one half of their total social support from the Internet. In addition, Wright, Rains, and Banas (2010) examined four dimensions of weak tie support among participants in online health-related support groups and found that weak tie network preference was related to the desire to obtain objective information and to the perception of reduced risk when communicating about health issues with group members. Moreover, higher weak tie network preference scores were predictive of reduced stress among these participants.

Access to weak ties, such as online support groups, can also allow individuals to seek more anonymous support and reduce the pressure on the person's network of strong ties to provide all the needed support for the individual. Just because an individual has a social support network in place does not mean that he or she will receive helpful support from these individuals (Blythe, 1983). For instance, illnesses, especially chronic illnesses, change family dynamics. Families may not understand limitations caused by illness and place unreasonable expectations on the individual (Evans, Connis, Bishop, Hendricks, & Haselkorn, 1994) or may not want to talk about a person's illness. Individuals may wish to keep family members' anxiety levels low or continue stable family functioning. For example, Dakof and Taylor (1990) found that cancer patients reported that family members sought to minimize cancer's impact on their lives, perhaps wishing to help the patient feel less stressed; many patients, however, found this unhelpful. Therefore, the ability to reach out to weak ties through online support groups offers individuals another option through which they may seek needed support if their strong tie network is unable to provide it. This advantage of weak tie support may partially explain why Madden and Fox (2006) found that 36% of caregivers found advice or emotional support from people in online support groups to be helpful.

Optimal Matching Model

The Optimal Matching Model posits that an optimal match between the needs of support seekers and the resources/abilities of support providers is important in terms of coping with the many relational challenges associated with communicating social support (Cutrona & Russell, 1990). For example, if an individual is seeking emotional support and validation for an eating disorder and he or she perceives that members of his or her support network have competently listened, expressed empathy, and acknowledged the severity of the issue, then this would be considered an example of an optimal match between the support seeker and support providers. Conversely, if an individual desires emotional support, and members of his or her support network provide unwanted advice (a negative form of informational support), then this would be considered a bad (or less than optimal) match. Goldsmith (2004) contends that optimal matches in supportive episodes may lead to more positive perceptions of the relational partners and the type of support that is being offered, and this, in turn, may ultimately influence positive health outcomes.

While this model has been applied to a variety of face-to-face supportive contexts (see Goldsmith, 2004), relatively few researchers have used this framework to investigate computer-mediated support (some exceptions exist, e.g., Wright & Muhtaseb, 2005). Yet, this perspective may help to provide important insights into the supportive needs of individuals who seek computer-mediated support. For example, drawing upon an optimal matching theory framework, Eichhorn (2008) found that informational support through shared experiences was the most common type of support for members of an online support group for eating disorders (followed by emotional support). Moreover, Sullivan (2003) found that men were more likely to seek informational support within online support groups, whereas women were more likely to seek emotional support and validation.

Social Comparison Theory

Social Comparison Theory (Festinger, 1954) is another potentially useful framework for understanding how perceptions of others within computer-mediated networks provide individuals with relevant information for their health decision-making processes. According to this theory, individuals make assessments about their own health and coping mechanisms by comparing themselves to others in their social network (Helgeson & Gottlieb, 2000).

Helgeson and Gottlieb (2000) argue that *lateral comparisons,* that is, comparisons to similar others, may normalize people's experiences and reduce uncertainty and stress for those dealing with health concerns. Lateral comparisons appear to validate people's experiences (e.g., interactions with providers, fears, frustrations, etc.) and reduce a person's sense of social isolation when coping with health concerns. However, it is often the case that when individuals compare themselves to others in online environments, it leads to positive or negative self-assessments. For example, if a person with cancer feels that he or she is coping with problems less effectively than others in the online support network, this may create *upward comparisons*, which could produce feelings of frustration or, more productively, could provide inspiration to cope more effectively by emulating the successful behaviors of those other members. Conversely, *downward comparisons* to others in the online network, such as when an individual feels that he or she is coping better than other members, can lead to positive self-assessments or to negative feelings about the people or the group if interaction with the other members is perceived as being unhelpful.

Participants often glean information about the status of their health issues through social comparisons that take place when following online support group interactions (Davison, Pennebaker, & Dickerson, 2000). According to Sarasohn-Kahn (2008), the second most popular reason people seek health information through online social networks is to research other participants' experiences with a health condition. Such social comparison processes do not even require actual participation in the online group; rather, individuals may engage in these practices even if they do not actively contribute to the group discussion. However, the vast majority of studies using this framework have investigated face-to-face support groups (Davison et al., 2000), despite its potential utility for investigating social support processes within computer-mediated support groups.

Social Information Processing Theory

One theory that was formed to describe computer-mediated communication that is relevant to online social support is social information processing theory (Walther, 1996). This theory argues that in computer-mediated communication, message senders portray themselves in a socially favorable manner to draw the attention of message receivers and foster anticipation of future interaction. Message receivers, in turn, tend to idealize the image of the sender due to overvaluing minimal, text-based cues. In addition, the asynchronous format of most computer-mediated interaction (and to some extent in synchronous formats, such as chat rooms) gives the sender and the receiver more time to edit their communication, making computer-mediated interactions more controllable and less stressful compared to the immediate feedback loop inherent in face-to-face interactions. Idealized perceptions and optimal self-presentation in the computer-mediated communication process tend to intensify in the feedback loop, and this can lead to what Walther (1996) labeled as "hyperpersonal interaction," or a more intimate and socially desirable exchange than in typical face-to-face interactions.

Hyperpersonal interaction is enhanced when no face-to-face relationship exists, so that users construct impressions and present themselves "without the interference of environmental reality" (Walther, 1996, p. 33). Hyperpersonal interaction has been found to skew perceptions of relational partners in positive ways, and, in some cases, computer-mediated relationships may exceed face-to-face interactions in terms of intensity, including within online support groups (King & Moreggi, 1998; Walther, 1996). The next section will talk more about current research that has examined how participation in online support groups is related to health outcomes in participants.

Linking Computer-Mediated Support to Health Outcomes

A growing number of studies within the medical, nursing, psychology, and communication disciplines have measured psychological and physical health outcomes related to participation in computer-mediated support groups. There is empirical evidence that these groups provide a wide variety of health benefits for users (such as individuals with cancer, diabetes, and substance abuse problems), including reduced stress, increased positive coping, increased quality of life, increased self-efficacy in terms of managing one's health problems, reduced depression, and increased physical health benefits (Beaudoin & Tao, 2007; Fogel, Albert, Schnabel, Ditkoff, & Neugut, 2002; Gustafson et al., 2005; Houston et al., 2002; Jones et al., 2008; Owen, Klapow, Roth, Shuster, & Bellis, 2005; Rains & Young, 2009; Shaw, Hawkins, McTavish, Pingree, & Gustafson, 2006; Wright, 1999, 2000). Wright (2000) provided evidence that participation in a computer-mediated support community for older adults predicted reduced stress and increased coping skills. Owen et al. (2005) discovered that participation within an online support group for cancer patients predicted higher quality of life and reduced stress. In addition, in a recent meta-analysis of 28 computer-mediated support group studies, Rains and Young (2009) found that participation in computer-mediated social support groups led to increased social support, decreased depression, increased quality of life, and increased self-efficacy in terms of managing health conditions.

The mechanisms behind these benefits are beginning to be explored in computer-mediated support group research. Early studies indicated that the actual written expression of thoughts about emotionally traumatic events was linked to positive physical and mental health outcomes (see Pennebaker, 1997). In terms of supportive communication, Shaw et al. (2006) discovered that insightful self-disclosure from a cancer support group had an impact on emotional well-being, although it did not affect self-reported physical health outcomes.

Beaudoin and Tao (2007) showed that asynchronous online communication, such as discussion groups and e-mail, predicted perceptions of online social support, which predicted stress, coping, and depression in cancer patients. In their study, synchronous communication did not predict these outcomes. The authors suggest this may be due to a lack of member continuity. Research by Houston et al. (2002) indicates that those participants who reported using an online depression support group more often were more likely than lighter users to experience significant recovery from depression. Wright et al. (2010) discovered computer-mediated support group users who had higher weak tie support network preference scores had reduced levels of stress, although terminally ill participants were more likely to prefer strong tie support than non-terminally ill individuals.

Online support groups can also affect health outcomes by changing how individuals interact with their physicians. Houston et al. (2002) found that 63% of individuals who used online support groups for depression said that they had been influenced by their experience to ask their doctor a question and 26% had been influenced to change medications that they were taking.

Yet, there are many mediating variables that influence the relationship between social support and health outcomes, including an individual's coping abilities (Kohn, 1996), the communication competence of both support providers and receivers (Query & Wright, 2003), and perceptions of the support provider and type of support offered (Albrecht & Goldsmith, 2003).

In addition to considering the effects of computer-mediated support groups, researchers have sought to understand why individuals choose to utilize these groups. The next section will discuss advantages and disadvantages of using computer-mediated support groups.

Advantages of Computer-Mediated Support Groups

Computer-mediated support groups allow people a means to overcome a number of barriers that often present in the face-to-face world. This section briefly discusses some of the major interpersonal benefits of computer-mediated support groups.

Access to Multiple Perspectives

One advantage of computer-mediated support groups appears to be greater access to multiple perspectives on stressful situations through an extended support network capable of providing emotional, informational, and (in some cases) instrumental support. The online medium facilitates communication among a concentrated number of individuals sharing similar specific concerns. For example, Finn and Lavitt (1994) were some of the first to identify interpersonal advantages to meeting online through their study of a computer-mediated sexual abuse survivors group. They reported that participants were able to communicate with a wider variety of people than in the face-to-face world and were able to diffuse dependency needs that would normally be fulfilled through face-to-face interaction. Moreover, members were able to talk to many people and receive information from an assortment of people instead of relying on a small circle of friends or family. Later studies, such as Walther and Boyd (2002) and Wright (2002), indicated that members of computer-mediated support groups mentioned both the diverse experiences of group members and access to a larger network of people with more information about problems than would be possible to form in the face-to-face world as major advantages of online support groups over traditional sources of social support. For instance, Houston et al.'s (2002) sample of 100 people who used online support groups for depression included people from over 30 states and three continents (North American, Europe, and Australia).

These groups/communities also introduce a more diverse social network than is typical in the face-to-face world (Wright & Bell, 2003). In most face-to-face networks, individuals seek support from family members and close friends. These individuals are somewhat homogenous in terms of demographic, attitude, and background similarity. By contrast, online support groups/communities help people transcend the limitations of their face-to-face networks and introduce them to a more heterogeneous network of individuals who happen to share a similar health concern (Walther & Boyd, 2002). According to Adelman et al. (1987), access to a more diverse social network is one of the features of weak tie networks, although it is likely that some of these weak ties may eventually develop into stronger ties.

In the face-to-face world, individuals tend to rely heavily on in-group/out-group differences (Giles, Mulac, Bradac, & Johnson, 1987) when comparing themselves to people who appear to be members of a different social group (e.g., based on sex, race, age, background, etc.). In the computer-mediated environment, many of these social cues are unavailable due to the reduced nonverbal information in most contexts (e.g. virtual groups/communities). People may be more likely to judge individuals on the quality of their verbal messages (i.e., postings, etc.) rather than making snap judgments based on visible social cues. As a result, participants can often receive more unique and novel viewpoints about the health issue they are facing compared to what they are able to obtain in traditional face-to-face support networks. This interaction provides individuals with more opportunities for social comparisons with other individuals facing similar health concerns.

Collective Expertise of Participants

Houston et al. (2002) discovered that, after emotional support, receiving information was the second most popular reason individuals reported using a depression social support group. Through the access provided by the online environment, individuals may obtain a level of emotional support that is difficult to achieve from fewer face-to-face contacts or even the limited contact most individuals have with their health care providers. According to Tanis (2008), "at least part of the users of forums are 'experiential experts,' which can make them a good source of information: people can find or ask for information or advice, and learn from the first-hand experience of others" (p. 699). Tanis (2008) found that quality of emotional support from other group members as well as convenience were the best predictors of coping physically with one's health conditions.

Anonymity/Reduced Stigma

Another advantage for members of an online support group is the ability to discuss topics that would be difficult in the face-to-face environment, which is often a problem for people who have been traumatized by some type of disorder or illness (Finn & Lavitt, 1994; Wright & Bell, 2003). This increased anonymity and limited number of social cues within computer-mediated interaction tend to spur increased self-disclosure within online support groups

(Parks & Floyd, 1996; Wright, 2000). Through sharing information, stories, and feelings and emotions within a relatively anonymous environment, members are able to develop a social network, and discuss sensitive topics without the embarrassment of revealing personal information to strangers in face-to-face encounters (Furger, 1996).

One advantage of this increased anonymity is that individuals who never would have utilized a face-to-face support group may seek support. For instance, only one third of the individuals surveyed by Houston et al. (2002) who used an online support group for depression had ever used a face-to-face support group, and 40% preferred the online support group to face-to-face counseling. In addition, people may be more willing to use online social support groups because members tend to be judged based on the quality of their ideas rather than their physical appearance (Tanis, 2008; Wright & Bell, 2003), which may have suffered due to a health issue (e.g., following surgery). Stigmatization and limited mobility among computer-mediated support group members also predict the need for greater anonymity, the wish for more text-based communication, and the desire to extend one's social network. Each of these features of the computer-mediated support groups predicts participant coping abilities (Tanis, 2008). Both weak tie network theory and social information processing theory may be helpful frameworks for understanding the advantages of social support in an environment with less social-integrated relationships and reduced social cues (due to channel restrictions) in terms of helping to reduce the stigma/judgment that often accompanies certain diseases or physical conditions.

Similarity of Participants

Another advantage of online support groups is the sense of similarity people feel with other members of these groups (Walther & Boyd, 2002; Wright, 2000; Wright & Bell, 2003). In many cases, people who participate in online support groups have mentioned the feeling of being part of a larger community of individuals who are dealing with similar concerns as an important source of validation, emotional support, and comfort (Braithwaite, Waldron, & Finn, 1999; Lieberman & Goldstein, 2005; Sharf, 1997). Turner, Grube, and Meyers (2001) found that similarity among participants often leads to optimal matching of support within online groups, which is why optimal matching as well as social comparison frameworks may be helpful to investigate online support groups' participant similarity in future research.

Convenience

The convenience of forming supportive interpersonal relationships with people difficult to locate face-to-face is also a major advantage of online support groups (Eichhorn, 2008). Many online support groups/communities feature both asynchronous communication (e.g., bulletin boards, e-mail) and synchronous communication capabilities (e.g., chat rooms or chat applications) so that participants can obtain support from others in real time or post messages to the group. This provides people with access to support when they are facing immediate concerns (although the number of people using synchronous applications tends to be relatively small), or they can make comments or pose questions to the larger group/ community by posting comments via bulletin board or mass e-mail at their convenience. Tanis's (2008) study of motives for using health-related computer-mediated support groups in the Netherlands concluded that the convenience of computer-mediated support groups and the sense of inclusion they provide to members best predicted social coping with health concerns.

Other Advantages

Expressing thoughts in e-mails, bulletin boards, and chat applications appears to allow psychological distance between a person and his or her thoughts (Diamond, 2000). This perspective provides opportunities for individuals to reflect, reexamine their ideas and concerns, and rearticulate them prior to sending messages to the group. Recent research suggests that the very act of sending affectionate messages in supportive online exchanges is related to reduced total cholesterol levels and cortisol levels (Floyd, Mikkelson, Hesse, & Pauley, 2007). Both cholesterol and cortisol are physiological products of stress and have been linked to heart disease and strokes among individuals facing long-term stressful situations. This research provides an important empirical link between computer-mediated supportive communication and physical health outcomes and suggests fruitful future avenues of research.

Disadvantages of Computer-Mediated Social Support Groups

Computer-mediated support groups/communities also have a number of potential disadvantages for participants. Wright (2000, 2002), in a survey of many types of health-related online support groups, identified a number of these disadvantages. One problem is the relatively short-term membership that is typical in health-related groups. Participants often join online groups/communities when they are initially worried about a health problem or when they have been recently diagnosed with an illness. However, members often stop using these groups/communities after a few weeks. Such short-term membership may lead to several problems, including difficulty locating specific members and fewer "old-timers," or individuals who have been using the group/community to deal with an illness/health concern over a long period. Chronic illnesses require sustained lifestyle changes, and members may lose the ability to obtain continuing support for these lifestyle changes from the online community if they only interact with the group for a short period of time. Beaudoin and Tao (2007) suggest that such limitations of short-term membership explain why asynchronous communication but not synchronous communication predicts stress, difficulty coping, and depression for cancer patient members of an online support group.

In addition, despite greater access to individuals who share similar health concerns in online support groups/communities, participants often find the lack of immediacy frustrating (associated with reduced social presence) when they are communicating with others. For instance, Wright (2002) noted that online support group members missed the ability to engage in haptic communication (e.g., hugs, and other expressions of supportive touch) with fellow participants.

Other disadvantages of computer-mediated support groups include off-topic remarks from participants, spam messages, privateers (people who try to use the group/community for their own selfish purposes), and flaming (i.e., antisocial behavior). These behaviors increase negative perceptions of the group/community and may curtail membership if they occur frequently. Early computer-mediated communication researchers posited that the reduced social cues associated with the medium may encourage antisocial behaviors due to the lack of physical presence of other participants (Walther, 1996). In other words, it is much easier to be disruptive online because a person is in little danger of physical retaliation from other members. Hwang et al. (2007), in a content analysis of messages posted in 18 computer-mediated support groups, discovered that erroneous advice within these groups often contained harmful suggestions, such as the use of inappropriate medications.

However, the majority of advice given in the postings was not harmful and most incorrect advice was corrected by other members.

Moreover, the medium may facilitate deceptive practices. The anonymity can lead individuals to misrepresent themselves, to pretend to have an illness in order to receive attention from others, or to use the group/community for a variety of other reasons unrelated to the stated purpose of the group/community.

Theoretical/Methodological Limitations and Directions for Future Research

Computer-mediated social support groups are an important and growing context in which to study supportive relationships and health outcomes. The current literature suggests that these groups clearly have potential health benefits for many of the individuals who use them. However, despite some of the advantages of using these resources, there may be several pitfalls associated with them that could potentially have a negative influence on health outcomes. In addition, more research is needed to understand social support processes within this new environment, particularly in terms of physical and psychological health outcomes. In the following sections, we discuss several theoretical and methodological limitations of current research as well as fruitful directions for research in this area.

Limitations of Current Research

Wright and Bell (2003) concluded that the majority of computer-mediated support group studies have been largely descriptive in nature and have not sufficiently linked findings to a broader theoretical framework. Similarly, Eysenbach, Powell, Englesakis, Rizo, and Stern (2004) contend "the lack of measurable evidence from controlled studies is in sharp contrast to the increasing body of anecdotal and descriptive information on the self-helping processes in virtual communities" (p. 5).

Although, as discussed earlier, general theories regarding social support have been applied to online social support groups, much less research has used theories related to computer-mediated communication to examine these groups. While some scholars have used Social Information Processing Theory (Walther, 1996) in studies of computer-mediated support groups (see Walther & Boyd, 2000; Wright, 2000, 2002), future studies would benefit from using this theory further to examine computer-mediated support groups. In addition, other CMC-based theories, including media richness theory, social network analyses, and a variety of other frameworks may increase our knowledge of channel-related characteristics of computer-mediated social support processes.

Methodological Limitations

Several methodological limitations of current research on computer-mediated support are apparent from this review. For example, existing measures of social support developed to assess perceived support in face-to-face interactions may not be appropriate to use among members of computer-mediated support groups. Beaudoin and Tao (2007) and Wright et al. (2010) developed or edited social support measures specific to the online environment. However, most researchers have relied on existing social support measures when studying computer-mediated support groups rather than focusing on developing new measures designed for online exchanges.

Online research is plagued by sampling issues, such as a lack of demographic variables (Wright, 2005) and the ability to obtain a reliable sampling frame (Dillman, 2000). For instance, should lurkers, those who observe but do not participate in a group, fill out surveys related to the support group? Will sporadic participation in the group affect who fills out the survey and whether the resulting sample is representative of group membership? Such issues lower the validity of current data related to online support groups and decrease our ability to make accurate predictions about health outcomes. Finally, with any online group, one faces a variety of questions related to research ethics. Some online groups ask that researchers obtain permission before using communication between members for research (Barnes, 2001), and some university Institution Review Boards require researchers to post a notice that any communication posted to the online discussion board may be used for research purposes.

Directions for Future Research

Despite the growing body of research on computer-mediated support, there remain many areas needing further development. For example, what happens when members of an online social support group meet in person? This might happen if, for instance, one were to attend a conference related to one's health issue and to meet individuals with whom one has interacted online. Whether weak ties encountered within computer-mediated support groups develop into stronger ties in the face-to-face world, and whether this process will negate some of the advantages of computer-mediated support (i.e., reduced stigma, fewer role obligations, etc.) are questions for future research.

Another direction for future research involves the interface between online social support groups and health care providers. Is interaction affected by members' participation in these online groups? Are health care providers open to considering the impact of online support groups when considering how to interact with their patients? Suggestions regarding this issue for health providers include (a) monitoring their patients' use of online support groups (Houston et al., 2002), (b) suggesting that patients use frequently used sites rather than less frequently used sites, as advice on more popular sites is less likely to contain wrong or harmful information (Hwang et al., 2007), and (c) convincing their patients to be skeptical of information regarding medication on websites, as this information is more likely than other types of information to be incorrect (Hwang et al., 2007).

Whether a theory unique to computer-mediated support groups is needed is another interesting question for future research. How individuals use both face-to-face and online social support resources to obtain their desired level of social support for health-related concerns is also unanswered. How does interaction with those online affect individuals' face-to-face relationships and vice versa? How do individuals take the information they obtain in an online forum and integrate it into their face-to-face interactions with their families and friends?

Finally, scholars would benefit from understanding how characteristics of computer-mediated communication affect relationships between members of online support groups. As we have seen, these groups offer a number of advantages and disadvantages to participants. However, most studies have been cross-sectional, and relatively little is known about the development and maintenance of long-term supportive relationships within these groups, relational dilemmas in giving and receiving computer-mediated social support, and a host of other interpersonal communication concerns within this environment.

Conclusion

Computer-mediated social support groups are an important context within which to study supportive relationships and health outcomes. Most of the previous research suggests that online support has potential health benefits for those individuals who use computer-mediated support groups/communities or who engage in other types of online support. However, despite some of the advantages of using these resources, there are also problems associated with them. Theoretically based studies are needed in the future to help researchers better understand the supportive processes, health outcomes, and problems associated with these groups.

References

Adelman, M. B., Parks, M. R., & Albrecht, T. L. (1987). Beyond close relationships: Support in weak ties. In T. L. Albrecht, M. B. Adelman, & Associates (Eds.), *Communicating social support* (pp. 126–147). Newbury Park, CA: Sage.

Albrecht, T. L., & Goldsmith, D. J. (2003). Social support, social networks, and health. In T. L. Thompson, A. M. Dorsey, K. I. Miller, & R. Parrott (Eds.), *Handbook of health communication* (pp. 263–284). Mahwah, NJ: Erlbaum.

Barnes, S. B. (2001). *Online connections: Internet interpersonal relationships.* Cresskill, NJ: Hampton Press.

Barrera, M. (1986). Distinctions between social support concepts, measures, and models. *American Journal of Community Psychology, 14,* 413–445.

Beaudoin, C. E., & Tao, C. C. (2007). Benefiting from social capital in online support groups: An empirical study of cancer patients. *CyberPsychology & Behavior, 10,* 587–590.

Blythe, B. J. (1983). Social support networks in health care and health promotion. In J. K. Whittaker & J. Garbarino (Eds.), *Social support networks: Informal helping in the human services* (pp. 107–133). New York: Aldine De Gruyter.

Braithwaite, D. O., Waldron, V. R., & Finn, J. (1999). Communication of social support in computer-mediated groups for people with disabilities. *Health Communication, 11,* 123–151.

Cutrona, C. E., & Russell, D. W. (1990). Type of social support and specific stress: Toward a theory of optimal matching. In B. R. Sarason, I. G. Sarason, & G. R. Pierce (Eds.), *Social support: An interactional view* (pp. 319–366). Oxford, England: Wiley.

Dakof, G. A., & Taylor, S. E. (1990). Victims' perceptions of social support: What is helpful from whom? *Journal of Personality and Social Psychology, 58,* 80–89.

Darcy, A., & Dooley, B. (2007). A clinical profile of participants in an online support group. *European Eating Disorders, 15,* 185–195.

Davison, K. P., Pennebaker, J. W., & Dickerson, S. S. (2000). Who talks? The social psychology of illness support groups. *American Psychologist, 55,* 205–217.

Diamond, J. (2000). *Narrative means to sober ends: Treating addiction and its aftermath.* New York: Guilford Press.

Dillman, D. A. (2000). *Mail and Internet surveys: The tailored design method.* New York: Wiley.

Eichhorn, K. C. (2008). Soliciting and providing support over the Internet: An investigation of online eating disorder groups. *Journal of Computer-Mediated Communication, 14,* 67–78.

Evans, R., Connis, R., Bishop, D., Hendricks, R., & Haselkorn, J. (1994). Stroke: A family dilemma. *Disability and Rehabilitation, 16,* 110–118.

Eysenbach, G., Powell, J., Englesakis, M., Rizo, C., & Stern, A. (2004). Health related virtual communities and electronic support groups: Systematic review of the effects of online peer to peer interactions. *British Medical Journal, 328,* 1166–1172.

Festinger, L. (1954). A theory of social comparison processes. *Human Relations, 7,* 117–140.

Finn, J., & Lavitt, M. (1994). Computer-based self-help groups for sexual abuse survivors. *Social Work with Groups, 17,* 21–47.

Floyd, K., Mikkelson, A. C., Hesse, C., & Pauley, P. M. (2007). Affectionate writing reduces total cholesterol: Two randomized, controlled trials. *Human Communication Research, 33,* 119–142.

Fogel, J., Albert, S. M., Schnabel, E., Ditkoff, B. A., & Neugut, A. I. (2002). Internet use and social support in women with breast cancer. *Health Psychology, 21,* 398–404.

Furger, R. (1996). I'm okay, you're on-line. *PC World, 14*, 310–312.

Giles, H., Mulac, A., Bradac, J. J., & Johnson, P. (1987). Speech accommodation theory: The next decade and beyond. *Communication Yearbook 10*, 13–48.

Goldsmith, D. J. (2004). *Communicating social support*. New York: Cambridge University Press.

Granovetter, M. (1973). The strength of weak ties. *American Journal of Sociology, 78*, 1360–1380.

Granovetter, M. (1983). The strength of weak ties: A network theory revisited. *Sociological Theory, 1*, 201–233.

Gustafson, D. H., McTavish, F. M., Stengle, W., Ballard, D., Hawkins, R., Shaw, B. R., ... Landucci, G. (2005). Use and impact of ehealth system by low-income women with breast cancer. *Journal of Health Communication, 10*, 195–218.

Helgeson, V. S., & Gottlieb, B. H. (2000). Support groups. In S. Cohen, L. G. Underwood, & B. H. Gottlieb (Eds.), *Social support measurement and intervention* (pp. 221–245). New York: Oxford University Press.

Houston, T. K., Cooper, L. A., & Ford, D. E. (2002). Internet support groups for depression: A 1-year prospective cohort study. *American Journal of Psychiatry, 159*, 2062–2068.

Hwang, K. O., Farheen, K., Johnson, C. W., Thomas, E. J., Barnes, A. S., & Bernstam, E. V. (2007). Quality of weight loss advice on internet forums. *American Journal of Medicine, 120*, 604–609.

Im, E., Chee, W., Lim, H., Liu, Y., Guevara, E., & Kim, K. S. (2007). Patients' attitudes toward internet cancer support groups. *Oncology Nursing Forum, 34*, 705–712.

Jones, M., Luce, K. H., Osborne, M. L., Taylor, K. Cunning, D., Doyle, A. C., ... Taylor, B. (2008). Randomized, controlled trial of an Internet-facilitated intervention for reducing overeating and overweight in adolescents. *Pediatrics, 121*, 453–462.

King, S. A., & Moreggi, D. (1998). Internet therapy and self-help groups: The pros and cons. In J. Gakenbach (Ed.), *Psychology and the Internet: Intrapersonal, interpersonal, and transpersonal implications* (pp. 77–109). San Diego, CA: Academic Press.

Kohn, P. M. (1996). On coping adaptively with daily hassles. In M. Zeidner & N. S. Endler (Eds.), *Handbook of coping* (pp. 181–201). New York: Wiley.

Lieberman, M. A., & Goldstein, B. A. (2005). Self-help on-line: An outcome evaluation of breast cancer bulletin boards. *Journal of Health Psychology, 10*, 855–862.

Madden, M., & Fox, S. (2006). Finding answers online in sickness and in health. *Pew Internet and American Life Project*. Retrieved from http://www.pewinternet.org/pdfs/PIP_Health_Decisions_2006.pdf

Monnier, J., Laken , M., & Carter, C. L. (2002). Patient and caregiver interest in internet-based cancer services. *Cancer Practice, 10*, 305–310.

Neuhauser, L., & Kreps, G. L. (2003). Rethinking communication in the e-health era. *Journal of Health Psychology, 8*, 7–23.

Owen, J. E., Klapow, J. C., Roth, D. L., Shuster, J. L., & Bellis, J. (2005). Randomized pilot of a self-guided Internet coping group for women with early-stage breast cancer. *Annals of Behavioral Medicine, 30*, 54–64.

Parks, M. R., & Floyd, K. (1996). Making friends in cyberspace. *Journal of Communication, 46*, 80–97.

Pennebaker, J. W. (1997). Writing about emotional experiences as a therapeutic process. *Psychological Science, 8*, 162–166.

Pull, C. (2006). Self-help Internet interventions for mental disorders. *Current Opinion in Psychiatry, 19*, 50–53.

Query, J. L., Jr., & Wright, K. B. (2003). Assessing communication competence in an online study: Toward informing subsequent interventions among older adults with cancer, their lay caregivers, and peers. *Health Communication 15*, 203–218.

Rains, S. A., & Young, V. (2009). A meta-analysis of research on formal computer-mediated support groups: Examining group characteristics and health outcomes. *Human Communication Research, 35*, 309–336.

Sarasohn-Kahn, J. (2008). *The wisdom of patients: Health care meets online social media*. Retrieved from http://www.chcf.org/documents/chronicdisease/Health careSocialMedia.pdf

Sharf, B. F. (1997). Communicating breast cancer on-line: Support and empowerment on the Internet. *Women & Health, 26*, 65–84.

Shaw, B. R., Hawkins, R., McTavish, F., Pingree, S., & Gustafson, D. H. (2006). Effects of insightful disclosure within computer mediated support groups on women with breast cancer. *Health Communication, 19*, 133–142.

Sullivan, C. F. (2003). Gendered cybersupport: A thematic analysis of two on-line cancer support groups. *Journal of Health Psychology, 8*, 83–103.

Tanis, M. (2008). Health-related on-line forums: What's the big attraction? *Journal of Health Communication, 13*, 698–714.

Turner, J. W., Grube, J. A., & Meyers, J. (2001). Developing an optimal match within online communities: An exploration of CMC support communities and traditional support. *Journal of Communication, 51*, 231–251.

Walther, J. B. (1996). Computer-mediated communication: Impersonal, interpersonal, and hyperpersonal interaction. *Communication Research, 23*, 3–43.

Walther, J. B., & Boyd, S. (2002). Attraction to computer-mediated social support. In C. A. Lin & D. Atkin (Eds.), *Communication technology and society: Audience adoption and uses* (pp. 153–188). Cresskill, NJ: Hampton Press.

Walther, J. B., & Parks, M. R. (2002). Cues filtered out, cues filtered in: Computer-mediated communication relationships. In M. L. Knapp, J. A. Daly, & G. R. Miller (Eds.), *The handbook of interpersonal communication* (3rd. ed., pp. 529–563). Thousand Oaks, CA: Sage.

Wright, K. B. (1999). Computer-mediated support groups: An examination of relationships among social support, perceived stress, and coping strategies. *Communication Quarterly, 47*, 402–414.

Wright, K. B. (2000). Perceptions of on-line support providers: An examination of perceived homophily, source credibility, communication and social support within on-line support groups. *Communication Quarterly, 48*, 44–59.

Wright, K. B. (2002). Social support within an on-line cancer community: An assessment of emotional support, perceptions of advantages and disadvantages, and motives for using the community. *Journal of Applied Communication Research, 3*, 195–209.

Wright, K. B. (2005). Researching Internet-based populations: Advantages and disadvantages of online survey research, online questionnaire authoring software packages, and web survey services. *Journal of Computer-Mediated Communication, 10*. Retrieved July 15, 2009, from http://onlinelibrary.wiley.com/doi/10.1111/j.1083-6101.2005.tb00259.x/full

Wright, K. B., & Bell, S. B. (2003). Health-related support groups on the Internet: Linking empirical findings to social support and computer-mediated communication theory. *Journal of Health Psychology, 8*, 37–52.

Wright, K. B., & Muhtaseb, A. (2005, May). *Perceptions of on-line support in health-related computer-mediated support groups.* Paper presented to the Health Communication Division at the annual International Communication Association Convention, New York.

Wright, K. B., Rains, S., & Banas, J. (2010). Weak-tie support network preference and perceived life stress among participants in health-related, computer-mediated support groups. *Journal of Computer-Mediated Communication, 15*, 606–624.

23

INSIGHTS ABOUT HEALTH FROM FAMILY COMMUNICATION THEORIES

Loretta L. Pecchioni and Maureen P. Keeley

Families and how they communicate matter in health communication. Making sense of the ways in which families matter is complicated and at times overwhelming because many studies focus on a particular illness, family structure, or stage in life. While each of these approaches is valuable and informative, they do not present the complex and multifaceted relationship that exists in family–health scholarship. Thus, in an attempt to provide a more holistic understanding of the symbiotic relationship between family communication and health communication, we thought about the role of family theories in helping to understand family dynamics and how those theories provide a framework for examining this important body of family–health scholarship. As a consequence, the goal of this chapter is not to provide an exhaustive review of the family–health scholarship; instead, we hope to highlight the important role that family plays in health processes; as well as offer insights into health communication that arise when family communication theories are used to examine these dynamics.

In this chapter, we present arguments for why families matter to health communication and briefly highlight some of the many contingencies that can influence and be influenced by families and health. Next, we present our arguments about how theories focusing on family communication can bring insight and understanding to the wide range of findings regarding the intersections of family and health communication. Then we review select examples of family communication theories, ranging from well-established to new and promising, as a way to illustrate how these theories have been or can be used in health communication to extend the readers' understanding of those intersections. Certainly other theories could have been chosen and the authors hope that these illustrations provide a spark for further theoretical examinations of family and health communication.

Why Families Matter to Health

From the perspective of health communication, examining the role of families in health is valuable because of pragmatic health outcomes. Across the family life cycle, family members provide the bulk of care on both a day-to-day basis or during an illness, contributing significant time, energy, and financial resources (Albrecht & Adelman, 1987). Research from a broad range of disciplines consistently finds that "better" communication results in more positive outcomes related to physical and mental health (Pecchioni, Thompson, &

Anderson, 2006). In addition to providing care, the ways in which families talk about (or avoid talking about) health-related issues impact attitudes and behaviors (Parrott, 2009). Individuals first learn about health behaviors and attitudes in their families of origin, influencing everyday behaviors and lifestyle choices, as well as current and future health outcomes (Geist Martin, Berlin Ray, & Sharf, 2003). These health-related behaviors may reflect family cultural norms related to religion, ethnic background, gender norms, or socioeconomic status. Family practices also reflect what are considered appropriate and inappropriate topics for conversation (Ormondroyd et al., 2008).

Family talk about health helps individuals to cope with and make sense of a health crisis. While medical personnel serve an array of valuable purposes during a health crisis, families provide much of the day-to-day care and emotional support that results in a strong, positive link to health outcomes (Pecchioni et al., 2006). Research consistently finds that individuals who receive sufficient social support cope better with a wide range of illnesses, emotional challenges, and life transitions (Burleson & MacGeorge, 2002).

We know that how families talk about health has an impact on health outcomes (Parrott, 2009), but not all families must talk about health in the same ways in order to have positive outcomes. Even families that appear to be quite similar may have very different experiences with regard to a health crisis; and families that appear to be very different from each other may have quite similar experiences. It is challenging to try to understand this variability and identify meaningful patterns. In the area of families and health, the number of variables is overwhelming since they can be related to the individual (e.g., demographic and personality characteristics), family (e.g., structure, culture), health issue (e.g., lifestyle, acute or chronic illness, prognosis), or a combination of these factors.

These variables, while wide ranging, are suggestive rather than exhaustive of the possibilities. The number of iterations when combining these factors is probably not infinite, but sufficiently large to make it appear overwhelming to identify and understand them on all these levels. Individuals are embedded in families and families are embedded in larger social groups, making the nature of any health-related issue multilayered. Therefore, attempting to understand the complexity of issues and draw meaningful conclusions about what generates positive outcomes is best accomplished by applying theories that can help make sense of these complex interactions.

Why Theories of Family Communication Matter to Health Communication

Theories about family processes and functioning help to make sense of the inherent variability in families in meaningful ways. In general, family communication theories examine the social unit and the mutual influences of individuals within that unit, although different theories place different weight on the balance between the individual and the family (Noller & Fitzpatrick, 1993). Theories of family communication focus particularly on the functions of families, the roles of individuals within the family, and the interaction patterns and relational dynamics among the family members, as well as individual and family unit outcome measures (Baxter, 2006; Segrin & Flora, 2005). Successful theories of family communication help us to understand the experiences and events of individuals and family units.

Within the context of a family, health should be considered as more than "just a topic of conversation" but as something that plays a central role in family functioning. From teen risk behaviors, to lifelong lifestyle choices, to coping with illnesses and bereavement, research consistently finds that "better" communication leads to better health outcomes (Pecchioni et al., 2006). What constitutes better communication, however, is not always made clear. One barrier to determining what makes for better communication across this wide range of situations is that the researchers focus on a single, albeit important, issue. Findings across the range of studies are insufficiently collated to identify what counts as effective and competent communication and often fail to take into consideration the range of contingencies evident in any given situation. Focusing on family theories as a framework can potentially point out the behaviors that produce positive outcomes, explaining why they do so; this allows for greater generalizability, and for maintaining sensitivity to the contingencies of a specific situation.

Well-Developed Family Communication Theories: Insights for Health Communication

Systems Theory and Models of Family Stress, Coping, and Adaptation

Segrin and Flora (2005) stated that "[f]amily systems theory is the dominant paradigm in family science" (p. 32); similarly, Galvin, Dickson, and Marrow (2006) reported that the assumptions of systems theory have become so deeply embedded in our thinking about families that family theorists and scholars do not always explicitly acknowledge their influence. Due to space limitations, a thorough history and review of General Systems Theory and its influence in family studies are beyond the scope of this chapter (see Broderick, 1993). For the purposes of this chapter, a very brief review of the major assumptions and concepts of systems theory is provided and then two models of family systems with applications to health communication are examined.

Because family members are interdependent in the family systems perspective, one person's health impacts the other members of the family. Health can be an ongoing part of the interactions in the system or reflect an event that produces stress and potential change in the system. On a day-to-day basis, families develop patterned ways of interacting around health issues, whether they are discussing nutrition, engaging in joint activities, or sharing poor health habits. On the other hand, if one member experiences a health crisis, that stressor challenges the family's stability as its rules for interaction are called into question. Families, however, also have rules for how to behave during a crisis. While the family will likely have to adapt its behaviors to meet the new conditions surrounding the illness, the family will take action to return to some sense of stability.

As the models of family systems will more fully demonstrate, "healthy" family functioning results in "healthy" family outcomes. Research on family functioning has particularly focused on mental health because psychologists, psychiatrists, and mental health therapists were among the first to apply systems theory to families as they shifted from treating individuals to addressing the family system (Galvin et al., 2006; Segrin & Flora, 2005). While most of the research has focused on family functioning with regard to coping with stress and mental health, physical health issues have also been examined. The family systems perspective provides a meaningful way to organize the wide range of variables that were mentioned above as we examine a complex, dynamic system that is moving through a transition point.

Pragmatic Models of Family Systems

Olson's Circumplex Model In Olson's Circumplex Model (1993; Olson, Sprenkle, & Russell, 1979), three dimensions are identified for assessing family functioning: flexibility, cohesion, and communication. Flexibility, originally called adaptability, reflects a family's ability to make adaptive changes that inherently arise through developmental changes and life experiences. Cohesion reflects a family's emotional bonding. Communication serves as the facilitating dimension through which families adapt and grow or constrain each other. Positive communication includes such behaviors as self-disclosure, attentive listening, and demonstrating empathy. Negative communication includes such behaviors as criticism, denial of feelings, and excessive conflict.

Olson's circumplex model quickly came to be applied by family therapists working to help families cope with and adapt to change; examples include dealing with children and adolescents who were experiencing substance abuse (Friedman, Utada, & Morrissey, 1987) or mental health issues (Kashani, Allan, Dahlmeier, Rezvani, & Reid, 1995), or with a member who suffered a traumatic brain injury (Kosciulek, 1996). The goals of these studies were to identify patterns of family interaction and to offer recommendations for therapeutic intervention based on these different patterns.

Of particular interest to health communication scholars is the focus on communication as a resource suggesting specific behaviors that enhance or hinder family functioning. By acknowledging the complex dynamics of families, this model helps to create a framework for understanding both the uniqueness of each family's situation and the commonalities of their experiences.

Double ABC-X Model Hill (1949) proposed the ABC-X Model of Family Stress and Coping to examine how families adapt to stress by focusing not only on the stressful event, but the family's characteristics, interactions, and experiences in reaction to that event. In brief, the elements include: (A) = the stressful event; (B) = family resources; (C) = family's perceptions of the situation; (X) = outcome variable, which is the stress or the crisis experienced by the family. McCubbin and Patterson (1982) modified Hill's model (adding the double to the title), arguing that family stress unfolds over time and that no single stressful event occurs in isolation from other stressors. It may be expressed succinctly as: (aA) = stress pileup; (bB) = new resources added to the existing resources; (cC) = a redefinition of the crisis to find new meaning; (xX) = ultimate adaptation resulting in better or poorer functioning.

With its focus on coping with stress, the Double ABC-X Model has been widely used to examine issues related to health. A sampling of studies reveals that this model applies across the family life course from dealing with perinatal loss (Thomas & Striegel, 1995), to children with disabilities (Stuart & McGrew, 2009), or cancer (Han, 2003), to adults with health issues (Chapin, 2004), to elder abuse by family caregivers (Lee, 2009).

As with the Circumplex Model, the Double ABC-X acknowledges the complex dynamics of families and helps to create a framework for understanding both the uniqueness of each family's situation and the commonalities of their experiences. The role of communication as a resource should be further examined, especially during the time of a crisis, as emotions may negatively impact an individual or a family's ability to engage in positive communication. In addition, scholars should continue exploring the role of communication following the crisis to see how the family reframes the experience to produce more positive outcomes or fails to reframe it, leaving the family members damaged or worse off than they were prior to the health crisis.

Relational Dialectics Theory

Individuals make sense and give meaning to their world through competing discourses often referred to as relational dialectical tensions (Baxter, 2006). Family relationships and health care systems only exist because of the interaction of opposing voices exposed through communication. Without the interaction, specifically the talk, individuals would have no way of coming to an agreement as to the meaning of symbols. Individuals are constantly challenged to make sense of health issues in the midst of conflicting conversations among family and friends, among contradictory media images of different treatments for the same health concern, and in the middle of evolving solutions for health issues (Parrott, 2009). Consequently, meaning is made amid the communication process of engagement, thus Relational Dialectics Theory (RDT) is valuable for examining the dialogues evident in family-health scholarship (Baxter, 2006).

Three core propositions of the theory build a framework for understanding and using RDT in family-health studies (Baxter & Braithwaite, 2008): First, "meanings emerge from the struggle of different, often opposing, discourses" (p. 351). Consequently, understanding comes from the simultaneous blending and separation of dissimilar symbols (i.e., both verbal and nonverbal communication). Second, "the interpretation of discourse is both synchronic [in the moment] and diachronic [over time]" (p. 353). The third proposition emphasizes that, "the interpenetration of competing discourses constitutes social reality" (p. 355). Thus, communication is not merely a reflection of the relationship or institution, but rather it creates the relationship or institution. Family relationships and health organizations are made through competing, ongoing, and discursive discourses that are inherent in everyday interactions.

Between birth and death, individuals encounter countless health issues that are interfaced with their family's modeling, expectations, values, and lessons; they are the epitome of dialectical tensions. Utilizing RDT, scholars have shed light on family health issues across the life-span. For instance, mothers-to-be participate in tension-filled talk regarding alcohol use during pregnancy (Baxter, Hirokowa, Lowe, Nathan, & Pearce, 2004); and parents process the discord of premature birth through talk (Golish & Powell, 2003). Contradictory messages exist concerning the necessity and benefits of sun exposure to prevent rickets (Rowe, 2003); as well as the dangers of sun because of skin cancer risks (Brash, 1997). Researchers have also explored the contradictory interactions of wives with husbands suffering from Alzheimer's (Baxter, Braithwaite, Golish, & Olson, 2002).

When dialectical tensions such as these are ignored both family and health professionals are set up for conflict, failed health messages, and poor health outcomes. Opposing dialectical tensions are abundant when looking at the family. For instance, health care is expensive and many families are uninsured, thus they may be at odds when a member of the family becomes sick and needs treatment. Subsequently, if a family is not insured, the family member may choose not to go to the doctor or hospital, even when very sick, because doing so impacts the whole family (i.e., the choice becomes one about paying for the hospital fees or paying that month's mortgage; Committee on the Consequences of Uninsurance, 2002). The dialectical tension is negotiated through discussions such as: (a) what is truly valued in the family (health or financial security); (b) the meaning of the word "sick"; (c) whether the norm in the family becomes one of an individual family member not admitting that he or she is sick.

While there are potentially an infinite number of dialectical tensions in the intermingling of family and health, to date there have still been relatively few studies utilizing RDT theory to explain the failure or success of family-health initiatives and health outcomes in society.

Baxter and Braithwaite (2008) suggest a more complex, three level analysis for exploring a "chain of discourse" (p. 360), which should increase scholars' understanding about a given health–family phenomenon. First, what have the family members talked about regarding this health issue in the past? This type of data is called "discursive history" (p. 360), and it contextualizes their current talk in the framework of their past talk. Communication about health issues is rarely a one-time discussion; often health dialogues are a stream of discussions until a clear meaning is achieved. The second type of dialectical discourse is called "broader cultural discourse" (p. 360), which acknowledges that family members bring to their current dialogue information from outside of their familial boundaries that impact their sense-making. The third and final type of dialectical discourse is identified as "anticipated response talk" (p. 360). This type of dialogue recognizes that others (in the family, in the medical field, in society as a whole) will react, often "providing parties with a moral anchor by which to assess the appropriateness of their utterances in the present" (p. 360). Conflicting dialogues are complex, but they hold valuable information for scholars looking to understand individuals' and families' meaning of health events and health outcomes in their lives. Individuals rarely make sense of their health in isolation; it is most often done through dialogue with their family.

Communication Privacy Management Theory

Communication focusing on health issues is often perceived by patients and family members as a personal, private, and sensitive matter (Parrott, 2009). Revealing information about health issues can make the patient or family members feel vulnerable (Petronio, 1991) and can impact an individual's sense of identity (Parrott, 2009). Petronio's (2000, 2002) work on privacy and communication highlights the fact that revealing private information is risky because it makes people feel susceptible to harm, embarrassment, and a loss of control. Communication Privacy Management Theory (CPM; Petronio, 2000, 2002) provides a way to explain and predict the privacy factors that impact communication research in family and health communication.

CPM explains that how people handle private information is dependent upon the interaction of boundary structures and a rule-based management system (Petronio, 2000, 2002). Boundary structures are created to protect individuals from being hurt. The four dimensions of boundary structures include "ownership, control, permeability, and levels" (p.38). *Ownership* highlights who owns the private information. In the case of health issues, the owner of the information begins with the patient and then extends to the family member with whom the patient shares the information, that individual thereby becoming a co-owner of the information. Ownership within the realm of health topics can become complicated when some family members are in the "know" and others are not because it can also communicate messages about their relationships within the family. *Control* acknowledges that people have the right to manage what kind, and how much, personal information is divulged or hidden. Control of health-related information has been legalized and rigorously controlled in the medical professions through the HIPAA Privacy Rule (USDHSS, 2009), but within the family it becomes more complex due to factors such as issues pertaining to face threats (Cupach & Metts, 1994) and social support needs (Cutrona, 1996). *Permeability* addresses what private topics may be shared or concealed. Family norms and expectations often impact the permeability factor regarding health topics (Parrott, 2009). The last dimension of *levels* highlights the negotiation of restricting and concealing information along a continuum and is often dynamic as both the patient and family members may need to renegotiate numerous times during the health crisis. Ultimately, the management and negotiation regarding the sharing of the private information will be dependent upon the rule-based management system that regulates the flow of information between the patient, family, and health professionals.

The four components of the rule-based management system include boundary rules: usage, coordination, turbulence, and formation (Petronio, 2000, 2002). Rule usage highlights under what conditions and when rules for revealing or concealing are enacted. Revealing a sensitive and private topic should be a voluntary choice, made without any coercion by health professionals or family members. But what if telling one's health story in the family can help to save or protect others in the family who may be at a similar health risk (Parrott, 2009)? Rule coordination focuses on the fact that co-owners of the information mutually share the responsibility for sharing, regulating, and managing disclosed information. Boundary turbulence occurs when boundaries have been attacked, thereby jeopardizing ownership and control of the private information. Major life events such as a health crisis often trigger a change in privacy rules (Pennebaker, 1990). People often need to talk about events to give meaning to them (Petronio, 2000, 2002). Therefore, it is boundary turbulence and people's subsequent efforts to restore order that often motivate people to reveal or conceal information from others. Lastly, rule formation is the creation of privacy rules based on culture, individual characteristics, self-esteem, and motivations.

People often formulate privacy rules based on cultural norms and expectations (Benn & Gaus, 1983). Culture's influence on whether or not the topic is taboo often dictates the communication that is acceptable regarding the nature and type of issue (Parrott, 2009). Some personal issues that are commonly taboo include addictions (Le Poire, 1992), marital abuse, mental illness, sexually related health issues (Sandelowski & Jones, 1986), terminal illness (Keeley, 2007), and death (Keeley & Yingling, 2007).

Lastly, "compathy," which Morse and Mitchum (1997) define as the contagion of physical distress, is a real phenomenon of which family members and health professionals alike should be aware, especially insofar that it may stimulate the formation of a rule boundary. This phenomenon may be especially relevant to women because women have more permeable ego boundaries that allow them to more easily empathize with others' emotional experiences (Hartmann, 1991).

In summary, family members must deal with the tensions that they experience in regard to their choice to reveal or conceal private information about their health or their illness. The management of personal boundaries is a dynamic and ongoing struggle and is especially relevant when dealing with health issues in the family.

New and Promising Family Communication Theories: Implications for Health Communication

Inconsistent Nurturing as Control Theory

Two central functions of family are nurturance and control (Le Poire, 2006). Nurturance "includes the provision of care, warmth, and an environment capable of encouraging the growth and development of family members" (Le Poire, 2006, p. 58). Control includes "limiting behavioral options of other family members" (Le Poire, 2006, p. 63). These two functions can be at odds with each other, especially if one member exhibits compulsive behaviors that impact the functioning of the individual and the family. Le Poire (2006) proposed Inconsistent Nurturing as Control (INC) Theory to account for these paradoxes and to provide guidance for treating families when one member demonstrates compulsive behaviors, such as substance abuse, eating disorders, gambling, or depression.

Based in systems theory, INC focuses on the interdependence of family members and the ways in which they influence each other, highlighting the importance of relational contexts and communicative behaviors within the family (Le Poire & Dailey, 2006). The theory focuses on dyadic interactions within the family with one member being identified as the afflicted party and one member as the functional party. Three propositions are central to the theory. First, while the functional party seems to exhibit power in the relationship by exercising control over the afflicted party, the latter actually holds more power because he or she is the one who triggers both controlling and nurturing behaviors on the part of the functional party. Second, the functional party nurtures the afflicted party through a crisis, often making personal sacrifices that lead to the afflicted party feeling obligated to the functional party. As a result, the functional party has power based on this sense of obligation. Third, the functional party wants to maintain the relationship, but also wants the compulsive behaviors to stop. Caretaking is rewarding. If the compulsive behaviors disappear, the functional party may find the relationship to be less satisfying as the need to provide nurturing diminishes.

The consequences of this complex dance frequently are inconsistent nurturing and control behaviors (Le Poire & Dailey, 2006). INC is based in learning theory, which argues that reinforcement (positive reward) and punishment drive behavior. When the functional party provides nurturing, it may unintentionally reinforce the compulsive behavior and encourage its repetition in the future. When the compulsive behaviors are again exhibited, the functional party may become resentful and withhold nurturing as a form of punishment. The dependent party becomes even more helpless with regard to controlling the undesirable behavior. Intermittent reinforcement and punishment result in reinforcing the behavior.

Le Poire first proposed INC based on the family dynamics surrounding substance abuse (Le Poire, 1992; 1995; 2004), but has extended the theory to eating disorders (Prescott & Le Poire, 2002) and depression (Duggan & Le Poire, 2006). Thus, INC has clear implications for health issues within families by focusing on the ways in which family members communicate about undesirable behaviors and how to modify behaviors.

While INC has not been applied to issues of physical health, it might well prove enlightening with regard to the complex family dynamics that arise as the result of a chronic illness. Stepping back from the pathologizing nature of compulsive behaviors, individuals with chronic diseases often are more dependent on others than are those who do not have such conditions. The management of a chronic illness requires vigilance and yet the person with the illness may not maintain that vigilance. A partner may step in. For example, an adult with diabetes may be inconsistent about monitoring his or her glucose levels. The partner may know about this inconsistency, as well as the potential resulting health problems, and phone regularly to check for warning signs and to encourage testing or eating. The interplay of nurturing and controlling the partner's behavior in this case seems quite similar to that of the kinds of behaviors already examined through the lens of INC. These cases offer another location in which to examine the conflicting nature of nurturance and control and the impact on health outcomes.

Affection Exchange Theory

"Five hugs a day keeps the doctor away" is an adage in American society that highlights people's perception of the importance of affection in their daily lives; but, until the last decade, this belief had little scientific support. Research that explores the exchange of affection between individuals (primarily family members and couples) endeavors to investigate the consequences of affection, as well as offer an explanation as to why people communicate affection to one another (Floyd, 2001; Floyd, Judd, & Hess, 2008). Affection is defined as "those behaviors that encode feelings of fondness and intense positive regard...is shaped by cultural norms, is constrained by contextual demands;...and is evolutionarily derived" (Floyd et al., 2008, p. 288). Affectionate behavior can be transmitted in three ways: (1) verbally (i.e., "I love you"); (2) through direct nonverbal behaviors (i.e., kissing, hugging); or (3) through indirect nonverbal actions (i.e., behaviors that connote affection by providing social or material support). A comprehensive framework for understanding the link between affection exchanged in the family and health consequences is Affection Exchange Theory (AET) (Floyd, 2006a; Floyd & Mormon, 2002).

AET (Floyd, 2006a; Floyd & Mormon, 2002) is grounded in three fundamental assumptions (Floyd et al., 2008, p. 286): First, "the need and capacity for affection are inborn" or innate and come with measurable benefits when affection needs are met. Second, "affectionate feelings and affectionate expressions are distinct experiences that often, but not always covary." Hence, feelings and expressions do not have to both be present at the same time. Individuals may feel liking without expressing affection out of fear of rejection or social constraints; as well, individuals may express affection without feeling it when it is beneficial or polite to do so. Third, "affectionate communication is adaptive with respect to human viability and fertility." So, the expression and exchange of affection promotes survival and procreation success.

Research exploring the relationship between affectionate communication that is expressed within families and real-life outcomes related to health issues include: reproductive success, physical health, and mental health. Specifically, men are more affectionate with sons that will potentially have more successful reproductive outcomes (i.e., biological sons, heterosexual sons) (Floyd & Mormon, 2002). On mental health issues, highly affectionate individuals have more positive self-esteem, better general mental health, higher life satisfaction, more social engagements, and are less susceptible to depression and stress (Floyd, Hess et al., 2005). On physical health outcomes, higher levels of affection behavior are related to substantial (and healthy) variation in the adrenal hormone cortisol (Floyd, 2006b), and aid neuroendocrine stress recovery (Floyd, Mikkelson, et al., 2007) as well as lower blood pressure, healthier average blood glucose levels (Floyd, Hesse, & Haynes, 2007), and potentially reduced serum cholesterol levels (Floyd, Hesse, & Haynes, 2007). Parrott (2009) highlights the fact that humans are innately oriented with nerves in their brains connected to the body's arousal system (including heart rate, blood pressure, sweating, and breathing) and that these signs of arousal and brain activity are triggered by rewards and punishments, and punishments are related to feelings of worry, fear, anxiety, and stress (Parrott, 2009). The physiological reactions to rewards and punishments are closely linked to numerous health issues (Carver & White, 1994; Gray, 1982); and indicate that more research exploring the expression of affection in marriages and in the family and health outcomes is warranted. AET offers a direct link between communication in the family and health.

Theory of Negotiated Morality

Health and family concerns are often entangled with issues pertaining to topics of morality and human dignity (e.g., right to life, right to die, use of alternative medicines, IVF, use of contraception). Morality is an important component in families (M. P. Johnson, 1999) and in health care (Callahan & Jennings, 2002); therefore, a brand new theory emerging in the field of family communication merits a brief mention in this chapter. The Theory of Negotiated Morality (NMT), originally developed from Waldron and Kelley's (2008) work exploring forgiveness in family relationships, found that "at its core, forgiveness is fundamentally about issues of morality—questions of right and wrong, relational justice, and human dignity" (p. 78).

While NMT revolves around the concept of forgiveness, its logical, pragmatic, and theoretically sound assumptions offer a solid foundation that could provide some clarity regarding the complex interaction of numerous value laden health and family issues. Waldron and Kelley's (2008) NMT has eight basic assumptions: First, human relationships are interpreted based on a system of implicit or explicit values. Second, values result from community, personal, and relational (familial) sources. Third, the desire to preserve moral codes motivates behavior. Fourth, values that are socially sanctioned, individually internalized, and relationally shared, provoke behavior. Fifth, values with long relational, familial, and cultural histories are more motivating than values with brief histories. Sixth, behaviors that threaten significant values elicit emotional responses from those with a vested interest in maintaining those values. Seventh, the communication process is the primary way that moral codes are expressed, negotiated, and restored in human relationships. Eighth, the communication process in the midst of the negotiations influences the quality of the relationships after the value threatening episode is completed, including the extent to which the process is experienced as trustworthy, intimate, and just.

In the rapidly changing world of medicine in which (a) genetic testing is no longer a theory but a reality and impacts family medical decisions (Juengst, 1999); (b) where premature babies are living at a younger gestational age than was previously the case (Ertelt, 2009); and (c) during a time when life expectancies are continuing to be extended, but the quality of that life may not be (C. S. Johnson, 2008), values and morality need to be considered and addressed. Simply because science progresses does not always mean that society and families are prepared to embrace these changes. Morality is negotiated within every culture (Waldron & Kelley, 2008). Often the first and last place of negotiation regarding health issues is in individuals' homes and families (Parrott, 2009). Ultimately, NMT highlights the notion that it is the communicative process of these negotiations that will determine the resulting impact on the relationships and the health outcomes of individuals.

Why Family Communication Theories Matters to Health Communication

Families and health are intertwined in meaningful ways and communication is central to these processes and outcomes. Family and health do not occur in separate spheres, they co-exist in the same way that a helix exists in the world, in a spiral coil that cannot or should not be separated. The complexity of families by their very nature makes studying families and health together both daunting and critical for researchers.

Considerable research, some of it cited in this chapter, demonstrates the role of family communication in health. Data, however, are less meaningful without a theoretical framework. Theory highlights what is being examined, explains how to make sense of the findings, and provides an underlying mechanism for the identified relationships. Family Communication Theories place the focus on the communication that is occurring in the family about health issues—where the majority of sense-making is occurring for patients (in their homes with their families).

Sense-making is often talked about as a dyadic act (Koenig Kellas, 2005). The complexity of interactions that revolve around health communication suggests that a dyadic perspective may be too simplistic. Currently, the majority of communication research focuses primarily on the interaction between the patient and their health providers (e.g., doctor, nurse, social worker, etc.; see Duggan and Thompson; Politi and Street, this volume); while others explore the communication between the patient and family members (Keeley, 2007); yet, the more realistic picture of health communication interactions is that most are three-way conversations between the patient, health provider, and family member(s). In the 21st century, it is more common for family members to become directly or indirectly involved in all health-related interactions, such as being in the hospital room or the doctor's office, or after the fact at home, after completing Internet research regarding the health issue. Ultimately, a three-party interaction is occurring in the health conversation and decision-making process regarding the patient's health (Parrott, 2009). Thus, a complex piece of the puzzle is still largely unexplored: the interaction that occurs within the triad of the patient, the health provider, and the family member(s). The use of family communication theories allows examination of communication interactions that occur within "health triads."

For instance, Systems Theory could provide a more holistic view of the interaction that acknowledges the interdependence and mutual influence of all three participants in the health interaction. Communication Privacy Management Theory may be able to give some insight regarding the tensions and rules surrounding inherently private health issues that occur from each of the three perspectives. The Theory of Negotiated Morality presents a framework that makes it viable to explore the impact of each member of the triad's values and morality on the decisions made and health outcomes achieved. While these three theories are offered for demonstration, all of the family theories identified in this chapter could be used to explore the complex communication that occurs within patient–health-provider–family member interactions. Ultimately, to explore only two parts of the triad is to miss an important part of the interaction if the goal is to improve the health outcomes of the patient. Theories of family communication help us to not only develop a deeper understanding of unique experiences, but to collect that depth of understanding to identify common patterns, ultimately offering practical advice for helping individuals and their families navigate the complexities of health and life.

Future research should aim to examine family communication in and about health in this broader context. Studies that focus on particular diseases or family structures should be tied back into a larger theoretical framework so that the combination of factors that impact a particular situation can be examined in ways to produce insight into patterns of interaction that are more likely to produce positive outcomes. Identification of what constitutes "good" communication is only one part of the process and theoretical models provide help in generating an understanding of *why* certain communicative behaviors better meet individual and family needs, consequently producing better outcomes.

Family matters because health issues begin the moment people are conceived into a family, continue as family members learn and live healthy or risky daily health behaviors, are magnified by all family members' reactions to a health crisis, and only come to an end with death (that is often taken with family members as witnesses to the end of life journey). Communication is the process through which all health decisions are made and enacted in the family. Consequently, it is through the examination of the communication that is occurring in the family about health issues that a better understanding of the symbiotic relationship of family and health can be reached.

References

Albrecht, T. L., & Adelman, M. B. (1987). Communicating social support: A theoretical perspective. In T. L. Albrecht & M. B. Adelman (Eds.), *Communicating social support* (pp. 18–39). Newbury Park, CA: Sage.

Baxter, L. (2006). Relational Dialectics Theory: Multivocal dialogues of family communication. In D. O. Braithwaite & L. A. Baxter (Eds.), *Engaging theories in family communication: Multiple perspectives* (pp. 130–145). Thousand Oaks, CA: Sage.

Baxter, L. A., & Braithwaite, D. O. (2008). Relational Dialectics Theory: Crafting meaning from competing discourses. In L. A. Baxter & D. O. Braithwaite (Eds.), *Engaging theories in interpersonal communication: Multiple perspectives* (pp. 349–361). Thousand Oaks, CA: Sage.

Baxter, L. A., Braithwaite, D. O., Golish, T. D., & Olson, L. N. (2002). Contradictions of interaction for wives of elderly husbands with adult dementia. *Journal of Applied Communication Research, 30,* 1–26.

Baxter, L. A., Hirokowa, R., Lowe, J. B., Nathan, P., & Pearce, L. (2004). Dialogic voices in talk about drinking and pregnancy. *Journal of Applied Communication Research, 32,* 224–248.

Benn, S. I., & Gaus, G. F. (1983). The public and the private: Concepts and action. In S. I. Benn & G. F. Gaus (Eds.), *Public and private social life* (pp. 113–134). New York: St. Martin's Press.

Brash, D. E. (1997). Sunlight and the onset of skin cancer. *Trends in Genetics, 13,* 410–414.

Broderick, C. (1993). *Understanding family processes: Basics of family systems theory.* Newbury Park, CA: Sage.

Burleson, B. R., & MacGeorge, E. L. (2002). Supportive communication. In M. L. Knapp & J. A. Daly (Eds.), *Handbook of interpersonal communication* (3rd ed., pp. 374–424). Thousand Oaks, CA: Sage.

Callahan, D., & Jennings, B. (2002). Ethics and public health: Forging a strong relationship. *American Journal of Public Health, 92,* 169–176.

Carver, C. S., & White, T. L. (1994). Behavioral inhibition, behavioral activation, and affective responses to impending reward and punishment: The BIS/BAS scales. *Journal of Personality and Social Psychology, 67,* 319–333.

Chapin, M. G. (2004). Violence exposure in home and community: Influence on posttraumatic stress symptoms in army recruits. *Journal of Community Psychology, 32,* 527–541.

Committee on the Consequences of Uninsurance. (2002). *Health insurance is a family matter.* Washington, DC: National Academies Press

Cupach, W. R., & Metts, S. (1994). *Facework.* Thousand Oaks, CA: Sage.

Cutrona, C. E. (1996). Social support as a determinant of marital quality: The interplay of negative and supportive behaviours in marriage. In G. Pierce, B. Sarason, & I. Sarason (Eds.), *Handbook of social support and the family* (pp.173–194). New York: Plenum.

Duggan, A., & Le Poire, B. (2006). One down, two involved: An application and extension of inconsistent nurturing as control theory to couples including one depressed individual. *Communication Monographs, 73,* 379–405.

Ertelt, S. (2009). New medical study shows more premature babies surviving, living longer. Retrieved from www.lifenes.com/int1222.html/id on 7/1/2009

Floyd, K. (2001). Human affection exchange: I. Reproductive probability as a predictor of men's affection with their sons. *Journal of Men's Studies, 10,* 39–50.

Floyd, K. (2006a). *Communicating affection: Interpersonal behavior and social context.* Cambridge, England: Cambridge University Press.

Floyd, K. (2006b). Human affection exchange XII. Affectionate communication is associated with diurnal variation in salivary free cortisol. *Western Journal of Communication, 70,* 47–63.

Floyd, K., Hess, J. A., Miczo, L. A., Halone, K. K., Mikkelson, A. C., & Tusing, K. J. (2005). Human affection exchange: VIII. Further evidence of the benefits of expressed affection. *Communication Quarterly, 53,* 285–303.

Floyd, K., Hesse, C., & Haynes, M. T. (2007). Human affection exchange: XV. Metabolic and cardiovascular correlates of trait expressed affection. *Communication Quarterly, 55,* 19–94.

Floyd, K., Judd, J., & Hess, C. (2008). Affection exchange theory. In L. Baxter & D. O. Braithwaite (Eds.), *Engaging theories in interpersonal communication: Multiple complexities* (pp 285–293). Los Angeles, CA: Sage.

Floyd, K., Mikkelson, A. C.,Tafoya, M. A., Farinelli, L., La Valley, A. G., Judd, J., … Wilson, J. (2007). Human affection exchange: XIII. Affectionate communication accelerates neuroendo-crine stress recovery. *Health Communication, 22,* 123–132.

Floyd, K., & Mormon, M. T. (2002). Human affection exchange VII. Affectionate communication in the sibling/spouse/sibling in-law triad. *Communication Quarterly, 51,* 247–261.

Friedman, A. S., Utada, A., & Morrissey, M. R. (1987). Families of adolescent drug abusers are "rigid": Are these families either "disengaged" or "enmeshed," or both? *Family Process, 26,* 131–148.

Galvin, K. M., Dickson, F. C., & Marrow, S. R. (2006). Systems theory: Patterns and (w)holes in family communication. In D. O. Braithwaite & L. A. Baxter (Eds.), *Engaging theories in family communication: Multiple perspectives* (pp. 309–324). Thousand Oaks, CA: Sage.

Geist Martin, P., Berlin Ray, E., & Sharf, B. F. (2003). *Communicating health: Personal, cultural, and political complexities.* Belmont, CA: Wadsworth.

Golish, T. D., & Powell, K. A. (2003). "Ambiguous loss": Managing the dialectics of grief associated with premature birth. *Journal of Social and Personal Relationships, 20,* 309–334.

Gray, J. A. (1982). *The neuropsychology of anxiety: An enquiry into the functions of the septo-hippocampal system.* New York: Oxford University Press.

Han, H. R. (2003). Korean mothers' psychosocial adjustment to their children's cancer. *Journal of Advanced Nursing, 44,* 499–506.

Hartmann, E. (1991). *Boundaries in the mind: A new psychology of personality.* New York: Basic.

Hill, R. (1949). *Families under stress.* New York: Harper.

Johnson, C. S. (2008). Aging and healthy life expectancy: Will the extended years be spent in good or poor health? *Journal of the Indian Academy of Geriatrics, 4,* 64–67.

Johnson, M. P. (1999). Personal, moral, and structural commitments to relationships: Experiences of choice and constraint. In J. M. Adams & W. H. Jones (Eds.), *Handbook of interpersonal commitment and relationship quality* (pp. 73–87). New York: Plenum.

Juengst, E. T. (1999). Genetic testing and the moral dynamics of family life. *Public Understanding of Science, 8,* 193–205.

Kashani, J. H., Allan, W. D., Dahlmeier, J. M., Rezvani, M., & Reid, J. C. (1995). An examination of family functioning utilizing the circumplex model in psychiatrically hospitalized children with depression. *Journal of Affective Disorders, 35,* 65–73.

Keeley, M. P. (2007). "Turning toward death together": The functions of messages during final conversations in close relationships. *Journal of Social and Personal Relationships, 24,* 225–253.

Keeley, M. P., & Yingling, J. (2007). *Final conversations: Helping the living and the dying talk to each other.* Acton, MA: VanderWyk & Burnham.

Koenig Kellas, J. (2005). Family ties: Communicating identity through jointly told stories. *Communication Monographs, 72,* 365–389.

Kosciulek, J. F. (1996). The Circumplex Model and head injury family types: A test of the balanced versus the extreme. *Journal of Rehabilitation, 62,* 49–54.

Lee, M. (2009). A path analysis on elder abuse by family caregivers: Applying the ABCX Model. *Journal of Family Violence, 24,* 1–9.

Le Poire, B. A. (1992). Does the codependent encourage substance dependent behavior? Paradoxical injunctions in the codependent relationship. *The International Journal of Addiction, 27,* 1465–1474.

Le Poire, B. A., (1995). Inconsistent nurturing as control theory: Implications for communication-based research and treatment programs. *Journal of Applied Communication Research, 23,* 1–15.

Le Poire, B. A. (2004). The influence of drugs and alcohol on family communication: The effects that substance abuse has on family members and the effects that family members have on substance abuse. In A. Vangelisti (Ed.), *Handbook of family communication* (pp. 609–628). Thousand Oaks, CA: Sage.

Le Poire, B. A. (2006). *Family communication: Nurturing and control in a changing world.* Thousand Oaks, CA: Sage.

Le Poire, B. A., & Dailey, R. M. (2006). Inconsistent nurturing as control theory: A new theory in family communication. In D. O. Braithwaite & L. A. Baxter (Eds.), *Engaging theories in family communication: Multiple perspectives* (pp. 82–98). Thousand Oaks, CA: Sage.

McCubbin, H. I., & Patterson, J. M. (1982). Family adaptation to crisis. In H. I. McCubbin, A. E. Cauble, & J. M. Patterson (Eds.), *Family stress, coping, and social support* (pp. 26–47). Springfield, IL: Thomas.

Morse, J. M., & Mitchum, C. (1997). Compathy: The contagion of physical distress. *Journal of Advanced Nursing, 26,* 649–657.

Noller, P., & Fitzpatrick, M. A. (1993). *Communication in family relationships.* Englewood Cliffs, NJ: Prentice-Hall.

Olson, D. H. (1993). Circumplex model of marital and family systems: Assessing family functioning. In F. Walsh (Ed.), *The family on the threshold of the 21st century: Trends and implications* (pp. 259–280). Mahwah, NJ: Erlbaum.

Olson, D. H., Sprenkle, D. H., & Russell, C. S. (1979). Circumplex model of marital and family systems: I. Cohesion and adaptability dimensions, family types, and clinical applications. *Family Processes, 18,* 3–28.

Ormondroyd, E., Moynihan, C., Ardern-Jones, A., Eeles, R., Foster, C., Davolls, S., & Watson, M. (2008). Communicating genetics research results to families: Problems arising when the patient participant is deceased. *Psycho-Oncology, 17,* 804–811.

Parrott, R. (2009). *Talking about health: Why communication matters.* Oxford, England: Wiley-Blackwell.

Pecchioni, L. L., Thompson, T. L., & Anderson, D. J. (2006). Interrelations between family and health communication. In L. H. Turner & R. West (Eds.), *The family communication sourcebook* (pp. 447–468). Thousand Oaks, CA: Sage.

Pennebaker, J. W. (1990). *Opening up: The healing power of confiding in others.* New York: Morrow.

Petronio, S. (1991). Communication boundary management: A theoretical model of managing disclosure of private information between married couples. *Communication Theory, 1,* 311–335.

Petronio, S. (2000). *Balancing the secrets in private disclosures.* Mahwah, NJ: Erlbaum.

Petronio, S. (2002). *Boundaries of privacy: Dialectics of disclosures.* Albany, NY: SUNY Press.

Prescott, M., & Le Poire, B. (2002). Eating disorders and mother–daughter communication: A test of inconsistent nurturing as control theory. *Journal of Family Communication, 2,* 59–78.

Rowe, P. (2003). Why is rickets resurgent in the USA? *The Lancet, 357,* 1100.

Sandelowski, M., & Jones, L. C. (1986). Social exchanges of infertile women. *Mental Health Nursing, 8,* 173–189.

Segrin, C., & Flora, J. (2005). *Family communication.* Mahwah, NJ: Erlbaum.

Stuart, M., & McGrew, J. H. (2009). Caregiver burden after receiving a diagnosis of an autism spectrum disorder. *Research in Autism Spectrum Disorders, 3,* 86–97.

Thomas, V., & Striegel, P. (1995). Stress and grief of a perinatal loss—Integrating qualitative and quantitative methods. *Omega: Journal of Death and Dying, 30,* 299–311.

U.S. Department of Health & Human Services. (2009). *Health Insurance Portability and Accountability Act (HIPAA) Privacy Rule.* Retrieved from http://www.hhs.gov/ocr/privacy/hipaa/administrative/privacyrule/index.html

Waldron, V. R., & Kelley, D. L. (2008). *Communicating forgiveness.* Thousand Oaks, CA: Sage.

24

EVERYDAY INTERPERSONAL COMMUNICATION AND HEALTH

Rebecca J. Welch Cline

Health communication, as an area of theory, research, and practice, focuses on the relationships between communication and health, health beliefs, and health and risk behavior. Health communication research has focused more on formal than informal contexts and on planned than incidental or everyday messages. When investigating informal contexts and everyday messages, researchers have attended more to mass than to interpersonal communication. The purpose of this chapter is to address the "missing box," the role of everyday interpersonal interaction as an arena of health communication. The chapter presents a rationale and a social influence framework for exploring everyday interpersonal communication and health. A review of the literature on various roles of everyday interpersonal communication and HIV/AIDS clarifies the potentially powerful and often neglected influence of everyday interaction on health and provides road signs for future research and practice.

Rationale for Exploring Everyday Interpersonal Communication and Health

A cursory overview of the status of health communication scholarship identifies patterns of phenomena that researchers have addressed and neglected. Initial explorations yield glimpses of the role of everyday interpersonal communication and health and hint at the possibilities.

Status of Health Communication Scholarship

Communication increasingly is recognized as a significant factor in health care and promotion. Health communication has become a vital part of national public health efforts (e.g., Office of Disease Prevention and Health Promotion, 2009). However, a critical look at the field points simultaneously to limitations and directions for future research.

Health communication emphasizes some phenomena to the neglect of others. From a systemic perspective, health communication occurs in both formal and informal everyday contexts; however, formal contexts have been studied to the relative neglect of informal contexts. Large bodies of research address formal interpersonal contexts (most frequently physician–patient interaction; see, e.g., Roter & Hall, this volume). Similarly large bodies of research address formal attempts to change the public's health behavior via health communication campaigns, with substantially more focus on the role of mass media than on interpersonal communication, although researchers agree that interpersonal communication plays a powerful role in changing health behavior and is requisite to campaign success (see, e.g., Silk, Atkin, & Salmon, this volume).

When health communication scholars *have* addressed the roles of everyday informal communication and incidental messages in influencing health, they have attended more to mass than interpersonal communication, particularly the roles of television (see, e.g., Kline this volume), news, and advertising of health-related products (e.g., prescription drugs; see DeLorme, Huh, Reid, & An, this volume) with less attention to incidental health messages in other forms of popular culture (e.g., advertising of non-health products, such as alcohol and tobacco; movies; billboards; magazines; and musical lyrics).

When health communication is construed as occurring in a matrix of *formal and informal communication contexts* in which *planned and incidental everyday messages* abound, in both *mediated and interpersonal forms,* everyday interpersonal communication emerges as "the neglected box." When addressed, this topic often has been explored in fragments.

Glimpses of the Role of Everyday Interpersonal Communication in Health

A wide array of illustrations, cutting across numerous health and disease contexts, provides glimpses of the significance of everyday interpersonal interaction in health. Just "plain talk" has health-related functions (Lynch, 1985). Simply talking changes one's heart function, raising blood pressure, with more emotional talk having a relatively greater effect. Risk-taking behavior (e.g., taking drugs, drinking) may influence interpersonal communication. Drinking alcohol affects verbal and nonverbal behavior in ways that both facilitate and disrupt interpersonal interaction.

Everyday interaction plays a significant role in labeling illness. Research on mass psychogenic illness indicates that people can become ill by suggestion or due to social factors (see, e.g., Lorber, Mazzoni, & Kirsch, 2007). In fact, deciding whether one is "ill," and the timing of that labeling, often are influenced by social interaction.

Everyday social networks disseminate health information. For example, health is a commonly observed conversational topic in beauty salons. Conversely, everyday social networks may reinforce risk-taking behavior as a social norm.

One commonly investigated phenomenon of everyday interpersonal communication with implications for health is helpful and unhelpful communication. Typically studied under the rubric of "social support" (see Goldsmith & Albrecht, this volume), this area focuses on the functions of everyday interaction in helping people manage uncertainties.

Ironically, communication with those closest to us sometimes *endangers* well-being. Much adolescent risk-taking may be attributed to peer influence. In social contexts, communication can function to recruit others to engage in risky behavior, such as smoking or drug use *and* to resist recruitment. Although explanations of adolescent risk-taking tend to focus on peer influence, research also indicts family communication as sometimes risk-promoting.

Understanding that everyday interpersonal communication plays a significant role in teens' risk behavior, health educators and public health professionals created interpersonal skills interventions for teens. Such typical public health advice often fails to address how they can negotiate multiple goals in the context of a social situation without violating social norms. Indeed, the diverse though scant literature on the role of everyday interpersonal communication in health reinforces the primacy of identity and relational goals over instrumental goals. For example, adolescents who smoke regularly use smoking to forge new identities and to meet new friends. In refusal situations, although adolescents may be able to "just say no" to strangers, doing so with friends and acquaintances is unlikely. Thus, identity and relational goals tend to compete with health-related instrumental goals.

In summary, everyday interpersonal talk plays a significant role in health. Influences of everyday communication on health: (a) are anchored more in the social reality and social norms of participants than in health knowledge, health information, and traditionally defined health beliefs and behaviors; (b) are embedded in social situations that can be understood only through the realities of the participants; (c) may be positive or negative; and (d) may be planned or incidental. Taken as a whole, this potpourri points to social influence as a framework for the organizing and understanding of health-related roles of everyday interpersonal communication.

Everyday Interpersonal Communication and Health as a Matter of Social Influence

Historically, social psychological and communication approaches to social influence would not have included the study of everyday interpersonal communication vis-à-vis health-related outcomes. However, over time, social influence evolved to include the role of "everyday" interpersonal communication (Cline, 2003).

Contemporary Social Influence Theory

Contemporary social influence theory focuses on the social realities of participants with implications for understanding social influence messages and meanings from their viewpoint. Social psychologists contributed a focus on "social reality" and social norms. Communication scholars offered the significance of *messages, meanings*, and a *transactional* perspective as they moved from an emphasis on persuasion to social influence. That transition shifted focus from persuading the public to interpersonal compliance-gaining, and from there to recognizing that (a) social influence does not require intention or conscious awareness; in fact, much social influence may involve "mindless" communication; and (b) the multifunctionality of communication. Clark and Delia (1979) identified three kinds of objectives that are explicitly or implicitly embedded in every communicative transaction: (a) instrumental objectives, involving completing a task, (b) identity objectives, related to managing self-presentation and facilitating the other's identity management, and (c) interpersonal objectives that involve establishing or maintaining a relationship. Historically, instrumental or task-oriented goals received greatest attention, while identity and relational objectives received scant attention.

Social Reality and Social Norms: The Basis for Everyday Interaction

The concepts of socially constructed reality and social norms are central to understanding social influence. As both products of and templates for everyday interpersonal interaction, socially constructed realities provide blueprints for formulating meaning and guiding behavior.

The Social Construction of Reality.   Berger and Luckmann (1966) cast everyday interaction as significant in creating a "shared reality." "Everyday knowledge," or what "everyone knows," flows from continuously validating everyday interaction that creates "intersubjective" realities. Socially constructed realities are so unconsciously and continuously reinforced that they come to be experienced as "objective." Socially constructed realities become the template for human behavior. Reality hardened by intersubjectivity makes "evident" what is "real" and, in turn, "appropriate" behavioral responses. That sense of "appropriateness" constitutes what we term "social norms." Thus, everyday talk and everyday language play powerful roles in constructing realities and social norms for operating within those realities.

The Centrality of Language.   The only means for "knowing" anything is through experience and all experience is mediated through language. From a health perspective, social interaction provides the basis for the "reality" and "meanings" of such basic concepts as "health," "illness," "disease," and "risk." Within social contextual boundaries (whether family, peer group, or culture), social interaction yields social norms regarding the meaning of and reactions to specific health states and diseases. Language surrounding a particular disease not only labels it, but also frames the disease in larger perspectives and builds relationships with other concepts, yielding networks of meaning.

Meanings We Live By: Metaphors as Behavioral Blueprints.   "Metaphor is pervasive in everyday life" (Lakoff & Johnson, 1980, p. 3). In everyday talk, we constantly refer to one thing in terms of another; what we know about the second phenomenon provides some understanding of the first. The power of language rests in its metaphoric nature; we do not process symbols as discrete phenomena, rather we use symbols in patterns, invoking whole *systems of meanings* beyond apparent referents. Thus, a single word can come to stand for a fully developed metaphoric blueprint for the situational reality and serve as a model to guide human action.

The Meanings of Everyday Interaction vis-à-vis Health

Traditional approaches to social influence focused on intentional phenomena and instrumental goals to the exclusion of other sometimes competing goals. A contemporary perspective on the reviewed glimpses of everyday interpersonal health communication indicates that health-influencing messages are not necessarily (nor even likely) to be *intended* to influence health nor to contain explicit health content. Messages and meanings that lead to health outcomes often have little to do with health content in actors' minds. From a *public health* perspective, instrumental goals are primary (i.e., changing health behaviors). Thus, a teen offering another teen a cigarette is understood as recruiting risk-taking; the outcome is understood in terms of enhanced or diminished risks to health. However, from the *participants'* perspective, offering a cigarette may symbolize friendliness and sharing. To understand the functions of everyday interpersonal communication in health, researchers need to expand the frames of meaning for investigation to include identity and relational management.

Everyday Interpersonal Communication in the HIV/AIDS Epidemic

Understanding the roles of everyday interpersonal communication in health may help to discover points of intervention and to develop efficacious strategies for health-promoting and disease-preventing social influence. HIV/AIDS provides a territory for exploring those roles.

HIV/AIDS as a Territory for Exploring Everyday Interpersonal Communication and Health

In the past 25 years, no disease has captured the American public's attention more than HIV/AIDS. By virtue of its magnitude and the tentacles of its meanings, HIV/AIDS emerged as the number one health problem in the public's mind and the most stigmatizing disease in contemporary times (see, e.g., Smith, this volume). The more than 1,030,832 cases diagnosed and 562,793 deaths attributable to AIDS in the United States by the end of 2007 (Centers for Disease Control and Prevention [CDC], 2009) are only suggestive of impact. The magnitude of impact includes health care costs and social, psychological, relational, and economic effects on partners, family, friends, coworkers, neighbors, schoolmates, and health care providers. From early in the epidemic, the disease was associated with an array of social and health problems and marginalized populations. The tapestry of meanings of HIV/AIDS was woven with the threads of drug use, unwanted and teen pregnancy, other sexually transmitted diseases, and violence. Gay men, prostitutes, drug-users, ethnic minorities, and the poor dominated the HIV-population constructed in the public's mind.

Over time, HIV/AIDS emerged as an interpersonal epidemic both in etiology and social impact. HIV infection occurs most often in interpersonal if not intimate contexts (sexual encounters, needle-sharing, maternal care). Prevention messages were quickly framed as interpersonal advisories: "know your partner," "negotiate condom use," and "don't share needles." Interpersonal dilemmas driven by stigma characterize experiences associated with the disease, as HIV/AIDS became defined as a disease of "us" versus "them," (the other). As more effective highly active antiretroviral therapy (HAART) emerged, HIV/AIDS became understood as a chronic disease and—with this new meaning—public attention (e.g., news coverage) diminished, despite continued growth of the epidemic. However, many previous social dynamics remained.

The social reality and resultant consequences of HIV/AIDS grew directly from the meaning-laden nature of the disease. With reactions driven more forcefully by schema associated with AIDS than by biomedical/clinical information, AIDS became "one of the most meaning-laden of diseases" (Sontag, 1990, pp. 179–180). Thus, HIV/AIDS, in its inseparable health and social contexts, offers a window into understanding the significance and varied roles of everyday interpersonal communication in health and risk contexts.

The Social Construction of HIV/AIDS

The social construction of HIV/AIDS is both a product and process of everyday talk. The social construction emerging from everyday talk provides a framework of meaning that, in turn, drives everyday interaction associated with the disease.

The Socially Constructed Identity of AIDS. The course of the development of the AIDS epidemic in the United States, and responses to it by both the public and policy makers, contributed to a socially constructed identity in which the disease has both gender and sexual orientation. Historical accounts of how the epidemic was reported both in epidemiological and social circles clarify how AIDS came to be "a gay man's disease" in everyday vocabulary (see, e.g., Kinsella, 1989; Shilts, 1987).

Despite the fact that officials at the Centers for Disease Control and Prevention thought they were alerting the public via routine reporting channels (i.e., the *Morbidity and Mortality Weekly Report* [MMWR]) about early and as yet unlabeled cases of AIDS, both health and news professionals ignored the emerging epidemic due to its association with gay men. Press response to the first AIDS-related *MMWR* (CDC, 1981, June) was nominal (Kinsella, 1989). By late 1981, *MMWR* had run several articles on what the CDC termed the "epidemic of immunosuppression" (Kinsella, 1989, p. 15), with little resulting media attention. Thus, early in the epidemic, AIDS was virtually ignored in the news media, and therefore was largely unknowable by the public.

Much early news coverage proved harmful by reflecting a polarity of realities, ranging from anyone can get AIDS and easily, to only gay men are at risk. Neither reality was helpful in constructing health risks for the public. The competing realities contributed to unnecessary panic and fear or to a glib "not me" reality. At the same time, what could have been helpful information to the public was missing. Notably absent was "any guidance concerning action the public could take to avoid transmission of the virus" (Roth, 1990, p. 7). The process of labeling the disease went hand-in-hand with news coverage (and its absence) in developing and hardening a reality in which the disease was delimited by gender and sexual orientation. That social construction permitted denial of vulnerability among every other population.

The Language of AIDS: Labeling an Emerging Epidemic, an Epidemic of Labels. Early labels explicitly associated AIDS with gay men. Additional dysfunctional language emerged that reinforced moral judgments and interfered with rational understanding of risk and efficacious approaches to prevention.

Among the terms that emerged for AIDS by 1982 were "gay cancer," "gay pneumonia," "the gay plague," and WOGS (wrath of God syndrome). Doctors unofficially used terms like ACIDS (acquired *community* immune deficiency syndrome), and CAIDS (*community* acquired immune deficiency syndrome); the first official label was GRID (gay-related infectious disease). These labels focused attention on "communities" or groups of people and posed AIDS as a "gay disease." This "group" identity functioned to define AIDS as a disease of "others." Such labels shifted public attention and everyday discourse away from the causes of the disease and risk-taking behaviors, to attention on "*who* has the disease." The public came to accept and use language that cast judgment on people with the disease; the *infected people* rather than the *risk behaviors* emerged as *what was to be avoided*.

Additional dysfunctional language surrounding AIDS interfered with understanding risk and efficacious prevention (Shilts, 1987). Use of the term "bodily fluids" to summarize routes of disease transmission, functioned to avoid explicit language (e.g., "semen," "vaginal fluids") in public discourse but implied that AIDS could be contracted through casual household contact (e.g., via tears or sweat). Use of the term "exposed to the virus," to explain a positive HIV test, simultaneously hid the reality that having the antibodies meant having the virus and fed the myth of HIV as airborne.

Failure to use explicit language played a significant role in failing to provide clear prevention guidelines to the public once modes of transmission were identified. Unwillingness to use terms like "penis," "vagina," "condom," and "anal intercourse" disallowed clear public discourse that influences private behavior. For example, *The New York Times* failed to print the word "penis" until the 1993 Bobbitt case. Network television refused to air condom advertising. Debates about using the word "condom," condom advertising, and teaching condom use as prevention contributed to a social construction in which "condoms" themselves came to have stigmatizing moral overtones in everyday interpersonal contexts.

Metaphors of AIDS: An Emerging Epidemic of Meaning. Metaphors provide conceptual maps for thinking about diseases. Each identifies the role of the infected person and implies a prototype of responses both to the disease and the infected.

Sontag (1978) analyzed metaphors of cancer and uncovered patterns of language in which cancer was associated with punishment, energy, warfare, death, and pollution. AIDS provided a yet more stigmatizing disease. With the early identification of Kaposi's sarcoma as an indicator, AIDS took on metaphors of cancer and more. The emerging metaphors functioned to polarize concepts and people, and to stereotype both the disease and the infected. Metaphors of AIDS so commonplace as to be invisible to the everyday person include associations with: war/military, pollution, plague, crime, and otherness/civic divisiveness (Sontag, 1990; see Cline, 2003). In turn, these metaphors further stigmatized people with HIV disease as the enemy, pollutants, sinners, criminals, and the socially and morally distanced "them." These metaphors abound in the everyday language of the public at large, health care professionals, and public figures, with significant implications for everyday interaction.

How Everyday Meanings and Communication "Direct" Behavior

A major premise of the present analysis is that human beings act in accordance with meanings associated with message-affiliated behaviors and anticipated interpretations of those actions by others. Thus, understanding the array of meanings associated with HIV risk-taking behavior is necessary to predicting and influencing those behaviors.

The Tapestry of Meanings of HIV Risk-Taking Behaviors. Meanings associated with HIV-risk behavior are embedded in a larger array of messages and meanings associated with sexuality and drug use. Those messages and meanings hold clues for why risks are taken and efficacious prevention behaviors are avoided.

The Meanings of Unsafe Sex. Public health officials tend to see sexuality in terms of risk. The term "unsafe sex" (sex without a condom) mirrors that perspective. But from participants' perspectives, "unsafe sex" is replete with identity and relational meanings, and thus with risk avoidance meanings.

Identity Meanings. Sexual choices, including unsafe sex, function to define the self. Among the identity-related meanings associated with unsafe sex are: (a) a dialectic of invincibility (e.g., East, Jackson, O'Brien, & Peters, 2007) and fatalism, (b) judgments of unhealthiness or "uncleanness" (Masaro, Dahinten, Johnson, Ogilvie, & Patrick, 2008), (c) trustworthiness, (d) ability to judge a partner's safety (e.g., Downing-Matibag & Geisinger, 2009), (e) judgments of gender appropriateness for women (e.g., Bell, 2009) and machismo for men, (f) disconnectedness with one's ethnic community, (g) personal conservatism, (h) embarrassment (Bell, 2009), (i) rebelliousness or liberation among gay men, and (j) dissatisfaction with body image. Engaging in unsafe sex also is associated with being "out of control" due to "the heat of the moment" (Downing-Matibag & Geisinger, 2009). This attribution functions to buffer identity by absolving the actor of responsibility.

Relational Meanings. Sexuality invokes relational meanings in terms of both affiliation and control. Affiliative meanings commonly associated with sexual intercourse in Western culture include connectedness, emotional involvement, commitment, love, caring, romance, intimacy, and trust. Women, more than men, associate intercourse with romantic love (e.g., East et al., 2007). In the typical scenario, women prefer condom use; men resist. Having unsafe sex is seen as more affiliative than using a condom, an indicator of love, loyalty, honesty, and trust (e.g., Downing-Matibag & Geisinger, 2009), attributes generally valued more by women than men. For people who are HIV-infected, having unsafe sex may signify acceptance. "'Having a relationship' is protection" emerges as a theme in research. For both gay men and heterosexual couples (East et al., 2007), having unsafe sex may be taken as evidence of emotional connectedness and that emotional connectedness may be taken as evidence of the "safety" of having unsafe sex. For people who are HIV-infected, having unsafe sex may signify acceptance as "normal" (i.e., absent stigma).

Engaging in sex also can be understood in terms of relational control. Concepts associated with sex as relational control include sex as power or conquest. In this context, having sex may amount to exerting one's will with a partner. These relational meanings provide the backdrop for understanding risky sexual behavior. Men do not need to negotiate condom use but women do. However, gender-based power imbalances may constrain a woman's ability to negotiate condom use (East et al., 2007). The man who insists on or physically forces unsafe sex not only dominates his partner, he also reinforces his identity as masculine and in control. Women's claims to engage in unsafe sex by mutual consent may shroud the reality of their submission; these accounts, often after a woman planned to use a condom, permit denial of relational powerlessness and dependence.

In summary, identity and relational meanings may largely account for decisions not to use a condom. These meanings also help to explain HIV risk-taking behavior in other contexts.

The Meanings of Prostitution. As a matter of *public health*, prostitution is replete with meanings of risk. However, *participants'* meanings are symbolic worlds away. For sex workers, intercourse represents a business transaction. Sex represents money and unsafe sex may represent more money when preferred by clients (e.g., Gysels, Pool, & Nnalusiba, 2002). For a client, having sex with a prostitute may mean easy access, lack of emotional involvement, and company, fun, or variety.

Despite the socially constructed association of AIDS with prostitution, in the United States sex workers are more likely to use condoms with clients than in personal relationships (i.e., boyfriends). Accounts of both male and female sex workers portray the meanings of unsafe sex in dramatically different terms, depending on the meaning of the encounter. Although condom use may be mandated or at least desirable for work, it is not expected in personal relationships where engaging in unsafe sex signifies familiarity and trust. Unsafe sex with clients is associated with urgency to earn money (Gysels et al., 2002) and loss of relational control (i.e., lack of bargaining power, fear of violence).

In summary, the meanings of behavior in sex work can be explained better in terms of identity and relational meanings than risk. Sex workers tend to use condoms when engaging in what they construe as "not real sex" and not to use them for "real sex," where they see themselves as "protected by relationships."

The Meanings of IV Drug Use and Sharing Works. In terms of public health, sharing needles for IV drug use represents a major risk for HIV infection. But for intravenous drug users (IVDUs) relational meanings tend to dominate drug use. Drug use symbolizes an array of positive interpersonal phenomena including the romantic initiation, social bonding, and shared instrumental goals. In this context, needle sharing is associated with close and emotionally supportive relationships.

Availability of sterile equipment is the greatest factor that influences sharing of injecting equipment (Des Jarlais & Semaan, 2008). However, sharing needles has significant social meanings, including giving and reciprocity. For example, the process of one IVDU injecting another may be a ritual associated with emotional bonding. Not surprisingly, then, research has clarified that IVDUs do not share needles randomly nor indiscriminately. Instead, they are more likely to share needles if they have large social networks, or if their closest friends and sexual partners are IVDUs. Both men and women are more likely to share needles with partners who have provided emotional support, have injected them or who they injected, and with whom they have had sex. This selectivity may be based on the perception that people they know better are at lesser risk for HIV.

Needle sharing also may be associated with relational control. Younger IVDUs dependent on partners for drugs or injection equipment may not feel empowered to insist on clean needles. Women who are dependent on male partners for instrumental support (money, housing, physical protection) may be similarly disempowered.

Clearly, interpersonal relationships play a significant role in drug use behaviors. Understanding the social context, social norms, and meanings associated with drug practice can inform HIV prevention efforts.

The Tapestry of Meanings of HIV Prevention. The federal government was slow to respond to the AIDS epidemic. Five years into the epidemic the U.S. Surgeon General (1986) released a 35-page report that served as the primary source for AIDS prevention messages. Two primary messages advised the public about interpersonal communication for the purpose of AIDS prevention. Stated in ambiguous terms ("know with absolute certainty, that neither you nor your sexual partner is carrying the virus of AIDS," or "you must use protective behavior," p. 16), they were widely disseminated as: "know your partner" and "negotiate safe sex." Both messages are problematic in interpretation and practice.

"Know Your Partner" as Prevention Advice: The Meanings and Practice of "Safe Sex Talk." The message to "know your partner" was translated to mean that sexual partners should talk openly for the purposes of AIDS prevention. Partners were advised to disclose their sexual histories and past risk behaviors and to discuss certain intimate topics (monogamy, condom use). Substantial evidence supports wide dissemination and practice of the advice (e.g., Cline, Johnson, & Freeman, 1992).

Unfortunately, both the logic and interpretation of the advice to talk to a partner as a means of risk reduction can be indicted. The advice to use "talk-as-prevention" can be critiqued as follows: no amount of talk, unless it leads to condom use, constitutes efficacious HIV risk reduction. Not only is this advice simply inefficacious, the advice is potentially dangerous.

Difficulty of Implementation. Talking with a partner for the purpose of AIDS prevention poses several challenges: (a) the high level of communication skills required to simultaneously manage health, identity, and relational goals; (b) violating relational norms by discussing taboo topics; (c) managing competing frames of discourse (romantic versus clinical, trust versus distrust); (d) managing identity goals while implicitly questioning a partner's character; and (e) not knowing a partner well enough to engage in intimate talk (Cline et al., 1992). The challenges are so daunting that talking about AIDS prevention in efficacious ways may be ineffable.

The Logic of Talk as Risk-Assessment. A second criticism involves the efficacy of talk as prevention. The advice to "know your partner" fosters belief in the efficacy of personal judgment as risk assessment. Few people perceive that they "do not know" their partners; "knowing" may mean identifying by name, being acquainted, or having made judgments based on superficial information. Those who attempt talk for risk assessment are stymied by two factors: (a) a partner cannot know reliably the risk behaviors of his or her previous partners or the partners of those partners (i.e., the sexual family tree), and (b) the potential for partner deception.

Competing Goals: Managing Images and Relationships. To the extent that "talk" leads to condom use, talk is a worthwhile prevention effort. However, talking in order to use condoms is relatively unlikely as that advice simultaneously jeopardizes identity and relational goals. The most dominant reasons for "not talking" to a partner about AIDS, even though desiring to do so, reflect struggles with identity and relational management.

Practicing the advice may jeopardize partners' identity management or identity management may jeopardize prevention. Individuals are likely to see themselves as wise or credit themselves with being "careful" or "selective." Following this logic, partners may substitute personal perceptions for talk, or if talk occurs, substitute conversation for condom use. A potential sexual partner may reason, "If he talks about intimate topics, he must be honest"; that "honesty" can be extended to additional character judgments, including low disease risk, and obviate the need for condoms. In either case, no efficacious risk reduction occurs. At worst, the advice is dangerous when it becomes a substitute for condom use.

Meanings associated with AIDS-prevention talk may jeopardize the relationship or relational meanings may jeopardize talk. A desire to talk suggests lack of trust; in turn, partners may reason, "If I trust you, I don't have to ask." Ironically, the perception of having a "trusting relationship" may be construed as evidence of "safety" and preclude engaging in safe sex talk.

"Know Your Partner" Research. Numerous findings argue that attempts to practice the "know your partner" advice are associated with increased reliance on personal judgment and decreased probability of condom use, and, thus, ultimately with greater risk. Evidence of assessing risk intuitively, by appearance and conversation, and thereby precluding the need to actually talk about using condoms includes: judging "known partners" as "safe"; judging risk by observing personal attributes (e.g., social circles, appearance, and attire); liking (e.g., Masaro et al., 2008); perceived monogamy; perceiving being in a loving and caring relationship (e.g., Masaro et al., 2008); perceiving the *possibility* of a long-term relationship; and invoking trust.

Evidence indicates that conversation specifically about condoms increases the probability of their use in certain limited circumstances, particularly via "bullying" strategies, in uncommitted relationships, and for contraceptive purposes. Some evidence indicates that communication specifically about a partner's sexual history or condom use is related to safer behavior (Noar, Morokoff, & Harlow, 2004). However, the "know your partner" advice focused on *talk* as *prevention*. Rather than specifying that partners should use conversation in order to insist on condom use, the advice implied that *conversation itself* might be the endpoint in the prevention process. Relatively little research has systematically examined the nature of *actual attempts* to influence partners to use condoms (see Noar et al., 2004 as an exception).

In summary, by advocating conversation as prevention, the advice to "know your partner" may inadvertently reinforce the view that being in a relationship is protective. The end result is that the advice likely has done more harm than good.

Condom Use and Meanings, The second interpersonal message was to "negotiate safe sex" or "negotiate condom use." A wealth of evidence suggests limited condom use in most populations, with identity and relational meanings as major prohibiting factors.

Evidence Regarding Condom Use. Although people are knowledgeable about condoms' efficacy, most do not use condoms. Among those most likely to use condoms are sex workers with their clients and serodiscordant couples. About 20% of U.S. adults aged 18 and older report using condoms at last intercourse, although the rate is lower for "ongoing relationships" than for "other partners" (Andersen, 2003). Condom use is low among adolescents and use declines with age. Condom use is low among college students, despite most having multiple partners. Condom use is low among heterosexual adults (aged 18 and older) regardless of gender and ethnicity; rates of never using condoms typically exceed those of college students. Further, studies of varied populations show that as numbers of partners increase, condom use decreases.

Meanings Associated with Condoms. Because condom use occurs in dyadic contexts, behavior is fraught with identity and relational meanings. Substantial evidence indicates that condoms are condemned and avoided by both men and women for psycho-physical reasons (issues of pleasure, spontaneity, and comfort; e.g., Bauman & Berman, 2005). However, identity and relational reasons may be even stronger deterrents.

Risks to Identity. Meanings commonly associated with condoms pose threats to identity. Jeopardy is attached to procuring, carrying, and using condoms. Both young males and females are embarrassed by buying condoms. Women report greater embarrassment than men in buying (e.g., Bell, 2009) and carrying condoms (e.g., Marston & King, 2006), although often men are more embarrassed to use them (Cline & McKenzie, 1994).

Gender norms pose a double standard in which being sexual is positive for men and negative for women. Men are dominant and sexually active; sexual intercourse is sometimes understood as conquest and an indicator of manliness. In contrast, women often are expected to be passive and chaste. To buy, carry, or suggest using condoms may challenge a woman's reputation or denote lack of sexual innocence (Frankel & Curtis, 2008); mark her as sexually active (Marston & King, 2006) or promiscuous; result in stigma associated with casual sex, promiscuity, and infidelity (Frankel & Curtis, 2008); and jeopardize cultural (Marin & Marin, 1992) as well as gender identity (e.g., East et al., 2007).

Suggesting condom use may jeopardize one's *own* character. A person may fear being seen as having poor judgment, being unwise, careless, diseased, sexually active, promiscuous (Marston & King, 2006); or having cheated or being untrustworthy or unfaithful (e.g., Bralock & Koniak-Griffin, 2009); or being labeled homosexual or bisexual, a drug user, or a prostitute. Similarly, proposing condom use may threaten a *partner's* character by calling into question the partner's honesty (e.g., Khan, Hudson-Rodd, Saffers, Bhuiyan, & Bhuiya, 2004), fidelity, trustworthiness, faithfulness (East et al., 2007), or implying the partner is at high risk for an STD. These meanings are enough to motivate condom avoidance.

The power of identity meanings in the context of relating is clear: many people fear risk of rejection more than they fear STDs (e.g., Bralock & Koniak-Griffin, 2009). More than simple rejection, to use or suggest the use of condoms is potentially stigmatizing (Marston & King, 2006). Because relational meanings are so closely associated with identity meanings, they, too, often result in condom avoidance.

Relational Meanings of Condoms. Meanings commonly associated with condoms pose significant relational threats. In fact, condoms evoke images that defy relational well-being.

Condoms represent a relational barometer: not using a condom becomes a tangible indicator of intimacy, trust, and the developmental stage of a relationship. Using a condom signifies relational distance, questionable trust, limited commitment, or an early stage of a relationship.

Condoms often are associated with one-night stands and casual sex (e.g., Frankel & Curtis, 2008). They signify suspicion (Khan et al., 2004) and mistrust (East et al., 2005). Condoms are associated with the lack of relational involvement—the absence of love, trust, intimacy, and commitment. They are, in fact, relatively more likely to be used as contraception among the young (East et al., 2007), in short-term relationships, in casual rather than steady relationships, and with lovers rather than husbands (East et al., 2005). Because condoms symbolize extra-relational activity, partners may avoid their use in order to sustain positive relational values (East et al., 2005). In short, condoms are equated with lack of relational connectedness.

Condoms also are associated with relational control. Women's ability to effect condom use with a male partner requires interpersonal empowerment (Soet, Dudley, & DiIorio, 1999). Women who report being in male-dominated relationships exhibit less confidence in their abilities to negotiate condom use and report fearing the negative consequences of attempts to do so (Soet et al., 1999). In contrast, women with high levels of relational power are far more likely than those with low power to report consistent condom use. Due to the power differential in many heterosexual relationships, women often are ill-equipped to negotiate condom use (e.g., East et al., 2007). Beyond losing prized relational values (e.g., commitment, and trust), women may fear relational control costs (e.g., anger, emotional and physical abuse). Women often cite partners' dislike of condoms to justify not using them. Given that men tend to be more negative about condoms' meanings than women (e.g., Cline & McKenzie, 1994) and in greater control, condom use is improbable among unequal partners (East et al., 2007). Many women at highest risk have little or no bargaining power, as they rely on partners for money, drugs, food, or housing. Women may be more likely to perceive risk and desire to use condoms, but men are likely to hold greater relational control. In such cases, condom use requires the submission of the man to a woman's request.

In summary, the meanings and practice of the "negotiate safe sex" or "negotiate condom use" advice are daunting. Condoms, associated with safety from a public health perspective, have become equated with risks to identities and relationships in the minds of participants.

The Meanings of an HIV Test. From a public health perspective, the meanings of HIV testing are associated with risk assessment and prevention. Although testing rates have increased dramatically in recent years due to medical advances and policy changes, interpersonal meanings associated with being tested continue to serve as a barrier to universal testing.

Earlier research indicated that people often were tested for interpersonal rather than health or risk-related reasons (Cline, 2003). Testing was sometimes used to negotiate a new relationship (i.e., as evidence of the seriousness of a relationship) or to bring symbolic closure to a terminated relationship. A negative test result often was used to justify not using condoms. Most people driven by these relational meanings assumed that they would test negative. As a result, they often failed to return for test results and tended not to seek follow-up tests despite engaging in recent risky behavior.

Several factors have changed the landscape of HIV testing and *perhaps* some of its meanings. The recognition of efficacious treatment of HIV/AIDS has effectively transformed AIDS from a fatal illness into a chronic disease. That transformation has been accompanied by greater institutional efforts at routine "opt-out" testing as a part of medical care for patients aged 13 to 64 years in all health care settings. "Opt-out" testing preserves the patient's right to decline testing; a patient who does not decline is assumed to assent to the test. Being tested under an "opt-out" versus the previous "opt-in" model may be seen as less stigmatizing (i.e., fewer negative character judgments are made about the person). In addition, the recent development of rapid testing procedures allows a less time-consuming and less distressing process that may have been a barrier to testing. These factors may have changed the very meanings of HIV testing and thereby affected who gets tested and for what reasons.

At the same time, the call for mandatory testing—previously fraught with an array of ethical concerns—has been renewed for some populations (e.g., pregnant women, health care workers). However, patients are generally accepting of routine HIV testing and repeat testing. Likelihood of being tested is associated with: seeking other medical services, including having or testing for other sexually transmitted diseases; females who are pregnant; having engaged in high risk sexual or drug use behavior; awareness of efficacious treatment (Nanin et al., 2009); being symptomatic; and identifying as gay or bisexual.

However, large proportions of people living with HIV remain unaware of their infection. Early diagnosis of HIV disease permits timely clinical intervention and reduces cases of unknowing transmission of HIV to partners. Despite increased testing and greater access to rapid testing, the interpersonal meanings of HIV testing continue to remain a major barrier to more widespread testing in an era when early diagnosis can prolong when and improve the quality of life.

Identity issues continue to serve as barriers to HIV testing. In particular, stigmatizing processes deter HIV testing (Nanin et al., 2009). Belief that a positive HIV test is a death sentence persists despite efficacious treatment (Nanin et al, 2009); thus fear of testing positive deters people from gettingg tested. Some avoid being tested for any sexually transmitted diseases due to embarrassment and fears of being perceived as "loose," "dirty," "stupid," and "irresponsible." Us–them perceptions, homophobia, and the related belief that one is at low risk for HIV infection are barriers to testing (e.g., Nanin et al., 2009). Others believe that they can accurately judge their sexual partners as HIV negative despite the lack of a test.

Little is known about the process of disclosing a positive HIV test result to clients. With changes in policy to include HIV testing as part of routine medical care, people who test HIV positive may be less likely to anticipate a positive diagnosis and less likely to receive their results from a person specifically trained to help them understand and respond to their diagnosis. In fact, the provider's own distress over disclosing the diagnosis may add to the patient's distress. The diagnosed person's longer term adjustment is dependent on the immediate attention of the health care professional to facilitate addressing identity and relational (e.g., disclosing to partners) as well as health concerns.

Managing the Meanings of Having the Disease. A positive HIV test result forever changes how one manages one's life. Despite advances in medical treatment, many people equate AIDS, and thus a positive HIV test, with death (e.g., Nanin et al, 2009). The initial reaction to an HIV diagnosis may include shock, fear, and an overwhelming sense of uncertainty about their disease as well as about others' responses to their disclosure of a diagnosis. And despite advances in medical treatment, the social meanings of HIV disease remain (Scott, 2009), and thus also the dynamics of stigma and resulting discrimination against people with HIV disease persist (Dowshen, Binns, & Garofolo, 2009). In fact, people with HIV disease report stigma as among their most pressing concerns. The interpersonal dynamics of stigma associated with HIV/AIDS cut across gender, ethnic, age, and sexual orientation lines.

The Dilemma of Disclosure. HIV disclosure decisions pose a major dilemma and source of recurring stress. The dilemma emerges immediately upon diagnosis, when people tend to maintain silence. The stressor recurs as the need for social support emerges in coping with the meanings and emotional turmoil of diagnosis and treatment, if not disease progression. The major stressor lies in uncertainty about others' responses to the disclosure. People with HIV disease face the choice of risking stigma or denying themselves opportunities for social support (e.g., Smith, Rossetto, & Petersen, 2008), as the prospects for others' reactions range from wholehearted and unconditional love, acceptance, and support to rejection, condemnation, ostracism, abandonment, or violence. The end result of an HIV diagnosis is enhanced need for social support at the very time that access to that social support likely is jeopardized by disclosing the very reason for its need.

As a result, people with HIV disease face uncertainty about to whom and under what conditions to make disclosures. Social uncertainties include others' judgments about one's identity and character and impact of disclosure on relationships. Perceived stigma is inversely associated with disclosing one's HIV status (Smith et al., 2008). The extent that people with HIV disease experience stigma is negatively correlated with availability and satisfaction with social support. The reasons for engaging in HIV disclosures include identity and relational meanings. For example, being responsible/ethical may result in disclosures to partners (Arnold, Rice, Flannery, & Rotheram-Borus, 2008). Other disclosures may occur in anticipation of gaining social support. However, the social meanings of HIV disease pose significant threats that inhibit the very disclosure that is requisite to obtaining social support. Those meanings also pose threats to physical well-being and access to health care.

Threats of Disclosure: The Social Meanings of Having HIV Disease. Beyond its health impact, being diagnosed HIV positive carries identity and relational meanings. In turn, the interpersonal dynamics surrounding HIV/AIDS have consequences for interpersonal and mental well-being, as well as health care. People with HIV disease fear for their reputations, their relationships, and their very livelihoods.

Identity Meanings. Being stigmatized or rejected is prima facie evidence of failure to achieve identity management goals. The implications of AIDS can be summarized in one word: stigma. The impact of stigma associated with AIDS is multiplied by its associations with an array of stigmatizing features including: terminal illness, IV drug use, promiscuity, prostitution, and disenfranchised populations.

HIV represents a massive attack on one's identity, both internally and externally. People with HIV disease often internalize stigma and experience shame due to their diagnosis, which can pose immediate damage to their self-concept (Dowshen et al., 2009). Psychological consequences of an HIV positive test include psychological distress and poorer mental health status, in general, and depression in particular (e.g., Dowshen et al., 2009). The stigma, associated stress, and resulting depression go beyond people with HIV/AIDS to include their informal caregivers.

Having HIV is the most reputation-damaging diagnosis among sexually transmitted infections. Some people with HIV disease report being seen by others as contaminated ("dirty," "poisoned,"), judged as reckless or irresponsible, and viewed as dying rather than living with a chronic disease. Scott (2009) reports that some women with HIV disease associate HIV/AIDs with death and distinguish between having "just HIV" versus "AIDS," in an effort to construct illness meanings to protect themselves from stigma. Not surprisingly, then, the fear of being stigmatized is a motive for keeping one's diagnosis private.

Maintaining secrecy often is directed toward protecting others as well as one's own identity (Smith et al., 2008). Decisions to not disclose to family members are designed to protect the family's singular and collective identities and to protect them from worry and distress (e.g., Arnold et al., 2008).

Relational Meanings.   In light of the transition of HIV disease from a fatal to a chronic disease, the impact of a diagnosis on interpersonal relationships may be of even greater concern both because those relationships will last longer and they may affect quality of life, social support, and ultimately the quality of care received. As an interpersonal syndrome, people with HIV disease commonly fear and experience relational rejection, betrayal, abandonment, and, at best, uncomfortable interaction. A large number of individuals living with HIV report having experienced rejection from friends, family, church members, service providers, and potential sexual partners. Accounts include refusal to hold hands during prayer and preventing patients from seeing their grandchildren. Perhaps the most devastating relational consequence of having an HIV diagnosis is the impact of stigma on social support. Studies generally find stigma and social support inversely related (e.g., Smith et al., 2008). Not surprising, given the identity and relational meanings of their diagnosis, people with HIV face significant dilemmas about disclosing their health status.

Threats to Lifestyle and Well-Being.   Disclosure of HIV disease endangers physical well-being. What many take for granted, such as spousal and family support, everyday protection by law against discrimination, employment, housing, education, insurance, and access to health care, may be jeopardized (e.g., Arnold et al., 2008). Ironically, the need to engage in disclosure often keeps HIV-infected people away from the services they most need.

Access to Health Care.   As HIV has shifted from a terminal illness to a chronic disease, increasing attention is being paid to factors that influence access to and quality of health care. Stigma is a significant barrier to access to health care among some living with HIV (e.g., IVDUs). But larger issues of access to care loom across the varied populations of people who are living with HIV. Case managers report difficulty in gaining access to non-HIV-related care for their patients. They report refusal of care, being referred elsewhere, future visits being discouraged, and stigmatizing comments. These dynamics may account for why patients are inconsistent in their HIV disclosures to health care professionals (Arnold et al., 2008).

Patients report interactions with health care professionals as awkward. This experience should not be surprising in light of stigmatizing and prejudicial beliefs held by many health care professionals. Actual stigmatizing behaviors by health care professionals reported by American military veterans living with HIV included: nonverbal nonimmediacy and verbal abuse (e.g., anger, blame, ridicule). Some report acts of physical abuse. With regard to health care, participants report use of excessive precautions (e.g., protective gear for conversations not involving procedures), scaring patients ("You're gonna die"), denying care, and ignoring patients in great need or providing substandard care.

Adherence to Treatment. In light of internalized stigma, stigma in personal relationships, and stigmatizing responses in the health care system, perhaps it should not be surprising that lack of adherence to treatment regimens has become a significant issue. In the era of HIV as a disease to be managed, increasing research attention is being paid to adherence issues. Psychosocial factors emerging as playing a role in nonadherence include: stigma; fearing discovery of their disease by friends and family; depression, a factor associated with lack of social support; and the quality of the doctor–patient relationship.

Not coincidentally, the risks associated with disclosing HIV-status reflect the same frames of meaning that drive HIV risk- and prevention-behavior: threats to identities and relationships, physical and functional well-being, and access to and consistent use of health care services. Although the meanings of HIV disease have been influenced by the advent of HAART, studies across developed and developing countries of varied cultures (Marston & King, 2006) show consistently that the stigmatizing meanings of HIV, particularly with regard to identity and relational meanings (e.g., character judgments, condoms' association with absence of trust, social expectations), remain largely unchanged (Marston & King, 2006) and continue to hamper communication about sex in ways that interfere with promoting HIV prevention as well as social justice.

Summary: Interpersonal Messages and Meanings Frame Behavior

Patterns of interpersonal communication in the HIV/AIDS epidemic support four primary conclusions. First, *everyday interpersonal interaction constructs a framework of meaning that functions to direct behavior with regard to AIDS.* The language, labels, and metaphors of AIDS create meanings that reflect and predict interpersonal behavior across many contexts. A reality built on themes of stigmatizing identities and divisiveness in relationships yields social norms that guide risk and prevention behavior and responses to people with HIV/AIDS. Predictably, these behaviors are designed more to avoid character judgments and relational discord than to promote health and supportiveness.

Second, across populations and contexts, across behaviors associated with risk, prevention, and responses to people with HIV disease, *the primary frameworks of meaning that drive participants' behaviors are social rather than health-related.* Actions tend to be framed by meanings associated more with identity and relational management than with health issues. Whatever actions are taken, whether in response to others, in taking risks, in understanding prevention messages, or in managing one's own illness, occur with consistent sensitivity to maintaining positive impressions among peers and partners and positive relationships with significant others. Logically, intervention efforts must be framed in terms of the participants' social objectives rather than solely in terms of public health objectives or likely they will fail; worse, they may encourage enhanced risk-taking.

Third, in the case of AIDS, *most risky behavior and, thus, most of the desired behavior changes, occur in an interpersonal context.* Drug and sexual partners influence risk behavior and their cooperation and participation are necessary to enact prevention behavior. Risk, prevention, and supportive responses occur in dyadic or group contexts; interpersonal transactions rather than personal behavior become the unit of analysis and the point of intervention.

Interventions must account for the transactional nature of the context; unless interventions permit interactants to meet their immediate and longer-term interpersonal goals, they are likely to fail. Worse, ignoring the interpersonal context in which risk-taking occurs will yield ineffective and potentially dangerous prevention messages.

Finally, this review underscores the nature of communication as systemic. Although we get more health and risk messages via everyday interpersonal communication than in clinical settings or in the media, everyday interpersonal communication is further influenced by both discriminating and efficacious health care and media messages (e.g., direct-to-consumer advertising (DTCA) of HIV medications and the diminishing news attention to the epidemic). The development of HAART has had some unintended consequences for the meaning of HIV/AIDS. Some evidence indicates that viewing HIV as chronic rather than fatal may have reduced concern about HIV among both gay men and heterosexual men and women. Knowledge of the efficacy of HAART may be accompanied by a willingness to take greater sexual risks, including among those who are HIV-infected. Being on HAART is not associated with disclosing HIV status to sexual partners. Greater exposure to DTCA of HIV medications also is associated with greater likelihood to engage in unprotected sex.

Everyday Interpersonal Communication and Health: Directions for Future Research and Practice

The present review of everyday interpersonal communication and health makes several arguments regarding future research and practice. First, more systematic and theoretically driven research is needed. The present review provides glimpses of the varied and significant roles interpersonal communication plays every day in health-related outcomes; the case of AIDS illustrates the pervasiveness of those roles across populations and contexts. As a field, we need to attend to the sometimes more difficult-to-capture factors that influence health. We have long known and accepted, in the realm of public health communication campaigns, that interpersonal communication tends to precede behavior change. We have long understood the significance of interpersonal communication in health care transactions for outcomes (e.g., satisfaction, compliance, probability of malpractice suits, and significant medical outcomes). But as a field, we have little attended to the particular dynamics of that interpersonal communication and have little attempted to understand the role of *everyday* interpersonal communication as it influences health and risk behavior. By focusing on messages and meanings from the perspectives of those engaged in symbolic behavior, social influence offers one theoretical framework around which to conduct research.

Second, as researchers in the arena of health, we tend to look at our research topics and questions in a way that overattends to frames of meaning invoked from a public health perspective. That is, we overemphasize the significance of explicit health information and themes of risk in understanding health communication problems. Ironically, as communication scholars, one of the first lessons we likely learned as part of our training was the value of "audience analysis." That lesson is often set aside in health communication research and practice. Instead of attempting to understand messages and meanings from the perspectives of those participating in health-significant interpersonal transactions, we tend to impose frames of meaning that drive public health policy, interventions, and sources of research funding. That is, we tend not only to frame our research questions from the vantage point of instrumental goals and health as communication content, but also our methods and interpretations of results. In so doing, *we enter a different sphere of reality and speak a different language from the one used by the individuals we hope to influence.* As a result, the messages and meanings likely to be most influential in affecting health-related behavior often are ignored. The present review calls for researchers to understand health and risk behaviors in terms of the frames of meaning used in the interpersonal contexts in which the behavior occurs. More specifically, we can begin this shift in perspective by investigating the identity and relational meanings associated with health- and risk-behaviors. In turn, we can build interventions on these messages and meanings.

A warning is in order. Researchers' failure to be finely sensitized to participants' meanings jeopardizes the very validity of our research. For example, the language surrounding HIV everyday talk and mirrored in research that provides the foundation for future prevention efforts remains ambiguous. A study of college students revealed than 59% of respondents did not consider oral–genital contact as "having sex" (Sanders & Reinisch, 1999). Terms such as "promiscuous" and "sleeping around" may be meaningful only when applied to the behavior of *others* and not to one's own behavior. What constitutes being in a committed ("established") relationship may be defined by as few as 21 days among adolescents (Fortenberry, Tu, Harezlak, Katz, & Orr, 2002). "Monogamy" may commonly be used to describe "serial monogamy." And individuals who have had multiple partners of the same sex may self-identify as "heterosexual."

Third, in terms of both research and practice, the implications of understanding the social realities, social norms, messages, and meanings from participants' points of view go beyond effectiveness to issues of ethics. Like health care professionals, health communication specialists ought to adhere to the principles of medical ethics, beginning with "first do no harm." The principle of *nonmaleficence* is not simply the inverse of the principle of *beneficence*. In the name of "doing good," that is, acting with moral certitude, many in the fields of medicine, public health, and health communication risk doing harm. When public health officials design and disseminate messages for the public with more consideration for their political and moral acceptability than how those messages will be interpreted and practiced *within the social realities in which various targeted publics live,* they risk doing more harm than good. In the case of AIDS, the failure to attend to participants' meanings for the message "know your partner," yielded danger. Messages that framed condoms in positive terms (rather than avoiding the word, and, worse, explicitly arguing their inefficacy), and talk, *only to the extent that it related to condom use,* would have been clearer, more internally consistent, and potentially more effective. Instead, the widely disseminated messages appear to have done substantial harm. In a very real sense, as we begin the fourth decade of the epidemic, the solution (many widely disseminated prevention messages) has become the problem. Public health efforts to invoke change essentially often have promoted "more of the same" risky behaviors that promoters intended to prevent.

Finally, implicit in the present review is a plea to pursue an understanding of the significant role that social norms play in behavior; social realities establish the "oughtness" of behavior and interpretations of behavior. As argued here, health communication researchers need to understand the implications of the sources of social norms, their role in interpersonal contexts, and their implications for producing effective behavior change messages. At the same time, planned change messages are only a very small part of the mountain of everyday messages that influence various publics' social norms. The interrelationships between interpersonal and public influences on social norms need to be better understood. Public health officials, educators, religious leaders, community leaders, practitioners, politicians, news representatives, producers of popular culture, and institutional representatives need to understand that their messages also play a key role in establishing and maintaining social norms. Often their messages work against efficacious prevention. For example, rancorous public debate regarding shown-to-be efficacious prevention behaviors (e.g., education regarding condoms and condom use, needle cleaning and exchange programs) serves to *undermine* these practices as social norms. When university administrators debated making condoms available on campus, when news editors refused to use the explicit language needed to clearly identify prevention behaviors, when television networks refused condom advertising, when politicians contended, against prevailing evidence, that education about condoms and cleaning needles promotes drug use and sex, they all played a role in promoting norms that encourage risk and in denying the very social norms that may be most effective as prevention. One avenue of change for health communication specialists is to address the audiences (e.g., agenda setters, opinion leaders, gatekeepers) who have significant power to influence social norms.

References

Andersen, J. E. (2003). Condom use and HIV risk among US adults. *American Journal of Public Health, 93,* 912–914.

Arnold, E. M., Rice, E., Flannery, D., & Rotheram-Borus, M. J. (2008). HIV disclosure among adults living with HIV. *AIDS Care, 20,* 80–92.

Bauman, L. J., & Berman, R. (2005). Adolescent relationships and condom use: Trust love, and commitment. *AIDS and Behavior, 9,* 211–222.

Bell, J. (2009). Why embarrassment inhibits the acquisition and use of condoms: A qualitative approach to understanding risky sexual behavior. *Journal of Adolescence, 32,* 379–391.

Berger, P. L., & Luckmann, T. (1966). *The social construction of reality.* Garden City, NY: Anchor.

Bralock, A., & Koniak-Griffin, D. (2009). What do sexually active adolescent females say about relationship issues? *Journal of Pediatric Nursing, 24,* 131–140.

Centers for Disease Control and Prevention. (1981, June 5). Pneumocystis pneumonia—Los Angeles. *Morbidity and Mortality Weekly Report, 30,* 250–252.

Centers for Disease Control and Prevention. (2009). *HIV/AIDS surveillance report, 2007* (Vol. 19). Atlanta, GA: Department of Health and Human Services, Centers for Disease Control and Prevention. Retrieved from http://www.cdc.gov/hiv/topics/surveillance/resources/reports/#supplemental

Clark, R. A., & Delia, J. D. (1979). *Topoi* and rhetorical competence. *The Quarterly Journal of Speech, 65,* 187–206.

Cline, R. J. W. (2003). Everyday interpersonal communication and health. In T. L. Thompson, A. Dorsey, K. I. Miller, & R. Parrott (Eds.), *Handbook of health communication* (pp. 285–313). Mahwah, NJ: Erlbaum.

Cline, R. J. W., Johnson, S. J., & Freeman, K. E. (1992). Talk among sexual partners about AIDS: Interpersonal communication for risk reduction or risk enhancement? *Health Communication, 4,* 39–56.

Cline, R. J. W., & McKenzie, N. J. (1994). Sex differences in communication and the construction of HIV/AIDS. *Journal of Applied Communication Research, 22,* 322–337.

Des Jarlais, D. C., & Semaan, S. (2008). HIV prevention and infection drug users: The first 25 years and counting. *Psychosomatic Medicine, 70,* 606–611.

Downing-Matibag, T. M., & Geisinger, B. (2009). Hooking up and sexual risk taking among college students: A health belief model perspective. *Qualitative Health Research, 19,* 1196–1209.

Dowshen, N., Binns, H. J., & Garofalo, R. (2009). Experiences of HIV-related stigma among young men who have sex with men. *AIDS Patient Care and STDs, 23,* 371–376.

East, L., Jackson, D., O'Brien, L., & Peters, K. (2007). Use of the male condom by heterosexual adolescents and young people: Literature review. *Journal of Advanced Nursing, 59,* 103–100.

Fortenberry, J. D., Tu, W., Harezlak, J., Katz, B. P., & Orr, D. P. (2002). Condom use as a function of time in new and established adolescent sexual relationships. *American Journal of Public Health, 92,* 211–213.

Frankel, A., & Curtis, D. A. (2008). What's in a purse? Maybe a woman's reputation. *Sex Roles, 59,* 615–622.

Gysals, M., Pool, R., & Nnalusiba, B. (2002). Women who sell sex in a Ugandan trading town: Life histories, survival strategies and risk. *Social Science and Medicine, 54,* 179–192.

Khan, S. I., Hudson-Rodd, N., Saffers, S., Bhuiyan, M. I., & Bhuiya, A. (2004). Safer sex or pleasurable sex? Rethinking condom use in the AIDS era. *Sexual Health, 1,* 217–225.

Kinsella, J. (1989). *Covering the plague: AIDS and the American media.* New Brunswick, NJ: Rutgers University Press.

Lakoff, G., & Johnson, M. (1980). *Metaphors we live by.* Chicago, IL: University of Chicago Press.

Lorber, W., Mazzoni, G., & Kirsch, I. (2007). Illness by suggestion: Expectancy, modeling, and gender in the production of psychosomatic symptoms. *Annals of Behavioral Medicine, 33,* 112–116.

Lynch, J. J. (1985). *The language of the heart: The human body in dialogue.* New York: Basic Books.

Marin, B. V., & Marin, G. (1992). Predictors of condom accessibility among Hispanics in San Francisco. *American Journal of Public Health, 82,* 592–595.

Marston, C., & King, E. (2006). Factors that shape young people's sexual behavior: A systematic review. *Lancet, 368,* 1581–1586.

Masaro, C. L., Dahinten, V. S., Johnson, J., Ogilvie, G., & Patrick, D. M. (2008). Perceptions of sexual risk partner safety. *Sexually Transmitted Diseases, 35,* 566–571.

Nanin, J., Osubu, T., Walker, J., Powell, B., Powell, D., & Parsons, J. (2009). "HIV is still real": Perceptions of HIV testing and HIV prevention among black men who have sex with men in New York City. *American Journal of Men's Health,* 150–164.

Noar, S. M., Morokoff, P. J., & Harlow, L. L. (2004). Condom influence strategies in a community sample of ethnically diverse men and women. *Journal of Applied Social Psychology, 34,* 1730–1751.

Office of Disease Prevention and Health Promotion. (2009, January). *Healthy people 2020: Proposed objectives: Health communication and health IT.* Washington, DC: U.S. Department of Health and Human Services. Retrieved from http://www.healthypeople.gov/HP2020/Objectives/ViewObjective.aspx?Id=285&TopicArea=Health+Communication+and+Health+IT&Objective=HC%2FHIT+HP2020%E2%80%936&TopicAreaId=25

Roth, N. L. (1990, November). *The paradox of silence: Suppressed fantasy themes in Sullivan's first HIV/AIDS speech.* Presented to the annual meeting of the Speech Communication Association, Chicago, IL.

Sanders, S. A., & Reinisch, J. M. (1999). Would you say you "had sex" if …? *Journal of the American Medical Association, 281,* 275–277.

Scott, A. (2009). Illness meanings of AIDS among women with HIV: Merging immunology and experience. *Qualitative Health Research, 19,* 454–465.

Shilts, R. (1987). *And the band played on.* New York: St. Martin's Press.

Smith, R., Rossetto, K., & Peterson, B. L. (2008). A meta-analysis of disclosure of one's HIV-positive status, stigma, and social support. *AIDS Care, 20,* 1266–1275.

Soet, J. E., Dudley, W. N., & DiIorio, C. (1999). The effects of ethnicity and perceived power on women's sexual behavior. *Psychology of Women Quarterly, 23,* 707–723.

Sontag, S. (1978). *Illness as metaphor.* New York: Vintage Books.

Sontag, S. (1990). *Illness as metaphor and AIDS and its metaphors.* New York: Anchor Books.

U.S. Surgeon General. (1986). *Surgeon General's report of acquired immune deficiency syndrome.* Rockville, MD: U.S. Department of Health & Human Services.

SECTION V

[Un]intended Outcomes of Health Communication

25

PATIENT-CENTERED COMMUNICATION DURING COLLABORATIVE DECISION MAKING[1]

Mary Politi and Richard L. Street, Jr.

In June 2008, Joe, a father of three and a highly successful teacher and researcher, received devastating news. He was diagnosed with Stage 4 non-Hodgkin's lymphoma. Dr. Smith, Joe's oncologist, informed Joe that there was only one treatment option for his lymphoma— eight cycles of chemotherapy. Joe learned similar information through his search on the Internet, so he trusted Dr. Smith and began treatment. He suffered moderate to severe side effects, but hoped that the treatment would be successful and would outweigh the temporary discomfort. Joe and Dr. Smith were thrilled to learn that after six chemotherapy treatments, radiographic imaging showed no signs of the tumor.

The joy of this news quickly waned when Dr. Smith announced that he was moving out of state, and that an oncologist named Dr. Jones would continue to monitor Joe's progress. Although the tumor appeared to be in remission, Dr. Smith stated that it would be best to follow through on the final rounds of chemotherapy.

Much to Joe's confusion, in their first meeting, Dr. Jones disagreed with Dr. Smith's previous recommendation. Dr. Jones cited two recent studies that showed no added benefit from additional chemotherapy in Joe's situation. In fact, he argued, it could be harmful by increasing risk for long term effects of treatment. Dr. Jones recommended against additional chemotherapy, but gave Joe an option of choosing additional chemotherapy based on his preferences.

Joe was stressed and worried over these differences of expert opinion. On the one hand, he did not want more chemotherapy given the side effects. On the other hand, he was afraid that forgoing additional treatment would lead to a greater risk of recurrence. Joe could not find a clear answer from Internet searches. He made a decision—that he wanted the two doctors to discuss the latest research studies, come to agreement on the best course of action, and tell him what to do. Joe felt relieved when the doctors agreed to his request. The two doctors conferred, and decided that Joe should proceed with two more rounds of chemotherapy, which he did.

The scenario above is based on a real life event and captures the complexities of decision making in medical care. The clinical evidence suggests multiple, potentially viable treatment options. Clinicians have different opinions on the best course of action. The patient has some familiarity with the clinical evidence through outside searching. Patients and physicians actively discuss their understanding of the risks and benefits of each option. Within the context of conversations and professional and personal relationships, a decision is made, the outcome of which is unknown. The patient and family experience considerable stress and worry about whether the treatment will work, how debilitating the effects of chemotherapy will be, and how/if a family should plan for their future. Even when there is good news following treatment, uncertainty remains about whether the additional treatment is necessary, the long term effects of treatment, and the possibility of recurrence.

In this case, did Joe and Drs. Smith and Jones make a good decision? The answer to that question depends on one's perspective on a "good" decision—"yes" since all parties agree continued chemotherapy would be the best option, "no" since the doctors made the decision for the patient, and "it depends" because the clinical outcome of the decision is unknown. In this chapter, we present a communication perspective on how to better understand the quality of decisions and the decision-making process with particular attention to one of the most problematic aspects of decision making: the management of uncertainty.

Good Decisions and Good Decision Making

While a pragmatist might argue that a good medical decision is one that worked, such a conception fails at two levels. First, decisions may be both good and bad at multiple levels. For example, a decision to continue life sustaining treatments might add days or months to living, but significantly lower quality of life. Second, judging decision quality based on outcome is completely retrospective and does not inform how to determine quality at the time a decision is made. Thus, we adopt a perspective embraced by a number of scholars (Elwyn, Edwards, Kinnersley, & Grol, 2000; Epstein & Street, 2007; Sepucha, Ozanne, Silvia, Partridge, & Mulley, Jr., 2007) that quality medical decisions are those that (a) are based on the best clinical evidence, (b) incorporate the patient's values and preferences, (c) involve the patient in the decision-making processes to the extent that the patient wants or needs to be, and (d) are feasible to implement. While few would argue with such a conceptualization, engaging in a quality decision making process presents challenges in practice.

In clinical encounters, medical decision making is much more than a cognitive process. It is also a social event, one defined by the nature of the communication and the relationship between the clinician and patient/family (Street, 2007). The term "shared decision making" has been used to describe a model of collaboration between patients and clinicians to reach an agreement about a health decision (Charles, Gafni, & Whelan, 1997; Edwards & Elwyn, 2006; O'Connor et al., 2003). We will use the term "collaborative" rather than "shared" decision making because collaboration connotes a process of mutual participation and cooperation among clinicians, patients, and family members whereas shared decision making connotes that participants made the decision together. While this distinction may seem pedantic, it actually is quite important. As demonstrated in Joe's example above, patients can be highly involved in the processes of decision making (e.g., sharing information, deliberating, stating preferences) yet defer the actual decision to the doctor.

Collaborative decision making aims to help patients make medical choices by improving knowledge and helping patients to clarify values for the risks and benefits of options (O'Connor, Llewellyn-Thomas, & Stacey, 2005). This model places importance on incorporating preferences into health decisions and encourages a patient–provider discussion that goes beyond factual information giving. Through these discussions, providers can support and guide patients through decisions by giving them opportunities to ask questions, state concerns, and share socio-cultural information that might influence their decision.

Accomplishing Shared Mind during Collaborative Decision Making

Epstein and Peters (2009) use the term "shared mind" to reflect the ideal situation where clinicians and patients have a shared understanding of the patient's health condition, have an accurate understanding of the other's perspective, and are in agreement on the best treatment option. For example, in managing hypertension, shared mind occurs when patient and clinician agree that the patient's blood pressure is a problem, the patient understands treatment options, the doctor understands the patient's values (e.g., willing to tolerate light-headedness rather than frequent urination, two possible side effects of treatment), both agree to try one medication first, and both agree to a follow-up visit to check whether the medication is working with tolerable side effects. In the context of quality decision making, communication leading to shared mind would need to focus on the *clinical evidence, the patient's values and preferences, and implementation of the treatment plan*.

Achieving shared mind requires more patient-centered communication from both clinicians *and* patients. For the clinician, patient-centered communication involves (a) making efforts to elicit, understand, and validate, the patient's perspective; (b) understanding the psychosocial context of the patient's health; (c) involving the patient in care and decision making to the extent he or she needs or wants to be; (d) providing clear, understandable explanations; and (e) fostering a relationship characterized by trust and commitment (Epstein & Street, 2007). For the patient, communication reflects involvement in consultation and the decision-making process when the patient asks questions, states preferences, expresses concerns, conveys understandings, and offers opinions (Street & Millay, 2001). In order to achieve shared mind, clinicians and patients also need to work together to identify common ground, reconcile differences in opinion, and if necessary, negotiate a common understanding and agreement on treatment plan (Epstein & Street, 2007).

The Clinical Evidence

Achieving shared mind on the clinical evidence can range from simple to extremely complex. In its simplest form, the evidence strongly supports a particular diagnosis or treatment option. The clinician's tasks are to explain the diagnoses or treatment options using clear language, check for understanding, and provide further clarification or additional information if the patient expresses confusion. In the scenario above, shared mind occurred when the oncologist reported the diagnosis of non-Hodgkin's lymphoma in a way Joe understood, described the nature and course of the disease, identified eight rounds of chemotherapy as the best treatment given the clinical evidence, explained how the treatment could be curative, disclosed possible side effects, and satisfactorily answered Joe's questions and concerns. However, although Joe and Dr. Smith may have achieved shared mind about the diagnosis, treatment plan, and its potential risks and benefits, the uncertainty about whether the treatment would work still lurked heavily in Joe's thoughts.

In more complex cases, achieving shared mind about the clinical evidence can be challenging, particularly under three conditions. First, there can be a clash between an analytical understanding of disease and treatment (typically the clinician's view based on the clinical evidence) and an experiential understanding (often the patient's view based on personal experiences; Fagerlin, Wang, & Ubel, 2005). For example, even if the clinical evidence strongly supports chemotherapy for non–Hodgkin's lymphoma, Joe's understanding of the best treatment could have differed based on memories of a family member who suffered through chemotherapy side effects and died from the cancer shortly thereafter.

A second challenge occurs when the evidence is complicated or difficult to comprehend by a lay audience. Confusion can result from risk framing (absolute vs. relative; Lipkus, 2007), conditions under which the evidence might not apply (e.g., an early stage breast cancer than cannot be treated with breast conservation because of a diffuse tumor), or limitations associated with patients with low health literacy (Davis, Williams, & Marin, 2002).

Third, the clinical evidence may be inconsistent or insufficient to confidently establish a diagnosis or recommend a particular course of action. This occurred in Joe's case when Drs. Smith and Jones differed in their opinions about whether additional chemotherapy was needed once there was no evidence of the tumor. Under these more complex conditions, achieving shared mind about the clinical evidence depends on much more than simply providing a clear explanation, using appropriate formats for conveying the evidence, and allowing the patient to share his or her understanding. It also requires communication that is about exploring, clarifying, and tolerating uncertainty about the known and unknown aspects of the decision.

The Patient's Values and Preferences

Quality medical decisions are not only based on the best clinical evidence, they are consistent (to the degree possible) with the patient's values and preferences. However, clinicians are often not aware of patients' goals, values, understandings, and preferences (DesHarnais, Carter, Hennessy, Kurent, & Carter, 2007; Janz et al., 2004). When patients more actively participate in clinical encounters by asking questions, expressing concerns, and stating preferences, and clinicians encourage these discussions, it can increase the likelihood that clinicians and patients achieve agreement on the severity of the patient's symptoms and the potential benefits of treatment.

Active patient participation alerts clinicians to the patient's beliefs, concerns, and desires. Clinicians can then use this information to provide more personalized care and achieve a better understanding of the patient's perspective. This alone could lead to good quality decision making for decisions that are preference-sensitive with multiple, equally viable treatment options from an evidenced-based standpoint (Elwyn et al., 2000). However, for many health conditions, the clinical evidence will tilt toward one option more than another. Achieving shared mind will be more difficult when patient preferences are counter to the strongest clinical evidence. In Joe's example, Joe could have requested radiation treatment instead of chemotherapy because of his aversion to the side effects of chemotherapy. Under these circumstances, quality decision making will depend not only on clinician and patient becoming aware of and understanding the other's position, but also engaging in a dialogue to find common ground, identify and reconcile differences, and negotiate or compromise to reach a collaborative, agreed-upon decision.

A final complication related to integrating a patient's values into the decision is that patients might not have previously formed preferences because they find themselves in new, changing, emotionally intense situations. For instance, before his diagnosis, Joe had not formed preferences about cancer treatments. After diagnosis, his preferences could have fluctuated as his mind worked through cognitive (chemotherapy leads to the best chance of cure) and affective (aversion to side effects, fear of functional limitations) reactions. Thus, clinicians may need to help patients identify values (Epstein & Peters, 2009; E. J. Johnson,

Steffel, & Goldstein, 2005) through guided values clarification exercises or careful discussions, allowing the patient time to process the information. Clinicians should be mindful of the way in which information is presented because patients may have difficulty forming preferences when subjected to information overload. Patient preferences also could be influenced by the clinicians' message framing (e.g., chance of survival vs. chance of death).

Implementation: Action Plans, Goal Setting, and Follow-Up

Although a considerable amount of work has focused on decision making with respect to the clinical evidence and patient preferences, less has focused on feasibility as a criterion of decision. Some elements of implementation feasibility may be related to economic issues (e.g., insurance coverage), but others are behavioral and involve whether the patient is capable of carrying out a treatment plan. Although the implementation of some decisions may seem straightforward (e.g., taking chemotherapy treatments), others may be more complex (e.g., pain management). Even decisions that are simple to understand may face a number of complications in implementation. For example, Joe's decision to undergo eight chemotherapy treatments required coordination of several activities: arranging travel to a clinic that is 90 miles away, scheduling time off from work, coordinating transportation for children that needed to get to and from school, canceling vacation plans, and finding a substitute to take his place as regular coach for a Little League team.

One approach to address implementation issues in decision making is through collaborative goal setting and developing action plans. Collaborative goal setting refers to the process by which clinicians and patients negotiate and agree on a health-related goal and a plan by which that goal can be achieved (Bodenheimer & Handley, 2009). Although clinician–patient goal setting might take additional time in the consultation, establishing goals and action plans often helps patients with chronic disease achieve desired changes in behaviors (Shilts, Horowitz, & Townsend, 2004). In Joe's case, planning related to managing work and domestic responsibilities mostly occurred outside the clinic. However, clinicians can facilitate implementation through helping patients navigate complex health care systems (e.g., location and scheduling of treatment) and serving as an advocate for obtaining needed services (Epstein & Street, 2007).

Managing Uncertainty during Collaborative Decision Making to Achieve Shared Mind

In the previous section, we mentioned that one of the key aspects of good quality decisions is that they are based on the best clinical evidence. The next section will highlight in more detail one of the key challenges in achieving shared mind: *that most medical choices involve uncertain or unknown evidence about risk/benefit information guiding clinical decisions* (BMJ Clinical Evidence, 2007). Even experts can disagree based on uncertainty, as seen in Joe's scenario when he shifted his care from Dr. Smith to Dr. Jones. Collaborative decision making assumes that the uncertainty that complicates medical decisions is explicitly discussed with patients (O'Connor et al., 2005), either through decision support tools or through decision discussions in medical consults to achieve shared mind. However, discussion of uncertainty rarely occurs in decision tools or clinical practice (Braddock, Edwards, Hasenberg, Laidley, & Levinson, 1999; Politi, Han, & Col, 2007). Physicians may be hesitant to communicate uncertainty for several reasons. They may have been trained to display confidence to patients and emphasize an illusion of certainty to increase patients' trust in the information presented (C. G. Johnson, Levenkron, Suchman, & Manchester, 1988). Physicians also fear that the complexity of uncertainty might lead to confusion and anxiety (Babrow & Kline, 2000; Brashers, 2001) and could lead patients to delay or reject decision making as a result, as occurred in Joe's case when he deferred the decision to his doctors. Physicians' own discomfort with uncertainty might also lead them to engage in a more paternalistic style of decision communication (Légaré, O'Connor, Graham, Wells, & Tremblay, 2006).

Physicians' communication about decisions and uncertainty is an important component of decision quality. Below we will describe communication strategies that can facilitate discussions and tolerance of uncertainty during collaborative decision making. We will then propose a testable, theory-based model that can aid future studies on the dynamic decision communication process that occurs during patient–provider consults.

Defining Uncertainty in Collaborative Decision Making

There are numerous sources of uncertainty about medical decisions, and experts have conceptualized uncertainty in several ways. The most common definition of uncertainty in medical settings is the fundamental *stochastic uncertainty* about the future occurrence of an outcome (Edwards, Elwyn, & Mulley, 2002). This type of uncertainty includes general information about the chance of an unknown future event. For instance, the risk of developing a side effect from a treatment could be 5%, or 5 out of 100, but that risk does not specify for an individual patient whether he/she will be in the 5 affected or the 95 unaffected. In Joe's case, uncertainty about whether he would benefit from treatment, and whether he would develop short- or long-term side effects from chemotherapy, were both sources of stochastic uncertainty. Stochastic uncertainty and general risk information is the most widely studied source of uncertainty, with various strategies created to simplify risks and facilitate its understanding (e.g., Gigerenzer & Edwards, 2003; Reyna & Adam, 2003). However, both doctors and patients struggle to communicate about this type of uncertainty in practice settings.

Another type of uncertainty can be classified as *ambiguity* or *probabilistic uncertainty*, or the strength of the scientific evidence used to generate risk numbers. Ambiguity results from missing or inconsistent empirical data, differences in study design of randomized or observational trials used to generate recommendations, and multiple other scientific factors (Politi et al., 2007). It is often expressed graphically through confidence intervals (CIs) in visual displays of risk (Han et al., 2007; Ibrekk & Morgan, 1987), but involves much more than confidence intervals including varied timing, frequency, dose, and duration of medical interventions tested in research and used to generate risks. In Joe's situation, ambiguity resulted from difficulty integrating previous evidence with new trials, leading to conflicting recommendations about treatment. Although Joe's physicians discussed this evidence with him, ambiguity is typically not communicated to patients. Out of 131 tools reviewed in a Cochrane review of decision aids (O'Connor et al., 2003), few addressed probabilistic uncertainty, and preliminary evidence in real practice settings shows that discussing this type of uncertainty occurs in a minority of patient consultations (Politi, Clark, Ombao, Dizon, & Elwyn, 2010).

Multiple additional sources of uncertainty can arise during the patient–provider interaction, such as failure to recall family or personal history with an illness, lack of applicability of population based studies to individual patients, and co-morbid illnesses that are common in patients with chronic conditions and can complicate risk estimates (Politi et al., 2007).

Research is needed on the best ways to incorporate discussions of the multiple sources of uncertainty with patients during shared decision making.

Communicating about Uncertainty to Achieve Shared Mind: Past Problems and Future Suggestions

One of the goals of collaborative decision making is to help patients reduce their uncertainty and conflict about decisions (O'Connor et al., 2005). Decision tools are often evaluated based on whether patients report lower decisional conflict. However, uncertainty about risks and benefits of treatments, including ambiguity about the evidence used to develop guidelines for treatments, is non-modifiable. Communicating facts about most medical decisions necessitates acknowledging this to patients, and decisional conflict and uncertainty may be natural outcomes of a true understanding of the complexity of decisions. In fact, one of the initial theories used to develop widely used decision support frameworks is a psychological theory called the Decisional Conflict Theory (Janis & Mann, 1977). This theory suggests that individuals actually need some level of anxiety or conflict in order to deliberate about options and recognize the significance of the choice.

As a result, it may be beneficial to move toward a decision framework that emphasizes helping patients to *tolerate and cope* with uncertainty and decisional conflict, rather than to reduce it (Babrow & Kline, 2000; Brashers, 2001). Decision frameworks could move away from anxiety and conflict reduction, back toward a focus on their additional goals as targeted outcomes of decision support: improved patient knowledge, provider support for patient involvement in decisions, and providers' patient-centered behaviors that encourage choices that are consistent with patients' values and preferences.

The idea of tolerating instead of reducing or eliminating non-modifiable cognitions and emotions is not new in the field of clinical psychology. In psychological studies of general anxiety, "intolerance of uncertainty" is often defined as the tendency to react negatively to an uncertain event or situation, an inability to act under uncertainty, and a belief that unexpected events are negative and should be avoided (Buhr & Dugas, 2002; Ladouceur, Gosselin, & Dugas, 2000). Individuals who are intolerant of uncertainty tend to experience significant worry and physiological arousal in response to uncontrollable situations. They often report inaccurate, elevated estimations of risk (Butler & Mathews, 1987), and may be slow to make decisions when confronted with ambiguous stimuli (Ladouceur et al., 2000). Many psychotherapy techniques propose a shift from uncertainty-reduction to a focus on tolerating uncertainty and making behavioral changes consistent with values and goals (e.g., Hayes, Luoma, Bond, Masuda, & Lillis, 2006) in order to help patients to cope with risks and ambiguity.

These strategies could be applied to collaborative decision making during medical consultations. Rather than focusing on uncertainty reduction in order to achieve desired decision outcomes, physicians might be able to help patients cope with uncertainty to make necessary health decisions through supporting patients' natural discomfort with uncertainty, and modeling their own process of making medical recommendations despite treatment uncertainty. Values and goals clarification with patients can help physicians and patients to discuss the aspects of a medical decision that are salient and relevant to patients' needs when there is a point of equipoise about a best medical option from an evidence-based standpoint. Additionally, patient-centered communication strategies could help to reduce the potential negative impact of communicating uncertainty on patients' satisfaction, trust in their provider, and confidence in their medical treatment. The aim might not be reduction of decisional conflict, but managing conflict in order to make decisions that are consistent with patients' values, which is already a key outcome of decision support interventions.

In Joe's case, uncertainty was communicated through conflicting opinions between two treating physicians and an explanation of emerging research evidence that could challenge past guidelines. Joe's coping strategy was to take away the burden of making the choice, which some can argue was still a "good quality decision" because he was informed, supported, involved in the initial decision discussions, and the decision was ultimately made in a way that was consistent with his preferences. Although uncertainty still remained about whether the subsequent two chemotherapy rounds would lead to more short- or long-term side effects, and Joe might still have felt some decisional conflict about whether he needed more chemotherapy, he and his physicians achieved shared mind, and felt satisfied with their collaborative choice.

The next section will describe several strategies for encouraging patient-centered, values-based discussions during the patient–provider consultation that might help patients and providers tolerate the uncertainty inherent in medical decisions to achieve shared mind.

Incorporating Uncertainty into Successful Decision Communication Interventions during the Medical Consultation

There is a paucity of research on communicating uncertainty in the context of collaborative decision making (Politi et al., 2007). Evidence suggests that involving patients in decisions might help them to tolerate uncertainty. For instance, one recent study found that uncertainty communication was negatively related to decision satisfaction among patients making decisions about breast cancer (Politi et al., 2010). Patients who made challenging decisions about breast cancer were less satisfied when they learned about the uncertainty complicating the decisions. However, in the same study, there was an interaction between patient involvement in decisions and communicating uncertainty. Patients who were more involved in the decisions felt less dissatisfied when presented with information about uncertainty than were passive patients.

Although tolerance of uncertainty was not measured in the study, qualitative analysis showed that tolerance of uncertainty might be related to patient involvement and satisfaction with decisions. Below are two examples in which providers communicated uncertainty that resulted in different responses to uncertainty from patients. In the first example, the patient reported feeling comfortable making a decision, despite the fact that there was uncertainty about her choice:

Physician: "If the test is negative, there is a less than 1% chance that your cancer has spread. But it is not zero. All tests have some uncertainty involved.... What are your thoughts about the treatment options we discussed, given this information?"

This patient was encouraged to share concerns and questions, and to participate in the treatment decision-making process through the open-ended question. The decision discussion began by recognizing uncertainty and facilitating communication about the decision in spite of the non-modifiable uncertainty.

In the second example below, the patient reported feeling confused and uncomfortable with the uncertainty about whether she had cancer, and her provider's recommendation to repeat an ultrasound:

Physician: "I strongly feel in my clinical opinion that this is nothing, but we can't be sure without repeating your ultrasound. And maybe we'd have to biopsy if it looked suspicious after that, but, again, it's probably nothing. Let's just start here, ok?"

This clinician was attempting to reduce uncertainty to comfort the patient and reduce anxiety. However, the clinician's communication had the opposite effect, and the patient felt more anxious about the possibility of having cancer. She was also not given a clear opportunity to ask questions or state these fears.

To our knowledge, there are no other specific studies of uncertainty communication and collaborative decision making in clinical practice. However, studies of uncertainty during the patient–provider interaction more broadly have found that expressing uncertainty is related to positive rapport and information exchange between patients and clinicians (Gordon, Joos, & Byrne, 2000). When uncertainty is explicitly communicated, physicians tend to use more positive talk, engage in more partnership building behaviors, and provide more information to patients (Gordon et al., 2000). Patients might report feeling more satisfied with the interaction with their clinicians as a result of these patient-centered behaviors, even when difficult, uncertain information about decisions is presented. These behaviors could help patients to tolerate uncertainty through trust in their provider and observation of their providers' decision-making process under uncertainty.

Studies have also examined expressions of uncertainty that might hinder patients' confidence. One study using hypothetical clinical scenarios (C. G. Johnson et al., 1988) examined expressions of uncertainty that ranged from an illusion of certainty to a full disclosure of uncertainty during multiple aspects of the encounter. The study found that patients were most satisfied when there was an illusion of certainty and uncertainty was never discussed, although failing to acknowledge uncertainty when it is present is an ethical option in real practice. Patients were the least satisfied when physicians disclosed uncertainty, and then ignored it or failed to incorporate it into subsequent parts of the consultation. Explicit disclosure of uncertainty should be followed by additional patient-centered behaviors to build rapport and allow patients to manage this uncertainty in order to make informed decisions.

Interventions designed to increase patient involvement in decisions, improve physicians' patient-centered communication, and help patients to clarify their values have been shown to improve decision support during medical consultations. Although they have not explicitly targeted sources of uncertainty, they often incorporated uncertainty by encouraging discussions about decisions to achieve shared mind. For instance, one successful intervention used "issues cards" to encourage a discussion about diabetes self-management in a primary care setting (Breslin, Mullan, & Montori, 2008). Patients and providers were given cards organized by attributes of the illness and medication options. Patients could select the attribute of the illness or treatment that would most impact their decision to try a diabetes intervention—clarifying their values about the decision. The intervention created a more patient-centered consultation by increasing patients' involvement, helping patients express preferences, and highlighting the stochastic uncertainty about the decision. These cards also facilitated shared mind by allowing physicians to share their unique expertise about diabetes, and patients to share their unique knowledge about their personal values. As a result, the two reached collaborative, mutually agreed upon goals for coping with the illness. More explicit presentations of other types of uncertainty could be added to the intervention and tested in subsequent trials.

Another intervention (Belkora, Edlow, & Aviv, 2008) has focused on training patients to actively communicate with their providers about decisions and uncertainty. The intervention involved a facilitator who met with a patient immediately prior to his/her appointment. The facilitator used a template to help patients brainstorm questions or concerns to ask their physician. The patients, physicians, and family members involved received copies of the consultation plan for use during the medical visit to foster a discussion about patients' unique concerns. The intervention helped build collaborative decision making by engaging patients prior to their appointment, and communicating their questions and concerns about decisions to clinicians and family members involved in the decision. Future studies using this intervention could incorporate more explicit patient preparation exercises to help them discuss multiple sources of uncertainty. Studies might also consider providing some complementary training for providers, since providers' response to uncertainty influences their willingness to engage in collaborative decision making (Légaré et al., 2006), and provider-delivered interventions can improve the efficacy of decision support (Jones et al., 2009).

Although optimal strategies to improve communication about decisions and uncertainty should incorporate the patient–provider conversation during the medical visit, most tools were developed for use outside of the consultation. More research is needed to determine whether these tools can be used in conjunction with patient–physician tools, or on their own prior to health care visits, to increase patient-centered decision discussions, facilitate collaborative decision making, and achieve shared mind in situations with multiple sources of uncertainty.

Testable Model of Communicating Uncertainty during Shared Decision Making

Behavioral models focusing on the dynamic relationship between patients and providers could facilitate research and interventions to improve communication between patients and providers during collaborative decision making. From this standpoint, research should incorporate the communication patterns of both providers and patients when developing an intervention to support management of uncertainty during collaborative decision making. Based on theories of decision making and patient-centered communication, Figure 25.1 displays one possible model that incorporates reactions to uncertainty in order to engage in collaborative decision making and achieve shared mind.

This model emphasizes the interaction between patients and clinicians during decision making, including variables that can influence communication and tolerance of uncertainty. Discussing clinical evidence, values clarification, and goal-setting are all components of collaborative decision making and are already included in many measures of patient involvement in decisions. Communicating uncertainty is assumed to be a component of collaborative decision making, but was separated out in this model given the evidence that it is rarely done in practice (Braddock et al., 1999; Politi et al., 2007) and is not always included in measures of patient decision involvement (Elwyn et al., 2001). This model can be used to conduct exploratory studies of the variables that might influence physician behaviors, patient behaviors, and key decision outcomes. It can also be used to foster the development of improved measures of constructs relevant to decision outcomes.

Future Research Directions

In previous sections, we have alluded to several areas for future research development to help patients manage uncertainty and achieve shared mind during collaborative decision making. We have proposed a testable model that can be used to guide studies. In addition, the areas discussed below require further research to determine efficacy of decision interventions with these goals.

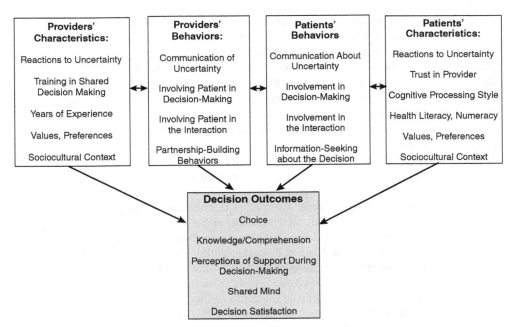

Figure 25.1 Communicating uncertainty during shared decision-making.

Measuring Reactions to Uncertainty

Measurement of patients' reactions to uncertainty about medical decisions is a key aspect of learning how to communicate it to patients. Patients' cognitive and affective reactions to uncertainty impact their perception of uncertainty and the decision-making process. However, there is very little research examining ways to measure patients' reactions to uncertainty. A lack of a well-defined measure may contribute to the variable cognitive and emotional responses to uncertainty found in clinical studies. Appropriate measures for patients, tested with patients who face an actual decision involving uncertainty, are necessary in order to determine whether reactions to uncertainty impact their health choices.

In addition to measuring patients' reactions to uncertainty, measures are needed to assess clinicians' response to uncertainty and its impact on their clinical communication. The Physicians' Reactions to Uncertainty Scale (Gerrity, White, DeVellis, & Dittus, 1995) is one valid and reliable measure of clinicians' cognitive and affective response to uncertainty in medical care. Adapting this measure to focus on the context of collaborative decision making, or building on this measure to address the dynamic communication between patients and providers in response to uncertainty, might provide useful insight into the ways in which reactions to uncertainty impact collaborative decision-making processes and outcomes.

Individual Patient Variation and Preferences

More research is needed to determine how individual patients with various characteristics (e.g., education, gender, culture) understand and cope with various sources of uncertainty during shared decision making. This research is essential to determining the best ways to communicate uncertainty in practice. Information might need to be tailored to individuals' unique context. For instance, less educated patients have been found to perceive information about ambiguity as "vague" or "wishy-washy," and might report decreased trust in the information source when ambiguity is presented (Ibrekk & Morgan, 1987). More educated patients might be more accepting of ambiguity, and might actually seek out information about uncertainty (Ibrekk & Morgan, 1987). Gender could also influence patients' response to uncertainty (Peters, Dieckmann, Dixon, Hibbard, & Mertz, 2007). Thus, additional studies should assess individual patients' interest in, and reactions to, communication about scientific uncertainty in order to develop interventions to improve tolerance and management of uncertainty.

Culture might also affect patients' response to uncertainty in the context of collaborative decision making. There is some evidence to show that Latino patients (particularly those who prefer speaking Spanish to English) may experience higher levels of decision dissatisfaction and decision regret than those from other cultural and ethnic groups, independent of clinical outcomes (Hawley et al., 2008). Additionally, Latino patients may also involve family members more heavily in decision making than those from other cultural or ethnic backgrounds (Maly, Umezawa, Ratliff, & Leake, 2006), thus complicating discussions by requiring providers to communicate with the family unit about uncertainty. Family members' responses to uncertainty could differ greatly from those of the patient. Acculturation among Latino patients could also impact their uncertainty management and role preference in decision making. Greater acculturation among Latinos can increase perceived autonomy in medical decision making (Maly et al., 2006) and might lead to a desire for more information about uncertainty. Non-Spanish-speaking providers may have more difficulty communicating uncertainty with Spanish-speaking Latino patients because of language barriers and the challenges of using a translator during the medical consult (Schapira et al., 2008). These complexities should be explored in future research to determine optimal ways to address uncertainty and achieve shared mind during decision making.

Patients' cultural background could also affect providers' behavior in the context of decision making, and providers might need to be made aware of these potential biases in communication before uncertainty management and shared mind can be achieved. For instance, objective observation and analysis of physicians' communication has found race-based disparities in patient-centered communication (R. L. Johnson, Roter, Powe, & Cooper, 2004). Physicians may be more dominant and less patient-centered with African American patients than with White patients (R. L. Johnson et al., 2004), which is not conducive to collaborative decision making or uncertainty management. In addition, African American patients may perceive negative attitudes or stereotypes in a clinician's communication (Cooper & Roter, 2003), which could make them less trusting of uncertain information when it is communicated. Without addressing these disparities in patient-centered communication with African American patients, collaborative decision making will not occur.

Conclusion

It is a challenge to communicate about decision making during medical consultations. Managing uncertainty to achieve shared mind requires patient-centered communication from both clinicians and patients. Physicians must build a partnership with patients and family members, present recommendations, check for understanding and agreement to ensure that patients' informational, emotional, and decisional needs are met, and foster a relationship characterized by trust and commitment, all during a time-limited health care visit. Patients must actively communicate their preferences, concerns, opinions, and questions in order to contribute to this collaboration. More research is needed to examine the fundamental aspects of the conversation between physicians and patients about decisions and uncertainty that can influence tolerance of uncertainty and shared mind during collaborative decision making.

Note

1. This chapter is an expansion of an earlier paper. Politi, M. C., & Street, R. L. (2010). The importance of communication in collaborative decision-making: Facilitating shared mind and the management of uncertainty. *Journal of Evaluation in Clinical Practice.* (epub ahead of print).

References

Babrow, A. S., & Kline, K. N. (2000). From "reducing" to "coping with" uncertainty: Reconceptualizing the central challenge in breast self-exams. *Social Science and Medicine, 51,* 1805–1816.

Belkora, J., Edlow, B., & Aviv, C. (2008). Training community resource center and clinic personnel to prompt patients in listing questions for doctors: Follow-up interviews about barriers and facilitators to the implementation of consultation planning. *Implementation Science, 3,* 6.

BMJ Clinical Evidence. (2007). Retrieved from http://www.clinicalevidence.com/ceweb/about/guide.jsp

Bodenheimer, T., & Handley, M. A. (2009). Goal-setting for behavior change in primary care: An exploration and status report. *Patient Education and Counseling, 76,* 174–180.

Braddock, C. H., Edwards, K. A., Hasenberg, N. M., Laidley, T. L., & Levinson, W. (1999). Informed decision making in outpatient practice: Time to get back to basics. *Journal of the American Medical Association, 282,* 2313–2320.

Brashers, D. E. (2001). Communication and uncertainty management. *Journal of Communication, 51,* 477–497.

Breslin, M., Mullan, R., & Montori, V. (2008). The design of a decision aid about diabetes medications for use during the consultation with patients with type 2 diabetes. *Patient Education and Counseling, 73,* 465–472.

Buhr, K., & Dugas, M. J. (2002). The intolerance for ambiguity scale: Psychometric properties of the English version. *Behaviour Research and Therapy, 40,* 931–945.

Butler, G., & Mathews, A. (1987). Anticipatory anxiety and risk perception. *Cognitive Therapy and Research, 11,* 551–565.

Charles, C., Gafni, A., & Whelan, T. (1997). Shared decision-making in the medical encounter: What does it mean? (or it takes at least two to tango). *Social Science and Medicine, 44,* 681–692.

Cooper, L. A., & Roter, D. L. (2003). Patient–provider communication: The effect of race and ethnicity on process and outcomes of health care. In B. D. Smedly, A. Y. Stith, & A. R. Nelson (Eds.), *Unequal treatment: Confronting racial and ethnic disparities in health care* (pp. 552–594). Washington, DC: National Academies Press.

Davis, T. C., Williams, M. V., & Marin, E. (2002). Health literacy and cancer communication. *CA: A Cancer Journal for Clinicians, 52,* 134–149.

DesHarnais, S., Carter, R. E., Hennessy, W., Kurent, J. E., & Carter, C (2007). Lack of concordance between physician and patient: Reports on end-of-life care discussions. *Journal of Palliative Medicine, 10,* 728–740.

Edwards, A., & Elwyn, G. (2006). Inside the black box of shared decision making: Distinguishing between the process of involvement and who makes the decision. *Health Expectations, 9,* 307–320.

Edwards, A., Elwyn, G., & Mulley, A. (2002). Explaining risks: Turning numerical data into meaningful pictures. *British Medical Journal, 324,* 827–830.

Elwyn, G., Edwards, A., Kinnersley, P., & Grol, R. (2000). Shared decision-making and the concept of equipoise: the competences of involving patients in healthcare choices. *British Journal of General Practice, 50,* 892–899.

Elwyn, G., Edwards, A., Mowle, S., Wensing, M., Wilkinson, C., Kinnersley, P., … Grol R. (2001). Measuring the involvement of patients in shared decision making: A systematic review of instruments. *Patient Education and Counseling, 43,* 5–22.

Epstein, R. M., & Peters, E. (2009). Beyond information: Exploring patients' preferences. *Journal of the American Medical Association, 302*, 195–197.

Epstein, R. M., & Street, R. L. (2007). *Patient-centered communication in cancer care: Promoting healing and reducing suffering* (NIH Publication No. 07-6225). Rockland, MD: National Cancer Institute.

Fagerlin, A., Wang, C., & Ubel, P. A. (2005). Reducing the influence of anecdotal reasoning on people's health care decisions: Is a picture worth a thousand statistics? *Medical Decision Making, 25*, 398–405.

Gerrity, M. S., White, K. P., DeVellis, R. F., & Dittus, R. S. (1995). Physicians' reactions to uncertainty: Refining the constructs and scales. *Motivation and Emotion, 19*, 175–191.

Gigerenzer, G., & Edwards, A. (2003). Simple tools for understanding risks: From innumeracy to insight. *British Medical Journal, 327*, 741–744.

Gordon, G. H., Joos, S. K., & Byrne, J. (2000). Physician expressions of uncertainty during patient encounters. *Patient Education and Counseling, 40*, 50–65.

Han, P. K., Korbrin, S. C., Klein, W. M. P., Davis, W. W., Stefanek, M., & Taplin, S. H. (2007). Perceived ambiguity about screening mammography recommendations: Association with future mammography uptake and perceptions. *Cancer Epidemiology Biomarkers and Prevention, 16*, 458–466.

Hawley, S. T., Lantz, P. M., Hamilton, A., Griggs, J. J., Alderman, A. K., Mujahid, M., & Katz, S. J. (2008). Latina patient perspectives about informed treatment decision making for breast cancer. *Patient Education and Counseling, 73*, 363–370.

Hayes, S. C., Luoma, J. B., Bond, F. W., Masuda, A., & Lillis, J. (2006). Acceptance and commitment therapy: Model, processes and outcomes. *Behavior Research Therapy, 44*, 1–25.

Ibrekk, H., & Morgan, M. J. (1987). Graphical communication of uncertain quantities to nontechnical people. *Risk Analysis, 7*, 519–529.

Janis, I. L., & Mann, L. (Eds.). (1977). *Decision making: A psychological analysis of conflict, choice, and commitment.* New York: Free Press.

Janz, N. K., Wren, P. A., Copeland, L. A., Lowery, J. C., Goldfarb, S. L., & Wilkins, E .G. (2004). Patient–physician concordance: Preferences, perceptions, and factors influencing the breast cancer surgical decision. *Journal of Clinical Oncology, 22*, 3091–3098.

Johnson, C. G., Levenkron, J. C., Suchman, A. L., & Manchester, R. (1988). Does physician uncertainty affect patient satisfaction? *Journal of General Internal Medicine, 3*, 144–149.

Johnson, E. J., Steffel, M., & Goldstein, D. G. (2005). Making better decisions: From measuring to constructing preferences. *Health Psychology, 24*(Supplement), S17–S22.

Johnson, R. L., Roter, D., Powe, N. R., & Cooper, L. A. (2004). Patient race/ethnicity and quality of patient-physician communication during medical visits. *American Journal of Public Health, 94*, 2084–2090.

Jones, L. A., Weymiller, A. J., Shah, N., Bryant, S. C., Christianson, T. J. H., Guyatt, G. H., … Gafni, A. (2009). Should clinicians deliver decision aids? Further exploration of the statin choice randomized trial results. *Medical Decision Making, 29*, 468–474.

Ladouceur, R., Gosselin, P., & Dugas, M. J. (2000). Experimental manipulation of intolerance of uncertainty: A study of a theoretical model of worry *Behaviour Research and Therapy, 38*, 933–941.

Légaré, F., O'Connor, A. M., Graham, I. D., Wells, G. A., & Tremblay, S. (2006). Impact of the Ottawa Decision Support Framework on the agreement and the difference between patients' and physicians' decisional conflict. *Medical Decision Making, 26*, 373–390.

Lipkus, I. M. (2007). Numeric, verbal, and visual formats of conveying health risks: Suggested best practices and future recommendations. *Medical Decision Making, 27*, 696–713.

Maly, R. C., Umezawa, Y., Ratliff, C. T., & Leake, B. (2006). Racial/ethnic group differences in treatment decision-making and treatment received among older breast carcinoma patients. *Cancer, 106*, 957–965.

O'Connor, A. M., Llewellyn-Thomas, H., & Stacey, D. (2005). *IPDAS Collaboration Background Document.* Retrieved from http://www.informedhealthchoice.com/pdf/IPDAS_background_2005.pdf

O'Connor, A. M., Bennett, C. L., Stacey, D., Barry, M., Col, N. F., Eden, K. B., … Entwistle, V. A. (2009). Decision aids for people facing health treatment or screening decisions. *Cochrane Database of Systematic Reviews, 3*. (CD001431).

Peters, E., Dieckmann, N., Dixon, A., Hibbard, J. H., & Mertz, C. K. (2007). Less is more in presenting quality information to consumers. *Medical Care Research and Review, 6*, 169–190.

Politi, M. C., Clark, M. A., Ombao, H., Dizon, D. S., & Elwyn, G. (2010). Communicating uncertainty and its impact on patients' decision satisfaction: Are we measuring the right outcomes of a good quality decision? *Health Expectations.* (epub ahead of print).

Politi, M. C., Han, P. K. J., & Col, N. C. (2007). Eisenberg Center 2006 White Paper Series: Communicating the uncertainty of harms and benefits of medical interventions. *Medical Decision Making, 7,* 681–695.

Reyna, V. F., & Adam, M. B. (2003). Fuzzy-trace theory, risk communication, and product labeling in sexually transmitted diseases. *Risk Analysis, 23,* 325–342.

Schapira, L., Vargas, E., Hidalgo, R., Brier, M., Sanchez, L., Hobrecker, K., … Lynch, T. (2008). Lost in translation: Integrating medical interpreters into the multidisciplinary team. *The Oncologist, 13,* 586–592.

Sepucha, K., Ozanne, E., Silvia, K., Partridge, A., & Mulley, Jr., A. G. (2007). An approach to measuring the quality of breast cancer decisions. *Patient Education and Counseling, 65,* 261–269.

Shilts, M. K., Horowitz, M., & Townsend, M. S. (2004). Goal setting as a strategy for dietary and physical activity behavior change: A review of the literature. *American Journal of Health Promotion, 19,* 81–93.

Street, R. L. (2007). Aiding medical decision making: A communication perspective. *Medical Decision Making, 27,* 550–553.

Street, R. L., & Millay, B. (2001). Analyzing patient participation in medical encounters. *Health Communication, 13,* 61–73.

26

PROVIDER–PATIENT INTERACTION AND RELATED OUTCOMES

Ashley P. Duggan and Teresa L. Thompson

One of the many reasons that the study of health communication is inherently fascinating is the real-world, bottom-line impact that we as scholars who study the interrelationships between health and communicative processes are privileged to examine in our work. None of the areas of health communication are more important than the interrelationship between provider and patient interaction and its various outcomes. It is crucial to understand that we study interaction between health care providers and patients not just out of an esoteric interest in the topic, but because it both impacts and is impacted by such variables as satisfaction, adherence, quality of life/health outcomes, and malpractice suits. Our focus in this chapter is to both survey this body of literature and to discuss the inherent limitations in such a survey. Although there are, indeed, links between outcomes and provider–patient interactions, there are also limitations to predicting outcomes from analyzing interactions. We then explore the nature of patient-centered and relationship-centered care, and move on to discuss explanatory frameworks to help the reader understand why links to outcomes do or do not exist. This discussion leads to a consideration of such issues as obstacles to care, knowledge–understanding considerations, decision-making processes, social systems, disclosure, emotions-bias, and communication interventions.

Of the many outcomes of provider–patient interaction, the variable that is most commonly studied is satisfaction level. Although this variable is not necessarily the most important outcome, it likely serves as a moderator between interactions and other, more inherently important, outcomes. We thus begin our discussion of outcomes with this variable.

Patient Satisfaction

Since Korsch and her colleagues' seminal work that documented mothers' dissatisfaction with pediatricians' lack of warmth, consideration for parent concerns, and clarity of diagnosis, as well as their use of medical jargon (Korsch, Gozzi, & Francis, 1968), patient satisfaction has remained a key construct for understanding patient perceptions of health care. Research since that time has continued to focus on parents' perceptions of physicians' caring and interest and suggests higher satisfaction associated with increased physician–parent collaboration (Galil et al., 2006). Not surprisingly, research documents the importance of interpersonal dimensions (physician rapport and patient disclosure) of the encounter over organizational dimensions (physical facilities and structure).

Research on patient satisfaction demonstrates that it is largely determined by interpersonal elements that vary across interactions with the same physician and that require cooperation and coordination between providers and patients (Hausman, 2004). Higher perceptions of competence and caring in physicians, nurses, and support staff predict higher patient satisfaction (Paulsel, McCroskey, & Richmond, 2006). Similarly, higher levels of information-giving from the care provider and question-asking from the patient lead to satisfaction, as does more demonstration of positive affect between providers and patients (Ong, Visser, Lammes, & de Haes, 2000; Pieterse, van Dulmen, Beemer, Bensing, & Ausems, 2007). Ong et al. and Pieterse et al. also noted that increased satisfaction is associated with length of visit, increased rapport (i.e., through nonverbal communication), more psychosocial discussion, and lower physician dominance.

Although the causal direction of the relationships is not necessarily clear, it is apparent that, within established relationships, satisfaction is positively associated with better health, more positive affect, more favorable patient ratings, and more mutual liking (Hall, Horgan, Stein, & Roter, 2002). Patients report more satisfaction with more patient-centered physicians if patient-centeredness matches patient preference (Krupat, Yeager, & Putnam, 2000).

Other provider or patient characteristics also either moderate the relationship between communicative variables and satisfaction or directly impact satisfaction. Sicker patients tend to be less satisfied than healthier patients regardless of the provider communication (Hall, Milburn, Roter, & Daltroy, 1998), and patients whose health problems negatively and strongly impact their quality of life may evaluate treatment less positively than do other patients. Disability is similarly associated with dissatisfaction and frustration with unmet health care needs (Veltman, Stewart, Tardif, & Branigan, 2001), with disappointed expectations regarding physician relationships (Shapiro, Mosqueda, & Botros, 2003), and with lack of physician questioning of patients about their needs (Duggan, Bradshaw, & Altman, 2010).

Communication processes associated with lower patient satisfaction also include unclear communication about treatment benefits, side effects and symptom control, and patients' feelings of constraint due to physician behaviors (Butow, 2001). Importantly, research indicates that combining physician and patient communication skills training improves patient satisfaction more than does training just the patient or just the physician (Haskard et al., 2008). Satisfaction itself, however, is also related to more fundamental outcome variables—adherence with treatment suggestions and health outcomes/quality of life.

Health Outcomes, Quality of Life, and Medical Adherence

An important goal of most provider–patient interaction is the generation of treatment recommendations. Whether cooperation with treatment suggestions occurs is determined in part by communicative issues related to the recommendations. It is hoped that ultimate quality of life issues are then also associated with such adherence. Levels of satisfaction with providers and with provider communication are positively related to adherence; more satisfaction and improved communication lead to more adherence. We thus see two processes operating: satisfaction directly impacting health outcomes and quality of life; and satisfaction impacting both variables through the moderating influence of patient cooperation with treatment recommendations as influenced by provider communication.

In regard to the first of these, research indicates that specific aspects of physician–patient communication are associated with "better health" as measured physiologically (blood pressure or blood sugar), behaviorally (functional status), or more subjectively (overall health status) (Kaplan, Greenfield, & Ware, 1989). Patient satisfaction has been found to change over time along with patient changes in health status (Jackson & Kroenke, 2001). When patient–provider dialogue is structured to focus on patients' views, it has a positive influence on quality of life and treatment satisfaction (Priebe et al., 2007), and more positive perceptions of physicians on the part of patients predicts smaller health status decline (Franks et al., 2005). Provider communicative competence is even related to such specific outcomes as glucose control in diabetic patients (Parchman, Flannagan, Ferrer, & Matamoras, 2009).

When the focus is more directly on adherence, research shows that patients who perceive that their doctors know them as people, rather than just as patients (Beach, Keruly, & Moore, 2006), adhere to treatment recommendations more consistently and experience more positive health outcomes. Similarly, provider communication that is rated by hypertensive African American patients as more collaborative is associated with better adherence (Schoenthaler et al., 2009). Cancer screening adherence is improved when doctors more positively endorse screening through their communication (Fox et al., 2009). Adherence is also improved when physicians demonstrate more warmth, openness, and interest (Fox et al.), engage in more shared decision making with patients (Lakatos, 2009; Schoenthaler et al., 2009), and demonstrate less discord with and control over patients (Lakatos, 2009).

The research on physician communication and patient adherence is most thoroughly summarized in Zolnierek and DiMatteo's (2009) meta-analysis of 106 studies on this topic from 1948 to 2008. Their results indicate a significant, positive correlation between effective physician communication and patient adherence, with the data demonstrating "a 19% higher risk of non-adherence among patients whose physicians communicate poorly" (p. 826). Their analysis also confirmed the positive relationship between satisfaction and adherence. When physician behaviors are coded, Roter and Hall's (2009) commentary on this study notes that the effect is even stronger than when patient reports of physician behaviors are utilized.

Malpractice

Perhaps the outcome that attracts the most attention from providers is the relationship between better provider communication and decreased malpractice. However, these research studies must be looked at within the time frame in which they were conducted, particularly when considering the vast changes in the organization and delivery of health care that have occurred in the United States in the last two decades. Patients and relatives who sue doctors say they want greater honesty, an appreciation of the severity of the trauma suffered, and assurances of lessons learned from negative experiences, but research suggests that many malpractice claims are initiated without evidence of quality lapse or medical injury. Other variables seem to be more relevant. For instance, some research in primary care suggests that longer routine visits are associated with fewer malpractice claims (Levinson, Roter, Mullooly, Dull, & Frankel, 1997). Similarly, families who file medical malpractice claims following prenatal injuries express dissatisfaction with physician–patient communication, and believe that physicians would not listen, would not talk openly, attempted to mislead them, or did not warn about long-term neuro-developmental problems (Hickson, Clayton, Githens, & Sloan, 1992). Mothers who have experienced a child's death are more likely to sue when they also offered more complaints, felt rushed, did not receive explanations for tests, or felt ignored (Hickson, Clayton, Entman, et al., 1994). Higher ratings of dominance and lower ratings of concern in the voices of surgeons are associated with increased likelihood of malpractice suits (Ambady et al., 2002). Malpractice lawyers consistently advise physicians about the relevance of their communicative behaviors to litigation (Nichols, 2003). Hickson and Entman (2008) have also noted that collaboration amongst members of the health care team is negatively related to malpractice litigation—more collaboration is associated with less litigation.

Vukmir's (2004) examination of medical malpractice research from 1976 to 2003 found that the likelihood of legal action was not related to severity of medical outcomes or any patient profile or socio-demographic variables, but was related to patient–provider interaction and communication variables. Likelihood of legal action was negatively related to length of visit and patient satisfaction. These findings are consistent with Beckman's (1995) analysis of 45 malpractice suits, which showed that patients and families who felt abandoned, discounted, or uninformed by their care providers were those that were most likely to sue. Doctors who are dominant and less patient centered are most likely to be sued, although gender and ethnic factors moderate this relationship (Wissow, 2004). Even in areas such as pathology, which was not traditionally a field that attracted a lot of malpractice attention, research within the last couple of decades indicates the essential role of the communication of diagnostic uncertainty when performing such procedures as breast fine-needle aspirations and cervical smears (Skoumal, Florell, Bydalek, & Hunter, 1996). More recently, the responsibility to communicate diagnoses directly to patients has been extended to radiologists, who traditionally had little interaction with the patient. It is now apparent that there is a relationship between their communication with patients and malpractice litigation (Berlin, 2007).

Interventions

Many accreditation agencies and medical educators have noted the literature linking communication process with health outcomes and now integrate communication as a core competency in medical education. For instance, the Accreditation Council for Graduate Medical Education (ACGME) requires documentation that physicians are able to (a) create and sustain a therapeutic and ethically sound relationship with patients; (b) use effective listening skills and elicit and provide information using effective nonverbal skills, explanatory questioning, and writing skills; and (c) work effectively with others as members or leaders of a health care team or other professional group. Similarly, the Royal College of Physicians recommends that teaching communication skills should continue to be highlighted as a priority in medical education and training at all levels. Although these steps allow for building new bridges between researchers, medical educators, and clinicians, the possibilities for large-scale, theory-based research that allows for conclusions about patient populations is still in the early stages. Similarly, the range of possibilities for training and evaluation leave much to be desired.

Reviews of evaluation studies suggest methodological deficiencies in many cases (Chant, Jenkinson, Randle, Russell, & Webb, 2002), and studies with the most adequate designs report the fewest positive training effects (Hulsman, Ros, Winnubst, & Bensing, 1999). Although research and medical education suggest a general consensus about the importance of communication in the medical encounter, informing best practice is much more difficult. The available evidence that links communication processes and health outcomes is currently limited by issues of definition and measurement, including different ways of measuring outcomes, small sample sizes, and lack of cohesiveness and language across academic disciplines and clinical specialties. Rigorous randomized clinical trials would allow for establishing causality, but systematic review of clinical trials suggests that less than half of the studies provide evidence linking communication and outcomes, that similar interventions predict different outcomes, and that the ways of measuring outcomes and small sample sizes further limit overall conclusions from clinical trials (Griffin et al., 2004). The state of research on interpersonal processes and health outcomes does, however, provide a foundation to begin to explicate the breadth and depth of communication constructs (such as patient-centered behavior), to place communication behavior within the context of the interactions, and to formulate theoretical explanations for the relationship between communication and health. The construct that has received the most focus is patient-centered care.

Explicating the Health Care Context: Patient-Centered/Relationship-Centered Care

Based on a new philosophy of shared power, the last 15 years of provider–patient research documents a shift in the interaction and promotes a more relationship-centered perspective on communication. The construct was first described as shifting from a paternalistic model of provider power to shared power between the provider and patient and was initially defined as patient-centered care. A subsequent interdisciplinary group of researchers and practitioners later made a case for relationship-centered care. This conceptualization (a) recognizes the personhood of both participants, (b) acknowledges the importance of affect and emotion, (c) places all health care relationships in the context of reciprocal influence, and (d) infers moral value in the formation and maintenance of genuine relationships in health care (Beach, Roter, Wang, Duggan, & Cooper, 2006). Relationship-centered care emphasizes that both physicians and patients bring unique perspectives, emotions, and expectations to the interaction (Roter, Frankel, Hall, & Sluyter, 2006). The term "relationship-centered" is consistent with relational communication literature that places interactions within a context of mutual influence, and acknowledges that relationship development, multiple goals, and identities influence the communication process. The term "patient-centered" moves beyond a paternalistic model of providers as the primary source of influence and is also consistent with current dialogue in health care reform about the "patient-centered medical home" (Barr, 2008). Both "relationship-centered" and "patient-centered" continue to be seen in the literature and depend more on the writer than on competing assumptions, but "patient-centered" is used more consistently in the research literature and also implies more of a focus on a goal-oriented interaction than does the term "relationship-centered."

Acknowledging mutual influence rather than a solely physician-driven model poses implications for the ways psychosocial concerns and the organization and delivery of health care are communicated and validates the role of actively encouraging patient input (Duggan & Parrott, 2001). A fundamental assumption is that patients must be able to describe their concerns, but patients' concerns are most often interrupted after the first expressed point and after a mean time of only 18 seconds (Beckman & Frankel, 1984). The classic study documenting this also found that only one patient ever returned to his or her agenda to describe additional concerns (Beckman & Frankel, 1984). Subsequent research reports physician solicitation of patient concerns in 75% of interviews and redirecting patients after a mean of 23.1 seconds; when patients were allowed to completely state their concerns, however, the interactions lasted on average only 6 seconds longer (Marvel, Epstein, Flowers, & Beckman, 1999).

Five principal domains of patient-centeredness have been identified: exploring the illness experience or expectations, understanding the whole patient experience, finding common ground, health promotion, and definitive interaction about illness (Little et al., 2001). Building on these notions, an observational study using covert standardized patient visits with primary care physicians found that asking about patients' needs, perspectives, and expectations, attending to psychosocial context, and encouraging patient involvement in decisions predicted lower diagnostic testing expenditures and lower total hospital and ambulatory care expenditures (Epstein et al., 2005). Epstein et al. articulated four patient-centered communication domains that included integrating the patient's perspective, acknowledging the psychosocial context, and encouraging both shared understanding and shared power/responsibility. Furthermore, this research team described the interrelationships amongst patient factors (i.e., personality, values, emotions), relationship factors (i.e., concordance of race and expectations, relationship duration and trust, expectations), health system factors (access to care, environment, visit length), and clinician factors (personality, risk aversion, visit frequency). Patient-centered consulting skills are increasingly seen as crucial for the delivery of effective primary care (Mead & Bower, 2002), but definitions and measurement of patient-centered care will continue to evolve.

The notion of patient-centered communication recognizes patient involvement in medical decision making, but also encompasses other issues. It includes notions ranging from exploring patients' ideas and expectations, tailoring information, checking reactions, or discussing decisions (Elwyn et al., 2001). Others suggest a more global approach to communication goals that includes fostering relationships, information gathering and provision, decision making, enabling disease and treatment-related behavior, and responding to emotions (de Haes & Bensing, 2009). Overall, research in patient-centered care continues to examine the role of communication in immediate outcomes (stress level), intermediate outcomes (improved diagnosis, trust, ordering diagnostic tests), and long-term health (a disease course or length of survival).

When patient-centered care is integrated into training and practice a potential discrepancy is again highlighted between the concepts of patient-centered care and the ways the communication behaviors are translated into clinical practice. Patients of doctors and nurses who completed training to improve care and skills in providing patient-centered care report better communication with providers and greater treatment satisfaction and well-being. However, objective measures indicate their body mass index and triglyceride concentrations are higher and their knowledge skills are lower than the control group (Kinmonth, Woodcock, Griffin, Spiegal, & Campbell, 1998). Relationship-centered care provides a context for understanding the ways provider–patient communication predicts outcomes, and poses questions for the pathways linking process and outcomes.

Pathways Linking Communication Processes and Health Outcomes

Researchers, medical educators, and clinicians have also explored why/how communication predicts health outcomes. Street, Makoul, Arora, and Epstein (2009) propose careful consideration of pathways linking provider–patient communication to improved health, connections explored in greater detail in cancer care but applicable to other contexts. When the pathways are articulated, the role of patient understanding and perceptions is recognized and this allows for more complete explication of the ways communication foundations translate into health outcomes. When pathways are explicated it builds shared understanding of the ways terms are used across studies and across disciplines and increases depth and clarity of constructs.

Access and Obstacles to Care. In the United States and some other countries, patients face disparities in access to health care. For instance, underserved women with breast cancer who are able to frequently utilize online information services demonstrate more positive appraisals of their providers (Shaw et al., 2007). Individuals with disabilities are especially vulnerable to adverse health care experiences, including little time to address complex health issues, sensory and cognitive communication barriers, limited financial resources, physically inaccessible care sites, and erroneous assumptions from physicians (Iezzoni, 2006).

Research also demonstrates variation in medical procedures by race, even when insurance status, income, age, and severity of conditions are comparable, and indicates that racial and ethnic minorities receive fewer routine medical procedures and experience lower quality health care (Institute of Medicine, Committee on Quality of Health Care in America, 2001; also, see Ndiaye et al., this volume). Older Latinas receiving breast cancer treatment report less support and poorer quality of life than do white women (Maly, Stein, Umezawa, Leake, & Anglin, 2008). Black patients and patients in race-discordant interactions use fewer behaviors to prompt doctors for information. Doctors, in turn, provide less information to these patients, thus perpetuating passivity and limiting information exchange (Gordon, Street, Sharf, Kelly, & Souchek, 2006). Sohler, Fitzpatrick, Lindsay, Anastos, and Cunningham (2007) found that racial concordance was associated with lower mistrust in the health care system, but not with trust in the provider, suggesting that racial–ethnic concordance might be important for helping patients navigate the health care system. Health literacy further limits access, in that some patients lack the skills and competencies required to find, comprehend, evaluate, and use health information, or to make educated choices, reduce health risks, or improve quality of life (Zarcadoolas, Pleasant, & Greer, 2003; see also Cameron, Wolf, & Baker, this volume).

Patient and Provider Knowledge and Understanding. Acknowledging the role of both the provider and the patient assumes that both bring knowledge and understanding to the interaction, but they do not necessarily share the same framework or expectations. This is particularly true when the etiology of symptoms is unclear. Patients and providers frequently disagree about patients' needs and decision-making preferences, and physicians are often unable to accurately predict their patients' decision-making preferences (Bruera, Sweeney, Calder, Palmer, & Benisch-Tolley, 2001).

Some research suggests that videotaping the interaction can be helpful for patients in terms of knowledge and understanding. Cancer patients provided with such tapes are more satisfied and recall more information, enhancing satisfaction in younger patients and diagnosis recall in older patients (Ong et al., 2000). Disparate prognostic and survival expectations between patients with cancer and their physicians may be a result of physicians' lack of full disclosure. Even when patients with cancer request survival estimates, physicians provide a frank estimate only 37% of the time and provide no estimate, a conscious overestimate, or a conscious underestimate most (63%) of the time (Lamont & Christakis, 2001). Overall, research suggests patients overestimate the probability of curing illness.

Quality and Process of Decision Making. Reaching consensus in medical decision making involves disclosure and negotiation, and should be grounded in a clear understanding of what providers and patients desire from the interaction. The process of collective decision making first involves relationship-centered care, mutual trust, access to care, and shared knowledge and understanding. Thus, quality decision making functions as a unique construct that involves a process of shared information and deliberation continuously shaped throughout the interaction. Overall, decision-making research suggests a need for preference-sensitive decision making, where patient preferences are an integral part of treatment (see Politi and Street, this volume for a more complete analysis of medical decision making).

Social Systems. For patients, illness occurs within a context of family expectations, social relationships, and everyday roles and responsibilities. Provider–patient interactions may include talk about these relationships, and may even include friends or family attending visits with the patient. Beyond patient networks, relationships among patients' multiple providers can result in the patients feeling respected and cared for, or on the contrary, leave the patient feeling isolated. A conceptual model of health care communication should involve collaboration among patients, providers, and significant family members. However, a systematic review of original research suggests that physicians typically spend less than one minute discussing treatment and planning, that informed patient decision making occurs in only 9% of outpatient office visits, that physicians ask patients if they have questions in less than half of the interactions, and that patients recall only a fraction of the information transmitted (Epstein, Alper, & Quill, 2004). This hardly equates to the kind of collaboration advocated above.

An extension of these concerns to include family members, interpreters, and multiple care providers as well as the uncertainty of complex issues poses additional constraints. Family members bring a range of emotional reactions, interpersonal dynamics, and expectations for the care the patient receives.

Older patients' social alliances further complicate the processes but also illustrate the links between interaction variables and health outcomes. Elderly health care consumers who take a proactive role in coordinating multiple health services indicate higher satisfaction, higher adherence to preventative and corrective recommendations, and higher quality of life (Kahana & Kahana, 2003). In geriatric medicine, lack of coordination among the interdependent systems of patient, family members, multiple health specialists, and organizations can result in misdiagnoses, decreased trust, provider reluctance to continue the relationship, and even increased mortality (Nussbaum & Fisher, 2009). Caregivers of older individuals are also affected by the act of providing care. A lack of social alliances in both their lives and the lives of those for whom they are providing care may decrease their ability to cope. For example, women without close relatives, friends, or living children indicate elevated risks of breast cancer mortality and of all-cause mortality compared with those with the most social ties (Kroenke, Kubzansky, Schernhammer, Holmes, & Kawachi, 2006). Research suggests a need to integrate family communication into interactions with providers and highlights advantages of integrating additional alliances. Involvement of other individuals, of course, also increases the complications due to disclosure and trust issues.

Disclosure and Privacy in Building Trust. Exchanging health information involves assumptions about sharing information and negotiating privacy. At the core, patients' health files encompass private information, but privacy also extends to psychological, social, physical, and relational dimensions. Patients expect to control their levels of affect, attitudes, beliefs, and values, and to determine circumstances for revealing intimate information; they also expect social privacy in managing interactions and maintaining status divisions. Importantly, patients expect physical privacy in controlling who has access to them

(Ong, de Haes, Hoos, & Lammes, 1995). The untangling of patient, provider, and family members' competing needs for information and disclosure can be conceptualized in terms of boundaries and the ways privacy rules manage the flow of information (Petronio, 2002). Situational needs can function as a catalyst for shifting privacy rules; patients and their families may be surprised at what they are willing to disclose or withhold. Providers face disclosure challenges that affect patient outcomes and their own relationships (Petronio, 2006). Disclosure may depend on how the providers and health care teams ask the questions. The provider–patient relationship may also be influenced by family and friends as informal health care advocates, where patient disclosure is shaped by social networks beyond the provider–patient interaction. Physician–patient boundary violations are described as violations of social norms that can range from the communication of uncomfortable or unkind comments to outright exploitation (Beach & Roter, 2005). Disclosure about prognosis poses a communicative dilemma. Although the general medical consensus is that patients have a moral and legal right to know the truth about their illness, patients may not actually want to know all the details of their illness (Schofield et al., 2003). Perceptions of support and partnering may either encourage, or may sacrifice, patient trust, in that some patients do not want all the details of their illness.

Emotions and Bias.   Patients' emotions are a central component of illness and of coping, and represent a potential pathway for responsiveness and concern as a cornerstone of relationship-centered care. Physicians miss opportunities to respond to patient emotions in 38% of surgical cases and 21% in primary care (Levinson, Gorawara-Bhat, & Lamb, 2000). Research also suggests that it is rare for patients to overtly express their true concerns. They instead disclose their concerns and expectations through implied "clues," subtle disclosures that include expressions of concern or worry, attempts to understand or explain symptoms, speech clues (i.e., repeating an illness statement), personal narratives, and suggesting unresolved concerns (i.e., seeking a second opinion or implying unresolved care with another provider; Lang, Floyd, & Beine, 2000). It is increasingly accepted as integral to medical curricula that empathy be taught.

Communication-Based Interventions

Research does indeed document the efficacy of communication interventions for both providers and patients. Senior cancer care providers who receive any type of intervention (written feedback followed by a course, a course alone, or written feedback alone) indicate more focused and open questions, expressions of empathy, appropriate response to patient cues, and lower rates of leading questions (Fallowfield et al., 2002). Subsequent research indicates that the physicians also integrate their newly acquired communication skills into clinical practice (Fallowfield, Jenkins, Farewell, & Solis-Trapala, 2003). Interventions are also aimed at patients. Mishel et al.'s (2005) theoretically based uncertainty management intervention utilizing a randomized controlled design delivered to older long-term breast cancer survivors predicted better cognitive reframing, cancer knowledge, patient–provider communication, and a variety of coping skills. Other interventions address patient communication skills training and report a positive effect on patient adherence and clinical health outcomes. Work in this area also calls, however, for patient training that addresses underserved populations, patients' preferences for involvement, and assesses the effects of training on health outcomes (Cegala, 2006).

Moving beyond the Threshold: Future Directions

To move beyond the threshold of what we know about provider–patient interaction and its outcomes, researchers, medical educators, policy makers, and clinicians will have to work toward clearer consensus in definition and measurement of constructs that are used across relevant disciplines. Current research provides guidance in regard to training providers, patients, and standardized patient educators/actor patients. Communication processes identified in the literature provide fertile ground for training providers in recognizing and using reflective practice to continue to work toward relationship-oriented care that considers the pathways through which communication processes are linked to outcomes. Similarly, the literature identifies areas for patient training, including the facilitation of shared decision making and understanding, and for recognizing the mutual influence process between providers and patients. Standardized patient educators/actor patients used in medical education provide both evaluative and reflective opportunities for student providers to experience and personally attempt patient scenarios and to receive feedback on their communication after the interaction. Theoretical explanations have not kept pace with the provider–patient research, but the research does allow for competing explanations of causality when provider and patient variables are considered. Thus, a broader application of theory as explanatory framework may be more appropriate given the unique dynamics of provider–patient interaction.

An integration in research is taking shape, as studies integrate multiple stakeholders, including providers, researchers, theorists, public health experts, and social epidemiologists, and involve them in each step of the design and implementation of research. This line of research has the potential to move beyond what we now know. It can examine the ways that communication processes influence, and are influenced by, the health and illness outcomes across populations. Similarly, communication has been identified as a core theme in leading medical schools and in accreditation agencies. International organizations that bridge disciplines and geographical limitations are taking a lead role in encouraging the ongoing dialogue among researchers, clinicians, and policy makers. Designs to measure communication and health outcomes are increasingly recognizing and accounting for the reciprocal roles of provider and patient in intervention designs, methods, and measures. Future research also must address the ways in which technology may shape the interaction, adding flexibility to the form and content of the message but perhaps discouraging responsiveness and even challenging core assumptions of the relationship. For example, communication via computer operates almost exclusively in the realm of the content of the message and ignores context, including the ways nonverbal communication and emotional expression shape relationship development. Similarly, disclosures about psychosocial aspects of illness that are not necessarily part of the medical record are easily forwarded to others when patient information is shared through technology. Underdeveloped norms and standards for the nature and content of the provider–patient relationship further challenge the interpersonal aspects of negotiating relationships. The ways that relationships between health personnel, providers, and patients are organized and navigated pose additional challenges for future researchers interested in this important area.

Conclusion

It is evident from the research summarized herein that communicative behaviors do indeed have important impacts on numerous outcomes of the health care interaction. These outcomes include those that are desirable but not essential, such as satisfaction, as well as those that are more important, such as health status, quality of life, adherence, and malpractice litigation. We have attempted to provide some discussion of the pathways through which communicative behaviors impact these variables. It is these pathways that should be the focus of future, theoretically based research.

References

Ambady, N., LaPlante, D., Nguyen, T., Rosenthal, R., Chaumeton, N., & Levinson, W. (2002). Surgeons' tone of voice: A clue to malpractice history. *Surgery, 132,* 5–9.

Barr, M. S. (2008). The need to test the patient-centered medical home. *Journal of the American Medical Association, 300,* 834–835.

Beach, M. C., Keruly, J., & Moore, R. D. (2006). Is the quality of the patient–provider relationship associated with better adherence and improved health outcomes for patients with HIV? *Journal of General Internal Medicine, 21,* 661–665.

Beach, M. C., & Roter, D. L. (2005). Interpersonal expectations in the patient–physician relationship. *Journal of General Internal Medicine, 15,* 825–827.

Beach, M. C., Roter, D. L., Wang, N. Y., Duggan, P. S., & Cooper, L. A. (2006). Are physicians' attitudes of respect accurately perceived by patients and associated with more positive communication behaviors? *Patient Education and Counseling, 62,* 347–354.

Beckman, H. (1995). Communication and malpractice: Why patients sue their physicians. *Cleveland Clinic Journal of Medicine, 62*(2), 85–89.

Beckman, H. B., & Frankel, R. M. (1984). The effect of physician behavior on the collection of data. *Annals of Internal Medicine, 101,* 692–696.

Berlin, L. (2007). Communicating results of all diagnostic radiological examinations directly to patients: Has the time come? *American Journal of Radiology, 189,* 1275–1282.

Bruera, E., Sweeney, C., Calder, K., Palmer, L., & Benisch-Tolley, S. (2001). Patient preferences versus physician perceptions of treatment decisions in cancer care. *Journal of Clinical Oncology, 19,* 2883–2885.

Butow, P. (2001). The importance of communication skills to effective cancer care and support. *NSW Public Health Bulletin, 12*(10), 272–274.

Cegala, D. J. (2006). Emerging trends and future directions in patient communication skills training. *Health Communication, 20,* 123–129.

Chant, S., Jenkinson, T., Randle, J., Russell, G., & Webb, C. (2002). Communication skills training in healthcare: A review of the literature. *Nurse Education Today, 22,* 189–202.

de Haes, H., & Bensing, J. (2009). Endpoints in medical communication research, proposing a framework of functions and outcomes. *Patient Education & Counseling, 74,* 287–294.

Duggan, A. P., Bradshaw, Y. S., & Altman, W. (2010). How do I ask about your disability? An examination of interpersonal communication processes between medical students and patients with disabilities. *Journal of Health Communication, 15,* 334–350.

Duggan, A. P., & Parrott, R. L. (2001). Physicians' nonverbal rapport building and patients' talk about the subjective component of illness. *Human Communication Research, 27,* 299–311.

Elwyn, G., Edwards, A., Mowle, S., Wensing, M., Wilkinson, C., Kinnersley, P., & Grol, R. (2001). Measuring the involvement of patients in shared decision-making: A systematic review of instruments. *Patient Education and Counseling, 43,* 5–22.

Epstein, R. M., Alper, B. S., & Quill, T. E. (2004). Communicating evidence for participatory decision making. *Journal of the American Medical Association, 291,* 2359–2366.

Epstein, R. M., Franks, P., Sheilds, C. G., Meldrum, S. C., Miller, K. N., Campbell, T. L., ... Fiscella, K. (2005). Patient-centered communication and diagnostic testing. *Annals of Family Medicine, 3,* 415–421.

Fallowfield, L., Jenkins, V., Farewell, V., Saul, J., Duffy, A., & Eves, R. (2002). Efficacy of a cancer research UK communication skills training model for oncologists: A randomised controlled trial. *Lancet, 359,* 650–655.

Fallowfield, L., Jenkins, V., Farewell, V., & Solis-Trapala, I. (2003). Enduring impact of communication skills training: Results of a 12-month follow-up. *British Journal of Cancer, 89,* 1445–1449.

Fox, S. A., Heritage, J., Stockdale, S. E., Asch, S. M., Duan, N., & Reise, S. P. (2009). Cancer screening adherence: Does physician–patient communication matter? *Patient Education and Counseling, 75,* 178–184.

Franks, P., Fiscella, K., Shields, C. G., Meldrum, S. C., Duberstein, P., Jerant, ... Epstein, R. M. (2005). Are patients' ratings of their physicians related to health outcomes? *Annals of Family Medicine, 3,* 229–234.

Galil, A., Bachner, Y. G., Merrick, J., Flusser, H., Lubetzky, H., Heiman, N.,& Carmel, S. (2006). Physician–parent communication as predictor of parent satisfaction with child development services. *Research in Developmental Disabilities, 27,* 233–242.

Gordon, H. S., Street Jr., R. L., Sharf, B. F., Kelly, P. A., & Souchek, J. (2006). Racial differences in trust and lung cancer patients' perceptions of physician communication. *Journal of Clinical Oncology, 24,* 904–909.

Griffin, S. J., Kinmonth, A, Veltman, M. W. M., Gillard, S., Grant, J., & Stewart, M. (2004). Effect on health-related outcomes of interventions to alter the interaction between patients and practitioners: A systematic review of trials. *Annals of Family Medicine, 2,* 595–608.

Hall, J. A., Horgan, T. G., Stein, T. S., & Roter, D. L. (2002). Liking in the physician–patient relationship. *Patient Education and Counseling, 48,* 69–77.

Hall, J. A., Milburn, M. A., Roter, D. L., & Daltroy, L. H. (1998). Why are sicker patients less satisfied with their medical care? Tests of two explanatory models. *Health Psychology, 17,* 70–75.

Haskard, K. B., Williams, S. L., DiMatteo, M. R., Rosenthal, R., White, M. K., & Goldstein, M. G. (2008). Physician and patient communication training in primary care: Effects on participation and satisfaction. *Health Psychology, 27,* 513–522.

Hausman, A. (2004). Modeling the patient–physician service encounter: Improving patient outcomes. *Journal of the Academy of Marketing Science, 32,* 403–417.

Hickson, G. B., Clayton, E. W., Entman, S. S., Miller, C. S., Githens, P. B., Whetten-Goldstein, K., & Sloan, F. A. (1994). Obstetricians' prior malpractice experience and patients' satisfaction with care. *Journal of the American Medical Association, 272,* 1583–1587.

Hickson, G. B., Clayton, E. W., Githens, P. B., & Sloan, F. A. (1992). Factors that prompted families to file medical malpractice claims following perinatal injuries. *Journal of the American Medical Association, 267,* 1359–1363.

Hickson, G. B., & Entman, S. S. (2008). Physician behavior and litigation risk: Evidence and opportunity. *Clinical Obstetrics & Gynecology, 51,* 688–699.

Hulsman, R. L., Ros, W. J. G., Winnubst, J. A. M., & Bensing, J. M. (1999). Teaching clinically experienced physicians communication skills: A review of evaluation studies. *Medical Education, 33,* 655–668.

Iezzoni, L. I. (2006). Make no assumptions: Communication between persons with disabilities and clinicians. *Assistive Technology, 18,* 212–219.

Institute of Medicine, Committee on Quality of Health Care in America. (2001). *Crossing the quality chasm: A new health system for the 21st century.* Washington, DC: National Academy Press.

Jackson, J. L., & Kroenke, K. (2001). Effect of unmet expectations among adults presenting with physical symptoms [Supplement]. *Annals of Internal Medicine, 134*(Part 2), 889–897.

Kahana, E., & Kahana, B. (2003). Patient proactivity enhancing doctor–patient–family communication in cancer prevention and care among the aged. *Patient Education and Counseling, 50,* 67–73.

Kaplan, S. H., Greenfield, S., & Ware, J. E. (1989). Assessing the effects of physician–patient interactions on the outcomes of chronic disease. *Medical Care, 27*(Supplement), S110–S127.

Kinmonth, A. L., Woodcock, A., Griffin, S., Spiegal, N., & Campbell, M. J. (1998). Randomised controlled trial of patient centered care of diabetes in general practice: Impact on current well being and future disease risk. *British Journal of Medicine, 317,* 1202–1208.

Korsch, B. M., Gozzi, E. K., & Francis, V. (1968). Gaps in doctor–patient communication. *Pediatrics, 42,* 855–871.

Kroenke,C. H., Kubzansky, L. D., Schernhammer, E. S., Holmes, M. D., & Kawachi, I (2006). Social network, social support, and survival after breast cancer diagnosis. *Journal of Clinical Oncology, 24,* 1105–1110.

Krupat, E., Yeager, C. M., & Putnam, S. (2000). Patient role orientations, doctor–patient fit, and visit satisfaction. *Psychology and Health, 15,* 707–719.

Lakatos, P. L. (2009). Prevalence, predictors, and clinical consequences of medical adherence in IBD: How to improve it? *World Journal of Gastroenterology, 15,* 4234–4239.

Lamont, E. B., & Christakis, N. A. (2001). Prognostic disclosure to patients with cancer near the end of life. *Annals of Internal Medicine, 134,* 1096–1105.

Lang, F., Floyd, M. R., & Beine, K. L. (2000). Clues to patients' explanations and concerns about their illnesses. *Archives of Family Medicine, 9,* 222–227.

Levinson, W., Gorawara-Bhat, R., & Lamb, J. (2000). A study of patient clues and physician responses in primary care and surgical settings. *Journal of the American Medical Association, 284,* 1021–1027.

Levinson, W., Roter, D. L., Mullooly, J. P., Dull, V. T., & Frankel, R. M. (1997). Physician–patient communication: The relationship with malpractice claims among primary care and surgeons. *Journal of the American Medical Association, 277,* 553–559.

Little, P., Everitt, H., Williamson, I., Warner, G., Moore, M., Gould, C., … Payne, S. (2001). Observational study of effect of patient centredness and positive approach on outcomes of general practice consultations. *British Medical Journal, 323,* 908–911.

Maly, R. C., Stein, J. A., Umezawa, Y., Leake, B., & Anglin, M. D. (2008). Racial/ethnic differences in breast cancer outcomes among older patients: Effects of physician communication and patient empowerment. *Health Psychology, 27,* 728–736.

Marvel, M. K., Epstein, R. M., Flowers, K., & Beckman, H. B. (1999). Soliciting the patient's agenda: Have we improved? *Journal of the American Medical Association, 281,* 283–287.

Mead, N., & Bower, P. (2002). Patient-centred consultations and outcomes in primary care: A review of the literature. *Patient Education and Counseling, 48,* 51–61.

Mishel, M. H., Germino, B. B., Gil, K. M., Belyea, M., Laney, I. C., Stewart, J., … Clayton, M. (2005). Benefits from an uncertainty management intervention for African-American and Caucasian older long-term breast cancer survivors. *Psycho-Oncology, 14,* 962–978.

Nichols, J. D. (2003). Lawyer's advice on physician conduct with malpractice cases. *Clinical Orthopaedics and Related Research, 407,* 14–18.

Nussbaum, J. F., & Fisher, C. L. (2009). A communication model for the competent delivery of geriatric medicine. *Journal of Language and Social Psychology, 28,* 190–208.

Ong, L. M. L., de Haes, J. C. J. M., Hoos, A. M., & Lammes, F. B. (1995). Doctor–patient communication: A review of the literature. *Social Science and Medicine, 40,* 903–918.

Ong, L. M. L., Visser, M. R. M., Lammes, F. B., & de Haes, J. C. J. M. (2000). Doctor–patient communication and cancer patients' quality of life and satisfaction. *Patient Education and Counseling, 41,* 145–156.

Parchman, M. L., Flannagan, D., Ferrer, R. L., & Matamoras, M. (2009). Communication competence, self-care behaviors, and glucose control in patients with type 2 diabetes. *Patient Education & Counseling, 77,* 55–59.

Paulsel, M. L., McCroskey, J. C., & Richmond, V. P. (2006). Perceptions of health care professionals' credibility as a predictor of patients' satisfaction with their medical care and physician. *Communication Research Reports, 23,* 69–76.

Petronio, S. (2002). *Boundaries of privacy: Dialectics of disclosure.* Albany, NY: SUNY Press.

Petronio, S. (2006). Impact of medical mistakes: Negotiating work–family boundaries for physicians. *Communication Monographs, 73,* 462–467.

Pieterse, A. H., van Dulmen, A. M., Beemer, F. A., Bensing, J. M., & Ausems, M. G. (2007). Cancer genetic counseling: Communication and counselees' post-visit satisfaction, cognitions, anxiety, and needs fulfillment. *Journal of Genetic Counseling, 16,* 85–96.

Priebe, S., McCabe, R., Bullenkamp, J., Hansson, L., Lauber, C., Martinez-Leal, R., … Wright, D. J. (2007). Structured patient–clinician communication and 1-year outcome in community mental health care: Cluster randomised controlled trial. *British Journal of Psychiatry, 191,* 420–426.

Roter, D., Frankel, R. M., Hall, J. A., & Sluyter, D. (2006). The expression of emotion through nonverbal behavior in medical visits: Mechanisms and outcomes. *Journal of General Internal Medicine, 21*(Supplement), S28–S34.

Roter, D. L., & Hall, J. A. (2009). Communication and adherence: Moving from prediction to understanding. *Medical Care, 47,* 823–825.

Schoenthaler, A., Chaplin, W. F., Allegrante, J. P., Fernandez, S., Diaz-Gloster, M., Tobin, J. N., & Ogedegbe, G. (2009). Provider communication effects medication adherence in hypotensive African Americans. *Patient Education and Counseling, 75,* 185–191.

Schofield, P. E., Butow, P. N., Thompson, J. F., Tattersall, M. H. N., Beeney, L. J., & Dunn, S. M. (2003). Psychological responses of patients receiving a diagnosis of cancer. *Annals of Oncology, 14,* 48–56.

Shapiro, J., Mosqueda, L., & Botros, D. (2003). A caring partnership: Expectations of ageing persons with disabilities for their primary care doctors. *Family Practice, 20*, 635–641.

Shaw, B. R., Han, J. Y., Hawkins, R. P., Stewart, J., McTavish, F., & Gustafson, D. H. (2007). Doctor–patient relationship as motivation and outcome: Examining uses of an interactive cancer communication system. *International Journal of Medical Informatics, 76*, 274–282.

Skoumal, S. M., Florell, S. R., Bydalek, M. K., & Hunter, W. J. (1996). Malpractice protection: Communication of diagnostic uncertainty. *Diagnostic Cytopathology, 14*, 385–389.

Sohler, N. L., Fitzpatrick, L. K., Lindsay, R. G., Anastos, K., & Cunningham, C. O. (2007). Does patient–provider racial/ethnic concordance influence ratings of trust in people with HIV infection? *AIDS Behavior, 11*, 884–896.

Street, R. L., Makoul, G., Arora, N. K., & Epstein, R. M. (2009). How does communication heal? Pathways linking clinician–patient communication to health outcomes. *Patient Education and Counseling, 74*, 295–301.

Veltman, A., Stewart, D. E., Tardif, G. S., & Branigan, M. (2001). Perceptions of primary healthcare services among people with physical disabilities. Part 1: Access issues. *Medscape General Medicine, 3*, 1–4.

Vukmir, R. B. (2004). Medical malpractice: Managing the risk. *Medicine and Law, 25*, 495–513.

Wissow, L. S. (2004). Patient communication and malpractice: Where are we now? *Patient Education & Counseling, 52*, 3–5.

Zarcadoolas, C., Pleasant, A., & Greer, D. S. (2003). Elaborating a definition of health literacy: A commentary. *Journal of Health Communication, 8*, 119–120.

Zolnierek, K. B. H., & DiMatteo, M. R. (2009). Physician communication and patient adherence to treatment: A meta-analysis. *Medical Care, 47*, 826–834.

27

STRESS, BURNOUT, AND SUPPORTIVE COMMUNICATION

A Review of Research in Health Organizations

Eileen Berlin Ray and Julie Apker

> As demands increase and become chronic and resources decrease, stress increases and leaves care providers especially vulnerable to a variety of negative personal and professional outcomes.
>
> Halbesleben (2008, p. xi)

Stress and social support among employees and caregivers in health organizations remain enduring subjects of interest for health organization researchers and practitioners. Researchers have investigated a variety of issues related to these subjects, ranging from identifying the communicative antecedents of burnout, to determining the "bottom-line" outcomes of stress in areas such as reduced worker commitment and increased turnover, to studying the messages and structures that may help employees cope with workplace stress and burnout. These various lines of scholarship reveal that stress, burnout, and social support are communicative processes that are central to our understanding of health organizations and their members. This literature shows that stress and burnout present ongoing challenges to health providers and their institutional employers. While there is no one "silver bullet" that will solve these problems, social support offers a promising avenue through which individuals and organizations can deal effectively with stress and burnout.

Over the past two decades, we have witnessed massive changes in health care in the United States. It is critical to note these changes because it is impossible to discuss job stress without acknowledging their impact. Previous research on stress in health organizations has often drawn an arbitrary boundary around the organization, giving only a passing nod to exigencies in the external environment. Among these external factors are organizational restructuring and managed care and their subsequent impact on providers. In our previous *Handbook of Health Communication* chapter (Apker & Ray, 2003) we argued that these forces affect the experience of work in health organizations and must be considered when exploring job stress and burnout. This current chapter, which updates the research literature, demonstrates the continued importance of the implications of these external factors and includes issues that further impact providers' job stress and the role of social support.

We examine job stress due to (1) the nature of health care work; (2) structural issues and managed care; (3) changing roles; (4) emotional labor; and (5) home/work conflict. We then discuss social support and how supportive communication may mediate or exacerbate job stress. Finally, we consider implications for future research and examine the relationship between job stress, burnout, and social support.

Job Stress within Health Care Professions

Health care work is inherently stressful. Care providers experience ongoing, life-challenging health issues as they care for those who suffer from health problems. Health care work seems to attract people who exhibit certain characteristics: they talk about wanting to make a difference in people's lives and often see their career choice as a calling. They are aware of the intrinsic stress of health care work, at least cognitively. Once in the field, however, they are likely to experience additional stressors such as workload (underload and overload), role conflict, role ambiguity, scarce resources, understaffing, physical strain (e.g., lifting and moving patients), and a lack of participation in decision making (see Ford & Ellis, 1998). The effects may be physical, behavioral, or attitudinal. At the individual level, increases in substance abuse, physical illness, relationship conflict, and psychological problems are not uncommon. At the organizational level, increases in absenteeism, turnover, poor job performance, and job dissatisfaction are common results.

For patients, the impact of care provider job stress can be, literally, a matter of life and death. The category "preventable medical errors" is the eighth most common cause of death in the United States, killing between 44,000 and 98,000 people each year (Sexton, Thomas, & Helmreich, 2000). A study of surgery staff and intensive care unit staff found that poor communication and teamwork were frequent contributors to these errors, complicated by the fact that medical staff may deny their high stress levels or refuse to acknowledge their mistakes. High patient-to-nurse ratios and extended shifts result in provider fatigue and may lead to decreases in patient safety, medical care, patient satisfaction, and burnout. Health care providers' stress also impacts patients' level of satisfaction with their hospital stay and patients who have more cynical nurses report less satisfaction with medical care (Halbesleben & Rathert, 2008).

Within health care organizations, numerous stressors have been identified in various care occupations. For example, for hospital nurses these stressors include work overload, patient death and separation, the emotional demands brought about by patients and their families, poor communication with coworkers, and low social support. Nurses are faced with sicker patients, long hours, increased patient load, and less autonomy (Breaux, Meurs, Zellars, & Perrewe, 2008). Specifically, nurses who perceive low stressors, high social support, and high patient contact report low burnout, while nurses who experience patient decay and suffering, conflict with coworkers, low social support, fewer patients, and moderate stress levels report high burnout (Hillhouse & Adler, 1997). Stressors also appear to vary depending on the degree of status differences. For example, peer conflict may be easier to resolve and less threatening, while asymmetrical relationship (e.g., nurse–doctor) conflict, combined with heavy work and patient loads, may magnify nurses' stress (Hayhurst, Saylor, & Stuenkel, 2005). Nurses also report that role ambiguity, role conflict, workload, daily pressure (Ford & Ellis, 1998; Lee & Ashforth, 1996) and high patient-to-nurse ratios (Aiken, Clarke, Sloane, Sochalski, & Silber, 2002) are stressors that affect their work lives.

Stressors including time pressure and emotional and conflicting demands are pronounced for nurses caring for dementia patients (Josefsson, Sonde, Winblad, & Wahlin, 2007), while critical care nurses (Meltzer & Huckabay, 2004) and those working with the terminally ill (Breaux et al., 2008) also report increased emotional exhaustion. For medical residents, stress has been related to burnout, suicidal ideation, and suicide (Dyrbye et al., 2008).

This line of scholarship, then, illustrates that health care professionals experience many different kinds of job stress, some of which are tied to particular occupational characteristics, skills, or work settings. However, it is important to avoid taking an exclusively microlevel perspective when examining workplace stressors and burnout in health care organizations (Ray & Miller, 1990). Thus, we next address the more overarching sources of job stress that affect health care professionals regardless of medical specialty or occupation.

Sources of Job Stress

Numerous health communication scholars (e.g., Ray & Miller, 1990; Wright, Sparks, & O'Hair, 2007) advocate adopting a systems perspective that highlights the critical nature of the interdependencies between all components within the organization and their impact on the provision of care. When the system works efficiently and effectively, it remains in balance. However, if this balance is disrupted, the outcome is potentially dangerous for both care providers and recipients. It is critical to understand the context within which job stress occurs. We provide this context by first discussing hospital restructuring and managed care. We then discuss their impact on three types of stressors: role stress, emotional labor, and home–work conflict.

Hospital Restructuring

Hospital nurses experience a great deal of chronic stress. These stressors have been exacerbated by major hospital restructuring, which requires nurses to continue to provide quality patient care with fewer resources and results in high levels of burnout. The use of mandatory or voluntary overtime to cover staff nurse vacancies has become common but increases the likelihood of medical errors, nurse fatigue, and burnout (Garrett, 2008).

This restructuring also includes a shift in responsibilities to allied health care occupations such as medical assistants, cardiovascular technologists, diagnostic medical sonographers, physician assistants, and respiratory therapy technicians. According to the Bureau of Labor Statistics, allied health care occupations are expected to increase over 25% annually. The use of these workers decreases organizations' costs but also forces a redistribution of job responsibilities. This workforce shift may increase interdisciplinary collaboration but at the same time heighten stressors such as role conflict and role ambiguity as providers may experience overlapping responsibilities (Kovner & Jonas, 2002). The provision and receipt of care are impacted by these changes in ways that are both positive and negative.

Managed Care

It is likely that the structural change that has most dramatically transformed U.S. health care has been managed care. Popular cost-cutting measures in recent decades have included increasing workers' administrative and clinical workload, downsizing staff, and redefining conventional caregiver roles (Apker, 2001). Doctors employed by managed care organizations in the United States (currently about 88%) report greater job dissatisfaction and turnover due to reduced autonomy, pressure to limit referrals, higher patient load, and problematic communication with managed care organizations.

Changes due to managed care also impact provider and patient roles and communication. Patients must take on the role of "health consumer" and take more responsibility for gathering health information, and choosing medical services and providers. They may often find themselves more dehumanized, with little care continuity. Communication with physicians who adhere to their managed care organization's rules is likely to become more formal, and potentially adversarial; but for doctors who attempt to bypass these regulations, communication is likely to become more conspiratorial.

While the original goal of managed care focused on preventive, accessible, and cost effective care, it has led to increased job stress by combining high job demands with low control, subsequently reducing providers' emotional resources and leading to burnout. Next, we discuss three types of stressors: (a) interorganizational and interpersonal role stress; (b) emotional labor; and (c) home–work conflict.

Role Stress

Role stress, including its relationship to various negative outcomes, gained notoriety because of the early work of Kahn and colleagues (Kahn, Wolfe, Quinn, Snoek, & Rosenthal, 1964). The term *role* has been defined as the behavioral expectations of individuals who occupy a particular position. Role stress has traditionally been divided into role conflict (having to engage in two or more incompatible roles simultaneously) and role ambiguity (a lack of clarity regarding the definition and expectations for a role). In health organizations, research suggests that worker role stress rises at both interorganizational and interpersonal levels.

Interorganizational Role Stress

Perhaps the most visible way in which we see interorganizational role stress is when experts in health care find themselves fighting regulations put in place by those who view health care as a business as opposed to focusing on appropriate care coordination. Cost containment strategies result in outside organizations dictating the length of hospital stays, coverage of treatments, and care. Both nurses and doctors are affected by this type of interorganizational role stress, as they must negotiate with third-party managed care or government systems over the care to be provided to their patients.

Similar interorganizational stressors have resulted from the institution of diagnosis related groups (DRGs), designed to contain costs for Medicare patients. DRGs determine reimbursement for hospitals to care for specific illnesses before the care is needed for a specific patient. The rate is based on the average cost of providing treatment for that particular illness. If costs exceed the reimbursement rate, hospitals lose money, but if costs are consistently below the rate, hospitals share in the profit. Thus, there is an incentive for hospitals to stay below the reimbursement level (Goldfield, 2010).

The implications for communication in health organizations are pervasive. For example, explaining how DRGs will impact a patient's care is considered "dirty work" that no one wants to perform (Hughes, 1971), and usually falls to the nurses. Thus, those providers having the most frequent and intense contact with patients and their families, and usually the strongest interpersonal relationships, are faced with explaining the intricacies of the managed care system.

Interpersonal Role Stress

Role stress related to interpersonal relationships is another common source of stress. RNs report feeling more stress as they care for more highly acute patients (Letvak, 2001), who must be the "sickest of the sick" before being admitted. Nurses have new role sets in a managed care environment that involve more (and increasingly complex) responsibilities. RNs must also communicate with allied health personnel and third-party payers as part of their nursing roles.

Nurses are increasingly expected to perform traditional bedside care in addition to conducting administrative duties and managing unlicensed staff. This struggle to balance clinical and nonclinical work roles often results in nurses reporting greater job stress, less personal accomplishment, and reduced time to spend with patients. Furthermore, research indicates that nurses who attempt to negotiate traditional clinical responsibilities with new work roles, such as case manager and discharge planner, experience ambiguity in the process of role development.

Health care professionals may experience stress related to role conflict even when their jobs are purposefully redesigned to reduce role-related stressors. Role conflict may also occur as part of the equal–subordinate dialectic, requiring nurses to juggle the contradiction of attempting to be viewed as competent peers of doctors while simultaneously conforming to the traditional hierarchical structure.

Experiencing role-related conflict also affects those employed in allied health and support staff positions. Similarly, nondirect care professionals report role stress. A study of those working in a retirement center found that food service, housekeeping, and administrative workers experienced role stress similar to their direct care counterparts (Miller, Zook, & Ellis, 1989). In sum, then, although some scholars warn against spreading caregivers too thinly in times of increased patient acuity and reduced patient lengths of stay, today's health care workers serve increasing numbers of patients and, in the process of delivering medical care, they perform more (and more varied) tasks. As health organizations downsize personnel and restructure job tasks, health care professionals may be in positions where they experience multiple and potentially conflicting roles. In addition, care providers are expected to present a certain front when enacting their role. This enactment, through emotional labor, may, in fact, act as an additional stressor.

Emotional Labor

The term *emotional labor* refers to "the management of feelings to create a publicly observable facial and bodily display" that is "sold for a wage" and where workers must "induce or suppress feeling in order to sustain the outward countenance that produces the proper state of mind in others" (Hochschild, 1983, p. 7). Miller, Stiff, and Ellis (1988) differentiate between human service workers who are able to maintain "empathic concern" (feeling *for* the other) versus "emotional contagion" (feeling *with*, or parallel to, the other). While empathic concern is more likely to have positive outcomes, emotional contagion is more likely to result in burnout.

In the context of health organizations, the notion of emotional labor is certainly applicable to caregivers because much of their communication involves affective content as they provide medical services. Health workers may perform emotional labor to potentially reduce workplace stress and burnout brought about by highly emotional circumstances. Nursing home caregivers use a wide range of emotional expressions to achieve numerous goals and functions at work (Sass, 2000), while caregivers in a cardiac center use established organizational rules regarding emotional labor to perform scripted work roles and necessary job activities (Morgan & Krone, 2001). From these studies, it appears that emotional labor may buffer or protect health professionals from work-related stressors.

Emotional labor can be a significant source of stress and burnout for caregivers, however.

Not only must health care workers manage their emotions when caring for patients but also when interacting with families, doctors, coworkers, and support staff. The efficiency of interdependent action among the various staff and departments, coupled with juggling symmetrical and asymmetrical roles, requires careful management of emotions. Workers must also maintain a positive face even when forced into a double bind by their employer (de Castro, Agnew, & Fitzgerald, 2004). For example, trying to persuade a patient that a less expensive treatment (which happens to be covered by managed care) is preferable to the more expensive (but not covered) treatment requires substantial presentation and persuasion skills.

In the realm of medical and nursing education, for instance, emotion management is an unspoken topic. Health care professionals-in-training must learn emotional labor strategies through unspoken rules and trial-and-error processes (Apker & Eggly, 2004). According to Hafferty (1988), medical training such as cadaver labs is a forum in which students and residents learn either to enact coping mechanisms such as displaying detached concern or suffer ridicule and isolation from their peers and supervisors. Hafferty (1988) argues that this type of emotional socialization promotes "maladaptive coping strategies," which may negatively affect physicians and their patients (p. 354). Smith and Kleinman (1989) found that medical residents and students informally learned affective neutrality from more experienced peers and supervisors, leading to problematic physician communication behaviors such as depersonalizing, blaming, and mocking patients. The negative effect of concealing emotions continues well beyond medical education.

Juggling these emotions is likely to exacerbate other stressors and increase levels of burnout. It is unrealistic, however, to suggest that job stressors are confined to health care organizations. Stress impacts, and is impacted by, life within and outside the workplace, often resulting in conflict between home and work spheres.

Home–Work Conflict

Over the past two decades, there has been an increase in research on the impact of home–work role conflict on health care providers. Role conflict between work and child or elder care has become a concern as many parents find themselves members of the "sandwich generation," caught between simultaneously caring for their children and their aging parents. These individuals report high levels of stress from their multiple caregiving roles. Others, such as single parents, must juggle their work and home responsibilities, a difficult task in the best of circumstances.

In a study of nurses, Bacharach (1991) found that work-based role conflict was an important antecedent to work–home conflict, observing that work-based role conflict spilled over into work–home conflict, leading to greater burnout. Miller and Gilles's (1996) research on the work–home stress experienced by oncology and HIV health staff also indicated that work stress negatively affected workers' domestic and social lives.

Physicians also find themselves caught in home–work role conflict. Although women comprise about 45% of medical students, they are still disproportionately in the lower-status, lower-pay medical specialties such as family medicine and internal medicine. These women are faced with two major decisions. The first is whether they are willing to put in the long, intense years necessary to reach the top tier of their profession (i.e., surgery, neurology, orthopedics). The implications of this decision are clear; aiming for this type of career will require a level of commitment not conducive to maintaining personal relationships or raising children. However, even female physicians in other specialties often find that they are not experiencing the career they originally had in mind. Instead, many arrange to work less and have more flexible hours. A quarter of female doctors report that they work less than 40 hours per week, compared to 12% of male doctors. Seventeen percent of female doctors said they worked 30 hours per week or less, while only 8% of male doctors worked this little (Steinhauer, 1999). The principal sources of stress for women doctors are conflict between personal life and work and being torn between professional duties and family responsibilities. Female doctors identify balancing work and family commitments as a greater determinant of job satisfaction than their male counterparts.

It is important for health organizations to understand the causes and consequences of workplace stress in order to avoid increased worker turnover, reduced productivity, and rising absenteeism. For communication scholars, though, a primary focus of job stress research has been consideration of the role of social support in reducing stress and influencing burnout and turnover.

Supportive Communication

Kahn (1993) argued that primary caregivers (e.g., nurses, physicians, social workers) are often the individuals who require the greatest caregiving themselves because their jobs encourage them to provide substantial emotional resources to others. Unfortunately, in the absence of supportive communication from coworkers and supervisors, caregivers' own emotional resources may be depleted in ways that place them at greater risk of burnout. We begin by considering the functions of supportive communication within health organizations.

Functions of Supportive Communication

Uncertainty is a significant component of the illness experience, as individuals struggle to make sense of the physical, social, emotional, and psychological signs associated with disease. While some have argued that social support acts to reduce uncertainty (see Goldsmith & Albrecht, this volume), other scholars assert that it is more likely that support can help us to manage, rather than reduce, uncertainty. According to Babrow and colleagues (see Babrow & Mattson, this volume), the theory of problematic integration (PIT) provides a useful framework for understanding how supportive communication enables people to manage uncertainty in health and illness situations.

In addition to this shift in the conceptual framework for the supportive communication–stress relationship, communication research has focused on two levels. At the individual level, the emphasis is on recipient perceptions of support or categories of support and linking workplace phenomena with health care issues. This approach establishes social support as a coping mechanism or as a buffer of workplace stress and burnout and has been linked to workplace role ambiguity and attachments to health organizations and professions. At the macro level, scholars have examined supportive ties within a network analytic framework (Ray, 1991), explicating how supportive communication is interactively constructed and may play a role in the stress and burnout experienced by health care workers.

Zimmermann and Applegate (1994), for example, suggest a message-centered approach, viewing support as an interactional accomplishment with an emphasis on how it is strategically created in talk. Miller and Ray (1994) discuss ways to identify supportive messages and their meaning among organizational members. At the individual level, they suggest adapting the memorable message concept (Knapp, Stohl, & Reardon, 1981) to identify health care workers' specific supportive and unsupportive messages. At the macro level, they investigated how nursing home assistants are linked through semantic networks, where linkages are not based on interaction patterns but on shared meaning and interpretation.

Sources of Support

At the interpersonal level, supportive communication can occur between and among all levels in health care organizations. Outside the organization, support may come from friends, spouses, partners, family members, and even acquaintances. For example, physicians who receive support from colleagues and professional networks, spouses, friends, and support groups report better health, with female physicians seeking and benefitting more from this support (Voltmer & Spahn, 2009).

Coworkers often have the benefit of shared knowledge, context, and experiences that contributes to social support in the workplace. Lee and Ashforth (1996) highlight the importance of coworker support by suggesting that workers' experience of emotional and physical strain is related to poor social support in their work environment. Metts, Geist, and Gray (1994) found that work relationships offered greater tangible assistance (e.g., providing needed goods and services) than nonwork relationships, and emotional support offered during work episodes was more effective than when it was offered outside of work settings.

Researchers studying health care workers in particular have identified the importance of support from coworkers, particularly peers and supervisors, as coping mechanisms for job-related stress (Deelstra et al., 2003; Halbesleben, 2008; Ray & Miller, 1994). Miller et al. (1989) found that coworker support lessened nurses' experience of burnout by reducing their emotional exhaustion and depersonalization, and supervisory support reduced nurses' depersonalization. Nurses who feel supported by their coworkers are more likely to identify with their hospital and profession, which may lower turnover. Nurse aides who report more supervisory support also report less stress and job dissatisfaction (McGilton, McGillis Hall, Wodchis, & Petroz, 2007), as do nurses who receive administrative support and have positive relationships with doctors (Rosenstein, 2002). For nurse manager–staff nurse relationships, supervisors who use a rhetorical message design approach (one that is designed to build consensus and harmony) experience the highest levels of relational support and lowest levels of burnout (Peterson & Albrecht, 1996). In their study of supportive and nonsupportive messages communicated among nurses, Ford and Ellis (1998) note that "RNs as peers and nursing supervisors as superiors continue to be a reliable source of organizational support for nurses under stress" (p. 53).

However, the content of the messages is important; while more positive messages may buffer burnout, communication in the form of gripe sessions is more likely to increase stress and burnout (Breaux et al., 2008). The intent of the messages is also critical and may result in dysfunctional "support." Ray (1993) notes that those in power may strategically manipulate supportive messages in ways that mask hidden agendas, maintain hierarchical control, and preserve the status quo. Thus, communication that may appear to be support may actually be a stressor. Health care organizations based on asymmetrical relationships, competition for resources, and capitation can provide fertile breeding ground for such communication.

Research regarding issues such as assertiveness, personal control, and participation in decision making also shows that such factors are important in creating a supportive communication environment for health workers. Ellis and Miller (1993) found that nurse assertiveness and participation in decision making with physician colleagues was important in increasing RNs' feelings of personal control which, in turn, reduced perceptions of burnout.

A study of nurse managers found that nurses perceive participation in decision making as a form of social support, one that bolstered their ability to cope with role stress (Apker, 2002).

Among social workers, research shows mixed findings. Jayaratne, Himle, and Chess (1988) found coworker support significantly mediated the relationship between the stressors of role ambiguity and role conflict and the burnout characteristics of depersonalization and emotional exhaustion. They also found that supervisor support was not helpful in reducing burnout. In contrast, Kim and Lee (2009) report that job relevant and position relevant communication with supervisors has a negative correlation with social worker burnout whereas upward communication buffers the effect of role stress on burnout.

Thomas and Ganster's (1995) study of work–family role conflict among health care professionals found that supervisor behaviors that were seen as supportive of employees' nonwork demands were instrumental in reducing worker stress and strain. While this line of research has underscored the importance of social support, it has focused on recipients' perceptions of accessible and available support or on characteristics of ongoing support networks (Miller & Ray, 1994). What has typically not been considered are actual support messages and their shared meaning between support providers and recipients.

In addition to emotional support, managers and administrators can provide instrumental and informational support by implementing organizational structures and policies that help workers minimize and cope with job-related stressors. Organizational programs such as flexible scheduling practice increased health care workers' perceptions of control over work, and reduced the negative physical and mental health outcomes typically associated with stress and strain (e.g., Keeton, Fenner, Johnson, & Hayward, 2007). An organizational environment that promotes social support is also important. A study conducted by Hullett, McMilan, and Rogan (2000) found that health care workers in a nursing home felt higher levels of personal accomplishment when they perceived their organizational culture as valued and that it rewarded supportive communication.

The scholarship reviewed in this chapter illustrates that job stressors and supportive communication in health organizations are fruitful subjects for researchers to explore. To conclude our discussion of this literature, we briefly identify issues that we believe are promising topics for future study. Specifically, we consider issues of managed care, alternative health care settings, and lay caregiving.

Implications for Future Research

Health professionals work in an increasingly complex environment, one characterized by constant change at systemic, organizational, and individual levels. The effects of managed care policies and initiatives have dramatically transformed the delivery of health care in the United States and shifted health care workers' job roles and practices (e.g., Halbesleban, 2008; Sultz & Young, 2009). By all accounts, the managed care era is far from over and health care systems will continue to adapt and respond to managed competition in a variety of ways (Miller, 2003).

Cost containment, capitation, HMOs, preferred provider organizations, and changes in Medicare have impacted not only what and how care is provided but also the communication between and among providers and recipients. Research reviewed in this chapter reveals that managed care is a significant job stressor. One interesting area for scholars to investigate is the relationship between communication about managed care (e.g., sources of information, quantity and quality of communication, patterns of communication between caregivers) and health care providers' experience of stress. For example, does talk about managed care heighten caregiver stress or does it manage uncertainty and give caregivers a greater sense of control over managed care changes? Moreover, where and from whom (e.g., coworkers, supervisors, patients, the media) do caregivers receive information about managed care and how do these sources influence subsequent communication about managed care changes? How does such communication help (or hinder) health care providers' sense making of and coping with managed care changes in their work lives and relationships? Communication scholars are well suited to study these research topics.

A second area for researchers to consider is to extend the study of stressors and supportive communication into more varied organizational contexts such as outpatient clinics, long term care settings, and holistic care provider practices. Although hospitals remain an important component of health care delivery and a significant setting in which to continue the study of stress and social support, economic changes and shifting health care, consumer preferences have led to more and more patients seeking medical care outside of inpatient settings (du Pré, 2010). We encourage researchers to investigate job stressors and supportive communication within the wide range of health care organizations and occupations that exist. As people are living longer with chronic diseases and medical costs continue to rise, many people who are not health care professionals (e.g., family, friends) are taking on caregiving responsibilities for others. Future research should examine communication issues between health organizations, these lay caregivers, and their coordination of care. As du Pré (2010) argues, lay caregivers may experience the same stress related to caregiving as their professional counterparts, but they often lack the training and supportive communication to help them cope. What are the physical, psychological, and communicative effects for lay caregivers who have insufficient medical training? How can supportive communication buffer their stress and reduce the likelihood of burnout? These questions will be of increasing significance as lay caregiving becomes more common.

Finally, with the increase in hospital restructuring and managed care has come an increase in the use of interdisciplinary health care teams. Despite the assumption that interdisciplinary health care team members will have positive experiences, resulting in less burnout and turnover and greater job satisfaction, Apker, Propp, and Ford (2009) note that research to date has not supported this assumption. In fact, team membership may increase stress. Teams can only be effective to the extent that members are able to coordinate and collaborate through clear, explicit communication. This is often a difficult goal to achieve (e.g., Coopman, 2001; Kreps & Bonaguro, 2009) for many reasons, including "backstage" communication by team members that may negatively impact team functioning and communication with care recipients (Ellingson, 2003). An additional concern has been voiced by Kovner and Jonas (2002), who warn that concurrent with the shift toward collaboration is a move toward competition within and between professions. Care provided by primary care physicians, nurse practitioners, and physician assistants is likely to overlap, while the roles of psychiatrists, psychologists, and social workers regarding mental health care may be blurred (Pecukonis, Doyle, & Bliss, 2008). Thus, well-functioning teams are likely to act as a stress buffer and provide social support to team members while conflicts with collaboration or competition are likely to become, rather than ameliorate, a stressor. Health care team communication is critical to organizational functioning and patient care and is fertile ground for communication scholars.

Conclusion

This chapter has reviewed research from the past three decades regarding stress and social support in health organizations. The literature presented here indicates that the health care landscape has become increasingly complex for health care providers, and significant stressors often accompany these complexities in health care delivery and systems. Research suggests that health professionals experience many different types of jobs stress, but issues of organizational restructuring, managed care, role changes, emotional labor, and home–work conflict have been particularly noteworthy. As researchers' conceptualization of job stress has evolved, so has their understanding of supportive communication. Scholarship suggests that social support serves a variety of helpful functions for caregivers. However, other scholars speculate that supportive communication may also negatively affect health care organizations by furthering the communicative dysfunctions that may already exist among health care professionals.

The field of stress and supportive communication has a rich research history among organizational and health communication scholars. It may seem that there is not much more to unearth about these topics, but we would argue that the research reviewed in this chapter indicates otherwise. Topics such as managed care, and all of its systemic, organizational, and individual implications, present researchers with myriad opportunities for new discoveries about the job stressors and supportive communication that occur in health care. It is through continued scholarly investigation that we will better understand the demands that impact health care professionals and the communication processes that characterize the delivery of care.

References

Aiken, L. H., Clarke, S. P., Sloane, D. M., Sochalski, J., & Silber, J. H. (2002). Hospital nurse staffing and patient mortality, nurse burnout, and job dissatisfaction. *Journal of the American Medical Association, 288,* 1987–1993.

Apker, J. (2001). Role development in the managed care era: A case of hospital-based nursing. *Journal of Applied Communication Research, 29,* 117–136.

Apker, J. (2002). Front-line nurse manager roles, job stressors, and coping strategies in a managed care hospital. *Qualitative Research Reports in Communication, 3,* 75–81.

Apker, J., & Eggly, S. (2004). Communicating professional identity in medical socialization: Considering the ideological discourse of morning report. *Qualitative Health Research, 14,* 411–429.

Apker, J., Propp, K. M., & Ford, W. S. Z. (2009). Investigating the effect of nurse-team communication on nurse turnover: Relationships among communication processes, identification, and intent to leave. *Health Communication, 24,* 106–114.

Apker, J., & Ray, E. B. (2003). Stress and social support in health care organizations. In T. L. Thompson, A. M. Dorsey, K. I. Miller, & R. Parrott (Eds.), *Handbook of health communication* (pp. 347–368). Mahwah, NJ: Erlbaum.

Bacharach, S. B. (1991). Work-home conflict among nurses and engineers: Mediating the impact of role stress on burnout and satisfaction at work. *Journal of Organizational Behavior, 12,* 39–53.

Breaux, D. M., Meurs, J. A., Zellars, K. L., & Perrewe, P. L. (2008). Burnout in health care: When helping hurts. In J. R. B. Halbesleban (Ed.), *Handbook of stress and burnout in health care* (3rd ed., pp. 39–50). Hauppauge, NY: Nova Science.

Coopman, S. J. (2001). Democracy, performance, and outcomes in interdisciplinary health care teams. *Journal of Business Communication, 38,* 261–284.

de Castro, A. B., Agnew, J., & Fitzgerald, S. T. (2004). Emotional labor: Relevant theory for occupational health practice in post-industrial America. *American Association of Occupational Health Nursing Journal, 52,* 109–115.

Deelstra, J. T., Peeters, M. C., Schaufeli, W. B., Stroebe, W., Zijlstra, F. R. H., & van Doornen, L. P. (2003). Receiving instrumental support at work: When help is not welcome. *Journal of Applied Psychology, 88,* 324–331.

du Pré, A. (2010). *Communicating about health: Current issues and perspectives* (3rd ed.). New York: Oxford University Press.

Dyrbye, L. N., Thomas, M. R., Massie, F. S., Power, D. V., Eacker, A., Harper, W., ... Shanafelt, T. D. (2008). Relationshiop between burnout and suicidal ideation among U. S. medical students. *Annals of Internal Medicine, 149*, 334–341.

Ellingson, L. L. (2003). Interdisciplinary health care teamwork in the clinic backstage. *Journal of Applied Communication Research, 31*, 93–117.

Ellis, B. H., & Miller, K. I. (1993). The role of assertiveness, personal control, and participation in the prediction of nurse burnout. *Journal of Applied Communication Research, 21*, 327–342.

Ford, L. A., & Ellis, B. H. (1998). A preliminary analysis of memorable support and nonsupport messages from three research studies. *International Journal of Social Psychiatry, 42*, 102–111.

Garrett, C. (2008). The effect of nurse staffing patterns on medical errors and nurse burnout. *Association of periOperative Registered Nurses, 87*, 1191–1204.

Goldfield, N. (2010). The evolution of diagnosis-related groups (DRGs): From its beginnings in case-mix and resource use theory, to its implementation for payment and now for its current utilization for quality within and outside the hospital. *Quality Management in Health Care, 19*(1), 3–16.

Hafferty, F. W. (1988). Cadaver stories and the emotional socialization of medical students. *Journal of Health and Social Behavior, 29*, 344–356.

Halbesleben, J. R. B. (2008). (Ed.). *Handbook of stress and burnout in health care* (3rd ed.). Hauppauge, NY: Nova.

Halbesleben, J. R. B., & Rathert, C. (2008). Linking physician burnout and patient outcomes: Exploring the dyadic relationship between physicians and patients. *Health Care Management Review, 33*(1), 29–39.

Hayhurst, A., Saylor, C., & Stuenkel, D. (2005). Work environmental factors for the retention of nurses. *Journal of Nursing Care Quality, 20*, 283–288.

Hillhouse, J., & Adler, C. (1997). Investigating stress effect patterns in hospital staff nurses: Results of a cluster analysis. *Social Science & Medicine, 45*, 1781–1788.

Hochschild, A. R. (1983). *The managed heart: Commercialization of human feelings*. Berkeley: University of California Press.

Hughes, E. (1971). *The sociological eye*. Chicago, IL; Aldine.

Hullett, C. R., McMilan, J. J., & Rogan, R. G. (2000). Caregivers' predispositions and perceived organizational expectations for the provision of social support to nursing home residents. *Health Communication, 12*, 277–300.

Jayaratne, S., Himle, D., & Chess, W. A. (1988). Dealing with work stress and strain: Is the perception of support more important than its use? *Journal of Applied Behavioral Science, 24*, 191–202.

Josefsson, K., Sonde, L., Winblad, B., & Robins Wahlin, T. B. (2007). Work situation of registered nurses in municipal elderly care in Sweden: A questionnaire survey. *International Journal of Nursing Studies, 44*, 71–81.

Kahn, R. L., Wolfe, D. M., Quinn, R. P., Snoek, J. D., & Rosenthal, R. A. (1964). *Organizational stress: Studies in role conflict and ambiguity*. New York: Wiley.

Kahn, W. A. (1993). Caring for the caregivers: Patterns of organizational caregiving. *Administrative Science Quarterly, 38*, 539–563.

Keeton, K., Fenner, D. C., Johnson, T. R., & Hayward, R. A. (2007). Predictors of physician career satisfaction, work–life balance, and burnout. *Obstetrics & Gynecology, 109*, 949–955.

Kim, H., & Lee, S. Y. (2009). Supervisory communication: Burnout and turnout intention among social workers in health care settings. *Social Work in Health Care, 48*, 364–385.

Knapp, M. L., Stohl, C., & Reardon, K. K. (1981). "Memorable" messages. *Journal of Communication, 31*, 27–42.

Kovner, A. R., & Jonas, S. (2002). *Health care delivery in the United States* (7th ed.). New York: Springer.

Kreps, G. L., & Bonaguro, E. W. (2009). Health communication as applied communication inquiry. In. L. R. Frey & K. N. Cissna (Eds.), *Routledge Handbook of Applied Communication Research* (pp. 380–404). New York: Routledge.

Lee, R. T., & Ashforth, B. E. (1996). A meta-analytic examination of the correlates of the three dimensions of job burnout. *Journal of Applied Psychology, 81*, 123–133.

Letvak, S. (2001). Nurses as working women. *Association of periOperative Registered Nurses, 73*, 675–676, 678, 680–682.

McGilton, K.S., McGillis Hall, L., Wodchis, W. P., & Petroz, U. (2007). Supervisory support, job stress, and job satisfaction among long-term care nursing staff. *Journal of Nursing Administration, 37*(7/8), 1–6.

Meltzer, L. S., & Huckabay, L. M. (2004). Critical care nurses' perceptions of futile care and its effect on burnout. *American Journal of Critical Care, 13*, 202–208.

Metts, S., Geist, P., & Gray, J. L. (1994). The role of relationship characteristics in the provision and effectiveness of supportive messages among nursing professionals. In B. R. Burleson, T. L. Albrecht, & I. G. Sarason (Eds.), *Communication of social support: Messages, interactions, relationships, and community* (pp. 229–246). Thousand Oaks, CA: Sage.

Miller, D., & Gilles, P. (1996). Is there life after work? Experiences of HIV and oncology health staff. *AIDS Care, 8*, 167–182.

Miller, K. I. (2003). Organizational Issues. In T. L. Thompson, A. Dorsey, K. I. Miller, & R. Parrott (Eds.), *Handbook of health communication* (pp. 315–317). Mahwah, NJ: Erlbaum.

Miller, K. I., & Ray, E. B. (1994). Beyond the ties that bind: Exploring the "meaning" of supportive messages and relationships. In B. R. Burleson, T. L. Albrecht, & I. G. Sarason (Eds.), *Communication of social support: Messages, interactions, relationships, and community* (pp. 215–228). Thousand Oaks, CA: Sage.

Miller, K. I., Stiff, J. B., & Ellis, B. H. (1988). Communication and empathy as precursors to burnout among human service workers. *Communication Monographs, 55*, 250–265.

Miller, K. I., Zook, E. G., & Ellis, B. H. (1989). Occupational differences in the influence of communication on stress and burnout in the workplace. *Management Communication Quarterly, 3*, 166–190.

Morgan, J. M., & Krone, K. J. (2001). Bending the rules of "professional" display: Emotional improvisation to caregiver performances. *Journal of Applied Communication Research, 29*, 317–340.

Pecukonis, E., Doyle, O., & Bliss, D. L. (2008). Reducing barriers to interprofessional training: Promoting interprofessional cultural competence. *Journal of Interprofessional Care, 22,* 417–428.

Peterson, L. W., & Albrecht, T. L. (1996). Message design, logic, social support, and mixed-status relationships. *Western Journal of Communication, 60*, 291–309.

Ray, E. B. (1991). The relationship among communication network roles, job stress, and burnout in educational organizations. *Communication Quarterly, 39*, 91–102.

Ray, E. B. (1993). When the links become chains: Considering dysfunctions of supportive communication in the workplace. *Communication Monographs, 39*, 106–111.

Ray. E. B., & Miller, K. I. (1990). Communication in health care organizations. In E. B. Ray & L. Donohew (Eds.), *Communication and health: Systems and applications* (pp. 92–107). Hillsdale, NJ: Erlbaum.

Ray, E. B., & Miller, K. I. (1994). Social support, home/work stress, and burnout: Who can help? *Journal of Applied Behavioral Science, 30*, 357–373.

Rosenstein, A. H. (2002). Nurse–physician relationships: Impact on nurse satisfaction and retention. *American Journal of Nursing, 102*(6), 26–34.

Sass, J. S. (2000). Emotional labor as cultural performance: The communication of caregiving in a nonprofit nursing home. *Western Journal of Communication, 64*, 330–358.

Sexton, B., Thomas, E. K., & Helmreich, R. L. (2000). Errors, stress, and teamwork in medicine and specialist physicians. *Journal of the American Medical Association, 288*, 1447–1450.

Smith, A. C., & Kleinman, S. (1989). Managing emotions in medical school: Students' contacts with the living and the dead. *Social Psychology Quarterly, 52*, 56–69.

Steinhauer, J. (1999, April 2). Life vs. work: For female doctors, a difficult choice. *San Diego Union Tribune*, p. E-3.

Sultz, H. A., & Young, K. M. (2009). *Health care USA: Understanding its organization and delivery* (6th ed.). Boston, MA: Jones & Bartlett.

Thomas, L. T., & Ganster, D. C. (1995). Impact of family-supportive work variables on work–family conflict and strain: A control perspective. *Journal of Social Psychology, 80*, 6–15.

Voltmer, E., & Spahn, C. (2009). Social support and physicians' health. *Zeitschrift für Psychosomatische Medizin und Psychotherapie, 55*(1), 51–69.

Wright, K., Sparks, L., & O'Hair, D. (2007) (Eds.), *Health communication in the 21st century*. New York: Wiley-Blackwell.

Zimmermann, S., & Applegate, J. (1994). Communicating social support in organizations: A message-centered approach. In B. R. Burleson, T. L. Albrecht, & I. G. Sarason (Eds.), *Communication of social support: Messages, interactions, relationships, and community* (pp. 50–70). Thousand Oaks, CA: Sage.

28

LIFE SPAN AND END-OF-LIFE HEALTH COMMUNICATION

Joy Goldsmith, Elaine Wittenberg-Lyles, Sandra Ragan, and Jon F. Nussbaum

Life span scholars investigate the numerous, inevitable changes that occur as we age. These changes are physiological, biological, psychological, sociological, and even spiritual. Most obvious are the physiological changes that each of us observe as we progress from infancy through childhood, adolescence, young adulthood, middle adulthood, and older adulthood. We grow taller; we jump higher and run faster. We recover from various injuries rather quickly, and then we notice that our jumps aren't quite so high and our pace is not so quick. Our hair comes and goes, we begin to develop wrinkles as our skin loses its moisture and smoothness, we experience pains that never occurred before and we actually begin to shrink. Similar positive and negative changes occur in our ability to process and remember information, to communicate effectively in a variety of formal and informal social contexts, in our desire to initiate and maintain close relationships, and generally in our motivation and ability to adapt to the multiple environmental contingencies that challenge us as we attempt to maintain our desired lifestyles (Pecchioni, Wright, & Nussbaum, 2005). Surprisingly, these inevitable life changes are often overlooked or ignored by communication scholars and, therefore, are not accounted for in the possible explanations of competent or appropriate interactive behavior. Much worse than ignoring the often predictable change related to normal aging is the stereotypic notion that the aging process is entirely negative, that youth is always preferred over age, and that any sign of aging must be avoided at all costs (Nussbaum, Miller-Day, & Fisher, 2009).

As we age, and especially if we are faced with life-threatening or life-limiting illness, we require health care communication that includes communication competencies that are likely absent in many patients and health care providers. An additional complexity of communication at various specific phases of the life span (most notably in childhood and in old age) is the preeminence of the family as the recipient of diagnoses, prognoses, medical information, and the like. The inclusion of the family is central to the end-of-life experience for the patient, especially as the family shares in the illness journey of anxiety, depression, and the numerous losses accompanying critical illness (Ragan, Wittenberg-Lyles, Goldsmith, & Sanchez-Reilly, 2008). Within this chapter, we propose that palliative care—medical care designed to simultaneously offer curative and comfort care, to relieve suffering, and to improve quality of life for both patients and their families—is a needed intervention for all patients facing the end of their life span.

This chapter first introduces the perspective of life span health communication by identifying five important principles that focus our attention toward the process of change in our understanding of health communication. Next, we turn to a discussion of serious/terminal illness as a unique context in which life changes are dramatically highlighted. End-of-life communication and more specifically palliative care communication are areas within the health communication discipline that are largely unexplored. Here we identify palliative care in the landscape of health communication and discuss current deficits and challenges in communication within the context of serious, chronic, and terminal illness. We conclude by considering the work ahead in mapping competencies of communication across the life span in this most challenging arena.

Five Principles of Life Span Health Communication

The fundamental principles of the Life Span Developmental perspective have been outlined by Baltes (1987) within the discipline of psychology and have subsequently been adapted by Nussbaum (1989) and Pecchioni et al. (2005) within the discipline of communication. These fundamental principles can be further adapted to provide a foundation for our effort to describe health communication across the life span and the interrelated issue of complicated illness that often accompanies increased age.

The first important principle of life span health communication—*Change is inevitable*—restates the introductory comment that change is an ongoing process as we age. Change is the one constant in our lives. To understand health communication, we must first come to understand that competent health communication may be very different at different points in the life span. Just as certain diseases are more likely to occur at certain ages (e.g., breast cancer, prostate cancer, and pancreatic cancer are all more likely to occur in middle to late adulthood and certain types of leukemia are much more likely to occur in childhood and adolescence), the very nature of communication and the functions of that communication may change in rather dramatic ways as we age. This first principle should motivate health communication scholars to ask research questions that attempt to uncover age appropriate health campaign strategies or age appropriate communicative competencies that both health care providers and patients must utilize to communicate about diagnosis, plans of care, and treatment plan.

The second principle—*No one point in the life span is more significant than any other point in the life span*—complements the initial principle in that it forces us to study or at least to consider change across the entirety of the life span rather than focusing all our attention on phases or segments of the aging process. Developmental psychologists have a rather long history of focusing on childhood, and many nonscholars refer to this period of life as the most important for all cognitive, physical, and even spiritual development. Certain therapies attempt to trace all later life "issues" to early infant interactions with parents. While this may be true for specific aspects of language development, for instance, life span scholars view each phase of life to be as important as any other life phase with critical adaptations and processes related to well-being. Health communication scholars can concentrate their investigations within a limited age range. These same investigators, however, should never forget that their findings may not be generalizable beyond the age limitations of their participants. For example, certain interactive strategies that prove effective for college aged students who are attempting to deal with a chronic or terminal illness may not work as well, or at all, for middle aged or elderly adults.

The third principle of life span health communication—*Gains and losses occur throughout the life span*—speaks to the myth that aging is a period of universal decline. It is true that numerous normal indicators of physical and mental aging do decline. Many other normal aging indicators have been found to change in a positive direction. For instance, vocabulary increases with age; wisdom has been shown to increase with age; competencies in decision making and strategic planning have been shown to increase with age as does our ability to communicate effectively across numerous novel situations (see Pecchioni et al., 2005 for more information on specific communication competencies that decline and increase with age). The important point here is that until the very end of the life span we change in both positive and negative ways. The stereotype that old age is a time of significant decline in all areas of our lives is simply not supported by the social scientific literature. These negative stereotypes related to the aging process have been shown to cause significant harm within older adult–health care provider interactions (Nussbaum & Fisher, 2009). Aging is not a disease. The ability of the brain to change and grow (brain plasticity) in later life has dramatically changed the way all of us should view the aging process as a time of communicative adaptability, relational maintenance, and positive growth (Nussbaum, Federowicz, & Nussbaum, 2009).

The fourth principle highlights the importance of social interaction throughout our lives—*Family and friends play a significant yet changing role in our ability to maintain good health across the entire life span.* When we interact with the health care system as a child, as an adolescent, and as an older adult, we are often accompanied by a family member, though medical education and scholars are still slow to address this reality. Parents typically initiate and serve as conversational proxies for their children during any medical interaction. Adolescents are often accompanied by parents but learn to act on their own during specific medical encounters such as an appointment addressing birth control. Young adults often underutilize the health care industry; middle adults reconnect with former health providers during preventative encounters; and older adults utilize the health care system more often than any other age category (Nussbaum & Fisher, 2009), and are often accompanied to their various medical appointments by a spouse or an adult child. The role a family member plays in health discussions, the understanding of possible health issues, and ultimately adherence to the prescribed medications or behavioral change can significantly impact positive health outcomes (see Pecchioni & Keeley, this volume). Older adults tend not to ask as many questions within the medical encounter as younger adults. Older adults can leave the medical encounter without mentioning the major reason they actually visited the physician. A family companion can intervene so that appropriate questions are asked. Of course, the health care provider must be able to competently interact with multiple individuals and should understand that once the patient leaves their office the network of family and friends who support the patient will have a significant effect on how the plan of care is followed. Our social networks of family and friends play a significant yet varying role in our lives as we age. It is, therefore, not hard to imagine that our interaction with the health care system will be quite different as we age.

The final principle of a life span health perspective involves the appropriate training of health care practitioners—*Medical education should incorporate a life span perspective that emphasizes the physical, psychological, and communication changes that occur throughout the aging process.* Accurate diagnosis and appropriate treatment require knowledge of normal aging processes and communication with patient and family. While it is certainly true that significant health crises can occur at any point in the life span and that these health crises will require frequent visits to physicians and therapists, the majority of us will lead healthy lives with infrequent formal medical encounters until we age beyond the seventh decade of life. Once we enter our seventies, many of us will begin to experience numerous, often complex, simultaneous chronic conditions. Multiple pharmaceuticals may be needed to help us cope with these various chronic ailments. These drugs can interact and may cause an entirely new set of medical challenges. Nussbaum and Fisher (2009) have developed a communication model for the competent delivery of geriatric medicine that is based on the premise that health care workers attempting to practice competent medicine with older adults need to reframe their traditional methods.

Communication researchers have concentrated on the impact of the stereotyping process as a major barrier to effective, competent interaction within intergenerational encounters. Older patients spend the great majority of their time interacting with much younger health care providers and family members as they attempt to cope with the health care system. The Communication Predicament Model of Aging (Ryan, Giles, Bartolucci, & Henwood, 1986) and the Communication Enhancement Model of Aging (Ryan, Meredith, MacLean, & Orange, 1995) were developed within the health care context to capture both the negative and positive effects of the stereotyping process within intergenerational interactions. Briefly, these models describe a process that begins with a younger individual recognizing old age cues that subconsciously activate stereotyped expectations that directly lead to communicative behaviors such as patronizing speech that in turn directly cause changes in the psychological well-being of the older adult. Hummert (1994) and Hummert, Garstka, Ryan, and Bonnesen (2004) have developed the Age Stereotypes in Interaction Model to further refine both the positive and negative effects of intergenerational stereotyping on not only the communicative behavior of older adults but also on the general well-being of older adults facing chronic health problems.

Nussbaum and Fisher (2009) argue that the health care context is a communicative arena rich with negative stereotyping and the negative consequences of that stereotyping behavior. At the very least, all health care workers and all family caregivers should be made aware of the possibly severe consequences of stereotyped expectations and patronizing talk. Baltes and Wahl (1996) clearly showed that the independent behavior of well functioning older adults can be extinguished within older patients by the dependency reinforcing communicative actions of nursing home staff. All geriatric health education and training programs should emphasize the significance of eliminating inappropriate patronizing speech and behavior and emphasize communicative caring scripts that reinforce psychological and physical well-being.

While the research on communication competencies across the life span has received close examination and development in the last several years, human communication competency across the life span in the context of serious and terminal illness has not. To discuss these unknowns, we begin with a foundational understanding of this end-of-life context.

Palliative Care

Serious, chronic, and terminal illness can strike at any point in the life span. Palliative care is offered simultaneously with all other appropriate (curative or noncurative) medical treatments and thus is for all patients of any age suffering from stressful, painful, or debilitating symptoms (Ragan et al., 2008). A definition of the tenets of palliative care would include considering the patient and family as the unit of care, recognizing suffering to include physical, psychological, social, and spiritual pain, valuing communication as critical to the delivery of care, and administering coordinated care through a team of interdisciplinary clinicians (Ragan et al., 2008). In contrast, hospice care is a service that *excludes* curative treatment of primary illness and is limited to comfort care only for terminally ill patients. The primary goal in hospice care is pain and symptom management at the end of disease progression. An essential mission of hospice is to provide patients with the opportunity to die where they would like to die, surrounded by loved ones, in the greatest comfort possible.

While hospice care is initiated in the patient's last six months of life, a significant point of confusion in the practice of palliative care is *when* it should begin (Ragan, Wittenberg & Hall, 2003). The World Health Organization states that palliative care is intended for all seriously ill patients, not just the actively dying. Palliative care "is applicable early in the course of illness, in conjunction with other therapies that are intended to prolong life, such as chemotherapy or radiation therapy, and includes those investigations needed to better understand and manage distressing clinical complications" (World Health Organization, n.d., para. 3). Essentially, palliative care is the large umbrella sheltering modern protocols of treatment (curative and noncurative in nature) in addition to hospice care services.

Palliative and hospice care programs conserve money. A facility can find itself saving anywhere from $1,700.00 to $4,900.00 per admission (Morrison et al., 2008); individual families can save up to 35.7% in care costs during the last week of life (Zhang et al., 2009). In addition to financial benefits, palliative and hospice care also ensure a higher quality of life in the dying process as well as less complicated grief for the surviving family (Bakitas et al., 2009; Zhang et al., 2009), two areas that are problematic for dying patients and families who do not benefit from this class of medical care (SUPPORT, 1995). Palliative care generally improves the serious and terminal illness experience for patients and families by combining curative treatment alongside comfort care.

Patient and Family Communication in Serious and Terminal Illness

In the United States, a common way of managing privacy during terminal illness is *not* to talk about death and dying (Callahan, 2009). A mutual pretense of cure becomes the drama family members and patients perform; in other words, no one is dying (Glaser & Strauss, 1965; Ragan & Goldsmith, 2008). This mutual pretense includes anyone who interacts with the family and the patient and their abnegation of the terminal context. It is enacted verbally and nonverbally by pretending life is "normal," that there will be a restored future, and that dying is not taking place. The drama of mutual pretense might be more prolific at various stages of the patient's life span (i.e., neonatal, infancy, youth, or young adulthood) and further research is needed to understand the specific challenges of bad health news at each of these life phases for patients and families. Because privacy is jointly enacted it entails many elements of the combined (patient–family member) dying experience. As news of the prognosis is shared within the family, and as the patient's body begins to decline, families can and do create and enact many, many layers of denial.

The absence of end-of-life conversations among family members and with clinicians, coupled with a patient's uncontrolled pain, dementia, and display of imminent dying (i.e., reduced function, dysphagia, weight loss, reduced overall intake and output) can result in family crisis (Lau, Downing, Wesperance, Shaw & Kuziemsky, 2006; Wittenberg-Lyles, Goldsmith, Ragan, & Sanchez-Reilly, 2010a). Distressed family members and their guilt lead to difficult decision making, the tendency to emphasize treatment, and the overestimation of survival (Holst, Lundren, Olsen, & Ishøy, 2009; Matsuyama, Reddy, & Smith, 2006).

Palliative resistance, the reluctance of patients and families to be cared for by a palliative or hospice care team, becomes an interference for clinicians extending comfort care

(Wittenberg-Lyles et al., 2010a). When palliative care is not introduced at diagnosis and becomes an option only when patients are acutely terminally ill, patients and families are caught in the dialectical tension between science (length of life) and humanism (quality of life) and face difficult and often ethically challenging decision-making dilemmas. Awareness of the dialectic juxtaposes curative and comfort care, requiring palliative and hospice care teams to facilitate family communication among family members who vary on this continuum (King & Quill, 2006). This shift is especially salient when families are tasked with making a decision about treatment withdrawal—family conflict with clinicians arises from unmet communication needs and minimal transitory communication between aggressive treatment to palliative care (Norton, Tilden, Tolle, Nelson, & Eggman, 2003).

What communication failures are taking place that enable families and patients in the United States to opt for highly aggressive and medically futile therapies even days before death—therapies that complicate suffering and grief for many families? One major contributor is that our systems of communication have not shifted with the literacy needs of our culture (Ratzan, 2008). Health literacy assessments of U.S. adults indicate that only 12% (and only 3% of seniors, the sickest group) operate at a proficient level of health literacy (Kutner, Greenberg, Jin, & Paulsen, 2006), with half of the American population limited in its proficiency (Reisfield & Wison, 2008). Though the average reading level of U.S. adults is believed to be 8th grade (Doak, Doak, & Root, 1996), most health/medical websites are written at an undergraduate level and assume an elevated degree of knowledge on health matters. The populations at highest risk for chronic and terminal illness are similarly at the highest risk for low literacy skills, further marginalizing their ability to obtain comprehensible health information that could enable them to make crucial decisions about the best type of care (Riffenburgh, 2008). In addition, Matsuyama et al. (2006) point out that web sources considered rigorous and sponsored by research organizations do not provide the information patients and families need to make decisions about curative-only versus palliative treatment.

Health literacy moves beyond the tenets of literacy alone, to the applicability of (a) cultural and conceptual knowledge, (b) oral skills, (c) writing and reading, and (d) numeracy (Villagran & Sparks, 2010). The health literacy complexities of interacting, retaining, discerning, clarifying, self-advocating, analyzing, and negotiating are demands few are prepared for or possess the ability to immediately administer upon initiation into the journey of serious or terminal illness (Kreps & Sparks, 2008; Sparks & Nussbaum, 2008).

Patient/Family and Provider Communication in Serious and Terminal Illness

Families and patients facing the most difficult news of their lives would rather know the news, receive it from their primary care physician, and maintain a relationship of care with that clinician throughout their illness (Back et al., 2009). A recent study of 1,042 Americans found that most are fearful of futile interventions (e.g., vasopressors, life support), pain at the end of life, and not being able to communicate their end-of-life desires. Most respondents know little about end-of-life medical care and have not talked about dying or care at the end of life with anyone (Scharader, Nelson, & Eidsness, 2009).

Another likely producer of this antithetical world of extreme intervention at the end of life, despite our preferences to avoid it, is the still minimal communication education and training clinicians receive throughout their medical school journey. Recent research indicates that the primary physician managing a patient case is the number one determinant of treatment intensity for patients/families near the end of life. When end-of-life treatment depends on a clinician, patient and family preferences might be neglected (Larochelle, Rodriguez, Arnold, & Baranato, 2009). For this reason, communication education for health practitioners seems essential in shifting the tide of intervention futility for serious and terminally ill patients.

As health communication professionals, we lament that the medical community frequently fails to incorporate communication research into its writing and teaching about communication. The commonly used and physician-developed protocol for breaking bad medical news (SPIKES) that is much heralded by the medical community has been critiqued by communication researchers for conceptualizing communication as mechanistic and formulaic rather than as a complex, nonscripted process that requires constant adaptation (Eggly et al., 2006; Wittenberg-Lyles, Goldsmith, Sanchez-Reilly, & Ragan, 2008). Medical students continue to view communication as a naturally occurring element in their practice—one that is "unlearnable," but at the same time are aware of their shortcomings in the most challenging communication contexts, such as breaking bad news about terminal illness, discussing advance directives, coordinating care, and talking about death (Wittenberg-Lyles, Goldsmith, Ragan, & Sanchez-Reilly, 2010b). Postgraduate physicians who feel competent to communicate in the context of noncurative care and dying make more end-of-life recommendations to patients and family and feel they can impact coping with dying, while those unable to engage in these communications report a more distant role with their patients and the patients' families (Jackson et al., 2008). Similarly, clinicians who feel underprepared for these communication challenges with terminally ill patients and families suffer from early career burnout, admit to offering unnecessary interventions instead of engaging in difficult conversations, and overtreat patients too close to death (Back, Arnold, Tulsky, Baile, & Fryer-Edwards, 2003). As with physicians, family members and interdisciplinary palliative care teams must also exhibit competent communication in navigating the shifting sands of end-of-life care.

During chronic/terminal illness family members become the nucleus of patient care; end-of-life conversations are aimed at ensuring that families understand a patient's goals of care so that decision making and at-home caregiving support are consonant (Haley et al., 2002). Family meetings are an identifying feature of palliative and hospice care, emphasizing communication as an inclusive, focalized act in the practice of medicine. In these communications, families are heralded as central in palliative care. Meetings are initiated by members of the interdisciplinary health care team (physician, nurse, chaplain, social worker) to develop an individualized, personal care plan based on the values, needs, and preferences of the patient and family (Hickman, 2002). Individualized care plans match patient goals of care with appropriate treatment and the inclusion of the family demonstrates application of the biopsychosocial approach to medicine (Engel, 1977). Family meetings are necessary to reposition patients' and families' master narrative, one based on societal norms about death and dying, which emphasizes treatment and cure. By remixing the master narrative to include death and dying, health communication gaps among specialty clinicians (e.g., oncologists), patients, and families are unveiled, and explicit communication about these topics facilitates discussion about such challenging matters as withdrawal of artificial nutrition, nursing home placement, and hospice care.

For many patients and families, the family meeting is the first context for learning bad news about the prognosis and a turning point for understanding that the care trajectory does not include cure (Wittenberg-Lyles, 2010a). Education about disease and prognosis in the family meeting setting allows the health care team to address health literacy issues, explain medical and technical jargon, and set expectations based on disease progression.

Given the prevalence and inclination for cure-driven health communication, the family meeting precipitates an exigent shift in the patient–family understanding of the illness narrative toward one that includes palliative and end-of-life care by (a) facilitating patient–family education, (b) supporting decision making, and (c) mediating among family members (Wittenberg-Lyles, 2010a). The palliative/hospice triad (patient, team member, and family member) is influenced by family dysfunction (Holst et al., 2009) as well as tensions in the interdisciplinary team (Goldsmith, Wittenberg-Lyles, Rodriguez, & Sanchez-Reilly, 2010a).

A chill still exists between clinicians and social scientists when it comes to blending ways of knowing in order to create the most effective interventions. We view communication in the clinical setting as a particularly challenging arena for this "blending" process. A small camp of clinicians offers a preponderance of "skills" training presented mechanically through rubrics and algorithms that do not address the complexities of communication competency, but rather provide a scripted guide for the practitioner (Wittenberg-Lyles, Goldsmith, Sanchez-Reilly, & Ragan, 2008; Wittenberg-Lyles et al., 2010b). Recent publications from the biomedical sector of the academy promote new "communication strategies" to facilitate communications that are terminal, including the use of metaphors (Casarett et al., 2009; Wittenberg-Lyles et al., 2010a), silence (Back, Bauer-Wu, Rushton, & Halifax, 2009), and exercising what we understand to be the practice of strategic ambiguity (Wittenberg-Lyles, Goldsmith, Ragan, & Sanchez-Reilly, 2010a). All of these clinically advocated "communication skills" are designed to ease the experience of the clinician and do little to facilitate the breaking of terminal prognostic news and the discussion points that must follow (i.e., fear, loss, identity questions, care plan, etc.).

The absence of a family meeting at the end of life results in family difficulties and increases the likelihood for misunderstandings (Holst et al., 2009). Inviting family members into the care process can help them feel supported, prepared, and connected to the health care team that asks them to make life-and-death decisions; exclusion from this process and the absence of communication about these decisions can leave family members feeling responsible for the death of their loved one (Hickman, 2002). Feelings of guilt, anger, and frustration are common for family members who are dissatisfied with their loved one's end-of-life care (Thompson, Menec, Chochinov, & McClement, 2008). This guilt manifests when a loved one is dying and can contribute to the unwillingness to make decisions (Goold, Williams, & Arnold, 2000). Family meetings which directly address the patient's physical changes, discuss discrepancies in information from multiple clinicians, and give family members the opportunity to ask questions and be heard, foster trust and create a sustainable balance between the clinician, patient, and family member (Holst et al., 2009).

Although family meetings are a powerful tool in the provision of palliative care, few clinicians are prepared to conduct them effectively (Fineberg, 2005). To facilitate a family meeting requires appropriate skills in group work, therapeutic communication, and palliative care (Hudson, Quinn, O'Hanlon, & Aranda, 2008). To date, there has been no known comprehensive exploration of the conduct and utility of family meetings in palliative care (Hudson et al., 2008). The feasibility of an educational intervention has been tested in palliative care curricula (Fineberg, 2005), but training remains focused on increasing the clinician's confidence in the ability to lead a family meeting and assumes that such confidence will lead to greater success in facilitating family conferences (Gueguen, Bylund, Brown, Levin, & Kissane, 2009).

As communication scholars we know that the targeted goal of collaboration and shared decision making assumes a degree of equity in conversation (Apker, Propp, & Ford, 2005);

however, dialectic tensions are present as health care providers deliver expertise and family members and patients utilize relational history as knowledge. This dichotomy creates a tension that subordinates the traditional clinician role and thus requires substantive training to unravel the complicated factors that are embedded in patient and family relationships (Apker et al., 2005; Keeley, 2007).

Advancing Life Span Communication to Address the Palliative Care Imperative

Since Dame Cecily Saunders (1967), founder of hospice, introduced the notion of total pain, both palliative and hospice care recognize, respect, and manage the multiple dimensions of human pain (including psychological, social, and spiritual pain) rather than focusing solely on physical pain. This holistic approach to pain—and the recognition that it cannot merely be measured as a vital sign on a 10-point scale—profoundly complicates communication for the health provider, the patient, and the family. Communication competencies heretofore unexplored or undeveloped are all called into play. They include clinicians' fear of losing control of a communication interaction if death is discussed (Friedrichsen, Lipkin, & Hall, 2006) and their fear of the collateral costs of truth-telling when it comes to prognostic disclosures (Hancock et al., 2007). Also to be considered is the palliative care team's ability to talk about the patient's existential fear of death; the patient's need to disclose highly personal information about unresolved relationship issues; and the family's conflict resolution skills in reconciling disparate preferences for treatment. Whereas a younger person/patient only rarely experiences such complex communication exigencies, the aging and dying elderly, along with their caregivers, confront a formidable challenge in negotiating health care and in holistically managing many types of pain.

One of the primary barriers to the dissemination and utilization of palliative care is the medical community's own ignorance and lack of health literacy concerning both palliative and hospice care, in addition to their ignorance regarding the effective communication of palliative care (Fadul et al., 2007; Ferrell, 2005; Johnson, Girgis, & Paul, 2008). Yet, because we subscribe to dyadic communication as reciprocal and mutually influential, we also believe that patients and families must enhance their health literacy in palliative and end-of-life care and must develop the communication competencies to address their changing communication needs over the life span.

While palliative care and hospice are now board-certified subspecialties in medicine, a lack of qualified physicians in palliative medicine is a fundamental issue that threatens the promulgation of palliative care. In 2007, there were only 2,883 physicians board-certified in palliative medicine, or 1 per 31,000 persons living with serious and life-threatening illness. Further complicating this dearth of trained physicians, medical education fails to adequately train clinicians in end-of-life issues, including communication, interdisciplinary group communication, pain management, hospice, palliative care, and death and dying. Both palliative care communication and communication in general are shortchanged in current medical school curricula.

In stark contrast to the "communication manual" approach of many physicians writing about communication, we laud the narrative medicine movement in which patients' and family members' stories are solicited and valued. Coined as "Narrative Medicine" by Dr. Rita Charon, Professor of Clinical Medicine and Director of the Program in Narrative Medicine at Columbia University, narrative knowledge is believed to be at the core of humane and effective medical practice. Narrative knowledge is characterized by an understanding of the meaning and significance of stories (Charon, 2001). Narratives offer physicians an invaluable opportunity to witness the human side of medicine and to understand illness and medicine from the perspective of their patient; emotion and subjectivity are at the core of narrative medicine (Charon, 2001). In fact, Saunders's (1967) concept of total pain was born from listening to thousands of dying patients tell their stories of suffering that encompassed more than physical pain. We would hope that more medical school curricula adopt this humanistic, patient-centered approach to end-of-life care.

Yet we also advocate for increased health literacy concerning end-of-life issues for patients and families. Further, we believe that our death-denying culture inhibits such literacy, instead advancing the notion that life can be forever prolonged—that old age is a disease to be cured. The life span perspective demands that we develop communication competencies in planning for and managing the end of life, including the critical patient–provider and patient–family discussions of our preferences for dying (e.g., advance directives). Without these competencies, we are destined to die in precisely the ways that we claim we want to avoid: in hospitals or other institutions, hooked up to invasive machines, and without the benefit of palliative care or hospice.

The practice of palliative care appears uniquely appropriate for the life span perspective: as opposed to biomedical care, which treats the disease exclusively (with little attention to patient needs other than the biological and nearly no regard for the patient's social milieu), palliative care opens the door to biopsychosocial medical care and holistic communication. Palliative care privileges rather than dismisses patients' relationships, emotions, values, and beliefs. In conjunction with this unique class of care that promises to reduce emotional and financial costs, the incorporation of narrative medicine offers invaluable benefits for those in the medical field, including a humanistic focus, narrative skills, exposure to other experiences and realities, self-reflection, and emotional release—all quintessential practices in the facilitation of interdisciplinary team communication as well as family communication (Ragan, Mindt, & Wittenberg-Lyles, 2005).

Palliative care not only provides one productive solution to the current oppressions of our health care system, but it advances opportunities for the convergence of social science and medical science. Translational research is a relative newcomer to the world of communication research, although it is a practiced and well-integrated concept in medical research. It seems a logical matter-of-course that health communication scholars would herald this class of inquiry. Parrott's (2008) description identifies translational research as work that is implemented "in ways that function as pathways to improve lives.... [I]t depends upon the willingness of researchers from different disciplines to collaborate.... For scholars and colleagues from other disciplines sitting at the translational research table, there must be some consensus about which evidence is most persuasive in pointing to viable intervention" (pp. 1–2). Palliative care and end-of-life communication as an area of study is well-positioned to exploit the multivoiced nature of cross-disciplinary research teams committed to identifying and practicing interventions that improve the experience of patients and families at the end of life.

Conclusion

We note the convergence of the five principles of the life span perspective with our advocacy for successful end-of-life communication advanced specifically through palliative care. At end of life, or in cases of life-threatening or life-limiting illness, patients, their medical care providers, and their families must recognize the inevitability of change—palliative care seeks to help the involved parties in their quest to make that change more palatable for patients and families while also recognizing that physical decline does not have to be accompanied by psychological, relational, or spiritual decline. Concomitantly, communication competencies gained throughout the life span can aid patients and their families in negotiating the difficulties of serious illness and even of impending death. The skills of the aged relative to communication adaptability, relational maintenance, and positive growth can be enlarged and enhanced at the end of life, particularly through the offering and implementation of palliative care that addresses the patient holistically. Certainly the expanded role of family and friends is showcased when patients must face severe or life-threatening illness. New communication skills must be acquired for all involved. Lastly, medical care providers should be educated from a life span perspective that would include communication competencies required for dealing with the physical, psychological, and communication changes of their patients at end of life. In sum, the end-of-life context and the advocacy of palliative care provide an intriguing set of research challenges specific to the life span perspective.

References

Apker, J., Propp, K. M., & Ford, W. S. Z. (2005). Negotiating status and identity tensions in health-care team interactions: An exploration of nurse role dialectics. *Journal of Applied Communication Research, 33*, 93–115. doi:10.1080/00909880500044620

Back, A., Arnold, R. M., Tulsky, J. A., Baile, W. F., & Fryer-Edwards, K. (2003). Teaching communication skills to medical oncology fellows. *Journal of Clinical Oncology, 21*, 2433–2436. Retrieved from http://jco.ascopubs.org

Back, A., Bauer-Wu, S., Rushton, C., & Halifax, J. (2009). Compassionate silence in the patient–clinician encounter: A contemplative approach. *Journal of Palliative Medicine, 12*, 1113–1117. doi: 10.1089/jpm.2009.0175

Back, A., Young, J., McCown, E., Engelberg, R., Vig, E., & Reinke, L. (2009). Abandonment at the end of life from patient, caregiver, nurse, and physician perspectives. *Archives of Internal Medicine, 169*, 474–479. Retrieved from http://archinte.ama-assn.org

Bakitas, M., Lyons, K., Hegel, M., Balan, S., Brokaw, F., Seville, J., & Ahles, T. (2009). Effects of a palliative care intervention on clinical outcomes in patients with advanced cancer. *Journal of the American Medical Association, 302*, 741–749. Retrieved from http://jama.ama.assn.org

Baltes, P. B. (1987). Theoretical propositions of life-span developmental psychology: On the dynamics between growth and decline. *Developmental Psychology, 23*, 611–626. doi: 10.1037/0012-1649.23.5.611

Baltes, M., & Wahl, H. (1996). Patterns of communication in old age: The dependence-support and independence-ignore script. *Health Communication, 8*, 217–231.

Callahan, D. (2009). Death, mourning, and medical progress. *Perspectives in Biological Medicine, 52*, 103–115. doi: S1529879508100060 [pii]10.1353/pbm.0.0067

Casarett, D., Pickard, A., Fishman, J., Alexander, S., Arnold, R. M., Pollak, K., & Tulsky, J. (2009). Can metaphors and analogies improve communication with seriously ill patients? *Journal of Palliative Medicine. Advance online publication.* doi: 10.1089/jpm.2009.0221

Charon, R. (2001). Narrative medicine: A model for empathy, reflection, profession, and trust. *JAMA, 286*, 1897–1902. doi: 10.1001/jama.286.15.1891

Doak, C., Doak, L., & Root, J. (1996). *Teaching patients with low literacy skills* (2nd ed.). Philadelphia, PA: J. B. Lippincott.

Eggly, S., Penner, L., Albrecht, T., Cline, R., Foster, T., Naugton, M., & Ruckdeschel, J. (2006). Discussing bad news in the outpatient oncology clinic: Rethinking current communication guidelines. *The Journal of Clinical Oncology, 24*, 716–719. doi: 10.1200/JCO.2005.03.0577

Engel, G. (1977). The need for a new medical model: A challenge for biomedicine. *Science, 196*, 129–136. doi:10.1126/science.847460

Fadul, N., Elsayem, A., Palmer, L., Zhang, T., Braitheh, F., & Bruera, E. (2007). Predictors of access to palliative care services among patients who died at a comprehensive cancer center. *Journal of Palliative Medicine, 10,* 1146–1152. doi: 10.1089/jpm.2006.0259

Ferrell, B. (2005). Late referrals to palliative care. *Journal of Clinical Oncology, 23,* 2588–2589. doi: JCO.2005.11.908 [pii] 10.1200/JCO.2005.11.908

Fineberg, I. C. (2005). Preparing professionals for family conferences in palliative care: Evaluation results of an interdisciplinary approach. *Journal of Palliative Medicine, 8,* 857–866. doi: 10.1089/jpm.2005.8.857

Friedrichsen, M., Lipkin, M., & Hall, A. (2006). Concerns about losing control when breaking bad news to terminally ill patients with cancer: Physicians' perspective. *Journal of Palliative Medicine, 9,* 673–682. doi: 10.1089/jpm.2006.9.673

Glaser, B., & Strauss, A. (1965). *Awareness of dying.* San Francisco, CA: Aldine.

Goldsmith, J., Wittenberg-Lyles, E. M., Rodriguez, D., & Sanchez-Reilly, S. (2010). Interdisciplinary geriatric and palliative care team narratives: Collaboration practices and barriers. *Qualitative Health Research, 20,* 94–104. doi: 10.1177/1049732309355287

Goold, S. D., Williams, B., & Arnold, R. M. (2000). Conflicts regarding decisions to limit treatment. *Journal of the American Medical Association, 283,* 909–914.

Gueguen, J. A., Bylund, C. L., Brown, R. F., Levin, T. T., & Kissane, D. W. (2009). Conducting family meetings in palliative care: Themes, techniques, and preliminary evaluation of a communication skills module. *Palliative and Supportive Care, 7,* 171–179. doi: S1478951509000224 [pii] 10.1017/S1478951509000224

Haley, W. E., Allen, R., Reynolds, S., Chen, H., Burton, A. M., & Gallagher-Thompson, D. (2002). Family issues in end-of-life decision making and end-of-life care. *American Behavioral Scientist, 46,* 284–298. doi: 10.1177/000276402236680

Hancock, K., Clayton, J. M., Parker, S. M., Walder, S., Butow, P. N., Carrick, S., & Tattersall, M. H. (2007). Truth-telling in discussing prognosis in advanced life-limiting illnesses: A systematic review. *Palliative Medicine, 21,* 507–517. doi: 10.1177/0269216307080823

Hickman, S. (2002). Improving communication near the end of life. *American Behavioral Scientist, 46,* 252–267. doi: 10.1177/000276402236677

Holst, L., Lundren, M., Olsen, L., & Ishøy, T. (2009). Dire deadlines: Coping with dysfunctional family dynamics in an end-of-life care setting. *International Journal of Palliative Nursing, 15,* 34–41. Retrieved from http://www.ijpn.co.uk

Hudson, P., Quinn, K., O'Hanlon, B., & Aranda, S. (2008). Family meetings in palliative care: Multidisciplinary clinical practice guidelines. *BMC Palliative Care, 7,* 12. doi: 1472-684X-7-12 [pii]10.1186/1472-684X-7-12

Hummert, M. L. (1994). Stereotypes of the elderly and patronizing speech. In M. L. Hummert, J. M. Wiemann, & J. F. Nussbaum (Eds.), *Interpersonal communication in older adulthood: Interdisciplinary theory and research* (pp. 162–184). Newbury Park, CA: Sage.

Hummert, M. L., Garstka, T. A., Ryan, E. B., Bonnesen, J. L. (2004). The role of age stereotypes in interpersonal communication. In J. F. Nussbaum & J. Coupland (Eds.), *Handbook of communication and aging research* (2nd ed., pp. 91–121). Mahwah, NJ: Erlbaum.

Jackson, V., Mack, J., Matsuyama, R., Lakoma, M. D., Sullivan, A. M., Arnold, R. M., … Block, S. D. (2008). A qualitative study of oncologists' approaches to end-of-life care. *Journal of Palliative Medicine, 11,* 893–906. doi: 10.1089/jpm.2007.2480

Johnson, C., Girgis, A., Paul, C., & Currow, D. C. (2008). Cancer specialists' palliative care referral practices and perceptions: Results of a national survey. *Palliative Medicine, 22,* 51–57. doi: 10.1177/0269216307085181

Keeley, M. (2007). "Turning toward death together": The functions of messages during final conversations in close relationships. *Journal of Social and Personal Relationships, 24,* 225–253. doi: 10.1177/0265407507075412

King, D. A., & Quill, T. (2006). Working with families in palliative care: One size does not fit all. *Journal of Palliative Medicine, 9,* 704–715. doi: 10.1089/jpm.2006.9.704

Kreps, G., & Sparks, L. (2008). Meeting the health needs of immigrant populations. *Patient Education and Counseling, 71,* 328–332. doi: 10.1016/j.pec.2008.03.001

Kutner, J., Greenberg, E., Jin, Y., & Paulsen, C. (2006). *The health literacy of America's adults: Results from the 2003 National Assessment of Adult Literacy* (National Center for Education Statistics #2006483). Retrieved from http://bookstore.gpo.gov

Larochelle, M. R., Rodriguez, K., Arnold, R. M., & Baranato, A. E. (2009). Hospital staff attributions of the causes of physician variation in end-of-life treatment intensity. *Palliative Medicine, 23,* 460–470. doi: 10.1177/026216309103664

Lau, F., Downing, M., Lesperance, M., Shaw, J., & Kuziemsky, C. (2006). Use of Palliative Performance Scale in end-of-life prognostication. *Journal of Palliative Medicine, 9,* 1066–1075.

Matsuyama, R., Reddy, S., & Smith, T. (2006). Why do patients choose chemotherapy near the end of life? A review of the perspective of those facing death from cancer. *Journal of Clinical Oncology, 24,* 3490–3496. doi: 10.1200/JCO.2005.03.6236

Morrison, R. S., Penrod, J. D., Cassel, J. B., Caust-Ellenbogen, M., Litke, A., Spragens, L., & Meier, D. E.; Palliative Care Leadership Centers' Outcomes Group. (2008). Cost savings associated with United States hospital palliative care consultation programs. *Archives of Internal Medicine, 168,* 1783–1790. Retrieved from http://archinte.ama-assn.org

Norton, S. A., Tilden, V. P., Tolle, S. W., Nelson, C. A., & Eggman, S. T. (2003). Life support withdrawal: Communication and conflict. *American Journal of Critical Care: An Official Publication, American Association of Critical-Care Nurses, 12,* 548–555. Retrieved from http://ajcc.aacnjournals.org

Nussbaum, J. F. (Ed.). (1989). *Life-span communication: Normative processes.* Hillsdale, NJ: Erlbaum.

Nussbaum, J. F., Federowicz, M., & Nussbaum, P. D. (2009). *Brain health and optimal engagement in older adulthood.* Girona, Spain: Editorial Aresta.

Nussbaum, J. F. & Fisher, C. L. (2009). A communication model for the competent delivery of geriatric medicine. *Journal of Language and Social Psychology, 28,* 190–208. doi: 10.1177/0261927X08330609

Nussbaum, J. F., Miller-Day, M., & Fisher, C. (2009). *Communication and intimacy in older adulthood.* Girona, Spain: Editoria Aresta.

Parrott, R. (2008). A multiple discourse approach to health communication: Translational research and ethical practice. *Journal of Applied Communication Research, 36,* 1–7. doi: 10.1080/00909880701799345

Pecchioni, L., Wright, K., & Nussbaum, J. F. (2005). *Life span communication.* Mahwah, NJ: Erlbaum.

Ragan, S., & Goldsmith, J. (2008). End-of-life communication: The drama of pretense in the talk of dying patients and their M.D.s. In K. Wright & S. Moore (Eds.), *Applied health communication* (pp. 207–228). Cresskill, NJ: Hampton Press.

Ragan, S., Mindt, T., & Wittenberg-Lyles, E. (2005). Narrative medicine and education in palliative care. In L. Harter, P. Japp & C. Beck (Eds.), *Narratives, health, and healing: Communication theory, research, and practice* (pp. 259–276). Mahwah, NJ: Erlbaum.

Ragan, S., Wittenberg-Lyles, E. M., Goldsmith, J., & Sanchez-Reilly, S. (2008). *Communication as comfort: Multiple voices in palliative care.* New York: Routledge.

Ragan, S., Wittenberg, E., & Hall, H. T. (2003). The communication of palliative care for the elderly cancer patient. *Health Communication, 15,* 219–226. Retrieved from http://www.tandf.co.uk/journals/hhth

Ratzan, S. (2008). Our challenge: Beware of a-literacy. *Journal of Health Communication, 13,* 307–308. doi: 10.1080/10810730802138801

Reisfield, G., & Wison, G. (2008). Health literacy in palliative medicine. *Journal of Palliative Medicine,* 105–106. doi: 10.1089/jpm.2008.9990

Riffenburgh, A. (2008, February). *Health websites and users with low health literacy.* Paper presented at the Western States Communication Association, Denver, CO.

Ryan, E. B., Giles, H., Bartolucci, G., & Henwood, K. (1986). Psycholinguistic and social psychological components of communication by and with the elderly. *Language and Communication, 6,* 1–24.

Ryan, E. B., Meredith, S. D., MacLean, M. J., & Orange, J. B. (2004). Changing the way we talk with elders: Promoting health using the communication enhancement model. *International Journal of Aging and Human Development, 41,* 87–105.

Saunders, C. (1967) *The management of terminal illness.* London: Hospital Medicine Publications Limited.

Scharader, S., Nelson, M., & Eidsness, L. (2009). Dying to know: A community survey about dying and end-of-life care. *Omega, 60,* 33–50. doi: 10.2190/OM.60.1.b

Sparks, L., & Nussbaum, J. F. (2008). Health literacy and cancer communication with older adults. *Patient Education and Counseling, 71,* 345–350. doi: 10.1016/j.pec.2008.02.007

SUPPORT. (1995). A controlled trial to improve care for seriously ill, hospitalized patients: The Study to Understand Prognoses and Preferences for Outcomes and Treatments (SUPPORT). *Journal of the American Medical Association, 274,* 1591–1598. Retrieved from http://jama.ama-assn.org

Thompson, G. N., Menec, V. H., Chochinov, H. M., & McClement, S. E. (2008). Family satisfaction with care of a dying loved one in nursing homes: What makes the difference? *Journal of Gerontological Nursing, 34,* 37–44. Retrieved from http://www.jogonline.com

Villagran, M. M., & Sparks, L. (2010). *Patient and provider interaction: A global health communication perspective.* Boston, MA: Polity Press.

Wittenberg- Lyles, E., Goldsmith, J., Ragan, S., & Sanchez-Reilly, S. (2010a). *Dying with COMFORT: Family narratives and early palliative care.* Cresskill, NJ: Hampton.

Wittenberg-Lyles, E. M., Goldsmith, J., Ragan, S., & Sanchez-Reilly, S. (2010b). Medical students' views and ideas about palliative care communication training. *American Journal of Hospice and Palliative Medicine.*

Wittenberg-Lyles, E. M., Goldsmith, J., Sanchez-Reilly, S., & Ragan, S. L. (2008). Communicating a terminal prognosis in a palliative care setting: Deficiencies in current communication training protocols. *Social Science and Medicine, 66,* 2356–2365. doi: S0277-9536(08)00066-X [pii]10.1016/j.socscimed.2008.01.042

World Health Organization. (n.d.). WHO definition of palliative care. *World Health Organization.* Retrieved from http://www.who.int/cancer/palliative/definition/en/

Zhang, B., Wright, A. A., Huskamp, H. A., Nilsson, M., Maciejewski, M. L., Earle, C. C., ... Prigerson, H. G. (2009). Health care costs in the last week of life: Associations with end-of-life conversations. *Archives of Internal Medicine, 169,* 480–488. Retrieved from http://archinte.ama-assn.org

29

STIGMA, COMMUNICATION, AND HEALTH

Rachel A. Smith

Stigma processes are considered a leading barrier to health promotion, treatment, and social support for those facing health challenges (e.g., World Health Organization, 2001) and may well be the least understood (e.g., UNAIDS, 2004). Stigma has been linked to delays in seeking treatment, prolonged risk of transmission, poor treatment adherence, and increased risks of recurrence of health problems (e.g., Heijnders & Van der Meij, 2006) among other things. What is a stigma? It is a socialized, simplified, standardized image of the disgrace of a particular social group (Smith, 2007a). Thus, being marked as the member of a stigmatized group does more than designate someone as different (Thompson & Seibold, 1978); it denotes them as profoundly discredited, devalued, and disgraced (Goffman, 1963). The relationship between stigma, health, and communication is complex, dynamic, and multifaceted. This chapter discusses these relationships in four sections, describing toxic messages, communicative reactions, health consequences of stigma, and stigma-reduction interventions.

Stigma Defined

Stigmas are based in stereotypes, defined as formulaic and simplified conceptions of a group and its members (Ashmore & Del Boca, 1981). The disgrace embedded in a stigma relates to a taboo, which is defined as a prohibited condition or act (*Oxford English Dictionary*, 2010). Stigmas and taboos can be viewed as helping to protect group survival, because "people will stigmatize those individuals whose characteristics and actions are seen as threatening or hindering the effective functioning of their groups" (Neuberg, Smith, & Asher, 2000, p. 34). Stigmas, then, are social constructions (e.g., Brown, Macintyre, & Trujillo, 2003) shared among community members to socialize them as to how they can recognize the stigmatized and enact the required devaluation of them (Smith, 2007a).

Many relationships exist between stigmas and health. Goffman (1963) argued that stigmas generate an intense form of devaluation such that a member of a stigmatized group is no longer considered to be human. Due to the dehumanization, communities exercise a number of discrimination choices that ultimately limit stigmatized people's quality of life and possibly the length of their lives (Goffman, 1963). Further, specific health conditions or acts may be related to the taboo or the disgrace embedded in a stigma. Finally, managing

455

stigma may present its own health-related challenges for stigmatized persons as well as their supporters, such as loved ones or even health providers. Thus, stigma may be based on one's health condition; being stigmatized may further compromise one's health and well-being; and caring for a stigmatized person may provide unique challenges above and beyond the health issue.

Toxic Messages: Stigmatizing Health through Communication

Two assumptions of this chapter are that stigmas are socialized (Goffman, 1963) and they must be communicated. The effect of this communication is specific: People need to be able to recognize those who pose threats to their community's way of life and how to limit this stigmatized group's access to group resources and future interactions. Consequently, stigma communication needs to include content that quickly gains attention, encourages grouping and stereotyping, and provides reasons and emotional motivation to engage in devaluation and discrimination. To achieve these message effects, efficient stigma communication includes four types of content cues: marks, labels, responsibility, and peril. The next few paragraphs describe each content cue with health examples.

Marks

Marks are the cues used to recognize members of a stigmatized group. The most effective marks facilitate quick recognition, are easy to learn, and evoke emotions that trigger functional behavioral responses, such as wanting to remove someone from the situation. To more easily categorize someone as a member of a stigmatized group, it helps if the mark is harder to conceal (Deaux, Reid, Mizrahi, & Ethier, 1995; Frable, 1993; Jones, Farina, Hastorf, Markus, Miller, & Scott, 1984) and disgusting (Goffman, 1963; Jones et al., 1984). Why disgust? Disgust results in an action tendency to avoid or reject the marked target and eventually to remove it from one's presence (Mackie & Smith, 2002). It also results in an evaluative tendency to make moral judgments about the "disgusting" person (Looy, 2004). Marks may be affixed to people by placing a temporary or permanent (e.g., a brand) symbol on a target or placing attention on attributes already attached to the target. For example, one health care organization required HIV positive and AIDS patients to wear blue wrist bands to identify them—a stigmatizing practice that was further reinforced by listing their names on bulletin boards and placing a little red dot next to them—"it didn't take too long before the people there in the ward figured it out. I heard the talk about AIDS. So some of it got out" (Vanderford, Smith, & Harris, 1992, p. 142).

In medical practice, some conditions inherently evoke disgust more easily than others (see Haidt, McCauley, & Rozin, 1994 for a review of disgust cues); lack of treatment for them can generate social distancing effects. For example, in the "stigma of smell," Emma Price (1996) describes the critical need for nurses to address fungating wounds. Patients withdraw from others, including family and other patients, and feel disgusted and embarrassed by the smell coming from such wounds. The smell, in contrast to other symptoms such as pain or breathlessness, is associated with greater levels of physical pain and greater pessimism on the part of patients about their prognosis. More recent reports indicate that the smell makes it seemingly impossible to be physically proximate to others (Lund-Nielsen, Muller, & Adamsen, 2005). Price claims that, although the odor from a malignant fungating lesion may seem like a small part of a patient's medical condition, it has significant and dramatic effects on the patient's quality of life and deserves greater attention by health providers.

Labels

The process of labeling a stigmatized group plays a key role in stigmatization, facilitating the process of considering the stigmatized group as a coherent, distinct entity. Bringing the group into existence (i.e., entitativity) makes the group appear structured and its members homogeneous and subject to a common fate (e.g., Hogg & Reid, 2006). The process also encourages the development of stereotypes and stereotype-consistent interpretation of group members' behavior (Hogg & Reid, 2006).

The word selected for the group's label can bring attention to the stigma by using the mark or stigmatizing condition in the label. A salient example can be found in the discussion of illnesses (Link & Phelan, 2001) or genetics (Smith, 2007b) as either conditions or labels (Link & Phelan, 2001). For example, a person can have a cold, diabetes, epilepsy, or schizophrenia. In contrast, a person could say that "I saw one of those *epileptics* in town today": "The second statement denotes that the person is the disease and a member of a separate group from the rest of society" (Smith, 2007a, p. 470). In a different example, people may self-reflectively state that "I have a genetic mutation" or "I am a genetic mutant" (Smith, 2007b). Indeed, one risk of genetic testing may be an increase of stigma due to labeling. Meiser, Mitchell, McGirr, Van Herten, and Schofield (2005) quoted one worried participant as stating, "You could be labeled—you get the stigma. If you've got that chance that you are going to get it, you will be treated like that" (p. 112).

Sometimes labels result from translating medical terminology into lay language. For example, the word "carrier" may be a new label coming from genetic testing (e.g., Phelan, 2005). One example of its use is an advertisement for genetic testing that states "Are you a carrier?" (Gollust, Hull, & Wilfond, 2002, p.1762). The fact that carriers share genes that differentiate them from others can further bolster the notion that the carriers differ fundamentally from other people. Biological differences are seen as more elemental, real, and immutable than those due to the environment (Mehta & Farina, 1997). By using the word "carrier" as a social category, people may be more easily grouped and then labeled by their genetic test results.

Responsibility

Responsibility in this context refers to information that is included in messages to imply blame by making attributions about a person's choice or control. In other words, it is used to argue that those within a stigmatized group made decisions that put the community at risk. Marked, labeled members of a stigmatized group may be thought of as *choosing* their stigmatized condition (Jones et al., 1984) due to an immoral character (Goffman, 1963). For example, since late in the 20th century, US smokers have been blamed for making a deviant, personal health choice that threatens public health through secondhand smoke. Choice has powerful consequences: Empathy, which can reduce stigmas, is difficult to evoke for those seen as choosing their labeling condition (e.g., Batson et al., 1997). The notion of responsibility also encompasses how much *control* the person has in eliminating the threat (Deaux et al., 1995; Frable, 1993). In other words, even if people did not choose to contract swine flu, they have control over how quickly they get better and how much they infect others in the community. Goffman (1963) wrote about the triple stigmas with illnesses: (a) its physical symptoms (such as erupting sores), (b) one's tarnished character, and (c) one's choice to associate with groups who carry it. Thus, stigma communication about those who contract an illness may convey the belief that the marked, labeled members *intentionally* put the community's health and well-being at risk.

The language of blame helps to evoke anger. Anger is thought to motivate people to aggressive acts to destroy or remove the obstacle and regain access to a desired outcome (Mackie & Smith, 2002). For example, armed with anger, people may be motivated to speak out and to command a smoker to move out of their airspace or put the cigarette out.

Peril

Peril refers to information that links the marked, labeled, responsible individuals to a physical or social danger that threatens the community's way of life (Deaux et al., 1995; Frable, 1993; Jones et al., 1984). For example, the media portray characters with mental illnesses as volatile (e.g., Wahl, Wood, & Richards, 2002), twisted and deranged, and behaving in irrational and criminal ways (Wilson, Nairn, Coverdale, & Panapa, 2000). Highlighting this danger evokes fear, and fear is thought to encourage actions to escape from the threat (Cottrell & Neuberg, 2005). Thus, danger helps to remind citizens to avoid the stigmatized and spurs the unstigmatized to collective efforts to eliminate the stigmatized people's ability to threaten them.

In some cases, changing responsibility for a health condition, such as schizophrenia, may have implications for perceptions of peril. For example, genetic arguments for schizophrenia may eliminate perceptions that people choose the condition, but it can also make them seem more threatening and dangerous than when the condition was seen as a choice (Schnittker, 2008). Other contextual effects, such as uncertainty related to novel health conditions, may exacerbate a feeling of fear and a sense of danger.

An Integrated Perspective

Together, messages that include information about marks, labels, responsibility, and peril allow listeners (a) to access relevant social mores and attitudes, (b) to access and develop stereotypes, and (c) to feel disgust, anger, and fear. These cognitive and emotional reactions encourage listeners to develop or maintain stigma beliefs, stereotypes, and attitudes. They inspire actions such as tracking, isolating, and removing the stigmatized from community interactions. These message features also encourage people to share stigma messages throughout the community's social network.

While these content choices have been associated with socializing stigmatization, it does not mean that the lack of such content is unproblematic. Coopman (2003), for example, lists a topology of metaphors associated with disability, and how each can generate some form of oppression. When a disability is seen as a medical condition, then the condition is seen as needing to be fixed, and defines people in terms of what they are not (i.e., abled). Even if people attempt to repair their conditions, they may not regain a "normal" status, but be redefined as those with corrected conditions (Goffman, 1963). This also affects the way that communication takes place.

Communicative Reactions to Stigmatization

Health stigmas are formed, sustained, and socialized through communication. Others respond to stigma via communication.

Interactions

Interactions between marked, labeled people and "normal" ones (those not categorized as members of a stigmatized group) are thought to be stressful (Goffman, 1963). Such conversations are filled with impression management challenges (Goffman, 1963), and sometimes conflicting obligations to uphold expectations to watch for and to protect the community from stigmatized members (Cottrell & Neuberg, 2005), and yet to not appear too inhumane (Thompson & Seibold, 1978). For example, the Ad Council and the American Legacy Foundation released the "Don't pass gas" campaign in January 2005 (http://www.adcouncil.org/default.aspx?id=58). The campaign showed family members expressing disgust and encouraging family members to leave the room as if they had passed human gas. The gas, however, is secondhand smoke. The website included multiple materials to download and print out, such as door hangers with instructions to "make gagging sounds and repeat, 'You're killing me here'" when they detect secondhand smoke. A small poster, made to look like homemade needlework, was a pledge: the third item stated, "I vow to make passing gas in public a social taboo" (see www.dontpassgas.org) and to do so "politely."

"Normal" persons report feelings of uncertainty, discomfort, and anxiety about interacting with labeled ones (Kelley, Hastorf, Jones, Thibaut, & Usdane, 1961). Thus, it is not surprising that "normal" persons avoid contact (Thompson, 1982), shorten interactions (e.g., Thompson & Seibold, 1978), and increase interpersonal distance from labeled people (Kleck, Ono, & Hastorf, 1966). These feelings and reactions appear consistently across different stigma conditions (Goffman, 1963); they appear more strongly for more stigmatized conditions. Indeed, Thompson and Seibold (1978) found similar nonverbal displays of tension, repulsion, and rejection to those in wheelchairs, wearing "gay liberation" buttons, or displaying Star of David necklaces. Participants exhibited more of these nonverbal displays when interacting with marked confederates in comparison to "normal" confederates.

For those in the medical profession, these conversational changes could challenge doctor–patient interactions. If practitioners shorten their conversations, increase personal distance, and avoid contact with stigmatized patients, they may not provide the same quality of care. For example, some dentists refuse dental care to those living with HIV or AIDS (McCarthy, Koval, & MacDonald, 1999). Stigma can impact practitioners' examinations and guidance. For example, physicians report fewer pelvic exams for obese versus non-obese women (Adams, Smith, Wilbur, & Grady, 1993). In a different example, many general practitioners (64%) would recommend that a 50-year-old patient diagnosed with lung cancer file a worker's compensation claim after 20 years of working at a location known for high asbestos exposure levels; fewer (33%) would make this recommendation if the patient was also described as a heavy smoker (Verger et al., 2008). Moreover, although medical assistance can double the odds of quitting smoking successfully, few providers help patients quit. A reason for providers' reluctance is a negative attitude toward smokers (Schroeder, 2005).

Coping with Stigmatization

Labeled Responses.   Bruce Link and colleagues (e.g., Link, Mirotznik, & Cullen, 1991; Link, Struening, Neese-Todd, Asmussen, & Phelan 2002) have argued that those labeled as members of a stigmatized group attempt to cope with the stress of impending devaluation, rejection, and discrimination through three coping strategies: withdrawal, secrecy, and education. Withdrawal is action taken to selectively expose oneself to only those people who accept the conditions associated with the stigma label (e.g., Link et al., 2002). Secrecy refers to action taken to conceal the marks and labeling conditions that could trigger categorization into a stigmatized group (Goffman, 1963; Herek, 1996; Jones et al., 1984; Link et al., 1991; Smith, 2007a). Education, in contrast, is active and intentional disclosure of one's marked and labeled status, and providing information about the conditions associated with it (Link et al., 1991; Peters et al., 2005). This is done to persuade others to change their stereotypes, to generate acceptance, and to ward off rejection. For example, a positive HIV diagnosis often places people into a stigmatized group (Herek, 1996; Herek, Capitanio, & Widaman, 2002). Aware of this potential, a person newly diagnosed with HIV may select either (a) to withdraw from interacting with anyone except for those who would accept this diagnosis, (b) to attempt to conceal the positive status, or (c) to share it with others (e.g., Smith, Rossetto, & Peterson, 2008).

Label Management.   Until recently, the research on coping with stigmatization has focused on the labeled person. But what happens when labeled people disclose their situation to a confidant? Does the confidant advise the labeled person to engage in withdrawal, secrecy, or education? Instead of presuming that labeled persons come up with these coping strategies without assistance, Label Management theory (LM; Smith & Hipper, 2010) argues that confidants may advise labeled persons to engage in withdrawal, secrecy, or education to help the labeled person avoid future stigmatization and discrimination.

A basic premise of LM theory is that the labeled person has disclosed his/her labeling condition to an unlabeled confidant. Intentional disclosures are common: People seek help with challenging situations by turning for advice to those with whom they have close relationships (Feng & Burleson, 2008).

LM theory presumes that when a person discloses his/her labeling condition to an unlabeled confidant, the two become co-owners of this information (Petronio, 2002; Petronio, Sargent, Andea, Reganis, & Cichocki, 2004). Co-owners share in the knowledge of the discloser's labeled status, regulation of this knowledge, and its consequences. Once the news is shared, family members and cancer survivors may decide together who else will know and not know about a cancer diagnosis. For example, spousal pairs may decide not to tell their children about a cancer diagnosis until they must (e.g., Hallowell et al., 2005; Mellon, Berry-Bobovski, Gold, Levin, & Tainsky, 2006).

In LM theory, it is argued that confidants consider the label, its stereotypes, and potential consequences in similar fashion to those bearing the label, because stigma is socialized among all members of a community (Link, Cullen, Struening, Shrout, & Drohrenwend, 1989; Scheff, 1966; Smith, 2007a). Moreover, Goffman's (1963) notion of a courtesy stigma suggests that confidants may co-own not just the information of one's labeled status, but its consequences as well. Through *courtesy stigma*, the community does the courtesy of extending supporters the same stigma as their labeled loved one, thus treating both labeled persons and their supporters as though they all have been labeled (Goffman, 1963). As predicted by

LM theory, multiple studies in the United States and southern Africa show that unlabeled confidants report greater intentions to advise their labeled loved ones to use secrecy to cope with stigmatization if they held more devaluation–discrimination beliefs about the labeling condition and felt that the labeling condition was more personally relevant (Smith & Hipper, 2010; Smith, Moore, Catona, & Johnson, 2009; Smith & Niedermyer, 2009). Although secrecy, withdrawal, and education have received a great deal of theoretical attention and empirical testing, Meisenbach (2009) notes that a labeled person may use a variety of communication strategies, such as humor, denial, or ignoring, to manage stigma communication. These strategies deserve attention in future research.

These conversations do not need to contain advice in order to influence how labeled persons manage potential stigmatization. Romantic partners, family members, friends, children, and coworkers may be eager to get past the disruptions created by discovery of an illness and its treatment so that life can return to normal (Lewis & Deal, 1995). This has frequently been observed by those diagnosed with cancer, being treated for cancer, and living as survivors of cancer. These significant others may discourage discussions, leaving labeled persons to work through their unresolved questions and feelings in isolation (Lewis & Deal, 1995).

Toxic Consequences: Stigmatization and Health

A full discussion of all of the ways stigmatization can influence health is outside of the boundaries of one chapter. This discussion focuses on two consequences: social networks and patient confidentiality.

Challenged Social Networks

Motivations exist for both unlabeled and labeled persons to avoid conversations with each other. Although avoidance of conversation can limit stress for the unlabeled person and possible stigmatization for the labeled one, it has its own negative consequences. For example, as labeled persons' networks shrink, they have fewer chances to develop their communication skills (Kleck, 1968), which may further perpetuate stereotypes associated with the stigma (Thompson, 1981). Labeled children, in particular, may have fewer opportunities to interact with others, and these few interactions may provide a limited, challenging environment in which to learn appropriate social skills (Thompson, 1981).

As labeled persons restrict their networks to those who will accept them, they may be found on the periphery of a community's social network, isolated due to their few group memberships (Smith, 2008). Stigma, then, may alter a community's network structure, and people's positions within it. This restructuring may, in fact, create the tight pockets of 2-core networks found by Friedman et al. (1997) and Lovell (2002) as the most at risk for problematic health behaviors, HIV acquisition, and HIV transmission. If people are drawn together via a taboo activity, it may exacerbate social norms to engage in it. For example, injection drug users are less likely to reduce needle-sharing with close, supportive injecting partners as compared to other drug use partnerships (Latkin, Sherman, & Knowlton, 2003).

Stress-Inducing. Aversive reactions, secrecy, stigma, and social isolation can increase stress. Sometimes stress or depression results from maintaining relationships with people who present conflicts, stigma, or discrimination (e.g., Riggs, Vosvick, & Stallings, 2007).

For example, for each additional, quarrelsome relationship injection drug users reported, the likelihood of high depressive symptoms for that group rose 57% higher (Knowlton & Latkin, 2007). Depression in persons living with HIV has been related to faster CD4 decline (Burack et al., 1993), progression to AIDS (Leserman, 2003; Leserman, Jackson, et al., 1999; Lesserman, Petitto, et al., 2002; Page-Sharfer, Delorenze, Satariano, & Winkelstein, 1996), and mortality (Ickovies et al., 2001; Mayne, Vittinghoff, Chesney, Barrett, & Coates, 1996).

Supporter Synchronicity. Caregivers and health care providers of those facing stigmatization may not only encourage their labeled loved ones and patients to use withdrawal, secrecy, and education to cope with stigmatization; they may use it as well to address their own experiences with courtesy stigmatization (e.g., Green, 2003). As they restrict their own networks, caregivers report more caregiver burden (e.g., Goldstein et al., 2004) and compromised immune regulation (Miller, Cohen, & Ritchey, 2002). Further, intending to keep the labeling condition secret may induce physical stress reactions in the labeled person as well as their confidants (Smith et al., 2009).

Patient Confidentiality

One communication-related difference in health practices appears in a legal tension involving the Tarasoff principles (*Tarasoff v. Regents of the University of California*, 1976). The Tarasoff principles cover the conditions under which a patient's confidentiality may be broken to protect others, such as disclosing people's HIV-positive status to their partners. Unfortunately, breaches of confidentiality have eroded patients' trust in and disclosure to providers (e.g., Cline & McKenzie, 2000; Parrott, Duncan, & Duggan, 2000).

Multiple experiments show that psychotherapists are more likely to report intentions to violate the confidentiality of patients testing positive for HIV and not cooperating in taking steps to protect their partner (Kozlowski, Rupert, & Crawford, 1998; McGuire, Nieri, Abbot, Sheridan, & Fisher, 1995), especially if they have stronger homophobic attitudes (McGuire et al., 1995) and stronger belief in an HIV/AIDS stigma (Simone & Fulero, 2001). Reported actions include warning someone (McGuire et al., 1995), such as the patient's partner (Kozlowski et al., 1998), or even detaining their HIV-positive clients (McGuire et al., 1995). Legally, the 2005 Texas Health and Safety Code states that spouses of persons testing positive for HIV may be informed without the patient's consent. Mental health professionals in Texas are not allowed to notify spouses if their patients have threatened to do these spouses bodily harm (Barbee, Combs, Ekleberry, & Villalobos, 2007).

One hope is to reduce or eliminate the stigmas attached to health conditions. The next section provides a brief description of the communication alternatives used to influence stigmas and their efficacy.

Communication Interventions to Mitigate the Negative Effects of Stigma

If stigma relies on marks, labeling, responsibility, and peril, then stigma-reduction campaigns would need to alter these features. Further, as noted earlier, stigmas are stereotype-based phenomena, so communication would need to undermine these stereotypes. Stigma-reduction campaigns may be placed into three categories: protest, education, and contact (Corrigan & Penn, 1999).

Protest campaigns highlight the injustice of stigma through moral appeals that shame those who enact the stigma. As explained by psychological reactance theory (Brehm, 1966), appeals that limit one's freedom to believe, to feel, or to act often result in pushing listeners to reassert their freedom by continuing to believe, to feel, or to act in the decried manner. Accordingly, these types of campaigns often result in no change or stronger stigmas (e.g., Corrigan, River, et al., 2001). On the other hand, protest campaigns have been useful in leveraging institutional changes, such as protests to television stations that show stigmatizing materials (Corrigan, 2004).

Education campaigns focus on changing beliefs about responsibility and peril. For example, these campaigns may provide facts indicating that those in the stigmatized category are not responsible for the threatening concern or that they may not pose a danger. Education, in general, has been the most popular strategy reported by labeled persons (Link, Cullen, et al., 1989) and recommended for labeled persons to use (Smith & Hipper, 2010), but its predictors and consequences are not well understood empirically (Smith & Hipper, 2010). Campaigns using these techniques exhibit short-term success in changing attitudes about mental illness (e.g., Holmes, Corrigan, Williams, Canar, & Kubiak, 1999; Penn, Guynan, Daily, & Spaulding, 1994), but no research has investigated their success in sustaining attitude change or affecting behavior (Corrigan, 2004). Education campaigns that focus on increasing empathy with the stigmatized through role taking or simulations have shown little influence on increasing acceptance of those with hearing or physical disabilities (Burgstahler & Doe, 2004; French, 1992). In fact, such exercises have been shown to reinforce myths and stigma-related stereotypes even if they generate feelings of sympathy (Burgstahler & Doe, 2004). Unfortunately, although education, and even simple disclosure, seems like a very positive strategy, disclosure may have very little impact on how unlabeled persons talk with labeled ones (Thompson & Seibold, 1978).

Contact interventions encourage contact between stigmatized and nonstigmatized people, and show some promise in producing sustainable attitude changes and related behavior change (e.g., Corrigan, River, et al., 2001; Corrigan, Rowan, et al., 2002). Theoretically, the contact could make a person question if the group truly exists (i.e., as a separate social entity) or if the out-group members could be included into their own groups. Specific conditions are needed for contact to make a positive impact on stereotypes and social categorization (e.g., Pettigrew & Tropp, 2000); recent interventions show that virtual contact with media characters can generate similar outcomes (e.g., Schiappa, Gregg, & Hewes, 2005; Vaughan & Hansen, 2004). One concern about contact interventions is that people may be forced to disclose their labeling condition, and that disclosure can have negative consequences (Heijnders & Van der Meij, 2006).

Final Thoughts

This chapter has been a brief introduction to the relationship between stigma and health communication by reviewing (a) how communication can be used to socialize stigmas, (b) how communication is used to manage stigmatization, (c) how management can have its own health effects and interfere with health practices, and (d) how communication may attenuate existing health stigmas. The existing literature provides a grim portrayal of how easily and effectively stigmas may be socialized, how challenging they are to manage, how many facets of health and health management are compromised, and how difficult it is to attenuate them. The dynamics between stigma and health communication need to appear in research and policy, such as the benefits of prevention messages that come with the cost of generating or bolstering stigmas. One may recommend that communication about health issues purge stigma communication cues altogether, employ social support and mobilization cues, and watch for unintended consequences. As noted earlier, world health agencies argue that stigma may well be the leading and least understood impediment to health promotion, treatment, and support. This chapter presents a preliminary discussion of these communication issues, with the acknowledgment that there is much more work to be done to understand the pragmatic and ethical consequences of stigma for health communication.

References

Adams, C. H., Smith, N. J., Wilbur, D. C., & Grady, K. E. (1993). The relationship of obesity to the frequency of pelvic examinations: Do physicians and patient attitudes make a difference? *Women & Health, 20,* 45–57.

Ashmore, R. D., & Del Boca, F. K. (1981). Conceptual approaches to stereotypes and stereotyping. In D. L. Hamilton (Ed.), *Cognitive processes in stereotyping and intergroup behavior* (p. 16). Hillsdale, NJ: Erlbaum.

Barbee, P. W., Combs, D. C., Ekleberry, F., & Villalobos, S. (2007). To warn and protect: Not in Texas. *Journal of Professional Counseling, Practice, Theory, & Research, 35,* 18–25.

Batson, C. D., Polycarpou, M. P., Harmon-Jones, E., Imhoff, H. J., Mitchener, E. C., Bednar, L., ... Highberger, L. (1997). Empathy and attitudes: Can feelings for a member of a stigmatized group improve feelings toward the group? *Journal of Personality and Social Psychology, 72,* 105–118.

Brehm, J. W. (1966). *A theory of psychological reactance.* New York: Academic Press.

Brown, L., Macintyre, K., & Trujillo, L. (2003). Interventions to reduce HIV/AIDS stigma: What have we learned? *AIDS Education and Prevention, 15,* 49–69.

Burack, J. H., Barrett, D. C., Stall, R. D., Chesney, M. A., Ekstrand, M. L., & Coates, T. J. (1993). Depressive symptoms and CD4 lymphocyte decline among HIV-infected men. *Journal of the American Medical Association, 270,* 2568–2573.

Burgstahler, S., & Doe, T. (2004). Disability-related simulations: If, when, and how to use them in professional development. *The Review of Disability Studies, 1,* 8–18.

Cline, R. J. W., & McKenzie, N. J. (2000). Dilemmas of disclosure in the age of HIV/AIDS: Balancing privacy and protection in the health care context. In S. Petronio (Ed.), *Balancing the secrets of private disclosures* (pp. 71–82). Mahwah, NJ: Erlbaum.

Coopman, S. J. (2003). Communicating disability: Metaphors of oppression, metaphors of empowerment. *Communication Yearbook, 27,* 337–394.

Corrigan, P. (2004).Target-specific stigma change: A strategy for impacting mental illness stigma. *Psychiatric Rehabilitation Journal, 28*(2), 113–121.

Corrigan, P., & Penn, D. (1999). Lessons from social psychology on discrediting psychiatric stigma. *American Psychologist, 54,* 965–776.

Corrigan, P. W., River, L. P., Lundin, R. K., Penn, D. L., Uphoff-Wasowski, K., Campion, J., ... Kubiak, M. A.(2001). Three strategies for changing attributions about severe mental illness. *Schizophrenia Bulletin, 27,* 187–195.

Corrigan, P. W., Rowan, D., Green, A., Lundin, R., River, P., Uphoff-Wasowski, K., ... Kubiak, M. A. (2002). Challenging two mental illness stigmas: Personal responsibility and dangerousness. *Schizophrenia Bulletin, 28,* 293–310.

Cottrell, C. A., & Neuberg, S. L. (2005). Different emotional reactions to different groups: A socio-functional threat-based approach to "prejudice." *Journal of Personality and Social Psychology, 88,* 770–789.

Deaux, K., Reid, A., Mizrahi, K., & Ethier, K. A. (1995). Parameters of social identity. *Journal of Personality & Social Psychology, 68,* 280–291.

Feng, B., & Burleson, B. R. (2008). The effects of argument explicitness on responses to advice in supportive interactions. *Communication Research, 35,* 849–874.

Frable, D. E. (1993). Dimensions of marginality: Distinctions among those who are different. *Personality & Social Psychology Bulletin, 19,* 370–380.

French, S. (1992). Simulation exercises in disability awareness training: A critique. *Disability, Handicap and Society, 7,* 257–266.

Friedman, S. R., Neaigus, A., Jose, B., Curtis, R., Goldstein, M., Ildefonso, G., ... Des Jarlais, D. C. (1997). Sociometric risk networks and HIV Risk. *American Journal of Public Health, 87,* 1289–1296.

Goffman, E. (1963). *Stigma: Notes on the management of spoiled identity.* Englewood Cliffs, NJ: Prentice-Hall.

Goldstein, N. E., Concato, J., Fried, T. R., Kasl, S.V., Johnson-Hurzeler, R., & Bradley, E. H. (2004). Factors associated with caregiver burden among caregivers of terminally ill patients with cancer. *Journal of Palliative Care, 20,* 38–43.

Gollust, S. E., Hull, S. C., & Wilfond, B. S. (2002). Limitations of direct-to-consumer advertising for clinical genetic testing. *Journal of the American Medical Association, 288,* 1762–1767.

Green, S. E. (2003). "What do you mean 'what's wrong with her?'": Stigma and the lives of families of children with disabilities. *Social Science & Medicine, 57,* 1361–1374.

Haidt, J., McCauley, C. R., & Rozin, P. (1994). Individual differences in sensitivity to disgust: A scale sampling seven domains of disgust elicitors. *Personality and Individual Differences, 16,* 701–713.

Hallowell, N., Ardern-Jones, A., Eeles, R., Foster, C., Lucassen, A., Moynihan, C., & Watson, M. (2005). Communication about genetic testing in families of male BRCA1/2 carriers and non-carriers: Patterns, priorities and problems. *Clinical Genetics, 67,* 492–502.

Heijnders, M., & Van der Meij, S. (2006). The fight against stigma: An overview of stigma-reduction strategies and interventions. *Psychology, Health, & Medicine, 11,* 353–363.

Herek, G. M. (1996). Why tell if you're not asked? Self-disclosure, intergroup contact, and heterosexuals' attitudes toward lesbians and gay men. In G. M. Herek, J. Jobe, & R. Carney (Eds.), *Out in force: Sexual orientation and the military* (pp. 197–225). Chicago, IL: University of Chicago Press.

Herek, G. M., Capitanio, J. P., & Widaman, K. F. (2002). HIV-related stigma and knowledge in the United States: Prevalence and trends, 1991–1999. *American Journal of Public Health, 92,* 371–377.

Hogg, M. A., & Reid, S. A. (2006). Social identity, self-categorization, and the communication of group norms. *Communication Theory, 16,* 7–30.

Holmes, E., Corrigan, P., Williams, P., Canar, J., & Kubiak, M. (1999). Changing public attitudes about schizophrenia. *Schizophrenia Bulletin, 25,* 447–456.

Ickovics, J. R., Hamburger, M. E., Vlahov, D., Schoenbaum, E. E., Schuman, P., Boland, R. J., Moore, J. (2001). Morality, CD4 cell count decline, and depressive symptoms among HIV-seropositive women: Longitudinal analysis from the HIV Epidemiology Research Study. *Journal of the American Medical Association, 285,* 1460–1465.

Jones, E. E., Farina, A., Hastorf, A. H., Markus, H., Miller, D. T., & Scott, R. A. (1984). *Social stigma: The psychology of marked relationships.* New York: W. H. Freeman.

Kelley, J. J., Hastorf, A. H., Jones, E. E. S., Thibaut, J. W., & Usdane, W. M. (1961). Some implication of social psychological theory for research on the handicapped. In L. H. Lofquist (Ed.), *Psychological research and rehabilitation* (pp. 172 – 204). Washington, DC: American Psychological Association.

Kleck, R. (1968). Physical stigma and nonverbal cues emitted in face-to-face interactions. *Human Relations, 21,* 19–28.

Kleck, R., Ono, H., & Hastorf, A. H. (1966). The effects of physical deviance on face-to-face interaction. *Human Relations, 19,* 425–436.

Knowlton, A. R., & Latkin, C. A. (2007). Network financial support and conflict as predictors of depressive symptoms among a highly disadvantaged population. *Journal of Community Psychology, 35,* 13–28.

Kozlowski, N. F., Rupert, P. A., & Crawford, I. (1998). Psychotherapy with HIV-infected clients: Factors influencing notification of third parties. *Psychotherapy, 35,* 105–115.

Latkin, C. A., Sherman, S., & Knowlton, A. (2003). HIV prevention among drug users: Outcome of a network-oriented peer outreach intervention. *Health Psychology, 22,* 332–339.

Leserman, J. (2003). HIV disease progress: Depression, stress, and possible mechanisms. *Biological Psychiatry, 54,* 295–306.

Leserman, J., Jackson, E., Petitto, J., Golden, R. N., Silva, S. G., Perkinds, D. O., … Evans, D. L. (1999). Progression to AIDS: The effects of stress, depressive symptoms, and social support. *Psychosomatic Medicine, 61,* 397–406.

Lesserman, J., Petitto, J. M., Gu, H., Gaynes, B. N., Barroso, J., Golden, R. N.,…Evans, D. L. (2002). Progression to AIDS, a clinical AIDS condition and mortality: Psychosocial and physiological predictors. *Psychological Medicine, 32,* 1059–1073.

Lewis, F. M., & Deal, L. W. (1995). Balancing our lives: A study of the married couple's experience with breast cancer recurrence. *Oncology Nursing Forum, 22,* 943–953.

Link, B. G., Cullen, F. T., Struening, E. L., Shrout, P. E., & Dohrenwend, B. P. (1989). A modified labeling theory approach to mental disorders: An empirical assessment. *American Sociological Review, 54,* 400–423.

Link, B. G., Mirotznik, J., & Cullen, F. T. (1991). The effectiveness of stigma coping orientations: Can negative consequences of mental illness labeling be avoided? *Journal of Health and Social Behavior, 32,* 302–320.

Link, B. G., & Phelan, J. C. (2001). Conceptualizing stigma. *Annual Review of Sociology, 27,* 363–385.

Link, B. G., Struening, E. L., Neese-Todd, S., Asmussen, S., & Phelan, J. C. (2002). On describing and seeking to change the experience of stigma. *Psychiatric Rehabilitation Skills, 6,* 201–231.

Looy, H. (2004). Embodied and embedded morality: Divinity, identity, and disgust. *Zygon, 39,* 219–235.

Lovell, A. M. (2002). Risking risk: The influence of types of capital and social networks on the injection practices of drug users. *Social Science & Medicine, 55,* 803–821.

Lund-Nielsen, B., Muller, K., & Adamsen, L. (2005). Malignant wounds in women with breast cancer: Feminine and sexual perspectives. *Journal of Clinical Nursing, 14,* 56–64

Mackie, D. M., & Smith, E. R. (2002). *From prejudice to intergroup relations: Differentiated reactions to social groups.* New York: Psychology Press.

Mayne, T. J., Vittinghoff, E., Chesney, M. A., Barrett, D. C., & Coates, T. J. (1996). Depressive effect and survival among gay and bisexual men infected with HIV. *Archives of Internal Medicine, 156,* 2233–2238.

McCarthy, G. M., Koval, J. J., & MacDonald, J. K. (1999). Factors associated with refusal to treat HIV-infected patients: The results of a national survey of dentists in Canada. *American Journal of Public Health, 89,* 541–545.

McGuire, J., Nieri, D., Abbott, D., Sheridan, K., & Fisher, R. (1995). Do *Tarasoff* principles apply in AIDS-related psychotherapy? Ethical decision making and the role of therapist homophobia and perceived client dangerousness. *Professional Psychology: Research and Practice, 26,* 608–611.

Mehta, S. I., & Farina, A. (1997). Is being "sick" really better? Effect of the disease view of mental disorder on stigma. *Journal of Social and Clinical Psychology, 16,* 405–419.

Meisenbach, R. J. (2009). *Stigma management communication: A typology of strategies used by stigmatized individuals.* Paper presented at the annual meeting of the International Communication Association: Chicago, IL.

Meiser, B., Mitchell, P. B., McGirr, H., Van Herten, M., & Schofield, P. R. (2005). Implications of genetic risk information in families with a high density of bipolar disorder: An exploratory study. *Social Science & Medicine, 60,* 109–118.

Mellon, S., Berry-Bobovski, L., Gold, R., Levin, N., & Tainsky, M. A. (2006). Communication and decision-making about seeking inherited cancer risk information: Findings from female survivor-relative focus groups. *Psycho-Oncology, 15,* 193–208.

Miller, G. E., Cohen, S., & Ritchey, A. K. (2002). Chronic psychological stress and the regulation of pro-inflammatory cytokines: A glucocorticoid-resistance model. *Health Psychology, 21,* 531–541.

Neuberg, S. L., Smith, D. M., & Asher, T. (2000). Why people stigmatize: Toward a biocultural framework. In T. F. Heatherton, R. E. Kleck, M. R. Hebl, & J. G. Hull (Eds.), *The social psychology of stigma* (pp. 31–61). New York: Guilford Press.

Page-Shafer, K., Delorenze, G. N., Satariano, W. A., & Winkelstein, W. Jr. (1996). Comorbidity and survival in HIV-infected men in the San Francisco Men's Health Survey. *Annals of Epidemiology, 6,* 420–430.

Parrott, R., Duncan, V., & Duggan, A. (2000). Promoting patients' full and honest disclosure during conversations with health caregivers. In S. Petronio (Ed.), *Balancing the secrets of private disclosures* (pp. 137–147). Mahwah, NJ: Erlbaum.

Penn, D. L., Guyan, K., Daily, T., & Spaulding, W. D. (1994). Dispelling the stigma of schizophrenia: What sort of information is the best? *Schizophrenia Bulletin, 20,* 567–578.

Peters, K. F., Apse, K. A., Blackford, A., McHugh, B., Michalic, D., & Biesecker, B. B. (2005). Social and behavioral research in clinical genetics. Living with Marfan syndrome: Coping with stigma. *Clinical Genetics, 68,* 6–14.

Petronio, S. (2002). *Boundaries of privacy: Dialectics of disclosure.* New York: State University of New York Press.

Petronio, S., Sargent, J., Andea, L., Reganis, P., & Cichocki, D. (2004). Family and friends as health-care advocates: Dilemmas of confidentiality and privacy. *Journal of Social and Personal Relationships, 21*, 33–52.

Pettigrew, T. F., & Tropp, L. R. (2000). Does intergroup contact reduce prejudice? Recent meta-analytic findings. In S. Oskamp (Ed.), *Reducing prejudice and discrimination* (pp. 93–114). Mahwah, NJ: Erlbaum.

Phelan, J. C. (2005). Geneticization of deviant behavior and consequences for stigma: The case of mental illness. *Journal of Health and Social Behavior, 46*, 307–322.

Price, E. (1996, May 15-21). The stigma of smell. *Nursing Times, 92*, 70–72.

Riggs, S. A., Vosvick, M., & Stallings, S. (2007). Attachment style, stigma and psychological distress among HIV+ adults. *Journal of Health Psychology, 12*, 922–936.

Scheff, T. J. (1966). *Being mentally ill: A sociological theory.* Chicago, IL: Aldine.

Schiappa, E., Gregg, P. B., & Hewes, D. E. (2005). The parasocial contact hypothesis. *Communication Monographs, 72*, 92–115.

Schnittker, J. (2008). An uncertain revolution: Why the rise of a genetic model of mental illness has not increased tolerance. *Social Science & Medicine, 67*, 1370–1381.

Schroeder, S. A. (2005). What to do with a patient who smokes. *Journal of the American Medical Association, 294*, 482–487.

Simone, S. J., & Fulero, S. M. (2001). Psychologists' perceptions of their duty to protect uninformed sex partners of HIV-positive clients. *Behavioral Sciences and the Law, 19*, 423–436.

Smith, R. A. (2007a). Language of the lost: An explication of stigma communication. *Communication Theory 17*, 462–485.

Smith, R. A. (2007b). Picking a frame for communicating about genetics: Stigmas or challenges. *Journal of Genetic Counseling, 16*, 289–298.

Smith, R. A. (2008, January). *Social influences in diagnosis, treatment, and survivorship.* Invited presentation at the seminar series of the Center for Infectious Disease Dynamics, University Park, PA.

Smith, R. A., & Hipper, T. (2010). Label management: Investigating how confidants encourage the use of communication strategies to avoid stigmatization. *Health Communication, 25*, 410–422.

Smith, R. A., Moore, J, Catona, D., & Johnson, J. (2009). *Understanding confidants' advice to use communication to avoid stigmatization and its effects on stress.* Paper presented at the annual meeting of the National Communication Association: Chicago, IL.

Smith, R. A., & Niedermyer, A. J. (2009). Keepers of the secret: Desire to conceal a family member's HIV+ status in Namibia, Africa. *Health Communication, 24*, 459–447.

Smith, R. A., Rossetto, K., & Peterson, B. L. (2008). A meta-analysis of perceived stigma, disclosure of one's HIV+ status, and perceived social support. *AIDS Care, 20*, 1266–1275.

Tarasoff v. Regents of the University of California, 17 Cal. 3d 425, 551 P.2d 334, 131 Cal. Rptr. 14 (Cal. 1976).

Texas Health and Safety Code. (2005). Title II; Section 81.051 and 81.103. Retrieved from http://www.statutes.legis.state.tx.us/Docs/HS/htm/HS.81.htm#81.050

Thompson, T. L. (1981). The development of communication skills in physically handicapped children. *Human Communication Research, 8*, 312–324.

Thompson, T. L. (1982). Gaze toward and avoidance of the handicapped: A field experiment. *Journal of Nonverbal Behavior, 6*, 188–196.

Thompson, T. L., & Seibold, D. R. (1978). Stigma management in "normal"–stigmatized interactions: Test of the disclosure hypothesis and a model of stigma acceptance. *Human Communication Research, 4*, 231–242.

UNAIDS. (2004, September). *Epidemiological fact sheets on HIV/AIDS and sexually transmitted infections.* Geneva, Switzerland: Author.

Vanderford, M. L., Smith, D. H., & Harris, W. S. (1992). Value identification in narrative discourse: Evaluation of an HIV education demonstration project. *Journal of Applied Communication Research, 20*, 123–160.

Vaughan, G., & Hansen, C. (2004). "Like minds, Like mine": A New Zealand project to counter the stigma and discrimination associated with mental illness. *Australian Psychiatry, 12*, 113–117.

Verger, P., Arnaud, S., Ferrer, S., Iarmarcovai, G., Saliba, M., Viau, A., & Souville, M. (2008). Inequities in reporting asbestos-related lung cancer: Influence of smoking stigma and physician's specialty, workload and role perception. *Occupational & Environmental Medicine, 65*, 392–397.

Wahl, O. F., Wood, A., & Richards, R. (2002). Newspaper coverage of mental illness: Is it changing? *Psychiatric Rehabilitation Skills, 6,* 9–31.

Wilson, C., Nairn, R., Coverdale, J., & Panapa, A. (2000). How mental illness is portrayed in children's television: A prospective study. *British Journal of Psychiatry, 176,* 440–443.

World Health Organization (2001). *The world health report 2001—Mental health: New understanding, new hope.* Geneva, Switzerland: Author.

30

COMMUNICATION AND HEALTH DISPARITIES

Khadidiatou Ndiaye, Janice L. Krieger, Jennifer R. Warren, and Michael L. Hecht

Introduction

As the first decade of the 21st century draws to a close, *Healthy People 2010* goals for reducing/eliminating health disparities remain unmet. Health care often remains inaccessible based on qualifiers such as income, geography, and other factors with clear implications not only for disadvantaged populations but also for those who are exposed to increased risks through contagious diseases. In this chapter, we explore health disparities from a multilevel perspective. The first section presents the significance of the problem and then discusses the role of communication in health disparities. Next, various disparities are presented followed by potential solutions. But first, what is the scope of the problem?

The Role of Communication for Understanding Health Disparities

This chapter offers just a glimpse at the stark nature of health disparities around the world. The '10/90 gap' is a classic description. Around the world, $70 billion is spent annually on health care, but only 10% of that is allocated to poor countries where 90% of the world's disease burden is felt (Lown & Banerjee, 2006). Even in wealthier nations such as the United States, health care is not uniform. Large health differences exist based on cultural factors such as age, region, race/ethnicity, and economics (U.S. Department of Health and Human Services [DHHS], 2008) resulting in pervasive health disparities. For example, among all groups, African Americans have the highest age-adjusted death rate for cardiovascular disease, cancer, and diabetes (Centers for Disease Control [CDC], 2005); minority ethnic groups are more likely than majority group members to report having cancer diagnosed at an advanced stage because they lack preventive cancer screenings (U.S. Department of Health and Human Services [DHHS], 2008).

These disparities are not restricted to race/ethnicity; there are geographic disparities as well (Ndiaye, Krieger, Warren, Hecht, & Okuyemi, 2008). Compared with residents of metropolitan areas, those living in rural areas are less likely to receive treatment for cancer, recommended preventive services, and report fewer visits to health providers (DHHS, 2008). These examples demonstrate the pervasiveness of disparities between those in dominant groups and all "others." Health resources and outcomes are better for those who control resources and this is evident across a range of socio-demographic indicators. Communication has been posited as an important tool for narrowing the aforementioned gaps, but its relationship to disparities is a complex one.

Communication's Role in Health Disparities

Communication is both part of the problem and the solution to health disparities (Wang, 1998). While communication may play a role in preventing and treating health problems, inadequate communication patterns, poor message choices, lack of intercultural competence, and unequal access to information all contribute to disparities. For instance, misunderstandings can occur when physicians are interacting with patients of different backgrounds. Examples of communication increasing health disparities can be found in culturally based misunderstandings (Fadiman, 1998) and the propensity for ill-conceived messages to stigmatize groups (Parrott, 2004). There is a delicate balance between creating messages that highlight groups at high risk of HIV/AIDS and messages that suggest that they are responsible for contracting or spreading the disease. Thus, group differences present a complex and problematic communication task, in both relieving as well as intensifying disparities. A multilevel perspective offers an opportunity to resolve these problematic realities and address disparities.

A Multilevel Framework for Understanding Health Disparities

Cultural differences exist at many levels and play a critical role in health disparities. A multilevel cultural lens suggests that health disparities exist at levels ranging from individual choices to social relations to societal norms. Each of these levels holds the potential for health disparities. Dominant culture dictates the approach to health that is privileged. Individuals and groups who are unfamiliar with, unconforming or unexposed to such an approach may be disadvantaged. The complex relationships between the biological and social environments demand that efforts to understand and alleviate health disparities acknowledge the multiple levels at which health disparities occur and the various factors that contribute to poorer health outcomes for vulnerable populations (Holmes et al., 2008). We conceptualize these levels as personal, relational, and communal (Hecht, Warren, Jung, & Krieger, 2004).

The health care system provides an excellent illustration of these three levels. At the personal level are the individual or personal influences on health. Patient characteristics such as being un/underinsured, low-income, or belonging to a minority group, all influence treatment quality (Sedlis et al., 1997). Next, patient–provider relationships are one of the key influences on health care quality. Provider attitudes toward minorities, social stereotypes, the health care provider's ability to understand a patient's report of symptoms (Weisse, Sorum, Sanders, & Syat, 2001), as well as the overall quality of medical interactions (van Ryn & Burke, 2000) are all key aspects of this relationship. Finally, there are a number of health care systems (i.e., communal) factors that might impede quality care, including a shortage of health care providers or medical facilities in underserved areas (Kahn et al., 1994).

Personal Influences on Health Disparities

There are myriad personal factors that influence health disparities, including demographic characteristics (e.g., age, education, income), identity (e.g., group membership, social role), and previous health care experiences (Warren, Allen, Hopfer, & Okuyemi, 2010; Warren, Kvansy, et al., 2010). For instance, lower income and older patients tend to have lower health literacy and are less likely to seek cancer screening. Social influences also play an integral role for many communities. Research has demonstrated that African Americans usually seek health information first from family and friends (Spink & Cole, 2001). While tapping into the expertise of these informal health care networks can contribute to resilience among African Americans (Russell & Jewell, 1992), heavy reliance upon peer and family networks in one's health care also can interrupt timely participation in health screening or interfere with physician-informed medical decision making.

Another personal factor that influences health disparities is social group membership or identity. Identities based on membership in race/culture, class, and other social groups are both self-selected and ascribed by society (Hecht et al., 2004) and impact motivation (Oyserman, Fryberg, & Yoder, 2007). They are often the basis for self-regulation and self-perception, serving to organize and guide perceptions of health realities, including health care providers and interaction (Warren, Kvansy, et al., 2010). Groups that do not fit into the dominant culture in American society have their health concerns treated differently from those who do (Ford & Yep, 2003). For example, the ways in which many African Americans' racial, cultural, and class-based identities are perceived by both health care providers and patients contribute to ineffective health communication that results in unequal access to and quality of care (Institute of Medicine, 2009).

Racial/Ethnic Identities. Racial identity refers to identification with an historical, cultural, sociopolitical, and economic context (Hecht, 1998). Many racial/ethnic groups perceive that the U.S. medical system is not supportive of their group membership and practices. Hispanics generally report dissatisfaction with health care, feeling that health providers communicate little respect or interest in their concerns (Merrill & Allen, 2003). Both Asians and Hispanics report lower levels of cultural sensitivity in health care encounters (Saha, Arbelaez, & Cooper, 2003) and African American patients believe they are judged unfairly by health practitioners. Unfortunately, an individual's appraisal of a situation as discriminatory is a source of chronic stress that complicates health status (Penner et al., 2009).

Socioeconomic Identity. Race-based disadvantages are compounded when socioeconomic status is involved (King & Williams, 1995). Social class differentiates individuals' experiences, practices, and how they perceive the world (Aries & Seider, 2005). Stereotypes of lower income groups negatively influence their quality of health information and medical care (Ford & Yep, 2003), particularly for those receiving public health assistance (McCann & Weinmann, 1996). In health encounters, lower income patients are perceived as less rational or intelligent than are higher income patients (van Ryn & Burke, 2000), which interferes with treatment and medical decision making for both practitioner and patient. Additionally, low income patients' mistrust of the health professionals in clinic settings has been reported (Becker & Newsom, 2003).

Sexual Orientation Related Disparities. Sexual orientation is another salient personal factor. In general, there are limited data on health concerns of lesbian, gay, bisexual, and transgender (LGBT) individuals. Less than 1% of articles in the Medline database address LGBT medical concerns and most of those that do so focus on sexually transmitted diseases (Boehmer, 2002). This lack of attention is a form of disparity because it impedes the development of treatments. The recognition that LGBT individuals may experience health differently is a first step in addressing these health disparities. Next, one must recognize that limiting research involving the LGBT community to their sexual behaviors is stigmatizing and neglects other health issues. For instance, LGBT populations tend to have a higher incidence of issues such as smoking. Archer, Hoff, and Snook (2009) explained that smoking in LGBT populations coexists with such issues as depression and victimization. It is clear, then, that LGBT health issues are broader than those related to sexual behaviors and must be dealt with in their full complexity.

Relational Influences on Health Disparities

Patient–Physician Relationships. Patient–physician relationships are central to patients' quality of health care (Saha et al., 2003) and can contribute to health disparities (van Ryn & Burke, 2006). Providers may communicate racial, ethnic, and class biases when interacting with patients and patients, too, may play a role. Generally, physicians expect to view each patient objectively (Kleinman, Eisenberg, & Good, 2006). However, they are more likely to apply stereotypes to out-group members (Burgess, Fu, & van Ryn, 2004), as when physicians' perceptions of Black patients as failing to comply with medical advice and as more likely to abuse drugs were found to influence their recommendations for heart surgery (van Ryn, Burgess, Malat, & Griffin, 2006).

Furthermore, population statistics that inform clinical decision making also may function like stereotypes (Balsa & McGuire, 2003). For example, physicians may or may not ask certain questions related to optional medical procedures based on race rather than based on what the individual patient is telling them (Burgess et al., 2004).

Family Relationships. Kinship networks have both positive and negative influences on health behaviors and health disparities (Freimuth & Quinn, 2004) and the influence of families in health decision making may be even more pronounced among underserved populations (Coyne, Demian-Popescu, & Friend, 2006). For example, rural Appalachian women report that extended family members are important stakeholders in the decision to have a young girl vaccinated against HPV (Katz et al., 2009). The literature focuses on two major themes: family lifestyle and family influences on health information and decision making.

Family Lifestyle Factors. Health disparities exist in a number of lifestyle areas, especially occupational injury and illness. Many Hispanic, African, and Native Americans as well as people living in rural areas are employed in industries associated with extreme health hazards, such as agriculture, mining, construction, and textiles (Myers, Layne, & Marsh, 2009). Family members may be directly harmed through secondary exposure to work-related toxins if workers fail to wear protective gear or remove contaminated shoes and clothing before entering the home (McCauley et al., 2001). Family health also may be harmed when work-related illness or death indirectly alter family communication as a result of income loss, changing family dynamics, and depression (Lipscomb, Loomis, McDonald, Argue, & Wing, 2006).

The physical nature of these occupations has important implications for the way health is conceptualized and communicated within the family. Physical ability is a dominant health value among social groups employed in occupations requiring heavy labor, which also tend to be hazardous (Elliot-Schmidt & Strong, 1997). Consequently, "health" in these communities is often socially constructed to mean the absence of disease, and acute care and chronic disease management is prioritized over preventive care (Coster & Gribben, 1999). For example, a family that conceptualizes health as the absence of the disease may be more supportive of physical injuries (e.g., broken leg) and remain silent about social, emotional, or mental difficulties.

This is particularly true because of the cultural importance of family among many medically underserved groups (Gil, Wagner, & Vega, 2000). The nuclear and extended family can serve as a valuable source of social support, which may buffer the negative effects of low SES (Chen, Martin, & Matthews, 2006). However, family members also may encourage behaviors known to increase risk of illness, such as unhealthy diet, inactivity, and substance use (Jones, Chilton, Hajek, Iammarino, & Laufman, 2006). Similarly, substance use may be encouraged as part of cultural rites of passage or other family traditions (Moreland, Krieger, Miller-Day, & Hecht, 2009).

In other cases, family members may wish to encourage healthy behavior, but not have control of the circumstances that may lead to poor outcomes. For example, the presence of parents at the evening meal is associated with healthier eating habits among adolescents because it provides an opportunity for parents to model healthy eating habits for their children (Videon & Manning, 2003). However, lower-income parents may be forced to choose between being present at mealtimes and working. Similarly, time, cost, and access to exercise equipment are barriers to physical activity among the underserved (Schrop et al., 2006). Thus, communication that blindly promotes these sorts of approaches to health and healthy habits reinforces the gaps between the haves and the have-nots.

Medical Information and Decision Making. A second important consideration is the substantial cultural variation in how families negotiate health and well-being (Pecchioni, Krieger, Sparks, Pitts, & Ota, 2008). Family medical discussions are important because relatives often are the primary source of family health history information (Weiner, Silk, & Parrott, 2005) and play an active role in health decision making (Ross et al., 1999). Thus, it is important to consider family discussions about health among medically underserved groups (Coyne et al., 2006; Pecchioni et al., 2008).

The recent mapping of the human genome has accentuated the importance of family health history for providing effective medical care (Guttmacher, Collins, & Carmona, 2004). What is often overlooked, however, are the significant challenges associated with discussing personal health information with family members. One challenge is identifying what information is appropriate and necessary. For example, individuals vary regarding the degree to which they attribute health outcomes to genetics, personal behaviors, the social environment, and spirituality (Parrott et al., 2004). Other families may have difficulty sharing health information about socially stigmatizing conditions (Weiner et al., 2005). In sum, formal and informal interpersonal contexts both play important roles in health disparities. However, individuals and families do not exist in a vacuum. Communities are another site for exploring health disparities.

Communal-Level Health Disparities

Health Disparities in Rural Communities. Health disparities in geographically isolated areas are widely documented (Glasgow, Wright Morton, & Johnson, 2004). Rural residents are more likely to suffer from health problems such as smoking-related illnesses, female adult obesity, child and young adult deaths, male suicide rates, limitation in activity due to chronic health conditions, and total tooth loss (Eberhardt et al., 2001). Discrimination against people in rural areas and its influence on health is multifaceted, including economic issues, cultural values, and availability of clinicians and health care facilities (Haynes & Smedley, 1999). Rural communities may distrust and even resist efforts to reduce disparities due to poor communication and failure to involve rural communities in the process (Krieger, Parrott, & Nussbaum, 2011).

Sociocultural components of health and well-being contribute to rural health inequities. The social marginalization of rural residents is apparent through the use of cultural labels such *hick*, *hillbilly*, and *redneck* (Krieger, Moreland, & Sabo, 2010). These labels reflect a larger network of stereotypes associated with rurality, leading to stigma (see Smith in this volume). These stereotypes influence rural health inequities in a number of ways. For example, a physician may assume that a rural breast cancer patient would be unwilling to make repeated trips for radiation treatment and recommend a more invasive initial treatment (Tropman et al., 1999). Both positive and negative stereotypes of members of "other" groups can have harmful consequences because they can lead to communication that is adapted based on membership in a group, not on individual characteristics (Nussbaum, Pitts, Huber, Raup Krieger, & Ohs, 2005).

One of the most common rural health problems is a lack of access to quality health care (Glasgow et al., 2004; Pande & Yazbek, 2003; Rahman, 2006). There is a severe shortage of health care providers, especially specialists, in U.S. rural areas (Gamm, Castillo, & Pittman, 2003). It is common for people who have HIV in some parts of the United States, for example, to travel 250 miles round trip to see an infectious disease specialist (Heckman et al., 1998). As a result, primary care providers have limited time to address patient needs (Ricketts, 2000). Furthermore, patients may choose to forgo seeking health care if they are unsatisfied with the communication skills of their provider and have few other options available. Despite this reality, few public communication campaigns address this issue and too few political debates about health care reform reflect awareness of the implications of rurality on well-being.

Access to quality health care for rural residents also is a problem on a global scale. For example, Bangladesh's public health expenditures are highest for urban, nonpoor males, while low-income rural residents receive the least services from the government health facilities (Rahman, 2006). In India, rural children are more likely to be underimmunized or not immunized at all (Pande & Yazbek, 2003). In remote areas of Canada, community health nurses are often the only local health care service provider (Leipert & Reutter, 1998). Limited opportunity to interact with health care providers restricts rural residents' access to an important source of health information.

Health Disparities in World Communities. Disparities are magnified when examined in the larger scale of world communities. Inequalities are not only limited to resources, they are very apparent in the burden of disease. For instance, the African continent bears the burden of the HIV/AIDS epidemic but receives a disproportionately small share of prevention and treatment (UNAIDS, 2006). The magnitude of these differences is also felt when comparing different European regions (Mackenbach et al., 2008).

Culturally defined health paradigms present yet another potential for health disparities. The biomedical approach is privileged, especially in Western cultures, but is not the sole approach to health. Traditional healing in Africa is a great illustration as it reaches 80% of people and is generally useful, cost conscious, personal, and culturally sensitive (Morris, 2001). Sometimes called 'alternative medicine,' a term that some find stigmatizing, traditional medicine is defined as "health practices, approaches, knowledge and beliefs incorporating plant, animal, and mineral based medicines, spiritual therapies, manual techniques, applied singularly or in combination to treat, diagnose, and prevent illness or maintain well-being" (WHO, 2002, p. 7). Individuals who wish to use traditional healing face many barriers. Lack of regulation and recognition may make it difficult to make informed choices and many insurance companies refuse to cover traditional healers. As a result, the failure to legitimize traditional healing leaves many patients without much choice about health care paradigms.

Health Disparity Solutions

Communication is involved in all aspects of health and is thus central to any proposed solutions. Accurate health information is needed for healthy behaviors. However, health promotion messages, whether mass or interpersonally communicated, frequently do not reach the groups we discuss in this chapter because they often are poorly designed in content and form. In general, we argue that culturally appropriate messages must be designed to inform diverse groups about susceptibility to particular ailments as well as for health information in general. This is true of media campaigns, interactions between health care providers and patients, or informal communication about health.

This chapter illustrated the complex layers of health disparities, ranging from those that involve individuals or relationships to those inherent to communities. Stark numbers are associated with the lack of health access, quality of care, and other issues related to disparities throughout the health system. While some patients do not have the basic access to the health care they need, others choose to avoid it based on negative experiences. Unequal medical treatment fosters feelings of helplessness or lack of control over one's health (Oyserman et al., 2007). The complex relationship between communication and health disparities mentioned earlier in this chapter might hold one key to addressing these disparities.

Personal Influences

At the most basic level communication can play an important role in ensuring that personal influences in disparity are recognized. Unique experiences associated with particular identities (whether avowed or ascribed) should be recognized. For instance, the recognition that LGBT individuals may experience health differently is a first step in addressing their health disparities. Next, it is important to take steps to recognize that LBGT research limited to sexual behavior is stigmatizing and essentially a discriminatory oversight (Boehmer, 2002). Unfortunately, stereotypes are difficult to overcome. Research suggests that providing counterexamples often does little to impact the impression of the overall group (Hecht, 1998). What is required is a more systematic and pervasive intervention in which contact is amongst those of equal status involving cooperation and interdependence, perhaps forming a "common in-group identity" (Hecht, 1998, p. 21). For example, diversity training in organizations has proven effective, especially when there is support from top management and it is integrated in organizational practices (Hecht, 1998).

Relational Influences

If disparities are addressed at the relational level it highlights the role of interpersonal communication in both formal and informal health contexts. For instance, family therapy (Willerton, Dankoski, & Sevilla Martir, 2008) can be an important tool for reducing stigma related to certain health conditions. Training for health care providers about ageism and geriatrics could help providers accurately determine what symptoms can be considered part of normal aging and what are not.

It is also imperative that health providers begin to challenge the communication of negative stereotypes linked to stigmatized social identities (Brown, Stewart, & Ryan, 2003). Providers who have at least some control over how their particular clinic or facility is run can work to create an identity-safe environment by signaling that they value racial and ethnic diversity (Burgess, Warren, Phelan, Dovidio, & van Ryn, 2010). Burgess et al. suggest four identity-safe strategies:

1. Elicit the patient's values and strengths; 2. Invoke high standards and assurance of the patient's ability to meet those standards; 3. Provide external attributions for patients' anxiety and difficulties; and 4. Provide cues that diversity is valued.

Communal Influences

Finally, it also is important to see the community as a locus of intervention (Canino et al., 2008). Communal influences play out in subtle ways, requiring culturally competent communication strategies. For example, what is considered good or equitable health differs from one culture to another (McLachlan, Maynard, & Culyer, 1982). For some, the Western biomedical perspective is the norm, while others would turn to traditional methods of healing for primary care. It is then imperative for researchers interested in addressing these inequities to steer away from the myth of universal notions of health and study what the concept means within a particular context. The lack of such particular attention could lead to further disparities.

Increased cultural competence may be achieved by careful consideration about whether community involvement is the goal of the health intervention or the strategy for achieving intervention outcomes (Guttman, 2000). Cultural disconnect is likely to be higher when communities are considered simple vehicles for delivering interventions, as opposed to active stakeholders. Communication interventions should be particularly well suited to emphasizing community involvement as both a goal and strategy when they emphasize the mastery of skills that can be used to facilitate social change. For instance, the idea of "culturally grounding" interventions, akin to community-based participatory research strategies, refers to both microstrategies of community input as well as the more communal notion of what health is and how it is attained (Hecht & Krieger, 2006).

A culturally grounded approach to a health intervention can facilitate appropriate message design as well as reveal the underlying barriers and facilitators to improved health in a given community. Intended audiences can help determine the ways in which racial, ethnic, and regional culture should influence a health message. For example, community members can identify when informal medical terminology clashes with local understanding, and generate examples of metaphorical language that is congruent with cultural values and ways of knowing (Krieger et al., 2011). This approach also acknowledges the importance of the social and physical environment on health behavior. For poor neighborhoods where less expensive food options are often high in calories and cholesterol, an intervention targeted toward the "food environment" is likely to be more successful than one based on nutrition knowledge alone (Sloane et al., 2003).

Finally, recent advances have seen the emergence of truly community-level interventions (Antin, Moore, Lee, & Satturland, 2008; Miller, Holden, & Voas, 2009). The idea of planned communities that are structured to maximize activity has great potential to advance health and reduce disparities (Sallis & Owen, 2002). Another communal approach seeks to enhance "social capital," the resources a community can utilize to encourage healthy practices (see Dearing et al., in this volume). Social capital has been linked to health behaviors, including smoking behavior (Patterson, Eberly, Ding, & Hargreaves, 2004) and recent evidence suggests that urban renewal projects that reconfigure public spaces can enhance community involvement and social capital in urban communities (Semenza & March, 2009). There remains, however, much work to be done in the development of strategies to facilitate social capital and other community-level processes.

Summary of Proposed Solutions

These examples, although not exhaustive, illustrate the central role communication plays in reducing health disparities. In essence, communication can facilitate interactions between different groups, mitigate misunderstandings, improve relationships, and alter health care delivery systems. It facilitates the process of prevention through messages that make audiences aware of health issues and changes health environments to facilitate healthier eating and exercise.

Conclusion

In this chapter we examine the role of communication in personal, relational, and communal influences on health disparities. Our multilevel approach leads us to conceptualize these levels as overlapping. Health disparities are a pervasive and significant social problem that impacts the lives of those most vulnerable and least able to overcome their effects. We suggest strategies for changing or eliminating communication that creates disparities as well as using communication as a prosocial force. On the positive side, the recognition of health disparities is clearly emerging along with a movement that is anticipated to reduce them in the not too distant future. The chapter is intended as a reflection of the hopeful voice of the authors, a voice that is realistic about the scope of the problem without losing sight of the possibilities for improvement. It is easy to be overwhelmed by the scope of health disparities as well as past failures to overcome them. We end with the quest for improvement and the belief that the readers of this handbook have a role to play in this journey.

References

Antin, T. M. J., Moore, R. S., Lee, J. P., & Satterlund, T. D. (2008). Law in practice: Obstacles to smoke-free workplace ordinances in bars serving Asian immigrants. *Journal of Immigrant and Minority Health*. Retrieved October 25, 2009, from http://www.springerlink.com/content/10v553m3804128p1/fulltext.pdf

Archer, R., Hoff, G. L., & Snook, W. D. (2009). Tobacco use and cessation among men who have sex with men. *American Journal of Public Health, 95,* 929.

Aries, E., & Seider, (2005). The interactive relationship between class identity and the college experience: The case of lower income students. *Qualitative Sociology, 28,* 419–443.

Balsa, A. I., & McGuire, T. G. (2003). Prejudice, clinical uncertainty and stereotyping as sources of health disparities. *Journal of Health Economics, 22,* 89–116.

Becker, G., & Newsom, E. (2003). Socioeconomic status and dissatisfaction with health care among chronically ill African Americans. *American Journal of Public Health, 93,* 742–748.

Boehmer, U. (2002). Twenty years of public health research: Inclusion of lesbian, gay, bisexual, and transgender populations. *American Journal of Public Health, 92,* 1125–1130.

Brown, J. B., Stewart, M., & Ryan B. L. (2003). Outcomes of patient–provider interaction. In T. L. Thompson, A. M. Dorsey, K. I. Miller, & R. Parrott (Eds.), *Handbook of Health Communication* (pp. 141–163). London: Erlbaum.

Burgess, D. J., Fu, S. S., & van Ryn, M. (2004). Why do providers contribute to disparities and what can be done about it? *Journal of General Internal Medicine, 19,* 1154–1159.

Burgess, D., Warren, J. R., Phelan, S., Dovidio, J., & van Ryn, M (2010). Stereotype threat and health disparities: What medical educators and future physicians need to know. *Journal of Internal General Medicine* (34)Supplement 2, 169–177.

Canino, G., Vila, D., Normand, S., Acosta-Pérez, E., Ramirez, R., Garcia, P., & Rand, C. (2008). Reducing asthma health disparities in poor Puerto Rican children: The effectiveness of a culturally tailored family intervention. *Journal of Allergy and Clinical Immunology, 121,* 665–670.

Centers for Disease Control. (2005). Health disparities experienced by racial/ethnic minority populations—United States, *Morbidity and Mortality Weekly Report, 54,* 1–3.

Chen, E., Martin, A. D., & Matthews, K. A. (2006). Understanding health disparities: The role of race and socioeconomic status in children's health. *American Journal of Public Health, 96,* 702–708.

Coster, G., & Gribben, B. (1999). *Primary care models for delivering population-based health outcomes.* Wellington, New Zealand: National Advisory Committee on Health and Disability.

Coyne, C. A., Demian-Popescu, C., & Friend, D. (2006). Social and cultural factors influencing health in southern West Virginia: A qualitative study. *Preventing Chronic Disease, 3,* A124.

Eberhardt, M. S., Ingram, D. D., Makuc, D. M., Pamuk, E. R, Freid, V., M., Harper, S. B., ... Xia, H. (2001). *Urban and rural health chartbook. Health, United States, 2001.* Hyattsville, MD: National Center for Health Statistics.

Elliot-Schmidt, R., & Strong, J. (1997). The concept of well-being in a rural setting: Understanding health and illness. *Australian Journal of Rural Health, 5,* 59–63,

Fadiman, A. (1998). *The spirit catches you and you fall down: A Hmong child, her American doctors, and the collision of two cultures.* New York: Farrar, Straus & Giroux.

Ford, A. L., & Yep, G. A. (2003). Working along the margins: Developing community-based strategies for communicating about health with marginalized groups. In T. L. Thompson, A. M. Dorsey, K. I. Miller, & R. Parrott (Eds.), *Handbook of health communication* (pp. 241–262). Mahwah, NJ: Erlbaum.

Freimuth, V., & Quinn, S. C. (2004). The contributions of health communication to eliminating health disparities. *American Journal of Public Health, 94,* 2053–2055.

Gamm, L., Castillo, G., & Pittman, S. (2003). Access to quality health services in rural areas—Primary care. In L. D. Gamm, L. L. Hutchison, B. J. Dabney, & A. Dorsey (Eds.), *Rural healthy people 2010: A companion document to healthy people 2010* (Vol. 1, pp. 45–51). College Station, TX: The Texas A&M University System Health Science Center, School of Rural Public Health, Southwest Rural Health Research Center.

Gil, A. G., Wagner, E. F., & Vega, W. A. (2000). Acculturation, familism, and alcohol use among Latino adolescent males: Longitudinal relations. *Journal of Community Psychology, 28,* 443–458.

Glasgow, N., Wright Morton, L., & Johnson, N. E. (2004). *Critical issues in rural health.* Ames, Iowa: Blackwell.

Guttmacher, A. E., Collins, F. S., & Carmona, R. H. (2004). The family health history—More important than ever. *The New England Journal of Medicine, 351,* 2333–2336.

Guttman, N. (2000). *Public health communication interventions: Values and ethical dilemmas.* Thousand Oaks, CA: Sage.

Haynes, A., & Smedley, B. D. (1999). *The unequal burden of cancer: An assessment of NIH research and programs for ethnic minorities and the medically underserved.* Washington, DC: National Academies Press.

Hecht, M. L. (Ed.). (1998). *Communicating prejudice*. Newbury Park, CA: Sage.

Hecht, M. L., Warren, J. R., Jung, E., & Krieger, J. (2004). The communication theory of identity: Development, theoretical perspective, and future directions. In W. B. Gudykunst (Ed.), *Theorizing about intercultural communication* (pp. 257–278). Newbury Park, CA: Sage.

Hecht, M. L., & Krieger, J. R. (2006). The principle of cultural grounding in school-based substance abuse prevention. *Journal of Language and Social Psychology, 25*, 301–319.

Heckman, T. G., Somlai, A. M., Peters, J., Walker, J., Otto-Salaj, L., Galdabini, C. A., & Kelly, J. A. (1998). Barriers to care among persons living with HIV/AIDS in urban and rural areas. *AIDS Care, 10*, 365–375.

Holmes, J. H., Lehman, A., Hade, E., Ferketich, A., Gehlert, S., Rauscher, G. H., … Bird, C. E. (2008). Challenges for multilevel health disparities research in a transdisciplinary environment. *American Journal of Preventive Medicine, 35*, 128–192.

Institute of Medicine. (2009). *Race, ethnicity, and language data: Standardization for health care quality improvement*. Report from the Subcommittee on Standardized College of Reace/Ethnicity Date for Health Care Quality Improvement, Institute of Medicine. Retrieved from http://www.iom.edu/~/media/Files/Report%20Files/2009/RaceEthnicityData/Race%20Ethnicity%20report%20brief%20FINAL%20for%20web.ashx

Jones, L. A., Chilton, J. A., Hajek, R. A., Iammarino, N. K., & Laufman, L. (2006). Between and within: International perspectives on cancer and health disparities. *Journal of Clinical Oncology, 24*, 2204–2208.

Kahn, K. L., Pearson, M. L., Harrison, E. R., Desmond, K. A., Rogers, W. H., Rubenstein, L. V., … Keeler, E. B. (1994). Health care for Black and poor hospitalized medicare patients. *Journal of the American Medical Association, 271*, 1169–1174.

Katz, M., Reiter, P., Heaner, S., Ruffin, M., Post, D., & Paskett, E. (2009). Acceptance of the HPV vaccine among women, parents, community leaders, and health care providers in Ohio Appalachia. *Vaccine, 27*, 3945–3952.

King, G., & Williams. D. R. (1995). Race and health: A multi-dimensional approach to African American health. In D. W. S. Levine, B. C. Amick, & A. R. Tarlov (Eds.), *Society and health: Foundation for a nation* (pp. 93–130). New York: Oxford University Press.

Kleinman, A., Eisenberg, L., & Good, B. (2006). Culture, illness and care: Clinical lessons from anthropologic and cross-cultural research. *American Psychiatric Association, 4*, 140–149.

Krieger, J. L., Moreland, J., & Sabo, J. (2010, November). *Hillbilly or redneck? Linguistic stereotypes of rural Americans*. Paper presented to the Intercultural Division at the annual meeting of the National Communication Association, San Francisco, CA.

Krieger, J. L., Parrott, R. L., & Nussbaum, J. F. (2011). Metaphor use and health literacy: A pilot study of strategies to explain randomization in cancer clinical trials. *Journal of Health Communication, 16*, 3–16.

Leipert, B., & Reutter, R. (1998). Women's health and community health nursing practice in geographically isolated settings: A Canadian perspective. *Health Care for Women International, 19*, 575–588.

Lipscomb, H. J., Loomis, D., McDonald, M. A., Argue, R. A., & Wing, S. (2006). A conceptual model of work and health disparities in the United States. *International Journal of Health Services, 36*, 25–50.

Lown, B., & Banerjee, A. (2006). The developing world in *The New England Journal of Medicine*. *Globalization and Health, 2*, 3–8.

Mackenbach J. P., Stirbu, I., Roskam. A. J., Menvielle, G., Leinsalu, M., & Kunst, A. E. (2008). Socioeconomic inequalities in health in 22 European countries. *New England Journal of Medicine, 358*, 2468–24681.

McCann, S., & Weinmann, J. (1996). Empowering the patient in the consultation: A pilot study. *Patient Education and Counseling, 27*, 227–234.

McCauley, L. A., Lasarev, M. R., Higgins, G., Rothlein, J., Muniz, J., Ebbert, C., & Phillips, J. (2001). Work characteristics and pesticide exposures among migrant agricultural families: A community-based research approach. *Environmental Health Perspectives, 109*, 533–538.

McLachlan, G., Maynard, A., & Culyer, A. J. (1982). *Nuffield trust for research and policy studies in health services. The Public/private mix for health: The relevance and effects of change essays*. London: Nuffield Provincial Hospitals Trust.

Merrill, R. M., & Allen, E. W. (2003). Racial and ethnic disparities in satisfaction with doctors and health providers in the United States. *Ethnicity & Disease, 13,* 492–498.

Miller, B. A., Holder, H., & Voas, R. (2009). Environmental strategies for prevention of drug use and risks in clubs. *The Journal of Substance Use, 14,* 19–38.

Moreland, J., Krieger, J. L., Miller-Day, M., & Hecht, M. (2009, November). *Conceptualizing adolescent risky behavior in the rural Appalachian context.* Paper presented to the Health Communication division at the annual meeting of the National Communication Association, Chicago, IL.

Morris, K. (2001). Treating HIV in South Africa: A tale of two systems. *The Lancet, 357,* 1190.

Myers, J. R., Layne, L. A., & Marsh, S. M. (2009). Injuries and fatalities to U. S. farmers and farm workers 55 years and older. *American Journal of Industrial Medicine, 53,* 185–194.

Ndiaye, K., Krieger, J., Warren, J., Hecht, M., & Okuyemi, K. (2008). Health disparities and discrimination: Three perspectives. *Journal of Health Disparities Research and Practice, 2,* 53–72.

Nussbaum, J., Pitts, M., Huber, F., Raup Krieger, J., & Ohs, J. (2005). Ageism and ageist language across the life span: Intimate relationships and non-intimate interactions. *Journal of Social Issues, 61,* 287–305.

Oyserman, D., Fryberg, S. A., & Yoder, N. (2007). Identity–based motivation and health. *Journal of Personality and Social Psychology, 93,* 1011–1027.

Pande, R. P., & Yazbek, A. S. (2003). What's in a country average? Wealth, gender, and regional inequalities in immunization in India. *Social Science & Medicine, 57,* 2075–2088.

Parrott, R. L. (2004). Emphasizing "communication" in health communication. *Journal of Communication, 54,* 751–787.

Parrott, R. L., Silk, K., Weiner, J., Condit, C., Harris, T., & Bernhardt, J. (2004). Deriving lay models of uncertainty about genes' role in illness causation to guide communication about human genetics. *Journal of Communication, 54,* 105–122.

Patterson, J. M., Eberly, L. E., Ding, Y., & Hargreaves, M. (2004). Associations of smoking prevalence with individual and area level social cohesion. *Journal of Epidemiology and Community Health, 58,* 692–697.

Pecchioni, L. L., Krieger, J. L., Sparks, L., Pitts, M. J., & Ota, H. (2008). Investigating cancer and aging from a cultural perspective. In L. Sparks, D. O'Hair, & G. Kreps (Eds.), *Cancer, communication, and aging* (pp. 239–257). Cresskill, NJ: Hampton Press.

Penner, L. A., Dovido, J. F., Edmonson, D., Dailey, R. K., Markova, T., Albrecht, T. L., & Gaertner, S. L. (2009). The experience of discrimination and black–white health disparities in medical care. *Journal of Black Psychology, 35,* 180–203.

Primack, B. A., Bost, J. E., Land, S. R., & Fine, M. J. (2007). Volume of tobacco advertising in African American markets: Systematic review and meta-analysis. *Public Health Reports, 122,* 607–615.

Rahman, R. M. (2006). Human rights, health and the state in Bangladesh. *BMC International Health and Human Rights, 6.* Retrieved from http://www.biomedcentral.com/1472-698X/6/4.

Ricketts, T. C., III. (2000). The changing nature of rural health care. *Annual Review of Public Health, 21,* 639–657.

Ross, S., Grant, A., Counsell, C., Gillespie, W., Russell, I., & Prescott, R. (1999). Barriers to participation in randomized controlled trials: A systematic review. *Journal of Clinical Epidemiology, 52,* 1143–1156.

Russell, K., & Jewell, N. (1992). Cultural impact of health-care access: Challenges for improving the health of African Americans. *Journal of Community Health Nursing, 9,* 161–169.

Saha, S., Arbelaez, J. J., & Cooper, L. A. (2003). Patient–physician relationships and racial disparities in the quality of health care. *American Journal of Public Health, 93,* 1713–1719.

Sallis, J. F., & Owen, N. (2002). Ecological models of health behavior. In K. Glanz, B. K. Rimer, & F. M. Lewis (Eds.), *Health behavior and health education: Theory, research, and practice* (pp. 462–484). San Francisco, CA: Jossey-Bass.

Schrop, S. L., Pendleton, B. F., McCord, G., Gil, K. M., Stockton, L., McNatt, J., & Gilchrist, V. J. (2006). The medically underserved: Who is likely to exercise and why? *Journal of Health Care for the Poor and Underserved, 17,* 276–289.

Sedlis, S. P., Fisher, V. J., Tice, D., Esposito, R., Madmon, L., & Steinberg, E. H. (1997). Racial differences in performance of invasive cardiac procedures in a department of veterans' affairs medical center. *Journal of Clinical Epidemiology, 50,* 899–901.

Semenza, J. C., & March, T. L. (2009). An urban community-based intervention to advance social interactions. *Environment and Behavior, 41,* 22–42.

Sloane, D. C., Diamant, A. L., Lewis, L. B., Yancey, A. K., Flynn, G., Nascimento, L. M., ... Cousineau, M. R. (2003). Improving the nutritional resource environment for healthy living through community-based participatory research. *Journal of General Internal Medicine, 18,* 568–575.

Spink, A., & Cole, C. (2001). Information and poverty: Information-seeking channels used by African American low-income households. *Library & information Science Research, 23,* 45–65.

Tropman, S. E., Ricketts, T. C., Paskett, E., Hatzell, T. A., Cooper, M. R., & Aldrich, T. (1999). Rural breast cancer treatment: Evidence from the Reaching Communities for Cancer Care (REACH) project. *Breast Cancer Research and Treatment, 56,* 59–66.

UNAIDS—Joint United Nations Programme on HIV/AIDS. (2006). *Report on the HIV/AIDS epidemic.* Geneva, Switzerland: Author.

U.S. Department of Health and Human Services. (2008). *National health care disparities report* (AHRQ Publication No. 09-0002). Rockville, MD: Author.

van Ryn, M., Burgess, D., Malat, J., & Griffin, J. (2006). Physicians' perceptions of patients' social and behavioral characteristics and race disparities in treatment recommendations for men with coronary artery disease. *American Journal of Public Health, 50,* 351–367.

van Ryn, M., & Burke, J. (2000). The effect of patient race and socio-economic status on physicians' perceptions of patients. *Social Science and Medicine, 50,* 813–828.

Videon, T. M., & Manning, C. K. (2003). Influences of adolescent eating patterns: The importance of family meals. *Journal of Adolescent Health, 32,* 365–373.

Wang, C. (1998). Portraying stigmatized conditions: Disabling images in public health. *Journal of Health Communication, 3,* 149–159.

Warren, J. R., Allen M. L., Hopfer, S. & Okuyemi, K. S. (2010). Contextualizing single parent–preadolescent drug use talks. *Qualitative Research Reports in Communication, 11*(1), 29–36.

Warren, J. R., Kvansy, L., Hecht, M. L., Burgess, D., Ahluwalia, J. S., & Okuyemi, K. S. (2010). Barriers, control and identity in health information seeking: Listening to lower income African American women. *Journal of Health Disparities Research and Practice, 3*(3), 68–90.

Weiner, J., Silk, K., & Parrott, R. (2005). Family communication and genetic health: A research note. *The Journal of Family Communication, 5,* 313–324.

Weisse, C. S., Sorum, P. C., Sanders, K. N., & Syat, B. L. (2001). Do gender and race affect decisions about pain management? *Journal of General Internal Medicine, 16,* 211–217.

Willerton, E., Dankoski, M. E., & Sevilla Martir, J. F. (2008). Medical family therapy: A model for addressing mental health disparities among Latinos. *Families, Systems, and Health, 2,* 196–206.

World Health Organization (WHO). (2002). *Traditional medicines strategy 2002–2005.* Geneva, Switzerland: Author.

31

HEALTH COMMUNICATION AND HEALTH INFORMATION TECHNOLOGY

Priority Issues, Policy Implications, and Research Opportunities for Healthy People 2020

Linda M. Harris, Cynthia Baur, Molla S. Donaldson, R. Craig Lefebvre, Emily Dugan, and Sean Arayasirikul

Healthy People: A Participatory Public Health Policy Process

In her book, *Policy Paradox*, Deborah Stone (1997) argues that policy making is not always a rational process of cool-headed decision making among people seeking to maximize their individual self-interests and well-being in an orderly sequence of stages. Rather, she offers a model of policy making that invokes metaphor and category making to persuade other people to adopt a particular policy. The essence of policy making, in her view, is the struggle over ideas to create shared meaning about the public interest and the nature of the community. Rather than being a marketplace of individuals maximizing self-interest, she considers it to be communities trying to achieve something as communities—motivating people to collective action (Stone, 1997).

Healthy People is an example of policy making as collaborative work to establish shared meaning and achieve community-level goals. It is a federally led process for creating national health goals and objectives that reflects available evidence and stakeholders' views on the most important issues in public health. The process tracks data over time to establish progress and tries to generate collective actions at multiple levels to improve the public's health. The process involves thousands of stakeholders interested in all aspects of public health. At the beginning of every decade, these stakeholders set national health goals and measurable objectives for the 10 years ahead; these goals and objectives comprise the Healthy People agenda for the decade. Over the course of each decade, stakeholders also periodically assess progress toward achieving the objectives of improved health and reductions in disparities.

The year 2010 marks the launch of Healthy People 2020, including a new framework with national health goals, health determinants, and an expanded set of measurable objectives. The Healthy People 2020 framework explicitly adopts a multiple determinants of health perspective to understand and address the main causes of illness, disability, and premature death.

The Federal Lead

Beginning in 1980 with the release of the first set of national disease prevention and health promotion objectives (U.S. Public Health Service, 1980), and each decade thereafter, the U.S. Department of Health and Human Services (HHS) has been the lead cabinet agency in the federal government for Healthy People.[1] HHS once again leads the development of Healthy People 2020. In 2008, HHS convened a Federal Interagency Workgroup (FIW) to lead the development of the prevention framework, goals, and objectives. The FIW membership reflects a multidisciplinary approach to prevention policy making. Representatives from a variety of HHS offices and agencies, as well as from many other federal agencies (such as the U.S. Departments of Agriculture, Education, Housing and Urban Development, Justice, Interior, and Veterans Affairs, and the Environmental Protection Agency), joined the effort. This diverse participation is consistent with a social determinants approach that links issues of housing, transportation, education, and other social factors in an ecological model of health improvement.

What Makes the Healthy People Policy Process Participatory?

Healthy People has a long tradition of involving the public in developing national health goals and objectives. Although the governing body of Healthy People 2020 is made up of federal agencies, the goals and objectives are not determined solely by federal officials. The goals and objectives emerge from collaboration, not only among federal departments but also with the nation's citizens in all sectors of society. The launch of Healthy People 2020 reflects the contributions of federal, state and local governments, individuals, communities, organizations, businesses, and universities working in collaboration for almost two years. The objectives also reflect the state of evidence about public health issues. If proposed objectives cannot be supported by data, they are not included in Healthy People.

Health Communication and Healthy People 2010

Whether a topic is included as an objective or set of objectives in Healthy People reflects consensus about the perceived value and evidence of its contribution to improving the nation's health. In the earliest iterations of the Healthy People initiative, diseases, risk factors, and preventive services were recognized as critical aspects of national health objectives. These were also the topics that had data from surveillance systems and surveys that could be reported in Healthy People.

Some topic areas and objectives are cross-cutting and relate to effective interventions and actions to help affect rates and prevalence of diseases and risk factors. Early examples of cross-cutting topic areas are community, workplace, and school-based health promotion programs that could be adapted and used to address other risk behaviors or public health practice.

In Healthy People 2010, for the first time, HHS recognized health communication as a distinct, cross-cutting topic area. The HHS Office of Disease Prevention and Health Promotion (ODPHP) was designated the lead agency to manage the topic area. The inclusion of discrete objectives for a health communication topic area confirmed the importance of communication as an intellectual framework, a scientific endeavor, and a set of processes and interventions for health improvement in public health policy making. This landmark action was the result of a number of factors, including:

- the actions of HHS staff to propose health communication objectives and solicit stakeholder feedback;
- the participation of external advocates in workgroups and public meetings to give feedback on proposed objectives;
- the robustness of the research literature that supported the contribution of communication to public health improvements;
- a high profile initiative at the National Cancer Institute that fostered new communication research and funded Centers of Excellence;[2] and
- secular trends that accelerated the role of technologies, such as the Internet and interactive consumer e-health applications, in consumer and patient health behaviors.

In addition, a number of HHS agencies had extensive experience addressing a variety of health topics that used health communication and social marketing strategies. These included the National High Blood Pressure and Cholesterol Education Programs of the National Heart, Lung and Blood Institute (Bellicha & McGrath, 1990); the National Cancer Institute's 5 A Day for Better Health program (Lefebvre et al., 1995); and the integration of health communication with many prevention programs at the Centers for Disease Control and Prevention (Roper, 1993). In addition, most agencies within HHS, including each of the Institutes of the National Institutes of Health, had Offices of Communication that included public, patient, and professional education programs in addition to public affairs and public inquiry activities.

In developing Healthy People 2010 health communication objectives, a health communication Workgroup was created; it was made up of representatives from these Offices of Communication as well as several health communication and social marketing professionals from outside the federal government. The goal of the group was to create a rationale for including health communication objectives in Healthy People 2010 and draft the proposed objectives. ODPHP staff played the role of conveners and facilitators of the process over 18 months.

The 2010 health communication objectives were conceived in 1999 when health information was expanding exponentially as a result of the recent global adoption of the World Wide Web. Health information portals were introduced into the health IT landscape. The portals were developed to extend the reach of medical science to the public. The appearance of "snake oil information" not vetted by doctors and scientists was of great concern to the medical community (Silberg, Lundberg, & Musacchio, 1997). These objectives reflected the concerns of their time, especially concerns about how "the digital divide" would affect information access and quality.

The Workgroup's deliberations and the resulting public comment and review produced a set of six objectives about information access, equity, and quality; health literacy; provider–patient communication; and communication research and evaluation. Only one objective had reportable data when the objectives were issued in 2000. By 2006, all six health communication objectives had reportable data, ensuring their continuity in the process.

The six objectives were deliberately broad to convey how health communication can contribute to all aspects of disease prevention and control, health promotion, and medical and dental care including:

- how people are exposed to, search for, and use health information;
- individuals' ability to reduce or eliminate unhealthy behaviors and adopt healthy behaviors;

Table 31.1 Health Communication Objectives for Healthy People 2010

11-1.	Increase the proportion of households with access to the Internet at home.
11-2	Improve the health literacy of the population.
11-3	Increase the proportion of health communication activities that include research and evaluation.
11-4	Increase the proportion of health-related World Wide Web sites that disclose information that can be used to assess the quality of the site.
11-5	Increase the number of centers for excellence that seek to advance the research and practice of health communication.
11-6	Increase the proportion of persons who report that their health care providers have satisfactory communication skills.

- their ability to gain access to the public health and health care systems and understand clinical recommendations and expected outcomes;
- how to disseminate information about individual and population health risks and craft public health messages and campaigns; and
- the development of e-health applications, including online personal health records, health Web sites, interactive personal health tools, and telemedicine systems.

The 2010 health communication objectives are shown in Table 31.1.

The Beginnings of Healthy People 2020

Healthy People 2020 carries on the tradition of participation and transparency in selecting health objectives. Technology played a role in fostering participation because of the availability of online public comment tools. The first way the process involved people outside the government was through a first-of-its-kind external federal advisory committee made up of 13 nationally known experts with diverse expertise in public health. This committee, the Secretary's Advisory Committee on National Health Promotion and Disease Prevention Objectives, is a fully public-member advisory committee, charged with providing advice and consultation to the Secretary of HHS on the development and implementation of the national objectives. The Committee met regularly and a record of its deliberations is available to the public (healthypeople.gov).

The authoritative body for Healthy People is the Federal Interagency Workgroup (FIW) that is made up of representatives of multiple federal agencies. The FIW obtains additional public input throughout the development process to ensure that Healthy People 2020 reflects the needs and warrants the commitment of a broad spectrum of stakeholders. Stakeholders in Healthy People 2020 formed a consortium for the purpose of staying abreast of the process and accessing resources such as tools for planning, collaboration, and learning for achieving the targets set for the next decade. Stakeholders participated in the process of developing recommendations for the framework and objectives:

- through a series of nine regional meetings across the country; some engaging the public in the development of a Healthy People 2020 Framework and others for gathering suggestions about Healthy People 2020 objectives.
- via a public comment Website where anyone could post ideas or comments;

- during a public meeting of the Advisory Committee; and
- through a request for public comment published in the *Federal Register*.

First Results of the Healthy People 2020 Process

The development of Healthy People 2020 occurred in two phases. The first phase yielded a vision statement and a set of four overarching goals. The vision for Healthy People 2020 is "a society in which all people live long healthy lives." These goals are to:

- Attain high quality, longer lives free of preventable disease, disability, injury, and premature death;
- Achieve health equity, eliminate disparities, and improve the health of all groups;
- Create social and physical environments that promote good health for all; and
- Promote quality of life, healthy development, and healthy behaviors across all life stages.

Healthy People 2020, Health Communication, and Health Information Technology

Lest anyone doubt the fast pace of changes in the information and communication landscape consider some of the parallel historical touch points of Healthy People and information technologies:

- When Healthy People 2000 was launched in 1990, the World Wide Web was 1 year old.
- When Healthy People 2010 was launched in 2000 Google was 2 years old.
- In 2010, the year Healthy People 2020 was launched, SMS and MMS usage on mobile phones surpassed minutes of voice calling for the first time.

Federal Leadership

The leadership of the Health Communication Focus Area in Healthy People 2010 expanded for 2020. ODPHP was joined by the HHS Office of the National Coordinator for Health Information Technology (ONC) and the Centers for Disease Control and Prevention (CDC) as lead agencies to create a Health Communication and Health IT Topic Area.[3] The leadership group recruited representatives from 14 federal agencies across the government to become a Workgroup of the FIW. The Workgroup's charge was the same as for the 2010 process: make recommendations to the FIW regarding measurable health communication and health IT objectives for the next decade.

In 2008 the Workgroup leadership met with other federal colleagues who have responsibilities for food and drug regulations, substance abuse, mental health, cancer and other chronic conditions, the environment, communication regulation, IT standards, health services for American Indians, for veterans and those who are in the nation's safety net (e.g., community health centers, Medicaid), and the elderly. The consultations focused on developing what became 20 user-centered futuristic (2020) scenarios to project the utility of the health communication and health IT objectives far enough into the future. The meetings also yielded a set of themes that helped set the stage for nationwide conversations over the following months.

The dominant theme from these federal meetings was the need to change health systems and services to become more prevention oriented. Making these changes will likely require new data about how health systems work and new policies to institutionalize the changes. Specifically, meeting participants wanted to see:

- A change from silos of clinical and public health practices to integrated prevention driven systems including communication and information services;
- A change from managing national health problems with sparse local data and in a reactive mode to nationwide localized anticipatory surveillance and information systems;
- A change from dependence on long-ago formal training in a professional program to real time decision support; and
- A change from provider-centric to person-centered communication and self-management support.

Conversations Beyond the Beltway and Online

In addition to consulting with federal colleagues, the Workgroup leadership engaged health communication, health IT, and public health experts in academe, industry, community and non-profit organizations, and state and local governments. Participants included researchers, practitioners, program managers, policy makers, consultants, software developers, telecommunications providers, advocates, and instructors. Their comments and discussions helped confirm or challenge the themes from the federal discussions. The conversations played a significant role in the topics selected for measurable objectives. The Workgroup, which started with 14 federal agency representatives, grew to approximately 400 members over the course of the two-year process of objectives development.

Public Meetings

Representatives of the Workgroup held open discussions with:

- Principal Investigators of the Centers of Excellence in Health Communication at the American Public Health Association (APHA) Annual Meeting in Washington DC, November, 2007;
- Participants at CDC's National Conference on Health Communication, Marketing and Media in Atlanta, Georgia, August, 2007;
- Members of the Disparity Reducing Advances Project Partners meeting, Alexandria, VA, September 25, 2007;
- Participants at the 6th and 7th Annual Information Therapy Conferences, Park City, Utah, October 8, 2007 and Washington, DC, June 12, 2008;
- Members of APHA at their annual meeting, San Diego, California, October 25, 2008;
- Participants at the Health 2.0 Conference, Boston, April 23, 2009;
- Participants at the meeting of The Institute for the Future and the AMA, Chicago, August, 2009;
- Members of the National Committee on Vital and Health Statistics Subcommittee on Quality, Hyattsville, Maryland, October 13, 2009;
- Technology experts in the academic and private sectors including representatives from the Institute of the Future, Scripps Health Genomics Medicine Program, Qualcomm, Navigenics, 23 and Me, Stanford University, Intel, Johnson and Johnson, Google, and

Cisco. These stakeholders were convened, along with selected Workgroup members, at a Roundtable on Personalized Population Health at the California Institute for Telecommunications and Information Technology of the University of California, San Diego on March 30, 2009.

Conference Calls and Webinars

When technology is involved, thinking a decade at a time is a special challenge. The Workgroup tried to be both realistic and futuristic to capture known changes in health communication and health IT in the short-term and allow for new developments that cannot be fully anticipated in the medium and long-term. To do so, the Workgroup leadership and the Workgroup sought help from those in the forefront of change by hosting conference calls with Frank Moss, Director of the MIT Media Lab (Boston, MA) and conference calls and Webinars on topics such as health literacy, social marketing, media and information seeking, information prescription, personal health records, and systems views of health communication.

Online Outreach

Each conference call encouraged participants to comment, ask questions, and add to the conversation either in real-time or asynchronously via an online workspace, a Website comprised of a bulletin board, discussion threads, blogs, and file sharing functionalities. This online workspace provided colleagues, constituents, and partners with an open process for the continued development of potential objective topics. Workgroup members could discuss with one another the viability and potential impact of a proposed objective topic or suggest new objectives and allow others to critique or fine-tune their proposals.

Health IT and Healthy People

Healthy People 2010 included two objectives related to information technology: Internet access at home and quality Websites (see Table 31.1). However, the health IT landscape has changed dramatically in the last decade and continues to change at a rapid pace, warranting an additional set of priority issues for 2020. Also, there can be significant synergies between health communication and health IT. Health IT offers the opportunity to enhance patient–provider interactions in ways that evolve into continuous productive relationships.

A metamorphosis toward participatory health creates mass potential for autonomy and confident self-maintenance using secure technology tools and health promotion methods. Health IT can also facilitate efficient information seeking and the creation of digital social networks. This potential, especially in the context of the significant public financial investment underway to increase the adoption of health IT in clinical care, was an important consideration in expanding health IT and making it an explicit part of the health communication topic area for Healthy People 2020.

Office of the National Coordinator for Health Information Technology (ONC)

The Federal Office of the National Coordinator for Health Information Technology (ONC) was allocated approximately $61 million for 2009–2010 to provide federal oversight of health IT. An additional $2.0 billion in American Recovery and Reinvestment Act

(ARRA) funds are being used to support the adoption and meaningful use of health IT. One-third of the ARRA dollars were allocated for the Office of Provider Adoption Support (OPAS), the office driving the meaningful use of health IT.

The health IT objectives proposed for Healthy People 2020 derive from the ONC Strategic Plan (ONC, 2008). The Plan calls for a broad diffusion of EHRs, among other priorities.[4] The plan revolves around private and secure, interoperable, highly adoptive, and collaboratively governed patient-focused health care and population health (ONC, 2008). As a result of this plan, electronic health information will become more patient-centric and enable beneficial biomedical research, quality improvement, and emergency preparedness.

Meaningful Use

Federal policy makers recognize that the broad use of health IT has the potential to improve health care quality, improve patient safety, increase the efficiency of care, and improve the public health information infrastructure (Health Information Technology for Economic and Clinical Health [HITECH] Act, 2009). The HITECH Act codifies in legislation that the large public investment in EHRs is sub-optimal if technology is not used to improve health outcomes. In other words, the adoption, implementation, or upgrading of health IT would be ineffective if the technology is not used to benefit the health of the public.

The criteria for "meaningful use" of health IT is an area of substantial public debate. As the use of health IT is as important as its widespread adoption, the Centers for Medicare and Medicaid Services (CMS) drafted a definition of 'meaningful use' in order to assure its use for the improvement of individual and population health. Eligible providers and hospitals must meet three criteria to be considered meaningful users:

- Demonstrate use of certified EHR technology in a meaningful manner (electronic prescribing);
- Demonstrate that the exchange of certified EHR technology is connected in a manner to improve quality of care (care coordination); and
- Submit information on clinical quality measure using certified EHR technology to the Secretary of HHS (Centers for Medicare and Medicaid Services [CMS], 2010).

Having a clear understanding of what constitutes 'meaningful use' of health IT will ensure that eligible providers and hospitals can effectively use electronic health information to achieve six key health outcomes priorities. The priorities identify ways to facilitate effective communication and improve health:

- improve quality, safety, efficiency;
- reduce health disparities;
- patient and family engagement;
- care coordination;
- public and population health;
- privacy and security of personal health information.

These criteria for using EHRs in meaningful ways bring the adoption of health IT in line with the vision and goals of Healthy People 2020.

Systems Thinking and Determinants of Health

An important premise of Healthy People 2020 is that health status is affected in multiple ways that require understanding of various systems that determine how healthy a person can become. A systems approach to health considers the interaction of multiple factors to understand a single health outcome. Some of the most widely acknowledged determinants of health include individual behaviors, mediated and unmediated health interactions, social and physical environments, and health care and public health services.

The potential synergies between the strategic use of health communication and health IT become most apparent when viewed in the context of these health determinants. Differential access to accurate, actionable, and trusted health information and health IT is a factor in health disparities (Viswanath et al., 2006). In the late 1990s, there was a visible public policy focus on lowering barriers to access to information technologies such as computers with Internet access (National Telecommunications and Information Administration, 2000; Science Panel on Interactive Communication and Health, 1999). The barriers— social, economic, and technical—were characterized as creating a "digital divide" among population groups (National Telecommunications and Information Administration, 1995).

A higher income is linked to higher health awareness and a higher rate of health information acquisition (Baur, 2004; Fox, 2009; Fox & Fallows, 2003). Although people without computers and Internet connections in their homes often could use community locations such as libraries and schools, home-based access was the "gold standard" for many years because of the assumed personal and immediate nature of health information. The rapid diffusion of mobil digital devices could dramatically alter this equation.

In summary, health IT holds great promise as a facilitator of productive interactions between providers and individuals and among professionals across the contexts in which they strive to achieve longer, healthier lives for all Americans.

Priority Topics for Health Communication and Health IT for 2020

The topics listed below consistently appeared as priorities in both the face-to-face and online discussions and meetings to develop health communication and health IT objectives. More research on each of these broad topics is needed to understand the dynamic relationships among health communication, health IT, and health determinants. More research also will set the stage for measuring progress on the objectives during the next decade.

The priority topics for Healthy People 2020 objectives include:

- build supportive relationships and shared decision making;
- encourage engaging, efficient, and convenient delivery of care with personalized, interactive self-management support tools and health information resources;
- provide social support networks;
- foster interactions between health professionals and the public using accurate, accessible health information that is targeted or tailored, culturally sensitive, respectful, clear, and actionable;
- facilitate the meaningful use of health IT and productive health interactions among health care and public health professionals;
- design programs that effectively address incentives, opportunities and access for interactive products and services that result in healthier behaviors;

- use best practices in crafting messages that lead to quick and informed action in public health emergencies;
- increase health literacy skills; and
- increase Internet access, including broadband and mobile.

Data Requirements for Healthy People 2020

A set of priority topics is only part of the Healthy People objective development process. A set of topics must be translated into measurable objectives that meet the following criteria. They must:

- have an identified national data source;
- be national in scope (typically using survey data);
- include operational definitions for how the objective will be measured and an evidence-based justification for how impact will be documented; and
- follow one of the approved target setting methodologies for expected change over the decade. The default target setting method is an increment of 10% change in the desired direction.

Ideal data sources have the following characteristics:

- if the objective is population-level, provide demographics (such as race, age, sex, education, income);
- provide a minimum of three data points during the decade; and
- report the standard error.

During the two years when the Health Communication and Health IT Workgroup met, a broad net was cast for possible data sources for each of the priority topics. The Workgroup consulted with researchers in universities, non-profit organizations, think tanks, and government agencies to identify the most appropriate, accurate, comprehensive, and stable data sets available. In some cases, the data sources from the 2010 objectives will continue to be used for the 2020 objectives. An example is the Medical Expenditure Panel Survey (MEPS) fielded by the federal Agency for Health care Research and Quality (AHRQ). MEPS data were used for the 2010 objective on provider–patient communication and will continue to provide data for the same objective for 2020. AHRQ has added three questions to the MEPS to replace the U.S. Department of Education as a source of health literacy data.

Some objectives will not have an identified source when they are launched. These objectives have been deemed of sufficient importance to public health, however, that they should be included and efforts made to develop or modify data sources to support the objective. Each objective is expected to be measurable by mid-decade at the latest.

Final Approval and Release of Healthy People 2020 Objectives

In early 2010, the Health Communication and Health IT Working Group recommended 13 measurable objectives, which were approved by the FIW. They went through an HHS-wide clearance process before the Secretary approved them. The launch date for the entire set of Healthy People 2020 objectives was December 3, 2010. Readers should refer to the Healthy People Web site (www.healthypeople.gov) for the objectives.

Unlike the Healthy People 2010 process, Healthy People 2020 is designed to provide opportunities to add objectives during the coming decade using the data requirements outlined above. This new approach keeps Healthy People interactive, participatory and responsive to new and emerging public health opportunities and threats. The research questions below provide guides to the topics of greatest interest for additional objectives and intervention strategies.

Implementation of Strategies to Support Objectives

Another new dimension of Healthy People 2020 is an emphasis on identifying and sharing implementation strategies to help reach the targets for the objectives. This focus on implementation will be supported by:

- an interactive Website;
- a relational database of health indicators at all levels, including national, state, and county;
- tools for planning, learning, and collaborating; and
- a collection of interventions.

Readers should check healthypeople.gov for current information on implementation strategies and guidance.

Implementation Evidence Requirements for Healthy People 2020

It is likely the levels of evidence for including implementation research in Healthy People 2020 will evolve over the next few years. Many groups have attempted to grade evidence according to the research design, intended use, and quality of research implementation. Evidence from clinical trials, for example, is graded differently from evidence for population-based health interventions.

The interventions included in the Healthy People 2020 Website are those recommended in the *Guide to Clinical Preventive Services* and the *Guide to Community Preventive Services*. *The Guide to Clinical Preventive Services* is made up of recommendations of The US Preventive Services Task Force (http://www.ahrq.gov/) and has a well-accepted grading system (A,B,C,D,I) that grades evidence for clinical preventive services such as screening, vaccination, and tobacco use cessation. The *Guide to Community Preventive Services* (www.thecommunityguide.org) grades evidence for public health interventions as strong, sufficient, or based on expert opinion. Execution can be characterized as good, fair, or variable for its intended purpose. Additional considerations are the number of studies done, consistency of results, and effect sizes.

Implications for Health Communication and Health IT Research

The focus upon implementation is an opportunity for health communication and health IT researchers to conduct research that will inform policy in the next decade. The accompanying table offers illustrative research questions that emerge by juxtaposing the priority health communication and health IT topics with three categories of health determinants. These opportunities include:

- conducting national level surveys for identifying new health communication or health IT objectives and supporting and monitoring progress on existing ones;
- intervention research, both quantitative and qualitative, that informs how health communication and health IT can impact health outcomes and disparities; and
- design research, focusing upon user-centered design of interfaces, interactive tools, service systems, and processes.

Health communication derives from the basic human dynamic that facilitates learning, planning, and collaboration for the purpose of creating and sustaining good health. The meaningful use of health IT offers tools that can extend the reach, timeliness and impact of these interactions. As the strategic use of health communication and health IT becomes pervasive throughout the systems that impact health all Americans can expect to live longer, healthier lives. That day is in sight but much is still to be learned before this goal can be achieved.

Research questions that emerge from the juxtaposition of the priority topics in health communication and health IT and three determinants of health are presented in Table 31.2. They have been generated for the purpose of encouraging researchers to apply their curiosities and skills of inquiry to answers that will move our nation closer to achieving our health objectives and goals.

Table 31.2 Health Communication, Health IT, and Determinants of Health Illustrative Research and Evaluation Questions

Priorities	Personal Behavior	Social Environment	Public Health & Health Care Services
Building supportive relationships and shared decision-making between individuals and professionals	What is the role of trust in building and sustaining productive shared decision making?	How do professionals support family and community systems with reliable, real-time health guidance?	How do we incorporate new technologies that facilitate real time clinical decision-making and care coordination? How can the Expanded Care Model inform shared decision making among health professionals and between health professionals and patients?
Providing personalized self-management tools and resources	How do we design health guidance to help people sustain healthy behaviors (e.g. physical activity, smoking cessation, weight loss, etc)?	What factors influence patient decision making about how much health information to share, with whom, how, and under what circumstances?	How do we design and use public health systems to collect, synthesize, package and disseminate population level knowledge that supports personal self management?

(continued)

Table 31.2 Continued

Priorities	Personal Behavior	Social Environment	Public Health & Health Care Services
Building social support networks	How do we capture and share the creative ways individuals make sense of health information while maintaining the integrity of the scientific basis for that information?	How can health and communication professionals engage with members of collaborative and social sharing networks and community organizations to encourage evidence based health promotion?	How can social support be prescribed, referred and encouraged by health professionals? How can outcomes be safely and securely exchanged between social support groups and professionals recommending them?
Delivering accurate, accessible health information that is targeted or tailored	How do we target and tailor ongoing decision support over a life time?	How can we design EHRs so that they link patients and their families with healthy community based activities?	How can we design EHRs to be used in meaningful ways?
Communicating in culturally sensitive, respectful, clear, and actionable ways	How can public users of health data, information, guidance, and interactive tools be involved in their design?	How can cross-cultural comparisons inform strategies for communicating in culturally meaningful ways?	How can professional users of health data, information, guidance, and interactive tools be involved in their design? How can we test various marketing strategies to increase and maintain health provider engagement and/or involvement?
Facilitating the meaningful use of health IT and exchange of health information among health care and public health professionals	How can cultural and environmental differences among providers be bridged and inform meaningful use criteria?	How can members of social networks be engaged in communication with professionals in meaningful ways?	What health systems changes are needed in order to enable socioeconomically disadvantaged populations to achieve meaningful use? How can the Expanded Care Model inform the definition of meaningful use of Health IT?
Enabling quick and informed action in public health emergencies	What are the most salient features of public health emergency situations that prompt information seeking?	How do communities with differential access to information resources and technologies share and circulate public health emergency information?	How much understanding of basic scientific processes does the public need to comprehend and act on recommendations in different types of public health emergencies?

Priorities	Personal Behavior	Social Environment	Public Health & Health Care Services
Increasing health literacy skills	How can we develop instruments to assess public and professional skills that are sensitive to language, culture, and experience?	How can health professionals work with community organizations to improve health literacy?	How can we instill health literacy best practices, including guidelines, standards, outcome measures, and innovative approaches, in diverse public health and health care settings?
Providing new opportunities to connect with culturally diverse populations	How do we develop tools and strategies aimed at reducing communication inequalities?	How do health and communication professionals collaborate with community members to reduce communication inequalities?	How do we increase and enhance effective cross disciplinary collaborations in health promotion and disease prevention? What health systems changes are needed to enable socioeconomically disadvantaged populations to achieve meaningful use?
Designing programs that improve incentives, opportunities and access for products and services that result in healthier behaviors	How do we develop strategies aimed at reducing communication inequalities that may exist in terms of people's access to and use of information channels and resources to enable them to act on health information?	How do we nurture healthy interactions among families and neighborhoods?	How can productive relationships between social marketers and health professionals be developed and sustained?
Increasing Internet access, including broadband and mobile	How does strategic communication mediate the potential for health IT to improve personal health, population health, and health care? How can we develop and scale public education and action models to increase user monitoring and validation of health information from various digital sources, including social network sites?	How can informal online and person to person interactions inform and be informed by population knowledge bases of best practices and outcomes.	How can digitized and mobilized health information enhance teamwork and coordinated care?

Conclusion

As we observed with Stone (1997) in the introduction to this chapter, policy making is a collaborative process with wide-reaching effects on communities. Healthy People objectives are the core of an iterative, interactive process that benefits from the fullest participation of the multiple disciplines intersecting with health communication and health IT issues. As such, public health policy may be both a driver and reflection of the evolution of our community of practitioners and researchers of health communication and health IT. This chapter provides a wide-angle view of the many health communication and health IT topics that are being addressed and still need to be considered in the context of a social determinants of health approach. Health communication and health IT may be relatively new to health policy making but they are now firmly established as an integral part of the present and future of comprehensive approaches to public health.

Two well-known and likely over-used phrases characterize policy making, including health policy making: (a) Policy making is like sausage-making. You might like the product but you don't really want to see how it's done. (b) What gets measured, gets done. The Healthy People 2020 process for developing health communication and health IT objectives has tried to avoid the messiness of the former and focus on the latter. The Workgroup used participatory and transparent methods to engage a very broad collection of the public from academe, industry, government, non-profit, and community-based organizations to develop a forward-looking view of health communication and health IT for public health.

The proposed Healthy People 2020 health communication and health IT objectives highlight important factors affecting the public's health and break new ground in measuring factors that have not been studied or reported before. The research opportunities for expanding on and pioneering new topics for objectives and new methods and data sources are limitless. The Workgroup invites all researchers to join the community of people actively working to develop and use measurable health communication and health IT objectives to improve the public's health. Visit healthypeople.gov frequently to get updates on funding, learning, planning, and collaboration opportunities that support health communication and health IT.

Notes

1. The office of Disease Prevention and Health Promotion (ODPHP), in the office of the Assistant Secretary for Health, HHS, is the office that coordinates the Healthy People process.
2. See the National Cancer Institute's Health Communication and Informatics Research Branch for more information. Retrieved from http://dccps.nci.nih.gov/hcirb/index.html.
3. Harris, Baur, and Dugan, three of the authors of this chapter, are from ODPHP, CDC, and ONC respectively.
4. The plan was supported in 2009 with expanded funding to reach the EHR objectives by 2014.

References

Baur, C. (2004). Using the Internet to move beyond the brochure and improve health literacy. In J. G. Schwartzberg, J. VanGeest, & C. C. Wang (Eds.), *Understanding health literacy: Implications for medicine and public health* (pp. 141–154). Chicago: AMA Press.

Bellicha, T., & McGrath, J. (1990). Mass media approaches to reducing cardiovascular disease risk. *Public Health Reports, 105*, 245–252.

Bower, J. L., & Christensen, C. M. (1995, January–February). Disruptive technologies: Catching the wave. *Harvard Business Review*, 43–53.

Centers for Medicare & Medicaid Services (CMS). (2010). *Medicare and Medicaid programs; Electronic health record incentive program; Proposed rule.* Washington, DC: U.S. Department of Health and Human Services. Retrieved from http://edocket.access.gpo.gov/2010/E9-31217.htm.

Fox, S. (2009, October). *Trends: The social life of health information.* Presented at the e-Patient Connections Conference, Philadelphia, PA.

Fox, S., & Fallows, D. (2003). *Internet health resources.* Washington, DC: Pew Research Center, Pew Internet and American Life Project. Retrieved from http://www.pewinternet.org/Reports/2003/Internet-Health-Resources.aspx

Health Information Technology for Economic and Clinical Health (HITECH) Act. (2009, February 17). Title XIII of Division A and Title IV of Division B of the American Recovery and Reinvestment Act of 2009 (ARRA), Pub. L. No. 111-5.

Lefebvre R. C., Doner, L., Johnston, C., Loughrey, K., Balch, G., & Sutton, S. M. (1995). Use of database marketing and consumer-based health communication in message design: An example from the Office of Cancer Communications' "5 a Day for Better Health" program. In E. Maibach & R. Parrott (Eds.), *Designing health messages: Approaches from communication theory and public health practice* (pp. 217–246). Thousand Oaks, CA: Sage.

National Telecommunications and Information Administration. (1995). *Falling through the net: A survey of the "have nots" in rural and urban America.* Washington, DC: U.S. Department of Commerce. Retrieved from http://www.ntia.doc.gov/ntiahome/fallingthru.html

National Telecommunications and Information Administration. (2000). *Falling through the net: Toward digital inclusion.* Washington, DC: U.S. Department of Commerce. Retrieved from http://www.ntia.doc.gov/ntiahome/fttn00/contents00.html

Office of the National Coordinator for Health Information Technology. (2008). *The ONC-coordinated federal health IT strategic plan: 2008–2012.* Washington DC: U.S. Department of Health and Human Services. Retrieved from http://healthit.hhs.gov/portal/server.pt/gateway/PTARGS_0_10731_848083_0_0_18/HITStrategicPlan508.pdf.

Public Health Service. (1980). *Promoting health/preventing disease: Objectives for the nation.* Washington, DC: U.S. Department of Health and Human Services.

Roper, W. L. (1993). Health communication takes on new dimensions at CDC. *Public Health Reports, 108,* 179–183.

Science Panel on Interactive Communication and Health. (1999). *Wired for health and well-being: The emergence of interactive health communication* (T. R. Eng & D. H. Gustafson, Eds.). Washington, DC: U.S. Department of Health and Human Services, U.S. Government Printing Office. Retrieved from http://www.health.gov/scipich/pubs/finalreport.htm

Shekelle, P. G., Morton, S. C., & Keeler, E. B. (2006). Costs and benefits of health information technology. *Evidence Report Technology Assessment, 132,* 1–71.

Silberg, W. M., Lundberg, G. D., & Musacchio, R. A. (1997). Assessing, controlling, and assuring the quality of medical information on the Internet: Caveat lector et viewor—Let the reader and viewer beware. *Journal of the American Medical Association, 277,* 1244–1245.

Stone, D. (1997). *Policy paradox: The art of political decision making.* New York: Norton.

Viswanath, K., Breen, N., Meissner, H., Moser, R., Hesse, B., Steele, W., & Rakowski, W. (2006). Cancer knowledge and disparities in the information age. *Journal of Health Communication, 11,* 1–17.

SECTION VI

Methods in Health Communication

32

CONVERSATION ANALYSIS AND HEALTH COMMUNICATION

Jeffrey D. Robinson

Conversation Analysis (CA) originated at the University of California during the 1960s, and it is now the dominant, contemporary, theoretical, and methodological framework for the analysis of social interaction (Heritage, 2009). CA represents a naturalistic and inductive approach to the study of generalizable patterns of interaction that are ultimately amenable to quantification (Robinson, 2007). Although the term 'conversation analysis' reflects the origins of CA in studies of everyday casual conversation, CA is widely used to study communication in health care settings. Within numerous health-related fields, the bulk of CA research focuses on communication between health care providers (e.g., physicians, psychotherapists, nurses) and their clients (e.g., patients). As such, this chapter reviews CA findings relevant to provider–client interaction.

A critical piece of the puzzle of explaining health care outcomes is understanding associated provider–client interaction (Stewart, 1995). Prior to CA, and still today, the predominant method for studying such interaction is the use of pre-existing coding schemata (such as the *Roter Interaction Analysis System*; Roter & Larson, 2002) to divide interaction into component speech acts and place them into mutually exclusive categories, which allows for the generation of frequency counts that can be statistically associated with other variables (for review, see Heritage & Maynard, 2006). On the one hand, despite the fact that traditional coding methods are commonly referred to as methods of 'interaction process analysis'—as in Bales's (1950) *Interaction Process Analysis* schema, which was used early on by Korsch and Negrete (1972) to study pediatrics, and later tailored to primary care by Roter (1977)—traditional coding is not itself a method for describing and explaining the social organization of interaction; that is the *modus operandi* of CA. On the other hand, in its basic-science form, CA does not produce findings that naturally accord with the statistical assumptions required by most statistical-modeling techniques (Robinson, 2007; Schegloff, 1993). That is an essential function of traditional coding methods. Thus, there has been a social-scientifically pragmatic and symbiotic relationship between CA and traditional coding methods, the former qualitatively bringing validity to the latter, and the latter quantitatively empowering the former. This relationship is clearly visible in coding schemata developed by Donald Cegala (e.g., Cegala, Street, & Clinch, 2007), Richard Street (e.g., Street & Millay, 2001), and Richard Kravitz (e.g., Kravitz, Bell, & Franz, 1999), all of which are, in different ways, heavily informed by CA.

CA is generally concerned with how people create, maintain, and negotiate meaning. Two of CA's core assumptions are as follows. First, in contrast (but not necessarily opposition) to approaches that treat communication as a process of information-transmission driven by social-cognitive variables (for review, see LeBaron, Mandelbaum, & Glenn, 2003), CA assumes that people produce and understand communication primarily in terms of the social action(s) it accomplishes (Schegloff, 1995). Admittedly, this assumption is also embodied, in a very general fashion, in many contemporary coding schemata. However, as detailed below, one unique contribution of CA is its attention to how turns of talk establish nuanced action agendas that affect members' understanding and production of talk in ways that are not always or fully captured by traditional coding methods. Second, CA assumes that the production and understanding of action are not only influenced by traditional forms of context (e.g., sex, race/ethnicity, self-monitoring), but also by interactional forms of context (Goffman, 1983). Relating to these core assumptions, this chapter has three goals. First, the bulk of this chapter is dedicated to reviewing how interactional forms of context can shape the production and understanding of action during health care provider–client interaction. Second, this chapter reviews the relationship between CA-derived patterns of interaction and post-interaction medical outcomes. Third, this chapter briefly reviews efforts to 'translate' CA research for providers and intervene in their practice for the purpose of improving medical outcomes.

How Different Types of Interactional Context can Shape Communication

This section reviews how interactional forms of context can shape the production and understanding of health care provider–client communication. Three types of context are reviewed: (1) the constraints imposed by immediately preceding talk/action; (2) the position of an action relative to the sequence of action in which it participates; (3) the position of an action relative to larger-scale medical activities.

Interactional Context 1: Immediately Preceding Talk/Action

Health care provider–client communication is, like ordinary conversation, organized on a turn-by-turn basis (Sacks, Schegloff, & Jefferson, 1974). Current turns of talk embody many different types of context that shape and constrain next turns of talk. For two major examples, current turns of talk establish action agendas and 'preference' agendas. Both of these types of context are reviewed in the following sub-sections.

Establishing Action Agendas.   CA has powerfully demonstrated that, and how, the details of turn organization—that is, the nature and ordering of sounds and words, intonation patterns, and a variety of rules for their production and understanding (e.g., pragmatic rules, turn-taking rules, etc.)—establish action agendas that constrain subsequent talk. Action agendas are different from grammatical forms. For instance, the grammatical form of an 'interrogative' (or, vernacularly, a 'question') can implement actions other than (or in addition to) 'questioning' or 'information seeking' (Schegloff, 1984). Furthermore, even when interrogatives do primarily seek information, they can nonetheless embody different action agendas that differentially constrain responses. For example, take the case of primary-care physicians soliciting patients' chief medical concerns (Heritage & Robinson, 2006b), represented in both Extracts 1–2 at line 1. Many traditional coding schemata, which tend to conflate grammatical form and action by operationalizing code categories according to the former, would effectively (but incorrectly) represent these questions as accomplishing 'the same' action; That is, they would be coded as 'direct questions,' and in many cases, 'open-ended' questions.

Extract 1
```
01   DOC:   What can I do for you today.
02          (0.5)
03   PAT:   We:ll- (0.4) I fee:l like (.) there's something
04          wro:ng do:wn underneath here in my rib area.
```

Extract 2
```
01   DOC:   Sounds like you're uncomfortable.
02          (.)
03   PAT:   Yeah. My e:ar,=an' my- s- one side=of
04          my throat hurt(s).
```

However, Heritage and Robinson (2006b) demonstrated that these questions embody different action agendas that have dramatically different consequences for patients' responses. In Extract 1, the question "What can I do for you today." is a *Wh*-interrogative that encourages patients, *as a first order of business*, to present their chief complaint. Furthermore, as designed, this question tacitly claims that the physician lacks information about the patient's concerns, which encourages expanded problem presentation. In contrast, the question in Extract 2 ("Sounds like you're uncomfortable.") is a request for confirmation that encourages patients, *as a first order of business*, to produce tokens of either confirmation or disconfirmation, which the patient does: "Yeah." (line 3). Only then does the patient present her chief concern: "My e:ar,=an' my- s- one side=of my throat hurt(s)." Furthermore, requests for confirmation tacitly claim that physicians possess (at least some) information about the patients' concerns (e.g., information previously solicited and documented by nurses), which discourages expanded problem presentation. Finally, the rules of turn taking (Sacks, Schegloff, & Jefferson, 1974) provide physicians with a formal opportunity to speak immediately after patients' (dis)confirmations, which can result in patients losing the opportunity to present their problems according to their own agenda. This is what happens in Extract 3.

Extract 3
```
01   DOC:   You're having knee problems since Ju::ne.
02   PAT:   Yes.
03   DOC:   Okay what have you done for that. (.) since then.
```

In response to the physician's request for confirmation, "You're having knee problems since Ju::ne." (line 1), the patient produces a confirmation, "Yes." (line 2), at which point the physician begins to take the patient's medical history (line 3). Heritage and Robinson (2006b) demonstrated that, relative to question types represented in Extracts 2–3, those in Extract 1 resulted in *patients presenting their concerns for longer periods of time and presenting more discrete medical symptoms.*

Many traditional coding schemata make the distinction between 'open-ended' and 'closed-ended' questions. However, this distinction is not sufficient to capture the nuance of action agendas. Different action agendas, again with important consequences for patients' responses, can be instantiated by 'open-ended' solicitations of patients' chief concerns. For example, the *Tell me*-format, as seen in Extract 4 (drawn from Clemente et al., 2008), encourages patients to produce *narratives* (Clemente et al., 2008; Coupland, Robinson, & Coupland, 1994).

Extract 4
```
01  DOC:  Tell me a little bit from you:r point of
02        view (.) what's going on.
03        (0.7)
04  PAT:  Well, (0.3) uhm (0.5) since I was twelve
05        years old I- (0.2) produced- (.) uhm (0.2)
06        ovarian cysts so I have (0.2)
07  DOC:  Mm hm,
08  PAT:  Pain from that. .hhh And then (.) it kinda
09        just got outta hand and they did a laparoscopy ...
```

Note that the patient begins by presenting past-tense medical information, which projects a narrative (which the patient continues at lines 8–9), and that this is oriented to by the physician with his continuer (Schegloff, 1982): "Mm hm" (line 7).

Alternatively, Robinson (2006) examined the *How are you feeling?* format, seen in Extract 5.

Extract 5
```
01  DOC:  How are you feelin' to[da:y.]
02  PAT:                         [.hhhh]h Better,
03  DOC:  And your sinuses?
```

Robinson (2006) discovered that the *How are you feeling?* format performs the action of soliciting an evaluation of a particular, recipient-owned, currently experienced condition that is known about by the speaker and typically related to physical health. In Extract 5 (above), the patient responds by saying "Better," (line 2), which is a report of improvement on, and thus a positive evaluation of, the state of a particular and ongoing health condition. When asked by physicians, contrary to being open-ended, *How are you feeling?* is actually narrow and biomedically focused, and tailored to visits in which patients are following up on problems for which they have already been treated. In sum, categories of grammatical form (e.g., 'open-ended questions') do not sufficiently capture the action agenda imposed by a turn of talk.

A chief goal of CA is the inductive discovery of particular social actions and their social organization (Heritage, 1984). 'Actions' include things like: soliciting a patient's chief concern, giving a diagnosis of upper respiratory infection, making a treatment recommendation for antibiotics, persuading a patient to stop smoking, advising a patient how to lose weight, empathizing with a patient's cancer diagnosis, and reassuring a patient about their cancer prognosis (and, of course, actions associated with patients' responses, such as resisting physicians' diagnoses). However, the nature of action is not always intuitively obvious. In this regard, traditional coding schemata are criticized in two ways. First, they embody finite sets of pre-specified categories of action. Second, at least originally in the study of health care (e.g., Korsch & Negrete, 1972), coding schemata operationalized action based on theory rather than on empirical conceptualizations drawn from participants' lifeworlds and the study of actual interaction (Patton, 1989). The result is that many coding schemata necessarily exclude actions, and frequently mis-represent the actions they are designed to capture (Stiles & Putnam, 1995).

One exemplary discovery of action is what Heritage and Stivers (1999) termed physicians' 'online commentary,' or communication that is produced while examining patients and that "describes or evaluates what the physician is seeing, feeling or hearing" (p. 1501). Online commentary affords patients at least some access to physicians' diagnostic reasoning. As such, online commentary has the capacity to foreshadow the existence of medical problems (or lack thereof) and thus, ultimately, whether or not physicians will provide treatment (or not). For example, see Extract 6 (this Extract is also analyzed by Heritage & Stivers, 1999), in which a patient has presented with upper-respiratory concerns.

Extract 6

```
01            DOC: An:' we're gonna have you look s:traight ahea:d,=h
02                 (0.5)
03            DOC: J's gonna check yer thyroid right no:w,
04                 (9.5) ((physician examines patient))
05    —>      DOC  .hh That feels normal?
06                 (0.8)
07    —>      DOC: I don't feel any: lymph node: swelling, .hh in yer
08                 neck area,
09            DOC: .hh Now what I'd like ya tuh do I wantchu tuh
10                 breath: with yer mouth open....
```

After instructing the patient to "look s:traight ahea:d," (line 1), after explaining the imminent examination procedure, "J's gonna check yer thyroid" (line 3), and after examining the patient (line 4), the physician produces online commentary: "That feels normal?...I don't feel any: lymph node: swelling, .hh in yer neck area," (lines 5–8). Insofar as lymph-node swelling is commonly recognized as a sign of infection (or at least a medical problem), the physician's online commentary contributes to foreshadowing at least 'no treatable problem,' and at most 'no problem at all.'

Online commentary can be generally categorized as that which foreshadows 'no problems,' including utterances such as *That feels normal* (see Extract 6, line 5, above), versus that which foreshadows 'problems,' including utterances such as *There's inflammation there* and *That ear looks terrible* (Mangione-Smith, Stivers, Elliott, McDonald, & Heritage, 2003). Heritage and Stivers (1999) argued that online commentary has at least three functions. First, it is used to reassure patients about their health status (especially in the case of 'no-problem' online commentary). Second, at least 'problem' online commentary is used to legitimize patients' decisions to seek medical treatment. Third, at least 'no-problem' online commentary is used to tacitly build a case, prior to physicians' official diagnoses, that patients' medical problems are not in need of medical treatment (e.g., antibiotics). Regarding this last function, Heritage, Elliott, Stivers, Richardson, and Mangione-Smith (2010) found that, *compared to physicians' provision of 'problem' online commentary, the provision of exclusively 'no-problem' commentary significantly reduced the likelihood of patients subsequently resisting or challenging physicians' treatment recommendations, which is important because such resistance can lead to physicians' inappropriate prescription of antibiotics.*

The nature of online commentary exposes another limitation of traditional coding methods. The mathematical reliability of any coding schema used for statistical purposes relies on the assumption of an independence of measures. Coding schemata are necessarily constructed as groupings of mutually exclusive categories that represent single meanings and actions. However, talk (and body deployment) are polysemic; communication behavior simultaneously contains multiple dimensions of meaning. Different types of online commentary have the capacity to serve two or more of the functions noted above (i.e., reassuring, legitimizing, and case-building).

Incorporating Preferences.   There is a large CA literature on the notion of preference organization (Heritage, 1984). Put simply, different action agendas establish different social biases for particular types of responses. Part and parcel of CA's goal of documenting action agendas is that of documenting their preference organizations. For one illustration, take physicians' treatment recommendations. Stivers (2005b) demonstrated that pediatricians' treatment recommendations, as actions, not only make relevant their acceptance or rejection by parents, but *prefer acceptance*, which is normatively required in order to progress to the next medical activity (i.e., closing the visit). For example, just prior to Extract 7 (this Extract is analyzed in greater detail by Stivers, 2005b), the pediatrician diagnoses the child with a cold, and here produces the treatment recommendation (RX>). The patient accepts the recommendation with Oh okay (line 4) and Okay (line 7).

Extract 7
```
01  RX>   DOC:  .hh So wha- what I can do is give her uhm
02    >          .h(ml) cough medication 't=has a little bit
03    >          of combination of uhm .h decongestan:t, and
04    >          also clearing up the [.hh
05          MOM:                    [Oh okay.
06          DOC:  no:se, dry it up uh little bit so .h at night
07                she can: sleep a little better .h[h
08          MOM:                                  [Okay.
```

Alternatively, Stivers (2005b) found that patients can 'resist' physicians' treatment recommendations by withholding the preferred response of acceptance. Resistance can be passive, as in the case of patients' silences and unmarked acknowledgement tokens, such as *Mm hm* and *Yeah*, or active, as in the case of patients questioning or challenging the appropriateness or effectiveness of the treatment recommendation (e.g., *What I'm worried about is…*, *Are you going to give her antibiotics?*). For example, in Extract 8 (this Extract is analyzed in greater detail be Stivers, 2005b), a different child is again diagnosed with a cold. The physician produces the treatment recommendation at lines 1–2 (RX>). This time, though, the mom resists this recommendation by producing an unmarked acknowledgement token, "Yeah." (line 3), inquiring about an additional diagnostic test, "Did you want her tuh get that ultra sound?" (line 3), and reporting her husband's concern that 'something must be wrong' (lines 8–11).

Extract 8
```
01  RX>   DOC:  But in the meanti::me no:: antibiotics or
02    >          anything yet. Okay?
03          MOM: Yeah. Did you want her tuh get that ultra sound?
04          DOC:  Yes I want her [to get thuh ultra-sound too.
05          MOM:                 [Okay.
06          MOM: Okay. (       ) ((to girl/patient))
```

```
07        DOC: [Alright see: [(      ) not so scary,
08        MOM: [So          [Should we- bring her i:n? See e- my
09              husband gets just rea:l insistent that- (.) "there's
10              some'in wrong with her" because she keeps getting
11              sick.
```

Importantly, Stivers (2005b) demonstrated that, when patients withhold acceptance, physicians routinely work to pursue it by accommodating patients, which can lead to deleterious medical outcomes. For instance, when patients resist treatment recommendations of no-antibiotics, physicians can secure acceptance by 'caving' and inappropriately prescribing antibiotics (i.e., prescribing for a viral, versus bacterial, condition).

Given the observation that, as actions, pediatricians' treatment recommendations prefer 'acceptance,' Stivers (2005a) further demonstrated that such recommendations can be designed in ways that promote their acceptance. Stivers found that "A treatment recommendation is generally treated as insufficient...if it (1) fails to provide an affirmative action step, (2) is nonspecific, or (3) minimizes the significance of the problem" (p. 956). Thus, treatment recommendations that affirmatively discuss what patients can do to treat the problem, as in Extract 8 (above, lines 1–4), are more likely to secure patient acceptance compared to recommendations that negatively discuss what patients cannot do or what will not work, as in Extract 8 (above, lines 1–2).

For a second example of preference organization, the inclusion of certain *polarity items* in *Yes/No*-interrogatives can establish an additional preference for either a *Yes*-answer or *No*-answer (for review, see Heritage, 2010). The polarity items *any* and *at all* (e.g., *Any chest pain? Do you smoke at all?*) are negative polarity items that embody an additional preference—that is, beyond other sources of preference, including grammar (Sacks, 1987) and socio-medical issues (Heritage, 2010)—for a *No*-type answer, and the polarity items *some* and *still* (e.g., *Do you have some chest pain? Are you still taking your medicine?*) embody an additional preference for a *Yes*-type answer. Heritage, Robinson, Elliot, Beckett, and Wilkes (2007) demonstrated that, compared to the negative-polarity question, *Are there any other issues you would like to address during the visit today?*, the positive-polarity question, *Are there some other issues you would like to address during the visit today?*, is significantly more likely to elicit as-of-yet-unstated concerns from patients.

Interactional Context #2: Sequence Organization

There is wide agreement across disciplines and methodological perspectives that health care provider–client interaction is organized sequentially; for example, as questions and answers (Robinson, 2001). Sequential position is an important type of context that shapes the meaning of actions and, thus, subsequent talk. Admittedly, sequentiality is partially built into the fabric of traditional code categories, such as 'provider/client question.' However, very few coding schemata distinguish between actions that are produced either under, or out from under, response-obligatory constraints of prior actions. For example, most coding schemata include 'information giving' as a category, but do not distinguish between self-initiated, versus solicited, information (for exceptions, see Cegala et al., 2007; Street & Millay, 2001).

This sequential distinction has important consequences for topics such as client participation (Robinson, 2001) and providers' responsiveness to clients' concerns. For example, a consistent criticism of providers is that they systematically disattend or ignore the psychosocial aspects of clients' medical concerns, which can have consequences for medical outcomes (Robinson & Nussbaum, 2004). However, this criticism relies, at least partially, on the claim that patients raise such concerns to be taken up, and that physicians are interactionally accountable for taking them up. However, patients frequently raise psychosocial concerns as part of *responses* to physicians' actions that pertain to other, more biomedically focused matters, and these responses frequently do not hold physicians (strongly) accountable for responding in turn. This issue was addressed by Beach and Mandelbaum (2005, pp. 347–348), who examined Extract 9. The medical interviewer's question at lines 1–2 refers to the patient's previous comments (data not shown) that she drinks alcohol every night.

Extract 9

```
01  INT:   >But you've been doing that everyday< (.) for
02         the past four or five ye[ars?
03  PAT:                           [Pretty mu:ch.
04         (.)
05  INT:   °Okay.°
06         (.)
07  PAT:   My mom had a stroke (.) five years ago and
08         u:h I have to go every night after work and
09         help (.) my dad out with her so:=hh when I
10         come home just to unwind $I have a few drinks$
11         and then >go to bed<.
12  INT:   Have you ever noticed any blo:od in your stools
13         or bla:ck stools?
```

The patient initially responds with a hedged agreement: "Pretty mu:ch." (line 3). After the interviewer's "°Okay.°" (line 5), which proposes to close the question–answer sequence and move forward (Beach, 1995), the patient initiates more response to the interviewer's initial question in the form of an account for her frequent drinking. The patient designs her account as 'more response' by using the same time frame as that in the interviewer's question (i.e., "five years;" line 7), and by addressing her drinking (e.g., "I have a few drinks"; line 10), which was referred to by the interviewer's "that" (line 1). The patient's account proposes a psychosocial cause of her drinking, that being stress induced by family. However, as a response, the patient's account does not hold the interviewer interactionally accountable for a response, that is, for 'taking up' the psychosocial concern. Indeed, the interviewer proceeds to a next history-taking question (lines 12–13).

Even if an action is designed to hold providers accountable for a response, and even if providers provide a response, that response is not always immediately forthcoming. This is because there can be a range of contingencies that prevent people from being able to produce a relevant response, such as not hearing or understanding the initiating action, or finding fault with it. In these cases, a single action is accomplished over multiple sequences of talk (Schegloff, 2007). For example, see Extract 10 (this Extract is analyzed In greater detail by Coupland et al., 1994), which is between a physician and an eighty-one-year-old patient. At line 1, the physician asks "How young are you?", and at line 6, the patient answers with "Eighty one." However, before answering, the patient twice initiates repair (Schegloff, Jefferson, & Sacks, 1977) on the physician's question (lines 2–3 and 4–5).

Extract 10

```
01  Q->  DOC:  How young are you?
02       PAT:  Pardon?
03       DOC:  May I ask you how young are you?
04       PAT:  How young?
05       DOC:  Yes
06  A->  PAT:  Eighty one
```

One of many consequences of the sequential nature of interaction is that the physician's question at line 3, "May I ask you how young are you?" is *not* a fundamentally different question from that in line 1, but rather a redoing of it in response to the patient's "Pardon?" (line 2), which embodies a claim to have not heard/understood the initial question. Coding schemata that do not attend to sequential positioning are prone to counting/coding the physician as having asked two separate questions, which is invalid. (A trickier issue is: If only one question is counted, which one should it be?)

Interactional Context #3: The Organization of Medical Activities

A defining feature of institutional, as opposed to ordinary, interaction is its organization by the participants around particular and recurrent goals (Drew & Heritage, 1992). One effect of this goal orientation is that medical interactions are characteristically structured into standard sets and orders of goal-organized, task-oriented phases, which comprise larger-scale medical activities. For example, primary-care visits organized around dealing with acute medical problems (e.g., new rash, new flu, etc.) are regularly comprised of six ordered phases: (1) opening the visit; (2) problem presentation; (3) information gathering (i.e., history taking and physical examination); (4) diagnosis; (5) treatment; and (6) closing the visit (Robinson, 2003). In many cases, the existence and nature of this normative phase organization is understood by both providers and clients, and provides a type of context that shapes the production and understanding of communication throughout interactions. This sub-section reviews findings pertaining to three phases: opening the visit, problem presentation, and history taking.

Opening the Visit. The activity of opening primary-care visits is organized around the goal of initiating patients' concerns (Robinson, 1998). Achieving this goal involves the negotiation of a transition, or lack thereof, from a state of non-co-participation to talking about patients' concerns. Openings are constructed through the accomplishment of various tasks (social, interactional, and bureaucratic) that prepare physicians and patients for dealing competently with patients' concerns, including: (1) greeting; (2) embodying readiness; (3) securing patients' names; (4) retrieving and reviewing patients' records; and (5) initiating patients' concerns (Robinson, 1998). Tasks 1–4 are preparatory for dealing with patients' concerns, and openings are normatively organized such that tasks 1–4 get accomplished before dealing with patients' concerns (Robinson, 1999). Importantly, tasks 1–4 do not merely occur before the medical business of visits, but rather are constitutive of that business. One consequence of this normative organization is that *the exact same physician question can be understood differently by patients—that is, can accomplish an entirely different action—depending on its location within openings.* For instance, when physicians ask the question *How are you? before they have accomplished tasks 1–4, it is not typically understood medically (i.e., as a solicitation of patients' problems), but rather 'socially' (i.e., as a solicitation of patients' current and general state of being; Sacks, 1975).* This can be seen in Extract 11 (for more detail, see Robinson, 1999). Note that the patient is visiting for numerous palpable lumps in both of his breasts.

Extract 11

```
01         DOC: Hi.
02              (.)
03         DOC: M[ister Bald]win,
04         PAT:      [Hello.   ]
05         PAT: Ye:s.
06         DOC: Hi. I'm doct'r Mulad I'm one o' thuh interns
07              he:re?
08              (.)
09         PAT: <Okay,>
10              (1.1)
11   —>   DOC: *How are you today. ((* closes door))
12   —>   PAT: Alright,
13              (1.7)
14         DOC: Okay. So. >Can I ask< you what brings you in
15              today?
16              {(.)/ˈh}
17   —>   PAT: Yeah. I have lumps, in my uh breasts:.
```

After the doctor opens the door, he greets the patient (lines 1–4) and then confirms his name (lines 3–5). As the doctor introduces himself (lines 6–7) he begins to close the door. The doctor asks "How are you today." (line 11) just after closing the door. Although the doctor has greeted the patient, confirmed the patient's name, and introduced himself, he is standing across the room from his desk and chair, and thus has not yet embodied readiness to deal with the patient's concern. Insofar as the doctor has neither sat down nor read the records, he is not sufficiently prepared to deal with the patient's concerns. Note that the patient responds with "Alright," (line 12), despite the fact that he is visiting the doctor for potentially cancerous "lumps, in my uh breasts:." (line 17). Thus, the patient orients to the doctor's "How are you today." as a request for an evaluation of his current and general state of being rather than as a solicitation of his medical problems.

In contrast, when physicians ask the question *How are you?* after they have accomplished tasks 1–4, it is typically understood medically. See, for example, Extract 12 (for more detail, see Robinson, 1999).

Extract 12

```
01   PAT: ((Knock Knock Knock))
02   DOC: COME IN.
03        (1.7)
04   DOC: Hello: Come in.
05        (0.6)
06   DOC: Mister Ha:ll?
07        (0.5)
08   PAT: Yes ((gravel voice))
09        (0.2)
10   PAT: Mmhhm ((throat clear))
```

```
11          (1.9)
12   DOC:  Have a seat
13          (2.4) ((doctor reads records; patient sits down))
14   DOC:  I'm doctor Masterso[n.
15   PAT:               ['h I: believe so.
16   DOC:  How are you.
17   PAT:   hhhhhh I call down fer som::e=uh::(m) (0.6)
18          breeth- eh: (musname) tablets: water tablets....
```

Before the doctor produces "How are you." (line 16), the patient has entered the room and sat down (line 13) and the doctor has greeted the patient (line 4), confirmed his name (lines 6–8), read his records (line 13), and introduced himself. When the doctor asks "How are you?", he is gazing at the patient. At this point, both the doctor and the patient have performed the typical preliminary opening actions and thus have sufficiently prepared for dealing with the patient's concerns. In sum, due to its positioning within the activity of opening, the exact same question, *How are you?*, accomplishes a different action. The distinction between *How are you?* as, for example, 'social talk' or 'medical question,' is not typically captured by traditional coding schemata, whose code categories are operationalized largely according to content alone.

Problem Presentation. Stivers (2002) demonstrated that patients have at least two different practices for presenting their medical problems, which convey different stances toward the problems' doctorability (Heritage & Robinson, 2006a) and treatability, and which place differing amounts of pressure on physicians to treat the problems, for example with antibiotics. Relative to the six-phase structure of acute-care visits (outlined above), the first practice is 'unmarked' and is one of presenting 'symptoms only' (i.e., describing the problem without speculating about a particular diagnosis, which is the purview of physicians). This practice conveys a stance that patients are, first and foremost, seeking the physician's evaluation (i.e., diagnosis and treatment) of the problem. For example, see Extract 13 (this Extract is analyzed in greater detail by Stivers, 2002). Here, in a pediatric context, a mother presents her daughter as having a *cough, stuffy nose,* and *really goopy eyes.*

Extract 13
```
01   DOC:  And so: do- What's been bothering her.
02          (0.4)
03   MOM: Uh:m she's had a cou:gh?, and stuffing- stuffy
04          no:se, and then yesterday in the afternoo:n she
05          started tuh get really goopy eye:s,
```

The second practice is 'marked' and is one of (additionally) presenting a 'candidate diagnosis,' which "pushes forward across the physician's medical judgment by anticipating this judgment" (Stivers, 2002, p. 322) and thereby conveys a stance that the problem warrants treatment. For example, see Extract 14 (this Extract is analyzed in greater detail by Stivers, 2002). The pediatrician solicits the mother's problem presentation (i.e., this is not history taking) with "So how long has she been sick." (line 1). After presenting symptoms (i.e., *four days* and *headaches*), the mother produces a candidate diagnosis: "So I was thinking she had like uh sinus infection er something." (lines 10–12).

Jeffrey D. Robinson

Extract 14

```
01   DOC:  .hh So how long has she been sick.
02         (1.2)
03   MOM: Jus:t (.) I came down with it last Wednesday, so
04         she's probably had it (0.2)
05   DOC:  °Uh huh_°
06   MOM: (Like) over- four days?
07         (1.0)
08   MOM:  An' she's been complaining of headaches.
09         (.)
10   MOM: So I was thinking she had like uh sinus in[fection=
11   DOC:                                           [.hhh
12   MOM: =er something.=
13   DOC:  =Not necessarily:, Thuh basic uh: this is uh virus
14         basically:, an'=uh: .hh (.) thuh headache seems tuh
15         be:=uh (0.5) pretty prominent: part of it at fir:st...
```

Stivers demonstrated that, during the activity of problem presentation, pediatricians perceive parents' candidate-diagnosis as applying 'pressure' to prescribe antibiotics, and this is at least partially (if not largely) due to the positioning of the phase of problem presentation within the larger six-phase structure of visits. One consequence of such positioning is that it, once again, affects the nature of the action being accomplished, this time by the parent. For example, whereas the parent's talk at lines 3–6 (i.e., *She's probably had it over four days*) and line 8 (*She's been complaining of headaches*) grossly accomplishes 'giving medical information,' the parent's candidate diagnosis at lines 10–12 accomplishes 'applying pressure to prescribe.' This is supported by the fact that the pediatrician responds by disagreeing, "Not necessarily:,", and then justifies his disagreement by asserting "this is uh virus" (line 13), which is not effectively treated by antibiotics.

History Taking. The normative organization of the phase of history taking—wherein providers, as medical experts, seek information preparatory to making official diagnoses—shapes the extent and nature of patient participation (Street & Millay, 2001), which is concerned with: (1) whether or not patients 'participate,' that is, independently produce actions outside of the sequential constraints of providers' actions that 'require' particular responses; and (2) whether or not patients' actions themselves 'require' providers to respond. During history taking, patients participate relatively infrequently (Robinson, 2001), and when they do, they tend to format their actions in ways that do not (strongly) require providers to respond (Gill, 1998). This produces an analytically frustrating situation in which patients refrain from asking for things (e.g., information, services) explicitly, but rather do so tacitly. For example, Gill examined what she termed 'speculative explanations,' where clients use "I don't know..." or "I wonder..." formats to speculate on causes of problems during history taking. For example, see Extract 15 (Drawn from Gill, 1998, p. 350).

Extract 15

```
01        PAT:  Also (1.3) my stools lately have seemed dark?
02   -->  PAT:  And I'm wondering if that's because I did
03   -->        start taking the vitamins with iron too
04              (0.3)
```

512

```
05  —>    PAT:   .hh An' I'm wondering if the iron in those
06               vitamins could be doing it.
07        DOC:   (Possibly)    ((nods his head))
```

CA has demonstrated that actions can be designed so as to place differing amounts of pressure on addressees to respond (Stivers & Rossano, 2010). Each of the following design features contributes to this pressure: (1) interrogative syntax; (2) interrogative (e.g., final-rising) intonation; (3) gazing at addressee at action's end; and (4) framing the addressee as having epistemic authority over the matter at hand. Although speculative explanations frame providers as having epistemic authority over the diagnostic information, they frequently do not contain interrogative syntax or intonation, nor action-final gaze at providers. In some cases, speculative explanations do (ultimately) get responses. For example, in Extract 15 (above), although the patient's initial speculative explanation (at lines 2–3) is not responded to (see the silence at line 4), the patient's second attempt (at lines 5–6) is responded to with "Possibly" (line 7). In other cases, though, physicians do not respond. For instance, see Extract 16 (drawn from Gill, 1998, p. 345).

Extract 16
```
01           PAT:   I still ha::ve my: ordinary::: migraine
02                  headaches, which I've ha:d for yea::rs?
03                  (1.3)
04  —>       PAT:   And ah: (.) they come and go so badly I: just
05  —>              have to really wonder what triggers that.
06           PAT:   I know I do have some allergies.
07           PAT:   So [that's] s:ome possibilities
08           DOC:      [>M hm<]
```

At lines 4–5, the patient tacitly solicits a diagnostic explanation with "I: just have to really wonder what triggers that." At this point, the physician could relevantly speak (Sacks et al., 1974). Instead, the patient continues to produces a possible explanation: "I know I do have some allergies." (line 6). At line 8, the physician acknowledges the patient's explanation with "M hm," but otherwise does not respond with his own diagnostic evaluation.

The practice of soliciting diagnostic information speculatively—that is, in ways that place relatively low 'pressure' on providers to respond with diagnostic information, and thus hold providers relatively less accountable for responding—serves at least two functions. First, "[w]ith speculative explanations, patients exhibit caution in displaying their knowledge about causation" (Gill, 1998, p. 346), which is traditionally the purview of providers. Second, and simultaneously, speculative explanations are frequently done while physicians are gathering diagnostic information, such as taking a verbal history from, or physically examining, patients. In this case, they are a practice for not disrupting providers' fact-gathering actions/activities by making providers accountable for answering (Gill, 1998). Speculative explanations are designed to be "trial balloons" that providers can opt to attend to, or not. Because turns can be designed with varying amounts of 'pressure' to respond, the notion of client participation is not binary (which is an assumption embodied in most coding schemata). For instance, speculative explanations are relatively less 'participatory' than more explicit questions. Furthermore, when providers do not respond to speculative explanations (i.e., with diagnostic information) they are relatively less accountable for 'ignoring' patients than if posed with more explicit questions.

Although it was recognized, early on, that different phases of visits contain different distributions of different types of communication behaviors/actions (Stiles, Putnam, Wolf, & James, 1979), strikingly few studies have coded for the location of actions relative to such phases. Doing so, though, has produced tremendous analytic payoff. For example, in post-surgical visits, cancer specialists' psycho-social information giving, which is otherwise positively associated with patients' satisfaction, is negatively associated with satisfaction when it occurs during the phase of physical examination (Eide, Graugaard, Holgersen, & Finset, 2003).

From Interaction Process to Medical Outcomes

The previous section briefly reviewed research showing that various forms of interactional context shape the production and understanding of health care provider–client communication, and thus are consequential for understanding interaction-process outcomes. *However, do these findings demonstrably matter with respect to post-interaction health outcomes?* Common sense suggests that they do, but this case is neither easily nor convincingly made from qualitative analyses alone (Robinson, 2007). Here, operationalization, coding, and statistical analysis are required, which involves sacrificing a measure of CA detail for 'larger-picture' features of interaction that translate across individual cases, as well as sacrificing some CA methodological and theoretical assumptions (Heritage, 2008; Schegloff, 1993) for those of statistical analysis. Procedurally, this process of translation is always preceded by basic CA research that exposes generalizable practices of interaction (Robinson, 2007), and individual cases are always kept nearby so as to retain an awareness of what is 'lost in translation.' One hallmark of quantitative CA research (at least so far) is that it involves the analysis (and thus coding) of single actions or sequences of action; Stated negatively, this research does not attempt to code every bit of talk during health care encounters, as do many contemporary coding schemata (because this would involve a systematic understanding of every possible type of medical action). This CA philosophy has informed several contemporary coding schemata, such as that by Kravitz (Kravitz et al., 1999), which focuses on patient requests (for information and services), and Street (Street & Millay, 2001), which focuses on patient participation.

Because the application of CA to medicine is a relatively recent phenomenon, quantitative analyses are recent and comparatively sparse. Nonetheless, these studies strongly indicate the value of CA. For the first of three examples, Boyd (1998) examined interactions in which board-certified physicians working for an insurance company (i.e., insurance agents) call physicians who are proposing surgical procedures, interview them about the details of the case, and then approve or deny insurance reimbursement for such procedures. Boyd found that agents initiated calls with at least two different types of actions, including a 'bureaucratic opening,' wherein the agent stresses a need for specific missing information (e.g., *I don't have any documentation of any problems at all*), and a 'collegial opening,' wherein the agent asks for information in an open-ended fashion as if consulting a colleague on a case (e.g., *Can you tell me something about this youngster*). Boyd found that, compared to calls initiated with bureaucratic openings, those initiated with collegial openings were significantly more likely to result in procedures being approved.

For a second example, patients' post-visit satisfaction with physicians' communication is consistently and robustly associated with myriad beneficial health outcomes (Robinson, Krieger, Burke, Weber, & Oesterling, 2008). Robinson and Heritage (2006) found that patients are significantly more satisfied with physicians' listening behavior and positive affective-relational communication when physicians' initiate the phase of problem presentation with 'genuine' solicitations of patients' concerns (e.g., *What can I do for you?*) as compared to requests for confirmation of patients' concerns (e.g., *Sore throat, huh?*).

For a third example, pediatrician's inappropriate prescription of antibiotics—e.g., prescribing antibiotics for children's' viral (vs. bacterial) upper-respiratory-tract infections—has led to increased antibiotic resistance by many strains of bacteria, which poses a significant health risk to both individuals and communities (Stivers, 2007). One reason why pediatricians inappropriately prescribe is because they perceive parents, as measured after visits, as having expected antibiotics for their children-patients (Stivers, 2007). This finding contributed to Stivers (2007) titling her book: *Prescribing under Pressure*. Pediatricians' perceived 'pressure' to prescribe is largely generated by, and has been statistically associated with, particular practices of parents' communication during visits, including parents providing 'candidate diagnoses' (vs. 'symptoms only') while presenting their children's' problems (Stivers, Mangione-Smith, Elliott, McDonald, & Heritage, 2003), and parents resisting pediatricians' treatment plans (Mangione-Smith, Elliot, et al., 2006; Stivers, Mangione-Smith, Elliott, McDonald, & Heritage, 2003). Pediatricians are not entirely without defenses. Heritage et al. (2010) demonstrated that pediatricians' use of exclusively 'no problem' (vs. problematic) online commentary is significantly associated with a reduction in their inappropriate-prescription rates.

Conversation Analysis as Intervention

The present author teaches required continuing-medical-education (CME) courses to practicing physicians as part of their annual license-renewal process. One recurrent difficulty encountered with translating traditional coding-based findings for physicians is that individual code categories (e.g., 'asks open-ended question,' 'provides medical information') are 'blunt instruments,' and dulled even further when, as is frequently the case during analysis, categories are collapsed to meet the requirements of statistical analysis (e.g., when 'asks open-ended question' and 'asks closed-ended question' are collapsed into 'asks questions'). During CME training, recommendations to, for example, 'provide patients with more medical information' are frequently and arduously resisted by physicians who want to know 'exactly what to say' and 'exactly where to say it.' Admittedly, this translation problem is diminishing as coding schemata are developed and refined according to CA principles.

The question is: Can physicians be trained, within realistic parameters (e.g., one half-day or less), to employ specific interactional practices as identified by CA? Heritage, Robinson, Elliott et al. (2007) designed a study to reduce the frequency with which patients leave visits with unmet medical concerns, or concerns that patients intend/want to have addressed during visits but that do not get addressed. Through a five-minute training CD that physicians watched alone on their office computers prior to seeing patients, Heritage et al. achieved 75% success in training physicians to ask one of two specifically formatted questions immediately after patients finished presenting their chief concern: (1) *Is there <u>anything</u> else you want to address in the visit today?*; or (2) *Is there <u>something</u> else you want to address in the visit today?* Compared to the control condition (in which physicians were not trained), the *Some*-question condition, which involves a linguistic preference for a *Yes*-type answer, significantly reduced the occurrence of unmet concerns (The *Any*-question condition, which involves a linguistic preference for a *No*-type answer, was not significantly different from the control condition.)

Discussion

This chapter reviewed contributions of the analytic approach known as Conversation Analysis (CA) to the sub-field of Health Communication regarding the domain of health care provider–client interaction. CA represents a naturalistic and inductive approach to the study of action in interaction, and is generally concerned with how people create, maintain, and negotiate meaning. This chapter demonstrated that providers' and clients' production and understanding of meaning is shaped by a variety of types of interactional context, such as constraints imposed by immediately preceding talk/action and the position of an action relative to larger-order sequences and medical activities. This chapter also argued that CA-derived patterns of interaction are amenable to quantification, are associated with post-interaction medical outcomes, and are translatable to providers for the purpose of health-care intervention. CA is an extremely valuable complement to, and is equally complemented by, the predominant approach for studying provider–client interaction, which involves the use of pre-existing coding schemata (e.g., Roter & Larson, 2002). This chapter attempted to demonstrate how CA can constructively inform the traditional coding approach, and vice versa, and productive syntheses of these two approaches are beginning to emerge (e.g., Cegala, Street, & Clinch, 2007; Robinson & Heritage, 2006).

Author Note

The author thanks John Heritage for his comments on an earlier draft of this chapter.

References

Bales, R. F. (1950). *Interaction process analysis: A method for the study of small groups*. Reading, MA: Addison-Wesley.

Beach, W. A. (1995). Preserving and constraining options: 'Okays' and 'official' priorities in medical interviews. In B. Morris & R. Chenail (Eds.), *Talk of the clinic: Explorations in the analysis of medical and therapeutic discourse*. Hillsdale, NJ: Erlbaum.

Beach, W. A., & Mandelbaum, J. (2005). "My mom had a stroke": Understanding how patients raise and providers respond to psychosocial concerns. In L. H. Harter, P. M. Japp, & C. M. Beck (Eds.), *Narratives, health, and healing: Communication theory research* (pp. 343–364). Mahwah, NJ: Erlbaum.

Boyd, E. (1998). Bureaucratic authority in the "company of equals": The interactional management of medical peer review. *American Sociological Review, 63*, 200–224.

Cegala, D. J., Street, R. L., Jr., & Clinch, C. R. (2007). The impact of patient participation on physicians' information provision during a primary care medical interview. *Health Communication, 21*, 177–185.

Clemente, I., Lee, S., & Heritage, J. (2008). Children in chronic pain: Promoting pediatric patients' symptom accounts in tertiary care. *Social Science and Medicine, 66*, 1418–1428.

Coupland J., Robinson, J. D., & Coupland, N. (1994). Frame negotiation in doctor–elderly patient consultations. *Discourse and Society, 5*, 89–124.

Drew, P., & Heritage, J. (1992). *Talk at work: Interaction in institutional settings*. Cambridge, England: Cambridge University Press.

Eide, H., Graugaard, P., Holgersen, K., & Finset, A. (2003). Physician communication in different phases of a consultation at an oncology outpatient clinic related to patient satisfaction. *Patient Education and Counseling, 51*, 259–266.

Gill, V. (1998). Doing attributions in medical interaction: Patients' explanations for illness and doctors' responses. *Social Psychology Quarterly, 61*, 342.

Goffman, E. (1983). The interaction order. *American Sociological Review, 48*, 1–17.

Heritage, J. (1984). *Garfinkel and ethnomethodology*. Cambridge, England: Polity Press.

Heritage, J. (2008). Conversation analysis as social theory. In B. Turner (Ed.), *The new Blackwell companion to social theory* (pp. 300–320). Oxford, England: Blackwell.

Heritage, J. (2009). Conversation analysis as an approach to the medical encounter. In J. B. McKinlay & L. Marceau (Eds.), *E-Source: Behavioral and social science research interactive textbook*. Office of Behavioral and Social Science Research. Retrieved from http://www.esourceresearch.org/

Heritage, J. (2010). Questioning in medicine. In A. Freed & S. Ehrlich (Eds.), *"Why do you ask?" The function of questions in institutional discourse* (pp. 42–68). New York: Oxford University Press.

Heritage, J., Elliott, M., Stivers, T., Richardson, A., & Mangione-Smith, R. (2010). Reducing inappropriate antibiotics prescribing: The role of online commentary on physical examination findings. *Patient Education and Counseling, 81*, 119–125.

Heritage, J., & Maynard, D. (2006). Problems and prospects in the study of doctor–patient interaction: 30 years of research in primary care. *Annual Review of Sociology, 32*, 351–374.

Heritage, J., & Robinson, J. D. (2006a). Accounting for the visit: Giving reasons for seeking medical care. In J. Heritage & D. Maynard (Eds.), *Communication in medical care: Interaction between primary care physicians and patients* (pp. 48–85). Cambridge, England: Cambridge University Press.

Heritage, J., & Robinson, J. D. (2006b). The structure of patients' presenting concerns 1: Physicians' opening questions. *Health Communication, 19*, 89–102.

Heritage, J., Robinson, J. D., Elliot, M. N., Beckett, M., & Wilkes, M. (2007). Reducing patients' unmet concerns in primary care: A trial of two question designs. *Journal of General Internal Medicine, 22*, 1429–1433.

Heritage, J. C., & Stivers, T. (1999). Online commentary in acute medical visits: A method of shaping patient expectations. *Social Science and Medicine, 49*, 1501–1517

Korsch, B. M., & Negrete, V. F. (1972). Doctor–patient communication. *Scientific American, 227*, 66–74.

Kravitz, R. L., Bell, R. A., & Franz, C. E. (1999). A taxonomy of request by patients (TORP): A New system for understanding clinical negotiation in office practice. *The Journal of Family Practice, 48*, 872–878.

LeBaron, C. D., Mandelbaum, J., & Glenn, P. J. (2003). An overview of language and social interaction research. In P. Glenn, C. D. LeBaron, & J. Mandelbaum (Eds.), *Studies in language and social interaction: In honor of Robert Hopper* (pp. 1–39). Mahwah, NJ: Erlbaum.

Mangione-Smith, R., Elliott, M. N., Stivers, T., McDonald, L. L., & Heritage, J. (2006). Ruling out the need for antibiotics: Are we sending the right message? *Archives of Pediatrics & Adolescent Medicine, 160*, 945–952.

Mangione-Smith, R., Stivers, T., Elliott, M. N., McDonald, L. L., & Heritage, J. (2003). Online commentary on physical exam findings: A communication tool for avoiding inappropriate antibiotic prescribing? *Social Science & Medicine, 56*, 313–320.

Patton, M. J. (1989). Problems with and alternatives to the use of coding schemes in research on counseling. *The Counseling Psychologist, 17*, 490–506.

Robinson, J. D. (1998). Getting down to business: Talk, gaze, and body orientation during openings of doctor–patient consultations. *Human Communication Research, 25*, 97–123.

Robinson, J. D. (1999). The organization of action and activity in primary-care, doctor–patient consultations. *Dissertation Abstracts International*, 60(10), 3800. (UMI No. AAT 9947036)

Robinson, J. D. (2001). Asymmetry in action: Sequential resources in the negotiation of a prescription request. *Text, 21*, 19–54.

Robinson, J. D. (2003). An interactional structure of medical activities during acute visits and its implications for patients' participation. *Health Communication, 15*, 27–59.

Robinson, J. D. (2006). Soliciting patients' presenting concerns. In J. Heritage & D. Maynard (Eds.), *Communication in medical care: Interaction between primary care physicians and patients* (pp. 22–47). Cambridge, England: Cambridge University Press.

Robinson, J. D. (2007). The role of numbers and statistics within conversation analysis. *Communication Methods and Measures, 1*, 65–75.

Robinson, J. D., & Heritage, J. (2006). Physicians' opening questions and patients' satisfaction. *Patient Education and Counseling, 60*, 279–285.

Robinson, J. D., Krieger, J., Burke, G., Weber, V., & Oesterling, B. (2008). The relative influence of patients' pre-visit global satisfaction with medical care on patients' post visit satisfaction with physicians' verbal communication. *Communication Research Reports, 25*, 1–9.

Robinson, J. D., & Nussbaum, J. F. (2004). Grounding research and medical education about religion in actual physician–patient interaction: Church attendance, social support, and older adults. *Health Communication, 16*, 63–85.

Roter, D. (1977). Patient participation in the patient–provider interaction: The effects of patient question asking on the quality of interaction, satisfaction, and compliance. *Health Education Monographs, 5,* 281–315.

Roter, D., & Larson, S. (2002). The Roter interaction analysis system (RIAS): Utility and flexibility for analysis of medical interactions. *Patient Education and Counseling, 46,* 243–251.

Sacks, H. (1975). Everyone has to lie. In B. Blount & M. Sanches (Eds.), *Sociocultural dimensions of language use* (pp. 57–79). New York: Academic Press.

Sacks, H. (1987). On the preference for agreement and contiguity in sequences in conversation. In G. Button & J. R. Lee (Eds.), *Talk and social organization* (pp. 54–69). Clevedon, England: Multilingual Matters.

Sacks, H., Schegloff, E. A., & Jefferson, G. (1974). A simplest systematics for the organization of turn-taking for conversation. *Language, 50,* 696–735.

Schegloff, E. A. (1982). Discourse as an interactional achievement: Some uses of 'uh-huh' and other things that come between sentences. In D. Tannen (Ed.), *Analyzing discourse: Text and talk* (pp. 71–93). Washington, DC: Georgetown University Press.

Schegloff, E. A. (1984). On some questions and ambiguities in conversation. In J. M. Atkinson & J. Heritage (Eds.), *Structures of social action: Studies in conversation analysis* (pp. 28–52). Cambridge, England: Cambridge University Press.

Schegloff, E. A. (1993). Reflections on quantification in the study of conversation. *Research on Language and Social Interaction, 26,* 99–128.

Schegloff, E. A. (1995). Discourse as an interactional achievement III: The omnirelevance of action. *Research on Language and Social Interaction, 28,* 185–211.

Schegloff, E. A. (2007). *Sequence organization in interaction: A primer in conversation analysis.* Cambridge, England: Cambridge University Press.

Schegloff, E. A., Jefferson, G., & Sacks, H. (1977). The preference for self correction in the organization of repair in conversation. *Language, 53,* 361–382.

Stewart, M. A. (1995). Effective physician–patient communication and health outcomes: A review. *Canadian Medical Association Journal, 152,* 1423–1433.

Stiles, W. B., & Putnam, S. M. (1995). Coding categories for investigating medical interviews: A metaclassification. In M. Lipkin Jr., S. M. Putnam, & A. Lazare (Eds.), *The medical interview: Clinical care, education and research* (pp. 489–494). New York: Springer-Verlag.

Stiles, W. B., Putnam, S. M., Wolf, M. H., & James, S. A. (1979). Interaction exchange structure and patient satisfaction with medical interviews. *Medical Care, 17,* 667–681.

Stivers, T. (2002). 'Symptoms only' and 'candidate diagnoses': Presenting the problem in pediatric encounters. *Health Communication, 14,* 299–338.

Stivers, T. (2005a). Non-antibiotic treatment recommendations: Delivery formats and implications for parent resistance. *Social Science & Medicine, 60,* 949–964.

Stivers, T. (2005b). Parent resistance to physicians' treatment recommendations: One resource for initiating a negotiation of the treatment decision. *Health Communication, 18,* 41–74.

Stivers, T. (2007). *Prescribing under pressure: Parent–physician conversations and antibiotics.* Oxford, England: Oxford University Press.

Stivers, T., Mangione-Smith, R., Elliott, M. N., McDonald, L., & Heritage, J. (2003). Why do physicians think parents expect antibiotics? What parents report vs. what physicians believe. *Journal of Family Practice, 52,* 140–147.

Stivers, T., & Rossano, F. (2010). Mobilizing response. *Research on Language and Social Interaction, 43,* 3–31.

Street, R. L., & Millay, B. (2001) Analyzing patient participation in medical encounters. *Health Communication, 13,* 61–73.

33

SOCIAL NETWORKS AND HEALTH COMMUNICATION

Thomas W. Valente

Introduction

Public health and other agencies throughout the world promote many types of health behaviors, including immunizations, HIV/AIDS prevention, family planning, reproductive health, sanitation and hygiene, tobacco/substance use prevention, and adoption of healthy lifestyles and eating habits. Implemented in many forms, these health promotion programs are often accompanied by extensive research about their planning and effectiveness. Typically, many programs use a single medium, either radio or television, to communicate messages to mass audiences. As communication technology has advanced, experts are increasingly using multimedia approaches when communicating health promotion messages in order to accelerate behavior change. This chapter discusses how health communication programs and research can incorporate social network analytic methods to better inform the interpersonal processes inherent in health communication programs. Social networks are the connections among people in a group, society, community, or any defined population. Diffusion of innovations theory provides the foundation for this article and we begin by discussing its principles, followed by an explanation of its use in evaluating mass media campaigns. Throughout, we will highlight the importance and role played by interpersonal communication and social networks.

Behavior Change and the Diffusion of Innovation

Diffusion of innovation theory examines how new ideas and practices spread within and between populations (Rogers, 2003). This theory describes the mechanisms through which opinions, new ideas, attitudes, and behaviors spread throughout a community (Katz, Levine, & Hamilton, 1963; Rogers, 2003; Ryan & Gross, 1943; Valente, 1993, 1995; Valente & Rogers, 1995). Diffusion theory has at least five major components: (a) people pass through stages in the adoption process; (b) diffusion takes time, often a long time; (c) people can modify the innovation and sometimes discontinue its use; (d) perceived characteristics of the innovation influence adoption; and (e) individual characteristics influence adoption. The first two components, the stages of adoption and the time it takes for diffusion to spread are discussed at length.

Researchers hypothesize five stages in the adoption process: knowledge, persuasion, decision, trial, and adoption (Rogers, 2003). Other models of behavior change also specify stages in the change process. For example, Prochaska, Diclemente, and Norcross (1992) proposed five stages of change in their research on tobacco cessation: precontemplation, contemplation, preparation, action, and maintenance. The diffusion stages signify a person's progress toward adopting a healthy behavior, while the stages of change were often used to indicate a person's progress toward quitting a harmful one (Prochaska & DiClemente, 1986). Also, the diffusion stages emphasize the role of information and sources of influence, while the stages of change emphasize cognitive dispositions (see Valente, 2002, p. 42, for a comparison of stage models).

People become aware of new behaviors at different times based in part on their social networks and this creates variation in adoption times. In addition, because they pass through the stages of adoption at varying rates, this furthers the variation in adoption times, creating a considerable gap between the earliest and latest adopters. For instance, Ryan and Gross (1943) showed that in spite of hybrid seed corn's superior attributes, it took 14 years for it to spread from the first to last farmer in two Iowa counties. Communication media are thought to play different roles at each stage of change. Specifically, the mass media are often thought to spread awareness about new products and ideas, although many people also report social networks as sources of awareness. As individuals progress from early to later stages of adoption, the importance of interpersonal influence and social networks increases substantially. As individuals seek more information about the behavior, they increasingly rely on the advice of friends and close associates. Making the commitment to change behavior and ultimately continue the new behavior often requires the support and aid of strong, close family, friends, and acquaintances. Later stages of adoption require more cognitive effort, causing more reliance on interpersonal communications and support.

The spread of new ideas and practices can be graphed as the cumulative percent of adopters, which typically follows a growth or S-shaped curve (Figure 33.1). Because diffusion frequently occurs through personal networks, and personal networks are shaped by ethnic, socioeconomic, and geographic factors, the diffusion of the innovation has a propensity to be shaped by these factors as well. As a result, it takes time for ideas and practices to spread between the groups formed by social network affinities defined on these characteristics. And, further, there may be different diffusion trajectories for different subgroups (e.g., faster diffusion for high SES segments of the population and slower diffusion for lower ones).

When the diffusion of a new behavior occurs, there are few adopters and the growth in new adoption is slow. Research has found that individuals who adopt an innovation early ("early adopters") are more often persuaded by mass media and other targeted media that provide information that is relevant to the behavior. It is also believed that these early adopters are occasionally less constrained by social norms that would otherwise inhibit them from adopting a new behavior. Whatever the case may be, because new behaviors are uncertain and risky, early adopters have to perceive some reason or benefit in order to adopt the new behavior.

Figure 33.1 also illustrates projected rates of the spread of awareness (knowledge), positive attitude (attitude), and behavior (practice). Expected levels for each can be determined by looking at any point in time. The expected lag between knowledge and practice can be attained by reading across the graph (a straight line from any point on the y-axis). This general model, where awareness (K) eventually leads to a positive attitude (A), which in turn leads to use of the behavior (P), is known as the learning hierarchy. Even though this K-A-P sequence occurs often, other researchers argue that different sequences are possible (Chaffee

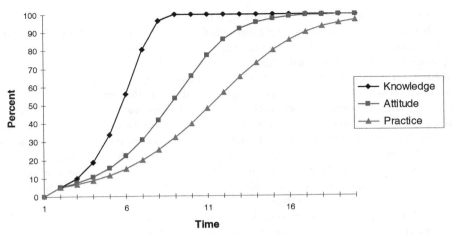

Figure 33.1 Typical knowledge, attitude, and practice diffusion curves used to predict the rate of diffusion and the time lag between knowledge and practice.

& Roser, 1986; Valente, Paredes, & Poppe, 1998). For example, some behaviors may be adopted before knowledge of or positive attitudes toward that behavior are developed. For instance, people may use condoms because they want to protect themselves from pregnancy or sexually transmitted diseases (practice) even though they may not like to use them (low positive attitude), and with little knowledge about their effectiveness (knowledge), thus resulting in the behavioral change sequence to P-A-K (Valente, Paredes, & Poppe, 1998).

Few studies have examined the relative influences of mass and interpersonal communication within a specific study (Hornik, 1989a, 1989b; Valente, Poppe, & Merritt, 1996). As a result, there are few models that integrate mass media and interpersonal communication influences. This lack of integration helps continue an underappreciation of the role of mass media in creating sustainable behavior change. It has also contributed to an underappreciation of the link between mass media and interpersonal communication.

Interpersonal Communication and Social Networks

Media campaigns are often thought of as broadcasts to a population of individuals, yet the audience is a network of human relationships, connected to one another in complex and nonrandom ways (Valente, 2010). As a result, mass media messages are not received in a vacuum; instead, they are filtered and interpreted within people's social networks. People often receive messages while in the company of others, and this may directly influence how the message is interpreted and reinterpreted. In addition, people usually converse with others about the health promotion messages, thereby influencing the way the messages are interpreted. Consistently, the topics of media campaigns are designed with the goal of generating interpersonal discussion. Such was the case in a national family planning campaign conducted in Bolivia (Valente & Saba, 2001).

Researchers would benefit from the inclusion of variables that measure networks of interpersonal communication about media content. Such questions can focus on with whom the respondent watched the media or program, or with whom they participated in project activities. Researchers should also ask the respondent whether the other individuals in attendance approved of the message or activities, and, most importantly, whether they discussed the messages or activities. Finally, if the message was discussed, it is important to ask what they said to each other. Obtaining information about how and with whom they discussed the messages and what was said may provide valuable information for understanding program effects and designing future activities.

One significant network influence is the behavior of opinion leaders. Opinion leaders have been shown to be effective change agents (Valente & Pumpuang, 2007) and over 20 studies to date have used network methods to identify such leaders. Relying only on opinion leaders to disseminate information may be an oversimplification of their influence and how networks mediate media effects. It may be that media communications influence opinion leaders, who then influence others, and these others then influence others—a three-step or even multistep flow. Furthermore, it may be that some opinion leaders influence only one or a few others, whereas other opinion leaders may have much higher multiplier effects, influencing five, ten, or hundreds of others.

In addition, opinion leader models do not take into consideration a number of other factors regarding the behavior change process. First, it is likely that opinion leaders are influenced by others just as much as others are influenced by them and that media messages are designed to be compatible with audience members' attitudes and beliefs. Essentially, to state that media communications influence A, who influences B, may be an oversimplification of the media influence process. Individuals are embedded within complex social network structures. Some people have small networks, whereas others have quite large ones. Some social networks are integrated (their friends know each other) whereas others are radial (their friends do not know one another). Given these complexities, we describe three potential ways in which social network structures can affect media effects processes.

First, social networks are a function of homophily, the tendency for people to form relationships with others like themselves (McPherson, Smith-Lovin, & Cook, 2001). Evidence indicates that for both social and psychological reasons, social networks tend to form among people who are like one another on sociodemographic, attitudinal, and practice characteristics. Further, it is believed that information flow and persuasion occur more readily among homophilous dyads, rather than among nonhomophilous ones (Rogers, 2003). Consequently, diffusion, as mentioned earlier, tends to occur along sociodemographic lines because social networks are contoured by sociodemographic characteristics.

Second, personal networks and social networks vary in their degree of cohesion or integration. Personal network density measures the degree an individual's set of ties know and nominate one another. Dense personal networks provide reinforcement for prevailing norms and practices and can provide protection from outside sources of influence or risk. Conversely, radial personal networks provide access to more information or influence that may be circulating in the network. Radial networks can be advantageous or disadvantageous depending on the topic or behavior being studied and its prevalence in the community or network. Social networks with high rates of personal network densities are characterized by having many subgroups and behaviors may circulate rapidly within groups yet require bridges to spread between groups (Watts, 1999).

Third, normative perceptions of behaviors and actions have strong influences on individual behavior and these may interact with the media influence process. When a majority of one's personal network favors a behavior it is easy for that person to adopt and embrace the practice. Perceptions of personal network support and approval may be required for many behaviors, thus media influences may depend on individual perceptions of what is normative for the individual's peer group. In general, these three network properties influence health behavior outcomes and potentially mediate the influence of exposure to media

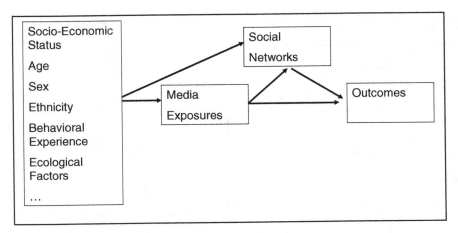

Figure 33.2 A general mediation model of social network influences.

messages. Figure 33.2 illustrates a general theoretical model proposing that networks mediate the direct effects of communication campaigns on behavior.

Personal (Egocentric) Networks

The challenge, of course, is to determine how to measure network properties and which kinds of network properties may influence the outcomes of interest. Egocentric network techniques are used to measure individual personal networks from the respondent's perspective. Egocentric data can be used to include network variables in any type of study design and are analyzed using standard statistical software (i.e., SAS, SPSS, STATA). Burt (1984) proposed a set of egocentric questions that were included in the General Social Survey, fielded in 1985 by the National Opinion Research Corporation. The survey consisted of a random digit dial sample of US households and included for the first time a measure of social networks. After extensive pilot testing, Burt proposed the survey items reproduced in Figure 33.3. These questions were designed to measure Americans' close personal networks derived from responses to the name generator: "Who do you talk to about important matters?" There are other questions one might use to generate egocentric names such as, "Who do you talk with most frequently?" or "Who are your closest friends?" depending on the specific research questions and settings. The respondent only needs to provide the first names, nicknames, or initials since the researcher will not attempt to contact the persons named. The named persons are often referred to as alters.

Once the names are generated, the researcher asks a series of questions about each person named. For example, researchers generally measure sociodemographic characteristics of each alter, such as their gender, ethnicity, age, marital status, and how the respondent, ego, is related to each alter (e.g., family, friend, or colleague). The researcher can then assess substantive issues specific to the research, such as whether the person supports a political candidate, is a smoker, uses substances, practices safe sex, supports gun control legislation, or whatever the research issue. Once the personal networks have been measured, the researcher can characterize people's immediate close social networks and determine whether the network characteristics are associated with substantive phenomenon.

Please provide the first names or initials of up to 5 people you talk to about **important matters.**

	Name 1	Name 2	Name 3	Name 4	Name 5
a. How do you know _____ ?	1. Family member 2. Friend 3. Neighbor 4. School mate 5. Other _____	1. Family member 2. Friend 3. Neighbor 4. School mate 5. Other _____	1. Family member 2. Friend 3. Neighbor 4. School mate 5. Other _____	1. Family member 2. Friend 3. Neighbor 4. School mate 5. Other _____	1. Family member 2. Friend 3. Neighbor 4. School mate 5. Other _____
b. Does he/she live within ½ mile of your home?	No Yes	No Yes	No Yes	No Yes	No Yes
c. Is _____ male or female)?	Male Female	Male Female	Male Female	Male Female	Male Female
d. How long have you known him/her	____ mos ____ yrs.	____ mos ____ yrs.	____ mos ____ yrs.	____ mos ____ yrs	____ mos ____ yrs.
e. How often do you see him/her?	1. once/year 2. 1x/month 3. 1x/week 4. Everyday	1. once/year 2. 1x/month 3. 1x/week 4. Everyday	1. once/year 2. 1x/month 3. 1x/week 4. Everyday	1. once/year 2. 1x/month 3. 1x/week 4. Everyday	1. once/year 2. 1x/month 3. 1x/week 4. Everyday
f. What do you usually discuss with this person?	1. Family life 2. Politics 3. The neighborhood 4. Work 5. Other _____	1. Family 2. Politics 3. Neighbor-hood 4. Work 5. Other _____	1. Family 2. Politics 3. Neighbor-hood 4. Work 5. Other _____	1. Family 2. Politics 3. Neighbor-hood 4. Work 5. Other _____	1. Family 2. Politics 3. Neighbor-hood 4. Work 5. Other _____
g. Have you ever exercised with this person?	No Yes	No Yes	No Yes	No Yes	No Yes
h. How often have you exercised together?	1. Once 2. Once/month 3. Once/week 4. 2+/week	1. Once 2. Once/month 3. Once/week 4. 2+/week	1. Once 2. Once/month 3. Once/week 4. 2+/week	1. Once 2. Once/month 3. Once/week 4. 2+/week	1. Once 2. Once/month 3. Once/weekv4. 2+/week
i. If yes, what kind of exercise do you usually discuss with this person?	1. Walk 2. Jog/run 3. Go to a gym 4. Play sport 5. Other _____	1. Walk 2. Jog/run 3. Go to a gym 4. Play sport 5. Other _____	1. Walk 2. Jog/run 3. Go to a gym 4. Play sport 5. Other _____	1. Walk 2. Jog/run 3. Go to a gym 4. Play sport 5. Other _____	1. Walk 2. Jog/run 3. Go to a gym 4. Play sport 5. Other _____

Figure 33.3 Draft ego-centric questionnaire for physical activity.

When constructing an egocentric survey, it is typical to measure the following characteristics:

1. Strength of relationship (e.g., closeness, acquaintance, stranger; how long known);
2. Frequency of interaction (e.g., how often talk to, how often consult);
3. Type of relation (e.g., family, friend, coworker);
4. Socioeconomic characteristics (e.g., educational attainment, wealth, income);
5. Demographic characteristics (e.g., age, residential location);
6. Substantive characteristics (e.g., smoke, practice safe sex, practice family planning, support a candidate);
7. Content of communication (e.g., discuss politics, health, child rearing) or risk behavior (e.g., unprotected sex, share syringes).

Typical egocentric variables are size, personal network exposure, tie strength, concurrency, density, and constraint. Personal network size is a simple count of the number of persons named in response to the question and is associated with many outcomes. Network size provides an estimate of the number of people the focal person can access for social support and other needs. Although network size is important, the specific attitudes and behaviors of a person's social network is perhaps more important because it indicates the degree of exposure to those attitudes and behaviors.

Personal network exposure is the workhorse variable in network research. Exposure is the degree to which a focal individual's alters or network partners (the people named) engage in a particular behavior. Egocentric data can also be used to show that people who engage in certain behaviors are more likely to have close personal network associates who also engage in those behaviors. For example, in a study of factors associated with the adoption of contraceptive methods in Bolivia, people who reported using a current contraceptive method noted that 63% of their personal networks also used contraception, while those who did not use contraception reported only 37% of their personal network used it ($p<.001$, $N = 5,691$). This difference persisted but diminished when the respondent's partner was removed from the calculation (54.4% versus 38.3%, respectively, $p<.001$; $N = 4,156$). Thus, Bolivians who use contraception to limit their family size are more likely to have people in their network who also use contraception. This finding is not surprising given that people usually associate with others like themselves (the homophily principle) and that information about contraceptive availability and use would pass through social networks.

Personal network exposure is a fundamental and critical variable to be calculated in network research. It captures social influence by measuring the extent to which one's network engages in a behavior. There is often an assumption that the networks influence the respondent given that the respondent knows these alters engage in the behavior. This social influence and the assumption that alters are influenced by their peers can be tested in at least two ways. First, social influence can be tested by asking the respondent to indicate whether he/she was influenced by each alter. For example, after eliciting network nominations to measure social influence on smoking, the researcher can ask, "Did this person (name) offer you a cigarette?" Of course, specific question wording or construction is likely to be highly dependent on cultural norms and conventions. Second, social influence can be tested by weighting exposure by tie strength or communication frequency. In this case, the behavior of the tie is multiplied by the frequency of communication or contact. Frequency of communication is used as a proxy or indicator for tie strength. Social influence for behavior change is thought to pass through strong ties, whereas information is thought to flow more readily from weak ties (Granovetter, 1973).

Egocentric data can be used to test many other hypotheses regarding network influences on behavior. For example, Morris and Kretzshamer (1997) have shown that concurrency in a community, degree of the overlap in sexual relationships, affects the prevalence of HIV. Burt (2005) created a measure of constraint which indicates the extent to which a person's network inhibits him/her from reaching out into a network. Burt (2005) has shown that constraint is negatively associated with outcomes (such as job promotions).

Sociometric Social Networks

Although personal networks can provide considerable information useful for understanding network influences on behavior, many researchers prefer analysis of sociometric data because they consist of reports or information on the linkages between all members of a community, organization, society, or otherwise bounded set of nodes. Sociometric data can be used to draw maps of the connections among people and analytic properties using mathematical analysis extracted. Like personal network data, sociometric data can be used to calculate the extent of network exposure to behaviors, only with sociometric data the calculations can be based on alters' self-reports since the alters are also study participants.

An example of a sociometric network is presented in Figure 33.4. It uses data from adolescents' reports of their closest friends in class. We asked students to name their closest friends by selecting them from a class roster. There was a unique number (1 to 34) for each student that he/she wrote on a form, which included a space for the student's own identifica-

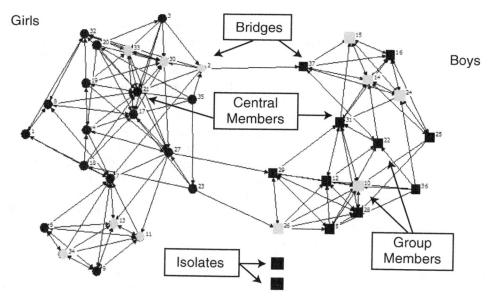

Figure 33.4 The network of friendship choices among 6th grade students who named their five closest friends in the class. Girls are depicted as circles and boys as squares. The data can be used to identify positions in the network such as isolates, central members, group members, bridges, and so on. In addition the network can be characterized as dense or sparse, centralized or decentralized, and so on. (Graph made with Netdraw.)

tion (ID) number. The list of ID numbers is entered into a spreadsheet and the friendships are then mapped using widely available social network analysis software. Each circle or square represents a student, boys are depicted as squares and girls as circles. The ID number for each student is shown next to their circle or square and lines connecting them indicate who nominated whom. In this example, the boundary of the network is the classroom whereas in other cases it might be grade in school, or even the entire school.

The lines have arrows indicating the direction of the nomination. For example, 27 named 3 as a friend, but 3 did not name 27. The length or width of the arrows in this graph do not have meaning, although it is possible to make graphs which vary line properties (color, width, or style) to represent strength of relation or type of relation. The graphs are usually drawn with the people who are most central being in the center and then their connections placed near them. There are many different ways to place people in the graph and many different techniques to arrange everyone in the graphing space. You can also use colors or shapes to represent different properties of the people. There are up to four attributes of the nodes that can be included in a network graph by using color (or shading), shape, labels, and size; there are also three attributes of the relations using line color, size, or style.

There are specific positions in a network and most people instinctively look to see who is at the center of a network. There are, however, deceptively numerous ways to define and hence identify central members. It might also be useful to determine isolates, people with no connections, or peripheral members, people with one or few links on the outside of the network. It should be emphasized that while many people equate being on the periphery or isolated in a network as a negative quality, often peripheral members have connections to other people and other networks in which they may occupy important positions. It is also true that peripheral members may act as bridges connecting different networks. In Figure 33.4 we can also identify people (numbers 3 and 27) who occupy bridging positions within the network.

In this network there are also two groups defined by sex (boys and girls). It is also possible to categorize people as being members of specific groups and there are numerous ways to define groups and positions in a network (Valente, 2010). The considerations of centrality, bridging, groups, and positions in the past few paragraphs can influence how behaviors are distributed in networks. In the network in Figure 33.4, no students were smokers in sixth grade, but some students were susceptible to smoking (indicated by refusing to state they would not smoke in the future; Pierce, Choi, Gilpin, Farkas, & Merritt, 1996). Susceptibility to smoking increased from three of these students to eight within two years. Figure 33.4 shades the eight students who became susceptible to smoking during the study period and shows considerable clustering. Everyone who became susceptible to smoking was connected to someone who already reported being susceptible.

The overall configuration or pattern of relationships can also be important. So, although each person's connections may affect his/her behavior, the influence of these connections may vary depending on the overall pattern of relations in the whole network. The pattern of links in the whole network is referred to as the network structure, and structure matters. For example, this network can be described by its density (the number of links in the network expressed as a proportion of the total possible links), the amount of reciprocity, the number of subgroups, and so on. The network analysis field has created a standard set of metrics to use when describing a network (Valente, 2010). Describing networks by these metrics is interesting, but it is also possible to study whether these network properties are associated with outcomes. For example, does behavior spread more rapidly in a dense or sparse network (Valente, 1995; Valente, Chou, & Pentz, 2007)?

The network information can be used to understand how information, ideas, and communications flow within and between communities. At the individual level, network position may be related to when and how one learns about new ideas. Peripheral members are often more open to new information than integrated members because they are less constrained by group norms. Central members have more sources of interpersonal information given their privileged position and access to many others in the network. To maintain their position of prestige in the network, leaders will rarely be the earliest adopter of a new idea. Because they have more information, they are in a position to make an informed adoption decision earlier than most and be an early adopter (but not the earliest).

Behavioral adoption by central members does two things: (1) it signals to many others the acceptance of the idea and thus accelerates the rate of adoption in the community; and (2) because of the leaders' greater number of links, it dramatically increases the number of interactions between users and nonusers (Valente, 2010). Leaders thus play an integral role in getting behaviors to "go critical," as their adoption is often tantamount to reaching critical mass. After this point the diffusion should be self-sustaining, and communication program staff can switch from message dissemination to message monitoring. Of course, rather than waiting for passive uptake of the communicated material, researchers can use social networks to identify key players and key network structural features that can be exploited to accelerate change.

Social Networks as a Vehicle for Message Delivery

Peer influence and peer modeling are significant correlates of behavior and behavior change. Therefore, harnessing the power of peer influence for health promotion is logical. This power is most likely to be harnessed by allowing peer leaders to deliver health messages. Although peer leaders are defined in different ways (Borgatti, 2006; Valente & Pumpuang, 2007), peers have been used in many settings with generally favorable results (Kelly et al., 2004; Singhal & Rogers, 2003; Valente, 2010; Valente & Davis, 1999; Valente & Pumpuang, 2007).

There are two recently proposed approaches to improving peer delivery of health messages in ways that capitalize on the local nature of opinion leadership. The group model involves identifying groups within social networks first (these can include subgroups and cliques), and then identifying peer opinion leaders within each of those groups. This model was proposed and pilot-tested in a school-based tobacco use prevention program (Wiist & Snider, 1991) and was further developed and implemented in a worksite nutrition promotion program (Buller, Buller et al., 2000; Buller, Morrill et al., 1991). This model begins with identifying subgroups or cliques within a network and then selecting peer opinion leaders from each clique. The peer opinion leaders are identified as those people who received the most nominations in response to the question: "To whom do you go for advice?"

Another method of improving peer delivery of health messages is the network leader model. This model begins with identifying peer opinion leaders first and then grouping network members to each leader, thereby creating new cliques. This model was proposed by Valente and Davis (1999) and tested in a school-based smoking prevention program (Valente, Hoffman, Ritt-Olson, Lichtman, & Johnson, 2003). Opinion leaders were defined as those members of a network who received the most nominations as people others wanted to lead a group project. Once the leaders are identified, other network members are matched to each leader based on their "closeness" in the social network.

Studies using social networks as delivery vehicles have reported considerable success (Amirkhanian, Kelly, Kabakchieva, McAuliffe & Vassileva, 2003; Valente & Davis, 1999; Valente et al., 2003). The approach is both intuitively appealing and is supported by behavior change theories that stress the importance of opinion leadership, homophily, and group dynamics. The main limitation to these approaches is that they are used primarily in closed settings, such as schools, workplaces, and organizations and these approaches may not be feasible in large community and population settings. In a city of tens of thousands, it is not feasible to identify leaders and assign them to those who nominated them or to identify networks/cliques based on social network ties.

Conclusion

This article used social networks and diffusion of innovation theory to explore how interpersonal communication can function during the behavior change process. Following an introduction of the principles behind the diffusion of innovation theory, the history of media campaigns and other methods of communication were discussed. The importance of incorporating interpersonal communication into health promotion interventions in order to obtain enhanced campaign effects was stressed throughout the chapter.

Early models of the association between interpersonal communication and mass media were introduced, including a review of the two-step and multiflow hypotheses. The two-step flow hypothesis proposed that media influence opinion leaders who in turn influenced their less attentive peers. Support for the two-step flow hypothesis has yet to be provided, mostly because individuals inhabit multiple and complex social networks. Given the complexity of social network and interpersonal dynamics, the chapter described some common models and metrics used in the field. Personal network methods are likely to be useful for understanding the impact of mediated communications as the personal network will modify message input and interpretation.

Sociometric data, however, provide considerably more power by providing information used to predict when certain members of the network will learn about and hence adopt the new idea. The network information is also useful for identifying key change agents such as central or bridging nodes and using them as program advocates. Sociometric segmentation, developing media messages based on sociometric position, was presented as an extension of geographic, sociodemographic, and psycho-graphic segmenting. Sociometric segmentation recommends the identification of audiences based on their position within a social network, whether an opinion leader, isolate, or bridge (an individual who connect two or more networks). In addition, it can be used to tailor messages to those with many adopters in their network or those with few. Again, interventions should strive to generate interpersonal communication within these social networks.

The messenger is as important as the message and so using naturally occurring social network structures to deliver health promotion messages is essential. Two similar models were reviewed: a group model and a networked leader model. In the group model, subgroups are identified and leaders chosen from within each subgroup. In the networked leader model, opinion leaders are identified first and then social network members are assigned to leaders based on who these networks nominate. Using social network data to determine the most appropriate change agents is a novel but theoretically grounded approach. Although many studies have used opinion leaders to accelerate behavior change, the full powers of network analytic techniques has yet to be deployed in the service of behavior change programs.

Understanding who delivers the message and the context of interpersonal consumption media may be just as important, if not more so, than the message itself. The field of communication and the analysis of media and communication campaign effects have long been characterized by a bifurcation between mass and interpersonal levels of influence. Yet this distinction is increasingly being blurred by the advent of new media and new forms of communication that provide different behavior change dynamics. All mass media are personal media and can be used in interpersonal ways.

References

Amirkhanian, Y. A., Kelly, J. A., Kabakchieva, E., McAuliffe, T. L., & Vassileva, S. (2003). Evaluation of a social network HIV prevention intervention program for young men who have sex with men in Russia and Bulgaria. *AIDS Education and Prevention, 15*, 205–220.

Borgatti, S. (2006). Identifying key players in a social network. *Computational and Mathematical Organization Theory, 12*, 21–34.

Buller, D., Buller, M. K., Larkey, L., Sennott-Miller, L., Taren, D., Aickin, M., ... Morrill, C. (2000). Implementing a 5-a-day peer health educator program for public sector labor and trades employees. *Health Education & Behavior, 27*, 232–240.

Buller, D. B., Morrill, C., Taren, D., Aickin, M., Sennott-Miller, L., Buller, M. K., ... Wentzel, T. M. (1999). Randomized trial testing the effect of peer education at increasing fruit and vegetable intake. *Journal of the National Cancer Institute, 91*, 1491–1500.

Burt, R. (1984). Network items and the general social survey. *Social Networks, 6*, 293–339.

Burt, R. S. (2005). *Brokerage and closure: An introduction to social capital.* Oxford, England: Oxford University Press.

Chaffee, S. H., & Roser, C. (1986). Involvement and the consistency of knowledge, attitudes, and behaviors. *Communication Research, 13*, 373–399.

Granovetter, M. (1973). The strength of weak ties. *American Journal of Sociology, 78*, 1360–1380.

Hornik, R. C. (1989a). Channel effectiveness in development communication programs. In R. E. Rice & C. K. Atkin (Eds.), *Public communication campaigns* (2nd ed.). Newbury Park, CA: Sage.

Hornik, R. C. (1989b). The knowledge-behavior gap in public information campaigns: A development communication view. In C. T. Salmon (Ed.), *Information campaigns: Balancing social values and social change* (pp. 113–138). Newbury Park, CA: Sage Annual Reviews.

Katz, E., Levine, M. L., & Hamilton, H. (1963). Traditions of research on the diffusion of innovation. *American Sociolological Review, 28*, 237–253.

Kelly, J. A., St. Lawrence, J., Stevenson, L., (2004). Popular opinion leaders and HIV prevention peer education: Resolving discrepant findings, and implications for the development of effective community programmes. *AIDS Care, 16*, 1483–1489.

McPherson, M., Smith-Lovin, L., & Cook, J. M. (2001). Birds of a feather: Homophily in social networks. *Annual Review of Sociology, 27*, 415–444.

Morris, M., & Kretzschmar, M. (1997). Sexual networks and HIV. *AIDS, 11*(Supplement), S209–S216.

Pierce, J. P., Choi, W. S., Gilpin, E. A., Farkas, A. J., & Merritt, R. K. (1996). Validation of susceptibility as a predictor of which adolescents take up smoking in the United States, *Health Psychology, 15*, 355–361.

Potterat, J. J., Rothenberg, R. B., & Muth, S. Q. (1999). Network structural dynamics and HIV transmission. *International Journal of STD AIDS, 10*, 182–185.

Prochaska, J. O., & DiClemente, C. C. (1986). Toward a comprehensive model of change. In W. R. Miller & N. Neather (Eds.), *Treating addictive behaviors: Processes of change* (pp. 3–27). New York: Plenum.

Prochaska, J. O., Diclemente, C. C., & Norcross, J. C. (1992). In search of how people change: Applications to addictive behaviors. *American Psychologist, 47*, 1102–1114.

Rogers, E. M. (2003). *Diffusion of innovations* (5th ed.). New York: Free Press.

Ryan, B., & Gross, N. (1943). The diffusion of hybrid seed corn in two Iowa communities. *Rural Sociology, 8*, 15–24.

Singhal, A., & Rogers, E. M. (2003). *Combating AIDS: Communication strategies in action.* Thousand Oaks, CA: Sage.

Valente, T. W. (1993). Diffusion of innovations and policy decision-making. *Journal of Communication, 43*, 30–45.

Valente, T. W. (1995). *Network models of the diffusion of innovations.* Cresskill, NJ: Hampton Press.

Valente, T. W. (2002). *Evaluating health promotion programs.* Oxford, England: Oxford University Press.

Valente, T. W. (2010). *Social networks and health: Models, methods, and applications.*Oxford, England: Oxford University Press.

Valente, T. W., Chou, C. P., & Pentz, M. A. (2007). Community coalition networks as systems: Effects of network change on adoption of evidence-based prevention. *American Journal of Public Health, 97*, 880–886.

Valente, T. W., & Davis, R. L. (1999). Accelerating the diffusion of innovations using opinion leaders. *The Annals of the American Academy of the Political and Social Sciences, 566*, 55–67.

Valente, T. W., Hoffman, B. R., Ritt-Olson, A., Lichtman, K., & Johnson, C. A. (2003). The effects of a social network method for group assignment strategies on peer led tobacco prevention programs in schools. *American Journal of Public Health, 93*, 1837–1843.

Valente, T. W., Paredes, P., & Poppe, P. R. (1998). Matching the message to the process: The relative ordering of knowledge, attitudes and practices in behavior change research. *Human Communication Research, 24*, 366–385.

Valente, T. W., Poppe, P. R., & Merritt, A. P. (1996). Mass media generated interpersonal communication as sources of information about family planning. *Journal of Health Communication, 1*, 247–266.

Valente, T. W., & Pumpuang, P. (2007). Identifying opinion leaders to promote behavior change. *Health Education & Behavior, 34*, 881–896.

Valente, T. W., & Rogers, E. M. (1995). The origins and development of the diffusion of innovations paradigm as an example of scientific growth. *Science Communication: An Interdisciplinary Social Science Journal. 16*, 238–269.

Valente, T. W., & Saba, W. (1998). Mass media and interpersonal influence in a reproductive health communication campaign in Bolivia. *Communication Research, 25*, 96–124.

Watts, D. (1999). *Small worlds: The dynamics of networks between order and randomness.* Princeton, NJ: Princeton University Press.

Wiist, W. H., & Snider G. (1991). Peer education in friendship cliques: prevention of adolescent smoking. *Health Education Research, 6*, 101–108.

34

QUALITATIVE METHODS

Bridging the Gap between
Research and Daily Practice

Athena du Pré and Sonia J. Crandall

> The world is very complex. There are no simple explanations for things. Rather, events are the result of multiple factors coming together and interacting in complex and unanticipated ways. Therefore any methodology that attempts to understand experience and explain structures will have to be complex.
>
> (Corbin & Strauss, 2008, p. 8)

Qualitative research approaches are oriented largely to the idea of multiple realities shaped by the interplay of social forces, cultural expectations, personal experiences, knowledge, and more. Likewise, clinicians must understand patients' complex perspectives if they are to be effective. For example, Mrs. J comes to the clinic every three months to have her A1c (an indicator of blood sugar control) checked, but it consistently runs higher than average. Mrs. J and her provider agree on steps to improve her blood sugar control. However, at the next visit her A1c is still high. Why are "things not working"? Gaining insight into the lifeworld of the patient requires an understanding of her health beliefs, including what she believes about the medication's side effects, how diabetes affects her body, how to control blood sugar, and how she conceives the social implications of being diabetic. Her health literacy (discussed in the Cameron et al. chapter, this volume) is an issue as well. Understanding these factors requires active listening to the social and emotional cues embedded in the patient's account. Thus, medicine is not simply a matter of empirical evidence or medical history. It is a process in which both the caregiver and patient, with all their experiences and expectations, are active agents in cocreating and cointerpreting what occurs.

Qualitative researchers' interface with social phenomena leads some to assume that the resulting analysis is a collection of idiosyncratic impressions. But qualitative research, done well, involves rigorous, methodical investigation based on evidence that can readily be demonstrated. With the development of grounded theory, Glaser and Strauss (1967) established a method of examining qualitative data that involves constant, ongoing comparison between an observer's impressions and patterns demonstrated by the data. This back-and-forth inductive/deductive process permeates the practice of medicine and medical education as well. As Crandall and Marion (2009) put it:

Clinicians who will thrive in their work will have the capacity for being able to toggle back and forth between objectivity and receptivity. In essence, effective clinicians attend to the patient's whole story in tandem with clinical reasoning, which leads to a mutually satisfactory process and outcome.

(p. 1175)

Qualitative research typically recognizes that the activities of everyday life do not occur as discrete units but within a sophisticated web of factors (Denzin & Lincoln, 1994, 2005). Similar complexities affect medical encounters. For example, a patient may want to quit smoking, but for the past several generations his family's business has been connected to the tobacco industry, income from which "put my kids through college." Recognizing the complexity behind seemingly straightforward decisions, qualitative researchers often blend methods and simultaneously focus on a variety of phenomena. It is useful, although not always easy, to distinguish between qualitative research *methods,* which may include observation, introspection, interviewing, recording, and studying conversation, and so on, and qualitative *perspectives* such as ethnography, grounded theory, ethnomethodology, and phenomenology, which may involve multiple combinations of the methods just listed. In a sense, one *does* ethnography in many of the same ways one *does* ethnomethodology, but with a different set of objectives and assumptions.

Grounded Theory

Grounded theory was originally proposed by sociologists Barney Glaser and Anselm Strauss (1965, 1967) to identify patterns and assumptions that help explain why people behave as they do. The approach is appealing because it articulates a disciplined way to follow the processes we naturally employ as we attempt to make sense of the world around us. Another advantage is that it allows researchers to systematically examine large amounts of data for patterns that members themselves may be unable to articulate because they are known only tacitly. Grounded theory proposes that researchers focus on questions such as these: What is happening here? What patterns or words or behaviors can I identify? What might be functioning below the surface to give rise to these patterns? (Charmaz, 2006).

For example, when Zubia Mumtaz and Sarah Salway (2007) explored decisions surrounding antenatal care in Pujab, Pakistan, they lived in the village for 5 months. Their data ultimately included field notes and transcripts from more than 200 observations, interviews, and focus groups. To identify patterns within such a large corpus, they applied grounded theory. As they addressed the questions What is going on here? and What words or behaviors can I identify? the researchers became aware of cultural mores that privileged the opinions of older female relatives in making decisions about pregnancy and childbirth. "Normatively, the pregnant woman is not supposed to voice her opinion or have any personal desires," the researchers observed (p. 9). In looking below the surface, they found that, although young women adhered to such traditions on the surface, they were becoming increasingly discontented with them. They resented being silenced about their own medical care, and they were frustrated that men were culturally distanced from the process. Many women reported that pregnancy and childbirth were considered so "off limits" to men that their husbands avoided them while they were pregnant.

From a medical school perspective, Crandall (1993) used a grounded theory approach to explore how highly regarded medical educators perceived their own efforts to model patient

533

care experiences and reflective practices for medical residents. She asked residents to identify "expert teachers," that is, teachers the residents considered to be "better than average." Then she studied those teachers' experiences using a Critical Incident Technique (Flanagan, 1954). Such a technique involves asking people to think about, then talk about, episodes they consider pivotal in some way. Researchers have used the Critical Incident Technique to study the circumstances (usually involving perceived lack of communication) that lead to patient complaints (Hsieh, 2010); instances in which medical students find it difficult to be patient-centered, such as times of intense emotion or disagreement (Bower et al., 2009); episodes in which doctors feel pressured by patients or coworkers to prescribe medication they are not sure will help the patient (Lewis & Tully, 2009); and a range of other circumstances involving health communication.

Crandall (1993) employed the Critical Incident Technique by asking 13 physician educators to describe a teaching encounter that, in their opinion, went exceptionally well and one that went exceptionally poorly. After interviewing the doctors, she compared and contrasted their responses, looking for themes, patterns, and assumptions within them. She found consistent evidence that, overall, the physician educators most highly esteemed by their students regarded medical practice as an inherently uncertain and ambiguous enterprise in which learning is best accomplished through continual learning-in-the-doing and learning-in-reflection.

Crandall's discovery process was iterative in that it involved looking for patterns within each interview transcript and then collectively throughout all of the transcripts. Once she had identified themes, Crandall conducted member checks, asking the doctors to review her conclusions to be sure they accurately reflected their perceptions. The doctors agreed with her observation that, from their perspective, reflective learning "makes uncertainty, uniqueness, and surprise a positive part of medical practice, instead of something to dread" (p. 97).

Grounded theory helps to identify patterns of behavior. Such patterns are more prevalent in health communication than people might assume. For example, in a review of qualitative research about intensive care units, Sinuff, Cook, and Giacomini (2007) present consistent themes voiced by patients' family members. One theme is that a single episode of reassurance is not enough to quell their fears. The families appreciate being told multiple times that their loved ones are being carefully monitored, and that, should they die, they will not be alone (Sinuff et al., 2007). Using grounded theory, Sparks, Villagran, Parker-Raley, and Cunningham (2007) identified four common patterns of bad news delivery: an indirect approach in which the health professional largely avoids talking about the issue; straightforward, direct strategies; comforting strategies involving touch and immediacy; and empowering strategies that present a range of choices and options for the patient. The researchers found that patient preferences for various strategies depended largely on the severity of the news and the patients' sex, age, cultural background, and education. Using similar means, researchers have found consistent patterns of emotional support offered by nurse aides to patients in long-term care facilities. These range from assistance with meals and tasks, to conversations, to words of praise and support (Carpiac-Claver & Levy-Storms, L., 2007). Most of these studies make it evident that, despite the range of options available, individuals tend to overrely on particular strategies and underutilize others. Perhaps, by explicitly identifying the patterns, researchers and careful observers can expand their communication repertoires to be more flexible and adaptive.

For more guidance on grounded theory, see Bryant and Charmaz (2010) and Charmaz (2006) in addition to the works already cited.

Ethnography

> When I arrive at Dorothy's apartment today, she is having one of her "spells," as Terry calls them. I am glad that Terry is home this time, because Dorothy's confusion is much worse. As I greet Dorothy and take her hand, Dorothy smiles warmly, but she also seems distracted and confused about who I am.
>
> (Foster, 2007, p. 133)

The above excerpt from Elissa Foster's book, *Communicating at the End of Life,* describes one of her experiences as a hospice volunteer and ethnographic researcher. Ethnography is characterized primarily by a focus on naturally occurring social phenomena. The premise is that cultural assumptions and values are made available in the way people behave and interact (Atkinson & Hammersley, 1994). Ethnographers typically immerse themselves in communities to learn through direct observation or experience. As Patricia Adler and Peter Adler (1994) explain, naturalistic observation "enjoys the advantage of drawing the observer into the phenomenological complexity of the world, where connections, correlations, and causes can be witnessed as they unfold" (p. 378).

By virtue of being present in the social situations they study, ethnographers are almost always, to some degree, participants in what occurs. At one end of a continuum, researchers seek to remain unobtrusive, affecting participants' behavior as little as possible. At the other end, researchers are more than silent observers. Indeed, they may be integral parts of the scenarios. Autoethnographies such as Leah Vande Berg and Nick Trujillo's (2008) book, *Cancer and Death: A Love Story in Two Voices,* provide poignant insights into the experiences of people who are both the main characters in the story and reflective storytellers who make available aspects of the experience that no third-party observer could adequately capture. In the book, Vande Berg and Trujillo describe where they were raised, how they met and fell in love, their hopes for a child, their love for their dogs, and their different impressions and experiences once she is diagnosed with ovarian cancer. The book includes passages written by both of them, interspersed with comments and letters from loved ones. Here's a sample by Nick:

> When I kissed Leah goodbye in the hallway near the preop area, I honestly wondered whether I would ever see her again. Unlike Leah, I was worried that she might not survive surgery. Neither of us had ever gone through a major operation, and this procedure seemed as major as it could get.... On the drive home, I prayed "Dear God," I said. "If you're going to take her anyway, take her now rather than make her have a long painful death."
>
> (p. 58)

In a review of the book, Elizabeth Gill (2009) calls it a "beautifully written story of love and loss and an extremely honest account of the cancer and death experience" (p. 308) as well as a powerful example of narrative and autoethnography. She recommends it both for scholars and for laypeople experiencing health crises. As Gill's (2009) review illustrates, an appealing quality of ethnography is insight about real-life experiences. Ethnographic reports often have the rich, readable quality of novels. "I think of ethnography as being very organic in a way," says Foster.[1] "It's trying to capture everyday ways of thinking and taking it up a notch by being very conscious of how you're doing it."

This is not achieved without effort. Conducting an ethnography involves a great deal of time, discipline, and careful thought. Foster's process of discovery followed several steps replicable in other ethnographic research. She began by considering the role she might play. "My initial idea was to visit patients or to follow the team somehow," she says. But even shadowing a professional would require that she master, to some extent, the vocabulary and processes that help define the process. Foster met with local hospice leaders, who were enthusiastic about hosting her research and agreed to enroll her in a hospice volunteer training program. The more she learned in the training program, Foster says, the more she realized that she actually wanted to volunteer, not just watch others.

Assumptions everyday participants take for granted may be apparent to researchers who are looking closely for them and for whom the occurrences are novel rather than routine. When researcher Jennifer Laws (2009) sought to understand the dynamics of an alternative self-help group for recipients of mental health services in England, she obtained permission to attend support group meetings over a 10-month period. Although she was originally interested in listening behaviors, the notion of physical space and healing landscapes emerged as central to the participants' experience and became the focus of Laws's study. Participants frequently addressed the notion of being sequestered or confined to particular spaces such as "madhouses"; hospital grounds; and locked, limited-access psychiatric wards. But as Laws became familiar with group practices she realized that they conceived of a different space as well—in this case, a literal healing *landscape* in the form of a city park, which—although it had a reputation as a dangerous, disreputable place—was appealing to group members because it was a nontechnical space in which they felt a sense of agency and freedom from social judgment. Laws arrived at the unexpected conclusion that the carefully controlled, "pleasant," and "clean" atmosphere that mental health professionals typically cultivate is not necessarily regarded as healthy or inviting by people seeking care.

For ethnographers, venturing into unfamiliar situations has advantages, but it can also be intimidating. Says Foster: "I was really scared about *getting it*, about being inadequate and trying to be one of what I thought of as 'those amazing hospice people.'" Looking back, she says the process involved both unexpectedly comfortable and frightening experiences. Foster worked mainly with Dorothy, a petite, energetic woman in the last stages of chronic obstructive pulmonary disease (COPD). The two women struck up a warm friendship. But even once she had known Dorothy for some time, Foster says she experienced moments of dread and uncertainty, as when she first drove Dorothy in her car. "I had to get over my fear that she would have respiratory arrest and I wouldn't know what to do," Foster says. "And my car was so dodgy—a typical grad student car. Having someone in the car with a terminal illness scared the crap out of me, quite frankly!" In an effort to "get it right," Foster relied on regular feedback and guidance from hospice staff members.

Other experiences presented ethical issues. Foster quickly realized that being in a person's home involves exposure to intimate details not meant for public disclosure. "I needed to make decisions about what to include and what not to include in ways that made sense to me," Foster recalls. She established an ethical code for herself that distinguished her study from a reality TV show. "Something in all our lives would make for titillating reading, but it can be completely irrelevant to the point of the study," Foster says. Instead, "I kept asking myself: *What is relevant to the research question? What is core? What is the real thing that I am pursuing?* I used those questions as the key to crafting the narrative."

Good ethnographers are sensitive to a range of ethical concerns. For one, although they typically try not to change the dynamics they are studying, doing nothing may seem irresponsible when the participants are engaged in risky or illegal behaviors. Hemmings (2009) explores this issue in relation to studies of adolescents, who may trust researchers not to "tattle" on them. Whether to intervene or not is a difficult decision, best made on a case-by-case basis by researchers who have carefully thought through ethical principles (Hemmings, 2009). Another ethical issue involves the "harm" or "innocence" of considering public behaviors fair game for undeclared ethnographical observation (Schrag, 2009).

In her case, Foster made Dorothy aware of her status as a researcher, but she felt that their interactions should focus on Dorothy's needs, not on the research. She put it this way:

> My patient knew what I did and knew that I was studying hospice. But she wasn't really that interested, and it wasn't that important for her to read what I was writing. I didn't want to impose that in our sessions. I felt a little protective of her, too. I had to find a way to write about my relationship with her so it was really about me and my experience of her and my visits and it wasn't really about her life, her family, her environment so much.

The result is a rich, insightful account of Foster's discovery process, culminating in her feelings about Dorothy's death.

Foster says her ethnographic experience serves her well as a medical educator in the Department of Family Medicine at Lehigh Health Network in Allentown, Pennsylvania. As she works with staff members and medical students to design a team-oriented, patient-centered process she keeps extensive field notes about the experience and writes up narratives that allow her and others to chart their progress and evaluate what people are experiencing along the way. The narrative includes descriptions of people's verbal and nonverbal behaviors and how they describe their feelings about the process. Foster says the ongoing narrative is a way to step back from the "moments of everyday life" and become aware of larger patterns. One of those patterns involves the realization that becoming more patient-centered does not mean only that caregivers interact differently with patients. Almost without realizing or predicting it, Foster says, staff members began interacting differently with each other. Looking at episodes and changes over time, "we realized that imbedded in the systems are power differences and relationships that are all impacted," she says, adding:

> We can look at what is happening to see how that plays out—if we are actually empowering people or making a difference and to see if our behavior is in tune with the values we espouse. I see this as an essential strength of ethnography—to capture what is happening in particular instances and look at it from the perspective of individuals and groups embedded in a larger context.

In this way, ethnography is not only a tool of researchers but a means of charting and better understanding changes within an organization or community.

For more on conducting an ethnographic study, we recommend Angrosino (2007), Fetterman (2009), Hymes (1962), Spradley (1979), Taylor (2002), and Van Maanen (1988). We turn now to a form of inquiry that shares many of the goals of ethnography but approaches social interaction from a different perspective.

Phenomenology

Phenomenology concentrates on people's *experience* of the world. As a philosophy, it is not much concerned with how elements of the physical world may exist separately from people's perceptions of them. Instead, the focus is on the way that people constitute those experiences within consciousness. Because it is not limited to the corporeal, phenomenology makes it possible to study phenomena such as love, beauty, courage, and oppression. As with most qualitative approaches, the means of accomplishing such an investigation vary a good deal.

Edmund Husserl, widely regarded as the founder of phenomenology, prescribed a method of eidetic reduction or bracketing. Following such a process, a person seeks to imagine a thing or concept and "bracket" out all nonessential elements of it. The objective is to arrive at its essential properties, those that ultimately define it as being different from other phenomena (Husserl, 1970). A simple example helps illustrate: Picture in your mind a chair.

> *How do you know this thing you imagine is a chair and not something else?*
> Because it has four legs.
> *Ah, so it wouldn't be a chair if it had three legs?*
> Well that's not exactly correct. I have seen three-legged chairs.
> *Then four legs isn't essential to the experience of a thing as a chair. What else might define it?*
> It has a flat portion on which to sit.
> *So anything with a flat portion suitable for sitting is a chair?*
> No, there are stools and benches and rocks and any number of other things that are not chairs.
> *It's not so easy, strictly speaking, to say what makes a chair a chair is it? But it is possible. Let's keep going....*

Arriving at the essential elements of an experience—whether it be "chairness," love, health, or any other experience—is more challenging than you might initially assume. However, it is possible. Indeed, we do it constantly within what Husserl (1970) calls "the natural attitude" of life. To wit, you may not know, in words, how you define the essence of a chair. Yet you can distinguish between a chair and a stool without conscious effort. At some level, there *is* an understanding of what, essentially, makes a chair a chair. Phenomenology focuses on that process.

Opening one's eyes to the essential properties of constituted experiences while bracketing out sediment (suppositions and theories that are not essential) is part of a larger process Husserl (1970) called epoché. Relevant to health, we may seek to understand how people experience some caregivers as *good, friendly, rude,* or so on.

We might also examine the very notion of being *healthy* or *ill*. Integrative health theory proposes that health is, essentially, the experience of alignment between three factors: interpretive accounts (our assumptions and explanations about life), performance (what we are able to do), and self-image (Lambert, Street, Cegala, Smith, Kurtz, & Schofield, 1997). For example, say Lambert and colleagues, if a man interprets that being a loving husband properly involves having sex with his wife but blood pressure medication renders him impotent, there is likely to be a sense of misalignment between his self-image (a good husband), his account of what it means to be a good husband (having sexual intercourse), and the extent to which he is able to fulfill those expectations. The theorists suggest that he is healthy to the extent that he experiences alignment between these factors and unhealthy to the extent that he experiences misalignment. Of course, there are multiple ways to threaten alignment just as there are multiple ways it might be restored. The man might go off the medication, change his ideas about sex or being a good husband, and so on. Health is not a static or easily predicted state of being. Neither is health care or health communication. As this example illustrates, health concerns often evoke fear, embarrassment, and threats to identity. Talking about issues such as impotence and self-image is not typically simple or straightforward. Some people are relatively comfortable raising sensitive subjects, whereas others may benefit from the chance to write down questions or keep a journal in which they explore and articulate how they feel.

The conventional Western perspective holds that, whether the patient realizes it or not, his health is probably improved once he is on medication. It's an idea that holds water to a certain extent, but from a phenomenological perspective, it doesn't tell the whole story. After all, two people with the same measurable condition can feel different and experience different outcomes. One may be incapacitated by pain the other is able to tolerate. One may die from a condition that doesn't kill another. Physical indicators are one way to gauge health, but their utility is limited, and they usually fail to take into account a person's *experience* of being healthy or unhealthy. From a pragmatic perspective, understanding how people *experience* being healthy or unhealthy can help us understand why they behave as they do. With knowledge of integrative health theory, it's not hard to understand why the man might stop taking his medication, particularly if we do not help him identify alternative options that will lessen the sense of misalignment. It's also useful to know if patients perceive diagnoses or treatments to be inconsistent with their self-image, performance, or interpretations. Otherwise, we may assume they are merely being difficult, negligent, disrespectful, or nonadherent to treatment. Caregivers may be frustrated and even refuse to care for such people. And patients may leave medical encounters feeling less healthy than when they arrived.

Phenomenology is accomplished through other methods as well. Claire Wilkinson and Sue McAndrew (2008) interviewed people whose loved ones had been admitted to psychiatric units. Following the tenets of qualitative interviewing (Kvale & Brinkmann, 2009), they planned some of the interview questions in advance, but they mostly let interviewees set the tone and focus on topics of interest to them personally. By listening intently and asking only open-ended questions the researchers sought to avoid imposing their own interests or agendas. With the participants' permission, the researchers taped the interviews and later made transcripts of them. Using a form of constant comparative method, they identified common themes and patterns. One theme was especially prevalent. Everyone interviewed reported an experience of *powerlessness* in which others were now in control and could either recognize and partner with them or exclude them and make them feel unnecessary and isolated. Said one participant:

> I felt inferior, I didn't know what was going on, I didn't know how to make things right. The doctors and nurses were the experts and I had to trust them. I didn't have any choice because I just felt that things were beyond my control.
>
> (p. 395)

In other studies, health communication researchers have used qualitative interviews to gauge what is most important to patients and their loved ones. For example, although physicians typically frame dialysis treatment options in terms of predicted life expectancy, patients allowed to speak candidly often say their more immediate concerns are how autonomous they can remain and how convenient the treatment plans will be for themselves and others (Morton et al., 2010). In another interview-based study, family members of people with aphasia (a compromised ability to communicate) said the hardest part was feeling lonely and isolated from others (Nätterlund, 2010). Insights such as these lead some theorists to call for an "integration of research, practice, and teaching" (Newton, McKenna, Gilmour, & Fawcett, 2010, p. 1). Newton and collaborators trained students in a midwifery program to conduct unstructured interviews with women who had recently given birth via cesarean section. The students analyzed the interview transcripts and reflected on what they learned. Most said they were surprised by the wide range of attitudes they encountered among women, and they vowed to be attentive to patients' unique needs and perspectives. One student said: "It opened my eyes to the reality of the individual" (p. 7; for more about qualitative interviewing, we suggest Kvale & Brinkmann, 2009; Rubin & Rubin, 2005; Wengraf, 2001.)

Similar techniques may be employed to speak with groups of individuals who share common interests. In practice, such a group may constitute family members and loved ones brought together to discuss their views about a patient's treatment or imminent death. From a research angle, it might involve focus group discussions, as in Macdonald and colleagues' (2010) study of women with family histories of breast cancer (Macdonald, Sarna, Weitzel, & Ferrell, 2010). They found that the women were frequently not able to speak with providers well schooled in genetic medicine, and they often felt overwhelmed when asked to make quick decisions about treatment options. Such insights are not typically considered central to evidence-based medicine, but they add a qualitative understanding of patients' experiences that can be useful in managing their care (for more on focus groups, see Krueger & Casey, 2009; Stewart, Shamdasani, & Rook, 2007).

Another form of phenomenology involves the use of narratives. Narrative analysis is well covered in the Sharf et al. chapter (this volume), so we will confine our remarks to the way participants in medical education sometimes employ narrative principles. As mentioned in the chapter on narratives, Rita Charon, a general internal medicine physician who also has a doctorate in English and directs the Program in Narrative Medicine at Columbia University, is a leader of the narrative medicine movement. The program she directs for third-year medical students highlights the concept of narrative competence, using "parallel charts" in which learners write about, and share with other students, their feelings and reactions to patients—aspects not allowed in conventional medical charts. These reflective writings include "deep attachments to patients, their awe at patients' courage, their sense of helplessness in the face of disease, their rage at disease's unfairness, the shame and humiliation they experience as medical students, and the memories and associations triggered by their work" (Charon, 2006, p. 156). Charon emphasizes that this process is not designed to be a support group but "to increase the students' capacity for effective clinical work" (p. 156).

Researchers and practitioners interested in learning more about phenomenology and narrative analysis may wish to consult Atkinson and Heritage (1985), Charon (2006), Harter, Japp, & Beck (2005), Husserl (1970), and Spiegelberg (1981).

Ethnomethodology

Ethnomethodology is concerned primarily with the methods by which people generate and perpetuate a sense of orderliness in life circumstances. John Heritage (1984) describes ethnomethodology as the study of:

> the body of common-sense knowledge and the range of procedures and considerations by which the ordinary members of society make sense or, find their way about in, and act on the circumstances in which they find themselves.

(p. 4)

This differs from ethnography in that, from an ethnomethodological perspective, *meaning* and *order* are not seen as products of culture that are communicated to members. Rather, social actors are considered to be active agents in rendering as sensible what occurs to them and in collaboratively perpetuating what they consider to be sensible actions-in the–doing (Zimmerman & Boden, 1991). For example, if you see someone walking backward down the sidewalk, your first response is likely to involve an effort at sense-making. You might say, "Ah, she's crazy!" or "He's probably acting on a dare." The point is that you render the situation "sensible" in some way. Let's take that idea a step further.

The founder of ethnomethodology, Harold Garfinkel (1967), proposed that we are involved in the enterprise of sense-making all of the time, but our efforts frequently take on a tacit, unmindful quality. Because people *usually* walk forward down the sidewalk you may not find yourself puzzling over it when it happens. Indeed, in such cases, orderliness seems to exist externally to our efforts to create it. People walk that way because it's "normal" or "how you're supposed to walk." Look a bit deeper, however, and you realize that such patterns are only "sensible" because we interpret and enact them within a common understanding. In other words, order in the social world doesn't simply happen. People are collaboratively involved in enacting behaviors that are, as Garfinkel (1967) put it, "visibly-rational-and-reportable-for-all-practical-purposes" (p. vii). That is, we are involved, not only in making sense of the world around us, but in creating a sense of order by acting consistently with tacitly agreed-upon expectations. What's more, such behaviors tend to be attributed a moral quality such that people who violate them may seem to be bad, crazy, rude, or stupid.

This is not to say that social actors are confined to narrowly defined rules or that they are somehow brainwashed into following them. It's more to say that, within the complexities of a social situation, participants subtly campaign for the salience of different interpretive modes. And within that collaboratively created context, particular options for behavior are presented as preferable to others. It is socially permissible to act in novel ways if the context and participants support it or there is an explanation that excuses the violation (i.e., you might walk backward with impunity if you are carrying furniture or joking around). The emphasis in ethnomethodology is not on the rules, but on everyday actors' roles in manufacturing and interpreting them (Holstein & Gubrium, 1994).

A case in point is a medical educator who asks an open-ended question in class, then remains silent until someone speaks. Typically, the silence will extend only so long before someone feels compelled to break it with a comment. This is predictable because people in the predominant American culture are typically uncomfortable with silence. Because of its dispreferred status, silence tends to feel awkward. The second author (Crandall) puts medical students in this situation and then asks them to consider how their discomfort with silence might influence their interactions with patients. She points out that clinicians rarely tolerate silence during medical interviews. Indeed, they seldom wait more than a few seconds for a patient to answer one question before they ask another. Becoming aware of this tendency may help future clinicians avoid acting on the same impulse. Likewise, with an attenuated sense of the boundaries most people consider socially acceptable (concerning silence, appropriateness, modesty, and so on) medical professionals may more readily comprehend patients' behavior, including the subtle ways they demonstrate reluctance, fear, and trust.

From a researcher's perspective, there are a number of ways to do ethnomethodology relevant to health communication. One is conversation analysis (CA). The idea is that preferred modes of social interaction are negotiated, and thus made available for inspection, in the way people talk to each other. This perspective is covered in the Robinson chapter (this volume). Therefore we will limit our focus here to an example of how CA can function as both a research tool and a guide to practical application.

In a 2007 study, John Heritage and colleagues adopted a simple plan: Train doctors to ask patients either *"Is there anything else you want to address in the visit today?"* or *"Is there something else you want to address in the visit today?"* They put "stickie notes" with one question or the other in patient charts to remind the doctors what to ask. They found that the wording did matter. Patients who were asked *"Is there something else…?"* typically left the doctor's visit with about half as many unmet concerns as patients randomly assigned to the *"Is there anything else…?"* group (Heritage, Robinson, Elliot, Beckett, & Wilkes, 2007). The "some" question was more effective at eliciting patients' concerns. In the end, many physicians who had been reluctant to try the experiment paid to have reminders with the "some" question on them created for their patient charts in the future. Previously, says Robinson, "the doctors had recognized the importance of asking the question, just not the importance of exactly *how* they asked it."

In this case and many others, studies of naturally occurring transactions are as interesting to practitioners as they are to researchers. For more on ethnomethodology and conversation analysis, see Atkinson and Heritage (1985), Garfinkel (1967), Heritage (1984), Schegloff (2007), and ten Have (2007).

Conclusion

In this chapter we have sought to provide a rich, contextual understanding of qualitative explorations of health communication through the eyes of trained researchers and the experiences of people involved in health education and health encounters. As you have seen, many people are engaged in "qualitative research" more than they realize.

In daily life, we ground our ideas about people and experiences in data that are constantly presented to us. Researchers build upon that discovery process by imposing a rigor that overcomes many of the perceptual biases that tempt social actors. For example, ethnography provides a means of appreciating the cultural and situational factors that underlie much of human behavior. From Foster's story of befriending a dying woman we learn about hospice care, but also something about ourselves and the human condition. This perspective is underscored by phenomenology, which emphasizes that much of what a health experience *means* lies in our consciousness of it. Storytelling, and narrative analysis of those stories, provides a window into people's experiences and perceptions. At the same time, ethnomethodology reminds us that social patterns are shaped, not only by what we are conscious of, but what we know at a tacit level and the way we respond to subtle (and not-so-subtle) cues such as the way a question is worded or how the furniture is arranged.

Together, these perspectives reflect the intuitive ways that we seek knowledge, and they prod us to go a little further toward understanding and examining our own assumptions about health and healing and how those assumptions are shaped by culture, experience, individuality, the desire to please others, and our need for human connection. As Charon (2006) observed so poignantly, in health communication, the listening and the telling are sometimes emotionally charged and frightening. But the rewards of paying close attention are powerful.

Note

1. The information presented here was collected during a personal interview with Foster by the first author (du Pré) in October 2009.

References

Adler, P. A., & Adler, P. (1994). Observational techniques. In N. K. Denzin & Y. S. Lincoln (Eds.), *Handbook of qualitative research* (pp. 377–392). Thousand Oaks, CA: Sage.

Angrosino, M. (2007). *Doing ethnographic and observational research.* Thousand Oaks, CA: Sage.

Atkinson, P., & Hammersley, M. (1994). Ethnography and participant observation. In N. K. Denzin & Y. S. Lincoln (Eds.), *Handbook of qualitative research* (pp. 248–261). Thousand Oaks, CA: Sage.

Atkinson, J. M., & Heritage, J. (Eds.). (1985). *Structures of social action.* New York: Cambridge University Press.

Bower, D. J., Young, S., Larson, G., Simpson, D., Tipnis, S., Begaz, T., & Webb, T. (2009). Characteristics of patient encounters that challenge medical students' provision of patient-centered care [Supplement]. *Academic Medicine, 84,* S74–S78.

Bryant, A., & Charmaz, K. (2010). *The Sage handbook on grounded theory.* Thousand Oaks, CA: Sage.

Carpiac-Claver, M. L., & Levy-Storms, L. (2007). In a manner of speaking: Communication between nurse aides and older adults in long-term care settings. *Health Communication, 22,* 59–67.

Charmaz, K. (2006). *Constructing grounded theory: A practical guide through qualitative analysis.* London: Sage.

Charon, R. (2006). *Narrative medicine: Honoring the stories of illness.* New York: Oxford University Press.

Corbin, J., & Strauss, A. (2008). *Basics of qualitative research* (3rd ed.). Los Angeles: Sage.

Crandall, S. J. (1993). How expert clinical educators teach what they know. *Journal of Continuing Education in the Health Professions, 13,* 85–98.

Crandall, S. J., & Marion, G. S. (2009, September). Commentary. Identifying attitudes towards empathy: An essential feature of professionalism. *Academic Medicine, 84,* 1174–1176.

Denzin, N. K., & Lincoln, Y. S. (1994). Introduction: Entering the field of qualitative research. In N. K. Denzin & Y. S. Lincoln (Eds.), *Handbook of qualitative research* (pp. 1–17). Thousand Oaks, CA: Sage.

Denzin, N. K., & Lincoln, Y. S. (Eds.). (2005). *The Sage handbook of qualitative research* (3rd ed.). Thousand Oaks, CA: Sage.

Fetterman, D. M. (Ed.). (2009). *Ethnography: Step-by-step* (3rd ed.). Thousand Oaks, CA: Sage.

Flanagan, J. C. (1954). The critical incident technique. *Psychological Bulletin, 51,* 327–358.

Foster, E. (2007). *Communicating at the end of life: Finding magic in the mundane.* Mahwah, NJ: Erlbaum.

Garfinkel, H. (1967). *Studies in ethnomethodology.* Cambridge, MA: Polity Press/Basil Blackwell.

Gill, E. (2009). Book Review. *Cancer and death: A love story in two voices. Journal of Health Communication, 14,* 308–310.

Glaser, B. G., & Strauss, A. L. (1965). *Awareness of dying.* Chicago, IL: Aldine.

Glaser, B. G., & Strauss, A. L. (1967). *The discovery of grounded theory: Strategies for qualitative research.* Chicago, IL: Aldine.

Harter, L. M., Japp, P. M., & Beck, C. S. (2005). *Narratives, health, and healing: Communication theory, research, and practice.* Mahwah, NJ: Erlbaum.

Hemmings, A. (2009). Ethnographic research with adolescent students: Situated fieldwork ethics and ethical principles governing human research. *Journal of Empirical Research of Human Research, 4*(4), 27–38. doi: 10.1525/jer.2009.4.4.27

Heritage, J. (1984). *Garfinkel and ethnomethodology.* Cambridge, MA: Polity.

Heritage, J., Robinson, J. D., Elliot, M. N., Beckett, M., & Wilkes, M. (2007, October). Reducing patients' unmet concerns in primary care: A trial of two question designs. *Journal of General Internal Medicine, 22,* 1429–1433.

Holstein, J. A., & Gubrium, J. F. (1994). Phenomenology, ethnomethodology, and interpretive practice. In N. K. Denzin & Y. S. Lincoln (Eds.), *Handbook of qualitative research* (pp. 262–272). Thousand Oaks, CA: Sage.

Hsieh, S. Y. (2010). The use of patient complaints to drive quality improvement: An exploratory study in Taiwan. *Health Services Management Research, 23*, 5–11.

Husserl, E. (1970). *The crisis of the European sciences and transcendental phenomenology* (D. Carr, Trans.). Evanston, IL: Northwestern University Press.

Hymes, D. (1962). The ethnography of speaking. In T. Gladwin & W. C. Sturtevant (Eds.), *Anthropology and human behavior* (pp. 13–53). Washington, DC: The Anthropology Society of Washington.

Krueger, R. A., & Casey, M. A. (2009). *Focus groups: A practical guide for applied research* (4th ed.). Thousand Oaks, CA: Sage.

Kvale, S., & Brinkmann, S. (2009). *InterViews: Learning the craft of qualitative research interviewing* (2nd ed.). Thousand Oaks, CA: Sage.

Lambert, B. L., Street, R. L., Cegala, D. J., Smith, D. H., Kurtz, S., & Schofield, T. (1997). Provider–patient communication, patient-centered care, and the mangle of practice. *Health Communication, 9*, 27–43.

Laws, J. (2009). Reworking therapeutic landscapes: The spatiality of an "alternative" self-help group. *Social Science & Medicine, 69*, 1827–1833. doi: 10.1016/j.socscimed.2009.09.034

Lewis, P. J., & Tully, M. P. (2009). Uncomfortable prescribing decisions in hospitals: The impact of teamwork. *Journal of the Royal Society of Medicine, 102*, 481–488.

Macdonald, D. J., Sarna, L., Weitzel, J. N., & Ferrell, B. (2010). Women's perceptions of the personal and family impact of genetic cancer risk assessment: Focus group findings. *Journal of Genetic Counseling, 19*, 148–160.

Morton, R. L., Devitt, J., Howard, K., Anderson, K., Snelling, P., & Cass, A. (2010). Patient views about treatment of stage 5 CKD: A qualitative analysis of semistructured interviews. *American Journal of Kidney Diseases, 55*, 431–440.

Mumtaz, Z., & Salway, S. M. (2007). Gender, pregnancy and the uptake of antenatal care services in Pakistan. *Sociology of Health & Illness, 29*, 1–26. doi: 10.1111/j.1467-9566.2007.00519.x

Nätterlund, B. S. (2010). Being a close relative of a person with aphasia. *Scandinavian Journal of Occupational Therapy, 17*, 18–28.

Newton, J. M., McKenna, L. G., Gilmour, C., & Fawcett, J. (2010). Exploring a pedagogical approach to integrating research, practice and teaching. *International Journal of Nursing Education Scholarship, 7*(1), 1–13.

Rubin, H. J., & Rubin, I. S. (2005). *Qualitative interviewing: The art of hearing data* (2nd ed.). Thousand Oaks, CA: Sage.

Schegloff, E. A. (2007). *Sequence organization in interaction: Vol. 1. A primer on conversation analysis.* New York: Cambridge University Press.

Schrag, B. (2009). Piercing the veil: Ethical issues in ethnographic research. *Science and Engineering Ethics, 15*, 135–160.

Sinuff, T., Cook, D. J., & Giacomini, M. (2007). How qualitative research can contribute to research in the intensive care unit. *Journal of Critical Care, 22*, 104–111. doi: 10.1016/j.jcrc.2007.03.001

Sparks, L., Villagran, M. M., Parker-Raley, J., & Cunningham, C. B. (2007). A patient-centered approach to breaking bad news: Communication guidelines for health care providers. *Journal of Applied Communication Research, 35*, 177–196.

Spiegelberg, E. (Ed.). (1981). *The phenomenological movement: A historical introduction (Phaenomenologica)* (3rd ed. rev.). New York: Springer.

Spradley, J. P. (1979). *The ethnographic interview.* New York: Holt, Rinehart, and Winston.

Stewart, D. W., Shamdasani, P. N., & Rook, D. W. (2007). *Focus groups: Theory and practice* (2nd ed.). Thousand Oaks, CA: Sage.

Taylor, S. (Ed.). (2002). *Ethnographic research: A reader.* Thousand Oaks, CA: Sage.

ten Have, P. (2007). *Doing conversation analysis* (2nd ed.). Thousand Oaks, CA: Sage.

Vande Berg, L., & Trujillo, N. (2008). *Cancer and death: A love story in two voices.* Cresskill, NJ: Hampton.

Van Maanen, J. (1988). *Tales of the field: On writing ethnography.* Chicago: University of Chicago Press.

Wengraf, T. (2001). *Qualitative research interviewing: Biographic narrative and semi-structured methods.* Thousand Oaks, CA: Sage.

Wilkinson, C., & McAndrew, S. (2008). "I'm not an outsider, I'm his mother!" A phenomenological enquiry into career experiences of exclusion from acute psychiatric settings. *International Journal of Mental Health Nursing, 17*, 392–401.

Zimmerman, D. H., & Boden, D. (1991). Structure-in-action: An introduction. In D. Boden & D. H. Zimmerman (Eds.), *Talk and social structure: Studies in ethnomethodology and conversation analysis* (pp. 3–21). Berkeley: University of California Press.

35

COMMUNITY ORGANIZING
RESEARCH APPROACHES

James W. Dearing, Bridget Gaglio, and Borsika A. Rabin

A broad perspective on what constitutes a community means that "the community" can refer to a neighborhood or town or city block, as well as to the people who live and work there. Community also refers to the social interactions among those individuals, to the identification that they feel toward the place and each other, and to the normative expectations and consequent behaviors in which they engage as members of a commons. When individuals feel involved, when they feel that others listen to them, when they perceive that they share things in common with a defined group of others, they feel a sense of community. Residents can share a neighborhood and never know one another, thus feeling a low degree of community, just as members of a breast cancer discussion board scattered throughout the world can develop strong affect and feel a high degree of community.

For many years, community organizing has been a valued approach for the betterment of communities. This means of social change has been practiced worldwide by rural outreach workers and urban residents, paid staff of government change agencies, as well as outraged unpaid social movement activists, and researchers who ostensibly seek to explain efforts at change and, more often than not, also try to intervene with the observed community. More recently, community organizing has become recognized as an approach to social change that can produce community-level capabilities which can be deployed again and again as new problems or opportunities arise. These capabilities include knowing who in each organization to contact to invite into new improvement efforts, knowing which organizations have technologies and infrastructure that can be accessed for a community-wide effort, and understanding which of these people and organizations can best bring a broad range of stakeholders to focus on a topic and draw out their continued participation. Process capabilities like these transcend the topically defined objectives of health campaigns, programs, and policies in affecting substantive problems such as infant mortality, health disparities, and unjust living conditions.

The Carter Center is a case in point. The Carter Center has become an important international philanthropy in "waging peace, fighting disease" in Africa. As its primary means of getting effective public health innovations to the people who most need them, the center worked to recruit, train, and support thousands of community-based volunteers in Ethiopia for the control of Guinea worm. Center staff, led by Donald Hopkins, vice president of health programs, didn't pursue the creation of a network of community-based volunteers as a transferable skill set. But Guinea worm control worked well. Staff quickly perceived that the capacity they had built among community members could be tapped again, this time for the control of onchocerciasis, or river blindness, a black fly-based parasitic disease caused by tiny worms that multiply in humans. Control of river blindness is very challenging because it most infects the poorest of the poor who cannot afford protection against flies. The volunteer network proved perfectly suited to reaching out into poor communities. Then the center tapped the same volunteer network to fight trachoma, again with success, and then malaria, by having the volunteers distribute millions of bed nets, focusing on homes with pregnant women and children younger than five.

When it works best, capacity building results in a renewable resource of transferable skills that can be applied again and again. The Carter Center's work is a strong example of community organizing by first building the capacity of the community in question by training them with new skills so that they can then carry out new coordinated activities.

In this chapter, we illustrate the range of community organizing through several examples, and focus on four dimensions of transferable process capabilities: readiness, organizational process, capacity building, and social capital. Each of these dimensions can be measured for the purpose of research or evaluation of community organizing.

The Problem: Weak Communities, Strong Organized Systems

A *community* has traditionally been understood as an informally organized set of loose associations among residents. Based on intrinsic and shared interests, people gather in voluntary association. As citizens (a political term meaning "one who controls") rather than clients (with the Greek root "one who is controlled"), residents are free to be creative, communicate together, express feelings, and over time develop and reflect shared norms. This use of the term "community" is consistent with classical definitions in the community development literature in which people, place, social interaction, and psychological identification are described as necessary elements of a community (Christenson & Robinson, 1989). We consider mediated spaces, too, to be places in which people engage in social interaction and with which they may psychologically identify. Thus, for example, we include online and virtual discussion boards in our definition of community organizing.

Communities coexist with organized systems (transportation systems, health care systems, restaurant associations, etc.). *Organized systems* function to control resources in order to produce standardized practices and outcomes. Organized systems depend upon consumers (i.e., clients) to buy or use their products and services. For example, a local education system may include public and private schools, school districts and policy boards, state, county, and city jurisdictions that provide funding and maintain oversight of school curricula and performance, parent–teacher organizations, and teacher unions as well as children and their parents. An organized system does not have to be either efficient or effective in order to be powerful. A local government can, by virtue of formalized rules and procedures, discourage understanding and stifle participation by residents, thus maintaining centralized control. Yet some organized systems are both efficient and effective; communities rarely are either.

The U.S. Environmental Protection Agency's Technical Outreach Services for Communities (TOSC) Program illustrates the challenges of community organizing when representatives of organized systems seek to help communities. In partnership with universities, TOSC worked in 21 heavily contaminated communities to help residents understand the links between toxic waste in their communities, health outcomes, and options for cleanup. One community designated by the EPA as a TOSC site was Boston's Dudley

Street neighborhood. Dudley Street was characterized by heavy and light industry, low income residents, and more than 1,000 houses burnt by arsons and vandals. The resulting 1,300 vacant lots attracted nighttime trash haulers who illegally dumped mounds of garbage. Dudley Street was the poorest neighborhood in Massachusetts, with Boston's highest rates of unemployment and violent crime. In 1993, the state listed 54 hazardous waste sites along Dudley Street. TOSC staff at two universities decided to work through a progressive neighborhood association, the Dudley Street Neighborhood Initiative (DSNI), to involve residents in understanding their toxic waste problems, and in making decisions about what to do. But involvement by community residents other than community-based organization staff and representatives from the Mayor's Office was elusive. Community attendance at meetings was low; organizing of residents, unsuccessful. DSNI staff did credit the TOSC program and its university staff with providing money that helped in reaching out to other community organizations and thus raising the issue of toxic waste contamination on city agendas. But the TOSC aims for Dudley Street went unfulfilled.

Many efforts at community organizing are directed toward contacting voluntary associations. An absence of zoning standards may serve the interests of realtors and of the construction industry; a lack of green space may serve the commercial interests of shopping mall developers and retail business owners; a poor performing mass transit system may serve the interests of automobile sales and repair shops. A high rate of crime in some neighborhoods generates business sales of home security systems, auto alarms, and enrollment in self-defense courses. Conditions like these reflect degrees of community-level *disorganization*. Conditions like these provide the spark that ignites the social process of community organizing. Conditions like these also explain why the social process of community organizing can be political, economic, and polarizing. Communication theorists and researchers recognize the opportunities associated with applied and translational science in these situations, acknowledging the critical core issue associated with organizing communities.

Community Organizing Basics

What does the organizing of a community involve? Is intention on the part of an organizer necessary? Can initiative originate from multiple points inside as well as outside of a community? How participative must community members be for community organizing to have occurred? And must the result of organizing be collective action or can individual behavior change be considered an organizing outcome?

Organizing in communities occurs in response to perceived need. The perception of need may arise from the experience of a private resident, unaffiliated with any particular solution within the community, as when a neighbor gets fed up with her daily walk by a vacant lot where children play among garbage and rodents. This type of community resident may be considered especially "authentic" and be highly valued by others because, presumably unlooked for, she experiences the problem in her daily life. She volunteers her time to address the problem; she is accorded special status in the process of organizing. Her lack of affiliation with a particular nonprofit or governmental organization means that others perceive her as being able to validly speak for other residents who are presumed homophilous in some important ways. Frequently, however, the local community members who come to be involved in addressing a felt need do so by virtue of their professional role as public health workers, city planners, or university professors. Their professional role does not preclude them from feeling strong affect about a problem or its solution or from being personally affected by either. Yet a professional role can lead others to call into question the local professional's objectivity or, more often, her authenticity as a member of the community.

The perception that a community has a problem which should be solved can also arise from outside the community in a *change agency*, an organization with a mission of improving some aspect of community life and from which some of those with professional roles who align with an issue may come. A state epidemiologist might rank-order counties by percent of immunization refusals, and based on that could then decide which counties have a need for education about the importance of immunization for children. A national rural health association may produce a report that identifies areas of the country where residents are especially disadvantaged by disparities in access to health services. This concern of locus of control in the identification of and solution to community problems is often at issue during community organizing processes. Sometimes, in not very transparent social change processes, locus of control can be ambiguous, oftentimes strategically so. Locus of control over community organizing can also be dynamic. An external change agency such as a private foundation commits to a community organizing effort for a limited period of time, anticipating that a community-based partnership or organization will take over the responsibility. Similarly, when a research team's study period ends, their organizing effort typically stops.

Community organizing can be conceptualized as one of four types of social action according to where problems and solutions are believed to exist. When individual community members help each other to solve individual but commonly experienced problems (as in our breast cancer discussion board example), individuals help themselves on the basis of what community members suggest to them. When community members see themselves as the solution to a problem for which they blame institutions, community organizing is grassroots activism. When technical experts working in institutions identify behavioral changes that need to occur among a population segment in order to improve community conditions, a behavior change campaign is mounted. When experts in institutions identify system or policy changes that need to occur, community organizing takes the form of a social ecology intervention bringing stakeholders together in a decision-making partnership that seeks interinstitutional answers to institutional problems. So our broad perspective on community organizing spans cases from Internet-based collective action to grassroots social movements to externally initiated social planning and community development projects (Walter, 1997). In some cases, "the community" is the generative source of change and fully involved; in others, it is only involved through representative members in an advisory or expert role. Table 35.1 summarizes these four types of social action.

Many studies of community organizing have focused on how well institutions are able to mobilize communities to address problems, especially place-bound communities in which internal or external change agencies seek to improve conditions such as poor access to health care services by low-income residents. Many times in such a case, a monitoring agency such as a city department of public health or a technical expert such as a state department epidemiologist identifies an unmet need in an underserved population segment. Identification of the problem is made by people external to the affected community, whether they live locally or not. The technical expert, often inclusive of health communication researchers, is someone whose access to affected members of a community cannot be assumed. They may be perceived as trusted if they share enough behavioral, experiential, and demographic traits with an affected community. Often, even for the insider, trust must be earned through a process of engagement which requires a skill set lacking in many researchers (Horowitz, Robinson, & Seifer, 2009).

Table 35.1 Locus of Problems and Solutions in Community Organizing

	The Solution is....	
	In Individuals	In Institutions
The Problem is...		
In Individuals	Self-Help	Behavior Change Campaigns
In Institutions	Grassroots Activism	Social Ecology Interventions

Source: Dearing (2003).

A number of scholars have identified similar steps in the process of community organizing or mobilization:

- Community assessment;
- Creation of a core leadership group;
- Development of a plan of action;
- Attraction of mass support;
- Implementation of the action plan;
- Organizational maintenance and change institutionalization; and
- Evaluation of projects and outcomes.

Since organizing in such cases is not initiated by affected community members but rather by technical experts, many interventionists and scholars of citizen mobilization emphasize the importance of community-based participatory research, community engagement, local ownership over change processes, and the building of community capacity. These are efforts to move the locus of control into the community. Doing so can heighten the likelihood that solutions will be compatible with community context and that solutions will be sustained because of felt ownership.

More problematic and at least as prevalent is community organizing that is begun for a broad range of local challenges and for which local organized systems such as school systems or health care networks will contribute to solutions. This type of social ecology or comprehensive community intervention typically forms a broad-based partnership of representatives from an array of organizations that then give rise to a series of interventions such as an afterschool program for youth, a bicycle helmet distribution program, a youth leadership academy, health education curriculum for schools, and the introduction of municipal policies for more bike lanes and playgrounds (Dearing, 2003). Social ecology interventions that try to take comprehensive approaches to a broad problem-set (such as adolescent health) depend heavily on citizen and representative input to identify issues, decide on solutions, and prioritize both. When the group process does not reflect the community input, conflict can result. For example, when citizens are asked to rank priorities for improvements to guide the expenditures of tax dollars aimed at decreasing youth access to harmful substances but the activities undertaken reflect none of the citizen input, it is likely to create hostility in those who volunteered their opinions. Tensions persist and, rather than dissipate, lie latent to resurface in the wake of other, later efforts at community organizing (Medved et al., 2001).

While it is common to assess organizing efforts according to developmental stages such as problem identification, convening of a stakeholder governance group, decisions about and implementation of a series of health interventions, and so on, we group our suggestions about research approaches according to four intermediate outcomes of organizing. While scholars have titled these four intermediate outcomes differently, we find their meanings of these four intermediate outcomes to be quite consistent. They are:

- *Readiness,* including that of individuals and their community, and of the change agency (if any) and the initiative or intervention;
- *Organizational process,* including group process measures of inclusion, participation, and decision making;
- *Capacity building,* in which individuals, organizations, and communities can be measured in terms of empowerment and new capacities; and
- *Social capital,* in which relational measures of communication networks among stakeholders can reflect lasting collective efficacy.

Readiness

Prior to engaging in a community organizing effort, many researchers and external change agencies want an indication of the extent to which a particular community is prepared, psychologically and organizationally, for change. The operative assumption is that only a community that is cognizant of a problem, and agrees that the problem should be seen as an important public issue deserving of solution, has the capability, and is motivated to do so, is likely to do well in organizing for action and demonstrating positive results. Results from a readiness assessment can, for example, suggest which of a set of communities—each preselected on the basis of high need—will most likely respond favorably to a community organizing invitation and be capable of marshaling local resources to address the problem.

The idea of assessing readiness grew out of theorizing about how people change and general support for stage-based models of individual behavior change. Stages of change have been shown to be good predictors of, for example, smoking cessation outcomes (Prochaska, DiClemente, Velicer, & Rossi, 1993) with multiple questionnaire instruments demonstrating favorable psychometric properties.

At the level of a geographic community, additional variables become important for assessing readiness. Psychometric measurement of an individual's readiness to engage in community organizing change cannot be taken as a valid indicator of a community's likely success at changing a problem. Even motivated individuals who are excited to organize a community around a problem and possible solutions often face challenging organizational and public policy barriers due to the multilevel complexity of our communities (Schensul, 2009). Community readiness is better assessed on the basis of understanding prior community efforts at addressing a problem, the degree of awareness in the community of the problem, perceived salience of the problem, extant leadership and its involvement in the problem, community climate, the extent to which knowledge about the problem is available and shared in the community, and community resources available to address the problem (Kelly et al., 2003). Answers to questions about these dimensions of readiness can then be used to categorize a community into one of a series of stages each of which is associated with different strategies for community organizing activity (Edwards, Jumper-Thurman, Plested, Oetting, & Swanson, 2000). The answers to questions about readiness dimensions can also be used to surface minority community perspectives about a particular problem and the community's prior organizing efforts.

A community health improvement project initiated by the W. K. Kellogg Foundation illustrates the use of readiness criteria. Led by Gloria Smith and Pat Babcock, health policy experts at the foundation, a test was conceived to study whether broad-based community partnerships could become sustainable means for generating new and effective public health and clinical services projects to better serve disadvantaged populations. This effort became the foundation's $23 million eight-year Comprehensive Community Health Models (CCHMs) initiative. Foundation staff, along with a technical services intermediary organization created just for CCHMs grantees, conducted a readiness assessment of Michigan counties to identify those counties to invite into the CCHM's initiative. After selecting three counties, the foundation helped to establish and then worked with a community partnership in each county to hire an entrepreneurial team that could implement the work decided upon by each partnership, and generate new projects to improve community health. Key process objectives were to broaden the representativeness of the stakeholders "around the table" making decisions about health and to increase their voice in planning decisions.

Ultimately, local stakeholders contributed more than a 1:1 match of the monies spent in their counties by the foundation. A number of novel projects were created, such as Miles of Smiles, a bus outfitted as a dental clinic which partnered with local McDonald's restaurants to screen and treat children on the spot. CCHMs were part of a wave of community organizing investments by private foundations to test the relationship between the creation of community partnerships and their ability to produce effective community improvement projects.

Several community readiness assessment tools have been developed and validated as semistructured telephone-based interview protocols for use with key informants (e.g., Slater et al., 2005). This approach to data collection can be used for pre–post comparison, and was designed to gather the perspectives of diverse persons within a community who are especially knowledgeable and influential regarding a particular issue. Sampling for such an approach to interview data collection can use a snowball procedure in which the first participants are contacted on the basis of their broad knowledge of the community; they are asked for their recommendations of who should be interviewed so that the snowball begins with the second set of contacted persons. Each set of interviewees is asked the protocol questions as well as for their suggestions of who else should be interviewed. An example of this type of sociometric question is: "Who in this community do you go to for advice about new ideas in environmental conservation?" When the names generated are mostly those of people who have already been interviewed, the snowball procedure data collection is complete.

Another example of a readiness tool is the Community Healthy Living Index (Kim et al., 2009) created to measure support for physical activity and healthy eating by cataloguing current community conditions and suggesting opportunities for community improvement. The tool, based in literature and expert panel reviews, has five subindices assessing schools, after-school child care settings, work sites, neighborhoods, and the community as a whole. Community organizing teams of key stakeholders are the intended users of the Index, which has been shown to help community planners engage in improvement activities. As of February 2009, more than 150 communities had been trained in use of the Index.

Departments of community health often have epidemiological archival data as well as lists of community-based service providers for specific health problems that can, in conjunction, serve as a basis for conducting a gap analysis of local population needs, on the one hand, and service provision to address that need, on the other. Gap analyses can suggest not only extent of need (service "gaps") but also overcapacity in the case of too many local agencies targeting the same problem for the same population segment, or extensive organizational responses to what are only minor health problems at a community level.

Organizational Process

Organizational process refers to the convening of a decision-making group such as a community coalition and how it functions as a goal-directed group in deciding upon and implementing specific health improvement projects. Community health improvement efforts, in which an external or internal change agency plays a determining and a convening role, can be assessed in terms of the interorganizational process that they put into motion. An example of this role is the Carter Center's work to control malaria and other diseases in Africa.

Organizational process consists of the group functions of inclusion (who is at the meeting table), participation (the extent to which those at the table contribute their ideas), and decision making (the style of facilitation and procedures of voting). How the conveners, staff, and leaders of a group plan for and structure these aspects of group process can make or break an attempt at organizing a community. If an organizational process is very inclusive, some of the stakeholders to an organizing effort will not be prior collaborators, so a period during which the group members are allowed to become comfortable with one another is often necessary. Prior collaborations may have been limited to interorganizational relationships within but not across political and social divisions, which can mean that the larger group may exhibit factions. Highly inclusive organizing efforts bring together competitors. For example, private health care organizations are oftentimes invited to take part in community organizing efforts by philanthropic or governmental conveners. Community-based organizations that serve different disadvantaged segments of a community and compete for grants are also sought out as representatives of minority populations into which they presumably have access. As a result, stakeholders often engage in community organizing efforts with something less than enthusiasm. Prior negative experiences shape their expectations; ulterior motives are presumed; and trust is low with surveillance more the norm than the sharing of information.

Multiple methods are available for studying organizational processes of inclusion, participation, and decision making. These include evaluative forms that ask participants for their opinions of coalition objectives, meeting effectiveness, leadership and meeting facilitation, and checklists that prompt participants to think through what should be a part of each specific health improvement project decided upon by a coalition. Monthly tracking of organizational processes, some objective indicators of achievements, and subjective assessments of participant opinions can serve both as measures of organizational progress and diagnostics for members to periodically assess and improve their group performance (Goodman, Wandersman, Chinman, Imm, & Morrissey, 1996). Doing a good job at inclusion, participation, and decision making takes diligence. These are dynamic group-level relational variables that may ebb and flow partly in reaction to external conditions, partly in reaction to changes in personnel, and also as a result of learning by the group. Because of the passionate desire of many participants in community organizing efforts to make tangible progress in problem reduction, frustration with the deliberate pace of group process is common. Participants may respond to frustration with putting in place efficiency practices in the organizational process, such as less inclusive meetings, abbreviated discussion, and authoritative decision making.

Researchers and evaluators of coalition organizational process are well-advised to collect data over time so that changes in inclusion, participation, and decision making can be documented and explained. At the overarching level of a coalition, the effective group may be that partnership which intentionally keeps things difficult; that is, the processes of inclusion, participation, and decision making are not short-circuited for the sake of efficiency. Action is, of course, of paramount importance to participants; but efficiency is more desirable in the delimited province of the goal-directed projects that are spun-off from the community partnership. At the broad level of the coalition, having realistic expectations about the time required to create and operate functional community partnerships is important. Realistic expectations are especially important when inclusiveness is achieved and maintained since diversity appears to negatively affect certain aspects of group member interactions (George & Chattopadhyay, 2008).

Inclusion can be operationalized by combining background interviews with key stakeholders to illuminate political divisions and organizational alliances in a community; survey results with organizational representatives who have been invited to participate in an organizing effort to learn about their prior involvement with others in the community; and archival records of who was invited to join an organizing effort and who is present at meetings. Many community coalitions see declining diversity over time in the people who take part in meetings. Simple over-time tracking of attendance and types of stakeholders present at meetings and events can suggest the extent to which an effort at community organizing is able to remain inclusive rather than become exclusive.

Because so much of community organizing often occurs in group meetings, behavioral indicators of participation and decision making can be observed by researchers. Leaders' attempts to draw out and motivate participants; clarity and understanding of messages and objectives; meeting facilitators' relevancy to the task at hand; conflict resolution skill, perceptions of fairness and respect; boredom with lack of progress: many aspects of participation and decision making can be qualitatively noted by process observers or quantitatively assessed on the spot using structured coding forms. Seeing can too easily be believing, so observation depends on careful training and systematic technique, and interpretive follow-up through circular validation with participants and informants (Dearing, Waters, & Rogers, 2005).

Capacity Building

In terms of community organizing, a *capacity* is a resource that can be used to achieve an objective. The topic of capacity building has been operationalized expansively as: dimensions of citizen participation and leadership, skills, resources, social and interorganizational networks, sense of community, understanding of community history, community power, and community values. We take a narrower perspective based in empowerment, a learning process by which individuals, organizations, and communities acting in concert gain mastery over their affairs. Engagement in community organizing can be either empowering or disempowering to individuals depending on the nature of the organizing experience.

Zimmerman (2000) defines empowerment at three levels: psychological, organizational, and community. Psychological empowerment includes beliefs about one's own competence, behaviors to exert the self, and an awareness of obstacles to one's greater control over and ability to work within circumstances. Psychological empowerment also includes the learning of group process skills and decision-making skills, practice participating in group meetings, and understanding how resources are managed, all of which can lead to a greater sense of control, critical awareness, and participatory behaviors (Zimmerman, 2000). Measurement of individual-level empowerment can reflect both theses empowering processes and outcomes of becoming empowered. Measurement is well-suited to close-ended questionnaires with scaled response categories, though alternative approaches are possible, including observation of individuals and personal narratives (Narayan, 2006).

At the organizational level of a social movement, a decision-making group, or a broad-based community coalition, processes of empowerment can be conceptualized and measured as shared beliefs, shared expectations or intentions for betterment, shared sense of responsibilities or internalized locus of control, and shared acceptance of leadership responsibilities. Organization-level empowerment outcomes can include the organization's success in applying for and receiving grants and contracts, communication, cooperation, and collaboration with other organizations, and the extent to which the organization is able to affect policy agendas and decision making.

Community empowerment processes can be operationalized as access to resources, the extent to which local government is open to citizen participation, and tolerance for diversity (Zimmerman, 2000). Outcomes at the community level can include the tangible programs and projects to which community organizing can give birth, and changed practices and policies of local government. Both organization-level and community-level empowerment can be measured through tracking of organizational and community records that can be content-analyzed, and interviews with key stakeholders.

Social Capital

Social capital can be defined as resources embedded in a social structure which are accessed or mobilized in purposive actions. A community's social capital is both its network of relations and what is available through that network. Availability of social capital is dependent on one's position within a network; network structure both enables and constrains one's opportunity to access and use resources. While social capital is often written about as a "public" good (Coleman, 1988), clearly some actors have differential access to more of it than others, based on who they are and who they know.

Social capital can be put to a range of productive uses, from good to bad. A community that is high in social capital can be a community that is insular, closed, and isolationist, as manifest in a dominant "old boy's network." In general, communities as a whole benefit the most when their networks are diverse, inclusive, flexible, horizontal (linking those of similar status or in similar structural positions), vertical (linking those of different status or in different structural positions), tie together organizations, and have links to people and organizations in other communities. So the goal for a community is not simply more social capital, but better social capital by including more diverse individuals and organizations that might not normally be a part of planning processes.

Informal relational assets include the personal contacts that can be accessed through community members' social networks, as well as the routinized but not institutionalized relationships between people in agencies and organizations. Formal relational assets include interagency agreements, memorandums of understanding between organizations, and contracts. Interorganizational relations can be distinguished, for example, by their extensiveness and how committed each organization is to a relationship or to the network. The social capital accumulated through these relationships can be of two types: it can result from "reciprocity transactions," when people do favors for others, and from "enforceable trust," when people act in response to system or community norms that prescribe their action for the benefit of others.

Social network analysis is a perspective and method that is well-suited to measuring social capital (see Valente in this volume). Social network analysis can be used to describe by mapping the nature of local communication, advice-seeking, or collaboration among organizations for a certain topic such as health care or public health improvement, all of which has demonstrated advantages for both the organizations and the individuals concerned. For example, board members and executive staff involved in interlocking directorates share strategic information and advice; technical staff and specialists engage in know-how trading to solve on-the-job problems even if it means sharing proprietary information across direct competitors in the same city. And leaders decrease organizational risk and personal uncertainty when confronted with innovations from outside the organization by seeking out the opinions and experiences of other leaders in functionally similar organizations.

Increasingly, the social network perspective, its set of analytic tools, and network analysis programs are being seen as useful for the planning, monitoring, and assessment of community health organizing interventions when objectives are greater collaboration and joint problem solving across organizations, or the involvement of organizations serving diverse segments of the population that are not typically involved in health planning in the community (Luke & Harris, 2007). Network mapping can reveal how organizational engagement in community organizing is related to resource allocation, political factions, and the dynamics of organizational legitimacy.

Network analysis is well-suited to capture the expansion of a successful grassroots social movement, such as MADD. When a five-time convicted drunk driver struck Candy Lightner's 13-year-old daughter Cari so hard that his car knocked the teenager out of her shoes and immediately killed her, disbelief and sadness gave way to outrage that became one of the fastest growing grassroots social movements in U.S. history. The nascent Mothers Against Drunk Drivers, from its organizational home in Cari's still decorated bedroom, grew into MADD—with emphasis on the harmful behavior rather than stigma toward those committing the act. Chapters in all 50 states, a prominent presence with federal and state legislators, a massive volunteer force and courtroom adjudication monitoring network, and institutionalized relationships with the largest corporations have organized around this movement.

Candy Lightner and her new collaborators each had a passionate reason for joining together. Broadcast again and again through emotional mass media stories, their intensity was a signal to similarly affected siblings, mothers, fathers, and grandparents of how they too could get involved to right a societal wrong. By 2009, MADD had proven instrumental in the passage of hundreds of laws raising the minimum drinking age, requiring blood alcohol concentration testing, establishing sobriety checkpoints, lowering blood alcohol concentration levels for determining intoxication, and requiring revocation of driving licenses. The annual number of deaths in the United States due to drunk driving has fallen from 30,000 in 1980 when Cari Lightner was killed to about 17,000 per year now, a saving of 350,000 lives.

Intermediate Processes as Organizing Outcomes

Seen in terms of readiness to engage in change, organizational processes of inclusion, participation, and decision making, capacity in terms of individual, organizational, and community empowerment, and social capital via interorganizational relationships in a community, community problems such as crime or teenage pregnancy can be understood as problems of community disorganization. Organizing through heightened readiness and more inclusive group processes, and the nurturing of empowerment and enabling broader access to networked resources become the solutions. And community organizing can proceed in multiple ways, as we have shown in several case-examples (see Table 35.2).

An emphasis on community organizing variables as important outcomes of people acting in concert can be expected to be a hard sell to communities as well as to change initiative

Table 35.2 Types of Social Action, Locus of Control, and Community Organizing Dimensions in Four Examples

	Community Organizing Examples			
	TOSC	Carter Center	CCHMs	MADD
Types of Social Action				
Self-Help	No	No	No	No
Grassroots Activism	No	No	No	Yes
Behavior Change Campaigns	No	Yes	No	No
Social Ecology Interventions	Yes	No	Yes	No
Locus of Control				
External Initiation	Yes	Yes	Yes	No
Community Residents Involved	No	Yes	No	Yes
Community Organizations Involved	Yes	Yes	Yes	No
Diffusion Beyond Initial Site	No	Yes	No	Yes
Community Organizing Dimensions				
Readiness	Yes	Yes	Yes	No
Organizational Process	Yes	No	Yes	No
Capacity Building	Yes	Yes	No	Yes
Social Capital	No	No	No	Yes

sponsors. The latter are focused on health outcomes. Reducing the rate of sexually transmitted disease or improving the nutrition of single mothers are, to most people, more intuitively important objectives than, say, increasing the level of trust within an interorganizational network of community health workers. Yet readiness, organizational process skills, capacities to address problems, and the nurturing of productive social capital are generic core assets that, once developed, can be applied again and again to community challenges across the health communication spectrum. Research has shown positive relationships between these types of processes and health-related behaviors. This is the first of two rationales for emphasizing the importance of intermediate processes as outcomes worthy of measuring and reporting. The second rationale for focusing on intermediate processes as important outcomes of community organizing is that they are logically and directly related to institutionalization and sustainability. Skills, capacities, and tools for improving readiness, group processes, capacities, and relational capital *stay with the individual*. External and internal change agencies necessarily end their involvement with community organizing efforts, but the positive process benefits of community organizing can be sustained through skill learning and retention by individuals. This perspective requires health communication researchers to argue for the importance and inclusion of process variables in their study designs, not just as explanatory variables for observed outcomes of organizing, but as key transferable capabilities in their own right.

Innovations in Community Organizing

Health communication researchers are subject to the dominant paradigms in evidence-based medicine and evidence-based public health. Both medicine and public health have adopted the top-down, center-outward metaphor of translational science as a narrowing funnel. Basic scientists conduct many efficacy trials designed to assess internal validity; that subset of devices, drugs, practices, and processes found to work to improve some outcome under controlled laboratory conditions may then proceed to effectiveness trials that move from the lab to the clinic, thereby introducing degrees of uncontrolled factors into the tests to assess their external validity (so-called practical trials). Externally validated innovations then can be tested one against another in comparative effectiveness research designs.

One contribution that health communication researchers interested in the study of community organizing can make is to question this metaphor of research-to-practice translation. Are formal research tests really the source of what occurs in real-world health care and public health practice? Or is the degree of program or intervention adaptation sometimes so considerable that the users are as much creators as were the initial researchers? Do most health care providers and public health officers really look first to distant researchers when they see an opportunity for improving the health of their constituents? Some public health researchers have suggested that if we want more evidence-based practice we might start with more practice-based evidence. This is good advice. Yet in many cases it does not go far enough. To what extent do health care providers and public health workers first look to each other for innovations in health care and disease prevention? To what extent do new approaches to community organizing move from community to community without any research involvement? Health communication researchers can empirically explore these questions of social networking, diffusion of innovation, and communities of practice. Health communication researchers could also study the relative worth of new practices. Is the research-based innovation inherently more effective due to its internal validity than is the community-generated innovation with its proven external validity? Innovations in community organizing that spring from communities are steeped in community context; only the ones that are most compatible with community life will survive. But should they? Are they effective means of organizing for better health? We believe that health communication researchers can bring real value to answering questions such as these and in so doing bring a critical perspective to dominant assumptions about how we can best improve health care delivery and public health in communities.

References

Christenson, J. A., & Robinson, Jr., J. W. (Eds.). (1989) *Community development in perspective*. Ames, Iowa: Iowa State University Press.

Coleman, J. S. (1988). Social capital in the creation of human capital. *American Journal of Sociology, 94* (Supplement), S95–S120.

Dearing, J. W. (2003). The state of the art and the state of the science of community organizing. In T. L. Thompson, A. M. Dorsey, K. I. Miller, & R. Parrott (Eds.), *Handbook of health communication* (pp. 207–220). Mahwah, NJ: Erlbaum.

Dearing, J. W., Waters, W. F., & Rogers, E. M. (2005). Observational research in global health communications. In M. Haider (Ed.), *Global public health communication: Challenges, perspectives, and strategies* (pp. 67–89). Sudbury, MA: Jones & Bartlett.

Edwards, R. W., Jumper-Thurman, P., Plested, B. A., Oetting, E. R., & Swanson, L. (2000). Community readiness: Research to practice. *Journal of Community Psychology, 28*, 291–307.

George, E., & Chattopadhyay, P. (2008). Group composition and decision making. In G. P. Hodgkinson & W. H. Starbuck (Eds.), *The Oxford handbook of organizational decision making* (pp. 361–379). Oxford, England: Oxford University Press.

Goodman, R. M., Wandersman, A., Chinman, M., Imm, P., & Morrissey, E. (1996). An ecological assessment of community-based interventions for prevention and health promotion: Approaches to measuring community coalitions. *American Journal of Community Psychology, 24*, 33–61.

Horowitz, C. R., Robinson, M., & Seifer, S. (2009). Community-based participatory research from the margin to the mainstream: Are researchers prepared? *Circulation, 119,* 2633–2642.

Kelly, K. J., Plested, B .A., Edwards, R. W., Jumper-Thurman, P., Comello, M. L. G., & Slater, M. D. (2003). The community readiness model: A complementary approach to social marketing. *Marketing Theory, 3,* 411–425.

Kim, S., Adamson, K. C., Balfanz, D. R., Brownson, R. C., Wiecha, J. L., Shepard, D., ... Alles, W. F. (2009). Development of the community health living index: A tool to foster healthy environments for the prevention of obesity and chronic disease [Supplement 1]. *Preventive Medicine,* S80–S85.

Luke, D. A., & Harris, J. A. (2007). Network analysis in public health: History, methods, and applications. *Annual Review of Public Health, 28,* 69–93.

Medved, C. E., Morrison, K., Dearing, J. W., Larson, R. S., Cline, G., & Brummans, B. H. J. M. (2001). Tensions in community health improvement initiatives: Communication and collaboration in a managed car environment. *Journal of Applied Communication Research, 29,* 137–152.

Narayan, D. (2006). *Measuring empowerment: Cross-disciplinary perspectives.* Oxford, England: Oxford University Press.

Prochaska, J. O., DiClemente, C. C., Velicer, W. F., & Rossi, J. S. (1993). Standardized, individualized, interactive, and personalized self-help programs for smoking cessation. *Health Psychology, 12,* 399–405.

Schensul, J. J. (2009). Community, culture and sustainability in multilevel dynamic systems intervention science. *American Journal of Community Psychology, 43,* 241–256.

Slater, M. D., Edwards, R. W., Plested, B. A., Thurman, P. J., Kelly, K. J., Comello, M. L. G., ... Keefe, T. J. (2005). Using community readiness key informant assessments in a randomized group prevention trial: Impact of a participatory community-media intervention. *Journal of Community Health, 30,* 39–53.

Walter, C. L. (1997). Community building practice. In M. Minkler (Ed.), *Community organizing and community building for health* (pp. 68–83). New Brunswick, NJ: Rutgers University Press.

Zimmerman, M. A. (2000). Empowerment theory. In J. Rappaport & E. Seidman (Eds.), *Handbook of community psychology* (pp. 43–63). New York: Kluwer Academic.

36

ADVANCING HEALTH COMMUNICATION RESEARCH

Issues and Controversies in Research Design and Data Analysis

Michael T. Stephenson, Brian G. Southwell, and Marco Yzer

We have seen remarkable growth in the amount of health communication literature over the past decade. Recent editorial experiences at two of the leading journals in this area—*Health Communication* and the *Journal of Health Communication*—illustrate this point. *Health Communication* began its run in 1989 with four issues; today, it publishes eight issues and recently increased the physical size of the journal yet again so that more articles could be included in each issue. In 1996, *Journal of Health Communication* had only four issues per volume; in 2009 it published eight. Despite the increase, the acceptance rates have remained low. Indeed, researchers are more likely than ever now to label their work as being relevant to "health communication" while more and more researchers are attempting to contribute to the literature.

If such increased volume represented increasingly fine efforts to focus on a stable set of questions and phenomena, we might expect that new health communication researchers would need only to understand a limited number of basic research tools; the action would be in subtle advances in theory development. At first glance, however, the growth in health communication literature seems to have expanded in breadth rather than having narrowed our gaze in terms of research questions. At the same time, we also have an expanding chest of statistical tools available, giving authors both helpful resources but also, frankly, sometimes unhelpful temptation.

The increasingly complicated array of methods employed by health communication scholars is not solely a function of trendiness, of course. Rather than focusing solely on "communication" projects, for example, health communication researchers are increasingly working in interdisciplinary teams, as discussed by Parrott and Kreuter in this volume. Health communication researchers are now challenged to keep up with the statistical and methodological innovations that are increasingly central to other disciplines and subfields. For example, we have recently seen applications of neuroimaging techniques to understand health message processing (e.g., Anderson et al. 2006). Moreover, statistical advancements have informed new norms and standards that slowly, but steadily, are being adopted by health communication researchers. There are many such advancements: consider examples such as using multilevel modeling for campaign evaluation (Southwell, 2005); reporting effect sizes in addition to statistical significance levels (DeVaney, 2001); using bootstrap methods in small sample mediation analysis (Shrout & Bolger, 2002); avoiding principal component analysis for factor analysis (Fabrigar, Wegener, MacCallum, & Strahan, 1999); or conducting a priori power analysis (Cohen, 1992). All such innovations are noteworthy for their departure from previous health communication literature, but, as separate methodological tools and advice, such innovations will only be part of an appropriate strategy to take health communication research to a higher level.

Chapter Overview

In our view, a chapter on methodological and statistical issues in a handbook of health communication should not address these patterns by simply cataloging what's new in the toolkit for health communication researchers. Instead, we opt to focus on some prevalent dilemmas that are not only resolvable, but that also help to point the way toward theory development.

For the purpose of this chapter, we interpret health communication as the processes through which an individual or an audience engages, either directly or indirectly, information that can influence health-relevant beliefs and behavior, regardless of whether that information was or was not intended to affect health outcomes. In our interpretation, those processes occur as a function of both individual-level and higher-level variables. These definitional choices imply that, across studies, analyses of health communication effects necessarily should be able to address a time component (because a process orientation implies lagged effects), multiple possible outcome variables, and both direct and indirect effects.

Building on these considerations, we address three themes that are of particular importance for health communication researchers in recent years and into the foreseeable future: measurement problems related to key variables, issues in model development and testing, and statistical issues. All of these sections have theoretical underpinning and implications.

I. Measurement Problems Related to Key Variables

Across the wide scope of current health communication scholarship involving individuals (leaving aside purely cultural-, structural-, or other macro-level work in the present discussion), several central variables are paramount, such as information exposure, beliefs and summative perceptions (such as attitudes and norms), and health-related behavior. We start with the surprising but reasonable assertion that our measurement of many of these variables is weak, thereby limiting our ability to detect anything other than simple main effect relationships. It was Schmidt and Hunter (1996) who observed that "every psychological variable yet studied has been found to be imperfectly measured, as is true throughout all other areas of science" (p. 199). This means simply that health communication researchers have much in common with other social scientists.

Therefore, what should be important in any survey of methodological innovations are solutions, or at least discussions of potential solutions, to those fundamental problems of measurement. A variable that is central to most conceptual and empirical frameworks in health communication is exposure. Whether it be worksite interventions, mediated messages, intervention components, or interpersonal interactions, accurately capturing one's level of exposure is critically important to health communication research. Note, however, that not only is there concern about how to best conceptualize and measure exposure, but there is equal interest in determining its influence on important health outcome variables. It is to these issues that we first turn.

Independent Variables Tied to Information Exposure

Health communication research has long been complicated by the elusive nature of information exposure. Left to their own devices, people sometimes selectively expose themselves to information (see Zillmann & Bryant, 1985), but this possibility is typically not addressed in analyses of exposure to health messages (Morris, Rooney, Wray, & Kreuter, 2009). Moreover, we know that measuring exposure is not as straightforward as one might think (Hornik, 2002; Slater, 2004). Most self-report measures of exposure are vulnerable to the dynamics of human memory (Southwell, 2005). As a result, our effort to understand the impact of information on health behavior or the patterns of information-seeking among various groups has often hinged on our ability to accurately measure and subsequently harness variance in exposure. Insofar as a health communication research project fails to produce variation in exposure among people, it is virtually impossible to detect any project impact (Hornik & Kelly, 2007). Failing to measure real exposure that actually occurred, moreover, tells us no more about project impact than instances in which real exposure to materials and messages never happened.

Methodologically, then, what can be done to improve our study of exposure? One approach to improving assessment of exposure is to exchange the commonly employed method of self-report for a researcher-controlled approach of randomly assigning people to an exposure or control condition. For example, Leshner and colleagues (Leshner, Bolls, & Thomas, 2009) manipulated exposure to one of two different messages. Then, the researchers assessed attention to messages using continuous physiological measurement of heart rate and message recognition with keyboard response to message prompts. Exposure in that study was assigned and monitored rather than simply reported by participants. Moreover, researchers were able to gain a more nuanced assessment of exposure by gauging participants' attention to the content. Importantly, Chaffee and Schleuder (1986) discuss the intricacies and importance of distinguishing exposure from attention.

This move away from self-reported exposure does not need to be limited to the laboratory. Albeit more costly on a larger scale, the experimental method also has proven successful in field settings. For example, Southwell and Torres (2006) randomly assigned regular TV news viewers to one of two conditions where they were asked to watch health and science news stories from a different media market. Researchers mailed a DVD or VHS tape containing stories from one of two conditions that varied by dosage of news content and then assessed effects. In a different example, the AIDS Community Demonstration Projects randomly assigned at-risk communities to intervention conditions to receive media material and engage in conversations with peers from their communities regarding HIV-relevant practices, or to control conditions to receive referrals to HIV services (Fishbein et al., 1996). In both field studies, exposure was controlled by researchers, thereby solving the problem of self-report data (although admittedly introducing other methodological issues related to forced exposure).

Longitudinal designs are also a useful alternative as they offer within-individual variance in exposure over time that can allow one to draw causal inferences without contriving experimental designs. For example, analyzing Dutch STD prevention media campaigns, Yzer, Siero, and Buunk (2000) modeled levels of campaign exposure over a four-year period such that the likelihood of engaging in preventive behavior at the final observation was a function of cumulative and varying exposure to different campaigns conducted in preceding years. Recent developments in latent growth modeling offer the health communication researcher even more options for longitudinal analysis. Perhaps most importantly, latent growth modeling is based on the idea that individuals have unique growth trajectories over time; put differently, how individuals change over time is different for different people. Latent growth modeling allows the researcher not only to identify individual growth trajectories, but also to explain them as a function of a set of intra-individual and inter-individual variables, including exposure to health messages (McArdle, 1998). Although not widely adopted yet in the health communication domain, Schemer, Matthes, and Wirth (2009) have demonstrated the usefulness of latent growth modeling for longitudinal analysis of media effects. Schemer and colleagues modeled change in attitude in the context of media attention for a proposed tightening of the Swiss asylum law and found that latent growth modeling was able to demonstrate media effects on attitude change whereas a more conventional regression approach could not. The explanation for this important difference is that, in contrast to conventional regression methods, latent growth methods allow the researcher to model media effects on attitude change as time-variant and different for different people, which is more in line with what we would theoretically expect.

Validity Issues in Measuring Exposure and Some Creative Solutions.

It is important to note that measurement recommendations should be based on a broad interpretation of what it is to which an audience is exposed. Health researchers are often interested in understanding how messages used in a health intervention work, and for this purpose, exposure measures are designed that ask about exposure to and engagement with the health message of interest. However, this practice may not always be optimal. We know, after all, that the overall diet of content available in the media market in which a person lives is a crucial, if obvious, predictor of his or her engagement with relevant messages, and those relevant messages include much more than a single or few messages that are part of a planned health intervention (Southwell, 2005). Hornik (2002) explained that evaluations of public health interventions often fail to demonstrate intervention success not necessarily because exposure measures were flawed, but because interventions were not able to produce enough exposure relative to the thousands of health-relevant messages people get each day from advertising, entertainment media, personal experience, and so on.

Building on this idea, much research has focused on effects of media information that was not planned as health-relevant, such as food advertising and food media portrayals (e.g., Greenberg, Rosaen, Worrell, Salmon, & Volkman, 2009). One possibility for such research efforts is to ask people how often they have seen health-relevant information in, for example, entertainment media. From a measurement validity standpoint, we should be concerned, however, with the very real possibility that self-reported exposure to relevant health information may not be accurate because of memory issues or because of other biases. One approach that recognizes both the reality of complex media diets and the validity concerns associated with recall exposure measures is to obtain non-self-reported indicators of group exposure likelihood. These indicators include, but are not limited to, gross rating point estimates from advertising buys, television program audience ratings, or content analysis data. Then, researchers can compare groups that likely have been more or less exposed to key content.

Recent work in the smoking and sexual behaviors domains suggests another approach, which creatively integrates a subjective assessment of the types of media people use with an independent, objective assessment of the health-relevant content of those media. The rationale for this approach comes from Brown and colleagues (Brown & Pardun, 2005). They argued that whereas self-reported data on exposure to different media classes (such as television and magazines) and vehicles (such as the *American Idol* TV program and *People* magazine) usefully suggest patterns of adolescent media consumption, such frequency usage data are not optimally informative because they cannot speak to the kind of information to which adolescents were exposed. These authors have demonstrated that weighing media use data with the extent to which those media contain sexual content offers a much more powerful predictor of sexual behaviors than simple self-reports of either general media use or exposure to sexual content. In a similar vein, Sargent and colleagues (2005) asked adolescents which movies they had seen and then weighed these responses by objective counts of smoking references in those movies obtained in separate content analyses. Their research not only showed powerful relationships between watching movies rich in smoking episodes and smoking initiation, but also effectively removed concerns about the validity of self-reported exposure to media information.

These lines of research illustrate how thinking about how people use the media can inform creative solutions to measurement development. Importantly, attempts to improve measures of exposure will not produce better prediction if the underlying conceptual model of exposure effects does not accurately reflect how health information reaches and is used by relevant audience segments.

Dependent Variables Derived from Critical Health Outcomes

The "gold standard" outcome for many health communication projects is behavior, either in terms of change or maintenance. Essentially, at issue is whether the communication event (e.g., message, nonverbal behavior, verbal interaction) influenced behavior. For example, Palmgreen and colleagues (Palmgreen, Donohew, Lorch, Hoyle, & Stephenson, 2001) conducted antimarijuana media campaigns and the primary outcome variable was 30-day marijuana use. Similarly, Morgan, Miller, and Arasaratnam (2002) evaluated how many individuals signed an organ donor card as a result of a worksite communication intervention. Finally, work by the Centers for Disease Control, AIDS Community Demonstraction Projects (CDC ACDP Research Group; 1999) examined condom use and bleach use to clean needles before injecting drugs in response to community-based HIV-prevention efforts. In each of these cases, the primary dependent variable was behavior (marijuana use, signing an organ donor card, using condoms, cleaning needles). Behavioral outcomes are critical because, first, the ultimate objective of many health interventions is to contribute to behavior change, and second, and related, behavioral responses are arguably the most immediate antecedent of public health issues such as obesity, STDs, and certain forms of cancer.

Despite the clear significance of behavioral outcomes in health communication research, they may neither be feasible to measure nor may they be appropriate. Feasibility issues stem from the necessity of prospective analysis (as behavior effects are lagged relative to their causes) and include lack of funding or resources for longitudinal data collection. Similarly, with experimental studies, it may be useful to focus more on the mechanisms that influence variables earlier in the hierarchy of effects, such as time spent communicating with family or friends (e.g., Stephenson et al., 2009), beliefs, attitudes, efficacy, or behavioral intent (e.g., Roberto, Meyer, Johnson, & Atkin, 2000). This latter point also speaks to the inappropriateness of a singular focus on behavioral outcomes. The hierarchy of effects proposed by the behavioral theories that are most frequently used as a foundation for health communication research do not simply reflect an opportunity to examine multiple or alternative dependent variables. In fact, hierarchy of effects models propose mechanisms by which health information ultimately affects behavior. The idea is that health information does not directly change behavior, but instead changes determinants of behavior, and those in turn affect behavior (e.g., Stephenson, Quick, & Hirsch, 2010).

For instance, using HIV programs as an example, Yzer, Fishbein, and Hennessy (2008) argued that

> behavioral theory informs HIV prevention programs by identifying important predictors of the relevant behavior. Changes in those predictors brought about by program messages should theoretically translate into behavior change. Program evaluation, however, may examine only whether message exposure is associated with behavior change, assuming that if people changed their behavior, the intervention must have effectively changed the determinants. This practice obscures how intervention programs work in the field.
>
> (p. 456)

They reanalyzed condom use data from the AIDS Community Demonstration Projects and demonstrated that program effects on condom use, which had previously published as the sole dependent variable (CDC ACDP Research Group, 1999), could in fact be explained by program effects on self-efficacy. Obviously, such explanatory findings are much more meaningful if we are to advance our understanding of *how* communication programs work, and not just our decision *that* they work.

We should heed, though, the notion that true understanding of communication processes requires an examination of both behavioral antecedents and actual behavior. As argued, a singular focus on behavior is not helping us very much in explaining communication processes. Neither, however, is a focus on behavioral determinants absent behavior. Using intention-behavior models as an example, it is not good enough to argue that tests of communication processes insofar they affect intention are sufficient because intention should lead to behavior. Although we readily acknowledge a common reality of budget, time, and other resource constraints, claims about communication effects on health behavior are most convincing when based on a prospective study design. This does not mean that cross-sectional analysis is not useful, but rather serves to remind us to take seriously the limitations in scope of our conclusions based on cross-sectional work.

A second, more general issue related to dependent variables in health communication research pertains to construct validity. Although we teach our students to consider construct validity, the literature gives good reason to repeat here a call to consider whether the dependent measure is a valid indicator of the concept of interest. For instance, in Witte's (1992) early work on the extended parallel process model, she critiqued earlier fear appeal research for its "interchangeable use of conceptually distinct terms" that ultimately "muddied the fear appeal waters considerably" (p. 329). Specifically, Witte (1992) found that earlier research had conflated fear with threat when in fact the two variables produced different outcomes. Fear is an emotional response whereas threat is more of a cognitive appraisal. Similarly, Quick and Stephenson (2007) published a scale designed to measure the boomerang effect theorized to occur when one was experiencing psychological reactance. These authors argued that previous research in this area used attitudes, behavioral intentions, and source and message evaluations to demonstrate the presence of a boomerang effect. While a reasonable approach, the authors argued that these constructs only partially represented earlier conceptualization of reactance restoration.

The argument here is that measures need to be valid representations of the concept of interest. There are many opportunities for scale development in health communication. For example, although quite often health communication research uses many different operationalizations as a measure for the same concept, very little attention is being paid to the question of whether such variability matters. Indeed, there is a paucity of validation research in the health communication literature. For example, whereas scale development validation research using approaches such as the multimethod multitrait matrix are common in other disciplines, they rarely appear in health communication journals. When there is no consensus on valid measures of a concept, for example because rigorous validation work has not been done, choice for a particular operationalization of that concept should be explicitly justified. Relevant work published in health communication journals typically does not include those arguments.

Meta-analysis is potentially useful for validation, especially in terms of predictive validity. If a variable is theorized to predict another, and if across many studies that variable in fact is associated with the criterion variable, even though the predictor variable was operationalized in different ways, then one could argue that different operationalizations tap the same construct. We offer two cautionary notes, however. First, because meta-analysis is a method of weighed averages, an analysis across all available studies can obscure meaningful differences between studies. It is possible that meta-analytic research that examines predictor–criterion associations for different operationalizations finds that some operationalizations work better than others, suggesting that not all operationalizations perform equally well. Second, just as a high reliability coefficient does not mean that we are necessarily measuring what we think we are measuring, an association between two different sets of measures is not enough to conclude that we are measuring the construct of interest.

II. Issues in Model Development and Testing

Communication as a Process

Stephenson, Holbert, and Zimmerman (2006) reintroduced the argument that communication is inherently a *process*. They cite earlier work by Cappella (1991) who wrote that "processes ... are the guts of any substantive theory" (p. 168), and that "how messages are understood (read, interpreted, comprehended, etc.) is a process question fundamental to all forms of human communication" (p. 169). To view communication as a process suggests that there are antecedents to the communication of interest as well as outcomes that will naturally follow said communication. For instance, Stephenson (2003) argued that an antecedent variable called sensation seeking would subsequently influence the way individuals responded to antimarijuana television ads. In turn, the cognitive and emotional responses to this communication would subsequently influence one's attitudes toward marijuana. This process—that one's need for sensation would influence the way the individuals responded cognitively and affectively to the ad, and that in turn would influence antimarijuana attitudes—was captured in the method and subsequently the statistical analyses used in the cross-sectional study.

Many theoretical assumptions are more complex than the phenomena studied by Stephenson (2003). Take for instance Street's (2003) three-stage model for using interactive media in health services. To illustrate how patients interact with health communication technology, Street advances the three stages that capture the process of patients interacting with technology: *implementation* (comprised of institutional, technological, and user factors), *use* (utilization of technology and intermediate outcomes such as knowledge and efficacy), and *health outcomes* (health improvement, lifestyle change, preventive action). Implementation of the technology influences its use, which in turn may increase knowledge and efficacy, and culminates in healthy behavior change. At each stage, Street makes the point that communication is central to this process where communication is influenced by antecedent variables and subsequently influences health outcomes.

The two example research studies noted above differ in method. Stephenson's (2003) study is a traditional cross-sectional study conducted in the research lab. Once at the lab, participants completed a paper and pencil personality measure (sensation seeking), watched the ads, then completed a paper and pencil measure of their responses. In contrast, the method required to assess Street's (2003) entire three-stage model required a longitudinal design so that researchers could observe the subsequent changes in health. The important point is this: communication is a process in which careful choices must be made about how to best capture phenomena of interest.

Processes as Mediated

If we think of communication as a process, then multiple variables are involved and methodology becomes critical to the assessment of the process. For example, if a communication act is designed to elicit a set of processes that culminate in a specified outcome, measurement of these constructs must occur in a fashion that is consistent with the process. Careful methodological choices are a necessity.

First, at the most basic level, the questionnaire must be designed in a way that antecedent variables are answered before outcome variables. For example, we may be interested in the question whether an evaluation of a health message informs attitude toward the particular health behavior. For this purpose we could show the health message and then ask how good or bad the message was, followed by questions about attitude toward the particular health behavior addressed in the message. The sequence of questions is meaningful. If the attitudinal questions would precede the message evaluation questions, study participants could use their attitudinal response to indicate their evaluation of the message ("I said that wearing a seat belt is a good thing, so I guess the seat belt message was good"). It is important for researchers who utilize multiple survey orders to eliminate response bias and not unintentionally create new problems where, for example, behaviors precede attitudes.

Second, data collection may need to occur at multiple levels. Hannawa (2009) describes a three-step model illustrating how physicians disclose mistakes. The exogenous variable, physician defensiveness, is negatively related to the physician's disclosure competence, which in turn, influenced beneficial outcomes for both the physician and the patient. Hannawa notes that "whereas the effects of physician defensiveness on disclosure competence may be assessed on an individual level, the outcome variables can be examined only as dyadic effects because they integrate the patient's reactions" (p. 397).

Similarly, data collection may need to employ multiple types of data. In Leshner et al. (2009), the authors examine the effects of messages containing either fear appeals or disgust appeals on attention, as well as the effects of attention on recognition. They manipulated exposure to one of the two message appeals, measured attention to the messages using continuous physiological measurement of heart rate, and then assessed recognition using a computer keyboard. Exposure leads to heart rate acceleration or deceleration, which subsequently leads to recognition. The process itself is easily recognized because of the temporality involved in the assessment of effects.

Finally, an interpretation of communication as a process should have consequences for analytical choices. For example, for the purpose of this discussion, let us oversimplify and agree that a media health message does not directly change behavior, but it might do so indirectly by first affecting beliefs about the message, which in a stepping stone manner in turn would affect beliefs about the particular health behavior, and change in those health behavior beliefs would ultimately change behavior. The theorized process in this example is one of mediated effects. Therefore, an analysis that examines effects of message exposure on beliefs about the message, on beliefs about the health behavior, and on the health behavior does not match with our theorized idea of mediated effects because it assumes that message exposure affects all three dependent variables directly. Yet, analyses similar to this example are prominent in the literature. The problem is one of incorrect inferences. If our illustrative analysis does not demonstrate a direct message exposure effect on health beliefs, we should not conclude that the message failed to affect health beliefs but instead consider that this result is indicative of full mediation. The general point here is that the appropriate analytical move is to use mediation analysis when mediation is theorized (Holbert & Stephenson, 2003).

Multiple Regression and Structural Equation Modeling

In further discussion of how communication is a process that involves a series of antecedent variables and outcomes, Stephenson et al. (2006) suggest that it could be theoretically useful and enlightening to investigate such phenomena of interest by looking at the "big picture." There are, minimally, two ways one can do so. One can examine the relationships between multiple variables of interest through path analysis via ordinary least squares regression or through structural equation modeling which uses a host of estimators, the most common being maximum likelihood.

Full Information versus Partial Information Estimation. Prior to the availability of user-friendly structural equation modeling (SEM) software, regression-based path analysis was (and still is) an accepted approach to analyzing systems of equations. Depending upon the complexity of the model, a path analysis involves running regression analyses for each dependent variable in the model. Most researchers stop after running the regression equations, although the next appropriate step would be to compare the predicted regression coefficients to the observed correlation matrix in order to determine the fit of the model. In contrast, SEM examines the entire system of equations simultaneously. Because SEM is based on covariances and not correlations as well as different estimators, SEM programs are utilized to determine the fit of the model.

The first difference between the two procedures is that SEM uses full-information estimators while regression uses partial information estimators. What is the difference? Quite simply, full information estimators allow individuals to analyze simultaneously a system of equations that represent a theoretical process. Street's model (discussed earlier) is but one theoretical process, but there are others in the health domain, among them are Witte's (1992) extended parallel process model, Fishbein's (2000) integrative model of behavioral prediction, or Petty and Cacioppo's (1986) elaboration likelihood model. Full-information estimators allow a theoretical model to be compared to the data for the sample, and to the extent to which there is discrepancy, the model is said to be inconsistent with the data. The point here is that the *entire model* is tested simultaneously using SEM. In contrast, general linear model-based analyses such as multiple regression use partial information estimators (e.g., ordinary least squares) where equations are solved one at a time. So when one reads about a "regression-based path analysis," the researcher has been limited to specifying one dependent variable at a time. SEM is not limited in that manner and the entire theoretical model is tested simultaneously.

Latent Variables. The second difference between the two statistical procedures is that SEM allows researchers to extract measurement error due to the measure's unreliability. For example, if researchers use a five-item measure to assess attitudes toward skin cancer and coefficient alpha is .72, then there is considerable measurement error embedded in that construct. However, SEM allows researchers to establish a measurement model that, in effect, isolates random error: "In this way, uniqueness and random error are divorced from commonality in such a way that the reliability ... is in effect 1.0" (Hoyle & Kenny, 1999, p. 203). As a result, the parameter between the measured variables and their respective latent variable reflects the systematic (true) relationship of measurement corrected for unreliability). Once measurement error has been extracted, only the systematic relationship between these latent variables remains.

Time-Based Modeling

Increasingly, health communication scholars are recognizing the utility of conceiving of time period as a unit of analysis and looking at longitudinal changes in beliefs and behaviors related to health as a function of available media content and campaign efforts. Instead of associating individual-level variables in cross-sectional fashion, some have successfully demonstrated how we look at trends in media content and relate them to trends in relevant beliefs or behaviors. This move resonates with much of our discussion thus far, as it often allows for adequate variation in exposure and reflects communication dynamics as part of an unfolding process. The disadvantages of such an approach include the costs of aggregating data to produce data points for each time period and also difficulty of finding appropriate longitudinal data stretching back in time. Successful studies that have adopted this approach have assessed the predictive ability of media content trends in explaining outcomes such as marijuana abstinence (Stryker, 2003) or drunk driving (Yanovitzky & Bennett, 1999).

Linking Multiple Levels of Variables

While undoubtedly not a panacea and certainly not necessary for all sorts of health communication hypothesis testing, our discussion of new methodological directions would not be complete without further comment on multilevel modeling. (We earlier touched on latent growth modeling, which can be interpreted as a special case of multilevel modeling.) On a technical level, we know that people in samples are often nested within higher-level units (such as families, communities, or countries) in ways that are not completely independent, leaving many regression approaches vulnerable to underestimated standard errors (Raudenbush & Bryk, 2002). Even aside from such considerations, however, researchers need to consider multilevel approaches because the questions they are asking involve both variables and mechanisms that reside at different levels of organization (e.g., Hwang & Southwell, 2009).

As Luke (2004) notes, the most important justification for using multilevel statistical models is theoretical. Southwell (2005) has argued for the specific theoretical utility of multilevel modeling for communication research, noting that many of our conceptualizations of media effects implicitly or explicitly involve more than simple bivariate relationships at one level of analysis and often suggest cross-level interactions. Multilevel models allow the simultaneous estimation of equations at different levels of analysis in a way that permits variance in a key outcome to be a function of both macrolevel and microlevel predictors. For example, a person's tendency to smoke might be predictable as a function of not only that individual person's perceptions about smoking but also as a function of the market-level availability of cigarettes, country-level presence or absence of large-scale health campaigns, and other factors at various levels of analysis. Moreover, these factors might interact so as to amplify or curtail individual beliefs.

III. Some Additional Statistical Challenges

Missing Data

It is inevitable that data will be missing. The question, then, is how to handle the issue. Surprisingly, Harel, Zimmerman, and Dekhtyar (2008) found that communication scholars avoided or sidestepped the issue. They reviewed journals from 2005 and 2006 that are known to publish quantitative research in communication and found that only one in five articles mentioned anything about missing data. When researchers did mention it, 75% of those used listwise deletion, a "method that is known to be one of the worst available" (p. 351). What follows is an overview of the missing data options available to researchers, beginning with the less-desirable unprincipled solutions.

Unprincipled Solutions

Three solutions to missing data, listwise deletion, pairwise deletion, and single imputation procedures, are used frequently but are perhaps least desirable with regard to how the statistical properties of the data change as a result of their use. Equally problematic is that some of these procedures are the default in our commonly used statistical packages such as SPSS and SAS. As a result, it is important that researchers understand how these procedures impact the results of their data analysis.

Listwise deletion is frequently the default in statistical packages. Consider a research scenario where a researcher gathers survey data from 200 undergraduate college students, but 80 of the 200 individuals did not respond to the question about income (perhaps because some college students are not employed, get money from parents or student loans, or in general just don't know how to answer the question). Therefore, when the researcher conducts a simple independent-samples *t*-test to see if female students make more than male college students, only 120 of the 200 cases are included in the analysis. In listwise deletion, the statistical program simply omits the cases on which data are missing.

Pairwise deletion is similar though the implications are slightly different. Here, data are deleted when there is missing data on one or both of the variables in the analysis. For example, the researcher who collected the data set with the 200 undergraduate college students wants to produce a correlation matrix that includes gender, income, and grade point average. Therefore, in the correlation matrix, there would be three sets of correlations—gender and income, gender and grade point average, and income and grade point average. The problem occurs when there is data missing on one of the variables and not the others. So, if an individual provides his gender and income but not his grade point average, he is included in the correlational data for the first outcome but not the second. The problem is that the researcher literally has different sets of data for each analysis.

Finally, single imputation procedures are options available in most statistical packages. Single imputation merely implies that a new single value is derived (imputed) to replace all the missing values for that variable. One single imputation approach, called mean substitution, occurs when the researcher computes the mean value of the variable and replaces all the missing values with the mean. So, in our fictional research scenario above, the researcher wanted to replace all 80 missing values on the income variable and did so by computing the mean for the other 120 cases. Then, the researcher would replace the missing value for income with the mean value from the other 120 cases. The result is that the researcher now has 200 values for the income variable (though there are obviously problems with this approach, which we discuss shortly). A second single imputation procedure, similar to the first, is to use a regression-based approach to estimate the missing value and then replacing the missing value with the estimate obtained from the regression analysis (e.g., Harel et al., 2008). While at first glance this approach may appear better than mean value substitution, it is not much of an improvement largely because the regression-based approach imputes a value that lies squarely on the regression line.

Unprincipled solutions are problematic primarily for three reasons. First, no matter how you look at the problem, both listwise and pairwise deletion mean the researchers lose valuable data and statistical power to detect statistically significant effects. Additionally, listwise and pairwise deletion may yield results that are biased. For example, if those whose data are missing are similar (e.g., limited literacy levels or high income), the analysis will be limited in generalizability, and potentially misleading, because the results fail to consider those individuals whose data are missing. Finally, the liability with single imputation is a loss in statistical variance. Variance is ultimately what we as researchers are trying to explain with the analyses. By substituting missing data with the variable's mean value or an estimate obtained from a regression-based approach, we also restrict the variance in the variable.

Principled Solutions

Given the limitations with unprincipled solutions, researchers have designed a couple of options to replacing missing data without compromising the statistical properties of the data set. The two approaches widely recommended include the use of an algorithm called expectation maximization (EM). EM is based on full information maximum likelihood estimators. The second recommended approach is called multiple imputation (MI). Because both are based on statistical theory (and hence the term "principled solutions"), each yields an outcome that is unbiased. As a result, these approaches are superior to the unprincipled solutions described earlier. That said, the computational details of each approach are complex and beyond the scope of this chapter. It is most appropriate, then, to provide a conceptual explanation of the approach as well as how to implement each in your data sets.

The first principled approach uses statistical theory based on full information maximum likelihood (FIML) estimators. FIML estimation allows researchers to fit a specific model to the data one has obtained. Data set in hand, researchers can specify a model and the FIML estimators will iteratively generate the parameters for that model that are maximally likely; that is, they are the most optimal parameters for the proposed model given the data that the researcher has obtained (Curran, West, & Finch, 1996). A widely used FIML-based algorithm for estimating missing data is called expectation maximization, or EM (Dempster,

Laird, & Rubin (1977): "Intuitively, what EM does is to iteratively 'augment' the data by 'guessing' the values of the hidden variables and to re-estimate the parameters by assuming that the guessed values are the true values" (Zhai, 2004, p. 1). As the iterations approach convergence, the EM algorithm is assessing the most likely value for the missing data, and that value is based not only on the individual's other nonmissing data but also on the distribution of all variables in the data set. Implementing EM is fairly straightforward, depending upon how accessible the software is to the researcher. The procedure is available in AMOS, EQS, LISREL, and MPlus. SAS and SPSS also make the EM algorithm available but typically only in advanced modules.

In addition to the FIML-based EM approach, researchers can utilize multiple imputation (MI) in order to replace missing data. Unlike the EM-based approach, which generates only one set of missing values, the MI approach involves the imputation of missing values multiple times—anywhere from 3 to 100—depending upon the statistical power needed to detect a significant effect (Graham, Olchowski, & Gilreath, 2007). This approach is often referred to as a simulation.

The procedures are fairly straightforward. First, one uses statistical software to replace the missing values. Second, the data analytic procedures are carried out. Third, the parameter estimates from the data analysis are then saved into a separate file. This process is repeated between 3 and 100 times (see Graham et al., 2007). The output from each analysis is saved and the parameter estimates are then averaged to determine the value of the output. MI can be conducted with SAS using PROC MI or through LISREL. Additionally, researchers may download free software called NORM from the methodology center at Penn State (methodology.psu.edu).

Nonlinear Relationships

Many health communication researchers continue to rely on linear statistics when the possibility of nonlinear relationships and non-normal distributions are theoretically relevant to consider. One manifestation of this tendency is the use of simple linear correlations to assess relationships when curvilinear possibilities are likely. Consider, for example, the relationship of fear induced by a message and protective responses. Initial work suggested a linear relationship where increased fear is associated with weaker protective responses (Janis & Feshbach, 1953). Because other findings suggested a positive relationship, such that increased fear produced consistent gains in protective responses (Leventhal & Watts, 1966), that view was subsequently replaced by a curvilinear interpretation where increased fear produces healthy responses up to the point where fear becomes too strong, after which we should see decreasing protective responses (Janis, 1967). Using linear statistics to test such relationships would overlook this theoretical nuance.

Another related problem is a tendency to overlook the distribution of dependent variables and the potential for violating assumptions of normality. We have seen the widespread adoption of logistic regression to address instances of dichotomous outcome variables. Less prevalent is the acknowledgment of issues associated with relatively rare outcomes and the problems of zero-clustered data. Consider, for example, family conversation about certain health topics, such as indoor tanning. We know that such conversations are relatively rare (Friedenberg, Wang, Choi, Southwell, & Lazovich, 2009). In instances in which we attempt to model zero-clustered dependent variables, approaches such as Tobit regression that predict asymptotes as one approaches zero rather than straight-line relationships might be more appropriate than OLS regression (e.g., Shen & Dillard, 2009).

These observations extend to tests of interactions. The complexity of communication processes makes straightforward main effects the exception rather than the rule, and processes are often better conceptualized as conditional. In other words, the best description of a relationship often begins with "it depends."

Take, for example, health risk communication. Building on conceptual propositions developed in the context of the protection motivation theory (Rogers, 1975) and the extended parallel processing model (Witte, 1992), a large body of work has shown that a message that increases perceived risk to a health threat only produces healthy responses if the message also improves self-efficacy regarding performing such responses. Staying with this example, a perceived risk by self-efficacy interaction can very well be demonstrated in experimental work, because experiments allow the researcher to create situations where the interaction should be most visible, in effect, the four most extreme positions in a perceived risk–efficacy space (low risk, weak efficacy; low risk, strong efficacy; high risk, weak efficacy; high risk, strong efficacy; see McClelland & Judd, 1993). Health communication research, however, very often relies on nonexperimental methods, such as surveys. The distribution of survey data is likely to be unipolar, clustered, and skewed. The result is diminished statistical power for the detection of small interaction effects (e.g., Yzer, 2007).

This reality appears to encourage the discomforting practice of underreporting interaction effects because such results failed to reach statistical significance even though conceptually such interaction effects make sense and hold much promise for a deeper understanding of explanatory processes. Researchers should be wary of being blinded by statistical significance levels and make more use of diagnostic analyses. For example, even if solutions to the problem of detecting interaction effects, such as greatly increasing sample size, are not feasible, the health researcher can nonetheless inspect descriptive and distribution statistics to assess whether the lack of an apparent interaction stems from the nature of the sample rather than from the theoretical bankruptcy of the idea.

Concluding Thoughts

In an increasingly crowded arena, new methods offer a way of making one's research stand out. Yet, embracing methods simply because they are trendy can distract scholars from fundamental considerations, such as "What is the question I want to answer in this research?" and potentially obfuscate the original research question.

We have reviewed a series of challenges that have recently faced health communication scholars. Some published work suffers from these limitations, whereas other recent pieces have shown useful paths forward. The most useful work, in our estimation, has applied statistical models that match the explicit or implied theoretical propositions in question, acknowledge that communication is a process that unfolds over time, and reflects the fact that there are important questions to be asked at different levels of analysis using different units of analysis. Ideally, the method section in our papers should be generating research questions and theoretical debate rather than simply being mundane recitation of details.

In closing, our next steps methodologically and statistically need to be driven by theoretical priorities. Whereas the premise that theoretical questions are the basis of, and therefore should precede, methodological considerations is by no means new, a tendency for researchers to simply employ known and preferred techniques persists. As a result, crucial health communication questions may remain untapped as we churn out papers that tell the same story while making only modest new contributions. Methodological and statistical advancement alone will not lead to advanced understanding of questions pertinent to health communication if innovative conceptual ideas do not come first. The analogy comes to mind of a spontaneous drive without a roadmap: it may be fun or stimulating, but we do not really know where we are headed or, perhaps, even how to replicate the journey. Theory should be our hypothetical map; methods and statistical procedures, such as those we describe in this chapter, can be our new telescopes and compasses to explore the terrain of communication and health in the 21st century, inordinately useful devices but dependent on what one wants to measure and analyze.

References

Anderson, D. R., Bryant, J., Murray, J. P., Rich, M., Rivkin, M., & Zillmann, D. (2006). Brain imaging—An introduction to a new approach to studying media processes and effects. *Media Psychology, 8,* 1–6.

Brown, J. D., & Pardun, C. J. (2005). Little in common: Racial and gender differences in adolescents' television diets. *Journal of Broadcasting and Electronic Media, 48,* 266–278.

Cappella, J. N. (1991). Review of Stephen W. Littlejohn, *Theories of human communication* (3rd ed.). *Communication Theory, 1,* 165–171.

Centers for Disease Control, AIDS Community Demonstration Projects (CDC ACDP) Research Group (1999). Community-level HIV intervention in 5 cities: Final outcome data from the CDC AIDS Community Demonstration Projects. *American Journal of Public Health, 89,* 336–345.

Chaffee, S., & Schleuder, J. (1986). Measurement and effects of attention to media news. *Human Communication Research, 13,* 76–107.

Cohen, J. (1992). A power primer. *Psychological Bulletin, 112,* 155–159.

Curran, P. J., West, S. G., & Finch, J. F. (1996). The robustness of test statistics to nonnormality and specification error in confirmatory factor analysis. *Psychological Methods, 1,* 16–29.

Dempster, A. P., Laird, N. M., & Rubin, D. B. (1977). Maximum likelihood from incomplete data via the EM algorithm. *Journal of the Royal Statistical Society, Series B, 39,* 1–38.

DeVaney, T. A. (2001). Statistical significance, effect size, and replication: What do the journals say? *The Journal of Experimental Education, 69,* 310–320.

Fabrigar, L. R., Wegener, D. T., MacCallum, R. C., & Strahan, E. J. (1999). Evaluating the use of exploratory factor analysis in psychological research. *Psychological Methods, 4,* 272–299.

Fishbein, M. (2000). The role of theory in HIV prevention. *AIDS Care, 12,* 273–278.

Fishbein, M., Guenther-Grey, C., Johnson, W., Wolitski, R. J., McAlister, A., Rietmeijer, C.A., ... the AIDS Community Demonstration Projects (1996). Using a theory-based community intervention to reduce AIDS risk behaviors: The CDC's AIDS Community Demonstration Projects. In S. Oskamp & S. C. Thompson (Eds.), *Understanding and preventing HIV risk behavior: Safer sex and drug use* (pp. 177–206). Thousand Oaks, CA: Sage.

Friedenberg, L. M., Wang, Y., Choi, T. C. K., Southwell, B. G., & Lazovich, D. (2009, November). *Family communication constraints as health intervention challenge: Parent–child conversation about indoor tanning.* Paper presented at the American Public Health Association Annual Meeting, Philadelphia, PA.

Graham, J. W., Olchowski, A. E., & Gilreath, T. D. (2007). How many imputations are really needed? Some practical clarifications of multiple imputation theory. *Prevention Science, 8,* 206–213.

Greenberg, B. S., Rosaen, S. F., Worrell, T. R., Salmon, C. T., & Volkman, J. E. (2009). A portrait of food and drink in commercial TV series. *Health Communication, 24,* 295–303.

Hannawa, A. F. (2009). Negotiating medical virtues: Toward the development of a physician mistake disclosure model. *Health Communication, 24,* 391–399.

Harel, O., Zimmerman, R., & Dekhtyar, O. (2008) Approaches to the handling of missing data in communication research. In A. F. Hayes, M. D. Slater, & L. B. Snyder (Eds.), *The SAGE sourcebook of advanced data analysis methods for communication research* (pp. 349–372). Thousand Oaks, CA: Sage.

Holbert, R. L., & Stephenson, M. T. (2003). The importance of analyzing indirect effects in media effects research: Testing for mediation in structural equation modeling. *Journal of Broadcasting & Electronic Media, 47,* 556–572.

Hornik, R. C. (2002). Exposure: Theory and evidence about all the ways it matters. *Social Marketing Quarterly, 8*(3), 30–37.

Hornik, R., & Kelly, B. (2007). Communication and diet: An overview of experience and principles. *Journal of Nutrition Education and Behavior, 39,* S5–S12.

Hoyle, R. H., & Kenny, D. A. (1999). Sample size, reliability, and tests of statistical mediation. In R. H. Hoyle (Ed.), *Statistical strategies for small sample research* (pp. 195–222). Thousand Oaks, CA: Sage.

Hwang, Y., & Southwell, B. G. (2009). Science TV news exposure predicts science beliefs: Real world effects among a national sample. *Communication Research, 36,* 724–742.

Janis, I. L. (1967). Effects of fear arousal on attitude change: Recent developments in theory and experimental research. *Advances in Experimental Social Psychology, 3,* 167–225.

Janis, I. L., & Feshbach, S. (1953). Effects of fear-arousing communications. *Journal of Abnormal and Social Psychology, 48,* 78–92.

Leshner, G., Bolls, P., & Thomas, E. (2009). Scare 'em or disgust 'em: The effects of graphic health promotion messages. Health Communication, 24, 447–458.

Leventhal, H., & Watts, (1966). Sources of resistance to fear-arousing communications on smoking and lung cancer. *Journal of Personality, 34,* 155–175.

Luke, D. A. (2004). *Multilevel modeling.* Thousand Oaks, CA: Sage.

McArdle, J. J. (1998). Modeling longitudinal data by latent growth curve methods. In G. A. Marcoulides (Ed.), *Modern methods for business research* (pp. 359–406). Mahwah, NJ: Erlbaum.

McClelland, G. H., & Judd, C. M. (1993). Statistical difficulties of detecting interactions and moderator effects. *Psychological Bulletin, 114,* 376–390.

Morgan, S. E., Miller, J., & Arasaratnam, L. A. (2002). Signing cards, saving lives: An evaluation of the Worksite Organ Donation Promotion Project. *Communication Monographs, 69,* 253–273.

Morris, D. S., Rooney, M. P., Wray, R. J., & Kreuter, M. W. (2009). Measuring exposure to health messages in community-based intervention studies: A systematic review of current practices. *Health Education and Behavior, 36,* 979–998.

Palmgreen, P., Donohew, D., Lorch, E. P., Hoyle, R. H., & Stephenson, M. T. (2001). Television campaigns and adolescent marijuana use: Tests of sensation seeking targeting. *American Journal of Public Health, 91,* 292–296.

Petty, R. E., & Cacioppo, J. T. (1986). Communications and persuasion: Central and peripheral routes to attitude change. New York: Springer-Verlag.

Quick, B. L., & Stephenson, M. T. (2007). The reactance restoration scale (RRS): A measure of direct and indirect restoration. *Communication Research Reports, 24,* 131–138.

Raudenbush, S. W., & Bryk, A. S. (2002). *Hierarchical linear models. Applications and data analysis models* (2nd ed.). Thousand Oaks, CA: Sage.

Roberto, A. J., Meyer, G., Johnson, A. J., & Atkin, C. K. (2000). Using the extended parallel process model to prevent firearm injury and death: Field experiment results of a video-based intervention. *Journal of Communication, 50,* 157–175.

Rogers, R.W. (1975). A protection motivation theory of fear appeals and attitude change. *Journal of Psychology, 91,* 93–114.

Sargent, J. D., Beach, M. L., Adachi-Mejia, A. M., Gibson, J. J., Titus-Ernstoff, L. T., Carusi, C. P., ... Dalton, M. A. (2005). Exposure to movie smoking: Its relation to smoking initiation among US adolescents. *Pediatrics, 116,* 1183–1191.

Schemer, C., Matthes, J., & Wirth, W. (2009). Applying latent growth models to the analysis of media effects. *Journal of Media Psychology, 21,* 85–89.

Schmidt, F. L., & Hunter, J. E. (1996). Measurement error in psychological research: Lessons from 26 research scenarios. *Psychological Methods, 1,* 199–223.

Shen, L., & Dillard. J. P. (2009). Message frames interact with motivational systems to determine depth of message processing. *Health Communication, 24,* 504–514.

Shrout, P. E., & Bolger, N. (2002). Mediation in experimental and nonexperimental studies: New procedures and recommendations. *Psychological Methods, 7,* 422–445.

Slater, M. D. (2004). Operationalizing and analyzing exposure: The foundation of media effects research. *Journalism and Mass Communication Quarterly, 81,* 168-183.

Southwell, B. G. (2005). Between messages and people: A multilevel model of memory for television content. *Communication Research, 32,* 112–140.

Southwell, B. G., & Torres, A. (2006). Connecting interpersonal and mass communication: Science news exposure, perceived ability to understand science, and conversation. *Communication Monographs, 73,* 334–350.

Stephenson, M. T. (2003). Examining adolescents' responses to antimarijuana PSAs. *Human Communication Research, 29,* 343–369.

Stephenson, M. T., Holbert, R. L., & Zimmerman, R. S. (2006). On the use of structural equation modeling in health communication research. *Health Communication, 20,* 159–167.

Stephenson, M. T., Quick, B. L., & Hirsch, H. A. (2010). Evidence in support of a strategy to target authoritarian and permissive parents in anti-drug media campaigns. *Communication Research, 37,* 73–104.

Stephenson, M. T., Quick, B. L., Witte, K., Vaught, C., Booth-Butterfield, S., & Patel, D. (2009). Conversations among coal miners in a campaign that promotes hearing protection. *Journal of Applied Communication Research, 37,* 317–337.

Street, R. L., Jr. (2003). Communication in medical encounters: An ecological perspective. In T. Thompson, A. M. Dorsey, K. J. Miller, & R. Parrott (Eds.), *Handbook of health communication* (pp. 63–93). Mahwah, NJ: Erlbaum.

Stryker, J. E. (2003). Media and marijuana: A longitudinal analysis of news media effects on adolescents' marijuana use and related outcomes, 1977–1999. *Journal of Health Communication, 8,* 305–328.

Witte, K. (1992). Putting the fear back into fear appeals: The extended parallel process model. *Communication Monographs, 59,* 329–349.

Yanovitzky, I., & Bennett, C. (1999). Media attention, institutional response, and health behavior change—The case of drunk driving, 1978–1996. *Communication Research, 26,* 429–453.

Yzer, M. C. (2007). Does perceived control moderate attitudinal and normative effects on intention? A review of conceptual and methodological issues. In I. Ajzen, D. Albarracin, & R. Hornik (Eds.), *Prediction and change of health behavior: Applying the reasoned action approach* (pp. 107–123). Mahwah, NJ: Erlbaum.

Yzer, M, Fishbein, M., & Hennessy, M. (2008). HIV interventions affect behavior indirectly: Results from the AIDS Community Demonstration Projects. *AIDS Care, 20,* 456–461.

Yzer, M. C., Siero, F. W., & Buunk, B. P. (2000). Can public campaigns effectively change psychological determinants of safer sex? An evaluation of three Dutch safer sex campaigns. *Health Education Research, 15,* 339–352.

Zhai, C. (2004). *A note on the expectation-maximization (EM) algorithm.* Unpublished manuscript, University of Illinois at Urbana-Champaign.

Zillmann, D., & Bryant, J. (Eds.). (1985). *Selective exposure to communication.* Hillsdale, NJ: Erlbaum.

Additional References for Web Page

Ahmed, S., & Mosely, W. H. (2002). Simultaneity in the use of maternal–child health care and contraceptives: Evidence from developing countries. *Demography, 39,* 75–93.

Bollen, K. A. (1989). *Structural equations with latent variables.* New York: Wiley.

Brehm, J. W. (1966). *A theory of psychological reactance.* New York: Academic Press.

Brown, J. D., L'Engle, K. L., Pardun, C. J., Guo, G., Kenneavy, K., & Jackson, C. (2006). Sexy media matter: Exposure to sexual content in music, movies, television and magazines predicts Black and White adolescents' sexual behavior. *Pediatrics, 117,* 1018–1027.

Cohen, J. (1969). Statistical power analysis for the behavioral sciences. New York: Academic Press.

Cudeck, R., du Toit, S., & Sörbom, D. (2001). *Structural equation modeling: Present and future.* Chicago, IL: SSI Scientific Software.

Dalton, M. A., Sargent, J. D., Beach, M. L., Titus-Ernstoff, L., Gibson, J. J., Ahrens, M. B., … Heatherton, T. F. (2003). Effect of viewing smoking in movies on adolescent smoking initiation: A cohort study. *Lancet, 362,* 281–285.

Duncan, O. D. (1975). *Introduction to structural equation models.* New York: Academic.

Hayes, A. F. (2006). A primer on multilevel modeling. *Human Communication Research, 32,* 385–410.

Hertog, J. K., & Fan, D. P. (1995). The impact of press coverage on social beliefs—The case of HIV transmission. *Communication Research, 22,* 545–574.

Hoenig, J. M., & Heisey, D. M. (2001). The abuse of power: The pervasive fallacy of power calculations for data analysis. *The American Statistician, 55,* 19–24.

Jöreskog, K. G. (1973). A general method for estimating a linear structural equation system. In A. S. Goldberger & O. D. Duncan (Eds.), *Structural equation models in the social sciences* (pp. 85–112). New York: Seminar Press.

Kline, R. B. (2009). *Becoming a behavioral science researcher: A guide to producing research that matters.* New York: Guildford Press.

Kreft, I., & De Leeuw, J. (1998). *Introducing multilevel modeling.* Thousand Oaks, CA: Sage.

Langleben, D. D., Loughead, J. W., Ruparel, K., Hakun, J. G., Busch-Winukur, S., Holloway, M. B., ... Lerman, C. (2009). Reduced prefrontal and temporal processing of high "sensation value" ads. *NeuroImage, 46,* 219–225.

L'Engle, K. L., Brown, J. D., & Kenneavy, K. (2006). Mass media are an important context for adolescents' sexual behavior. *Journal of Adolescent Health, 36,* 186–192.

Shen, L., & Bigsby, E. (in press). Behavioral activation/inhibition systems and discrete emotions: A test of valence vs. action tendency hypotheses. *Communication Monographs, 11,* 1–26..

Snyder, L., Fleming-Milici, F., Slater, M. D., Sun, H., & Strizhakova, Y. (2006). Effects of alcohol advertising exposure on youth drinking. *Archives of Pediatric and Adolescent Medicine, 160,* 18–24.

Southwell, B. G., Hornik, R. C., Fan, D. P., Yanovitzky, I., & Lazili, P. (2000, June). *Can news coverage predict mammography use? A time series analysis to predict health behavior using the ideodynamic model.* Paper presented at the International Communication Association annual conference, Acapulco, Mexico.

Story, M., & French, S. (2004). Food advertising and marketing directed at children and adolescents in the US. *International Journal of Behavioral Nutrition and Physical Activity, 1,* 3.

Tobin, J. (1958). Estimation of relationships for limited dependent variables. *Econometrica, 26,* 24–36.

Wei, R., & Lo, V-h. (2008). News media use and knowledge about the 2006 U.S. midterm elections: Why exposure matters in voter learning. *International Journal of Public Opinion Research, 20,* 347–362.

37

USING NEW TECHNOLOGIES TO ENHANCE HEALTH COMMUNICATION RESEARCH METHODOLOGY

Susan E. Morgan, Andy J. King, and Rebecca K. Ivic

New technologies provide unique opportunities to design, execute, and evaluate studies that improve upon commonly accepted methodological standards for health communication research (Eng, 2002). For example, interactive computer technology can be used to conduct focus groups where people may feel at greater liberty to express controversial opinions about a topic, or to confess to participating in stigmatized health-related behaviors (Campbell et al, 2001). This additional information may prove critical to the development of an intervention aimed at changing health risk behaviors of a targeted population. Similarly, computer technology can assure the fidelity of an intervention by delivering precisely customized health messages to all members of a particular audience via tailoring, a task nearly impossible to do when using face-to-face (and most other) channels of communication.

In this chapter, we address specific ways that new technologies have been used to conduct basic and formative research, improve the delivery of health communication interventions, and create new opportunities for evaluation. Additionally, we discuss some of the ethical issues raised by the use of new technologies in the delivery and evaluation of interventions. Finally, we outline some of the limitations and opportunities that new technologies present for researchers.

The Use of New Technologies to Conduct Basic and Formative Research

In order to develop solid health communication interventions and campaigns, scholars and practitioners must first conduct formative research to determine the knowledge, attitudes, and behaviors that might be targeted by a program's health messages. In addition, researchers must either work from existing theories that have been demonstrated as effective in generating health-related behavior change, or they must work from the ground up to develop those theories, subsequently testing underlying principles. Once an intervention has been developed, pre-testing and formative evaluation can confirm its technological usability and functionality (see Connell et al., 2003 for an excellent example). Preliminary evidence finds new technologies useful in conducting both basic and formative research.

Online Focus Groups

The use of the Internet to purposefully conduct focus groups, rather than monitor discussion groups, constitutes a newer approach to conducting research. Traditionally, focus groups are conducted in face-to-face settings. The Internet provides a different versatility as a medium. Unrestricted by geography, new technologies provide researchers with great flexibility; able to support rich content (any combination of audio, video, and text) while maintaining confidential and secure conversation environments (Cheng, Krumwiede, & Sheu, 2009). These technical options make it possible for researchers to adapt focus groups to their specific needs. Online focus groups can be conducted via instant messaging, in a chat room, or in an online discussion group. They can be done using videoconferencing (Clapper & Massey, 1996), audio (Cheng et al., 2009), or through typing (Campbell et al., 2001). The Internet provides the opportunity to interact with hard-to-reach populations, such as those who are geographically dispersed (O'Lear, 1996), or individuals who may not have the ability to travel to a meeting (Campbell et al., 2001).

Similarly, many benefits exist for online focus group participants. Notably, greater anonymity is possible in online focus groups than face-to-face groups. Face-to-face groups can be problematic at times, as members may feel uncomfortable discussing sensitive issues with strangers. Online focus groups can help people feel more at ease, resulting in greater self-disclosure (Campbell et al., 2001). Some research has found that online focus groups using only audio produce higher quality responses, greater satisfaction, and more openness compared to face-to-face focus groups (e.g., Cheng et al., 2009). However, depending on the communication method used and the number of participants, it may be more difficult to determine who participated and who did not in online focus groups. One possible solution is for the researcher to ask each participant in turn to answer a question (e.g., Campbell et al., 2001), although this could limit the natural conversation dynamic in which researchers might want individuals to engage.

Online Discussion Groups, Listservs, and Bulletin Boards

Previous research in health communication has explored the role of online discussion groups and forums, website bulletin boards, and managed e-mail lists (e.g., listservs). Extant research has focused on the function of these communication outlets for different subpopulations (e.g., Ginossar, 2008), as well as the utility of these channels for social support (e.g., Sharf, 1997). As there are few empirical examples of research translating virtual community data into intervention formative research, we proffer suggestions of how current research might provide a springboard for future studies.

Identifying dissemination channels for an intervention is an important consideration during the formative research phase. Monitoring online discussion groups, joining topic-specific managed e-mail lists, and posting questions to certain website bulletin boards might allow researchers to gain great insight into channel preferences and media consumption patterns of a targeted population. Virtual communities can also act as sources for messages designed for interventions. For example, van Uden-Kraan et al. (2008) found that some participants engaging in online support groups felt empowered by their participation. By determining the language used by participants, and what types of information are transferred between online community members, researchers might be able to more efficiently create intervention materials. This could streamline message development for a campaign or intervention, as source material would be coming directly from the target audience just as it would through focus groups or interviews, but cut down on access and cost issues.

Geographic Information Systems (GIS) Technology

Public health researchers regularly use geographic information systems (GIS) to analyze disease clustering, environmental hazards, spread of infectious diseases, access to health services, and other aspects of public health care policy and practice (Cromley & McLafferty, 2002; Maheswaran & Craglia, 2004). GIS technology is far less common in health campaigns or health communication research in general. A growing body of scholarship on GIS demonstrates the potential of this technology to be used in the formative, dissemination, and evaluation stages of an intervention. More specifically, health communication intervention research can use GIS technology to identify geographic areas most in need of interventions, determine the most efficient means of intervention delivery, use the maps produced by GIS data as visual communication, and use existing systems to evaluate the impact of interventions.

Using GIS technology for formative research can assist in determining what areas are most affected by a particular set of risk factors, a disease cluster, or lack of health care services access. In the case of cancer control, GIS maps might assist intervention planners to advance particular components before others (Parrott, Hopfer, Ghetian, & Lengerich, 2007), or identify populations with the greatest need for intervention (e.g., Lubenow & Tolson, 2001; see also Parrott et al., 2010). Similarly, researchers interested in promoting cancer clinical trials might use GIS technology to determine if trials are being offered in areas with the highest cancer incidence. The utilization of GIS for formative research is mostly an extension of the epidemiological mapping being done by public health researchers. Collaborating with those individuals will likely allow communication researchers to be more efficient at using GIS during the formative phase.

New Technologies to Enhance the Delivery of Health Communication Interventions

The capacity of new technologies to incorporate a steady stream of novel elements into interventions can be seen as a strong methodological advantage over traditional delivery methods. There are several predominant uses of new technology that are used to deliver health interventions. These include web-based delivery, health message tailoring, freestanding computer kiosks, mobile communication devices, and serious gaming.

Web-Based Delivery of Health Interventions

Delivering interventions through the use of web-based content via computer is increasingly easy to do as technologies become more affordable. One advantage of web-based interventions is enhanced fidelity; multiple messages are delivered systematically and in a uniform fashion, using the same protocol with every participant even if they are widely dispersed geographically (see Glang, Noell, Ary, & Swartz, 2005). Web delivery also allows for the inclusion of multimedia components, which has enhanced the effectiveness of programs designed to enhance pedestrian safety, skin cancer prevention, and health behavior change counseling (Glang et al., 2005; Glasgow, Bull, Piette, & Steiner, 2004). In addition to being accessible any time of the day, web-based interventions can better segment populations than traditional, geographically bound interventions. The interactivity and multimedia options of web browsers also make these interventions promising because of the potential for increased levels of participant involvement.

Web-based health interventions are becoming increasingly common, and a meta-analysis revealed that web-based interventions were at least as effective as non-web-based interventions on behavioral change (Wantland, Portillo, Holzemer, Slaughter, & McGhee, 2004). A variety of randomized control trials on website interventions (e.g., Buller et al., 2008; Kypri et al., 2009) further inform researchers about how—or if—to utilize, and maximize the efficacy of, web-based efforts.

Health Message Tailoring

Tailoring interventions to specific populations is made easier through the use of web-based technologies (Buller et al., 2008). Because of the increasing availability of tailoring software discussion of the methodological implications and advances is warranted for this chapter. The information provided to an individual in interventions using tailoring is intended to reach only that individual specifically (Kreuter, Farrell, Olevitch, & Brennan, 1999). Traditionally, tailored interventions used software programs and message libraries to generate messages that were delivered after an initial wave of data collection. Providing instant, tailored health information, feedback, or persuasive messages is advantageous by standardizing dose and exposure rates to individuals, allowing for more rigorous evaluation of what message components, narrative structures, or specific types of information are advantageous in reaching intervention goals.

As Kreuter et al. (1999) predicted it, appears as though "software developed specifically for the purpose of automating tailored message[s]" *is* "the future of tailored health communication programs" (p. 199). The recent creation and release of the Michigan Tailoring System (MTS) presents one example of such a software platform (Center for Health Communication Research, 2009). This open source software package is one example of what will likely be a wide variety of open source code that will circumvent the need, for researchers or practitioners, to commission computer programmers to create tailoring software.

The availability of tailoring software and tailoring delivery methods will improve the ability to manipulate what elements result in the greatest effect sizes for tailored interventions (see Noar, Benac, & Harris, 2007). Using advances in tailoring research could go beyond population-level interventions as well. Focusing research on tailoring messages to policy makers or community representatives with the power to engage in major social change related to health issues could greatly advance health communication scholars' public health agenda. The key to major advances in tailoring is methodologically advancing available algorithms that will allow communication researchers to focus more on message design, resulting in improved intervention and campaign quality.

Free-Standing Computer Kiosks

Free-standing computer kiosks are touch-screen computers that can be programmed to display carefully selected information for targeted populations or individuals (see Jones, 2009). They can also track user activity (e.g., Connell et al., 2003), and have been used to promote children's health (Thompson, Lozano, & Christakis, 2007), encourage breast cancer screening (Kreuter et al., 2006), provide information on diabetes management (Lewis & Nath, 1997), and teach safe sex tactics to adolescents (Thomas, Cahill, & Santilli, 1997).

Typically, kiosks have been used as vital parts of large-scale health interventions. The Michigan Interactive Health Kiosk Project started in 1996, and has led to numerous communication interventions utilizing text, audio, video, and multimedia formats at kiosks across the state (Suggs, 2006; Thompson, Lozano, & Christakis, 2007). Similarly, Lin, Neafsey, and Strickler (2009) investigated the utility of a personal education program (PEP) system for older adults on a regimen for hypertension. The system was easy to use and helped participants avoid harmful self-medication errors, improving medical adherence. These results point to the utility of kiosks to deliver information to users with limited health literacy and computer experience.

There are numerous aspects to consider when delivering an intervention via kiosks. For instance, the location of a kiosk is crucial. Opportunistic sites must be used help ensure success of the intervention. Self-selection biases are prevalent drawbacks in research using kiosks. In the aforementioned kiosk projects in Michigan, for instance, the average user was 32 years old, and the highest usage rates were found among teens and young adults (see Connell et al., 2003). This was problematic as older adults were a target population for the kiosks. The researchers concluded that older adults were likely hesitant to approach kiosks because they mistakenly believed that computer experience was required to access health information.

Geographic Information Systems

Another way to use geographic information systems (GIS) is to determine the most efficient means of intervention delivery. A GIS analysis of health education kiosk use found that two community settings, laundromats and libraries, had greater localized reach than other community settings like beauty salons, churches, health fairs, neighborhood health centers, and social service agencies (Alcaraz, Kreuter, & Bryan, 2009). More research needs to be done to determine how GIS technology can be used to specify intervention sites or settings, such as laundromats or primary care practices, within communities and geographic locales identified as being at-risk. Additionally, researchers must remember that mapping technology "is useful in identifying *where* to intervene but provides little guidance about *how* to intervene" (Alcaraz et al., 2009, p. 55).

Serious Gaming

Gaming research simultaneously provides an intervention dissemination channel that is both a delivery method and a site for health communication interventions. Games allow for a storyline-based interaction(s) between intervention participants and customizable interfaces, with the added benefit of the game's ability to remember, store, and recall play history and information about participants. This allows video games to have narrativity, simulation, interactivity, and intelligence (Ritterfeld & Weber, 2006), diversity that seemingly no other delivery method can provide. The interactive nature of gaming also allows for personalized content (e.g., targeted or tailored messages), user control, multiple presentation modes (i.e., video, audio, and text), and portability (Lieberman, 2000). These traits make games ideal for all sorts of messages and message components, adaptable for a variety of health issues, groups, and individuals.

There is also potential for gaming research to directly increase healthy behaviors, like physical activity. "Exergames" refer to games compelling users to engage in some type of physical activity while playing the game, breaking from the traditional "sedentary pastime" of gaming (Lieberman, 2006, p. 1). Evaluations of these interventions have demonstrated mixed results, ranging from minimal improvements in physical activity (Madsen, Yen, Wlasiuk, Newman, & Lustig, 2007), to claims that *Dance Revolution* provides a rigorous enough workout according to exercise guidelines (Tan, Aziz, Chua, & Teh, 2002). There is also some research into using Nintendo's *Wii*™ gaming console, which utilizes wireless remote control technology to help enhance individual interactivity during game play. One case study examined the potential of *Wii Fit*™, a particular game for the console, to assist in the rehabilitation process of an adolescent with cerebral palsy with promising results (Deutsch, Borbely, Filler, Huhn, & Guarrera-Bowlby, 2008).

Perhaps the most involved of all gaming research is that which includes an entirely interactive environment for participants/users. Real-time virtual worlds allow individuals to create avatars, which act as virtual personas (Centers for Disease Control and Prevention [CDC], 2008). The CDC recently developed two virtual worlds as part of their e-Health marketing plan: *Whyville* and a space in *Second Life*. *Whyville* is intended for tweens (8- to 15-year-olds), and allows participating youth to create their own avatar, a Whyvillian, to vicariously experience things in the fictitious town. The site promotes influenza prevention by offering participating youth virtual vaccinations (CDC, 2008). The CDC reports virtually vaccinating 40,000 *Whyville* users, and holding a virtual event with thousands of participants (CDC, 2008). Another CDC initiative focused on developing a space inside of the popular *Second Life* computer game. The CDC's space in the game includes interactive content, as well as streaming video, historical public health posters, and links to information on the organizations website. Currently, the CDC is developing a *Second Life*-island that will contain a virtual lab, conference center, and other interactive activities (CDC, 2008).

Gaming research is promising, but not all studies find that games improve health-related outcomes with individuals or find significant advantages for the use of this technology (e.g., Huss et al., 2003; Silk et al., 2008). Other research indicates the potential boomerang effects of games on psychosocial variables (i.e., lowering response efficacy and intention to receive treatment if diagnosed with cancer; see Prestin, So, Lieberman, Kang, & Anderson, 2008). Additionally, the majority of health gaming studies focus on children and adolescents (see Baranowski, Buday, Thompson, & Baranowski, 2008) rather than adults (see Peng, 2009; Read et al., 2006; Thomas et al., 1997 for adult gaming research examples).

The Use of New Technologies to Improve Intervention Evaluation Methodology

One of the most exciting applications for new technologies is evaluation research. For example, new technologies used for summative evaluation research can be highly efficient when compared to administering paper-and-pencil surveys (Supple, Aquilino, & Wright, 1999). Because there is little if any data entry, surveys administered using personal digital assistants (PDAs) and laptops are likely to yield more accurate data and have the potential to be less expensive because respondents themselves enter the data. New technologies are also useful for assessing the reach and success of interventions that aim to improve patient–provider interactions. In particular, analysis of e-mail exchanges between providers and patients can reveal whether campaigns and interventions are working as intended. How each type of new technology has been used for evaluation research is further described in this section.

Telephones and Mobile Communication Devices

Mobile communication devices are useful in the delivery of health communication intervention messages because they are widely available and easy to use (Weaver et al., 2007), creating a relative methodological advantage over other forms of new technology. These technologies allow researchers access to a target population more freely than traditional methods. Some interventions employing these devices show considerable promise. These evaluations may include real-time patient assessments conducted via phone (e.g., Weaver et al., 2007), and use handheld computers (Denny et al., 2008) or PDAs (Stroud, Smith, & Erkel, 2009). Mobile devices present a useful opportunity for research because they can aid populations who may otherwise lack access to technology (Quilin et al., 2009).

Interestingly, the mere use of phone technology itself may enhance the effectiveness of health interventions. In a comparison of delivery methods for messages designed to increase mammography, tailored telephone messages generated by a computer algorithm (but read by a female physician) increased adherence over identical messages delivered in print format (Lipkus, Rimer, Halabi, & Strigo, 2000). The mechanism underlying the increased effect is not clear; however, it is possible that receivers perceived printed messages to be more impersonal.

Use of PDAs to Collect Data

PDAs, generally, organize personal information such as memos and lists and can use software programs to manage patient information and clinical care references (Stroud et al., 2009). In recent years, PDAs have developed faster processors, increased storage capacity, wireless capability, and easier portability. This makes them ideal for mobile research laboratories, because they can integrate multiple databases, providing instant access to schedules, lab reports, and patient and pharmacy records (Vishwanath, Brodsky, & Shaha, 2009). Additionally, PDAs can serve as data collection instruments for researchers interested in gathering data for a project on site (e.g., a workplace participating in a worksite campaign).

Advances in PDAs make them useful tools for health interventions and research. For example, researchers have collected various types of data from HIV patients and, in turn, have delivered counseling protocol training to nurses involved in HIV care (Kurth et al., 2007). In another example, Fowles and Gentry (2008) provided a sample of women with PDAs to track their dietary intake. The researchers found that women who used the PDA to record their eating habits in real time were more accurate than those who later tried to recall their consumption from memory. More research should examine the use of PDAs as supplemental tools in self-care health studies. To this end, PDAs are also useful in conjunction with web-based tools in health interventions. Kurth et al. (2007) developed web-based tools for use on PDAs to collect information from HIV patients and to deliver counseling protocol training to nurses involved with HIV care. Based on the information patients entered in the tool, the PDAs provided participants with tailored feedback.

PDAs are also useful in collecting data from hard-to-reach populations and for reaching underserved or low-income populations (e.g., Fowles & Gentry, 2008). PDAs should not be limited to only serving as a handheld electronic survey. For example, interventions aimed at improving fruit and vegetable consumption, general nutrition, and exercise might consider providing participants with PDAs to track outcomes of interest such as changes in consumption patterns, saturated fat intake, and frequency of exercise.

Use of Laptop Computers to Collect Data

Researchers have found that computerized data collection offers improved privacy, confidentiality, and portability over paper-and-pencil methods (Bobula et al., 2004; Supple et al., 1999). Laptops have also been useful for health interventions in the homes of targeted populations (Barrera, Glasgow, McKay, Boles, & Feil, 2002) and in schools (Denny et al., 2008). A further advantage of using laptops to administer surveys involves the potential to improve the validity of self-reported data (e.g., Denny et al., 2008; Supple et al., 1999).

Studies have collected survey data via laptops targeting youth and adolescents, particularly because formative research has found that these populations are comfortable using laptops (Bobula et al., 2004; Denny et al., 2008; Supple et al., 1999). For instance, Supple et al. (1999) brought laptops to the homes of adolescents to collect sensitive self-report data from them about their smoking, alcohol, and illegal drug use, either by pencil and paper or via provided laptops. Participants who used laptops were more likely to admit to illicit drug use, perceived more anonymity during the study, and had a more favorable attitude toward using their respective laptops than those who used pencil and paper (Supple et al., 1999). Other research also revealed higher self-disclosure from adolescents when using laptops but the size of laptops used in data collection might influence adolescent perceptions of privacy and confidentiality (Denny et al., 2008). Interestingly, tablet laptops (smaller versions of laptop computers) were reported as being more private and confidential. The size of the laptop, then, can be important when using laptops for survey administration, especially when addressing sensitive information in campaign evaluation.

Although laptops have been used for data collection and health interventions, they can also be useful in conjunction with web-based interventions. For example, the National Cancer Institute's Cancer Information Service (CIS) provided laptop and Internet access to improve the quality of life for underserved breast cancer patients (Gustafson et al., 2005). Similarly, Barrera et al. (2002) installed computers in the homes of individuals with Type 2 diabetes to assess the ability of online social support interventions to change participants' perceptions of social support. Participants under the social support condition perceived social support to be more readily available. The three-month study interval may have been too short to see the full effects of computer-mediated social support, and a longer study may have yielded different, and perhaps stronger, results.

There is major overlap between the potential of PDAs and laptops in improving the quality and types of data available in campaign evaluation. Generally, researchers should consider how laptops might be able to provide different types of data than collected in the past. For example, during the course of an intervention, with appropriate consent obtained, researchers could include software that determines what health information people seek or scan during an intervention or campaign period. This would provide a concrete behavioral measure for information seeking or scanning that might be otherwise difficult or inefficient to measure through other means (e.g., recall measures).

GIS as an Evaluation Tool

Some researchers have suggested that GIS can be used as an evaluation tool (Renger, Cimetta, Pettygrove, & Rogan, 2002). Applying the evaluation possibilities of GIS to health communication campaigns and interventions has not been explored, but there is great potential. For example, GIS data could allow researchers to examine how continued intervention efforts, policy changes, and new program implementation waves might decrease risk factors for a particular geographic region over time. Collecting zip code data from participants when conducting intervention evaluations could allow researchers to more accurately track the reach of campaign messages; although, researchers should be aware of issues between using ZIP codes compared to ZIP code tabulation areas (ZCTAs), which are used by the U.S. Census (see Grubesic & Matisziw, 2006). There is great potential for GIS technology to influence research at all intervention phases, but considerably more research is needed.

Patient–Provider Communication for Intervention/Campaign Evaluation

Analyzing physician–patient e-mail exchange might be one outlet for intervention or campaign evaluation that has not previously been considered. A content analysis of e-mails between patients and health care providers participating in a test study of an electronic communication system demonstrated the potential of such communication for intervention and campaign researchers; many patients provided their physicians with information updates (41.4%), health questions (13.2%), questions about test results (10.9%), and referrals (8.8%; White, Moyer, Stern, & Katz, 2004).

The use of any technology to investigate or improve the patient–physician interaction potentially suffers from issues of gaining access to appropriate samples. Even though research demonstrates that many individuals with access to e-mail are interested in using that communicative tool to interact with their doctors, studies do not report improvement in communication satisfaction scores for patients who do or do not use e-mail (Stalberg, Yeh, Ketteridge, Dellbridge, & Dellbridge, 2008).

Ethical Issues of New Technologies in Health Communication Research

New technologies have considerable potential to improve public health outcomes by improving the methodologies researchers use to create, implement, and evaluate the effectiveness of health interventions. There are, however, several ethical issues that should be considered before research is undertaken. First, it is important that special precautions are taken to protect the privacy and confidentiality of audience members or participants (Eng, 2002). One study reported that after a patient entered information it was saved onto the hard drive of the computer in the clinic waiting room (Prochaska, Zabininski, Calfas, Sallis, & Patrick, 2000); in such situations it would be critical to encrypt files and programs to keep other patients or non-study personnel from accessing confidential information. Protecting privacy and confidentiality of respondents is especially important because studies show that people feel freer to confess to illegal drug use or risky sexual behavior when data collection is done via computer (Palmgreen, Donohew, Lorch, Hoyle, & Stephenson, 2002), which is a significant methodological strength of using computers.

A second possible ethical issue is the difficulty of knowing about adverse events if they occur. New technology offers distance and anonymity for participants and researchers alike. While this can be a benefit for both parties, breaches of privacy and confidentiality may not be known or may be known only after it is too late to mitigate potential damage. Similarly, researchers may not be able to readily observe unintended consequences of interventions mediated by technology. For example, weight control websites offer means for people to meticulously record food consumption and exercise as a way to assess the intake and expenditure of calories. For people prone to eating disorders, such websites might exacerbate or enable dysfunctional behaviors. As Fogg (2003) points out, computers cannot shoulder responsibility for adverse events or unintended consequences; it is up to researchers to anticipate them and to try to incorporate mechanisms that will increase the likelihood that we can intervene in a timely manner.

A third ethical issue arises if new technologies that are designed to improve public health are used in the surveillance of individuals, particularly if individuals face punishment for noncompliance (Fogg, 2003). For example, Fogg describes a surveillance technology program called Hygiene Guard, which monitors employee hand washing. Sensor technology reads employee badges and measures the amount of time the employee stands at a restroom sink; any period less than 30 seconds is recorded as an infraction of hygiene guidelines. While this technology may prove to be a useful evaluation tool to assess whether a hand washing campaign has been successful, it may prove to be a far too draconian strategy for assessing employee behavior if misused.

Finally, researchers need to consider the ways in which the use of new technologies may leave out underserved populations (Eng, 2002). Although the digital divide has narrowed, the rural and urban poor and the elderly still lack the access and skills needed to use many forms of new technology (Wright & Hill, 2009). While some studies have done admirable work in creating highly accessible forms of technology that require few or no computer skills (Lin et al., 2009), these remain the exception rather than the standard. Without conscious efforts to reach underserved populations with our strongest, most innovative interventions we only exacerbate existing health disparities (Hay et al., 2009).

Limitations of Research Using New Technologies

New technologies are important tools that can be used by health communication researchers, but there are certain limitations that warrant consideration. First, new technologies cannot magically improve a poorly constructed intervention. Second, it is unclear whether interventions that are delivered using new technologies would be more powerful if combined with face-to-face communication. New technologies offer the capacity to tailor to individual attitudes, traits, and behavioral risk factors, but they cannot respond "on the fly" to questions and objections that have not been anticipated by researchers well in advance. In contrast, peer health educators are able to read subtle nonverbal cues that indicate the need to clarify a concept or to address an issue at a deeper level. Additionally, research on the use of hand-held devices to gather patient information seems to indicate that pairing this technology with live interpersonal feedback is an effective means of creating health behavior change (Glasgow et al., 2004; Leeman-Castillo et al., 2007; Lin et al., 2009). Perhaps research should consider how to include a virtual face-to-face component in interventions utilizing highly technological delivery or evaluation methods.

It is also unclear in what ways new technologies fundamentally change the way people interact. Previous research has indicated that face-to-face support groups appear to differ in systematic ways from online social support groups (Klemm & Hardie, 2002), and these issues logically extend to other forums where people disclose and respond to personal information. Researchers should keep this in mind if they are basing interventions on current theories about interpersonal interaction and self-disclosure, which may not be entirely applicable when new technologies are introduced into the mix. This, however, can be viewed as an opportunity for theory development and testing in a new context.

Fourth, when conducting certain types of evaluation that compare a new technology to deliver an intervention compared to more traditional methods, researchers may find that it is difficult, if not impossible, to create a truly parallel "traditional" intervention (Brug, Steenhuis, van Assema, & de Vries, 1996; Lipkus et al., 2000). This may also be true when researchers and practitioners try to create interventions for populations that do not have the access, ability, or motivation required to use new technologies. In other words, the intervention may be, in part, promoting the technology itself. In either case, evaluating the success of the intervention when attempting to combine or contrast methods of delivery may face a serious confound.

Fifth, self-selection bias may be a problem when attempting to recruit participants to participate in an intervention or health communication research that is mediated by new technologies. Only people with a particular skill set and the motivation to engage with new technologies are likely to be willing to participate. Research has demonstrated that even when interventions are adapted for naïve users of technology, self-selection bias occurs (Wantland et al., 2004).

Finally, attrition may be greater in studies that rely on technology (Eysenbach, 2005). Many traditional types of health intervention that involve a face-to-face element create a sense of personal connection or responsibility. When engaged with an intervention that is wholly mediated by technology, this sense of responsibility to continue with participation would not be present. Attrition is a serious methodological issue because it decreases the statistical power needed to conduct a valid evaluation of an intervention. Thus, it is especially important to seek ways to keep participants actively involved.

New Directions for Research Using New Technologies

There are several challenges facing researchers who are considering using new technologies. First and foremost, new methods will undoubtedly have to be further developed and the strengths and weaknesses of those methods will need to be evaluated by the scholarly community. One way to begin to assess what is gained and what is lost through new technologies is to conduct rigorous studies that closely compare traditional research methods with methods that integrate (or rely wholly upon) new technologies (Noell & Glasgow, 1999). As these comparative evaluations occur, it will be important to attempt to identify the underlying sociological, psychological, or physiological mechanisms that might be responsible for the increased effectiveness of interventions, such as increased elaboration or stimulation from an interactive intervention delivered via new technologies. For example, most current intervention studies using new technologies focus solely on the effects of these interventions on individuals without consideration of other influences. Future research should consider the role of important others in targeted populations' lives that could be moderating or mediating the outcomes of interest. Additionally, intervention effects could extend beyond the individual to affect others within a receiver's network of relationships. Looking past the individual will allow for a deeper understanding of how technologies can efficiently promote health.

Of course, the integration of new technologies to improve research practice does not entail an either–or choice. In addition to combining interpersonal or face-to-face communication with some form of mediated communication, and assessing the relative effectiveness of different forms of new technology for conducting formative evaluation, intervention implementation, and summative evaluation, it is important that we evaluate the cost-effectiveness of the use of these technologies. In some cases, such as downloading messages from an online bulletin board, there may be enormous cost advantages over traditional methods like interviewing. However, in the case of intervention delivery, we have to address the question of whether the costs for development, implementation, and maintenance of certain intervention types are reasonable relative to the impact on health outcomes, health care quality, and access (Eng, 2002; Noell & Glasgow, 1999).

There are some areas where future research challenges are much the same as with the use of traditional means of conducting and evaluating health interventions. For example, it is not clear whether interventions delivered via new technology are effective over the long term. As with all types of health communication interventions, longitudinal studies are needed (Wantland et al., 2004). Similarly, interventions must consider the importance of maximizing exposure; simply "putting the message out there" does not guarantee that members of the target audience will encounter it (Snyder & Hamilton, 2002). There seems to be an opportunity to greatly increase the number of longitudinal studies conducted as new technologies allow greater access to participants. While traditional longitudinal studies are expensive to conduct, the ability to use online surveys and the declining costs of new technologies could improve the likelihood of increases in longitudinal studies.

There appears to be a certain level of giddiness over the potential of social networking to reach audiences (e.g., Eysenbach, 2008), but there is still limited evidence to suggest how social networking platforms can improve the delivery of health campaigns or interventions. Messages delivered via these channels should still contain new information presented in ways that are perceived as novel and interesting by audience members for these messages to make a significant impact (Snyder & Hamilton, 2002). This is not to say that we should not always be searching for new ways to strengthen the field of health communication by using these new technologies. Perhaps researchers should consider how to use these social networking sites to study how to effectively disseminate health messages between individuals, maximizing frequency of message exposure through network ties while using a platform that can facilitate instant feedback about perceived message quality, attitude toward the ad, and other relevant message design constructs. Researchers should also study the phenomenon of illness-specific social networking sites, and the impact of these sites on health outcomes, social support, and the quality of life of individuals with certain medical conditions.

Researchers should also consider how they might assist in diffusing new technologies to underserved populations. For example, interventions using message tailoring in underserved urban populations are not uncommon, but interventions with rural populations receiving tailoring appear less frequently in the literature. One reason for this may be that for urban populations, interactive kiosks can be used by large numbers of people at high traffic areas. In rural populations, there are far fewer high traffic areas, making kiosks less ideal. Considering how to put together a mobile research lab for rural data collection and intervention delivery would allow researchers to test the effects of tailoring on previously unexplored vulnerable populations.

In addition to looking for ways to "adopt new technologies as they become available to meet the changing health information needs of Americans, as well as Internet users worldwide" (Bright, 2005, p. 11), we should be looking for corresponding ways to meet the needs of researchers to strengthen formative and summative evaluations of innovative interventions designed to improve the health of the population.

References

Alcaraz, K. I., Kreuter, M. W. & Bryan, R. P. (2009). Use of GIS to identify optimal settings for cancer prevention and control in African American communities. *Preventive Medicine, 49*, 54–57.

Baranowski, T., Buday, R., Thompson, D. I., & Baranowski, J. (2008). Playing for real: Video games and stories for health-related behavior change. *American Journal of Preventive Medicine, 34*, 74–82.

Barrera, M., Glasgow, R., McKay, H. G., Boles, S. M., & Feil, E. G. (2002). Do Internet-based support interventions change perceptions of social support? An experimental trial of approaches for supporting diabetes self-management. *American Journal of Community Psychology, 30*, 637–654.

Bobula, J. A., Anderson, L. S., Riesch, S. K., Canty-Mitchell, J., Duncan, A., Kaiser-Krueger, H. A., ... Angresano, N. (2004). Enhancing survey data collection among youth and adults. *Computers Informatics Nursing, 22*, 255–265.

Bright, M. A. (2005). The National Cancer Institute's Cancer Information Service: A new generation of service and research to the nation. *Journal of Health Communication, 10*, 7–13.

Brug, J., Steenhuis, I., van Assema, P., & de Vries, H. (1996). The impact of a computer-tailored nutrition intervention. *Preventive Medicine, 25,* 236–242.

Buller, D. B., Woodall, W. G., Zimmerman, D. E., Slater, M. D., Heimendinger, J., Waters, E., … Cutter, G. R. (2008). Randomized trial on the 5 a day, the Rio Grande way website: A web-based program to improve fruit and vegetable consumption in rural communities. *Journal of Health Communication, 13,* 230–249.

Campbell, M. K., Meier, A., Carr, C., Enga, Z., James, A. S., Reedy, J., & Zheng, B. (2001). Health behavior changes after colon cancer: A comparison of findings from face-to-face and on-line focus groups. *Family & Community Health, 24,* 88–103.

Center for Health Communication Research. (2009). *Michigan tailoring system* [computer software]. Ann Arbor, MI: University of Michigan.

Centers for Disease Control and Prevention (CDC). (2008, April 14). *Virtual world: eHealth marketing.* Retrieved from http://www.cdc.gov/healthmarketing/ehm/virtual.html

Cheng, C. C., Krumwiede, D., & Sheu, C. (2009). Online audio group discussions: A comparison with face-to-face methods. *International Journal of Market Research, 51,* 219–241.

Clapper, D., & Massey, A. (1996). Electronic focus groups: A framework for exploration. *Information and Management, 30,* 43–50.

Connell, C. M., Shaw, B. A., Holmes, S. B., Hudson, M. L., Derry, H. A., & Strecher, V. J. (2003). The development of an Alzheimer's disease channel for the Michigan interactive health kiosk project. *Journal of Health Communication, 8,* 11–22.

Cromley, E. K., & McLafferty, S. L. (2002). *GIS and public health.* New York: Guilford Press.

Denny, S. J., Milfont, T. L., Utter, J., Robinson, E. M., Ameratunga, S. N., Merry, S. N., … Watson, P. D. (2008). Hand-held Internet tablets for school-based data collection. *BMC Research Notes, 1,* 1–4.

Deutsch, J. E., Borbely, M., Filler, J., Huhn, K., & Guarrera-Bowlby, P. (2008). Use of a low-cost, commercially available gaming console (Wii) for rehabilitation of an adolescent with cerebral palsy. *Physical Therapy, 88,* 1196–1207.

Eng, T. R. (2002). eHealth research and evaluation: Challenges and opportunities. *Journal of Health Communication, 7,* 267–272.

Eysenbach, G. (2005). The law of attrition. *Journal of Medical Internet Research, 7,* e11.

Eysenbach, G. (2008). Medicine 2.0: Social networking, collaboration, participation, apomediation, and openness. *Journal of Medical Internet Research, 10,* e22.

Fogg, B. J. (2003). *Persuasive technology: Using computers to change what we think and do.* San Francisco, CA: Morgan Kaufmann.

Fowles, E. R., & Gentry, B. (2008). The feasibility of personal digital assistants (PDAs) to collect dietary intake data in low-income pregnant women. *Journal of Nutrition Education and Behavior, 40,* 374–377.

Ginossar, T. (2008). Online participation: A content analysis of differences in utilization of two cancer communities by men and women, patients, and family members. *Health Communication, 23,* 1–12.

Glang, A., Noell, J., Ary, D., & Swartz, L. (2005). Using interactive multimedia to teach pedestrian safety: An exploratory study. *American Journal of Health Behavior, 29,* 435–442.

Glasgow, R., Bull, S., Piette, J., & Steiner, J. (2004). Interactive behavior change technology: A partial solution to the competing demands for primary care. *American Journal of Preventive Medicine, 27,* 80–87.

Grubesic, T. H., & Matisziw, T. C. (2006). On the use of ZIP codes and ZIP code tabulation areas (ZCTAs) for the spatial analysis of epidemiological data. *International Journal of Health Geographics, 5,* 58.

Gustafson, D. H., McTavish, F. M., Stengle, W., Ballard, D., Jones, E., Julesberg, K., … Hawkins, R. (2005). Reducing the digital divide for low-income women with breast cancer: A feasibility study of a population-based intervention. *Journal of Health Communication, 10,* 173–193.

Hay, J., Harris, J. N., Waters, E. A., Clayton, M. F., Ellington, L., Abernethy, A. D., & Prayor-Patterson, H. (2009). Personal communication in primary and secondary cancer prevention: Evolving discussions, emerging challenges. *Journal of Health Communication, 14,* 18–29.

Huss, K., Winkelstein, M., Nanda, J., Naumann, P. L., Sloand, E. D., & Huss, R. W. (2003). Computer game for inner-city children does not improve asthma outcomes. *Journal of Pediatric Health Care, 17*(2), 72–78.

Jones, R. (2009). The role of health kiosks in 2009: Literature and informant review. *International Journal of Environmental Research and Public Health, 6,* 1818–1855.

Klemm, P., & Hardie, T. (2002). Depression in internet and face to face cancer support groups: A pilot study. *Oncology Nursing Forum, 29,* 45–51.

Kreuter, M. W., Black, W. J., Friend, L., Booker, A. C., Klump, P., Bobra, S., & Holt, C. L. (2006). Use of computer kiosks for breast cancer education in five community settings. *Health Education Behavior, 33,* 625–642.

Kreuter, M. W., Farrell, D., Olevitch, L., & Brennan, L. (1999). *Tailored health messages: Customizing communication with computer technology.* Mahwah, NJ: Erlbaum.

Kurth, A. E., Curioso, W. H., Ngugi, E., McClelland, L., Segura, P., Cabello, R., & Berry, D. L. (2007). Personal digital assistants for HIV treatment adherence, safer sex behavior support, and provider training in resource-constrained settings. *AMIA Annual Symposium Proceedings* (p. 1018). Bethesda, MD: AMIA.

Kypri, K., Hallett, J., Howat, P., McManus, A., Maycock, B., Bowe, S., & Horton, N. J. (2009). Randomized controlled trial of proactive web-based alcohol screening and brief intervention for university students. *Archives of Internal Medicine, 169,* 1508–1514.

Leeman-Castillo, B. A., Corbett, K. K., Aagaard, E. M., Maselli, J. H., Gonzales, R., & Mackenzie, T. D. (2007). Acceptability of a bilingual interactive computerized educational module in a poor, medically underserved patient population. *Journal of Health Communication, 12,* 77–94.

Lewis, D., & Nath, C. (1997). Feasibility of a kiosk-based patient education system in a busy outpatient clinic setting. *Diabetes Educator, 23,* 577–586.

Lieberman, D. A. (2000). Using interactive media in communication campaigns for children and adolescents. In R. Rice & C. Atkin (Eds.), *Public communication campaigns* (3rd ed., pp. 373–388). Thousand Oaks, CA: Sage.

Lieberman, D. A. (2006, April). *Dance games and other exergames: What the research says.* Retrieved from http://www.comm.ucsb.edu/faculty/lieberman/ exergames.htm

Lin, C. A., Neafsey, P. J., & Strickler, Z. (2009). Usability testing by older adults of a computer-mediated health communication program. *Journal of Health Communication, 14,* 102–118.

Lipkus, I. M., Rimer, B. K., Halabi, S., & Strigo, T. S. (2000). Can tailored interventions increase mammography use among HMO women? *American Journal of Preventive Medicine, 18,* 1–10.

Lubenow, A., & Tolson, K. (2001). GIS technology helps pinpoint patients. *Health Management Technology, 22,* 54–55.

Madsen, K. A., Yen, S., Wlasiuk, L., Newman, T. B., & Lustig, R. (2007). Feasibility of a dance videogame to promote weight loss among overweight children and adolescents. *Archives of Pediatric & Adolescent Medicine, 161,* 105–107,

Maheswaran, R., & Craglia, M. (Eds.). (2004). *GIS in public health practice.* Boca Raton, FL: CRC.

Noar, S. M., Benac, C. N., & Harris, M. S. (2007). Does tailoring matter? Meta-analytic review of tailored health behavior change interventions. *Psychological Bulletin, 133,* 673–693.

Noell, J., & Glasgow, R. E. (1999). Interactive technology applications for behavioral counseling: Issues and opportunities for health care settings. *American Journal of Preventive Medicine, 17,* 269–274.

O'Lear, R. M. (1996). Using electronic mail (e-mail), surveys for geographic research: Lessons from a survey of Russian environmentalists. *Professional Geographer, 48,* 209–217.

Palmgreen, P., Donohew, L. Lorch, E. P., Hoyle, R. H., & Stephenson, M. T. (2002). Television campaigns and sensation seeking targeting of adolescent marijuana use: A controlled time series approach. In R. C. Hornik (Ed.), *Public health communication: Evidence for behavior change* (pp. 35–56). Mahwah, NJ: Erlbaum.

Parrott, R., Hopfer, S., Ghetian, C., & Lengerich, E. (2007). Mapping as a visual health communication tool: Promises and dilemmas. *Health Communication, 22,* 13–24.

Parrott, R., Volkman, J., Lengerich, E., Ghetian, C., Chadwick, A., & Hopfer, S. (2010). Using geographic systems to promote community involvement in comprehensive cancer control. *Health Communication, 25,* 276–285.

Peng, W. (2009). Design and evaluation of a computer game to promote a health diet for young adults. *Health Communication, 24,* 115–127.

Prestin, A., So, J., Leiberman, D. A., Kang, P., & Anderson, G. (2008, November). *Involvement as a moderator of the effects of a cancer education video game.* Paper presented at the annual meeting of the National Communication Association, San Diego, CA.

Prochaska, J. J., Zabinski, M. F., Calfas, K. J., Sallis, J. F., & Patrick, K. (2000). PACE+: Interactive communication technology for behavior change in clinical settings. *American Journal of Preventive Medicine, 19,* 127–131.

Quillin, J. M., Tracy, K., Ancker, J. S., Mustian, K. M., Ellington, L., Vishwanath, V., & Miller, S. M. (2009). Health care system approaches for cancer patient communication. *Journal of Health Communication, 14,* 85–94.

Read, S. J., Miller, L. C., Appleby, P. R., Nwosu, M. E., Reynaldo, S., Lauren, A., ... Putcha, A. (2006). Socially optimized learning in a virtual environment: Reducing risky sexual behavior among men who have sex with men. *Human Communication Research, 32,* 1–34.

Renger, R., Cimetta, A., Pettygrove, S., & Rogan, S. (2002). Geographic information systems (GIS) as an evaluation tool. *American Journal of Evaluation, 23,* 469–479.

Ritterfield, U., & Weber, R. (2006). Video games for entertainment and education. In P. Vorderer & J. Bryant (Eds.), *Playing video games: Motives, responses, & consequences* (pp. 399–413). Mahwah, NJ: Erlbaum.

Sharf, B. F. (1997). Communicating breast cancer on-line: Support and empowerment on the Internet. *Women & Health, 26,* 65–84.

Silk, K. J., Sherry, J., Winn, B., Keesecker, N., Horodynski, M. A., & Sayir, A. (2008). Increasing nutrition literacy: Testing the effectiveness of print, Web site, and game modalities. *Journal of Nutrition Education and Behavior, 40,* 3–10.

Snyder, L. B., & Hamilton, M. A. (2002). Meta-analysis of U.S. health campaign effects on behavior: Emphasize enforcement, exposure, and new information, and beware the secular trend. In R. C. Hornik (Ed.), *Public health communication: Evidence for behavior change* (pp. 357–383). Mahwah, NJ: Erlbaum.

Stalberg, P., Yeh, M., Ketteridge, G., Dellbridge, H., & Dellbridge, L. (2008). E-mail access and improved communication between patient and surgeon. *Archives of Surgery, 143,* 164–168.

Stroud, S. D., Smith, C. A., & Erkel, E. A. (2009). Personal digital assistant use by nurse practitioners: A descriptive study. *Journal of the American Academy of Nurse Practitioners, 21,* 31–38.

Suggs, L. S. (2006). A 10-year retrospective of research in new technologies for health communication. *Journal of Health Communication, 11,* 61–74.

Supple, A. J., Aquilino, W. S., & Wright, D. L. (1999). Collecting sensitive self-report data with laptop computers: Impact on the response tendencies of adolescents in a home interview. *Journal of Research on Adolescence, 9,* 467–488.

Tan, B., Aziz, A. R., Chua, K., & Teh, K. C. (2002). Aerobic demands of the dance simulation game. *International Journal of Sports Medicine, 23,* 125–129.

Thomas, R., Cahill, J., & Santilli, L. (1997). Using an interactive computer game to increase skill and self-efficacy regarding safer sex negotiation: Field test results. *Health Education & Behavior, 24,* 71–86.

Thompson, D. A., Lozano, P., & Christakis, D. A. (2007). Parent use of touchscreen computer kiosks for child health promotion in community settings. *Pediatrics, 119,* 427–434.

van Uden-Kraan, C. F., Drossaert, C. H. H., Taal, E., Shaw, B. R., Seydel, E. R., & van de Laar, M. A. F. J. (2008). Empowering processes and outcomes of participation in online support groups for patients with breast cancer, arthritis, or fibromyalgia. *Qualitative Health Research, 18,* 405–417.

Vishwanath, A., Brodsky, L., & Shaha, S. (2009). Physician adoption of personal digital assistants (PDA): Testing its determinants within a structural equation model. *Journal of Health Communication, 14,* 77–95.

Wantland, D. J., Portillo, C. J., Holzemer, W. L., Slaughter, R., & McGee, E. M. (2004). The effectiveness of web-based vs. non-web-based interventions: A meta-analysis of behavioral change outcomes. *Journal of Medical Internet Research, 6,* e40.

Weaver, A., Young, A. M., Rowntree, J., Townsend, N., Pearson, S., Smith, J., ... Tarassenko, L. (2007). Application of mobile phone technology for managing chemotherapy-associated side-effects. *Annals of Oncology, 18,* 1887–1892.

White, C. B., Moyer, C. A., Stern, D. T., & Katz, S. J. (2004). A content analysis of e-mail communication between patients and their providers: Patients get the message. *Journal of the American Medical Informatics Association, 11,* 260–267.

Wright, D.W., & Hill, T. J. (2009). Prescription for trouble: Medicare Part D and patterns of computer and internet access among the elderly. *Journal of Aging and Social Policy, 21,* 172–186.

SECTION VII

Overarching Issues in Health Communication

38

TRANSLATING HEALTH COMMUNICATION RESEARCH INTO PRACTICE

The Influence of Health Communication Scholarship on Health Policy, Practice, and Outcomes

Gary L. Kreps

Health communication is an inherently applied area of social scientific inquiry that examines the powerful roles performed by human and mediated communication in delivering health care and promoting health. Health communication research is typically problem-based, focused on explicating, examining, and addressing important and troubling health care and health promotion problems. These problems might include difficulties in promoting active coordination and collaboration in the delivery of care, demands to eliminate inadvertent errors made that jeopardize quality of care, attempts to meet unmet health information needs to guide health decisions, and the quest to overcome serious inequities in care that lead to poor health outcomes. The applied nature of health communication inquiry is firmly grounded in the implicit goal to facilitate improvements in the delivery of care and the promotion of health, ultimately enhancing health outcomes. This chapter focuses on evaluating where we are as health communication scholars in achieving this important translational goal and what we need to do to really make a significant positive difference in enhancing the delivery of health care and the promotion of public health.

To improve health care and health promotion, health communication scholars must take their work very seriously and go the extra mile to translate health communication research into practice. Taking health communication scholarship seriously means conducting relevant, rigorous, and far-reaching studies that generate valid, reliable, and generalizable data that can ably inform health care and health promotion practices. It means working to actively transform raw health communication research findings into practical and usable health care/promotion interventions and policies. It means carefully testing the efficacy and monitoring the outcomes (both positive and negative outcomes) of evidence-based health communication interventions within actual health care systems. It also means developing meaningful public partnerships with health care providers, consumers, administrators, government agencies, support organizations, and policy makers to effectively design, implement, and institutionalize the best evidence-based health communication interventions within society. Health communication scholarship has come a long way over the past several decades, but there is great potential to go even farther!

Going the Extra Mile with Health Communication Scholarship

To really make a difference, health communication scholarship must provide important insights into best practices for delivering health care and promoting health. Research must chronicle what works well and what is causing problems in the delivery of care and promotion of health. The quality of the research that health communication scholars conduct is directly related to its potential to inform health policies and practices. Care must be taken to rigorously design and conduct health communication studies to generate the most accurate, valid, and revealing data to demystify the many complexities of health care and health promotion. New models and theories need to be developed, tested, and refined to help describe and predict the intricate influences of communication within the health system. Innovative methods need to be employed to study the complex communication processes that enable the effective delivery of care and promotion of health. To this end, there have been calls to advance communication as a "big science" to make a difference in society (Kreps, Viswanath, & Harris, 2002, p. 372).

From a big science perspective, scholars strive to ask important research questions that address serious and challenging social issues. Health communication scholars should design ambitious studies to directly address serious problems that limit the effectiveness of health care and health promotion. Scholars should take great care to meticulously design their studies and carefully operationalize research variables to accurately measure key health communication concepts, processes, and outcomes with both precision and depth. This often means designing new and innovative measures and measurement tools. It also often means using multiple research methods and measurement tools, including triangulating qualitative and quantitative measures, to generate robust and revealing data. It means both focusing in to study the critical parts, while also examining the larger societal, institutional, and cultural influences on health and health care. While there is a plethora of cross-sectional, one point in time studies, there is a tremendous need for health communication studies that collect data over time to avoid myopia and reflect the emergent nature of health practices.

It is also imperative for health communication scholars to study the most relevant research populations involved in health care and health promotion to collect meaningful and usable data. In the past, too many health communication studies depended on data gathered from convenient samples that often did not reflect very well the actual experiences of the health care providers and consumers that the studies purported to generalize to. If we do not study the specific populations we want to help, we will not generate data that will result in useful interventions, practices, and policies. This is stated quite clearly,

> While it is reasonable to and even legitimate to use small or convenient sample-based studies, the applied nature of health communication, and other applied areas of focus, forces us to confront the reality of the field. This reality raises many questions. First are population issues. Who are we studying? Do the samples of humans we use have the background, knowledge, and orientation to really answer the big questions we are asking? Do the samples we use provide representative data?
>
> (Kreps et al., 2002, pp. 371–372)

To gather data that will inform health policies and practices, we need to study patients, providers, and administrators who have the in-depth experiences and insights to guide evidence-based interventions.

Many studies have also used unrealistic conditions and artificial questions that do not fully represent the complexities of health care and health promotion situations. The "law of the hammer" can encourage scholars to use popular and easy to administer research tools that may not accurately measure the key issues under investigation in health communication studies. These research practices pose serious threats to the ecological validity of health communication studies. "Ecological validity refers to research that describes what actually occurs in real-life circumstances. To the extent that research procedures reflect what people do in the contexts in which their behavior normally occurs, confidence in the generalizability of findings to other people and situations is increased" (Frey, Botan, & Kreps, 2000, p. 133). It is imperative that health communication researchers design and conduct studies that provide valid, reliable, and generalizable data for guiding solutions to the problems that health care consumers and providers face.

The Translational Value of Health Communication Inquiry

A large and developing body of health communication scholarship has already begun to powerfully illustrate the centrality of communication processes in achieving important health care and health promotion goals. For example, Kreps and O'Hair (1995) reported a series of seminal studies illustrating the powerful influences of communication strategies and programs on health knowledge, behaviors, and outcomes. Research by Greenfield, Kaplan, and Ware (1985) clearly demonstrates the positive influences of increased patient/provider participation in directing health care treatment on achieving desired health outcomes. Kreps and Chapelsky Massimilla (2002) also report a number of studies that illustrate the positive effects of communication interventions on cancer-related health outcomes.[1] Communication research has been increasingly used to inform the development of public health policies and legislation, including policies to prevent and respond to serious health risks, promote equity in health care, and improve media coverage of important health issues (cf., Atkin & Smith, 2010; Guttman, 2010; Kunkel, 2010; National Cancer Institute, 2008, Noar, Palmgreen, Chabot, Dobransky, & Zimmerman, 2009; Siu, 2010). Yet, there is so much more that can be done by health communication scholars to improve public health and wellness.

Translational Health Communication Campaigns

Perhaps the greatest positive impact that health communication research has had on society is in the development and implementation of health-promotion campaigns, even given limitations in the sophistication of many communication campaigns (Noar, Harrington, & Helme, 2010). Communication theory, research, and practice has guided the development of robust health-promotion campaigns focused on the prevention and control of serious health threats, such as HIV/AIDS, cancer, and heart disease. These campaigns often employed a broad set of communication strategies to disseminate relevant and compelling information that can help at-risk populations resist serious health threats. For example, Dearing et al. (1996) illustrated the positive applications of social marketing and diffusion-based communication campaign strategies for encouraging adoption of behaviors for resisting HIV infection. Similarly, evaluations of several large-scale, longitudinal communication intervention programs, such as the Stanford Five City Heart Health Program (Flora, Maccoby, & Farquhar, 1989), the Minnesota Heart Health Program (Pavlik et al., 1993), and the Pawtucket Heart Health Program (Lefebvre, Lasater, Carleton, & Peterson, 1987) demonstrated that these campaigns reduced gaps in public health knowledge and influenced adoption of lifestyle changes to prevent cardiovascular disease. These classic health promotion research programs provided early evidence about the tremendous potential for using strategic communication campaigns to influence health behaviors and promote public health.

While health communication campaigns are generally designed to educate target audiences about important health threats and risky behaviors, it is important to recognize that a primary goal of most health campaigns is also to move target audiences to action in support of public health. For example, communication campaigns often encourage target audiences to engage in healthy behaviors to help them resist serious health threats. Behaviors that are often advocated include adopting healthy lifestyles (e.g., exercise, nutrition, and stress reduction), avoiding dangerous situations and substances (e.g., poisons, carcinogens, or other toxic substances), engaging in early screening and diagnosis for serious health problems (enrolling in recommended early detection and screening tests), and seeking health care services, when appropriate, to minimize harm. Several well-known persuasion theories have been fruitfully used to guide campaign efforts to influence health behaviors, although there have been calls to develop more refined and powerful models to guide campaigns (Dutta-Bergman, 2005; Fishbein & Cappella, 2006).

Successful health communication campaigns have been designed to address a range of important health issues (Noar, Harrington, & Helme, 2010). Tobacco use, for example, has been identified as the single-most preventable cause of morbidity and mortality within society and is a primary target for public health promotion (World Health Organization, 1997). Health communication campaigns have been used successfully to educate the public about the dangers of tobacco use, provide information about how to break the tobacco habit, and encourage public officials to develop powerful tobacco control policies (such as taxing tobacco products and instituting no-smoking laws; National Cancer Institute [NCI], 2008; Shopland, 1993). As a result of these tobacco-control communication campaigns, tobacco use has steadily declined across the Unites States, extending many lives (Shopland, 1993). However, the battle against big tobacco is far from over, as the industry employs increasingly sophisticated marketing strategies for promoting its dangerous products targeted at new and vulnerable populations. The challenge for health communicators is to counter the sophisticated advertising and marketing strategies employed by the well-heeled tobacco industry with more frugally funded strategic health communication campaigns.

Communication campaigns have also been used effectively to encourage the use of safer sexual practices for decreasing the spread of serious sexually transmitted diseases (STDs), such as HIV/AIDS. For example, successful campaigns have promoted condom use for reducing HIV transmission. Other effective campaigns have discouraged sharing of intravenous needles by intravenous drug users (Noar, Palmgreen, et al., 2009). These communication efforts have helped to prevent the spread of HIV within high-risk populations, ultimately saving many lives (Dearing et al., 1996). However, there is evidence that the gains made in promoting HIV prevention have not been sustained well over time and there is still much to do to address the threat of HIV infection and control (Noar, Palmgreen, et al., 2009).

A number of high profile public communication campaigns have been used to promote healthy dietary and exercise behaviors. Several national and international campaigns have been mounted to encourage low-fat, high-fiber diets that are rich in fruits and vegetables.

For example, the 5-A-Day Program for Better Health has been successful in increasing public awareness about the importance of including fruits and vegetables in daily diets (Potter et al., 2000). Similarly, campaigns to increase physical activity have been introduced to improve public health and increase resistance to a host of diseases, including heart disease, diabetes, and many cancers (Flora et al., 1989; Pavlik et al., 1993). Once again, while progress has been made, the current epidemic of growing obesity in the United States suggests the need for more and better campaigns to promote healthy nutrition and exercise regimens (Pratt, 2007).

Communication campaigns have also been successfully employed to promote child immunization (Centers for Disease Control [CDC], 1999). Several campaigns have been used to encourage public support for vaccinating children, supported by federal, state, and local health departments across the United States. These campaign efforts have protected children from a host of diseases, and virtually eliminated widespread incidences of serious health threats, such as diphtheria, tetanus, measles, polio, and smallpox, in the United States (Smith, 1997). Our more recent experience with difficulties promoting vaccination against the H1NI influenza suggests the need for improved campaigns to promote immunization.

Federally Funded Translational Health Communication Programs

There have been a number of prominent large-scale translational health communication research programs introduced over the last decade by major U.S. federal agencies, such as the National Cancer Institute (as well as other NIH Institutes and Centers), the Centers for Disease Control and Prevention (CDC), and the Health Resources and Services Administration (HRSA). These big-science research programs serve as powerful models of the potential for developing translational health communication inquiry.

The National Cancer Institute (NCI), for example, has been a leader in developing large-scale health communication research programs designed to improve cancer prevention, detection, treatment, and survivorship. One of the most important NCI health communication research programs is the far-reaching Health Information National Trends Survey (HINTS), that provides longitudinal, nationally representative data about health information seeking and utilization behaviors that have been used to guide evidence-based public health interventions.[2] NCI's innovative open-source promotion and presentation of the HINTS dataset and research instruments have spurred a wide array of supplemental health information research projects and public health applications (Finney Rutten, Hesse, Moser, & Kreps, 2010). The NCI actively tracks these supplemental studies and disseminates information about the growing body of HINTS-related research through its websites, publications, and meetings.

Another influential NCI health communication research program that made a difference in society is the Digital Divide Pilot Projects.[3] Four regional field intervention studies were conducted with different at-risk populations to test computer-based strategies for disseminating cancer information to these vulnerable populations and track program influences on consumer knowledge and behaviors. The studies documented strong connections between information access (the digital divide) and health disparities, while establishing evidence-based models for institutionalizing community-based programs for disseminating relevant health information to promote the health of vulnerable populations. Many of these intervention programs have been sustained and expanded within host communities.

NCI's innovative Small Business Innovation Research program on Multimedia Technology and Health Communication has funded the development of a range of important cancer control communication products and services for use by health care consumers, providers, and researchers (National Cancer Institute, 2010b). These products include print materials, computer-based programs, and radio and television media to support cancer education, prevention, treatment decision making, and promotion of quality of life that are rigorously developed, tested, and marketed to key audiences. The NCI presents information about these products at SBIR product showcase meetings, on their online directory of SBIR products, and on their Cancer Control Planet website (National Cancer Institute, 2010c, 2010d).

The NCI also supported the far-reaching Cancer Information Service (CIS) Research Program to test innovative uses of a mediated health information program (the CIS) on promoting cancer prevention and control.[4] This research program supported a number of key studies that illustrated the powerful uses of multiple communication media (print, telephone, and Internet) administered by the CIS to influence relevant health behaviors, promote cancer prevention and early detection, and support informed health care decision making for cancer treatment and survivorship. Robust findings from this research program were adopted and implemented by the CIS to improve NCI information dissemination, cancer prevention, and health promotion programs.

The large-scale Centers of Excellence in Cancer Communication Research program was designed to support in-depth research for advancing health communication science, while extending the reach and improving the effectiveness of cancer communication practices (see National Cancer Institute, 2010a). In 2003 the NCI funded for five years four regional transdisciplinary research centers, each with a unique focus on cancer communication, to conduct programmatic health communication studies to expand knowledge, inform health policies/practices, and train the next generation of health communication scientists (National Cancer Institute, 2010a). In 2008 the NCI re-funded for another five years the original four centers and added an additional research center (National Cancer Institute, 2010a). These centers have generated an impressive body of health communication research and cancer communication interventions concerning media coverage of cancer, consumer information seeking, cancer risk prevention, early detection of cancer, reduction of cancer health disparities, e-health applications for cancer survivors, and quality of cancer care to help reduce the national cancer burden.

Similarly, in 2003 the NCI in collaboration with the National Institute for Environmental Health Sciences funded four transdisciplinary Breast Cancer and the Environment Research Centers to study environmental factors that cause breast cancer (National Institute for Environmental Health Sciences, 2010). One of these centers was designated as the hub for applied health communication research (Atkin & Smith, 2010). This research center has conducted important research about the dissemination of information about promising new approaches for preventing breast cancer that has informed breast cancer campaign messages and strategies. The center has also worked closely with breast cancer advocates to educate them about effective health communication strategies and practices.

The Centers for Disease Control and Prevention followed the lead of the NCI in funding three Centers of Excellence in Health Marketing and Health Communication (Centers for Disease Control and Prevention, 2010a). Each of these research centers developed their own unique research focus, including reducing disparities in health outcomes for African Americans living in the southern United States, improving health outcomes in health promotion/chronic disease prevention, and informing the design and dissemination of health communication and marketing interventions for at-risk populations. The CDC also established five Centers of Excellence in Public Health Informatics in 2005 (Centers for Disease

Control and Prevention, 2010b) to examine the development, expansion, and evaluation of health information technology applications to promote public health in different regions of the United States.

The Department of Transplantation at the Health Resources and Services Administration (HRSA) funded a series of health communication studies examining strategies for promoting organ donations through media advocacy and innovative communication campaign strategies (Morgan & Harrison, 2010).[5] Communication campaign interventions to promote organ donation have been tested in a variety of settings, including at universities (Feeley, Tamburlin, & Vincent, 2008), worksites (Morgan & Miller, 2002), and motor vehicle departments (Harrison, Morgan, & Di Corcia, 2008). This applied research has influenced national and local organ donation practices and policies.

HRSA has also applied health communication research to inform development of an innovative new online program for training health care providers to communicate effectively with consumers from diverse backgrounds. Their Unified Health Communication program addresses issues of health literacy, cultural competency, and limited English proficiency (Health Resources and Services Administration, 2010). This educational program is now required as mandatory in-service training for health care providers serving indigent health care consumers in the more than 1,000 clinics funded by HRSA's Bureau of Primary Care. This training program is also available free of charge online (open source) and is being used by students and health care professionals around the world. So far, this training program has helped more than 4,000 health care professionals and students improve patient–provider communication, and it has the potential to influence the quality of communication for many health care consumers and providers (Health Resources and Services Administration, 2010).

Ripe Areas for Translational Health Communication Inquiry

While health communication scholarship has already made important contributions to improving health care and health promotion, health communication inquiry has the potential to make even more important and wide-ranging contributions to improving public health. Three research areas that have shown great promise for enhancing health communication are particularly ripe for expanded applied research: e-health, strategic health campaigns, and consumer–provider participation.

E-Health

We are in the midst of an information revolution where new media and information technologies are becoming increasingly central to the advancement of health care delivery and public health promotion goals. The development, adoption, and implementation of a broad range of new e-health communication applications within the modern health care system (such as ubiquitous online health information websites, innovative interactive electronic health records, powerful health decision support programs, tailored health education programs, health care system portals, and advanced telehealth applications) holds tremendous promise to increase access to relevant health information, enhance quality of care, reduce health care errors, increase collaboration, and encourage adoption of healthy behaviors. Yet, with the growth of new and exciting health information technologies, comes the daunting responsibility to design interoperable, easy to use, engaging, and accessible e-health applications that communicate the right information needed to guide health care and health promotion for diverse audiences. Health communication scholars have the opportunity to provide the evidence-base for guiding development and utilization of new health information technologies.

Health information technologies, such as the Internet, have been shown to be particularly important sources of relevant health information for consumers and providers confronting serious life threatening diseases, such as cancer, heart disease, and AIDS, where the demand for accurate and up-to-date health information is especially crucial. Research has shown that online support groups and communities provide individuals confronting serious health problems with relevant and timely information for managing their condition (Ginossar, 2008; Query & Wright, 2003). Similarly, Robinson, Turner, Levine, and Tian (2010) describe the effective use of the MyCareTeam® online health management web portal to provide health information about diabetes and track the Native American participants' diabetes treatment, exercise, and diet. Data have shown that this e-health system helps at-risk consumers effectively manage their blood sugar levels (Levine, Turner, Robinson, Angelus, & Hu, 2009; Smith, Levine, Clement, Hu, Alaoui, & Mun, 2004). Online information systems have great potential to provide people with quick and easy access to relevant health information (Eysenbach & Kohnler, 2002). However, there are many unanswered questions about consumer and provider use of e-health technologies that need to be carefully examined.

Health communication researchers can help answer important questions about the best ways to design, implement, and utilize e-health applications. For example, how accurate and current is the health information available via the Internet? Eysenbach, Powell, Kuss, and Sa (2002) argued that more sophisticated research is needed to determine the accuracy and quality of health information. Another important research question that needs to be addressed concerns who has access to health information and who is left out. The NCI Digital Divide Pilot Projects showed that online health information can be successfully disseminated to diverse audiences with adequate training, support, and design. More research is needed to test communication strategies to effectively provide health information to those who do not have access and to evaluate the potential impact this information can have on health outcomes. Moreover, research should examine how the positive influences of health information available via the Internet and other new communication technologies can be maximized, while negative outcomes, such as information overload and misinformation, can be minimized. Programmatic health communication research is needed to answer these and other important questions to guide the development and implementation of new health information technologies for enhancing health care and health promotion.

Strategic Health Communication Campaigns

While there is a long history of strategic health communication campaigns (as reviewed in this chapter), additional research is needed to enhance the strategic design of sophisticated evidence-based health communication campaigns so these campaigns can have the strongest positive influences on health beliefs, attitudes, values, and behaviors (Randolph & Viswanath, 2004). The effectiveness of health communication campaigns has been shown to be influenced by numerous variables, beginning with audience members' perceptions of targeted health behaviors, the design of campaign communication messages and strategies, the employment of appropriate communication channels, the sources of health information, the effective applications of formative evaluation data to guide campaigns, and the use of guiding theories of communication and social influence (Hornik, 2002; Kiwanuka-

Tondo & Snyder, 2002). However, too many campaigns have not demonstrated strong and lasting health promotion influences on target audiences (Snyder et al., 2004). Early health communication interventions were developed with general message strategies that were designed to appeal to broad audiences, whereas more sophisticated campaigns carefully segment target audiences based on shared demographics, personality predispositions, beliefs and attitudes, media use, and other factors, and then create effective messages to appeal to those segmented audiences (Noar, Harrington, & Helme, 2010; Slater, 1996). Evaluation research is needed to inform campaign planning and implementation, as well as to identify the campaign strategies that work most and least effectively for guiding future health communication campaigns.

Growing evidence supports the use of tailored health communication campaign interventions to promote behavior changes, especially cancer-prevention and control behaviors (Kreps & Chapelsky Massimilla, 2002; Rimer & Glassman, 1998). Tailored message strategies identify key individual factors to personalize health-promotion messages to appeal to the unique interests and backgrounds. Rimer and Glassman (1998) found that tailored interventions facilitated positive patient–provider interactions, fostered behavioral changes conducive to health, enhanced health-evaluation processes (by requiring collection of patient-specific information), and offered opportunities to expand the reach of health professionals, especially by sending personalized, individualized messages to patients. Advances in the use of tailored messages for health promotion, however, have raised concerns about accessing information that identifies the specific health behaviors of an individual, leading to questions about the appropriate level of analysis for audience segmentation in health communication campaigns (Kreuter & Wray, 2003). There are also calls to develop tailored interventions specifically for vulnerable consumers to help reduce health disparities (Campbell & Quintiliani, 2006). Future research is needed to test the best strategies for tailoring health communication campaign interventions for different audiences.

There are a number of campaign design and implementation factors that deserve close examination by health communication scholars. Salmon and Atkin (2003), for example, pointed out that health communication campaigns should be examined according to the dose of health information given, duration of message exposure, degree of media richness, vertical integration of communication channels, and the horizontal integration of approaches to social change. Randolph and Viswanath (2004) describe how the crowded media environment demands strategic placement of campaign messages to promote message exposure and influence with targeted audiences. Careful study of these campaign design and implementation factors can help guide future interventions.

Health communication scholars should recognize the multidimensional nature of health campaigns, evaluating the use of communication strategies that incorporate multiple levels and channels. Health communication planning should focus on a wide range of campaign messages and intervention strategies targeted or tailored to specific (well segmented) audiences. Health communication scholars can help increase the sophistication of health promotion campaigns by drawing on relevant theories, methods, and communication technologies and integrating multiple communication channels—including interpersonal, group, organizational, and societal communication—to effectively target well-segmented, at-risk, and marginalized populations. Scholars need to measure accurately the effectiveness of health communication campaigns to determine what works and why.

Health communication campaigns can be fruitfully examined according to implementation stages. For instance, the four health communication campaign phases (pre-campaign, campaign/message development, post-campaign, and ongoing/ad hoc) that guided the

"America Responds to AIDS" campaign have unique demands and functions (Nowak & Siska, 1995). Future research can profitably examine critical campaign processes and issues such as strategic planning, needs assessment, target-audience analysis, formative and sum-mative evaluation, and message efficacy. Moreover, research can identify new planning strategies for improving the design, implementation, and evaluation of health communica-tion campaigns. For example, Parrott and Steiner (2003) recommended that campaigns be planned jointly with health communication researchers and public health practitioners, to promote "more linkages between academic health communicators and public health profes-sionals" (p. 647).

Health communication scholars should be increasingly concerned with the role of culture on health care and health promotion. Cultural affiliation frames the ways that individuals interpret health promotion messages and should be a primary focus when designing health campaign communication strategies and messages. Scholars should examine the influences of culture on the significant disparities that exist in health outcomes between majority and minority populations in the United States. These disparities have been linked both to the quality of health communication experienced and to access to health information. Future campaign communication research should carefully examine the health communication needs of marginalized cultural groups and identify evidence-based strategies for enhancing health campaign communication. Health communication scholars have the opportunity to develop the evidence base for advancing the science of strategic health communication campaigns.

Focus on Consumer–Provider Participation

There is a growing societal emphasis on public advocacy, consumerism, and empower-ment in health communication research that has the potential to revolutionize health care systems by equalizing power between providers and consumers and by relieving a great deal of strain on the system through a greater focus on disease prevention, self-care, and encouraging consumers to be active partners in the health care enterprise. To promote more active participation in health care and health promotion, communication researchers should study consumers' information needs and suggest strategies for encouraging consumers to take control of their health and health care. Ideally, health communication research should identify appropriate sources of information available to consumers and gather data from them about the challenges and constraints they face within health care systems, as well as develop and field test educational media programs for enhancing consumers' medical lit-eracy. Such research has the potential to help consumers negotiate their ways through health care bureaucracies and to help them develop the strategic communication skills needed for interacting effectively with health care providers.

Consumers and providers develop interpersonal relationships that define the ways they interact with one another. These relationships guide individual responses to communica-tions. Communication scholars should embrace a relational orientation to the study of con-sumer–provider communication to examine the ways the exchange of messages influences the establishment, development, and maintenance of interpersonal relationships in health care. This suggests that research should examine the perspectives of both consumers and providers in health communication research, and resist the tendency to glorify the provid-er's communication, while ignoring the consumer's communication perspective. Research should carefully examine the natural conversations that health care consumers engage in within their personal and professional networks when adapting to serious health threats, such as cancer (Beach, 2010).

There are many important relational communication issues that merit careful examination in consumer/provider interactions. For example, relational control and dominance are critical communication issues in health care delivery that must be better understood. Closely related to the issues of dominance and control are the ways relational conflict is expressed and managed communicatively in health care. It is also imperative that the expression and relational development of empathy, therapeutic communication, social support, and psycho-social adjustment be examined in consumer–provider interactions. Translational health communication research focused on the relational communication factors related to consumer participation in health care holds the promise to inform training interventions (for both consumers and providers), health care delivery practices, and health policies for enhancing the quality of health care services and health care outcomes.

Potential Influences of Translational Health Communication

Health communication scholars are finding new pathways for enhancing the quality of health practices and outcomes as health communication research grows in sophistication. As health communication scholarship has grown in institutional credibility in recent years, we have seen expanded outreach opportunities, including opportunities for external research and intervention funding, opportunities for exciting new health communication collaborations and partnerships, and new health communication job opportunities in government agencies, research firms, and health care organizations. Health communication scholars should eagerly seek and leverage these new opportunities for applying health communication research to health care and health promotion practice.

With help from external funding, health communication scholars can focus on conducting "big science" studies that can provide relevant and compelling research results. They can garner the resources necessary to mount ambitious, robust, and rigorous longitudinal, multi-methodological field studies with large real-world health system populations. They can develop new and improved research methods for conducting health communication research and innovative theoretical frameworks for guiding health communication inquiry. They can vigorously disseminate the findings of health communication research to health policy makers, health care delivery system administrators, health care providers and consumers, as well as to media representatives. They can also develop and implement new programs, practices, and interventions based upon strong health communication research findings, and work with community partners to institutionalize the best programs to be sustained over time.

It is time for health communication scholars to move out of their ivory academic towers and develop more meaningful collaborations with community partners from government agencies, health care delivery systems, non-profit associations, social service agencies, advocacy organizations, and corporations. It is only through these community collaborations that we can effectively translate compelling research findings into products, programs, policies, and practices that will be adopted by the modern health care system. Community partners have the embedded health system expertise that scholars need to collaboratively introduce new health communication programs into health systems and help to refine these programs so they will work effectively.

Community participative research and intervention programs have shown great potential to facilitate applications of research results into health care practices (Minkler, 2000; Minkler & Wallerstein, 2002). Community partners can help health communication scholars learn the best inside strategies for gathering meaningful data from respondents, for interpreting research results within the framework of cultural contexts, and for implementing research recommendations within social systems (Neuhauser, 2001). Actively engaging community partners in the applied research process can impart a strong sense of ownership in the research and intervention processes, minimizing potential community resistance and encouraging cooperation.

The Future of Translational Health Communication

The field of health communication is rapidly moving toward a sophisticated, multi-dimensional agenda for applied research that has the potential to inform enlightened health care delivery and health promotion practices. Modern, evidence-based health communication practices should be designed to integrate human and mediated channels of communication in the delivery of health care and the promotion of public health. Scholars need to carefully examine the multi-faceted influences of communication on health at multiple levels of analysis and across a wide range of health care contexts. There is a powerful need to carefully evaluate the use of a broad and evolving range of communication strategies in delivering care and promoting health to assess the influences of communication on important health outcomes. Such inquiry can provide important information about the development of cooperative relationships between interdependent participants in the modern health care system, encourage the use of sensitive and appropriate communication in health care and health promotion, empower those affected by illness to work collaboratively with caregivers to make their best health decisions, enhance the dissemination of relevant health information and the use of strategic communication campaigns to promote public health, and suggest adaptive strategies for using communication to accomplish desired health outcomes. Health communication scholars need to go the extra mile to ask important research questions, gather rigorous and insightful data, disseminate relevant findings, and build meaningful community research and intervention partnerships to guide the translation of data into practice.

Notes

1. See the 100th anniversary issue of the scholarly journal, *Health Communication* (2010), for a review of major contributions of health communication research to health outcomes. Several articles from that issue are cited in this chapter.
2. See the following website for more information about the HINTS research program: http://www.google.com/search?q=HINTS+nci&rlz=1I7GGLD_en&ie=UTF-8&oe=UTF-8&sourceid=ie7.
3. See the following website for more information about the Digital Divide Pilot Projects research program: http://cancercontrol.cancer.gov/cancer_resources-digdivide.html#projects.
4. See the following website for more information about the CIS Research Program: http://cis.nci.nih.gov/research/research.html.
5. See the following website for more information about the HRSA organ donation research program: http://organdonor.gov/research/index.htm.

References

Atkin, C. K., & Smith, S. W. (2010). Improving communication practices to reduce breast cancer environmental rsks. *Health Communication, 25,* 587–588.

Beach, W. A. (2010). Communicating about cancer in families and clinics. *Health Communication, 25,* 599–600.

Campbell, M. K., & Quintiliani, L. M. (2006). Tailored interventions in public health: Where does tailoring fit in interventions to reduce health disparities? *American Behavioral Scientist, 49*, 775–793.

Centers for Disease Control and Prevention. (1999). Achievements in public health, 1900–1999: Impact of vaccines universally recommended for children–United States. *MMWR Morbidity and Mortality Weekly Report, 48*, 243–248.

Centers for Disease Control and Prevention. (2010a). Centers of Excellence in Health Marketing and Health Communication (P01). Retrieved from http://www.cdc.gov/od/science/PHResearch/grants/fy2005_108.htm.

Centers for Disease Control and Prevention. (2010b). Centers of Excellence in Public Health Informatics (P01). Retrieved from http://cdc.gov/od/science/PHResearch/grants/fy2005_109.htm

Dearing, J. W., Rogers, E. M., Meyer, G., Casey, M. K., Rao, N., Campo, S., & Henderson, G. M. (1996). Social marketing and diffusion-based strategies for communicating with unique populations: HIV prevention in San Francisco. *Journal of Health Communication, 1*, 342–364.

Dutta-Bergman, M. J. (2005). Theory and practice in health communication campaigns: A critical interrogation. *Health Communication, 18*, 103–122.

Eysenbach, G., & Kohnler, C. (2002). How do consumers search for and appraise health information on the world wide web? Qualitative study using focus groups, usability tests, and in-depth interviews. *British Medical Journal, 324*, 573–577.

Eysenbach, G., Powell, J., Kuss, O., & Sa, E. R. (2002). Empirical studies assessing the quality of health information for consumers on the World Wide Web: A systematic review. *Journal of the American Medical Association, 287*(20), 2691–2700.

Feeley, T. H., Tamburlin, J., & Vincent, D. E. (2008). An educational intervention on organ and tissue donation for first-year medical students. *Progress in Transplantation, 18*, 103–108.

Finney Rutten, L, Hesse, B., Moser, R., & Kreps, G.L. (Eds.). (2010). *Building the evidence base in cancer communication.* Cresskill, NJ: Hampton Press.

Fishbein, M., & Cappella, J. N. (2006). The role of theory in developing effective health communications [Supplement]. *Journal of Communication, 56*, S1–S17.

Flora, J. A., Maccoby, N., & Farquhar, J. W. (1989). Communication campaigns to prevent cardiovascular disease: The Stanford community studies. In R. E. Rice & C. K. Atkin (Eds.), *Public communication campaigns* (2nd ed., pp. 233–252). Newbury Park, CA: Sage.

Frey, L. R., Botan, C. H., & Kreps, G. L. (2000). *Investigating communication: An introduction to research methods* (2nd ed.). Boston, MA: Allyn & Bacon.

Ginossar, T. (2008). Online participation: A content analysis of differences in utilization of two online cancer communities by men and women, patients and family members. *Health Communication, 23*, 1–12.

Greenfield, S., Kaplan, S., & Ware, J. Jr. (1985). Expanding patient involvement in care: Effects on patient outcomes. *Annals of Internal Medicine, 102*, 520–528.

Guttman, N. (2010). Using communication research to advance the goals of the National Health Insurance law in Israel. *Health Communication, 25*, 613–614.

Harrison, T. R., Morgan, S. E., & Di Corcia, M. J. (2008). The impact of organ donation education and communication training for gatekeepers: DMV clerks and organ donor registries. *Progress in Transplantation, 18*, 301–309.

Health Resources and Services Administration. (2010). HRSA health literacy. Retrieved from http://www.hrsa.gov/healthliteracy/default.htm

Hornik, R. C. (2002). *Public health communication: Evidence for behavior change.* Mahwah, NJ: Erlbaum.

Kiwanuka-Tondo, J., & Snyder, L. B. (2002). The influence of organizational characteristics and campaign design elements on communication campaign quality: Evidence from 91 Ugandan AIDS campaigns. *Journal of Health Communication, 7*, 59–77.

Kreps, G. L., & Chapelsky Massimilla, D. (2002). Cancer communications research and health outcomes: Review and challenge. *Communication Studies, 53*, 318–336.

Kreps, G. L., & O'Hair, D. (Eds.). (1995). *Communication and health outcomes.* Cresskill, NJ: Hampton Press.

Kreps, G. L., Viswanath, K., & Harris, L. M. (2002). Advancing communication as a science: Opportunities from the federal sector. *Journal of Applied Communication Research, 30*, 369–381.

Kreuter, M. W., & Wray, R. J. (2003). Tailored and targeted health communication: Strategies for enhancing information relevance. *American Journal of Health Behavior, 27*(Supplement 3), S227–S232.

Kunkel, D. (2010). Media research contributes to the battle against childhood obesity. *Health Communication, 25,* 595–596.

Lefebvre, R.C., Lasater, T.M., Carleton, R.A., & Peterson, G. (1987). Theory and delivery of health programming in the community: The Pawtucket Heart Health Program. *Preventive Medicine, 16*(1), 80–95.

Levine, B. A., Turner, J. W., Robinson, J. D., Angelus, P., & Hu, M. (2009). Communication plays a critical role in web based monitoring. *Journal of Diabetes Science and Technology, 3,* 461–467.

Minkler, M. (2000). Using participatory action research to build healthy communities. *Public Health Reports, 115,*191–197.

Minkler, M., & Wallerstein, N. (Eds.). (2002). *Community based participatory research for health.* San Francisco, CA: Jossey-Bass.

Morgan, S. E., & Harrison, T. R. (2010). The impact of health communication research on organ donation outcomes in the United States. *Health Communication, 25,* 589–592.

Morgan, S. E., & Miller, J. (2002). Communicating about gifts of life: The effect of knowledge, attitudes, and altruism on behavior and behavioral intentions regarding organ donation. *Journal of Applied Communication Research, 30,* 163–178.

National Cancer Institute. (2008). *The role of the media in promoting and reducing tobacco use* (Tobacco Control Monograph No. 19, NIH Pub. No. 07-6242). Bethesda, MD: U.S. Department of Health and Human Services, National Institutes of Health, National Cancer Institute.

National Cancer Institute. (2010a). Centers of Excellence in Cancer Communication Research Initiative. Retrieved from http://cancercontrol.cancer.gov/hcirb/ceccr/ceccr-index.html

National Cancer Institute. (2010b). The Multimedia Technology Health Communication Research Program. Retrieved from http://cancercontrol.cancer.gov/hcirb/sbir/

National Cancer Institute. (2010c). The Multimedia Technology Health Communication Research Program Catalog of Products. Retrieved from http://cancercontrol.cancer.gov/hcirb/sbir/products/catalog-of-products.html

National Cancer Institute. (2010d). Cancer Control Planet. Retrieved from http://cancercontrol-planet.cancer.gov/

National Institute for Environmental Health Sciences. (2010). Breast Cancer and the Environment Research Centers. Retrieved from http://www.niehs.nih.gov/research/supported/centers/breast-cancer/index.cfm

Neuhauser, L. (2001). Participatory design for better interactive health communication: A statewide model in the USA. *The Electronic Journal of Communication, 11*(3&4), retrieved from http://www.cios.org/EJCPUBLIC/011/3/01134.html

Noar, S. M., Harrington, N. G., & Helme, D. W. (2010). The contributions of health communication research to campaign practice. *Health Communication, 25,* 593–594.

Noar, S. M., Palmgreen, P., Chabot, M., Dobransky, N., & Zimmerman, R. S. (2009). A 10-year systematic review of HIV/AIDS mass communication campaigns: Have we made progress? *Journal of Health Communication, 14,* 15–42.

Nowak, G. J., & Siska, M. J. (1995). Using research to inform campaign development and message design. In E. W. Maibach & R. L. Parrott (Eds.), *Designing health messages: Approaches from communication theory and public health practice* (pp. 169–246). Thousand Oaks, CA: Sage.

Parrott, R., & Steiner, C. (2003). Lessons learned about academic and public health collaborations in the conduct of community-based research. In T. L. Thompson, A. M. Dorsey, K. I. Miller, & R. Parrot (Eds.), *Handbook of health communication* (pp. 637–649). Mahwah, NJ: Erlbaum.

Pavlik, J. V., Finnegan, J. R., Strickland, D., Salman, C. T., Viswanath, K., & Wackman, D. B. (1993). Increasing public understanding of heart disease: An analysis of the Minnesota heart health program. *Health Communication, 5,* 1–20.

Potter, J. D., Finnegan, J. R., Guinard, J.-X., Huerta, E. E., Kelder, S. H., Kristal, A. R., ... Sorensen, G. (2000). *5 A Day for Better Health program evaluation report* (NIH Publication No. 01-4904). Bethesda, MD: National Institutes of Health, National Cancer Institute.

Pratt, C. (2007). Crafting campaign themes (and slogans) for preventing overweight and obesity. *Public Relations Quarterly, 52*(2), 2–8.

Query, J. L., & Wright, K. B. (2003). Assessing communication competence in an online study: Toward informing subsequent interventions among older adults with cancer, their lay caregivers, and peers. *Health Communication, 15,* 203–218.

Randolph, W., & Viswanath, K. (2004). Lessons learned from public health mass media campaigns: Marketing health in a crowded media world. *Annual Review of Public Health, 25,* 419–437.

Rimer, B. K., & Glassman, B. (1998). Tailoring communication for primary care settings. *Methods of Information in Medicine, 37,* 171–177.

Robinson, J. D., Turner, J. W., Levine, B., & Tian, Y. (2010). Patient-provider interaction in the regulation of diabetes-mellitus. *Health Communication, 25,* 597–598.

Salmon, C. T., & Atkin, C. (2003). Using media campaigns for health promotion. In T. L. Thompson, A. M. Dorsey, K. I. Miller, & R. Parrot (Eds.), *Handbook of health communication* (pp. 449–472). Mahwah, NJ: Erlbaum.

Shopland, D. R. (1993). Smoking control in the 1990's: A National Cancer Institute model for change. *American Journal of Public Health, 83,* 1208–1210.

Siu, W. (2010). Fear appeals and public service advertising: Applications to influenza in Hong Kong. *Health Communication, 25,* 580.

Slater, M. D. (1996). Theory and method in health audience segmentation. *Journal of Health Communication, 1,* 267–284.

Smith, K., Levine, B., Clement, S., Hu, M. Alaoui, A., & Mun, S. (2004). Impact of MyCareTeam for poorly controlled diabetes mellitus. *Diabetes Technology & Therapeutics 6,* 828–835.

Smith, S.L. (1997). The effective use of fear appeals in persuasive immunization: An analysis of national immunization intervention messages. *Journal of Applied Communication Research, 25,* 264–292.

Snyder, L. B., Hamilton, M. A., Mitchell, E. W., Kiwanuka-Tondo, J., Fleming-Milici, F., & Proctor, D. (2004). A meta-analysis of the effect of mediated health communication campaigns on behavior change in the United States. *Journal of Health Communication, 9*(Supplement 1), 71–96.

World Health Organization. (1997). *Tobacco or health: A global status report.* Geneva, Switzerland: Author.

39

(RE)VIEWING HEALTH COMMUNICATION AND RELATED INTERDISCIPLINARY CURRICULA

Towards a Transdisciplinary Perspective

Nichole Egbert, James L. Query Jr., Margaret M. Quinlan,
Carol A. Savery, and Amanda R. Martinez

As the other chapters in this volume readily reveal, health communication is the systematic study of message behavior, across a rich array of contexts, with the overarching goals of facilitating positive health outcomes, as well as reducing the prevalence and likelihood of a myriad of health threats. Since its institutional inception in 1972 via the "Therapeutic Communication" interest group in the International Communication Association (see Kreps, Bonaguro, & Query, 1998; Sharf, 1993), this area of study has achieved several milestones and evolved significantly (see Kreps et al., 1998; Ratzan, 1994; Rogers, 1994, 1996; Thompson, Robinson, Anderson, & Federowicz, 2008). Considered collectively, the overall magnitude of these achievements and growth led Ratzan (1994) to conclude that "effective communication between participants, advocates, and publics becomes the currency to achieve optimal health" (p. 202). Widespread recognition of the pivotal role of health communication in health promotion and health care has been institutionalized through centers of excellence, as well as through external funding from NIH, CDC, numerous foundations, and nongovernment organizations, thereby contributing "directly to the increased effectiveness of health promotion activities" (Rogers, 1994, p. 210; see also Kreps, 2003; Kreps & Bonaguro, 2009; Kreps, Vishwanath, & Harris, 2002; Rogers, 1997). These contributions are also evidenced by the identification of health communication in the Healthy People 2010 report, recognizing "communication as a critical core competency of public health practice" (Institute of Medicine, 2003, p. 6). This 2003 Institute of Medicine (IOM) Report, *The Future of the Public's Health in the 21st Century*, and the Centers for Disease Control and Prevention's (CDC) Office of Workforce Policy and Planning (2001) report, *A Collection of Competency Sets of Public Health-Related Occupations and Professions*, both identify health communication as a vital set of key competencies. Both of these influential documents include communication competency domains such as effective management and distribution of information, relating to the public, as well as other professional advocacy and health literacy skills.

In light of the preceding growth, it would seem reasonable to suggest that health communication-driven curricula, inside and outside the communication discipline, would reflect a similar progression. There have been several nationwide studies of a variety of communication courses, but as of this date, there has been no systematic and comparative investigation into health communication-related curricula in public health, nursing, or medicine. The nationwide studies include intercultural communication (Beebe & Biggers 1986); speech communication in secondary schools (Book & Pappas, 1981); graduate courses in argumentation theory (Benoit & Follert, 1986); quantitative and qualitative communication research methods (Frey, Anderson, & Friedman, 1998; Frey & Botan, 1988); oral communication in K-12 grades (Hall, Morreale, & Gaudino, 1999); and health communication (Query, Wright, Bylund, & Mattson, 2007). And although there has been an increase in the number of health communication courses offered within some communication departments, comprehensive health communication programs with more than two or three courses remain relatively sparse (see Query et al., 2007)—73% of 77 respondents indicated their department offered a health communication course in 2007 (Query et al., 2007), compared to 20% of 148 participants who indicated a similar course was offered in 1999 (Waldrope, 1999). An examination of key communication pedagogical references further supports the dearth of information concerning the development and growth of health communication curricula within the field (see Daly, Friedrich, & Vangelisti, 1990; Friedrich, 1981; Friedrich & Boileau, 1990; Harter, Dutta, & Cole, 2009; Johnson, 1992; Lederman, 1992).

At least three pressing questions then arise: how can health communication or new health communication-related curricula be encouraged in light of such a paucity of information? How can faculty, both new and seasoned members, in communication, nursing, public health, and medicine, best dedicate their time and coordinate their efforts to develop and then sustain relevant and interdisciplinary health communication curricula? The IOM (2003) clearly champions such curricular developments, stating: "Academic institutions should increase interdisciplinary learning opportunities for students in public health and other related health science professionals" (IOM, 2003, p. 16). The chapter thus attempts to address these pressing and thorny issues by conducting a comprehensive analysis of communication, nursing, public health, and medicine academic websites.

The purpose of this chapter is to provide readers with a comparative analysis of how health communication is currently incorporated in communication, nursing, public health, and medical programs of higher education.[1] To achieve the preceding purpose, program goals, course names, and course descriptions were collected from the World Wide Web and analyzed for communication content. Although there are several limitations to relying upon web-based content, this approach simultaneously presents advantages. One such strength is that searching only publicly available information obtained through Web-based sources provides the perspective that is available to other users when they desire information about any of these fields separately (or comparatively). Thus, this review employs an audience-centered approach by analyzing the material that often provides the fundamental basis of understanding for students, parents, professors, as well as other lay and professional audiences. In addition, college and university faculty members commonly turn to online sources (such as other institutions' websites) when generating their own content for program descriptions, course names, and course content. This chapter incorporates qualitative information from the websites of 600 academic programs (websites for 26 of the programs, which are directly cited in this chapter, are to be found at the end of the reference list). Although not every appropriate academic program may have been included in this analysis, this investigation of these four disciplines noted above should be representative due to the breadth of the analysis.

Method Used to Represent Health Communication Curricula

Between September 2009 and March 2010, 600 U.S. college and university websites were searched for health communication-related curricula in the four fields of communication, nursing, public health, and medicine. The twelve types of degree programs included in the searches were: communication (Bachelor of Arts, BA; Master of Arts, MA; Master of Science, MS; Doctor of Philosophy, PhD); medicine (Doctor of Osteopathic Medicine DO; Medical Doctor, MD); nursing (Registered Nurse, RN; Bachelor of Science in Nursing, BSN; Master of Science in Nursing, MSN; Doctor of Nursing Practice, DNP; and Doctor of Philosophy, PhD); and public health (Master of Public Health, MPH; Doctor of Public Health, DrPH; and Doctor of Philosophy, PhD). Lists of programs for each of the four fields were generated through several means. For the field of communication, the health communication programs found in the National Communication Association's (NCA) searchable list of programs and the list of graduate programs found on the homepage of the Coalition for Health Communication were included. In addition, a request was sent out using the disciplinary listserv "Communication Research and Theory Network" (CRTNET) for names of colleges and universities with a programmatic focus in health communication. A list of graduate programs in public health was found on the website of the Council on Education in Public Health. The American Association of Medical Colleges (1998) maintains a list of current programs in medicine, and the nursing list was generated from Allnursingschools. com.

Once the lists of programs were compiled, the authors began to search each college or university's publicly accessible website for program descriptions and course offerings that contained content related to health communication. For the communication websites, "health communication" was the specific search term. For the other three fields, researchers searched for the term "communication," but also for closely related terms such as "relationship," "interpersonal," "interaction," or "campaign." Many times, other terms or the course description would cause the related course name to be included due to overlap with health communication principles and content. The goal of the process was to be as inclusive and descriptive as possible while still maintaining some definitional boundaries that privilege communication-related content. Once it appeared that health communication-related course names and descriptions were reaching the point of data saturation (i.e., unique course names and course descriptions were seldom being found), the researchers ceased searching that program list and began the next. A total of 600 programs was analyzed (communication = 120; nursing = 205; public health = 152; medicine = 123).

Course names for each of the twelve program types were subjected to open coding where emerging categorical themes based on the course names were identified (Lindlof & Taylor, 2002). During axial coding, the codes were then applied to one program's list of course names to develop a codebook, which was subsequently used to categorize the remaining course names. Once the codebooks were developed, two authors independently coded each list.[2] Any disagreements on the fit of codes were discussed between the two authors until consensus was reached. The following is a summary of the results of this systematic analysis, as well as a discussion of how these results could be utilized by faculty members in any of these four disciplines.

Health Communication Course Names and Descriptions

As described earlier, health communication course names and descriptions were culled from lists of academic programs found on the websites of the National Communication Association and the Coalition for Health Communication. In addition, program names were solicited via the CRTNET listserv. However, only the online, publicly accessible material was included from programs discovered through the listserv. There were 43 undergraduate programs with a focus in health communication, 46 MA programs, and 31 PhD programs (see Table 39.1). With the exception of the MS in Health Communication program at Tufts University School of Medicine, all of the programs were housed in communication or journalism units.

As would be expected, the most common course name across all three program levels (BA, MA, and PhD) was a general course in health communication. Some programs designated this course specifically as a "Survey in Health Communication." Seminars, special topics, and "Topics in Health Communication" were also found in many programs across all curricular levels.

Health campaigns and patient–provider communication were the most frequent specialized health communication offerings across the 120 programs that were reviewed. With regard to the former, the term "campaign" was typically included somewhere in the course name. For the courses focusing on clinical interactions between patients and providers, a range of terms, including "patient," "provider," "doctor," and "consumer" could be found. San Diego State University has a course called "Medical Interaction" that focuses

Table 39.1 Health Communication Courses: Thematic Analysis with Examples

Themes	Example Course Names	BA (43)	MA (46)	PhD (31)
Survey in Health Communication	Health Communication	X	X	
	Advanced Health Communication			
	Survey in Health Communication			
Seminar	Seminar in Health Communication	X	X	X
	Colloquium			
	Topics in Health Communication			
Health Campaigns	Health Campaigns	X	X	X
	Health Communication Campaigns			
	Development and Evaluation of Health Communication Campaigns			
Patient-Provider Communication	Doctor–Patient Communication	X	X	X
	Health Provider–Consumer Communication			
	Medical Interviewing and Information Dissemination			
Health Communication & Culture	Multicultural Health Communication	X	X	X
	Health Advocacy in a Multicultural Society			
	Health Communication for Diverse Populations			

(continued)

Table 39.1 Continued

Themes	Example Course Names	BA (43)	MA (46)	PhD (31)
Health Communication and Technology	E-Health Communication	X	X	X
	Health Communication & the Web			
	Online Consumer Health			
Interpersonal Health Communication	Interpersonal Health Communication	X	X	X
	Relational Issues in Health			
Health Care and Organizations	Communication in Health Organizations		X	X
	Health Care Organization: Budgeting and Management			
	Health Communication Organizational Issues			
Health Communication & Media	Mass Media & Health		X	X
	Health Communication in Mass Media			
	Behavior Change Through Entertainment			
Research Methods	Research Methods for Health Communication		X	
	Research Methodology: Communication in Allied Health			
Health Communication Theory	Health Communication Theory		X	
	Health Communication Theory & Research			
	Theories of Health Communication			
Health Literacy	Health Literacy	X	X	
Communication Skills	Oral Communication		X	
	Writing about Health & Medicine			
	Health & Science Writing			
Public Health & Health Promotion	Public Health Communication	X	X	X
	Health Promotion Evaluation			
	Public Health Practice and Healthcare: Politics, Policies, and Programs			
Risk Communication	Health & Risk Communication		X	
	Risk Communication in Public Health Practice			
	Risk Communication			
On-site training	Internship	X	X	X
	Practicum			
	Cooperative Field Experience			
Other Examples	Communicating Grief, Loss, & Illness			X
	Rhetoric of Health	X		
	Communication in Healthcare Contexts	X		
	Science/Health Communication		X	
	Training & Consulting in Healthcare		X	
	Health Behavior & Health Communication		X	

on medical interviewing, whereas the University of Georgia uses the title, "Medical Interviewing and Information Dissemination," to refer to a similar graduate course with the following description:

> Theoretical foundations and interpersonal processes in medical interviewing. Information-seeking and dissemination strategies of consumers and providers; the use of conventional and new technologies; communicating bad news; health literacy; the depiction of illness, health, and disease in media and society; and media relations training will be addressed.
>
> (University of Georgia, para. 59)

It is essential to note, however, that not all communication between patients and their providers would be characterized as an interview, which may be why some programs such as Ohio State University and University of Illinois at Urbana-Champagne have developed courses with titles such as "Health Communication in Interpersonal Contexts" and "Interpersonal Health Communication."

In addition to interpersonal contexts, many health communication programs include courses devoted to organizational and mediated communication environments. The applied fields of organizational communication and health communication are joined in courses such as "Communication in Health Organizations" at the University of Oklahoma. With regard to media, some courses, such as "Seminar in Mass Media and Health" at the University of Florida, were specifically designed to broaden the scope of study beyond that of health communication campaigns:

> Mass communication and health communication theories are examined as they related to intended and unintended effects on individual behavior and on public health policy. Focus on effects *other* than those associated with mass mediated public health campaigns.
>
> (University of Florida Graduate School, para. 46)

Culture, technology, and risk communication are often the subject of seminars in health communication programs. These topics are more common at the graduate level, but are also present in more developed undergraduate curricula, such as the one at the University of Houston.

Although the focus of most health communication programs is on theory and research, communication skills and on-site training can also be found in these curricula. For example, the School of Medicine's Health Communication program at Tufts University offers a graduate course titled, "Writing about Health and Medicine." Most BA programs offer internships. Applied projects and practicums are frequently encouraged at the MA level.

Health communication programs, by and large, favor a social science orientation, although some programs, like the University of Illinois at Urbana-Champaign, offer courses that would be considered more humanistic, such as "Rhetoric of Health." Graduates of the BA and MA programs are prepared for careers in academe, as well as in corporate, nonprofit, and governmental organizations (see Edgar & Hyde, 2005; Fowler, Celebuski, Edgar, Kroger, & Ratzan, 1999). Doctoral students trained in health communication, in contrast, specialize in one or more theoretical areas and take many courses in research methods to be proficient in conducting independent research.

The findings of this study reflect the campaign-related themes present in the influential review conducted by Maibach, Parrott, Long, and Salmon (1994), where the authors asked experts in health communication, public health, and social and media advocacy to identify competency areas for health communication specialists. The results of their study underlined "the importance of the ability to apply relevant theories to program development and evaluation efforts at both the individual and the societal level" (p. 353). In their discussion, Maibach et al. (1994) expanded these survey results to include competencies as they relate to both the theoretical and applied levels for individuals and society.

Health communication programs are not bound by accrediting agencies as are the programs in nursing, public health, and medicine; however, a recent assessment by Edgar and Hyde (2005) identified what recent MA graduates perceived to be the most valuable competencies of their program. Recent graduates with an MA in health communication ranked knowledge of campaign planning and communication theory as the top two competencies, followed by presentation skills, medical knowledge, and research methods (Edgar & Hyde, 2005). Respondents to this survey would have liked their curriculum to have included more content related to new technologies, health care finance/business skills, and marketing skills.

Communication-Related Course Names and Course Descriptions in Nursing

Five types of nursing programs were reviewed: Registered Nurse (RN), Bachelor of Science in Nursing (BSN), Master of Science in Nursing (MSN), Doctor of Nursing Practice (DNP), and Doctor of Philosophy in Nursing (PhD) (see Table 39.2). Although there were a few courses with "communication" explicitly included in the title, many of the topics overlapped with communication content, but were not named as such.

For example, in the BSN programs that were reviewed, except for the basic introductory communication course required of several programs (e.g., "Fundamentals of Speech Communication," "Introduction to Speech Communication"), only two courses ("Communication in Health care" and "Advanced Nursing Communication") displayed names that included the term, "communication." However, several other courses, such as "Tools for Interpersonal Effectiveness," and "Nursing Situations with Individuals" clearly hint at communication-related content. Other names, more obliquely related to communication, included "Culture and Health," and "Nurse Educator as Leader."

It was a challenging task to choose which courses to include as representative of communication content in nursing curricula because many course descriptions and names refer to the term, "communication." For example, "Psychiatric Mental Health Nursing," bears the following course description: "Examination of psychiatric mental health needs of individuals, families, and groups across the life span, emphasizing communication, neurobiology and psychosocial nursing with clinical experiences in acute and community mental health care settings" (Ida V. Moffett School of Nursing, Samford University, p. 190). Part of the difficulty in choosing and interpreting names is the inconsistent use of terminology across universities. For instance, although identifying the course requirements related to pharmacology is a straightforward task, determining the communication-related content in a course title such as "Nursing as a Societal Interpersonal Profession" is more precarious.

Nursing curricula on the whole, however, *are* replete with communication-related content. Consider one of the most common themes found among the BSN programs reviewed: leadership. As an example, this course at the undergraduate level at Norwich University bears the following course description:

Table 39.2 Communication-Related Nursing Courses: Thematic Analysis with Examples

Themes	Example Course Names	RN (10)	BSN (76)	MSN (72)	DNP (20)	PhD (27)
Leadership/ Professional Development	Professional Role Development	X	X	X	X	X
	Principles of Nursing Leadership					
	The Healthcare Workforce—Issues and Leadership Strategies					
Clinical Skills and Patient Care	Foundations for Clinical Nursing Practice	X	X	X	X	X
	Pharmacology for Nurses					
	Advanced Pathophysiology					
Public Health and Health Promotion	Public Health Nursing	X	X	X	X	X
	Health Promotion/Disease Prevention					
	Nursing and Health Promotion					
Healthcare Quality	Health & Health Care/ Quality and Cost Effective Outcomes	X	X	X	X	X
	Caring for the Community					
	Community Nursing					
Community Health	Community Health Nursing	X	X	X	X	X
	Health Care Policy and Ethics for Contemporary Nursing Practice					
	Health Policy Development & Implementation					
General Communication	Intro to Speech; Strategies for Communication in Health Care	X	X	X	X	X
	Interpersonal Communication					
	Communication for Health Care Professionals					
Care of Special Patient Groups	Mental Health Nursing	X	X	X	X	X
	Maternal–Child Nursing					
	Acute Care of Children					
Health Policy	Health Policy: Issues & Process		X	X	X	X
	Healthcare Delivery Systems					
	Quality Improvement and Patient Safety					
Technology/ Information systems	Information Systems in Health Care	X	X	X		
	Information and Knowledge Management					
	Introduction to Health Informatics					
Culture and Health	Cultural Issues in Health Care Delivery		X	X		X
	Cultural Dimensions of Nursing					
	Concepts in Health & Culture					

(continued)

Table 39.2 Continued

Themes	Example Course Names	RN (10)	BSN (76)	MSN (72)	DNP (20)	PhD (27)
Research Methods	Scholarly Inquiry in Nursing		X	X		X
	Methods for Evidence-Based Practice					
	Advanced Qualitative Research Methods					
Other Examples	Case Management and Evidence Based Practice			X		
	Living with Dying			X		X
	Collaborative Health Care	X				
	Management and Response for Disasters and Mass Casualty Incidents					X
	Spirituality in Health Care		X			
	Contextual Nature of Health and Health Behaviors				X	

This course examines the leadership process in nursing. The student studies the effects of leadership theory in the management of people and tasks within the health care environment, such as teaching assistive personnel the requirements of ensuring security of patient's medical information and professional ethics. Emphasis is placed on a humanistic model for teaching and learning that stresses interpersonal communication as an essential component of nursing and leadership.

(Nursing Course Descriptions, para. 13)

Thus, although the course category and name reflect leadership, communication is central to most curricula in nursing at many levels.

Apart from formal coursework, a fundamental component of nursing curricula emphasizes communication skills and practices through clinical experiences. When observing and shadowing nursing professionals in a variety of clinical contexts, students are exposed to faculty role models engaging in communication on the job, and are able to raise questions about effective strategies to employ across a wide range of nursing contexts with patients/families. Later, when students are engaged in more of the hands-on care in clinical settings, these experienced faculty members can provide individualized guidance regarding communication practices to their students.

A desire for standardization across curricula was the impetus for a project sponsored by the American Association for Colleges of Nursing (AACN, 2008) titled *The Essentials of Baccalaureate Education for Professional Nursing Practice* (see Table 39.3). This comprehensive set of nine core standards was developed by a task force that held regional meetings with over 300 colleges of nursing, addressing the Institute of Medicine's recommendations for the core knowledge, as well as the recommendations of other professional stakeholders in health care (IOM, 2003).

The AACN's *Essentials* series (1996, 2006, 2008) assists educators by detailing guidelines for evaluating students in their knowledge, clinical skills, liberal education, professional values, and role development (a toolkit is also provided.) Of these nine core standards, eight

Table 39.3 American Association of Colleges of Nursing Essentials for Professional Nursing Practice

The Essentials of Baccalaureate Educaiton for Professional Nursing Practice (2008)	The Essentials of Master's Education for Advanced Practice Nursing	The Essentials of Doctoral Education for Advanced Nursing Practice
• Essential I: Liberal Education for Baccalaureate Generalist Nursing Practice • Essential II: Basic Organizational and Systems Leadership for Quality Care and Patient Safety • Essential III: Scholarship for Evidence Based Practice • Essential IV: Information Management and Application of Patient Care Technology • Essential V: Health Care Policy, Finance, and Regulatory Environments • Essential VI: Interprofessional Communication and Collaboration for Improving Patient Health Outcomes • Essential VII: Clinical Prevention and Population Health • Essential VIII: Professionalism and Professional Values • Essential IX: Baccalaureate Generalist Nursing Practice	I. Research II. Policy, Organization, and Financing of Health Care III. Ethics IV. Professional Role Development V. Theoretical Foundations of Nursing Practice VI: Human Diversity and Social Issues VII: Health Pomotion and Disease	• Essential I: Scientific Underpinnings for Practice • Essential II: Organizational and Systems Leadership for Quality Improvement and Systems Thinking • Essential III: Clinical Scholarship and Analytical Methods for Evidence-Based Practice • Essential IV: Information Systems/Technology and Patient Care Technology for the Improvement and Transformation of Health Care • Essential V: Health Care Policy for Advocacy in Health Care • Essential VI: Interprofessional Collaboration for Improving Patient and Population Health Outcomes • Essential VII: Clinical Prevention and Population Health for Improving the Nation's Health • Essential VIII: Advanced Nursing Practice

of the descriptions explicitly mention communication as being fundamental to the success of the student in meeting the core expectancies.

At the higher graduate degree levels, the situation is similar. Although there is less emphasis on the basic sciences of biology and chemistry, with more courses devoted to research and specialized practice, communication-related course content (as reflected in course names and descriptions) is found throughout the curricula. Courses such as "Effective Communication" and "Nursing Communication" clearly denote communication content, whereas other course names such as "Ethical and Culturally Competent Health Care Professional" refer to content that often overlaps considerably with communication studies courses such as "Intercultural Communication." At the graduate level, this course specialization is understandable, as professional licensure becomes less of an issue, and academic institutions concentrate more on developing relevant research programs. Similar to the BSN, The American Association of Colleges in Nursing (AACN) has developed *The Essentials of Master's Education for Advanced Practice Nursing* (1996) and *The Essentials of Doctoral Education for Advanced Nursing Practice* (2006), both of which include multiple references to communication content that should be standard for graduate education in nursing (see Table 39.3).

Communication-Related Course Names and Course Descriptions in Public Health

As shown in Table 39.4, the public health programs that were searched for communication-related content included: Master of Public Health (MPH; 100 programs), Doctor of Public Health (DrPH; 16 programs), and Doctor of Philosophy (PhD; 37 programs).[3]

Similar to the communication programs, many public health programs featured general and specific courses with the term, "communication," in the course name. As one might expect, some of these course names also included the term "public health" (e.g., "Public Health Communication"). Compared with the other three disciplines, public health course names more often highlighted the term, "theory." For example, the course "Health Communications: Theory and Practice" from the University of Alabama at Birmingham bears this course description:

> This course is designed to investigate the role of communication *theories* and methods in promoting public health and preventing disease. Both theoretical background in communication and behavioral science and practical communication/intervention development methods will be addressed.
>
> (University of Alabama at Birmingham, 2009)

It is worth noting that public health programs often explicitly emphasize theory when constructing communication curricula. Although theory is certainly central to health communication programs that are housed in communication studies, the term was less prominent in those course names relative to course names in public health.

One of the most common communication-related courses was communication campaigns. Every level of public health program included courses in this category. Some

Table 39.4 Communication-Related Public Health Courses: Thematic Analysis with Examples

Theme	Example Course Names	MPH (99)	DPH (16)	PhD (37)
Health Communication	Health Communication Research	X	X	X
	Health Communication			
	Communication Strategies			
Communication Theory	Health Communication Theory & Practice	X	X	X
	Introduction to Persuasive Communication Theories			
	Theories of Mediated Communication			
Mass Communication/ Media	Mass Communication & Public Health	X	X	X
	Media & Health Communication			
	Communication in Popular Media			
Health Communication Campaigns	Health Communication Campaigns	X	X	X
	Monitoring & Evaluation of Communication Programs			
	Persuasive Communication Campaigns			

Theme	Example Course Names	MPH (99)	DPH (16)	PhD (37)
Managerial & Leadership Communication	Communication Skills of Public Health Leaders	X	X	X
	Managerial Communication			
	Strategic Communication in Health Policy & Management			
Public Health Communication	Public Health Communication	X	X	
	Strategies for Public Health			
	Communication in Public Health Practice			
Risk Communication	Introduction to Health Risk Communication	X		X
	Risk Assessment, Communication & Management			
	Risk Assessment, Communication & Management			
Disaster Communication	Communication Issues in Disaster Preparedness	X	X	
	Disaster Communication & Media Relations			
Communication & Technology	High Tech Approaches to Health Communication	X	X	
	Communication & Info Tech. Tools for Public Emergencies			
	Future Health Communication – New Media & Emerging Technologies			
Organizations and Communication	Communication in Health Organizations	X		X
	Organizational Health Communication			
	Organizational Communication & Conflict Mgmt			
Environmental Communication	Advanced Environmental Health Communication	X		
	Environmental Mgmt & Risk Communication			
Communication & Informatics	Informatics for Health Care	X		
	Information & Communication Systems			
	Public Health Communication & Informatics			
Other Examples	Narrative Public Health	X	X	
	Persuasion & Health	X		X
	Communication & Conflict	X		
	Challenges for Health Literacy Communication	X		
	Workshop in Scientific Communication	X		
	Communication Values & Behavior	X		

programs divided the campaigns content into formative stages (e.g., "Designing & Implementing Public Health Campaigns") and later stages (e.g., "Monitoring & Evaluation of Communication Programs"). Other programs were designed more as an overview and did not specify campaign design or evaluation (e.g., Health Communication Campaigns").[4]

Course names in public health courses also reflected an emphasis on communication campaigns that utilized mass media. The course descriptions represented mass media broadly, ranging from traditional broadcasting channels to social media and entertainment venues. In a related vein, course names and titles using the term, "informatics," were also unique to public health offerings. Although in some cases, the term "informatics" may represent a specific mediated communication topic (such as in bioinformatics), in other cases programs linked communication and informatics content together in one course. In the end, this focus on media and informatics further demonstrates how public health characterizes health communication as being persuasive, mediated, information-based, and part of the public sphere.

Although the preceding focus is widely represented in the public health curriculum content, a review of professional and accrediting agencies reveals that communication is considered a core competency across specializations and central to the professional practice of public health (see Table 39.5).

Not only does the Association for Schools of Public Health (ASPH) name communication specifically as a core competency for both the MPH and DrPH degrees, but the descriptions of the other competencies include communication activities such as "partnering," "articulating," "translating," and "interacting" (Calhoun, Ramlah, McGean Weist, & Shorteil, 2008). These terms suggest that the content of academic training in public health programs may be transitioning toward a framework that is more similar to that of nursing in terms of how communication is diffused throughout the curriculum. As such, communication is not always used as a persuasive tool (e.g., when partnering), and can be face-to-face (e.g., when interacting).

Communication-Related Course Names and Course Descriptions in Medicine

The vast majority of medical degrees offered beyond the undergraduate level do not explicitly require many health communication courses (see Table 39.6). Rather, the only ascertainable health communication classes (with varied course titles) that are included in medical degree curricula are focused on the doctor–patient relationship and are often housed under a more general course title, such as a shadowing experience of clinical preparation. The

Table 39.5 Association for Schools of Public Health Core Competency Models

MPH Interdisciplinary/Cross-Cutting Competencies	DrPH Core Competencies
COMMUNICATION AND INFORMATICS	ADVOCACY
DIVERSITY AND CULTURE	COMMUNICATION
LEADERSHIP	COMMUNITY/CULTURAL ORIENTATION
PUBLIC HEALTH BIOLOGY	CRITICAL ANALYSIS
PROFESSIONALISM	LEADERSHIP
PROGRAM PLANNING	MANAGEMENT
SYSTEMS THINKING	PROFESSIONALISM AND ETHICS

Table 39.6 Communication-Related Medical Courses: Thematic Analysis with Examples

Theme	Example Course Names	DO (17)	MD (106)
Clinical Skills & Patient Care	Essentials of Patient Care I, II, III	X	X
	Integrative Clinical Skills		
	Foundations of Patient Care: Physical Diagnosis		
On-site training	Internal Medicine Preceptorship	X	X
	Competence-Based Apprenticeship in Primary Care		
	Longitudinal Generalist Mentorship		
Interviewing	Medical Interviewing	X	X
	Interviewing & Communication		
	Foundations of Patient Care: Interviewing & the Doctor–Patient Relationship		
Professional Development	Business & Professional Communications	X	X
	Being a Physician 1 & 2		
	Professionalism & the Practice of Medicine		
Ethics	Ethical & Social Issues in Medicine	X	X
	Online Ethics and Communication		
	Healthcare Ethics, Law & Policy		
Patient-Doctor Communication	Doctor–Patient Relationship	X	X
	Doctor–Patient Communication & Culture Matters		
	Advanced Patient Doctor (2 wks)		
Hospice & Palliative Care	Palliative & Hospice Care	X	X
	Palliative Medicine: End-of-Life Care		
	Hospice & Palliative Care: A Continuum of Caring		
Public Health	Population-Based Medicine	X	X
	Principles of Preventive Medicine & Clinical Research		
	Population Health/ Epidemiology/ Evidence-Based Medicine		
Community Medicine	Community & Behavioral Medicine	X	X
	Patients, Doctors, & Communities		
Special patient groups	Women's Health	X	X
	Introduction to Multi-Disciplinary Geriatrics		
	Clinical Management of HIV/AIDS Infection		
Family medicine	Family Medicine & Family Practice	X	X
	Interdisciplinary Family Health		
	Family Medicine Elective		
General Communication	Communication Skills for Health Professionals	X	X
	Interpersonal & Communication Skills		

(continued)

Table 39.6 Continued

Theme	Example Course Names	DO (17)	MD (106)
Medicine & Society	Medicine in Contemporary Society	X	X
	Social Issues in Medicine		
	Physician, Patient & Society		
Other Examples	Medical Humanities & Human Values		X
	Medical Humanities		X
	Religious Perspectives in Bioethics	X	
	Narrative Medicine		X
	Medical Spanish	X	

doctor–patient content is typically only part of this type of on-site course, although some courses include a doctor–patient focus over the span of two or three years of the degree plan. Other courses required of medical students that appear related to health communication include medical interviewing, health promotion and disease prevention, medical ethics, community and rural medicine specializations, as well as cultural and spiritual segments. The following summary is based on the examination of 17 Doctor of Osteopathic Medicine programs and 106 medical doctor curricula found online.

Although the majority of osteopathic medicine degree curricula include a doctor–patient communication emphasis, these courses are not always specifically listed. Oftentimes, the doctor–patient exploration occurs through an on-site shadowing experience. For example, at Michigan State University, the shadowing experience is designed for students to observe the physician–patient interaction, answer questions when asked by the supervising physician, and to "observe the milieu in which the patient care is provided, and understand that it takes many people to provide care to one patient" (Michigan State University, para. 8). Doctor–patient communication is studied during a one-time course listing the first year, or as a series of courses throughout the first two or into the third year (though the latter is rare). In Midwestern University's Introduction to Human Behavior I, II, and III courses, medical students are introduced to the doctor–patient relationship and interviewing techniques. Similarly, Tulane University's Foundations in Medicine I course covers human behavior, community–preventive medicine, community service learning, medical ethics, medical interviewing, and nutrition. Other universities, such as Pennsylvania State University, Creighton University, and the University of Pittsburgh, offer medical interviewing as a stand-alone course.

Courses where medical students learn about communicating with patients are also labeled in the following various ways, such as "Essentials of Patient Care," "Clinical Skills and Development," "Patient-Centered Medicine," and "Patients, Physicians, and Society." In some programs, the doctor–patient courses are discussed in terms of skills, such as "Physical Examination Skills," Manipulative Techniques," and "Processes of Obtaining Documentation." In these instances, communication content is embedded in the course description along with other pertinent skills. For example, at Thomas Jefferson University's "Introduction to Clinical Medicine," topics include: professionalism, medical ethics, system-based care, interprofessional care, medical informatics, evidence-based medicine, cultural diversity, and behavioral science. Also, the clinical skills portion of training includes history-taking, communication and interpersonal skills, as well as basic physical exam skills.

Health promotion is another theme that includes techniques for interaction with patients. However, health promotion courses are typically listed as distinct from doctor–patient interaction and interviewing. For example, at the Philadelphia College of Osteopathic Medicine, the recognition that medical practice is more than science is a prominent or clearly discernible rationale that shapes instruction. The program description argues that coursework in ethics and patient communication helps students relate well to patients, with content in medical law and public health preparing students for private practice.

Medical ethics courses have their own specific emphasis in the medical programs. Ethics overlap with many areas of medical education, including medicine, science, research, and society. In the Edward Via Virginia College of Osteopathic Medicine, the Primary Care/Osteopathic Manipulative Medicine course includes a segment titled, "Effective Communication." More specifically, a family medicine course teaches students communication skills, such as how to listen attentively and compassionately, and to communicate clearly with patients, families, and other health care team members. It is noted that clinical experiences where students are given the opportunity to use and assess their communication skills are included.

Other course offerings specifically pertain to the community context with many programs emphasizing rural medicine. More general courses are mainly entitled "Medicine and Society." At the Oklahoma State University Center for Health Sciences, College of Osteopathic Medicine, "the patient as a whole individual, not just a body system, is considered in context with the social and family unit" (Oklahoma State University Center for Health Sciences, para. 17). In a wider societal context, other medical program curricula focus on the interactive, overlapping domain of doctor–patient coping beyond scientific decision making. For example, Yale University offers a course named, "Professional Responsibility," which may also overlap with medical ethics and legal knowledge. Texas A&M University's medical program requires first and second year students to take a course called "Physician Heal Thyself," demonstrating an emphasis on physician well-being.

In general, the osteopathic medicine degrees focused more on topics such as culture and spirituality than general medical degrees did. For example, at Nova Southeastern University, a cultural competency course and multicultural health course are listed. Competency-type courses often cover health literacy foci and language issues. Nova Southeastern University was among the only programs to include an ethnocultural medicine course and a medical Spanish course, although the latter is listed as an elective. The University of Pennsylvania combines doctor–patient communication with a "Culture Matters" emphasis. This series includes discussions of spirituality and patient care, complementary and alternative medicine, and linguistic barriers to health care.

This review is further evidence of the many variations in how medical schools provide communication training. Although some programs have courses solely dedicated to communication, others rely predominantly upon standardized patient programs or clinical experiences. Changes in the licensing examination that medical students have to pass have likely led to curricular changes in recent years (Makoul, 2003). In 2004, these changes included requiring medical students to pass a clinical skills examination with twelve standardized patients. Medical program accreditation is also contingent upon the delivery of communication training: "There must be specific instruction in communication skills as they relate to physician responsibilities, including communication with patients, families, colleagues, and other health professionals" (Liaison Committee on Medical Education,

2008, p. 9). These changes are in part an outgrowth of the Association of American Medical Colleges' (AAMC) first report on the Medical School Objectives Project (MSOP) in 1998. These are the related communication objectives from this report:

> For its part, the medical school must ensure that, before graduation, a student will have demonstrated, to the satisfaction of the faculty:
> - The ability to obtain an accurate medical history that covers all essential aspects of the history, including issues related to age, gender, and socio-economic status
> - The ability to communicate effectively, both orally and in writing, with patients, patients' families, colleagues, and others with whom physicians must exchange information in carrying out their responsibilities
> - Knowledge about relieving pain and ameliorating the suffering of patients
> - Knowledge of the important non-biological determinants of poor health and of the economic, psychological, social, and cultural factors that contribute to the development and/or continuation of maladies
> - Compassionate treatment of patients, and respect for their privacy and dignity

Discussion

In concert with the overarching goal of this chapter, the information presented in this review provides a basis for readers to compare how communication content is represented in the four disciplines of health communication, nursing, public health, and medicine. With the exception of communication studies, nursing courses overwhelmingly incorporated the largest amount of communication content, although one must search the various course descriptions as opposed to the course titles to find it. Although public health courses traditionally have focused on planned, mediated, public communication messages, many of these programs seem to be moving more toward the integrated communication content that was characteristic of nursing. Finally, communication content in medical programs was the scarcest, and was predominantly found in clinical and patient care courses, medical interviewing courses, and as part of on-site training such as apprenticeships and preceptorships. However, recent changes to licensing examinations have emphasized communication skills and may lead to the generation of new curricula.

For many experienced academics from any of these four disciplines, the distinctions between and among these fields in terms of how communication is viewed are likely to be self-evident. For others, appreciating the different emphases between and among the disciplines (as well as between and among the different degrees), may help better contextualize their current teaching or research in health communication. Certainly, understanding how accrediting bodies direct the curricula of nursing, public health, and medicine is vital for anyone developing inter- or cross-disciplinary programs. This comprehensive review of course names and descriptions should be valuable for course and program designers as a similar comparative discussion does not exist.

Another benefit of this comparison is that it can provide a starting place for conversations about interdisciplinary pedagogy. In some situations, it may be important not only for one to have a strong grasp of the disciplinary overlaps and distinctions, but also to provide this contextual background to the other stakeholders in the discussion. Although the breadth of the field of health communication allows for countless exciting applications, it can, at times, be challenging to articulate how health communication is similar to and different from other disciplines, such as the professional fields represented here. On college and university campuses, units often become territorial about the terminology used to describe course content. Terms such as "communication" and "health" are especially problematic as they defy exclusive categorizations. Clearly, all four of these disciplines have a vested interest in both of these terms. Course designers could add the terms "nursing," "public health," and "medical" to any course title to distinguish ownership, but perhaps a more interdisciplinary approach would serve key publics and students better. This systematic comparison is but a first step toward diffusing a more sophisticated understanding of health communication theories, contexts, and applications across disciplinary boundaries.

The present review's approach of surveying only online course titles and descriptions is limited in several key ways. First, the information described here is current at the time of writing, but may have been changed the day after the websites were accessed. By reviewing content from 600 websites, however, this limitation is somewhat offset in light of the comprehensive assessment of the online content. It is also well-established that most academic institutions are relatively slow when reviewing and approving new curricula. Thus, many newer programs or programs still in development would not be represented in this discussion if they were not listed on the disciplinary lists that were consulted, or if their course information was not available online.

Finally, most college and university websites are very difficult to navigate. Locating course names and descriptions is challenging; moreover, some institutional websites made this content password-protected or did not post it at all. It is not unusual for a single website to require over fifteen minutes of searching before the user encounters course names and descriptions for a particular program of study. This point is raised not so much as justification for the effort required by this review, but as a strong suggestion for educational institutions to make their websites more user-friendly. Perhaps individual programs will also discern the benefit in developing individual websites apart from their respective college or university if the size of the organization makes the program content too complicated to find.

As argued earlier, however, the major benefit of a comprehensive review of web-based information is that it provides a broad view of what one might experience when investigating the role of communication in these four disciplines. The major conclusion to be drawn from this comparative investigation is that communication is central to all four of these disciplines; however, each discipline places a slightly different emphasis on communication when developing programs and courses. Understanding these variations can assist curriculum designers in proposing inter- and cross-disciplinary courses that maximize the strengths of each academic field. Although encroachment issues are important to consider, they should not quash interdisciplinary collaboration and the design of cutting-edge curricula. In the end, this type of careful and constructive education programming can be a powerful change agent to enhance health care delivery, develop health campaigns, and ultimately, promote societal wellness.

Similar to Parrott and Kreuter (this volume), we argue that this chapter can be used to stimulate transdisciplinary linkages by identifying common points of interest and demonstrating the potential for cross-discipline fertilization in pedagogy and inquiry. For example, some of the areas in public health most ready for these types of transdisciplinary approaches include interactive health communication technologies (see Alverson, Saiki, & Caudell, 2004), global public health communication issues, and health informatics (Kreps & Maibach, 2008). In developing cutting-edge curricular programs, these emergent areas can be combined with the foundational theories and practice-oriented skills (see Calhoun et al., 2008; Maibach et al., 1994) that both health communication specialists and public health professionals need.

Another area in need of development is the incorporation of resources from other disciplines when developing and choosing course-related materials. Although nursing and communication studies share a great deal of common ground, the two fields seem hesitant to cross-pollinate their textbooks and other supporting materials. Nursing textbooks primarily include ideas from other nursing publications, and health communication textbook authors are likewise prone to cite their own. Even reference lists from communication-specific texts in nursing almost exclusively include only references to other nursing or other health-related sources, and although popular health communication textbooks also make reference to research in medicine and other health-related fields, nursing literature is typically only cited when nurses are specifically being discussed. Understandably, organizational pressures to publish in one's own discipline may dictate some of these choices; however, if there is to be significant growth in the research and education of health professionals with regard to communication, there needs to be more cooperation and interaction between communication and these other academic disciplines. Team-taught classes would be another way to address this deficit, as would interdisciplinary research teams and guest lectures.

When examining the course titles and descriptions of health communication and medicine, the two seem to have the least amount of overlap. For medical curriculum designers, desire to reduce medical errors (Richardson, Berwick, & Bigard, 2000) and increase patient satisfaction (Buller & Buller, 1987) have been the main justifications for including communication content. Merely including some form of communication content, however, may not help students gain a sound appreciation of communication dynamics and complexities (Dutta & Zoller, 2008). Although passing a clinical skills examination is now required of anyone seeking a medical license in the United States, some fear that this requirement rewards "acting" for the test as opposed to effective communication skills and practices (Henry, 2005). Wright et al. (2006) discovered that when medical students had a positive attitude toward communication skills training, they also perceived communication skills as more important, had higher confidence when communicating with patients, and demonstrated a greater knowledge of effective provider communication (Wright et al., 2006). Wright et al. suggested that affective learning strategies may be a route to motivating students to pursue better clinical communication skills.

As the 21st century further unfolds, it seems reasonable to suggest that educators, across the various disciplines, continue to seek out collaborative pedagogical and research paths to crystalize the central role of communication training and scholarship in carrying out professional and clinical practices—especially when combined with salient literature and insights gleaned from public health, nursing, and medicine. Such endeavors are likely to resemble a windy road with many twists and turns; yet, the overarching goal of enhancing health care delivery can and should serve as a powerful beacon to guide transdisciplinary initiatives.

Authors' Note

The authors would like to thank Benjamin Efrid, graduate student at University of North Carolina at Charlotte, for his assistance with this chapter.

Notes

1. Many other academic disciplines could be included in this analysis; however, these four were chosen due to their ubiquity on college and university campuses, their political stature within these institutions, and the frequency with which health communication courses have been cross-listed in these disciplines.
2. The first author coded all four lists to maintain consistency.
3. Some colleges and universities also offered a Bachelor of Science (BS) in Public Health and several types of combined degrees; however, these were not as common and thus were not included in this analysis.
4. "Social Marketing" is another term often included in campaign-related courses in Health Promotion.

References

Alverson, D. C., Saiki, Jr., S. M., & Caudell, T. P. (2004). Telehealth in cyberspace: Virtual reality for distance learning in health education and training. In P. Whitten & D. Cook (Eds.), *Understanding health communication technologies* (pp. 212–224). San Francisco, CA: Jossey-Bass.

American Association of Colleges of Nursing. (1996). *The essentials of master's education for advanced practice nursing.* Retrieved from http://www.aacn.nche.edu/Education/pdf/MasEssentials96.pdf

American Association of Colleges of Nursing. (2006). *The essentials of doctoral education for advanced nursing practice.* Retrieved from http://www.aacn.nche.edu/DNP/pdf/Essentials.pdf

American Association of Colleges of Nursing. (2008). *The essentials of baccalaureate education for professional nursing practice.* Retrieved from http://www.aacn.nche.edu/Education/pdf/BaccEssentials08.pdf

American Association of Medical Colleges. (1998). *Learning objectives for medical student education: Guidelines for medical schools.* Retrieved from https://services.aamc.org/publications/showfile.cfm?file=version87.pdf&prd_id=198&prv_id=239&pdf_id=87

Beebe, S. A., & Biggers, T. (1986). The status of the introductory intercultural communication course. *Communication Education, 35,* 56–60.

Benoit, W. L., & Follert, V. F. (1986). Graduate courses in argumentation theory. *Communication Education, 35,* 61–66.

Book, C, L., & Pappas, E. J. (1981). The status of speech communication in secondary schools in the United States: An update. *Communication Education, 30,* 200–208.

Buller, M., K., & Buller, D. B. (1987). Physicians' communication style and patient satisfaction. *Journal of Health and Social Behavior, 28,* 375–388.

Calhoun, J. G., Ramlah, K., McGean Weist, E., & Shorteil, S. M. (2008). Development of a core competency model for the Master of Public Health Degree. *American Journal of Public Health, 98,* 1598–1607.

Centers for Disease Control and Prevention. (2001). *A collection of competency sets of public health-related occupations and professions.* Retrieved from http://www.dphhs.mt.gov/PHSD/MPHTI/docs/compgrid.pdf

Daly, J. A., Friedrich, G. W., & Vangelisti, A. L. (Eds.). (1990). *Teaching communication: Theory, research and methods.* Hillsdale, NJ: Erlbaum.

Dutta, M. J., & Zoller, H. M. (2008). Theoretical foundations: Interpretive, critical, and cultural approaches to health communication. In H. M. Zoller & M. J. Dutta (Eds.), *Emerging perspectives in health communication: Meaning, culture, and power* (pp. 1–27). New York: Routledge.

Edgar, T., & Hyde, J. N. (2005). An alumni-based evaluation of graduate training in health communication: Results of a survey on careers, salaries, competencies, and emerging trends. *Journal of Health Communication, 10,* 5–25.

Fowler, K., Celbuski, C., Edgar, T., Kroger, F., & Ratzan, S. C. (1999). An assessment of the health communication job market across multiple types of organizations. *Journal of Health Communication, 4,* 327–342.

Frey, L. R., Anderson, S., & Friedman, P. G. (1998). The status of instruction in qualitative communication research methods. *Communication Education, 47,* 246–260.

Frey, L. R., & Botan, C. H. (1988). The status of instruction in introductory undergraduate communication research methods. *Communication Education, 37,* 249–256.

Friedrich, G. W. (Ed.). (1981). *Education in the 80's: Speech communication.* Washington, DC: National Education Association.

Friedrich, G. W., & Boileau, D. M. (1990). The communication discipline. In J. A. Daly, G. W. Friedrich, & A. L. Vangelisti (Eds.), *Teaching communication: Theory, research, and methods* (pp. 3–18). Hillsdale, NJ: Erlbaum.

Hall, B. I., Morreale, S. P., & Gaudino, J. L. (1999). A survey of the status of oral communication in the K-12 public education system. *Communication Education, 48,* 139–148.

Harter, L., Dutta, M. J., & Cole, C. E. (Eds.). (2009). *Communicating for social impact: Engaging theory, research and pedagogy.* Cresskill, NJ: Hampton Press.

Henry, S. G. (2005). Playing doctor. *Journal of the American Medical Association, 294,* 2139–2140.

Institute of Medicine. (2003). *Health professions education: A bridge to quality.* Washington, DC: National Academies Press.

Johnson, F. L. (1992). Continuities and imperatives in communication education. In L. C. Lederman (Ed.), *Communication pedagogy: Approaches to teaching undergraduate courses in communication* (pp. 39–54). Norwood, NJ: Ablex.

Kreps, G. L. (2003). Opportunities for health communication scholarship to shape public health policy and practice: Examples from the National Cancer Institute. In T. L. Thompson, A. M. Dorsey, K. I. Miller, & R. Parrott, (Eds.), *Handbook of health communication* (pp. 609–624). Mahwah, NJ: Erlbaum.

Kreps, G. L., & Bonaguro, E. W. (2009). Health communication as applied communication inquiry. In L. R. Frey & K. N. Cissna (Eds.), *Routledge handbook of applied communication research* (pp. 380–404). New York: Routledge.

Kreps, G. L., Bonaguro, E. W., & Query, J. L., Jr. (1998). The history and development of the field of health communication. In L. D. Jackson & B. K. Duffy (Eds.), *Health communication research: A guide to developments and directions,* (pp. 1–15). Westport, CT: Greenwood Press.

Kreps, G. L., & Maibach, E. W. (2008). Transdisciplinary science: The nexus between communication and public health. *Journal of Communication, 58,* 732–748.

Kreps, G. L., Vishwanath, K., & Harris, L. M. (2002). Advancing communication as a science: Research opportunities from the federal sector. *Journal of Applied Communication Research, 30,* 369–381.

Lederman, L. C. (Ed.). (1992). *Communication pedagogy: Approaches to teaching undergraduate courses in communication.* Norwood, NJ: Ablex.

Liaison Committee on Medical Education. (2008, June). *Structure and function of a medical school.* Retrieved from: http://www.lcme.org/functions2008jun.pdf

Lindlof, T. L., & Taylor, B. C. (2002). *Qualitative communication research methods* (2nd ed.). Thousand Oaks, CA: Sage.

Maibach, E., Parrott, R. L., Long, D. M., & Salmon, C. T. (1994). Competencies for health communication specialist for the 21st century. *American Behavioral Scientist, 38,* 351–360.

Makoul, G. (2003). Communication skills education in medical school and beyond. *Journal of the American Medical Association, 289,*93.

Query, J. L., Jr., Wright, K. B., Bylund, C. L., & Mattson, M. (2007). Health communication instruction: Toward identifying common learning goals, course content, and pedagogical strategies to guide curricular development. *Health Communication, 21,* 133–141.

Ratzan, S. C. (1994). Editor's introduction: Communication—The key to a healthier tomorrow. *American Behavioral Scientist, 38,* 202–207.

Richardson, W. C., Berwick, D. M., & Bisgard, J. C. (2000). The Institute of Medicine report on medical errors. *New England Journal of Medicine, 342,* 663–664.

Rogers, E. M. (1994). The field of health communication today. *American Behavioral Scientist, 38,* 208–214.

Rogers, E. M. (1996). The field of health communication today: An up-to-date report. *Journal of Health Communication: International Perspectives, 1,* 15–23.

Rogers, E. M. (1997). Foreword. In P. T. Piotrow, D. L. Kincaid, J. G. Rimon, II, & W. Rinehart (Eds.), *Health communication: Lessons from family planning and reproductive health* (pp. xiii–xv). Westport, CT: Praeger.

Sharf, B. F. (1993). Reading the vital signs: Research in health care communication. *Communication Monographs, 60,* 35–41.

Thompson, T. L., Robinson, J. D., Anderson, D. J., & Federowicz, M. (2008). Health communication: Where have we been and where can we go? In K. B. Wright & S. Moore (Eds.), *Applied Health Communication* (pp. 3–33). Cresskill, NJ: Hampton Press.

Waldrope, W. J. (1999). A curricular profile of U. S. communication departments. *Communication Education, 48*, 256–258.

Wright, K. B., Bylund, C. B., Ware, J. Parker, P., Query, J. L., Jr., & Baile, W. (2006). Medical student attitudes toward communication skills training and knowledge of appropriate provider–patient communication: A comparison of first-year and fourth-year medical students. *Medical Education Online, 11*(18). Retrieved from www.med-ed-online.org

College and University Websites Cited

Creighton University, http://medschool.creighton.edu/gme/programs/pathology/index.php

Edward Via Virginia College of Osteopathic Medicine, http://www.vcom.vt.edu/

Michigan State University, College of Osteopathic Medicine, http://www.com.msu.edu/ss/Elective_Course_Listing.html

Midwestern University, http://www.midwestern.edu/Documents/Registrar/Curriculums/DM%20 2012%20landscape.pdf

Ida V. Moffett School of Nursing, Samford University, http://www4.samford.edu/nursing/

Norwich University, Course Descriptions, http://www.norwich.edu/academics/mathScience/nursing/courses.html

Nova Southeastern University Health Professions Division, http://hpd.nova.edu/catalog/forms/hpd_catalog_full.pdf

Ohio State University School of Communication, http://www.comm.ohio-state.edu/

Oklahoma State University Center for Health Sciences College of Osteopathic Medicine, http://www.healthsciences.okstate.edu/college/course_descriptions.cfm

Pennsylvania State University, http://cas.la.psu.edu/grad/gradcourses.htm

Philadelphia College of Osteopathic Medicine, http://www.pcom.edu/index.html

San Diego State University, http://arweb.sdsu.edu/es/catalog/0910/webfolder/Communication.pdf

Texas A&M University, http://www.medicine.tamhsc.edu/institutional-advancement/communications/news/23march2009.html

Thomas Jefferson University Medical College, http://www.aboutmedicalschools.com/medical/unitedstates/pennsylvania/philadelphia/93.asp

Tufts University School of Medicine MS in Health Communication, http://www.tufts.edu/med/education/phpd/mshealthcomm/

Tulane University School of Medicine, Foundations in Medicine 1, http://www.som.tulane.edu/courses/fimI.html

University of Alabama at Birmingham School of Public Health, Health Behavior Courses, https://www.soph.uab.edu/node/213

University of Florida College of Journalism and Communications, http://www.jou.ufl.edu/

University of Florida Graduate School, http://gradschool.ufl.edu/

University of Georgia, Department of Speech Communication, course descriptions, http://bulletin.uga.edu/bulletin/courses/descript/SPCM.html

University of Houston, Jack J. Valenti School of Communication, http://www.valenti.uh.edu/

University of Illinois at Urbana-Champaign, Department of Communication, http://www.communication.illinois.edu/

University of Oklahoma Department of Communication, http://www.ou.edu/cas/deptcomm/

University of Pennsylvania Medical Education Program, http://www.med.upenn.edu/culture/history.shtml

University of Pittsburgh Internal Medicine Residency, http://www.residency.dom.pitt.edu/

Yale University School of Medicine Office of Education, http://www.med.yale.edu/education/

40

ETHICS IN COMMUNICATION FOR HEALTH PROMOTION IN CLINICAL SETTINGS AND CAMPAIGNS

New Challenges and Enduring Dilemmas

Nurit Guttman

Introduction

Whether through national mass media campaigns, local community projects, or clinical settings, the use of health communication to promote people's health by changing their health beliefs or behaviors is invariably inundated with ethical issues. Increasingly, health care providers in clinical settings are expected to influence patients to adopt health promotion practices, while public health organizations and government agencies use information campaigns to amplify their efforts to influence the public to adopt these practices. When the purpose is to influence people to adopt health-promoting practices, recent developments in communication technology, health care policy, and new manifestations of infectious diseases present new ethical dilemmas along with the ongoing ones. Identifying ethical issues in clinical and public health communication interventions has become a critical challenge because they are widely pervasive and increasingly used by governments and public organizations as a means to influence people's health-related practices. For example, persuasive strategies are employed by health care providers in clinical settings and by public health agencies to urge reluctant parents to vaccinate their children. Regardless of the beneficent intentions of the appeals used to convince parents, their use raises various ethical concerns. For example, should strong emotional appeals be employed? Is it more convincing to present the risk of not vaccinating a child in an exaggerated manner or would a lower key approach be as effective, or more so? Ethical issues are involved in most, if not all, decisions that relate to the goals, design, implementation, and evaluation of any health communication intervention. These include decisions regarding which health issues to tackle, which populations should be 'targeted' by the intervention, and whether to employ highly persuasive tactics. These ethical issues are often implicit and embedded in subtle decision-making processes, and their delineation requires an assessment of unintended impacts.

Why should health communicators seek to identify ethical issues? One argument is that when goals are noble, the means to achieve them must be noble as well (Kirby & Andreasen,

632

2001). It has become imperative to identify and address ethical issues as health interventions take place in multicultural settings, and because commercial marketing tactics and new information technologies are widely embraced and exploited. There are also pragmatic implications to addressing ethical issues: Interventions that are sensitive to ethical concerns are more likely to gain the trust and respect of intended populations and collaborators. Thus, identifying ethical issues needs to become a routine part of any purposive attempt to influence people to change their health-related attitudes or behaviors. This chapter presents a brief overview of ethical frameworks, followed by a discussion of the types of ethical issues that can inadvertently emerge in the goals and tactics of persuasive health communication. The chapter concludes with new and enduring challenges associated with developments in communication technologies.

Ethical Frameworks and Principles

Philosophers have presented ethical theories and principles that define moral duties and obligations, some with particular relevance to the health care and health promotion context (Veatch, 1999). The bioethics literature typically notes two major theoretical approaches broadly labeled as *deontological* and *teleological*. Deontological approaches—as implied by the Greek word *deon*, duty—hold that some actions are intrinsically right or wrong, regardless of the consequences they may lead to, and that individuals should not be treated as a means to an end. The *teleological* perspective—as indicated by the word *telos*, end—focuses on consequences as the main criteria for determining moral worth. A utilitarian perspective, which adopts a teleological approach, emphasizes the importance of efficiency and effectiveness in terms of maximizing the greatest good to the greatest number of people within society's limited resources. When health care providers or health communicators adopt particular goals and communication strategies, these reflect the adoption of a particular moral approach, even if done unintentionally.

Two central moral obligations noted by bioethicists that have a particular relevance to health communication interventions are the obligations to *do good* and to *do no harm* (Beauchamp & Childress, 1994). Since the days of Hippocrates, the obligation to avoid doing harm (while intending to do good) is often considered the foremost ethical maxim for health providers and includes physiological, psychological, social, and cultural aspects of harm. In the context of health communication in clinical settings or in information campaigns, harmful effects may occur when the communication between them and health care providers or when campaign messages create undue anxiety, label or stigmatize people, and when they trigger the opposite of what the message was intended to do. The obligation to do good (*beneficence*), or prevent people from being harmed, is another basic tenet of the helping professions. However, the obligations to promote people's health by encouraging them to adopt health promoting behaviors may conflict with the obligation to respect their autonomy.

Respect for personal autonomy and privacy is a central ethical obligation, based on the premise that people have an intrinsic right to make decisions for themselves on any matter that might affect them, at least so far as such decisions do not bring harm to others. It is rooted in a liberal Western tradition that places high importance on individual choice, both regarding political life and personal development. It underlies democratic forms of government and self-determination and has been the foundation for the development of medical care codes such as patients' rights, informed consent, and confidentiality. Health communicators, according to this precept, are obligated to honor the dignity of individuals and communities as autonomous, free actors. In practice, health communicators may need to choose to uphold one moral principle at the expense of another, which creates an ethical dilemma. In multicultural settings a contentious issue concerns moral relativism: whether to respect certain cultural values, cherished by members of a cultural group, which conflict with moral precepts considered as universal (Cortese, 1990). Another central ethical precept is the notion of *justice* that typically encompasses the moral requirement of a just society to eliminate or reduce barriers that prevent equal opportunities to good health (Beauchamp & Childress, 1994; Daniels, 1985).

It should be noted that despite the wide use of these principles in the medical and health promotion context, they have also been criticized as representing mainly a Western approach to moral issues, with its strong emphasis on individualism and universalism. Critics maintain that these principles may be too removed from actual situations that elicit moral choices, and do not reflect diversity in moral reasoning (Makau & Arnett, 1997). Thus, additional ethical approaches may be highly relevant. One such approach is the Ethic of Care, which draws from feminist studies and emphasizes the moral importance of maintaining relationships, connectedness, and attentiveness to needs over principles of impartial justice (Manning, 1992; O'Brien-Hallstein, 1999). Other perspectives that emphasize harmony and interdependence as moral imperatives are found in Communitarian or community-oriented approaches, and non-Western cultures (Cortese, 1990; Etzioni, 1993). Casuistry presents yet another type of moral reasoning that does not rely on abstract principles. Casuistry (from *casus* the Latin root for "case") is grounded in an appeal to reasoning that derives from analogical cases, and it focuses on the specific circumstances of each case (Beauchamp & Childress, 1994). Each of these ethical perspectives may proffer tools to articulate, identify, and address ethical issues embedded in the health communication intervention as a whole or in its particular facets.

Ethical Precepts in Communication and the Presentation of Persuasive Health Information

Ethics in health communication campaigns can be informed by the stipulations posed by communication ethics scholars (e.g., Johannensen, 1996). The most prominent may be the adherence to *truth*, considered one of the tenets of Western morality (Beauchamp & Childress, 1994), even if distorting the truth is done for what health communicators would consider a good cause. Truthful communication also requires that all relevant information should be provided, as indicated by the ethical standard of *completeness*, according to which it may be unethical to present a one-sided argument, to select only favorable supporting evidence, or to present scientific findings as certain when they are considered tentative (Johannensen, 1996). This is a challenge health communicators often need to address, especially when they believe that in order to be effective, they need to present brief and nontentative information. A similar challenge is the stipulation to ensure that the information disseminated is 'correct,' but this information depends on current research data, which may be based on recommendations that are tentative, incomplete, or subject to different interpretations (Marshall, 1995). Another obligation is to ensure that the topic is truly relevant to the intended population and not just made to seem that way (McLeroy et al., 1995). This can be related to the standard of *sincerity*. Reasons for the communicative initiative need to be made clear, including goals and implicit agendas of sponsors. Sincerity may be particularly important to members of groups who feel they have been discriminated against or exploited in the past, or who feel that the interventional messages serve hidden agendas

(Myrick, 1998). Highly relevant to health communication interventions is the stipulation of *comprehensibility*: to ensure that the information, recommendations, and claims made in messages can be fully understood by all members of the intended audiences. When developing messages for populations with low levels of literacy or different types of cognitive skills, the information provided needs to be adapted to individuals' capacities.

Finally, associated with the moral obligation to respect people's autonomy and self-determination, is the standard of *inclusion*. It underscores the importance of involving diverse members of the populations whose behavior the intervention aims to influence. Inclusion may also be important for strategic reasons: Messages developed with those who are its intended audiences are more likely to create a sense of ownership. However, even when practitioners emphasize the pragmatic importance of inclusion, the methods they use may not fulfill principles of democratic discourse and they may not give voice to the intended population. This raises ethical issues regarding people's right to self-determination (Brenkert, 2002).

Ethical Issues in Goals, Strategies, and Tactics

Who Has the Mandate to Influence?

Consider messages that urge parents to vaccinate their children, or to make their children follow a certain diet. Who has the moral right to tell people to follow such recommendations (and to make them feel inadequate if they do not)? Do health care providers, community organizations, or government agencies have the mandate to intervene in people's lives through health claims and persuasive messages? These questions represent ethical concerns associated with the issue of mandate and entitlement (Paisley, 1989). Health communication activities are often initiated by government agencies and organizations that come from outside the intervention community or represent only particular sectors. Similarly, health care providers may come from different ethnic groups, whose values and life circumstances differ from those of the people whom they are trying to influence. In certain communities there may be a residue of distrust of governmental agencies because of a history of prejudice and abuse. Thus, the moral mandate to intervene cannot be taken for granted. It may need to be justified and earned.

Defining Goals and Obtaining Consent

The choice of goals and objectives also raises ethical issues because there may be alternative ways of understanding causes and solutions to health-related problems. For example, certain cultural groups may believe that what health communicators describe as a problem is in fact a normal part of aging, or they may emphasize the role of fate or of a supreme being in resolving particular health problems. Individuals or groups may feel they have alternative priorities that should be pursued by the intervention. Another ethical concern associated with program goals is whether the health recommendations can be readily adopted by all population members. If they are not accessible to all, the communication intervention helps only those who can adopt them, and may frustrate those who are unable to do so (Smith, 2000).

In addition, health communicators face the challenge of how to respect the autonomy of individuals and groups by obtaining the consent of the intended population that is to be the object of the intervention. In health communication campaigns, because health messages are typically disseminated to populations with whom the communicators do not have direct contact and in clinical settings, health care providers may display printed and audiovisual health-promotion materials. Therefore, it is not feasible to obtain direct consent from each individual to be exposed to this type of communication. One approach is to engage community advisory boards as representatives. However, its members may not necessarily represent the various perspectives in the community and it may hinder the implementation of the intervention (Myrick, 1998). In certain situations it is difficult to disclose the actual topic of the health communication intervention before a certain level of trust is established with members of the population. In addition, the notion of consent raises the dilemma regarding who should give their consent in the case of children and youth.

Ethics in Tailoring, Targeting, and Cultural Sensitivity

Customizing information that is meant to influence people's health in a way that fits their cultural beliefs, practices, and needs is referred to as 'tailoring.' The goal is to be 'culturally sensitive' and to provide equivalent but culturally appropriate information to populations with diverse sociocultural backgrounds and levels of literacy (Campbell & Quintiliani, 2006; Kreps, 1996). In clinical settings, practitioners may need to obtain highly personal information in order to effectively 'tailor' the health information, and this may infringe on people's privacy and autonomy. Practitioners may also choose to devote more time and effort to try to 'tailor' the health communication to people from particular social groups, compared to others. This kind of a decision may be based on ethical considerations of need as well as utility.

When designing health communication campaigns, health communication practitioners often adopt both the terminology and practice of commercial marketers. 'Segmentation' and 'targeting' are accepted as essential strategic approaches even within ethnic populations (Hornik & Ramirez, 2006). Yet, the mere decision to 'segment' a population contains within it moral judgments typically associated with considerations of equity and utility (Rothschild, 2001). For example, some interventions target those who are most likely to adopt recommendations or seem to possess a higher degree of readiness to do so (a utilitarian approach). Others may choose to target those with the greatest need, even when it is believed they are least likely to adopt the recommendations (De Jarlais, Padian, & Winkelstein, 1994). This can occur in clinical settings as well: Practitioners may decide to divide their limited time by devoting relatively more of it to communicate health recommendations to people whom they think are more likely to adopt these recommendations than to people whom they assume are not likely to do so.

In addition to ethical considerations of utility, needs, and fairness, three ethical concerns associated with segmentation and 'targeting' are noted here. First, communication campaigns that focus on segmentation may come at the expense of fostering community norms and consensus, and thus would not focus on changing norms, on collaborations, or on diffusion of goals, and would not encourage public debate (Hornik & Ramirez, 2006). Second, when information is tailored for particular individuals or groups, others may feel excluded or disadvantaged. A third concern is that though a cultural sensitivity approach may advance the well-being of individuals, critics maintain it will mainly serve the establishment's agenda, and will not help change the position of socioeconomically marginalized groups. A proposed alternative to the culturally sensitive approach is a 'culturally centered' approach, that emphasizes providing members of marginalized groups with opportunities to engage in critical dialogues and have their voices heard by their own community and by decision makers outside their community (Dutta, 2007).

The Tools of Persuasion: Exaggeration, Omission, and Strong Emotional and Fear Appeals

Perhaps the most debated issue in health communication—whether in the interpersonal context or in mass media campaigns—is the ethics of using persuasive appeals: Is it ethical to even slightly distort probabilities of risk in order to persuade people to avoid potentially harmful practices? Is it ethical to use highly emotional appeals, to scare people by showing graphic images that will be etched in their memory, or to use analogies that frame risk in an exaggerated way? The debate pits arguments that aim to justify the use of manipulative 'tools of persuasion' with arguments that this infringes on the moral principle of respecting people's autonomy. For example, some may argue that 'strong' or scary appeals are needed in order to "break through the clutter" of so many competing messages (Smith, 2000). The dilemma regarding the use of strong emotional or scary appeals is particularly vexing when this is commonly suggested by members from the intervention's population. Yet, increasingly researchers oppose using such appeals both on the basis of pragmatic and moral arguments (Hastings, Stead & Webb, 2004). Strong emotional and scary appeals may fail to meet stipulations for correctness and accuracy by inflating the probability or magnitude of the risk. They may also mainly scare those who already are scared, thus not producing desired protective practices or norms (Muthusamy, Levine, & Weber, 2009). Further, theory and research on the use of risk messages to persuade people to change their behaviors emphasize the crucial role played by people's self-assessment of their capacity to address the risk. If their self-assessment is low, they are less likely to adopt the recommended protective practices and such messages could foster a feeling of fatalism (Ruiter, Verplanken, Kok, & Werrij, 2003; Witte, 1994). Therefore, to be both ethical and pragmatic, communication interventions that aim to elicit people's sense of vulnerability to risk by appealing to their emotions of fear and dread, would need to include information that enhances their capacities to adopt the recommendations.

Despite the inclination to use strong emotional and fear appeals, both in clinical encounters or mediated communication, health-promoting information can be presented in more factual, dialogical, or deliberative methods. This can be applied in both clinical settings and in the design of communication campaigns. Participative and deliberative strategies for message production are increasingly adopted in health communication initiatives, particularly in community programs (e.g., Laub, Somera, Gowen, & Diaz, 1999; Rudd & Comings, 1994). But even appeals disseminated through mass media channels can represent a dialogical approach (Johannesen, 1996). For example, the purposive use of drama and entertainment programs to influence audiences' health behaviors (the Edutainment approach) can employ dialogue and plot to present different perspectives or value orientations and can model how to overcome barriers for personal and collective action. It should be noted, however, that this approach raises its own slew of ethical concerns (Singhal & Rogers, 1999).

Cultural Themes: Co-Optation, Appropriation, and Confrontation

It has become one of the staples in health communication to take into consideration the cultural heritage of minority and ethnic populations. The underlying rationale is that incorporating cultural symbols and themes in health messages can serve as a source of pride, increase identification with the message, and increase the likelihood of people adopting the health recommendations. Ethical concerns, however, are raised when cultural themes or symbols are co-opted by detaching them from their original meaning, and using them as a persuasive tactic. Also, an emphasis on particular cultural values (e.g., values associated with *machismo* that can appeal to men from particular cultural groups) raises ethical concerns because it can inadvertently serve to perpetuate traditional gender roles. This raises another moral dilemma: Should certain cultural norms be challenged? Practitioners described such dilemmas when they tried to promote personal empowerment and found that they had to challenge dominant cultural norms related to gender or conceptions of authority (Sabogal, Oterso-Sabogal, Pasick, Jenkins, & Pe'rez-Stable, 1996).

A related ethical issue is associated with cultural sensitivity in references to particular body organs, intimate practices, or in the use of images that may be deemed offensive by some. Whereas there is an ethical obligation to avoid being offensive, practitioners may feel obligated to refer to them to promote health goals. For example, only a decade ago it was considered offensive to mention oral or anal sexual practices or impotency, but, although certain groups find mentioning them offensive, it is nonetheless essential to discuss them for health-promotion purposes.

The use of images considered culturally appropriate may also serve to perpetuate negative stereotypes held within this culture. This was illustrated in the case of messages developed for older U.S. minority women who shared a belief that breast cancer risk is mainly associated with what they considered "loose" or promiscuous behavior. To dispel this perception, printed material intended to be culturally oriented showed women in different apparent lifestyles, including a woman in clerical robes and one in a tight-fitting low-cut dress (Skinner et al., 1998). This approach may serve to further entrench negative stereotypes in this population of women who dress in a traditional way. Thus, as health communication for health promotion increasingly incorporates cultural symbols and themes, practitioners face the challenge to develop sensitivity not only regarding which themes may be culturally appropriate, but the ethical implications of using them.

Blame, Shame, Culpability, and Responsibility

Personal responsibility as "the key to good health" is central in modern discourse on health promotion, and is used extensively (Guttman & Ressler, 2001; Kirkwood & Brown, 1995). A common persuasive approach is to warn individuals that if they do not prevent illness or disability they will become a burden to their family or society as a whole. This appeal may resonate with the precept of fairness (it is not fair to burden others), but it may elicit strong feelings of shame and guilt among individuals who are not able to adopt the recommended practices (Bayer, 1996; Finerman & Bennet, 1995). Although health messages may not explicitly blame individuals for their illness, they may frame the notion of responsibility for disease prevention as if it were primarily under the control of individuals, when, in fact, they may have only partial control. As such, they deemphasize institutional and structural factors such as work and housing conditions, access to health care, or pollution that contribute to the etiology of health-related problems. This has been referred to as 'victim blaming': locating the causes of social problems within the individual, rather than in social and environmental forces (Wikler, 1987).

Stigmatization has been used in clinical settings as well as in communication campaigns as a means to influence people to avoid practices that can cause them or others harm. For example, proponents of vaccination in the 1920s used appeals to shame in order to persuade parents to have their children immunized. More recently, some campaigns sought to stigmatize drunk drivers or to "de-normalize" and marginalize smoking, and indirectly to stigmatize people who smoke (Stuber, Galea, & Link, 2008). Ethical objections to the purposive use of stigmatization as a health communication tactic include the argument that it fails to meet the ethical obligation to respect human dignity and that its deterrent effects are likely not to be experienced equally across different socioeconomic and racial/ethnic subgroups (Burris, 2008).

Personal Responsibility and Public Opinion on Health Insurance Coverage

When health communications emphasize lifestyle factors and personal responsibility they may implicitly characterize those who do not adopt recommended practices as unwilling and at fault for a detrimental medical condition. Evidence on such notions of culpability can be found in research data that show that the general public and decision makers tend to accept the proposition that people should be obligated to pay more for the expenses of particular health conditions believed to be a result of what has been determined as irresponsible behavior (Sachs,1996). It is also reflected in priority setting of health care services (Bowling, 1996). These sentiments raise concerns among ethicists who maintain that health care policies should be based on the values of equity and solidarity. Further, discourse on risk, like any other discourse that relates to the human body, can be viewed as ideologically and culturally based. What is considered irresponsible depends, therefore, on each society's selection of what it considers risky and on its definition of social roles, behavioral obligations, legal responsibility, what is or is not covered by health insurance, and sanctions and rewards (Douglas, 1994; Lupton, 1993).

Persuasive messages may appeal to people's sense of moral obligations associated with their social roles. However, the moral bases of appeals to personal responsibility may be contested by those who hold alternative conceptions of social roles and obligations. This can happen in clinical settings when health care providers try to convince women to adopt a certain practice in order to be a 'good wife' as well as in campaigns. One example is a message developed to promote breast cancer screening among women from low-income ethnic populations. It appealed to them as wives, mothers, grandmothers, and friends on whom others depend; therefore they needed to undergo screening for the sake of others (Earp et al., 1997).

Another kind of an appeal to responsibility is that individuals may be called upon to help promote or protect the health of significant others. Common examples are appeals to help one's spouse maintain a healthy diet or to quit smoking. Such messages may reinforce social values of solidarity or moral commitments to be responsive to others, and kindness, as emphasized in the ethic of care. Ethicists point out that we express moral disapproval, even outrage, toward people who do not warn, protect, or come to the aid of others who are at risk, even if they are not related to them (Douard & Winslade, 1994). Anti-drunk driving messages utilized the appeal that "Friends don't let friends drive drunk" basing this proclamation on the responsibility people feel for others. But what does this responsibility entail? Are friends responsible when the individual drinks beyond what is believed to be safe, resists the friends' pleas, chooses to drive, and is involved in a crash?

Inadvertent Cultural and Personal Adverse Effects

The ethical principle most emphasized in medical ethics is to refrain from doing harm, and it can serve as a reminder that even persuasive talk in clinical settings or the dissemination of information through health campaigns can result in unintended adverse outcomes (Cho & Salmon, 2007). Interventions in clinical settings are notorious for being susceptible to the prospect of detrimental *iatrogenic* outcomes (an adverse condition that comes from or is caused by healing or medical treatment). In his critique of modern institutionalized medicine, Illich (1975) extends the concept of physiological *iatrogenesis* to include social and cultural harm. This framework can help characterize potential adverse effects of health communication interventions. Potential physiological harmful effects may include injuries sustained when individuals engage in recommended physical activities or the tendency for eating disorders reinforced by messages on dieting (Seedhouse, 1991). Similarly, psychological harmful effects should be considered as well, because individuals may be made to feel guilty about not taking good care of their health or find they are living in a constant state of worry about it (Barsky, 1988).

At the social and cultural levels, communication in clinical settings and in health communication campaigns may increase medical control over various domains of human behaviors as described by the notion of *medicalization*, a term that refers to the social phenomenon that occurs when various life domains become incorporated within medical definitions and control. Critics maintain that medical ways of labeling and framing issues have come to play a central role in contemporary social discourse, contribute to people redefining life events in medical terms, and may turn health into the focus of human existence (Verweij, 1999).

These concerns regarding the potentially adverse effects of health communication interventions are not meant to dismiss the contribution of health communication efforts to the promotion of the welfare of individuals and populations. Rather, they are meant to sensitize health communicators to the possibility that communication regarding health promotion, although it may help urge people to adopt health-promoting practices, may also have a negative cumulative impact in cultural and psychological terms.

Labeling, Stigmatizing and Stereotyping

Despite the sophistication of current scientific understanding of the etiology of diseases, people often seek explanations for devastating illnesses in moral frameworks and social stereotypes (Douglas, 1994). Throughout history, individuals or groups associated with threatening diseases were feared and stigmatized, and at times even quarantined (Crawford, 1994). Health messages that warn against the risk of contracting a stigmatized medical condition may inadvertently serve to reinforce prejudice and damage the self-esteem of those who have these conditions. One societal-level effect of stigmatization is people's support of coercive measures against those who have the stigmatized medical condition and discrimination. Even school-based programs for weight loss can stigmatize overweight children (McLeroy et al., 1995). Thus, health communicators face the challenge to portray risks and ways to avoid them without making negative attributions. In addition, *labeling* may also affect individuals' or groups' identities. When a person's persona is connected to the medical condition it can lower the individual's self-esteem or place the person in an almost constant state of anxiety (Barsky, 1988). Similarly, humorous uses of presumably harmless stereotypes in health messages may need to be scrutinized for ethical implications. For example, messages that use humorous images of the nagging mother-in-law or a wife's bad cooking when a man returns from work can contribute to gender-role stereotypes.

Inequity in Health Communication

Communication for health promotion typically entails the moral obligation to promote equity across social groups. Yet health communication campaigns as well as health communication in clinical settings may inadvertently reinforce existing social disparities. Inequity in communication has been defined as differences in the generation, manipulation, and distribution of information among social groups and the impact of structural determinants and socioeconomic factors on differences in people's access, attention, retention, and capacity to act on relevant information to enhance their health (Viswanath & Emmons, 2006). Communication studies have noted the knowledge gap phenomenon, which can be found both in the dissemination and in people's adoption of health recommendations. Research findings indicate that populations from higher socioeconomic groups are more likely to increase their knowledge relevant to the health issue after the dissemination of health information; they are also more likely to adopt recommended practices, though motivation to do so may be similar across different populations (Winkleby, Taylor, Jatulis, & Fortmann, 1996). Further, as public health and social critics point out, even when people adopt certain health recommendations as a result of health communication, institutional, social, and structural factors may prevent them from attaining more permanent behavioral changes. The same kind of phenomenon may occur in clinical settings when people with limited means are less likely to realize providers' health recommendations.

Another type of ethical concern associated with inequity is that certain practices considered unhealthy might offer members of vulnerable groups not only pleasure but also an important coping mechanism for which substitutes are not easily found (MacAskill, Stead, MacKintosh, & Hastings, 2002). Thus, the less privileged are likely to have fewer options for healthier substitutions. An example can be found in an antismoking program developed for Vietnamese American men whose practice was to carry a pack of cigarettes and offer one to a friend in social encounters. When offered a cigarette, the men reported that they felt obliged to accept it. This sharing of cigarettes appears to be an important social practice that serves to reinforce social ties and solidarity in this immigrant community. Other minority communities, for example, Arab men in Israel, appear to share this practice as well. Messages that aim to challenge this norm and state that offering someone a cigarette is like offering them cancer raise ethical concerns. First, if they do not quit, it can make them feel guilty. Second, if they do quit, it may serve to deprive these socially and economically disadvantaged men of a gratifying social practice that involves a fraternal gesture and shared activity. This example raises the question whether health communicators are morally obligated to help find alternative practices when they aim to eliminate 'risky' practices that may serve to enhance social solidarity or represent generosity, kinship, friendship, and bonding.

Health as a Moral Phenomenon and a Value

From ancient times the notion of health has essentially been represented in moral and ideological dimensions that are related to what people believe is good and what they believe is responsible. Health has been associated with moral virtue, to such an extent that critics maintain that health becomes a significant feature in people's aspirations and personal goals and that the pursuit of health is identical to the pursuit of moral personhood (Crawford, 1994). Communication about health both in the clinical context and in communication campaigns can contribute to this process through an agenda-setting function. Focusing on certain health issues can lead to prioritization on both public and personal agendas (Dearing & Rogers, 1996) and influence some people to think those issues are more prominent than others. The ethical concerns that follow draw on these theoretical conceptions and concern the moral impact of health-promotion messages on culture and society.

One ethical concern is associated with the obligation to promote equity. It draws on the assumption that an emphasis on health as a value contributes to people's escalating expectations from medicine and health care. The assumption is that the more powerful groups could demand that the health care system meet their escalating needs, whereas members of vulnerable groups will continue to receive relatively fewer services (Daniels, 1985). A related concern is that a cultural preoccupation with personal health may result in distracting people from other social issues and contribute to fostering individualism and self-interest at the expense of values of connectedness to others. Similarly, another concern is that it will increase values of consumerism and of a culture that emphasizes youth and health and degrades aging and those who are ill (Callahan, 1990). An example of this issue would be antismoking messages aimed at youth that emphasize that smoking increases the formation of wrinkles. This position reinforces the notion of youthful looks as an ideal for attractiveness (Kirby & Andreasen, 2001).

Finally, a growing ethical concern is that good health increasingly is associated with virtue. Thus, those who are not healthy may be made to feel that they have been punished or are unworthy (Callahan, 1990; Fitzgerald, 1994). They may be viewed as social deviants because they lack the necessary willpower to be admirable members of society (Crawford, 1994). As Becker (1993), a prominent health promotion scholar, declared: Health promotion messages may turn the pursuit of health into a crusade with moral overtones that may harm people more than it helps them.

New and Enduring Challenges

Communication to promote people's health is inundated with ethical issues and dilemmas precisely because it aims to benefit people. Some of the ethical precepts regarding the use of persuasive tactics were discussed by ancient health care practitioners and endure until today. Other ethical concerns have emerged from current social and technological developments. This chapter concludes with four such challenges: an increasing emphasis on personal responsibility as it relates to health care insurance policies; the authoritative voice in health promotion messages; commercial organizations as a health promotion resource; and advances in new communication technologies.

1. *Health communication about personal responsibility and health care insurance policies*: Health care delivery and health promotion are increasingly on the social and political agenda. Health issues such as obesity have been identified not only as health concerns, but as threats to the economy because of escalating health care costs. Communication that emphasizes personal responsibility for health can contribute to the current cost-control social climate, which is reflected in changing provisions in health insurance policies for conditions considered to be dependent on people's lifestyle choices. Some insurance companies (both public and private) have created 'patient charters' that outline patient obligations. This raises ethical concerns regarding the ability of people from different socioeconomic backgrounds to meet these obligations (Schmidt, 2007; Steinbrook, 2006). The challenge is how to address issues of responsibility for one's health as empowering rather than blaming or discriminatory.

2. *The authoritative voice?* Health communication campaigns have increasingly become an important tool for government to influence public views and behaviors. The authoritative voice often used in campaigns that tells people what they should do has been described by critics as paternalistic or as the voice of the 'Nanny state.' This raises

questions about the ethics of government approaches in presenting health information in a prescriptive manner, instead of developing communication campaigns that rely less on telling people what to do and more on providing them with information and resources to make informed decisions and with opportunities to choose healthier solutions (Henley, 2006). Similarly, in clinical contexts, health care providers face the challenge of how to avoid a prescriptive tone and offer patients the information and resources that enable them to make informed decisions.

3. *Commercial organizations as a health promotion resource:* Promoting health is a growing business, with substantial profits to commercial companies that sell health-related products and services. Commercial companies are also interested in contributing to communication campaigns as part of the growing trend labeled 'corporate social responsibility.' Numerous ethical issues emerge when health care providers and not-for-profit or government agencies partner with commercial organizations to disseminate health information. For example, should health care providers use health promotion materials produced by for-profit organizations? Should commercial organizations' resources be used to help increase the impact of the campaign, which otherwise could be limited? Which companies can be considered appropriate partners? Should companies whose products contribute directly or indirectly to unhealthy factors such as obesity, consumerism, pollution, or images of thinness and eating disorders be considered as potential partners because of their ability to provide needed resources? Additional new challenges emerge with the growing trend of direct marketing of medical products and services (e.g., medications to prevent illnesses or diagnostic tests) to the public, which previously were only addressed to health care providers. Whereas the dissemination of this type of information by commercial companies can provide people with beneficial information, clearly it raises concerns that it is meant to serve commercial interests. One challenge is to articulate and enforce the ethical obligations of for-profit organizations that market health-related products directly to the public. Another challenge is the obligation of health care providers and public health organizations to help people critically assess information from a for-profit source.

4. *New communication technologies:* The rapid growth in the availability of health-related information through channels that several years ago seemed unimaginable poses new challenges and opportunities in communication for health promotion, as well as ethical dilemmas. Can new capacities of communication technologies (e.g., in cell phone technology and the Internet) and the growth of new types of social networks address health-related social disparities and knowledge gaps or will they contribute to what has been characterized as 'the digital divide'? Can new communication technologies help promote self-determination, public discourse, and mobilize public action to promote health issues, or will they create enhanced opportunities for commercial interests to exploit dissemination of products and services associated with health risks?

Both the use of more traditional and newer modes of communication for the purpose of promoting health suggest that ethical issues in communication about health promotion play an important role in daily routines in clinical settings and in the design of communication campaigns. Some of these ethical issues present familiar and enduring challenges associated with truth-telling or avoiding manipulative communication tactics when trying to influence people to adopt health promoting practices. Others present newer challenges associated with cultural and institutional factors. Ethics in communication to promote health thus entails not only consideration of the ethics in persuasive approaches to influence people to better their health, but it also has moral implications regarding broad social values associated with equity, gender roles, and health care services policy.

References

Barsky, A. J. (1988). *Worried sick: Our troubled quest for wellness.* Boston: Little, Brown.

Bayer, R. (1996). AIDS prevention: Sexual ethics and responsibility. *New England Journal of Medicine, 334,* 1540–1542.

Beauchamp, T. L., & Childress, J. F. (1994). *Principles of biomedical ethics* (4th ed.). New York: Oxford University Press.

Becker, M. H. (1993). A medical sociologist looks at health promotion. *Journal of Health and Social Behavior, 34,* 1–6.

Bowling, A. (1996). Health care rationing: The public's debate. *British Medical Journal, 312,* 670–674.

Brenkert, G. G. (2002). Ethical challenges of social marketing. *Journal of Public Policy and Marketing, 21*(1), 14–25.

Burris, S. (2008). Stigma, ethics and policy: A commentary on Bayer's "Stigma and the ethics of public health: Not can we but should we." *Social Science & Medicine, 67,* 473–475.

Callahan, D. (1990). *What kind of life: The limits of medical progress.* New York: Simon & Schuster.

Campbell, M. K., & Quintiliani, L. M. (2006). Tailored interventions in public health: Where does tailoring fit in interventions to reduce health disparities? *American Behavioral Scientist, 49,* 775–793.

Cho, H., & Salmon, C. T. (2007). Unintended effects of health communication campaigns. *Journal of Communication, 57,* 293–317.

Cortese, A. (1990). *Ethnic ethics: The restructuring of moral theory.* Albany, NY: SUNY Press.

Crawford, R. (1994). The boundaries of the self and the unhealthy other: Reflections on health, culture and AIDS. *Social Science and Medicine, 38,* 1347–1356.

Daniels, N. (1985). *Just health care.* New York: Cambridge University Press.

Dearing, W. J., & Rogers, E. M. (1996). *Agenda-setting.* Thousand Oaks, CA: Sage.

De Jarlais, D. C., Padian, N. S., & Winkelstein, W. (1994). Targeted HIV-prevention programs. *New England Journal of Medicine, 331,* 1451–1453.

Douard, J. W., & Winslade, W. J. (1994). *Tarasoff* and the moral duty to protect the vulnerable. In J. F. Monagle & D. C. Thomasa (Eds.), *Health care ethics: Critical issues* (pp. 316–324). Gaithersburg, MD: Aspen.

Douglas, M. (1994). *Risk and blame: Essays in cultural theory.* London: Routledge.

Dutta, M. J. (2007). Communicating about culture and health: Theorizing culture-centered and cultural sensitivity approaches. *Communication Theory, 17,* 304–328.

Earp, J. A., Viadro, C. I., Vincus, A. A., Altpeter, M., Flax, V., Mayne, L., & Eng. E. (1997). Lay health advisors: A strategy for getting the word out about breast cancer. *Health Education and Behavior, 24,* 432–451.

Etzioni, A. (1993). *The spirit of community.* New York: Crown

Finerman, R., & Bennet, L. A. (1995). Guilt blame and shame: Responsibility in health and sickness. *Social Science and Medicine, 40,* 1–3.

Fitzgerald, F. T. (1994). The tyranny of health. *New England Journal of Medicine, 331,* 196–198.

Guttman, N., & Ressler, W. H. (2001). On being responsible: Ethical issues in appeals to personal responsibility in health campaigns. *Journal of Health Communication, 6,* 117–136.

Hastings, G., Stead, M., & Webb, J. (2004). Fear appeals in social marketing: Strategic and ethical reasons for concern. *Psychology and Marketing, 21,* 961–986.

Henley, N. (2006) Free to be obese in a 'Super Nanny State'? *Media and Culture Journal, 9*(4). Retrieved from http://journal.media-culture.org.au/0609/6-henley.php

Hornik, R., & Ramirez, A. S. (2006). Racial/ethnic disparities and segmentation in communication campaigns. *American Behavioral Scientist, 49,* 868–884.

Illich, I. (1975). *Medical nemesis.* London: Calder & Boyars.

Johannesen, R. L. (1996). *Ethics in human communication* (4th ed.). Prospect Heights, IL: Waveland Press.

Kirby, S. D., & Andreasen, A. R. (2001). Marketing ethics to social marketers: A segmentation approach. In A. R. Andreasen, (Ed), *Ethics in social marketing* (pp. 160–183). Washington, DC: Georgetown University Press.

Kirkwood, W. G., & Brown, D. (1995). Public communication about the causes of disease: The rhetoric of responsibility. *Journal of Communication, 45*(1), 55–76.

Kreps, G. L. (1996). Communicating to promote justice in the modern health care system. *Journal of Health Communication, 1*, 99–109.

Laub, C. L., Somera, D. M., Gowen, L. K., & Diaz, R. M. (1999). Targeting "risky" gender ideologies: Constructing a community-driven, theory-based HIV prevention intervention for youth. *Health Education and Behavior, 26*, 185–199.

Lupton, D (1993). Risk as moral danger: The social and political functions of risk discourse in public health. *International Journal of Health Services, 23*, 425–435.

MacAskill, S., Stead, M., MacKintosh, A. M., & Hastings, G. (2002). "You cannae just take cigarettes away from somebody and no' gie them something back": Can social marketing help solve the problem of low-income smoking? *Social Marketing Quarterly, 8*, 19–34.

Makau, J., & Arnett, R. (1997) (Eds.). *Communication ethics in an age of diversity*. Urbana: University of Illinois Press.

Manning, R. (1992) *Speaking from the heart: A feminist perspective on ethics*. Lanham, MD: Rowan & Littlefield.

Marshall, J. R. (1995). Improving Americans' diet—Setting public policy with limited knowledge [Editorial]. *American Journal of Public Health, 85*, 1609–1611.

McLeroy, K. R., Clark, N. M., Simons-Morton, B. G., Forster, J., Connell, C. M., Altman, D., & Zimmerman, M. A. (1995). Creating capacity: Establishing a health education research agenda for special populations. *Health Education Quarterly, 22*, 390–405.

Muthusamy, N., Levine, T., & Weber, R. (2009). Scaring the already scared: Some problems with HIV/AIDS fear appeals in Namibia. *Journal of Communication, 59*, 317–344.

Myrick, R. (1998). In search of cultural sensitivity and inclusiveness: Communication strategies used in rural HIV prevention campaigns designed for African Americans. *Health Communication, 10*, 65–85.

O'Brien-Hallstein, D. L. (1999). A postmodern caring: Feminist standpoint theories, revisioned caring, and communication ethics. *Western Journal of Communication, 63*, 32–56.

Paisley, W. (1989). Public communication campaigns: The American experience. In R. E. Rice & C. K. Atkin (Eds.), *Public communication campaigns* (2nd ed., pp. 15–38). Newbury Park, CA: Sage.

Rothschild, M. L. (2001). Ethical considerations in the use of marketing for the management of public health and social issues. In A. R. Andreasen (Ed), *Ethics in social marketing* (pp. 39–69). Washington, DC: Georgetown University Press.

Rudd, R. E., & Comings, J. P. (1994). Learner developed materials: An empowerment product. *Health Education Quarterly, 21*, 313–327.

Ruiter, R. A., Verplanken, B., Kok, G., & Werrij, M. Q. (2003). Do we need threat information? *Journal of Health Psychology, 8*, 465–474.

Sabogal, F., Oterso-Sabogal, R., Pasick, R., Jenkins, C. N., & Pe'rez-Stable, E. J. (1996). Printed health education materials for diverse communities: Suggestions learned from the field [Supplement]. *Health Education Quarterly, 23*, S123–S141.

Sachs, L. (1996). Causality, responsibility and blame—Core issues in the cultural construction and subtext of prevention. *Sociology of Health and Illness, 18*, 632–652.

Schmidt, H. (2007). Patients' charters and health responsibilities. *British Medical Journal, 335*, 1187–1189.

Seedhouse, D. (1991). *Ethics: The heart of health care*. New York: Wiley.

Singhal, A., & Rogers, E. M. (1999). *Entertainment-education: A communication strategy for social change*. Mahwah, NJ: Erlbaum.

Skinner, C. S., Sykes, R. K., Monsees, B. S., Andriole, D. A., Arfken, C. L., & Fisher, E. B. (1998). Learn, share, and live: Breast cancer education for older, urban minority women. *Health Education and Behavior, 25*, 60–78.

Smith, W. A. (2000). Ethics and the social marketer: A framework for practitioners. In A. R. Andreasen, (Ed), *Ethics in social marketing* (pp. 1–16). Washington, DC: Georgetown University Press.

Steinbrook, R. (2006). Imposing personal responsibility for health. *New England Journal of Medicine, 355*, 753–756.

Stuber, J., Galea, S., & Link, B. G. (2008). Smoking and the emergence of a stigmatized social status. *Social Science & Medicine, 67*, 420–430.

Veatch, R. M. (1999). The foundation of bioethics. *Bioethics, 12,* 206–217.

Verweij, M. (1999). Medicalization as a moral problem for preventive medicine. *Bioethics, 13,* 89–105.

Viswanath, K., & Emmons, K. M. (2006) Message effects and social determinants of health: Its application to cancer disparities. *Journal of Communication, 56*(Supplement 1), S238–S264.

Wikler, D. (1987). Who should be blamed for being sick? *Health Education Quarterly, 14,* 11–25.

Winkleby, M., A., Taylor, B., Jatulis, D., & Fortmann, S. P. (1996). The long-term effects of a cardiovascular disease prevention trial: The Stanford Five-City Project. *American Journal of Public Health, 86,* 1773–1779.

Witte, K. (1994). Fear control and danger control: A test of the extended parallel process model (EPPM). *Communication Monographs, 61,* 113–132.

INDEX

Page numbers in italic refer to figures or tables.

THE ROUTLEDGE HANDBOOK
OF HEALTH COMMUNICATION

The Routledge Handbook of Health Communication brings together the current body of scholarly work in health communication. With its expansive scope, it offers an introduction for those new to this area, summarizes work for those already learned in the area, and suggests avenues for future research on the relationships between communicative processes and health/health care delivery.

This second edition of the *Handbook* has been organized to reflect the goals of health communication: understanding to make informed decisions and to promote formal and informal systems of care linked to health and well-being. It emphasizes work in such areas as barriers to disclosure in family conversations and medical interactions, access to popular media and advertising, and individual searches online for information and support to guide decisions and behaviors with health consequences.

This edition also adds an overview of methods used in health communication and the unique challenges facing health communication researchers applying traditional methods to efforts to gain reliable and valid evidence about the role of communication for health. It introduces the promise of translational research being conducted by health communication researchers from multiple disciplines to form transdisciplinary theories and teams to increase the well-being of not only humans but the systems of care within their nations.

Arguably the most comprehensive scholarly resource available for study in this area, *The Routledge Handbook of Health Communication* serves an invaluable role and reference for students, researchers, and scholars doing work in health communication.

Teresa L. Thompson is Professor of Communication at the University of Dayton, USA. She edits the journal *Health Communication*, and has authored or edited seven books and over 70 articles on various aspects of health communication. She was the 2009 National Communication Association/International Communication Associaton Health Communication Scholar of the Year.

Roxanne Parrott is a Distinguished Professor in the Department of Communication Arts & Sciences at The Pennsylvania State University, USA, with a joint appointment in Health Policy & Administration. She was the recipient of the ICA/NCA Outstanding Health Communication Scholar Award in 2004.

Jon F. Nussbaum is a Professor of Communication Arts & Sciences and Human Development & Family Studies at The Pennsylvania State University, USA. He is a Fellow and Past President of the International Communication Association, and former editor of the *Journal of Communication*. He received the 2007 Outstanding Health Communication Scholar Award from ICA/NCA.

ROUTLEDGE COMMUNICATION SERIES

Jennings Bryant/Dolf Zillman, General Editors

THE ROUTLEDGE HANDBOOK
OF HEALTH COMMUNICATION

Second Edition

Edited by:

Teresa L. Thompson

Roxanne Parrott

Jon F. Nussbaum

Routledge
Taylor & Francis Group

NEW YORK AND LONDON

First Edition published 2003
By Lawrence Erlbaum Associates

This edition published 2011
by Routledge
711 Third Avenue, New York, NY 10017

Simultaneously published in the UK
by Routledge
2 Park Square, Milton Park, Abingdon, Oxon OX14 4RN

Routledge is an imprint of the Taylor & Francis Group, an informa business

Library of Congress Cataloging in Publication Data
The Routledge handbook of health communication / edited by Teresa L. Thompson, Roxanne Parrott, Jon F. Nussbaum. — 2nd ed.
p. ; cm.
Includes bibliographical references.
1. Communication in medicine—Handbooks, manuals, etc.
2. Physician and patient—Handbooks, manuals, etc.
I. Thompson, Teresa L. II. Parrott, Roxanne. III. Nussbaum, Jon F.
[DNLM: 1. Communication—Review. 2. Physician-Patient Relations—Review.
3. Delivery of Health Care—organization & administration—Review.
4. Health Promotion—methods—Review.
5. Patient Education as Topic—methods—Review. W 62]
R118.H26 2011
613—dc22
2010042511

ISBN 13: 978-0-415-88314-6 (hbk)
ISBN 13: 978-0-415-88315-3 (pbk)
ISBN 13: 978-0-203-84606-3 (ebk)

Typeset in Bembo and Minion by
EvS Communication Networx, Inc.

To Alyse and Tony … Again, and always
And to Annie — save a place for me!
TT

In honor of my sisters, Cyndi, Tammy, and Karen ...
who bring me love and laughter
RP

To Mary Ann whose smile heals all
JFN

Dedicated to Dale Brashers